THE
ENGLISH NOTEBOOKS
BY
NATHANIEL HAWTHORNE

THE
ENGLISH NOTEBOOKS

BY

NATHANIEL HAWTHORNE

BASED UPON THE ORIGINAL MANUSCRIPTS
IN THE PIERPONT MORGAN LIBRARY

AND EDITED BY

RANDALL STEWART

PROFESSOR OF ENGLISH IN
BROWN UNIVERSITY

NEW YORK

RUSSELL & RUSSELL · INC

1962

PREFACE

THIS volume continues the work which was begun with my edition of *The American Notebooks* (Yale University Press, 1932) and which will be completed with an edition of *The Italian Notebooks*, now being prepared by Mr. Norman Holmes Pearson, namely, the presentation of the true texts of Hawthorne's journals based upon the original manuscripts. Since readers and students of Hawthorne heretofore have been seriously misled by Mrs. Hawthorne's extremely bowdlerized texts (1868-71), it has seemed desirable that the true texts of these basic works be made available.

Mrs. Hawthorne's expurgations and revisions were even more extensive in the English notebooks than in the American. The discussion of these alterations in the first chapter of the Introduction to the present work serves the double purpose of demonstrating the necessity of the new text and of bringing into strong relief certain traditionally obscured characteristics of Hawthorne himself. The second chapter of the Introduction attempts to present Hawthorne's complex and conflicting reactions to England, his irritations and resentments, and his deep-seated affection for "our old home." The notes on the text describe peculiarities of the manuscript, identify quotations, persons, and obscure references, and indicate the uses of the notebooks in Hawthorne's other writings.

The notebooks themselves, composed in England between 1853 and 1857, and comprising more than 300,000 words, are perhaps the fullest and richest book ever written by an American about England. They were written when Hawthorne was at the height of his powers and they were the only literary work which he did during those four years. Acute in observation, pungent in phrase, the English notebooks are an important contribution to the comparative study of the English and the American modes of life. No other American man of letters has studied the respective characteristics of the two countries so painstakingly.

Although his American patriotism was strong, and his English experience often disconcerting, Hawthorne could never rid himself of the profound consciousness of the tie that binds America to England, nor did he really wish or endeavor to do so. It seems a strange accident of history that his manuscript should have waited, unaccountably, for complete publication until a time when a similar consciousness is felt, perhaps more than ever before, by many Americans, and when so many of the things which he described with meticulous and loving care are either already destroyed, or threatened with destruction. Hawthorne's descriptions of the old English landmarks, which might have seemed tedious and almost irrelevant in another, happier time, now acquire, with the tragic change of circumstances, a relevancy new and poignant.

* * * *

The plan of the present edition follows closely that of *The American Notebooks*. I have tried to reproduce the original manuscripts with exactness, preserving all peculiarities of paragraphing, punctuation, and spelling, except for a single departure: namely, in order to avoid possible confusion, I have taken the liberty of regularizing the spelling (occasionally heterodox) of proper names. What was said in the Preface to *The American Notebooks* of the history and general appearance of the manuscripts is applicable here, except that the inked-out passages are somewhat fewer. As in the former volume, manuscript page numbers are enclosed in brackets, page references to the present work are printed in italics, and all references to Hawthorne's works, unless otherwise indicated, are to the Riverside edition, edited by George Parsons Lathrop.

I am extremely grateful to the trustees of the Pierpont Morgan Library for permission to publish the original manuscripts and to Miss Belle da Costa Greene and other members of the staff of the Pierpont Morgan Library for their generous aid; to Mr. H. W. L. Dana, the Rev. Mr. U. S. Milburn, and the Henry E. Huntington Library for permission to quote from manuscript letters by Hawthorne, and to the New York Public Library for permission to quote from manuscript letters by Una Hawthorne; to Mr. Norman Holmes Pearson and Professors J. B. Hubbell and Stanley T. Williams for helpful suggestions; to Brown University and the American Council of Learned Societies for grants-in-aid which made publication possible; and to the Modern Language Association of America, particularly to the Committee on Research Activities, for the Association's sponsorship of this volume.

Brown University   R. S.
  January, 1941.

CONTENTS

INTRODUCTION

CHAPTER I

Mrs. Hawthorne's Revisions of the English Notebooks

DURING his residence of four years in England (from 1853 to 1857) Hawthorne did no creative writing. Perhaps he had written himself out, for the time being (for *The Scarlet Letter, The House of the Seven Gables,* and *The Blithedale Romance* had appeared between 1850 and 1852), and needed a period of recuperation. Or possibly new scenes and experiences in England (he had never been abroad before), together with his duties as American consul at Liverpool, left no room for creative effort. But he did find abundant time for his journal: "In the evening," he wrote on April 14, 1857, "I scrawled away at my Journal till past ten o'clock; for I have really made it a matter of conscience to keep a tolerably full record of my travels."[1] This tolerably full record comprises more than 300,000 words.

Hawthorne's attitude toward the journal is interestingly revealed in several letters to his friends. His record of observations and impressions was too plain-spoken in its treatment of England and the English, he thought, to publish, at least during his lifetime: "I keep a journal of all my travels and adventures," he wrote to W. D. Ticknor, "and I could easily make up a couple of nice volumes for you; but, unluckily, they would be much too good and true to bear publication. It would bring a terrible hornet's nest about my ears."[2] Of his journal written during a visit in London in 1856, Hawthorne said to Ticknor: ". . . [it] would be worth a mint of money to you and me, if I could let you publish it."[3] And to Ticknor, once more, he wrote: "Everything that I see in my travels goes down into my journal; and I have now hundreds of pages, which I would publish if the least of them were not too spicy."[4] To Miss Elizabeth Peabody, Hawthorne expressed the same opinion: ". . . it [the journal] is written with so free and truth-telling a pen that I never shall dare to publish it. Perhaps parts of it shall be read to you, some winter evening, after we get home."[5]

When Hawthorne left England, in 1857, to go to Italy, where he was to spend more than a year, he entrusted the manuscript to the care of his good friend, Henry Bright, an Englishman, with the following note of instruction and prophecy: "Here are these journals. If unreclaimed by myself, or by my heirs or assigns, I consent to your breaking the seals in the year 1900—not a day sooner. By that time, probably, England will be a minor republic, under the protection of the United States. If my country-men of that day partake in the least of my feelings, they will treat you generously."[6]

Well, 1900 is already in the distant past; and the present editor be-lieves that the English journals may now be published in their entirety with Hawthorne's full approval.

Most of the material in these journals, of course, is no longer new. In the writing of *Our Old Home* (published in 1863), Hawthorne himself drew upon large portions of the manuscript. And Mrs. Hawthorne pub-lished in 1870 a work entitled *Passages from the English Note-Books*,[7] in the Preface to which she said: "The Editor has transcribed the manu-scripts just as they were left, without making any new arrangement or altering any sequence—merely omitting some passages, and being es-pecially careful to preserve whatever could throw any light upon his [Hawthorne's] character."[8] Mrs. Hawthorne's edition, with a few ex-ceptions, indicates only two kinds of omissions: the omission of passages which Hawthorne had re-worked in writing *Our Old Home;* and the omission of passages or portions of passages describing certain persons of importance who were still living. Except for alterations of these two kinds, the reader is led to believe that, in the main, "the Editor has tran-scribed the manuscripts just as they were left." But a collation of Mrs. Hawthorne's edition with the original manuscripts (now in the possession of the Pierpont Morgan Library) reveals that the English Notebooks (like the American Notebooks)[9] underwent a pretty thorough revision at the editor's hands. The changes, nearly always amusing and occasionally en-lightening, are so numerous that only a comparatively few representative examples can be given here; nor does their importance seem to warrant a complete tabulation.

An attempt to classify these revisions, which are of almost infinite variety, and which spring from complex and subtle editorial motives, is likely to yield unsatisfactory results. But the following rough divisions must perforce serve the present purpose: stylistic revisions; and the omis-sion or revision of passages which dealt with trivial, unpleasant, or indeli-cate subjects; or which described certain contemporaries with uncircum-spect freedom; or which expressed uncomplimentary opinions of England;

or which had to do, in too personal a way, with Hawthorne and the members of his family.

The stylistic revisions. Hawthorne frequently allowed himself a colloquial freedom, all traces of which the editor was careful to remove:

speechifying: making speeches
a pretty smart frost: a pretty hard frost
fix: predicament
boozy: intoxicated
tots: babes
itch ("some New Englander with the itch for reform"): rage
soft soap: praise
doctor (the verb, taking as object "wine"): adulterate
clockwork (the mechanism of the human body; "always something has
    gone wrong with their clockwork"—referring to the ill-health of
    English women): them
youngish: rather young
pigged in: lived in
queer: absurd
a little shrimp of a man: a little man
in a strange pickle: in a strange trim
play the deuce: play me false[10]

Mrs. Hawthorne often substituted a generic term for a specific one:

squint: look
peeping: looking
puddle: pool
smelt: perceived
hovels: houses
muttons (of sheep in a painting): creatures
sprawled (of artists' models): sat
sixpence (the precise amount of Hawthorne's charity on one occasion):
    a piece of silver
puckery-faced: wrinkled face
bug: insect
scabby (of a child's mouth): defaced[11]

Or a word of Latin derivation for the Anglo-Saxon:

feelers: antennae
cross-breed: interfuse
harsh: dissonant
done: executed[12]

Many stylistic alterations seem owing to the editor's ignorance of good English idiom:

> good-looking: comely looking
> nick of time: moment
> out of sorts: out of tune
> would not have past muster (of a sermon in an English Cathedral, if delivered in a New England meeting house): would not have been considered of any account
> betimes: early
> right (one object right above another): exactly
> party walls: partition walls[13]

There are, moreover, nice little emendations which improved the social tone of the journals: the "eating cellar" or "eating house" where Hawthorne picked up a hurried lunch was metamorphosed into an "inn."[14] Other examples of this kind of revision are:

> well-victualled: a good table
> victualling department: table
> mattress: ottoman
> clean shirt: clean linen[15]

An old-fashioned "parlour" became a "drawing-room,"[16] which was more *à la mode;* and a "sideboard" became a "beaufet,"[17] which was, I suppose the correct word for the thing referred to.

And of course we find, as we should expect to find, the stock Victorian euphemisms:

> legs: limbs
> leg: knee
> female: wife
> females: women
> female children: little girls
> bottoms (of chairs): seats
> broad-bottomed (of the Chancellor's chair at Oxford): broad
> at meal-time and at bed-time (Hawthorne expressed a desire to observe some itinerant musicians at such times): in their social relations
> went to bed: retired
> got into bed: composed myself to sleep
> rears (of lions): backs
> backside (of London, as seen from the Thames): back side
> smell: odor
> smells of cigar smoke: was scented with
> slops: rubbish

straddled: strode
stark naked: nude
soaked: drenched
being once on my legs (the author had got up, somewhat reluctantly, to make a speech): being once started
was brought to bed of: gave birth to
on the raw ("if we wish to hit England on the raw"): to the quick[18]

The word "bosom" was omitted, even though, in one instance, the bosom referred to was that of an Egyptian mummy[19]; and likewise the word "strumpet," which occurs in a passage quoted from one of the old county histories, but for which the editor apparently could not find a decorous synonym.[20]

Many other usages were objectionable to the editor for one reason or another:

snort (of John Bull): roar
a Jewish cast of features (said of Henry Bright's father): Oriental
a first rate ship (technically correct as applied to a war vessel): stately, full-rigged
the Gothic quaintnesses which pimple out over the grandeur and solemnity of this and other cathedrals: blotch
old maids: old maiden ladies
her (referring to Queen Victoria): her Majesty[21]

Perhaps the most amusing of all these stylistic revisions is one by means of which Mrs. Hawthorne exonerated her sex though in so doing she was forced both to place the onus squarely upon the other sex and to violate a long-established mythological and literary tradition:

troubles are a sociable sisterhood: brotherhood[22]

A second category includes passages which were either completely omitted or extensively revised because their subjects seemed trivial, or unpleasant, or even indelicate.

Mrs. Hawthorne omitted a very interesting passage (interesting, not intrinsically, but for what it reveals of Hawthorne's literary aims) in which Hawthorne enumerated the vehicles which, during a half-hour period, passed on the road before the house where he happened to be staying—for the sake, he said, of "knowing the character of the travel along this road."

A man wheeling a small hand-cart in the direction from Manchester; an omnibus, pretty full, to do [ditto]; a cab to do; a man on horseback, leading another horse, from do; a dog-cart to do; a two-horse carriage to do. . . .[23]

These are trivial details. But Hawthorne's chief object in writing the English journals was that he might accumulate materials some of which at least might be used later "for the side-scenes and backgrounds and exterior adornment of a work of fiction"[24] (the English Romance, that is, which he never quite finished to his satisfaction). And in the English Romance, he doubtless hoped to achieve by the elaboration of externals a greater verisimilitude than his previous works had possessed. "It is odd enough. . . ," Hawthorne wrote to Fields, "that my own individual taste is for quite another class of works than those which I myself am able to write. . . . Have you ever read the novels of Anthony Trollope? They precisely suit my taste; solid and substantial. . . ."[25] Motivated, then, by his admiration of the Trollopean solidity, Hawthorne resolved at least to know "the character of the travel along this road":

> a one-horse carriage from do; an omnibus to do, full; a Hansom cab to do; . . .

Omissions of the kind just mentioned are few; but there are many passages which the editor omitted or revised because she found them unpleasant or indelicate.

Hawthorne was greatly interested in the social and economic conditions of the poorest classes in England. There was nothing in the New England of the 1850's, he thought, even remotely approaching the squalor and misery which he saw in the streets of Liverpool and London. His notebooks contain a good deal of material on this subject, part of which he used in writing that trenchant and compassionate chapter, "Glimpses of English Poverty." He studied street-scenes with avidity: dirty children, women barefooted in mid-winter carrying baskets in which they collected horse-dung, spirit-vaults with placards advertising "beds," street-walkers, and so on.[26]

He described the inmates of the Derby Workhouse with a realism which is worthy of our modern adjective "stark."[27] Moreover, it was sometimes part of Hawthorne's consular duty to visit seamen in Liverpool hospitals, and some of his descriptions of what he saw there shocked the editor by their realistic force; this, for example—an amputated arm, "looking just like a small lump of butcher's meat."[28]

Not only city-slums and poor-houses and hospitals, but picture-galleries sometimes yielded descriptions which required editing. A "Venus, naked and asleep, in a most lascivious posture" is only a "Venus" in the revised version.[29] Likewise, the following passage describing the women in the paintings of Etty was deleted almost entirely away:

The most disagreeable of English painters is Etty, who had a diseased appetite for woman's flesh, and spent his whole life, apparently, in painting them with enormously developed bosoms and buttocks. I do not mind nudity, in a modest and natural way; but Etty's women really thrust their nakednesses upon you so with malice aforethought, and especially so enhance their posteriors, that one feels inclined to kick them.[30]

In both of the examples just cited, the objectionable words were not only omitted from the purified text but were inked out in the original manuscript.

There are miscellaneous examples. This brief entry was omitted: "A child's caul is advertised for sale in the Liverpool paper of today, price £8."[31] (A curious omission, especially when one remembers that David Copperfield "was born with a caul, which was advertised for sale in the newspaper at the low price of fifteen guineas.") Omitted, too, or seriously mutilated, were an extraordinarily vivid description of a monkey[32]; an account of the manuring of an English garden[33]; a reference to the promiscuity of priests in York in the time of Henry VI[34]; a speculative comment upon a woman of extraordinary largeness, the author wondering if there might be a correlation between the lady's enormous size and the "connubial bliss" which she afforded[35]; the story of a terrier bitch—praised for her faithfulness in poems by Wordsworth and Scott—who actually (so Hawthorne was told) ate the body of her dead master[36]; a grimly humorous anecdote of the retreat of the British at New Orleans:

In their retreat, many of the enemy would drop down among the dead, then rise, run a considerable distance, and drop again, thus confusing the riflemen's aim. One fellow had thus got about 450 yards from the American line; and thinking himself secure, he displayed his rear to the Americans, and clapt his hand on it derisively. "I'll have a shot at him anyhow!" cried a rifleman; so he fired, and the poor devil dropt.[37]

There is a third large class of revisions which the editor thought it imperative to make because Hawthorne often wrote with uncircumspect freedom of certain people whom he met, or saw, or heard stories about. Most of these people were still living in 1870, the date of Mrs. Hawthorne's edition; and the editor can hardly be censured, in these instances, for exercising an editorial discretion.

Little gossipy stories about the Queen and the Prince Consort were of course omitted. Victoria, according to Ambassador Buchanan, was "a fiery little devil."[38] According to a certain Mr. Durham, a sculptor, she requested that a considerable thickness of clay be removed from the shoulders of a bust which he had made—"thereby," commented Hawthorne, "improving the bust, though injuring the likeness."[39] Albert, the author was told, was not well liked by those who knew him.[40] Miscellaneous comments, authentic or apochryphal, about members of the aristocracy or people otherwise prominent in English social and political life, were either omitted or emended. The editor withheld from Hawthorne's readers such items as the following: that a young lord, while at Rugby, stole a five-pound note[41]; that Lord and Lady Palmerston (it was rumored) had been intimate before the death of the lady's first husband[42]; that Sir Robert Peel had never heard of James Sheridan Knowles or Alfred Tennyson[43] (the date of Sir Robert's ignorance is not given); that the Duke of Cambridge looked "punchy . . . on horseback" and a ludicrous effect was produced by his bald head when he removed his hat[44]; that Monckton Milnes's chin had "magnified itself considerably" since Hawthorne last saw him[45]; that Lord Lansdowne was the original of Thackeray's Lord Steyne[46]; that Lady Waldegrave was a "Brummagem kind of countess"[47]; that Disraeli was an "adventurer," who had risen by "quackish" methods[48]; that Bulwer, on one occasion, had exclaimed: "Oh that somebody would invent a new Sin, that I might go in for it!"[49] The editor also kept private the following tidbits: that Sir Thomas Birch's house was "in no very good order" (emended to read, "in very nice order")[50]; that Mr. Bramley-Moore "circulated his wines more briskly than is customary at gentlemen's tables" and Mrs. Bramley-Moore was an "under-bred woman"[51]; that Barry Cornwall was "a small, though elegant poet, and a man of no passion or emphasized intellect"[52]; that W. C. Bennett, another poet, aspirated his *h's* in good Cockney style[53]; that Martin Tupper was "an absurd little man"[54]; that Alexander Ireland (a friend of Emerson's) "talked earnestly in favor of the Maine Liquor law, while quaffing sherry, champagne, hock, port, and claret"[55]; that a guest of Mrs. Ainsworth's, next to whom the author sat at table, "had a great pimple on one side of her nose."[56] The editor did not permit Hawthorne to say that the collar of Tennyson's shirt "might have been clean the day before,"[57] or that he liked Mrs. Browning better than her poetry.[58] There are little comments on Americans, also, which the editor saw fit to leave out: Stephen A. Douglas, who, when Hawthorne saw him in Washington, wore "a very dirty shirt-collar"[59]; George Bradford, a Brook Farmer, whose "conscientiousness seems to be a kind of itch—keeping him always uneasy and inclined to scratch"[60]; Ambassador Buchanan, who carried "his head in a very awkward way, in consequence, as the old scandal says, of having once attempted to cut his throat,"[61] and whose handkerchief "ought to have gone into this week's wash"[62]; Miss

Lane, the Ambassador's charming niece, whose gown at a dinner-party was "terribly low across the shoulders"[63]; Mr. Dallas, a "stale old fogy,"[64] who succeeded Mr. Buchanan. But details of this sort might be multiplied indefinitely; and those which have been given will more than suffice. Moreover, these brief descriptive phrases are misleading when considered apart from their contexts. In most instances, one finds balanced and sympathetic portraits of the persons named above and of many others. Conspicuous among these portraits are those of Tennyson,[65] Melville,[66] Francis Bennoch,[67] and the beautiful Jewess[68] who suggested Miriam in *The Marble Faun*—all of which were radically revised by Mrs. Hawthorne.

A fourth division has to do with Mrs. Hawthorne's revisions of those passages which expressed uncomplimentary opinions of England or compared England with America to the former's disadvantage. Hawthorne's irritations in England found expression, of course, in *Our Old Home;* but he had allowed himself an even greater freedom and sharpness of language in the journals.

The editor in some instances was able to temper the author's acerbity by means of slight alterations:

> his English surliness (said of a waiter at a hotel): his surliness
> such dolt-heads, scamps, rowdies, and every way mean people as most of the English sovereigns have been: many (and "scamps" was omitted)
> the picture of a man beside whom . . . any English nobleman would look like common beef or clay (said of Washington): any English nobleman whom I have seen (and "beef" was omitted)[69]

But alterations like these were often inadequate: in general, editorial discretion required a more extensive revision of passages in which the author disparaged England and asserted or implied American superiority. And America, Hawthorne liked to think, was superior in many respects, ranging from the important to the trivial. American women were more attractive than English women (Hawthorne's unchivalrous description of the English dowager in *Our Old Home*[70] had, according to Lowell, "sent a spasm through all the journals of England"[71]; and Mrs. Hawthorne dared not publish the even less restrained passages in the notebooks on that subject).[72] American manners were at once more democratic and more refined.[73] Agriculture and commerce in America were more progressive,[74] and religion was more sincere.[75] American hotels were more commodious and American food was more palatable.[76] The American army (Hawthorne thought after visiting a military camp in England) surpassed the English army in maneuvers and sham-fights.[77] Americans made better after-dinner speeches.[78] American mountebanks at country fairs were more lively and resourceful than English mountebanks![79]

These, and other items of a similar nature, if taken alone, would give a distorted view of Hawthorne's attitude toward England. There are many passages in the journals in which the author surrendered to the charm of things English and gave full and rich expression to that charm[80]; but these passages were retained in Mrs. Hawthorne's edition, and, therefore, do not concern us here.

A final group comprises revisions of passages which had to do more or less intimately with Hawthorne himself or with Mrs. Hawthorne and the children.

The numerous references to Mrs. Hawthorne's ill health were omitted: "the Doctor . . . after due examination, gave hopeful opinions respecting Sophia's case"[81]; "poor Mamma having caught cold . . . and being confined to her bed"[82];—are examples. Often a sight-seeing trip had to be cut short because of Mrs. Hawthorne's fatigue: "it being desirable to get home betimes, on account of Sophia's cough"[83]; "we wandered through the rest of the Bazaar . . . till Sophia was quite wearied out, and we resumed our way home"[84]; "and thence turned back, and took a cab homeward, on Sophia's account."[85] We can understand Mrs. Hawthorne's unwillingness to include references as personal as these, especially in view of the obvious irony in the fact that the invalid therein described lived to edit her husband's posthumous papers. Omitted also was a rather prosaic reference to their married life: "our union has turned out to the utmost satisfaction of both parties, after fifteen years' trial"[86]; though the editor interpolated, after the date, July 9, 1856, the phrase in parentheses, "Our wedding-day,"[87]—thus correcting her husband's forgetfulness.

Many omitted passages affect our conception of Hawthorne himself.

There are a great many references in the journal to eating, drinking, and smoking. These references were either omitted or drastically revised. In the bowdlerized edition, Hawthorne was allowed ordinarily to have tea but not mutton-chops or beef-steak.[88] He was not permitted to drink ale, porter, or stout[89]; or to express his enthusiasm in the discovery at Oxford of two "new articles of drink": "Hop-champagne"[90] and "Arch Deacon" (a superior kind of ale, named in honor of its inventor, "with a richer flavor and of a mightier spirit")[91]; or to reveal his unregenerate delight in finding "how little progress tee-totalism has yet made" in certain parts of England[92]; or to confess that when he was called upon to make a speech on a certain public occasion, he "stood up with a careless, dare-devil feeling, being indeed rather pot-valiant with champagne."[93] (The last phrase

was not only omitted from the text but inked out in the original manuscript.) Hawthorne was not allowed to smoke cigars in his journals,[94] either
alone or with other men (not even with Herman Melville)[95]; or, so much as
to express his desire of an opportunity to smoke in the company of that
admirable smoking companion, Tennyson[96] ("the best man in England
to smoke a pipe with," Carlyle told Emerson).[97] Indeed, Hawthorne's social and convivial instincts suffer serious abatement in Mrs. Hawthorne's
edition. The restoration of two passages alone—one describing a convivial evening with the sons of Burns,[98] the other giving a circumstantial
account of Hawthorne's interested conversation with Mrs. Blodgett's boarders, mostly American sea-captains[99] (whom the editor doubtless regarded
as "low company")—contributes much toward the humanizing of an author who, I am inclined to believe, has been too persistently represented as
coldly aloof.

Other revisions suppressed evidence of Hawthorne's legitimately appreciative eye for female beauty:

Tom Taylor, who had a very pretty wife with him: Mr. Taylor[100]
Good, round (for she is very round) Mrs. Hall: Mrs. Hall[101]

Revisions like these, of course, were made partly out of deference to the
persons named. But anonymous ladies were omitted also: for example, a
nurse in a hospital who was described as "a comely young woman."[102] One
passage required deletion because it seemed to connote an almost domestic
intimacy: it is simply a reference to a "young lady's feet, which she was
toasting at the fire"[103]; another, because it implied a thought too bold:
"I never should have thought of touching her," Hawthorne said of the
"miraculous Jewess" whom he saw at the Lord Mayor's Dinner, "nor
desired to touch her."[104]

Other revisions still further subtracted from Hawthorne's humanity by
concealing quite human moods of impatience, or mildly humorous irreverence, or quiet skepticism. Hawthorne remarked that children were an
impediment to travel[105]; that a certain cathedral was "a great, old, dreary
place enough"[106]; that "almost everything" (emended to "very many
things") in the British Museum was rubbish.[107] He said (tongue in cheek)
that he declined an invitation to church, pleading his wife's illness as an
excuse[108]; he noted that the light which came through the stained glass
windows of a cathedral and fell upon the persons in the congregation tinged
"some of their cheeks and noses with crimson" (the emendation is "tinging
them"; there was a little malice in "noses").[109] Hawthorne observed that
"all the misery we endure here constitutes a claim for another life—and

still more, all the happiness"; the misery was made less personal by the emendation "all the misery endured here" and the passage was brightened up considerably by italicizing "all the happiness."[110] From a description of the dome and pinnacles of St. Paul's, which a dense fog so obscured that "the statues of Saints looked down dimly from their stand-points on high," Mrs. Hawthorne omitted the skeptical commentary: "faintest, as spiritual consolations are apt to be, when the world was darkest."[111] Finally, Hawthorne questioned the wisdom of Christ in cursing the fig-tree: "it seems most unreasonable to have expected it to bear figs out of season." The editor deftly changed skepticism to faith by italicizing "seems."[112] (Seems, madam! nay, it is!) Mrs. Hawthorne did what she could to keep her husband sober, grave, reverent, and optimistic about life, whatever evidence there might be in the tales and novels to the contrary.

Only one other revision will be mentioned—a revision that is of especial interest because of its political implications. Having noticed admiringly "the hearty meed of honor" which the English bestowed upon the soldiers returning from the Crimean War, Hawthorne continued:

Whereas, in America, when our soldiers fought as good battles in the Mexican War, with as great proportionate loss, and far more valuable triumphs, the country seemed rather ashamed than proud of them.

By deleting the phrase "in the Mexican War,"[113] the editor in one stroke effaced an unpleasant reminder of Hawthorne's connection with the Democratic party of James K. Polk and Franklin Pierce, destroyed an extraordinarily vivid bit of contemporary evidence of the unpopularity of the Mexican War in New England, and rendered the passage meaningless.

Although scarcely a tithe of the total, the revisions which have been cited are of sufficient number and variety to demonstrate the need of a true text of the English journals. Moreover, the emphasis which I have given the subject of this chapter has another and more important justification: namely, that a study of these revisions reveals once more in bold relief certain traditionally obscured aspects of Hawthorne's personality. It becomes increasingly clear that out of the restored journals and letters a new Hawthorne will emerge: a more virile and a more human Hawthorne; a more alert and (in a worldly sense) a more intelligent Hawthorne; a Hawthorne less dreamy, and less aloof, than his biographers have represented him as being.

It would be both an error and an injustice, from the point of view of the biographer and historian, to censure Mrs. Hawthorne. She was a woman of rare refinement and high cultivation, a devoted wife and an inspiration to her husband. If, to the modern reader, she seems to have been misguided and even unethical in her emendations and excisions, it should be remembered that editors in the Nineteenth Century—especially when those editors happened to be relatives or friends—often took similar liberties with the manuscripts which Fate entrusted to their care. Mrs. Hawthorne carried an enormously laborious task to completion in accordance, I have no doubt, with this high principle: to print no more than Hawthorne himself would have printed had he been revising the manuscript for publication, and to make such verbal alterations as he would have made[114] (or, in her not too humble judgment, ought to have made). Though false, of course, to the canons of modern textual scholarship, she was true to the Victorian ideal of decorum. In the words of another Victorian paradox, "faith unfaithful kept her falsely true."

CHAPTER II

Hawthorne in England

THE subject of Hawthorne's reactions to England during and immediately following his residence there is such a complex one that an analysis of his attitude requires a careful weighing of conflicting thoughts and emotions. He wrote, with obvious understatement, in *Our Old Home:* "An American is not very apt to love the English people, as a whole, on whatever length of acquaintance."[115] At the same time, he confessed to "an unspeakable yearning towards England"[116] and a "singular tenderness" for her institutions.[117] His was a divided mind, for reasons which this chapter will attempt to show.

There were several reasons ("good" for him, if not always valid for his readers) why Hawthorne entertained, at times, an unfriendly and even hostile feeling toward England. Born only twenty-one years after the close of the Revolutionary War, and nearly eleven years of age when Jackson defeated the British at New Orleans, he had thought of England from childhood as the foe and oppressor of America. His great admiration of Jackson was owing in large measure, no doubt, to Jackson's brilliant military victory; and he was embarrassed, almost to the point of humiliation, when, upon a visit to Chelsea Hospital, he saw the American flags which had been captured in the War of 1812.[118] His notions of the American Revolution, we may be sure, were quite "unreconstructed": not until the present century did American historical scholarship redress the balance by establishing, to the satisfaction of most Americans, the view that there was some measure of justice in Britain's demands upon the colonies. In what is perhaps his finest patriotic composition, "The Gray Champion," the symbolical hero, who is described as "the type of New England's hereditary spirit,"[119] led a revolt against the tyranny of Andros, the Royal Governor; he appeared again, we are told in the epilogue to the tale, at Lexington and at Bunker Hill. In brief, Hawthorne's patriotism was bound up inextricably with a traditional and deep-seated feeling of enmity toward England.

This traditional enmity, inherited from colonial times, had been aggravated by the concerted detraction of American institutions and manners in many books written by English visitors to America during the first half of the Nineteenth Century. Although Hawthorne nowhere referred by name to the *Domestic Manners of the Americans* of Mrs. Trollope or the *American Notes* of Dickens or other works of that school, he had read them, and he remembered them unpleasantly. "Not an Englishman of them all," he declared with vehemence in *Our Old Home,* "ever spared America for courtesy's sake or kindness."[120]

It is not surprising, therefore, that with a background so "conditioned," Hawthorne, while in England, should have been sensitive, even hypersensitive perhaps, to criticisms of America in the current English press and to unflattering and untactful remarks which he heard on every side.

The English press seemed to him deliberately unfriendly. No sooner was Sebastopol reported taken than the London *Times* began "to throw out menaces against America," which evoked the grim comment: "There is an account to settle between us and them for the contemptuous jealousy with which (since it has ceased to be unmitigated contempt) they regard us."[121] More irritating than "menaces," however, was the ridicule which Americans in England seemed only too liable to lay themselves open to, and which the English press seemed all too eager to inflict. When Professor Mahan of West Point, attired in "frock coat, black neckcloth, and yellow waistcoat," sought admittance to the Queen's levee and was turned away, the *Times* asked, with fine rhetorical sarcasm: "When will Americans learn manners? Who shall teach our Transatlantic cousins how to behave?"[122] The Manchester *Guardian* saw in the incident another confirmation of the "vulgarity and arrogance" reported by Mrs. Trollope and Dickens, and struck home (unwittingly at Hawthorne himself!) with the suggestion that the reputation of America might be improved if the President would appoint one or two civilized persons to European diplomatic posts.[123] Employing, for the occasion, good Grub-street satire, Mr. Punch recommended to the American embassy a clothing establishment in Hounsditch, where a court "outfit" including "pants" could be had cheap.[124] Hawthorne was sufficiently disturbed by these journalistic sallies to call upon Dallas, the American minister, in order to ascertain "the facts about the American gentleman's being refused admittance to the Levee."[125]

Punch, which may doubtless be taken as a trustworthy barometer of English opinion on the present subject, was, it would seem, particularly offensive. An article entitled "Barnum for President," which purported to have been copied from an American newspaper, began as follows:

It is with no ordinary pleasure that we announce a new candidate for the Presidential chair of this great and enlightened Republic; and we shall be much surprised if the news that the individual in question is about to tender himself for this, the most honorable office in creation, does not at once cause the heart of every true American to leap with rapture. . . .

The honorable candidate . . . says: "I own, not with shame, but with pride, that my character is truly American. I glory in the thought that my nature reflects that of the millions to whom I now appeal. I admit that I have the true American admiration for all that I have myself achieved, and the true American disbelief in the achievements of others. So thinks the nation of herself and of her contemporaries. . . . I am an American, and I dauntlessly say, that he best represents America who is bound by no tyrannic fetter, but who bends his knee alone at the shrine of progress and enlightenment."[126]

"Rachel and Jonathan" (to select only one other article from many articles of the same tenor which appeared in *Punch* during the years of Hawthorne's stay in England) was hardly calculated to increase an American's fondness for the mother country:

Rachel—France will be happy to hear it—has given satisfaction in America. Just before her debut, the Yankee critics very properly remarked, that a most important epoch in her life was approaching, and that the question, whether she were "clever" or not, was to be settled by "an audience as intellectual and subtle as that which first sat in judgment upon her." Indeed, the value of the test was increased by the fact—recorded in the same papers—that the American mind was a *tabula rasa* in regard to her, and that the intellectual and subtle audience assembled in some doubt as to what they were to see or hear, one journal having described her as "a great *danseuse*," and another, having congratulated "the lovers of good music" upon her arrival. However, New York has now found out—and of course talks as glibly of the discovery as if it were of ancient date—that there were some French dramatists called Racine and Corneille, who wrote "the most boring plays ever heard in America," and that Rachel really delivers their language brilliantly, and with a very pure French accent. Nay, rushing into extremes, as usual, the Americans actually find histrionic merit in the bundle of Hebrew sticks whom Rachel takes about with her to fill the other characters, the innocent Yankees being unaware that all the acting permitted to those articles is the acting as foils to herself. Let it be added, that Rachel's slight figure has been duly appreciated, and that the leading New York critic describes it as "very light physical timber."[127]

From time to time, it is true, *Punch* wrote of America in a less satirical vein; but even protestations of friendship and admiration were often so phrased as to inflict once more, though obliquely, the old sting of ridicule. The following verses, which were written at a time of diplomatic tension between the two countries, could hardly have improved appreciably the American feeling toward England; for the author, even while professing

to make amends for ancient wrongs, maliciously contrived to recapitulate
the ancient accusations:

> How can you think, you Yankee fellows,
> That of your progress we are jealous?
> Why, Middlesex as well might worry,
> Herself because of thriving Surrey.
>
> We know the spread of your dominion
> Is likewise that of free opinion,
> Which bowie-knife, revolver, rifle,
> And Lynch-law but in small part stifle. . . .
>
> Against us why are you so bitter?
> Because we sometimes grin and titter
> A little at your speech and manners?
> Therefore must ours be hostile banners? . . .
>
> Are you enraged with us for joking?
> Are you indeed for bayonets poking
> Against our fun in sober sadness?
> Or have we bantered you to madness?
>
> Say is it your intent to wallop
> Us on account of Mrs. Trollope?
> Or are we by you to be smitten
> For something Dickens may have written?
>
> For you we have the kindest feeling;
> Add Stars on Stars—by honest dealing—
> To those which now your striped flag spangle;
> 'Twill be no cause why we should jangle.
>
> Great Nation!—still keep getting bigger,
> All of you, saving what is Nigger,
> We shall rejoice—not envy nourish—
> The more you go ahead and flourish. . . .[128]

Whatever contribution such an equivocal composition might have made
toward removing "the American misunderstanding" was more than offset
by two cartoons which appeared in the same issue. One, "The Spoilt Child,"
showed Jonathan in a tantrum, scattering his toys about him, while John
Bull, with a look of exhausted patience, remarked: "I don't like to cor-

rect him just now, because he's about his teeth, and sickening for his measles—but he certainly deserves a clout on the head." The other, "Life in an American Hotel," showed two men at a dinner-table, one of whom was pointing a pistol at the other and commanding, "Pass the Mustard!"

If it was difficult for Hawthorne to ignore the English press, it was also difficult for him (as it was for Lowell later) to be unmindful of a certain condescension in the English people whom he met. This "condescension," he discovered, was capable, on occasion, of taking the form of open ridicule to one's face. At a dinner-party at Smithell's Hall, Mrs. Ainsworth, his hostess and the wife of a member of Parliament, told an anecdote which Hawthorne described as "very characteristic of the English people generally." The account in the journal deserves full quotation:

One anecdote which she told was very characteristic—not of the hero of it —but of herself and of the English people generally, as showing what their tone and feeling is, respecting Americans. Mr. Bancroft, while Minister here, was telling somebody about the effect of the London atmosphere on his wife's health. "She is now very delicate," said he: "whereas, when we lived in New York, she was one of the most *indelicate* women in the city!" And Mrs. Ainsworth had the face to tell this foolish story for truth, and as indicating the mistakes into which Americans are liable to fall in the use of the English language. In other instances, I have heard stories equally ridiculous about our diplomatic people, whom the English seem determined to make butts of, reason or none. It is very queer, this resolute quizzing of our manners. . . .[129]

Less flagrantly discourteous, but hardly less distressing because equally derogatory, by implication, to America was the assumption, which Hawthorne often encountered, that he was either an Englishman who had traveled in America or an American who had lived for a long while in England. The rector at Stanton Harcourt inquired, Hawthorne recorded in the journal, "whether I had spent much time in America; appearing to think that I must have had an English breeding, if not birth, to be so much like other people."[130] If, on the other hand, Hawthorne's American past should have been disclosed at the outset, his English interlocutor (in one instance, a casual acquaintance in the Coffee Room of a hotel at Gloucester) would seize upon (as it seemed to him) the only alternative: "But I suppose you have now been in England some time?" "He meant," Hawthorne explained, "(finding me not absolutely a savage) that I must have been caught a good while ago."[131]

These examples sufficiently illustrate Hawthorne's personal experience of the condescension of the English, their resolute quizzing of American manners, which is, of course, a familiar story in the history of Anglo-American relations in the last century. Matthew Arnold averred, a little apologetically perhaps, that Hawthorne had been particularly unfortunate in his English associates, that he was "so situated in England that he was perpetually in contact with the British Philistine," and that (as no one knew better than Arnold himself) "the British Philistine is a trying personage."[132] But Hawthorne was convinced that the contemptuous attitude toward America was universal in England: "This insular narrowness," he declared, "is quite as much a characteristic of men of education and culture as of clowns."[133] "And Philistines," he would almost certainly have added, if he had lived to read Arnold's essay.

However foolish and even reprehensible from one point of view, a perfectly human and understandable reaction in Hawthorne's case to such influences as I have attempted to describe in the foregoing paragraphs was a flare-up of patriotism. Scarcely an opportunity was lost in the journals of asserting a point wherein America was superior to England. (Whether an alleged superiority was real or only imagined it is not, of course, the business of the editor of these journals to determine.) A complete list of such comparative statements would comprehend a wide variety of items: aspects of nature (clouds, trees, fruits, lakes, and rivers); conveniences of travel (railways, hotels, food, and eating places); the people themselves (their appearance, speech, and manners); social and economic conditions among the poorer classes; achievements in agriculture, industry, and commerce; social, political, and religious institutions. On all of these topics, and many more besides, Hawthorne at one time or another expressed his belief in the superiority of the American manifestation.[134]

This general position, however, was by no means consistently maintained. The writer's mood was variable: subsequent to a patriotic assertion, one is likely to find a partial retraction, or, not infrequently, a whole-hearted recognition of something quite admirable in English life which America could not hope to match. The accumulated result (as exhibited in the journals and letters, in *Our Old Home* and the posthumous novels) is a comparative weighing of the English and the American civilizations, which can scarcely be equaled elsewhere for its painstaking detail.

Scores of petulant remarks can be set down to the irritation of the moment and need not be taken too seriously. Even the notorious passages on English women may appear less prejudiced, though hardly less flagrant, when compared with certain passages on American women: if, from Hawthorne's point of view, English women were too fat, American women, by his own admission, were too thin. "As a point of taste," he confided to his journal, "I prefer my own countrywomen; though it is a pity that we must choose between a greasy animal and an anxious skeleton."[135] In these matters, it would seem that Hawthorne, like Aylmer in "The Birth-mark," was a perfectionist; late in life he complained, a little querulously, that he had never seen a woman whom he thought quite beautiful.[136]

The question of manners vexed him continually. If the English ridiculed American crudity, he would assert American refinement. After the visit to Smithell's Hall, noted above, he wrote: ". . . we are really and truly much better figures, and with more capacity of polish, for drawing-room or dining-room, than they [the English] themselves are."[137] He numbered among his acquaintance a few Englishmen, notably Monckton Milnes and Leigh Hunt, whose manners pleased him. But Milnes had "not quite so polished an address" as Longfellow[138]; and Hunt owed his exquisite manners to "his American blood (his mother was a Pennsylvanian)."[139]

And yet Hawthorne was fully aware that many Americans were fair game for English satire and his awareness of this unpleasant fact was progressively enlarged by his observation of Americans in England. Almost the first itinerant American to visit the new consul at Liverpool was a Mr. Lilley from Ohio, whom Hawthorne discovered to be "a very un-favorable specimen of American manners—an outrageous tobacco-chewer and atrocious spitter on carpets."[140] Even an American of superior education and social advantages (Mr. John Appleton, who was a native of Beverly, Massachusetts, a graduate of Bowdoin College, and a member of the American Legation at London) was so unmindful of the proprieties, on one occasion, as to put on his hat in St. Paul's; whereupon Hawthorne hastily excused himself because he "was ashamed of being seen in company with a man who could wear his hat in a Cathedral."[141] These and other experiences of a similar nature led Hawthorne, after his four years' residence in England, to conclude reluctantly: "I begin to agree partly with the English, that we are not a people of elegant manners."[142]

In a discriminating passage in *Doctor Grimshawe's Secret,* he reviewed the whole subject somewhat, apparently, to his final satisfaction. The imperfections of American manners were real enough as seen through English eyes:

An American, be it said, seldom turns his best side outermost abroad; and an observer, who has had much opportunity of seeing the figure which they make, in a foreign country, does not so much wonder that there should be severe criticisms on their manners as a people. I know not exactly why, but all our imputed peculiarities—our nasal pronunciation, our ungraceful idioms, our forthputtingness, our uncouth lack of courtesy—do really seem to exist on a foreign shore; and even, perhaps, to be heightened of malice prepense. The cold, unbelieving eye of Englishmen, expectant of solecisms in manners, contributes to produce the result which it looks for. Then the feeling of hostility and defiance in the American must be allowed for; and partly, too, the real existence of a different code of manners, founded on, and arising from, different institutions; and also certain national peculiarities, which may be intrinsically as good as English peculiarities; but being different, and yet the whole result being just too nearly alike, and, moreover, the English manners having the prestige of long establishment, and furthermore our own manners being in a transition state between those of old monarchies and what is proper to a new republic,—it necessarily followed that the American, though really a man of refinement and delicacy, is not just the kind of gentleman that the English can fully appreciate.[143]

But having conceded this much, Hawthorne asserted once more his belief in a finer quality, potential in Americans and certain of fulfilment, if not actually achieved at the moment:

. . . We are bold to say, when our countrymen are developed, or any one class of them, as they ought to be, they will show finer traits than have yet been seen. We have more delicate and quicker sensibilities; nerves more easily impressed; and these are surely requisites for perfect manners; and, moreover, the courtesy that proceeds on the ground of perfect equality is better than that which is a gracious and benignant condescension—as is the case with the manners of the aristocracy of England.[144]

Hawthorne weighed comparatively not only the "manners" of England and America but their institutions as well. Though basically a Puritan and a democrat, he was not impervious to the attractions of the Anglican church and of the hereditary aristocracy of England. These matters were dealt with repeatedly in his writings.

Of creeds and church polity, he had almost nothing to say. He deeply appreciated, of course, the English cathedrals, both for their architectural beauty and their religious symbolism. "A Gothic cathedral is surely the most wonderful work which mortal man has yet achieved,"[145] he wrote in a passage on the Cathedral at Lichfield; and this appreciation was in a sense religious as well as aesthetic. He was impressed, also, by the availability of the great English churches to the daily life of the people. Of St. Paul's, he wrote: "It is a beautiful idea enough, that, several times in the course of the day, a man can step out of the thickest throng and bustle of London, into this religious atmosphere, and hear the organ, and the music of young, pure voices. . . ."[146]

But his sympathy did not extend to the Episcopal service; indeed, he retained, with little abatement, the antipathy of his New England ancestors to religious ceremonial. In the passage just quoted, he went on to say: ". . . after all, the rites are lifeless in our day." And after having been present in York Cathedral on Easter Sunday, he wrote:

The spirit of my Puritan ancestors was mighty in me, and I did not wonder at their being out of patience with all this mummery, which seemed to me worse than papistry, because it was a corrupton of it.[147]

Moreover, the Anglican sermon was a disappointment. At York,

. . . a Canon gave out the text, and preached a sermon of about twenty minutes long, the coldest, dryest, most superficial rubbish; for this gorgeous setting of the magnificent Cathedral, the elaborate music, and the rich ceremonial, seems inevitably to take the life out of the sermon—which, to be anything, must be all. The Puritans showed their strength of mind and heart by preferring a sermon of an hour and a half long, into which the preacher put his whole soul and spirit, and lopping away all these externals, into which religious life had first gushed and flowered, and then petrified.[148]

Though farther in the same entry he wrote a partial retraction of this harsh judgment, admitting the possibility of another view as to the relative importance of the sermon, he retained his preference for the New England way and his admiration of "the elaborate intellectual efforts of New England ministers."[149]

Political and social questions were treated with a somewhat more open mind, though the author's deep-seated preference for American patterns is sufficiently obvious throughout. He could note, for example, a point of English superiority in politics:

In America, people seem to consider the government merely as a political administration; and they care nothing for the credit of it, unless it is the administration of their own political party. In England, all people, of whatever party, are anxious for the credit of their rulers. Our government, as a knot of persons, changes so entirely, every four years, that the institution itself has come to be considered a temporary thing.[150]

This clear advantage, however, was perhaps more than offset in Hawthorne's mind by a later discovery, namely, that knowledge of political affairs, and an active interest in them, were much less widely diffused in England than in America:

The rural people [he wrote while in the Lake District] really seem to take no interest in public affairs; at all events, they have no intelligence ["news"] on

such subjects. . . . If they generally know that Sebastopol is besieged, that is
the extent of their knowledge. The public life of America is lived through
the mind and heart of every man in it; here, the people feel that they have
nothing to do with what is going forward, and, I suspect, care little or nothing
about it. Such things they permit to be the exclusive affair of the higher
classes.[151]

This confidence in the higher classes, he was willing to concede, was not
altogether misplaced. Many of the English nobility seemed still to live
up to the ancient motto, *Noblesse oblige.* Such a nobleman was Lord
Stanley, of whom Hawthorne wrote with sympathy and admiration:

He has adopted public life as his hereditary profession, and makes the very
utmost of all his abilities, cultivating himself to a determined end, knowing
that he shall have every advantage towards attaining his object. . . . I felt, in
his person, what a burthen it is upon human shoulders, the necessity of keeping
up the fame and historical importance of an illustrious house; at least, when
the heir to its honors has sufficient intellect and sensibility to feel the claim
that his country, and his ancestors, and his posterity, all have upon him.[152]

During the Crimean War, moreover, the conduct of English noblemen in
positions of responsibility led Hawthorne to declare that "the nobles were
never positively more noble than now."[153]

Charmed by the beauty of the ancestral estates of the nobility, he
would have liked to believe that beautiful surroundings inevitably produce
beautiful lives. After a visit to Blenheim, he wrote:

Really, the garden of Eden could not be more beautiful than this garden of
Blenheim. . . . The world is not the same within that garden fence, that it is
without; it is a finer, lovelier, more harmonious Nature. . . . What a good
and happy life might be spent there! . . . Republican as I am, I should still love
to think that noblemen lead noble lives, and that all this stately and beautiful
environment may serve to elevate them a little above the rest of us.[154]

And yet, it was still too easy to find depraved individuals in noble families
that had enjoyed hereditary advantages for centuries. The Marquis of
Lansdowne—so Henry Bright told Hawthorne—was "a most disreputable
character."[155] And while Hawthorne and his companions were viewing the
lovely garden of Blenheim in the morning sunshine, "the besotted Duke
was in that very garden . . . and perhaps was thinking of nothing nobler
than how many ten-shilling tickets had that day been sold!"[156] Hawthorne
felt tempted to draw a stern Calvinistic moral: such instances would seem
to prove that "more favorable conditions of existence" do not suffice to
"eradicate our vices and weaknesses."[157] He could draw a good republican

moral, too, from this phase of his comparison of the Old World and the New: when one came to think about it, the hereditary aristocracy of all Europe had not produced more illustrious men than Washington and Franklin, "whom America gave to the world in her nonage."[158]

To royalty, Hawthorne shared, for the most part, the old Revolutionary antipathy. More than one passage in the journals recalls the strident tone of Paine: "These kings thrust themselves impertinently forward, by bust, statue, and picture, on all occasions; and it is not wise in them to show their shallow foreheads among men of mind."[159] Hawthorne was not ignorant, to be sure, of the great argument for royalty, and he presented that argument, fairly and persuasively, through an English character in *Doctor Grimshawe's Secret,* who reasoned as follows with his American guest:

How can you feel a heart's love for a mere political arrangement like your Union? How can you be loyal, where personal attachment—the lofty and noble and unselfish attachment of a subject to his prince—is out of the question? Where your sovereign is felt to be a mere man like yourselves, whose petty struggles, whose ambition—mean before it grew to be audacious—you have watched, and know him to be just the same now as yesterday, and that tomorrow he will be walking unhonored amongst you again? Your system is too bare and meagre for human nature to love, or to endure it long. These stately decrees of society, that have so strong a hold upon us in England, are not to be done away with so lightly as you think.[160]

Good reasons these, and not without their appeal to Hawthorne. But good reasons must, of force, give place to better; and the reply of Redclyffe, the young American in the story, may fairly be taken as presenting Hawthorne's own convictions:

I do aver that I love my country, that I am proud of its institutions, that I have a feeling unknown, probably, to any but a republican, but which is the proudest thing in me, that there is no man above me,—for my ruler is only myself, in the person of another, whose office I impose upon him,—nor any below me. If you would understand me, I would tell you of the shame I felt when first, on setting foot in this country, I heard a man speaking of his birth as giving him privileges; saw him looking down on laboring men, as of an inferior race. And what I can never understand, is the pride which you positively seem to feel in having men and classes of men above you, born to privileges which you can never hope to share. It may be a thing to be endured, but surely not one to be absolutely proud of. And yet an Englishman is so.[161]

England, Hawthorne believed, was already decadent. Of Westminster Hall he wrote in the journal:

I cannot help imagining that this rich and noble edifice has more to do with the past than with the future; that it is the glory of a declining empire; and that the perfect bloom of this great stone flower, growing out of the institutions of England, forebodes that they have nearly lived out their life. It sums up all. Its beauty and magnificence are made out of ideas that are gone by.[162]

A less attractive symbol of decadence was a pervasive "bad smell," which his American nostrils detected in old towns and in old churches: "I never smelt it before crossing the Atlantic. It is the odor of an old system of life; the scent of the pine-forests is still too recent with us for it to be known in America."[163] If England was to survive, England would have to be refashioned after the American pattern. "I have had a feeling of coming change," Redclyffe said to his English friend, "among all that you look upon as so permanent, so everlasting; and though your thoughts dwell fondly on things as they are and have been, there is a deep destruction somewhere in this country, that is inevitably impelling it in the path of my own."[164]

Thus Hawthorne in passage after passage compared the manners and institutions of England and America with care and patience and as much open-mindedness as he could muster, and this comparative study confirmed and even strengthened his confidence in the present and future greatness of America. The American lot, the young woman in *The Ancestral Footstep* said to the hesitant American, "is such a lot as the world has never yet seen, and . . . the faults, the weaknesses, the errors, of your countrymen will vanish away like morning mists before the rising sun."[165] Such was Hawthorne's belief and affirmation.

If the evidence thus far presented conveys the impression that Hawthorne in England was little more than a patriotic American, with an unconquerable bias for American ways and American institutions, many passages in the journals and other writings give a very different impression, namely, that in the depth of his nature, he felt drawn to England by certain powerful, attractive forces. For Hawthorne was not only the patriotic American tourist; he was also the literary artist whose imagination had been nourished on English literature; and more strongly perhaps than any other American writer of his generation he felt the many attractions of England.

In general, nature in England was a joy and a delight. There are, it is true, passages of disparagement. The diminutiveness of English lakes and rivers seemed almost ludicrous to this American, whose country possessed these objects on a much ampler scale. Of Rydal Lake he wrote: "It certainly did look very small; and I said, in my American scorn, that I could carry it away bodily in a porringer."[166] And upon being told that a weed of American origin, brought to England with imported timber, was about to choke the English rivers, he exclaimed: "I wonder it does not try its obstructive powers upon the Merrimack, the Connecticut, or the Hudson —not to speak of the St. Lawrence or the Mississippi!"[167] But such passages express only a mood, and by no means an habitual one. In the journal kept in the Lake Country, he wrote more often in the following vein: "I question whether any part of the world looks so beautiful as England —this part of England, at least—on a fine summer morning."[168] Wordsworth's house he found "so delightfully situated, so secluded, so hedged about with shrubbery and adorned with flowers, so ivy-grown on one side, so beautified with many years of the personal care of him who lived in it and loved it—that it seemed the very place for a poet's residence."[169] Of a scene near Lodore, he observed that it "might be characterized—without lauding it a great deal too much—as stern grandeur with an embroidery of rich beauty."[170] He admitted "the great superiority of these mountains over those of New England" in "variety and definiteness of shape,"[171] though the Notch of the White Mountains seemed, in recollection, "more wonderful and richly picturesque."[172]

If America might rival, and even surpass, England in scenes of grandeur —in rivers, lakes, and mountains—the English domesticated landscape (described best, Hawthorne thought, in the poetry of Tennyson) assuredly possessed a unique beauty. In his rural walks, he enjoyed without reservation "the rich verdure of the fields," "the stately wayside trees and carefully kept plantations of wood," "the old and high cultivation that has humanized the very sods by mingling so much of man's toil and care among them."[173] The objects of the landscape, he discovered, "take hold of the observer by numberless minute tendrils":[174] a tree covered with moss and ivy; a hedge, filled with wild flowers—the very flowers, some of them, which the original settlers brought to New England and which their descendants have faithfully cultivated; a stone fence, to which was imparted "a charm of divine gracefulness" by its covering of vegetation;[175] a footpath, by means of which one could wander "from stile to stile, along hedges, and across broad fields, and through wooded parks" "to little hamlets of thatched cottages, ancient, solitary farm-houses, picturesque old mills, streamlets, pools, and all those quiet, secret, unexpected, yet strangely familiar features of English scenery."[176] The English landscape is the subject of scores of passages remarkable for their sensitivity and their descriptive art.

Another strong attraction for Hawthorne in England consisted of the architectural monuments and the works of art which he saw there. In these matters he was by no means a connoisseur or critic; but he visited, and wrote many descriptions, at once meticulous and appreciative, of abbeys and cathedrals, and he studied patiently a number of pictures in the galleries and exhibition-rooms. In his understanding of painting, he never progressed, perhaps, beyond the stage of novice, though he read Ruskin,[177] and, after having spent several days at the Manchester Exhibition, he could record a growing appreciation: ". . . pictures are certainly quite other things to me, now, from what they were at my first visit; it seems even as if there were a sort of illumination within them that makes me see them more distinctly."[178] His enjoyment of cathedrals and abbeys, however, did not need to be laboriously acquired; it was natural and instinctive. For Hawthorne was, in some ways, a child of the romantic revival (which was, in part, a mediaeval revival), and a life-long reader and admirer of Walter Scott. Despite his Puritan inheritance, therefore, he was able to surrender to the beauty and the spiritual influences of these monuments of old Catholic times.

He described the abbeys in characteristically romantic fashion. "Neglect," he observed, "wildness, crumbling walls, the climbing and conquering ivy, masses of stone lying where they fell, trees of old date growing where the pillars of the aisles used to stand; these are the best points of ruined Abbeys."[179] He pronounced Melrose Abbey "a very satisfactory ruin,"[180] and he found Dryburgh Abbey in "a delightful state of decay," yet "not so far gone but that we had hints of its former grandeur, in the columns and broken arches."[181] Indeed, from the romantic point of view, the abbeys were more inspiring in their present state than they could possibly have been in their original integrity. Of the ruins of Furness Abbey he wrote: "They suggest a greater majesty and beauty than any human work can show—the crumbling traces of the half-obliterated design producing somewhat of the effect of the first idea of anything admirable, when it dawns upon the mind of an artist or a poet—an idea, which, do what he may, he is sure to fall short of."[182]

Even more completely, Hawthorne came under the spell of England's great cathedrals. A Gothic cathedral seemed to him, he said in a fine passage on the subject,

. . . so vast, so intricate, and so profoundly simple, with such strange, delightful recesses in its grand figure, so difficult to comprehend within one idea, and yet all so consonant that it ultimately draws the beholder and his universe into its harmony. It is the only thing in the world that is vast enough and rich enough.[183]

Lincoln Cathedral affected him so powerfully that he felt its influence as a "thraldom":

... as the weather was very unpropitious, and it sprinkled a little now and then, I would gladly have felt myself released from further thraldom to the Cathedral. But it had taken possession of me, and would not let me be at rest; so at length I found myself compelled to climb the hill again between daylight and dusk.[184]

Hawthorne felt strongly also the attraction of scenes of historical and literary associations. A special, and quite understandable, interest in the Cromwellian period, for example, is revealed by many references, of which the following passage is representative:

There are three or four towers and other prominent points, in the course of the circuit [of the wall at Chester]; the most interesting being one from the top of which King Charles the First is said to have seen the rout of his army, by the Parliamentarians.[185]

Aside from this Puritan preference, however, Hawthorne's approach to English history would seem to have been largely through English historical literature, notably, the historical plays of Shakespeare and the novels of Scott. The journals abundantly attest his familiarity with scenes portrayed by these writers, and, in general, his imaginative interest in the pageantry and wars of feudal times.

Among the places of literary associations, he was drawn first of all, of course, to Stratford, though he found the experience disappointing: "I felt no emotion whatever in Shakespeare's house," he frankly confessed; "not the slightest—nor any quickening of the imagination."[186] "The Shakespeare whom I met there . . . had not his laurels on."[187] In visiting the scenes of Scott's novels and poems, he experienced the pleasure of recognition; but Abbotsford was almost as disappointing in its evocations as Stratford:

On the whole, there is no simple and great impression left by Abbotsford; and I felt angry and dissatisfied with myself for not feeling something which I did not and could not feel. But it is just like going to a museum, if you look into particulars; and one learns from it, too, that Scott could not have been really a wise man, nor an earnest one, nor one that grasped the truth of life;— he did but play, and the play grew very sad towards its close. In a certain way, however, I understand his romances the better for having seen his house; and his house the better, for having read his romances. They throw light on one another.[188]

The pilgrimage to the haunts of Burns was much more satisfying:

We shall appreciate him better as a poet, hereafter; for there is no writer whose life, as a man, has so much to do with his fame, and throws such a necessary light upon whatever he has produced. Henceforth, there will be a personal warmth for us in everything that he wrote; and, like his countrymen, we shall know him in a kind of personal way, as if we had shaken hands with him, and felt the thrill of his actual voice.[189]

Although Shakespeare, Scott, and Burns, and the places associated with them, received fuller treatment in the journals, many other writers were mentioned, in one connection or another, and were treated with varying degrees of enthusiasm. The account of the visit to Leigh Hunt reveals a warm personal admiration;[190] the passage on Wordsworth's cottage was written with a mild, though genuine, sympathy;[191] the description of Newstead Abbey reflects primarily the curiosity of the writer, and in only a limited degree a romantic interest.[192]

Hawthorne's admiration for the great writers of the Eighteenth Century comes out repeatedly in the journals. After one of his many excursions among the streets of London, he wrote: "I think what interests me most here is the London of the writers of the Queen Anne age—whatever Pope, the Spectator, De Foe, and down as late as Johnson and Goldsmith have mentioned."[193] He noted, with a heightened interest, the houses where Addison had lived in Lichfield and London,[194] the cloisters where he had meditatively composed "one of his most beautiful pieces in the Spectator,"[195] the essay on Westminster Abbey, and the tombstone in the Abbey inscribed with Tickell's lines to his memory.[196] The kitchen at Stanton Harcourt seemed as familiar as his grandmother's, for he remembered Pope's description of it—"one of the most admirable pieces of description in the language"[197]—in a letter to the Duke of Buckingham. For Dr. Johnson, his admiration was as great, and more affectionate. He recorded having seen Dr. Johnson's pencil-case, appropriately stalwart,[198] and having dined at the Mitre Tavern, "in memory of Johnson and Boswell."[199] He climbed "Dr. Johnson's Staircase" in the Temple, "passing my hand over a heavy, ancient-looking, oaken balustrade, on which, no doubt, Johnson's hand had often rested."[200] He journeyed to Lichfield "partly to see its beautiful cathedral, and still more . . . because it was the birthplace of Dr. Johnson."[201] From Lichfield he went on to Uttoxeter ("one of the few purely sentimental pilgrimages that I ever undertook")[202] to visit the scene of Dr. Johnson's penance, the story of which he invested with a tender and poignant beauty.[203]

So high, indeed, was Hawthorne's regard for the Eighteenth Century (for the three writers already mentioned, and for others also, notably Swift) that it no doubt equalled, and possibly exceeded, his regard for any other period, taken as a whole, in English literature. The fact is of some importance for Hawthorne and his writings. He had a much sounder appreciation of the great English Augustans than one usually meets with in his century, either in America or in England. At a time when it was almost the universal fashion to disparage those literary values of which Dr. Johnson was the completest epitome, Hawthorne could commend "London" and "The Vanity of Human Wishes" for their "stern and masculine" qualities and Dr. Johnson's morality as "wholesome food even now."[204] Moreover, the influence of the Augustans (and a salutary influence it was) is seen everywhere in his writings: his prose was firm-textured like theirs; he had their sense of structure, and their penchant for criticism and satire.

The sensuous enjoyment of English landscape, the appreciation, aesthetic and moral, of English abbeys and cathedrals, the interested, and often heart-warming recognition of the relics and mementos of English writers whose works had been familiar to him from childhood—these were some of the ties which bound Hawthorne to England. There remains to be considered another tie, less tangible but stronger even than any of these, namely, the almost mystic feeling of inheritance: England was, above all else, our old home.

The hereditary sense was preternaturally strong in Hawthorne. So deeply did he feel his own inheritance from his early New England ancestors, William Hathorne, the persecutor of the Quakers, and John Hathorne, the witch-judge, that, in *The Scarlet Letter,* he had taken shame upon himself for their sakes, and had prayed that any curse incurred by them might be henceforth removed.[205] The first American ancestor, to whom Hawthorne felt so closely bound, had grown to maturity in England before settling in Massachusetts, and *his* ancestors, for unnumbered generations, had lived in England before him. "Of all things," Hawthorne wrote to Fields, "I should like to find a gravestone in one of these old churchyards, with my own name upon it."[206] Hawthorne sometimes felt that he was himself William Hathorne, living again:

My ancestor left England in 1635. I return in 1853. I sometimes feel as if I myself had been absent these two hundred and eighteen years—leaving England just emerging from the feudal system, and finding it on the verge of Republicanism. It brings the two far separated points of time very closely together, to view the matter thus.[207]

While visiting English scenes, he often had "a singular sense of having been there before":

Of course [he wrote in *Our Old Home*] the explanation of the mystery was that history, poetry, and fiction, books of travel, and the talk of tourists, had given me pretty accurate preconceptions of the common objects of English scenery, and these, being long ago vivified by a youthful fancy, had insensibly taken their places among the images of things actually seen. Yet the illusion was often so powerful, that I almost doubted whether such airy remembrances might not be a sort of innate idea, the print of a recollection in some ancestral mind, transmitted, with fainter and fainter impress through several descents, to my own.[208]

The same thought was expressed in the journal, but without nearly so strong an implication of its illusoriness:

I had a feeling as if I had seen this old church before, and dimly remembered; so well did it correspond with my idea, from much reading about them, of what English rural churches are. Or perhaps the image of them, impressed into the minds of my long-ago forefathers, was so deep that I have inherited it; and it answers to the reality.[209]

In his English romances, Hawthorne gave this hereditary feeling to his central character, the American who returned to England. Middleton, in *The Ancestral Footstep*, "felt as if he were the original emigrant who, long resident on a foreign shore, had now returned, with a heart brimful of tenderness, to revisit the scenes of his youth."[210] And likewise, in *Doctor Grimshawe's Secret*, Redclyffe's visit to Braithwaite Hall, the residence of his English ancestors, "seemed to him like a coming home after an absence of centuries."[211]

But while rejecting as quite irrational the strange feeling that he was the original emigrant who had returned to claim his own, Hawthorne was aware that in a certain large sense England was a common American inheritance—at least, that historical portion of England which antedated the English settlements in America. "An American," he declared, "has a right to be proud of Westminster Abbey; for most of the men who sleep in it are our great men, as well as theirs."[212] "What a wonderful land!" he wrote near the end of his four years in England; "It is our forefathers' land; our land; for I will not give up such a precious inheritance."[213] From this point of view, the "titles manifold" of Wordsworth's sonnet belong to Americans as well as to Englishmen

> who speak the tongue
> That Shakespeare spake; the faith and morals hold
> Which Milton held.

In a fine and revealing passage in *Dr. Grimshawe's Secret,* Hawthorne described Redclyffe's feeling for England:

... he began to feel the deep yearning which a sensitive American—his mind full of English thoughts, his imagination of English poetry, his heart of English character and sentiment—cannot fail to be influenced by,—the yearning of the blood within his veins for that from which it has been estranged; the half-fanciful regret that he should ever have been separated from these woods, these fields, these natural features of scenery, to which his nature was moulded, from the men who are still so like himself, from these habits of life and thought which (though he may not have known them for two centuries) he still perceives to have remained in some mysterious way latent in the depths of his character, and soon to be reassumed, not as a foreigner would do it, but like habits native to him, and only suspended for a season. This had been Redclyffe's state of feeling ever since he landed in England, and every day seemed to make him more at home; so that it seemed as if he were gradually awakening to a former reality.[214]

The passage describes Hawthorne's own experience.

The subject of England and America occupied a large place in Hawthorne's thinking and writing during the last eleven years of his life. While in England, he recorded his observations and comparisons voluminously in his journals; and later, with the journals before him, he wrote a rich comparative study in *Our Old Home,* and elaborated the theme of the American in England in two unfinished romances. I have attempted to present some of the facets of the subject as they appear in these writings.

England both attracted and repelled: attracted (it may not be too misleading to say) the imaginative writer, and repelled the American patriot; for Hawthorne was, somewhat diversely, both of these. He was, as we have seen, sensitively responsive to the charms of England's storied and poetical associations; he was also loyal to America's institutions, and, on occasion, indignant toward America's detractors. England, therefore, was an object at once of love and of resentment. The psychological result for Hawthorne was an acute mental conflict, for

> ... to be wroth with one we love
> Doth work like madness in the brain.

Matthew Arnold said truly that *Our Old Home* was "the work of a man chagrined."[215] The chagrin, and the mental conflict which underlay it, contributed not a little to the unhappiness of Hawthorne's last years.

NOTES

1. P. *456*.
2. May 23, 1856. (Quotations from Hawthorne's letters to Ticknor are taken from *Letters of Hawthorne to William D. Ticknor,* Newark, 1910.)
3. June 20, 1856.
4. June 5, 1857.
5. Rose Hawthorne Lathrop, *Memories of Hawthorne,* Boston and New York, 1897, p. 336.
6. Julian Hawthorne, *Nathaniel Hawthorne and his Wife,* Boston, 1885, II, 168-9.
7. A good many hitherto unpublished passages were printed in Julian Hawthorne, *Hawthorne and his Wife,* II, *passim.*
8. I, 412.
9. See *The American Notebooks by Nathaniel Hawthorne,* ed. Randall Stewart, New Haven, 1932, xiii-xxi.
10. For the revisions in this list, see pp. *36* (I, 464), *43* (I, 476), *186* (II, 62), *187* (II, 65), *231* (II, 128), *267* (II, 173), *312* (II, 227), *374* (II, 317), *376* (II, 319), *44* (I, 477), *105* (I, 561), *166* (II, 26), *459* (II, 418), *458* (II, 415), *454* (II, 407).
The reference preceding the parentheses is to the present text, and the reference within the parentheses is to *Passages from the English Note-Books.* The references follow the sequence of the items in the list.
11. See pp. *26* (I, 450), *337* (II, 260), *336* (II, 259), *337* (II, 262), *361* (II, 304), *550* (II, 526), *561* (II, 542), *35* (I, 462), *312* (II, 226), *328* (II, 245), *276* (II, 185).
12. See pp. *77* (I, 518), *192* (II, 71), *209* (II, 99), *238* (II, 137).
13. See pp. *297* (II, 212), *413* (II, 359), *438* (II, 381), *37* (I, 466), *239* (II, 138), *249* (II, 155), *556* (II, 533).
14. See pp. *4* (I, 417), *252* (II, 158).
15. See pp. *21* (I, 441), *163* (II, 21), *245* (II, 148), *46,* I, 478).
16. See pp. *616* (II, 595).
17. See pp. *558* (II, 538).
18. See pp. *18* (I, 437), *602* (II, 575), *563* (II, 543), *564* (II, 545), *13* (I, 429), *181* (II, 54), *413* (II, 358), *184* (II, 59), *198* (II, 81), *198* (II, 81), *176* (II, 45), *216* (II, 110), *200* (II, 85), *9* (I, 424), *537* (II, 503), *258* (II, 164), *293* (II, 206), *18* (I, 436), *12* (I, 429), *78* (I, 521), *11* (I, 427).
19. See pp. *243* (II, 145).
20. See pp. *34* (I, 461).
21. See pp. *186* (II, 62), *188* (II, 66), *205* (II, 94), *450* (II, 402), *452* (II, 404), *608* (II, 582).
22. See pp. *591* (II, 560).
23. See pp. *546-7* (II, 520).
24. *Our Old Home,* p. 15.
25. February 11, 1860. The letter is in the Huntington Library.
26. See, as examples, pp. *271* (II, 179), *232* (II, 129).
27. See pp. *273-7* (II, 184-5), and *Our Old Home,* 344-59.
28. See pp. *61* (I, 498).
29. See pp. *293* (II, 206).
30. See pp. *556* (II, 535).
31. See pp. *116* (I, 576).
32. See pp. *209* (II, 99).
33. See pp. *8* (I, 421).
34. See pp. *450* (II, 401).
35. See pp. *353* (II, 289).
36. See pp. *189* (II, 68).
37. See pp. *438* (II, 380).
38. See pp. *237* (II, 134).
39. See pp. *400-1* (II, 347).
40. See pp. *189* (II, 68).
41. See pp. *53* (I, 488).
42. See pp. *55* (I, 490).
43. See pp. *89* (I, 538).
44. See pp. *297* (II, 212).
45. See pp. *457* (II, 413).
46. See pp. *385* (II, 334).
47. See pp. *421* (II, 361).
48. See pp. *325* (II, 242).
49. See pp. *349* (II, 283).
50. See pp. *52-3* (I, 487).
51. See pp. *55-6* (I, 490).
52. See pp. *62* (I, 498).
53. See pp. *222-3* (II, 115).
54. See pp. *393* (II, 338).
55. See pp. *351* (II, 286).
56. See pp. *197* (II, 80).
57. See pp. *553* (II, 530).
58. See pp. *382* (II, 328).

59. See pp. *35* (I, 464).
60. See pp. *77* (I, 518).
61. See pp. *221* (II, 113).
62. See pp. *234* (II, 131).
63. See pp. *100* (I, 553).
64. See pp. *280* (II, 190).
65. See pp. *553-4* (II, 530).
66. See pp. *432-3* (II, 374).
67. See pp. *605-6* (II, 578).
68. See pp. *321* (II, 238).
69. See pp. *30* (I, 456), *286* (II, 198), *225* (II, 119).
70. See pp. 66-8.
71. "On a Certain Condescension in Foreigners," *The Works of James Russell Lowell,* Standard Library Edition, Boston and New York, 1890, III, 231. For examples of the journalistic "spasm" alluded to by Lowell, see the reviews of *Our Old Home* in *The Illustrated London News,* Oct. 3, 1863, and in *Punch,* Oct. 17, 1863. The following passage from the review in *Punch* will strike the modern reader as extraordinary, even for an age when reviewers could be as "personal" as they pleased:

"Not content with smashing up our "male population in the most everlasting "manner, you make the most savage on- "slaught upon our women. This will be "doubly pleasant to your delicate-minded "and chivalrous Countrymen. And we "are the more inclined to give you credit "here, because you do not write of ladies "whom you have seen at a distance, "or in their carriages, or from the point "of view of a shy and awkward man who "skulks away at the rustle of a crinoline, "and hides himself among the ineligibles "at the ball-room door. Everybody knows "that you have had ample opportunity of "cultivating ladies' society, and have "availed yourself of that opportunity to "the utmost. Everybody in the world "knows that the gifted American Consul "at Liverpool is an idolizer of the ladies, "and is one of the most ready, fluent, ac- "complished talkers of lady-talk that ever "fascinated a sofa-full of smiling beau- "ties. His gay and airy entrance into a "drawing-room, his pleasant assurance "and graceful courtesy, his evident revel "in the refined atmosphere of perfume "and *persiflage,* are proverbial, and there- "fore he is thoroughly acquainted with "the nature and habits of English women. "Consequently his tribute has a value "which would not appertain to the criti- "cisms of a sheepish person, either so in- "spired with a sense of his own infinite su- "periority, or so operated on by a plebeian "*mauvaise honte,* that he edges away from "a lady, flounders and talks nonsense "when compelled to answer her, and es- "capes with a red face, like a clumsy "hobbadehoy, the moment a pause allows "him to do so. No, this is the testimony "of the lady-killer, the sparkling yet "tender Liverpool Lovelace, Nathaniel "Hawthorne, to the merits of our English "women."

For further information on the English reception of *Our Old Home,* see Bertha Faust, *Hawthorne's Contemporaneous Reputation,* Philadelphia, 1939, pp. 132-134.

72. See pp. *27-8* (I, 452), *88-9* (I, 537).
73. See pp. *62* (I, 499), *197* (II, 80), *87* (I, 536).
74. See pp. *227* (II, 123), *216* (II, 110).
75. See pp. *198* (II, 81).
76. See pp. *185* (II, 61-2), *345* (II, 277).
77. See pp. *297* (II, 212).
78. See pp. *440* (II, 384).
79. See pp. *431* (II, 374).
80. See the following chapter.
81. See pp. *374* (II, 317).
82. See pp. *604* (II, 578).
83. See pp. *239* (II, 138).
84. See pp. *241* (II, 142).
85. See pp. *399* (II, 346).
86. See pp. *537* (II, 502).
87. See pp. *375* (II, 317).
88. See pp. *445* (II, 391), *591* (II, 560).
89. See pp. *83* (I, 530), *86* (I, 534), *87* (I, 536), *205* (II, 92), *206* (II, 95), *223* (II, 116), *232* (II, 129), *248* (II, 154), *252* (II, 158).
90. See pp. *401* (II, 348).
91. See pp. *413* (II, 357).
92. See pp. *345* (II, 277).
93. See pp. *90* (I, 539).
94. For references to smoking in addition to those included in note 89, see pp. *208* (II, 97), *218* (II, 111), *236* (II, 133), *243* (II, 146), *244* (II, 147).

95. See pp. *432* (II, 374).
96. See pp. *554* (II, 531).
97. *Journals of Ralph Waldo Emerson*, Boston and New York, 1912, VII, 447.
98. See pp. *31-2* (I, 456-7).
99. See pp. *227*ff. (II, 122ff.).
100. See pp. *377* (II, 321).
101. See pp. *375* (II, 317).
102. See pp. *61* (I, 498).
103. See pp. *42* (I, 474).
104. See pp. *321* (II, 239).
105. See pp. *184-5* (II, 60), *210* (II, 101).
106. See pp. *29* (I, 453).
107. See pp. *242* (II, 143).
108. See pp. *401* (II, 348).
109. See pp. *37-8* (I, 466).
110. See pp. *101* (I, 555).
111. See pp. *615* (II, 594).
112. See pp. *278* (II, 185).
113. See pp. *97* (I, 548).
114. In adapting material from the English journals in *Our Old Home*, Hawthorne occasionally, though by no means regularly, made verbal alterations similar to Mrs. Hawthorne's refinements. I have noticed the following instances:
smelling of tobacco smoke (p. *474*): scented with (*Our Old Home*, p. 187)
stink (p. *500*): odor (*Our Old Home*, p. 231)
vomited (p. *503*): belched (*Our Old Home*, p. 238)
infernally (p. *500*): intolerably (*Our Old Home*, p. 233)
louse (p. *502*): unmentionable parasite (*Our Old Home*, p. 237)
For similar revisions by Hawthorne of his earlier journals, see *The American Notebooks by Nathaniel Hawthorne*, pp. xli-xlii.
115. p. *83*.
116. *Ibid.*, p. *33*.
117. *Ibid.*, p. *79*.
118. See p. *250*.
119. *Twice-Told Tales*, p. 31.
120. p. *17*.
121. pp. *91-2*.
122. See n. 365, p. *648*.
123. *Ibid.*, pp. *648-9*.
124. *Ibid.*, p. *649*.
125. p. *374*.
126. Issue of September 1, 1855. A casual reference in the journals (p. *158*) indicates Hawthorne's familiarity with *Punch*.
127. Issue of October 6, 1855.
128. "The American Misunderstanding," issue of June 28, 1856.
129. p. *197*.
130. p. *416*.
131. pp. *367*.
132. "Emerson," *Discourses in America*, London, 1912, pp. 173-4.
133. *Our Old Home*, p. 218.
134. For a treatment of the patriotic aspect of the English journals, see Randall Stewart, "Hawthorne in England: The Patriotic Motive in the Notebooks," *New England Quarterly*, VIII (March, 1935), 3-13.
135. p. *89*.
136. See W. D. Howells, *Literary Friends and Acquaintance*, New York and London, 1911, p. 53.
137. p. *197*.
138. p. *87*.
139. p. *255*.
140. p. *35-6*.
141. p. *224*.
142. p. *568*.
143. pp. *208-9*.
144. p. *208*.
145. *Our Old Home*, p. 153.
146. p. *257*.
147. p. *451*.
148. *Ibid.*
149. p. *37*. For evidence of Hawthorne's extensive reading in the Puritan sermons of New England, see "Books Read by Nathaniel Hawthorne, 1828-1850," *The Essex Institute Historical Collections*, LXVIII (January, 1932), 65-87.
150. p. *97*.
151. p. *163-4*.
152. pp. *457*.
153. p. *99*.
154. p. *409-10*.
155. p. *385*.
156. p. *410*.
157. *Our Old Home*, p. 212.
158. p. *612*.
159. p. *413*.
160. pp. *198-9*.
161. pp. *199-200*.
162. p. *246*.
163. p. *337*.
164. *Doctor Grimshawe's Secret*, p. 199.

165. p. 489. This passage was written presumably about 1858. Three years later, his faith was profoundly disturbed by the outbreak of the Civil War, the termination of which he did not live to see, and his fears for the future of his country are reflected in many passages in *Our Old Home* (1863). For a treatment of the effects of the Civil War upon Hawthorne, see Randall Stewart, "Hawthorne and the Civil War," *Studies in Philology*, XXXIV (January, 1937), 91-106.

166. p. *165*.
167. *Our Old Home*, p. 224.
168. p. *172*.
169. p. *166*.
170. p. *176*.
171. *Ibid.*
172. p. *173*.
173. *Our Old Home*, p. 113.
174. *Ibid.*, p. 115.
175. *Ibid.*, pp. 115-7.
176. *Ibid.*, pp. 68-9.
177. See n. 478, p. *654*.
178. p. *562*.
179. p. *448*.
180. p. *338*.
181. p. *340*.
182. p. *157*.
183. *Our Old Home*, p. 153.
184. *Ibid.*, p. 182.
185. p. *29*.

186. p. *132*.
187. *Our Old Home*, p. 123.
188. p. *343-4*.
189. *Our Old Home*, p. 253.
190. See pp. *254-6*.
191. See pp. *165-7*.
192. See pp. *486-91*.
193. p. *204*.
194. See pp. *151*, *282*.
195. p. *247*.
196. See p. *220*.
197. *Our Old Home*, p. 219.
198. See p. *101*.
199. p. *252*.
200. p. *293*.
201. *Our Old Home*, p. 149.
202. *Ibid.*, p. 162.
203. See n. 192, p. *636*.
204. *Our Old Home*, pp. 150-1.
205. p. 25.
206. James T. Fields, *Yesterdays with Authors*, Boston, 1882. p. 74.
207. p. *92*.
208. pp. 82-3.
209. p. *124*.
210. p. 493 (see also pp. 447, 510).
211. p. 273 (see also p. 278).
212. p. *213*.
213. p. *495*.
214. pp. 180-1.
215. "Emerson," *Discourses in America*, London, 1912, p. 173.

1853

Thursday, August 4th.

A MONTH, lacking two days, since we left America;—a fortnight, and some odd days, since we arrived in England. I began my services (such as they are) on Monday last, August 1st; and here I sit in my private room at the Consulate, while the Vice Consul and clerk are carrying on affairs in the outer office. Every morning, I find the entry thronged with the most rascally set of sailors that ever were seen—dirty, desperate, and altogether pirate-like in aspect. What the devil they want here, is beyond my present knowledge; but probably they have been shipwrecked, or otherwise thrown at large on the world, and wish for assistance in some shape. Daily, half a dozen or so of these rogues are distributed among the American vessels to be sent back to their native country;—or rather, to their adopted one; for not one in ten of them are really Americans, but outcasts of all the maritime nations on earth, in a uniform of dirty red-baize shirts.

[2] The pleasantest incident of the day, is when Mr. Pierce (the vice-consul or head-clerk) makes his appearance with the account books, containing the receipts and expenditures of the preceding day, and deposits on my desk a little rouleau of the Queen's coin, wrapt up in a piece of paper. This morning, there were eight sovereigns, four half-crowns, and a shilling—a pretty fair day's work, though not more than the average ought to be.

This forenoon, thus far, I have had two calls, not of business—one from an American captain, Foster and his son, a boy—another from Mr. H. A. Bright,[1] whom I met in America, and who has shown us great attention here. He has arranged for us to go [to] the Theatre with his family, this evening.

My office consists of two rooms in an edifice called Washington buildings, and so named from the circumstance of the consulate being located here. It is near the docks, and on the corner of Brunswick-street; and from my window, across the narrow street, I have a view of a tall, dismal, smoke-blackened, ugly brick ware-house, [3]—uglier than any building I ever saw in America; and from one or another of the various stories, bags of salt are often being raised or lowered, swinging and vibrating in the air. There is a continual rumble of heavy wheels, which makes conversation rather difficult, although I am gradually getting accustomed to it. My apartment (about twelve feet by fifteen, and of a good height) is hung with a map of the United States, and another of Europe; there is a hideous colored lithograph of General Taylor,[2] life-size, and one or two smaller engraved portraits; also three representations of American naval victories; a lithograph of the Tennessee State-house, and another of the Steamer Empire State. The mantel-piece is adorned with the American Eagle, painted on the wood; and on shelves there are a number of volumes, bound in sheepskin, of the laws of the United States and the Statutes at Large. Thus the consular office is a little patch of America, with English life encompassing it on all sides. One truly English object, however, is the Barometer hanging on the wall, and which, to-day, [4] for a wonder, points to Fair.[3] Since I have been in Liverpool, we have hardly had a day, until yesterday, without more or less of rain; and so cold and shivery that life was miserable. I am not warm enough, even now, but am gradually getting acclimated in that respect.

Just now, I have been fooled out of half-a-crown by a young woman, who represents herself as an American, and destitute—having come over to see an Uncle, whom she found dead, and she has no means of getting back again. Her accent is not that of an American; and her appearance is not particularly prepossessing, though not decidedly otherwise. She is decently dressed, and modest in deportment; but I do not quite trust her face. She has been separated from her husband, as I understand her, by course of law, and probably for infidelity; has had two children, both dead. What she war s is, to get back to America; and perhaps arrangements may be made with some shipmaster to take her as stewardess or in some subordinate capacity. My judgement on the whole is, that [5] she is an Englishwoman, married to, and separated from, an American husband,—of no very decided virtue, yet not abandoned. I might as well have kept my half-crown; and yet I might have bestowed it worse. She is very decent in her manner, cheerful—at least, not despondent.

At two °clock, I went over to the Royal Rock Hotel, about fifteen or twenty minutes steaming from this side of the river. We are going there on Saturday to reside for a while. Returning, I found that Mr Barber, from the American Chamber of Commerce, had called to arrange the time and place of a visit to the consul from a delegation of that body. Settled for tomorrow at 1/4 past one, at Mrs. Blodgett's.[4]

AUGUST 5TH.

AN invitation, this morning, from the Mayor to dine at the Town Hall on Friday next. Heaven knows, I had rather dine at the humblest eating-cellar in the city; inasmuch as a speech will doubtless be expected from me. However, things must be as they may.

[6] At 1/4 past one, I was duly on hand at Mrs. Blodgett's to receive the deputation from the Chamber of Commerce. They arrived pretty seasonably in two cabs, and were ushered into the drawing-room—seven or eight gentlemen, two or three of whom I had met before. Hereupon ensued a speech from Mr. Barber, the chairman of the delegation, short and sweet, alluding to my literary reputation, and other laudatory matters, and occupying only a minute or two. The speaker was rather embarrassed, which encouraged me a little; and yet I felt more diffidence on this occasion, than in my effort at Mr. Crittenden's[5] lunch—where, indeed, I was perfectly self-possessed. But here, there being less formality, and more of a conversational character in what was said,

my usual diffidence could not so well be kept down. However, I did not break down to an intolerable extent; and winding up my eloquence as briefly as possible, we sat down and had a social talk. Their whole stay could not have been much more than a quarter of an hour.[6]

[7] In the evening (about 8 °clock) I went to the Waterloo Hotel, whither my wife had preceded me; and we there found Grace Greenwood, who had come from London, to take passage in the America. Grace looked much older for the year's wear and tear through which she has passed; her health seems not good, nor her spirits buoyant. This, doubtless, is partly due to her regret in leaving England, where she has met with great kindness, and the manners and institutions of which she likes rather better, I suspect, than an American ought. She speaks rapturously of the English hospitality and warmth of heart. I likewise, have already experienced something of this, and apparently have a good deal more of it at my option. I wonder how far it is genuine, and in what degree it is better than the superficial good-feeling with which Yankees receive foreigners—a feeling not calculated for endurance, but a good deal like a brushwood fire. We shall see.

We staid an hour or more; and in the course of it, two or three visitors called in to see Grace, so [8] that her little parlor had as many as it could conveniently hold; while she sipped her tea and talked. She was expecting Miss Cushman, who did not, however, arrive. Mr. Montgomery Neale (an Englishman, of no very striking characteristics), Mr. Jeny, an American artist, seven years resident in Italy, and a Mrs. Eames—these, with ourselves, made up the party. I think Grace's manners are improved by her residence abroad—not so theatrical, more natural; she has had the nonsense somewhat taken out of her. She goes home, I fear, with a good deal of sadness at heart; after a year's comparative freedom, she goes back to take up again the weary burthen of her life—to break off, I am pretty sure, the engagement with Lippincott, after which it is hard to say what else she will be other than a hopeless old maid—with a very capacious heart cold and empty; a great yearning for admiration, never to be half-gratified.

AUGUST 6th.

THIS morning, at seven or little after, went to the Waterloo with Una and Julian, to see Grace, who was to go on board the steamer at nine. [9] After a little delay, we were admitted to her parlor. She certainly looked very sallow, and woefully mature—a little on the wrong side of ripeness. Grace Greenwood is an alias that turns her into ridicule. She kissed the children, and seemed very glad to see them; there is a good deal of good in this woman; but I doubt whether she be not deeply morbid, and incapable of ever being comfortable. If her residence in England were for life, instead of a holiday, she would not be contented here; her only happiness will be in little excursions from the real track of her life, during which she throws the burthen down. We talked about England and America; and while telling how much she loved this country, she drew her shawl about her shoulders, and looked shivery and miserable.[7] There ought to be an extraordinary warmth in the people's hearts, to make up for the chill of such a climate.

A call, this morning, at the consulate, from Doctor Bowring, who is British minister, or something of the kind, in China, and now absent on a twelve-month's leave. [10] The Doctor is a brisk man, with the address of a man of the world, free, quick to smile, of agreeable manners—not exactly a gentleman; and, indeed, what Englishman is? He has a good face, rather American than English in aspect, and does not look much above fifty, though he says he is between sixty and seventy. I should take him rather for an active lawyer or a man of business, than for a scholar and literary man. He talked in a lively way (saying nothing, however, at all remarkable) for ten or fifteen minutes, and then took his leave—offering me any service in his power in London, as, for instance, in introducing me to the Athenaeum Club.

AUGUST 8th.

DAY before yesterday, I escorted my family to Rock Ferry, two miles either up or down the Mersey (and I really don't know which) by steamer, which runs every half-hour. There are other steamers going continually to Birkenhead and other landings, and almost always a great many passengers on the transit. On this occasion the boat was crowded so as to afford scanty standing room; it being Saturday, and therefore a kind of gala-day. I think I have never seen a populace before coming to England; but this [11] crowd afforded a specimen of one, both male and female. The women were the most remarkable; there is almost always something ladylike and delicate about an American woman; but in these, though they seemed not disreputable, there was a coarseness, a freedom, an—I don't know what—that was purely English. In fact, men and women do things that would at least make them ridiculous in America; they are not afraid to enjoy themselves in their own way, and have no pseudo gentility to support. Some girls danced upon the crowded deck, to the miserable music of a little fragment of a band, which goes up and down the river on each trip of the boat. Just before the termination of the voyage, a man goes round with a bugle turned wide and upward, to receive the half ele[e]mosynary pence and half-pence of the passengers. I gave one of them, the other day, a silver four-pence; which fell into the vitals of the instrument, and compelled the man to take it to pieces. At Rock Ferry, there was a great throng, forming a scene not unlike one of our muster-days or Fourth of July; and there were bands of music, and [12] banners, with small processions after them; and there [was] a school of charity-children, I believe, enjoying a festival; and there was a club of respectable persons playing at bowls on the bowling-green of the hotel; and there were children infants riding on donkies, at a penny a ride, while their mothers walked alongside, to prevent a fall.

Yesterday (Sunday) while we were at dinner, Mr. Barber came in his carriage, to take us to his place at Poulton Hall. He had invited us to dine; but

I misunderstood him, and thought he only intended to give us a ride. Poulton Hall is about three miles from Rock Ferry; the road passing through some pleasant rural scenery, and one or two villages, with houses standing close together, and old stone or brick cottages, with thatched roofs, and now and then a better mansion, apart among trees. We passed an old church, with a tower and spire, and, half-way up, a patch of ivy, dark-green, and some yellow wall-flowers in full bloom, growing out of the crevices of the stone. Mr. Barber told us that the tower was formerly quite clothed with ivy, from bottom to top; but that it had [13] fallen away, for lack of the nourishment that it used to find in the lime, between the stones. This old church answered to my trans-atlantic fancies of England, better than anything I have yet seen. Not far from it was the Rectory, behind a deep grove of ancient trees; and there lives the Rector, enjoying a thousand pounds a year and his nothing-to-do, while a curate does the real duty on a stipend of eighty pounds.

We passed through a considerable extent of private road, and finally drove through a lawn, shaded with trees, and closely shaven, and reached the door of Poulton Hall. Part of the mansion is three or four hundred years old; another portion is some hundred and fifty; and still another has been built during the present generation, and looks much like a stone jail. The house is two stories high, with a sort of beetle-browed roof in front; it is not very striking, and does not look older than many wooden houses which I have seen in America. Within, there is [a] curious, old, stately staircase, with a twisted balustrade, much like that of the old Province House in Boston. The drawing-room looks like a very [14] handsome modern room, being beautifully painted, gilded, and paper-hung, with a white-marble fire-place, and rich furniture; so that the impression is of newness, not of age. It is the same with the dining-room, and all the rest of the interior, so far as I saw it.

Mr. Barber did not inherit this old hall, nor, indeed, is he now the owner, but only the tenant of it. He is a merchant of Liverpool, formerly resident in New Orleans—a bachelor, with two sisters keeping house for him. They are maturely ripe, not handsome or pretty, but seem to be sensible and good ladies. In the entrance hall, there was a stuffed fox with glass eyes, which I never should have doubted to be an actual, live fox, except for his keeping so quiet;—also, some grouse and other game. Mr. Barber seems to be a sports-man, and is setting out this week on an excursion to Scotland, moor-fowl shooting.

While the family and two or three guests went to dinner, we (wife, Una, Julian, and I) walked out to see the place. The gardener, an Irishman, showed us through the garden, which is large, and well cared-for. They certainly get everything from Nature which she can possibly be persuaded to give them, here [15] in England. There were peaches and pears (miserably enough they looked, too) growing against the high, brick, southern walls—the trunk and branches of the trees being spread out perfectly flat against the wall, very much like the skin of a dead animal nailed up to dry—and not a single branch protruding. Figs were growing in the same way. The brick-wall, very probably, was heated within, by means of pipes, in order to re-inforce the insufficient heat of the sun. It seems as if there must be something unreal and unsatisfactory in fruit that owes its existence to such artificial methods; it is, at best, no more than half natural.[8]

Squashes were growing under glass, poor things. There were immensely large gooseberries in the garden; and in this particular berry, I believe the English have decidedly the advantage over ourselves. The raspberries, too, were large and good. I espied one gigantic hog-weed in the garden; and really my heart warmed to it, being strongly reminded of the principal product of my own garden at Concord. After viewing the garden sufficiently, the gardener led us to other points of the estate, and we had [16] glimpses of a delightful valley, its sides shady with beautiful trees, and a rich grassy meadow at the bottom. By means of steam-engine, and subterranean pipes, and hydrants, the liquid manure from the barn yard is distributed wherever it is wanted, over the estate—being spouted in rich and filthy showers from the hydrants. Under this influence, the meadow at the bottom of the valley had already been made to produce three crops of grass, during the present season, and would produce another. By the by, manure is such an essential article here, that I smell it continually in walking past the fields, although there be none in sight.

The lawn around Poulton Hall, like thousands of other lawns in England, is very beautiful, but requires great care to keep it so, being shorn every three or four days. No other country will ever have this charm, nor the charm of lovely verdure, which almost makes up for the absence of sunshine; without the constant rain and shadow which strikes us [as] so dismal, these lawns would be as brown as an Autumn leaf. I have not, thus far, found any such magnificent trees as I expected. Mr. Barber told [17] me that three oaks, standing in a row on his lawn, were the largest in the county; they were very good trees, to be sure, and perhaps four feet through the trunk near the ground, but with no very noble spread of foliage. In Concord, there are, if not oaks, yet certainly elms, a great deal more stately and beautiful. But, on the whole, this lawn, and the old hall in the midst of it, went a good way towards realizing some of my fancies of English life.

By-and-by, a footman, looking very quaint and queer in his livery-coat, drab breeches, and white stockings, came to invite me to the table; where I found Mr. Barber, and his sisters and guests, sitting at the fruit and wine. There was port, sherry, madeira, and one bottle of claret, all very good; but they addict themselves, here, to much heavier wines than we now drink in America. After a tolerably long session, we went to the tea-room, where I drank some coffee; and about the edge of dusk, the carriage came to the door to take us home. Mr. Barber and his sisters have shown us genuine kindness; and they give us a hearty invita[18]tion to come and ramble over the house, whenever we please, during their absence in Scotland. They say that there are many legends and ghost-stories connected with the house; and there is an attic-chamber, with a sky light, which is called the Martyr's chamber, from the fact of its having in old times been tenanted by a lady, who was imprisoned there and persecuted to death for her religion. There is an old black-letter library in the house; but the room containing it is shut, barred, and padlocked—the owner of the house refusing to let it be opened, lest some of the books should be stolen. Meanwhile the rats are devouring them, and the damps destroying them.

AUGUST 9th.

A PRETTY comfortable day, as to warmth; and I believe there is sunshine overhead; but a cloud, composed of fog and coal-smoke, envelopes Liverpool. At Rock Ferry, when I left it at 1/2 past nine, there was promise of a cheerful day. A good many gentlemen (or, rather, respectable business people) came in the steamer; and it is not unpleasant, on these fine mornings, to take the breezy atmosphere of the river. The [19] huge steamer Great Britain, bound for Australia, lies right off the Rock Ferry landing; and at a little distance, too, are two old hulks of ships of war, dismantled, roofed over, and anchored in the river, formerly for quarantine purposes, but now used chiefly or solely as homes for old seamen, whose light labor it is to take care of these condemned ships. There are a great many steamers, plying up and down the river, to various landings in the vicinity; and a good many steam tugs; also, many boats, most of which have dark red or tan-colored sails, being oiled to resist the wet; also, here and there a yacht or pleasure boat; also, a few ships riding stately at their anchors, and probably on the point of sailing. The river, however, is by no means crowded; because the immense multitude of ships are ensconced in the docks; where their masts make an intricate forest for miles up and down the Liverpool shore. The small black steamers, whizzing industriously along, and many of them crowded with passengers, make up the chief life of the scene. The Mer[20]sey has the color of a mud-puddle; and no atmospheric effect, so far as I have seen, ever gives it a more agreeable tinge.

Visiters, to-day, thus far, have been H. A. Bright, with whom I have arranged to dine with us at Rock Ferry, and then to take us on board the Great Britain, of which his father is part owner; secondly, Monsieur Hitier, the French Consul, who can speak hardly any English, and who smells more powerfully of cigar smoke than any man I ever encountered; a polite, gray-haired, red-nosed gentleman, very courteous and formal. Heaven keep him from me!

At one °clock, or thereabouts, I walked out into the city, down through Lord Street, Church Street, drank a glass of porter, and back to the Consulate through various untraceable crookednesses. Coming to Chapel-street, I crossed the church-yard of the old church of St Nicholas. This is, I suppose, much the oldest sacred site in Liverpool; a church having stood here ever since the Conquest; though probably there is little or nothing of the old edifice in the present one. Either the whole of the edifice—or else the steeple, [21] being thereto shaken by a chime of bells—or perhaps both, at different times—has tumbled down; but the present church is what we Americans should call venerable. When the first church was built, and long afterwards, it must have stood on the grassy verge of the Mersey; but now there are pavements, and warehouses, and the thronged Prince's and George's Docks, between it and the river; and all around it is the very busiest bustle of commerce, rumbling wheels, hurrying men, porter-shops—everything that pertains to the grossest and most practical life. And, notwithstanding, there is the broad church-yard, extending on three sides of it, just as it used to a thousand years ago. It is absolutely paved from border to border with flat tombstones, on a level with the soil and with each other, so that it is one floor of stone over the whole space, with grass here and there sprouting between the crevices. All these stones, no doubt, had formerly inscriptions; but as many people continually pass in various directions across the church-yard, and as the tomb-stones are not of a [22] very hard material, the records on many of them are effaced. I saw none very old;—a quarter of a century is sufficient to obliterate the letters, and make all smooth, when the direct pathway from gate to gate lies over the stones. The climate, and casual footsteps, rub out any inscription in less than a hundred years. Some of the monuments are cracked. On many is merely cut "The burial-place of" so and so.—on others, there is a long list of half-readable names;—on some few, a laudatory epitaph, which, however, it were far too tedious to pick the meaning out of. But it really is interesting and suggestive, to think of this old church, first built when Liverpool was a small village, and remaining there, with its successive dead of ten centuries around it, now that the greatest commercial city of the world has its busiest centre there. I suppose people still continue to be buried in this cemetery. The greatest upholders of burials in cities are those whose progenitors have been deposited around or within the city-churches. If this spacious church-yard stood in a similar position in one of our American cities, I rather suspect that, long ere [23] now, it would have run the risk of being laid out in building lots and covered with warehouses; and if the church itself escaped—but it would not escape, longer than till its disrepair afforded excuse for tearing it down. And why should it?—when its purposes might be better served in another spot.

M. Hitier remarked—"I understand English with my eyes, but not with my ears"—he could read it, but not comprehend it easily when spoken. The same is true of my French.

We went on board the Great Britain before dinner, between five and six °clock;—a great affair, as to convenient arrangement and adaptation, but giving me a strong impression of the tedium and misery of the long voyage to Australia. By way of amusement, she takes over £50 worth of playing cards, at 2s. per pack, for the use of passengers. Also, a small, well-selected library. After a considerable time spent on board, we returned to the hotel, and dined; and Mr. Bright took his leave at nine °clock. I then went into the tap-room of the hotel, a large, stone-paved room, with pine tables and long wood[24]en benches, and at one end a coal-fire burning, with a kettle of hot-water over it—a pot, rather. Some Englishmen (mechanics, I should think, or the lower class of tradesmen,) were sitting over their beer, and smoking pipes.

AUGUST 10th.

I LEFT Rock Ferry for the city, at 1/2 past nine. In the boat which arrived thence, there were several men and women with baskets on their heads; for this is a favorite way of carrying burthens; and they trudge onward beneath them, without any apparent fear of an overturn, and seldom putting up a hand to steady them. One woman, this morning, had a heavy load of crockery; another, an immense basket of turnips, freshly gathered, that seemed to me as much as a man could well carry on his back. These must be a stiff-necked people. The women step sturdily and freely, and with not ungraceful strength. The trip up to town was pleasant; it being a fair morning, only with a low-hanging fog. Had it been in America, I should have anticipated a day of burning heat.

Visiters this morning, Mr Ogden of Chicago, or somewhere in the western States, who arrived in England a fortnight [25] or thereabouts ago, and who called on me at that time. He has since been in Scotland, and is now going to London and the Continent; secondly, the Captain of the Collins Steamer Pacific, which sails to-day; thirdly, an American shipmaster, who complained that he had never, in his heretofore voyages, been able to get a sight of the American Consul.

Mr Pearce's customary matutinal visit was unusually agreeable to-day; inasmuch as he laid on my desk nineteen golden sovereigns, and thirteen shillings. It being the day of the Steamer's departure, an unusual number of Invoice certificates had been required—my signature to each of which brings me two dollars. The autograph of a living author has seldom been so much in request at so respectable a price. Colonel Crittenden told me that he had received as much as £50 in a single day. Heaven prosper the trade between America and Liverpool!

AUGUST 15th.

MANY scenes which I should have liked to record have occurred; but the pressure of business has prevented me from recording them from day to day. [26] On Thursday, I went, on invitation from Mr. Bright, on the pro-digious steamer Great Britain, down the harbor and some miles into the sea, to see her off on her voyage to Australia. There is an immense enthusiasm amongst the English people, about this ship, on account of her being the largest in the world. The shores were lined with people to see her sail; and there were innumerable small steamers, crowded with people, all the way out into the ocean. Nothing seems to touch the English nearer than this question of nautical superiority; and if we wish to hit them on the *raw*, we must hit them there.

On Friday, at 7 P.M. I went to dine with the Mayor. It was a dinner given to the Judges and the Grand Jury. The Judges of England, during the time of holding an Assize, are the persons first in rank in the Kingdom. They take precedence of everybody else—of the highest military officers—of the Lord Lieutenants—of the Archbishops—of the Prince of Wales—of all except the Sovereign; whose authority and dignity they represent. In case of a royal dinner, the Judge would lead the Queen to the table.

[27] The dinner was at the Town-Hall; and the rooms, and the whole affair, were all in the most splendid style. Nothing struck me more than the footmen in the city-livery; they really looked more magnificent, in their gold-lace, and breeches, and white silk stockings, than any officers of state whom I have ever seen. The rooms were beautiful; gorgeously painted and gilded, gorgeously lighted, gorgeously hung with paintings, gorgeously illuminated— the plate gorgeous, the dinner gorgeous, in the English fashion. As to the company, they had a kind of roughness, that seems to be the characteristic of all Englishmen so far as I have yet seen them;—elderly John Bulls—and there is hardly a less beautiful object than the elderly John Bull, with his large body, protruding paunch, short legs, and mottled, double-chinned, irregular-featured aspect. They are men of the world, at home in society, easy in their manners, but without refinement; nor are they especially what one thinks of, under the appel[l]ation of gentleman.

After the removal of the cloth, the Mayor gave [28] various toasts, prefacing each with some remarks—the first of course, the Sovereign, after which "God Save the Queen" was sung; and there was something rather ludicrous in seeing the company stand up and join in the chorus, their ample faces glowing with wine, enthusiasm, perspiration, and loyalty. There certainly is a vein of the ridiculous running through these people; nor does it take away from their respectability. Afterwards the Bar, and various other dignities and institutions were toasted; and by-and-by came a toast to the United States and me as their representative. Hereupon, either "Hail Columbia" or "Yankee Doodle," or some other of our national tunes (but Heaven knows which) was played; and at the conclusion—being cornered, and with no alternative—I got upon my legs and made a response. They received me and listened to my nonsense with a good deal of rapping; and my speech seemed to give great satisfaction. My chief difficulty lay in not knowing how to pitch my voice to the size of the room; as for the matter, it is not of the slightest consequence. Any body may make an after-dinner speech, [29] who will be content to talk onward without saying anything. My speech was not more than two or three inches long;—and considering that I did not know a soul there, except the Mayor himself, and that I am wholly unpractised in all sorts of oratory, and that I had nothing to say, it was quite successful. I hardly thought it was in me; but being once on my legs, I felt no embarrassment, and went through it as coolly as if I were going to be hanged.[9]

August 20th.

This being Saturday, there early commenced a throng of visitants to Rock Ferry. The boat, in which I came over, brought from the city a multitude of factory-people, male and female. They had bands of music, and banners inscribed with the Mills they belonged to, and other devices; pale-looking people, but not looking exactly as if they were underfed. They are [30] brought on reduced terms by the railways and steamers, and come from considerable distances in the interior. These, I believe, were from Preston. I have not yet had an opportunity of observing how they amuse themselves during these excursions.

Almost every day, I take walks about Liverpool; preferring the darker and dingier streets, inhabited by the poorer classes. The scenes there are very picturesque in their way; at every two or three steps, a gin-shop; also[10] [fil]thy in clothes and person, ragged, pale, often afflicted with humors; women, nursing their babies at dirty bosoms; men haggard, drunken, care-worn, hopeless, but with a kind of patience, as if all this were the rule of their life; groups stand or sit talking together, around the door-steps, or in the descent of a cellar; often a quarrel is going on in one group, for which the next group cares little or nothing. [31] Sometimes, a decent woman may be seen sewing or knitting at the entrance of her poor dwelling, a glance into which shows dismal poverty. I never walk through these streets without feeling as if I should catch some disease; but yet there is a strong interest in such walks; and moreover there is a bustle, a sense of being in the midst of life, and of having got hold of something real, which I do not find in the better streets of the city. Doubtless, this noon-day and open life of theirs is entirely the best aspect of their existence; and if I were to see them within doors, at their meals, or in bed, it would be unspeakably worse. They appear to wash their clothes occasionally; for I have seen them hanging out to dry in the street.[11]

At the dock, the other day, the steamer arrived from Rock Ferry with a countless multitude of female children in coarse blue-gowns, who, as they landed, formed in procession and walked up the dock. These girls had been taken from the work-houses, and educated at a charity-school, and would by-and-by be apprenticed [32] as servants. I should not have conceived it possible that so many children could have been collected together, without a single trace of beauty, or scarcely of intelligence, in so much as one individual; such mean, coarse, vulgar features and figures, betraying unmistakeably a low origin, and ignorant and brutal parents. They did not appear wicked, but only stupid, animal, and soulless. It must require many generations of better life to elicit a soul in them. All America could not show the like.

August 22^d.

A Captain Auld, an American, having died here, yesterday, I went with my clerk and an American shipmaster, to take an inventory of his effects. His boarding-house was in a mean street; an old, dingy-house, with narrow entrance—the class of boarding-house frequented by mates of vessels, and inferior to those generally patronized by masters. A fat, elderly landlady, of respectable and honest aspect, and her daughter, a likely young woman enough, received us, and ushered us into the deceased's bed-chamber. It was a dingy, back-room, plastered and painted yellow; its one window looking into the very narrowest [33] of back-yards or courts, and out on a confused multitude of back buildings, appertaining to other houses; most of them old, with rude chimneys of wash-rooms and kitchens, the bricks of which seemed half-loose.

The chattels of the dead-man were contained in two trunks, a chest, a sail-cloth bag, and a barrel, and consisted of clothing, suggesting a thickset, middle-sized man; papers relative to ships and business; a spy-glass, a loaded iron-pistol, some books of navigation; some charts; several great pieces of tobacco, and a few cigars; some little plaster images, that he had probably bought for his children; a cotton umbrella; and other trumpery of no great value. In one of the trunks we found about £20's worth of English and American gold and silver, and some notes of hand, due in America. Of all these things, the clerk made an inventory; after which we took possession of the money, and affixed the consular seal to the trunks, bag, and chest.

While this was going [on], we heard a great noise of men quarrelling in an adjoining court; and, altogether, it [34] seemed a squalid and ugly place to live in, and a most undesirable one to die in. At the conclusion of our labors, the young woman asked us if we would not go into another chamber and look at the corpse, and appeared to think that we should be rather glad than otherwise of the privilege. But, never having seen him during his life-time, I declined to commence his acquaintance now.

His bills for board and nursing amount to about the sum which we found in his trunk; his funeral expenses will be about £10 more; the surgeon has sent in a bill of £8, odd shillings; and the account of another medical man is still to be rendered. As his executor, I shall pay the landlady and nurse; and for the rest of the expenses, a subscription must be made, (according to custom in such cases) among the ship-masters, headed by myself. The funeral pomp will consist of a hearse, one coach, four men with hat-bands, and a few other items; together with a grave at £5, over which his friends will be entitled to place a stone, if they choose to do so, within twelve months.

As we left the house, we looked into the dark and [35] squalid dining-room, where a lunch of cold meat was set out for the surviving boarders; but, having no associations with the house except through this one dead man, it seemed as if his presence and attributes pervaded it wholly. He appears to have been a man of reprehensible habits, though well advanced in years. I ought not to forget a brandy-flask (empty) among his other effects.[12] The landlady and daughter made a good impression on me, as honest and respectable persons.

August 24th.

YESTERDAY, in the forenoon, I received a note, and shortly afterwards a call at the Consulate, from Miss Fanny Haworth,[13] whom I apprehend to be a lady of literary tendencies. She said that Miss Lynch[14] had promised her an introduction, but that, happening to be passing through Liverpool, she had snatched the opportunity to make my acquaintance. She seems to be a mature demoiselle, rather plain, but with an honest and intelligent face enough. It was rather a queer freedom, methinks, to come down upon a perfect stran[36]ger in this way—to sit with him in his private office an hour or two, and then walk about the streets with him, as she did;—for I did the honors of Liverpool, and showed her the public buildings. Her talk was sensible, but not particularly brilliant or interesting;—a good, solid personage, physically and intellectually.

In the afternoon, at three °clock, I attended the funeral of Captain Auld. Being ushered into the dining-room of his boarding-house, I found brandy, gin, and wine, set out on a tray, together with some little spice-cakes. By-and-by came in a woman, who asked if I were going to the funeral; and then proceeded to put a mourning hat-band on my hat—a black-silk band, covering the whole hat, and streaming nearly a yard behind. After waiting the better part of an hour, nobody else appeared, although several shipmasters had promised to attend. Hereupon, the undertaker was anxious to set forth; but the landlady (who was arrayed in shining black silk) thought it a shame that the poor man should be buried with such small attendance. So we waited a little longer; during which interval, I heard the [37] landlady's daughter sobbing and wailing in the entry; and but for this tender-hearted lass, there would have been no tears at all. Finally, we set forth—the undertaker, a friend of his, and a young man, perhaps the landlady's son, and myself, in a black-plumed coach, and the landlady, her daughter, and a female friend, in another coach behind. Previous to this, however, everybody had taken some wine and spirits; for it seemed to be considered disrespectful not to do so.

Before us went the plumed hearse, a stately affair, with a bas-relief of funereal figures upon its sides. We proceeded quite across the city to the Necropolis, where the coffin was carried into a chapel, in which we found already another coffin, and another set of mourners, awaiting the clergyman. Anon, he appeared, a stern, broad-framed, large and bald-headed man, in black silk gown; he mounted his desk, and read the service in quite a feeble and unimpressive way, though with no lack of solemnity. This done, our four bearers took up the coffin and car[38]ried it out of the chapel; but descending the steps (and perhaps having taken a little too much brandy) one of them stumbled, and down came the coffin—not quite to the ground, however; for they grappled with it, and contrived, with a great struggle, to prevent that misadventure. But I really expected to see poor Captain Auld burst forth among us in his grave-clothes.

The Necropolis is quite a handsome burial-place, shut in by high walls, so overrun with shrubbery that no part of the brick or stone is visible. Part of the space within is an ornamental garden, with flowers and green turf; the rest is strewn with flat grave-stones, and a few raised monuments; and straight avenues run to-and-fro between. Captain Auld's grave was dug nine-feet deep; it is his own for twelve months; but if his friends do not choose to give him a stone, it will become a common grave at the end of that time; and four or five more people may then be piled upon him. Everybody seemed greatly to admire this grave; the undertaker praised it, and also the dryness of its site, which he took credit to himself for [39] having chosen; the grave-digger, too, was very proud of its depth and the neatness of his handiwork. The clergyman (who had marched in advance of us from the chapel) now took his stand at the head of the grave, and lifting his hat, proceeded with what remained of the service, while we stood bare-headed around. When he came to a particular part ('ashes to ashes, dust to dust,' I think) the undertaker lifted a handful of earth, and threw it rattling on the coffin; so did the land-lady's son, and so did I.

After the funeral, the undertaker's friend (an elderly, coarse-looking man) looked around him, and remarked that the grass had never yet grown on the graves of the "parties" who died in the cholera-year; but at this the under-taker laughed in scorn.

As we returned to the gate of the cemetery, the Sexton met us, and pointed to a small office, on entering which, we found the clergyman, who was waiting for his burial-fees. There was now a dispute between the clergyman and the undertaker; the former wishing to receive the whole amount for the grave-stone, which the un[40]dertaker of course refused to pay. I explained how the matter stood; on which the clergyman acquiesced, civilly enough; but it was very queer to see the worldly, business-like a [sic] way in which he entered into this squabble, so soon after burying poor Captain Auld.

During our ride back in the mourning-coach, the undertaker, his friend, and the landlady's son, still kept descanting on the excellence of the grave— 'such a fine grave!'—'such a nice grave!'—'such a splendid grave!'—and, really, they seemed almost to think it worth while to die, for the sake of being buried there. They deemed it an especial pity that such a grave should ever become a common grave. "Why," said they to me, "by paying the extra price you may have it for your own grave, or for your family!"—meaning that we should have a right to pile ourselves over the defunct captain. I wonder how the English ever attain to any conception of a future existence, since they so overburthen themselves with earth and mortality, in their ideas of funerals. A ride with an undertaker in a sable-plumed coach!—talking about graves!—and yet he was a jolly [41] old fellow, comfortably corpulent, with a smile breaking out easily all over his face—although, once in-a-while, he looked professionally lugubrious.

From 1 °clock till 2, to-day, I have spent in rambling along the streets, Tithe Barn Street, Scotland road, and that vicinity. I never saw, of course, nor imagined from any description, what squalor there is in the inhabitants of these streets, as seen along the sidewalks. All these avenues (the quotation occurs to me continually; and I suppose I have made it two or three times already) are "with dreadful faces thronged."[15] Women with young figures, but old and wrinkled countenances; young girls, without any maiden neatness and trimness, barefooted, with dirty legs,[16]

Women of all ages, even elderly, go along with great, bare, ugly feet; many have baskets and other burthens on their heads. All along the street, with their wares at the edge of the sidewalk, and their own seats fairly in the carriage-way, you see women with fruit to sell, or combs and cheap jewelry, [42] or[17] coarse crockery, or oysters, or the devil knows what; and sometimes the woman is sewing, meanwhile. This life and domestic occupation in the street is very striking, in all these meaner quarters of the city—nursing of babies, sewing and knitting, sometimes even reading. In a drama of low life, the street might fairly and truly be the one scene where everything should take place—courtship, quarrels, plot and counter-plot, and what not besides. My God, what dirty, dirty children! And the grown people are the flowers of these buds, physically and morally. At every ten steps, too, there are "Spirit Vaults," and often "Beds" are advertised on a placard, in connection with the liquor-trade.

Little children are often seen taking care of little children; and it seems to me that they take good and faithful care of them. To-day, I heard a dirty mother laughing and priding herself on the pretty ways of her dirty infant—just as a Christian mother might in a nursery or drawing-room. I must study this street-life more, and think of it more deeply.[18]

[43] All the time, the scent of that horrible mourning coach is in my nostrils; and I breathe nothing but a funeral atmosphere.

AUGUST 25th.

FURTHER items of street-rambles:—little gray donkies, dragging along disproportionately large carts[19];—the anomalous aspect of cleanly dressed and healthy looking young women, whom one sometimes sees talking together in the street, evidently residing in some contiguous house;—the apparition, now and then, of a bright, intelligent, merry, child's face, with dark, knowing eyes, gleaming through the dirt like sunshine through a dusty window-pane; at provision-shops, the little bits of meat, ready for poor customers, and little heaps of selvages and corners, snipt off from points and steaks;—the kindliness with which a little boy leads and lugs along his little sister;—a pale, hollow-cheeked, large-eyed girl of 12, or less, paying a sad, cheerless attention to an infant;—a milkwoman, with a wooden yoke over her shoulder, and a large pail on each side;—in a more reputable street, res[44]pectably dressed women going into an ale and spirit-vault, evidently to drink there;—the police-men loitering along, with observant eye, holding converse with none, and seldom having occasion to interfere with anybody;—the multitudinousness and continual motion of all this kind of life. The people are as numerous as maggots in cheese; you behold them, disgusting, and all moving about, as when you raise a plank or log that has long lain on the ground, and find many vivacious bugs and insects beneath it.[20]

Rec^d, today, a watch for my wife from Bennett of London—selected by Mr. Ticknor.

AUGUST 27th.

THIS (Saturday) being the gala-day of the manufacturing people about Liverpool, the steam boats to Rock Ferry were seasonably crowded with large parties of both sexes. They were accompanied with two numerous bands of music, in uniform; and these bands, before I left the hotel, were playing in competition and rivalry with each other, in the court-yard—loud, martial strains from shining brass-instruments. A prize is to be assigned to one or other of these bands; and I [45] suppose this was a part of the competition. Meanwhile, the merry-making people, who thronged the court-yard, were quaffing coffee from blue earthen-mugs, which they brought with them— as likewise they brought the coffee, and had it made in the hotel.

It had poured with rain about the time of their arrival—notwithstanding which, they did not seem disheartened; for, of course, in this climate, it enters into all their calculations to be soaked through and through. By and by, the sun shone out; and it has continued to shine and shade, every ten minutes, ever since. All these people were decently dressed; the men generally in dark clothes, not so smartly as in America, on a festal day, but so as not to be greatly different as regards dress. They were paler, smaller, less wholesome looking, and less intelligent, and, I think, less noisy, than so many Yankees would have been. The women and girls differed much more from what our girls and women would be, on a pleasure excursion;—being so shabbily dressed, with no kind of smartness, no silks, nothing but cotton gowns, I believe, and ill-looking bon[46]nets—which, however, was the only part of their attire that they seemed to care about guarding from the rain. As to their persons, they generally, I think, looked better developed and healthier than the men; but there was a woeful lack of beauty and grace—not a pretty girl among them —all coarse and vulgar. How different would this be in Yankee-land. Their bodies, it seems to me, are apt to be very lengthy, in proportion to their legs; in truth, this kind of make is rather characteristic of both sexes in England. The speech of these folks, in some instances, was so broad Lancashire that I could not well understand it.

AUGUST 29th.

YESTERDAY (Sunday), wife, the children, and I, took a walk into the country, after a dinner at 1/2 past one. It was a fine afternoon—with clouds, of course, in different parts of the sky; but a clear atmosphere, bright sunshine, and altogether a Septembrish feeling. The ramble was very pleasant, along the hedge-lined roads, in which there were flowers blooming, and the varnished holly—certainly one of the most beautiful shrubs in the world, so far as foliage goes. We [47] saw one cottage which I suppose was several hundred years old; it was of stone, filled into a wooden frame, the black oak of which was visible, like an external skeleton; it had a thatched roof and was white-washed. We passed through a village (Higher Bebington, I believe) with narrow streets, and mean houses, all of brick or stone, and not standing wide apart from each other, as in American country villages, but conjoined. There was an immense alms-house in the midst; at least, I took it [to] be so. In the center of the village, too, we saw a moderate-sized brick house, built in imita-tion of a castle, with a tower and turret, in which an upper and an under row of small cannon were mounted, and now green with moss; there were also battlements along the roof of the house, which looked as if it might have been built eighty or a hundred years ago. In the centre of it, there was the dial of a clock; but the inner machinery had been removed, and the hands, hanging listlessly, moved to-and-fro in the wind. It was quite a novel symbol of decay and neglect. On the wall, close to the street, there were certain eccentric in-scrip[48]tions cut into slabs of stone; but I could make no sense of them. At the end of the house opposite the turret, we peeped through the bars of an iron gate-way, and beheld a little paved courtyard, and at the farther side of it, a small piazza, beneath which seemed to stand the figure of a man. He appeared well advanced in years, and was dressed in blue coat and buff breeches, with a white or straw hat on his head. Behold, too, in a kennel beside the porch, a large dog sitting on his hinder legs, chained! Also, close beside the gate-way, another man seated under a kind of arbor! All these were wooden images, and the whole castellated, small, village dwelling, with the inscriptions, and this queer statuary, was probably the whim of some half-crazy person, who has now, no doubt, been long asleep in Bebington church-yard. (The church, described below, seems to be St. Andrews Church in Lower Bebington, built in 1100.)[21]

The bell of the old church was ringing, as we went along, and many re-spectable looking people, and cleanly dressed children were moving towards the sound. Soon, we reached the church; and I have seen nothing in England that so completely answered my idea of what such a thing was, as this old village-church of Bebington. [49] It is quite a large edifice, built in the form of a cross, with a low peaked-porch in the side, over which, rudely cut in stone, is the date 1300 and something. The steeple has ivy on it, and looks old, old, old; so does the whole church, though portions of it have been renewed, but not so as to impair the aspect of heavy, substantial endurance, and long, long decay (which may go on hundreds of years longer, before the church is a ruin) that belongs to the whole. There it sits among the surrounding graves, looking just the same as it did in Bloody Mary's days; just as it did in Crom-well's time. A bird (and perhaps many birds) had its nest in the steeple, and flew in and out of the loop-holes that were opened into it. The stone frame-work of the windows looked particularly old.

There were monuments about the church, some lying flat on the ground, others elevated on low pillars, or on cross-slabs of stone, and almost all looking dark, moss-grown, and very antique. But, on reading some of the inscriptions, I was surprised to find them very recent; for, in fact, twenty years of this climate [50] suffices to give as much, and more, antiquity of aspect, whether to grave-stone or edifice, than a hundred years of our own;— so soon do lichens creep over the surface; so soon does it blacken; so soon do the edges lose their sharpness—so soon does time gnaw away the records. The only really old monuments (and those not very old) were two standing close together, and raised on low, rude arches, the dates on which were 1684 and 1686. On one a cross was rudely cut into the stone. But there may have been hundreds older than this, the records on which had been quite obliterated, and the stones removed, and the graves dug over anew. None of the monuments commemorated people of rank; on only one the buried person was commemorated as "Gent."

While we sat on one of the flat slabs, resting ourselves, several little girls, healthy-looking, and prettily dressed enough, came into the church-yard, and began to talk and laugh, and to skip merrily from one tomb-stone to another. They stared very broadly at us; and one of them, by-and-by, ran up to Una and Julian, and [51] gave each of them a green apple. Then they skipped upon the tomb-stones again; while, within the church, we heard the singing, sounding pretty much as I have heard it in our pine-built New England meeting-houses. Meantime, the Rector had heard the voices of these naughty little girls, and perhaps had caught glimpses of them through the stained windows; for, anon, out came the sexton, and addressing himself to me, asked whether there had been any noise or disturbance in the church-yard. I should not have borne testimony against these little villagers; but my wife was so anxious to exonerate our own children, that she pointed out those poor little sinners to the sexton, who forthwith turned them out of the churchyard. He would have done the same to us, no doubt, had my coat been worse than it was; but, as the matter stood, his demeanor was rather apologetic than menacing, when he informed us that the Rector had sent him out.

We staid a little longer, looking at the graves, some of which were between the buttresses of the church, and quite close to the wall, as if the sleepers anticipated [52] greater comfort and security, the nearer they could get to the sacred edifice. One or two of these monuments were especially moss-grown; and a bright green moss had grown into the letters of the inscription, and entirely filled them up, so that the lines of the inscription were embossed in living green on the gray or brown slab of stone. It was a bas-relief of green letters, and thereby the more legible—"HERE Lieth the body"—cut very long ago, no doubt, but just as fresh as the present summer, with this ever-new moss. The letters, when just cut, were never half so legible as now.[22]

As we went out of the church-yard, we passed the aforesaid little girls, who were sitting behind the mound of a tomb; and busily babbling together. They called after us, expressing their discontent that we had betrayed them to the sexton, and saying that it was not they who made the noise. Going homeward, we went astray in a green lane, that terminated in the midst of a field, without outlet, so that we had to retrace a good many of our footsteps. We reached home at about 1/2 past 6, having had a pleasant walk.

[53] Close to the wall of the church, beside the door, there was an ancient baptismal font of stone; in fact it was a pile of roughly hewn stone-steps, five or six feet high, with a block of stone at the summit, in which was a hollow about as big as a wash-bowl. It was full of rain-water.

SEPTR. 1st, 1853.

TODAY, we leave the Rock Ferry Hotel, where we have spent nearly four weeks. It is a comfortable place; and we have been well-victualled, and kindly treated. We have occupied a large parlor, extending through the whole breadth of the house, and with a projecting window looking towards Liverpool, and adown the intervening river, and to Birkenhead on the hither side. The river would be a pleasanter object, if it were blue and transparent, instead of such a mud-puddly hue;—also, if it were always full to its brims; whereas it generally presents a margin, and sometimes a very broad one, of glistening mud, with here and there a small vessel aground on it.

Nevertheless, the parlor-window has given us a [54] pretty good idea of the nautical business of Liverpool; the constant objects being the little black steamers, puffing unquietly along, sometimes to our own ferry, sometimes beyond it to Eastham; and sometimes towing a long string of boats from Runcorn, or otherwhere up the river, laden with goods;—and sometimes gallanting in or out a tall ship. Some of these ships lie for days together in the river, very majestic and stately objects, with often the flag of the stars and stripes waving over them. Now and then, after a blow at sea, a vessel comes in with her masts broken short off in the midst, and marks of rough handling about the hull. Once a week, comes a Cunard steamer, with its red funnel pipe whitened by the salt-spray; and firing off some cannon to announce her arrival, she moors to a large iron-buoy in the middle of the river, and a few hundred yards from the stone-pier of our ferry. Immediately comes puffing towards her a little mail-steamer, to take away her mail-bags, and such of the passengers as choose to land; and for several hours afterwards, the Cunarder lies with the smoke [55] and steam coming out of her, as if she were smoking her pipe after her toilsome passage across the Atlantic. Once a fortnight, comes an American steamer of the Collins-line; and then the Cunarder salutes her with some cannon, to which the American responds, and moors herself to another iron buoy, not far from the Cunarder. When they go to sea, it is with similar salutes;—the two vessels paying each other the more ceremonious respect, because they are inimical and jealous of each other.

Besides these, there are other steamers of all sorts and sizes, for pleasure excursions, for regular trips to Dublin, the Isle of Man, and elsewhither; and vessels which are generally stationary, as floating-lights, but seem to relieve one another at intervals; and small vessels with sails looking as if made of tanned leather; and schooners; and yachts; and all manner of odd-looking craft; but none so odd as the Chinese Junk, which lies by our pier, and looks as if it were copied from some picture on an old tea-cup. Beyond all these objects, we see the other side of the Mersey, with the delectably green fields opposite [56] to us; while the shore becomes more and more thickly populated, until two miles off, or thereabouts, we see the dense center of the city, with the dome of the Custom House, and steeples and towers, and close to the water, the spire of St Nicholas; and above and intermingled with the whole city-scene, the duskiness of the coal-smoke, gushing upward. Along the bank, we see the warehouses of the Albert Dock, and the Queen's Tobacco Warehouses, and other docks; and, nigher to us, a ship-yard or two. In the evening, all this sombre picture gradually darkens out of sight; and we see only the lights of the city kindling into a galaxy of earthly stars, for a long distance up and down the shore; and, in one or two spots, the bright red gleam of a furnace, like the "red planet Mars"[23]; and, once in a while, the bright wandering star gliding along the river, as a steamer comes or goes between us and Liverpool.

SEPT[r] 2[d].

WE got into our new house in Rock Park, yesterday. It is quite a good house, with three apartments, besides kitchen and pantry, on the lower floor; and three stories high, with four good chambers in each story. It is a stone [57] edifice, like almost all the modern English houses, and handsome in its design—much more so than most of the American houses. The rent, without furniture, would probably have been £100;—furnished, it is £160. Rock Park, as the locality is called, is private property, and is now nearly covered with residences for professional people, merchants, and others of the upper middling class; the houses being mostly built, I suppose, on speculation, and let to those who occupy them. It is the quietest place imaginable; there being a police station at the entrance; and the officer on duty admits no ragged or ill looking person to pass. There being a toll, it precludes all unnecessary passage of carriages; and never were there more noiseless streets than those that give access to these pretty residences. On either side, there is thick shrubbery, with glimpses through it at the ornamented portals, or into the trim gardens, with smooth shaven lawns, of no large extent, but still affording reasonable breathing space. They are really an improvement on anything save what the very rich can enjoy, in America. The former occupants (a Mrs. Campbell [58] and family) of our house having been fond of flowers, there are many rare varieties in the garden; and we are told that there is scarcely a month of the year in which a flower will not be found there.

The house is respectably, though not elegantly furnished. It was a dismal rainy day, yesterday; and we had a coal fire in the sitting-room; beside which I sat, last evening, as twilight came on, and thought rather sadly how many times we have changed our home, since we were married. In the first place, our three years at the Old Manse; then a brief residence at Salem, then at Boston, then two or three years at Salem again; then at Lenox, then at West Newton, and then again at Concord, where we imagined that we were fixed for life, but spent only a year. Then this farther flight to England, where we expect to spend four years, and afterwards another year in Italy—during all which time we shall have no real home. For, as I sat in this English house, with the chill, rainy English twilight brooding over the lawn, and a coal-fire to keep me comfortable on the first evening of September; and the picture of a stranger (the dead hus[59]band of Mrs. Campbell) gazing down at me from above the mantel-piece, I felt that I never should be quite at home here.[24] Nevertheless, the fire was very comfortable to look at; and the shape of the fire-place, an arch, with a deep cavity, was an improvement on the square, shallow opening of an American coal-grate.

SEPT 7th

IT appears by the annals of Liverpool, (contained in Gore's Directory) that in 1076, there was a baronial castle, built by Roger de Poictiers, on the site of the present St. George's Church. It was taken down in 1721. The church now stands at one of the busiest points of the principal street of the city; the old church of St Nicholas, founded about the time of the Conquest, and more recently re-built, stood within a quarter of a mile of the castle.

In 1150, Birkenhead Priory was founded, on the Cheshire-side of the Mersey. The monks used to ferry passengers across to Liverpool, until 1282, when Woodside Ferry was established—2[d] for a horseman, 1/4 d for a foot-passenger. Steam ferry boats now cross to Birkenhead, Monks ferry, and Woodside, every ten minutes; and I believe there are [60] large hotels at all these places, and many of the business men of Liverpool have residences there.

In 1252, a tower was built by Sir John Stanley, which continued to be a castle of defence to the Stanley family for many hundred years, and was not finally taken down until 1820, when its site had become the present Water-street, in the densest commercial centre of the city.

There appear to have been other baronial castles and residences in different parts of the city, as a hall in old Hall street, built by Sir John de la More; a counting-house now stands on its site. This knightly family of de la More sometimes supplied Mayors to the city; as did the family of the Earls of Derby.

1361, a plague was in the town, which was often subject to such visitations.

1522, John Crosse of Crosse Hall, south side of Dale street; he founded a grammar-school free for all children.

About 1532, Edward, Earl of Derby, used to maintain 250 citizens of Liverpool, "fed 60 aged persons twice a day, and provided 2700 persons with meat, drink, and money every Good Friday."

[61] So late as 1561, there were only seven streets of the city inhabited, with 138 cottages, & 690 inhabitants:—Chapel-street, (so called from St Nicholas church being at the end of it)—Bancke-street and Moor-street, (now Water street and Tithe Barn street)—Castle-street, Dale-street, High-street, and what is now called Old Hall street.

In 1644, Prince Rupert besieged the town for 24 days, and finally took it by storm. This was June 26th; and the Parliamentarians, under Sir John Meldrum, re-possessed it the following October.

In 1669, the Mayor of Liverpool kept an inn.

In 1730, there was only one carriage in town; and no stage-coach came nearer than Warrington, the roads being impassable

In 1734, the Earl of Derby gave a great entertainment in the tower in Water-street.

In 1737, the Mayor was George Norton, a saddler, who frequently took the chair with his leather apron on. His immediate predecessor seems to have been the Earl of Derby, who gave the above mentioned entertainment during his Mayoralty.

[62] Where George's Dock now is, there used to be a battery of 14 eighteen-pounders for the defense of the town; and the old sport of bull-baiting was carried on in that vicinity, close to St Nicholas Church.

In 1778, the royal regiment of Liverpool Blues was raised, received its colors, and sailed for Jamaica, 1100 strong; in 1784, the regiment returned, numbering only 84 men, and deposited its colors in the Exchange.

Septr 12th.

ON Saturday, a young man was found wandering about in West Derby (a suburb of Liverpool) in a state of insanity; and being taken before a magistrate, he proved to be an American. As he seemed to be in a respectable station of life, the magistrate sent the master of the work-house to me, in order to find out whether I would take the responsibility of his expenses, rather than have him put in the work-house. My clerk went to investigate the matter, and brought me his papers. His name proves to be George Ruggles, belonging in Providence, twenty-five years of age. One of the papers was a passport from our legation in Naples; likewise a power of attorney from his mother (who seems to have been [63] married again) to dispose of some property of her's [sic] here abroad; a hotel-bill, also, of some length, in which were various charges for wine; and among other evidences of low funds, a pawn-brokers receipt for a watch, which he had pledged at five pounds. Then there was a ticket for his passage to America by the screw-steamer Andes, which sailed on Wednesday last. The clerk found him to the last degree incommunicative; and nothing could be got out of him, save what the papers disclosed. Besides those above mentioned, there were about a dozen utterly unintelligible notes, written by himself since his derangement

I decided to put him into the insane hospital, where he now accordingly is; and tomorrow (by which time he may be in a more conversible mood) I mean to pay him a visit.

The clerk tells me, that there is now, and has been for three years past, an American lady in the Liverpool almshouse, in a state of insanity. She possesses great accomplishments, especially in music; but [64] in all this time, it has been impossible to find out who she is, or anything about her connections or previous life. She calls herself Jenny Lind, and as for any other name or identity, she keeps her own secret. The physician of the alms-house has an idea that she was the mistress of some man who deserted her; but whether he deducts this from any hint that has fallen from herself, I know not.

SEPT 14th.

IT appears that Mr. Ruggles being unable to pay his bill at the inn where he was latterly staying the landlord had taken possession of his luggage, and satisfied himself in that way. My clerk has taken his watch out of pawn. It proves to be not a very good one, though doubtless worth more than the £5 for which it was pledged. The governor of the Lunatic Asylum wrote me, yesterday, stating that the patient was in want of a change of clothes, and that, according to his own account, he had left his luggage at the American Hotel. After office-hours, I took a cab, and set out, with my clerk, to pay a visit to the Asylum, taking the American Hotel in our way.

[65] The American Hotel is a small house, not at all such a one as American travellers, of any pretensions, would think of stopping [at]; but still very respectable, cleanly, and with a neat sitting-room, where the guests might assemble, after the American fashion. We asked for the landlady; and, anon, down she came, a round, rosy, comfortable-looking English dame of fifty, or thereabouts. On being asked whether she knew a Mr. Ruggles, she readily responded that he had been there, but had left no baggage—having taken it away before paying his bill; and that she had suspected him of meaning to take his departure, without paying her at all. Hereupon, she had traced him to the hotel before-mentioned, where she found that he had staid two nights in company with a lady, which she thought hardly proper, ("for, I am sure," quoth the landlady, "there was no lady with him at my house") but was then, I think, gone from thence. Afterwards, she encountered him again, and demanding her due, went with him to a pawnbroker's, where he pledged his watch, and paid her. This was about the [66] extent of the landlady's knowledge of the matter. I liked the woman very well, with her shrewd, good-humored, worldly, kindly disposition.

Then we proceeded to the Lunatic Asylum, to which we were admitted by a porter at the gate. Within doors, we found some neat and comely servant-women, one of whom showed us into a handsome parlor, and took my card to the Governor. There was a large book-case, with a glass-front, and containing handsomely bound books—many of which, I observed, were of a religious character. In a few minutes, the Governor came in, a middle-aged man, tall and thin, for an Englishman, kindly and agreeable enough in aspect, but not with the marked look of a man of force and ability. I should not judge, from his conversation that he was an educated man, or that he had any scientific acquaintance with the subject of insanity.

He said that Mr. Ruggles was still quite incommunicative, and not in a very promising state;—that I had perhaps better defer seeing him for a few days;—that it would not be safe, at present, to send him home to [67] America, without an attendant;—and this was about all. But, on returning home, I learned from my wife (who had had a call from Mrs. Blodgett) that Mrs. B. knew Mr. Ruggles and his mother, who has recently been re-married to a young husband, and is now somewhere in Italy. They seem to have been at her house, on their way to the continent; and within a week or so, an acquaintance and pastor of Mr. Ruggles, the Rev. Dr. Crocker, has sailed for America. If I could only have caught him, I would have transferred the care, expense, and responsibility of the patient to his shoulders. The Governor of the Asylum mentioned, by the way, that Mr. Ruggles describes himself as having been formerly a midshipman in the navy. Not improbably, he has been abusing his brain with drink, gambling, and dissipation of all kinds, and has thereby brought himself to his present state.

I walked through the St. James's Cemetery, yesterday. It is a very pretty place, dug out of the rock, having formerly, I believe, been a stone quarry. It is now a deep and spacious valley, with graves and mon[68]uments on its level and grassy floor, through which run gravel-paths, and where grows luxuriant shrubbery. On one of the steep sides of the valley, hewn out of the rock, are tombs, rising in tiers to the height of fifty feet or more; some of them cut right into the rock, and with arched portals, others built with stone. On the other side, the bank is of earth, and rises abruptly, quite covered with trees, and looking very pleasant with their green shade. It was a warm and sunny day, and the cemetery really had a most agreeable aspect. I saw several grave-stones of Americans; but what struck me most was one line of an epitaph on an English woman—"Here rests in *pease* a virtuous wife." The statue of Huskisson[25] stands in the midst of the valley, in a kind of mausoleum, with a door of plate-glass, through which you squint at the dead statesman's effigies.

Septr 22ᵈ.

Nothing very important has happened lately. Some days ago, an American captain came to the office, and told how he had shot one of his crew, shortly after sailing from New Orleans, and while the ship was still [69] in the river. As he described the event, he was in peril of his life from this man, who was an Irishman; and he only fired his pistol, when the man was coming upon him with a knife in one hand, and some other weapon of offence in the other;—the captain, at the same time, struggling with one or two more of the crew. At the time, he was weak, having just recovered from the yellow fever. The shot struck him in the pit of the stomach, and he only lived about a quarter of an hour.

No magistrate in England has a right to arrest or examine the captain, unless by a warrant from the Secretary of State on the charge of murder. After his statement to me, the mother of the slain man went to the police-officer, and accused him of killing her son. Two or three days since, moreover, two of the sailors came before me, and gave their account of the matter; and it looked very different from that of the captain. According to them, the man had no idea of attacking the captain, and was so drunk that he could not keep himself upright, without assistance. [70] One of these two men was actually holding him up, when the Captain fired two barrels of his pistol, one immediately after the other, and lodged two balls in the pit of his stomach. The man immediately sank down, saying, "Jack, I'm killed,"—and died very shortly. Meanwhile, the captain drove this man away, under threat of shooting him likewise. Both the seamen described the captain's conduct, both then and during the whole voyage, as outrageous; and I do not much doubt that it was so. They gave their evidence (under oath) like men who wished to tell the truth, and were moved by no more than a natural indignation at the captain's wrong.

I did not much like the captain, from the first; a hard, rough man, with little education—nothing of the gentleman about him; a red face, a loud voice. He seemed a good deal excited, and talked fast and much about the event, but yet not as if it had sunk deeply into him. He observed that he would not have had it happen for a "thousand dollars"—that being the amount of detriment which he conceives himself to suffer by [71] the ineffaceable blood-stain on his hand. In my opinion, it is little short of murder, if at all; but then what would be murder, on shore, is almost a natural occurrence, when done in such a hell on earth as one of these ships, in the first hours of her voyage. The men are then all drunk, some of them often in delirium tremens; and the captain feels no safety for his life, except in making himself as terrible as a fiend. It is the universal testimony, that there is a worse set of sailors in these short voyages between Liverpool and America, than in any other trade whatever.

There is no probability that the captain will ever be called to account for this deed. He gave, at the time, his own version of the affair in his log-book; and this was signed by the entire crew, with the exception of one man, who had hidden himself in the hold in terror of the captain. His mates will sustain his side of the question; and none of the sailors would be within reach of the American courts, even should they be sought for.

[72] SEPT 24.

THE women of England are capable of being more atrociously ugly than any other human beings; and I have not as yet seen one whom we should distinguish as beautiful in America. They are very apt to be dowdy. Ladies often look like cooks and housemaids, both in figure and complexion;—at least, to a superficial observer, although a closer inspection shows a kind of dignity, resulting from their quiet good opinion of themselves and consciousness of their position in society. I do not find in them those characteristics of robust health, in which they are said so much to exceed our countrywomen. Some have that appearance, and thereby are well repaid for the coarseness which it gives their figures and faces; others, however, are yellow and haggard, and evidently ailing women. As a general rule, they are not very desirable objects in youth, and, in many instances, become perfectly grotesque after middle-age;—so massive, not seemingly with pure fat, but with solid beef, making an awful ponderosity of frame. You think of them as composed of sirloins, and with broad and thick steaks on their immense [73] rears. They sit down on a great round space of God's footstool, and look as if nothing could ever move them; and indeed they must have a vast amount of physical strength to be able to move themselves. Nothing of the gossamer about them; they are elephantine, and create awe and respect by the muchness of their personalities. Then as to their faces, they are stern, not always positively forbidding, yet calmly terrible not merely by their breadth and weight of feature, but because they show so much self-reliance, such acquaintance with the world, its trials, troubles, dangers, and such internal means of defence;—such á plombe [sic]; —I can't get at my exact idea; but without anything salient and offensive, or unjustly terrible to their neighbors, they seem like seventy-four gun ships in time of peace;—you know that you are in no danger from them, but cannot help thinking how perilous would be their attack, if pugnaciously inclined,— and how hopeless the attempt to injure them. Really they are not women at all;—not that they are [74] masculine, either, though more formidable than any man I ever saw. They are invariably, I think, clad in black. I have not happened to see any thin, lady-like old women, such as are so frequent among ourselves; but sometimes, even in these broadly-developed old persons, you see a face that indicates cultivation, and even refinement, although, even in such cases, I am generally disturbed by the absence of sex. They certainly look much better able to take care of themselves than our women; but I see no reason to suppose that they really have greater strength of character than they. They are only strong, I suspect, in society, and in the common route of things.

I have not succeeded in getting my view of the English dowager into the above;—beefy, not pulpy.[26]

OCTOBER 1st.

ON Thursday I went with Mr. Ticknor[27] to Chester, by railway. It is quite an indescribable old town; and I feel, at last, as if I had had a glimpse of Old England. The wall encloses a large space within the town; but there are numerous houses and streets, or portions of streets, not [75] included within its precincts. Some of the principal streets pass under the ancient gateways; and at the side, there are flights of steps, giving access to the top. Around the top of the whole wall (a circuit of about two miles) there runs a walk, well paved with flag-stones, and broad enough for two or three to walk abreast. On one side of the wall, (the side towards the country) there is a parapet of red free-stone, about breast high. On the other side, there are houses, rising up immediately from the side of the wall, so that they seem a part of it. The height of the wall, I suppose, may be thirty or forty feet; and in some parts, you look down from the parapet into orchards, where there were tall apple-trees, and men in the branches gathering the fruit, and women and children down among the grass, filling bags or baskets. There are glimpses of the surrounding country among the buildings outside the wall; at one point, a view of the river Dee, with an old bridge of arches. It is all very strange; very quaint; very curious to see how the town has overflowed [76] its barrier, and how, like many institutions here, the ancient wall still exists, but is turned to quite another purpose than what it was meant for—so far as it serves any purpose at all. There are three or four towers and other prominent points, in the course of the circuit; the most interesting being one from the top of which King Charles the First is said to have seen the rout of his army, by the Parliamentarians. We ascended the short flight of steps that led up into this tower, where an old man pointed out the site of the battle-field, (now thickly studded with buildings) and told us what we had already learned from the guide-book.

After this we went into the Cathedral, which I will perhaps describe on some other occasion, when I shall have seen more of it, and to better advantage. The cloisters gave me most the impression of antiquity; the stone arches being so worn and so blackened with time. Still an American must always have imagined a better cathedral than this; although it is a great, old, dreary place enough. There were some immense win[77]dows of painted or stained glass, but all modern. In the chapter-house (a comfortless vault of dusky stone-work) we found a coal-fire burning in a grate, and a large heap of old books, the library of the cathedral, in a discreditable state of decay—mildewed, rotten, neglected for years. The sexton told us that they were to be arranged and better ordered. Over the door, within the chapter-house, hang two faded and tattered banners; being those of the Cheshire regiment.

The most utterly indescribable feature of Chester is the Rows, which every traveller has attempted to describe. At the height of several feet above some of the oldest streets, a walk runs through the front of the houses which project over it. Back of this walk, there are shops; on the outer side of the walk, a space of two or three yards, where the shopmen have their tables and stands and show cases; overhead, just high enough for persons to stand erect, a ceiling. At frequent intervals, little narrow passages go winding in among the houses, which all along are closely conjoined, and seem to have [78] no access or exit, except through the shops, or into these narrow passages, where you can touch each side with your elbows, and the top with your hand. We penetrated into one or two of them; they smelt ancient and disagreeable. At one of the doors stood a pale-looking but cheerful and good-natured woman, who told us that she had come to that house when first married, twenty-one years before, and had lived there ever since; and that she felt as if she had been buried through the best years of her life. She let us peep into her kitchen and parlor, small, dingy, dismal, but yet not wholly destitute of a home-look. She said that she had seen two or three coffins in a day, during cholera times, carried out of that narrow passage into which her door opened. These avenues put me in mind of those which run through ant-hills, or those which a mole makes, underground.

This fashion of Rows does not appear to be going out; and for ought I can see, it may last hundreds of years longer. When a house becomes so old as to be untenantable, it is rebuilt; and the new one is fash[79]ioned like the old, so far as regards the walk running through its front. Many of the shops are very good, and even elegant; and these Rows are the favorite places of business in Chester. Indeed, they have many advantages, the passengers being sheltered from the rain; and there being within the shops that dimmer light by which tradesmen love to exhibit their wares.

A large proportion of the edifices in the Rows must be comparatively modern; but there are some very old ones, with oaken frames visible on the exterior. The Row, passing through these houses, is railed with oak, so old that it has turned black and grown to be as hard as stone—which it might be mistaken for, if one did not see where names and initials have been cut into it with knives, at some by-gone period. Overhead, cross-beams project through the ceiling, so low as almost to hit the head. In the front of one of these buildings was the inscription—"GOD'S PROVIDENCE IS MINE INHERITANCE"—said to have [been] put there by the occupant of the house, two hun[80]dred years ago, when the plague spared this one house in the whole city. Not improbably, the inscription has operated as a safe-guard to prevent the demolition of the house, hitherto; but a shopman of an adjacent house told us that it was soon to be taken down.

Here and there, about some of the streets through which the Rows do not run, we saw houses of very aged aspect, with steep, peaked gables; the front gable-end was supported on stone-pillars, and the side walk passed beneath. Most of these old houses seemed to be taverns—the Black Bear—the Green Dragon—and such names. We thought of getting our dinner at one of them; but, on inspection, they looked rather too dingy, and close, and of questionable neatness. So we went to the Royal Hotel, where we probably fared just as badly, at much more expense, and where there was a particularly gruff and crabbed old waiter, who, I suppose, thought himself free to display his English surliness, because we arrived at the hotel on foot. For my part, I love to see John Bull show himself.

[81] I must go again and again and again to Chester; for I suppose there is not a more curious place in the world.

Mr. Ticknor (who has been staying at Rock Park with us since Tuesday) has steamed away in the Canada, this morning. His departure seems to make me feel more abroad—more dissevered from my native country—than before.

OCTOBER 3ᵈ 1853.

SATURDAY evening at 6, I went to dine with Mr. Aiken, a wealthy merchant here, to meet two of the sons of Burns.[28] There was a party of ten or twelve, Mr. Aiken and two daughters included. The two sons of Burns have both been in the Indian army, and have attained the ranks of colonel and major; one having spent thirty, and the other twenty-seven years in India. They are now old gentlemen of sixty and upwards; the elder with a gray head, the younger with a perfectly white one;—rather under than above the middle stature, and with a British roundness of figure—plain, respectable, intelligent-looking persons, with quiet manners, though not particularly refined. I saw [82] no resemblance in either of them to any portrait of their father. After the ladies left the table, I sat next to the Major (the younger of the two) and had a good deal of talk with him. He seemed a very kindly and social man, and was quite ready to speak about his father; nor was at all reluctant to let it be seen how much he valued the glory of being descended from the poet. By and by, at Mr. Aiken's instance, he sang one of Burns's songs; the one about Annie and the rigs of barley.[29] He sings in a perfectly simple style, so that it is little more than recitation; and yet the effect is very good as to humor, sense, and pathos. After rejoining the ladies, he sang another—"A posie for my ain dear May"[30]—and likewise "A man's a man for a' that." My admiration of his father, and partly, perhaps, my being an American, gained me some favor with him; and he promised to give me what he considered the best engraving of Burns, and some other remembrance of him. The Major is that son of Burns, who spent an evening at Abbotsford with Sir Walter Scott, when, as Lockhart writes, "the children sang the ballads of their sires."[31] He spoke [83] with vast indignation of a recent edition of his father's works by Robert Chambers; in which the latter appears to have wronged the poet by some misstatements.

Late in the evening, Mr. Aiken and most of the gentlemen retired to the smoking-room, where we found brandy, whiskey, and some good cigars. The sons of the poet showed, I think, an hereditary appreciation of good liquor, both at the dinner table (where they neglected neither sherry, port, hock, champagne, nor claret) and here in the smoking-room. Both of them, however, drank brandy, instead of the liquor which their father immortalized. The colonel smoked cigars; the major filled and refilled a German pipe. Neither of them (nor, in fact, anybody else) was at all the worse for liquor; but I thought I saw a little of the coarser side of Burns, in the rapturous approbation with which the Major responded to a very good but rather indecorous story from one of the gentlemen. But I liked them both, and they liked me,[32] and asked me to come and see them at Cheltenham, where they reside. We broke up at about midnight.

[84] The members of this dinner-party were of the more liberal tone of thinking, here in Liverpool. The colonel and major seem to be of similar principles; and the eyes of the latter glowed, when he sang his father's noble verse—The rank is but the guinea's stamp"&c. It would have been too pitiable, if Burns had left a son who could not feel the spirit of that verse.

OCTR 8th.

COMING to my office, two or three mornings ago, I found Mrs. Eaton, the mother of Mr. Ruggles, the insane young man whom I had taken charge of. She is a lady of fifty or thereabouts, and not very remarkable, any way, nor particularly ladylike, as I think my countrywomen are, oftener than Englishwomen. However, she was just come off a rapid journey, having come from Naples without taking rest, since my letter reached her, together with three small children. A son of about twenty had come with her to the consulate.

She was, of course, infinitely grieved about the young man's insanity, and had two or three bursts of tears while we talked the matter over. She said he was the hope of her life—the best, purest, most innocent child that [85] ever was, and wholly free from every kind of vice—(at which I could not but smile, knowing that the young gentleman had been in company with a lady, two nights, at a hotel here, and, from the items of his bill, had had a particularly jolly time)—but it appears that he had had a previous attack of insanity, lasting three months, about three years ago.

After I had told her all that I knew about him (including my personal observations, at a visit, a week or two since) we got into a cab and drove to the Asylum. It must have been a dismal moment to the poor lady, as we entered the gateway, through a tall, prison-like wall. Being ushered into the parlor, the Governor soon appeared, and informed us that Mr. Ruggles had had a relapse, within a few days, and was not now so well as when I saw him. He complains of unjust confinement, and seems to consider himself, if I rightly understand, under persecution for political reasons. The Governor, however, proposed to call him down; and I took my leave, feeling that it would be indelicate to be present at his first interview with his mother. So [86] here ended my guardianship of the poor young fellow.

In the afternoon I called at the Waterloo Hotel, where Mrs. Eaton was stopping, and found her in the Coffee Room with the children. She had determined to take a lodging in the vicinity of the Asylum, and was going to remove thither as soon as the children had had something to eat. They seemed to be pleasant and well-behaved children, and impressed me more favorably than the mother, whom I suspect to be rather a foolish woman; although her present grief makes her appear in a more respectable light than at other times. She seemed anxious to impress me with the respectability and distinction of her connexions in America; and I had observed the same tendency in the insane patient, at my interview with him. However, she has undoubtedly a mother's love for this poor shatterbrain; and this may weigh against the folly of her marrying an incongruously youthful second husband, and many other follies. This was day before yesterday; and I have heard nothing of her since.

[87] The same day, I had applications for assistance in two other domestic affairs;—one from an Irishman, naturalized in America, who wanted me to get him a passage to America, and to take charge of his wife and family here, at my own private expense, until he could remit funds to carry them across. Another was from an Irishman, who had a power of attorney from a country-woman of his in America, to find and take charge of an infant whom she had left in the Liverpool workhouse, two years ago. I have a great mind to keep a list of all the businesses I am consulted about and employed in; it would be so very curious. Among other things, all pennyless Americans, or pretenders to Americanism, look upon me as their banker; and I could ruin myself, any week, if I had not laid down a rule to consider every applicant for assistance an impostor, until he proves himself a true and responsible man—which it is very difficult to do. Yesterday, there limped in a very respectable-looking old man, who described himself as a citizen of Baltimore, who had [88] been on a trip to England and elsewhere, and being detained longer than he expected, and having had an attack of rheumatism, was now short of funds to pay his passage home, and hoped that I would supply the deficiency. He had quite a plain, homely, though respectful manner; and, for ought I know, was the very honestest man alive; but, as he could produce no kind of proof of his character and responsibility, I very quietly explained the impossibility of my helping him. I advised him to try to obtain a passage on board of some Baltimore ship, the master of which might be acquainted with him, or, at all events, take his word for payment after arrival. This he seemed inclined to do, and took his leave. There was a decided aspect of simplicity about this old man; and yet I rather judge him to be an impostor.

It is easy enough to refuse money to strangers and unknown people, or wherever there may be any question about identity. But it will not be so easy, when I am asked for money by persons whom I know, but do not like to trust. They shall meet the eternal 'No,' however.

[89] OCTOBER 13th.

IN Ormerod's History of Cheshire[33] (Vol 1, page 36) it is mentioned that Randal Earl of Chester having made an inroad into Wales (say about 1225) the Welshmen gathered in mass against him, and drove him into the castle of Rothelent, in Flintshire. The earl sent for succor to his Constable of Chester, Roger Lacy, surnamed "Hell," on account of his fierceness. It was then fairtime at Chester; and the Constable collected a miscellaneous rabble of fiddlers, players, cobblers, tailors, strumpets, and all manner of debauched people, and led them to the relief of the earl. At sight of this strange army, the Welshmen fled; and forever after, the earl assigned to the Constable of Chester power over all fiddlers, shoemakers, and strumpets, within the bounds of Cheshire. The Constable retained for himself and heirs the control of the shoemakers, and made over to his own steward, Dutton, that of the fiddlers and players; and, for many hundreds of years afterwards, the Duttons of Dutton retained this power. On midsummer-day, they used to ride through Chester, attended by all the minstrels playing on their [90] several instruments, to the Church of Saint John, and there renew their licenses. It is a good theme for a legend. Sir Peter Leycester (writing in Charles II's time) copies the Latin deed from the Constable to Dutton; rightly translated, it seems to mean, "the magisterial power over all the lewd people and whores in the whole of Cheshire"[34]; but the custom grew into what is above stated. In the time of Henry VII, the Duttons claimed, by prescriptive right, that the Cheshire minstrels should deliver them, at the feast of Saint John, four bottles of wine and a lance, and that each separate minstrel should pay four pence half-penny, and each whore of Chester four pence.

Another account says Ralph Dutton was the Constable's son-in-law, and a "lusty youth."[35]

OCTOBER 19th.

COMING to the ferry, this morning, a few minutes before the boat arrived from town, I went into the Ferry House (a small stone edifice) and found there an Irishman, his wife, and three children,—the oldest eight or nine years old, and all girls. There was a good fire burning in the room, and the family were clustered round it, apparently enjoying the warmth very much; [91] but when I came in, both husband and wife very hospitably asked me to come to the fire, although there was not more than room at it for their own party. I declined, on the plea that I was warm enough; and then the woman said that they were very cold, having been long on the road. The man was gray haired and gray-bearded, clad in an old drab over-coat, and had a huge bag, which seemed to contain bed-clothing or something of the kind. The woman was pale, with a thin, anxious, wrinkled face, but a good and kind expression. The children were quite pretty, with delicate faces, and a look of patience and endurance in them, but yet as if they had suffered as little as they possibly could. The two elder were cuddled up close to the father; the youngest, about four years old, sat in its mother's lap, and she had taken off its little shoes and stockings, and was warming its feet at the fire. Their little voices had a sweet and kindly sound, as they talked in low tones to their parents and one another. They all looked very shabby, and yet had a decency about them; and it was [92] touching to see how they made themselves at home at this casual fireside, and got all the comfort they could out of the circumstances. By and by, two or three market-women came in, and looked kindly at them, and said a word or two to the children.

They did not beg of me, as I partly expected they would; but after looking at them awhile, I pulled out a sixpence, and handed it to one of the little girls. She took it very readily, as if she partly expected it; and then the father and mother thanked me, and said they had been travelling a long distance, and had nothing to live upon, but what they picked up on the road. They found it impossible to live in England, and were now on their way to Liverpool, hoping to get a passage back to Ireland, where, I suppose, extreme poverty is rather better off than here. I heard the little girl say that she should buy a loaf with the money. There is not much that can be caught in the description of this scene; but it made me understand, better than before, how poor people feel, wandering about in such destitute circumstances, and how they suffer, and yet how they have a life not quite [93] miserable, after all; and how family love goes along with them. Soon, the boat arrived at the pier; and we all went on board; and as I sat in the cabin, looking up through a broken pane in the skylight, I saw the woman's thin face, with its anxious, motherly aspect, and the youngest child in her arms, shrinking from the chill wind, but yet not impatiently; and the eldest of the girls standing close by, with her expression of childish endurance—but yet so bright and intelligent, that it would evidently take but a few days to make a happy and playful child of her. Somehow or other, I got into the interior of this poor family, and understand, through sympathy, more of them than I can tell. They were much better, I think, and more delicate, than if they had been English.

I am getting to possess some of the English indifference as to beggars and poor people; but still, whenever I come face to face with them, and have any intercourse, it seems as if they ought to be the better for me. I wish, instead of sixpence, I had given this poor family ten shillings, and denied it to a begging subscriptionist,[36] [94] who has just fleeced me to that amount. How silly a man feels, in this latter predicament!

I have [had] a good many visitors at the consulate from the United States, within a short time past;—among others, Mr. D. D. Barnard,[37] our late minister to Berlin, returning homeward to-day by the Arctic. Mr. Sickles,[38] Secretary of Legation to London, a fine-looking, gentlemanly, intelligent young man, but, so I am told, very dissolute, and with some remarkably dark stains in his character. Unless belied, he has been kept by a prostitute, within a few years, and is now married to a woman whom he seduced, and who is not received into society at home. Be that as it may, in aspect and address he does us credit; and I cannot but think that he will yet outlive the evil that may be in him. With him came Judge Douglas,[39] the chosen man of young America. He is very short—extremely short—but has an uncommonly good head, and uncommon dignity of manner, without seeming to aim at it, being free and simple in manners. I judge him to be a very able man, with the Western sociability and free fellowship. When I saw him in Washington,[40] [95] he had on a very dirty shirt-collar. I believe it was clean, yesterday. At the Waterloo Hotel, there is a Mr. Lill[e]y,[41] who has the appointment of Consul to Pernambuco. He is from Ohio, I believe, and a very unfavorable specimen of American manners—an outrageous tobacco-chewer, and atrocious spitter on carpets; the appearance of a country trader; a politician, such as one meets with at home, often enough, without particular notice, but who stands out in strong relief here. Yet he seems to have associated on familiar terms with Secretary Marcey [*sic*][42], and even to have chatted confidentially with the President. Generally, I see no reason to be ashamed of my countrymen who come out here in public position, or otherwise assuming the rank of gentleman; but I doubt whether any English office-holder, of similar rank, could parallel Mr. Lill[e]y. Nevertheless, I suppose he will administer his office well; and the worst of him is probably on the outside. He is taking a thousand pounds of tobacco to Pernambuco, by way of speculation.

[96] OCTOBER 20th.

ONE sees incidents in the streets, here, occasionally, which could not be seen in an American city. For instance, a week or two since, I was passing a quiet-looking elderly gentleman, when, all of a sudden, and without any apparent provocation, he uplifted his stick and struck a blackgowned boy a smart blow over the shoulders. The boy looked at him ruefully and resentfully, but said nothing, nor can I imagine why the thing was done. In Tithe Barn street, to-day, I saw a woman suddenly assault a man, clutch at his hair, and cuff him about the ears. The man, who was of decent aspect enough, immediately took to his heels, full speed, and the woman after him; and as far as I could discern the pair, the chase continued.

In the same street, I met two women, bearing on their backs bundles of large chips, absolutely bulkier than themselves. The burthens which women carry on their heads are absolutely marvellous; and they step along the crowded streets with the utmost freedom and security, without touching the loads with their hands. I meet many women barefoot, even at this advanced season.[43]

[97] The ancient family of Aston, in Cheshire, bears for its crest an Ass's head—punning, I suppose, on the same—'Ass-ton.'[44]

OCTOBER 22[d].

AT a dinner-party, at Mr. Holland's, last evening, M[r] Littledale, in instance of Charles Dickens's unweariability, said that, during some theatrical performances in Liverpool, he played in play and farce, spent the rest of the night speechifying, feasting, and drinking at table, and ended at seven °clock in the morning by playing at leap-frog over the backs of the whole company.

In Moore's diary,[45] he mentions a beautiful Guernsey lily having been given to his wife, and says that the flower was originally from Guernsey [Japan]. A ship from thence had been wrecked on the coast of Japan [Guernsey], having many of the lilies on board; and, the next year, the flowers appeared—springing up, I suppose, on the wave-beaten strand.

Wishing to send a letter to a dead man, who may be supposed to have gone to Tophet—throw it into the fire.[46]

[98] Sir Arthur Aston had his brains beaten out, with his own wooden leg, at the storming of Tredagh, in Ireland, by Cromwell.[47]

In the county of Cheshire, many centuries ago, there lived a half-idiot, named Nixon, who had the gift of prophecy, and made many predictions about places, families, and important public events—since fulfilled. He seems to have fallen into fits of insensibility, previous to uttering his prophecies.[48]

The family of Hockenhull bore for their arms an Ass's head erased sable.[49]

Farquhar drew his character of Sir Harry Wildair from his friend Sir Henry Bunbury of Little Stanney, in Cheshire. His residence was called Rake Hall—the name being given it at a convivial meeting, the guests at which were inscribed on a pane of glass.[50]

The family of Mainwaring (pronounced Mannering) of Brombrorough had an Ass's head for a crest.[51]

"Richard Dawson being sick of the plague, and perceiving he must die at that time, rose out of his bed, and made his grave, and caused his nephew to cast [99] straw into the grave, which was not far from the house, and went and laid him down in the said grave, and caused clothes to be laid upon him, and so departed out of this world. This he did because he was a strong man, and heavier than his said nephew and another wench were able to bury. He died about the 24th of August. Thus much was I credibly told he did 1625." This was in the township of Malpas. The house had been infected by Ralph Dawson, who came sick of the plague from London, and died in his father's house. The whole family, father, mother, sons, daughters, & servants, appear to have died—the last being Rose Smyth, a servant. The son of the family (John Dawson—the same nephew mentioned above) "came unto his father when his father sent for him, being sick, and having laid him down in a ditch, died in it, the 29th day of August 1625, in the night." The above is from the parish register of Malpas.[52]

At Bickley Hall (taken down a few years ago) used to be shown the room where the body of an Earl of Leinster was laid for a whole twelvemonth, from 1659 to 1660—he having [100] been kept unburied all that time, owing to a dispute which of his heirs should pay his funeral expenses.[53]

Novʀ 5 Saturday.

My wife, Una, Julian, and I, together with Mr Squarey,[54] went to Chester, last Sunday, and attended the Cathedral service. A great deal of ceremony, and not unimposing, but rather tedious before it was finished—occupying two hours or more. The Bishop was present, but did nothing, except to pronounce the benediction. In America, the sermon is the principal thing; but, here, all this magnificent ceremonial of prayers, and chanted responses, and psalms, and anthems, was the setting to a little meagre discourse, which would not at all have past muster among the elaborate intellectual efforts of New England ministers. While this was going on, the light came through the stained-glass windows, and fell upon the congregation, tinging some of their cheeks

and noses with crimson. After service, we wandered about the aisles, and
looked at the tombs and monuments—the oldest of which was that of some
nameless Abbot, with a staff and miter half obliterated from his tomb, which
was under a [101] shallow arch in the wall of the cathedral. There were also
marbles on the walls, and lettered stones in the pavement under our feet;—
but chiefly, if not entirely, of very modern date. We lunched at the Royal
Hotel, and then walked round the walls;—also crossing the bridge (of a
great, single arch) over the Dee, and penetrating as far into Wales as the
entrance of the Marquess of Westminster's park at Eaton. It was, I think, the
most lovely day, as regards weather, that I have seen in England—although
rather cool in the morning and evening.

Chester has an ancient smell pervading it.

I passed, to day, a man chanting a ballad in a street, about a recent murder,
in a voice that had innumerable cracks in it, and was most lugubrious. The
other day, I saw a man who was reading, in a loud voice, what seemed to be
an account of the late riots and loss of life in Wigan. He walked slowly along
the street, as he read, surrounded by a small crowd of men, women, and children; and close by his elbow stalked a policeman, as if guarding against a
disturbance.[55]

[102] Arms of Manning, Gules, a Cross patonce, Or, between four trefoils
slipped of the second.

Inscription on a painted window—"Of your charity pray for the good
estate of Sir George Calveley and Elizabeth his wife, daughter of Piers
Dutton of Hatton who was at the cost of glasing this window, anno
MCCCCCXXXIII." Church of Aldford[56]

The family of Calveley of Lea bear three calves trippant, sable—a fesse, gules,
between them in a field, argent. Crest a calf's head, proper, issuing from a
ducal coronet.[57]

The family of Davenport bore as a crest a Felon's Head, with a halter
about the neck.[58]

Nov 14th.

THERE is a heavy, dun fog on the river, and over the city, to-day; the very
gloomiest atmosphere that ever I was acquainted with. On the river, the
steamboats strike gongs or ring bells, to give warning of their approach.
There are lamps burning in the counting-rooms and entries of the warehouses,
and they gleam distinctly through the windows.

The other day, at the entrance of the market-house, [103] I saw a woman
sitting in a small hand-wagon, apparently for the purpose of receiving alms.
There was no attendant at hand; but I noticed that one or two persons, who
passed by, seemed to inquire whether she wished her wagon to be moved.
Perhaps this is her mode of making progress about the city, by the voluntary
aid of boys and other people, who lend their aid to drag her. There is something in this (I don't yet well know what) that has impressed me, as if I

could make a romance out of the idea of a woman living in this manner a public life, and moving about by such means.

Novr 29th.

Mr BRIGHT told of his friend Mr. Synge (who was formerly attaché to the British Legation at Washington, and whom I saw at Concord) that his father, a clergyman, married a second wife. After the marriage, the noise of a coffin, being nightly carried down the stairs, was heard in the parsonage. It could be distinguished when the coffin reached a certain broad stair, and rested on it. Finally his father had to leave the parsonage for another resi[104]dence. Besides this, Synge had had another ghostly experience—having seen a dim apparition of an uncle, at the precise instant when the latter died, in a distant place. Synge is a credible and honorable fellow, and talks of these matters as if he positively believed them. But Ghostland lies beyond the jurisdiction of veracity.

In the garden of a house near Chester, in taking down a summer-house, a tomb was discovered beneath it, with a Latin inscription to the memory of an old Doctor of Medicine, William Bentley, who had owned the house long ago, and died in 1680. And his dust and bones had lain beneath all the merry times in the summer house.[59]

DECEMBER 1st.

IT is curious how many methods people put in practice here to pick up a half-penny. Yesterday I saw a man standing bareheaded and bare-legged, in the mud and misty weather, playing on a fife, in hopes to get a circle of auditors. Nobody, however, seemed to take any notice. Very often, a whole band of musicians will strike up—passing a hat round after playing a [105] tune or two. On board the ferry-boats, until the colder weather began, there were always some wretched musicians, with an old fiddle, an old clarionet, an old, verdigreased [sic] brass bugle, playing during the passage; and, as the boat neared the shore, sending round one of their number to gather contributions in the hollow of the brass bugle. They were a very shabby set, and must have made a very scanty living, at best. Sometimes, it was a boy with an accordion, and his sister, a smart little girl, with a timbrel—which, being so shattered that she could not play on it, she used only to collect half-pence in. Ballad-singers, or rather chanters, or croakers, are often to be met with in the streets. Hand-organ players are not more frequent than in our own cities.

I still observe little girls and other children bare legged and barefooted, on the wet sidewalks. There never was anything so dismal as the November weather has been; never any real sunshine; almost always a mist; sometimes a dense fog, like slightly rarefied wool, pervading the atmosphere.

[106] An epitaph on a person buried on a hill side in Cheshire, together with some others, supposed to have died of the plague, and therefore not admitted into the church-yards:—

> "Think it not strange our bones ly here,
> "Thine may ly thou knowest not where"
> Elizabeth Hampson.

These graves were near the remains of two rude stone crosses, the purport of which was not certainly known, although they were supposed to be boundary-marks. Probably, as the plague-corpses were debarred from sanctified ground, the vicinity of these crosses was chosen, as having a sort of sanctity.[60]

"Bang-beggar"—an old Cheshire term for a parish beadle.

Hawthorne Hall, Cheshire, Macclesfield Hundred, Parish of Wilmslow, and within the hamlet of Morley. It was vested at an early period in the Lathoms of Irlam, Lancaster Co. and passed through the Leighs, and possibly other families, to the Pages of Eardshaw. Thomas Leigh Page sold it to Mr. Ralph Bower of Wilmslow, whose children owned it in 1817. [107] The Leighs built a chancel in the Church of Wilmslow, where some of them are buried; their arms painted in the windows. The hall is said to be an "ancient, respectable mansion of brick.[61]

DEC 3ᵈ.

YESTERDAY—a chill, misty, December day—I saw a woman barefooted in the street; not to speak of children.

Chill and uncertain as the weather is, there is still a great deal of small trade carried on in the open air. Women and men sit in the streets, with a stock of combs and such small things to sell; the women knitting, as if they sat by a fireside. Cheap crockery laid out in the street, outside of the side walk, so that, without any great deviation from the regular track, a wheel might pass right through it. Stalls of apples are innumerable, but the apples not fit for a pig. In some streets, herrings are very abundant, laid out on boards. Coals seem to be for sale by the wheelbarrow-full. Here and there, you see children with some small article for sale; as, for instance, a girl with two linen caps. A somewhat overladen cart [108] of coal was passing along, and some small quantity of the coal fell off; no sooner had the wheels passed, than several women and children gathered to the spot, like hens and chickens round a handful of corn, and picked it up in their aprons.[62] We have nothing parallel to these street-women, in our country.

DECʳ 10th.

I DON'T know any place that brings all classes into contiguity, on equal ground, so completely as the waiting-room at Rock Ferry, on these frosty days. The room is not more than eight feet square, with walls of stone, and wooden benches ranged round them; and an open stove in one corner, generally well furnished with coal. It is almost always crowded; and I rather suspect that many persons, who have no fireside elsewhere, creep in here and spend the most comfortable part of their day.

This morning, when I looked into the room, there were one or two gentlemen and other respectable persons, male and female; but in the best place, close
to the fire, and crouching almost into it, was an elderly beggar—with the
raggedest of overcoats, two great rents on the shoulders, disclosing the dingy
lining, all bepatched with [109] various stuff, covered with dirt; and on his
shoes and trowsers the mud of an interminable pilgrimage. Owing to the
posture in which he sat, I could not see his face, but only the battered crown
and rim of the very shabbiest hat that ever was. Regardless of the presence of
women (which, indeed, Englishmen seldom do regard, when they wish to smoke)
he was smoking a pipe of vile tobacco; but, after all, this was fortunate, because the man himself was not personally fragrant. He was terribly squalid—
terribly—and when I had a glimpse at his face, it well befitted the rest of
his development; grizzled, wrinkled, weather-beaten, yet sallow, down-looking
with a watchful kind of eye, turning upon everybody and everything, meeting
the eyes of other people rather boldly, yet soon shrinking away;—a long, thin
nose, gray beard of a week's growth, hair not much mixed with gray, but
rusty and lifeless. A miserable object; but it was curious to see how he was
not ashamed of himself, but seemed to feel that he was one of the estates
of the kingdom, and had as much right to live [110] as other men. He did
just as he pleased, took the best place by the fireside, nor would have cared
though a nobleman were forced to stand aside for him. When the steamer's
bell rang, he shouldered a large and heavy pack, and hobbled down the pier,
leaning on a crook-staff, and looking like a pilgrim with his burden of sin, but
certainly journeying to hell, instead of heaven. On board, he looked round for
the best position, at first stationing himself near the boiler-pipe, but finding
the deck damp under foot, went to the cabin-door, and took his stand on the
stairs, protected from the wind, but very incommodiously to those who wished
to pass. All this was done without any bravado or forced impudence, but in
the most quiet way, merely because he was seeking his own comfort, and
considered that he had a right to seek it. It was an Englishman's spirit; but,
in our country, I imagine, a beggar considers himself a kind of outlaw, and
would hardly assume the privileges of a man, in any place of public resort.
Here, beggary is a system, and beggars are a numerous class, and make themselves, in a certain way, respected as such. [111] Nobody evinced the slightest
disapprobation of this man's proceedings. In America, I think, we should
have seen many aristocratic airs, on such provocation; and probably the ferry-
people would have rudely thrust the beggar-man aside;—giving him a shilling,
however—which no Englishman would ever think of doing. There would also
have been a great deal of fun made of this squalid and ragged figure; whereas,
nobody smiled at him, this morning, nor in any way evinced the slightest
disrespect. This is good; but it is the result of a state of things by no means
good.

For many days past, there has been a great deal of fog on the river; and
the boats have groped their way along, continually striking their bells, while
on all sides there are responses of bell and gong; and the vessels at anchor

look shadowlike as we glide past them; and the master of one steamer shouts a warning to the steamer which he meets. The Englishmen (who hate to run any risk without an equivalent object) show a good deal of caution and timidity, on these foggy days.

[112]Decr 13th.

CHILL, frosty weather;—such an atmosphere as forebodes snow in New England; and there has been a little here. Yet I saw a barefooted young woman, yesterday. The feet of these poor creatures have exactly the red complexion of their hands, acquired by constant exposure to the cold air.

At the Ferry-room, this morning, a small, thin, anxious-looking woman, with a bundle, looking in rather poor circumstances, but decently dressed, and eyeing other women, I thought, with an expression of slight ill-will and distrust; an elderly, stout, gray-haired woman, of respectable aspect; two young lady-like persons, rather pretty, one of whom was reading a shilling volume of James's "Arabella Stuart[63]; they talked to one another with that up and down intonation which English ladies practise, and which strikes an unaccustomed ear as rather affected, especially in women of size and mass. It is very different from an American lady's mode of talking;—there is the difference between color and no color;—the tone variegates it. One of these young ladies spoke to me, making some remark about the [113] weather;— the first instance I have met with of a gentle-woman's speaking to an unintroduced gentleman. Besides these, a middle-aged man of the lower classes; and also a gentleman's out-door servant, clad in a drab great-coat, corduroy breeches, and drab cloth gaiters buttoned from the knee to the ankle. He complained to the other man of the cold-weather, said that a glass of whiskey every half-hour would keep a man comfortable, and accidentally hitting his coarse foot against one of the young lady's feet (which she was toasting at the fire) said, "Beg pardon, Ma'am,—" which she acknowledged with a slight movement of the head. Somehow or other, different classes seem to encounter one another in an easier manner than with us;—the shock is less palpable. I suppose the reason is, that the distinctions are real, and therefore need not be continually asserted.

Humphrey Warren, son of an ancient family, blinded by shot out of a gun, accidentally fired by his half-brother; he invented a loom, very intricate and curious, and occupied himself with weaving silk in intricate and beautiful patterns. Specimens remained, as also fragments of the loom, 1816. Born 1671, died 1744.[64]

[114] In Ormerod's History of Cheshire (III, page 444) Richard Eaton is mentioned as the second vicar of Great Budworth. "He had a son Nathaniel, born 1609, who was first master of the college at New Cambridge in New England; he afterwards died in the King's Bench."

Nervous and excitable persons need to talk a great deal, by way of blowing off their steam.

On board the Rock Ferry steamer, a gentleman coming into the cabin, a voice addresses him from a dark corner—"How do you do, Sir?" "Speak again!" says the gentleman. No answer from the dark corner; and the gentleman repeats, "Speak again!" The speaker now comes out of the dark corner, and sits down in a place where he can be seen. "Ah," cries the gentleman, "very well, I thank you! How do you do? I did not recognize your voice." Observable, the queer English caution shown in the gentleman's not vouchsafing to say "Very well, thank you!" till he knew his man.

What was the after-life of the young man, whom Jesus, looking on, "loved him," and bade him sell all [115] that he had, and give to the poor, and take up the cross and follow him? Something very deep and beautiful might be made out of this.

Decr 31st.

AMONG the beggars of Liverpool, the hardest to encounter is a man without any legs, and, if I mistake not, likewise deficient in arms. You see him before you all at once, as if he had sprouted half-way out of the earth, and would sink down and re-appear in some other place, the moment he has done with you. His countenance is large, fresh, and very intelligent; but his great power lies in his fixed gaze, which is inconceivably difficult to bear. He never once removes his eye from you, till you are quite past his range; and you feel it all the same, although you do not meet his glance. He is perfectly respectful; but the intentness and directness of his silent appeal is far worse than any impudence. In fact, it is the very flower of impudence. I would rather go a mile about than pass before his battery. I feel wronged by him, and yet unutterably ashamed. There must be [116] great force in the man, to produce such an effect. There is nothing of the customary squalidness of beggary about him, but remarkable trimness and cleanliness. A girl of twenty or thereabouts, who vagabondizes about the city on her hands and knees, possesses, to a considerable degree, the same characteristics. I think they hit their victims the more effectually, from being below the common level of vision.[65]

The other day, there came to me, with an introduction from Governor Crosby of Maine, a Mr John A. Knight, who had come across the Atlantic in attendance on two ladies, claimants of the Booth estate in Cheshire. His information on the subject seems to be of a very vague character; and, no doubt, the claim is wholly untenable. The ladies assume to be of royal blood, and are apprehensive that the English lawyers will be the less willing to allow their pretensions from a disinclination to admit new members into the royal kin. I think I recorded the visit, a short time ago, of the lady who claims the most valuable part of Liverpool, including the Exchange and Docks.[66]

[117] JANUARY 3^d 1854.

NIGHT before last, there was a fall of snow, about three or four inches; following it, a pretty smart frost. On the river, the vessels at anchor, with the snow along their yards, and on every ledge where it could lie. A blue sky and sunshine overhead, and apparently a clear atmosphere close at hand; but, at distance, a mistiness became perceptible, obscuring the shores of the river, and making the vessels look dim and uncertain. The steamers ploughing along, smoking their pipes through the frosty air. On the landing stage and in the streets, hard-trodden snow, looking more like my New England home, than anything I have yet seen. Last night, the thermometer fell as low as 13°; nor, probably, is it above 20°, to-day. No such frost has been seen in England these forty years; and my junior clerk, Mr. Wilding, tells me that he never saw so much snow before.

If we were bad yesterday, we must be worse to-day, and worst tomorrow.

[118] JAN^y 6th, 1854.

I SAW, yesterday, stopping at a cabinet-maker's shop in Church-street, a coach with four beautiful dark horses, and a postillion on each near horse; behind, in the dickey, was a footman, and on the box a coachman, all dressed in uniform style. The coach-panel bore a coat of arms with a coronet, and I presume, must have been the equipage of the Earl of Derby. A crowd of people stood round, gazing at the coach and horses; and when any of them spoke, it was in a lower tone than usual. I doubt not they all had a kind of enjoyment of the spectacle; for these English are strangely proud of having a class above them.

At this season, how long the nights are—from the first gathering gloom of twilight, when the grate in my office begins to glow ruddier, all through dinner-time, and the putting to bed of the children, and the lengthened evening, with its books or its drowsiness,—our own getting to bed, the brief awakenings through the many dark hours, and then the creeping onward of morning. It seems an age between light and light.

[119] Every Englishman runs to "The Times" with his little grievance, as a child runs to his mother.

I was sent for to the Police-court, the other morning, in the case of an American sailor, accused of robbing a shipmate at sea. A large room, with a great coal-fire burning on one side; and above it the portrait of a Mr Rushton, deceased, a magistrate of many years continuance. A long table, with chairs; on one side, the witness-box. One of the borough-magistrates (a merchant of the city) sat at the head of the table, with paper and pen-and-ink before him; but the real judge was the clerk of the court, whose professional knowledge and experience governed all the proceedings. In the short time while I was waiting, two cases were tried, in the first of which the prisoner was discharged. The second case was of a woman—a thin, sallow, hard-looking, careworn, youngish woman—for stealing a pair of slippers out of a shop. The trial occupied five minutes or less; and she was sentenced to twenty-one days imprisonment—whereupon, without speaking, [120] she looked up wildly first into one policeman's face, then into another's, at the same time wringing her hands, with no theatric gesture, but because her torment took that outward shape—and was led away. The Yankee sailor was then brought up—an intelligent, but ruffianlike fellow; and as the case (being only for stealing a comforter) was out of the jurisdiction of the English magistrates, and as it was not worth my while to get him sent over to America for trial, he was forthwith discharged.

If mankind were all intellect, they would be continually changing, so that one age would be entirely unlike another. The great conservative is the heart, which remains the same in all ages; so that common-places of a thousand years standing are as effective as ever.

Lancashire tradition. When all the people of Amounderness were in fear of trouble, a cow presented herself ready to supply the inhabitants with milk, so long as no vessel was presented which she could not fill. At [121] last a mischievous old witch brought a sieve; "and the cow, not being able to fill it, wandered away sorrowfully to a hill near Preston, called Cow Hill to this day, and there died" *Proceeding of His. Soc. Lancashire & Cheshire. Ses IV*[67]

FEB^y 13th 1854, MONDAY.

VISITORS of inner office—Captain Libby, to be sworn to and sign a protest;—one of the second class of masters of vessels, plain, and without any dash or pretension.—A white sailor and a dark mulatto, to swear to some vessel's protest.—Towards 4 °clock, Captain Foster to subscribe and swear to a document.—I meant to have put down everybody who called on me, through the week; but there were too many for record, and too many interruptions to record them.

FEB 20th MONDAY.

AT the police-court on Saturday, attending the case of the 2^d mate and four seamen of the John and Albert, for assaulting, beating, and stabbing the chief-mate. The chief mate has been in the hospital, ever since the assault, and was brought into the court to-day to give evi[122][dence.] A man of thirty or upwards, black hair, black eyes, a dark complexion, disagreeable expression; sallow, emaciated, feeble, apparently in pain, one arm disabled; he sat bent and drawn upward, and had evidently been severely hurt, and was not yet fit to be out of bed. He had some brandy and water to enable him to sustain himself. He gave his evidence very clearly, beginning (sailor-like) with telling in what quarter the wind was at the time of the assault, and what sail was taken in. His testimony bore only on one man, at whom he cast a vindictive look; but I think he told the truth, as far as he knew and remembered it. Of the prisoners, the 2ᵈ mate was a mere youth, with long sandy hair, an intelligent and not unprepossessing face, dressed as neatly as a three or four weeks captive, with small or no means, could well be, in a frock coat, and with a clean shirt; the only linen or cotton shirt in the company. The other four were rude, brutish sailors, in flannel or red-baize shirts; three of them appeared to give themselves little concern; but the fourth, a red haired and red [123] bearded man (Paraman by name) evidently felt the pressure of the case upon himself. He was the one whom the mate swore to have given him the first blow; and there was other evidence of his having been [sic] stabbed him with a knife. The captain of the ship, the pilot, the cook, and the steward, all gave their evidence; and the general bearing of it was, that the chief mate had a devilish temper, and had misused the 2ᵈ mate and men, that the four seamen had attacked him, and that Paraman had stabbed him; while all but the steward concurred in saying that the 2ᵈ mate had taken no part in the affray. The steward swore to having seen him strike the chief-mate with a wooden marling-spike, which was broken by the blow. The magistrate dismissed all but Paraman, whom I am to send to America for trial. In my opinion, the chief mate got pretty nearly what he deserved, under the code of natural justice.

While business was going forward, the magistrate (Mʳ Mansfield) talked about a fancy-ball [124] at which he had been present the evening before, and of other matters grave and gay. It was very informal; we sat at the table, or stood with our backs to the fire; police-men came and went; witnesses were sworn on the greasiest copy of the gospels I ever saw, polluted by hundreds and thousands of perjured kisses; and for four hours the prisoners were kept standing at the foot of the table, interested to the full extent of their capacity, while all others were indifferent. At the close of the case, the police-officers and witnesses applied to me about their expenses.

Yesterday, I took a walk with wife and two children to Bebington-church. A beautifully sunny morning. Wife and Una attended church; Julian and I continued our walk. When we had got a little distance from the church, the bells suddenly chimed out with a most cheerful sound, as sunny as the morning. It is a pity we have no chimes of bells to give the churchward summons at home. People were standing about the ancient church-[125] porch, and among the tomb-stones. In the course of our walk, we past many old thatched cottages, built of stone, and with what looked like a cow-house or pig-stye, at one end, making part of the cottage; also, an old stone farm-house, which may have been a residence of gentility in its day. We passed, too, a small Methodist chapel, making one of a row of low brick edifices; there was a sound of prayer within. I never saw a more unbeautiful place of worship; and it had not even a separate existence for itself, the adjoining tenement being an ale-house.

The grass along the wayside was green, with a daisy or two. There was green holly in the hedges; and we passed through a wood, up some of the tree-trunks of which ran clustering ivy.

FEB 23ᵈ '54.

THERE came to see me the other day a young gentleman with a moustache and a blue cloak (of rather coarse texture) who announced himself as William Allingham,⁶⁸ and handed me a copy of his poems, in a thin volume with paper-covers, published by Rout[126]ledge. I thought I remembered hearing his name, but had never seen any of his works. His face was intelligent, dark, rather pleasing, and not at all John Bullish. He said that he had been employed in the Customs in Ireland, and was now going to London to live by literature— to be connected with some newspaper, I imagine. He had been in London before, and was acquainted with some of the principal literary people—among others, Carlyle and Tennyson. He seemed to have been on rather intimate terms with the latter; and I gathered from what he said that Tennyson is a moody man, though genial with his friends. He says Tennyson told him that, if he were sure there were no hereafter, he would go and fling himself over London bridge;—a foolish thing to do or to say; but perhaps he might have said a wiser thing to a wiser man. Tennyson is a very shy man, and thinks everybody stares at him on account of his strange appearance, on railways and everywhere else, even in the seclusion of his own garden. This, I judge, has no reference to the no[127]tice drawn on him by his poetry, but is the natural morbidness of a man who shirks society. Tennyson's wife seems to be a good person, not handsome, but cheerful, capable of appreciating him and fit to make him comfortable. Her mode seems to be a gentle and good-humored raillery of his peculiarities. Allingham says that they have a fine boy and that it would have been better for Tennyson to have been married fifteen years ago, instead of three or four. We talked awhile in my dingy and dusky consulate, and he then took leave. His manners are good, and he appears to possess independence of mind. On looking over his poems, I find some good things among them.

Yesterday, I saw a British regiment march down to George's Pier, to embark in the Niagara for Malta. The troops had nothing very remarkable about them; but the thousands of ragged and filthy wretches, who thronged the pier and streets to gaze at them, were what I had not seen before, in such masses. How unlike the well-dressed and [128] well-washed multitude in an American city. This was the first populace I have beheld; for even the Irish, on the other side of the water, acquire respectability of aspect.

John Bull is going with his whole heart into this Turkish war. He is a great fool. Whatever the Czar may propose to himself, it is for the interest of Democracy that he should not be easily put down.

The regiment, on its way to embark, carried the Queen's colours, and, side by side with them, the banner of the 28th, yellow, with the names of the peninsular, and other battles in which it had been engaged, inscribed on it, in a double column. It is a very distinguished regiment; and Mr. Henry Bright mentioned as one of its distinctions that Washington had formerly been an officer in it. I never heard of this, and don't believe it.

FEB 27th '54, MONDAY.

A MAN with his wife and child yesterday, on board the steamer, taking a Sunday-trip to Rock Ferry. He, thin and rather small, with a large beard; she, older than himself, and somewhat bony; their three children the largest and flabbiest little he and she-urchins [129] that ever were seen. I never saw such vast broadsides of cheek in my life. They were people of the lower-middle class. The husband had a cane (a bamboo with ivory head gone) and occasionally he smiled at his youngest girl and poked her jocosely with this stick; the little one taking it in excellent part. Never did paternal tenderness find a queerer medium than this stick.

Sophia, Una, Julian, and myself, were in the steamboat;—having walked to Woodside in the pleasant Sabbath forenoon, and thence crossed to Liverpool. On our way to Woodside, we saw the remains of the old Birkenhead Priory, built of the common red free-stone, much time-worn, with ivy creeping over it, and birds evidently at home in its old crevices. These ruins are pretty extensive, and seem to be the remains of a quadrangle. A handsome modern church (likewise of the same red-free stone) has been built on part of the site occupied by the Priory; and the organ was sounding within, while we walked about the premises. On some of the ancient arches, there were grotesquely carved stone-faces. The old walls have [130] been sufficiently restored to make them secure, without destroying their venerable aspect. It is a very interesting spot;—and so much the more, because a modern town, with its brick and stone houses, its flags and pavements, has sprung up about the ruins, which were new a thousand years ago. The station of the Chester railway is within a hundred or two of yards. Formerly, the monks of this Priory kept the only ferry that then existed on the Mersey.

FEB^y 28th

YESTERDAY afternoon, while waiting for the Rock Ferry boat to cross, a young man accosted me with a copy of the Times for sale—a single copy, and with an aspect of doubtful newness. He was the leanest poor-devil I ever saw, woefully ragged and rended, pretty evidently half-starved, and sickly besides. One is so beset by all sorts of beggars, here in England, that I shook my head, and he immediately went off, saying—"Well, upon my word, Sir, I'm in want of a bit of bread"—in a grave, bewildered kind of tone, not angry or reproachful;—in fact, I can't quite make out what the tone signified. Afterwards, [131] I watched him plying from one group or individual to another, with such activity that his rags fluttered in the wind, and offering his single poor copy of the Times, soiled as it was, and which nobody would buy. I have had a pang of conscience ever since, for not giving him something. They say that it does mischief, and that all these wretches can find a refuge somewhere, if they choose to acccept it;—but this poor, ragged devil upholds the other side of the question. He was certainly hungry and half-frozen, and could not have been so for his own pleasure. (P.S.) From subsequent observation, I think him a humbug.

Calling on a ship-master to take his oath to a protest, he being confined by illness to a Hotel. The cheerful and lively aspect of the front and lower regions of the hotel, with clerks and waiters in attendance; neat parlors, coffee-room &c. Ascending, and progressing towards the rear, the scenery of the house becomes dingy and shabby; the passages narrow, and I think, uncarpeted; staircases steep and narrow; glimpses on one [132] side and the other of small bed-rooms, furnished in the plainest style; house-maids flitting past, with broom and basket. At last we come to the captain's room, with a scanty carpet, and a wide margin of bare floor; a small, cheerless fire in the grate; a pine dressing table, a chair or two, and the captain himself in bed, with a weather beaten, sick face, his hands looking pale and sick, though they have evidently never worn gloves much. I speak to him cheerily; he responds with a dull kind of hopefulness; my clerk reads the protest, which the captain scrambles out of bed to sign, in his shirt and drawers, throwing back the bed clothes, which disclose a rather dingy pair of sheets. While the protest is being read, comes in a woman with a cup and saucer of tea or gruel, which she puts on the hob and retires,—glancing anxiously at us and the captain, as suspecting that he is making his will or doing some other ominous business. We retire, wishing him speedy health. His disease is probably partly on his spirits—he having lost his ship, the Australia, while endeavoring to get back into port, very soon [133] after sailing. Julian accompanied me, and clambering into an arm-chair, looked over its back at the sick man with great interest.

There came into my office, a few days ago, a man of about fifty, short and square, with a foreign look and tongue, rather shewily dressed, and with a forward demeanor, as of one accustomed to back up his own pretensions with strangers. He announced himself as an eradicator of corns, and produced two thick quarto volumes of testimonials from innumerable persons, among whom were many distinguished Americans—as Everett,[69] and the members of the present legation &c. Also, I had a glimpse of Thackeray's. Many of these were fortified with the wax-seals as well as signatures of the writers. He wished to know if I myself had any corns for him to operate upon; or if Madame, my lady, had any; and failing of these, he desired the addresses of any American houses in Liverpool—which I did not give him. A bold, showy, gentlemanly, vulgar humbug—a man whom I think I have heard [134] of in America; a Jew, who takes out any number of corns out of a foot, at half a dollar a-piece, and never fails to find an abundant harvest. His two books of testimonials would doubtless be valuable to autograph-collectors.

At a dinner at Mr Bramley-Moore's, a little while ago, we had a prairie-hen from the West of America. It was a most delicate bird; and a gentleman carved it most skillfully to a dozen guests, and had still a second slice to offer.

Englishmen are not made of polishable substance—not of marble, but rather of red free-stone. There is a kind of roughness and uncouthness in the most cultivated of them. After some conversance with them as a people, you learn to distinguish true gentlemen among them; but at first it seems as if there were none.

Aboard the ferry-boat, yesterday, a laboring man eating oysters; he took them, one by one, from his pocket in interminable succession, opened them with his jack[135]knife, swallowed the oyster, threw the shell overboard— and then for another. Having concluded his meal, he took out a clay tobacco pipe, filled, lighted it with a rush, and smoked it—all this while the other passengers were looking at him, and with a perfect coolness and independence, such as no single man can ever feel in America. Here, a man does not seem to consider what other people will think of his conduct, but whether it suits his convenience to do so and so. It may be the better way.

A French military man (a veteran of all Napoleon's wars) now living, with a false leg and arm, both moveable by springs, false teeth, a false eye, a silver nose with a flesh-colored covering, and a silver plate replacing part of the skull. He has the cross of the Legion of Honor.

FEB [MARCH] 13th

ON Saturday, I went with Mr Bright to the Dingle, a pleasant domain on the banks of the Mersey, about opposite to Rock Ferry. Walking home, we looked into Mr. Thom's[70] Unitarian chapel (in Renshaw Street, I think) where [136] Mr Bright's family-place of worship is. There is a little grave yard connected with the chapel; a most uninviting and unpicturesque square of ground, perhaps thirty or forty yards across, in the midst of back fronts of city buildings. About half the space was occupied by flat tomb-stones, level with the ground; the remainder being yet vacant. Nevertheless, there were perhaps more names of men generally known to the world, on these few tombstones, than in any other church-yard in Liverpool—Roscoe,[71] Blanco White,[72] and the Rev. William Enfield,[73] whose name has a classical sound in my ears, because, when a little boy, I used to read his Speaker, at school. In the vestry of the chapel, there were many books, chiefly old theological works in ancient print and binding, much mildewed and injured by the damp. The body of the chapel is neat, but plain; and being not very large, has a kind of social and family aspect, as if the clergyman and his people must needs have intimate relations among themselves. The Unitarian sect in Liverpool have, as a body, great wealth and respectability.

Yesterday, I walked with my wife and children to the [137] brow of a hill, overlooking Birkenhead and Tranmere, and having a fine view of the river, and Liverpool beyond. All roundabout, new and neat residences for city people are springing up, with fine names—Eldon Terrace, Rose Cottage, Belvoir Villas, &c &c &c—with little patches of ornamental garden or lawn in front, and heaps of curious rock-work, which the English are ridiculously fond of adorning their front-yards with. I rather think the middling classes—meaning shopkeepers, and other respectabilities of that level—are better lodged here than in America; and, what I did not expect, the houses are a good deal newer than in our new country. Of course, this can only be the case in places circumstanced like Liverpool and its suburbs. But, scattered among these modern villas, there are old stone cottages, of the rudest structure, and doubtless hundreds of years old, with thatched roofs, into which the grass has rooted itself and now looks verdant. These cottages are in themselves as ugly as possible, resembling a larger kind of pig-stye; but often, by dint of the verdure on their thatch, and the shrubbery clustering about them, they look picturesque.

[138] The old fashioned flowers in the gardens of New England (blue-bells, crocusses [sic], primroses, and many others) appear to be wild flowers here on English soil. There is something very touching and pretty in this fact, that the old Puritans should have carried these field and hedge-flowers, and nurtured them in their gardens; until, to us, they seem entirely the products of cultivation.[74]

MARCH 16th.

YESTERDAY, at the Coroner's court, attending the inquest on a colored sailor, who died on board an American vessel, after her arrival at this port. The court room capable of accommodating perhaps fifty people, dingy, with a pyramidal skylight above, and a single window on one side, opening into a gloomy back court. A private room, also lighted with pyramidal skylight, behind the court-room, into which I was asked, and found the Coroner—a gray headed, grave, intelligent, broad, red-faced man, with a due quantity of English beef in him, and an air of some authority, well-mannered and dignified, but not exactly a gentleman—dressed in a blue coat, with a black cravat [139] and no shirt collar above it. Considering how many and what a variety of cases of the ugliest death are constantly coming before him, he was much more cheerful than could be expected, and had a kind of formality and orderliness, which I suppose balances the exceptionalities with which he has to deal. In the private room with him was likewise the surgeon who professionally attends the court. We chatted about suicide and such matters—the surgeon, the Coroner, and I—until the American case was ready, when we adjourned to the court-room, and the Coroner began the examination. The American captain was a rude, uncouth Down Easterner, about thirty years old, and sat on a bench doubled and bent into an indescribable attitude, out of which he occasionally straightened himself—all the time toying with a ruler, or some such article. The case was one of no interest; the man had been frost-bitten, and died from natural causes, so that no censure was deserved or passed upon the captain. The jury, who had been examining the body, were at first inclined to think that the man had not been frost-bitten, but [140] that his feet had been immersed in boiling water; but, on explanation by the surgeon, readily yielded their opinion, and gave the verdict which the Coroner put into their mouths, exculpating the captain from all blame. In fact, it is utterly impossible that a jury of chance-individuals should not be entirely governed by the judgement of so experienced and weighty a man as this coroner. In the court-room, were two or three police-officers in uniform, and some other officials; a very few idle spectators, and a few witnesses waiting to be examined; and while the case was going forward, a poor-looking woman came in, and I heard her, in an under-tone, telling an attendant of a death that had just occurred. The attendant received the communication in a very quiet and matter of course way, said that it should be attended to; and the woman retired. *The Diary of a Coroner* would be a work likely to meet with large popular acceptance. A dark passage-way, only a few yards in extent, leads from the liveliest street in Liverpool to this Coroner's court-room, where all the discussion is about murder and suicide. It seems, [141] that, after a verdict of suicide, the corpse can only be buried at midnight, without religious rites.

"His lines are cast in pleasant places"[75]—applied to a successful angler.

A woman's chastity consists, like an onion, of a series of coats. You may strip off the outer ones without doing much mischief, perhaps none at all; but you keep taking off one after another, in expectation of coming to the inner nucleus, including the whole value of the matter. It proves, however, that there is no such nucleus, and that chastity is diffused through the whole series of coats, is lessened with the removal of each, and vanishes with the final one, which you supposed would introduce you to the hidden pearl.

MARCH 23ᵈ.

MR BRIGHT and I took a cab, Saturday afternoon, and rode out of the city in the direction of Knowsley. On our way, we saw many gentlemen's or rich people's places; some of them dignified with [142] the title of Halls—with lodges at their gates, and standing considerably removed from the road. The greater part of them were built of brick—a material with which I have not been accustomed to associate ideas of grandeur; but it was much in use here in Lancashire in the Elizabethan age,—more, I think, than now. These suburban residences, however, are of much later date than Elizabeth's time. Among other places, Mr. Bright called at the Hazles [*sic*], the residence of Sir Thomas Birch, a kinsman of his. It is a large, rather dreary and bare-looking brick mansion; and in America, if it stood in the center of a village, might pass for a town-hall. It has old trees and shrubbery about it, however—the latter very fine and verdant—hazles [*sic*], holly, rhododendron, &c. Mr. Bright went in, and shortly afterwards Sir Thomas Birch came out, a very frank and hospitable old gentleman, and pressed me to come in and take luncheon—which latter hospitality I declined. He is an old bachelor, and his house in no very good order—rather shabby, indeed, compared with most English houses; but he seemed to have a [143] good many pictures, and amongst them a small portrait of his mother, painted by Sir Thomas Lawrence when a youth. It is unfinished; and when the painter was at the height of his fame, he was asked to finish it. But Lawrence, after looking at the picture, refused to re-touch it, saying that there was a merit in this early sketch, which he could no longer attain. It was really a very beautiful picture of a lovely woman.

Sir Thomas Birch proposed to go with us and get us admittance into Knowsley Park, where we could not probably find entrance without his aid. So we went to the stables, where the old groom had already shown hospitality to our cabman by giving his horse some provender, and himself, I believe, some beer. There seemed to be a kindly and familiar sort of intercourse between the old servant and the old baronet—each of them, I presume, looking on their connection as indissoluble.

The gate-ward of Knowsley-park was an old woman, who readily gave us admittance at Sir Thom[144]as's request. The Derby family are not now at the Park. They do not seem to be at all popular with their neighbors, or with the gentry of Liverpool—being accused of arrogant and unsocial habits; and, in fact, it is rather a pity to see, that, after so many centuries of connection with the soil and neighborhood, they have not the slightest hold on the affections of the country. Moreover, all those centuries do not seem to have made the race truly noble, or else it has latterly degenerated; for the present Lord Stanley, a young man of twenty-six, eldest son of the Earl, is said to be a mean fellow. There is a story (averred to be true, though only mentioned in a whisper) that, while at Rugby School, he stole a five-pound note, and, I think, was compelled to leave the school for it. In his present character, so far as I can understand, there is nothing to obliterate this early stain.

It was a very bad time of year to see the park; the trees just showing the earliest symptoms of vitality, while whole acres of ground were covered with large, dry, brown ferns—which I suppose would look very [145] beautiful when green. Two or three hares scampered out of these ferns, and stood on their hind-legs looking about them, as we rode by. A sheet of water (artificial, no doubt,) had been drawn off in order to deepen its bed. The oaks did not seem [to] me so magnificent as they should be, in an ancient noble property, like this. A century does not do so much for a tree, in this slow region, as it does in ours. I think, however, that they were more individual and picturesque—with more character in their contorted trunks; therein somewhat resembling apple-trees. Our forest-trees have a great sameness of character, like our people;—because one and the other grow too closely.

In one part of the park, we came to a small tower, for what purpose I know not, unless as an observatory; and near it a marble statue on a high pedestal. The statue had been long exposed to the weather, and was overgrown and ingrained with moss and lichens; so that its classic beauty was in some sort gothicised. A half-mile or so from this point, we [146] saw the mansion of

Knowsley, in the midst of a very fine prospect, with a tolerably high ridge of hills, called (something) Pikes [Rivington Pike], in the distance. The house itself is exceedingly vast, a front and two wings, with suites of rooms, I suppose, interminable. The oldest part, Sir Thomas Birch told us, is a tower of the time of Henry VII. Nevertheless, the effect is not overwhelming, because the edifice looks low in proportion to its great extent over the ground; and, besides, a good deal of it is built of brick, with white window frames (whether marble or painted, I know not;) so that, looking at separate parts, I might think them American structures, without the smart addition of green Venetian blinds, so universal with us. Portions, however, were built of red free-stone; and if I had looked at the edifice longer, no doubt I should have admired it more. We merely rode round it from the rear to the front. It stands in my memory rather like a college or a hospital, than the ancestral residence of a great English noble.

We left the park in another direction, and passed through a part of Lord Sefton's property by a private [147] road. Lord Sefton seems to be a more affable man, and with more popular characteristics, than Lord Derby; and he does not so utterly exclude visitors from Croxteth as the latter does from Knowsley. By-the-by, we saw, I should suppose, half a dozen police-men, in their blue coats and embroidered collars, after entering Knowsley-park; but the Earl's own servants would probably have supplied their place, had the family been at home. The mansion of Croxteth (the seat of Lord Sefton) stands within a stone's throw of the public road, and though large, looked of rather narrow compass, after Knowsley.

Sir Thomas Birch took a kindly leave of us, and trotted home. Being a man of title (and I presume, fortune) we Americans would rank him with the higher classes; but I doubt whether he feels himself as belonging to them. This great Earl, his neighbor, keeps him within his shadow, and looks down upon him, as a giant looks at an ordinary man. Hanging on the skirts of the aristocracy, a baronet probably is oftener much sensible of his inferiority [148] to the few than of his elevation over the many. Indeed, his position is not one of real elevation. Nevertheless, Sir Thomas seems a kind-hearted man, a little wayward and peevish, at times, I should judge, and perhaps not over-happy in his bachelor solitude. He spends a good deal of time in London, Mr. Bright says, and has been a man of the world.

The rooks were talking together very loquaciously in the high tops of the trees, near his house; it being now their building time. It was a very pleasant sound; the noise being comfortably veiled by the remote height. Sir Thomas said that, more than half a century ago, the rooks used to inhabit another grove of lofty trees, close in front of the house; but being noisy, and not altogether cleanly in their habits, the ladies of the family grew weary of them, and wished to remove them. Accordingly, the colony was driven away, and made their present settlement in a grove behind the house. Ever since that time, not a rook has built in the ancient grove; every year, however, one or another pair of young [149] rooks attempts to build among the deserted tree-tops, but the old rooks tear the new nest to pieces as often as it is put together. Thus either the memory of aged individual rooks, or an authenticated tradition among their society, has preserved the idea that the old grove is forbidden and inauspicious to them.

Mr Bright told a funny story of the lady of a former American Ambassador to England. In London, one day, she went into a cheap shop, where the articles are ticketted [sic], and bought a shawl, which she wore pretty extensively about town. She had not taken care to remove the ticket from the shawl; so that she exhibited herself to the eyes of the metropolis with this label—"PER-FECTLY CHASTE 15/S."—certainly a moderate valuation of perfect chastity.

Also, another of a blunder of hers with regard to a son of Lady Palmerston by her former husband—there having been much scandal respecting the connection between Lord and Lady Palmerston, before her first husband's death. "There is no mistaking him," quoth [150] Mrs —— "He is the very image of Lord Palmerston!—" This being just what scandal said he was, though what he had no right to be; and therefore a somewhat astounding announcement to be made to Lady Palmerston.

MARCH 28th.

ON Friday last, I dined with Mr. Bramley Moore[76] at Aigburth, to meet Mr Warren,[77] author of "Ten thousand a Year." There were eight or ten gentlemen at dinner, principally lawyers now attending the assizes, and of no great interest. Mr. Warren is a man (on his own authority) of forty-six—not tall nor large, with a pale, rather thin, and intelligent face—American more than English in its aspect, except that his nose is more prominent than ordinary American noses; as most English noses are. He is Recorder of Hull, an office which he says brings him but little; nor does he get much practice as a barrister, on account of the ill-will of the attornies [sic], who consider themselves aggrieved by his depictures of Quirk, Gammon, & Snap.[78]

On the whole, the dinner was not a very agreeable one. I led in Mrs. Bramley-Moore (the only lady present) and found her a stupid woman, of vulgar tone, and [151] outrageously religious—even to the giving away of little tracts, and lending religious books. The family are virulent tories, fanatics for the Established Church, and followers of Dr. McNeill,[79] who is the present low-church Pope of Liverpool. I could see little to distinguish her from a rigidly orthodox and Calvinistic woman of New England; for they acquire the same characteristics from their enmity to the Puseyite movement and Roman Catholic tendencies of the present day. Mrs. Bramley-Moore must be an under-bred woman; it is indescribably evident in her whole tone and manner; and, I suspect, an Englishwoman does not so readily overcome such disadvantages as an American would.

The eatables and drinkables were very praiseworthy; and Mr. Bramley-

Moore circulated his wines more briskly than is customary at gentleman's tables. He, too, I suspect, is not quite a gentleman; nor of one of those ancient merchant-princely families, who form the century-old aristocracy of Liverpool. He seems to be rich, however, has property in the Brazils (where [152] he was at one time resident,) has been Mayor of Liverpool, an unsuccessful candidate for Parliament, and now lives at a very pretty place. But he alludes to the cost of wines, and of other things which he possesses; a frailty which I have not observed in any other Englishman of good station. He is a moderately bulky, and rather round-shouldered man, with a kindly face enough; and seems to be a passably good man; but I hope, on the whole, that he will not ask me to dinner any more—though his dinners are certainly very good.

Mr Warren, nevertheless, turned out agreeably; he sat opposite to me, and I observed that he took champagne very freely, not waiting till Mr Bramley-Moore should suggest it, or till the servants should periodically offer it, but inviting his neighbors to a glass of wine. Neither did he refuse hock, nor anything else that came round. He was talkative, and mostly about himself and his writings—which I have no objection to, in a writer—knowing that if he talks little of himself, he perhaps thinks the more. It is a trait of simplicity that ought not [153] to be so scouted as it generally is. Mr. Warren said nothing very brilliant; but yet there was occasionally a champagny frothiness of his spirits, that enlivened me more than anything else at table. He told a laughable story about an American who had seen a portrait of Warren's father, which was prefixed to an American edition of his works as his own; and was perplexed at the dissimilarity between this effigy of an old bewigged clergyman and the dapper, youthfullish personage before him. He appears to feel very kindly towards the Americans, and says somebody has sent him some of the Catawba champagne. Warren has a talent of mimicry, and gave us some touches of Sergeant Wilkins,[80] whom I met, several months ago, at the Mayor's dinner.

After Mrs. Bramley-Moore had retired, Warren began an informal little talk to Mr. Bramley-Moore (who sat between him and me) on my merits as a man and an author. Mr. B.-M. urged him to speak up and give the company the privilege of hearing his remarks; and though I remonstrated, it gradually grew into almost [154] a regular dinner-table speech, the audience crying (in rather a gentle tone, however) "Hear! Hear!" I have forgotten what he said, and also what I responded; but we were very laudatory on both sides, and shook hands in most brotherly fashion across the table. If either of us said too much, let Mr Bramley-Moore's first-rate champagne, and very agreeable hock, and excellent sherry, and forty-five year old madeira, and port genuine from the vineyard, and his magnum of admirable claret, bear as much of the blame as can anywise be attributed to them. Anon (but after a good while at table,) Mrs. Bramley-Moore sent to announce coffee and tea; and adjourning to the drawing-room, we looked, among other pretty things, at some specimens of bright autumnal leaves, which Mr. B. M. had brought with him from his recent visit to America. These were pasted on wooden screens and varnished, and were really very beautiful, though giving but an inadequate idea of their original splendors. Warren admired them greatly. His vanity (which those who know him speak of as a very prominent characteristic) kept peeping out in everything he said.[81]

[A son of General Arnold, named William Fitch Arnold, and born in 1794, now possesses the estate of Little Messenden Abbey, Bucks County, and is a magistrate for that county. He was formerly Captain of the 19th Lancers. He has now two sons and four daughters. The other three sons of General Arnold, all older than this one, and all military men, do not appear to have left children; but a daughter married to Colonel Phipps, of the Mulgrave family, has a son and two daughters. I question whether any of our true-hearted Revolu][82][157]tionary heroes have left a more prosperous progeny than this arch-traitor. I should like to know their feelings with respect to their ancestor.

Ridley of Hawthorn, Co. of Durham, tempore, 1816.

TUESDAY, APRIL 3ᵈ

ON Sunday morning, I walked with Julian to Eastham, a village on the road to Chester, and five or six miles from Rock Ferry. On our way, we passed through a small village, in the centre of which was a small stone pillar, standing on a pedestal of several steps, on which children were sitting and playing. I take it to have been an old Catholic cross; at least I know not what else. It seemed very antique. Eastham, I think, is the finest old English village I have seen, with many ancient houses, and altogether a picturesque and rural aspect; unlike anything in America, and yet possessing a kind of familiar look, as if it were something I had dreamed about. There were thatched stone cottages intermixed with houses of a better kind; and likewise a gateway and gravelled walk, that perhaps gave admittance to the Squire's house. It was [158] not merely one long, wide street, as in most New England villages, but several crooked streets, gathering the whole village into a pretty small compass. In the midst of it stood an old church of the common red free-stone (the same, I suppose, that Chester Cathedral is built of) with a most venera[b]l[e] air, considerably smaller than Bebington church, but more beautiful, and looking quite as old. There was ivy on the spire, and on other parts of the edifice. It looked very quiet and peaceful, and as if it had received the people into its low arched doors, every Sabbath, for many centuries. There were many tombstones about it, some level with the ground, some raised on blocks of stone, or low pillars, moss-grown, weather-worn; and probably these were but the successors of other stones that had quite crumbled away, or been buried by the accumulation of dead men's dust above them. In the center of the church-yard stood an old yew-tree of immense trunk, which was all decayed within, so that it is a wonder how the tree retained any life—which nevertheless it did. (This tree was noted as the Old Yew of Eastham, 600 years ago)[83]

After passing through the church-yard, we saw the village inn on the other side. The doors were fastened; but [159] a girl peeped out of the window at us, and let us in, ushering us into a very neat parlor. There was a cheerful fire in the grate, a straw carpet on the floor, a mahogany side-board, a mahogany table in the middle of the room; and on the walls the portraits of mine host, no doubt, and his wife and daughters;—a very neat parlor, and looking like what I might have found in a country parlor at home; only this was an older house; and there is nothing at home like the glimpse from the window at the church, and its old, red, ivy-grown tower. I got some sandwiches for Julian, and a glass of ale and cigar⁸⁴ for myself; being waited on by the girl, who was very neat, intelligent, and comely—almost as much so as a New England girl—and more respectful. Soon the people came out of the church; and some of them got into their wagons and rode off; while two or three old dames, with caps on their heads, and rustic attire, remained in the church-yard, sitting on the grave-stones. As we left the inn, some village urchins left their play, and came to me begging, calling me "Master!"—They turned at once from play to beg[160]ging; and as I gave them nothing, they turned to their play again.

This village is too far from Liverpool to have been much injured, as yet, by the novelty of cockney residences which have grown up almost everywhere else, so far as I have visited. About a mile from it, however, is the landing-place of a steamer, which runs regularly except in the winter-months, and where a large, new hotel is built. The grounds about it are extensive and well-wooded. We got some biscuits and another glass of ale⁸⁵ at the hotel; and I gave the waiter—a splendid gentleman in black—four half-pence, being the surplus of a shilling. He bowed and thanked me very humbly. An American does not easily bring his mind to the small measure of English liberality to servants; if anything is to be given, we are ashamed not to give more, especially to clerical looking persons in black suits and white neck-cloths.

We took the steamer at two °clock for Liverpool, and arrived in half an hour; and after waiting half an hour on the landing-stage, steamed back to Rock Ferry.

[161] I stood on the Exchange, at noon, to-day, to see the 88ᵗʰ regiment, or Connaught rangers, marching down to embark for the East. These were a body of young, healthy, and cheerful-looking men; and looked greatly better than the dirty crowd that thronged to gaze at them. The royal banner of England, quartering the lion, the leopard, and the harp, waved on the town-house, and looked gorgeous and venerable. Here and there, a woman exchanged greetings with an individual soldier, as he marched along; and gentlemen shook hands with officers, with whom they happened to be acquainted. Being a stranger in the land, it seemed as if I could see the future in the present, more than if I had been an Englishman; so I questioned with myself, how many of these ruddy-cheeked young fellows, marching so stoutly away, would ever tread English ground again!

The populace did not evince any enthusiasm; yet there could not possibly be a war to which the country could assent more fully than to this. I somewhat doubt whether the English populace really feels a vital interest in the nation. Mem. "March to Finchley."[86]

[162] Some years ago, a rude piece of marble sculpture, representing St George and the dragon, was found over the fire-place of a cottage near Rock Ferry, on the road to Chester. It was plastered over with pipe-clay; and its existence was unknown to the cottagers, (a boatman, by name Mathews, and his family) until a lady noticed the projection, and asked what it was. It was supposed to have originally adorned the walls of the Priory at Birkenhead. It measured 14 1/2 inches by 9 inches; in which space were the heads of the king and queen, with uplifted hands, in prayer, their daughter, also in prayer, and looking very grim, a lamb, the slain dragon, and St George proudly prancing on what looks like a donkey—brandishing a sword over his head. *Papers of Historic So. Lan. & Chesh. Session I*[87]

The following is a Legend inscribed on the inner margin of a curious old box.

> "From Birkenheden unto Hilbree,
> A squirrel might leap from tree to tree."[88]

I do not know where Hilbree is; but all round Birkenhead, a squirrel would scarcely find a single tree to climb upon. All is pavement and brick buildings.

[163] GOOD FRIDAY.

THE English and Irish think it good to plant anything on this day, because it was the day when our Savior lay in the grave. Seeds, therefore, are certain to rise again.

It is stated of Lt. Col. Craufurd of Craufurdland that, at the execution of Lord Kilmarnock for his share in the rebellion of 1745, Craufurd held one corner of the cloth that received his head when struck off—he being the earl's intimate and faithful friend. Craufurd was on the Hanover side of the question, and had served with distinction. For his friendship, his name was placed at the bottom of the army list.

At dinner, the other evening, Mrs. J. L. O'Sullivan mentioned the origin of Franklin's adoption of his customary civil dress, when going to court as a diplomatist. It was, simply, that his tailor had dissapointed [*sic*] him of his court-suit; and he wore his customary one, with great reluctance, because he had no other. After[164]wards, having great success and praise by his mishap, he continued to wear it from policy.

Mrs. O'Sullivan's grandmother died fifty years ago, at the age of twenty-eight. She had great personal charms, and among them a beautiful head of chestnut hair. After her burial (in a family tomb) the coffin of one of her children was laid on her own coffin; so that the lid seems to have decayed or been broken, from this cause;—at any rate, this was the case when the tomb was opened, about a year ago. The grandmother's coffin was then found to be filled with beautiful, glossy, living chestnut ringlets, into which her whole substance seems to have been transformed; for there was nothing else but this coffin-full of shining ringlets, the grcwth of half-a century in the tomb. An old man, with a ringlet of his youthful mistress treasured on his heart, might be supposed to witness this wonderful thing.[89]

Madam O'Sullivan (Mr. O'Sullivan's mother) who is now at my house, and very infirm, though not old, was once carried to the grave, and on the point of being buried. [165] It was in Barbary, where her husband was Consul General. He was greatly attached to her; and told the Arab bearers, at the grave, that he must see her once more. When her face was uncovered, he thought he discerned signs of life, and felt a warmth. Finally, she was restored to life, and for many years afterwards supposed the funeral procession to have been a dream;—she having been partially conscious throughout, and having felt the wind blowing on her and lifting the shroud over her feet; for I presume she was to be buried in Oriental style, without a coffin. Long after, in London, when she was speaking of this dream, her husband told her the facts; and she fainted away. Whenever it is now mentioned, her face turns white. She died 1860.[90]

O'Sullivan[91] was born on shipboard, on the coast of Spain, and claims three nationalities—those of Spain, England, and the United States—his father being a native of Great Britain, a naturalized citizen of the United States, and having registered his birth and baptism in a catholic church of Gibraltar, which gives him Spanish privileges. He has hereditary claims to a Spanish countship. His [166] infancy was spent in Barbary, and his lips first lisped in Arabic. There has been an unsettled and wandering character in his whole life.

Madam O'Sullivan's grandfather (who was a British officer) once horse-whipt Paul Jones—Jones being, it seems, a poltroon. How singular it is, that the personal courage of famous warriors should be so often called in question!

MAY 20th SATURDAY.

I WENT, yesterday, to the hospital to take the oath of a mate to a protest. He had met with a severe accident by a fall on shipboard. The hospital is a large edifice of red freestone, with wide, airy passages, resounding with footsteps passing through them. A servant or porter was waiting in the vestibule. We (Mr. Wilding and myself) were shown in the first instance to the parlor; a neat, plainly furnished room, with newspapers and pamphlets lying on the table and sofa. Soon the surgeon of the house came; a brisk, alacritous, civil, cheerful young man, by whom we were shown to the room where the mate was lying. As we went through the principal passage, a man was borne along in a chair, look[167]ing very pale, rather wild, and altogether as if he had just come through great tribulation, and hardly knew as yet whereabouts he was. I noticed that his left arm was but a stump, and was done up, it seemed, in red baize—at all events was of a scarlet hue. The surgeon shook the hand which the man had left, cheerily; and he was carried along. This was a patient who had just had his arm cut off. He had been a rough kind of a person, apparently; but now there was a kind of tenderness about him, through pain and helplessness.

In the room where the mate lay, there were seven beds, all of them occupied by persons who had met with accidents. In the centre of the room was a stationary pine table, about the length of a man, intended, I suppose, to extend patients upon for necessary operations. The furniture of the beds was plain and homely. I thought that the faces of the patients all looked remarkably intelligent, though they were evidently men of the lower classes;—suffering had educated them, for the time, morally and intellectually. [168] They looked curiously at us, but nobody said a word. In the next bed to the mate, lay a little boy, with a broken thigh. The surgeon observed that children generally did well, with accidents; and this boy certainly looked very bright and cheerful. There was nothing particular[l]y interesting about the mate.

After finishing our business, the surgeon showed us into another room of the surgical ward, of the same size as the former, and likewise devoted to cases of accident and injury. All these beds were occupied; and in two of them lay two American sailors who had recently been stabbed. They had been severely hurt, but were doing very well. The surgeon seemed to think that it was a good arrangement to have several cases together, and that the patients kept up one another's spirits—being often cheerful and merry together. Smiles and laughter may operate favorably enough from bed to bed; but dying groans, I should think, must be somewhat of a discouragement. Nevertheless, the previous habits and modes of life of such people as compose the most numerous [169] class of patients in a hospital must be considered before deciding this matter. It is very possible that their misery likes such bedfellows as it here finds.

As we were taking our leave, the surgeon asked us if we should not like to see the operating room; and before we could reply, he threw open a door, and behold there was a roll of linen—"garments rolled in blood"[92]—and a bloody fragment of a human arm, looking just like a small lump of butcher's meat. The surgeon glanced at me, and smiled, kindly, but as pitying my discomposure. At that moment, a comely young woman passed us into the operating room, to set it to rights, and scrub out the blood-stains, I suppose.

Gervase Elwes (son of Sir Gervase Elwes, Bart, of Stoke College, Suffolk) married Isabella, daughter of Sir Thomas Hervey, Knt. and sister of the first Earl of Bristol. This Gervase died before his father, but left a son, Hervey, who succeeded to the baronetcy. Sir Hervey died without issue, and was succeeded by his sister's son, John Meggott Twining, who assumed the name of Elwes. He was the famous miser, and [170] must have had Hawthorne blood in him, through his grandfather, Gervase, whose mother seems to have been a Hawthorne. It was to this Gervase that my ancestor, William Hawthorne, willed some land in Massachusetts, "if he would come over and enjoy it." My ancestor calls him his nephew; but I cannot at all make out the relationship, if his father married a Trigge, as Burke says.[93]

JUNE 12th '54.

BARRY CORNWALL[94] (alias Procter) called on me, a week or more ago; but I happened not to be in the office. Saturday last, he called again, and as I had crossed to Rock Park, he followed me thither. A plain, middle-sized, rather smallish, English-looking gentleman, elderly (sixty or thereabouts) with short white hair. Particularly quiet in his manners; he talks in a somewhat feeble tone and emphasis, not at all energetic, scarcely distinct. An American of the same intellectual calibre, would have more token of it in his manner and personal appearance, and would have a more refined aspect; his head, however, has a good outline, and would look well in marble; but the English complexion takes greatly from [171] its chasteness and dignity. I liked him very well; he talked unaffectedly, showing an author's regard to his reputation, and evidently was pleased to hear of his American celebrity. Nothing remains on my mind of what he said, except that, in his younger days, he was a scientific pugilist, and once made a journey to have a sparring-encounter with the Game Chicken.[95] Certainly, no one would have looked for a pugilist in this subdued old gentleman. He is now a Commissioner of Lunacy, and makes periodical circuits through the country, attending to the business of his office. He is slightly deaf; and this may perhaps be the cause of his feeble utterance—owing to his not being able to regulate his voice exactly, by his own ear. On the whole, he made a pleasant and kindly, but not a powerful impression on me— as how should he?—being a small, though elegant poet, and a man of no passion or emphasized intellect.[96] My wife and the children came into the drawing-room to see him; and all parties seemed to be pleased with one another. He is a good little man, and is much better expressed [172] by his real name, William [sic] Procter, than by his poetical one, Barry Cornwall. Every Englishman has an outward case of such undesirable flesh and blood, that I doubt whether it is best to see the poets of this country. Our pale, thin, Yankee aspect is the fitter garniture for poets. Mr. Procter took my hand in both of his, at parting, and walking with very short steps, left the house—being in a hurry to get to the Adelphi, where he expected a friend to dinner. I think the social rank of Englishmen (always conscious of somebody above them) prevents them from having any dignity in their manner. Barry Cornwall looks like a man who may have kept company with lords—not that he is mean, either, but neither is he of the first rank.

JUNE 17th

AT this season, the days seem to have no beginning, and no end. I wake up before it can even be called early, and find it broad daylight;—go to sleep, and after a long while, wake again, and see the gleam of sunshine—doze an hour or two longer—and at last get up in season for a timely breakfast. The unweariable sun is still shining at eight °clock in the evening or thereabouts; [173] we can sit reading by the daylight, comfortably, till between nine and ten; at eleven, and how much longer I know not, there is still a twilight. If we could only have such dry, deliciously warm evenings as we used to have in our own land, what enjoyment there might be in these interminable twilights. But, here, we close the window-shutters, and make ourselves cosy by a coal-fire.

All three of the children, and, I think, my wife and myself, are going through the [w]hooping-cough. The east-wind of this region and season is most horrible. There have been no really warm days; for though the sunshine is sometimes hot, there is never any diffused heat throughout the air;—on passing from the sunshine into the shade, we immediately feel too cool.

June 20th.

THE vagabond musicians about town are very numerous and miscellaneous. On board the steam-ferry boats, I think I have heretofore spoken of them; they infest them from May to November, for very little gain, apparently. A shilling a day, per man, must [174] be the extent of their emolument. It is rather sad to see somewhat respectable looking old men engaged in this way, with two or three younger associates. Their instruments look terribly the worse for wear, and even my unmusical ear can distinguish more discord than harmony. They appear to be a very quiet and harmless people. Sometimes there is a woman playing on a fiddle, with her husband playing a wind-instrument. There is an old blind fiddler, too. The greatest nuisance on board of these boats is a boy, playing an accordion. In the streets, it is not unusual to find a band of half a dozen performers, or more, who, without any provocation or reason whatever, sound their brazen instruments, till the houses re-echo. Sometimes, one passes a man who stands whistling a tune, most unweariably, though I never saw anybody give him anything. Then there are the Italian organ-grinders. The ballad-singers are the strangest, from the total lack of any kind of music in their cracked voices. Sometimes, you see a space cleared in the street, and a foreigner playing some instrument, while a girl—weather-beaten, tanned, freckled, and wholly uncomely in face, and shabby in attire, dan[175]ces some such dances as you may have seen on the stage. The common people look on, and never seem to criticise, or to treat any of these poor devils unkindly or uncivilly; but I do not observe that they give them anything.

A crowd—or, at all events, a moderate-sized group—is much more easily drawn together here, than with us. The people have a good deal of idle and momentary curiosity, and are always ready to stop when another man has stopt, so as to see what has attracted his attention. I hardly ever stop to look at a shop-window, without being immediately incommoded by boys and men, who stop likewise, and would forthwith throng the pavement, if I did not move on.

JUNE 30th.

IF it is not known how and when a man dies, it seems to make a kind of ghost of him for many years thereafter—perhaps for centuries. King Arthur is an example; the Emperor Frederic, and other famous men, who were thought to be alive ages after their disappearance. So with private individuals. I had an Uncle John, who went a voyage to sea, about the [176] beginning of the war of 1812, and has never returned to this hour. But, as long as his mother lived (as much as twenty years afterwards) she never gave up the hope of his return, and was constantly hearing stories of persons whose description answered to his;—some people actually affirmed that they had seen him in various parts of the world. Thus, so far as her belief was concerned, he still walked the earth. And even to this day, I never see his name (which is no very uncommon one) without thinking that this may be the lost uncle.[97]

Thus, too, the French Dauphin still exists—or a kind of ghost of him. The three Tells, too, in the Cavern of Uri.

I saw a blind man sitting on the pavement, the other day, reading aloud out of an embossed-printed book, to attract the notice and charity of passers-by. He read very slowly indeed. A woman was in attendance on him.

JULY 6th.

Mr CECIL, the other day, was saying that England could produce as fine peaches as any other country. I asked what was the particular excellence of a peach, and he answered, it's [sic] "cooling and refreshing quality, like that of a melon." Just think of this idea of the richest, [177] lusciousest of all fruits. But the untravelled Englishman has no more real idea of what fruit is, than of what sunshine is; he thinks that he has tasted the first, and felt the last;—but they are both watery alike. I heard a lady in Lord-street talking about the "broiling sun" (with a breadth and emphasis that sounded like bacon in a frying-pan) when I was almost in a shiver. They keep up their animal-heat by means of ale and wine; else they could not bear this climate.

JULY 19th '54.

A WEEK ago last Saturday, I made a little tour in North Wales with Mr. Bright. We left Birkenhead by railway for Chester, at 2 °clock; thence for Bangor;—thence by carriage over the Menai Bridge to Beaumaris. At Beaumaris, a fine old castle, quite coming up to my idea of what an old castle should be. A gray, ivy-hung exterior wall, with large round towers at intervals; within this, another wall, the place of the portcullis between; and again within the second wall, the castle itself, with a spacious green courtyard in front. The outer wall is so thick [178] that a passage runs between it, all round the castle, which covers a space of three acres. This passage gives access to a chapel, still very perfect, and to various apartments in the towers—all exceedingly dismal, and giving very unpleasant impressions of the way in which the garisson [sic] of the castle lived. The main building of of [sic] the castle is entirely roofless;

but the hall and other rooms are pointed out by the guide; and the whole is
tapestried with abundant ivy; so that my impression is of gray walls, with
here and there a vast green curtain; a carpet of green over the floors of halls
and apartments; and around all the outer battlement, with a narrow and rather
perilous footpath running round the top of it. There is a fine vista, through
the castle itself and the two gateways of the two encompassing walls. The
passage within the wall is very rude, both under foot and on each side; with
various ascents and descents of rough steps—sometimes so low that your
head is in danger; and dark except when a little light comes through a loop-
hole or window in the thickness of the wall. In part of the castle a tennis-
court was fitted up, by laying [179] a smooth pavement on the ground, and
casing the walls with tin or zinc, if I recollect rightly. All this was open to
the sky; and when we were there, some young men of the town were playing
at the game. There are only a very few of these tennis-courts in England; and
this old castle seemed a very strange place for one.

The castle is the property of Sir Richard Bulkel[e]y, whose seat (Baron
Hill) is in this vicinity, and who owns a great part of the island of Anglesey,
on which Beaumaris lies. The hotel where we stopt was the Bulkel[e]y Arms;
and Sir Richard seems to have a kind of feudal influence in the town.

In the morning, we set out and walked along a delightful road, bordering
on the Menai Straits, to Bangor Ferry. It was really a very pleasant road,
overhung by a young growth of wood, exceedingly green and fresh. English
trees are green all over their stems, owing to the creeping-plants that over-run
them. They [There] were some flowers in the hedges such as we cultivate in
gardens. At the ferry, there was a white-washed [180] cottage, or small-house;
a woman or two, and a child or two, and a fishermanlike personage, walking
to-and-fro before the door. The scenery of the strait is very beautiful and
picturesque; and directly opposite to us lay Bangor—the strait being here, I
believe, about a mile across. An American ship (from Boston) lay in the middle
of it. The ferry-boat was just putting off from the Bangor-side, and, by the
aid of a sail, soon neared the shore.

At Bangor we went to a handsome hotel (the Penrhyn arms, I think) and
hired a carriage and two horses for some Welsh place, the name of which I
forget; neither can I remember a single name of the places (nor could spell
them if I heard them pronounced, nor pronounce them, if I saw them spelt)
through which we posted, that day. It was a circuit, I believe, of about forty
miles, bringing us to Conway at last. I remember a great slate-quarry; and
also that many of the cottages, in the earlier part of our ride, were built of
blocks of slate. The mountains were very picturesque, thrusting themselves up
abruptly, and in [181] peaks—not of the dumpling formation which is somewhat too prevalent among the New England mountains. At one point, we saw
Snowdon, with its bifold summit. We also visited the Swallow waterfall (this
is the translation of an unpronounceable Welsh name [Rhaiadr-y-Wennol]),
which is the largest in Wales. It was a very picturesque rapid; and the guide-

book considers it equal in sublimity to Niagara.⁹⁸ Likewise, one or two lakes, which Mr Bright and the guide-book greatly admired, but which, to me, (who remembered a hundred blue sheets of water in New England) seemed nothing more than sullen and dreary puddles, with bare banks—and wholly destitute of beauty. I think they were no where more than a hundred yards across. But the hills were certainly very good; and though generally bare of trees, this served to make their outlines the stronger and more striking.

Many of the Welshwomen, particularly the elder ones, wear black beaver hats, high-crowned, and almost precisely like men's. It makes them look [182] ugly and witchlike. Welsh is still the prevalent language, and the only one of a great many of the inhabitants. I have had Welsh people in my office, on official business, with whom I could not communicate, except through an interpreter.

At some unutterable village [Bettws-y-Coed], we went into a little church, where we saw an old stone image of a warrior, lying on his back, with his hands clasped. It was the natural son (if I remember right) of David, Prince of Wales, and was doubtless the better part of a thousand years old. There was likewise a stone coffin of still greater age; some person of rank and renown had mouldered to dust within it, but it was now open and empty. Also, monumental brasses on the walls, engraved with portraits of a gentleman and lady, in the costume of Elizabeth's time. Also, on one of the pews, a brass record of some persons who slept in the vault beneath; so that, every Sunday, the survivors and descendants kneel and worship directly over their dead ancestors. In the churchyard, on a flat tombstone, there was the representation of a harp. I [183] supposed that it must be the resting place of a bard; but the inscription was in memory of somebody, a merchant, and skilful manufacturer of harps.

This was a very delightful tour. We saw a great many things which it is now too late to describe; the sharpness of the first impression being gone— but I think I can produce something of the sentiment of it hereafter.

We arrived at Conway, late in the afternoon, to take the rail for Chester. I must see Conway, with its old gray wall, and its unrivalled castle, again. It was better than Beaumaris; and I never saw anything more picturesque than the prospect from the castle-wall towards the sea.

We reached Chester at ten, or thereabouts, P.M. Next morning, Mr. Bright left for Liverpool, before I was up. I visited the Cathedral, where the organ was playing—sauntered through the rows—bought some playthings for the children, and left for home at ¼ past 12.

[SECOND MANUSCRIPT VOLUME]

1854

VISITING the Zoological gardens, the other day, with Julian, it occurred to me what a fantastic kind of life a person connected with them might be depicted as leading,—a child, for instance. The grounds are very extensive, and include arrangements for all kinds of exhibitions, calculated to attract the idle people of a great city. In one enclosure a bear, who climbs a pole to get cake and gingerbread from the spectators. Elsewhere, a circular building, with compartments for lions, wolves, tigers, &c. In another part of the garden, a colony of monkeys; the skeleton of an elephant; birds, of all kinds. Swans, and various rare waterfowl, swimming on a piece of water—which was green, by the by; and when the fowls dived, they stirred up black mud. A stork was parading along the margin, with melancholy strides of its long legs, and came slowly towards us, as if for companionship. In one apartment, was an obstreperously noisy society of parrots, macaws, &c, most gorgeous and diversified of hue. These different colonies of birds and beasts were scattered about in various parts of the grounds; so that you came upon them unexpectedly. Also, there was an archery-ground, a shooting-ground, a swing, and other such things. Also, a theatre, at which a rehearsal was going on—we standing at one of the exterior doors, and looking in towards the [2] dusky stage, where the company, in their ordinary dresses, were rehearsing something that had a good deal of dance and action in it. In the open air, too, there was an arrangement of painted scenery, representing a wide expanse of mountains, with a city at their feet, and before it the sea, with actual water, and large vessels upon it—the vessels having only the side that would be presented towards the spectator; but the scenery was so good that, at first casual glance, I almost mistook it for reality. There was a refreshment-room, with drinks, and cake and pastry, but, so far as I saw, no substantial victual. About in the centre of the garden, there seemed to be an actual, homely looking, small dwelling-house or cottage, where perhaps the overlookers of the concern live. Now, this might be wrought, in an imaginative description, into a pleasant sort of a fool's paradise, where all sorts of unreal delights should seem to cluster round some suitable personage; and it would relieve, in a very odd and effective way, the stern realities of life on the outside of the garden walls. I saw a little girl, simply dressed, who seemed to have her habitat within the garden. There was also a daguerreotypist, with his wife and family, carrying on his business in a little shed or shanty, and perhaps having his home in its inner-room. He seemed to be an honest, intelligent, pleasant young man, and his wife a pleasant woman; and I [3] got Julian's daguer[r]eotype, for three shillings, in a little brass frame. In the description of the garden, the velvet-turf, of a charming verdure, and the shrubbery, and shadowy walks under large trees, and the slopes and inequalities of ground, must not be forgotten. In one place, there was a maze and labyrinth, where perhaps a person might wander a long while in the vain endeavor to get out; although, all the time, looking at the exterior garden over the low hedges that border the walks of the maze. And this is like the inappreciable difficulties that often beset us in life.

I will see the garden again, before long, and get some additional record of it.

AUGUST 10th.

WE went to the Isle of Man, a few weeks ago, where Sophia and the children spent a fortnight. I spent a Sunday with them, and then returned; but went again to spend the ensuing Sunday.

I never saw anything prettier than the little church of Kirk Bradden. It stands in a perfect seclusion of shadowy trees; a plain little church, that would not be at all remarkable in another situation, but is most picturesque in its solitude and bowery environment. The church-yard is quite full and overflowing with graves, and extends down the gentle slope of a hill, with a dense mass of shadow above it. Some of the tombstones are flat on the ground, some erect, some [4] are laid horizontally on low pillars or masonry. There were no very old dates on any of these stones; for the climate soon effaces inscriptions, and makes a stone of fifty years look as old as one of five hundred—unless it be slate, or something harder than the usual red freestone. There was an old Runic monument, however, near the centre of the church-yard, that had some strange sculpture on it, and an inscription still legible by persons learned in such matters. Against the tower of the church, too, there is a circular stone, with carving on it, said to be of immemorial antiquity. There is likewise a tall marble monument, as much as fifty feet high, erected some years ago to the memory of one of the Atholl [Athol] family, by his brother-officers of a local regiment, of which he was colonel. At one of the side entrances of the church, and forming the threshold within the thickness of the wall, so that the feet of all who enter must tread over it, is a flat tombstone of somebody who felt himself a sinner, no doubt, and desired to be thus trampled upon. The stone is much worn.

The church is extremely plain within, and very small. On the walls, over the pews, are several monumental sculptures; a quite elaborate one to a Col. Murray of the Coldstream guards, his military profession being designated by banners and swords in marble; another was to a farmer.

[5] On one side of the church-tower, there was a little pent-house, or lean-to, —merely a stone-roof about three or four feet high, and supported by a single pillar—beneath which was deposited the bier.

I have let too much time pass before attempting to record my impressions of the Isle of Man; but as regards this church, no description can come up to its quiet beauty, its seclusion, its everything that one would like to find in an English country-church.

Last Sunday, I went to Eastham, and entering the church-yard, sat down on a tombstone under the yew-tree, which has been known for centuries as the Great Tree of Eastham. Some of the old village people were sitting on the graves near the church-door; and an old woman came towards me, and said, in a low, kindly, admonishing tone, that I must not let the Sexton see me, because he would not allow any one to be in the church-yard, in sacrament time. I inquired why she and her companions were there; and she said they were waiting for the sacrament. So I thanked her, gave her a sixpence, and departed. Close under the eaves of the church, I saw two upright stones, in memory of two old servants of the Stanley family—one over ninety, and the other over eighty years of age.

[6] AUGUST 12th.

JULIAN and I went to Birkenhead Park, yesterday. A large, ornamented gateway, to the Park; and the grounds within are neatly laid-out, with borders of shrubbery. There is a piece of water, with swans and other aquatic fowl, which swim about, and are fed with dainties by the visitors. Nothing can be more beautiful than a swan; it is the ideal of a goose—a goose beautified and beatified. There were not a great many visitors; but some children were dancing on the green, and a few lover-like people straying about. I think the English behave better than the Americans, at similar places; and yet I don't know.

There was a Camera Obscura, very wretchedly indistinct. At the refreshment-room, no more potent drink was to be obtained than ginger-beer and British wines.

AUGUST 21st.

IN the Crown-Court, on Saturday, sitting in the Sheriff's seat. The Judge, Baron Platt,[99] an old gentleman of upwards of sixty, with very large, long features; his wig helped him to look like some strange kind of animal—very queer, but yet with a sagacious and, on the whole, beneficent aspect. During the session, some mischievous young barrister occupied himself with sketching the Judge in pencil; and being handed about, it found its way to me. It was very like, and very laughable, but hardly caricatured. The judicial wig is an exceedingly odd affair; and as it covers [7] both ears, it would seem intended to prevent his lordship (and Justice in his person) from hearing anything of the case on either side—that thereby he may decide the better. It is like the old idea of blindfolding the statue of Justice.

It seems to me there is less formality—less distance between the Judge, jury, witnesses, and bar—in the English courts than in our own. The Judge takes a very active part in the trial—constantly putting a question to the witness on the stand—making remarks on the conduct of the trial—putting in his word on all occasions—and letting his own sense of the matter in hand be pretty

plainly seen; so that, before the trial is over, and long before his own charge
is delivered, he must have exercised a very powerful influence over the minds
of the jury. All this seems to be done, not without dignity, yet in a familiar
kind of way; it is a sort of paternal supervision of the whole matter, quite
unlike the cold awfulness of an American Judge. But all this may be owing
partly to the personal characteristics of Baron Platt. It appeared to me, however, that from this closer relation of all parties, truth was likely to be arrived
at, and justice to be done. As an innocent man, I should not be much afraid
to be tried by Baron Platt.

[8] AUGUST 24th.

I WENT to Eaton Hall, yesterday, with my wife and Mr G. P. Bradford, via
Chester. On our way, at the latter place, we visited St. John's Church. It is
built of the same red free-stone as the Cathedral, and looked exceedingly
antique and venerable—this kind of stone, from its softness, and its liability
to be acted on by the weather, being favorable to an early decay. Nevertheless,
I believe the church was built above a thousand years ago, some parts of it,
at least; and the surface of the tower and walls is worn away and hollowed,
in shallow scoops by the hand of time. There were broken niches, in several
places, where statues had formerly stood; all except two or three had fallen
or crumbled away, and those which remained were as much damaged as a
child's sugar image, when half dissolved by sucking it. The face and details
of the figure were half-obliterated, in just that way. There were many grave-
stones round the church; but none of them of any antiquity. Probably, as the
names become indistinguishable on the elder stones, the graves are dug over
again, and filled with new occupants, and covered with new stones—or perhaps
with the old ones, newly inscribed.

Closely connected with the church was the clergyman's house, a comfortable
looking residence; and likewise in the churchyard, with tombstones all about
it, even almost at the threshold (so that the doorstep itself might have been a
tombstone) was another house, of respectable size and aspect. We surmised
that this might [9] be the sexton's dwelling; but it proved not to be so; and
a woman, answering our knock, directed us to where he might be found. So
Mr. Bradford and I went in search of him, leaving Sophia seated on a tombstone. The sexton was a jolly-looking, ruddy-faced man—a mechanic of some
sort, apparently—and followed us to the church-yard with much alacrity. We
found Sophia standing at a gate way, which opened into the most ancient and
now quite ruinous part of the church; the present church covering much less
ground than it did some centuries ago. We went through this gate way, and
found ourselves in an enclosure of venerable walls, open to the sky, with old
Norman arches (or perhaps Saxon) standing about, beneath the loftiest of
which, the Sexton told us, the high altar used to stand. Of course, there were
weeds and ivy growing in the crevices, but not so abundantly as I have seen
it elsewhere. The sexton pointed out a piece of statue that had once stood in one

of the niches, and which he himself, I think, had dug up from several feet below the earth; also, in a niche of the walls, high above our heads, he showed us an ancient wooden coffin, hewn out of a solid log of oak, the hollow being made rudely in the shape of the human figure. This too had been dug up; and nobody knows how old it was. While we looked at all this solemn old trumpery, the curate (quite a young man) stood at the [10] back door of his house, elevated considerably above the ruins, with his young wife, I presume, and a friend or two, chatting cheerfully among themselves. It was pleasant to see them there.

After examining the ruins, we went inside of the church, and found it a dim and dusky old place, quite paved over with tombstones; not an inch of space being left, in the aisles, or near the altar, or in any nook or corner, uncovered by a tomb stone. There were also mural monuments and escutcheons; and close against the wall lay the mutilated statue of a Crusader, with his legs crossed, in the style which one has so often read about. The old fellow seemed to have been represented in chain armor; but he had been more battered and bruised, since death, than ever during his pugnacious life; and his nose was almost knocked away. This figure had been dug up, many years ago; and nobody knows whom it was meant to commemorate.

The nave of the church is supported by two rows of Saxon pillars, not very lofty, but six feet six inches (so the Sexton says) in diameter. They are covered with plaster, which was laid on ages ago, and is now so hard and smooth that I took the pillars to be really composed of solid shafts of gray stone. But, at one end of the church, the plaster had been removed from two of these pillars, in order to discover [11] whether they were still sound enough to support the church; and they prove to be made of blocks of red free-stone, just as new and sound as when it came from the quarry; for though this stone soon crumbles in the open air, it is as good as indestructible when sheltered from the weather. It looked very strange to see the fresh hue of these two pillars, amidst the dingy antiquity of the rest of the church.

The body of the church is covered with pews, the wooden enclosures of which seemed of antique fashion. There were also modern stoves; but the Sexton said that the church was rather a cold one, in spite of the stoves. It had, I must say, a disagreeable odor pervading it, in which the dead people of long ago had doubtless some share:—a musty fragrance, by no means amounting to a stench, but unpleasant, and, I should think, unwholesome. Old wood-work, and old stones, and antiquity of all kinds, moral and physical, go to make up this smell. I observed it in the Cathedral; and Chester generally has it, especially under the Rows. After all, the necessary damp and lack of sunshine, in such a shadowy old church as this, have probably more to do with it than the dead people have; although I did think the odor was particularly strong, over here and there one of the tomb-stones. Not [12] having shillings to give the Sexton, we were forced to give him half-a-crown—which no Englishman would have done.

The Church of St John is outside of the city-walls. Entering the east gate, we walked awhile under the Rows, bought our tickets for Eaton Hall and its gardens, and likewise some playthings for the children; for this old city of Chester seems to me to possess an unusual number of toyshops. Finally we took a cab, and drove to the Hall, about four miles distant, nearly the whole of the way lying through the wooded park. There are many sorts of trees, making up a "wilderness," which looked not unlike the woods of our own Concord, only less wild. The English oak is not a handsome tree, being short and sturdy, with a round, thick mass of foliage, lying all within its own bounds. It was a showery day; had there been any sunshine, there might doubtless have been many beautiful effects of light and shadow, in these woods. We saw one or two herds of deer, quietly feeding, a hundred yards or so distant. They appeared to be somewhat wilder than cattle, but, I think, not much wilder than sheep. Their ancestors have probably been in a half-domesticated state, receiving food at the hands of man, in winter, for centuries. There is a kind of poetry in this—quite as much as if they were really wild deer, such as their forefathers were when Hugh Lupus used to hunt them.

Our miserable cab drew up at the steps of Eaton Hall, [13] and ascending under the portico, the door swung silently open, and we were received very civilly by two old men—one a tall old footman in livery, the other in plain clothes. The entrance-hall is very spacious; and the floor, which is tessel[l]ated or somehow inlaid with marble, cost about seven thousand dollars. There was statuary in marble on the floor; and in niches stood several figures in antique armor, of various dates, some with lances, and others with battle-axes, swords &c. There was a two handed sword, as much as six feet long; but not nearly so ponderous as I have supposed this kind of weapon to be, from reading of it. I could easily have brandished it.

I don't think I am a good sight-seer; at least I soon get satisfied with looking at set-sights, and want to go on to the next. The plainly-dressed old man now led us into a long corridor, which goes, I think, the whole length of the house; about five hundred feet, arched all the way;—and lengthened interminably by a looking-glass at the end, in which I saw our own party approaching, like a party of strangers. But I have so often seen this effect produced in dry-good stores and elsewhere, that I was not much impressed. There were family portraits, and other pictures, and likewise pieces of statuary, along this arched corridor; and it communicated with a chapel, with a scriptural altar-piece, copied from Rubens, [14] and a picture of St Michael and the Dragon, and two, or perhaps three, richly painted windows. Everything here and all over the house (I mean, as regards the edifice itself) is entirely new and fresh; the house having been finished, I believe, this present year, and never yet inhabited by the family. This bran-newness makes it much less effective than if it had been lived in; and I felt pretty much as if I were strolling through any other new house. After all, the utmost force of man can do positively very little towards making grand things, or beautiful things; the imagination can

do so much more, merely on shutting one's eyes, that the actual effect seems
meagre; so that a new house, unassociated with the past, is exceedingly unsatisfactory—especially when you have heard that the wealth and skill of man
has here done its best. Besides, the rooms, as we saw them, did not look by
any means their best; the carpets not being down, and the furniture being
covered with protective envelopes. Moreover, such rooms cannot be seen to
advantage by daylight; it being altogether essential to the effect that they should
be illuminated by artificial light, which takes them somewhat out of the region
of bare reality. Nevertheless, there was undoubtedly great splendor—for the
details of which I refer to the guide-book. Among the family-portraits, there
was one of a lady famous for her beautiful hand; and she was holding it up
to notice in the funniest way—and very beautiful [15] it certainly was. The
private apartments of the family were not shown us. I should think it impossible
for the owner of this house to imbue it with his personality to such a degree
as to feel it to be his home; it must be like a small lobster in a shell much too
large for him.

After seeing what was to be seen of the rooms, we visited the gardens, in
which are noble conservatories and hot-houses, containing all manner of rare
and beautiful flowers,[100] and tropical fruits. I noticed some large pines [pine-
apples], looking as if they were really made of gold. The gardener (under
gardener I presume he was) who showed this part of the spectacle, was very
intelligent as well as kindly, and seemed to take an interest in his business.
He gave Sophia a purple everlasting-flower, which will endure a great many
years as a memento of our visit to Eaton Hall. Finally, we took a view of
the front of the edifice, which is very fine, and much more satisfactory than
the interior;—and returned to Chester.

We strolled about under the unsavory Rows, sometimes scudding from side
to side of the street, through the shower; took lunch in a confectioner's shop;—
and rode to the Railway Station in time for the three °clock train. It looked
picturesque to see two little girls, hand in hand, running along the ancient
passages of the Rows;—but Chester has a very evil smell. At the Railroad [16]
Station, Sophia saw a small edition of Twice-told Tales, forming a volume of
the Cottage Library; and opening it, there was the queerest imaginable portrait
of myself—so very queer that we could not but buy it. The shilling editions
of the Scarlet Letter and Seven Gables are at all the bookstalls and shop-
windows;—but so is the "Lamplighter,"[101] and still more trashy books.

August 26th.

Mr Bradford[102] has the blood of the Martyrs in him, through two channels;
and I doubt not that there is the substance in himself to make a martyr of;—
and yet he is a wonderfully small pattern of a man. He has a minute conscientiousness, which is continually stumbling over insignificant matters; and
trifles of all kinds seem to be matters of great moment with him. There is a
lack of strong will, that makes his conduct, when not determined by principle,

miserably weak and wavering; and he is so afraid of infringing upon somebody's else will, that he becomes exceedingly troublesome by the [*sic*] his very
anxiety not to give trouble. He is always uneasy what to do next; always regretting the last thing he did. He bothers and perplexes one with the re-iteration
of questions, the intent and importance of which cannot be seen, except by
himself. He wanders about the house like a cat, noiselessly, in slippers. The
homeliness of the New England middle-class pervades his habits; he has a
tendency to brush his own boots, either to save trouble to others, or because
they are not otherwise brushed to suit him. It [17] is very difficult to help him,
at table, because he seems to have scruples about not eating all that is given
him, for fear it should be wasted. This morning, he put back a piece of cold
chicken from his own plate into the dish;—to be sure, he had not begun to eat;
and I do not think him capable of anything really indelicate, though liable to
conventional indecorums. He is the best little man in the world; so incapable
of the slightest moral wrong that one pities him, and laughs at him, and is
inclined to despise him. He drinks half a glass of wine; he is fond of tea, and,
as his sole intemperance, is accustomed to take it rather strong. He does not
eat a great deal of meat, or other heavy viands, but, I think, is somewhat of
a gourmand in respect to lighter delicacies, when he can get them. He mentions
huckleberry-pudding, however, as his great passion. He takes shorter steps
than a man should, and seems to patter in his gait (though he wears thick,
creaking shoes) and goes about in an insignificant kind of way. There is such
a lack of dignity about him, and such an apparently inane inquisitiveness, that
all clerks, servants, and underlings of every sort, inevitably refuse to recognize
him as a gentleman. Good as he is, I cannot help thinking him rather selfish,
or self-involved, and tied down to self by a thousand little hair-lines; and yet
he feels regard for a good many people, and is of most social tendencies. With
all his lack of will, he [16] is wilful, or at least wayward;—or, at all events,
another man cannot make his own will operate over him. As an acquaintance,
there is a kindly warmth in his propinquity; but I do not think he could feel,
or sympathize with, any passionate emotion. His voice has somewhat of a
quaver. One can detect, by his continual references to it, by his restlessness, the
little trouble that happens at anytime to be agitating his mind. The "grass-
hopper" is already a "burden to him,"[103] though he has not yet made up his
half-century. I have not satisfactorily hit him off, with all these strokes. Fees
to servants and charges of cabmen occupy much of his thoughts.

  And yet this man is one of Emerson's most valued and trusted friends. He
is a scholar, with true cultivation; he has independence of thought, and keeps
his own thoughts distinctly, against whatever other man's. No originality,
certainly, but much good sense, and justness of view. His taste often appears
delicate. He is simple, natural, sincere, sees what is manly in others, and likes
nothing but that. He is an old bachelor; and I suppose he might have developed
into something better by marriage, and by coming into more earnest contact
with the joys, griefs, and business of the world, than he has. The paltriness

of his fortunes and hopes, too, as a girls' schoolmaster, has doubtless kept him small. One thing is remarkable—that I should see all these matters, now, so much more distinctly than ever before; but all past affairs, all home- [17] conclusions, all people whom I have known in America, and meet again here, are strangely compelled to undergo a new trial. It is not that they suffer by comparison with circumstances of English life, and forms of English manhood or womanhood; but, being free from my old surroundings and the inevitable prejudices of home, I decide upon them absolutely.

I think I neglected to record that I saw Miss Martineau,[104] a few weeks since. She is a large, robust (one might almost say bouncing) elderly woman, very coarse of aspect, and plainly dressed; but withal, so kind, cheerful, and intelligent a face, that she is pleasanter to look at than most beauties. Her hair is of a decided gray; and she does not shrink from calling herself an old woman. She is the most continual talker I ever heard; it is really like the babbling of a brook; and very lively and sensible too;—and all the while she talks, she moves the bowl of her ear-trumpet from one auditor to another, so that it becomes quite an organ of intelligence and sympathy between her and yourself. The ear-trumpet seems like a sensitive part of her, like the feelers of some insects. If you have any little remark to make, you drop it in; and she helps you to make remarks by this delicate little appeal of the trumpet, as she slightly directs it towards you; and if you have [18] nothing to say, the appeal is not strong enough to embarrass you. All her talk was about herself and her affairs; but it did not seem like egotism, because it was so cheerful and free from morbidness. And this woman is an Atheist, and thinks, I believe, that the principle of life will become extinct, when her great, fat, well-to-do body is laid in the grave. I will not think so, were it only for her sake;—only a few weeds to spring out of her fat mortality, instead of her intellect and sympathies flowering and fruiting forever!

Mr Bradford's conscientiousness seems to be a kind of itch—keeping him always uneasy and inclined to scratch.

SEPTEMBER 13th.

SOPHIA and the children went to Rhyl, last Thursday; and on Saturday I went thither to join them, in company with O'Sullivan, who arrived in the Bahama from Lisbon, that morning. We went by way of Chester, and found Sophia waiting for us at the Rhyl Station. Rhyl is a most uninteresting place— a collection of new lodging-houses and hotels on a long sand-beach, which the tide leaves bare almost to the horizon. The sand is by no means a marble pavement, but sinks under the foot, and makes very heavy walking; but there is a promenade in front of the principal range of houses, looking on the sea, where we have rather better footing. Almost all the houses were full; and Sophia had taken a parlor and two bed-rooms, and is living after [19] the English fashion, providing her own food, lights &c.—even to soap for the wash-stands. It is very awkward to our American notions; but there is an independence about it, which I think must make it agreeable, on better acquaintance. But the place is certainly very destitute of attraction; and life seems to pass very heavily. The English do not appear to have a turn for amusing themselves.

Sunday was a very bright and hot day; and in the forenoon I set out on a walk, not well knowing whither, over a terribly dusty road, with not a particle of shade along its dead level. The Welsh mountains were before me, at the distance of three or four miles, long, ridgy hills, descending pretty abruptly upon the plain; on either side of the road, here and there, an old white-washed, thatched stone-cottage, or a stone farm-house, with an aspect of some antiquity. I never suffered so much before, on this side of the water, from heat and dust, and should probably have turned back, had I not espied the round towers and walls of an old castle, at some distance before me. Having looked at a guide-book, previous to setting out, I knew that this must be Rhuddlan Castle, about three miles from Rhyl; so I plodded on, and by-an-by entered an antiquated village, on one side of which the castle [20] stands. This Welsh village is very much like old English villages, with narrow streets, and mean houses or cottages built in blocks, and here and there a larger old house standing alone— everything far more compact than in our rural villages, and with no grassy street-margins nor trees;—aged and dirty, and with dirty children staring at the passenger, and an undue supply of mean public-houses; most, or many, of the men in breeches, and some of the women, especially the elder ones, with black beaver hats, looking just as an old witch would look. The streets, I think, were paved with round pebbles, and looked squalid and ugly. Just think of a New England rural village in comparison.

The children and grown people looked lazily at me, as I passed, but showed no such alert and vivacious curiosity as a community of Yankees would. I turned up a street that led me to the castle, which looked very picturesque, close at hand—more so than at a distance, because the towers and walls have not a sufficiently broken outline against the sky. There are several round towers, at the angles of the wall—very large in their circles, built of gray stone, crumbling, ivy-grown, everything that one thinks of [in] an old ruin. I could not get into the inner space of the castle, without climbing over a fence, or clambering down into the moat; so I contented myself with walking round it, and viewing it from the [21] outside. Through the gateway, I saw a cow feeding on the green grass in the inner court of the castle. In one of the walls, there was a great triangular gap, where perhaps the assailants had made a breach; of course, there were weeds on the ruinous tops of the towers, and along the top of the wall. This, I believe, was the first castle built by Edward I in Wales; and he resided here while Conway Castle was being built; and here Queen Eleanor was brought to bed of a princess. Some few years since, a meeting of Welsh bards (I forget what the Welsh name for such an assemblage is) was held in this castle.

After viewing it awhile, and listening to the babble of some children who lay on the grass near by, I resumed my walk; and meeting a Welshman in the village-street, I asked him my nearest way back to Rhyl. "Dim Sassenach,"[105] said he, after a pause. How odd, that an hour or two on the Railway should have brought me amongst a people who speak no English. Just below the castle, there is an arched stone bridge over the river Clwyd; and the best view of the castle is from hence; it stands on a gentle eminence, commanding the passage of the river; and two twin round towers stand close beside one another, whence, I suppose, archers have often drawn their bows against the [22] wild Welshmen, on the river banks. Behind was the line of mountains; and this was the point of detence between the hill-country and the lowlands. On the bridge stood a good many idle Welshmen, leaning over the parapet, and looking at some small vessels that had come up the river from the sea. There was the frame of a new vessel on the stocks, near by.

As I returned through the village, on my way home, I again inquired my way of a man in breeches, who, I found, could speak English very well. He was kind, and took pains to direct me, giving me the choice of three ways— viz: the one by which I came,—another way across the fields;—and a third, by the embankment along the river-side. I chose the latter, and so followed the course of the Clwyd, which is a very ugly river, with a tidal flow, and wide, marshy banks. On its farther side was Rhuddlan marsh, where a battle was fought between the Welsh and Saxons, a thousand years ago. I have forgotten to mention that the castle and its vicinity was the scene of the famous battle of the fiddlers between De Blandeville, Earl of Chester, and the Welsh, about the time of the Conqueror. I reached Rhyl, pretty well tired, about two °clock.

On Monday, Sophia, O'Sullivan, Una, and I, went to Con[23]way Castle by rail. Certainly, this must be the most perfect specimen of a ruinous old castle, in the whole world; it quite fills up one's idea. We first walked round the exterior of the wall, at the base of which are hovels, with dirty children playing about them, and pigs rambling about, and squalid women visible in the door- ways; but all these things melt into the picturesqueness of the scene, and do not harm it. The whole town of Conway stands in what was once the castle- yard; and the whole circuit of the wall is still standing, in a delightful state of decay. At the angles, and at regular intervals along the extent of the wall, there are round towers, having half their ○ on the outside of the wall, and half within; most of these towers have a great crack pervading them irregu- larly from top to bottom; the ivy hangs upon them, the weeds grow on their tops. Gateways, three or four of them, open through the walls, and streets proceed from them into the town. At some points, very old cottages or small houses are built against the wall, and old as they are, they must have been built after the wall and castle were a ruin. In one place, I saw the sign of an ale-house painted on the gray stones of one of the old round towers. As we entered one of the gates, after making our circuit at the base of the walls, we saw an omnibus coming down the street toward us, with its horn sounding. Llandudno was [24] its place of destination; and knowing no more about it than that it was four miles off, we took our seats. It proved that Llandudno

is a watering village at the base of the Great Orme's Head, at the mouth of
the Conway river. In the omnibus, there were two pleasant looking girls who
talked Welsh together, a guttural, pleasant, childish kind of a babble; afterwards we got into conversation with them, and found them very agreeable.
One of them was reading Tupper's Proverbial Philosophy. On reaching
Llandudno, Sophia waited at the hotel, while O'S., Una, and I, ascended the
Great Orme's Head. There are copper-mines there, and we heard of a large
cave, with stalactites, but did not go so far as that. We found the old shaft of
a mine, however, and threw stones down it, and counted twenty before we
heard them strike the bottom. At the base of the Head, on the side opposite the
village, we saw a small church, with a broken roof, and horizontal grave-stones
of slate within the stone enclosure, around it. The view from the hill was most
beautiful—a blue summer sea, with the distant trail of smoke from a steamer,
and many snowy sails;—in another direction, the mountains, near and distant,
some of them with clouds below their peaks.

We went to one of the mines which is still worked; and boys came running
to meet us with specimens of the [25] copper-ore for sale. The miners were not
now hoisting ore from the shaft, but were washing and selecting the valuable
fragments from great heaps of crumbled stone and earth. All about this spot,
there are shafts and well-holes, looking fearfully deep and black, and without
the slightest protection, so that we might just as easily have walked into them
as not. Having examined these matters sufficiently, we descended the hill
towards the village, meeting parties of visitors mounted on donkeys, which
is a much more sensible way of ascending, in a hot day, than to walk. On the
sides and summit of the hill, we found yellow gorse,—heather, I think, of two
colors, and very beautiful—and here and there a hair-bell. Owing to the long
continued dry weather, the grass was getting dry and brown, though not so
much so as on American hill-pastures, at this season. Returning to the village,
we all went into a confectioners shop, and made a good luncheon of sandwiches,
cakes, and ginger beer, for eighteen pence. The two prettiest young ladies
whom I have seen in England came into the shop and ate cakes, while we were
there; they appeared to be living together in a lodging-house, and ordered some
of their house-keeping articles from the confectioner. Next, we went into the
village bazaar (a sort of tent, or open shop, full of knick-knacks and gew-
gaws) and bought [26] some playthings &c for the children. At 1/2 past one,
we took our seats in the omnibus to return to Conway.

We had as yet only seen the castle-wall, and the exterior of the castle; now
we were to see the inside. Right at the foot of the castle, an old woman has
her stand for the sale of lithographic views of Conway and other matters;
but these views are ridiculously inadequate;—so that we did not buy any. The
admittance into the castle is by a wooden door of modern construction; and
the present seneschal, I believe, is the sexton of a church. He remembered
me as having been there a month or two ago; and probably considering that
I was already initiated, or else because he had many other visitors, he left

us to wander about the castle at will. It is altogether impossible to describe
Conway Castle. Nothing ever can have been so perfect in its own style, and for
its own purposes, when it was first built; and now nothing else can be so
perfect as a picture of ivy-grown, peaceful ruin. The banquetting[sic]-hall,
all open to the sky, and with thick sheets of ivy tapestrying the walls, and grass
and weeds growing on the arches that over-pass it, is indescribably beautiful.
The hearth-stones of the great old fire-places, all about the castle, seem to be
favorite places for weeds to grow. There are eight of those great round towers
appertaining to this castle; and out of four of them I think, rise smaller towers,
ascending [27] to a much greater height, and once containing winding-stair-
cases, all of which are now broken and inaccessible from below, though, in
at least one of the towers, the stairs seemed perfect, high aloft. It must have
been the rudest of violence that broke down these stairs; for each step was a
thick and heavy slab of stone, built into the wall of the tower. There is no
such thing as a roof in any part of the castle; towers, hall, kitchen, all are open
to the sky. One round tower, directly overhanging the railway is so shattered
by the falling away of the lower part, that you can look quite up into it and
through it, while sitting in the cars; and yet it has stood thus, without falling
into completer ruin, for more than two hundred years. I think it was in this
tower that we found the castle oven, an immense cavern, big enough to bake
bread for an army. The railway passes right at the base of the high rock on
which this part of the castle is situated, and goes into the town through a
great arch that has been opened in the castle-wall. The tubular bridge across
the Conway has been built in a style that accords with the old architecture of
the castle; and I observed that one little sprig of ivy had rooted itself in the
new structure.

There are numberless intricate passages in the thickness of the castle-walls,
forming communications between tower and [28] tower—damp, chill passages,
with rough stone on either hand—darksome, and, likely as not, leading to dark
pitfalls. The thickness of the walls is amazing; and the people of those days
must have been content with very scanty light—so small were the apertures—
sometimes merely slits and loop-holes, glimmering through many feet thickness
of stone. One of the towers was said to have been the residence of Queen
Eleanor; and this was better lighted than the others, containing an oriel window, looking out of a little oratory, as it seemed to be, with groined arches and
traces of ornamental sculpture; so that we could dress up some imperfect
image of a queenly chamber, though the tower was roofless and floorless.
There was another pleasant little windowed nook, close beside the oratory,
where the Queen might have sat sewing, or looking down the Conway at the
picturesque headlands towards the sea. We imagined her stately figure, in
antique robes, standing beneath the groined arches of the oratory. There seem
to have been three chambers, one above another, in these towers; and the one
in which was the embowed window was the middle-one. I suppose the diameter
of each of these circular rooms could not have been more than twenty feet on

the inside. All traces of wood work and iron-work are quite gone from the whole castle. These are said to have been taken away by a Lord Conway, in the reign of Charles II.

[29] There is a grassy space under the windows of Queen Eleanor's tower— a sort of outwork of the castle, where, probably, when no enemy was near, the Queen used to take the open air, in summer afternoons like this. Here we sat down, on the grass of the ruined wall, and agreed that nothing in the world could be so beautiful and picturesque as Conway Castle, and that never could there have been so fit a time to see it as this sunny, quiet, lovely afternoon. Sunshine adapts itself to the character of a ruin, in a wonderful way; it does not "flout the ruins gray," as Scott says,[106] but sympathizes with their decay and saddens itself for their sake. It beautifies the ivy, too. We saw, at the corner of this grass plot around Queen Eleanor's tower, a real trunk of a tree, of ivy, with so stalwart a stem, and such a vigorous grasp of its strong branches, that it would be a very efficient support to the wall, were it otherwise inclined to fall. Oh, that we could have ivy in America! What is there to beautify us, when our time of ruin comes.

Before departing, we made the entire circuit of the castle, on its walls; and O'Sullivan and I climbed by a ladder to the top of one of the towers. While there, we looked down into the street beneath, and saw a photographist preparing to take a view of the castle, and calling out to some [30] little girl, in some niche or on some pinnacle of the walls, to stand still, that he might catch her figure and face. I think it added to the impressiveness of the old castle, to see the streets, and the kitchen-gardens, and the homely dwellings, that had grown up within the precincts of this feudal fortress, and the people of to-day following their little businesses about it. This does not destroy the charm; but tourists and idle visitors do impair it. The earnest life of to-day, however petty and homely it may be, has a right to its place alongside of what is left of the life of other days; and if it be vulgar itself, it does not vulgarize the scene. But tourists do vulgarize it; and I suppose we did so, just like others.

We took the train back to Rhyl, where we arrived at about four °clock; and having dined, again took the rail for Chester, and thence to Rock Park—that is, O'Sullivan and I. We reached home at about 10 °clock, and Emily came down in her night clothes to let us in.[107] O'Sullivan took his departure for London, the next day (yesterday) at five °clock.

Yesterday (Septr 13th) I began to wear a watch from Bennett's, 65, Cheapside, London. It costs £28, and W. C. Bennett warrants it as the best watch which they can produce. If it proves as good and as durable as he prophesies, Julian will find it a perfect time-keeper, long [31] after his father has done with time. If I had not thought of his wearing it hereafter, I should have been content with a much inferior one. No 39620

WEDNESDAY, SEPT^r 20th.

I WENT back to Rhyl, last Friday, in the steamer; a pleasant day. We arrived at the landing between three and four °clock (having started at 12) and I walked thence to our lodgings, 18, West Parade. The children and their mother were all out; and I sat sometime in our parlour, before anybody came.

The next morning, I made an excursion in the omnibus as far as Ruthin; passing through Rhuddlan, St. Asaph, Denbigh, and reaching Ruthin at about 1 °clock. All these are very ancient places. St Asaph has a cathedral, which is not quite worthy of that name, but is a very large and stately church, in excellent repair; its square, battlemented tower has a very fine appearance, crowning the clump of village-houses, on the hill-top, as you approach from Rhuddlan. The ascent of the hill is very steep; so it is at Denbigh and at Ruthin —the steepest streets, indeed, that I ever saw. Denbigh is a place of still more antique aspect than St Asaph; it looks, I think, even older than Chester, with its gabled houses, many of the windows opening on hinges; some of the edifices resting their fronts on pillars, with an open porch beneath. The castle makes an admirably [32] ruinous figure on the hill, higher than the village. I had come thither with the purpose of inspecting it; but as it began to rain, just then, I concluded to get into the omnibus and go on to Ruthin. There was another steep ascent from the commencement of the long street of Ruthin, till we reached the market-place, which is of nearly triangular shape, and certainly the oldest looking place I ever saw. Houses of stone, or plastered-brick; one or two with timber-frames. The roofs, of an uneven line, and bulging out, or sinking in; the slates moss-grown. Some of them had two peaks, or even three, in a row, fronting on the streets. An old stone market house, with a table of regulations. There is said to be a stone in the market-place, on which King Arthur beheaded one of his enemies; but this I did not see. All these old villages were very lively, as the omnibus drove in; and I rather imagine it was market-day in each of them—there being quite a bustle of Welsh people. The old women came round the omnibus, curtseying, and intimating their willingness to receive alms:—old, witch-like women, such as one sees in pictures or reads of in romances, and very unlike anything feminine in America. Their style of dress cannot have changed for a century. It was quite unexpected to me to hear Welsh so universally and familiarly spoken; everybody spoke it; the omnibus-driver could speak but imperfect English; there [33] was a gabble of Welsh all through the streets and market-places; and it seemed to flow out with a freedom quite different to the way in which they expressed themselves in English. I had had an idea that Welsh was spoken rather as a freak, and in fun, than as a native language; it was so strange to think of another language being the people's actual and earnest medium of thought, within so short a distance of England. But English seems to be scarcely more known to the body of the Welsh people, than to the peasantry of France. Moreover, they sometimes pretend to ignorance, when they might speak it fairly enough.

I took luncheon (a very good luncheon of cold-beef and a pint of ale) at the hotel where the omnibus stopt; and then went to search out the castle. It appears to have been once extensive; but the remains of it are now (so far as I could discover) very few; except a part of the external wall. Whatever other portion may still exist seems to have been built into a modern castellated mansion, which has risen within the wide circuit of the old fortress;—a handsome and spacious edifice of red free-stone, with a high tower, on which a flag was flying. The grounds were well laid out in walks; and really I think the site of the old castle could not have been turned to better account. I am getting tired of antiquity; it is [34] certainly less interesting, in the long run, than novelty; and so I was well content with the fresh, warm, red hue of the modern castellated house, and the unworn outline of its walls, and its cheerful, large windows; and was willing that the old ivy-grown ruins should exist now only to contrast with the modernisms. These old walls, by-the-by, are of immense thickness; there is a passage through the interior of a portion of them, the width, from this interior passage to the outer air being fifteen feet on one side, and I know not how much on the other.

It continued showery all day; and the omnibus was crowded. I had ridden on the outside from Rhyl to Denbigh, but, all the rest of the journey, imprisoned myself within. On our way home, an old lady got into the omnibus; an old lady of tremendous rotundity; and as she stumbled from the door to the farthest part of the carriage, she kept advising all the rest of the passengers to get out. "I don't think there will be much rain, gentlemen," quoth she. "You'll be much more comfortable on the outside." As none of us complied, she glanced along the seats—"What! Are you all Sass'nach?" she inquired. As we rode along, she talked Welsh with great fluency to one of the passengers, a young woman with a baby, and to as many others as could understand her. It has a strange, wild sound, [35] like a language half-blown away by the wind. The old lady's English was very good; but she probably prided herself on her proficiency in Welsh. My excursion to-day had been along the valley of the Clwyd;—a very rich and fertile tract of country. The hill-scenery around us was not particularly striking.

The next day, Sunday, we all took a long walk on the beach at Rhyl, picking up shells.

On Monday, Sophia, Una, Julian, and I, took an open car, and went to Rhuddlan; whence we sent back the car, meaning to walk back along the embankment of the river Clwyd, after inspecting the castle. The old fortress was the first, I think, which Edward I built in Wales, and he resided here while Conway was being built; and here his queen was brought to bed of a daughter. It is very ruinous; having been dismantled by the Parliamentarians. There are great gaps—two, at least, in the walls that connect the round towers, of which there were six; one on each side of a gateway in front, and the same at a gateway towards the river, whence there is a steep descent to a wall and square tower at the water-side. Great pains, and a great deal of gunpowder, must have been used in converting this castle into a ruin; there were one or two fragments lying near the walls, where they had fallen more than two hundred [36] years ago, which, though merely a conglomeration of small stones and mortar, were just as hard as if they had been solid masses of granite.

The substantial thickness of the walls is composed of these agglomerated small stones and mortar; the casing being hewn blocks of red free-stone. This stone is much worn away by the weather, wherever it has been exposed to the air; but, under shelter, it looks as it might if hewn only a year or two ago. Each of the round towers, I think, had formerly a small staircase-turret rising beside it and ascending above it, in which a warder might be posted; but all the towers have been so battered and shattered that it is impossible for an uninstructed observer to make out a satisfactory plan of them. The interior of each tower was a small room, not more than twelve or fifteen feet across; and of these there seem to have been three stories; with loop-holes for archery, and, I believe, not much other light than what came through them. Then there are various passages, and nooks and corners, and square recesses in the stone; some of which must have been intended for dungeons, and were the ugliest and gloomiest dungeons imaginable—for they could not have had any light or air. There is not the least splinter of wood-work remaining in any part of the castle; nothing but bare stone, and, if I remember aright, in one or two places, a little plaster on the [37] wall. In the front gateway, we looked at the groove on each side, where the portcullis used to rise and fall; and in each of the contiguous round towers there was a loop-hole whence an enemy, on the outer side of the portcullis, might be shot through with an arrow.

The inner court-yard of the castle is a parallelogram, nearly a square, and is about forty-five of my paces across. It is entirely grass-grown, and vacant, except for two or three trees that have been recently set out, and which are surrounded with palings to keep out the cows that pasture in and about the castle. No window looks from the walls or towers into this court-yard; nor are there any traces of buildings ever having stood within the enclosure, unless it be what looks something like the flue of a chimney, within one of the walls. I should suppose, however, that there must have been, when the castle was in its perfect state, a hall, a kitchen, and other commodious apartments and offices for the king and his train; such as there were at Conway and Beaumaris. But if so, all fragments have been carried away, and all hollows of the old foundations scrupulously filled up. The round towers could not have comprised all the accommodation of the castle. By the by, there is nothing more striking in these old ruins, than to look upward from the ruinous base, and see flights of stairs still com[38]paratively perfect, and by which you might securely ascend to the upper heights of the tower; although all traces of a staircase have disappeared below, and the upper portion cannot be come at. On three sides of the castle is a moat, about sixty feet wide, and cased with stone; it was probably of great depth in its day, but it is now partly filled up with earth, and is quite dry and grassy throughout its whole extent. On the inner side of the moat was the outer wall of the castle, portions of which still remain. Between the outer wall and the castle itself, the space, I think, is likewise about sixty feet.

The day was cloudy and lowering, and there were several little spatterings of rain, while we rambled about the castle. The two children ran shouting about, and were continually clambering into dangerous places, running along ledges of broken wall &c. At last, they alltogether [*sic*] disappeared for a good while; their voices, which had heretofore been loudly audible, were hushed; nor was there any answer when Sophia and I began to call them, making ready for our departure. But at last they made their appearance out of the castle-moat, where they had been picking and eating blackberries—which they said grew very plentifully there, and which they were very reluctant to leave. Before quitting the tower, I must not forget the ivy, which makes a perfect tapestry over a large [39] portion of the walls.

We walked about the village, which is older and uglier than anything that an American can conceive; small irregular streets, contriving to be intricate, though there are few of them; mean houses, joining on to each other. We saw, in the principal street, a house which (or a portion of it) was the parliament house in which Edward I gave a charter, or allowed rights of some kind or degree, to his Welsh subjects. The ancient part of the wall is easily distinguishable from what has since been built upon it.

We went into a small ale-house, by the river's side and close to a shipyard; where I drank a glass of porter while Sophia mended Una's straw-hat. Thence we set out to walk along the embankment, although the sky looked very threatening. The wind, however, was so strong, and had such a full sweep at us, on the top of the embankment, that we decided on taking a path that led from it across the moor. But we soon had cause to repent of this; for, whichever way we turned, we found ourselves cut off by a ditch or little stream; so that here we were, fairly astray on Rhuddlan moor, the old battle-field of the Saxons and Britons, and across which, I suppose, the fiddlers and mountebanks had marched to the relief of the Earl of Chester. Anon, too, it began to shower; and it [40] was only after various leaps and scramblings that we made our way to a large farm-house, and took shelter under a cart-shed. The back of the house, at which we gained access to it, was very dirty and ill-kept; some dirty children peeped at us as we approached; and nobody had the civility to ask us in; so we took advantage of the first cessation of the shower to resume our way. We shortly were overtaken by a very intelligent-looking and civil man, who seemed to have come from Rhuddlan, and said he was going to Rhyl. We followed his guidance over styles [*sic*], and along hedge-row paths, which we never could have threaded rightly by ourselves; but this mode of making one's way across the country, (almost unknown in America, but common here) is exceedingly pleasant; it is so much more picturesque, and adventurous in a harmless way, than the high road. These styles [*sic*] and by-paths (centuries old, no doubt) can never exist on our side of the water, where land is continually changing its owners and its enclosures.

By and by, our kind guide had to stop at an intermediate farm; but he gave us full directions how to proceed, and we went on till it began to shower again, pretty briskly, and we took refuge in a little bit of old stone cottage, which, small as it was, had doubtless a greater antiquity than any mansion in America. It had a thatched roof. The door was [41] open, and as we approached we saw several children gazing at us; and their mother, a pleasant-looking woman, who seemed rather astounded at the visit that was about to befall her, but tried to draw a tattered curtain over a part of her interior, which she fancied even less fit to be seen than the rest. To say the truth, the house was not a bit better than a pig-stye [sic]; and while we sat there, a pig came familiarly to the door, thrust in his snout, and seemed surprised that he should be driven away, instead of being admitted as one of the family. The floor was of brick; there was no ceiling, but only the peaked gable overhead. The room was kitchen, parlor, and, I suppose, bed room for the whole family; at all events, there was only the tattered curtain betwixt us and the sleeping accommodations. The good woman either could not or would not speak a word of English, only laughing when Sophia said "Dim Sassenach?"—but she was kind and hospitable, and found a chair for each of us. She had been making some bread, and the dough was on the dresser. Life, with these good people, is reduced to its simplest elements. It is only a pity that they cannot, or do not choose to, keep themselves cleaner; poverty, except in cities, need not be squalid. When the shower mitigated a little, we gave all the pennies we had to the children, and set forth again. By-the-by, there [42] were several colored prints stuck up against the walls; and there was a clock ticking in a corner; also some paper-hangings pinned up against the slanting roof.

It began to shower again before we got to Rhyl, and we we [sic] were driven into a small tavern, where I got another glass of ale. After staying here a while, we set forth between the drops; but the rain fell still heavier, and we got to our lodging-house pretty well damped. After dinner, I took the rail for Chester and Rock Park, where I arrived at about ten, P.M.; and Sophia and the children followed me the next day.

Septr 22d Friday.

I DINED on Wednesday evening at Mr John Heywood's, Norris Green; the company, among other people, Mr Monckton Milnes[108] and lady. Mr Milnes is a very agreeable, kindly, man of the world; rather under the medium height, but somewhat English in rotundity, though not decidedly so;—resembling Long-fellow a good deal in personal appearance, though of a thicker build, and (being an Englishman) with not quite so polished an address. He promotes, however, by his genial manners, the same pleasant sort of intercourse which is so easily established with Longfellow. He is said to be a very kind patron of literary men, and to do a great deal of good among young and neglected people of that class. He is considered one of the best conversationists at present in society; [43] and though one would hardly think of saying it, yet it may very well be so;—his style of talking being very simple and natural, anything but obtrusive, so that you might enjoy its agreeableness without suspecting it. He introduced me to his wife (a daughter of Lord Crewe) with whom and himself

I had a good deal of talk. I liked her very well; her manners being more like those of an American lady than those of any other Englishwoman whom I have met, most of whom seem to have little affectations of manner and tone. Also, like so many American ladies, she appears to be in delicate health.

Mr Milnes told me that he owns the land, in Yorkshire, whence some of the pilgrims of the Mayflower emigrated to Plymouth; and that Elder Brewster was the postmaster of the village. He takes pride in this ownership. He also said that, in the next voyage of the Mayflower, after she carried the pilgrims, she was employed in transporting a cargo of slaves from Africa—to the West Indies, I suppose.[109] This is a queer fact, and would be nuts for the Southern people

Mem. An American would never understand the passage in Bunyan about Christian and Hopeful going astray by a by-path into the grounds of Giant Despair—from there being no styles [*sic*] and footpaths in our country.

[44] SEPTEMBER 26th.

ON Saturday evening, my wife and I went to a soiree, given by the Mayor and Mrs. Lloyd at the Town Hall. It was quite brilliant; the public rooms being really magnificent; and adorned for the occasion with a large collection of pictures, belonging to Mr Naylor. They were mostly (I believe entirely) of modern artists, comprising some of Turner, Wilkie, Landseer, and others of the best English painters. Turner's seemed too airy to have been done by mortal hands.

The British scientific association being now in session here, many distinguished strangers were present. What chiefly struck me, however, was the lack of beauty in the women, and the horrible ugliness of not a few of them. I have heard a good deal of the tenacity with [which] English women retain their personal charms to a late period of life; but my experience is, that an English lady of forty or fifty is apt to become the most hideous animal that ever pretended to human shape. No caricature could do justice to some of their figures and features; so puffed out, so huge, so without limit, with such hanging dewlaps, and all manner of fleshly abomination—dressed, too, in a way to show all these points to the worst advantage, and walking about with entire self-satisfaction, unconscious of the wrong they are doing to one's idea of womanhood. They [45] are gross, gross, gross. Who would not shrink from such a mother! Who would not abhor such a wife? I really pitied the respectable elderly gentlemen whom I saw walking about with such atrocities hanging on their arms—the grim, red-faced monsters! Surely, a man would be justified in murdering them—in taking a sharp knife and cutting away their mountainous flesh, until he had brought them into reasonable shape, as a sculptor seeks for the beautiful form of woman in a shapeless block of marble. The husband must feel that something alien has grown over and incrusted the slender creature whom he married, and that he is horribly wronged by having all this flabby flesh imposed upon him as his wife. "Flesh of his flesh," indeed! And this ugliness surely need not be, at least to such a dreadful extent; it must be, in great part, the penalty of a life of gross feeding—of much ale-guzzling and beef-eating. Nor is it possible to conceive of any delicacy and grace of soul existing within; or if there be such, the creature ought to be killed, in order to release the spirit so vilely imprisoned.[110]

I really and truly believe that the entire body of American washerwomen would present more grace than the entire body of English ladies, were both to be shown up together. American [46] women, of all ranks, when past their prime, generally look thin, worn, care-begone, as if they may have led a life of much trouble and few enjoyments; but English women look as if they had fed upon the fat of meat, and made themselves gross and earthy in all sorts of ways. As a point of taste, I prefer my own countrywomen; though it is a pity that we must choose between a greasy animal and an anxious skeleton.[111]

SEPT[r] 29th.

MR. MONCKTON MILNES called on me at my office, day before yesterday. He is pleasant and sensible; but an intellectual and refined American is a higher man than he—a higher and a finer one. Speaking of American politicians, I remarked that they were seldom anything but politicians, and had no literary nor other culture, beyond their own calling. He said the case was the same in England, and instanced Sir Robert Peel, who once called on him for information when an appeal had been made to him (Sir Robert) respecting two literary gentlemen. Sir Robert had *never heard* the names of either of these gentlemen, and applied to Mr. Milnes, as being somewhat conversant with the literary class, to know whether they were distinguished, and what their claims. The names of the two literary men were James Sheridan Knowles, and Alfred Tennyson.

OCTOBER 5th, THURSDAY.

YESTERDAY, I was present at a *dejeuner* on board the "James Baines,"[112] on occasion of her coming [47] under the British flag—having been built for the Messrs Baines by Donald McKay of Boston. She is a splendid vessel, surely, and magnificently fitted up, though not with consummate taste. It would be worth while that ornamental architects and upholsterers should study this branch of art, since the ship-builders seem willing, at any rate, to expend a good deal of money on it. In fact, I do not see that there is anywhere else so much encouragement to the exercise of ornamental art. I saw nothing to criticise in the solid and useful details of the ship; the ventilation, in particular being free and abundant, so that the hundreds of passengers, who will have their berths between decks, and at a still lower depth, will have good air and enough of it.

There were four or five hundred people—principally Liverpool merchants and their wives—invited to the *dejeuner;* and the tables were spread between decks—the berths for passengers not being yet put in. There was not quite light enough to make the scene cheerful, it being an overcast day; and, indeed, there was an English plainness in the arrangement of the festal-room, which might have been better exchanged for the flowery American taste, which I have just been criticizing. By dint of flowers and the arrange-ment of flags, we should have made something very pretty of the space be[48]tween decks; but the English seem to have no faculty of this kind, so that there was nothing to hide the fact, that, in a few days hence, there would be crowded berths and sea-sick steerage passengers, where we were now feast-ing. However, the cheer was very good—cold fowl and meats, cold pies of foreign manufacture, very rich, and of mysterious composition—and cham-pagne in plenty, with other wines for those who liked them.

I sat between two ladies, one of them a Mrs. Schomberg, a pleasant young woman, who, I believe is of American provincial nativity, and whom I there-fore regarded as half a countrywoman. We talked a good deal together, and I confided to her my annoyance at the prospect of being called up to answer a toast; but she did not pity me at all, though she felt much alarm about her husband, Captain Schomberg, who was in the same predicament. Seriously, it is the most awful part of my official duty; this necessity of making dinner-speeches, at the Mayor's and other public or semi-public tables. However, my neighborhood to Mrs. Schomberg was good for me, inasmuch as, by laughing over the matter with her, I came to regard it in a light and ludicrous way; and so, when the time actually came, I stood up with a careless, dare-devil feeling, being indeed, rather pot-valiant with cham-pagne.[113] The chairman toasted the President immediately after the Queen, and did me the honor to speak of myself in a most flattering man[49]ner, something like this—"great by his position under the Republic—greater still, I am bold to say, in the Republic of letters!!" I made no reply at all to this dole of soft-sodder; in truth, I forgot all about it when I began to speak, and merely thanked the company, in behalf of the President and my countrymen, and made a few remarks, with no very decided point to them. However, they cheered and applauded, and I took advantage of the applause to sit down; and Mrs. Schomberg assured me that I had succeeded admirably. It was no suc-cess at all, to be sure; neither was it a failure; for I had aimed at nothing, and had exactly hit it.[114] But, after sitting down, I was conscious of an enjoy-ment in speaking to a public assembly, and felt as if I should like to rise again; it is something like being under fire,[115]—a sort of excitement, not ex-actly pleasure, but more piquant than most pleasures. I have felt this before, in the same circumstances; but, while on my legs, my impulse is to get through with my remarks and sit down again, as quickly as possible. The next speech, I think, was by Rev. Dr. Scoresby,[116] the celebrated Arctic gentleman, in reply to a toast complimentary to the clergy. He turned aside from the matter in hand to express his kind feelings towards America, where, he said, he had [50] been most hospitably received, especially at Cambridge Uni-versity; he also made allusions to me, and I suppose it would have been no more than civil for me to have answered with a speech in acknowledgement; but I did not choose to make another venture, so merely thanked him across the corner of the table; for he sat near me, with only his wife between. He is a venerable-looking, white haired gentleman, tall and slender, with a pale, intelligent, kindly, wrinkled face. If I mistake not, he has been a sea-captain; but there is nothing in [his] aspect either sea-captainish or John Bullish.

Other speeches were made; but, from beginning to end of the affair, there was not one breath of eloquence, nor even one neat sentence; and I rather imagine that the Englishman would avoid eloquence or neatness of after-dinner speeches, even were they capable of it. At any rate, it seems to be no part of their object. Yet any Englishman, almost (much more generally, I think, than with Americans) will get up and talk on, in a plain way, uttering one rough, ragged, and shapeless sentence after another, and will have expressed a sensible meaning, though in a very rude manner, before he sits down. And this is quite satisfactory to his audience; who, indeed, are rather prejudiced against the man who speaks too glibly.[117]

[51] The guests began to depart shortly after three °clock.[118] This morning I have seen two reports of my little speech—one, exceedingly incorrect; another, pretty exact, but not much to my taste; for I seem to have left out everything that would have been fittest to say.

OCTOBER 6th.

THE people, for several days, have been in the utmost anxiety, and latterly in the highest exultation, about Sebastopol; and all England, and Europe to boot, has been fooled by the belief that it had fallen. This, however, now turns out to be incorrect;[119] and the public visage is somewhat grim, in consequence. I am glad of it. In spite of his natural sympathies, it is impossible for a true American to be otherwise than glad. Success makes an Englishman intolerable; and, already, on the mistaken idea that the way was open to a prosperous conclusion of this war, the Times had begun to throw out menaces against America.[120] [52] I shall never love England till she sues to us for help; and, in the meantime, the fewer triumphs she obtains, the better for all parties. An Englishman in adversity is a very respectable character; he does not lose his dignity, but merely comes to a proper conceit of himself, and is thereby a great deal less ridiculous than he generally is. It is rather touching, to a mere observer like myself, to see how much the universal heart is in this matter;—to see the merchants gathering round the telegraphic messages, posted on the pillars of the Exchange news-room—the people in the streets, who cannot afford to buy a paper, clustering round the windows of the news-offices, where a copy is pinned up;—the groups of corporals and sergeants at the recruiting rendezvous, with a newspaper in the midst of them;—and all earnest and sombre, and feeling like one man together, whatever their rank. I seem to myself like a spy or a traitor, when I meet their eyes, and am conscious that I neither hope nor fear in sympathy with them, although (unless they detect me for an American by my aspect) they look at me in full confidence of sympathy. Their heart "knoweth its own bitterness"; and as for me, being a stranger and an alien, I "intermeddle not with their joy."[121] There is an account to settle between us and them for the contemptuous jealousy with which (since it has ceased to be unmitigated contempt) they regard us; [53] and if they do not make us amends by coming humbly to ask our assistance, they must do it by fairly acknowledging us as their masters.

OCTOBER 9th

My ancestor left England in 1635.[122] I return in 1853. I sometimes feel as if I myself had been absent these two hundred and eighteen years—leaving England just emerging from the feudal system, and finding it on the verge of Republicanism. It brings the two far separated points of time very closely together, to view the matter thus.[123]

OCTOBER 16th.

MAJOR Robert G. Scott[124] (the man whose famous interrogatory letter killed off so many presidential candidates, and left the field open for Pierce) arrived here last week. He is consul at Rio [de] Janeiro, but left his post to get married, and is now taking a round about way to get back, with his new wife. Major Scott is an exceedingly plain, somewhat yeomanlike man, dressed in gray, and looking as much like a country magistrate as anything;— quite different from the idea one forms of a Virginia gentleman. He is sensible, but heavy;—gray-headed, and a grandfather, though by no means infirm. His wife is a widow, a great deal younger than himself, rather handsome, and with a good deal of American dash. She is from Alabama, has a fortune, and no children. The poor old Major is fortunate—or otherwise.

[54] A day or two ago, arrived the sad news of the loss of the Arctic,[125] by collision with a French steamer off Newfoundland, and the loss of between three and four hundred people. I have seldom been more affected by anything quite alien from my personal and friendly concerns, than by the death of Captain Luce, and his son. The latter was a delicate lad; and it is said that he had never been absent from his mother till this time, when his father had taken him to England to consult a medical man about a complaint in his hip. So his father, while the ship was sinking, had to decide whether he would put the poor, weakly, timorous child on board the boat, to take his hard chance of life there, or keep him to go down with himself and the ship. He chose the latter;—and within half an hour, I suppose, the boy was among the child-angels. Captain Luce could not do less than die, for his own part, with the responsibility of all those lost lives upon him;—he may not have been in the least to blame for the calamity, but it was too heavy a one, certainly, for him to survive. He was a sensitive man;—a gentleman, courteous, quiet, with something almost melancholy in his address and aspect. Often-

times, he has come into my inner-office to say good-bye, before his departures; but I cannot precisely remember whether or no he took leave of me, on this latest voyage. I never exchanged a great many words with him, but those few were kind ones.

[55] OCTOBER 19th.

CAPTAIN Walter M. Gibson[126]—a man of romantic adventure from his very birth upward. He was born at sea, on board a Spanish vessel, off the coast of Gibraltar, I believe. Owing to some circumstances, he has been in doubt whether he was really the child of his reputed parents; they have not seemed to love him,[127] and, though both [are] still living, it is many years since he has seen or lived with them. Since he has been in England, he has been led to inquire into the subject, and finds that there were *two* births on board the Spanish vessel, nearly simultaneous; and the supposition is, that he himself was assigned to the wrong mother. He did not tell me the grounds of this belief; nor has he as yet fully examined into the matter; but he mentions that there is said to be a portrait in the family to which he supposes himself to belong, bearing a striking resemblance to himself. He has not as yet, I think, traced the child of the other birth; but he means to return to England, in a few months, to search fully into all these things. Meantime, he lost his passage in the Pacific, yesterday, owing to his lingering a little too long to follow out some inquiry which he had commenced. The family, to which he attributes himself, is that of a nobleman, whose name I do not precisely recollect. Most probably, the whole thing is another instance of the American fancy for connecting themselves with English property and lineage.

[56] Captain Gibson being thus left by the steamer, I invited him to dinner yesterday. He spent the night; and we found him a very interesting guest. He has been long in the Eastern Seas, at Sumatra and thereabouts, and there got into difficulties with the Dutch authorities, who confiscated his vessel, and confined him in prison for seventeen months;—whence he escaped by aid of some Malay friends. He has now been pressing a claim for damages on the government at the Hague; in the course of which enterprise, a voluminous mass of documents, respecting himself and his claim, have strangely come into his hands, through a blunder of the Dutch government; and these documents, much to his regret, have now gone in the Pacific, and (the package being directed to the State Department) will be carried to Washington, in his absence, and thus pass out of his own possession. Mr. Belmont,[128] our minister, has made a peremptory demand on the government of the Hague for $100,000, in satisfaction of his claim.

He told us of a visit to the island of Tristan d'Acunha, which had not been visited by civilized people for many years, and was supposed to be uninhabited; but he found there nearly a hundred inhabitants, living under the patriarchal rule of an old English sergeant, whose descendants they most of them were. It seems to be just such a colony, in all its [57] characteristics

of pure and happy simplicity, as that which was formed of the descendants
of the mutineers of the Bounty;[129] only the latter settlement was the larger
of the two. Captain Gibson seemed quite capable of appreciating the beauty
and poetry of the affair; but he has done his best to spoil it, I fear, by representing to our government the expediency of taking possession of the island, and
forming a naval station there. The United States can assert a plausible claim
to the territory; inasmuch as it [*sic*] its first occupant was an American
citizen, a native of Salem, who established himself there about half a century
ago, but had disappeared before the English sergeant came on the stage.

Captain Gibson's talk has a strange oriental fragrance breathing through it,
as if the smell of the Spice Islands were still in his garments. The Malays,
according to him, are a delightful people; and he thinks that the stories of
the Arabian Nights originated there. He has manuscripts of two or three
centuries' antiquity, written on strips of bamboo, which he obtained there.
He says that the Malay pirates follow their predatory and murderous warfare
on European ships as a profession, and, apart from this, are good and praiseworthy people, and are without blame in their other relations. But his strangest
stories are about a people who seem [58] exactly to realize Swift's fable of
the Yahoos—being so low in the scale of humanity that the Captain rather
inclines to doubt whether they have any souls. Hairy, with spots of fur,
filthy, shameless, weaponless, tool-less, house-less; with no language, but a
few guttural sounds—with no institutions of any kinds—beasts in all their attributes. I asked him whether they inspired a feeling of disgust in the spectator, from a sense that they were degraded human beings, or whether, looking
upon them as brute-beasts, he accepted their brutalities and was no more
shocked by them than by the natural habits of other beasts. I understood
him to answer that the latter was the case. These Orang-Cuboos [Kubus]
(as the Captain termed them) are hunted and caught in traps by the Malays,
and are put to the uses of beasts of burthen. He means to write and publish
a book of his adventures; so that I need not trouble myself with recording any
more of them.

He is a man, probably, of about thirty-five, slender, with a prominent nose
and, handsome, intelligent, moderately-bearded face, of a light complexion.
Like most men of an adventurous turn, he is of a very quiet deportment,
rather inclined to silence than conversation. He is gentlemanly, seems to have
read a good deal on such sub[59]jects as interest him, and shows signs of a
native fastidiousness of taste. The vicissitudes of his life appear to have
tinctured him with superstition, inclining him to look upon himself as
marked out for something strange. He diversified his accounts of strange
people, and "men whose heads do grow beneath their shoulders,"[130] with talking
of a little daughter, ten years old, who is now expecting him in America, and
will be on the pier to greet him when the Pacific arrives. His wife is dead.
Our little Rosebud made great friends with him, and was half ready to be persuaded to go off in his company. He says he has an instinctive love for,

and sympathy with the sea, which he attributes to its being his native element; and yet, after all his experience of it, he is liable to sea-sickness.

There is some similarity between his life and O'Sullivan's, who was likewise born at sea, near Gibraltar, and must be about Captain Gibson's age;—and who has also been a wanderer, a man of vicissitudes, as if his native waves were all the time tossing beneath him.

It appears to be customary for people of decent station, but in distressed circumstances, to go round among their neighbors and the public, accompanied by a friend, who explains the circumstances of the case. I have been accosted in the [60] street by persons on this errand; and to day there came to my office a grocer, who had become security for a friend, and who was threatened with an execution, with another grocer for supporter and advocate.[131] The beneficiary takes very little active part in the matter, merely looking care-worn, distressed, and pitiable, and throwing in a word of corroboration, or a sigh, or an acknowledgement, as the case may demand. In the present instance, the friend (a young, respectable-looking tradesman, with a Lancashire accent) spoke freely and simply of his client's misfortunes, not pressing the case unduly, but doing it full justice; and saying, at the close of the interview, that it was no pleasant business for himself. The broken grocer was an elderly man, of somewhat sickly aspect. This whole matter is very foreign from American habits. No respectable man would think of retrieving his affairs by such means, but would prefer ruin ten times over; no friend would take up his cause; no public would think it worth while to prevent the small catastrophe. And yet the custom is not without its good side, as indicating a closer feeling of brotherhood, a more efficient sense of neighborhood, than exists among ourselves; although, perhaps, we are more careless of a fellow-creature's ruin, because ruin with us is by no means the fatal and irretrievable affair that it is in England.

[61] Captain Gibson's Yahoos breed with the human race, and improve thereby. Among themselves, they breed in and in and have no scruple or restraint as to their intermixtures. Indeed, he says, incest is common, all over the East, and Princes marry their sisters, this being one of the princely privileges. As they are not brought up along with their sisters, but are quite as much strangers to them as to any other women, there is nothing to prevent the brother and sister being objects of natural desire.[132]

At the time when the Captain's vessel was seized by the Dutch, he was on the point of going in search of an immense buried treasure (amounting to two or three millions sterling) which he had heard of as having been left on one of the Eastern islands, by a South American cruiser. I did not suppose there was a man living who could talk, as a matter of fact, of so much wild and strange adventure. One looks into his eyes, to see whether he is sane or no. He states himself to be now but thirty-one years old.

The ponderous and imposing look of an English legal document—an assignment of real estate in America, for instance—engrossed on an immense sheet of the best paper, in a formal hand, beginning with "This Indenture," in German text, and with occasional phrases of form breaking out into large script—very lengthy and repetitious, fortified with [62] the Mayor of Manchester's seal, two or three inches in diameter, which is certified by a Notary Public—whose signature, again, is to have my Consular certificate and official seal.

Novr 2ᵈ '54

A YOUNG Frenchman of gentlemanly aspect, with a greyish cloak, or paletot, overspreading his upper person, and a handsome and well-made pair of black trowsers, and well-fitting boots, below. On sitting down, he does not throw off, or at all disturb, the cloak. Eyeing him more closely, one discerns that he has no shirt-collar, and that what little is visible of his shirt-bosom seems not to be of to-day, nor of yesterday;—perhaps not even of the day before. His manners are very good;—nevertheless, a coxcomb and a jackanapes. He avers himself a naturalized citizen of America, where he has been tutor in several families of distinction, and has been treated like a son of the family. Left America on account of his health; came near being tutor in the Duke of Norfolk's family, but failed for lack of testimonials; is exceedingly capable and accomplished; is reduced in funds, and wants employment here, or the means of returning to America, where he intends to take a situation under government, which he is sure of obtaining. Mentions a quarrel which he has recently had with an Englishman, in behalf of America; would have fought a duel, had such been the custom of the country; made the Englishman [63] foam at the mouth; told him that he had been twelve years at a military school, and could kill him. I tell him that I see little or no prospect of his getting employment here, but offer to inquire whether any situation as clerk or otherwise can be obtained him in a vessel returning to America; and ask his address. He has no address. Much to my surprise, he takes his leave without asking pecuniary aid, but hints that he shall call again. A very disagreeable young fellow, like scores of others who call on me in the like situation. His English is very good, for a Frenchman, and he says he speaks it the least well of five languages. He has been three years in America, and obtained his naturalization papers, he says, as a special favor, and by means of strong interest. Nothing is so absolutely abominable as the sense of freedom and equality, pertaining to an American, grafted on the mind of a native of any other country in the world. I do HATE a naturalized citizen; nobody has a right to our ideas, unless born to them.

Novr 9ᵗʰ.

I LENT the above Frenchman a small sum; he advertised for employment as a teacher; and has called, this morning, to thank me for my aid, and tells me that Mr Channing[133] has engaged him for his children, at a guinea a week; also, another engagement. The poor fellow seems [64] [to] have been brought to a very low ebb. He had pawned everything, even to his last shirt, save the one he had on, and had been living at the rate of two-pence a-day. I had procured him a chance to return to America; but he was ashamed to go back in such poor circumstances, so determined to seek better fortune here. I like him better than I did—partly, I suppose, because I have helped him.

Novr 14th

THE other day, I saw an elderly gentleman walking along Dale-street, apparently in a state of mania; for as he limped along (being afflicted with lameness) he kept talking to himself, and sometimes breaking out into a threat against some casual passenger. He was a very respectable-looking man; and I remember to have seen him, last summer, in the steamer returning from the Isle of Man, where he had been staying at Castle Mona. What a strange and ugly fix it must be, for a person of quiet and perfectly respectable habits to be suddenly smitten with lunacy at noon-day, in a crowded street, and to walk along through a dim maze of extravagancies—partly conscious of them, but unable to resist the impulse to commit them. A long repressed nature might be represented as bursting out in this way, for want of a safety-valve.

In America, people seem to consider the government merely as a political administration; and they care nothing for the credit of it, unless it is the administration of their own politi[65]cal party. In England, all people, of whatever party, are anxious for the credit of their rulers. Our government, as a knot of persons, changes so entirely, every four years, that the institution itself has come to be considered a temporary thing

Looking at the moon, the other evening Rosebud said, "It blooms out in the morning!"—taking the moon to be the blossom of the sun.

The English are a most intolerant people; nobody is permitted, now-a-days, to have any opinion but the prevalent one. There seems to be very little difference between their educated and ignorant classes, in this respect;—if any, it is to the credit of the latter, who do not show such tokens of intense interest in the war. It is rather agreeable, however, to observe how all Englishmen pull together; how each man comes forward with his little scheme for helping on the war—feeling themselves members of one family, and talking together about their common interest, as if they were gathered about one fireside. And then what a hearty meed of honor they award to their soldiers. It is worth facing death for! Whereas, in America, when our soldiers fought as good battles in the Mexican war, with as great proportionate loss, and far more valuable triumphs, the country seemed rather ashamed than proud of them.

[66] Mrs. Heywood tells me that there are many Catholics among the lower classes in Lancashire and Cheshire—probably the descendants of retainers of the old Catholic nobility and gentry, who are more numerous in these shires than in other parts of England. The present Lord Sefton's grandfather was the first of that race who became Protestant.

DECR 28th.

COMMODORE PERRY[134] called to see me, this morning—a brisk, gentlemanly, off-hand (but not rough) unaffected, and sensible man, looking not so elderly as he ought, on account of a very well-made wig.[135] He is now on his return from his cruise in the East Indian seas, and goes home by the Baltic, with a prospect of being very well received on account of his treaty with Japan. I seldom meet with a man who puts himself more immediately on conversible [sic] terms than the Commodore. He soon introduced his particular business with me—it being to inquire whether I could recommend some suitable person to prepare his notes and materials for the publication of an account of his voyage. He was good enough to say that he had fixed upon me, in his own mind, for this office, but that my public duties would of course prevent me from engaging in it. I spoke of Herman Melville, and one or two others; but he seems to have some acquaintance with [67] the literature of the day, and did not grasp very cordially at any name that I could think of; nor, indeed, could I recommend anyone with full confidence. It would be a very desirable labor for a young literary man, or, for that matter, an old one; for the world can scarcely have in reserve a less hacknied [sic] theme than Japan.

This is a most beautiful day of English winter; clear and bright, with the ground a little frozen, and the green grass, along the waysides at Rock Ferry, sprouting up through the frozen pools of yesterday's rain. England is forever green. On Christmas day, the children found wall-flowers, pansies, and pinks, in the garden; and we had a beautiful rose from the garden of the hotel—all grown in the open air. Yet one is as sensible of the cold here, as in the zero atmosphere of America. The chief advantage of England is, that we are not tempted to heat our rooms to so unhealthy a point as in New England.

I think I have been happier, this Christmas, than ever before,—by our own fireside, and with my wife and children about me. More content to enjoy what I had; less anxious for anything beyond it, in this life. My early life was perhaps a good preparation for the declining [68] half of life, it having been such a blank that any possible thereafter would compare favorably with it. For a long, long while, I have occasionally been visited with a singular dream; and I have an impression that I have dreamed it, even since I have been in England. It is, that I am still at college—or, sometimes, even at School—and there is a sense that I have been there unconscionably long, and have quite failed to make such progress in life as my contemporaries have; and I seem to meet some of them with a feeling of shame and depression that broods over me, when I think of it, even at this moment. This dream, recurring all through these twenty or thirty years, must be one of the effects of that heavy seclusion in which I shut myself up, for twelve years, after leaving college, when everybody moved onward and left me behind. How strange that it should come now, when I may call myself famous, and prosperous!—when I am happy, too!—still that same dream of life hopelessly a failure!

JANUARY 3ᵈ 1855.

THE progress of the age is trampling over the aristocratic institutions of England, and they crumble beneath it. This war has given the country a vast impulse towards democracy. The nobility will never hereafter, I think, assume, or be permitted, to rule the nation in peace, or command armies in war, on any ground except the [69] individual ability which may appertain to one of their number, as well as to a commoner. And yet the nobles were never positively more noble than now—never, perhaps, so chivalrous, so honorable, so highly cultivated; but, relatively to the rest of the world, they do not maintain their old place. The pressure of the war has tested and proved this fact, at home and abroad. At this moment, it would be an absurdity in the nobles to pretend to the position which was quietly conceded to them, a year ago. This one year has done the work of fifty ordinary ones;—or more accurately, perhaps, it has made apparent what has long been preparing itself.

JANUARY 6ᵗʰ 1855.

MR. BUCHANAN[136] called on me to-day, and staid a good while—an hour or two. He is now staying at Mr. Wᵐ Brown's[137] at Richmond Hill, having come to this region to bring his niece,[138] who is to be bridesmaid at a wedding of an American girl. I like Mr. Buchanan; he cannot exactly be called gentlemanly in his manners, there being a sort of rusticity about him;—moreover, a habit of squinting one eye, and an awkward carriage of his head; but, withal, a dignity in his large, white-headed person, and a consciousness of high position and importance, which gives him ease and freedom. Very simple and frank in his address; he may be as crafty as other [70] diplomatists are said to be; but I see only good sense and plainness of speech—appreciative, too, and genial enough to make himself conversible [*sic*]. He talked very freely of himself and other public people, and American and English affairs. He returns to America, he says, next October, and then retires forever from public life, being sixty-four years of age, and having now no desire except to write memoirs of his times—and especially of the administration of Mr. Polk. I suggested a doubt whether the people would permit him to retire; and he immediately responded to my hint as regards his prospects for the Presidency. He said that his mind was fully made up, and that he would never be a candidate, and that he had expressed this intention to his friends in such a way as to put [it] out of his own power to change it. He acknowledged that he should have been glad of the nomination for Presidency in 1852, but that it was now too late, and that he was too old;—and, in short, he seemed to be quite sincere in his nolo episcopari; although, really, he is the only Democrat, at this moment, whom it would not be absurd to talk of for the office. As he talked, his face flushed, and he seemed to get inwardly excited. Doubtless, it was the high vision of half his life time which he here relinquished. I cannot question that he is sincere; [71] but, of course, should the people insist upon having him for President, he is too good a patriot to disobey. I wonder whether he can have had any object in saying all this to me. He might see that it would be perfectly natural for me to tell it to General Pierce. But it is a very vulgar idea—this of seeing craft and subtlety, where there is a plain and honest aspect.

JANUARY 9th.

I DINED at Mr. W. Browne, M.P.'s, last evening, with a large party. Rather dull, as almost all Liverpool dinners are. The whole table & dessert-service was of silver. Speaking of Shakspeare, Mr Buchanan said that the Duke of Somerset (who is a man of nearly fourscore) told him, that the father of John and Charles Kemble had made all possible research into the events of Shakspeare's life, and that he had found reason to believe that Shakspeare attended a certain revel at Stratford, and, indulging too much in the conviviality of the occasion, he tumbled into a ditch on his way home, and died there! The Kemble patriarch was an aged man when he communicated this to the Duke; and their ages, linked on to each other, would extend back a good way;—scarcely to the beginning of the last century, however. If I mistake not, it was from the traditions of Stratford that Kemble had learnt the above. I do not remember ever to have seen it in print;[139]—which is more singular than anything else about it.

[72] Mr. Buchanan's niece (Miss Lane) has an English, rather than an American aspect—being of stronger outline than most of our girls, although handsomer than English women generally, and of better manners than of any I have seen. Extremely self-possessed and well-poised, without affectation or assumption, but quietly conscious of rank, as much as if she were an earl's daughter;—in truth, she probably felt pretty much as an earl's daughter would, towards the merchants wives and daughters who made up the feminine portion of the party. Her gown was terribly low across the shoulders. I should judge her to be twenty-five, or thereabouts. I talked with her, a little, and found her sensible, sufficiently vivacious, and seemingly firm-textured, rather than soft and sentimental. She paid me some compliments; but I don't remember paying her any.

Mr. Washington Jackson's daughters, two pale, handsome American girls, were present. One of them (whose wedding Miss Lane has come to assist at) is to be married to a grandson of Mr. Browne, a Mr. Hargreaves, who was also at the dinner. He is a small young man, with a thin and fair moustache, and of little or no apparent significance; but a lady who sat next me whispered me that his expectations are £6000 per annum. It struck me, that, being a country gentleman's son, he kept himself silent and reserved, as feeling himself too good for this commercial dinner-party; but perhaps (and I rather think so) he was [73] was [sic] really shy, and had nothing to say—being only twenty-one, and therefore quite a boy among Englishmen. The only man of cognizable rank present (except Mr. Buchanan and the Mayor of Liverpool) was a baronet, Sir Thomas Birch.

JANUARY 17th Wednesday.

SOPHIA and I were invited to be present at the wedding of Mr Washington Jackson's daughter, this morning; but we were also bidden to the funeral services of Mrs. Gandy, a young American lady, dead in childbed; and we went to the house of mourning, rather than to the house of feasting.[140] Her death was very sudden. I crossed to Rock Ferry on Saturday, and met her husband in the boat; he said his wife was rather unwell, and that he had been just sent for to come; but he did not seem at all alarmed;—and yet, on reaching home, he found her dead. The body is to be conveyed to America; and the funeral service was read over her, in the house, only a few neighbors and friends being present. We were shown into a darkened-room, where there was a dim gas-light burning, and a fire glimmering, and here and there a streak of sunshine struggling through the closed curtains. Mr Gandy looked pale, and quite overcome with grief—this, I suppose, being his first sorrow; and he has a young baby on his hands, and no doubt feels altogether forlorn in this foreign land. The clergyman came in in his canonicals, [74] and anon we walked in a little procession into another room, where the coffin was. Mr. Gandy sat down and rested his head on the coffin; the clergyman read the service; then knelt down (as did most of the auditors) and prayed, with great propriety of manner, but no earnestness—and we separated. Mr. Gandy is a small, smooth, and pretty young man, not emphasized in any way; but grief threw its awfulness about him to-day, in a degree which I should not have expected.

JANy 20th

MR. STEELE (an old gentleman of Rock Ferry) showed me, this morning, a pencil-case formerly belonging to Dr. Johnson. It is six or seven inches long, of large calibre, and very clumsily manufactured of iron, perhaps plated in its better days, but now quite bare;—indeed, it looks as rough as an article of kitchen furniture. The stamp on the end is a lion rampant. On the whole, it well became Dr. Johnson to have used such a stalwart pencil-case. It had a six-inch measure along part of its length; so that it must have been at least eight inches long. Mr. Steele says he has seen a cracked earthen tea-pot, of large size, in which Miss Williams used to make tea for Dr. Johnson.

God himself cannot compensate us for being born, in any period short of eternity. All the misery we endure here constitutes a claim for another life; —and, still more, all the happiness, because all true happiness involves something more than the earth owns, and [75] something more than a mortal capacity for the enjoyment of it.

After receiving an injury on the head, the person fancied, all the rest of his life, that he heard voices of people flouting, jeering, and upbraiding him

FEB 19th 1855

I DINED with the Mayor at the Town Hall, last Friday evening. Sat next to

Mr Washington Jackson, an old Irish-American merchant, who seems to be in very good standing here. He told me that he used to be very well acquainted with General Jackson, and that he was present at the street-fight[141] between him and the Bentons, and helped to take General Jackson off the ground. Colonel Benton shot at him from behind; but it was Jesse Benton's ball that hit him, and broke his arm. I did not understand him to infer any treachery or cowardice from the circumstance of Colonel Benton's shooting at Jackson from behind, but suppose it occurred in the confusion and excitement of a street fight. Mr. Washington Jackson seems to think that, after all, the reconciliation between Benton and the old General was merely external, and that they really hated one another as before. I don't think so.

These dinners of the Mayor are rather agreeable than otherwise, except for the annoyance, in my case, of being called up to speak to a toast; and that is less disagreeable [76] than at first. The suite of rooms at the Town Hall is stately and splendid; and all the Mayors, as far as I have seen, exercise hospitality in a manner worthy of the chief-magistrate of a great city. He is supposed always to spend much more than his salary (£2000) on these entertainments. The town provides the wines, I am told; and it might be expected that they should be particularly good—at least, those which improve by age, for a quarter-of-a-century should be only a moderate age for wine from the cellars of an age-long institution, like a corporate borough. Each Mayor might lay in a supply of the best vintage he could find, and trust his good name with posterity to the credit of that wine; and so he would be kindly and warmly remembered, long after his own nose had lost its rubicundity. In point of fact, the wines seem to be good, but not remarkable. The dinner was good, and very handsomely served, with attendance enough, both in the hall below (where the doors were wide open at the appointed hour, notwithstanding the cold) and at table—some being in the rich livery of the borough, and some in plain clothes. Servants, too, were stationed at various points from the hall to the reception-room; and the last one shouted forth the name of the entering guest. There were, I should think, about fifty guests at this dinner, mostly gray or baldheaded, of an English rotundity of shape, and very homely men, with no [77] polish of manner—being chiefly merchants and eminent professional men of this locality; but if they had been noblemen, I suspect they would have looked pretty much the same, externally. An Englishman's aspect and behavior never shocks, and never fascinates. Two bishops were present (Chester, & New South Wales) dressed in a kind of long tunic, and black breeches and silk stockings, insomuch that I at first fancied they were Catholics; also Dr. McNiel, in a stiff collared coat, looking more like a general than a divine. There were two officers (of a militia regiment, I believe) in blue uniforms; and all the rest of us were in black, with, I think, only two white waistcoats— my own being one—and a rare sprinkling of white cravats. How hideously a man looks in them. I should like to have seen such assemblages as must have gathered in that reception-room, and walked with stately tread to the dining-

hall, in times past—the Mayor and other civic dignities in their gowns, noblemen in their state dresses, the Consul in his olive-leaf embroidery—everybody
in some sort of bedizenment—and then the dinner would have been really a
magnificent spectacle, worthy of the gilded hall, the rich table-service, and the
powdered and gold-laced servitors. At a former dinner, I remember seeing a
gentleman in small clothes, and with a dress-sword; but all formalities [78]
of this kind are passing away. The Mayor's dinners, too, will no doubt be extinct, before many years go by. What should we think of them in America!

After dinner we had toasts, and "God Save the Queen" and other music.
The national anthem was sung with less energy and enthusiasm than I have
heretofore heard it; but this might be because the bishops and other clergymen
gave an extra amount of decorousness to the occasion. The speaking was better
than usual, being mostly from men accustomed to hear their own voices in
public. The Mayor toasted me by name, alluding to the foreign alliances of
England and expressing confidence in the good-will of the United States &c,—
whereupon, I got upon my legs and responded for my country rather more
decidedly than I might have found in my conscience to do, anywhere save at
an English Mayor's dinner-table. At least, the good will and applause, with
which my few words were received, made me suspicious that it was a little
too strong. After sitting down, as usual, I felt that there might be great
enjoyment in public speaking; but, while up, my great object is to get down
again as soon as possible.

I rode home from the Woodside Ferry in a cab, with Bishop Barker[142] (of
New South Wales) and two other gentlemen. The bishop is towards seven
feet high.

After writing the foregoing record of a civic banquet (where I ate turtle-
soup, salmon, woodcock, oyster-patties, and I know not what else, and might
have eaten twenty other things) I have been to the News-Room, and found the
Exchange pavement and its avenues densely thronged with people of all ages,
and of all manner of dirt and rags. They were waiting, I believe, for soup-
tickets, and waiting very patiently too, without outcry or disturbance, or even
sour looks—only patience and meekness. Well—I don't know that they have
a right to be impatient of starvation; but still there does seem to be an inso-
lence of riches and prosperity, which one day or another will have a downfall.
And this will be a pity, too. On Saturday, I rode with Mr. Bright to Otter[s]-
pool and to Larkhill, to see the skaters on the private pieces of water at those
two seats of gentlemen; and it is a wonder to behold—and it is always a new
wonder to me—how comfortable Englishmen know how to make themselves—
locating their dwellings far within private grounds, with secure gateways and
porter's lodges, and the smoothest roads, and trimmest paths, and shaven lawns,
and clumps of trees, and every bit of the ground, every hill and dell, made
the most of for convenience and beauty, and so well kept that even winter
cannot disarray it;—and [80] all this appropriated to the same family for
generation after generation; so that I suppose they come to think it created

exclusively and on purpose for them. And really the result seems to be good and beautiful—it is a home—an institution which we Americans have not—but then I doubt whether anybody is entitled to a home, in so full a sense, in this world.

The day was very cold, and the skaters seemed to enjoy themselves immensely. They were, I suppose, friends of the owners of the grounds; and Mr. Bright said they were treated in a jolly way, with hot luncheons. The skaters practise it more as an art, and can perform finer manoeuvres on the ice, than our New England skaters usually can, though the English have so much fewer opportunities for practice. A beggar-woman was haunting the grounds at Otter[s]pool, but I saw nobody give her anything. I wonder how she got inside of the gate.[143]

Mr. Washington Jackson spoke of General Jackson as having come from the same part of Ireland as himself, and perhaps being of the same family. I wonder whether he meant to say that the General was a born Irishman[144]— that having been suspected in America. Should opportunity offer, I will ask him.

FEBRUARY 21st.

YESTERDAY, two companies of work-people came to our house at Rock Park, asking assistance—being out of [81] work, and with no resource other than charity. There were a dozen or more in each party. Their deportment was quiet, and altogether unexceptionable—no rudeness, no gruffness, nothing of menace. Indeed, such demonstrations would not have been safe, as they were followed about by two policemen; but they really seem to take their distress as their own misfortune and God's will, and impute it to nobody as a fault. This meekness is very touching, and makes one question the more whether they have all their rights. There have been disturbances, within a day or two, in Liverpool, and shops have been broken open and robbed of bread and money; but this is said to have been done by idle vagabonds, not by the really hungry workpeople. These last submit to starvation meekly and patiently,[145] as if it were an every day matter with them, or, at least, nothing but what lay fairly within their horoscope. I suppose, in fact, their stomachs have the physical habit that makes hunger not intolerable, because customary. If they had been used to a full flesh-diet, their hunger would be fierce, like that of ravenous beasts;—but now, like the eels, they are "used to it."

I think that the feeling in an American, divided, as I am, by the ocean from his country, has a continual and immediate [82] correspondence with the national feeling at home; and it seems to be independent of any external communication. My thermometer stands at the same point where theirs does. Thus my ideas about this Russian war vary in accordance with the state of the public mind at home; so that I am conscious whereabouts public sympathy is.

MARCH 4th.

ON Sunday, Julian and I walked to Tranmere, and passed an old house which I suppose to be Tranmere Hall. Our way to it was up a hollow lane, with a bank and hedge on each side, and with a few thatched stone cottages (centuries old, I suppose, for their ridge-poles were crooked, and the stones time-worn) scattered along. At one point there was a wide, deep well, hewn out of the solid red free-stone, and with steps, also hewn in solid rock, leading down to it. These steps were much worn and hollowed by the feet of those who had come to the well; and they go down beneath the water, which was very high at the time. This well, not improbably, supplied water to the old cotters and retainers of Tranmere Hall, five hundred years ago. The Hall stands on the ridge of a long hill, which stretches behind Tranmere, and as far as Birkenhead; it is an old gray stone edifice, with a good many gables, and windows with mullions, and some of them extending the whole breadth of the gable. In parts of the house, the windows seem to have been built up, probably in the days when daylight was [83] taxed.[146] The form of the house is multiplex, the roofs sloping down and intersecting one another, so as to make the general result indescribable. There were two sun-dials on different sides of the house, both the dial-plates of which were of stone; and on one, the figures, so far as I could see, were quite worn away; but the gnomon still cast the shadow over it in such a way that I could judge that it was about noon. The other dial had some half-worn hour marks, but no gnomon. The house was very weedy in the chinks of the stones, and looked quaint and venerable; but it is now converted into a farm-house, with the farm-yard and out-buildings closely appended. A village, too, has grown up about it; so that it now seems out of place among modern stuccoed dwellings, such as are erected for trades-men and other moderate people, who have their residences in the neighborhood of a great city—rows of houses with such names as Belle Vue, Roslia Villas, &c, with little trim yards and grass plots before them, and in the centre of the grass plot some of the queer rock and shell work which the English love to put there. Among these, there are a few of the thatched cottages (the homeliest kind of house that ever mortals pigged in) that belonged to the old estate. Directly across the street from the hall is a wayside Inn, "licensed [84] to sell wine, spirits, ale, and tobacco." The street itself, no doubt, has been laid out since the land grew valuable by the increase of Liverpool and Birkenhead; for the old Hall would never have been built on the verge of a public way. A good many children, in their Sunday dresses, were playing merrily in the street.

I often see women or girls in the streets picking up fresh horse-dung with their hands, and putting it into a cloth—some accumulating large parcels of it.

In Chambers' work on America, he mentions that three British soldiers were discovered in attempting to desert into the States, across the Niagara river; and their bodies were carried down into the whirlpool, some miles below the falls; and there they were carried round and round, for as much as three weeks —and I know not how much more; probably till their bare skeletons sank down, perhaps bone by bone.[147]

MARCH 27th. MONDAY

I ATTENDED court to-day, at St. George's Hall, with my wife, Mr. Bright, and Mr. Channing—sitting in the High Sheriff's seat. It was the Civil side; and Judge Creswell presided. The lawyers, as far as aspect goes, seemed to me inferior to an American bar, judging from their countenances, whether as intellectual men or gentlemen. Their wigs and gowns do not impose on the spectator, though they strike him as an imposition. Their date is past. Mr Warren (of ten thousand a [85] year) was in court;—a pale, thin, intelligent face; evidently a nervous man, more unquiet than anybody else in court—always restless in his seat, whispering his neighbors, settling his wig, perhaps with an idea that people single him out. St. Georges Hall (the interior hall itself, I mean) is a spacious, lofty, and most rich and noble apartment, far more satisfactory than any other I ever saw. The pavement is made of mosaic tiles, and has a beautiful effect.

APRIL 7th, SATURDAY.

I DINED at Mr. J. P. Heywood's on Thursday; and met there Mr. and Mrs. Ainsworth of Smithell's Hall. The Hall is an old edifice of some five hundred years or so; and Mrs. Ainsworth says there is a bloody footstep in the entrance hall, at the foot of a staircase.[148] The tradition is that a certain martyr, in Bloody Mary's time, being examined before the then occupant of the Hall, and committed to prison, stamped his foot in earnest protest against the injustice with which he was treated. Blood issued from his foot, which slid along the stone pavement of the hall, leaving a long footmark printed in blood; and there it has remained ever since, in spite of the scrubbings of all after generations. Mrs Ainsworth spoke of it with much solemnity, real or affected; she says that they now cover the bloody impress with a [86] carpet, being unable to remove it. In a History of Lancashire,[149] which I looked at, last night, there is quite a different account—according to which, the footstep is not a bloody one, but is a slight cavity or inequality in the surface of the stone, somewhat in the shape of a man's foot with a peaked shoe. The martyr's name was George Marsh; he was a curate, and was afterwards burnt. Mrs. Ainsworth asked me to come and see the Hall and the footmark; and, as it is in Lancashire, and not a great way off, and a curious old place, perhaps I may.

APRIL 12th

THE Earl of Derby (whom I saw the other day at St. George's Hall) has a somewhat elderly look with spectacles—a pale and rather thin, or withered face, which strikes one as remarkably short, or compressed from top to bottom;—nevertheless, it has great intelligence,—sensitive, too, I should think—but a cold, disagreeable expression. I should take him to be a man of not very pleasant temper—not genial. He has no physical presence or dignity, yet one sees him to be a person of rank and consequence. But, after all, there is nothing about him which it need have taken centuries of illustrious nobility to produce, especially in a man of remarkable ability, as Lord Derby certainly is. Hundreds of American gentlemen, sons of their own good works, have full as noble an air, so far as that goes. But Englishmen are apt to look like anything but gentlemen, even when they most [87] unquestionably are so;—men of birth, rank, wealth, station having the aspect of—I don't know any class of Americans very similar in appearance—but jolly country tavern-keepers, as much as anything. Neither is there any degree of elegance of manner; but, after a while, you feel and acknowledge that they are really gentlemen. Lord Derby, however, is not at all of the jolly tavern-keeper order.

Sophia (who attended court all through the Hopwood trial,[150] and saw Lord Derby for hours together, every day) has come to conclusions quite different from mine. She thinks him a perfectly natural person, without any assumption—any self-presence to his own consciousness—any scorn of the lower world. She was delighted with his ready appreciation and feeling of what was passing around him—the quick enjoyment of a joke—the simplicity and naturalness of his emotion at whatever incidents excited his interest—the genial acknowledgement of sympathy, causing him to look round and exchange glances with those near him (not his individual friends, but barristers and other casual persons) who happened to sit near him. He seemed to her all that a nobleman ought to be, and naturally should be,—entirely simple, and free from all the pretence and self-assertion which persons of lower rank can hardly help be-devilling themselves with. [88] I saw him only for a very few moments;—so cannot put my observation against hers, more especially as I was prejudiced by what I have heard the Liverpool people say of his temper and manners.

I don't know whether I have mentioned that the handsomest man I have seen in England was a young footman at Mrs. Heywood's. In his rich livery, he was a perfect Joseph Andrews.

In my Romance,[151] the original emigrant to America may have carried away with him a family secret, whereby it was in his power (had he so chosen) to have brought about the ruin of the family. This secret he transmits to his American progeny, by whom it is inherited throughout all the intervening generations. At last, the hero of the Romance comes to England, and finds that, by means of this secret, he still has it in his power to procure the downfal[l] of the family. It would be something similar to the story of Meleager, whose fate depended on the firebrand that his mother had snatched out of the flames.

TUESDAY, APRIL 24th 55.

ON Saturday, I was present at a dejeuner on board the Donald Mackay (a new American ship, built for James Baines & Co) the principal guest being Mr. Layard, M.P.[152] There were several hundred people present, quite filling the between decks of the ship, which [89] was converted into a saloon for the nonce. I sat next to Mr. Layard at the head of the table—or rather, at the cross-table—and so had a good opportunity of seeing and getting acquainted with him. He is a man in early middle-age (with hair a very little frosted, I think) of a somewhat plebeian aspect, as Englishmen are so apt to be; of middle stature, with an open, frank, intelligent, kindly face, but no very intellectual or refined lines in it. His forehead is not expansive, but is prominent in the perceptive regions, and retreats a good deal; his mouth is fleshy. I liked him from the first, but, had I met him in America, should have set him down as an intelligent mechanic;—not that there is any lack of good-breeding, but only the usual English homeliness, and unpolished surface. Yet he has a French shrug; which I don't like to see. He was very kind and complimentary to me, and made me promise to come and see him in London.

It would have been a very pleasant entertainment; only that my pleasure in it was much marred by having to acknowledge a toast in honor of the President;—however, such things don't trouble me nearly so much as they did, and I came through it tolerably enough.[153] Mr. Layard's speech was the great affair of the day. He [90] speaks (though he assured me that he had to put great force upon himself to speak publicly) with much fluency; and, as he warms up, seems to speak with his whole moral and physical man, and to be quite possessed with what he has to say. His evident earnestness and good-faith make him eloquent, and stand him in stead of oratorical graces—of which (as a matter of study and acquisition) he does not seem to have any. His view of the position of England and the prospects of the war were as dark as well could be; in fact, there never was a better specimen of English grumbling than his whole speech—and it was exceedingly to the purpose, full of common sense, and with not one word of clap-trap. Judging from its effect upon the audience, he spoke the voice of the whole English people—although an English baronet, who sat next below me, seemed to dissent, or at least to think that it was not exactly the thing for a stranger to hear it. The speech concluded amidst great cheering. Mr. Layard appears to me a true Englishman, not remarkably bright intellectually, but with a moral force, and strength of character, and earnestness of purpose, and fullness of common sense, such as have always served England's turn in her past successes; but rather fit for resistance than for progress. No doubt, he is a good and very able man; but I question wheth[91]er he could get England out of the difficulties which he sees so clearly, or could do much better than Lord Palmerston, whom he so decries. The truth is, there is a spirit lacking in England, which *we* do not lack, and for the want of which she will have to resign a foremost position among the nations, even if there were not enough other circumstances to compel her to do so. Her good qualities are getting out of date;—at all events, there should be something added to them, in the present stage of the world.

We rose from table, I believe, about five °clock.

APRIL 25th.

TAKING the depositions of sailors, yesterday, in a case of alleged ill-usage by the officers of a vessel, one of the witnesses was an old seaman of sixty and upwards. In reply to some testimony of his, the captain said, "You were the oldest man in the ship; and we honored you as such." The mate also said, that he never could have thought of striking an old man like that. Indeed, the poor old fellow had a kind of dignity and venerableness about him, though he confessed to having been drunk, and seems to have been a mischief-maker— what they call a sea-preacher—promoting discontent and grumbling. He must have been a very handsome man in his youth, having regular features, of a noble and beautiful cast; his beard [92] was gray, but his dark hair had hardly a streak of white, and was abundant all over his head. He was deaf, and seemed to sit in a kind of seclusion, earless when loudly questioned or appealed to. Once, he broke forth from a deep silence, thus—"I defy any man!"—and then was silent again. It had a queer effect, this general defiance, which he meant, I suppose, in answer to some accusation that he thought was made against him. His general behavior throughout the examination was very decorous and proper; and he said he had never but once before been before a consul, and that was in 1819, when a mate had ill-used him, and "being a young man then, I gave him a beating"—whereupon his face gleamed with a quiet smile, like faint sunshine on an old ruin. "By many a tempest has his beard been shook";[154] —and now, I suppose, he must soon go into a workhouse, and thence shortly to his grave. He is now in a hospital, having, as the surgeon certifies, some ribs fractured; but there does not appear to have been any violence used upon him, aboard the ship, of such a nature as to cause this injury, though he swears it was a blow from a rope, and nothing else. What struck me in the case was the respect and rank that his age seemed to give him, in the view of the officers; and how, as the captain's expression signified, it lifted him out of his low position, and made him a person to be honored. The [93] dignity of his manner is perhaps partly owing to the Ancient Mariner, with his long experience, being an oracle among the forecastle-men.

THURSDAY, MAY 3ᵈ

IT rains to-day, after a very long period of east-wind and dry weather. The east-wind here, blowing across the island, seems to be the least damp of all the winds; but it is full of malice and mischief, of an indescribably evil temper, and sticks one like a cold, poisoned dagger. I never spent so disagreeable a spring as this, although almost every day for a month has been bright.

FRIDAY, MAY 11ᵗʰ.

A FEW weeks [ago], a sailor, a most pitiable object, came to my office to complain of cruelty from his captain and mate; they had beaten him shamefully, of which he bore grievous marks about his face and eyes, and bruises on his head and other parts of his person; and finally the ship had sailed, leaving him behind. I never in my life saw so forlorn a fellow, so ragged, so wretched; and he seemed as if his wits had been beaten out of him—if perchance he ever had any. He got an order for the hospital; and there he has

been, off and on, ever since, till yesterday, when I received a message that he
was dying, and wished to see the consul; so I went to the Hospital with Mr.
Wilding. We were ushered into the waiting-room [94] a kind of parlour,
with a fire in the grate, and a center table, wheron lay one or two medical
journals, with wood engravings of anatomies &c; and there was a young man,
who seemed to be an official of the hospital, reading. Shortly, the house-surgeon
appeared, a brisk, a cheerful, kindly sort of person, whom I have met there
on previous visits. He told us that the man was dying, and probably would
not be able to communicate anything; but nevertheless ushered us up to the
highest floor of the hospital, and into the room where he lay. It was a large,
oblong room, with, I should think, ten or twelve beds in it, each occupied by
a patient. The surgeon said that the Hospital was often so crowded that they
were compelled to lay some of the patients on the floor. The man whom we
came to see lay on his bed in a little recess, formed by a projecting window;
so that there was thus much of seclusion for him to die in. He seemed quite
insensible to outward things, and took no notice of our approach, nor responded
to what was said to him—lying on his side, breathing with short gasps, and
clutching a small earthen utensil in which to spit—his apparent disease being
inflammation of the chest; although the surgeon said that he might be found
to have sustained internal injury by bruises. He was restless, tossing his head
continually, mostly with his eyes shut, and much com[95]pressed and screwed
up, but sometimes opening them; and then they looked brighter and darker
than when I first saw them. I think his face was not any time so stupid as at
his first interview with me; but whatever intelligence he had was rather inward
than outward, as if there might be life and consciousness at a depth within,
while, as to external matters, he was in a mist. The surgeon felt of his wrist,
and said that there was absolutely no pulsation, and that he might die at any
moment, or might live perhaps an hour or more, but that there was no prospect
of his being able to communicate with me. He was quite restless, nevertheless,
and sometimes half raised himself in bed, sometimes turned himself quite over;
then lay gasping for an instant, then moved his head on the pillow. His woollen
shirt being thrust up on his arms, there appeared a tattooing of a ship, an
anchor, and other nautical emblems, on both of them, which another sailor-
patient, on examining them said, must have been done years ago. This might
be of some importance, because the dying man had told me, when I first saw
him, that he was no sailor, but a farmer, and that this being his first voyage,
he had been beaten by the captain for not doing a sailor's duty, which he had no
opportunity [96] of learning. These sea emblems indicated that he was probably a seaman of some years' service.

While we stood in the little recess, at his bedside, such of the other patients
as were convalescent gathered near the foot of the bed; and the nurse, too,
came and looked on, and hovered about the recess—a sharp-eyed, intelligent
woman, of middle-age, with a careful and not unkind expression, neglecting
nothing that was for the patient's good, yet taking his death as coolly as any

other incident in her daily business. Certainly, it was a very forlorn death-bed; and I felt—what I have heretofore been inclined to doubt—that it might be a comfort to have persons whom one loves to go with one to the threshold of the other world, and only leave us when we are fairly across it. This poor fellow had a wife and two children on the other side of the water.

At first, he did not utter any sound; but by-and-bye, he moaned a little, and gave tokens of being more sensible to outward concerns—not quite so misty and dreamy—as hitherto. We had been talking all the while,—myself in a whisper but the surgeon in his ordinary tones—about his state, without his paying any attention. But now the surgeon put his mouth down to the man's face, and said, "Do you know that you are dying?" At this, the patient's [97] head began to move upon the pillow; and I thought at first that it was only the restlessness that he had shown all along; but soon it appeared to be an expression of emphatic dissent—a negative shake of the head; he shook it with all his might, and groaned and mumbled, so that it was very evident how miserably reluctant he was, to die. Soon after this, a little more seeming insensibility, he absolutely spoke—"Oh, I want you to get me well! I want to get away from here!"—a groaning and moaning kind of utterance. The surgeon's question had revived him, but to no purpose; for, being told that the Consul had come to see him, and asked whether he had anything to communicate, he only said, "Oh, I want him to get me well!"—and the whole life that was left in him seemed to be distress and unwillingness to die. This did not last long; for he soon relapsed into his first state, only perhaps with his face a little more pinched and screwed up, and his eyes strangely sunken and lost in his head; and the surgeon said that there could be no use in my remaining; so I took my leave. Mr. Wilding had brought a deposition of the man's evidence, which he had already made at the Consulate, for him to sign; and this we left with the surgeon, in case there should be [98] such an interval of consciousness and intelligence, before death, as to make it possible for him to sign it. But of this there is no probability.

As we went down stairs, the surgeon showed us into several other wards, and discoursed about the various cases. The patients were all very quiet, some of them asleep, some looking listlessly at the visitors. They seemed to like to have their cases spoken of; and one man threw down the bedclothes to show us how his broken leg was bandaged. Over the head of each bed was a paper, with the name of the surgeon or doctor who attended the case, and the mode of treatment prescribed. In one of the rooms we saw the clown of an amphitheatre who had shattered his ankle in the performance of a feat; likewise a man whose arm had been cut off the day before.

I have just received a note from the Hospital, stating that the sailor (Daniel Smith) died about three quarters of an hour after I saw him.

TUESDAY, MAY 15th.

THE above-mentioned Daniel Smith had about him a bundle of letters, which

I have examined. They are all very yellow, stained too with sea-water or something else, smelling of bad tobacco smoke, and much worn and tearing at the folds. Never were such ill-written letters, nor such awfully [99] fantastic spelling. They seem to be from various members of his family—most of them from a brother, who purports to have been a deck-hand in the coasting and steam-boat trade between Charleston & other ports; others from female relatives; one from his father, in which he inquires how long his son has been in jail, and when the trial is to come on—the offense, however, of which he seems to have been accused, not being indicated. But from the tenor of his brother's letters, it would appear that he was a small farmer in the interior of South Carolina, sending butter, eggs, and poultry to be sold in Charleston by his brother, and receiving the returns in articles purchased there. This was his own account of himself; and he affirmed, in his deposition before me, that he had never had any purpose of shipping for Liverpool or anywhere else, but that, going on board the ship to bring a man's trunk ashore, he was compelled to remain and serve as a sailor. This was a hard fate, certainly, and a strange thing to happen in the United States, at this day—that a free citizen should be absolutely kidnapped, carried to a foreign country, treated with savage cruelty during the voyage, and left to die on his arrival. Yet all this has unquestionably been done, and will probably go unpunished.

In 1780, William Dawson, an old gentleman of Manchester,. was buried in a buffed shirt and cravat, a night-cap of brown fur, [100] a striped morning-gown (orange and white) deep crimson-colored silk waistcoat and breeches, white silk stockings, and red morocco slippers."

The seed of the long-stapled cotton, now cultivated in America, was sent thither in 1786 from the Bahama islands by some of the royalist refugees who had settled there. An inferior, short-stapled cotton had been previously cultivated for domestic purposes. The seeds of every other variety have been tried in America without success. The kind now grown was first introduced into Georgia. Thus, to the refugees, America owes as much of her prosperity as is due to the cotton crops, and much of whatever harm is to result from slavery.

Caresses are the foliage of affection; the plant dies at the root unless it has them.

TUESDAY, MAY 22ᵈ.

CAPTAIN Johnson says that he saw, in his late voyage to Australia, India &c, a vessel commanded by an Englishman, who had with him his wife and thirteen children. This ship was the home of the family; and they had no other. The thirteen children had all been born on board, and had been brought up on board, and knew nothing of dry land, except by occasionally setting foot on it.

Captain Johnson is a very agreeable specimen of the American shipmaster;— a pleasant, gentlemanly man, not at all refined, and yet with fine and honorable sensibilities. Very easy in manners [101] and conversation, yet gentle—talking on freely, and not much minding grammar, but finding a sufficient and picturesque expression for what he wants to say; very cheerful and vivacious; accessible to feeling—as yesterday, when talking about the recent death of his mother (which he had almost just heard of) his voice faultered [*sic*] and the tears came into his eyes, though, before and afterwards, he smiled merrily, and made us smile; fond of his little wife, and carrying her about the world with him, and mixing her up with all his enjoyments; an excellent and sagacious man of business; liberal in his expenditure; proud of his ship and of his flag; always well dressed, with some little touch of sailorlike flashiness, but not a whit too much; slender in figure, handsome face, and rather profuse brown beard and whiskers, active and alert—about thirty-two. A daguer[r]eotype sketch of any conversation of his would do him no justice; for its slang, its grammatical mistakes, its mistaken words (for instance, "portable," instead of "portly") would represent a vulgar man; whereas the impression he leaves is by no means that of vulgarity; but he is a character quite perfect within itself, fit for the deck and the cabin, and agreeable even in the drawing-room, though not amenable altogether to its rules. Being so perfectly natural, he is more of a gentleman for those little violations of rule which most men, with his opportunities, might escape.

[102] The men, whose appeals to the Consul's charity are the hardest to be denied, are those who have no country;—Hungarians, Poles, Cubans, Spanish Americans, French republicans. All exiles for liberty come to me, as if the representative of America were their representative. Yesterday came an old French soldier, and showed his wounds; to-day, a Spaniard, a friend of Lopez, bringing his little daughter with him. He said he was starving, and looked so. The little girl was in good case enough, and decently dressed. (May 23d '55)

MAY 24th

A WEEK or two ago, there called on me a Doctor of Divinity from New Orleans, who had just arrived in a sailing vessel; he was a good-looking, gentlemanly, middle aged man, and seemed all right, except perhaps a little excited, as most Americans are, on first setting foot in England. He took a large bundle of letters, which had come to hand in anticipation of his arrival, and went away. A day or two after, Captain Emerson (in whose vessel he had arrived) came to me and said that the Doctor had disappeared—not having been seen by him since his visit to my office. From the Captain's communications, I learned that the Reverend Doctor was a man of rather sad experience, having been divorced from his second wife, and having been in a lunatic asylum, and being also liable to fits of terrible intemperance. It was [103] therefore obvious to suppose that he had allowed himself to lapse into one of these fits. I had some thoughts of setting the police on his track, but concluded that it might be as well to let matters take their course, as he would probably turn up when his money was spent. Accordingly, precisely a week after his disappearance, he was brought back to Captain Emerson's ship, in a state of delirium tremens, by a woman of the town! He was in a filthy and horrible condition, the Captain told me, and said he had been robbed of five hundred dollars—which was more than he had ever had.

There is a Dr. Macauley, our Consul at Venice, now in Liverpool; and as he is likewise from New Orleans, I mentioned the Reverend Doctor's case in confidence to him. It turned out that Dr Macauley is an old acquaintance; and as he seems to be a most humane and good little, simple-hearted man, he immediately undertook to take charge of him, and get him back to America, if possible. Yesterday, while Dr. Macauley was sitting with me (having already visited Doctor R., and been joyfully received by him) there came into my office, a tall, middle-aged, mustach[i]oed gentleman, of rather a military aspect, in a blue sur[104]tout, closely buttoned. He addressed me as if previously acquainted; and at his first word, and my first glance at his face, I could see that he was under the influence of liquor—a very rowdy looking gentleman, indeed. I bowed coolly, and observed that I had not the pleasure of knowing him. "Am I then so changed!" he cried, with a vast depth of tragic intonation; and, after a little more blind talk, behold! I recognized him as the reverend gentleman himself. If I had meditated a scene, or a *coup de theatre,* I could not have contrived a more effectual one than by this simple non-recognition; for the poor man—his nerves being all in a devil's tremble—thought that he must have almost lost his personal identity in the space of one little week. To say the truth, he did look as if he had been dragged through hell, and changed from a decorous clergyman into a rowdy military man; but I should probably have known him, had I taken any particular note of his aspect, at our first interview. Seeing how good an effect had been produced, I maintained my austerity of manner, only granting him a cold recognition; and took occasion to represent to him the deplorable condition to which he had reduced himself, inasmuch as he could no longer be known for the same person whom I had seen a [105] week ago; and exhorted him to refrain from such evil courses hereafter—a lecture which I never dreamed of having an opportunity to bestow on a Doctor of Divinity. It was really a very tragic scene; and an actor might have taken a lesson in his art from him; for all his emotions, and all the external movement and expression of them, by voice, face, and gesture, were exaggerated by the tremendous vibration of nerves remaining from his delirium tremens. Poor, Reverend devil! Drunkard! Whoremaster[?]![155] Doctor of Divinity! He is very powerfully eloquent, I am told, in sermon and prayer.[156]

MAY 30th, WEDNESDAY.

THE two past days have been Whitsuntide Holidays; and they have been celebrated at Tranmere in a manner very similar to that of the old 'Lection' time in Massachusetts, as I remember it a good many years ago—though the festival, I think, has now almost or quite died out. Whitsuntide was kept up on our side of the water, I am convinced, under the pretence of rejoicing at the election of Governor; it occurred at precisely the same period of the year—

the same week—the only difference being, that Monday and Tuesday are the Whitsun festival-days, whereas, in Massachusetts, Wednesday was "Lection Day," and the acme of the merry-making.

I passed through Tranmere, yesterday afternoon, and [106] lingered awhile to see the sports. The greatest peculiarity of the crowd, to my eye, was, that they seemed not to have any best clothes, and therefore had put on no holiday suits;—a grimy people, as at all times, heavy, obtuse, with thick beer in their blood. Coarse, rough-complexioned women and girls were intermingled with them—fit females of such males—with no maiden-trimness in their attire, great blowsy things; how unlike the pretty, spruce little girls of our own country. Nobody seemed to have been washed, that day. All the enjoyment was of an exceedingly sombre character, so far as I saw it; though there was a richer variety of sports than at similar festivals in America. There were wooden horses and other animals, revolving in circles, to be ridden a certain number of rounds for a penny; also, swinging cars, gorgeously painted, and the newest named after Lord Raglan; and four cars balancing one another, and turned by a winch; and people with targets and rifles, the principal aim being to hit an apple bobbing on a string before the target; and other guns for shooting at a distance of a foot or two, for a prize of filberts; and a certain game, much in fashion, of throwing heavy sticks at earthen mugs, suspended on lines, three throws for a penny. Also, there was a posture-master, showing his art in the centre of a miscellaneous ring [107] of spectators, and handing round his hat after going through all his postures. The collection amounted only to one half-penny; and to eke it out, I threw in three more. There were some large booths, with tables placed the whole length, at which sat men and women drinking and smoking pipes; orange-girls a great many, selling the worst possible oranges, which had evidently been boiled to give them a shew of freshness; there were boys asking to black your boots. There were likewise two very large structures, the walls made of boards, roughly patched together, and roofed with canvass [sic], which seemed to have withstood a thousand storms. Theatres, these were; and in front they had pictures of scenes which were to be represented within; the price of admission being two pence to one theatre, and a penny to the other. While I stood looking, there came forth a man with a terribly lax drum, on which he thumped; and then appeared the whole dramatis personae, on a platform in front of the theatre, gentlemen and ladies, all dressed in character, and woefully shabby, with very dirty white tights, and all the gloss and glory gone from their theatrical costume, seen thus in the broad daylight, and after a long series of performances. They sang a song together, and then withdrew into the theatre; but, small as the price of tickets was, I could not see that anybody followed. Behind the thea[108]tre, close to the board wall, and perhaps serving as the general dressing-room, was the large, windowed wagon, in which I suppose the theatrical company travel and live together. Never, to my imagination, was the mysterious glory that has surrounded theatrical representations, ever since my childhood, brought into such dingy reality as this. The tragedy-queens were the same coarse and homely kind of women and girls that surrounded me on the green. I don't remember anything else, at all remarkable. Some of the people had evidently been drinking more than was good for them; but their drunkenness was silent and stolid, with no madness in it. No ebullition of any sort was apparent.

I never before felt it to be a marked characteristic of Americans, of both sexes and all classes, that every individual has a suit of Sunday clothes.[157]

MAY 31st.

LAST Sunday week, for the first time, I heard the note of the cuckoo. "Cuck-oo—Cuck-oo" he says, repeating the word twice, not in a brilliant, metallic tone, but low and flute-like, without the excessive sweetness of the flute—without an excess of saccharine juice in the sound. There are said to be always two cuckoos seen together. The note is very soft and pleasant. The lark I have not yet heard in the sky; though it is not infrequent to hear one singing in a cage, in the streets of Liverpool.

[109] I forgot to mention that I became responsible for Reverend Dr. Richards' passage to Boston, per Cunard steamer of May 26th, and sent him thither under the charge of Mr. Macauley. In my opinion, he has incurred sin no further than as a madman may.

Brewers' draymen are allowed to drink as much of their masters' brewage as they like, and they grow very brawny and corpulent—resembling their own horses in size, and presenting, one would suppose, perfect pictures of physical comfort and well-being. But the least bruise, or even the hurt of a finger, is liable to turn to gangrene or erysipelas, and become fatal.

A child's caul is advertised for sale in the Liverpool paper of to-day, price £8.[158]

When the wind blows violently (however clear the sky, the English say, "It is a stormy day." And, on the other hand, when the air is still and it does not actually rain, however dark and lowering the sky may be, they say, "The weather is fine!"

JUNE 2[d].

THE English women of the lower classes have a grace of their own (not seen in each individual, but nevertheless belonging to their order) which is not to be found in American women of the corresponding class. The other day, in the Police-court, a girl was put into the witness-box, [110] whose native graces of this sort impressed me a good deal. She was coarse, and her dress was none of the cleanest, and nowise smart; she appeared to have been up all night, too, drinking at the Tranmere wake, and had since ridden in a cart, covered up with a rug. She described herself as a servant-girl out of place; and her charm lay in all her manifestations, her tones, her gestures, her look, her way of speaking, and what she said, being so appropriate and natural in a girl of that class;—nothing affected;—no proper grace thrown away by attempting to appear ladylike—which an American girl *would* have attempted, and succeeded in, to a certain degree. If each class would but keep within itself, and show its respect for itself by aiming at nothing beyond, they would all be more respectable. But this kind of fitness is evidently not to be expected in the future; and something else must be substituted for it.[159]

These scenes at the Police-court are often well worth witnessing. The controlling genius of the court (except when the stipendiary magistrate presides) is the clerk, who is a man learned in the law. Nominally, the cases are decided by the aldermen, who sit in rotation; but, at every important point, there comes a nod or a whisper from the clerk; and it is that whisper which sets the prisoner free, or sends him [111] to prison. Nevertheless, I suppose the alderman's common sense and native shrewdness are not without their efficacy in producing a general tendency towards the right; and no doubt the decisions of the Police Court are quite as often just, as those of any other court whatever.

JUNE 3ᵈ.

THE old well near Tranmere hall, hewn through a ledge of solid rock, with steps descending into it, worn away from the sides to the centre, and the latter steps invisible in the not very pellucid water. The sides of the well are moist, green with moss, and with tufts and blades of grass springing out of chinks in the rock, and hanging down. Near it are white-washed cottages of stone, and thatched roofs—the roof-trees of some of them bowed with age. In one, there was a window with lozenge-shaped panes. All these cottages, I suppose, are of great antiquity. In one end of them dwell the human inhabitants; the other is for the cow, the pig, or the donkey. Tranmere Hall has three gables in a line, on one side; the middle one being ivy-grown. In the rear, connected with the house, are farm-buildings of brick, much more modern than the old, gray, stone edifice. It stands on an elevation, near the ridge of the long hill that extends behind Birkenhead; and around it is a village, almost entirely of modern houses.

[112] JUNE 7ᵗʰ THURSDAY.

THERE was one of the queerest cases of a foolish American that I have ever heard of, yesterday, in the person of a man who came to my office for assistance. I did not see him, but Mr. Wilding gave me an account of him. Some years ago, this man had two children, whom he named after Victoria and Prince Albert; and he sent the Queen daguerreotype-portraits of the children, his wife and himself. The gift was acknowledged by the Queen, in a letter from her equerry, or whoever her private secretary may be; and on the strength of this letter, the poor devil has come over to present himself to her Majesty, hoping, no doubt, for some great advantage from her friendship. During the voyage, he became acquainted with a German, who borrowed almost all his money under false pretences, and has lived upon him until the remainder is spent—and has now disappeared, leaving him penniless. In this condition, he presents himself at the Consulate. There certainly is something in royalty, and the institutions connected therewith, that turns the Republican brain.[160]

Elder ointment, prepared from the leaves of the tree, is stated to be an effectual preservative against musquito [*sic*] bites.

JUNE 11th.

WALKED with Julian, yesterday, to Bebington-church. When I first saw this church, nearly two years since, it seemed to me the fulfilment of my ideal of an old English country-church; it is not [so satisfactory now, although certainly a venerable edifice. There used some time ago to be ivy all over the tower; and at my first view of it, there was still a little remaining on the upper parts of the spire. But the main roots, I believe, were destroyed, and pains were taken to clear away the whole of the ivy, so that now it is quite bare,—nothing but homely gray stone, with marks of age, but no beauty. The most curious thing about the church is the font. It is a massive pile, composed of five or six layers of freestone in an octagon shape, placed in the angle formed by the projecting side porch and the wall of the church, and standing under a stained-glass window. The base is six or seven feet across, and it is built solidly up in successive steps, to the height of about six feet,—an octagonal pyramid, with the basin of the font crowning the pile hewn out of the solid stone, and about a foot in diameter and the same in depth. There was water in it from the recent rains,—water just from heaven, and therefore as holy as any water it ever held in old Romish times. The aspect of this aged font is extremely venerable, with moss in the basin and all over the stones; grass, and weeds of various kinds, and little shrubs, rooted in the chinks of the stones and between the successive steps.][161] [115] risen within the last few years. Dickens evidently is not liked nor thought well of by his literary brethren—at least, the more eminent of them, whose reputation might interfere with his. Thackeray is much more to their taste. Perhaps it is for his moral benefit to have succeeded late.

In my walk, Sunday afternoon, I heard larks in abundance, high up towards the sunny sky.

At each entrance of Rock Park, where we live, there is a small gothic structure of stone, each inhabited by a policeman and his family; very small dwellings indeed, with the main apartment opening directly to out-of-doors; and when the door is open, we can see the household fire, the good wife at work, perhaps the table set, and a throng of children clustering round, and generally overflowing the threshold. The policeman walks about the park in stately fashion, with his silver-laced blue uniform and snow-white gloves, touching his hat to gentlemen who reside in the park. In his public capacity, he has rather an awful aspect; but, privately, he is a humble man enough, glad of any little job, and of old clothes for his many children, or, I believe, for himself. One of the two policemen (perhaps both) is a shoemaker and cob[b]ler. His pay officially is somewhere about a guinea per week. The park, just now, is very agreeable to look at, shad[116]owy with trees and shrubs, and with glimpses of green lawns and flower-gardens through the branches and twigs that line the iron-fences. After a shower, the hawthorne-blossoms are delightfully fragrant. Golden tassels of the laburnum are abundant.

I think I have mentioned elsewhere the traditional prophecy, that when the ivy reached the top of Bebington-spire, the tower was doomed to fall.[162] It has still, therefore, a chance of standing for centuries. Mr. Turner tells me that the font now used is inside of the church, but that the one outside is of unknown antiquity, and that it was customary, in papistical times, to have the font without the church.

A banking-house in London (Messrs Strahan, Paul, & Co.) founded between 150 & 200 years ago, has just suspended payment. One of the members is a baronet. I should like to know whether the present partners are descendants of the original ones.

A little boy, often on board the Rock Ferry steamers, with an accordion— an instrument I detest; but nevertheless it becomes tolerable in his hands, not so much for its music, as for the earnestness and interest with which he plays it. His body and accordion together become one musical instrument, on which his soul plays tunes; for he sways and vibrates with the music, from head to foot, and throughout his frame, half-closing his eyes and uplifting his [117] face, as painters represent Saint Cecilia and other famous musicians;—and sometimes he swings his accordion in the air, as if in a perfect rapture. After all, my ears (though not very nice) are somewhat crucified by his melodies, especially when confined within the cabin. The boy is ten years old, perhaps, and rather pretty; clean, too, and neatly dressed, very unlike all other street and vagabond children whom I have seen in Liverpool. People give him their half-pence more freely than to any other musicians who infest the boats

English people say a great many more common-place and matter-of-course things, than people of similar respectability in America.

Julian, the other day, was describing a soldier-crab to his mother (he being much interested in natural history) and endeavoring to give as strong an idea as possible of its warlike characteristics, and power to harm those who molest it. Rosebud (now four years old) sat by, quietly sewing; and at last, lifting her head, she remarked, "I hope God did not hurt hisself when he was making him!"

LEAMINGTON, JUNE 21st 1855. THURSDAY.

WE left Liverpool and Rock Ferry on Monday, at 12½, by the rail, for this place; a very dim and rainy day, so that we had no pleasant prospect of the country; neither would the scenery [118] along the Great Western railway have been in any case very striking; though sunshine would have made the abundant verdure and foliage warm and genial. But a railway naturally finds its way through all the common-places of a country; it is certainly a most unsatisfactory way of travelling, the only object being to arrive. However, we had a whole carriage to ourselves, and the children enjoyed the earlier part of the ride very much. We skirted Shrewsbury; and I think I saw the old tower of a church near the station, perhaps the same that struck Falstaff's 'long hour.'163 As we left the town, I saw the Wrekin, a round, pointed hill, of regular shape;—and remembered the old toast, "To all friends round the Wrekin."164 As we approached Birmingham, the country began to look somewhat Brummagemish, with its manufacturing chimnies [sic], and pennons of flame quivering out of their tops; its forges; and great heaps of mineral refuse; its smokeiness [sic]; and other ugly symptoms. Birmingham itself we saw little or nothing of, except the mean and new brick lodging-houses, &c, on the outskirts of the town. Passing through Warwick, we had a glimpse of the castle,—an ivied wall and two turrets rising out of the embosoming foliage; one's very idea of an old gray castle. We reached Leamington at a little past six, and drove to the Clarendon Hotel, a very spacious and stately house, by far the most splendid ho[119]tel I have seen in England, though not equal in splendor or convenience to many in America; but then, in the latter, the accommodation is for the public in a mass, whereas here it is for individuals of the public. The landlady, a courteous old lady in black, showed my wife our rooms; and we established ourselves in an immensely large and lofty drawing-room, with red-curtains, and ponderous furniture, perhaps a very little out of date. The waiter brought us the book of arrivals, containing the names of all visitors for, I think, three to five years back; and there were not more entries than, in a popular American house, there might have been in a week. During two years, I estimated that there had been about three hundred and fifty; and, while we were there, I saw nobody but ourselves to support this great house. Among the names we saw princes, earls, countesses, baronets, and dignitaries of that sort; and when they learned from nurse that I too was a man of office, and held the title of Honorable in my own country, the people of the house greatly regretted that I had entered myself as plain Mister in the book.165 We found this Hotel very comfortable, and might doubtless have made it luxurious, had we chosen to go to perhaps five times the expense of similar luxuries in America; but we merely had comfortable things, and [120] so came off at no very extravagant rate—and with great honor, at all events, in the eyes of the waiters, to whom (as Americans are usually foolish enough to do) we gave more than Englishmen would, in like circumstances.

During the afternoon, we found lodgings, and established ourselves in them before dark. Leamington seems to be made chiefly of lodging-houses, and to be built with a view to a continually shifting population. It is a very beautiful town, with regular streets of stone or stuccoed houses, very broad pavements, and much shade of noble trees, in many parts of the town; parks and gardens, too, of delicious verdure; and throughout all an aspect of freshness and cleanness, which I despaired of ever seeing in England. The town seems to be almost entirely new. The principal street has elegant shops; and the scene is very lively, with throngs of people more gaily dressed than one is accustomed to see in this country; soldiers, too, lounging at the corners, and officers, who appear less shy of showing themselves in their regimentals than it is the fashion to be elsewhere.

This English custom of lodgings (which we had some experience of, at Rhyl, last year) has its advantages, but is rather uncomfortable for strangers, who, on first settling themselves down, find that they must undertake all the [121] responsibilities of house-keeping at an instant's warning, and cannot get even a cup of tea till they have made arrangements with the grocer. Soon, however, there comes a sense of being at home, and by our exclusive selves, which never could be attained at hotels or boarding houses. Our house is well situated and respectably furnished, with the dinginess, however, which I suppose is inseparable from lodging-houses—as if others had used these things and would use them after we are gone—a well-enough adaptation, but lack of peculiar appropriateness; and I think one puts off real enjoyment from a sense of not being really fitted.

Julian and I took walks yesterday forenoon and afternoon—very pleasant walks; but as I mean to take many more such, I defer a description of rural scenery for the present.

JUNE 22ᵈ THURSDAY.

IN the forenoon of yesterday, wife, Una and I took a walk through what looked like a park, but seemed to be a sort of semi-public tract on the outskirts of the town—hill and glade, with a fair gravel path through it, and most stately and beautiful trees overshadowing it. Here and there benches were set beneath the trees. These old, vigorous, well-nurtured trees, are fine beyond description; and in this leafy month of June,[166] they certainly surpass my recollections of [122] American trees—so tall, with such an aspect of age-long life. But I suppose what we know of English trees, of the care bestowed on them, the value at which they are estimated, their being traditional, and connected with the fortunes of old families—these moral considerations inevitably enter into physical admiration of them. They are individuals—which few American trees have the happiness to be. The English elm is more beautiful in shape and growth than I had imagined; but I think our own elm is still more so. Julian compared an English oak, which we saw on our journey, to a cauliflower; and its shape, its regular, compact rotundity, makes it very like one;—there is a certain John-Bullism about it. Its leaf, too, is much smaller than our own oak; and with similar advantages of age and cultivation, the latter would be far the noblest and most majestic form of a tree.[167] But in verdure, in the rich aspect of the country, nothing surely can equal England; and I never enjoyed weather anywhere so delightful as such a day as yesterday; so warm and genial, and yet not oppressive—the sun a very little too warm, while walking beneath it, but only enough too warm to assure us that it was warm enough. And, after all, there was an unconquered freshness in the atmosphere, which each little motion of the air made evident to us. I suppose there is still latent in us Americans (even of two centuries date, and [123] more, like myself) an adaptation to the English climate, which makes it like native soil and air to us.[168]

Beyond the park-like tract, we crossed a stile, and still followed the path, which led us through the midst of several fields and pastures. Men were whetting their scythes and mowing in adjacent fields. I delight in these English by-paths, which let a wayfarer into the heart of matters, without burdening him with the feeling of intrusiveness. Very likely, many, and most, of such paths are of more ancient date than the high roads; inasmuch as people tra- velled on foot before they had carriages or carts. In America, a farmer would plough across any such path, without scruple; here, the footsteps of centuries are sure to be respected.[169]

Soon, as we went along this path, we descried some brick farm-houses, looking rather venerable; and they proved to be ranged along a public road, leading from Leamington to some town to me unknown. These houses stood close together in one row; for it is to be noted that we seldom see scattered farm-houses here, as in New England;—they cluster themselves together in little hamlets and villages. These edifices were all of a ripe age, with roofs of tiles, and some of thatch; and, in two or three of them, the windows opened on hinges. Several of the houses were [124] good large dwellings, evidently inhabited by respectable people, well to do in the world; but others in the same range were the veriest old huts I have seen in England;—the thatch mossy, and in one case covered with a great variety of queer vegeta- tion—tufts of grass, house-leeks, and other plants, all differing in their shade of green. The windows were latticed (there was one little bit of a window right up in the eaves, half hidden by the thatch; the doors were time-worn; and this cottage, if I remember right, was built with its frame-work appear- ing through the stone and plaster, and painted black. I have seen several of these old houses hereabouts. The oaken frame seems to be more durable than the brick, stone, or plaster, which fills up the spaces; for, in some instances, these materials had evidently been renewed, while the frame-work still looked as solid as ever. As with an old man's back, however, so an old cottage betrays its decrepitude by the crookedness of its ridge-pole. Perhaps these huts may have descended from father to son, and remained in one hereditary line, longer than the castles and manor-houses of the nobles who hold the title- deeds of the estates over which they are strewn. These thatched cottages seem like something made by nature, or put together by instinct, like birds' nests, more than houses built by man. They have a great charm [125] for the observer; and artists, no doubt, like them better than the best edifices that could be built by rule and square; and yet they are as homely, and really ugly (if it were not for what decay and moss, and house-leeks, do for them in the way of beautification) as any pig-sty. No new stone and thatched cottages seem to be built, now-a-days; and, for the first hundred years, they would be eye-sores.

Beyond the first row of cottages, and on the opposite side of the road, there was another row—a block (as we should call it in America) of a dozen or more old brick cottages, all adjoining, with their thatched roofs forming one contiguity. The American idea of a cottage is, that it should be insulated; and I should not take it to indicate proper self-respect, and a due atmosphere of cleanly reserve, to have families growing in a mass, in this fashion. What an intimate community they must be, passing lives and generations, so near together. It is impossible, however, to think what a strangely rural and verdant scene was formed by this row of contiguous huts; for, in front of the whole was a hawthorne hedge, and betwixt the precincts of each was a dividing line of hedge; and belonging to each was a little square of garden, chock full—not of esculent vegetables—but of flowers and green [126] shrubs, flowers not of the conservatory, but of homely yellow and other bright colors, fit for cottage garden-plots. The sunshine fell warmly and brightly into these small enclosures, and into the old doors and small windows of the cottages; and the women and children were seen, looking very comfortable, and enjoying themselves. There was a great buzz, too, in the air, which we at first took to be the buzz of gnats, or musquitoes [sic], and which was very proper to the bright sunshine; but soon there came an old, witch-like woman out of one of the garden gates, holding forth a shovel, on which she clanged and clattered with a key; and then we discovered that a hive of bees had swarmed, and that the air was full of them, whizzing by our ears like bullets; and then we thought it best to retreat.[170]

Not far from these two congregations of houses and cottages, a green lane parted from the main-road, and we saw the square gray tower of a church, and wended thitherward to inspect it. It proved to be the very picture and ideal of a country-church and church-yard. A low, massive, turreted tower, of gray stone, and evidently of old date, as also were portions of the wall of the church, though it seemed to have been repaired no long time since. There was a stone platform, much worn and grass-grown, on which perhaps the font had stood (as at Beb[127]ington church) in past times. A path, well-trodden, led across the church-yard; and we went in, and looked at the graves and monuments. Most of them were head-stones, mossy, but none very old, so far as was discoverable by the dates; some of them, so far from being old, had glaring inscriptions in bright gold letters. Besides the headstones, there were a few monuments of granite or free stone, laid massively over the graves; one was to a former vicar, who died about twenty-five years ago. I suppose the ground must have been dug over and over, innumerable times, and that the soil is made up of what once was human clay. This church is but of humble size, and the eaves are so low that I think I could have touched them with my cane. I looked into the windows, and saw the dim and quiet interior, the nave being separated from the sides of the church by pointed Saxon arches, resting on very sturdy pillars. There was a small organ; and the pews looked very neat; and the woodwork seemed not to be of antiquity. On the opposite wall of the church, between two windows, was a mural tablet of white marble, with an inscription in black letters—the only one I could see within, though doubtless many dead people lay beneath. There were no painted windows, nor other [128] gorgeousness; and probably it is the worshipping-place of no more distinguished congregation than the farmers and peasantry who live in the houses and huts which we had been looking at. Had the lord of the manor been one of the parishioners, there would probably have been an eminent pew in the church.[171]

We rested ourselves on a flat tombstone, which somebody had been kind enough to place at just the height from the ground to make it a convenient seat. We observed that one of the head-stones stood very close to the church; so close that the droppings of the eaves must have fallen on it;—the pious inmate of that grave had doubtless wished to creep under the church-wall.[172] After a while, we arose and went our way; and I had a feeling as if I had seen this old church before, and dimly remembered; so well did it correspond with my idea, from much reading about them, of what English rural churches are. Or perhaps the image of them, impressed into the minds of my long-ago forefathers, was so deep that I have inherited it; and it answers to the reality. Part of our way home lay through a delightful shadowy lane; but we soon found ourselves getting into the brick work, and stuccoed lines of houses, and macadamized houses, of Leamington.

[129] June 23ᵈ, Saturday.

Nothing of note happened yesterday. We had purposed to go to Stratford on Avon, to celebrate Julian's birthday, who is nine years old; but he seemed not very well, and there were other incommodities; so we put off the expedition. In the forenoon, I took a little walk with Una and Rosebud, but saw only the useful [usual?] verdure and fertility, and a respectable old farm-house (large and handsome enough, however, to have been a gentleman's residence) of brick, with several gables, and with lattice-windows—broad windows, hinged on either side, and closing in the middle. The immediate vicinity of the house was laid out in a lawn and flower-beds, and with gravel walks, and beautiful old trees, all with great neatness and taste; but a few hundred yards off were the barn-yard and farm-offices. I should like to see the tenant of precisely such a farm-house as this. In New England, it would be thought a very handsome residence for a Senator, a Judge, or any dignitary of State.

About six °clock I took a walk alone, on a road which I know to lead to Warwick, though I think not the most direct road. The hedges here are very luxuriant, and all the better, I think, for not being trimmed so scrupulously as I have seen them elsewhere. It was almost, or quite, a sultry evening; or else I have forgot what sultriness is. At any [130] rate, it made me feel listless and languid. I sat down [on] a hospitable bench, a mile or so from the town, and smoked a cigar. A lady passed me on horseback, with her groom, with cockade in hat, riding at some distance behind; then two horsemen, looking like respectable farmers; an open phaeton, and various sorts of wagons and carts. Women and girls carrying baskets to or from the town, mostly, I thought, laundresses, with clothes for the gentry; a servant in livery; yeomen, in velveteen breeches, stout, shortish figures, in good flesh; and foot-travellers, with long staffs, one of whom observed to me—"Very warm, Sir!"—being the only words which I exchanged with anybody. In the course of my walk, I passed the Leam (pronounced *Lemon,* and Leamington Lemonington) by a bridge. It is a sluggish and dirty stream, about twenty-five to thirty yards across, but a pleasant object (unless you consider its muddiness too closely) on account of the verdure of its banks, fringed with grass right into the water, and the beautiful trees which see themselves in the placid current—though I could not perceive that there was any current. What one misses most in the scenery here is that which makes so great a charm in New England—the little sheets of water which there open their eyes out of the face of the country— and the little brooks and streamlets, every mile or two. I do not re[131]member having seen a single brook anywhere in England. If it were not for cultivation and trees, and old houses and churches, the country about Leamington would be very uninteresting; being flat and tame in its natural features.[173]

JUNE 24th, SUNDAY.

UNA, Julian, and I, took a walk out of town, yesterday forenoon; the road presenting the same features of hedge and stately trees, and broad green fields, elsewhere to be seen in this region. About a mile or more from Leamington, we came to a little rural village more picturesque and Old-English in its way, than anything we have seen yet. It seemed to be quite shut in by trees; and it was a cluster of a few old-fashioned cottages round a small ancient church. Not one of the dwellings appeared less than two or three centuries old, all being of the thatched, wooden-framed, and stone, brick, and plaster order, though the one nearest the church was quite a fair-sized and comfortable house, with several ends and gables. This, I suppose, may have been the vicarage; and it was most convenient to the scene of the clergyman's labors;— indeed, not more than a score of yards from the church-door, though with a small, narrow lane betwixt [it] and the church-yard wall. The church has the square, gray, battlemented tower, that seems to be the general form hereabouts; and it was much moss-grown, and time-gnawn, [132] and the arched window over the low portal was set with small panes of glass, cracked, dim, irregular, and evidently of old date. The frame of this window, and of the one over it towards the summit of the tower was of stone; and there were loop-holes up and down the sides of the tower, very narrow and small. No part of the church looked as if it had been repaired, for a very long time back; but masons were now at work in the churchyard, and in front of the tower, sawing a slab of stone, digging, building up bricks; and had we come a month or two later, no doubt we should have found the little edifice much sprucer, and not half so well worth looking at. They had dug an immense pit or vault on one side of the church, ten foot deep, at least;—yes, much more than ten—for I could see the depth of earth that was discolored by human decay, and the pit went far deeper than this. Probably they mean to enlarge the church. The grave stones had been much disturbed and scattered about, by these proceedings; they were mostly head-stones, some of them looking very old, but none that were legible were much over a hundred years old. The church-yard was very small, and surrounded by a gray stone fence, that looked as old as the church itself. On the outside of this fence, in front of the tower, was an elm of great circumference; and the children soon found out that it was hollow, and had opening large enough to admit them; [133] so they both got in and peeped forth at me with great delight. Examining it more closely, I found that there would have been room enough for me, too;—the whole trunk of the tree being a cavity, open to the sky at considerable height overhead. Besides the door into which the children had clambered, there was another opening that served for a window; and though its wooden heart was quite decayed and gone, the foliage of the tree was just as luxuriant as if it had been sound; and its great roots caught hold of the earth like gigantic claws, and, by their knots and knuckles, had doubtless afforded seats to the inhabitants, in summer evenings, and other idle times, from time immemorial. The little, rustic square of the hamlet lay in front and around the church, with all the cottage-doors opening into it—all visible and familiar to one another; and I never had such an impression of smugness, homeliness, neighborliness— of a place where everybody had known everybody, and forefathers, and foreforefathers and mothers had grown up together, and spent whole successions of lives, and died, and been buried under the same sods, so closely and conveniently at hand—the same family names, the same family features, repeated from generation to generation—as in this small village nook. And under that [134] gray church-portal, no doubt, young people had sat at midnight on mid-summer eve, to see who among their neighbors—whose apparitions— would pass into the church, because they were to die that year. And, long ago, mass had been said there; and the holy water had stood at the door. It is rather wearisome, to an American, to think of a place where no change comes for centuries, and where a peasant does but step into his father's shoes, and lead just his father's life, going in and out over the old threshold, and finally being buried close by his father's grave, time without end; and yet it is rather pleasant to know that such things are.[174]

I saw no public house in the village; there was a little shop, kept by an old woman, with papers of pins, cheap crockery, and other small matters, displayed in the window, where also I saw a wood engraving of the church (St. Margaret's, Whitnash) on a sheet of note-paper, to be sold towards paying the expenses of rebuilding the chancel. I bought six pence worth. Just out of the heart of the village, there was a tailor's sign over a cottage door. Probably there is no family of note or estate having its pew and place of worship in this church. The shadowiness and seclusion among the trees—and yet admitting sunshine into its little heart—is essential to the idea of this village. On our way home, we took [135] a by-path that led to Leamington through the fields, and met a gentleman, evidently clerical, who probably was the village-pastor. He seemed a staid, starched man, very conscious of being a priest.

JUNE 26th, TUESDAY.

YESTERDAY forenoon, Una, Julian, and I walked to Warwick, which is not above two miles from Leamington. We had hardly left the latter place, before two turrets of the castle, with trees rising high towards their summit, appeared in view; and likewise the tall tower of Saint Mary's Church. As we approached the town, we began to see antique houses; and near the beginning of the main street, we passed a venerable school-house (St John's School, I think it was called) a stone edifice, with a wide enclosure before it, surrounded by a high, antique fence. The front of the building had four gables in a row; and there was a large open porch, with seats under it. In the rear, the edifice seemed to be spacious, and adapted for domestic accommodation of the masters and scholars. It was striking to see a venerable house devoted to the youthful— to think how this old gray front had witnessed the sports of generations that had long ago grown decrepit and vanished. There was ivy on the wall of the playground and also here and there on the edifice itself. But I find it is getting to be [136] quite a common-place—this description of old, ivied and lichen-stained walls. It is entirely American; the English (unless professed antiq[u]aries) care nothing about a thing merely on account of its being old, and perhaps would rather see a house just erected, than one built a thousand years ago. And when one sees how much antiquity there is left, everywhere about England, and reflects how it may stand in the way of improvement, it is no great wonder that they should laugh at our estimate of it. An old thing is no better than a new thing, unless it [be] a symbol of something, or have some value in itself.

There are a good many modern houses in Warwick, and some of them handsome residences. It seems to be the fashion, now-a-days, to imitate the Elizabethan or some other old style of architecture; and the effect is good—only nobody seems to be building a house in real earnest, to live and die in, but rather as a sort of plaything. We are likely to leave no fashions for another age to copy, when we shall have become an antiquity. Getting further into the heart of the town, the old houses became more numerous; and I think Chester itself can hardly show such quaint architectural shapes as these;—such bowed, decrepit ridge-poles—such patched walls, such a multiplicity of peaked gables, such curious windows, some opening on the [137] roofs, and set in their own little gables; almost all opening lattice-wise, and furnished with twenty panes of glass, where one would suffice in a modern window. The style of visible oaken frame-work, showing the whole skeleton of the house (as if a man's bones should be arranged on the outside, with his flesh showing through the interstices) was prevalent. Some houses of this order were in perfect repair, and very spacious, and even stately, and probably presented quite adequate specimens of the aspect of the town, when this style was modern. About the centre of the town, we saw an arched gate way, with a church of [above] it, standing across the street; and this, I think, was the most ancient-look[ing] and picturesque portion of Warwick—all the adjacent houses being mediaeval, and evidently the abodes of old gentility; also, in near vicinity, there were public edifices of long ago. As we approached, we saw soldiers marching up the main-street, and turning a corner; and soon afterwards, when we found our way to the market-place, it was quite filled by a regiment, which was going through the drill. I suspect they were not regular soldiers, but a regiment of Warwickshire militia, commanded, I suppose by the earl. They were young men of healthy aspect, and looked very well in a body, but [138] individually had little of the soldier's mien—slouching into yeomanlike carriage and manners, as soon as dismissed. Their uniform was a red short-jacket and blue pantaloons. I saw an officer dressed in blue, and wearing embroidered on his collar the Warwick cognizance—the bear and ragged staff. The regiment being dismissed from drill, we afterwards saw squads of the soldiers everywhere about the streets, and sentinels posted here [and] there, perhaps before officers' quarters; and I saw one sergeant, with a great key in his hand (which might be a key of Warwick Castle) apparently setting a guard. Thus, centuries after feudal times have past, we find warriors still clustering under the old castle-walls, and under the command of the feudal lord. In the days of the Kingmaker, no doubt he often mustered his troops in the same market-place where we found this regiment.

Not far from the market-place stands the great church of St. Mary's—a huge church indeed, and almost worthy to be a cathedral. It is said not to be in any good and pure style of architecture, though designed by Sir Christopher Wren; but I thought it very striking, with its great, elaborate windows, its immense length, its tall towers, and a gray antiquity over the whole. While we stood gazing [139] up at the tower, the clock struck twelve, with a very deep voice; and immediately some chimes began to play, and kept up their music for five minutes. This was very pleasant, and seemed not unworthy of the huge church; although I have seen old-fashioned parlor-clocks that did just the same thing. We rambled round the town, finding old churches and other old matters everywhere, and wondering that the little children should look new, like other children, seeing they had come into existence under such old circumstances. We did, however, see one fresh, ruddy-cheeked, smiling urchin, who might have been taken for the child of a by-gone century; he was dressed in a collarless, wide skirted coat, and salmon colored breeches, and was probably a scholar of a charity-school in town.

The irregularity of old towns and villages is one of their most striking peculiarities. There is nothing square about them, and no street seems to have reference to any other street; and this absence of plan—this evident fact that the town has made itself, growing according to its necessities, from age to age—produces an effect worth all that science could do. There is a constant unexpectedness; and even after one is familiar with the twists and turns, I should think it never could grow tame. Now [140] as regards modern Leamington (though certainly a handsome town, and with many edifices which you perceive to be beautiful, when you force your attention to them) its streets soon get wearisome; and to have seen one, and only once, is as good as seeing all a thousand times.

We left Warwick[175] in the omnibus at one; not intending this as anything more than [an] exploratory visit, and meaning to return with mamma, and see the castle, and the interiors of churches, and many other things now left unnoticed. In about half an hour, we were at our lodging-house.

In the afternoon, I took a walk by myself to the village of Radford; a village of the customary thatched roof, wooden-framed cottages, very bowery and green-grassy. Most of these cottages stood alone, with its own little precincts about it; and this was much more agreeable to look at than the plan of several homesteads under one long roof. The doors of many of the houses were open, affording views of the stone or brick-floored kitchen, with its homely furniture. A man was repairing the thatch [of] one of the cottages with new straw, and scraping away the dust and dirt of ages from the part of the roof where the old thatch had been. Passing through this village, I turned [141] aside into a path that led across fields, expecting that it would bring me into the same road by which I had left Leamington. But, instead of this, the path led me through various gates, and over stiles, and along cart-tracks, and once across a broad ploughed field, where it threatened to become quite trackless (but still remained a path) until suddenly it came out directly behind the little old church of Whitnash, whither the children and I wandered the other day. Stopping to look at the tower, I saw that, at each extremity of the arched mullion[176] (if that be the proper phrase) over the great window, above the portal, there was a sculptured stone-face, very perfectly preserved. It shows how a general impression overcomes minor details, that—whereas, at my former visit, I saw nothing but old dwellings, and recorded that there were no others—I now found that there were several new brick cottages and outhouses in the village, directly in front of the church—and very ugly ones too, though they seemed to be built after the plan of old cottages, and perhaps were merely renewals of them. But their cold, meagre, and indeed ugly aspect (uglier than almost anything in an American village) showed how necessary is the mural ivy and moss of antiquity to make these dwellings pleasant to the eye.

[142] June 27th, Thursday.

This day promising to be a very fair one, we devoted it to our pilgrimage to Stratford-on-Avon; and Mamma, Una, Julian, and I, set out in a phaeton, at about ½ past 9. It was really a bright morning, warm, genial and delightful; so that we saw English scenery under almost an American sun, and the combination made something very like perfection. Our road lay through Warwick; and I observed, on the wall of an old chapel in the High-street, some foxglove flowers growing, as also grass and little shrubs, all at the height of perhaps twenty feet above the ground. Adjacent to this chapel (which stands almost across the street, with an archway for foot passengers beneath it, and causing the carriage track to swerve aside in passing it) there is an ancient edifice, in excellent repair, and with coats of arms and the cognizance of the Bear and Ragged Staff painted on its front. This turns out to be Leicester's Hospital, an institution for the support of twelve poor brethren; and I think we saw the better part of a dozen old faces, idly contemplating us from the windows or about the doors of the old house. I must try to get a better knowledge of this institution.

The road from Warwick to Stratford is most beautiful; not that it owes any remarkable features to Nature; for the country thereabouts is a succession of the gentlest swells and subsidences, here and there affording [143] wide and far glimpses of champagne [champaign] scenery; and near Stratford it becomes quite level. Altogether, throwing in a few higher hills, and opening the eye of the scene, here and there, by a sheet of water, like Walden-pond, it would look a good deal like the country near Concord—so far as its natural features are concerned. But the charm of the English scene is its old and high cultivation, its richness of verdure, its stately trees, with their trunks clustered about by creeping shrubs;—a great deal of which man has done, and in which he could be partly rivalled in America; but much, too, is due to the moisture of the climate, and the gentle sunshine. At any rate, the effect is beyond all description, and seen, as I have just said, under an American sun (that is to say, once or twice a year) nothing more could be asked by mortals, in the way of rural beauty. All along the way, there were cottages of old date, many so old that Shakspeare might have passed them in his walks, or entered their low doors; a few modern villas, too; and perhaps mansions of gentility or nobility hidden among the trees—for such houses seldom show themselves from the road.

There is nothing remarkable in the approach to [144] Stratford. The spire of Shakspeare's church shows itself among the trees, at a little distance from the town. Then come shabby old houses, intermixed with more modern ones, mostly mean-looking; and the streets being quite level, the effect on the whole is tame and quite unpicturesque. I think I might ride into such a town, even in America, and not be much struck by many peculiarities. Here and there, however, there are very queer dwellings, that seem to have been growing queerer and odder during the three or four centuries of their existence; and there appear to be more old people, tottering about and leaning on sticks—old people in breeches, and retaining all the traditional costume of the last century—than could be found anywhere on our side of the water. Old places seem to produce old people;[177] or perhaps the secret is, that old age has a natural tendency to hide itself, when it is brought into contact with new edifices, and new things, but comes freely out, and feels itself in sympathy, and is not ashamed to face the eye of man, in a decaying town. There is a sense of propriety in this.

We stopt at the Red Lion, a hotel of no great pretensions, and immediately set out on our rambles about town. After wandering through two or three streets, we [145] found Shakspeare's birth-place, which is almost a worse house than anybody could dream it to be; but it did not surprise me, because I had seen a full-sized fac-simile of it in the Zoological gardens at Liverpool. It is exceedingly small—at least, the portion of it which had anything to do with Shakspeare. The old, worn, butcher's counter, on which the meat used to be laid, is still at the window. The upper half of the door was open; and on my rapping at it, a girl dressed in black soon made her appearance and opened it. She was a ladylike girl, not a menial, but I suppose the daughter of the old lady who shows the house. This first room has a pavement of gray slabs of stone, which, no doubt, were rudely squared when the house was new, but they are all cracked and broken, now, in a curious way. One does not see how any ordinary usage, for whatever length of time, should have cracked them thus; it is as if the devil had been stamping on them, long ago, with an iron hoof,[178] and the tread of other persons had ever since been reducing them to an even surface again. The room is white-washed, and very clean, but woefully shabby and dingy, coarsely built, and such as it is not very [146] easy to idealize. In the rear of this room is the kitchen, a still smaller room, of the same dingy character; it has a great, rough fire-place, with an immense passage way for the smoke, and room for a large family under the blackened opening of the chimney. I stood under it, without stooping; and doubtless Shakspeare may have stood on the same spot, both as child and man. A great fire might of course make the kitchen cheerful; but it gives a depressing idea of the humble, mean, sombre character of the life that could have been led in such a dwelling as this—with no conveniences, all higgledy-piggledy, no retirement, the whole family, old and young, brought into too close contact to be comfortable together. To be sure, they say the house used to be much larger than now, in Shakspeare's time; but what we see of it is consistent in itself, and does not look as if it ever could have been a portion of a large and respectable house.

Thence we proceeded upstairs to the room in which Shakspeare is supposed to have been born, and which is over the front lower room, or butcher's shop. It has one broad window, with old irregular panes of glass; the floor is of very rudely hewn planks; the naked beams and rafters at the sides and over head bear all the marks [147] of the builder's axe; and the room, besides, is very small—a circumstance more difficult to reconcile one'self [sic] to, as regards places that we have heard and thought much about, than any other part of a mistaken ideal. I could easily touch the ceiling, and could have done so had it been a good deal higher; indeed, the ceiling was entirely written over with names in pencil, by persons, I suppose, of all varieties of stature; so was every inch of the wall, into the obscurest nooks and corners; so was every pane of glass—and Walter Scott's name was said to be on one of the panes; but so many people had sought to immortalize themselves in close vicinity to him, that I really could not trace out his signature. I did not write my own name.

This room, and the whole house, so far as I saw it, was white-washed and very clean; and it had not the aged, musty smell, with which Chester makes one familiar, and which I suspect is natural to old houses, and must render them unwholesome. The woman who showed us upstairs had the manners and aspect of a gentlewoman, and talked intelligently about Shakspeare. Arranged on a table and in chairs, there were various prints, views of [148] houses and scenes connected with Shakspeare's memory, editions of his works, and local publications relative to him—all for sale, and from which, no doubt, this old gentlewoman realizes a good deal of profit. We bought several shillings' worth, partly as thinking it the civilest method of requiting her for the trouble of shewing the house. On taking our leave, I most ungenerously imposed on Sophia the duty of offering an additional fee to the lady like girl who first admitted us; but there seemed to be no scruple, on her part, as to accepting it. I felt no emotion whatever in Shakspeare's house—[179] not the slightest—nor any quickening of the imagination. It is agreeable enough to reflect that I have seen it; and I think I can form, now, a more sensible and vivid idea of him as a flesh-and-blood man; but I am not quite sure that this latter effect is altogether desirable.

From Shakspeare's house (after doing a little shopping and buying some toys for Rosebud) we inquired out the church—the Church of the Holy Trinity—where he lies buried. The aspect of the edifice, as we approached it, was venerable and beautiful, with a great green shadow of trees about it, and the Gothic ar[149]chitecture and vast arched windows obscurely seen above and among the boughs. An old man in small clothes was waiting at the gate of the church-yard; he inquired whether we wished to go in, and preceded us to the church-porch and rapped—all which we could have done quite as well ourselves; but, it seems, the old men of the vicinity haunt about the churchyard, to pick up a half-elemosyanary [sic] sixpence from the visitors. We were admitted into the church by a respectable-looking man in black, who was already exhibiting the Shakspeare monuments to two or three visitors; and other parties came in while we were there. The poet and his family seem [to have] the best burial-places that the church affords— or, at least, as good as any. They lie in a row, right across the breadth of the chancel, the foot of each gravestone being close to the elevated floor about the altar. Nearest to the side wall, beneath Shakspeare's bust, is the slab of stone bearing an inscription to his wife; then his own, with the old anathematizing stanza upon it; then, I think, the stone of Thomas Nash, who married his granddaughter; then that of Dr. Hall, the husband of his daughter Susannah; then Susannah's [150] own. Shakspeare's grave stone is the commonest looking slab of all, just such a flag-stone as a side-walk of the street might be paved with. Unlike the other monuments of the family, it has no name whatever upon it; and I [do] not see on what authority it is absolutely determined to be his. To be sure, being in a range with his wife and children, it might naturally be guessed that it was his; but then he had another daughter, and a son, who would need a grave somewhere. Perhaps, however, as his name was on the bust, above, and as his wife, when he was buried, had not yet taken her place between him and the church-wall, his name was thought unnecessary. Fifteen or twenty feet behind this row of grave-stones is the great east-window of the Church, now brilliant with stained glass, of recent manufacture; and one side of this window, under an arch of marble, lies a full length marble figure of Shakspeare's friend John a Combe, dressed in what I take to be a robe of municipal dignity, and with his hands devoutly clasped—a sturdy English figure of a man, with coarse features. There are other mural monuments and altar-tombs in the chancel; but methinks one who cared about a monument would rather not have it overshadowed by Shakspeare's.

[151] Now, as for the bust of Shakspeare, it is affixed to the northern wall of the church, the base of it being about a man's height (or more) above the floor of the chancel. The bust is quite unlike any portrait, or any other bust of Shakspeare, that I have ever seen, and compels me to root up all old ideas of his aspect, and adopt an entirely different one. For my part, I am loth to give up the beautiful, lofty-browed, noble picture of him which I have hitherto had in my mind; for this bust does not represent a beautiful face or a noble head. And yet it clutches hold of one's sense of reality, and you feel that this was the man. I don't know what the phrenologists say to this bust; its forehead is but moderately developed, and retreats somewhat; the upper part of the skull seems rather contracted; the eyes are rather prominent. The upper lip is so long that it must have been almost a deformity; the showman of the church said that Sir Walter Scott's upper lip was longer, but I doubt it. On the whole, Shakspeare must have had a singular, rather than a striking face; and it is wonderful how, with this bust before its eyes, the world has insisted on forming an erroneous [152] idea of his appearance, permitting painters and sculptors to foist their idealized nonsense upon mankind, instead of the genuine Shakspeare. But as for myself, I am henceforth to see in my mind's eye a red-faced personage, with a moderately capacious brow, an intelligent eye, a nose curved very slightly outward, a long, queer upper lip, with the mouth a little unclosed beneath it, and cheeks very much developed in the lower part of the face. Sophia (when the sexton and other visitors were in a distant part of the church) seized the opportunity to clamber upon a nameless, oblong, cubic tomb, supposed to be that of a collegiate dignitary of the fourteenth century; she thus gained a near profile view of the bust. Afterwards we saw two identical casts from it, and made the observations above recorded. As to the length of the upper lip, it is possible that the sculptor

exaggerated it, in consideration that it was to be viewed from below, and thus would be foreshortened to the proper proportion.

In a side-chapel of the church, we saw a monument of a certain Clopton Esquire, and his wife, with their figures at full length upon it—he in armor, and she in stately robes. The material seemed to be some [153] kind of marble, but so highly polished that it looked like china, and was in excellent preservation;—excellently well manufactured, too. There was another monument, or two, to members of the same family, I believe, after it had been en[n]obled. The race is now extinct; and the sexton told us that interments have ceased to take place in any part of the church. This may be well; but it adds greatly to the impressiveness of a church to see it adorned with these mortuary memorials.

We had now done one of the things that an American proposes to himself as necessarily and chiefly to be done, on coming to England. Leaving the church, we walked about the church-yard, and at last sat down on the border of it, over the river, while the children and mamma ate each an orange. The Avon is a narrow and exceedingly sluggish river, with flags along its banks, and here and there some beautiful forget-me-nots growing among the flags, but quite out of reach from the banks. I do not know an American river so tame; in fact we have no river of just that size, or smallness;—if not bigger, it would be rather less, either a river or a brook. It is very lazy, and by [154] no means pellucid; and it loiters past Stratford Church as if it had been considering which way to flow, ever since Shakspeare used to paddle in it. Most of the grave-stones in the church-yard are modern.

From the church[180] we went back to the hotel, and there got a luncheon of cold lamb, cold ham, and Stratford ale, which does not seem to me a very good brewage. We then took leave of Stratford, directing the driver to pass by the grammar-school where Shakspeare was supposed (for his whole biography has nothing more tangible than suppositions, and more or less probabilities) to have been educated. Our road back to Leamington was different from that by which we came, and took us past Char[l]ecote Hall, the description of which (being very tired of this present writing) I must leave till another opportunity.

JUNE 30th, SATURDAY.

I SHOULD have done better to have continued my narrative, and described Charlecote forthwith; for the hues of a recollection fade as quickly as the colors of a dead dolphin. As we passed Charlecote Park, we saw the most stately elms, singly, in clumps, and in groves, scattered all about, in the sunniest, sleepiest, shadiest fashion—trees, all of which were civilized, all known to man, and befriended [155] by him, for ages past; not portions of wild nature, like our trees. There is an indescribable difference between this tamed, but by no means effete (on the contrary more luxuriant) Nature of England, and the shaggy and barbarous Nature of America. By and by, among the trees, we saw a large herd of deer, mostly reclining, some standing in picturesque attitudes—some running fleetly about, with here and there a little faun at its mother's heels. I never [saw] anything so like a picture; so perfectly fulfilling one's idea as this scene of an old English park. I thought so before I saw the deer; and they came in as all that was wanted to make it perfect—the want, too, not being felt till it was supplied. And these deer are in the same relation to their wild, natural state, that the trees are; they are not domesticated, not tamed, but yet how unlike forest-deer. They have held a certain intercourse with man for immemorial years;—very likely, the deer that Shakspeare killed was one of the progenitors of this very herd, and that deer was himself a humanized deer, like these. They are, perhaps, a good deal wilder than sheep; but still they do not snuff the air on the approach of human beings, nor feel alarmed at their pretty near proximity; although they toss their heads and take to their heels, in a kind of mimic terror, or something [156] like feminine skittishness, with a dim remembrance or tradition, as it were, of their having come of a wild race. But they have been fed and protected by man, ever since England had its institutions; and, I suppose, now, they could hardly get through a winter without human help. One rather despises them for this, but loves them too; and I think it was this partially domesticated state of the Charlecote deer that may have suggested to Shakspeare the tender and pitiful description of a wounded deer, in As You Like It.[181]

Arriving at the gate of the park, near the house, we alighted and went in; for the Lucies seem to be a kindly race of people, and do not throw any unreasonable obstacles in the way of curious tourists. The house, however, cannot be seen within, during the absence of the family (as was the case now) but we seemed to be at liberty to view on all attainable sides; and so we did. Before the front entrance, at the distance of some hundreds of yards, and almost hidden from passers-by by many trees between, is an old brick archway and porter's lodge, very venerable; and there appears to have been a wall and a moat in connection with this—the moat being still visible, a shallow, grassy scoop along at the base of an embankment of the lawn. Within this gateway, fifty yards off, per[157]haps, stands the house, forming, on this side, three sides of a square, surrounding a green ornamented space. Peaked gables, three in a row, one on each of the three sides; and there are several towers of quaint shape at different parts and angles of the house. All is in perfect repair, and there seem to have been large recent additions, which do not shock one by any incongruity. Over the gate way is the Lucy coat-of-arms, emblazoned in its proper colors. The impression is not of gray antiquity, but of stable and time-honored gentility, still as vital as ever. The mansion, I believe, was built in the early days of Elizabeth; and probably looked very much the same as now, when Shakspeare was brought before Sir Thomas Lucy for deer-stealing. All about the house, and the park, however, there is a perfection of comfort and domestic taste, and an amplitude of convenience, which it must have taken ages, and the thoughts of many successive generations, intent upon adding all possible household charm to the house which they loved, to produce. It is only so that real homes can be produced; one man's life is not enough for it; especially when he feels that he is probably making his house warm and delightful for a miscellaneous race of successors none of whom are likely to be of his blood. Looking at this estate, [158] it seemed very possible for those who inherit [it], and the many in England similar to it, to lead noble and beautiful lives, quietly doing good and lovely things, and deeds of simple greatness, should circumstances require such. Why should not the ideal of humanity grow up, like ideal trees, amid such soil and culture. I do not know anything about the private character of the Lucies; but I feel inclined to think well of them, from merely looking at their abode. Yet most of the aristocracy of England have as good or better.

Between the gateway and the church (only at a short distance, standing on the border of the Park) is an avenue of ancient elms, with a shadowy path only partially traced among the grass, running beneath. The church is new; the old one, if I mistake not, having recently been taken down. Much has escaped me that should have gone into the above sketch of Charlecote Park,[182] but the memory of it, and of the perfect day in which I saw it, is as beautiful as a dream. It seems to me there should have been a colony of rooks in the tree-tops of the churchward avenue.

SUNDAY, JULY 1st.

ON Friday, I took rail (at 10:55, with Julian for Coventry; a bright and very warm day; oppressively so, indeed; though I think that there is never, in this English climate, [159] the pervading warmth of an American day. The sunshine may be intensely hot, but an overshadowing cloud, or the shade of a tree or building, at once affords relief; and if the slightest breeze stirs, you feel the latent freshness of the air.

Coventry is some nine or ten miles from Leamington. The approach to it, from the railway, presents nothing very striking—a few church-towers and one or two tall steeples; and the houses that first present themselves are of modern and unnoticeable aspect. Getting into the interior of the town, however, you find the streets very crooked, and some of them very narrow. I saw one place where it seemed possible to shake hands from one jutting-storied old house to another. There are whole streets of the same kind of houses (one story impending over another) that used to be familiar to me in Salem, and in some streets of Boston. In fact, the whole aspect of the town, its irregularity and continual indirectness, reminded me very much of Boston, as I used to see it in rare visits thither, when a child. These Coventry houses, however, many of them, are much larger than any of similar style that I have seen elsewhere, and spread into greater bulk as they ascend, by means of one other jutting story. Probably the New Englanders continued to follow this fashion of architecture after it [160] had been abandoned in the mother-country. The old house built by Philip English, in Salem, dated not much earlier or later than 1692; and it was in this style, many gabled, and impending. Here, the edifices of such architecture seem to be Elizabethan, and earlier. A woman in Stratford told us that the rooms, very low on the ground flower [floor], grow loftier from story to story, to the attic. The fashion of windows in Coventry is such as I have not hitherto seen. In the highest story, a window, of the ordinary height, extends along the whole breadth of the house—ten, fifteen, perhaps twenty feet—just like any other window of a common-place house, except for this inordinate width. One does not easily see what the inhabitants want of so much window-light; but the fashion is very general, and in modern houses, or houses that have been modernized, this style of window is retained. Thus young people, who grow up amidst old people, contract quaint and old fashioned manners and aspects.

I imagine that these ancient towns—such as Chester, and Stratford, and Warwick and Coventry—contain even a great deal more antiquity than meets the eye. You see many modern fronts; but if you peep or penetrate inside, you see an antique arrangement, old rafters, intricate passages, ancient staircases, which have put on merely a new outside, and are likely still to prove good for the usual date [161] of a new house. They put such an immense and stalwart ponderosity into their old frame-work, that I suppose a house of Elizabeth's time if renewed has at least an equal prospect of durability with a house new in every part. All the hotels in Coventry, so far as I noticed them, are old houses with new fronts; and they have an arch-way for the admission of vehicles &c into the courtyard, and doors, admitting into the rooms of the hotel, on each side of the arch. You see maids and waiters darting across the arched passage, from door to door, and it requires (in my case, at least) a guide to show you the way to bar or coffee-room. I have never been up-stairs, in any of them, but can conceive of infinite bewilderment of zig-zag passages, between staircase and chamber.

It was fair-day, in Coventry, and this gave what no doubt is an unusual bustle to the old streets. In fact, I have not seen such crowded and busy streets in any English town; various kinds of merchandise being for sale in the open air, and auctioneers disposing of miscellaneous wares, pretty much as they do at musters and other gatherings in the United States. The oratory of the American auctioneer, however greatly surpasses that of the Englishman in vivacity and fun. But this movement and throng of [162] the street, together with the white glow of the sun on the pavements, make the scene, in my recollection, assume more of an American aspect than any other that I have witnessed in sluggish England;—a strange effect, in so antique and quaint a town as Coventry.

We rambled about, without any definite object, but found our way, I believe, to most of the objects that are worth seeing. Saint Michael's Church seemed to me most magnificent—all that I could conceive of, in the matter of a church; so old, yet so enduring, so huge, so rich, with such intricate minuteness in its finish, that, look as long as you will at it, you can always discover something new directly before your eyes. I admire this in Gothic architecture—that you cannot master it all at once—that it is not a naked outline, but as deep and rich as human nature itself, always revealing new little ideas, and new large ones. It is as if the builder had built himself up in it, and his age, and as if the edifice had life. Grecian edifices are very uninteresting to me, being so cold and crystalline. I think this is the only church I have seen, where there are any statues still left standing in the niches of the steeple. We did not go inside of the church. The steeple of St Michael's is three hundred & three feet high; and no doubt the clouds often envelope [*sic*] the tip of the spire. Trinity, another church with a tall [163] spire, stands near St Michael's, but did not attract me so much; though perhaps I might have equally admired it, had I seen it alone, or earliest. We certainly know nothing of church edifices in America; and of all English things that I have seen, methinks they are what disappoint me least. I feel, too, that there is something much more wonderful in them than I have yet had time to make myself know and experience.

In the course of the forenoon, poking about everywhere in quest of Gothic architecture, we found our way, I hardly know how, into St Mary's Hall.[183] The door was wide open; it seemed to be a public affair; there was a notice on the wall, desiring visitors to give nothing to attendants for showing the hall; and so we walked in. I observe in the guide-book that we should have obtained an order for admission from some member of the Town Council; but we had none such, and found no need of it. An old woman, and afterwards an old man, both of whom seemed to be at home on the premises, told us that we might enter, and troubled neither themselves nor us any further.

St. Mary's Hall is now the property of the corporation of Coventry, and seems to be the place where the Mayor and Council hold their meetings. It seems to have been built (early in Henry 6th's time) by one of the old guilds, or fra[164]ternities of merchants and tradesmen; and was the place where they held their annual feasts, and all their gatherings for pleasure and business;— being provided with kitchens and offices, and all conveniences for the exercise of public hospitality. The old woman shut the kitchen-door, when she saw me approaching; so that I did not see the great fire-places and huge cooking utensils which are said to be there. Whether these are ever used now-a-days— and whether the Mayor gives such hospitable banquets as the Mayor of Liverpool, I do not know.

I have forgotten all particulars about the exterior of the edifice, except that it looked exceeding venerable, and that I peeped into the basement (now used as a coal-cellar) and admired the massive stone arches, intersecting each other in all sorts of ways, on which the building rests. We passed up a black staircase, with an oaken balustrade, and entered the Great Hall, which is more than sixty feet long, and about half as wide, and, I should think, much more than half as high, from the floor to the angle of the roof. It has the original oaken roof, in shape like the roof of a barn, with all the beams and rafters visible; but carved, as the roof of barn never was nor will be, in beautiful style, with Gothic angels, and presenting, no doubt, the old artist's idea of the sky. The whole space of the hall is unimpeded by a single column, [165] and the roof supports itself with its proper strength. There were rows of benches (which I wished were away) on the floor of the room; and one side (on an elevated dais, if I mistake not) was an ancient Chair of State, looking very much like one of those old black settles which I have seen in America, and which are placed before the fire-place with the high back to the door, to keep off the wind. It was not so large as those to be sure, but would afford rather scanty accommodations for three persons; and is very straight, angular, and rigid in its make. Julian and I sat down in it, and did not know, till I read it in the Guide-Book, that English Kings and Queens (now heaps of dust for ages past) had sat there before us. I presume it was the old principle to manufacture chairs of state so that they should be as irksome and uncomfortable, physically, as they appear to be morally.

The great hall had an aged darkness diffused over its wood-work, and would have looked somewhat bare and lacking in adornment, but for a very large and magnificent arched-window at the northern end, full of old painted glass. It is in nine compartments, and represents the figures and coat-armories of many English monarchs. This window is very rich, and would be glorious no doubt, with the sun shining through it. There are also [166] windows of modern stained glass, which I did not much notice. Another ornament (or what must once have been so, is a piece of ancient tapestry, ten feet high, beneath the great painted window, and extending across the whole breadth of the hall. In it are wrought King Henry Sixth and his nobles, performing religious exercises, and above are saints, angels, and apostles, and Heaven itself; and the Deity was once there in person, but was long since taken out, and a figure of Justice sewed into the beatific vacuity. Julian says that the figures of Henry and his court are engraved in Markham's history of England.[184] The whole is now so faded that the design is not readily discernible; the whole, in the sombre light of the hall, appearing almost of one neutral tint; but when the whole hall was covered with such rare tapestry, and all was glowing in its pristine freshness of color, and when the carving of the vaulted roof had not been so obscured by the darkening of the wood, it must have been such a chamber of state and festivity as modern times cannot show.

There are full length pictures of English kings, from Charles II, downwards, hung up in the hall. At the southern end is a gallery for minstrels, and beneath it hang several suits of armor, with spears, pikes, and other such weapons; the armor has no brightness, being painted black, and probably was not intended for knights or persons of rank, but for men-at-arms in the pay and service of the city.[185] [We went to the Red Lion, and had a luncheon of cold lamb and cold pigeon-pie. This is the best way of dining at English hotels,—to call the meal a luncheon, in which case you will get as good or better a variety than if it were a dinner, and at less than half the cost. Having lunched, we again wandered about town, and entered a quadrangle of gabled houses, with a church, and its church-yard on one side. This proved to be St. John's Church, and a part of the houses were the locality of Bond's Hospital, for the reception of ten poor men, and the remainder was devoted to the Bablake School. Into this latter I peered, with a real American intrusiveness, which I never found in myself before, but which I must now assume, or miss a great many things which I am anxious to see.

Running along the front of the house, under the jut of the impending story, there was a cloistered walk, with windows opening on the quadrangle. An arched oaken door, with long iron hinges, admitted us into a school-room about twenty feet square, paved with brick tiles, blue and red. Adjoining this there is a larger school-room which we did not enter, but peeped at, through one of the inner windows, from the cloistered walk. In the room which we entered, there were seven scholars' desks, and an immense arched fireplace, with seats on each side, under the chimney, on a stone slab resting on a brick pedestal. The opening of the fireplace was at least twelve feet in width. On one side of the room were pegs for fifty-two boys' hats and clothes, and there was a boy's coat, of peculiar cut, hanging on a peg, with the number "50" in brass upon it. The coat looked ragged and shabby. An old school-book was lying on one of the desks, much tattered, and without a title; but it seemed to treat wholly of Saints' days and festivals of the Church. A flight of stairs,] [169] with a heavy balustrade of carved oak, ascended to a gallery, about eight or nine feet from the floor, which runs two sides of the room, looking down upon it. The room is without a ceiling, and rises into a peaked gable, about twenty feet high. There is a large clock on one side of the room, which is lighted by two windows, each about ten feet wide, one in the gallery, and the other beneath it. There were two benches, or settles with backs (on the plan of the Chair of State, only smaller and plainer) one on each side of the fire-place. An old woman in black passed through the room while I was making my observations, and looked at me, but said nothing. This school[186] was founded in 1563 by Thomas Wheatley, Mayor of Coventry; the revenue is about £900, and admits children of the working classes at eleven years old, clothes and provides for them, and finally apprentices them for seven years. We saw some of the boys playing in the quadrangle, dressed in long blue coats or gowns, with cloth caps on their heads. I know not how the atmosphere of antiquity, and massive continuance from age to age, which was the charm to me in this scene of a charity school-room, can be thrown over it in the description. After noting down these matters, I peeped into the quiet precincts of Bond's hospital, which, no doubt, was more than equally interesting; but the old men were lounging about, or lolling at length, looking [170] very quiet and drowsy, and I had not the heart or the face to intrude among them. There is something altogether strange to an American in these charitable institutions— in the preservation of antique modes and customs which is effected by them; insomuch that, doubtless without at all intending it, the founders have suc-ceeded in preserving a kind of model of their own long past age, down into the midst of ours, and how much later nobody can tell.

We were now rather tired and sated (for old things, and old houses, and all sorts of antiquity, pall upon the taste, after a little while) and went to the railroad, intending to go home. We got into the wrong train, however, and were carried by express, with hurricane speed, to Bra[n]don, where we alighted, and waited a good while for the return train to Coventry. There, too, we had more than an hour to wait, and therefore wandered wearily up into the city again, and took another look at its bustling old streets, in which there seems to be a good emblem of what England itself really is—with a great deal of antiquity in it, and what is new chiefly a modification of the old. The new things are based and supported on the sturdy old things, and often limited and impeded by them; but this antiquity is so massive that there seems to be no means of getting rid of it, without tearing the whole structure of society to pieces. We reached home between eight and nine; and so ends this book.

[171] Monday, July 2^d.

Here are some fly-leaves, however; so I may as well write down (what would else probably be lost) my observations during a visit to Warwick, on Saturday. I set out early in the forenoon, and walked thither, and passing Leicester's Hospital, at the end of the High-street, made bold to inspect it more closely. A small old stone church stands right above the street, compelling the latter to swerve aside in order to pass it; and there is also an arched passage-way (only for pedestrians, I think) through the foundation of the church. This foundation is very lofty; not less—probably more—than twenty feet; and weeds and foxgloves grow in the interstices of the stones, and wave above the street, the dust of which gives them soil to live in. This old gray church is the chapel of the brotherhood, and devoted to their religious services. The Hospital is adjacent to it, and consists of some old gabled edifices, in admirable repair, and ornamented with coats of arms, and devices, and with all the oaken beams of the framework nicely painted out—standing on one side of the street, on the same level with the chapel and surrounding a quadrangle. There were two or three of the brotherhood sitting sleepily on benches, and looking down on the street and whatever passed there—at me, among other objects. They said nothing, as I passed them, and after a moment's hesitation, entered an archway through the side of the front edifice, giving admission to [172] the quadrangle within. An old woman happened to be crossing it, and I asked her whether it was permitted me to enter. She was a plain, neat old woman, who seemed to be in some position of care and superintendance [sic]. She told me very readily and civilly "Oh yes, Sir, you can come in"—and said I was free to look about me—hinting a hope, however, that I would not open the private doors of the brotherhood, as some visitors were in the habit of doing. Under her guidance, I looked into a very spacious, raftered, barn-like hall, in which was an inscription, stating that King James I had here been feasted, in old days. It looks now not very fit for the exercise of princely hospitality, with its naked walls, and, if I remember right, red brick floor; but I presume it may have looked splendidly with its old adornments. It is now used as a wash-room, and for such miscellaneous purposes as occur in a large establishment.

The old lady now left me to myself, and I returned to the quadrangle. It was very quiet, very handsome, and must be a comfortable place for the old people to lounge in, when inclement winds make it inexpedient to be elsewhere. Opposite the arched entrance, the building rises into three ornamented gables; and along this front, a little above the level of the eye, were the following inscriptions—"Honor all men" "Love the Brotherhood"—"Fear God"—"Honor the King"—and over a door, at the side "He that ruleth over men must be just"—all in black letter. There are shrubs against the wall on one side; and on another is a cloistered walk, beneath a covered gallery, up to which leads a balustraded staircase. Three [173] stags' heads and antlers are fastened up against the house, in the cloistered walk. (One inscription—very necessary to be observed among these idle old people—I forgot to set down—"Be kindly affectioned one to another.") Everywhere on the walls—over windows and doors, and on every other place where the slightest reason for it, or no reason at all—were coats of arms, cognizances, and crests—especially the Bear and Ragged Staff was repeated over and over, and over again. All these were emblazoned in their proper colors; and there was likewise a large image of a porcupine, on a heraldic wreath, and apparently the crest of a family. Certainly, the founder, or founders of this old charity seem disposed to take all credit for their beneficence. The founder, originally, was Queen Elizabeth's Earl of Leicester; the hospital was intended for twelve poor men, native or inhabitants of Warwickshire or Gloucestershire, and must not possess more than £5 per annum of their own. They are to wear blue cloth gowns, with the bear and staff embroidered on them.

In the portion of the edifice opposite the entrance, is the residence of the master, a clergyman; and looking [in] at the window (as the old woman had said I might) I saw a low, but exceedingly comfortable looking parlor, very handsomely furnished—a really luxurious place. It had an immense arched fireplace, with all its ancient breadth (extending almost across the room) but so fitted up in modern style that the coal-grate looked very diminutive in the midst. On the cloistered side of the quadrangle, through a curtained window, I saw a great [174] blaze of what was doubtless the kitchen-fire, and heard the bubbling and squeaking of something that was being cooked.

As I was about to depart, another old woman, very plainly dressed, but fat, comfortable, and with a cheerful twinkle in her eyes, entered through the arch, and looked curiously at me. She asked me whether I wished to see the Hospital, and said that the porter was dead, and was to be buried that day; so that the whole could not conveniently be shown me. She offered, however, to show me the apartment occupied by herself and her husband; so we went up the antique staircase, and she led me into a small room, in the corner of the edifice, where sat an old man in a long blue garment, who arose and saluted me very civilly. They both seemed glad to have somebody to talk to; but, ever and anon, the old man nudged his wife—"Don't you be so talkative!" quoth he; and, indeed, he could hardly find space for a word. The old lady told me that they had their lodging and some other advantages free—I forget exactly what—but they appear to be placed, in some degree, on their individual responsibility. They carry on their household matters at their own pleasure, but can have their dinners cooked at the general kitchen, if they like; so that the immense old-fashioned cooking-establishment is probably used for frying, or stewing, or boiling, the humble and scanty messes which these poor people choose to provide for themselves. I must inquire further into this. The old woman told me that her husband had spent his [175] life in the marines. She seemed far more alive, and doubtless enjoyed life a great deal more, than he—partly, no doubt, because she has something to do, her little household matters to attend to, while he sits and mopes, and so has got all eaten up with rust;—not that he seemed miserable either. I mean to go to this Hospital[187] again, and carry my wife.

Afterwards, I went into a museum, chiefly of Natural History, but also containing some old coins and other antiquities. I saw an iron arrow-head, all rusty, which had been dug up in the church-yard of Radford Semele. Probably it had been buried in the body of some man slain in battle, and the rust on it was of his blood. It was fair-day in the town. I sat down to smoke a cigar and drink a glass of ale in an inn, looking on the market-place; and while so occupied, five or six butchers came in, all in white aprons, and each with a steel hanging at his girdle. They appeared to have been dining (it being between 12 & 1) and now took each a glass of gin and a pipe—occasionally looking through the window at their stalls (which were close to the inn) and numbering and naming what joints and other cuts they saw there.

On my way homeward, I took the road by the gate of Warwick Castle, and across the bridge of the Leam, whence is the magnificent view of it.

To day, I shall set out on my return to Liverpool, leaving my family here.

〖*THIRD MANUSCRIPT VOLUME*〗

1855

I LEFT Leamington on Monday, shortly after 12—having been accompanied to the Railway station by Una & Julian, whom I sent away before the train started. While I was waiting for the train, a rather gentlemanly, well-to-do, English-looking man—sat down by me and began to talk of the Crimea, of human affairs in general, of God and his Providence, of the coming troubles of the world, and of spiritualism—in a strange, free way for an Englishman, or, indeed, for any countryman whatever. It was easy to see that he was an enthusiast of some hue or other. He being bound for Birmingham, and I (in the first instance) for Rugby, we soon had to part; but he asked my name, and told me his own—which I did not much attend to, and immediately forgot.

My ride to Rugby, and thence to Lichfield presented nothing to be noted;—the same rich, verdant country, and old trees, which I had grown accustomed to, in a fortnight past. I reached Lichfield (which, I find, is Saxon for the "Field of Dead Bodies" refer[r]ing to two sons of a King of Mercia, who, being converted by Saint Chad, were martyred for their Christian faith)—I reached this scene of the old martyrdom, at, I think, not far [2] [from] four °clock, and put up at the Red Lion Hotel. In these old towns, all the hotels and inns are named after some animal or object, a Lion being as common as any—likewise deer, Bulls of all colors, Bull's Heads &c &c. It is the more modern fashion only to show the names of the Lion, the Bull, or what not; but in these old towns of Warwickshire and the Mid-land counties, you often see the thing or animal represented as the sign. Two or three centuries ago, when these signs were adopted, they would have been intelligible to very few persons in any other form. The Red Lion of Lichfield is a very good, old-fashioned, quiet house. The entrance from the street is by an archway, through which vehicles drive into the inn-yard; and in the two sides of the arch are the doors of the hotel. The interior arrangement is somewhat intricate. To finish off with the hotel, I may add that I got a very good supper, and good breakfast, dinner, and sherry, the next day—no, I forget, I did not get exactly a dinner on either day, but something like it on the day of arrival. The waiter was feminine, and greatly preferable to the male. The cream and butter of this part of England are greatly preferable to those articles in Lancashire, where, indeed, they are much inferior to what we have in America. At this house, I had the great, dull, dingy coffee-room (which did not look at all like a coffee-room) all to myself, and no books but the London Directory, and two Worcestershire, Staffordshire, and Midland Counties Directories, until I bought [3] a guide-book of Lichfield. There seemed to be no other guests;—at least, if so, they were in their private parlors. After all, I have made a mistake about the name of the house; it was not the

Red Lion, but the Swan, and had a picture of a Swan (black, if I remember right) hanging before it.

The streets of Lichfield are very crooked, and the town stands on an ascending surface. There are not so many old gabled houses as in Coventry, but still a great many of them;—and very few of the edifices, I suspect, are really and fundamentally new. They hide their age behind spruce fronts, but are old at heart. The people have an old-fashioned way with them, and stare at a stranger, as if the railway had not yet quite accustomed them to visitors and novelty. The old women, in one or two instances, dropt me a curtsey, as I passed them;—perhaps it was a mere obeisance to one whom, in their antique way, they acknowledged as their better;—perhaps they looked for sixpence at my hands. I gave them the benefit of the doubt, and kept my money.

The Swan Hotel stands, I believe, in Bird-street. At my first sally forth, I turned a corner at a venture, and soon saw a church before me. At this point, the street widens so much (though not very much either) as to be called Saint Mary's Square; and adjacent to it stands the market-house. In this [4] Square, not quite in the middle of it, is a statue of Dr. Johnson, on a stone pedestal, some ten or twelve feet high; the statue is colossal (though perhaps not much bigger than the mountainous Doctor, and sits in a chair, with big books underneath it, looking down on the spectator with a broad, heavy, benignant countenance, very like those of Johnson's portraits. The figure is immensely broad and massive—a ponderosity of stone, not fully humanized, nor finely spiritualized, but yet I liked it well enough, though it looked more like a great boulder than a man. On the pedestal were three bas-reliefs;—the first, Johnson sitting on an old man's shoulders, a mere baby, and resting his chin on the bald head which he embraces with his arms, and listening to Dr. Sacheverell preaching; the second, Johnson carried on the shoulders of two boys to school, another boy supporting him behind; the third, Johnson doing penance at Uttoxeter, the wind and rain beating hard against him, very sad and woe-begone, while some market-people and children gaze in his face, and behind are two old people with clasped hands, praying for him. I think these last must be the spirits of his father and mother; though, in queer proximity, there are dead and living ducks. I never heard of this statue before; it seems to have no reputation as a work of art, and probably may deserve none;—nevertheless, I found it somewhat touching and effective. The statue faces towards the house in which [5] Johnson was born, which stands not more than twenty to forty yards off, on the corner of a street which divides it from the church. It is a tall, three-story house, with a square front, and a roof rising steep and high; on a side view, the house appears to have been cut in two in the midst, there being no slope of the roof on that side. The house is plaistered [sic] and there was a high ladder against it, and painters at work on the front. In the basement corner apartment, what we should call a dry-good[s] store (and the English, I believe, a haberdasher's shop) is kept. There is a side, private entrance, on the cross-street between the house and the church, with much-worn stone steps, and an iron balustrade. I set my foot on the worn steps, and laid my hand on the wall of the house, because Johnson's hand and foot might have been in those same places. I forgot to say that the statue was sculptured by Lucas, and erected in 1838, at the expense of the Reverend Chancellor of the Diocese, Law.

From Saint Mary's Square, one passes by a piece of water, centuries old, but which appears to be artificial, and to occupy the cavity whence the stone for the Cathedral was taken. It makes a very pretty and quiet object, with its green bank, and the trees hanging over it, and a walk beside it; and I saw some boys and little children fishing in it; the latter, I [6] think, with pin-hooks. This pond (perhaps two hundred yards in diameter) is called the Minster Pool. Dam-street leads to it, and runs by the side of it, affording a partial view of the Cathedral; and it was in a house on one side of this street, that Lord Brook[e] was shot from the battlements of the Cathedral, which he was then assaulting, and which had been turned into a royalist fortress. There is said to be a stone, commemorating this fact, on the wall of the house in the porch of which he was shot; but I could see no such memorial.

The Cathedral of Lichfield seemed to me very beautiful indeed. I have heretofore seen no cathedral save that of Chester, and one or two little ones, unworthy of the name, in Wales. No doubt, there may be much more magnificent cathedrals, in England and elsewhere, than this of Lichfield; but if there were no other, I should be pretty well satisfied with this; such beautiful shapes it takes, from all points of view, with its peaks and pinnacles, and its three towers and their lofty spires, one loftier than its fellows; so rich it is with external ornament, of carved stone-work, and statues in a great many niches, though many more are vacant, which I suppose were once filled. I had no idea before (nor, possibly, have I now) what intricate and multitudinous adornment was bestowed on the front of a Gothic church. Above the chief entrance, there is a row of statues of saints, angels, martyrs, or kings, running along that whole front, [7] to the number, no doubt, of more than a score, sculptured in red stone. Then there are such strange, delightful recesses in the great figure of the Cathedral; it is so difficult to melt it all into one idea, and comprehend it in that way; and yet it is all so consonant in its intricacy— it seems to me a Gothic Cathedral may be the greatest work man has yet achieved—a great stone poem. I hated to leave gazing at it, because I felt that I did not a hundredth part take it in and comprehend it; and yet I wanted to leave off, because I knew I never should adequately comprehend its beauty and grandeur. Perhaps you must live with the Cathedral in order to know it; but yet the clerical people connected with it do not seem oppressed with reverence for the edifice.

In the interior of the Cathedral, there is a long and lofty nave, and a transept of the same height and considerable length; and side aisles, and chapels, and dim, holy nooks, which I cannot describe, and did not know the purport of. The nave, I thought, had not the naked, simple, aged majesty of that of Chester; the great pillars, made up of many smaller pillars in a cluster, seem to take away from the sense of a vast space; the great interior is too much broken into compartments, and goes up into a lofty narrowness. I should be more impressed by one great aisle, than by all these intersecting arches, with the rows of pil[8]lars, in long vistas up and down, supporting them. Still, it was good to be there; and I think it a noble fashion, this of erecting monuments in churches;—no matter if the people do not deserve a monument, still the sculptured marble is a good thing. There are a good many monuments in this Cathedral, though the greater part of them are of undistinguished people, clergymen connected with the establishment, or their relatives and families. I saw but two monuments to persons whom I remembered—one to Gilbert Walmsley,[188] and the other to Lady Mary Wortley Montagu,[189] erected by a lady in gratitude for having been benefitted [*sic*] by inoculation. But, then, the white marble sculpture on these old stone walls, in the shape of altars, obelisks, busts, and sarcophagi, has a beautiful effect, and speaks sadly and pleasantly of the dead people; and the white statues that stand or recline in the side chapels have a kind of real life, and you think of them as inhab[i]tants of the spot. Indeed, few spots have older inhabitants. I saw one upper half of a stone lady, the lower half having doubtless been demolished by Cromwell's soldiers; and she is still praying with clasped hands, as she reclines on her half of a slab. There is another very curious monument; it is a reclining skeleton in stone, apparently of great antiquity, and as faithfully represented as an empty anatomy could be in a solid material—very ghastly and Gothic; somewhat Egyptian, too, for it looked much like the mummy, with fleshless [9] arms and shanks, which I saw, the other day, in the Museum at Warwick.

The Cathedral service seems to be performed here twice a day, at 10 °clock and at four. When I first went into the room, the choristers, young and old, had just got through their duty, and came thronging forth from a side door upon the pavement of the Cathedral, dressed in white robes, and looking very fit to haunt and chaunt in that dim, holy edifice. All at once, one of the younger cherubs took off his white gown, and thus transformed himself into a youth of the day, in a modern frock coat and trousers. I do not know that I need to say any more of the Cathedral; except that the Canonical people seem to have made very creditable arrangements for the admittance of the public, and that visiters [*sic*] may enter (in service time) without being bothered with showmen, explaining everything that you do not care about knowing, or that you have learnt for yourself out of a guide-book, for a shilling.

The space about the Cathedral is called the Cathedral Close, and in it are the dwellings of the dignitaries of the Diocese, and perhaps some other respectable persons. The walk along the side of this Close, opposite the principal front of the Cathedral, is quite an illustrious spot;[190]—having been chosen by Farquhar as the locality of one [of] his principal scenes in the Beaux Stratagem, where Aimwell [10] and Archer make acquaintance with the ladies of the Comedy.

Here, too, was the favorite spot of Major André, where he used to walk before he went to America to be hanged. Addison, also, must have once resided here, in his father's house, when the latter was Dean of Lichfield. The house is still standing; and I take it to be a large edifice of brick, which looks stately enough to be the residence of the second di[g]nitary of the Diocese. The episcopal palace is a very noble-looking mansion of stone, built rather in the Italian style—not at all Gothic—and bears on its front the figures 1687. All this row of episcopal, canonical, clerical dwellings, have an air of the greatest quiet, repose, and dignified comfort, looking as if no disturbance or vulgar intrusion could ever come there—with fine, ornamented lawns in front, and beautiful gardens about them, and everything that a saint—and a great many things that a sinner—might desire. And before them, on the outside of their iron fences, lined with rich old shrubbery, extends this beautiful and shadowy walk, over-arched by noble trees, so that it is as good in its way as the arch of the Cathedral nave. From the end of the walk you have a fine view of sites known and noted in the life of Dr. Johnson.

Lichfield has several of those old charities—Hospitals for decayed men and women, schools &c—which form so singular and picturesque a feature in many of the antique English towns. [11] One edifice for the former purpose, at the extremity of Saint John-street, has a very aged aspect, and is supposed to have been one [of] the earliest structures erected after the introduction of chimneys [sic]. A line of half a dozen chimneys [sic] stand like buttresses against its wall, and rise high over its angular roof. Saint Michael's church, in which old Michael Johnson lies buried, stands just without the town, on a rising ground.

All these old, indirect streets, these old gabled houses, these churches, these hospitals, are contrasted with a great number of young soldiers, in red jackets, who lounge about, appear in the door-ways, and narrow passages that open between the houses, walk arm-in-arm smoking pipes, flirt with the girls, and always look as if they had had a little too much ale. Ever and anon, a bugle sounds at some street-corner. These soldiers seem to be new recruits of a militia regiment, and are mostly very youthful—mere boys, hardly grown. I talked with one of them; and he said he enlisted because he had "got a little of the drink" in him, but did not now regret it. He told me that his regiment was at Corfu, but he did not know the name of his commanding officer. Probably this poor, ruddy, thick-skulled English lad will volunteer into the regular army, go to the Crimea, and go to nourish the grass and weeds of that foreign soil. One likes the looks of these peasant boys [12] of old England—stupid, but kindly and homely, and with a suitable com[e]liness of aspect, and exceedingly wholesome.

At about 11, I left Lichfield[191] for Uttoxeter, on a purely sentimental pilgrimage, to see the spot where Johnson performed his penance. Boswell, I think, speaks of the town (pronounced Yute-oxeter) as being about nine miles from Lichfield; but the map would indicate a greater distance, and by rail, passing from one line to another, it was as much as eighteen. Johnson's father could hardly have performed the journey thither, transacted business through the day, and returned at night. I have always had an idea of his trudging thither on foot; but very likely he went in a cart or other vehicle, with his stock of books.

On arriving at the rail-way station, the first thing I saw, in a convenient vicinity, was the tower and tall gray spire of a church. It is but a very short walk from the station up into the town. It was my impression that the market-place of Uttoxeter lay round the church; and if I remember the incident aright, Johnson mentions that his father's bookstall had stood in the market-place, close by the church. But this is not the case. The church has a street, of ordinary width, passing around it; while the market-place, though near at hand, is not really contiguous to the church, nor would there probably be much of the bustle of the market about this edifice, now-a-days. Still a minute's walk would bring a person from the [13] centre of the market-place to the door of the church; and Michael Johnson may very well have had his stall in the angle of the tower and body of it;—not now, indeed, because there is an iron railing round it. The tower and spire of the church look old; but the walls have evidently been renewed since Johnson's time. The market-place is rather spacious, and is surrounded by houses and shops, some old, with red-tiled roofs, others with a pretence of newness, but probably as old as the rest. Unless it were by the church, I could not fix on any one spot more than another, likely to have been the spot where Johnson stood to do his penance.[192] How strange and stupid, that there should be no local memorial of this incident—as beautiful and touching an incident as can be cited out of any human life—no inscription of it on the wall of the church, no statue of the venerable and illustrious penitent in the market-place, to throw a wholesome awe over its earthly business. Such a statue ought almost to have grown up out of the pavement, (and thus have shown me the spot) of its own accord, in the place that was watered by his remorseful tears, and by the rain that dripped from him.

Uttoxeter-market is still held, Wednesday being market-day. The town has no manufactures, nor any business, except, I suppose, as a mart of agricultural produce. It seems [14] to contain some thousands (say two, three, or four) of inhabitants, and consists of indirect streets, paved (side walks and all) with little, round, uncomfortable stones, and bordered with gabled houses, almost entirely of red-brick, and with red brick-roofs. Here and there stands a loftier mansion; but the whole impression of the place is, that the inhabitants are in very moderate circumstances, but comfortable, and that the town undergoes small alteration from cycle to cycle, and may now look much as it did in Johnson's time. The people seemed very idle, in the warm afternoon, and clustered together, about the streets, in idle groups, and stared at me, as they would not, if strangers were more plentiful. I question if an American ever saw Uttoxeter before. What especially struck me was the abundance of inns— scores of them—at every step or two, the sign of the Red Lion, White Hart,

Bull's Head, Mitre, Cross keys—nobody knows which;—probably for the accommodation of the agricultural people on market-day; for if all the inhabitants drank at these inns from morning to night, it would do little towards supporting them.

I got some dinner at one of these rustic inns—bacon and greens and a chop, and a gooseberry pudding, altogether enough for six yeomen, besides ale—all for a shilling and sixpence. There was a man in the public room who seemed to be an artisan from Manchester, and we had some talk together—a shrewd, humorous man, [15] of good information, and making up his own ideas about matters;—loyal, too, I thought, and not caring about changes in church or state. Afterwards I drank a glass of ale at an old inn, called the Nag's Head, standing on the side of the market-place, in a very attainable position, and as likely as any inn could be to have entertained old Michael Johnson, on the days when he went to sell his books. He might have eaten his bacon and greens, and smoked his pipe, in the very room where I sat—a low, ancient room, with a red brick-floor, and a white-washed, cieling [sic], with the bare-rough beams running across—but all extremely neat, and adorned with prints of prize oxen, and other pretty engravings, and with figures of earthen-ware.

I spent I know not how many hours in Uttoxeter, and, to say the truth, was heartily tired of it; my penance being a great deal longer than Dr. Johnson's. It is a pity I did not take the opportunity to repent of my own sins; but I forgot all about them till it was too late. No train passed the town, by which I could get away, till five °clock. As I sat waiting for its appearance, I asked a boy who sat near me—(a school-boy, of some twelve or thirteen years, he seemed to me; and I should take him for a clergyman's son)—I asked him whether he had ever heard the story of Dr. Johnson's standing an hour by that church, whose spire rose before us. He said "no." I asked [16] if no such story was known or talked about in Uttoxeter. He answered, "No, not that he ever heard of!" Just think of the absurd little town, knowing nothing about the incident which sanctifies it to the heart of a stranger from three thousand miles over the sea!—just think of the fathers and mothers of the town, never telling the children this sad and lovely story, which might have such a blessed influence on their young days, and spare them so many a pang hereafter!

From Uttoxeter I rode in the first class to Crewe; thence in the second-class through Warrington to Liverpool, arriving at ½ past 9. P.M. It is foolish ever to travel in the first-class carriages, except with ladies in charge. Nothing is to be seen or learnt there; nobody to be seen but civil and silent gentlemen, sitting on their cushioned dignities. In the second class, it is very different.

N.B. The boy above-mentioned said he resided in Uttoxeter. I mentioned my pilgrimage to Mr. Bright, to-day; and neither had he any recollection of this incident in Johnson's life, nor seemed ever to have heard the name of Uttoxeter.

JULY 6th FRIDAY.

THE day after my arrival, the door of the Consulate opened, and in came the very sociable personage who had accosted me at the Railway Station, in Leamington. He was on his way towards Edinburgh, to deliver a lecture, or a course of lectures, and had called, he said, to talk with me about spiritualism, being [17] desirous of having the judgment of a sincere mind on the subject. In his own mind, I should suppose, he is past the stage of doubt and inquiry; for he told me that, in every action of his life, he is governed by the counsels received from the spiritual world, through a medium. I did not inquire whether the medium had suggested his visit to me. The medium is a small boy. My remarks to him were quite of a sceptical character, in regard to the faith to which he has surrendered himself. It seems he has lived in America, in times past, and had a son born there. He gave me a pamphlet written by himself, on the cure of consumption and other diseases by antiseptic remedies. The author's name is Dr. Washington Evans. I hope he will not bore me any more, though he seems to be a very sincere and good man; but these enthusiasts, who adopt such extragavant ideas, appear to me to lack imagination, instead of being misled by it, as they are generally supposed to be.

JULY 8th, SUNDAY.

AT the Consulate, yesterday, a queer, stupid, good-natured, fat-faced individual came in, dressed in a sky blue, coarse, cut-away coat, and mixed pantaloons, which (both coat and trowsers) seemed rather too small for his goodly size. He turned out to be the Yankee who came to England, a few weeks ago, to see the Queen, on the strength [18] of having sent her his own and his wife's daguerreotype, and having received a note of thanks from her secretary. Having been swindled by a fellow-passenger, he has loafed about here ever since his arrival, unable to get home—and, indeed, unwilling, until he shall have gone to London to see the Queen; and, to support himself, he has parted with all the clothes he brought with him, and thrusts himself into the narrow limits of this sky-blue coat and mixed pantaloons. It is certainly a very odd-looking court-dress; and he hinted, with a melancholy, stupid smile, that he did not look quite fit to see the Queen now. Of course, he wanted my assistance; but it is marvellous, the pertinacity with which he clings to his idea of going to court, and, though starving, will not think of endeavoring to get home, till that has been effected. I laid his absurdity before him, in the plainest terms. "My dear man!" quoth he, with good-natured, simple stubbornness, "if you could but enter into my feelings, and see the business from beginning to end, as I see it!" And this he repeated over and over again. He wished me, if I would not help him myself, to give him the names of some American merchants, to whom he might apply for means to get to London; but I refused to interfere with his affairs in any way, unless he promised to go back immediately to the United States, in case I could get him a passage. Besides his desire [19] to see the Queen, he has likewise (like so many of his countrymen) a fantasy that he is one of the legal heirs of a great English inheritance. No doubt, this dream about the Queen and his English estate has haunted his poor, foolish mind for years and years; and he deems it the strangest and mournfullest perversity of fate, and awfullest cruelty in me, that now—when he has reached England, and has wealth and royal honors almost within his grasp—he must turn back, a poor, penniless, be-fooled simpleton, merely because I will not lend him thirty shillings to get to London. I had never such a perception of a complete booby before, in my life; it made me feel kindly towards him, and yet impatient that such a fool should exist. Finally (as he had not a penny in his pocket, and no means of getting anything to eat) I gave him a couple of shillings, and told him not to let me see him again, till he had made up his mind to get back to America—when I would beg a passage for him if I could. He thanked me, and went away, half-crying, and yet with something like a dull, good-natured smile on his face; still fixed in his inveterate purpose of getting to London to see the Queen![193]

JULY 13th (FRIDAY) NEWBY BRIDGE.

I LEFT Liverpool at ½ past 1 on Saturday last, by the London and North-western railway, for Leamington, arrived between 8 & 9, P.M.; spent Sunday there, and started at [20] about 12 ½ on Monday, for the English lakes, taking the whole family. We should not have [taken] this journey, just now; but I had an official engagement, which it was convenient to combine with a pleasure excursion. The first night, we arrived at Chester, and put up at the Albion Hotel, where we found ourselves very comfortable. We took the rail at twelve, next day, and went as far as Milnthorpe station, where (at five or six °clock) we took seats in an old-fashioned English stage-coach, and came to Newby Bridge. I suppose there are not many of these machines now running on any road in Great Britain; but this appears to be the genuine article in all respects, and especially in the round, ruddy coachman, well-moistened with ale, good-natured, courteous, with a proper sense of his dignity and important position. Una, Julian, and I, mounted on top; Mamma, Nurse, and Rosebud, got inside; and we bowled off merrily up towards the hearts of the hills. It was more than half-past nine when we arrived at Newby Bridge, and alighted at the Swan Hotel, where we still are.

It is a very agreeable place; not striking as to scenery, but with a pleasant, rural aspect. A stone bridge, of five arches, crosses the river Leven (which is the communication between Windermere lake and Morecambe bay) close to the house, which sits low and well-sheltered in the lap of hills— an old-fashioned inn, where the landlord and his people have a simple and friendly way of dealing with [21] their guests, and yet provide them with all sorts of facilities for being comfortable. They load our supper and breakfast tables with trout, cold beef, ham, toast muffins, et cetera; and give us three fine courses for dinner, and excellent wine—the cost of all which remains to be seen. This is not one of the celebrated stations among the lakes; but twice a day the stage coach passes from Milnthorpe towards Ulverston, and twice returns; and three times a little steamer passes to-and-fro between our hotel and the head of the lake. Young ladies in broad-brimmed hats stroll about, or row on the river, in the light shallops of which there are abundance;—sportsmen sit on the benches under the windows of the hotel, arranging their fishing-tackle;—phaetons and post chaises, (with postillions in scarlet jackets and white breeches, with one white-topt boot, and the other leathered high in the leg, to guard against friction between the horses) dash up to the door;—morning and night comes the stage-coach, and we inspect the outside passengers, almost face to face with us, from our parlor window, up one pair of stairs;—little boys (and Julian among them) spend hours on hours, fishing in the clear, shallow river, for the perch, chubs and minnows that may be seen flashing, like gleams of light, over the flat stones with which the bottom is paved. I cannot answer for the other boys; but Julian catches nothing.

[22] There are a good many trees on the hills and roundabout; and pleasant roads loitering along by the gentle river-side; and it has been so sunny and warm, since we came here, that we shall have quite a genial recollection of the place, if we leave it before the skies have time to frown. The day after we came, Mamma, with Una, Julian, and myself, climbed a pretty high, and very steep hill, through a path shadowed with trees and shrubbery, up to a tower, from the summit of which we had a wide view of mountain scenery, and the greater part of Windermere. This lake is a lovely little pool among the hills, long and narrow, beautifully indented with tiny bays and headlands; and when we saw it, it was one smile (as broad a smile as its narrowness allowed) with really brilliant sunshine. All the scenery we have yet met with is in excellent taste, and keeps itself within very proper bounds—never getting too wild and ragged to shock the sensibilities of cultivated people, as American scenery is apt to do. On the rudest surfaces of English earth, there is seen the effect of centuries of civilization; so that you do not quite get at naked Nature anywhere. And then every point of beauty is so well known, and has been described so much, that one must need look through other people's eyes, and feels as if he were looking at a picture rather than a reality. Man has, in [23] short, got entire possession of Nature here; and I should think young men might sometimes yearn for a fresher draught. But an American likes it.

Yesterday, we took a phaeton and went to Furness Abbey—a ride of about sixteen miles, passing along the course of the Leven, to Morecambe bay, and through Ulverston, and other villages. These villages all look antique; and the smallest of them generally are formed of such close, contiguous clusters of houses, and have such narrow and crooked streets, that they give you the idea of a metropolis in miniature. The houses along the road (of which there are not many, except in the villages) are almost invariably old, built of stone, and covered with a light gray plaister [sic];—generally, they have a little flower garden in front, and, often, honeysuckle, roses, or some other sweet and pretty rustic adornment, is flowering over the porch. I have hardly had such images of simple, quiet, rustic comfort and beauty, as from the look of these houses; and the whole impression of our winding and undulating road, bordered by hedges, luxuriantly green, and not too closely clipt, accords with this aspect. There is nothing arid in an English landscape; and one cannot but fancy that the same may be true of English rural [24] life. The people look wholesome and well-to-do—not specimens of hard, dry, sunburnt muscle, like our yeomen—and are kind and civil to strangers, sometimes making a little inclination of the head in passing. Miss Martineau, however, does not seem to think well of their mental and moral condition.[194]

We reached Furness Abbey about 12. There is a railway-station close by the ruins; and a new hotel stands within the precincts of the Abbey-grounds; and continually there is the shriek, the whiz, the rumble, the bell-ringing, denoting the arrival of the trains, and passengers alight and step at once (as their choice may be) into the refreshment-room to get a glass of ale or cigar, or upon the gravelled paths of the lawn, leading to the old broken walls and arches of the Abbey. The ruins are extensive, and the enclosure of the Abbey is stated to have covered a space of sixty-five acres. It is impossible to describe them. The most interesting part is that which was formerly the church, and which, though now roofless, is still surrounded by walls, and has the remnants of the pillars that formerly supported the intermingling curves of the arches. The floor is all overgrown with grass, strewn with fragments and capitals of pillars. It was a great and stately edifice, the length of the nave and choir having been nearly three hundred feet, [25] and that of the transept more than half as much. The pillars along the nave were alternately a round, solid one, and a clustered one; now, what remains of some of them is even with the ground; others present a stump just high enough to form a seat, and others are perhaps a man's height from the ground—and all are mossy and with grass and weeds rooted in their chinks, and here and there a tuft of flowers giving its tender little beauty to their decay. The material of the edifice is a soft, red stone; and it is now extensively overgrown with a lichen, of a very light gray hue, which at a little distance makes the walls look as if they had long ago been white-washed, and now had partially returned to their original color. I never saw anything like the immense, the noble arches of the nave and transept; there were four of them together, supporting a tower which has long since disappeared—arches loftier than I ever conceived to have been made by man. Very possibly, in some cathedral that I have seen, or am yet to see, there may be arches as stately as these; but I doubt whether they can ever show to such advantage in a perfect edifice as they do in this ruin—most of them broken—only one, as far as I recollect, still completing its sweep. In this state, they [26] suggest a greater majesty and beauty than any human work can show—the crumbling traces of the half obliterated design producing somewhat of the effect of the first idea of anything admirable, when it dawns upon the mind of an artist or a poet—an idea which, do what he may, he is sure to fall short of.

In the middle of the choir is a much dilapidated monument of a cross-legged knight (a crusader, of course) in armor, very rudely executed; and up against the wall lie two or three more bruised and battered warriors, with square helmets on their heads, and visors down. Nothing can be uglier than these figures; the sculpture of those days seems to have been far behind the architecture. And yet they knew how to put a grotesque expression into the faces of their images, and we saw some fantastic shapes and heads at the lower points of arches, which would do to copy into Punch. In the chancel, just at the point below where the high altar stood, was the burial-place of the old barons of Kendal. The broken crusader perhaps represents one of them; and some of their stalwart bones might be found, by digging down. Against the wall of the choir, near the vacant space where the altar was, are some stone seats with canopies richly carved in stone, all quite perfectly preserved; these were where the priest used to sit [27] at intervals, during the celebration of mass. Conceive all these shattered walls, with here and there an arched door, or the great arched vacancy of a window—these broken stones and monuments scattered about—these rows of pillars up and down the nave—these arches, through which a giant might have stept, and not needed to bow his head, unless in reverence to the sanctity of the place—conceive it all with such verdure, and embroidery of flowers, as the gentle, kindly moisture of the English climate procreates on all old things, making them more beautiful old than new—conceive it with the grass for sole pavement of the long and spacious aisle, and the sky above for the only roof. The sky, to be sure, is more majestic than the tallest of those arches; and yet these latter perhaps make the stronger impression of sublimity, because they translate the sweep of the sky to our finite comprehensions. It was a most beautiful, warm, sunny day; and the ruins had all the pictorial advantage of bright light and deep shadows. I must not forget that birds flew in and out among the recesses, and chirped and warbled, and made themselves at home there. Doubtless, the birds of the present generation are the posterity of those who first settled in the ruins, after the [28] Reformation, and perhaps the old monks of a still earlier day may have watched them building about the Abbey, before it was a ruin at all.

We had an old description of the Abbey[195] with us, aided by which we traced out the principal parts of the edifice; such as the church, as already mentioned, and contiguous to this the Chapter House, which is better preserved than the church;—also the kitchen, and the room where the monks met to talk, and the range of wall where their cells probably were. I never before had given myself the trouble to form any distinct idea of what an abbey or monastery was—a place where holy rites were daily and continually to be performed, with places to eat and sleep contiguous and convenient, in order that the monks might always be at hand to perform those rites. They lived only to worship, and therefore lived under the same contiguity of roof with their place of worship, which, of course, was the principal object in the edifice, and hallowed the whole of it. We found, too, at one end of the ruins, what is supposed to have been a school-house for the children of the tenantry or villains of the Abbey; all round this room is a bench of stone against the wall, and the pedestal also of the master's seat. There are likewise the ruins of the mill; and the [29] mill-stream, which is just as new as ever it was, still goes murmuring and babbling past the abbey, and passes under two or three old bridges, consisting of a low, gray arch, overgrown with grass and shrubbery. That stream was the most fleeting and vanishing thing about the ponderous and high-piled Abbey; and yet it has outlasted everything else, and might still outlast another such edifice, and be none the worse for wear.

There is not a great deal of ivy upon the walls; and though an ivied wall is a beautiful object, yet it is better not to have too much—else it is but one wall of unbroken verdure, on which you can see none of the sculptured ornaments, nor any of the hieroglyphics of time. A sweep of ivy here and there, with the gray wall everywhere showing through, makes the better picture; and I think that nothing is so effective as the little bunches of flowers, a mere handful, that grow in spots where their seeds have been carried by the wind, ages ago.

I have made a miserable botch of this description; it is no description, but merely an attempt to preserve something of the impression it made on me— and in this I do not seem to have succeeded at all. I liked the contrast between the sombreness of the old walls, and the [30] sunshine falling through them and gladdening the grass that floored the aisles; also, I liked the effect of so many idle and cheerful people, strolling into the haunts of the dead monks, and going babbling about and peering into the dark nooks; and listening to catch some idea of what the building was, from a clerical-looking personage who was explaining it to a party of his friends. I don't know how well acquainted this gentleman might be with the subject; but he seemed anxious not to impart his knowledge too extensively, and gave a pretty direct rebuff to an honest man who ventured an inquiry of him. In short, I think that the railway, and the hotel within the abbey-grounds, add to the charm of the place. A moonlight, solitary visit might be very good, too, in its way; but I believe that one great charm and beauty of antiquity is, that we view it out of the midst of quite another mode of life;—and the more perfectly this can be done, the better. It can never be done more perfectly than at Furness Abbey, which is in itself a very sombre scene, and stands, moreover, in the midst of a melancholy valley, the Saxon name of which means the Vale of Deadly Night Shade.[196]

The entrance to the stable-yard of the hotel is [31] beneath an old pointed arch, of Saxon architecture; and on one side of this stands a little old building looking like a chapel, but which may, for aught I know, have been a porter's lodge. The abbot's residence was in this quarter; and the clerical personage before alluded to spoke of these as the oldest part of the ruins.

About half a mile on the hither side of the Abbey stands the village of Dalton, in which is a castle built on a Roman foundation, and which was afterwards used by the Abbots (in their capacity as feudal lords) as a prison. The

Abbey was founded about 1127, by King Stephen, before he came to the throne; and the faces of himself and his queen are still to be seen on one of the walls. I know not whose property it is now.

We had a very agreeable ride home (our ride thither had been uncomfortably sunny and hot) and stopt at Ulverston to buy a pair of shoes for Julian, and some drawing-books and stationery. As we passed through this little town in the morning, it was all alive with the throng and bustle of the weekly market; and though this had ceased, on our return, the streets still looked animated, because the heat of the day drew most of the population, I should imagine, out of doors. Old men look very antiqua[32]ted here, in their old fashioned coats and breeches, sunning themselves by the wayside. We reached home somewhere about eight °clock—home I see I have called it; and it seems as homelike a spot as any we have found in England, the old inn, close by the bridge, beside the clear river, pleasantly overshadowed by trees. It is entirely English, and like nothing that one sees in America; and yet I feel as if I might have lived here a long while ago, and had now come back because I retained pleasant recollections of it. The children, too, make themselves at home. Julian spends his time from morning to night, fishing for minnows or trout, and catching nothing at all; and Una and Rosebud have been riding between field and barn, in a hay-cart. The roads give us beautiful walks along the river-side, or wind away among the gentle hills; and if we had nothing else to look at in these walks, the hedges and stone-fences would afford interest enough—so many and pretty are the flowers, roses, honey-suckle, and other sweet things, and so abundantly does the moss and ivy grow among the old stones of the fences, which would never have a single shoot of vegetation on them, in America, till the very end of time. But here, no sooner is a stone fence built, than Nature sets to work to make it a part of herself; she adopts it, and adorns it as if it were her own child. A little sprig of ivy may be seen creeping up the side, and clinging fast with its many feet; [33] a tuft of grass roots itself between two of the stones, where a little dust from the road has been moistened into soil for it; a small bunch of fern grows in another such crevice; a deep, soft, green moss spreads itself over the top and all along the sides of the fence; and wherever nothing else will grow, lichens adhere to the stones and variegate their hues. Finally, a great deal of shrubbery is sure to cluster along its extent, and take away all hardness from the outline; and so the whole stone-fence looks as if God had had at least as much to do with it as man.[197] The trunks of the trees, too, exhibit a similar parasitical vegetation. Parasitical is an unkind phrase to bestow on this beautiful love and kindred which seems to exist here, between one plant and thing another [sic]; the strong thing being always ready to give support and sustenance, and the weak thing to repay with beauty, so that both are the richer;—as in the case of ivy and woodbine clustering up the trunk of a tall tree, and adding Corinthian grace to its lofty strength.[198]

Mr. White (our landlord) has lent us a splendid work with engravings,[199] illustrating the antiquities of Furness Abbey. I gather from it that the hotel must have been rebuilt or repaired from an old manor house, which was itself built by a family of Prestons, after the Reformation, and was a renewal from the Abbot's residence. Much of the edifice, probably, as it exists now, may have [34] formed part of the original one; and there are bas-reliefs of scripture-subjects, sculptured in stone, and fixed in the wall of the dining-room, which have been there since the Abbot's time. This author thinks that what we had supposed to be the school-house (on the authority of an old book) was really the building for the reception of guests, with its chapel. He says that the tall arches in the church are sixty feet high. The Earl of Burlington, I believe, is the present proprietor of the Abbey.

JULY 16th (MONDAY)

ON Saturday, we left Newby Bridge, and came by steamboat up Windermere lake to Lowwood Hotel, where we now are. The foot of the lake is just above Newby Bridge; and it widens from that point, but never to such a breadth that objects are not pretty distinctly visible from shore. The little steamer stops at two or three places in the course of its voyage;—the principal being Bowness, which has a little bustle and air of business about it, proper to the principal port on the lake. There were several small yachts on the lake, and many skiffs rowing about. The banks are everywhere beautiful, and the lake is one portion strewn with little islands, few of which are large enough to be inhabitable, but they all seem to be appropriated and kept in the neatest order. As yet, I have seen no wildness; everything is perfectly subdued and polished, and imbued with human taste; except, indeed, the outlines of the hills, which continue very much the same as God made them. As we ap[35]proached the head of the lake, the congregation of great hills in the distance became very striking. The shapes of these English mountains are certainly far more picturesque than those which I have seen (as I remember them) in America. There, their summits are almost invariably rounded; they are great hillocks—great bunches of earth, all very similar in their development. Here, they have great variety of shape, rising into peaks, falling in abrupt precipices, stretching along in zig-zag outlines; and thus making the most of their not very gigantic masses to produce a very striking effect.

We left Newby Bridge, and arrived at the Lowwood Hotel, (which is very near the head of the lake) not long after two °clock. This house stands almost on the shore of Windermere, with only a green and gravel-walked lawn between;—an extensive hotel, covering a good deal of ground, but low, and rather village-innlike, than lofty with four or five stories, like an American hotel. We found the house so crowded as to afford us no very comfortable accommodations, either as to parlor or sleeping-rooms; and we find nothing like the home-feeling into which we at once settled down at Newby Bridge. There is a very pretty vicinity; a fine view of mountains to the north-west, sitting together in a family group, sometimes in full sunshine, sometimes with only a golden gleam on one or two of them, sometimes all in a veil [36] of cloud, from which here and there a great dusky head creates itself, while you are looking at a dim obscurity. Nearer, there are high, green slopes, well-wooded, but with such decent and well-behaved wood as you perceive has grown up under the care of man; still no wildness, no raggedness;—as how should there be, when, every half-mile or so, a porter's lodge, or a gentleman's gateway, indicates that the whole region is used up for villas. On the opposite shore of the lake, there is a mimic castle (which I suppose I might have mistaken for a real one, two years ago) a great, foolish toy of gray stone.

A steamboat comes to the pier as much as six times a day; and stage-coaches and omnibusses [sic] stop at the door still oftener, communicating with Ambleside or the town of Windermere, and with the railway, which opens London and all the world to us. We get no knowledge of our fellow-guests, all of whom, like ourselves, live in their own circles, and are just as remote from us as if the lake lay between. The only word I have spoken since arriving here (except to my own family or a waiter) was to one of two young pedestrians, who met me on a walk, and asked me the distance to Lowwood Hotel. "Just beyond here," said I; and I might stay here for months, no doubt, without occasion to speak again.

Yesterday forenoon, Julian and I walked to Ambleside, distant barely two miles—a little town, chiefly of modern aspect, built on [37] a very uneven hillside, and with very irregular streets and lanes, which bewilder the stranger as much as those of a larger city. Many of the houses, as I remember, look old, and are probably the cottages and farm-houses, which composed the rude hill-side village, a century ago; but there are stuccoed shops and dwellings, such as may have been built within a year or two; and three hotels, one of which has the look of the good old village inn, and the others are fashionable or commercial establishments. Through the midst of the village comes tumbling and rumbling a mountain-streamlet, rushing through a deep, rocky dell, gliding under an old stone-arch, and turning (when occasion calls) the great, black wheel of a water-mill. This is the only very striking feature of the village (and this might very well have escaped my notice)—the stream from the steep hill-side taking its rough pathway to the lake, as it used to do before the poets had made this region fashionable.

In the evening, just before eight °clock, I took a walk alone, by a road which goes up the hill back of our hotel, and what I supposed might be the road to the town of Windermere. But it went up and higher, and, for the mile or two (or two or three) that it led me along, winding up the hillside, I saw no traces of a town; and at last the road turned into what seemed a valley between two high ridges, leading quite away [38] from the lake, within view of which the town of Windermere is situated. It was a very lonely road, though as smooth, hard, and well-kept, as any thoroughfare in the suburbs of a city; hardly a dwelling on either side, except one, half-barn, half farm-house; and one gentleman's gateway near the beginning of the road, and another more than a mile higher up. At two or three points, there were stone-barns, which are here built with great solidity. At one place, there was a painted board, announcing that a field of five acres was to be sold, and referring those desirous of purchasing to a solicitor in London. The lake-country is but a London-suburb. Nevertheless, this walk was lonely and lovely; the copse and the broad-hill-side, the glimpses of the lake, the great, misty company of pikes and fells, beguiled me into a sense of something like solitude; and the bleating of the sheep, remote and near, had a like tendency. Gaining the summit of the hill, I had the best view of Lake Windermere which I have yet obtained;—the best, I should think, that can be had, though, being towards the south, it brings the softer instead of the more striking features of the landscape into view. But it shows nearly the whole extent of the lake, all the way from Lowwood to just above Newby Bridge; and I think there can hardly be anything more beautiful in the world. The water was like a strip and gleam of sky, fitly set among lovely slopes of [39] earth. It was no broader than many a river; and yet you saw at once that it could be no river, its outline being so different from that of a running stream, not straight, nor winding, but stretching to one side or the other, as the shores made room for it;—a thing that could not make its own way through the world, but must take what was allowed it.

This morning, it is rainy; and we are not very comfortable or contented, being all confined to our little parlor, which has a broken window, against which I have pinned the "Times," to keep out the damp, chill air. Una has been ill with some kind of humor, resulting from her having been overheated at Newby Bridge. We have no books (except guide-books) no means of amusement, nothing to do. There are no newspapers; and I shall remember Lowwood not very agreeably;—as far as we are concerned, it is a scrambling, ill ordered hotel, with insufficient attendance, wretched sleeping accommodations, a pretty fair victualling-department, but German silver forks and spoons. Nothing that we eat tastes very good; and yet there is no really definite fault to be found.

Since writing the above, I have found the first volume (of seven) of Sir Charles Grandison, and two of G. P. R. James's works, in the Coffee-room. The days pass heavily here, and leave behind them a sense of having answered no very good purpose. They are long [40] enough, at all events; for the sun does not set till after eight °clock, and rises I know not when. One of the most remarkable distinctions between England and the United States is, the ignorance into which we fall of whatever is going on in the world, the moment we get away from the great thoroughfares and centres of life. In Leamington, we heard no news from week's end to week's end, and knew not where to find a newspaper; and here, the case is neither better nor worse. The rural people really seem to take no interest in public affairs; at all events, they have no intelligence on such subjects. It is possible that the cheap newspapers may, in time, find their way into the cottages; or, at least, in the country taverns; but it is not at all the case now. If they generally know that Sebastopol is besieged, that is the extent of their knowledge. The public life of America is lived through the mind and heart of every man in it; here, the people feel that they have nothing to do with what is going forward, and, I suspect, care little or nothing about it. Such things they permit to be the exclusive affair of the higher classes.

The arches of Furness Abbey owe their peculiar stateliness and impression of great height, to the tall pillars on which the arch is reared; all other arches, so far as I remember, are all sweep and segment of circles, and have no effect of lofty elevation.

[41] In front of our hotel, on the lawn between us and the lake, there are two trees which we have hitherto taken to be yews; but on examining them more closely, I find that they are pine-trees,²⁰⁰ and quite dead and dry, although they have all the aspect of dark, rich life. This is the verdure of two great plants of ivy, which have twisted like gigantic snakes round the pine-trees, and clambering up—perhaps throttling the life out of them—have put out branches, and made tops of thick verdure, so that, at a little distance, it is quite impossible not to mistake them for genuine trees. The trunks of the ivy-plants must be more than a foot in circumference; and the observer feels as if they had stolen the life that belonged to the pines. The dead branches of the pine stick forth horizontally, through the ivy-boughs, from one of the trees; the other has nothing but the ivy-boughs, and, in shape, a good deal resembles a poplar. When the pine-trunks shall have quite crumbled away, the ivy-stems will doubtless have gained sufficient strength to sustain themselves independently.

JULY 19ᵗʰ, THURSDAY.

YESTERDAY morning, Mamma went down the lake, in the steamboat, to take Una, baby, and Nurse, to Newby Bridge, where they are to stay while the three rest of us make a tour through the lake region. After Mamma's departure, and [42] when I had finished some letters, Julian and I set out on a walk which finally brought us—through much delightful shade of woods, and past beautiful rivulets, or brooklets, and over many uphills and down—to Bowness. This chief harbor of the lakes seemed all alive and bustling with tourists; it being a sunny and pleasant day, so that they were all abroad like summer-insects. The town is a confused and irregular little place, of very uneven surface; there is an old church in it, and nothing else that I remember particularly, unless it be two or three large hotels. We staid there perhaps half an hour, and then went to the steamboat pier, where, shortly, a steamer arrived, with music sounding, on the deck of which, with her back to us, sat a lady in a grey travelling-cloak. Julian cried out "Mamma, mamma!"—to which the lady deigned no notice; but he repeating it, she turned round, and was as much surprised, no doubt, at seeing her husband and son, as if this little lake had been the great ocean, and we encountering from opposite shores of it. We soon steamed back to Lowwood, and took a car thence for Rydal and Grasmere, after a cold luncheon. I forgot to say that, at Bowness, I met Miss Charlotte Cushman, who has been staying at the Lowwood hotel with us since Monday, without either party being aware of it.

Our road to Rydal lay through Ambleside, which is certainly a very pretty little town, and looks cheerfully in a sunny day. We saw Miss Martineau's residence, called the Knoll, standing high up on a [43] hillock, and having at its foot a Methodist chapel—for which, or whatever place of Christian worship, this good lady can have no great occasion. We stopt a moment in the street below her house, and deliberated a little whether to call on her; but concluded otherwise.

After leaving Ambleside, the road winds in and out among the hills, and soon brings us to a little sheet (or napkin rather than a sheet) of water, which the driver tells us is Rydal lake. We had already heard it was but three quarters of a mile long, and one quarter broad; still, having an idea of considerable size in our minds, we had inevitably drawn the ideal mass of its physical proportions on a somewhat corresponding scale. It certainly did look very small; and I said, in my American scorn, that I could carry it away bodily in a porringer.[201] It is nothing but a little, grassy-bordered pool, among the surrounding hills, which ascend directly from its margin; so that one might fancy it, not a permanent body of water, but a rather extensive accumulation of recent rain. Moreover, it was rippled with a breeze, and so, as I remember it (though the sun shone) looked dull and sulky, like a child out of humor. Now, the best thing these little ponds can do, is, to keep perfectly calm and smooth, and not to attempt to show off any airs of their own, but to content themselves with serving [44] as a mirror for whatever of beautiful or picturesque there may be in the scenery around them. The hills about Rydal-water are not very lofty, but are sufficiently so as objects of every day view—objects to live with;—and they are craggier than those we have hitherto seen, and more bare of wood; which, indeed, could hardly grow on some of their precipitous sides.

On the roadside, as we reach the foot of the lake (which is the part first reached from Ambleside) stands a spruce and rather large house, of modern aspect, but with several gables, and much overgrown with ivy; a most pretty and comfortable house, built, adorned, and seen to, with commendable taste. We inquired whose it was; and the driver said it was "Mr. Wardsworth's!"—and that Mrs. Wardsworth was still residing there. So we were much delighted to have seen his abode; and as we were to stay the night at Grasmere, about two miles farther on, we determined to come back and inspect as particularly as should be allowable. Accordingly, after taking quarters at Brown's Hotel (a very good house, on a retired and picturesque site, with fine mountain-views about it) we got into our return-car, and reaching the head of Rydal water, alighted to walk through this familiar scene of so many years of Wordsworth's life. We ought to have seen DeQuincey's former residence and Hartley Coleridge's cottage, I believe, on our way, but were not aware of it at the time. Near the lake there is a stone-quarry, [45] and a cavern of some extent, artificially formed, no doubt, by taking out the stone. Above the shore of the lake, not a great way from Wordsworth's residence, there is a flight of steps hewn in a rock, and ascending to a rocky seat, whence a good view of Rydal water, such as it is, may be attained; and as Wordsworth has probably sat there hundreds of times, so did we ascend and sit down, and look at the hills, and at the flags on the lake's shore.

Reaching the house that had been pointed out to us as Wordsworth's residence, we began to peer about, at its front and gables, and over the garden-wall, on both sides of the road—quickening up our enthusiasm as much as we could, and meditating to pilfer some flower or ivy-leaf from the house or its vicinity, to be kept as sacred memorials. At this juncture, a man approached who announced himself as the gardener of the place, and said that he could show us Wordsworth's garden;—and said, too, that this was not Wordsworth's house at all, but the residence of Mr. Ball, a Quaker gentleman;—but that his grounds adjoined Wordsworth's, and that he had liberty to take visitors through the latter. How queer, if we should have carried away ivy-leaves and tender recollections from this domicile of a respectable quaker. The gardener was an intelligent young man, of pleasant, sociable, and respectful [46] address; and as we went along, he talked about Wordsworth, whom he had known, and who, he said, was very familiar with the country-people. He led us through his master's grounds, up a steep hillside, by winding, gravelled walks, with summer-houses at points favorable for that purpose. It was a very shady and pleasant spot, containing about an acre of ground, and all turned to much account by the manner of laying out; so that it seemed more than it really is. In one place (on a little, smooth slab of slate, let into a rock) there is an inscription by Wordsworth, which I think I have read in his works, claiming kindly regards from those who visit the spot, after his departure, because many trees had here been spared, at his intercession.[202] Wordsworth's own grounds (or rather his ornamental garden) is separated from Mr. Ball's only by a wire-fence, or some such barrier; and the gates have no fastening; so that the whole appears like one possession, and doubtless was so as regarded the poet's walks and enjoyments. We approached by such winding paths that I hardly know how the house stands in relation to the road; but, after much circuity, we really did see Wordsworth's residence, an old house, with an uneven ridge-pole, built of stone, no doubt, but plaistered [sic] over of some neutral tint;—a house that would not have been remarkably pretty in itself, but so delightfully situated, so secluded, so hedged about with shrubbery and adorned with flowers, so ivy-grown on one [47] side, so beautified with many years of the personal care of him who lived in it and loved it—that it seemed the very place for a poet's residence; and as if, while he lived so long in it, his poetry had manifested itself in flowers, shrubbery, and ivy. I never smelt such a delightful fragrance of flowers as there was all through the garden. In front of the house, there is a circular terrace, of two ascents, in raising which Wordsworth had himself performed much of the labor; and here there are seats, from which is obtained a fine view down the valley of the Rothay, and Windermere in the distance—a view of several miles, and which we did not think of seeing, after winding among the hills so far from the lake. It is very beautiful and picturelike. While we sat here, Mamma happened to refer to the ballad of little Barbara Lewthwaite;[203] and the gardener said that little Barbara had died not a great while since, an elderly woman, leaving grown up children behind her. Her marriage name was Thompson; and the gardener believed that there was nothing remarkable in her character.

There is a summer-house at one extremity of Wordsworth's ground, in deepest shadow, but with glimpses of mountain views through trees which shut it in, and which have spread intercepting boughs since Wordsworth died. It is lined with pine-cones, in a pretty way enough, but of doubtful taste. I rather wonder [48] that people of real taste should help Nature out, and beautify her (or, perhaps, rather, *prettify*) so much as they do—opening vistas, showing one thing, hiding another, making a scene picturesque whether or no. I cannot rid myself of the feeling that there is something false—a kind of humbug—in all this. At any rate, the traces of it do not contribute to my enjoyment; and, indeed, it ought to be done so exquisitely as to leave no trace. But I ought not to criticise in any way a spot which gave me so much pleasure, and where it is good to think of Wordsworth, in quiet days past, walking in his home-shadow of trees which he knew, and training flowers, and trimming shrubs, and chaunting in an under-tone his own verses, up and down the undulating walks.

The gardener gave Julian a cone, from the summer-house (it had fallen on the seat) and Mamma got some mignionette [*sic*], and leaves of laurel and ivy; and we wended our way back to the hotel. Wordsworth was not the owner of this house; it being the property of Lady Fleming. Mrs. Wordsworth still lives there, and is now at home.

5 °clock. All day it has been cloudy and showery, with now and then thunder; the mists hang low on the surrounding hills, adown which, at various points, we can see the snow-white fall of little streamlets—forces, they call them here—swollen by the rain. An overcast day is not so gloomy in a hill-country as in the lowlands; there are [49] more breaks, more transfusion of sky-light, through the gloom, as has been the case to-day; and then, too, (as I found in Lenox) we get better acquainted with clouds by seeing at what height they lie on the hillsides, and find that the difference betwixt a fair day and a cloudy and rainy one is very superficial, after all. Nevertheless, rain is rain, and wets a man just as much among the mountains as anywhere else; so we have been kept within doors all day, till an hour or so ago, when Julian and I went down to the village in quest of the post-office.

We took a path that leads from the hotel across the fields, and coming into a road, crosses the Rothay by a one-arched bridge, and passes the village-church. The Rothay is very swift and turbulent to-day, and hurries along with foam-specks on its surface, filling its banks from brim to brim, a stream of perhaps twenty feet across. Perhaps more; for I am willing that the good little river should have all it can fairly claim; it is the Saint Lawrence of

several of these English lakes, through which it flows, and carries off their
superfluous waters. In its haste, and with its rushing sound, it was pleasant
both to see and hear; and it sweeps by one side of the old churchyard where
Wordsworth lies buried—the side where his grave is made. The Church of
Grasmere is a very plain structure, with a low body, on one side of which is a
low porch with a pointed arch; the tower is [50] square, and looks ancient; but
the whole is overlaid with plaister [sic] of a buff or pale yellow hue. It was
originally built, I suppose, of rough, shingly stones, as many of the houses
hereabouts are now; and, like many of them, the plaister [sic] is used to give a
sort of finish. We found the gate of the church-yard wide open; and the grass
was lying on the graves, having probably been mowed yesterday. It is but a
small churchyard, and with few monuments of any pretension in it, most of
them being slate headstones standing erect. From the gate at which we entered,
a distinct foot track leads to the corner nearest the river-side; and I turned
into it by a sort of instinct, the more readily as I saw a tourist-looking man
approaching from that point, and a woman looking among the grave stones.
Both of these persons had gone by the time I came up; so that Julian and I
were left to find Wordsworth's grave all by ourselves.

Right at this corner of the churchyard, there is a hawthorn-bush, or tree,
the extremest branches of which stretch as far as where Wordsworth lies.
This whole corner seems to be devoted to himself and his family and friends;
and they all lie very close together, side by side, and head to feet, as room
could conveniently be found. Hartley Coleridge lies a little behind, in the
direction of the church, his feet being towards Wordsworth's head, who lies
in the row of those of his own blood. I found out Hartley Coleridge's grave
sooner than [51] Wordsworth's; for it is of marble, and, though simple enough,
has more of sculptured device about it—having been erected, as I think the
inscription states, by his brother and sister. Wordsworth has only the very
simplest slab of slate with "William Wordsworth," and nothing else upon it.
As I recollect it, it is the midmost grave of the row. It is, or has been, well
grass-grown; but the grass is quite worn away from the top, though sufficiently
luxuriant at the sides; it looks as if people had stood upon it, and so does the
grave next to it, which I believe is one of his children. I plucked some grass
and weeds from it; and as he was buried within so few years, they may fairly
be thought to have drawn their nutriment from Wordsworth's mortal remains—
and I gathered them from just above his head. There is no fault to be found
with his grave—within view of the hills, within sound of the river murmuring
near by—no fault, except that he is packed so closely with his kindred; and,
moreover, that, being so old a churchyard, the earth over him must all have
been human once. He might have had fresh earth to himself; but he chose this
grave deliberately.[204] No very stately and broad-based monument can ever
be erected over it, without infringing upon, covering, and overshadowing, the
graves not only of his family, but of individuals who probably were quite
disconnected with him. [52] But it is pleasant to think and know—were it but

on the evidence of this choice of a resting-place—that he did not care for a stately monument.

After leaving the churchyard, we wandered about in quest of the post-office, and, for a long time, without success. This little town of Grasmere seems to me as pretty a place as ever I met with in my life. It is quite shut in by hills, that rise up immediately around it, like a neighborhood of kindly giants; these hills descend steeply to the verge of the level on which the village stands, and there they terminate at once, the whole site of the little town being as even as a floor. I call it a village; but it is no village at all, all the dwellings standing apart, each in its own little domain, and each, I believe, with its own little lane leading to it, independently of the rest. Most of these are old cottages, plaistered [sic] white, with antique porches, and roses and other shrubbery trained against them, or growing about them; some, too, are ivy-grown. There are a few edifices of more pretension, and of modern build, but not so strikingly as to put the rest out of countenance. The post-office, when I found it, proved to be an ivied cottage, with a good deal of shrubbery round it, having its own pathway, like the other cottages. The whole looks like a real seclusion, shut out from the great world by these encircling hills, on the sides of which, wherever [53] they are not too steep, you see the division lines of property, and tokens of cultivation—taking from them their pretensions to savage majesty, but bringing them nearer to the heart of man.

Since writing the above, I have been again with Sophia to see Wordsworth's grave; and finding the door of the church open we went in. A woman and little girl were sweeping at the farther end; and the woman came towards us out of the little cloud of dust which she had raised. We were surprised at the extremely antique appearance of the church. It is paved with bluish gray flag-stones, over which uncounted generations have trodden, leaving the floor as well laid as ever. The walls are very thick; and the arched windows open through them at a considerable distance above the floor. There is no middle aisle; but first a row of pews next either wall, and then an aisle on each side of the pews occupying the centre of the church—thus, two side aisles, but no middle one. And right down through the centre of the church runs a row of five arches, the rudest and the roundest-headed that I ever saw, all of rough stone, supported by rough and massive pillars, or rather, square stone blocks, which stand in the pews, and stood in the same place, probably, long before the wood of those pews began to grow. Above this row of arches is another row, built upon the same mass of stone, and almost as broad, but lower; and on this upper row rests the frame-work, the oaken [54] beams, the black skeleton of the church-roof. It seems a very clumsy contrivance for supporting the roof; and if it were modern, we should certainly condemn it as very ugly; but being a relic of a simpler age, it comes in well with the antique simplicity of the whole structure. The roof goes up, barn-like, into its natural angle, and all the rafters and cross-beams are visible. There is an old font; and in the chancel is a niche, where (judging from a similar one in Furness Abbey) the holy water used to be placed for the priest's use, while celebrating mass. Around the inside of the porch is a stone-bench, placed against the wall, narrow and uneasy, but where a great many people have sat, who now have found quieter resting-places.

The woman was a very intelligent looking person, not of the usual English ruddiness; but rather thin, and somewhat pale, though bright of aspect. Her way of talking was very agreeable. She inquired if we wished to see Wordsworth's monument, and at once showed it to us;—a slab of white marble, fixed against the upper end of the central row of stone arches, with a pretty long inscription, and a profile-bust in bas-relief of his aged countenance. The monument is placed directly over Wordsworth's pew, and could best be seen and read from the very corner-seat where he used to sit. The pew is the corner one of those occupying the centre of the church, and is just across the aisle from the pulpit, and is the best in the church for the pur[55]pose of seeing and hearing the clergyman, and likewise as convenient as any from its neighborhood to the altar. On the other side of the aisle, beneath the pulpit, is Lady Fleming's pew. This and one or two other pews are curtained. Wordsworth's was not. I think I can bring up his image, in that corner seat of his pew, and of the aisle, a white-headed, tall, spare man, plain in aspect—better than in any other situation. The woman said that she had known him very well, and that he had made some verses on a sister of hers.[205] She repeated the first lines (something about a lamb) but neither Sophia nor I remembered them.

On the walls of the chancel there are monuments to the Flemings and other people, and painted escutcheons of some of their arms; and along the side walls, too, and on the square pillars of the row of arches, there are other monuments, generally of white marble, with the letters of the inscriptions blackened. Along these pillars, likewise, and in many places on the walls, were hung verses from Scripture, painted on boards. At one of the doors was a poor box—an elaborately-carved little box, of oak—with the date of 1648, and the name of the Church (St. Oswald's) upon it. The whole interior of the edifice was ancient, plain, simple, almost to grimness—or would have been so, only that the foolish churchwardens, or whatever other authority, have washed it over with the same buff or salmon color with which they have overlaid [56] the exterior. It is a pity; it lightens it up and desecrates it horribly—especially as the woman says that there were formerly paintings on the old walls, now obliterated forever. I could have staid in the old church much longer, and could write much more about it; but there must be an end of everything. Pacing it from the farther end, to the elevation before the altar, I found that it was twenty-five paces long.

On looking again at the Rothay, I find I did it some injustice; for, at the bridge, in its present swollen state, it is nearer twenty yards than twenty feet across. Its waters are very clear, and it rushes along with a speed which is delightful to see, after an acquaintance with the muddy and sluggish Avon and Leam.

Since tea, I have taken a stroll from the hotel in a different direction than heretofore, and passed the Swan Inn, where Scott used to go daily to get a draught of liquor, when he was visiting Wordsworth, who had no wine or other inspiriting fluid in his house.[206] It stands right on the roadside, a small, white-washed house, with an addition in the rear that seems to have been built since Scott's time. Over the door is the painted sign of a swan, with "Scott's Swan Hotel." I went a considerable distance beyond it; but a shower coming up, I turned back, entered the inn, and following the mistress into a snug little room, was served [57] with a glass of bitter ale. It is a very plain and homely little inn; and certainly could not have satisfied Scott's wants, if he had required anything very far-fetched or delicate in his potations. I found two Westmore-land peasants in the room, with liquor before them. One went away almost immediately; but the other remained, and entering into conversation with him, he told me that he was going to New Zealand, and expected to sail in September. I announced myself as an American, and he said that a large party had lately gone from hereabouts to America; but he seemed not to understand that there was any distinction between Canada and the States. These people had gone to Quebec. He was a very civil, well-behaved, kindly sort of person, of a simple character, which I took to belong to the class and locality, rather than to himself individually. I could not very easily understand all that he said, owing to his provincial dialect; and when he spoke to his own countrymen, or to the women of the house, I really could but just catch a word here and there. How long it takes to melt England down into a homogeneous mass! He told me that there was a public library in Grasmere, to which he has access, in common with the other inhabitants, and a reading room connected with it, where he reads the "Times" in the evening. There was no American smartness in his mind. When I left the Swan [58] it was showering smartly; but the drops quite ceased, and the clouds began to break away before I reached my hotel; and I saw the new moon over my right shoulder.

JULY 21st SATURDAY.

WE left Grasmere yesterday, after breakfast, it being a delightful morning, with some clouds, but the cheerfullest sunshine on great part of the mountain-sides and on ourselves. We returned, in the first place, to Ambleside, along the border of Grasmere lake, which would be a pretty little piece of water, with its steep and high surrounding hills, were it not that a stubborn and straight-lined stone fence, running along the eastern shore, by the roadside, quite spoils its appearance. Rydal-water (though nothing can make a lake of it) looked prettier and less diminutive than at the first view; and, in fact, I find that it is impossible to know accurately how any prospect or other thing looks, until after at least a second view, which always essentially corrects the first. This, I think, is especially true in regard to objects which we have heard much about, and exercised our imagination upon; the first view being a vain attempt to reconcile our idea with the reality, and in the second we begin to accept the thing for what it really is. Wordsworth's situation is really a beautiful one; and Nab

Scar behind his house rises with a grand, protecting air. We passed Nab's cottage, in which DeQuincey formerly lived, and where Hartley Coleridge lived and died. It is a little, buff-tinted, plastered stone-cottage, right on the road[59]-side, and originally, I should think, of a very humble class; but it now looks as if persons of taste might sometime or other have sat down in it, and caused flowers to spring up about it. It is very agreeably situated, under the great, precipitous hill, and with Rydal water close at hand, on the other side of the road. An advertisement of lodgings to let was put up on this cottage.

I question whether any part of the world looks so beautiful as England—this part of England, at least—on a fine summer morning. It makes one think the more cheerfully of human life to see such a bright, universal verdure; such sweet, rural, peaceful, flower-bordered cottages; not cottages of gentility, but real dwellings of the laboring poor. Such nice villas along the roadside, so tastefully contrived for comfort and beauty, and adorned, more and more, year after year, with the care and after-thought of people who mean to live there a great while, and feel as if their children might live there after them—and so they plant trees to overshadow their walks, and train ivy and whatever beautiful thing will grow there, up against their walls; and so live for the future in another sense than we Americans do. And the climate helps them out, and makes everything so moist and green, and full of tender life, instead of being dry and arid; as human life and vegetable life is so apt to be with us. Certainly, England can present a more attractive face than we can; [60] even in its humbler modes of life; to say nothing of the beautiful lives that might, one would think, be led by the higher classes, whose gateways, with broad, smooth, gravelled tracks leading through them (but where none but the owner's carriage, or those of his friends, have a right to enter) you see every mile or two along the road, winding into some proud seclusion. All this is passing away; and society must assume new relations; but there is no harm in believing that there has been something very good in English life—good for all classes—while the world was in a state out of which these forms naturally grew.

Passing through Ambleside, we turned (that is, our phaeton and pair turned) towards Ullswater, which we were to reach through the pass of Kirkstone. This is some three or four miles from Ambleside; and as we approached it, the road kept ascending higher and higher; the hills grew more bare, and the country lost its soft and delightful verdure. At last, the road became so steep, that Julian and I alighted to walk. This is the "aspiring road," which Wordsworth speaks of in his ode;[207] it passes through the gorge of precipitous hills—or almost precipitous—too much so for even the grass to grow on many portions of their declivities, which are covered with gray shingly stones; and I think this pass, in its wilder part, must have looked just the same when the Romans marched through it,[208] as it does now. No trees could ever have grown on these steep hill-sides, where even the English climate can generate no [61] available soil. I do not know that I have seen anything more impressive than the stern, gray sweep of these naked mountain-sides, with nothing whatever to soften or adorn them. The notch of the White Mountains (as I remember it from my youthful days) is more wonderful and richly picturesque, but of quite a different character.

About the centre and at the highest point of the pass stands an old stone-house, of mean appearance, with the usual sign of an ale-house ("licensed to retail foreign spirits, ale, and tobacco") over the door; and another little sign, designating it as the highest inhabited house in England. It is a chill and desolate place for a residence. They keep a visitor's book here; and we recorded our names, and were not too sorry to leave, the mean little house, smelling as it did of tobacco smoke, and with whatever characterizes the humblest ale-house on the level earth.

The Kirk-stone, which gives the pass its name, is not seen in approaching from Ambleside, until some time after you begin to descend towards Brothers' Water. When the driver first pointed it out, a little way up the hillside on our left, it looked like little more than a boulder of a ton or two in weight, among a hundred others nearly as big; and I saw little or no resemblance to a church or church-spire, to which the fancies of past generation[s] have likened it. As we descended the pass, however, and left the stone farther [62] and farther behind, it continued to show itself, and assumed a more striking and prominent aspect, standing out clearly relieved against the sky; so that no traveller—where there were so few defined objects to attract notice, amid the naked monotony of the stern hills—could fail to observe it; though, indeed, if I had taken it for any sort of an edifice, it would be rather for a wayside inn or shepherd's hut, than for a church. We lost sight of this stone, and again beheld it more and more brought out against the sky, by the turns of the road, several times in the course of our descent. There is a very striking view of Brothers' Water, shut in by steep hillsides, as we go down Kirkstone pass.

At about ½ past twelve, we reached Patterdale, at the foot of Ullswater, and here had luncheon. The hotels are mostly very good, all through this region, and this appeared to deserve that character; a black-coated waiter, more gentlemanly than most Englishmen, yet taking a sixpence with as little scruple as a lawyer would his fee; the mistress, in lady like attire, receiving us at the door, and waiting upon us to the carriage-steps; clean, comely house-maids everywhere at hand—all appliances, in short, for being comfortable, and comfortable, too, within one's own circle. And, on taking leave, everybody who has done anything for you, or who might by possibility have done anything, is to be feed. You pay the landlord enough in all conscience, and then you pay all his servants, who have been your servants for the time. But, [63] to say the truth, there is a degree of the same kind of annoyance in an American hotel; although it is not so much an acknowledged custom. Here, in the house where attendance is not charged in the bill, no wages appear to be paid to those servants—chambermaid, waiter, and boots—who come into immediate contact with travellers. The drivers of the cars, phaetons, and flies, are likewise unpaid, except by travellers, and claim three pence per mile with the same sense of right as their masters, in charging for the vehicle and horses. When you come to understand this claim not as an appeal to your generosity, but as an actual and necessary part of the cost of the journey, it is yielded to with a more comfortable feeling; and the traveller has really option enough, as to the amount which he will give, to ensure civility and good behavior on the driver's part.

Ullswater is a beautiful lake, with steep hills walling it about; so steep, on the eastern side, that there seems hardly room for a road to run along. We passed up the western shore; and turned off from it, about midway, I believe, to take the road towards Keswick. We stopt, however, at Lyulph's tower (while the chariot went on, up a hill) and took a guide to show us the way to Aira Force, a little cataract which is claimed as private property, and out of which, no doubt, a pretty little revenue is raised. I do not think that there can be any [64] rightful appropriation, as private property, of objects of natural beauty. The fruits of the land, I suppose, and whatever human labor can produce from it, belong fairly enough to the person who has a deed or a lease; but the Beautiful is the property of him who can gather it and enjoy it. It is very unsatisfactory to think of a cataract under lock-and-key. However, we were shown to Aira Force by a tall and graceful mountain-maid, with a healthy cheek, and a step that had no possibility of weariness in it. The cascade is an irregular streak of foaming water, pouring through a rude, shadowy glen. I liked well enough to see it; but it is wearisome, on the whole, to go the rounds of what everybody thinks it necessary to see. It makes one a little ashamed; it is somewhat as if we were drinking out of the same glass and eating from the same dish as a multitude of other people.

Within a few miles of Keswick, we passed along at the foot of Blencathara, or Saddleback, and by the entrance of the Vale of Saint John; and adown the valley, on the side of one of the slopes, we saw the enchanted castle. Thence we drove along by the course of the Greta, and soon arrived at Keswick, which lies at the base of Skiddaw, and among a brotherhood of picturesque eminences, and is itself a compact little town, with a market-house (built from the old stones of the Earl of Derwentwater's ruined castle) standing in the centre, with the principal street forking into two, as it passes it. We alighted at the [65] King's Head, or King's Arms, or some such sign, and went in search of Southey's residence, which we found easily enough, as it lies just on the outskirts of the town. We inquired of a group of people, two of whom, I thought, did not seem to know much about the matter; but the third, an elderly man, pointed it out at once—a house surrounded by trees, so as to be seen only partially, and standing on a little eminence, a hundred yards or so from the road.

We went up a little private lane that led to the rear of the house, and so penetrated quite into the back-yard without meeting anybody, passing a small kennel in which were two hounds, who gazed at us, but neither growled nor wagged their tails. The house is three stories high, and seems to have a great deal of room in it, so as not to do discredit to its name of "Greta Hall";—a very spacious dwelling for a poet. The windows, I think, were all closed; there were no signs of occupancy, but a general air of neglect. Sophia (who is bolder than I, in these matters) ventured through what seemed a back-garden gate; and I soon heard her in conversation with some man, who now presented himself, and proved to be a gardener. He said that he had formerly acted in that capacity for Southey, although a gardener had not been kept by him as a regular part of his establishment. This was an old man with an odd crookedness of legs, and strange, disjointed limp. Sophia had told him that we were Americans; and he [66] took the idea that we had come this long distance over sea and land, with the sole purpose of seeing Southey's residence; so that he was inclined to do what he could towards exhibiting it. This was but little; the present occupant (a Mr. Radday,[209] I believe the gardener called him) being away, and the house shut up.

But he showed us about the grounds, and let us peep into the windows of what had been Southey's library, and those of another of the front apartments, and showed us the window of the chamber (in the rear of the house) where Southey died. The apartments into which we peeped looked rather small and low—not particularly so—but enough to indicate rather an old house; they are now handsomely furnished; and we saw over one of the fire-places an inscription about Southey, and in the corner of the same room stood a suit of bright armour. The front of the house is tall—taller than most gentlemen's houses in England are—and even stately. All about, in front, beside it, and behind—there is a great profusion of trees, most of which were planted by Southey, who came to live here more than fifty years ago; and they have of course grown much more shadowy now than he ever beheld them; for he died as much as fourteen years since. The grounds are well laid out, and neatly kept, with the usual lawn and gravelled walks, and quaint little devices in the ornamental way. These may be of later date than Southey's time. The gardener [67] spoke respectfully of Southey, and of his first wife; and observed that it was a "great loss to the neighborhood when that family went down."

The house stands right above the Greta, the murmur of which is audible all about it; for the Greta is a swift little river, and goes on its way with a continual sound, which has both depth and breadth in it. When we had seen the front of the house, the gardener led us to a walk along the bank of the river, close by the Hall, where he said Southey used to walk for hours and hours together. He might, indeed, get there out of his study in a moment. There are two paths, one above the other, well laid out on the steep declivity of the high bank; and there is such a very thick shade of oaks and elms (planted by Southey himself) over the bank, that all the ground and grass were moist, although it had been a sunny day. It is a very sombre walk; not many glimpses of the sky through those dense boughs. The Greta is here perhaps twenty yards across, and very dark of hue; and it[s] voice is melancholy, and very suggestive of musings and reveries, but I should question whether it were favorable to any settled scheme of thought. The gardener told us that there used to be a pebbly beach on the margin of the river; and that it was Southey's habit to sit and write there, using a tree of peculiar [68] shape for a table. An alteration in the current of the river has swept away the beach, and the tree, too, has fallen. All these things were interesting to me, although Southey was not, I think, a picturesque man, nor one whose personal character takes a strong hold of the imagination. In these walks, he used to wear a pair of shoes heavily clamped with iron; very ponderous they must have been, from the particularity with which the gardener mentioned them.

The gardener dismissed us through the front entrance of the grounds; and returning to the King's Arms, we took a one horse fly for the falls of Lodore. Our ride thither was along the banks of Derwentwater; and it is as beautiful a road, I imagine, as can be found in England, or any where else. I like Derwentwater the best of all the lakes, so far as I have yet seen them. Skiddaw lies at the head of a long even ridge of mountain, rising into several peaks, and one the highest; on the eastern side, there are many noble eminences; and on the west (along which we rode) there is, a part of the way, a lovely wood, and, nearly the whole distance, a precipitous range of lofty cliff, descending sheer down, without any slope except what has been formed, in the lapse of ages, by the fall of fragments and the washing down of smaller stones. The declivity thus formed, along the base of the cliffs, is in some places covered with [69] trees or shrubs; elsewhere it is quite bare and barren. The precipitous part of the cliffs is very grand; the whole scene indeed might be characterized—without lauding it a great deal too much—as stern grandeur with an embroidery of rich beauty. All the sternness of it is softened by vegetative beauty, wherever it can possibly be thrown in; and there is not here, so strongly as along Windermere, [evidence] that human art has been helping out Nature. I wish it were possible to give any idea of the shapes of the hills; with these, at least, man has had nothing to do, nor ever will. As we approached the bottom of this lake, and of the beautiful valley in which it lies, we saw one hill that seemed to crouch down, like a Titanic watch-dog, with its rear towards the spectator, guarding the entrance to the valley. The great superiority of these mountains over those of New-England (besides the abundance everywhere of water-prospects, which are wanting among our own hills) is their variety and definiteness of shape. They rise up decidedly; and each is a hill by itself; while ours mingle into one another; and, besides, have such large bases that you can tell neither where they begin nor end. These Cumberland mountains have, many of them, at least, a marked vertebral shape, so that they often look like a group of huge lions, lying down with their [70] rears turned towards each other. They slope down steeply from narrow ridges; hence these picturesque seclusions of valleys and dales, which subdivide the lake region into so many communities. Our hills, like apple dumplings in a dish, have no such vallies [sic] as these.

There is a good little inn at Lodore; a small, primitive, country-inn, which has latterly been enlarged and otherwise adapted to meet the convenience of the guests brought thither by the fame of the cascade; but it is still a country inn, though it takes upon itself the title of a Hotel. We found pleasant rooms here, and established ourselves for the night. From this point we have a view up the beautiful lake, and of Skiddaw at the head of it. The cascade, too, is within three or four minutes' walk, through the garden-gate, towards the cliff at the base of which the inn stands. The visitor would need no other guide than its own voice, which is said to be audible, sometimes, to the distance of four miles. As we were coming from Keswick, at some little distance from the inn, we caught glimpses of its white foam, high up the precipice; and it is only glimpses that can be caught anywhere, because there is no regular sheet of falling water. Once, I think, it must have fallen right over the edge of the long line of precipice that here extends along, parallel with the [71] shore of the lake; but, in the course of time, it has gnawed and sawn its way into the heart of the cliff—this persistent little stream—so that now it has formed a rude gorge, adown which it hurries and tumbles, in the wildest way, over the roughest imaginable staircase. Standing at the bottom of the fall, you have a far vista, sloping upward to the sky, with the water—everywhere as white as snow—pouring and pouring down, now [on] one side of the gorge, now on the other, among immense boulders which try to choke its passage. It does not attempt to leap over these huge rocks, but finds its way in and out among them, and finally gets to the bottom after a hundred tumbles. It cannot be better described than in Southey's verses,[210] though worthy of better poetry than that. After all, I do not know that the cascade is anything more than the beautiful fringe to the grandeur of the scene; for it is very grand—this fissure through the cliff, with a steep, lofty precipice on the right hand, sheer up and down, and on the other hand, too, another lofty precipice, with a slope of its own ruin, on which trees and shrubbery have grown. The right hand precipice, however, has shelves affording sufficient hold for small trees; but nowhere does it slant. If it were not for the white little stream, tumbling softly downward, and for the [72] soft verdure up and down either precipice, and even along the very pathway of the cascade, it would be a very stern vista up that gorge.

I shall not try to describe it any more; it has not been praised too much, though it may have been praised amiss. I went thither again in the morning; and climbed a good way up through the midst of its rocky descent; and I think I could have reached the top in this way. It is remarkable that the leaps of the water, from one step of its broken staircase to another, gives an impression of softness and gentleness; but there are black, turbulent pools, among the great boulders, where the stream seems angry at the difficulties which it meets with. Looking upward, in the sunshine, I could see a little rising mist; and I should not wonder if a speck of rainbow were sometimes visible. I noticed one small oak in the bed of the cascade; and there is a lighter vegetation scattered up and down.

About noon, we took a car for Portinscale, and rode thither, back along the road to Keswick, through which we passed (stopping to get a package of letters at the Post Office) and reached Portinscale, which is a mile from Keswick. After dinner, we walked over a bridge and through a green lane, to the church where Southey is buried. It is a white church (lime-plastered, I believe) of Norman architecture, with a low, square tower. As we approached, we saw two persons entering the porch; and following them [73] in, we found the sexton (a tall, thin old man, with white hair, and an intelligent, reverential face) showing the edifice to a stout, red-faced, self-important, good-natured John Bull of a gentleman. Without any question on our part, the old sexton immediately led us to Southey's monument, which is placed in a side-aisle, where there is not breadth for it to stand free of the walls; neither is it in a very good light. But it seemed to me a good work of art;—a recumbent figure of white marble, on a couch, the drapery of which he has drawn about him²⁴¹—being quite enveloped in what may be a sheet or a shroud. The sculptor has not intended to represent death; for the figure lies sidelong, and has a book in its hand, and the face is lifelike, and looks full of expression—a thin, high-featured, poetic face, with a finely proportioned head, and abundant hair. It represents Southey (and rightly, at whatever age he died) in the full maturity of manhood, when he was strongest and richest. I liked the statue, and wished that it lay in a broad aisle, or in the chancel, where there is an old tomb of a knight and lady of the Ratcliffe family, who have held the place of honor long enough to yield it now to a poet. Southey's sculptor was Lough. I must not forget to mention that John Bull, climbing on a bench to get a better view of the statue, tumbled off with a racket that resounded irreverently through the church.

The old, white headed, thin sexton was a model man of his [74] class, and appeared to take a loving and cheerful interest in the church, and those who, from age to age, have worshipped and been buried there. It is a very ancient and interesting church. Within a few years, it has been thoroughly repaired, as to the interior; and now looks as if [it] might endure ten more centuries; and I suppose we see little that is really old, except the double row of Norman arches, in a light free-stone, that support the oaken beams and rafters of the roof. All the walls, however, are old, and quite preserve the identity of the edifice. There is a stained-glass window of modern manufacture; and in one of the side-windows, set amidst plain glass, there is a single pane, five hundred years old, representing Saint Anthony, very finely executed, though it looks a little faded. Along the walls, on each side of the church, between the arched windows, there are marble-slabs, affixed, with inscriptions to the memories of those who used to occupy the seats beneath. I remember none of great antiquity, nor any old monument except that in the chancel, over the knight and lady of the Ratcliffe family. This consists of a slab of stone, on four small stone pillars about two feet high; the slab is inlaid with a brass-plate, on which is engraved the knight in armor, and the lady in the costume of Elizabeth's time, exceedingly well done and well preserved, and each figure as much as eighteen inches in length. The Sexton produced a rubbing of them, on paper. Under the slab—which, supported by the low stone pillars, forms a canopy for them—lie two sculptured figures of stone, of life-size and at full length, [75] representing this same knight and lady; but I think the sculptor was hardly equal in his art to the engraver.

The most curious antiquity in the church is the font. The bowl is very capacious, sufficiently so as to admit of the full immersion of a child of two or three months old. On the outside, in several compartments, there are bas-reliefs of scriptural and symbolic subjects—such as the Tree of Life—the Word proceeding out of God's mouth—the Crown of Thorns—in the quaintest taste, sculptured by some hand of a thousand years ago, and preserving the fancies of monkish brains in stone. The sexton was very proud of this font and its sculptures, and took a kindly personal interest in showing it, as he does whatever is interesting in the church. And when we had spent as much time as we could, inside, he led us to Southey's grave in the churchyard.

The old man told us that he had known Southey long and well, (he being only twenty-nine when he came to Keswick to reside) from early manhood to old age. He had known Wordsworth, too, and Coleridge, and Lovell;[212] and he had seen Southey and Wordsworth walking arm in arm together, in that churchyard. He seemed to revere Southey's memory, and said that he had been much lamented, and that there were as many as a hundred people in the churchyard, when he was buried. He spoke with great praise of Mrs. Southey, his first wife, telling of her charity to the poor, and how she was a blessing to the [76] neighborhood; but (for whatever reason) he said nothing in favor of the second Mrs. Southey, and only mentioned her selling the library and other things, after her husband's death, and going to London. Yet I think she was probably a good woman, and meets with less than justice, because she took the place of another good woman, and had not time and opportunity to prove herself as good.[213] As for Southey himself, my idea is, that few better or more blameless men have ever lived, than he; but he seems to lack color, passion, warmth, or something that should enable me to bring him into close relation with myself. The church-yard, where he lies, is not so rural and picturesque as that where Wordsworth lies buried; although Skiddaw rises behind it, and the Greta is murmuring at no very great distance away. But the churchyard itself has a somewhat cold and bare aspect; no shadow of trees, no shrubbery.

Over Southey's grave there is a ponderous, oblong block of slate, a native mineral of this region, as hard as iron, and which will doubtless last quite as long as Southey's works have any vitality in English literature. It is not a monument fit for a poet—there is nothing airy or graceful about it—and, indeed, there cannot be many men so solid and matter-of-fact as to deserve a tomb like this. Wordsworth's grave is much better, with only a simple head-stone, and the grass growing over his mortality—which, for a thousand years, at least, it never can over Southey's. Most of the monuments in the church[77]yard are of this same black slate; and some (erect head-stones) have curious sculptures, which seem to have been recently erected.

We now returned to the hotel, and took a car for the Valley of Saint John. The sky seemed to portend rain in no long time; and Skiddaw had put on his cap; but the people of the hotel and the driver said that there would be no rain this afternoon—and their opinion proved correct. After riding a few miles, we again came within sight of the enchanted ruin. It appears to stand rather more than midway adown the declivity of one of the ridges (to the left, as you go southward) that form the valley; and its site would have been a good one for a fortress intended to defend the lower entrance of this mountain defile. At a proper distance, it looks not unlike the gray dilapidation of a Gothic castle, which has been crumbling and crumbling away for ages, until Time might be supposed to have imperceptibly stolen its massive pile away from men, and given it back to Nature; its towers, and battlements, and arched entrances being so much defaced and decayed, that all the marks of human labor had nearly been obliterated; and the angles of the hewn stones rounded away; while mosses, and weeds, and bushes, grow over it as freely as over a natural ledge of rocks. It is conceivable that, in some lights, and in some states of the atmosphere, a traveller, at the entrance of the valley, might really imagine that he be[78]held a castle here; but, for myself, I must acknowledge that it required a willing fancy, to make me see it. As we drew nearer, the delusion did not immediately grow less strong; but at length we found ourselves passing at the foot of the declivity, with its mimic towers right above us; and, behold! it was nothing but an enormous ledge of rock, coming squarely out of the hill-side, with other parts of the ledge cropping out in its vicinity. Looking back, after passing, we saw a knoll or hillock, of which the castled rock is the bare face. There are two or three stone cottages along the road-side, beneath the magic castle, and within the enchanted ground. Scott, in the Bridal of Triermain, locates the castle right in the middle of the valley, and makes King Arthur ride around it;—which any mortal horseman would find great difficulty in doing.[214]

This Vale of Saint John is a very striking piece of scenery. Blencathara shuts it in to the northward, lying right across the entrance; and on either side, there are lofty crags and declivities, those to the west being more broken, as I remember, and better wooded, than the ridge to the eastward, which stretches along for several miles, steep, high, and bare, producing only grass enough for sheep pasture, until it rises into the dark brow of Helvellyn. Adown this ridge—seen afar, like a white ribbon—comes here and there a cascade, sending its voice before it, which distance robs of all its fury, and makes it the quietest [79] sound in the world; and while you see the foamy leap of its upper course, a mile or two away, you may see and hear the self-same little brook babbling through a field, and passing through the arch of a rustic bridge, beneath your feet. It is a deep seclusion, with mountains and crags on all sides.

About a mile beyond the castle, we stopt at a little wayside inn—the King's Head—and put up for the night. This, I believe, is the only inn which I have

found in England—the only one, I mean, where I have eaten and slept—
that does not call itself a hotel. It is very primitive in its arrangements; a long,
low, white-washed, unadorned, and ugly cottage of two stories. At one extremity is a barn and cow-house, and next to these the part of the inn devoted
to the better class of guests, where we had our parlor and sleeping chambers,
contiguous to which is the kitchen, and common room of the ale-house, paved
with flag-stones, and lastly another barn and stable—all which departments are
not under separate roofs, but under the same long contiguity, and forming
parts of the same building. Our parlor opens immediately upon the roadside,
without any vestibule. The house appears to be of some antiquity, with beams
across the low cielings [sic]; but the people made us pretty comfortable at
bed and board, and fed us with ham and eggs, veal-steaks, honey, oat-cakes,
gooseberry-tarts, and such cates and dainties—making a moderate charge when
we went away. The parlor was adorned [80] with rude engravings (I remember only a plate of the Duke of Wellington, at three stages of his life),
and there were minerals, delved doubtless out of the hearts of the mountains,
over the mantel-piece. The chairs were of an old fashion, and had very capacious bottoms. We were waited upon by two women-folks, who looked and
acted not unlike the country-folk of New England—say of New Hampshire—
except that they may have been a little more deferential.

While we remained here, I took various walks, to get a glimpse of Helvellyn,
and a view of Thirlmere—which is rather two lakes than one, being so
narrow, at one point, as to be crossed by a foot-bridge. Its shores are very
picturesque, coming down abruptly upon it, and broken into crags and prom-
inences, which view their shaggy faces in its mirror; and Helvellyn slopes
steeply upward from its southern shore into the clouds. On its eastern bank,
near the footbridge, stands Armboth House, which Miss Martineau says
is haunted;[215] and I saw a painted board, at the entrance of the road which
leads to it, advertising lodgings there. The ghosts, of course, pay nothing
for their accommodations.

At noon, on the day after our arrival, Julian and I went to visit the enchanted
castle; and we were so venturesome as to turn aside from the road, and ascend
the declivity towards its walls—which, indeed, we hoped to surmount. It
proved a very difficult undertaking, the site of the fortress being much higher,
and of steeper as[81]cent, than we had supposed; but we did clamber upon what
we took for the most elevated portion of the ruin, when, lo! we found that we
had only taken one of the outworks, and that there was a gorge of the hill betwixt us and the main walls, while the citadel rose high above, at more than
twice the elevation which we had climbed. Julian wished to go on; and I
let him climb, till he appeared to have reached so steep and lofty a height
that he looked hardly bigger than a monkey, and I should not at all have
wondered had he come rolling down to the base of the rock where I sat. But
neither did he get actually within the castle; though he might have done so,
but for a high stone-fence, too difficult for him to climb, which runs from the

rock, along the hillside. The sheep probably go thither much oftener than any other living thing; and to them we left the Castle of Saint John, with a shrub waving from its battlements instead of a banner.

After dinner, we ordered a car for Ambleside; and while it was getting ready, I went to look at the River of Saint John, which, indeed, flows close beside our inn, only just across the road, though it might well be overlooked, unless you specially looked for it. It is a brook, brawling over the stones, very much as brooks do in New England; only we never think of calling them rivers there. I could easily have made a leap from shore to shore; and Julian scrambled across on no better footing than a rail. I believe I have complained of the [82] want of brooks in other parts of England; but there is no want of them here, and they are always interesting, be they of what size they may.

We rode down the valley, and gazed at the vast slope of Helvellyn, and at Thirlmere beneath it, and at Eagle's Crag, and Raven's Crag, which beheld themselves in it; and we cast many a look behind, at Blencathara, and that noble brotherhood of mountains, out of the midst of which we came. But, to say the truth, I was weary of fine scenery; and it seemed to me that I had eaten a score of mountains, and quaffed down as many lakes, all in the space of two or three days;—and the natural consequence was a surfeit. There was scarcely a single place in all our tour, where I should not have been glad to spend a month; but, by flitting so quickly from one point to another, I lost all the more recondite beauties, and had come away without retaining even the surface of much that I had seen. I am slow to feel—slow, I suppose, to comprehend; and, like the anaconda, I need to lubricate any object a great deal, before I can swallow it and actually make it my own. Yet I shall always be glad of this tour, and shall wonder the more at England, which comprehends so much, such a rich variety, within its little bounds. If England were all the world, it still would have been worth while for the Creator to have made it; and mankind would have had no cause to [83] find fault with their abode —except that there is not room enough for so many as might be happy here.

We left the great inverted arch[216] of the valley behind us, looking back as long as we could at Blencathara, and Skiddaw over its shoulder; and the clouds were gathering over them, at our last glimpse. Passing by Dunmail Raise (a mound of stones over an old British King) we entered Westmoreland, and soon had the vale of Grasmere before us, with the church where Wordsworth lies, and Nab Scar and Rydal Water, farther on. At Ambleside, we took another car for Newby Bridge, whither we drove along the eastern shore of Windermere. The superb scenery through which we had been passing made what we now saw look tame, although, a week ago, we should have thought it more than commonly interesting. Hawkshead is the only village on our road; a little white-washed old town, with a white-washed old Norman Church, low, and with a low tower, on the same pattern with others that we have seen hereabouts. It was between seven and eight °clock when we reached Newby Bridge, and heard Una's voice greeting us, and saw her head, crowned with a wreath of flowers, looking down at us out of the window of our parlour.

And to-day (Monday, July 23ᵈ, I believe) I have finished this most incomplete and unsatisfactory record of what we have done and seen since Wednesday last. I am pretty well con[84]vinced that all attempts at describing scenery—especially mountain-scenery—are sheer nonsense. For one thing, the point of view being changed, the whole description which you made up from the previous point of view is immediately falsified. And when you have done your utmost, such items as those setting forth the scene in a play—"a mountainous country; in the distance a cascade tumbling over a precipice; in front a lake; on one side an ivy-covered cottage"—this dry detail brings the matter before one's mind['s] eye more effectually than all the art of word-painting.

JULY 27ᵗʰ, FRIDAY.

WE are still at Newby Bridge; and nothing has occurred of remarkable interest; nor have we made any excursions, beyond moderate walks. Two days—Tuesday and Wednesday—have been rainy; and to-day there is more rain. We find such weather as tolerable here as it would probably be anywhere; but it passes rather heavily with the children; and, for myself, I should prefer sunshine, though Mr. White's books afford me some resource, especially an odd volume of Ben Jonson's plays, containing "Volpone," "The Alchemist," "Bartholomew Fair," and others. The Alchemist is certainly a great play. We watch all arrivals, and other events, from our parlour window; —a stage-coach driving up, four times in the twenty-four hours, with its forlorn outsiders all saturated with rain;—the steamer from the head of the lake, landing a crowd of passengers, [85] who stroll up to the hotel, drink a glass of ale, lean over the parapet of the bridge, gaze at the flat stones which pave the bottom of the river, and then hurry back to the steamer again;— cars, phaetons, horsemen, all damped and disconsolate. There are a number of young men staying at the hotel, some of whom go forth in all the rain, fishing, and come back at night-fall, trudging heavily, but with creels on their backs that do not seem very heavy. Yesterday was fair, and enlivened us a good deal. Returning from a walk, in the forenoon, I found a troop of yeomanry Cavalry in the stable-yard of the hotel. They were the North Lancashire regiment, and were on their march to Liverpool, for the purpose of drill. Not being old campaigners, their uniform and accoutrements were in so much the finer order, all bright and looking span-new; and they themselves were a body of handsome and stalwart young men; and it was pleasant to look at their helmets, and red-jackets, and carbines, and steel-scabbarded swords, and gallant steeds—all so martial in aspect—and to know that they were only play-soldiers, after all, and were never likely to do any warlike mischief or suffer any. By-and-by, their bugles sounded, and they trotted away, wheeling over the ivy-grown stone-bridge, and disappearing behind the trees, on the Milnthorpe [86] road. Our host comes forth from his bar, with a bill, which he presents to an orderly-sergeant, or some such official. He (the Host) then tells me that he himself once rode many years a trooper in this regiment, and that all his comrades (I think he said all—the greater part, at least) were larger men than himself. Yet Mr. Thomas White is a good-sized man, and now, at all events, rather over-weight for a dragoon.

Yesterday, too, came one of those bands of music that seem to itinerate everywhere about the country. They consisted of a young woman who played the harp, a bass-violin player, a fiddler, a flutist, and a bugler, besides a little child, of whom, I suppose, the woman was the mother.[217] They sat down on a bench by the river-side, opposite the house, and played several tunes; and by-and-by, the waiter brought them a large pitcher of ale, which they quaffed with apparent satisfaction; though they seemed to be foreigners by their mustachios and sallow hue, and would perhaps have preferred a vinous potation. One would like to follow these people through their vagrant-life, and see them at meal-time and bed-time, and overhear their intercourse among themselves. All vagrants are interesting; and there seems to be a much greater variety of them here, than in America—people who cast themselves on fortune, and take whatever she gives, without a certainty of any[87]thing. I saw a travelling tinker, yesterday;—a man with a leather-apron, and a string of skewers hung at his girdle, and a pack over his shoulders in which, no doubt, were his tools and materials of trade.

It is remarkable what a natural interest everybody feels in fishing. An angler from the bridge immediately attracts a group to watch his luck; it is the same with Julian fishing for minnows, on the platform near which the steamer lands its passengers. By-the-by, Una caught a minnow, last evening, and im-mediately after a good-sized perch—her first fish.

JULY 30th, MONDAY.

WE left Newby Bridge, all of us, on Saturday at 12 °clock, and steamed up the river [lake] to Ambleside; a pretty good day, as to weather, but with a little bit of a tendency to shower. There was nothing new on the lake, and no new impressions, as far as I remember. At Ambleside, Mamma and Nurse went shopping; after which we took a carriage for Grasmere, and established our-selves at Brown's Hotel there. I find that my impressions from our previous sight of all these scenes do not change on revision. They are very beautiful; but, if I must say it, I am a little weary of them. We soon tire of things which we visit merely by way of spectacle, and with which we have no real and permanent connec[88]tion. In such cases, we very quickly wish this spec-tacle to be taken away, and another substituted;—at all events, I do not care about seeing anything more of the English lakes, for at least a year to come. Besides, a man with children in charge cannot enjoy travelling; he must content himself to be happy with them, for they allow him no separate and selfish possibility of being happy. Sophia, however, suffers far less from this impediment than I do, though she has to bear a great deal more of it.

Perhaps a part of my weariness of the lakes is owing to the hotel-life which we lead. At an English hotel, the traveller feels as if everybody, from the landlord downward, were in a joint and individual purpose of fleecing him; because all the attendants, who come in contact with him, are to be separately considered. So, after paying, in the first instance, a very heavy bill for what would seem to cover the whole indebtedness, there remain divers dues still to be paid, to no trifling amount, to the landlord's servants—dues not to be ascertained, and which you never even know whether you have properly satisfied. You can know, perhaps, when you have less than satisfied them, by the aspect of the waiter, which I wish I could describe;—not disrespectful, in the slightest degree, but a look of profound surprise, a gaze at the offered coin (which he nevertheless pockets) as if [89] he either did not see it, or did not know it, or could not believe his eyesight;—all this, however, with the most quiet forbearance, a Christian like non-recognition of an unmerited wrong and insult;—and, finally (all in a moment's space indeed) he quits you and goes about his other business. If you have given too much, too, you are made sensible of your folly by the extra amount of his gratitude, and the bows with which he salutes you from the door-step. But, generally, you cannot very decidedly say whether you have been right or wrong; but, in almost all cases, you decidedly feel that you have been fleeced. Then the living at the best of the English hotels (so far as my travels have brought me acquainted with them) deserves but moderate praise, and is especially lacking in variety. Nothing but joints, joints, joints; sometimes, perhaps, a meat-pie, which, if you eat it, weighs upon your conscience with the idea that you have eaten the scraps and rejected relics of other people's dinners. At the lake-hotels, the fare (with the exception of trout, which are not always fresh, and which one soon tires of, at any rate) is lamb and mutton. We pay like nabobs, and are expected to be content with plain mutton. The English seem to have no conception of better living than this. What must they think of the American hotels!

We spent the day, yesterday, at Grasmere in little quiet walks about [90] the hotel; and at a little past six, in the afternoon, I took my departure in the stage-coach for Windermere. The coach was awfully overburthened with outside passengers—fifteen, I think, in all, besides the four insiders—and one of the fifteen formed the apex of an immense pile of baggage on the top. It seems to me miraculous that we did not topple over; the road being so hilly and uneven, and the driver, I suspect, none the steadier for his visits to all the tap-rooms along the road from Cockermouth. There was a tremendous vibration of the coach, now and then; and I saw that, in case of our going over, I should be flung headlong against the high stone-fence, that, in English fashion, bordered most of the road. In view of this, I determined to muffle my head in the folds of my thick shawl, at the moment of overturn; and as I could do no better for myself, I awaited my fate with equanimity. As far as apprehension goes, I had rather travel from Maine to Georgia by rail, than from Grasmere to Windermere by stage-coach.

At Lo[w]wood, the landlady espied me from the window, and sent out a large packet that had arrived by mail; but as it was directed to some person of the Christian name of William, I did not venture to open it. She said, also, that a gentleman had been there who very earnestly desired to see me; [91] and I have since had reason to suppose that this was Allingham, the poet. We got to Windermere at about half past seven, and waited nearly an hour for the train to start. I took a ticket for Lancaster, and arrived there at ten; and talked about the war with a gentleman in the Coffee room, (who took me for an Englishman, as most people do, nowadays) and heard from him—as you may from all his countrymen—an expression of weariness and dissatisfaction with the whole business. These fickle islanders! How differently they talked a year ago! John Bull sees, now, that he never was in a worse fix in his life; and yet it would not take much to make him snort as bellicosely as ever. I went to bed at eleven, and slept unquietly on feathers. The English know as little how to sleep as to eat.

I had purposed to rise betimes, and see the town of Lancaster before breakfast. But here I reckoned without my host; for, in the first place, I had no water for my ablutions, and my boots were not brushed; and so I could not get down stairs till the hour I named for my coffee and chops;—and, secondly, the breakfast was delayed half an hour, though promised every minute. In fine, I'had but just time to take a hasty walk around Lancaster Castle, and see what [92] I could of the town on my way;—a not very remarkable little town, built of stone, with taller houses than in the middle shires of England, modern fronts, narrow streets, up and down an eminence on which the Castle is situated, with the town immediately about it. The castle is a satisfactory edifice, but so renovated that the walls look almost entirely modern, with the exception of the fine old front, with the statue of an armed warrior (John of Gaunt himself, very likely) in a niche over the Norman arch of the entrance. Close beside the Castle stands what looks like an old church.

The train left Lancaster at half past nine, and reached Liverpool (over as flat and uninteresting a country as I ever travelled) at twelve. I have betaken myself to the Rock Ferry Hotel, where I am as comfortable as I could be anywhere but at home; but it is rather comfortless to think of home as three years off and three thousand miles away. With what a sense of utter weariness —not fully realized till then—we shall sink down on our own threshold, when we reach it. The moral effect of being without a settled abode is very wearisome.

Our Coachman from Grasmere to Windermere looked like a great beerbarrel, oozy with his proper liquor. I suppose such solid soakers never get upset.

[93] AUGUST 2ᵈ THURSDAY.

MR. BRIGHT had urged me very much to go with his father and family to see the launch of a great ship which has been built for their firm, and afterwards to partake of a pic-nic; so, on Tuesday morning, I presented myself at the Landing Stage, and met the party, to take passage for Chester. It was a showery morning, and looked woefully like a rainy day; but nothing better is to be expected in England;—and, after all, there is seldom such a day that you cannot glide about pretty securely between the drops of rain. This, however, did not turn out one of those tolerable days, but grew darker and darker, and worse and worse; and was worst of all when we had passed about six miles beyond Chester, and were just on the borders of Wales, on the hither side of the River Dee, where the ship was to be launched. Here the train stopt, and absolutely deposited our whole party of excursionists, under a heavy shower, in the midst of a muddy potatoe [sic] field, whence we were to wade through mud and mire to the ship-yard, almost half a mile off. Some kind Christian (I know not whom) gave me half of his umbrella and half of his cloak, and thereby I got to a shed, near the ship, without being absolutely soaked through.

The ship had been built on the banks of the Dee [94] at a spot where it is too narrow (as, indeed, I do not think it would be anywhere wide enough) for her to be launched directly across; and so she lay lengthwise of the river, and was so arranged as to take the water parallel with the stream. She is, for aught I know, the longest ship in the world; at any rate, longer than the Great Britain; an iron screw-steamer, and looked immense and magnificent, and was gorgeously dressed out in flags. Had it been a pleasant day, all Chester and half Wales would have been there to see the launch; and in spite of the rain, there were a good many people on the opposite shore, as well as on our side, and one or two booths, and many of the characteristics of a fair;— that is to say, men and women getting boozy without any great noise or confusion.

The ship was expected to go off at about 12 °clock; and, at that juncture, all Mr. Bright's friends assembled under the bows of the ship, where we were a little sheltered from the rain by the projection of that part of the vessel over our heads. The bottle of port-wine, with which she was to be christened, was suspended from the bows to the platform where we stood, by a blue ribbon; and the ceremony was to be performed by Mrs. Bright, who, I could see, was very nervous in anticipation of the ceremony. Her [95] husband kept giving her instructions, in a whisper, and showing her how to throw the bottle; and as the critical moment approached, he took hold of it along with her. All this time, we were waiting in momentary expectation of her going off, everything being ready, and only the touch of a spring, as it were, needed to make her slide into the water. But the chief manager kept delaying a little longer and a little longer; though the pilot on board the ship sent to tell him that it was time she was off. "Yes, yes; but I want as much water as I can get," answered the manager; and so he held on till, I suppose, the tide had raised the river Dee to its very acme of height. At last the word was given; the ship began slowly to move; Mrs. Bright threw the bottle against the bow with a spasmodic effort that dashed it into a thousand pieces, and diffused the fragrance of the old port all around, where it lingered several minutes; and then spreading out her hands, she seemed to be praying for the good ship and the success of all her future voyages. I did not think that there could have been such a breathless moment in an affair of this kind.

The ship moved majestically down towards the [96] river; and unless it were Niagara, I never saw anything grander and more impressive than the motion of this mighty mass as she departed from us. We, on the platform, and everybody along both shores of the Dee, took off our hats in the rain, waved handkerchiefs, cheered—shouted—"Beautiful!"—What a noble launch!"— "Never was so fair a sight!"—and really it was so grand, that calm, majestic movement, that I felt the tears come into my eyes. The wooden pathway, adown which she was gliding, began to smoke with the friction; when all at once, when we expected to see her plunge into the Dee, she came to a full stop. Mr. Bright (the father, a gentleman with white hair, a dark expressive face, bright eyes, and a Jewish cast of features) immediately took the alarm; a moment before, his countenance had been kindled up with triumph; but now his under-jaw fell, he turned pale as death, looked furrowed, wrinkled, and haggard, and absolutely grew ten years older while I was looking at him. Well he might; for his noble ship was stuck fast in the mud of the Dee, and, without deepening the bed of the river, I do not see how her vast iron bulk is ever to be got out. (This steamer was wrecked most disastrously on the Welsh coast, after two or three years.[218])

There was no help for it. A steamboat was hitched on to [97] the stranded vessel, but broke two or three cables without stirring her an inch. So, after waiting long after we had given up all hope, we went to the office of the shipyard, and there got a lunch; and still the rain was pouring, pouring, pouring, and I never experienced a blanker affair in all my days. Then we had to wait a great while for a train to take us back; so that it was five o clock, almost, before we got to Chester, where I spent an hour in rambling about the old town, under the rows; and on the walls, looking down on the tree-tops directly under my feet, and through their thick branches at the canal, which creeps at the base; and in the Cathedral, walking under the black, intertwining arches of the cloisters (a good place to walk, on such a showery day) and looking up at the great cathedral-tower, so wasted away, externally, by time and weather, that it looks—save for the difference of color between white snow and red freestone—like a structure of snow, half dissolved by several warm days. At about ½ past six, I took the train for Birkenhead.

At the launch, I met with a graduate of Cambridge, (here in England) tutor of a grandson of Perceval[219] (the assassinated minister) with his pupil. I should not like this [98] position of tutor to a young Englishman; it certainly has an ugly twang of upper servitude. I observed that the tutor gave his pupil the best seat in the railway carriage, and, in all respects, provided for his comfort before thinking of his own; and this not as a father does for his child, out of love, but from a sense of place and duty, which I did not quite see how a gentleman could consent to feel. And yet this Mr. Clarke[220] was evidently a gentleman, and a quiet, intelligent, agreeable, and, no doubt, learned man. Kingsley being mentioned, Mr Clarke observed that he had known him well at college, having been his contemporary there. He did not like him, however—thought him a "dangerous man";—as well as I could gather, he thinks that there is some radical defect in Kingsley's moral nature; a lack of sincerity; and, furthermore, he believes him to be a sensualist (not, as far as I understood, that he practically sins in that way) in his disposition; in support of which view, he said that Kingsley had made drawings such as no pure man could have made, or could allow himself to show or look at. This was the only fact which Mr. Clarke adduced, bearing on his opinion of Kingsley; otherwise, it seemed to be one of those early impressions which a collegian gets of his fellow-students, and [99] which he never gets rid of, whatever the character of the person may turn out to be, in after years. I have judged several persons in this way, and still judge them so, though the world has come to very different conclusions. Which is right?—the world, which has the man's whole mature life on its side?—or his early companion, who has nothing for it but some idle passages of his youth.[221]

Mr. Melly[222] remarks of newspaper-reporters, that they may be known at all celebrations, and on any public occasion, by the enormous quantity of luncheon they eat.

August 12th, Sunday.

Mr. Bright dined with us at the Rock Ferry Hotel, day before yesterday. Speaking of Helvellyn, and the death of Charles Gough, which Wordsworth and Scott have both sung about,[223] Mr. B. mentioned a version of that story which rather detracts from the character of the faithful dog. People do say, it seems, that the terrier bitch lived literally upon her dead master, through those months before his body was discovered; and that, when found, she had a nice litter of pups with her! This quite solves Wordsworth's query as to how she had been nourished during the interval.[224] But, somehow, it lowers one's opinion of human nature itself, to be compelled so to lower one's standard of a dog's nature. [100] I don't intend to believe it; but it reminds me of the story of the New Zealander who was asked whether he loved a missionary that had been laboring for his soul and those of his countrymen,—"Love him, to be sure I did! Why I ate a piece of him for my breakfast, this morning!"

Mr. B. says that Prince Albert is very far from being liked by those who come into personal relations with him. This seems to be on account of his German character—cold, slow, heavy, undemonstrative, proud and stiff. He snubs the high nobility of England. There appeared to be a kindly feeling towards him among the people at large, when I first came here; but, I think, it has now passed into indifference.

For the last week or two, I have passed my time between the Hotel and the Consulate; and a weary life it is, and one that leaves little of profit behind it. I am sick to death of my office;—brutal captains and brutish sailors;—continual complaints of mutual wrong, which I have no power to set right, and which, indeed, seem to have no right on either side;—calls of idleness or ceremony from my travelling countrymen, who seldom know what they are in search of, at the commencement of their tour, and never have attained any desirable end, at the close of it;—beggars, cheats, simpletons, unfortunates, so mixed up that it is impossible to distinguish one from [101] another, and so, in self-defense, the consul distrusts them all. I see many specimens of mankind, but come to the conclusion that there is but little variety among them, after all.

At the hotel, yesterday, there was a large company of factory people, from Preston, who marched up from the pier with a band of military music playing before them. They spent the day in the gardens, and ball-room of the Hotel, dancing, and otherwise merry-making, but I saw little of them, being at the consulate. Towards evening, it drizzled, and the assemblage melted away gradually; and when the band marched down to the pier, there were few to follow, although one man went dancing before the musicians, flinging out his arms, and footing it with great energy and gesticulation. Some young women along the road (whether belonging to the Preston party I know not) likewise began to dance as the music approached.

Thackeray has a dread of servants, insomuch that he hates to address them, or to ask them for anything. His morbid sensibility, in this regard, has perhaps led him to study and muse upon them, so that he may be presumed to have a more intimate knowledge of the class than any other man. Carlyle dresses so badly and wears such a rough outside, [102] that the flunkies are rude to him, at gentlemen's doors.

In the afternoon (Sunday) Julian and I took a walk towards Tranmere Hall, and beyond, as far as Oxton, I believe. This part of the country (being so near Liverpool and Birkenhead) is all speckled over with what they call "Terraces," "Bellevues," and other pretty names for semi-detached villas, built to let to well-to-do tradesmen, besides separate villas (I saw on one gateway "Recluse Cottage") for a somewhat higher class. But the old, white-washed stone cottage is still frequent, with its roof of slate or thatch, which perhaps is green with weeds or grass; through its open door you see that it has a pavement of flag-stones, or perhaps of red free-stone; and hogs and donkies [sic] appear to be familiar with the threshold. The door always opens directly into the kitchen, without any vestibule; and glimpsing through, you see that a cottager's life must be the very plainest and homeliest that ever was lived by man and woman. Yet the flowers about the door often indicate a native capacity for the beautiful; but often, too, there is only a pavement of road stones, or of flag-stones, like those within. The villages, hereabouts, are all built in rows of contiguous houses, and most of them seem to be modern, with here and there an elder dwel[103]ling still surviving. At one point, where there was a little bay, as it were, let into the hedge-fence, we saw something like a small tent or wigwam—an arch of canvas, I think, three or four feet high, and open in front—under which sat a dark-complexioned woman and some little children. The woman seemed to be sewing. I took them for gypsies.

On our way home, we struck into a footpath,[225] as I always delight to do. These are probably the ancientest of ways—older than the Roman roads—older than towns or villages—old as the times when people first debarred themselves from wandering freely and widely, wherever they chose; and they swerve and linger along, and find pretty little vales and nooks of scenery where the high-road discloses nothing but the tiresomest blank. You can sometimes find these paths joining on to one another for miles and miles together. The right to them, on the part of the public, is highly valued and jealously guarded in England; and I saw, a little while ago, a notice of a meeting of a society, in the neighborhood of Manchester, for the "preservation of footpaths." The landowners, on each side of the way, put up sign-boards, threatening prosecution to whomsoever may encroach on their premises; but [104] they cannot abridge this liberty of the poor and landless to pass freely through the very heart of their territories; and thus the poorest man retains a kind of property in the oldest inheritance of the richest. Sometimes the stiles, over which you climb, are made of stone-steps, so worn that they are themselves a record of the antiquity of the path. I doubt whether I ever saw a dozen stiles in America—no; not half-a-dozen—not more than one or two.

AUGUST 17th FRIDAY.

YESTERDAY afternoon, Julian and I went to Birkenhead Park. It is a large enclosure, open to the public, and is pretty well beautified with shrubbery, and a pond, and pretty bridges, and here and there a statue, such as Mazeppa, and others of no particular merit, among the trees. There are broad open spaces, where people may play cricket and otherwise disport themselves; also, a camera obscura; and, of course a refreshment room—where, however, there is nothing better, of a drinkable order, than ginger-beer and British wines. And here the respectable middle-classes—the lower-middling—come to spend a summer afternoon, wandering up and down the winding gravel-paths, feeding the swans off the bridges, nibbling buns and gingerbread, and polka-ing (girls with girls) to the music of a hand-organ. It so happened that yesterday there was a large school spending its holiday there; a school of girls of the lower classes, to the num[105]ber of some hundred & fifty, who disported themselves on the green, under the direction of their schoolmistresses, and of an old gentleman. It struck me, as it always has, to observe how the lower orders of this country indicate their birth and station by their aspect and features. In

America, there would be a good deal of grace and beauty among one hundred and fifty children and budding girls, belonging to whatever rank of life; but here they had universally a most plebeian look—stubbed, and sturdy figures, round, coarse faces, snub-noses—the most evident specimens of the brown bread of human nature. They looked wholesome, and good enough, and fit to sustain their rough share of life; but it would have been impossible to make a lady out of any one of them. Climate, no doubt, has most to do with diffusing a slender elegance over American young-womanhood; but something, perhaps, is also due to the circumstance that classes are not kept apart there, as they are here; they cross-breed together, amid the continual ups-and-downs of our social life; and so, in the lowest stratum of life, you may see the refining influence of gentle blood. At all events, it is only necessary to look at such an assemblage of children as I saw yesterday, to be convinced that birth and blood [106] do produce certain characteristics. To be sure, I have seen no similar evidence, in England or elsewhere, that old gentility refines and elevates the race.

These girls were all dressed in black gowns, with white aprons and necker-chiefs, and white linen caps on their heads; a very dowdy-ish attire, and well suited to their figures. I saw only two of their games;—in one, they stood in a circle, while two of their number chased one another within and without the ring of girls, which opened to let the fugitive pass, but closed again to impede the passage of the pursuer. The other was blindman's buff on a new plan; several of the girls, sometimes as many as twenty, being blinded at once, and pursuing a single one, who rang a hand-bell to indicate her where-about. This was very funny; the bell-girl keeping just beyond their reach, and drawing them after her in a huddled group, so that they sometimes tumbled over one another and lay sprawling. I think I have read of this game in Strutt's English Sports and Pastimes.[226]

We walked from the Park home to Rock Ferry, a distance of three or four miles, a part of which was made delightful by a foot-path leading us through fields where the grass had just been mown, and others where the wheat-harvest had [107] been commenced. The path led us right into the midst of the rural labor that was going forward; and the laborers rested a moment to look at us; in fact, they seemed to be more willing to rest than American laborers would have been. Children were loitering along this path, or sitting down beside it; and we met one little maid passing from village to village, intent on some errand. Reaching Tranmere, I went into an ale-house nearly opposite the Hall, and called for a glass of ale. The door-step before the house, and the flag-stone floor of the entry and tap-room, were chalked all over in cork-screw lines; an adornment that gave an impression of care and neatness, the chalks being evidently fresh-made. It was a low, old-fashioned room, ornamented with a couple of sea-shells, and an earthen-ware figure, on the mantel-piece; also, with advertisements of Alsopp's Ale, and other drinks, and with a pasteboard handbill of "The Ancient Order of Foresters," any member of which, paying sixpence weekly, is entitled to ten shillings per week, and the attendance of a first-rate physician, in sickness, and twelve pounds to be paid to his friends, in case of death. Any member of the order, when travelling, is sure (the handbill says) to meet with a brother-member to [108] lend him a helping hand; there being nearly three thousand districts of the order, and more than 109000 members in Great Britain—whence, too, it has extended to Australia, and America, and other countries.

Looking up at the gateway of Tranmere Hall, after we left the alehouse, Julian discovered an inscription of [on] the red freestone lintel, and though much time-worn, I succeeded in reading it. "Labor omnia vincit. 1614." There were likewise some initials, which I could not satisfactorily make out. The sense of this motto would rather befit the present agricultural occupants of the house, than the idle old gentlefolks who built and formerly inhabited it.

AUGUST 25th, SATURDAY.

ON Thursday, I went by invitation to Smithell's Hall,[227] at Bolton le Moors, to dine and spend the night. The hall is two or three miles from the town of Bolton, where I arrived by railway from Liverpool, and which seems to be a pretty large town, though the houses are generally modern, or with modernized fronts of brick or stucco. It is a manufacturing town; and the tall brick chimnies [sic] rise numerously in the neighborhood, and are so near Smithell's Hall that, I suspect, the atmosphere is sometimes impregnated with their breath. Mr Ainsworth[228] comforts himself, however, with the rent which he receives from the [109] factories erected on his own grounds; and I suppose the value of his estate has greatly increased by the growth of manufactures; although, unless he wishes to sell it, I do not see what good this can do him.

Smithell's Hall is one of the oldest residences in England, and still retains very much the aspect that it must have had, several centuries ago. The house formerly stood around all four sides of a quadrangle, enclosing a court, and with an entrance through an archway. One side of this quadrangle was removed in the time of the present Mr. Ainsworth's father, and the front is now formed by the remaining three sides. They look exceedingly ancient and venerable, with their range of gables, and lesser peaks. The house is probably timber-framed throughout, and is overlaid with plaister [sic], and its generally light hue is painted with a row of trefoils, in black, producing a very quaint effect. The wing forming one side of the quadrangle is a chapel, and has been so from time immemorial; and Mr. Ainsworth told me, with some pride, that he had a clergyman, and was bishop in his own diocese. The drawing-room is on the opposite side of the quadrangle; and through an arched door, in the central portion, there is a passage to the rear of the house. It is [110] impossible to describe such an old rambling edifice as this, or to get any clear idea of its plan, even by going over it, without the aid of a map. Mr. Ainsworth has added some portions, and altered others, but with due regard to harmony with the original structure; and the great body of it is still mediaeval.

The entrance-hall opens right upon the quadrangular court; and is a large, low room, with a settle of old carved oak, and other old oaken furniture; a centre table, with periodicals and newspapers on it; some family pictures on the walls; and a large, bright coal-fire in the spacious grate. This fire is always kept up, throughout summer and winter; and it seemed to me an excellent plan, and rich with cheerful effects—insuring one comfortable place (and that the most central in the house) whatever may be the inclemency of weather. It was a cloudy, moist, showery day when I arrived; and this fire gave me the brightest and most hospitable smile, and took away my shivery feeling by its mere presence. The servant showed me thence into a low-studded drawing room, where soon Mrs Ainsworth made her appearance; and after some talk, brought me into the billiard-room (opening from the hall) where Mr. Ainsworth and a young gentleman were playing billiards, and two [111] ladies looking on. After the game was finished, the old gentleman took me round to see the house and grounds.

The peculiarity of this house is what is called "The Bloody Footstep."[229] In the time of Bloody Mary, a protestant clergyman (George Marsh by name) was examined before the then proprietor of the Hall (Sir Roger Barton, I think it was) and committed to prison for his heretical opinions, and ultimately burned at the stake. As his guards were conducting him from the justice-room, through the stone-paved passage that leads from front to rear of Smithell's Hall, he stamped his foot upon one of the flag-stones, in earnest protestation against the wrong which he was undergoing. The foot, as some say, left a bloody mark in the stone; others have it, that the stone yielded like wax under his foot, and that there has been a shallow cavity ever since. This miraculous footprint is still extant; and Mrs. Ainsworth showed it to me, before her husband took me round the estate. It is almost at the threshold of the door opening from the rear of the house, a stone two or three feet square, set among similar ones, that seem to have been worn by the tread of many generations. The footprint is a dark-brown stain in the smooth gray surface of the [112] flag-stone; and looking sidelong at it, there is a shallow cavity perceptible, which Mrs. Ainsworth accounted for as having been worn by people setting their feet just at this place so as to tread the very spot where the martyr wrought the miracle. The mark is longer than any mortal foot, as if caused by sliding along the stone, rather than sinking into it; and it might be supposed to have been made by a pointed shoe, being blunt at the heel, and decreasing towards the toe. The blood-stain version of the story is more consistent with the appearance of the mark, than the imprint would be; for if the martyr's blood oozed out through his shoe and stocking, it might have made his foot slide along the stone, and thus have lengthened the shape.

Of course, it is all a humbug—a darker vein cropping up through the gray flag-stone; but it is probably fact (and, for aught I know, may be found in Fox[230]) that George Marsh underwent an examination in this house; and the tradition may have connected itself with the stone within a short time after the martyrdom. Or perhaps, when the old persecuting knight departed this life, and Bloody Mary was also dead, people who had stood a little distance from the hall-door, and had seen George Marsh lift his hands and stamp his foot, just at this spot—perhaps they remembered this action and gesture, and [113] really believed that Providence had thus made an indelible record of it on the stone; although the very stone and the very mark might have lain there at the threshold, hundreds of years before. But, even if it had been always there, the footprint might, after the fact, be looked upon as a prophecy, from the time when the foundation of the old house was laid, that a holy and persecuted man should one day set his foot here, on the way that was to lead him to the stake. At any rate, the legend is a good one.

Mrs Ainsworth tells me that the miraculous stone was once taken up from the pavement and flung out of doors, where it remained many years; and in proof of this, it is cracked quite across, at one end. This is a pity, and rather interferes with the authenticity, if not of the stone itself, yet of its position in the pavement. It is not far from the foot of a staircase, leading up to Sir Roger Barton's examination-room, whither we ascended after examining the footprint. This room now opens sideways on the chapel, into which it looks down, and which is spacious enough to accommodate a pretty large congregation. On one of the walls of the chapel there is a marble tablet to the memory of one of the Ains[114]worths—Mr. Ainsworth's father, I suppose, he being the first of the name who possessed this estate. The present owners, however, seem to feel pretty much the same pride in the antiquity and legends of the house, as if it had come down to them in an unbroken succession of their own forefathers. It has, in reality, passed several times from one family to another, since the Conquest.

Mr. Ainsworth led me through a spacious old room (which was formerly panelled with carved oak, but which he has converted into a brew-house) up a pair of stairs, into the garret of one of the gables, in order to show me the ancient framework of the house. It is of oak, and preposterously ponderous— immense beams and rafters, which no modern walls could support—a gigantic old skeleton, which architects say must have stood a thousand years; and, indeed, it is impossible to ascertain the date of the original foundation of the house, though it is known to have been repaired and restored between five and six centuries ago. Of course, in the lapse of ages, it must continually have been undergoing minor changes, but without at all losing its identity. Mr. Ainsworth says that this old oak wood (though it looks as strong and as solid as ever) has really lost its strength, and that it would snap short off on any application of force.

[115] After this, we took our walk through the grounds, which are well wooded, though the trees will bear no comparison with those which I have seen in the midland parts of England. It takes, I suspect, a much longer time for trees to attain a good size, here, than in America; and these trees (I think Mr. Ainsworth told me) were principally set out by himself. He is a man

upwards of sixty, a good specimen enough of the old English country gentleman, not highly polished, pretty sensible, loving his land and his trees, and his dog and his game, doing a little justice-business, and showing a kind of fitness for his position, so that you feel rather satisfied than otherwise to have him keep it. He was formerly a member of parliament. I had met him, before, at dinner at Mrs. Heywood's, and thought him merely stupid; but he figures much more respectably here on his own estate, and would hardly be improved, I think, by brighter qualities.[231] He took pleasure, no doubt, in showing me his grounds, through which he has laid out a walk, winding up and down through dells and over hillocks, and now and then crossing a rustic bridge; so that you have an idea of quite an extensive domain. Beneath the trees, there is a thick growth of ferns, ser[116]ving as cover for the game. A little terrier-dog, who had hitherto kept us company, all at once disappeared; and soon afterwards we heard the squeak of of [sic] some poor victim in the cover—whereupon Mr. Ainsworth set out, with unexpected agility, and ran to the rescue. By-and-by, the terrier came back, with a very guilty look. From the wood, we passed into the open park, whence we had a distant view of the house; and returning thither, we viewed it in other aspects, and on all sides. One portion of it is occupied by Mr. Ainsworth's gardener, and seems not to have been repaired (at least as to its exterior) for a great many years—showing the old wooden frame, painted black, with plaister [sic] in the interstices; and the broad windows, extending across the whole breadth of the rooms, with hundreds of little diamond-shaped panes of glass.

Before dinner, I was shown to my room, which opens from an ancient gallery, lined with oak, and lighted by a row of windows along one side of the quadrangle. Along this gallery are the doors of several sleeping chambers, one of which—I think it is here—is called the "Dead Man's Chamber." It is supposed to have been the room where the corpses of persons connected with the household used to be laid out. My own room was called the "Beam Chamber," from an immense [117] cross-beam that projects from the cieling [sic], and seems to be an entire tree, laid across, and left rough-hewn, though at present white-washed. The but[t] of this tree (for it diminishes from one end of the chamber to the other) is nearly two feet square, in its visible part.

We dined at seven °clock, in a room some thirty five or forty feet long, and proportionably broad, all panelled with the old carved oak, which Mr. Ainsworth took from the room which he has converted into a brew-house. This oak is now of a very dark brown hue, and being highly polished, it produces a sombre, but rich effect. It is supposed to be of the era of Henry the Seventh; and when I examined it, next morning, I found it very delicately and curiously wrought. There are carved profiles of persons in the costume of the times, done with great skill; also, foliage, intricate puzzles of intersecting lines, sacred devices, anagrams, and, among others, the device of a bar across a tun, indicating the name of Barton. Most of the carving, however, is less elaborate and intricate than these specimens, being in a perpendicular style, and on one pattern. Before the wood grew so very dark, the beauty of the work must have been much more easily seen than now, as to particulars, though I hardly [118] think that the general effect could have been better—at least, the sombre richness that overspreads the entire square of the room is suitable to such an antique house. An elaborate Gothic cornice runs round the whole apartment. The sideboard and other furniture are of Gothic patterns, and, very likely, of genuine antiquity; but the fire-place is perhaps rather out of keeping, being of white-marble, with the arms of the Ainsworths sculptured on it.

Though hardly sunset when we sat down to dinner, yet, it being an overcast day, and the oaken room so sombre, we had candles burning on the dinner-table; and long before dinner was over, the candlelight was all we had. It is always pleasantest to dine by artificial light,—at least, unless [the dinner] be of the simplest order. Mrs. Ainsworth's dinner was a good one, though not magnificent, and Mr. Ainsworth's wines were very good, though it struck me that the supply was scantier than one usually sees at English tables. I had Mrs. Ainsworth on one side, and a round, bouncing woman, with an abundance of bust, on the other—a very ugly woman, uglier and grosser than an American woman could possibly be, and yet not absolutely unladylike. She had a great pimple on one side of her nose, and had very little to say. Mrs. Ainsworth talked rather copiously, but not particularly [119] well. She seems to have pretensions to a knowledge of literature, and to take an interest in literary people; but her talk is quite superficial, and, I must say, I think her a silly woman. One anecdote which she told was very characteristic—not of the hero of it—but of herself and of the English people generally, as showing what their tone and feeling is, respecting Americans. Mr. Bancroft, while Minister here, was telling somebody about the effect of the London atmosphere on his wife's health. "She is now very delicate," said he; "whereas, when we lived in New York, she was one of the most *indelicate* women in the city!" And Mrs. Ainsworth had the face to tell this foolish story for truth, and as indicating the mistakes into which Americans are liable to fall, in the use of the English language. In other instances, I have heard stories equally ridiculous about our diplomatic people, whom the English seemed determined to make butts of, reason or none. It is very queer, this resolute quizzing of our manners, when we are really and truly much better figures, and with much more capacity of polish, for drawing-room or dining-room, than they themselves are. I had been struck, on my arrival at Smithell's Hall, by the very rough [120] aspects of these John Bulls in their morning garbs, their coarse frock-coats, gray hats, checked pantaloons, and stout shoes. At the dinner-table, it was not at first easy to recognize the same individuals in their white waistcoats, muslin cravats, and their black coats, with silk facings, perhaps, as old Squire Ainsworth himself had; but, after awhile, you see the same rough figure through all this finery, and become sensible that John Bull cannot make himself fine, whatever he may put on. He is a rough animal, and incapable of high-polish; and his female is well adapted to him.[232]

After dinner, there were two card-parties formed in the drawing-room, at one of which there was a game of Vingt-un, and at the other a game of whist, at which Mrs. Ainsworth and I lost several shillings to a Mrs. Hutton and a Mr. Gaskill. It was amusing to observe the satisfaction with which the winners received and pocketed these little sums. I suppose they play at whist every night, and that the small vicissitudes of the game, and its petty results, are an essential part of their life. On the whole, I have been rather bored with these people, and with everything at Smithell's Hall, except the house itself. After finishing our games at cards, Mrs Hutton drove off in a pony-chaise to her own house; [121] the other ladies went to bed; and the gentlemen sat down to chat awhile over the hall-fire, occasionally sipping a glass of wine-and-water; and finally we all went off to our rooms. It was past twelve °clock when I got into bed; and I could not have slept long, when a tremendous clap of thunder awoke me, just in time to see a vivid flash of lightning. I saw no ghosts, though Mrs. Ainsworth tells me there is one, which makes a disturbance unless religious services are regularly kept up in the chapel.

In the morning, before breakfast, we had prayers (read by Mr. Ainsworth) in the oak dining-room, all the servants coming in, and everybody kneeling down. I should like to know how much true religious feeling is indicated by this regular observance of religious rites, in English families. In America, if people kneel down to pray, it is pretty certain that they feel a genuine interest in the matter, and their daily life is supposed to be in accordance with their morning devotion. But the Englishman goes from prayer to pleasure, and is a worldly man in all respects till morning prayer-time comes about again. If an American is an infidel, he knows it; but an Englishman is often so without sus[122]pecting it—being kept from that knowledge by this formality of family prayer and his other regularities of external worship. They feel nothing, and bring themselves no nearer to God when they pray, than when they play at cards.

There was a parrot in a corner of the dining-room; and when prayers were over, Mrs. Ainsworth praised it very highly for having been so silent;—it being Poll's habit, probably, to break in upon the sacred exercises with unseemly interjections and remarks. While we were at breakfast, Poll began to whistle and talk very vociferously, and in a tone and with expressions that surprised me, till I learned that the bird is usually kept in the kitchen and servant's hall, and is only brought into the dining-room at prayer-time and breakfast. Thus, its mouth is full of kitchen-talk, which flows out before the gentlefolks with the queerest effect.

After breakfast, I examined the carvings of the room. Mr. Ainsworth has added to its decorations the coats of arms of all the successive possessors of the house, with those of the families into which they married, including the Ratcliffes, Stanleys, and others. From the dining-room, I passed into the library, which contains books enough to [123] make a rainy day pass pleasantly. I remember nothing else that I need to record; and as I sat by the hall-fire, talking with Mr. Gaskill, at about 11 °clock, the butler brought me word that a fly, which I had bespoken, was ready to convey me to the railway. I took leave of Mrs. Ainsworth—her last request being that I would write a ghost-story for her house—and drove off, without at all caring to stay any longer. But I should think a week or two might pass very agreeably in an English country-house, provided the host and hostess and the guests were particularly pleasant people. Otherwise, I would rather possess myself in a hotel.

Septr 5th Wednesday, 1855.

YESTERDAY, we all of us (Mamma, Una, Julian, Rosebud, Fanny Wrigley, and I) set forth from Rock Ferry at ½ past 12, and reached Shrewsbury between three and four °clock, and took up our quarters at the Lion Hotel. We found Shrewsbury situated on an eminence, around which the Severn winds, making a peninsula of it, quite densely covered by the town. The streets ascend, and curve about, and intersect each other, with the customary irregularity of these old English towns; so that it is quite impossible to go directly to any given point, or for a stranger to find his way to a place which he wishes to [124] reach, though, by what seems singular good fortune, the sought for place is always offering itself when least expected. On this account, I never knew such pleasant walking as in old streets like those of Shrewsbury. And there are passages opening under archways, and winding up between high edifices, very tempting to the explorer, and generally leading to some court, or some queer old range of buildings, or piece of architecture, which it would be the greatest pity to miss seeing. There was a delightful want of plan in the laying out of these ancient towns; in fact, they never were laid out at all, nor were restrained by any plan whatever, but grew naturally, with streets as eccentric as the pathway of a young child toddling about the floor.

The first curious thing we particularly noticed, when we strolled out, after dinner, was the old market-house, which stands in the midst of an oblong square; a gray edifice, elevated on pillars and arches, and with the statue of an armed knight (it is Richard Plantaganet, Duke of York) in the central niche in its front. The statue is older than the market-house, having been removed thither from one of the demolished towers of the city wall, in 1795. The market-house was erected in 1596. There are other curious sculptures and carvings, and quirks of architecture about this building; and [125] the houses that stand about the square are, many of them, very striking specimens of what dwelling-houses used to be in Elizabeth's time, and earlier. I have seen no such stately houses, in that style, as we found here in Shrewsbury; there were no such fine ones in Coventry, Stratford, Warwick, Chester, nor anywhere else where we have been. Their stately height and spaciousness seem to have been owing to the fact that Shrewsbury was a sort of metropolis of the country round about, and therefore the neighboring gentry had their town-houses there, when London was several days journey off, instead of a very few hours; and, besides, it was once much the resort of kings, and the centre-point of great schemes of war and policy. One such house, formerly belonging to a now extinct family (that of Ireland) rises to the height of four stories, and has a front consisting of what look like four projecting towers; there are ranges of embowed windows, one above another to the full height of the house, and surmounted by peaked gables. The people of those times certainly did not deny themselves light; and while window-glass was an article of no very remote introduction, it was probably a point of magnificence and wealthy display, to have enough of it. One whole side of the room must often have [126] been formed by the window. This Ireland mansion (and so are all the rest of the old houses in Shrewsbury) is a timber-house; that is, a skeleton of oak, filled up with brick, plaister [sic], or other material, and with the beams of the timber marked out in black paint; besides which, in houses of any pretension, there are generally trefoils, and other Gothic-looking ornaments, likewise painted black. They have an indescribable charm for me;—the more, I think, because they are wooden;—but, indeed, I cannot tell why it is that I like them so well, and am never tired of looking at them. A street was a developement [sic] of human life, in the days when these houses were built; whereas a modern street is but the cold plan of an architect, without individuality or character, and without the human emotion which a man kneads into the walls which he builds on a scheme of his own.

We strolled to a pleasant walk under a range of trees, along the shore of the Severn. It is called the Quarry Walk. The Severn is a pretty river, the largest, I think, (unless it be such an estuary as the Mersey) that I have met with in England; that is to say, about a fair stone's throw across. It is very gentle in its course and winds along between grassy and sedgy banks, with a good growth of weeds in some part of its current. It has one stately bridge (called the [127] English bridge) of several arches; and, as we sauntered along the Quarry walk, we saw a ferry, where the boat seemed to be navigated across by means of a rope stretched from bank to bank of the river. After leaving the Quarry Walk, we passed an old tower of red free-stone, the only one remaining of those formerly standing at intervals along the whole course of the town-wall; and we also went along what little is now left of the wall itself. And, thence, through the irregular streets, which give no account of themselves, we found our way, I know not how, to our hotel. It is an uncheerful old house, which we should think very shabby in America, but which takes upon itself to be in the best class of English country-hotels, and charges the best price; very dark in the lower apartments, pervaded with a musty smell, but provided with a white neckclothed waiter, who spares no ceremony in serving the joint of mutton.

Julian and I afterwards walked forth again, and went this time to the castle, which stands right above the railway station. A path (from its breadth, it is quite a street) leads up to the arched gateway; but we found a board, giving notice that these are private grounds, and no strangers admitted; so that we only passed through [128] the gate, a few steps, and looked about us, and retired on perceiving a man approaching us through the trees and shrubbery. A private individual, it seems, has burrowed in this old warlike den, and turned the keep and any other available apartment into a modern dwelling, and laid out his pleasure grounds within the precinct of the castle wall, which allows verge enough for the purpose. The ruins have been considerably repaired. This castle was built at various periods, (the keep, by Edward I, and other portions at an earlier date) and it stands on the isthmus left by the Severn, in its winding course about the town. The Duke of Cleveland now owns it; I do not know who occupies it.

In the course of this walk, we passed Saint Mary's Church;—a very old church indeed—no matter how old—but, say, eight hundred or a thousand years. It has a very tall spire; and the spire is now undergoing repair, and seeing the door open, I went into the porch, but found no admission further. Then, walking around it, through the churchyard, we saw that all the venerable Gothic windows—one of them grand in size—were set with stained glass, representing coats of arms, and men in ancient armor, and kingly robes, and saints with glories about their heads, and scriptural people; but all of these (as far as our actual perception was concerned) quite [129] colorless, and with only a cold outline, dimly filled up. Yet, had we been within the church, and had the sunlight been streaming through, what a warm, rich, gorgeous, roseate, golden life would these figures have showed. It may be taken as a symbol of the difference of effect in Scripture history and doctrine, when viewed from the outside of the spiritual church, and when viewed from within. In the former case, how lifeless; in the latter, how imbued with the most vivid life![233]

In the churchyard, close upon the street, so that its dust must continually be scattered over the spot, I saw a heavy, gray tombstone, with a Latin inscription, purporting that Bishop Butler[234] (the author of the Analogy) in his life time, had chosen this as a burial place for himself and his family. There is a statue of him within the church. From the top of the spire of this church, a man (above a hundred years ago) attempted to descend by means of a rope, to the other side of the Severn; but the rope broke, and he fell in his midway flight, and was killed. It was an undertaking worthy of Sam Patch.[235] There is a record of the fact on the outside of the tower.

I remember nothing more that we saw, yesterday; but, before breakfast, Julian and I sallied forth again, [130] and inspected the gateway and interior court of the Council House; a very interesting place, both in itself, and for the circumstances connected with it;—it having been the place where the Councils for the Welsh Marches used to reside during their annual meetings; and Charles the First also lived here for six weeks, in 1642. James II likewise held his court here, in 1687. The house was originally built in 1501—that is, the Council House itself—the gate-way, and the house through which it passes, being of as late date as 1620. This latter is a fine old house, in the usual style of timber architecture, with the timber-lines marked out, and quaint adornments in black paint; and the pillars of the gateway (which passes right beneath the front chamber of the house) are of curiously carved oak, which has probably stood the action of English atmosphere better than marble would. Passing through this gateway we enter a court, and see some old houses (more or less modernized, but without destroying their aged stateliness) standing round three sides of it, with arched entrances, and bow windows, and windows on the roofs, and peaked gables, and all the delightful irregularity and variety that these houses have, and which make them always so fresh;—and with so much detail that, every minute, you see something heretofore unseen. It must have been no unfit [131] residence for a king and his court, when those three sides of the square (all composing one great, fantastic house) were in their splendor. The square itself, too, must have been a busy and cheerful scene, thronged with attendants, guests, horses, &c.

After breakfast, Mamma, Una, Julian, and I walked out, and crossing the English Bridge, looked at the Severn over its parapet. The river is here broader than elsewhere, and very shallow, and has an island covered with bushes about midway across. Just across the bridge, we saw an old church, of red free-stone, and evidently very ancient; this is the church of the Holy Cross, and is a portion of the ancient Abbey of Saint Peter and Saint John, which formerly covered ten acres of ground. We did not have time to go into the church; but the windows and other points of architecture (so far as we could discern them and knew how to admire them) were exceedingly venerable and beautiful. On the other side of the street, over a wide space, there are other remains of the old Abbey; and the most interesting was an old stone pulpit, now standing in the open air, (seemingly in a garden) but which originally stood in the Refectory of the Abbey, and was the station whence one of the monks read to his brethren, at their meals. The pulpit is much over[132]grown with ivy. We should have made further researches among these remains (though they seem now to be in private grounds) but a large mastiff came out of his kennel, and approaching us to the length of his iron chain, began barking very fiercely. Nor had we time to see half that we would gladly have seen and studied, here and elsewhere, about Shrewsbury. It would have been very interesting to visit Hotspur's and Falstaff's battlefield, which is four miles from the town;—too distant, certainly, for Falstaff to have measured the length of the fight by Shrewsbury clock. There is now a church, built there by Henry IV, and said to cover the bones of those slain in the battle.

Returning into the town, we penetrated some narrow lanes, where, as the old story goes, people might almost shake hands across from the top windows of the opposite houses, impending towards each other. Emerging into a wider street, at a spot somewhat more elevated than other parts of the town, we went into a shop to buy some Royal Shrewsbury Cakes, which we had seen advertised at several shop windows. They are a very rich cake, with plenty of eggs, sugar, and butter, and very little flour. A small public building of stone, of modern date, was close by; and asking the shopwoman what it was, she said it was the

Butter Cross, or market for butter, eggs, and [133] poultry. This is a memorable site; for here, in ancient times, stood a stone Cross, whence heralds used to make proclamation, and where criminals of state used to be executed. David, the last of the Welsh princes, was here cruelly put to death by Edward I; and many noblemen were beheaded on this spot, after being taken prisoners in the battle of Shrewsbury.

I can only notice one other memorable place in Shrewsbury, and that is the Raven Inn, where Farquhar wrote his comedy of the "Recruiting Officer," in 1704. The window of the room, in which he wrote, is said to look into the Inn-yard; and I went through the arched entrance to see if I could distinguish it. The ostlers were currying horses in the yard, and stared at me so that I gave but the merest peep. The Shrewsbury inns have not only the customary names of English inns—the Lion, the Stag's Head &c—but have also carved wooden figures of the object named; whereas, in all other towns, the name only remains.

We left Shrewsbury at half past ten, and arrived in London at about four in the afternoon. I ought to have mentioned a serious accident that occurred to us, on our first arrival in Shrewsbury, by the breaking of a bottle of port-wine on the stone-pavement of the Railway-station. We had brought [134] it for our travelling-store; and, indeed, so short are the stoppages on English railways, that people must carry their own meat and drink, or else go hungry and thirsty. This mishap, and the fragrance of the port-wine, caused the railway officials to gather round us like flies round a drop of molasses, and drew on us the smiling notice of a whole train of passengers, waiting to set off.

SEPTEMBER 7 FRIDAY

ON Wednesday, just before dark, Julian and I walked forth for the first time in London. Our lodgings are in George street, Hanover square, No. 24; and Saint George's Church, where so many marriages, in Romance and in fashionable life, have been celebrated, is a short distance below our house, in the same street. The edifice seems to be of white marble (now much blackened with London smoke) and has a Grecian pillared portico. In the square, just above us, is a statue of William Pitt. We went down Bond-street and part of Regent-street, just straying a little way from [our] temporary nest, and taking good account of landmarks and corners of streets, so as to find our way readily back again. It is long since I have had such a childish feeling; but all that I had heard, and felt, about the vastness of London, made it seem like swimming in a boundless ocean, to venture one step beyond the only spot I knew. My first actual impression of London was of stately and spacious streets, and by no means so dusky and grimy as I had expected—not [135] merely in the streets about this quarter of the town, which is the aristocratic quarter, but in all the streets through which we had passed from the Railway station. If I had not first been so imbued with the smoke and dinginess of Liverpool, I should doubtless have seen a stronger contrast betwixt dusky

London and the cheerful glare of our American cities. There are no red bricks here; all are of a dark hue, and whatever of stone or stucco has been white soon çlothes itself in mourning.

Yesterday forenoon, I went out alone, and plunged headlong into London, and wandered about all day, without any particular object in view, but only to lose myself, for the sake of finding myself unexpectedly among things that I have always read and dreamed about. The plan was pretty successful; for (besides vague and unsuccessful wanderings) I saw, in the course of the day, Hyde Park, the Regent's Park, Whitehall, the two new houses of Parliament, Charing Cross, St. Paul's, the Strand, Fleet-street, Cheapside, Whitechapel, Leadenhall-street, the Haymarket, and a great many other places, the names of which were classic in my memory. I think what interests me most here is the London of the writers of [the] Queen Anne age—whatever Pope, the Spectator, De Foe, and down as late as Johnson and Goldsmith have mentioned. The Monument, for instance, which is of no great [136] height or beauty, as compared with that on Bunker Hill, charmed me prodigiously. Saint Paul's appeared to me unspeakably grand and noble, and the more so from the throng and bustle continually going on around its base, without in the least disturbing the solemn repose of its great dome, and, indeed, of all its massive height and breadth. Other edifices may crowd close to its foundation, and people may tramp as they like about it, but still the great cathedral is as quiet and serene as if it stood in the middle of Salisbury plain. There cannot be anything else in the world so good, in its way, as just this effect of Saint Paul's in the very heart and densest tumult of London. I do not know whether the church is built of marble, or of whatever other white, or nearly white, material; but, in the time that it has been standing there, it has grown black with the smoke of ages, through which there are nevertheless gleams of white, that make a most picturesque impression on the whole. It is much better than staring white; the edifice would not be nearly so grand without this drapery of black.

I did not find these streets of old London so narrow and irregular as I expected. All the principal streets are sufficiently broad, and there are few houses that look antique, being, I suppose, generally modern fronted, when not actually of modern substance. There is little or no show or pretension in this part of the city; [137] it has a plain, business air; an air of homely, actual life, of a metropolis of tradesmen, who have been carrying on their traffic here, in sober earnest, for hundreds of years. You observe on the signboards— "established ninety years in Threadneedle-street"—"established in 1709"—denoting long pedigrees of silk-mercers and hosiers—De Foe's contemporaries still represented by their posterity, who handle the hereditary yardstick on the same spot.

I must not forget to say that I crossed the Thames over a bridge, which, I think, is near Charing Cross. Afterwards, I found my way to London bridge, where there was a delightful intensity of throng. The Thames is not so wide and majestic as I had imagined; nothing like the Mersey, for example. As a picturesque object, however, flowing through the midst of a city, it would lose by any increase of width.

I got a mutton-chop in the very meanest and dirtiest eating-place I ever chanced upon; a filthy table-cloth, covered with other people's crumbs; iron forks, a leaden salt cellar, the commonest earthen plates; a little dark stall, to sit and eat in. This place called itself the "Albert Dining Rooms." The charge for a chop, with bread, potatoes, and beans—each of which articles was proffered [sic] to me separately—together with a half-pint of ale—was a shilling; and, in order to be mag[138]nificent, I gave two pence to the girl who waited on me. This appeared not to be a disreputable place, but an honest place of resort for people whose circumstances were just adapted to that measure of comfort and luxury.

Omnibusses [sic] are a most important aid to wanderers about London. I reached home, well wearied, about six °clock. In the course of the day, I had seen one person whom I knew; the Mr. Clarke, to whom Henry Bright introduced me, when we went to see the great ship launched in the Dee. This, I believe, was in Regent-street. In that street, too, I saw a company of dragoons, beautifully mounted, and defensively armed in brass helmets and steel-cuirasses, polished to the utmost intensity of splendor. It was a pretty sight. At one of the public edifices, on each side of the portal, sat a mounted trooper, similarly armed, and with his carbine resting on his knee, just as motionless as a statue. This, too, as a picturesque circumstance, was very good, and really made an impression on me with respect to the power and stability of the government; though I could not help smiling at myself for it. But then the thought, that, for generations, an armed warrior has always sat just there, on his war-steed, and with his weapon in his hand, is pleasant to the imagination; although it is questionable whether his carbine is loaded; and, no doubt, if the authorities had any mes[139]sages to send, they would choose some other messenger than this heavy dragoon—the electric wire, for instance. Still, if he and his horse were to be withdrawn from their post, night or day (for I suppose the sentinels are on duty all night) it seems [as] if the monarchy would be subverted, and the British Constitution crumble into rubbish; and, in honest fact, it will signify something like that, when guard is relieved there for the last time.

SEPTEMBER 8th SATURDAY

YESTERDAY forenoon, Sophia, the two eldest children [, and I] went forth into London-streets, and proceeded down Regent street, and thence to Saint James Park, at the entrance of which is a statue of somebody, I forget whom. On the very spacious gravel-walk (covering several acres) in the rear of the Horse Guards, some soldiers were going through their exercise; and after looking at them awhile, we strolled through the park, along side of a sheet of water, in which various kinds of ducks, geese, and rare species of waterfowl, were swimming. There was one swan, of immense size, which moved about among the minor fowls like a first rate ship among gun-boats. By-and-by, we found ourselves near what we have since found to be Buckingham Palace, a long building in the Italian style, but of no impressiveness, and which one soon wearies of looking at. The Queen having gone to Scotland the day before, the palace now looked deserted, al[140]though there was a one-horse cab, of shabby aspect, standing at the principal front, where doubtless the carriages of princes and nobility drew up. There is a fountain playing before the palace; and waterfowl love to swim under its perpetual shower. These ducks and geese are very tame, and swim to the margin of the pond to be fed by visitors, looking up at you with great intelligence.

My wife asked a man in a sober sort of livery (of whom we saw several about the park) whose were some of the large mansions which we saw; and he pointed out Stafford House, the residence of the Duke of Sutherland, a very noble edifice, much more beautiful than the palace, though not so large; also one or two other residences of noblemen. I believe the house of Rogers,[236] the poet, is in the same row. This range of mansions, along the park, from the spot whence we viewed them, looks very much like Beacon street in Boston, bordering on the common, allowing for a considerable enlargement of scale, in favor of the park-residences. The park, however, has not the beautiful elms that overshadow Boston common, nor such a pleasant undulation of surface, nor the far-off view of the country, like that across Charles-river. I doubt whether London can show so delightful a spot as that common—always excepting the superiority of English lawns, which, how[141]ever, is not so evident in the London parks, there being less care bestowed on the grass than I should have expected.

From this place, we wandered into what I believe to be Hyde Park, attracted by a gigantic figure on horseback, which loomed up in the distance. The effect of this enormous steed and his rider is very grand, seen in the misty atmosphere of London. I do not understand why we did not see St. James['s] Palace, which is situated, I believe, at the extremity of the same range of mansions, of which Stafford House is at the opposite end. From the entrance of Hyde Park, we seem to have gone along Piccadilly; and, making two or three turns, and getting bewildered, I put Sophia and the children into a cab and sent them home. Continuing my wanderings, I went astray among squares of large, aristocratic-looking edifices, all apparently new, with no shops among them, some yet unfinished, and the whole seeming like a city built for a colony of gentlefolks who might be expected to emigrate thither in a body. It was a dreary business to wander there, turning corner after corner, and finding no way of getting into a less stately and more genial region. At last, however, I passed in front of the Queen's Mews, where sentinels were on guard, and where a jolly-looking man, in a splendidly laced scarlet coat and white-topt boots, was lounging at the entrance. He looked like the prince [142] of grooms or coachmen. Nearly on the opposite side of the street, there was a small, old-fashioned public-house, purporting to be the "Queen's Tavern and Tea Gardens," and there I called for a cigar and some ale, and went through the house to the garden in the rear, to refresh myself and smoke.

The tea-garden was not very beautifully adorned; a range of pent-houses along the wall, with benches and a table in each, and some wretched little straggly arbors in the middle. There was a shooting gallery connected with the garden, and I heard some shots of a pistol or rifle, while smoking my cigar. Two or three girls came and sat down in one of the arbors, talking and giggling; but I did not observe that they called for any refreshments. By the time I had done smoking, it was after one °clock; so I called for a chop, and ate it in the coffee-room, a neat little apartment enough. There was a notice of "Hot Joints from 1 till 3 °clock, daily"; and the waiter told me that the joint, that day, was boiled mutton. People certainly can dine very reasonably and very well, in London; for my chop—which was very good, though somewhat small, and very well served, together with bread, and two hot potatoes, and a glass of brandy-and-water, which I called for, because some call of the kind was expected—all came to eleven pence; and I gave the odd penny to the waiter.

[143] The corner of Hyde Park was within a short distance from the Queen's Tavern; and I took a Hansom at the cab-stand there, and drove to the American Despatch Agency (26 Henrietta-street, Covent Garden) having some documents of state to be sent by to-day's steamer. The business of forwarding despatches to America, and distributing them to the various legations and consulates in Europe, must be a pretty extensive one; for Mr. Miller has a large office, and two clerks in attendance. From this point, I went through Covent Garden market, and got astray in the city; so that I can give no clear account of my afternoon's wanderings. I passed through Holborn, however; and I think it was from that street that I passed through an archway (which I almost invariably do, whenever I see one) and found myself in a very spacious gravelled square, surrounded on the four sides by a continuous edifice of dark brick, very plain and of cold and stern aspect. This was Gray's Inn, all tenanted by a multitude of lawyers. Passing thence, I saw "Furnival's Inn," over another archway, but, being on the opposite side of the street, did not go in. In Holborn, still, I went through another arched entrance, over which was "Staples Inn"; and here likewise seemed to be offices; but, in a court opening inwards from this, there was a surrounding [144] seclusion of quiet dwelling-houses, with beautiful green shrubbery and grass-plots in the court, and a great many sun-flowers in full-bloom. The windows were open; it was a beautiful summer afternoon; and I have a sense that bees were humming in the court, though this may have been suggested by my fancy, because the sound would have been so well suited to the scene. A boy was reading at one of the windows. There was not a quieter spot in England than this; and it was very strange to have drifted into it so suddenly out of the bustle and rumble of Holborn, and to lose all this repose as suddenly, on passing through the arch of the outer court. In all the hundreds of years since London was built, it has not been able to sweep its roaring tide over that little island of quiet. In Holborn, I saw the most antique-looking houses that I have yet met with in London, but none of very remarkable aspect.

I think I must have been under a spell of enchantment, to-day, connecting me with Saint Paul's; for, trying to get away from it by various avenues, I still got bewildered, and again and again saw its great dome and pinnacles before me. I observe that the smoke has chiefly settled on the lower part of the edifice, leaving its loftier stories and its spires much less begrimed. It is very beautiful, very rich. I did not think that anything [145] but Gothic architecture could so have interested me. The statues, the niches, the embroidery, as it were, of sculpture traced around it—produced a delightful effect. In front of Saint Paul's, there is a statue of Queen Anne, looking rather more majestic, I doubt not, than that fat old dame ever did. St. Paul's Churchyard had always been a place of much interest in my imagination. It is merely the not very spacious street running round the base of the church; at least, this street is included as the churchyard, together with the enclosure immediately about the church, sowed with tombstones. I meant to look for the children's bookshop, but forgot it, or, I believe, neglected it, from not feeling so much interest in a thing near at hand, as when it seemed unattainable.

After this, I smoked a cigar in the smoking-room of the Queen's tavern, where were many cockneys, drinking brandy, gin, and punch, and smoking pipes and cigars, and where the waiter told me that they never brought any malt liquor up stairs; it being ungenteel, no doubt. While smoking, I watched a man tearing down the brick-wall of a house that did not appear very old; but it surprised me to see how crumbly the brick-work was, one stroke of his pick often loosening several bricks in a row. It is my opinion that brick houses, after a moderate term of years, stand more by habit and courtesy than through any adhesive force of the old mortar. When my cigar was out, [146] I recommenced my wanderings; but I remember nothing else particularly claiming to be mentioned, unless it be Paternoster Row, a little, narrow, darksome lane, in which (it being now dusk, in that density of the city) I could not very well see what signs were over the doors. In the Strand, or thereabouts, I got into an omnibus, and being set down near Regent's Circus, reached home well wearied.

SEPTEMBER 9th, SUNDAY.

YESTERDAY, having some tickets to the Zoological Gardens, we went thither with the two eldest children. It was a most beautiful sunny day; the very perfection of English weather,—which is as much as to say, the best weather in the world, except, perhaps, some few days in an American October. These gardens are at the end of Regent's Park, farthest from London, and are very extensive, though, I think, not quite worthy of London—not so good as one would expect them to be—not so fine and perfect a collection of beasts, birds, and fishes, as one might fairly look for, when the greatest metropolis of the world sets out to have such a collection at all. My idea was, that here every living thing was provided for, in the way best suited to its nature and habits, and that the refinement of civilization had here restored a Garden of Eden, where all the animal kingdom had regained a happy home. This is not quite the case; though, I believe, the creatures are [147] as comfortable as could be expected, and there are certainly a good many strange beasts here. The Hippopotamus, I believe, is the chief treasure of the collection; an immense, almost mis[s]hapen mass of flesh. At the moment, I do not distinctly remember anything that interested me, except a sick monkey—a very large monkey, and elderly, he seemed to be, and with a rear worn quite bare, by much sitting upon it. His keeper brought him some sweetened apple and water, and some tea; for the monkey had quite lost his appetite, and refused all ordinary diet. He came, however, quite eagerly, and smelt of the tea, and apple, the keeper exhorting him very tenderly to eat. But the poor monkey shook his head slowly, and with the most pitiable expression I ever saw, at the same [time] extending his hand to take the keeper's, as if claiming his sympathy and friendship. By and by, the keeper (who was rather a surly fellow) essayed harsher measures, and insisted that the monkey should eat what had been brought for him; and hereupon ensued somewhat of a struggle, and the tea was overturned upon the straw of the monkey's bed. Then the keeper scolded the monkey, and seizing him by one arm, drew him out of his little bed-room into the larger cage, upon which the wronged monkey began a loud, harsh, reproachful chatter, more expressive of a sense of injury than any words [148] could be. Observing the spectators in front of the cage, he seemed to appeal to them, and addressed his chatter thitherward, and stretched out his long, lean arm, and black hand, between the bars, as if claiming the grasp of any one friend he might have in the whole world. He was placable, however; for when the keeper called him in a gentler tone, he hobbled towards him, with a very stiff and rusty movement; and the scene closed with their affectionately hugging one another. But I fear the poor monkey will die. In a future state of being, I think it will be one my enquiries, in reference to the mysteries of this present state, why monkies [sic] were made. The Creator could not surely have meant to ridicule his own work. It might rather be supposed that Satan had perpetrated monkies [sic], with a malicious purpose of parodying the masterpiece of creation.

The aquarium, containing, in some of its compartments, specimens of the animal and vegetable life of the sea, and, in others, those of the fresh water, was richly worth inspecting, but nothing near so perfect as it might be. Now, I think we have a right to claim, in a metropolitan establishment of this kind, in all its departments, a degree of perfection that shall quite out-do the unpractised thought of any man, on that particular subject.

There were a good many well-dressed people and children in [149] the gardens, through the day; Saturday being a fashionable day for visiting them. One great amusement was feeding some bears, with biscuits and cakes, of which they seemed exceedingly fond. One of the bears (there were three) clambered to the top of a high pole, whence he invited the spectators to hand him bits of cake on the end of a stick, or to toss it into his mouth, which he opened widely for the purpose. Another, apparently an elderly bear, not having skill or agility for these gymnastics, sat on the ground, on his hinder end, groaning most pitifully. The third took what stray bits he could get, without earning them by any antics.

At four °clock, there was some music from the band of the First Life Guards;
a great multitude of chairs being set on the green-sward, in the sunshine and
shade, for the accommodation of the auditors. Here we had the usual exhibition
of English beauty, neither superior, nor otherwise, to what I have seen in other
parts of England. Before the music was over, we walked slowly homeward,
along beside Regent's Park, which is very prettily laid out, but lacks some last
touch of richness and beauty; though, after all, I do not well see what more
could be done with grass, trees, and gravel walks. The children—especially
[150] Julian, who had raced from one thing to another, all day long—grew
tired; so we put them into a cab, and walked slowly through Portland-place,
where are a great many noble mansions, yet no very admirable architecture;
none that possessed, or that ever can possess, the indefinable charm of some of
those poor old timber houses in Shrewsbury. The art of domestic architecture
is lost. We can rear stately and beautiful houses (though we seldom do) but
they do not seem proper to the life of man in the same way that his shell is
proper to the lobster;—nor, indeed, is the mansion of the nobleman proper to
him, in the same kind and degree that a hut is proper to a peasant.

From Portland-place, we passed I believe into Regent-street, and soon
reached home. This day has not been spent as my own taste would have inclined
me; but, when a man has taken upon himself to beget children, he has no longer
any right to a life of his own.

SEPTEMBER 10th, MONDAY.

YESTERDAY forenoon, we walked out with Una and children, intending for
Charing Cross; but missing our way, as usual, we went down a rather wide and
stately street, and saw before us an old brick edifice, with a pretty extensive
front, over which rose a clock-tower—the whole of dingy brick, and looking
both gloomy and mean. There was an arched entrance beneath the clock tower,
at which two guardsmen, in their bearskin-caps, were stationed as sentinels;
and [151] from this circumstance, and our having some guess at the locality, we
concluded the old brick building to be Saint James's Palace;—otherwise we
might have taken it for a prison, or for a hospital, which, in truth, it was at
first intended for. But, certainly, there are many paupers in England who live
in edifices of far more architectural pretension, externally, than this principal
palace of the English sovereigns.

Seeing other people go through the archway, we also went, meeting no impediment from the sentinels; and found ourselves in a large paved court, in the
centre of which a banner was stuck down, with a few soldiers standing near it.
This flag was the banner of the regiment of guards on duty. The aspect of the
interior court was as naked and dismal as the outside; the brick being of that
dark hue almost universal in England. On one side of the court, there was a
door which seemed to give admission to a chapel, into which several persons
went, and, probably we might have gone too, had we liked. From this court, we
penetrated into at least two or three others; for the palace is very extensive,

and all, so far as I could see, on the same pattern,—large, enclosed courts, paved, and quite bare of grass, shrubbery, or any beautiful thing—dark, stern brick walls, without the slightest show of architectural beauty, or even an ornament over the square, common-place windows, looking down on these forlorn [152] courts. A carriage-drive passes through it, if I remember right, from the principal front, emerging by one of the sides; and I suppose that the carriages roll through the palace, at the levees and drawing-rooms. There was nothing to detain us here any long time; so we went from court to court, and emerged through a side opening. The edifice is battlemented all round; and this—except somewhat of fantastic in the shape of the clock-tower—is the only attempt at ornament, in the whole.

Thence, we skirted along St. James' park, passing Marlborough House— a red brick building—and a very long range of stone edifices, which, whether it were public or private, and one house or twenty, we knew not. We ascended the steps by the York Column, and soon reached Charing Cross and Trafalgar Square, where there are more architectural monuments than in any other one place in London; besides two fountains playing in large reservoirs of water; and various edifices of note and interest. Northumberland House, now, and for a long while, the town residence of the Percies, stands on the Strand side, with a lion, very spiritedly sculptured, over the entrance, flinging out his long tail. On another side of the square is Morley's Hotel, exceedingly spacious, and looking more American than anything else in the Hotel line that I have seen in England. It is the site, too (viz. the very best in town) that Americans would choose for a principal hotel. The Nelson monu[153]ment, with himself in a cocked hat on its top, is very grand in its effect. All about the square, there were Sunday loungers, people looking at the bas-reliefs on Nelson's column, children paddling in the reservoirs of the fountains; and it being a sunny day, it was a cheerful and lightsome, as well as an impressive scene. On second thought, I do not know but that London should have a far better display of architecture and sculpture than this, on its finest site, and in its very centre; for, after all, there is nothing of the very best. But I missed nothing, at the time.

In the afternoon, Sophia and I set out to attend divine service in Westminster Abbey. On our way thither, we passed through Pall Mall, which is full of Club Houses; and we were much struck with the beauty of the edifice lately erected for Carlton Club. It is built of a buff-colored, or yellowish stone, with pillars or pilasters of polished Aberdeen granite, wonderfully rich and beautiful; and there is a running border of sculptured figures all round the upper part of the building, besides other ornament and embroidery, wherever there was room and occasion for it. The edifice being an oblong square, this smooth and polished aspect—this union of two rich colors in it—this delicacy and minuteness of finish—this lavish ornament—made me think of a lady's jewel-box; and if it could be reduced to the size [154] of about a foot square, or less, it would make the very prettiest one that ever was seen. I question whether it has any right to be larger than a jewel-box; but it is certainly a most beautiful edifice.

We turned down Whitehall, at the head of which (over the very spot where the Regicides were executed) stands the bronze equestrian statue of Charles I, the statue that was buried under the earth, during the whole of Cromwell's time, and emerged after the restoration. We saw the Admiralty, and the Horse Guards, and, in front of the latter, the two mounted sentinels, one of whom was flirting and laughing with some girls. On the other side of the street stands the banquetting[sic]-house, built by Inigo Jones, from a window of which King Charles stept forth, wearing a kingly head, which, within a few minutes afterwards, fell with a dead thump on the scaffold. It was nobly done—and nobly suffered. How rich in history is the little space around this spot.

I find that, the day after I reached London, I actually passed by Westminster Abbey, without knowing it; partly because my eye was attracted by the gaudier show of the new houses of Parliament, and partly because this part of the Abbey has been so much repaired and renewed that it has not the marks of age. Looking at its front, I now found it grand and venerable beyond my idea; but it is useless to attempt a description;—these things are [155] not to be translated into words; they can be known only by seeing them, and, until seen, it is well to shape out no idea of them. Impressions, states of mind, produced by noble spectacles of whatever kind, are all that it seems worth while to attempt reproducing with the pen. We entered the North transept, through a side entrance, and found a pretty large congregation assembled there, and in the central part of the nave, and service already begun. There were oaken benches arranged in the transept, with a passage between; and we seated ourselves on one of them, close by the pedestal of the statue of Canning. Next beyond this, was an antique tomb, on the top of which, side by side, reposed a marble lord and lady, whom I discovered by the inscription to be the Duke and Duchess of Newcastle, of the time of Charles I. In the inscription to the Duchess's memory, she is said to come of a family, of which "all the brothers were valiant, and all the sisters virtuous."[237] Next to this, was Sir John Malcolm's statue; and the monuments of Pitt and Fox, Lord Mansfield, and other statesmen and warriors, were distinguishable all around us; nor must I forget Sir Peter Warren[238] inasmuch as it was no merit of his own, so much as the valor and enterprise of the New Englanders—of old Massachusetts—that won him his place in Westminster Abbey.

The interior of the Abbey is of rich brown-stone; and the whole [156] of it—the lofty roof, the tall, clustered pillars, and the pointed arches—seems to be in perfect repair, the arches being strengthened with iron, so that I hope they may stand another thousand years at least. It was beautiful to see the sunshine falling in among them, and lightening up their aged gloom with the cheerfulness of the summer afternoon. In the South transept, directly opposite to us, there are painted glass windows, the uppermost of which is a large circle, painted with richly hued saints, whose figures form the rays of glory emanating from a cross in the midst. These windows are modern—only a very few years old—but wonderfully brilliant and beautiful, nevertheless. In the transept below, we saw monuments against the walls, looking darker and more ancient than those about us, most of which were to men of the present time;—that is to say, to men of the last fifty or a hundred years; for the present time may be taken to include at least a century gone by, in such a place as Westminster Abbey. I afterwards discovered that Poet's Corner is in this opposite transept.

I shall visit Westminster Abbey again—and again, and again, and again, I hope—so need not attempt to speak of its wonders now. We passed out through the nave, which is too noble to take into the mind, all at once—looking at what monuments we could; for the attendants were calling out to the spectators to quit [157] the Abbey, as they were about to close the doors. I had a glimpse of Major Andre's monument, which is a pretty little show of miniature-sculpture; but, indeed, the Abbey assimilates all monuments to its own grandeur and beauty, whatever may be their particular defects. They are all imbued—from the moment they take their place there—with the venerable and awful character of the spot. And how glad I am that England has such a church, its walls incrusted with the fame of her dead worthies, ever since she was a nation— their great deeds, and their beautiful deeds, crystallizing there—turning to marble there. An American has a right to be proud of Westminster Abbey;[239] for most of the men, who sleep in it, are our great men, as well as theirs.

After coming out of the Abbey, we looked at the two Houses of Parliament, directly across the way; an immense edifice, and certainly most splendid, built of a beautiful, warm-colored kind of stone. The building has a most elaborate finish, and delighted me, at first; but, by and by, I began to be sensible of a weariness in the effect—a lack of variety in the plan and ornament, a deficiency of invention; so that instead of being more and more interested, the longer one looks, as is the case with an old Gothic edifice, and continually reading deeper into it, you find that you have seen all in seeing a little piece, and that the magnificent structure has noth[158]ing further to show you, or to do for you. It is wonderful how the old weather-stained and smoke-blackened Abbey shames down this bran-newness;—not that the Parliament houses are not fine objects to look at, too.

SEPTR 11th, TUESDAY.

YESTERDAY morning, we walked to Charing Cross, with Una and Julian, and thence took a cab to the Tower, driving thither through the Strand, Fleet Street, past Saint Paul's, and amid all the thickest throng of the city. I have not a very distinct idea of the Tower; but remember that our cab drove within an outer gate, where we alighted at a ticket-office; the old royal fortress being now a regular show-place, at sixpence a head, including the sight of armory and crown-jewels. We saw about the gate several warders, or yeomen of the guard, or beef-eaters, dressed in scarlet-coats of an antique fashion, richly embroidered with golden crowns both on the breast and back, and other royal devices and insignia; so that they looked very much like the kings in a pack of cards, or regular trumps, at all events. I believe they are old soldiers, promoted to this position for good conduct. One of them took charge of us, and when a sufficient number of visitors had collected with us, he led us to see what very small portion of the tower is shown.

There is a great deal of ground within the outer precincts of the tower; and it has streets, and houses, and inhabitants, and a church, [159] within it; and, going up and down behind the warder, without any freedom of getting acquainted with the place by strolling about, I know little more about it than when I went in;—only recollecting a mean and disagreeable confusion of brick walls, barracks, paved courts, with here and there a low, bulky tower, of rather antique aspect; and, in front of one of the edifices, a range of curious old cannon, lying on the ground, some of them immensely large and long, and beautifully wrought in brass. I observe by a plan, however, that the White Tower, containing the armory, stands about in the centre of the fortress, and that it is a square, battlemented structure, having a turret at each angle. We followed the warder into this White Tower, and there saw, in the first place, a long gallery of mounted knights and men-at-arms, which has been so often described, that, when I wish to recall it to memory, I shall turn to some other person's account of it. I was much struck, however, with the beautiful execution of a good many of the suits of armor, and the exquisite detail with which it was engraved. The artists of those days attained very great skill in this kind of manufacture. The figures of the knights, too, in full armor, undoubtedly may have shown a combination of stateliness and grace which heretofore I have not believed in—not seeing how it could be compatible with iron garments. But it [160] is quite incomprehensible how, in the time of the heaviest armor, they could strike a blow, or possess any freedom of movement, except such as a turtle is capable of; and, in truth, they are said not to have been able to rise up, when overthrown. They probably stuck out their lances, and rode straight at the enemy, depending on upsetting him by their mass and weight. In this row of knights is Henry VIII; also, Charles Brandon, Duke of Suffolk, who must have been an immensely bulky man; also, a splendid suit of armor, gilded all over, presented by the city of London to Charles I; also, two or three suits of boy's armor, for the little princes of the house of Stuart. They began to wear these burthens betimes, in order that their manhood might be the more tolerant of them. We went through this gallery so hastily, that it would have been about as well not to see it at all.

Then we went up a winding stair to another room containing armor, and weapons, and beautiful brass cannon, that appeared to have been for ornament rather than use, some of them being quite covered with embossed sculpture, marvellously well done. In this room was John of Gaunt's suit of armor, indicating a man seven feet high; and the armor seems to bear the marks of much wear; but this may be owing to much scrubbing throughout the centuries since John of Gaunt died. Here, too, we saw the cloak in which Wolfe died, on the plains of Abraham; a coarse, faded, [161] threadbare, light-colored garment, folded up under a glass case. Many other things we might have seen, worthy of long attention, had there been time to look at them.

Following into still another room, we were told that this was Sir Walter Raleigh's apartment, while confined in the tower; so that it must have been within those walls that he wrote his History of the World. The room was formerly lighted by lancet windows, and must have been very gloomy; but, if he had the whole length of it to himself, it was a good space to walk and meditate in. On one side of the apartment is a low door, giving admittance, we were told, to the cell where Raleigh slept; so we went in, and found it destitute of any window, and so dark that we could not estimate its small extent except by feeling about. At the entrance of this sleeping-kennel, there were one or two inscriptions scratched in the wall, but not, I believe, by Raleigh.

In this apartment, among a great many other curious things, are shown the devilish instruments of torture which the Spaniards were bringing to England in their Armada; and at the end of the room sits Queen Elizabeth on horseback, in her high ruff, and faded finery. Very likely, none of these clothes were ever on her actual person. Here, too, we saw a headsman's block—not that on which Raleigh was beheaded, which I would have given gold to see—but [162] the one that was used for the three Scotch Lords, Kilmarnock, Lovat, and Balmerino, executed on account of the rebellion of 1745. It is a block of oak about two feet high, with a large knot in it, so that it would not easily be split by a blow of the axe; hewn and smoothed in a very workmanlike way, and with a hollow, to accommodate the head and shoulders, on each side. There were two or three very strong marks of the axe, in the part over which the neck lay, and several smaller cuts; as if the first strokes nearly severed the head, and then the chopping-off was finished by smaller blows, as we see a butcher cutting meat with his cleaver. A headsman's axe was likewise shown us, date unknown.

In the White Tower, we were shown the Regalia, under a glass case and within an iron cage. Edward the Confessor's golden staff was very finely wrought, and there were a great many pretty things; but I have a suspicion, I know not why, that these are not the real jewels;—at least, that such inestimable ones as the Kooh-i-noorh [Koh-i-Noor] or however it is spelt, are less freely exhibited.

The warder then led us into a paved court, which he said was the place of execution of all royal personages, and others, who, from motives of fear or favor, were beheaded privately. Raleigh was among these; and so was Anne Boleyn. We then followed him to the Beauchamp tower, where many state-prisoners of note were confined, and where, on the walls of one of the chambers, there are several [163] inscriptions, and sculptures of various devices, done by the prisoners, and very skilfully done, too, though perhaps with no better instrument than an old nail. These poor wretches had time and leisure enough to spend upon their work. This chamber is lighted by small lancet windows, pierced at equal intervals round the circle of the Beauchamp tower;

and it contains a large square fire-place, in which is now placed a small modern stove. We were hurried away, almost before we could even glance at the inscriptions; and we saw nothing else in the Tower, except the low, obscure doorway in the Bloody Tower, leading to the staircase under which were found the supposed bones of the little princes; and lastly the round Norman arch opening to the water-passage, called the Traitor's Gate. Finally, we ate some cakes and buns in the refreshment-room, connected with the ticket-office, and then emerged from the tower. The ancient moat, by the way, has been drained, within a few years, and now forms a great hollow space, with grassy banks, round about the fortress.

We now wished to see the Thames, and therefore threaded our way along Thames street, towards London Bridge, passing through a fish-market, which I suppose to be the actual Billingsgate, whence originated all the foul language in England. Under London Bridge, there is a station for steamers running to [164] Greenwich and Woolwich. We got on board one of them (not very well knowing, nor much caring, whither it might take us) and steamed down the river, which is bordered with the shabbiest, blackest, ugliest, meanest buildings I ever saw; it is the backside of the town; and, in truth, the muddy tide of the Thames deserves to see no better. There was a great deal of shipping in the river, and many steamers, and it was much more crowded than the Mersey, where all the shipping goes into dock; but the vessels were not so fine,—which I attribute to there being fewer Americans, and less influence of American example.[240] By and by, we reached Greenwich and went ashore there, proceeding up from the quay, past beer-shops and eating-houses, in great number and variety. Greenwich Hospital is here a very prominent object; and after passing along its extensive front, facing towards the river, we entered one of the principal gates, as we found ourselves free to do. There were many of the pensioners idling about, in their cocked hats and old-fashioned coats; and some of them had wooden legs, and seemed not at all bashful about protruding their timber-toes.

Greenwich Hospital does as much credit to the heart of England as any other thing that I have seen. As far as its material form goes, it is on a most liberal and beautiful plan, consisting of many separate edifices of stone, each of which is [165] finer, externally, than the Queen's palace. There are grassy squares, and gravel-walks, and long colonnades, under which the old tars may pace to-and-fro, in rainy days; and they may sit on benches, looking out at the passing ships, and tell their old sea-yarns, and be surly or kindly to one another, and smoke their pipes, I hope, and drink their allowance of grog, and so come quietly to the close of life. I fancied that they felt themselves a kind of petted children of the nation; and it was good to see them lounging in the sun, falling asleep, and waking in some small confusion, at the approach of footsteps. There is a real kindness and humorsomeness in the way in which England treats these old sailors, whom she loves, if she loves anything, for Nelson's sake.

Monday being a day when everything at Greenwich is open without fee to the public, we went first into a beautiful chapel, built in the classic style, and over the altar of which was a large picture of West['s]—whose works I hate to think of. Thence, we went to the painted Hall, a large and beautiful room, at least a hundred feet long, and half as high, and with a magnificent painted cieling [sic] by Sir James Thornhill. I had no idea, before of the exceedingly rich effect of this kind of adornment. The walls of this hall are quite covered with pictures, principally portraits of old admirals, distinguished in British naval [166] warfare, with a few representations of battles, one of which is by Turner. The upper part of this hall is separated and somewhat elevated above the rest, and is painted in fresco over the walls and cieling [sic]. Here we saw a golden astrolabe, presented by Queen Elizabeth to Sir Francis Drake; but the most interesting objects were two coats of Nelson, under separate glass-cases. One was the coat which he wore at the battle of the Nile, and is now much eaten by moths, which will quite destroy it in a few years, unless they adopt the plan pursued with Washington's coat, in America, by baking it occasionally. The other was the coat in which he received his death-wound, the bullet-hole being visible in the shoulder, where, also, a part of the epaulette has been torn away. On the breast of the coat are sewn three or four orders of knighthood, the glitter of which is supposed to have drawn the enemy's aim upon him. Over the coat is laid a white waistcoat, with a large bloodstain upon it, out of which all the redness has been discharged, in the fifty years since that blood gushed out. Yet it was once the reddest blood in England—Nelson's blood.

Adjoining the hall, there is a small room filled almost entirely with pictures illustrative of Nelson's life and victories. The English, I imagine, love him better than they ever did or ever will love anybody else, and would give up Shakspeare, New[167]ton, Bacon, and all their other worthies, rather than lose this one questionably great man out of their history. No man had more serious weaknesses than he; and yet I do not altogether quarrel with the English estimate. He was, and is, a most valuable man to them.

We now left the Hospital,[241] and steamed back to London Bridge, whence we went up into the city, and, to finish the labors of the day, ascended the Monument. This seems to be still a favorite adventure with the cockneys; for we heard one woman, who went up with us, saying that she had been thinking of going up all her life; and another said that she had gone up thirty years ago. There is an iron railing, or rather cage round the top, through which it would be impossible for people to force their way, in order to precipitate themselves; as six persons have heretofore done. There was a mist over London, so that we did not gain a very clear view, except of the swarms of people running about, like ants, in the street at the foot of the monument.

Descending, I put Sophia and the children into a cab, and myself wandered about the city. Passing along Fleet-street, I turned in through an archway, which I rightly guessed to be the entrance to the Temple. It is a very large space, containing many large, solemn, and serious edifices of dark brick; and no sooner do [168] you pass through the arch, than all the rumble and bustle of London dies away at once; and it seems as if a person might live there in perfect quiet, without suspecting that it was not always a Sabbath. People appear to have their separate residences here; but I do not understand what is the economy of their lives. Quite in the deepest interior of this region, there is a large garden, bordering on the Thames, along which it has a gravel walk, and benches where it would be pleasant to sit and smoke a cigar.[242] Along one border of this garden there is some scanty shrubbery, and flowers of no great brilliancy; and the green sward, with which the garden is mostly covered, is not particularly rich or verdant. This is the spot in which, according to Shakspeare,[243] the Plantaganets and the Lancastrians plucked their pale and bloody roses.

Emerging from the Temple, I stopt to smoke a cigar[244] at a tavern in the Strand, the waiter of which observed to me—"They say Sebastopol is taken, Sir!" It was only such an interesting event that could have induced an English waiter to make a remark to a stranger, not called for in the way of business.

The best view we had of the tower—in fact the only external view, and the only time we really saw the White Tower—was from the river, as we steamed past it. Here the high, square, battlemented, White Tower, with the four towers or turrets at its corners, [169] rises prominently above all other parts of the fortress.

SEPT^r 12th, WEDNESDAY.

YESTERDAY forenoon, my wife and I (taking Julian with us) went to Westminster Abbey. Approaching it down Whitehall and Parliament street, you pass the Abbey, and see "Poet's Corner"[245] on the corner-house of a little lane, leading up in the rear of the edifice. The entrance-door is at the south-eastern end of the South Transept—not a spacious arch, but a small, lowly door—and as soon as you are within it, you see the busts of poets looking down upon you from the wall. Great poets, too; for Ben Jonson is right behind the door; and Spenser's tablet is next; and Butler on the same wall of the transept; and Milton; (which you know at once by its resemblance to one of his portraits, though it looks older, more wrinkled, and sadder than the portrait) is close by it, with a profile medallion of Gray beneath it. It is a very delightful feeling, to find yourself at once among them;—the consciousness (mingled with a pleasant awe) of kind and friendly presences, who are anything but strangers to you, though heretofore you have never personally encountered them. I never felt this kind of interest in any other tomb-stones, or in the presence of any other dead people; and one is pleased, too, at finding them all there together, however separated by distant generations, or by personal hostility or other circumstances, while they lived.

The South Transept is divided lengthwise by a screen (as I think [170] they call these partition-walls in a church) and there are monuments against the wall of the screen, on both sides, as well as against those of the church. All are in excellent preservation—indeed, just as good as if put up yesterday—except that the older marbles are somewhat yellow. There seems to be scarcely an inch of space to put up any more; although room has been found, recently, for a bust of Southey, and a full length statue of Campbell. It is but a little portion of the Abbey, after all, that is dedicated to poets, literary men, musical composers, and others of that gentle breed; and even in Poet's Corner, and in the portion of it properest to poets, men of other kinds of eminence have intruded themselves; generals, statesmen, noblemen, at whom one looks askance, and would willingly turn them out, even if deserving of honorable graves elsewhere. Yet it shows aptly and truly enough what portion of the world's regard and honor has hitherto been awarded to literature, in comparison with other modes of greatness—this little nook in the vast Minster (nor even that more than half to themselves) the walls of which are sheathed and hidden behind the marble that has been sculptured for men once prominent enough, but now forgotten. Nevertheless, it would hardly be worth while to quarrel with the world on account of the scanty space and little honor it awards to poets; for even their own special Corner contains some whom one does not care to meet; and, I suppose, all the literary people who really make [171] a part of one's inner life—reckoning since English literature first existed—might lie together along one side of the Transept, and be separately and splendidly emblazoned against that one wall. But we must not look at the matter in just this way; and I should be willing that small poets, as well as great ones, all who are anywise known by tale or song, or who have even striven to be so, should meet here.

The chapels at the eastern end of the Abbey are not open to the public, but are shown to visitors, by people connected with the Abbey, at the cost of sixpence. We joined a party who were following a verger (or whatever the officer is called) and went through the chapels at such a pace that we scarcely saw anything, and brought away not a single distinct idea of any one object. But we were satisfied, at least, that there is enough in this one section of Westminster Abbey to employ one's mind for years; and, without seeing them, it is impossible to have the dimmest idea of what beautiful things the people of past centuries have planned and wrought. The Chapel of Henry VII—though it is in itself a large church, with a nave and side aisles of its own—is finished, as regards roof, walls, and pavement, with a gem-like elaboration, as if it were a curiosity to be kept under a glass-case. We have lost now, I think, this faculty of combining breadth of effect with minuteness of finish. In one of the aisles of this chapel, there is [172] a tomb erected by James I to his mother, Mary Queen of Scots, with a full length figure of Mary, reclining beneath an exquisite and intricate canopy. The face is said to be the best likeness of her, extant, and is very beautiful, though representing her as already past her youth. I cannot express the wonder with which I viewed the design and execution of this tomb, as well as of many other works of various ages (from Edward the Confessor downward) not one of which is there any use in particularizing, for I cannot get my feeling and idea of them into words. The state in which these things have come down to us is marvellous; they seem to have suffered no wrong at all from time, nor from chance, nor from the hands of violent and ignorant men. They came safely through the Reformation, and through Cromwell's time; being protected, I suppose, by their position right under the wing of King or Parliament, who would permit no harm to what was so precious. And, now, they have a good prospect of lasting as long as England does.

It was in Henry VII's Chapel, that I found my foot treading on a flat stone in the pavement, with Addison's name upon it, and Tickell's stately verse[246] in honor of him. No other English author sleeps amid such royal and noble companions; nor does he owe it to his literature, but to his official position as Secretary of State, and, partly no doubt, to his connection with [173] the Warwick family. There is a monument to him in Poet's corner; and he would have found better bedfellows there.

Henry VII's Chapel contains the stalls of the knights of the Bath, with their old banners hanging over them, and the seats of their esquires, each at the foot of his master's stall. These seats are designated by inscriptions on brasses; and on one (the only one that I chanced to examine) I read, (in old French, or Latin, I forget which) "the seat of the Esquire of Sir George Downing, Knt." If this were the famous Downing of New England birth and education,—and I do not see who else it could be, though I never heard of his being a knight of the bath—it is rather singular that I, a New England man, should have hit upon it.[247]

I so hate to be led round under the auspices of a showman, that I was glad when we got through with the Chapels; though we left behind us immense riches of architecture and monumental sculpture—crowds of royal and knightly tombs—which we appreciated no better than if we had never glanced at them. In the nave and transepts of the Abbey, the visitor is free to look at what he likes, and as long as he likes; so we strayed about here, and looked at one thing and another, but found few things, to say the truth, very good. I do not complain, however, that [174] the monuments are not all excellent, or that few of them rise above mediocrity, and some are little else than ridiculous. It is so much the truer representation of the taste and feeling of mankind, in its respective generations, here crystallized upon the wall. I mean to go back to the Abbey by myself—or, better, with Sophia alone—for Julian was by this time quite wearied and hungry, being altogether too young and unread to have any associations with the Abbey; so we hurried down one aisle and up another, and emerged at Poet's Corner.

When we first entered the Abbey, its bells were chiming joyously for the taking of Sebastopol; and while we were looking at the monuments, we heard the boom and rumble of a salute for this long delayed success, which, very likely, will add other laurelled tombstones to those which we saw there.

SEPT' 13th, THURSDAY.

MR BUCHANAN (American Minister) called on me, on Tuesday, and left his card; an intimation that I ought sooner to have paid my respects sooner [sic]; so, yesterday forenoon, I set out to find his residence, 56, Harley-street. It is a street out of Cavendish Square, in a fashionable quarter, although fashion is said to be ebbing away from it. The ambassador seems to intend some little state in his arrangements; but, no doubt, the establishment compares shabbily enough with the legations of other great countries, and with the houses of the English aristocracy. A servant not in livery (or in a very [175] unrecognizable one) opened the door for me, and gave my card to a sort of upper servant, who took it into Mr. Buchanan. He had three gentlemen with him; so desired that I should be shown into the Office of the legation, until he should be able to receive me. Here I found Mr. Moran,[248] a clerk or attache, who has been two or three years on this side of the water; an intelligent person, who seems to be in correspondence (I know not whether more than occasionally) with the New York "Courier and Enquirer."[249] By and by, came in another American to get a passport for the Continent; and soon the three previous gentlemen took leave of the Ambassador, and I was invited to his presence.

The tall, large figure of Mr Buchanan has a certain air of state and dignity; he carries his head in a very awkward way, (in consequence, as the old scandal says, of having once attempted to cut his throat) but still looks like a man of long and high authority, and, with his white hair, is now quite venerable. There is certainly a lack of polish, a kind of rusticity; notwithstanding which, you feel him to be a man of the world. I should think he might succeed very tolerably in English society, being heavy and sensible, cool, kindly and good-humored, and with a great deal of experience of life. We talked about various matters, politics among the rest; and he observed that if the President had taken the advice which he gave him in two [176] long letters,[250] before his inauguration, he would have had a perfectly quiet and successful term of office. The advice was, to form a perfectly homogeneous cabinet of Union men, and to satisfy the extremes of the party by a fair distribution of minor offices; whereas Pierce formed his cabinet of extreme men, on both sides, and gave the minor offices to moderate ones. But the anti-slavery people, surely, had no representative in the cabinet. Mr. Buchanan further observed, that he thought Pierce has a fair chance of re-nomination, for that the South could not in honor desert him;—to which I replied, that the South had been guilty of such things, heretofore.[251] He (Buchanan) thinks that the next Presidential term will be more important and critical, both as to our foreign relations and internal affairs, than any preceding one;—which I should judge likely enough to be the case, although I heard the same prophecy often made respecting the present term.

Mr. Buchanan was very kind in his inquiries about my wife, with whom he is acquainted, from having dined at our house, a year or two ago.[252] I always feel as if he were a man of heart, feeling, and simplicity, and certainly it would be unjust to conclude otherwise, merely from the fact (very suspicious, it is true) of his having been a life-long politician. After we had got through a little matter of business (respecting a young American who has enlisted, at Liverpool) the Minister rang his bell, and ordered another [177] visitor to be admitted; and so I took my leave. In the other room, I found

Mr. Appleton,[253] secretary of legation;—a tall, slender man, of about forty, with a small head and face—gentlemanly enough, sensible and well informed, yet, I should judge, not quite up to his place. There was also a Dr. Brown from Michigan present; and I rather guess the Ambassador is quite as much bored with visitors as the Consul at Liverpool. Before I left the office, Mr. Buchanan came in with Miss Sarah Clarke[254] on his arm. She had come thither to get her passport viséd; and, waiting till her business was concluded, we went out together.

She was going further towards the West End, and I into the city; so we parted, and I soon lost myself among the streets and squares, emerging at last into Oxford-street; though, even then, I did not know whether my face was turned cityward or in the opposite direction. Crossing Regent-street, however, I became sure of my whereabout, and went on through Holborn, and sought hither and thither for Grace Church street, in order to find the American Consul, General Campbell;[255] for I needed his aid to get a Bank post-bill cashed. But I could not find the street, go where I would; so, at last, I went to No. 65, Cheapside, and introduced myself to Mr. W. C. Bennett,[256] whom I already knew by letter, and by a good many of his poems [178] which he has sent me, and by two excellent watches which I bought of him. His establishment—though it has the ordinary front of dingy brick, common to buildings in the city—looks like a time-long stand, the old shop of a London tradesman, with a large figure of a watch over the door, a great many watches (and yet no gorgeous show of them) in the window, a low, dark front shop, and a little room behind, where was a chair or two. Mr. Bennett is a small, slender young man, quite un-English in aspect, with coal-black, curly hair, a thin, dark, colorless visage, very animated and of quick expression, a nervous temperament; he wore a dusty black suit, stooped a little, and looked like a clerk off his desk. In fact, he had dismounted from a desk, when my card was handed to him, and turned to me with a quick, glad look of recognition.

We talked in the first place about poetry and such matters, about England and America, and the nature and depth of their mutual dislike; and, of course, the slavery-question came up, as it always does in one way or another. Anon, I produced my Bank post-bill; and Mr. Bennett kindly engaged to identify me at the bank, being ready to swear to me, he said, on the strength of my resemblance to my engraved portrait. So we set out for the Bank of England, and, arriving there, were directed to the proper clerk, after much inquiry; but he told us that the Bill was not [179] yet due, having been drawn at seven days, and having two still to run—which was the fact. As I was almost shilling-less, however, Mr. Bennett now offered to cash the bill for me. He is very kind and good; and I hope there is no harm in saying that he is a Cockney, which he has the best possible right to be; for he was born, no doubt, in the paternal house, connected with the hereditary shop in Cheapside, right in the neighborhood of Bow-bells. It amused me to observe that, once, he firmly and strongly aspirated the *h* in some such word as "air," or atmosphere—as strongly as ever I heard it—and then quickly caught himself up, and gave the correct pronunciation. Arriving at his shop again, he went out to procure the money, and soon returned with it. At my departure, he gave me a copy of a new poem of his, entitled "Verdicts," somewhat in the manner of Lowell's satire (I forget the title at this moment) but wretchedly inferior. I think it is not yet published, and I do not see how it can fail to be damned—which I shall be sorry for. But it is too flat for a very brisk damnation. Mr. Bennett resides now at Greenwich, whither he hoped I would come and see him on my return to London. Perhaps I will; for I like him, though it seems strange to see an Englishman with so little physical ponderosity and obtuseness of nerve.

[180] After parting from him, it being three °clock or thereabouts, I got a chop and some stout at Dolly's Chop-house, and then resumed my wanderings about the city, of which I never weary, as long as I can put one foot before the other. Seeing that the door of St Paul's, under one of the semicircular porches, was partially open, I went in, and found that the afternoon service was about to be performed; so I remained to hear it, and to see what I could of the Cathedral. What a total and admirable contrast between this and a Gothic Church;—the latter so dim and mysterious, with its narrow aisles, its intricacy of pointed arches, its dark walls, and columns and pavement, and its painted glass-windows, bedimming even what daylight might otherwise get into its eternal evening. But this Cathedral was full of light, and light was proper to it; there were no painted windows, no dim recesses, but a wide and airy space beneath the dome; and even through the long perspective of the nave, there was no obscurity, but one lofty and beautifully rounded arch succeeding another, as far as the eye could reach. The walls were white; the pavement constructed of squares of gray and white marble. It is a most grand and stately edifice; and its characteristic seems to be, to continue forever fresh and new; whereas, such a church as Westminster must have been as venerable as it is now, from the first day when it grew to be an edifice at all. How wonder[181]ful man is in his works! How glad I am that there can be two such admirable churches, in their opposite styles, as St. Paul's and Westminster Abbey!

The organ played, while I was there; and there was an anthem beautifully chanted by voices that came from afar off, and remotely above us, as if out of a sunny sky. Meanwhile, I looked at such monuments as were near; chiefly to military or naval men, Picton, General Ponsonby, Lord St. Vincent, Admiral Duncan and others; but against one of the pillars stands a statue of Dr. Johnson, a noble and thoughtful figure, with a developement [*sic*] of muscle befitting an athlete. I doubt whether sculptors do not err, in point of taste, by making all their statues models of physical perfection, instead of expressing by them the individual character and habits of the man. The statue in the market-place at Lichfield has more of the homely truth of Johnson's actual personality, than this.

Saint Paul's, as yet, is by no means crowded with monuments; indeed, there is plenty of room for a mob of the illustrious, yet to come. But it seems to me that the character of the edifice would be injured by allowing the monuments to be clustered together so closely as at Westminster, by encrusting the walls with them, or letting the statues throng about the pedestals of columns. There must be no confusion in such [182] a cathedral as this; and I question whether the effect will ever be better than it is now, when each monument has its distinct place; and, as your eye wanders around, you are not distracted from noting each marble man in his niche against the wall, or at the base of a marble pillar. Space, distance, light, regularity, are to be preserved, even if the result should be a degree of nakedness.

I saw Mr. Appleton, of the Legation, and Dr. Brown, on the floor of the Cathedral. They were about to go over the whole edifice, and engaged a guide for that purpose; but, as I intend to go thither again with Sophia, I did not accompany them, but went away—the quicker that Mr. Appleton had put on his hat, and I was ashamed of being seen in company with a man who could wear his hat in a Cathedral. Not that he meant any irreverence, but simply felt that he was in a great public building—as big, almost, as all of out-doors— and forgot that it was a consecrated place of worship. The sky is the dome of a greater Cathedral than Saint Paul's, and built by a greater architect than Sir Christopher Wren; and yet we wear our hats unscrupulously beneath it.

I remember no other event of importance, except that I penetrated into a narrow lane or court, either in the Strand or Fleet-street, where was a tavern, calling itself the "Old Thatched House," and pur[183]porting to have been Nell Gwin's [sic] dairy. I met with a great many alleys and obscure archways, in the course of the day's wanderings.

The statue of Lord Mansfield, by Flaxman, in Westminster Abbey, has for one of its attendants a figure of Justice, holding—not a pair of scales—but an actual steelyard, such as butchers use for weighing meat, with a brass weight! I wonder how such an instrument came to be thrust into the hands of Justice. No judge could ever have needed it, since Portia's time, who might perhaps have used it to see that Shylock did not take more than his pound of flesh.[257]

Sept[r] 14th, FRIDAY.

YESTERDAY, in the earlier part of the day, it poured with rain; and I did not go out till four °clock in the afternoon; nor did I then meet with anything interesting. I walked through Albemarle-street for the purpose of looking at Murray's shop, but missed it entirely at my first inquisition. The street is one of hotels, principally, with only a few tradesmen's shops, and has a quiet, aristocratic aspect. On my return, down the other sidewalk, I did discover the famous publisher's locality, but merely by the name—"Mr. Murray"—engraved on a rather large brass plate, such as doctors use, on the door. There was no sign of a book, nor of its being a place of trade in any way; and I should have taken the house to be—if not a private residence—then a lawyer's of[184]fice. I think it vulgar in "Mr Murray" to be ashamed of his business.

At seven °clock, we (Mamma, Una, and I) went to dine with Mr. Russell Sturgis, in Portland-place. He is a partner with the Barings, and therefore a member of good society; though I have understood that the Barings are looked down upon by the body of London bankers, as being merely brokers. At any rate, Mr. Sturgis's house is a very fine one, and he gave us a very quiet, elegant, and enjoyable dinner, in much better taste and with less fuss than Liverpool dinners. Mr. Sturgis is a friend of Thackeray; and, speaking of the last number of the Newcomes—so touching that nobody can read it aloud without breaking down—he mentioned that Thackeray himself had read it to James Russell Lowell and William Story, in a cider-cellar! I read all the preceding numbers of the Newcomes to my wife, but happened not to have an opportunity to read this last, and was glad of it—knowing that my eyes would fill, and my voice quiver. Mr Sturgis likes Thackeray, and thinks him a good fellow.

Mr. Sturgis has a (I don't know but I ought rather to say the) beautiful full length picture of Washington, by Stuart;[258] and I was proud to see that noblest face and figure here in England; the picture of a man beside whom (considered merely as a physical man) any English nobleman would look like common beef or clay.

[185] Speaking of Thackeray, I cannot but wonder at his coolness in respect to his own pathos, and compare it with my emotions when I read the last scene of the Scarlet Letter to my wife, just after writing it—tried to read it, rather, for my voice swelled and heaved, as if I were tossed up and down on an ocean, as it subsided after a storm. But I was in a very nervous state, then, having gone through a great diversity and severity of emotion, for many months past. I think I have never overcome my own adamant in any other instance.

Tumblers, hand-organists, puppet-showmen, musicians, Highland bag-pipers, and all such vagrant mirthmakers, are very numerous in the streets of London. The other day, passing through Fleet-street, I saw a crowd filling up a narrow court, and high above their heads, a tumbler, standing on his head on the top of a pole that reached as high as the third story of the neighboring houses. Sliding down the pole, headforemost, he disappeared out of my sight. A multitude of Punches go the rounds continually. Two have passed through our street, this morning. The first asked two shillings for his performance; so we sent him away. The second demanded, in the first place, half-a-crown, but finally consented to take a shilling, and gave us the show at that price, though much maimed of its proportions. Besides the spectators in our windows, he had a little crowd on the sidewalk, to whom he [186] went round for contributions, but I did not observe that anybody gave him so much as a half-penny. It is strange to see how many people are aiming at the small change in your pocket; in every square, a beggar-woman meets you, and turns back to follow your steps with her miserable murmur; at the street-crossings, there are old men or little girls with their brooms; urchins propose to brush your boots; if you get into a cab, a man runs to open the door for you, and touches his hat for a fee, as he closes it again.

Septr 15th Saturday.

It was rainy yesterday, and I kept within doors till after four °clock, when Julian and I took a walk into the city. Seeing the entrance to Clement's Inn, we went through it, and saw the garden, with a kneeling bronze figure in it; and, when just in the midst of the Inn, I remembered that Justice Shallow was of old a student there.[259] I do not well understand these Inns of Court, or how they differ from other places. Anybody seems to be free to reside there (paying the rent of their office or tenement) and a residence does not seem to involve any obligation to study law, or any connection therewith. Clement's Inn consists of large brick houses, accessible by narrow lanes and passages, but, by some peculiar privilege or enchantment, enjoying a certain quiet and repose, though in close vicinity to the noisiest part of the city.

As has before happened to me, I got bewildered in the neighbor[187]hood of Saint Paul's; and, try how I might to escape from it, its huge, dusky dome kept showing itself before me, through one street and another. In my endeavors to escape it, I at one time found myself in Saint-John street, and was in hopes to have seen the old St John's Gate, so familiar for above a century on the cover of the Gentleman's Magazine.[260] But I suppose it is taken down; for we went through the entire street, I think, and saw no trace of it. Either afterwards, or before this, we came upon Smithfield; a large irregular square, filled up with pens for cattle, of which, however, there were none in the market, at that time. I leaned upon a post, at the western end of the square, and told Julian how the martyrs had been burnt at Smithfield, in Bloody Mary's days. Again we drifted back to Saint Paul's; and, at last, in despair of ever getting out of this enchanted region, I took a Hansom-cab to Charing Cross, whence we easily made our way hòme.

Sept 16th, Sunday.

I took the ten °clock train, yesterday morning, from the Euston Station, and arrived at Liverpool at about five, passing through the valley of Trent without touching at Birmingham. Nothing can be more monotonous and uninteresting than a journey on an English railway; very wearisome, too, from the brevity of the stoppages, hardly amounting to five minutes at any one place. [188] English scenery (except in such few regions as they have trumpeted to the wor[l]d) is the tamest of the tame; hardly a noticeable hill breaking the ordinary gentle undulation of the landscape; but still the verdure and finish of the fields and parks make it worth while to throw out a glance, now and then, as you rush by. Few separate houses are seen, as in America; but sometimes a village, with the square, gray battlemented tower of its Norman church, and rows of thatched cottages, reminding one of the clustered mud-nests of swallows under the eaves of a barn; here and there a lazy little river, like the Trent;—perhaps if you look sharply where the guide-book indicates, the turrets of an old castle in the distance;—perhaps the great steeple and spires of a cathedral;—perhaps the tall chimney of a manufactory;—but, on the whole, the traveller comes to his journey's end, unburthened with a single new idea. I observe that the harvest is not all gathered in, as yet; and this rainy weather must look very gloomy to the farmer. I saw gleaners, yesterday, in the stubble fields. There were two gentlemen in the same railway carriage with me, and we did not exchange half-a-dozen words, the whole way.

I am here established at Mrs. Blodgett's boarding-house, which I find quite full; insomuch that she had to send one of her sea-captains to sleep in another house, in order to [189] make room for me. It is exclusively American society;—four shipmasters, a Doctor from Pennsylvania,[261] who has been travelling a year on the continent, and who seems to be a man of very active intelligence, interested in everything, and especially in agriculture; two or three young men in business here; and ladies and children belonging to these various parties. As when I was here before, the little smoking-room is the resort of the gentlemen, in the evenings, and after breakfast; the ladies sometimes intruding, however, notwithstanding the odor of cigars. There we criticise and ridicule John Bull, and assert American superiority, in a way that it would probably chafe him a little to hear; because it goes to the very points on which he chiefly piques himself. The Doctor, for instance, asserted (and made out his assertion very fairly, so far as I could judge) that we are fifty years ahead of England in agricultural science, and that he could cultivate English soil to far better advantage than English farmers do, and at vastly less expense. Their heavy and cloddish tendency to cling to old ideas, which retards them in everything else, keeps them behindhand in this matter too. Really, I do not know any other place in England where a man can be made so sensible that he lives in a progressive world, as here in Mrs. Blodgett's boarding-house.

[190] The captains talk together about their voyages, and how they manage with their unruly mates and crews; and how freights are in America, and the prospects of business, and equinoctial gales; and the qualities of different ships and their commanders; and how crews, mates, and masters, have all deteriorated within their remembrance. Captain Johnson assigned as a reason for not boarding at this house, that the conversation made him sea-sick; and, indeed, the smell of tar and bilge-water is somewhat strongly perceptible in it. And yet these men are alive, and talk of real matters, and matters which they know. The shipmasters, who come to Mrs. Blodgett, are favorable specimens of their class; being all respectable men, in the employ of good houses, and raised by their capacity to the command of first-rate ships. In my official intercourse with them, I do not generally see their best side; as they seldom come before me except as complainants, or when summoned to answer to some

complaint made by a seaman. But hearing their daily talk, and listening to what is in their minds, and their reminiscences of what they have gone through, one becomes sensible that they are men of energy and ability, fit to be trusted, and retaining a hardy sense of honor, and a loyalty to their own country, the stronger because they have compared it with many others. Most of them are gentlemen, too, to a certain extent;—some more than others, per[191]haps;—and none to a very exquisite point;—or, if so, it is none the better for them, as sailors or as men.

Captain Knowles, this morning put his cigar into the mouth of his little boy, a child of two years and a half. The little fellow seemed not unused to it, and, I think, drew a whiff or two. I thought it rather early to begin; but, after all, the result may not be bad in the end.

SEPT^r 17th MONDAY.

IT is queer to feel a sense of my own country returning upon me, with the intercourse of the people whom I find here, and their talk and manners. Indubitably, they are alive, to an extent to which the Englishman never seems conscious of life. It would do John Bull good to come and sit at our table, and adjourn with us to our smoking-room; but he would be apt to go away a little crest-fallen.

The Doctor (I have not yet found out his name) is much the most talkative of our company, and sometimes bores me thereby, though he seldom says anything that is not either instructive or amusing. He tells a curious story of Prince Albert, and how he avails himself of American sharp-shooting. During the Doctor's tour in Scotland, which he has just finished, he became acquainted with one of the Prince's attaches, who invited him, very earnestly, to join his Royal Highness's par[192]ty, promising him a good gun, and a keeper to load it for him, two good dogs, besides as many cigars as he could smoke, and as much wine as he could drink; on the one condition that whatever game he shot should be the Prince's. "The Prince" says the attache, "is very fond of having Americans in his shooting parties, on account of their being such excellent shots; and there was one with him, last year, who shot so admirably that his Royal Highness himself left off shooting, in utter astonishment." The attache offered to introduce the Doctor to the Prince, who would be certain to receive him very graciously, and place him on his right hand, for the sake of glorifying himself by assuming the credit of the numerous head of game which he would be expected to shoot. The Doctor speaks very contemptuously of English shooting.

He told (I know not from what source) a story of the manner in which the young Queen intimated to Prince Albert that she had bestowed her heart on him. All the eligible young princes in Europe had been invited to England to visit the Queen—trotted out, as it were, for inspection—and all were suffered to take their leave, in due time—all but Prince Albert. When he came to pay his parting compliments, the Queen said to him, "It depends on your-self, whether you go!" This is rather pretty. I think, perhaps, we talk of kings and queens [193] more at our table, than people do at most other tables in England;—not, of course, that we like them better, or admire them more, but that they are curiosities. Yet I would not say that the Doctor may not be susceptible on the point of royal attentions; for he told us with great complacency how emphatically Louis Napoleon, on two or three occasions, had returned his bow, and the last time, had turned and made some remark (evidently about the Doctor) to the Empress. We certainly do talk a great deal about Princes and Potentates. The Doctor avers that Prince Albert's im-mediate attendants speak contemptuously ("lightly" was his precise word) of him, as a slow, common-place man.

Last evening (Sunday) two or three young men called in fortuitously to see some young ladies of our household, and chatted in parlor, hall, and smoking-room, just as they might have done in America. They staid to tea with us. In our party of perhaps half a dozen married women and virgins, there are two or three who may fairly be called pretty; an immense proportion compared with what one finds among the women of England, where, indeed, I could almost say I have found none. The aspect of my countrywomen, to be sure, seems to me somewhat peculiarly delicate, thin, pale, after becoming accustomed to the beefy rotundity and coarse complexions of the full-fed English [194] dames; but, slight as they look, they always prove themselves sufficient for the whole purpose of life. Then the lightness, the dance, the ebullition of their minds is so much pleasanter than the grim English propriety! I have not heard such a babble of feminine voices, on this side of the water, as I heard last night from these ladies, sitting round the table in the parlor—all busy—all putting in their word—all ready with their laugh.

I ought not to omit mentioning that the Doctor has been told, in France, that he personally resembles Louis Napoleon; and I suspect he is trying to heighten the resemblance by training his mustache on the pattern of that which adorns the imperial upper lip. This Doctor is a genuine American character, though modified by a good deal of travel;—a very intelligent man, full of various ability, with eyes all over him for any object of interest, a little of the bore, sometimes, quick to appreciate character, with a good deal of tact, gentlemanly in his manners, but yet lacking a deep and delicate refinement. Not but that Americans are as capable of this last quality as other people are; but what with the circumstances amid which we grow up, and the peculiar activity of our minds, we certainly do often miss it. By-the-by, he advanced a singular proposition, the other night;—viz, that the English people do not so well understand comfort, nor attain [195] it so perfectly in their domestic arrangements, as we do. I thought he hardly supported this opinion so satisfac-torily as some of his other new ideas.

I saw in an American paper, yesterday, that an opera (still unfinished) had been written on the story of the Scarlet Letter, and that several scenes of it had been performed successfully in New York.[262] I should think it might possibly succeed as an opera, though it would certainly fail as a play.

SEPT^r 24th MONDAY.

ON Saturday, at ½ past three °clock, I left Liverpool by the L. & N.W. railway, for London. Mrs. Blodgett's table had been thinned by several departures during the week; and Doctor and Mrs. Wickersham, with two American gentlemen, sailed by the Collins Steamer of Saturday. My mind had been considerably enlivened, and my sense of American superiority renewed, by intercourse with these people; and there is no danger of one's intellect becoming a standing pool, and a scum gathering over it, in such society. I think better of American shipmasters, too, than I did from merely meeting them in my office. They keep up a continual discussion of professional matters, and all things having any reference to their profession; the laws of insurance, the rights of vessels in foreign ports, the authority and customs of vessels of war with regard to merchantmen &c &c &c, together with stories and casual [196] anecdotes of their sea-adventures, gales, shipwrecks, ice-bergs, collisions of vessels, hair-breadth scapes. Their talk runs very much on the sea, and on the land as connected with the sea; and their interest does not seem to extend very far beyond the wide field of their professional concerns.

Nothing remarkable occurred on the journey to London. The greater part of the way, there were only two gentlemen in the same compartment with me; and we occupied each our corner, with little other conversation than in comparing watches, at the various stations. I got out of the carriage only once (at Rugby, I think;) and, for the last seventy or eighty miles, the train did not stop. There was a clear moon, the latter part of the journey; and the mist lay along the ground, looking very much like a surface of water—a moonlight lake. We reached London at about ten, and I found Sophia expecting me.

Yesterday, the children went with Fanny to the Zoological Gardens; and after sending them off, Sophia and I walked to Piccadilly, and thence took a cab for Kensington Gardens. It was a delightful day—the best of all weathers—the real English good weather; more like our Indian summer than anything else within my experience. A mellow sunshine, with great warmth in it; a soft, balmy air, with a little haze through it; if the sun made us a little too warm, we had but to go into the shade to be im[197]mediately refreshed. The light of these days is very exquisite; so gently bright, without any glare; a veiled glow; in short, it is the kindliest mood of Nature, and almost enough to compensate for chill and dreary months. Moreover, there is more of such weather than the English climate has ever had credit for.

Kensington Gardens form the most beautiful piece of artificial woodland and park-scenery that I have ever seen. The old palace of Kensington (now inhabited by the Dutchess [sic] of Inverness) stands at one extremity; an edifice of no great mark, anyhow, built of brick, covering much ground, and low in proportion to its extent. In front of it, at a considerable distance, there is a piece of water; and in all directions there are vistas of wide paths among noble trees, standing in groves, or scattered in clumps; everything being laid out with free and generous spaces, so that you could see long sheets of sunshine among the trees, and there was a pervading influence of quiet and remoteness. Tree did not interfere with tree; the art of man was seen, conspiring with Nature, as if she and he had consulted together how to make a beautiful scene, and had taken ages of quiet thought and tender care to accomplish it. We strolled slowly along these paths, and sometimes deviated from them to walk beneath the trees, many [198] of the leaves of which lay beneath our feet, yellow and brown, and with a pleasant smell of vegetable decay. These were the leaves of chestnut-trees; the other trees (unless elms) have yet hardly begun to shed their foliage, although you can discern a sober change of hue in the woodland masses; and the trees individualize themselves by assuming each its own tint, though in a very modest way. If these trees could have undergone the change of an American autumn, it would have been like putting on a regal robe. Autumn often puts on one in America, but it is apt to be very ragged.

There were a good many well-dressed people scattered through the grounds; young men and girls, husbands with their wives and children; nursery maids with little tots playing about on the grass. Anybody might have entered the gardens, I suppose; but only well-dressed people were there—not of the upper classes, but shopkeepers, I should think, clerks, apprentices, and respectability of that sort. It is pleasant to think that the people have the freedom (and therefore the property) of parks like this, more beautiful and stately than a nobleman can keep to himself. The extent of Kensington gardens, (when reckoned together with Hyde Park, from which it is separated only by a fence of iron-rods) is very great, comprising miles of green sward and woodland. The large sheet of artificial water, called the Serpentine river, lies [199] chiefly in Hyde Park, but comes partly within the precincts of the gardens. It is entitled to honorable mention among the English lakes, being larger than some that are world-celebrated;—some miles long, and perhaps a stone's throw across, in the widest part. It forms the paradise of a great many ducks of various breed, which are accustomed to be fed by visitors, and come flying from afar, touching the water with their wings, and quacking loudly, when bread or cake is thrown to them. I bought a bun of a little hunch-backed man, who kept a refreshment-stall near the Serpentine, and bestowed [it] piece-meal on these ducks, as we loitered along the bank. We emerged from the park by another gate, and walked along town-ward till we came to Tyburnia, and saw the iron memorial which marks where the gallows used to stand; thence we turned into Park Lane, then into Upper Grosvenor-street, and reached Hanover Square sooner than we expected.

In the evening, I walked forth to Charing Cross, and thence along the

Strand and Fleet-street, where I made no new discoveries, unless it were the Mitre Tavern. I mean to go into it, some day, and perhaps eat a chop and ale and smoke a cigar.[263] The streets were much thronged; and there seemed to be a good many young people—lovers, it is to be hoped—who had spent the day together, and were going innocently home. Perhaps [200] so—perhaps not. At every street corner, too, under archways, and at other places of vantage, or loitering along, with some indescribable peculiarity that distinguished her, and perhaps turning to re-tread her footsteps, was a woman; or sometimes two walked arm in arm—hunting in couples—and separated when they saw a gentleman approaching. One feels a curious and reprehensible sympathy for these poor nymphs; it seems such a pity that they should not each and all of them find what they seek!—that any of them should tramp the pavement the whole night through, or should go hungry and forlorn to their beds. They are much more tolerable than in Liverpool, where it is impossible to go out, after nightfall, without having to decline the overtures of some girl of the town.

SEPTEMBER 25th TUESDAY.

YESTERDAY forenoon, Julian and I walked out, with no very definite purpose; but seeing a narrow passage-way from the Strand down to the river, we went through it and gained access to a steamboat, plying thence to London Bridge. The fare was a half-penny a-piece, and the boat almost too much crowded for standing room. This part of the river presents the waterside of London in a rather pleasanter aspect than below London Bridge; the Temple with its garden, Somerset House, and generally a less tumble-down and neglected look about the buildings; although, after all, the metropolis [201] does not see a very stately face in its mirror. I saw Alsatia betwixt the Temple and Black-friars-bridge; its precincts looked very narrow, and not particularly distinguishable, at this day, from the portions of the city on either side of it. At London Bridge, we got aboard of a Woolwich steamer, and went farther down the river, passing the Custom House and the Tower, the only prominent objects rising out of the dreary range of shabbiness which stretches along close to the water's edge. At the Thames Tunnel (two miles, I believe, below London Bridge) we left the steamer.

The entrance to the Thames Tunnel[264] is beneath a large circular building, which is lighted from the top, so as to throw down the daylight into the great depth to which we descend, by a winding staircase, before reaching the level of the bore. A road must commence, I should think, at least a mile off on either side of the river, in order to make it possible for vehicles to go through the tunnel; so great is the descent. On reaching the bottom, we saw a closed door, which we opened, and passing through it, found ourselves in the Tunnel —an arched corridor, of apparently interminable length, gloomily lighted with jets of gas at regular intervals—plastered at the sides, and stone beneath the feet. It would have made an admirable prison, or series of dungeons, according to the old-time ideal of places of confinement; a good place, [202] for instance, for Sir Walter Raleigh to have paced to-and-fro, from end to end, meditating his history of the world; and, indeed, any man of meditative pursuits, might be profitably shut up here. There are people who spend their lives here, seldom or never, I presume, seeing any daylight; except perhaps a little in the morning. All along the extent of this corridor, in little alcoves, there are stalls or shops, kept principally by women, who, as you approach, are seen through the dusk, offering for sale views of the Tunnel, put up, with a little magnifying glass, in cases of Derbyshire spar; also, cheap jewelry and multifarious trumpery; also cakes, candy, ginger-beer, and such small refreshment. There was one shop that must, I think, have opened into the other corridor of the Tunnel, so capacious it seemed; and here were dioramic views of various cities and scenes of the daylight-world, all shown by gas, while the Thames rolled its tide and its shipping over our heads. So far as any present use is concerned, the Tunnel is an entire failure, and labor and immensity of money thrown away. I did not meet or pass above half a dozen passengers through its whole extent; whereas, no doubt, it would require a continual swarm, like that on London Bridge, besides horsemen, carts, carriages of all sorts, to pay anything like the interest of the money. Perhaps, in coming ages, the approaches to the Tunnel will be obliterated, its corridors choked [203] up with mud, its precise locality unknown, and nothing be left of it but an obscure tradition. Meantime, it is rather a pleasant idea, that I have actually passed under the bed of the Thames, and emerged into daylight on the other side.

The other side of the river is called Rotherhithe; a name which is familiar to me, either in Gulliver's Travels[265] or some other book relating to ships and sailors. We saw but little of it, beyond the interior of a beer-shop, the good woman of which advised us to recross the river (not beneath it, but on its surface) and take a steamboat in order to get back whence we came. So we did recross in the primitive fashion of the Thames, in an open boat; there being a ferry at this spot. There was an old lady in the boat, who was a little alarmed at the toss and swell caused by the wind, and by a passing steamer. "Never fear, mother!" said one of the boatmen, "we'll make the river as smooth as we can for you. We'll get a plane, and shave down the waves!" This was the only thing at all approaching to the old water-wit, for which the Thames used to be celebrated.[266]

We landed in Wapping,[267] where I was glad to be for once in my life, having read so much of it, and deeming it to be the most tarry and pitch-y spot on earth, swarming with old salts, and all sorts of *propria quae maribus*.[268] It is a very [204] dingy, shabby, and uninteresting region; and I don't think I saw a single sailor, though multitudes of 'long-shore people, who get their living, in one way or another, from business connected with the sea. Many ale and spirit-shops, apple-stands, fish and butcher's stalls, all on the poorest scale; and the people stared at me curiously, as if persons of respectable aspect seldom came there. On the whole, the place is dreary; no warm, bustling, coarse, homely life there—coarse and homely enough, it is true, but cold and torpid.

From this remote part of London, we walked towards the heart of the city; and, as we went, matters seemed to civilize themselves by degrees; and the streets grew crowded with cabs, omnibuses, drays, carts. We passed, I think, through Whitechapel; certainly through Fenchurch-street; and reaching Saint Paul's, got into an omnibus and rode to Regent-street, whence it was but a step or two home.

In the afternoon, at four °clock, Sophia and I went to call on Mr Buchanan and Miss Lane. The lady was not at home, but we went in to see Mr. Buchanan, and were shown into a stately drawing-room, the furniture of which was sufficiently splendid, but rather the worse for wear—being hired furniture, no doubt. The Ambassador shortly appeared, looking venerable, as usual—or rather more so than usual—benign and [205] very pale. His deportment towards ladies is highly agreeable and prepossessing, and he paid very kind attention to Sophia, thereby quite confirming her previous good feeling towards him. She thinks that he is much changed since she saw him last (at dinner, at our own house)—more infirm, more aged, and with a singular depression in his manner. I, too, think that age has latterly come upon him with great rapidity. He said that Miss Lane was going home on the 6th of October, and that he himself had long purposed it, but had received despatches which obliged him to put off his departure. The President, he said, had just written, requesting him to remain till April; but this he was determined not to do. I rather think he does really wish to return, and that not for any ambitious views upon the Presidency, but from an old man's natural desire to be at home, and among his own people. I like Mr. Buchanan.

Sophia spoke to him about an order from the Lord Chamberlain for admission to view the two Houses of Parliament; and the Ambassador drew from his pocket a colored silk handkerchief (which ought to have gone into this week's wash) and made a knot in it, in order to remind himself to ask the Lord Chamberlain. The homeliness of this little incident has a sort of propriety and keeping [206] with much of Mr. Buchanan's manner; but I would rather not have him do it before English people. He arranged to send a close carriage for us to come and see him socially, this evening.

After leaving his house (56, Harley-street) we drove around Hyde Park, and thence to Portland place, where we left cards for Mrs. Russell Sturgis,—thence into Regent's Park—thence home. Una and Julian accompanied us throughout these drives, but remained in the carriage during our call on Mr. Buchanan. In the evening, I strolled out, and walked as far as Saint Paul's—never getting enough of the bustle of London, which may weary, but can never satisfy me. By night, London looks wild and dreamy, and fills one with a sort of pleasant dread. It was a clear evening, with a bright English moon;—that is to say, what we Americans should call rather dim.

SEPTEMBER 26th, TUESDAY.

YESTERDAY, at eleven, I walked towards Westminster Abbey; and as I drew near, the Abbey-bells were clamorous for joy, chiming merrily, musically, and obstreperously—the most rejoicing sound that can be conceived; and we ought to have a chime of bells in every American town and village, were it only to keep alive the celebration of the Fourth of July. I conjectured that there might have been another victory over the [207] Russians—that perhaps the Northern side of Sebastopol had surrendered; but soon I saw the riddle that these merry bells were proclaiming. There were a great many private carriages, and a large concourse of loungers and spectators, near the door of the church that stands close under the eaves of the Abbey. Gentlemen and ladies, gaily dressed, were issuing forth; carriages driving away, and others drawing up to the door, in their turn; and, in short, a marriage had just been celebrated in the church, and this was the wedding-party. The last time I was there, Westminster was flinging out its great voice of joy for a national triumph; now, for the happy union of two lovers. What a mighty sympathyzer [sic] is the old Abbey!

I went round by Poet's Corner, and into the Abbey, where were a number of visitors. This time, I did not follow a guide through the Chapels, but wandered at leisure up and down the nave and aisles, and being in a more critical mood than at my first visit, I am afraid I came near concluding that Westminster Abbey is not the greatest imaginable thing, after all. There is such an immense preponderance of nobodies among the monumental worthies there!—forgotten people, with great piles of sculpture, often as high as the eaves of an ordinary house, built up [208] over their miserable bones; so that the visitor keeps saying to himself—"What right has this fellow among the Immortals?" It might be a good rule to permit no one to have a monument here, until his fame shall have been tried by the wear and tear of a term of years—say fifty years, or possibly a century, after the great man's decease. Two centuries, I think, must pass before a saint can claim canonization; but the shorter time would suffice to distinguish temporary from lasting reputations. But then how bare, had this rule been followed, would have been these marble-crusted walls! Poet's corner is about seven of my paces broad, by perhaps ten in length; the monumental tablets, busts, and statues are put up against three walls of this nook, and also against the other side of the screen, separating the Corner from the other half of the transept. There are several intrusive memorials of statesmen and generals within these narrow precincts; and yet, after all, there is quite room enough for every poet whom any man has room for in his heart. Yes; a great deal more than enough room; and much the greater number of the poets would never be remembered if you did not find them here. Westminster Abbey makes me feel—not how many great, wise, witty, and bright men there are—but how very few in any age, and how small a harvest of them for all the ages. The whole together, if they could rise up from under the pave[209]ment of the choir, the nave, the aisles, and the cloisters, would hardly make up the number of a modern dinner-party—not more than could dine together round one of the flat tombstones in Henry VII's chapel. But it is too bad to judge these poor dead folks—so hungry for fame while they lived—in this hard way. So let each century set up the monuments of those whom it admires and loves; and there is no harm, but, on the whole, much pleasure in having such a record before the world's eyes. Certainly, however, I should like to weed away some of the heroes; bullet-headed men, who defended a fort, or perhaps took a frigate, and have twenty square feet apiece of immortality awarded to them here.

It is pleasant to recognize the mould and fashion of English features through the marble of many of the statues and busts, even though they may be clad in Roman robes. I am inclined to think them, in many cases, faithful likenesses; and it brings them nearer to the mind to see these original sculptures—you see the man at but one remove, as if you caught his image in a looking-glass. The bust of Gay seemed to me very good; a thoughtful and humorous sweetness in the face. Goldsmith has as good a position as any poet in the Abbey, his bust and tablet filling [210] the pointed arch over a door that seems to lead towards the cloisters. No doubt he would have liked to be assured of so conspicuous a place. I [saw] one monument to a native American—"Charles [William] Wragg, Esq. of South Carolina"—the only one, I suspect in Westminster Abbey; and he acquired this memorial by the most un-American of qualities, his loyalty to his King. He was one of the refugees, leaving America in 1777, being shipwrecked on his passage; and the monument was put up by his sister. It is a small tablet, with a representation of Mr. Wragg's shipwreck at the base. Next to it is the large monument of Sir Cloudesley Shovel, which I think Addison ridicules[269]—the Admiral, in a full-bottomed wig and Roman dress, but with a broad, English face, reclining with his head on his hand, and looking at you with great placidity. I stood at either end of the Nave, and endeavored to take in the whole beauty and majesty of the edifice, but, apparently, was not in a proper state of mind; for nothing came of it. It is singular how like an avenue of over-arching trees are these lofty aisles of a cathedral.

Leaving the Abbey about one °clock, I walked into the city, as far as Gracechurch street, and there called on the American Consul, General Campbell, who had been warmly introduced to me, last year, by a letter from the President. I like [211] the General;—a kindly and honorable man, of simple manners, and large experience of life—somewhat slow and tedious withal, though very sensible. Afterwards I called on Mr. Oakford, an American, connected in business with Mr. Crosby, from whom I wanted some information as to the sailing of steamers from Southampton to Lisbon. Mr. Crosby was not in town; and after smoking a cigar with Mr. Oakford, I took my leave, and stumbling into a poor eating-house, dined shabbily on half-cold roast veal and green beans, with half-a-pint of stout, for a shilling. Then I went astray through Whitechapel; thence back to St. Paul's, and so home, pretty weary, at six °clock.

At eight °clock, Mr Buchanan (as per agreement) sent his carriage to take Sophia and me to spend the evening socially. Miss Lane received us with proper cordiality, and looked quite beamingly; more sweet and simple in aspect than when I have seen her in full dress. Shortly, the Ambassador appeared, and made himself highly agreeable; not that he is a brilliant conversationist; but his excellent sense, and good humor, and the much that he has seen and been a part of, are sufficient resources to draw upon. We talked of the Queen, whom he spoke of with high respect,—except that once he hinted that she is naturally a "fiery little [212] devil." Of the late Czar, whom he knew intimately while Minister to Russia; and he quite confirms all that has been said about the awful beauty of his person. Mr Buchanan's characterization of him was quite favorable; he thought better of his heart than most people, and adduced his sports with a school of children—twenty of whom, perhaps, he cause[d] to stand rigidly in a row, like so many bricks, then giving one a push would laugh obstreperously to see the whole row tumble down. He would lie on his back, and allow the little things to scramble over him. He admitted Mr. Buchanan to great closeness of intercourse, and informed him of a conspiracy which was then on foot for the Czar's murder. On the evening when the assassination was to take place, the Czar did not refrain from going to the public place where it was to be perpetrated, although, indeed, great precaution had been taken to frustrate the schemes of the conspirators. Mr. B said that, in case the plot had succeeded, all the foreigners (including himself) would likewise have been murdered;—the native Russians having a bitter hatred against foreigners. He observed that he had been much attached to the Czar, and had never joined in the English abuse of him. His sympathies, however, are evidently rather English than Russian, in this war. Speaking of the present Emper[213]or, he said that Lord Heytesbury (formerly English Ambassador in Russia) lately told him that he complimented the Czar Nicholas on the good qualities of his son, saying that he was acknowledged by all to be one of the most amiable youths in the world. "Too amiable, I fear, for his position," answered the Czar. "He has too much of his mother in him."

SEPTEMBER 27th, THURSDAY.

YESTERDAY (much earlier than English people ever do such things) General Campbell made us a call on his way to the Consulate, and sat talking a stricken hour or thereabout. Scarcely had he gone, when Mrs. Oakford and her daughter (a girl about twelve) came, while it was still earlier than the English verge of calling-hours. After sitting a long while, they took away Una to their house near St. John's Wood, to spend the night. I had been writing my Journal and official correspondence, during such intervals as these calls left me;

and, now concluding these businesses, Sophia, Julian, and I went out and took a cab for the terminus of the Crystal Palace railway—whither we proceeded over Waterloo Bridge, and reached the palace, I believe, not far from three °clock. It was a beautifully bright day, such as we have in wonderful succession, this month. The Crystal palace gleamed in the sunshine; but I do not think a very impressive edifice can be built of glass;—light and airy, to be sure, but still it will be [214] no other than an overgrown conservatory. It is unlike anything else in England; uncongenial with the English character, without privacy, destitute of mass, weight, and shadow; unsusceptible of ivy, lichens, or any mellowness from age.

The train of cars stop within the domain of the palace, whence there is a long, ascending corridor up into the edifice. There was a very pleasant odor of heliotrope diffused through the air; and, indeed, the whole atmosphere of the Crystal palace is sweet with various flower-scents, and mild and balmy, though sufficiently fresh and cool. It would be a delightful climate for invalids to spend the winter in; and if all England could be roofed over with glass, it would be a great improvement on its present condition.

The first thing we did, before fairly getting into the palace, was to sit down in a large ante-hall, and get some bread and butter, and a pint of Bass' pale-ale—together with a cup of coffee for Sophia. This was the best refreshment we could find, at that spot; but farther within the palace, we found abundance of refreshment-rooms, and John Bull and his wife and family at fifty little round tables, busily engaged with cold fowl, cold beef, ham, tongue, and bottles of ale and stout, and half-pint decanters of sherry. The English probably eat with more simple enjoyment than any other people;—not ravenously, [215] as we often do—and not exquisitely, and artificially, like the French—but deliberately, and vigorously, and with due absorption in the business, so that nothing good is lost upon them. They are a wise breed of animals. It is remarkable how large a feature the refreshment-rooms make, in the arrangements of the Crystal Palace.

The Crystal Palace is a gigantic toy, for the English people to play with. The design seems to be, to re-produce all past ages, by representing the features of their interior architecture, costume, religion, domestic life, and everything that can be expressed by paint and plaster; and likewise to bring all climates and regions of the earth within these enchanted precincts, with their inhabitants and animals in living semblance, and their vegetable productions, as far as possible, alive and real. Some part of this design is already accomplished to a wonderful degree. The Indian, the Egyptian, and especially the Arabic courts are admirably done. I never saw nor conceived anything so gorgeous as the Alhambra. There are Byzantine, and medi-aeval representations, too—reproductions of ancient apartments, decorations, statues from tombs, monuments, religious and funereal—that gave me new ideas of what antiquity has been. It takes down one's overweening opinion of the present [216] time, to see how many kinds of beauty and magnificence have heretofore existed, and are now quite past away and forgotten; and to find that we—who suppose that, in all matters of taste, our age is the very flower-season of time—that we are poor and meagre as to many things in which they were rich. There is nothing gorgeous now. We live a very naked life. This was the only reflection I remember making, as we passed from century to century through the succession of classic, oriental, and medi-aeval courts, adown the lapse of time— seeing all these ages in as brief a space as the Wandering Jew might glance along them in his memory. I suppose a Pompeian house, with its courts and interior apartments was as faithfully shown as it was possible to do it. I doubt whether I ever should feel at home in such a house.

In the pool of a fountain (of which there are several beautiful ones within the palace, besides larger ones in the garden before it) we saw tropical plants • growing, large water lilies of various colors, some white, like our own Concord pond-lily, only larger, and more numerously leaved. There were great, circular green leaves, lying flat on the water, with a circumference as large as that of a centre-table. Tropical trees, too—varieties of palm, and others—grew in immense pots or tubs, but [217] seemed not to enjoy themselves much. The atmosphere must, after all, be far too cool to bring out their native luxuriance; and this difficulty can never be got over, at a less expense than that of absolutely stewing the visitors and attendants. Otherwise, it would be very practicable to have all the vegetable world, at least, within these precincts.

The palace is very large, and our time was short, it being desirable to get home betimes, on account of Sophia's cough; so, after a stay of little more than two hours, we took the rail back again, and reached Hanover Square at about six. After tea, I wandered forth with some thought of going to the theatre; and passing the entrance of one, in the Strand, I went in, and found a farce in progress. It was one of the minor theatres—very minor, indeed—but the pieces, so far as I saw them, were sufficiently laughable. There were some Spanish dancers, too, very graceful and pretty. Between the pieces, a girl from the neighboring saloon came to the doors of the boxes, offering lemonade and ginger-beer to the occupants. A person in my box took a glass of lemonade, and shared it with a young lady by his side, both sipping out of the glass. The audience seemed rather heavy—not briskly responsive to the efforts of the performers—but good-natured, and willing to be pleased, especially with some patriotic dances, in [218] which much waving and intermingling of the French and English flags was introduced. Theatrical performances soon weary me, of late years; and I came away before the curtain rose on the concluding piece.

SEPTEMBER 28th FRIDAY.

SOPHIA and I walked to Charing Cross, yesterday forenoon, and thence took a Hansom cab to Saint Paul's Cathedral. It had been a thick, foggy morning, but had warmed and brightened into one of the balmiest and sunniest of noons. As we entered the Cathedral, the long bars of sunshine were falling from its upper windows through the great, interior atmosphere, and were made visible by the dust, or mist, floating about in it. It is a grand edifice, and I liked it quite as much as on my first view of it; although a sense of coldness and nakedness is felt, when we compare it with Gothic churches;—it is more an external affair than the Gothic churches are, and is not so made out of the dim, awful, mysterious, grotesque, intricate nature of man. But it is beautiful and grand. I love its remote distances and wide, clear spaces; its airy massiveness; its noble arches; its sky-like dome, which, I think, should be all over light with ground glass, instead of being dark, with only diminutive windows.

We walked round, looking at the monuments, which are so arranged at the bases of columns, and in niches, as to coincide with [219] the regularity of the Cathedral, and be each an additional ornament to the whole, however defective individually as works of art. We thought that many of these monuments were striking and impressive; though there was a pervading sameness of idea—a great many Victories, and Valors, and Britannias, and a great expenditure of wreaths, which must have cost Victory a considerable sum, at any florist's whom she patronizes. A very great majority of the memorials are to naval and military men, slain in Bonaparte's wars; men in whom one feels little or no interest, (except Picton, Abercrombie, Moore, Nelson, of course, and a few others really historic) having done nothing remarkable, save being shot, and shown no more brains than the cannon-balls that killed them. All the statues have the dust of years upon them, strewn thickly in the folds of their marble garments, and on any limb stretched horizontally, and on their noses; so that the expression is much obscured. I think the nation might employ people to brush away the dust from the statues of its heroes. But, on the whole, it is very fine to look through the broad area of the Cathedral, and see, at the foot of some distant pillar, a group of sculptured figures, commemorating some man and deed that (whether worth remembering or no) the nation is so happy as to reverence. [220] In Westminster Abbey, the monuments are so crowded, and so oddly patched together upon the walls, that they are ornamental only in a moral point of view; and, moreover, the quaint and grotesque taste of many of them might well make the spectator laugh—an effect not likely to be produced by the monuments in Saint Paul's. But, after all, a man might read the walls of the Abbey, day after day, with ever fresh interest; whereas the cold propriety of the Cathedral would weary him in due time.

We did not ascend to the galleries and other points of interest aloft, nor go down into the vaults, where Nelson's sarcophagus is shown, and many monuments from the old Gothic Cathedral, which stood on this site before the Great Fire. They say that these lower regions are comfortably warm and dry; but as we walked round in front of the Cathedral, within its iron railing, we passed an open door, giving access to the vaults, and it breathed out a chill like death upon us.

It is pleasant to stand in the centre of the Cathedral, and hear the noise of London, loudest all round that spot—how it is calmed into a sound as proper to be heard through the aisles, as the tones of its own organ. If Saint Paul's were to be burnt again (having already been burnt and risen again, three or four [221] times, since the sixth century) I wonder whether it would ever be re-built on the same spot! I doubt whether the city and the nation are still so religious as to consecrate their midmost heart for the site of a church, where land would be so valuable by the square inch.

Emerging from the Cathedral, we went through Paternoster Row, and saw Ave Mary Lane, and Amen Corner; all this locality appearing to have got its nomenclature from monkish passengers. We now took a cab for the British Museum, but found this to be one of the days on which strangers are not admitted; so we walked slowly into Oxford-street, where I left Sophia at a place of ladies' refreshment, and went myself to get a chop. We then strolled homeward, looking at the shop-windows and at the busy street; till coming to a sort of bazaar, we went in, and found a gallery of pictures. This bazaar proved to be the Pantheon (why called so, I know not) and the first picture we saw in the gallery was Haydon's "Resurrection of Lazarus"—a great height and breadth of canvas, right before you as you ascend the stairs. The face of Lazarus is very awful and not to be forgotten;—it is true as if the painter had seen it, or had been himself the resurrected man and felt it; but the rest of the picture signifies nothing, and is vulgar and disagreeable besides. There [222] are several other pictures by Haydon, in this collection; the Banishment of Aristides, Nero with his Harp, amid the conflagration of Rome; but this last is perfectly ridiculous, and all of them are exceedingly disagreeable. I should be sorry to live in a house that contained one of them. The best thing of Haydon's was a first hasty dash of a sketch for a small, full-length portrait of Wordsworth, sitting on the crag of a mountain. I doubt whether Wordsworth's likeness has ever been so poetically brought out. This gallery is altogether of modern painters; and it seems to be a receptacle for pictures by artists who can obtain places nowhere else;—at least, I never heard of their names before. They were very uninteresting, almost without exception; and yet some of the pictures were done cleverly enough. There is very little talent in this world, and what there is, it seems to me, is pretty well known and acknowledged. We don't often stumble upon geniuses in obscure corners.

Leaving the gallery, we wandered through the rest of the Bazaar, which is devoted to the sale of ladies' finery, jewels, perfumes, children's toys, and all manner of small and pretty rubbish; till Sophia was quite wearied out, and we resumed our way home. In the evening, I again sallied forth, and lost myself for an hour or two; at [223] last recognizing my whereabout in Tottenham Court Road. In such quarters of London, it seems to be the habit of people to take their suppers in the open air. You see old women at the corners, with kettles of hot water for tea or coffee; and as I passed a butcher's open shop, he was just taking out large quantities of boiled beef, smoking hot. Butcher's stands are remarkable for their profuse expenditure of gas; it belches forth from the pipes in a great, flaring jet of flame, uncovered by any glass, and broadly illuminating the neighborhood. I have not observed that London ever goes to bed.

SEPTEMBER 29th, SATURDAY.

YESTERDAY we walked to the British Museum—Sophia, Julian, and I. A centinel [sic] (or two) was on guard before the gateway of this extensive edifice, in Great Russell Street, and there was a porter at the lodge, and, I think, one or two police-men lounging about; but entrance was free, and we walked in without question. Officials and policemen were likewise scattered about the great entrance-hall; none of whom, however, interfered with us; so we took whatever way we chose, and wandered about the Museum at will. It is a hopeless—and to me, generally, a depressing—business to go through an immense, multifarious show like this (if there were any other like it) glancing at a thousand things, and con[224]scious of some little tittilation [sic] of mind from them, but really taking in nothing, and getting no good from anything. One need not go beyond the limits of the British Museum to be profoundly accomplished in all branches of science, art, literature; only it would take a lifetime to exhaust it in any one department; but, to see it as we did, and with no prospect of ever seeing it more at leisure, only impressed me with the old apothegm—"Life is short, and Art is long." The fact is, the world is accumulating too many materials for knowledge. We do not recognize for rubbish what is really rubbish; and under this head might be reckoned almost everything one sees in the British Museum; and as each generation leaves its fragments and potsherds behind it, such will finally be the desperate conclusion of the learned.[270]

We went first among some antique marbles—busts, statues, terminal gods &c—with several of the Roman emperors among them. We saw here the bust whence Haydon took his ugly and ridiculous likeness of Nero;—a foolish thing to do. Julius Caesar was there, too, looking more like a modern old man than any other bust in the series. Perhaps there may be a universality in his face that gives it this independence of race and epoch. We glimpsed along among the old marbles—Elgin, and others—which are esteemed such treasures of art;—the oddest fragments, many of [225] them, smashed by their fall from high places, or by being pounded to pieces by barbarians; or gnawed away by time so that the beautiful statues look like a child's sugar images, which it has sucked in its mouth; the surface roughened by being rained upon for thousands of years; almost always, a nose knocked off; sometimes, a headless form; a great deficiency of feet and hands;—poor, maimed veterans, in this hospital of incurables. The beauty of the most perfect of them must be rather guessed at, and seen by faith, than with the bodily eye; to look at the corroded faces and forms is like trying to see angels through mist and cloud. I suppose nine-tenths of those, who seem to be enraptured by these fragments, do not really care about them; neither do I. And if I were actually moved, I should doubt whether it were by the statues, or by my own fancy.

We passed, too, through Assyrian saloons, and Egyptian saloons—all full of monstrosities and horrible uglinesses, especially the Egyptian. They were surely an abominable people; and all the innumerable relics that I saw of them, in these saloons, and among the mummies, instead of bringing me closer to them, removed me farther and farther; there being no common ground of sympathy between them and us. Their gigantic statues are certainly very curious. I saw a hand and arm [226] up to the shoulder, fifteen feet in length, and made of some stone that seemed harder and heavier than granite, not having lost its polish in all the rough usage that it has undergone. There was a fist on a still larger scale, almost as big as a hogshead. Hideous, blubber-lipped faces of giants; human shapes with beast-heads on them;—the Egyptians controverted Nature in all things, only using it as a groundwork to depict the unnatural upon. Their mummifying process is a result of this tendency. We saw one very perfect mummy, a priestess, with apparently only one more fold of linen betwixt us and her antique flesh, and this fitting closely to her person, from head to foot, so that we could see the lineaments of her face, and the shape of her bosom and limbs, as perfectly as if quite bare. I judge that she may have been very beautiful in her day, whenever that was. One or two of the poor thing's toes (her feet were wonderfully small and delicate) protruded from the linen; and, perhaps not having been so perfectly embalmed, the flesh had fallen away, leaving only some little bones. I don't think this young woman has gained much by not turning to dust in the time of the Pharaohs. We also saw some bones of a king that had been taken out of a pyramid; a very fragmentary skeleton. Among the classic marbles, I peeped into an urn that once contained the ashes of dead people, and the bottom still had an ashy hue. I like [227] this mode of disposing of dead bodies; but it would be still better to burn them and scatter the ashes, instead of hoarding them up—scatter them over wheat-fields or flower-beds.

Besides these antique halls, we wandered through saloons of antediluvian animals, some set up in skeletons, others imprisoned in solid stone; also specimens of still extant animals, birds, reptiles, shells, minerals, the whole circle of human knowledge and guess-work; till I wished that the whole Past might be swept away—and each generation compelled to bury and destroy whatever it had produced, before being permitted to leave the stage. When we quit a house, we are expected to make it clean for the next occupant;—why ought we not to leave a clean world for the coming generation. We did not see the Library, of above half a million of volumes; else I suppose I should have found full occasion to wish that burnt or buried, likewise. In truth a greater part of it is as good as buried, so far as any readers are concerned.

Leaving the Museum, mamma got something to eat in a confectioner's shop, and Julian and I in a chop-house; and then we sauntered home. After a little rest, I set out for St. John's Wood, smoking a cigar by the way (a thing very common, in the street, in England, though no American gentleman, in a [228] northern city, at least, would think of it,) and arrived thither by dint of repeated inquiries. It is a pretty suburb, inhabited by people of the middling-class. Una met me joyfully, but seemed to have had a good time with Mrs Oakford and her daughter; and being pressed to stay to tea, I could not well help it. Before tea, I sat talking with Mrs. Oakford and a friend of hers, Miss Clinch, about the Americans and the English, especially dwelling on the defects of the latter—among which we reckon a wretched meanness in money-transactions, a lack of any embroidery of honor and liberality in their dealings; so that they require close watching, or they will be sure to take you at advantage. I hear this character of them from Americans on all hands; and my own experience confirms it, so far as it goes, not merely among tradespeople, but persons who call themselves gentlefolks. The cause, no doubt—or one cause— lies in the fewer chances of getting money here, the closer and sharper regulation of all the modes of life, nothing being left here to liberal and gentlemanly feeling—except fees to servants. They are not gamblers in England, as we, to some extent, are; and getting their money painfully, or living within an accurately known income, they are disinclined to give up so much as a sixpence that they can possibly get. But the result is, they are mean in petty things.

[229] By-and-by, Mr. Oakford came in, well-soaked with the heaviest shower that I ever knew in England, which had been rat[t]ling on the roof of the little side-room where we sat, and which had caught him on the outside of the omnibus. After he had changed his clothes, we had tea; then he invited me to smoke a cigar; and, a little before eight °clock, I got into a cab and came home with Una—the gas light glittering on the wet streets through which we drove, though the sky was now clear overhead.

SEPTEMBER 30th, SUNDAY.

YESTERDAY, a little before 12, we took a cab (mamma, Julian and I—Una being tired of sight-seeing) and went to the Two Houses of Parliament—the immensest building, methinks, that ever was built, and not yet finished, though it has now been occupied for years. Its exterior lies hugely along the ground, and its great unfinished tower is still climbing towards the sky; but the result (unless it be the river-front, which I have not yet seen) seems not very impressive. The interior is much more successful. Nothing can be more magnificent and gravely gorgeous than the Chamber of Peers; a large, oblong hall, panelled with oak, elaborately carved, to the height of perhaps twenty feet; then the balustrade of a gallery runs around the hall; and above the gallery are six arched windows on each side, richly painted with historic subjects. The roof [230] is ornamented and gilded; and everywhere, throughout the hall, there is embellishment of color and carving, on the broadest scale, and, at the same time, most minute and elaborate; statues of full size in niches aloft; small heads of kings, no bigger than a doll; and the oak is carved, in all parts of the panelling, as faithfully as they used to do it in Henry VII's time;— as faithfully, and with as good workmanship, but with nothing like the variety and invention which I saw in the dining-room of Smithell's Hall. There, the artist wrought with his heart and hand; but much of this work, I suppose, was done by machinery. Be that as it may, it is a most noble and splendid hall, and though so fine, there is not a touch of finery; it glistens and glows with even a sombre magnificence, owing to the rich, deep hues, and the dim light (bedimmed with rich colors) through the painted windows. In arched recesses, that serve as frames, at each end of the hall, there are three pictures by modern artists, from English history; and though it was not possible to see them well as pictures, they adorned and enriched the hall marvellously, as architectural embellishments.

The peers' seats are four rows of long sofas, on each side of the hall, covered with red morocco; comfortable seats enough, but not adapted to any other than a decorously erect position. The woolsack is between these two divisions of sofas, in the [231] middle passage of the hall, a great, square, cushion or mattress, covered with scarlet, and with a scarlet cushion stuck up perpendicularly, for the Chancellor to lean against. In front of this woolsack, there is another still larger scarlet mattress, on which he might lie at full length; for what purpose intended, I know not. I should take the woolsack to be not a very comfortable seat; though, I suppose, it was originally intended to be the most comfortable one that could be contrived, in view of the Chancellor's much sitting.

The Throne is the first object you see on entering the hall, being close to the door; an elbow chair of antique form, with a high, peaked back, and a square canopy above, the whole richly carved, and quite covered with burnished gilding, besides being adorned with rows of rock-crystals—which seemed to me of rather questionable taste. The throne is less elevated above the floor of the hall, than one imagines it ought to be. While we were looking at it, I saw two Americans (Western men, I should guess, and one with a true American slouch) talking to the police-man in attendance, and describing our senate-chamber in contrast with this House of Lords. The police-man smiled and ha-ed, and seemed to make as courteous and liberal responses as he could. There was quite a mixed company of spectators, and, I think, other Americans [232] present, besides the above two and ourselves. The Lord Chamberlain's tickets appear to be distributed with great impartiality; two or three were women of the lower middle-class, with children, or babies in arms, one of whom lifted up its voice loudly in the House of Peers.

We next (after long contemplating this rich hall) proceeded through passages and corridors to a great central room, very beautiful, which seems to be used for purposes of refreshment, and for electric telegraphs; though I should not suppose this could be its primitive and ultimate design. Thence we went into the House of Commons, which is larger than the chamber of peers, and much less richly ornamented, though it would have appeared splendid had it come first in order. The speaker's chair, if I remember rightly, is loftier and statelier than the throne itself. Both in this hall, and that of the lords, we were at first surprised by the narrow limits within which the great ideas of the

Lords and Commons of England are physically realized; they would seem to require a vaster space. When we hear of members rising on opposite sides of the house, we think of them as but dimly discernible to their opponents, and uplifting their voices so as to be heard afar;—whereas, they sit closely enough to feel each other's spheres, to note all expression of face, and to give the debate the character of a [233] conversation. In this view, a debate seems a much more earnest and real thing, than as we read it in a newspaper;—think of the debaters meeting each other's eyes, their faces flushing, their looks interpreting their words, their speech growing into eloquence, without losing the genuineness of talk. Yet, in fact, the chamber of peers is ninety feet long, and half as broad and high; and the Chamber of Commons still larger.

Thence we went to Westminster Hall, through a gallery with statues on each side, (beautiful statues too, I thought) six of them, principally from the times of the Civil Wars—Clarendon, Falkland, Hampden, Selden, Somers, Mansfield, Walpole. There is room for more in this corridor; and there are niches for hundreds of their marble brotherhood, throughout the edifice; but I suppose future ages will have to fill the greater part of them. But, yet, I cannot help imagining that this rich and noble edifice has more to do with the past than with the future; that it is the glory of a declining empire; and that the perfect bloom of this great stone flower, growing out of the institutions of England, forebodes that they have nearly lived out their life. It sums up all. Its beauty and magnificence are made out of ideas that are gone by.

We entered Westminster Hall (which is incorporated [234] into this new edifice, and forms an integral part of it) through a lofty arch-way, whence a double flight of broad steps descends to the stone pavement of the hall. After the elaborate ornament of the rooms we had just been viewing, this venerable hall looks extremely simple and bare; a gray stone floor, gray and naked stone walls, but a roof sufficiently elaborate, its vault being filled with carved beams and rafters of chestnut, very much admired and wondered at for their design and arrangement. I think it would have pleased me more to have seen a clear, vaulted roof, instead of this intricacy of wooden joists, by which so much sky-like space is lost. They make (be it not irreverently said) the vast and lofty hall look like the ideal of an immense barn. But it is a noble space, and all without the support of a single pillar. It is about eighty of my paces from the foot of the steps to the opposite end of the hall; and twenty-seven from side to side;—very lofty, too, though not quite proportionately to its other dimensions. I love it for its simplicity and antique nakedness, and deem it worthy to have been the haunt and home of History, through the six centuries since it was built. I wonder it does not occur to modern ingenuity to make a scenic representation, in this very Hall, of the ancient trials for life or death, pomps, feasts, coronations, and every great historic incident, in the [235] lives of Kings, Parliaments, Protectors, and all illustrious men, that have occurred here. The whole world cannot show another such a Hall, so tapestried with recollections of whatever is most striking in human annals.

Westminster Abbey being just across the street, we went thither from the Hall, and sought out the cloisters, which we had not yet visited. They are in excellent preservation, a broad walk, canopied with intermingled arches of gray stone, on which some sort of lichen, or other growth of ages, (which seems, however, to have little or nothing vegetable in it) has grown. The pavement under foot is entirely made of flat tombstones, inscribed with half-effaced names of the dead people beneath; and the wall all round bears the marble tablets which give a fuller record of their virtues. I think it was from a meditation in these cloisters that Addison wrote one of his most beautiful pieces in the Spectator.[271] It is a pity that the old fashion of a cloistered walk is not retained in our modern edifices; it was so excellent for shelter and for shade, during a thoughtful hour, this sombre corridor beneath an arched stone roof, with the central space of richest grass, on which the sun might shine or the shower fall, while the monk or student paced through the prolonged archway of his meditations.

[236] As we emerged from the cloisters, and walked along by the churchyard of the Abbey, a woman came begging behind us very earnestly—"A bit of bread," she said; "and I will give you a thousand blessings! Hunger is hard to bear. Oh, kind gentleman, and kind lady, a penny for a bit of bread! It is a hard thing that gentlemen and ladies should see poor people wanting bread, and make no difference whether they are good or bad." And so she followed us almost all round the Abbey, assailing our hearts in most plaintive terms, but with no success; for she did it far too well to be anything but an impostor, and, no doubt, she had breakfasted better, and was likely to have a better dinner, than ourselves. And yet the natural man cries out against the philosophy that rejects beggars. It is a thousand to one that they are impostors; but yet we do ourselves a wrong by hardening our hearts against them. At last, without turning round, I told her that I should give her nothing—with some asperity, doubtless, for the effort to refuse creates a bitterer repulse than is necessary. She still followed us a little farther, but at last gave it up, with a deep groan. I could not have performed this act of heroism on my first arrival from America.

Whether or no the beggar-woman had invoked curses on us, and Heaven saw fit to grant some slight response, I know not; [237] but it now began to rain on my wife's velvet; so I put her and Julian into a cab, and hastened to ensconce myself in Westminster Abbey, while the shower should last. Poet's Corner has never seemed like a strange place to me; it has been familiar from the very first;—at all events, I cannot now recollect the previous conception, of which the reality has taken the place. I seem always to have known that somewhat dim corner, with the bare brown stone-work of the old edifice aloft, and a window shedding down its light on the marble busts and tablets, yellow with time, that cover the three walls of the nook, up to a height of about twenty feet. Prior's is the largest and richest monument. It is observable that the bust and monument of Congreve are in a distant part of the Abbey. His Duchess probably thought it a degredation [*sic*] to bury a gentleman among the beggarly poets. I walked round the aisles, and paced the nave, and came to the conclusion that Westminster Abbey, both in itself, and for the variety and interest of its monuments, is a thousand times preferable to Saint Paul's. There is as much difference as between a snow-bank and a chimney-corner, in their relation to the human heart. By-the-by, the monuments and statues in the Abbey seem all to be carefully dusted.

The shower being over, I walked down into the city [238] where I called on Mr. Bennett, and left Sophia's watch to be examined and put in order. He told me that he and his brother had lately been laying out and letting a piece of land at Blackheath, that had been left them by their father; and that the ground-rent would bring them in two thousand pounds per annum. With such an independent income, I doubt whether any American would consent to be anything but a gentleman—certainly not an operative watchmaker. How sensible these Englishmen are in some things. From Mr. Bennett's, I went to Mr. Oakford's counting-room, and not finding him, ascended another flight of stairs to see General Campbell, who was likewise out. I then rambled forth in quest of a dinner, and found a better eating-house than those into which I usually stumble, and some roast-goose and a small bottle of stout, which put me in very good heart. Thence I went at adventure, and lost myself, of course. At one part of my walk, I came upon Saint Luke's Hospital, whence I returned to Saint Paul's, and thence along Fleet-street and the Strand. Contiguous to the latter is Holywell-street, a narrow lane, filled up with little bookshops and bookstalls, at some of which I saw sermons and other works of divinity, old editions of the classics, and all such serious matters; while, at stalls and windows close beside them (and, possibly, at the same stalls) there were books with [239] title pages displayed, indicating them to be of the most abominable kind.

OCTOBER 2ᵈ TUESDAY.

YESTERDAY forenoon, I went with Julian into the city—to 67, Gracechurch-street, to get a bank post-note cashed by Mr. Oakford, and afterwards to the offices of two lines of steamers, in Moorgate-street and Leadenhall-street. The city was very much thronged; it is a marvel what sets so many people agoing, at all hours of the day. Then it is to be considered that these are but a small portion of those who are doing the business of the city; much the larger part being occupied in offices, at desks, in discussions of plans of enterprise, out of sight of the public; while these earnest hurriers are merely the froth in the pot. After seeing the steamer-officials, we went to London Bridge, which always swarms with passengers more than any of the streets. Descending the steps that lead to the level of the Thames, we took passage in a steam-boat bound up the river to Chelsea; of which there is one starting every ten minutes, the voyage being of forty minutes' duration. It began to sprinkle a little just as we started; but, after a slight showeriness, lasting till we had passed Westminster Bridge, the day grew rather pleasant. Passing near the bridge nearest St. Paul's, (Southwark, I think) we saw a large and beautiful barge,[272] splendidly gilded and ornamented, and with an awning, waiting at the pier; it had the [240] royal banner of Great Britain displayed, besides being decorated with a number of other flags; and many footmen, in bright scarlet livery, with white silk stockings, were in attendance. It put me in mind of the old times when the sovereign and nobles were wont to make a high street of the Thames, and make pompous processions on it. This must have been some day of festival in the city;[273] for I saw a gorgeous state-coach, of an antique shape, but all over new with gilding and gingerbread work, waiting in the square near the bank. Coachmen and footmen are the grandest and gaudiest objects to be seen, at this day, in England. I doubt, however, whether their finery can endure much longer. People will recognize that it is nearly as bad taste to bedizen themselves with gay colors and gold lace, in the persons of their servants, as to wear these gew-gaws themselves. Meanwhile, I am glad the fashion has endured till my day; for I love to see it.

At Westminster Bridge, we had a good view of the river-front of the two Houses of Parliament,[274] which look very noble from this point of view; a long and massive extent, with a delightful promenade for the legislative people right above the margin of the river. This is certainly a magnificent edifice; and yet I doubt whether it is so impressive as it might and ought to have been made, considering its immensity. It makes no more impression than you can well account to yourself for, and rather wonder [241] that it is not more. The reason must be, that the architect has not "builded better than he knew";[275] there was no power higher and wiser than himself, making him its instrument; —he reckoned upon and contrived all his effects, with malice aforethought, and therefore missed the crowning effect—that being a happiness which God, out of his pure grace, mixes up with only the simple-hearted best efforts of men. On the opposite side of the river, almost directly across from the two Houses, is the ancient palace of Lambeth, the Archbishop of Canterbury's residence; a venerable group of halls and square towers, chiefly brick, but with at least one large tower of stone.

The Thames looks rather cleaner, in this upper part of its course, but still not tempting as the wherewithal to quench thirst. Its banks have not the ancient shabbiness that disfigures them all the way downward from Southwark Bridge; although there are few or no very striking objects, after passing Westminster. Chelsea is an old town with a vast number of pot-houses, and some gardens (the Cremorne) for public amusement. A great scenic exhibition, illustrative of the fall of Sebastopol, was advertised on the bills for the evening. After getting some dinner at an eating-house, we crossed Battersea Bridge, and took a stroll on the other side of the Thames, with some expectation of reaching the Crystal Palace, which was vis[242]ible at a far distance from the back streets of Chelsea. But we did not find our way to it. Returning, and wondering that we saw nothing of the Chelsea Hospital, I inquired its whereabout of a policeman, and finally discovered it, looking right upon the Thames. It must have been directly before my eyes, as the steamer passed, and a noticeable object, too; and yet I had not seen it.

It is a large quadrangle of brick edifices—the dark, sombre brick, which the English seemed to have used exclusively, from old times till the present—set off with stone-edgings and facings; edifices of three stories high, and with windows in the high roofs. There is no grandeur (which is somewhat of an attribute at Greenwich Hospital) but a venerable neatness. There is a large gateway at each extremity of the street-front; and, lounging about the gate which we first reached, we saw some of the pensioners; old, gray veterans, in long scarlet coats, of an antique fashion, and cocked hats, or sometimes a foraging cap. Almost all of them moved with an infirm gait; some stumped on wooden legs; and here and there an arm was missing. I asked one of them whether strangers could be admitted to see the grounds; and he answered with the heartiest hospitality—"Oh, yes, Sir, anywhere! Walk in, and go where you please;—up stairs or anywhere!" So we entered, and walked [243] along the inner side of the quadrangle, and came anon to the door of the chapel, which makes a part of the contiguity of edifice next the street. Here one of the pensioners touched his hat, and inquired if I wished to see the chapel; to which I assenting, he unlocked the door, and we went in.

The chapel is a large hall with a vaulted roof, in the farther portion of which, over the altar, there is a painting in fresco (I believe) the subject of which I could make nothing of. The more appropriate adornments of the place are the dusty and tattered banners, which hang from their staves all round the cieling [sic] of the chapel; banners of all the countries with which the British have had wars, since James the Second's time; French, Dutch, Indian, Prussian, and American; for the old pensioner failed not to show me the flags that had been captured at Washington, which hang, I think, a little higher than any of the rest. It is a comfort that they are already indistinguishable, or almost so, owing to dust and tatters, and will soon rot away from their staves. I suppose the moths do us a good office with these dishonored flags. There were two or three French eagles, which it might be as well to take down, in these days; and the latest trophies had been taken from the Chinese, though the old pensioner [244] smiled complacently at my suggestion that some Russian banners might soon hang from the walls. The pensioner was a meek-looking, kindly old man, with a humble affability that made it pleasant to converse with him. Old soldiers, I think, are much more accostable than old sailors. He told me that he had fought at a cannon, all through the battle of Waterloo, and escaped unhurt; that he had now been in the Hospital between four and five years; that he was married, but that his wife lived outside. To my inquiry whether the pensioners were comfortable and happy, he said—"Oh, yes Sir!"—afterwards qualifying his reply, however, by saying that some people could not be comfortable anywhere. In fact, it must be a life of too much torpor—too little occupation or variety—too little of the wholesome care and regulation of their own interests. From what I saw of them, I suspect there is little else for them to do, save to lounge in the sun;—and then there is so little sunshine in England!

I should have been glad to give this old pensioner half-a-crown, or thereabouts, for showing me the captured banners of my country, and then to tell him that I was an American; he having taken me for an Englishman, sharer in the glory, instead of the shame. But, feeling in my pocket, I found only [245] a few half-pence, which, with many apologies, I offered him, and he graciously accepted. I might have given him a sovereign, to be sure; but that would have been carrying the joke a little too far. My unavoidable shabbiness mortified me so much, however, that I did not ask to see the hall, or anything else; but wandered a little about the grounds (which seem to be a place of resort for nursery-maids and women with children) and then left the hospital. In the quadrangle, I observed a bronze classic figure, intended for Charles the Second.[276] We took an omnibus that was passing for London, and reached Regent street somewhere about six °clock.

OCTOBER 3ᵈ, WEDNESDAY.

I AGAIN went into the city, yesterday forenoon, to settle about the passages to Lisbon—taking Julian with me. From Hungerford bridge, we took the steamer to London bridge, that being an easy and speedy mode of accomplishing distances that take many footsteps through the crowded thoroughfares. After leaving the steamer office, we went back through the Strand, and crossing Waterloo Bridge, walked a good way on the Surrey side of the river; a coarse, dingy, disagreeable suburb, with shops apparently for country produce, for old clothes, second-hand furniture, for iron ware, and other things bulky and inelegant. How many scenes and sorts of life are comprehended within Lon[246]don. There was much in the aspect of these streets, that reminded me of a busy country-village in America, on an immensely magnified scale.

Growing rather weary anon, we got into an omnibus which took us as far as the Surrey Zoological Gardens, which Julian wanted very much to see. They proved to be a rather poor place of suburban amusement;—poor, at least, by daylight, their chief attraction for the public consisting in out-of-door representations of battles and sieges. The storming of Sebastopol (as likewise at the Cremorne Gardens) was advertised for the evening; and we saw the scenery of Sebastopol, painted on a vast scale, in the open air, and really looking like miles and miles of hill and water scenery;—with a space for the actual manoeuvering of ships on a sheet of real water in front of the scene, on which some ducks were now swimming about, in place of men-of-war. The climate of England must often interfere terribly with this sort of performance; and I can conceive of nothing drearier for spectators or performers than a drizzly evening. Convenient to this central spot of entertainment, there are liquor and refreshment-rooms, with pies and cakes, and this sort of thing, in which the English never produce anything very delicious. The menagerie, though the ostensible staple of the Gardens, is rather poor and scanty; pretty well provided with lions and lionesses, also a giraffe or two, some [247] camels, a polar bear, who plunges into a pool of water for bits of cake, and two black bears, who sit on their haunches, or climb poles; besides a wilderness of monkies [*sic*],²⁷⁷ some parrots and macaws, an ostrich, various ducks, and other animal and ornithological trumpery; some skins of snakes so well stuffed that I took them for live serpents, till Julian discovered the deception; and an aquarium, with a good many common fishes swimming among its seaweed.

The garden is shaded with trees, and set out with green sward and gravel walks, from which the people were sweeping the withered autumnal leaves, which every day now scatters down. Plaister [*sic*] statues stand here and there, one of them without a head, thus disclosing the hollowness of his trunk; there was a little drizzly fountain or two, with the water dripping over the rock-work of which the English are so fond; and the buildings for the animals and other purposes had a flimsy, pasteboard aspect of pretension. The garden was in its undress; few visitors, I suppose, coming hither at this time of day, and only here and there a lady and children, a young man and girl, or a couple of citizens, loitering about. I take pains to remember these small items, because they suggest the day-life or torpidity of what may look very brilliant at night; —these corked-up fountains, slovenly green sward, cracked casts of statues [248] pasteboard castles, and duck-pond bay of Balaclava [*sic*], then shining out in magic splendor; and the shabby attendants, whom we saw sweeping [and] shovelling, are probably transformed into the heroes of Sebastopol.

Julian thought it a delightful place; but I soon grew very weary, and came away about four °clock, I think; and getting into a city-omnibus, we alighted on the hither side of Blackfriar's bridge. Turning into Fleet-street, I looked about for a place to dine at, and chose the Mitre Tavern, in memory of Johnson and Boswell. It stands behind a front of modern shops, through which is an archway, giving admittance into a narrow court-yard, which, I suppose, was formerly open to Fleet-street. The house is of dark brick, and from a comparison of it with other London edifices, I should have taken it to have been at least re-fronted, since Johnson's time; but, within, we entered a low, sombre coffee-room, which might well enough have been of that era, or earlier. It seems to be a good, plain, respectable eating-house; and the waiter gave us each a plate of boiled beef, and, for dessert, a damson-tart, which made up a comfortable dinner; and, with a small bottle of stout, and sixpence to the waiter, cost four shillings.

After dinner, we zizzagged [*sic*] homeward through Clifford's Inn passage, Holborn, Drury Lane, the Strand, Charing Cross, Pall-mall, and [249] Regent-street; but I remember only an ancient brick gateway, as particularly remarkable. I think it was the entrance to Lincoln's Inn. We reached home at about six. There is a woman who has several times passed through our street, stopping occasionally to sing songs under the windows; and last evening, between 9 & 10 °clock, she came, and sang "Kathleen O'Moore,"²⁷⁸ richly and sweetly,—

a voice that rose up out of the dim, chill street, and made our heart throb in unison with it, here in our comfortable drawing-room. I never heard a voice that touched me more. Somebody told her to go away, and she stopt like a nightingale suddenly shot; but, finding that Sophia wished to know something about her, Fanny and one of the maids ran after her, and brought her into the hall. It seems she was brought up to sing at the opera, and married an Italian opera-singer, who is now dead;—lodging at a model lodging-house, at three pence a night; and being a penny short to-night, she tried this method in hope of getting that penny. She takes in plain sewing when she can get any, and picks up a trifle about the street by means of her voice, which, she says, was once sweet, but has now been injured by the poorness of her living. She is a pale woman with black eyes, Fanny says, and may have been pretty once, but is not so now. It seems very strange, that, with such a gift of heaven, so cultivated, too, as her voice is, and making even [250] an unsusceptible heart vibrate like a harp-string, she should not have some sort of an engagement among the hundred theatres and singing rooms of London;—that she should throw away her melody in the streets, for the mere chance of a penny, when sounds not a hundredth part so sweet are worth purses of gold from other lips.

OCTOBER 5ᵗʰ FRIDAY.

It rained, almost all day, Wednesday; so that I did not go out till late in the afternoon; and then only took a stroll along Oxford-street and Holborn, and back through Fleet-street and the Strand. Yesterday, at a little after ten, I went to the Ambassador's to get my wife's passport for Lisbon. While I was talking with the clerk, Mr. Buchanan made his appearance in a dressing-gown, with a morning cheerfulness and alacrity in his manner. He was going to Liverpool, last night or to-day, with his niece, Miss Lane, who returns to America by the steamer of Saturday. She has had a good deal of success in society here; being pretty enough to be remarked among English women, and with cool, self-possessed, frank, and quiet manners, which look very like the highest breeding.

I next went to Westminster Abbey, where I had long promised myself another quiet visit; for I think I could never be weary of it; and when I finally leave England, it will be this spot which I shall be most unwilling to quit forever. I found a [251] party going through the seven chapels, (or whatever their number may be) and again saw those stately and quaint old tombs; ladies and knights, stretched out on marble slabs, or beneath arches and canopies of stone, let into the walls of the Abbey, reclining on their elbows, in ruff and farthingale, or rivetted [*sic*] armor, or in robes of state, once painted in rich colors, of which only a few patches of scarlet now remain; bearded faces of stately knights, whose noses, in many cases, had been smitten off; and Mary Queen of Scots had lost two fingers (the fore and middle) from each of her beautiful hands, which she is clasping in prayer. There must formerly have been very free access to these tombs; for I observed that all the statues (so far as I examined) were scratched with the initials of visitors, some of the names being dated above a century ago. The old coronation-chair, too, is quite covered, over the back and seat, with initials cut into it with pocket-knives, just as Yankees would do it; only it is not whittled away, as would have been its fate in our hands. Edward the Confessor's shrine (what remains of which is chiefly of wood) likewise abounds in these inscriptions; although this was esteemed the holiest shrine in England;—so holy that (as an old lady in our party remarked, the very dust from it has been sold; and she said she had been told in Canterbury that pilgrims still come to kneel and kiss [252] this shrine. Our guide (a rubicund verger, of cheerful demeanor) said that this was true, though in few instances.

There is a beautiful statue in memory of Horace Walpole's mother; and I took it to be really her likeness, till the verger said that it was a copy of a statue which her son had admired in Italy, and so had transferred it to his mother's grave. There is something characteristic in this mode of filial duty and honor. In all these chapels, full of the tombs and effigies of kings, dukes, arch-prelates, and whatever is proud and pompous in mortality, there is nothing that strikes one more than the colossal statue of plain Mr. Watt, sitting quietly in a chair, in' Saint Paul's Chapel, and reading some papers; he dwarfs the warriors and statesmen; and as to the kings, we smile at them. Telford is in another of the chapels. This visit to the chapels was much more satisfactory than my former one; although I in vain strove to feel it adequately, and to make myself sensible how rich and venerable was what I saw. This realization must come at its own time, like the other happinesses of life. It is unaccountable that I could not now find the seat of Sir George Downing's Squire, though I examined particularly every seat on that side of Henry VII's chapel, where I before found it. I must try again. In the north aisle of the Nave, I found the square stone, inscribed "O rare Ben Jonson"; it is not the original [253] stone, but one substituted for it when the pavement was relaid. Ben Jonson's head, I suppose, (for he was buried upright,) is right under this stone.

When I reached home, at about ½ past two, I found Sophia awaiting me anxiously; for Mrs. Sturgis had notified Leigh Hunt that we were coming to visit him at Hammersmith, and she was to send her carriage for us at three o'clock. Barry Cornwall had likewise written me a note, and a note of introduction to Leigh Hunt. At three, the carriage came; and though the sky looked very ominous, we drove off, and reached Hammersmith in half an hour, or little more—the latter part of the drive in a real gush and pour of rain. Mr. Hunt met us at the door of his little house; a very plain and shabby little house, in a contiguous range of others like it, with no view but an ugly village-street, and nothing beautiful inside or out. But Leigh Hunt is a beautiful and venerable old man, tall and slender, with a striking face, and the gentlest and most naturally courteous manners. He ushered us into his little study, or parlor, or both; a very mean room, with poor paper-hangings and carpet, few books, and an awful lack of upholstery;—all which defects it is sad to see, because Leigh Hunt would so much enjoy all beautiful things, and would seem to be in [254] his place among them; nor has he the grim dignity that makes nakedness the better robe.

He is a beautiful man. I never saw a finer face, either as to the cut of the features, or the expression, or that showed the play of feeling so well. At my first glimpse of his face, when he met us in the entry, I saw that he was old, his long hair being quite white, and his wrinkles many; an aged visage, in short. But as he talked, and became earnest in conversation, I ceased to see his age; and sometimes a flash of youth came out of his eyes, and illuminated his whole face. It was a really wonderful effect. I have never met an Englishman whose manners pleased me so well;—with so little that was conventional, and yet perfect good-breeding, it being the growth of a kindly and sensitive nature, without any reference to rule. His eyes are dark, and very fine, and his voice accompanies them like music;—a very pleasant voice. He is exceedingly appreciative of what is passing among those who surround him. I felt that no effect of what he said—no flitting feeling in myself—escaped him; and, indeed, it rather confused me to see always a ripple on his face, responsive to any slightest breeze over my mind. His figure is very mobile; and as he talks, he folds his hands nervously, and betokens in many ways a nature delicate and immediately sensi[255]tive, quick to feel pleasure or pain. There is not an English trait in him, from head to foot, nor either intellectually or physically; no beef, no ale or stout; and this is the reason that the English have appreciated him no better, and that they leave this sweet and delicate poet poor, and with scanty laurels, in his old age. It is his American blood (his mother was a Pennsylvanian) that gives him whatever excellence he has—the fineness, subtlety, and grace that characterize him—and his person, too, is thoroughly American. I wonder that America has not appreciated him better, were it only for our own claims in him.

He loves dearly to be praised; that is, he loves sympathy as a flower likes sunshine; and in response to all that we said about his writings, (and, for my part, I went quite to the extent of my conscience) his face shone, and he expressed great delight. He could not tell us, he said, the happiness that such appreciation gave him; it always took him by surprise, he remarked, for— perhaps because he cleaned his own boots, and performed other little ordinary offices for himself—he never was conscious of anything wonderful in his own person. And then he smiled. It is usually very difficult for me to praise a man to his face; but [256] Mr. Hunt snuffs up the incense with such gracious satisfaction that it was comparatively easy to praise him; and, then, too, we were the representatives of our country, and spoke for thousands. The rain poured, while we were talking, the lightning flashed, and the thunder broke; but I fancy it was really a sunny hour for Leigh Hunt. He, on his part, praised the Scarlet Letter; but I really do not think that I like to be praised *viva voce;* at least, I am glad when it is said and done with, though I will not say that my heart does not expand a little towards the man who rightly appreciates my books. But I am of somewhat sterner stuff and tougher fibre than Leigh Hunt; and the dark seclusion—the atmosphere without any oxygen of sympathy—in which I spent all the years of my youthful manhood—have enabled me to do almost as well without as with it.

Leigh Hunt must have suffered keenly in his life, and enjoyed keenly; keeping his feelings so much upon the surface as he does, and convenient for everybody to play upon. But happiness has greatly predominated, no doubt. A light, mildly joyous nature, gentle, graceful, yet perhaps without that deepest grace that results from strength. I am inclined to imagine that he may be more beautiful, now, both in person and character, than in his earlier days; for the gravity of [257] age sheds a venerable grace about him, after all, and gives a dignity which he may have lacked at first. I was glad to hear him say, that he had most cheering views about a future life;[279] and there were many tokens of cheerfulness, resignation, enjoyment of whatever he had to enjoy, quiet relinquishment of what was denied him, and piety, and hope, that made me both like and respect him. I should delight to see him in a beautiful house, with a delightful climate and everything elegant about him, and a succession of tender and lovely women to praise him to his face, from morning till night. He is fitter for women's companionship than for men's because they can better give him the tender appreciation which he needs.

The sun shone out once, while we were talking, but was soon over-clouded; and it rained briskly again when we left his door. As we took leave he kissed Una's hand; for she had accompanied us, and sat listening earnestly, and looking very pretty, though saying not a word. He shook and grasped warmly both my hands, at parting; and seemed as much interested as if he had known us for years; and all this was genuine feeling, a quick, luxuriant growth out of his heart,—a soil in which to sow flower-seeds, not acorns—but a true heart, nevertheless. His dress, by [258] the by, was black, the coat buttoned up so high that I saw no sign of a shirt. His housemaid (my wife and Una say) was particularly slovenly in appearance. But Leigh Hunt himself is a beautiful object.[280]

OCTOBER 6th, SATURDAY.

YESTERDAY was not an eventful day. I took Julian with me to the city, called on Mr. Sturgis at the Barings' House, and got his checks for a bank-post-note. The house is at 8, Bishopsgate-street within; it has no sign of any kind, but stands back from the street, behind an iron-grated fence. The firm appears to occupy the whole edifice, which is spacious, and fit for princely merchants. Thence I went and paid for the passages to Lisbon (£32) at Peninsular Steam Co.'s office, and thence to call on General Campbell. I forgot to mention that, first of all, I went to Mr. Bennett's, whom I found kind and vivacious, as usual. After these callings, Julian and I had a dinner of roast chicken at an eating-house in Cheapside, among tradespeople and clerks of respectable aspect; during which time, it rained heavily; and being still showery when we emerged into

Cheapside again, we first stood under an archway (a usual resort with passengers through London streets,) and then betook ourselves to sanctuary, taking refuge in Saint Paul's Cathedral. The afternoon-service was about to begin; so, after looking at a few of the monuments, we sat down in the choir, the richest and most ornamented part of the Cathedral, with screens or partitions of oak, cunningly carved. Small white-robed choristers were flitting noiselessly about, making prepara[259]tions for the service, which by-and-by began. It is a beautiful idea enough, that, several times in the course of the day, a man can step out of the thickest throng and bustle of London, into this religious atmosphere, and hear the organ, and the music of young, pure voices; but they drew it out, methinks, a little too long. And, after all, the rites are lifeless in our day. We found, on emerging, that we had escaped a very heavy shower; and it still sprinkled and misted as we went homeward through Holborn and Oxford-street.

OCTOBER 11th, THURSDAY.

WE all left London, on Sunday morning, between ten and eleven, from the Waterloo Station, and arrived in Southampton about two, without meeting with anything very remarkable on the way. We put up at Chapple's Castle Hotel, which is one of the class styled commercial, and though respectable, not such a one as the nobility and gentry usually frequent. I saw little difference in the accommodation, except that young women attended us, instead of male waiters;—a pleasant change. It was a showery day; but Julian and I walked out to see the shore, and the town, and the docks, and, if possible, the ship in which mamma was to sail. The most noteworthy object was the remains of an old castle, near the waterside; the square, gray, weed-grown, ivied keep of which shows some modern chimney pots above its battlements; while remaining portions of the [260] fortress are made to seem as one of the walls for coal-depots and perhaps for small dwellings. The English characteristically patch new things into old things, in this manner, materially and physically, legally, constitutionally, and morally. Walking along the pier, we observed some pieces of ordnance, one of which was a large brass cannon of Henry VIII's time, about twelve feet long, and very finely made. The bay, or whatever it is called, of Southampton, presents a very pleasant prospect; and I believe it is the great rendezvous of the yacht-club. Old and young sea-faring people were strolling about, and lounging at corners, just as they do, on Sunday afternoons, in the minor seaports of America.

From the shore, we went up into town, which is handsome and of a cheerful aspect, with streets generally wide and well-paved;—a cleanly town, not smoke-begrimed. The houses, if not modern, are at least, with few exceptions, new-fronted. We saw one relic of antiquity; a fine mediaeval gateway across the principal street, much more elevated than the gates of Chester, with battlements at the top, and a spacious apartment over [under] the great arch for the passage of carriages, and the smaller one on each side for foot-passengers. There were two statues in armor [261] or antique costume, on the hither side of the gateway, and two old paintings on the other. This, so far as I know, is the only remnant of the old wall of Southampton.

On Monday, the morning was bright, alternating with a little showeriness. Una, Julian, and I, went into the town to do some shopping before the steamer sailed; and a little after twelve we drove down to the dock. The Madrid is a pleasant-looking ship enough, not very large, but accommodating, I believe, about seventy passengers. We looked at my wife's little state-room with its three berths for herself and the children; and then sat down in the saloon, and afterwards on deck, to spend the irksome and dreary hour or two before parting. Many of the passengers seemed to be Portuguese, undersized, dark, moustach[i]oed people, smoking cigars. John Bull was fairly represented, too. My wife behaved heroically, Una was cheerful; and Rosebud seemed only anxious to get off. Poor Fanny, our nurse, was altogether cast down, and shed tears, either from regret at leaving her native land, or dread of sickness, or general despondency, being a person of no hope, or spring of spirits. I waited till the captain came on board, (a middle-aged or rather el[262]derly man, with a sensible expression, but, methought a hard, cold eye) to whom I introduced my wife, recommending her to his especial care, as she was unattended by any gentleman; and then we thought it best to cut short the parting scene. So we bade one another farewell; and leaving them on the deck of the vessel, Julian and I returned to the hotel, and after dining at the table d'hôte, drove down to the railway. This is the first great parting that Sophia and I have ever had.

It was three °clock when we left Southampton. In order to get to Worcester (where we were to spend the night) we straddled, as it were, from one line of railway to another, two or three times, and did not arrive at our journey's end till long after dark. Julian bore the separation from his mother well; but took occasion to remind me that he had now no one but myself to depend upon, and therefore suggested that I should be very kind to him. There is more tenderness in his own manner towards me than ordinary, since this great event; and ever and anon he favors me with a little hug, or pressure of the hand; which I take as hints that I must now be father and mother both to him. For my own part, I [263] was not depressed, (trusting, in God's mercy, that we shall all meet again;) but yet the thought was not without a good deal of pain, that we were to be so long separated—so long a gap in life, during which Una will quite have passed out of her childhood, and Rosebud out of her baby-hood; for I shall not find them exactly such as I leave them, even if we are apart only two or three months. This will be a kind of era in their lives. My wife, I hope and pray, will meet me in better health and strength than for two years past.

At Worcester, we put ourselves into the hands of a cabman, who drove us to the Crown Hotel; one of the old-fashioned hotels, with an entrance through an arched passage, by which vehicles are admitted into the inn-yard, which has also an exit, I believe, into another street. On one side of the arch was the coffee-room, where (after looking at our sleeping-chamber on the other side of the arch) we had some cold pigeon-pie for supper, and for myself a pint of ale. The quality and character of ale differs widely in various parts of England; and I like this clear, brown, bitter ale of Worcester about as well as any. After seeing Julian to bed, I inquired for a smoking room, and was shown across the arched passage into [264] a pretty large apartment, which was quite misty with tobacco-smoke; there being at least a score of people sitting on the hair-cloth cushioned seats that were placed round the wall, and generally smoking pipes, which also lay numerously on the tables, together with glasses and tankards of various liquors. I never saw, in America or anywhere else, such an assemblage of smokers and topers, and at first fancied that I had intruded upon a club; but they received me courteously, made me welcome to a seat, and the waiting-maid brought me a cigar. My fellow-guests appeared to be tradesmen of the town, and farmers of the vicinity, with one Pole, named Zamouski, who (as I gathered from the conversation after his departure) is a quack-doctor and lecturer at Malvern, a few miles off. The deportment of these people was more courteous, I thought, and formal, than that of men of similar rank in the United States, sufficiently sensible, but without the raciness and humor that are to be met with in such society there. Their drink was mostly spirits, oftener whiskey with hot water and sugar than anything else, but one or two had brandy, and some a tankard of ale. For my part, I called for a glass of whiskey and cold water, and made myself as much at home as possible;—speaking to nobody, however, and spoken to by [265] none, after the first civilities of offering a seat. Some of the guests ever and anon took leave, civilly saluting the company as they retired; others came in; but I cannot say at what time their symposium finally broke up. I myself left them at eleven, or somewhat later;—and giving a fatherly and motherly glance at Julian, in his separate chamber, retired to bed.

It should be mentioned that, in the morning, before embarking Sophia and the children on board the steamer, I saw a fragment of a rainbow among the clouds, and remembered the old adage,[281] bidding "sailors take warning." In the afternoon, as Julian and I were railing from Southampton, we saw another fragmentary rainbow, which by the same adage, should be the "sailor's delight. The weather since has rather tended to confirm the first omen; but the sea-captains tell me that the steamer must have been beyond the scope of these winds.

【*FOURTH MANUSCRIPT VOLUME*】

OCTOBER 14th SUNDAY.

IN the morning of Tuesday, after breakfast in the coffee-room, Julian and I walked about to see the remarkables of Worcester. It is not a particularly interesting city, compared with other old English cities; the general material of the houses being red-brick, and almost all modernized externally, whatever may be the age of their original frame work. We saw a large brick jail, in castellated style, with battlements; a very barren and dreary-looking edifice; likewise, in the more central part of the town, a Guild hall, with a handsome front, ornamented with a statue of Queen Anne above the entrance, and statues of Charles I and Charles II on either side of the door, with the motto, "Floreat semper civitas fidelis." Worcester seems to pride itself upon its loyalty. We entered this edifice, and, in the large interior hall, saw some old armor hanging on the wall at one end; corselets, helmets, greaves, and a pair of breeches of chain-mail. An inscription told us that these suits of armor had been left by Charles II after the battle of [2] Worcester, and presented to the city, at a much later date, by a gentleman of the neighborhood. On the stone floor of the hall, under the armor, were two brass cannon, one of which had been taken from the French in a naval battle, within the present century; the other was a beautiful piece, bearing, I think, the date of 1632, and manufactured at Brussels for the Count de Burgh, as a Latin inscription testified. This likewise was a relic of the battle of Worcester, where it had been lost by Charles. Many gentlemen—connected with the city-government, I suppose— were passing through the hall; and looking through its interior doors, we saw stately staircases, and council-rooms panelled with oak or other dark wood. There seems to be a good deal of antique state in the government of these old towns.

Worcester Cathedral would have impressed me much had I seen it earlier; though its aspect is less venerable than that of Chester or Lichfield, having been faithfully renewed and repaired; and stone-cutters and masons were even now at work on the exterior. At our first visit, we found no entrance; but coming again at ten °clock, when the service was to begin, we found the door open, and the chorister-boys in their white robes standing in the [3] nave and aisles, with elder people in the same garb, and a few black-robed ecclesiastics, and an old verger. The interior of the cathedral has been covered with a light-colored paint, at some recent period; there is, as I remember, very little stained glass to enrich and bedim the light; and the effect produced is a naked, daylight aspect, unlike what I have seen in any other Gothic cathedral. The plan of the edifice, too, is simple; a nave and side aisles, with great, clustered pillars, from which spring the intersecting aisles; and, somehow or other, the venerable mystery, which I have found in Westminster Abbey and elsewhere, does not lurk in these arches and behind these pillars. The choir, no doubt, is richer and more beautiful; but we did not enter it. I remember two tombs, with recumbent figures on them, between the pillars that divide the nave from the side aisles; and there are also mural monuments against the walls; one, well executed, to an officer slain in the Peninsular war, representing him falling from his horse; another by a young widow to her husband, with an inscription of passionate grief, and a record of her purpose finally to sleep beside him. He died in 1803. I did not see on the monument [4] any record of the consummation of her purpose; and so perhaps, she sleeps beside a second husband. There are more antique memorials than these two, on the wall; and I should have been interested to examine them; but the service was now about to begin in the choir; and, at the far-off end of the nave, the old verger waved his hand to banish us from the Cathedral. At the same time, he moved towards us, probably to say that he would show us the Cathedral after service; but having little time, and being so moderately impressed with what I had already seen, I took my departure, and so disappointed the old man of his expected shilling or half-crown. The tomb of King John is somewhere in this Cathedral.

We renewed our rambles through the town, and passing the museum of the Worcester Natural History Society, I yielded to Julian's wish to go in. There are three days of the week, I believe, on which it is open to the public; but this being one of the close[d] days, we were admitted on payment of a shilling. It seemed a very good and well arranged collection in most departments of natural history; and Julian, who takes more interest in these matters than I do, was much delighted. We were left to examine the hall and galleries quite at our leisure. Be[5]sides the specimens of beasts, birds, shells, fishes, minerals, fossils, insects, and all other natural things, before the flood and since, there was a stone bearing a Roman inscription, and various antiquities, coins, and medals; and likewise portraits, some of which were old and curious.

Leaving the Museum, we walked down to the stone bridge over the Severn, which is here the most considerable river I have seen in England, except, of course, the Mersey and the Thames. A flight of steps leads from the bridge down to a walk along the river-side; and this we followed, till we reached the spot where an angler was catching chubs and dace, under the walls of the bishop's palace, which here faces the river. It seems to be an old building, but with modern repairs and improvements. The angler had pretty good success while we were looking at him, drawing out two or three silvery fish, and depositing them in his basket, which was already more than half full. The Severn is not a transparent stream, and looks sluggish, but has really movement enough to carry the angler's float along pretty fast. There were two vessels of considerable size (that is, as large as small schooners) lying at the bridge. [6] We now passed under an old stone archway, through a lane that led us from the river-side up past the Cathedral, whence a gentleman and lady were just emerging; and the verger was closing the door behind them.

We returned to our hotel, and ordered luncheon—some cold chicken (of which Julian ate the greater part), cold ham and ale; and after paying the bill (about fifteen shillings, to which I added five shillings for attendance) took our departure in a fly for the railway. The waiter (a young woman), chamber-maid, and boots, all favored us with the most benign and deferential looks, at parting; whence it was easy to see that I had given them more than they had any claim to. Nevertheless, this English system of fees has its good side; and I never travel without finding the advantage of it, especially on railways, where the officials are strictly forbidden to take fees, and where, in consequence, a fee secures twice as much good service as anywhere else. Be it recorded, that I never knew an Englishman to refuse a shilling—or, for that matter, a half-penny.

From Worcester we took tickets to Wolverhampton, and thence to Birkenhead. It grew dark before we reached Chester, and began to rain; and when we got to Birkenhead, it was [7] a pitiless, pelting storm, under which, on the deck of the steamboat, we crossed the abominable Mersey, two years trial of which has made me detest every day more and more. It being the night of rejoicing for the taking of Sebastopol, and the visit of the Duke of Cambridge, we found it very difficult to get a cab on the Liverpool side; but after much waiting in the rain, and afterwards in one of the refreshment-rooms on the Landing-Stage, we got into a Hansom and drove off. The cloudy sky reflected the illuminations, and we saw some gas-lighted stars and other devices, as we passed, very pretty, but much marred by the wind and rain. So we finally got to Mrs. Blodgett's and made a good supper of ham and cold chicken, like our luncheon; after which, wet as we were, and drizzly as the weather was, and though it was two hours beyond his bed-time, I took Julian out to see the illuminations. I wonder what his mother would have said. But the old boy must now begin to see life, and to feel it.

There was a crowd of people in the streets; such a crowd that we could hardly make a passage through them, and so many cabs and omnibusses [sic] that it was diffi[8]cult to cross. Some of the illuminations were very brilliant; but there was a woeful lack of variety and invention in the devices;—the star of the garter, which kept flashing out from the continual extinguishment of the wind and rain;—V. and A., or V. and N., in capital letters of light, were repeated a hundred times;—loyal and patriotic mottoes,—crowns, formed by colored lamps;—and, in some instances, a sensible tradesman, had illuminated his own sign, thereby at once advertising his loyalty and his business. Innumerable flags were suspended before the houses and across the streets; and the crowd plodded on, silent, heavy, and without any demonstration of joy, unless by the discharge of pistols close at one's ear. The rain, to be sure, was quite sufficient to damp any joyous ebullition of feeling; but the next day, when the rain had ceased, and when the streets were still thronged with people, there was the same heavy, purposeless strolling from place to place, with no more alacrity of spirit than while it rained. The English do not know how to rejoice; and, in their present circumstances, to say the truth, have not much to rejoice for.[282] We soon came home; but I believe it was nearly or quite eleven before Julian got to bed.

[9] At Mrs. Blodgetts, Mr Archer (surgeon to some prison or house of correction here in Liverpool) spoke of an Attorney, who, many years ago, committed forgery, and being apprehended, took a dose of prussic acid. Mr. Archer came with the stomach-pipe, and asked the patient how much prussic-acid he had taken; "Sir," he replied, attorney-like, "I decline answering that question!" He recovered, and afterwards arrived at great wealth in New South Wales.

Novr 14th.

At dinner at Mr. Bright's, a week or two ago, Mr. Robertson Gladstone spoke of a magistrate of Liverpool, many years since—Sir John Linkwater—or Drinkwater; but I think this last could not have been his name. Of a morning, sitting on the bench in the police-court, he would take five shillings out of his pocket, and say:—"Here, Mr. Clerk, so much for my fine—I was drunk last night!" Mr. Gladstone, a man under fifty, witnessed this personally.[283]

Novr 16th

I went to the North Hospital, yesterday, to take the deposition of a dying man, as to his ill-treatment by the second and third mates of the ship Assyria, on the voyage from New Orleans. This hospital is a very gloomy place, with its wide, bleak entries and staircases, [10] which may be very good for summer weather, but are most ungenial at this black November season. I found the physicians of the house talking and laughing very cheerfully with Mr. Wilding, who had preceded me. We went forthwith up two or three pairs of stairs, to the ward where the sick man lay, and where there were six or eight other beds, in almost each of which was a patient—narrow beds, shabbily furnished. The man whom I came to see was the only one who was not perfectly quiet; neither was he very restless. The doctor, informing him of my presence, intimated that his disease might be fatal, and that I was come to hear what he had to say as to the causes of his death. Afterwards, a Testament was sought for, in order to swear him; and I administered the oath, and made him kiss the book. He then (in response to Mr. Wilding's questions) told how he had been beaten and ill-treated, banged and thwacked, from the moment he came on board;—to which usage he ascribed his death. Sometimes his senses seemed to sink away, so that I almost thought him dead; but, by-and-by, the questions would appear to reach him, and bring him back, and he went on with his evidence;—interspersing it, however, with dying groans, and almost death rattles. [11] In the midst of whatever he was saying, he often recurred to a sum of four dollars and a half, which he said he had put into the hands of the porter of the hospital, and which he wanted to get back. Several times, he expressed his wish to get back to America (of which he was not a native), and, on the whole, I do not think he had any real sense of his precarious condition, notwithstanding that he assented to the doctor's hint to that effect. He sank away so much, at one time, that they brought him wine in a tin vessel, with a spout to drink out of; and he mustered strength to raise himself in bed and drink; then hemmed, with rather a disappointed air, as if it did not stimulate and refresh him, as drink ought. When he had finished his evidence (which Mr. Wilding took down in writing, from his mouth) he marked his cross at the foot of the paper; and we ceased to torment him with further question. His deposition will probably do no good, so far as the punishment of the persons implicated is concerned; for he appears to have come on board in a sickly state, and never to have been well during the passage. On a pallet close by his bed lay another seaman of the same ship, who had likewise been abused by the same men, and bore more [12] ostensible marks of ill usage than this man did, about the head and face. There is a most dreadful state of things aboard our ships. Hell itself can be no worse than some of them; and I do pray that some New Englander, with the itch of reform in him, may turn his thoughts this way. The first step towards better things—the best practicable step for the present—would be, to legalize flogging on shipboard; thereby doing away with the miscellaneous assaults and batteries, kickings, fisticuffings, rope's-endings, marlinspikings, which the inferior officers continually perpetrate, as the only mode of keeping up anything like discipline. As in so many other instances, Philanthropy has overshot itself by the prohibition of flogging, causing the captain to avoid the responsibility of solemn punishment, and leave his mates to make devils of themselves by habitual (and hardly avoidable) ill-treatment of the seamen.

Before I left the dying sailor, his features seemed to contract and grow sharp. Some young medical students stood about the bed, watching death creep upon him, and anticipating, perhaps, that, in a day or two, they would have the poor fellow's body on the dissecting-table. Dead patients, I believe, undergo this fate, unless somebody chooses [13] to pay their funeral expenses; but the captain of the Assyria (who seems to be respectable and kind-hearted, though master of a floating-hell) tells me that he means to bury this man at his own cost. This morning, there is a note from the surgeon of the hospital, announcing his death, and likewise the dangerous state of his shipmate, whom I saw on the pallet beside him.

Julian said to me, to day,—"Papa, you have bred a splendid son!"—said it with much gravity, and as if it were the thing most to my credit that he could find to say.

Sea-captains call a dress-coat a "claw hammer."

The phrase "three sheets in the wind"—meaning a man flustered with drink—does not convey any nautical idea.

Novr 22^d, THURSDAY

I WENT on board the ship William Tapscott, lying in the river, yesterday, to take depositions in reference to a homicide, committed in New York. I sat on a sofa in the cabin, and Mr. Wilding at a table with his writing materials before him, and the crew were summoned, one by one—rough, piratical-looking fellows, contrasting strongly with the gew-gaw cabin [14] in which I received them. There is no such finery on land, as in the cabin of one of these ships in the Liverpool trade, finished off with a complete panelling of rosewood, mahogany, and bird's eye maple, polished and varnished, and gilded along the cornices and the edges of the panels. It is all a piece of elaborate cabinet-work; and one does not altogether see why it should be given to the gales, and the salt-sea-atmosphere, to be tossed upon the waves, and occupied by a rude shipmaster, in his dreadnought clothes, when the finest lady in the land has no such boudoir. A tell-tale compass hung beneath the skylight, and a clock was fastened near it, and ticked loudly. A stewardess, with the aspect of a woman at home, went in and out of the cabin, about her domestic calls. Through the cabin door (it being a house on deck) I could see the arrangements of the ship. The first sailor that I examined was a black-haired, powerful fellow, in an oil-skin jacket, with a good face enough, though he, too, might have been taken for a pirate. In the affray, in which the homicide occurred, he had received a cut across the forehead, and another slantwise across his nose, which had quite cut it in two, on a level with his face, and had thence gone downward to his lower jaw. But neither he [15] nor anyone else could give any testimony elucidating the matter into which I had come to inquire. A seaman had been stabbed, just before the vessel left New York, and had been sent on shore, and died there. Most of these men were in the affray, and all of them were within a few yards of the spot where it occurred; but those actually present all pleaded that they were so drunk that the whole thing was now like a dream, with no distinct images; and, if any had been sober, they took care to know nothing that would inculpate any individual. Perhaps they spoke truth; they certainly had a free and honest-like way of giving their evidence, as if their only object was, to tell all the truth they knew. But I rather think, in the forecastle, and during the night-watches, they have whispered to one another a great deal more than they told me, and have come to a pretty accurate conclusion as to the man who gave the stab.

While the examination proceeded, there was a drawing of corks in a side-closet; and, at its conclusion the captain asked us to stay to dinner; but we excused ourselves, and drank only a glass of wine. The captain apologized for not joining us, inasmuch as he [16] had drunk no wine for the last seventeen years. He appears to be a particularly good and trustworthy man, and is the only shipmaster, whom I have met with, who says that a crew can best be governed by kindness. In the wine-closet, there was a cage containing two land birds, who had come aboard him, tired almost to death, three or four hundred miles from shore; and he had fed them and been tender of them, from a sense of what was due to hospitality. He means to give them to Julian.

Novr 28th WEDNESDAY.

I HAVE grown woefully aristocratic, in my tastes, I fear, since coming to England; at all events, I am conscious of a certain disgust at going to dine in a house with a small entrance-hall, and narrow staircase, parlor with chintz curtains, and all other arrangements on a similar scale. This is pitiable. However, I really do not think I should mind these things, were it not for the bustle, the affectation, the intensity, of the mistress of the house. It is certain, that a woman in England is either decidedly a lady, or decidedly not a lady. There seems to be no respectable medium. Bill of fare:—broiled soles, a half of a roast pig, a harico[t] of mutton, stewed oysters, a tart, pears, figs, with sherry and port-wine, both [17] good, and the port particularly so. I ate some pig, and could hardly resist the lady's importunities to eat more; though, to my fancy, it tasted of swill—had a flavor of the pig-stye [sic]. On the parlor table were some poor editions of popular books, Longfellow's poems, and others. The lady affects a literary taste, and bothered me about my own productions.

A beautiful subject for a Romance, or for a sermon, would be the subsequent life of the young man whom Jesus bade to sell all he had, and give to the poor; and he went away sorrowful, and is not recorded to have done what he was bid.

As regards the mystery of birth, we have told Julian and Una, at the advent of Rosebud, that she was sent from Heaven, as they themselves had been. Julian said, this morning, that he could not remember when he came down from Heaven, but that he was glad he happened to tumble into so good a family. It is queer that he is still satisfied with this first explanation of his origin— now in his tenth year.

Dec 11th TUESDAY.

THIS has been a foggy morning and forenoon, snowing a little, now and then, and disagreeably cold. The sky is of an inexpressibly dreary, dun color. It is so dark, at [18] times, that I have to hold my book close to my eyes; and then it lightens up a little. On the whole, disgustingly gloomy; and thus it has been for a long while past; although the disagreeableness seems to lie very near the earth, and, just above the steeples and house-tops, very probably, there may be a bright, sunshiny day. At about 12, there is a faint glow of sunlight, like the gleaming reflection from a not highly polished copper kettle.

DECEMBER 26th, WEDNESDAY.

ON Christmas eve, and yesterday, there were little branches of mis[t]letoe hanging in several parts of our house, in the kitchen, the entries, the parlor, and the smoking room—suspended from the gas-fittings. The maids of the house did their utmost to entrap the gentlemen-boarders, old and young, under these privileged places, and there to kiss them, after which they were expected to pay a shilling. It is very queer, being customarily so respectful, that they should assume this license now, absolutely trying to pull the gentlemen into the kitchen by main force, and kissing the harder and more abundantly, the more they were resisted. A little rosy-cheeked Scotch lass—at other times very modest—was the most active in this business. I doubt whether any gentleman but myself escaped.[284] I heard [19] old Mr. Smith parleying with the maids last evening, and pleading his age; but he seems to have met with no mercy, for there was a sound of prodigious smacking, immediately afterwards. Julian was assaulted, and fought most vigorously, but was outrageously kissed— receiving some scratches, moreover, in the conflict. The mis[t]letoe has white, wax-looking berries, and dull green leaves, with a parasitical stem.

Early in the morning of Christmas day, long before daylight, I heard music in the street, and a woman's voice, powerful and melodious, singing a Christmas hymn. Before bedtime, I presume one half of England, at a moderate calculation, was the worse for liquor. They are still a nation of beastly eaters and beastly drinkers; this tendency manifests itself at holiday time, though, for the rest of the year, it may be decently repressed. Their market-houses, at this season, show the national taste for heavy feeding; carcasses of prize oxen, immensely fat and bulky, fat sheep, with their woolly heads and tails still on, and stars and other devices ingeniously wrought on the quarters; fat pigs, adorned with flowers, like corpses of virgins; hares, wild fowl, geese, [20] ducks, turkies [sic]; and green boughs and banners suspended about the stalls—and a great deal of dirt and griminess on the stone-floor of the market-house, and on the persons of the crowd.

There are some English whom I like—one or two for whom, I might almost say, I have an affection;—but still there is not the same union between us, as if they were Americans. A cold, thin medium intervenes betwixt our most intimate approaches. It puts me in mind of Alnaschar, when he went to bed with the princess, but placed the cold steel blade of his scimitar between. Perhaps, if I were at home, I might feel differently; but, in this foreign land, I can never forget the distinction between English and American.

JANUARY 1st, 1856, TUESDAY.

LAST night, at Mrs. Blodgett's, we sat up till 12 °clock, to open the front-door, and let the New Year in. After the coming guest was fairly in the house, the back-door was to be opened, to let the Old Year out; but I was tired, and did not wait for this latter ceremony. When the New Year made its entrance, there was a general shaking of hands, and one of the shipmasters said that it was customary to kiss the ladies all round; but, to my considerable satisfaction, we did not proceed to such extremity. There was singing in the streets; and many voices of people passing; and [21] when twelve had struck, all the bells of the town, I believe, rang out together. I went up to bed, sad and lonely, and stepping into Julian's little room, wished him a happy New Year, as he slept, and many of them.

[To a cool observer, a country does not show to best advantage during a time of war. All its self-conceit is doubly visible, and, indeed, is sedulously kept uppermost by direct appeals to it. The country must be humbugged, in order to keep its courage up.]285

Sentiment seems to me more abundant in middle-aged ladies, in England, than in the United States. I don't know how it may be with young ladies.

I see nothing more disgusting than the women and girls here in Liverpool, who pick up horsedung in the streets—rushing upon the treasure, the moment it is dropt, taking it up by handsfull and putting it in their baskets. Some are old women; some marriageable girls, and not uncomely girls, were they well dressed and clean. What a business is this!

[22] The shipmasters bear testimony to the singular delicacy of common sailors, in their behavior in the presence of women; and they say that this good trait is still *strongly* observable even in the present race of seamen, greatly deteriorated as it is. On shipboard, there is never [an indecorous word or unseemly act said or done by sailors when a woman can be cognizant of it; and their deportment in this respect differs greatly from that of landsmen of similar position in society. This is remarkable, considering that a sailor's female acquaintances are usually and exclusively of the worst kind, and that his]285 intercourse with them has no relation whatever to morality or decency. For this very reason, I suppose, he regards a modest woman as a creature divine, and to be reverenced.

Jany 16th '56.

I HAVE suffered woefully from low spirits for sometime past; and this has not often been the case, since I grew to be a man, even in the least auspicious periods of my life. My desolate, bachelor condition, I suppose, is the cause. Really, I have no pleasure in anything; and I feel my tread to be heavier and my physical movement more sluggish than in happier times; a weight is always upon me. My appetite is not good. I [23] sleep ill, lying awake late at night to think sad thoughts, and to imagine sombre things, and awakening before light with the same thoughts and fancies still in my mind. My heart sinks always as I ascend the stairs to my office, from a dim augury of ill news that I may perhaps hear—of black-sealed letters—or some such horrors. Nothing gives me any joy. I have learned what the bitterness of exile is, in these days; and I never should have known it but for the absence of my wife. "Remote, unfriended, melancholy, slow—" I can perfectly appreciate that line of Goldsmith;[286] for it well expresses my own torpid, unenterprising, joyless state of mind and heart. I am like an uprooted plant, wilted and drooping. Life seems so purposeless as not to be worth the trouble of carrying it on any further.

I was at a dinner, the other evening (at Mr. Babcock's) where the entertainment was almost entirely American—New York oysters, raw, stewed, and fried; soup of American partridges, particularly good; also, terrapin-soup, rich, but not to my taste; American pork and beans, baked in Yankee style; a noble American turkey, weighing [24] thirty-one pounds; and, at the other end of the table, an American round of beef, which the Englishmen present allowed to be delicious, and worth a guinea an ounce. I forget the other American dishes, if there were any more. Oh, yes!—canvas-back ducks, coming on with the sweets, in the usual English fashion. We ought to have had Catawba wine, but this was wanting; although there was plenty of hock, champagne, sherry, madeira, port, and claret. Our host is a very jolly man, and the dinner was a merrier and noisier one than any English dinner within my experience.

FEBRUARY 8th, 1856.

I READ, to day, in the little office-Bible (greasy with perjuries) St. Luke's account of the agony, the trial, the crucifixion, and the resurrection; and how Christ appeared to the two disciples on their way to Emmaus, and afterwards to a company of disciples. On both these latter occasions, he expounded the Scriptures to them, and showed the application of the old prophecies to himself; and it is to be supposed that he made them fully (or at least sufficiently) aware what his character was, whether God, or Man, or both, or something between;—together with all other essential points of doctrine. But none of this doctrine, or of these expositions, are recorded; the mere facts being [25] most simply stated, and the conclusion to which he led them, that (whether God himself, or the Son of God, or merely the Son of Man) he was, at all events, the Christ foretold in the Jewish Scriptures. This last, therefore, must have been the one essential point.

FEB 18th, MONDAY.

ON Saturday, there called on me an elderly Robinson Crusoe sort of man, Mr Holbrook, a shipwright (I believe) of Boston, who has lately been travelling in the East. About a year ago, he was here, after being shipwrecked on the Dutch coast; and I assisted him to get home. Again I have supplied him with five pounds, and my credit for an outside garment. He is a spare man, with closely cropped gray, or rather white hair, close cropt whiskers fringing round his chin, and a close cropt white moustache, and his under lip and a portion of chin bare beneath; sunburnt and weather-worn. He has been in Syria and Jerusalem, and through the Desert, and at Sebastopol; and says he means to get Ticknor to publish his travels,[287] and the story of his whole adventurous life, on his return home. A free-spoken, confiding, hardy, religious, unpolished, simple, yet world-experienced man; very talkative, and boring me with longer visits than I like. [26] He has brought home, among other curiosities, a "lady's arm" as he calls it, two thousand years old—a piece of a mummy, of course; also, some coins, one of which, a gold coin of Vespasian, he showed me, and said he bought it of an Arab of the desert. The Bedouins possess a good many of these coins, handed down immemorially from father to son, and never sell them unless compelled by want. He had likewise a Hebrew manuscript of the book of Ruth, on a parchment-roll, which was given to his care to be delivered to Lord Haddo.

He was at Sebastopol during the siege, and nearly got his head knocked off by a cannon-ball; and his queerest statement is one in reference to the death of Lord Raglan. He says that an English officer told him that his lordship shut himself up, desiring not to be disturbed, as he needed sleep. When fifteen hours had gone by, his attendants thought it time to break open the door; and Lord Raglan was found dead, with a bottle of strychnine by the bedside. The affair (so far as the circumstances indicated suicide) was hushed up, and his death represented as a natural one. The English officer seems to have been an un-scrupulous sort of a fellow, jesting thus with the fresh memory of his dead com[27]mander; for it is impossible to believe a word of the story. Even if Lord Raglan had wished for death, he would hardly have taken strychnine, when there were so many chances of being honorably shot. In Wood's [sic] "Narrative of the Campaign,"[288] it is stated that he died surrounded by the members of his staff, after having been for some time afflicted with diarrhea. It appears, however, by the same statement, that no serious apprehensions had been entertained, until, one afternoon, he shut himself up, desiring not to be disturbed till evening. After two or three hours, he called Lord Burg-hersh—"Frank, Frank!"—and was found to be almost in a state of collapse, and died that evening. Mr. Holbrook's story may very well have been a camp-rumour.

––––––––––

It seems to me that the British Ministry, in its notion of a life-peerage, shows an entire mis-understanding of what makes people desire the peerage. It is not for the immediate personal distinction, but because it removes the peer and his consanguinity from the common rank of men, and makes a distinct order of them, as if they should grow angelic. A life-peer is but a mortal amid the angelic throng.

[28] FEBRUARY 28th THURSDAY.

I WENT yesterday with Mrs. Heywood and another lady, and Mr. Mansfield, to the West Derby Workhouse, which Mrs. Heywood, with some charitable purpose or other, had a desire to inspect. We were first shown into a room where paupers are received on their first arrival; and the superintendent of this room was a bright, cheerful old woman, between eighty and ninety years old. She has been a good many years in the Workhouse, and has learned to knit since she was seventy; and kept her fingers busily employed all the time she was talking to us. One of the ladies remarked, with great admiration, "Why, you can knit without looking at the stocking!" There were several other old women in the room; but Mrs. Heywood gave this oldest one half-a-crown, and thereby, no doubt, left heart-burnings and quarrelings behind her. In the next room, was the domicile of an old man and his wife; for the authorities sometimes allow old married people to live together, when there is no risk of their increasing the population of the Work-House.[289] In another room, there was an old lady, alone, and reading; a respectable-looking, intelligent old soul, with rather more refined manners than the others; so I took off my hat in her room. There was a row [29] of books on the mantel-piece, mostly religious, but with a romance among them. After we went out, the Governor of the House told us that she had ridden in her carriage not many years ago. She herself had told the same to Mrs. Heywood's friend, adding that she did not expect to stay long in the Workhouse, for she had rich friends who would remove her. She has been there a long while, however, and probably she deludes herself in expectations of being taken away. In my private belief, she never was absolutely a lady, though doubtless of a respectable class in life. We went into various other rooms, into which the women were variously classified; and everywhere there were comfortable coal-fires in the open fire-places, and the women sitting quietly about them, all knitting as fast as their fingers would go. They looked well-fed, and decently clothed in blue-checked gowns, all of one fashion; but none of them had a brisk, cheerful air, except two or three very old persons, to whom a childish vivacity seemed to have returned with their extreme age. In one room (where there were at least a dozen women) was an old lady in bed, who declared herself to be [30] more than a hundred years old, and the Governor said a hundred and four. She was positively the cheerfullest and jauntiest person in the house; it was as if she had long ago got through with all the real business of life, and had nothing else to do but to be as merry as she could, for the little while she stays here;—and so she seems to make herself a kind of old pet, whom people talk to as if she were a child, and she gives wayward, childish, half-playful answers. I believe she never gets out of bed. In the same room, there was a woman who had once been an actress, of some repute, but is now affected with a softening of the brain, which appears to make her half-idiotic. For some reason or other, she began to cry, and grimace, and wring her hands, while we were talking to the century-old woman; and Mrs. Heywood stayed behind to comfort her— with what effect I know not.

More women, and still more and more, we saw, all in the same homely blue-checked gowns, the same servant's caps, the same dowdy, English air, the same vulgar type of face. I asked the Governor whether he found any difficulty in keeping the peace among them; and he said they were more quarrelsome than men. Doubtless, [31] they do plague and pester one another from morning till night, though certainly all looked peaceable enough when we saw them. It was perceptible that some of them, at least, were acting for the Governor's eye. He is a man, I should judge, very fit for his situation; a bluff, ruddy-faced, hearty, kindly, yeomanlike Englishman, with no superfluous sensibility, but a warm, wholesome heart. He speaks to them in a loud, good-humored tone, and treats them in a simple, healthy way, which is much freer and better for them than any treatment which a man of nicer feelings would be able to bestow. An American, in similar position, would probably be a much superior man, better educated, with a far wider range of thought, more of a gentleman; but I doubt whether he would bring about better results.

We looked into a good many sleeping-rooms, where were rows of beds, most of them calculated for two, with sheets and pillow-cases that looked like sackcloth, or tow-cloth. Everything throughout the house was clean and perfectly neat. We went, too, into the laundry, where a great wash seemed to be going on, and the whole atmosphere of the room was almost steam, [32] in which (it was rather disagreeable to think) all the uncleanness of the pauper habiliments and bed clothes was resolved into a gaseous state. An old woman invited me to step into the room where the clothes were dried; and on doing so, I found myself immediately in a stew.

After this, we went to the ward where the children were kept; and on entering this, we saw, in the first place, two or three very unlovely and unwholesome little imps, who were lazily playing together. One of them (a child about six years old, but I know not whether girl or boy) immediately took the strangest fancy to me; it was a wretched, pale, half-torpid little thing, with a humor in its eyes, which the Governor said was the scurvy. I never saw (till a few moments afterwards) a child that I should feel less inclined to fondle. But this little, sickly, humor-eaten fright prowled around me, taking hold of my skirts, following at my heels; and at last held up its hands, smiled in my face, and standing directly before me, insisted on my taking it up! Not that it said a word (for I rather think the imp was underwitted, and could not talk) but its face expressed such [33] perfect confidence that it was going to be taken up and made much of, that it was impossible not to do it. It was as if God had promised the child this favor on my behalf, (but I wish He had not!) and that I must needs fulfil the contract. I held my undesirable burthen a little while; and after setting the child down, it still followed me, holding two of my fingers (luckily the glove was on) and playing with them, just as if (God save us!) it were a child of my own. It was a foundling; and out of all human kind, it chose me to be its father! We went up stairs into another ward; and on coming down again, there was this same child, waiting for me, with a sickly smile around its scabby mouth and in its dim, red eyes. If it were within the limits of possibility—if I had ever done such wickedness as could have produced this child—I should certainly have set down its affection to the score of blood-recognition; and I cannot conceive of any greater remorse than a parent must feel, if he could see such a result of his illegitimate embraces. I wish I had not touched the imp; and yet I never should have forgiven myself if I had repelled its advances.

[34] All the children in this ward were, I believe, invalids; and on going up stairs, we found more of them, with their mothers or other women in attendance. The matron of the ward (a middle-aged woman, very kind and motherly in aspect) was walking about, with an infant in her arms. She said she was very fond of the children; and certainly the tameness of all of them was sufficient proof that they never were harshly treated. It was a sort of tame familiarity, which I never saw among any other children; and which I account for partly by their nerveless, sickly, physical state, and partly by their never having known a private home, and therefore being without any homebred shyness.

In this room (which was large, containing a good many beds) there was a clear fire burning, as in all the other occupied rooms; and beside it sat a woman holding a baby, which was, beyond all comparison, the most horrible object I ever saw in my life. It really seems to lie upon the floor of my heart, and pollute my moral being with the recollection of it. The Governor said to me, apart, that it was the child of a diseased mother. True enough, it must have been. [35] This wretched infant had been begotten by Sin upon Disease— diseased Sin was its father, and sinful Disease its mother—and the offspring of their hideous embrace looked like a sucking Pestilence, which, if it could live to grow up, would make the world more accursed than ever heretofore. The baby did not seem more than two or three months old; it was all blotchy and strangely dark and discolored; it was withered away, quite shrunken and fleshless; it breathed only with pantings and gaspings, and moaned at every gasp. It appeared impossible that it should survive to draw many more of such miserable, moaning breaths; and it certainly would have been far less pitiable and heart-depressing to have it die, right before my eyes, than to go away and know that it was still living. I can by no means tell how horrible this baby was; neither ought I. And yet its pain and misery seemed to have given it a sort of intelligence; and its eyes stared at me out of their sunken sockets, knowingly, and appealingly—at least, I recollect them with that expression. Did God make this child? Has it a soul capable of immortality?—of immortal bliss? I am afraid not. At all events, [36] it is quite beyond my conception and understanding.

Thence we went to the school-rooms, which are in the rooms beneath the chapel. In one, there were children of twelve years old, or thereabouts, looking tolerably healthy. What their studies were, I cannot tell; but their teacher made them sing for our edification. We first saw the girls' school; then the boys' school; lastly the infant school. These infants (and probably all the rest of the children) are, in large proportion, foundlings—the offspring, no doubt, of servant-maids, and, in many cases, of common prostitutes. Almost without exception, they looked sickly, pale, or with marks of eruptive disease in their faces; and diseases of the eyes seemed remarkably prevalent. I saw only one child that looked healthy; and on pointing him out, the Governor said that this was not a foundling or work-house child, but that its father was one of the officers of the house. Almost every one of the rest, I should say, had tainted blood. And they appeared to be uneasy within their skins—poor little wretches! —they scratched, they screwed themselves about within their clothes. It would be a blessing to the world—a blessing to the human race, which they will contribute [37] to vitiate and enervate—a blessing to themselves, who inherit nothing but disease and vice—if every one of them could be drowned to-night, instead of being put to bed. If there be a spark of God's life in them, this seems the only chance of preserving it.

The Governor (or Mr. Mansfield, I forget which) remarked that boys, brought up in the work-house, had a tolerably good chance in life, because they are taught trades, and, if they behave well, can get employment and earn a livelihood. But it is different with girls, who have no resource but to go to service; and they can obtain no situations except among the poorest and lowest order of people who keep servants. They are never admitted into gentlemen's families. Thus they lead poor and precarious lives, and seldom come to any good.

From the schools, we went to the brew-house, and to the bake-house, and through the kitchens (where we saw an immense pot, with some kind of stew in it,) and afterwards to a tailor's shop, and a shoemaker's shop, where a number of men and small apprentices were at work. Finally (for it was almost the last thing he did) the Governor showed us a shed or outhouse, [38] inside of which were piled up an immense quantity of new coffins, of the plainest and cheapest description. They were made of pine-boards, not very nicely smoothed, not painted, nor stained with black, and with a loop of rope at either end to lift it by. Thus we had seen the whole establishment, from the cradle to the coffin; and I must say that I should be at a loss how to suggest any improvement. But the world, that requires such an establishment, ought to be ashamed of itself and set about an immediate reformation.

The paupers have a regular allowance of food, which seems abundant; also, daily beer, and other comforts more than the laboring classes can ordinarily provide themselves with.

After leaving the workhouse (we had come in Mrs. Heywood's handsome barouche) we drove to Norris Green; and Mrs. H. shewed me round the grounds, which are very good, and nicely kept. Oh, these English homes, what delightful places they are! I wonder how many people live and die in the workhouse, having no other home, because other people have a great deal more home than enough! However, Mrs. Heywood is a [39] good and kindhearted lady; and we had a very pleasant dinner, and Mr. Mansfield and I walked back (four miles and a half) to Liverpool, where we arrived just before midnight.

One character (to be found, I suppose, in every workhouse) should not have been left out of the foregoing sketch—the Idiot. In this case, it was a boy about fourteen years old, pale, uncouth, of awkward movement. He seemed to have understanding enough to run on little errands for the Governor, and clumped over the pavement of the court-yards, with queer flourishes of the legs, and noisy clatter of wooden-soled shoes.[290]

Why did Christ curse the fig-tree? It was not in the least to blame; and it seems most unreasonable to have expected it to bear figs out of season. Instead of withering it away, it would have been as great a miracle, and far more beautiful—and, one would think, of more beneficent influence—to have made it suddenly rich with ripe fruit. Then, to be sure, it might have died joyfully, having answered so good a purpose. I have been reminded of this miracle by a story of a man in Heywood (a town in Lancashire) who used such horribly [40] profane language, that a plane-tree, in front of his cottage, is said to have withered away from that hour.[291] I can draw no moral from the incident of the fig-tree, unless it be that all things perish from the instant when they cease to answer some divine purpose.

MARCH 6th 1856.

YESTERDAY, I lunched on board Captain Russell's ship, the Princeton. These daily lunches on shipboard might answer very well the purposes of a dinner; being in fact noontide dinners, with (as yesterday) soup, roast mutton, mutton chops, and a maccaroni pudding; a preliminary glass of brandy, and port and sherry wines. There were three elderly Englishmen at table, with white heads— which, I think, is oftener the predicament of elderly heads here, than in America. One of these was a retired Custom House officer, and the other two were connected with shipping in some way. There is a satisfaction in seeing Englishmen eat and drink, they do it so heartily, and on the whole so wisely— trusting so entirely that there is no harm in good beef and mutton, and a reasonable quantity of good liquor; and these three hale and hearty old men, who had acted on this wholesome faith for ever so long, were proofs that it is well, on earth, to live like earthly creatures. In [41] America, what squeamish- ness, what delicacy, what stomachic apprehensions, would there not be among three stomachs of sixty or seventy years' experience! I think this failure of American stomachs is partly owing to our ill-usage of our digestive powers, and partly to our want of faith in them.

After lunch, we all got into an omnibus and went to the Mersey Iron

Foundry, to see the biggest piece of ordnance in the world, which is there almost finished. The overseer of the works received us, and escorted us courteously throughout the establishment, which is very extensive, giving employment to a thousand men, what with night-work and day-work. The big gun is still on the axle, or turning-machine, by means of which it has been bored out. It is made entirely of wrought and welded iron, fifty tons of which were originally used; and the gun, in its present state, bored out and smoothed away, weighs nearly twenty-three tons. It has as yet no trunnions, and does not look much like a cannon, but only a huge iron cylinder, immensely solid, and with a bore so large that a young man of nineteen shoves himself into it, the whole length, with a light, in order to see whether it is duly smooth and [42] regular. I suppose it will have a better effect, as to the impression of size, when it is finished, polished, mounted, and fully equipped, after the fashion of ordinary cannon. It is to throw a ball of three hundred pounds weight, five miles; and woe be to whatever ship or battlement shall bear the brunt.

After inspecting the gun, we went through other portions of the establishment, and saw iron in various stages of manufacture. I am not usually interested in manufacturing processes, being quite unable to understand them, at least in cotton-machinery, or the like; but here there were such exhibitions of mighty strength, both of men and machines, that I had a satisfaction in looking on. We saw lumps of iron, intensely white hot, and all but in a melting state, passed through rollers of various size and pressure, and speedily converted into long bars, which came curling and waving out of the rollers, like great red ribbons, or like fiery serpents wriggling out of Tophet; and finally, straightened out, they were laid to cool in heaps. Trip-hammers are very pleasant objects to look at, working so massively as they do, and yet so accurately, chewing up, as it were, the hot iron, and fashioning it into shape, with a sort of [43] mighty and gigantic gentleness in their mode of action. What great things man has contrived, and is continually performing! What a noble brute he is!

Also, I found much delight in looking at the molten iron, boiling and bubbling in the furnace, and sometimes slopping over when stirred by the attendant. There were numberless fires on all sides, blinding us with their intense glow; and continually the pounding strokes of huge hammers, some wielded by machinery, others by human arms. I had a respect for these stalwart workmen, who seemed to be near kindred of the machines amid which they wrought— mighty men, sure enough, smiting stoutly, and looking at the fierce eyes of the furnace fearlessly, and handing the iron when it would have taken the skin off from ordinary fingers. They looked strong, indeed, but pale; for the hot atmosphere, in which they live, cannot but be deleterious, and I suppose their very strength wears them quickly out. But I would rather live ten years as an iron-smith than fifty as a tailor.

So much heat can be concentrated into a mass of iron, that a lump a foot square heats all the atmosphere about it, and burns the face at a considerable distance. As the trip ham[44]mer strikes this lump, it seems still more to intensify the heat by squeezing it together, and the fluid iron oozes out like sap or juice.

"He was ready for the newest fashions!"—This expression was used by Mrs. Blodget in reference to my predecessor, Crittenden, on his first arrival in England; and it is a tender way enough of signifying that a person is rather poorly off, as to apparel.

March 15th 1856.

Mr. Dallas, our new Ambassador, arrived on Thursday afternoon, by the Atlantic; and I called at the Adelphi Hotel, after dinner, to pay him my respects. I found him and his family (his wife, son, sister-in-law, and I know not precisely how many daughters) at supper, devouring beef stakes [sic], fish, and muffins, with great apparent relish. They seem to be plain, affable people, and one or two of the daughters are pretty enough to shine among English women. The Ambassador himself is a venerable old gentleman, with a full head of perfectly white hair, looking not unlike an old-fashioned wig; and this, together with his collarless white neckcloth, and his [45] brown coat, gave him precisely such an aspect as one would expect in a respectable person of pre-revolutionary days. There was a formal simplicity, too, in his manners, that might have belonged to the same era. He must have been a very handsome man in his youthful days, and is now a comely grandsire, very erect, moderately tall, not over-burthened with flesh; of benign and agreeable address, with a pleasant smile; but his eyes, which are not very large, impressed me as sharp and cold. He did not at all stamp himself upon me as a man of much intellectual or characteristic vigor. I found no such matter in his conversation; nor did I feel it in the indefinable way by which strength always makes itself acknowledged. Buchanan—though, somehow, plain and uncouth—yet vindicates himself as a large man of the world, able, experienced, fit to handle whatever difficult circumstances of life; dignified, too, and able to hold his own in any society. Mr. Dallas has a kind of venerable dignity; but yet, if a person could so little respect himself as to insult him, I should say that there was no innate force in Mr. Dallas to prevent it. It is very strange [46] that he should have made so considerable a figure in public life, filling offices that the strongest men would have thought worthy of all their ambition. There must be something shrewd and sly under his apparent simplicity; narrow, cold, selfish, perhaps. I fancied these things in his eyes. He has risen in life, by the lack of too powerful qualities, and by a certain tact which enables him to take advantage of circumstances and opportunity, and avail himself of his unobjectionableness just at the proper time. I suppose he must be pronounced a humbug, yet almost or quite an innocent one. Yet this stale old fogy is a queer representative to be sent from brawling and boisterous America, at such a critical period. It will be funny, if England sends him back again, on hearing (as she probably will) the news of Crampton's dismissal.

Mr. Dallas gives me the impression of being a very amiable man in his own family. He has brought his son with him as Secretary of Legation; a small young man, with a little moustache. It will be a feeble embassy.[292]

I called again the next morning, and introduced Mrs. Hawes, who, I believe, accompanied the ladies about town. This simplicity in Mr. Dallas's manner puzzles [47] and teases me; for, in spite of it, there was (or I imagine it) a sort of self-consciousness, as if he was being looked at—as if he were having his portrait taken.

Among other queer stories (doubtless, in many cases, fabulous) about our Ambassadors and their wives, the English tell the following of Mrs. Abbot Lawrence.[293] She was asking an invitation to a ball, or some favor of that kind, on behalf of Mrs. Augustus Peabody of Boston, and to show the lady's position in society at home, she observed—"On our side of the water, Mrs. Peabody is much more accustomed to grant favors, than to ask them!" I think it was of the same lady, she remarked, "The Peabodies hold the same position among us, that the Russells and the Stanleys do, with you."

MARCH 22ᵈ, SATURDAY.

YESTERDAY, at a quarter of four (no; it was day before yesterday) I left Liverpool for London, by rail, from the Lime-street station. The journey was a dull and monotonous one, as usual; three passengers were in the same carriage at starting; but they dropped off, and from Rugby I was alone, and availed myself of the [294]

Nothing can be more [48] tiresome than an English railway; the scenery, as viewed from the windows, having really no features; and the only incidents being the very brief stoppages at the intermediate stations. We reached London after ten °clock; and I took a cab for St. James's Place, No. 32, where I found Mr. Bowman expecting me. He had secured a bed-room for me at this lodging-house; and I am to be free of his drawing-room during my stay. I ate some biscuits, drank a glass of brandy, smoked a cigar,[295] and went to bed about midnight.

We breakfasted at nine, and then walked down to his counting-room, in old Bread street, in the city. It being a dim, dingy morning, London looked very dull; the more so as it was Good Friday, and therefore the streets were comparatively thin of people and vehicles, and had on their Sunday aspect. If it were not for the human life and bustle of London, it would be a very stupid place, with a heavy and dreary monotony of unpicturesque streets. We went up Bolt-court, where Dr. Johnson used to live; and this was, I think, the only interesting site we saw in the city. After spending some time at the counting-room, while Mr. Bowman read his letters, we went to London Bridge, and took the steamer for Waterloo Bridge, with partly an intent to go to Rich[49]mond; but the day was so damp and dusky, that we concluded otherwise. So we came home, visiting, on our way, the site of Covent Garden Theater, lately burnt down. The exterior walls still remain perfect, and look quite solid enough to admit of the interior being renewed; but I believe it is determined to take them down.

After a slight lunch, and a glass of wine, we walked out, along Piccadilly, and to Hyde Park, which already looks very green, and where there were a good many people walking and driving, and rosy, cabbage-faced children at play. Somehow or other, the shine and charm are gone from London, since my last visit; and I did not very much admire, nor feel much interest in, anything. We returned (and, for my part, I was much wearied) in time for dinner at five; some soles, roast mutton, and very pleasant sherry and port. The evening was spent at home, in various talk; and I find Mr. Bowman a very agreeable companion, and a young man of thought and information, with a self-respecting character, and, I think, a safe person to live with.

This St. James's place is in close vicinity to St. James's palace, the gateway and not very splendid front of which [50] we can see from the corner. The club-houses, and the best life of the town, are near at hand. Addison, before his marriage, used to live in St. James's place; and the house where Mr. Rogers recently died is up the court;—not that this latter residence excites much interest in my mind. I remember nothing else very noteworthy in this first day's experience; except that, on Sir Watkins Williams Wynn's door, not far from here, I saw a gold knocker, which is said to be unscrewed every night, lest it should be stolen. I don't know whether it is really gold; for it did not look so bright as the generality of brass ones.

I received a very good letter from Julian, this morning. He was to go to Mrs. Bright's, at Sandheys, yesterday, and remain till Monday.

After writing the above, I went out and walked along the Strand, Fleet-street, Ludgate-street, and Cheapside, to Wood-street; a very narrow street, insomuch that one has to press close up against the wall, to escape being grazed when a cart is passing. At No. 77, I found the place of business of Mr. Bennoch,[296] who came to see me at Rock Ferry, with Mr. Jerdan,[297] not long after my arrival in England. I found him in his office; but he did not at first recog[51] nize me, so much stouter have I grown during my English residence;—a new man, as he says. Mr. Bennoch is a kindly, jolly, frank, off-hand, very good fellow, and was bounteous in his plans for making my time pass pleasantly. We talked of Fields, from whom he has just received a letter, and who says he will fight for England, in case of war. I let Bennoch know that I, at least, should take the other side.[298] I inquired about Jerdan; and Mr. Bennoch spoke of him as a very disreputable old fellow, who had spent all his life in dissipation, and has not left it off even now in his old age. I do not see how such a man has attained vogue in society, as he certainly did; for he had no remarkable gifts, more than scores of other literary men, and his manners had, to my taste, no charm. Yet he had contrived to live amongst and upon whatever is exquisite in society, and in festivity, and had seduced (according to Bennoch's statement) innumerable women, and had an infinity of illegitimate children, besides an unconscionable number born in wedlock, of more than one wife. I asked Bennoch whether he supposed that there was any truth in the scan[52]dalous rumors in reference to Jerdan and L.E.L.[299] He replied that he did not think that they were true to the utmost extent, although he conceived that there had been great freedom, and even licentiousness, of intercourse between her and Jerdan—great looseness of behavior—only falling short of the one ultimate result. He said that Jerdan had assured him, on his honor, that L.E.L. had never yielded her virtue to him; and Bennoch thought he would not have denied it, had the case been otherwise. But, in short, the impression on my mind about Jerdan is, that he is a good-for-nothing old wretch, always disreputable, and now drunken and rowdyish on the edge of the grave. He is shameless even in begetting legitimate children; being now much above seventy, and his youngest child only about three years old. Bennoch exemplified the grossness of the English nature in the careless and unhorrified way in which he told these things.

After arranging to go to Greenwich Fair, and afterwards dine with Bennoch, I left him, and went to Mr. Bowman's office; and afterwards strayed forth again, and crossed London Bridge. Thence, I rambled rather drearily along through several shabby and unin[53]teresting streets on the other side of the Thames; and the dull streets in London are really the dullest and most disheartening in the world. By and by, I found my way to Southwark Bridge, and so crossed to Upper Thames-street, which was likewise very stupid; though I believe Clennam's paternal house, in Little Dorrit, stands thereabout. But many of Dickens's books have the odor and flavor of courts and localities that I stumble upon, about London. Next, I got into Ludgate-street, near St. Paul's; and being quite footweary, I took a Paddington-omnibus, and rode up into Regent-street, whence I came home, arriving at three °clock.

MARCH 24th, MONDAY.

YESTERDAY, being a clear day, (for England,) we determined on an expedition to Hampton Court; so walked out betimes towards the Waterloo Station; but first crossed the Thames by Westminster Bridge, and went to Lambeth palace. It stands immediately on the bank of the river, not far above the bridge. We merely walked round it, and saw only an old stone tower or two, partially renewed with brick, and a high connecting wall, within which appeared gables and other portions of the palace, all of an ancient plan and venerable aspect, though [54] evidently much patched up and restored in the course of the many ages since its foundation. There is likewise a church, part of which looks ancient, connected with the palace. The streets surrounding it have many old gabled houses, and a general look of antiquity, more than most parts of London. From the bank of the river, in front of the palace, there is a good view of the new houses of parliament, and a part of Westminster Abbey.

We then walked to the Waterloo station, on the same side of the river; and, at twenty minutes past one, took the rail for Hampton Court, distant some twelve or fifteen miles. On arriving at the terminus, we beheld Hampton palace, on the other side of the Thames; an extensive structure, with a front of red brick, long and comparatively low, with the great hall, which Wolsey built, rising high above the rest. We crossed the river (which is here but a narrow stream) by a stone bridge. The entrance to the palace is about half or a quarter of a mile from the railway, through arched gateways, which give a long perspective into the several quadrangles. These quadrangles, one beyond another, (I know not to what number) are paved with stone, and surrounded by the brick walls of the palace, the many windows of which look in upon them. Soldiers were standing sentinel at [55] the exterior gateways, and at the various doors of the palace; but they admitted everybody without question, and without fee. Policemen, or other attendants, were in most of the rooms, but interfered with nobody; so that, in this respect, it was one of the pleasantest places to visit that I have found in England. A good many people, of all classes, were strolling through the rooms.

We first went into Wolsey's Great Hall, up a most spacious staircase, the walls and cieling [sic] of which were covered with an allegorical fresco by Verrio, wonderfully bright and well-preserved; and without caring about the design or execution, I greatly liked the brilliancy of the colors. The Great Hall is a most noble and beautiful room, above a hundred feet long, and sixty high, and about the same breadth. Most of the windows are of stained or painted glass, with elaborate designs, whether modern or ancient I know not, but certainly most brilliant in effect. The walls, from the floor to perhaps half their height, are covered with antique tapestry, which, though a good deal faded, still retains color enough to be a most effective adornment, and to give an idea of how rich a mode of decking [56] out a noble apartment this must have been. The subjects represented were from Scripture, and the figures, I should think, colossal. On looking closely at this tapestry, you could see that it was thickly interwoven with threads of gold, still glistening. The windows, except one or two full length ones, do not descend below the top of this tapestry, and are therefore twenty or thirty feet above the floor; and this mode of lighting a great room seems to add much to the impressiveness of the enclosed space. The roof is very magnificent, of carved oak, intricately and elaborately arched, and still as perfect, to all appearance, as when it was first made. There are banners (so fresh in their hues, and so untattered, that I think they must be modern) suspended along beneath the cornice of the hall, and exhibiting Wolsey's arms and badges. On the whole, this is a very perfect sight in its way.

Next to the hall, there is a withdrawing-room, more than seventy feet long, and twenty five feet high. Its walls, too, are covered with ancient tapestry of allegorical design, but more faded than that of the hall. There is also a stained glass window, and a marble statue of Venus on a couch, very lean, and not very beautiful, and some cartoons of Carlo Cignani, which have left no impression on [57] my memory; likewise, a large model of a splendid palace of some East Indian nabob.

I am not sure, after all, that Verrio's frescoed Grand Staircase was not in another part of the palace; for I remember that we went from it through an immense suite of apartments, beginning with the Grand Chamber. All these apartments are wainscotted with oak, which looks just as good as new, being, I believe, of the date of King William's reign. Over many of the door ways, or around the panels, there are carvings in wood by Grinling Gibbons, representing wreaths of flowers, fruit, and foliage, the most perfectly beautiful that can be conceived; and the wood being of a light hue (lime-wood, I believe) it has a fine effect on the dark-oak panelling. The apartments open one beyond another, in long, long, long succession—rooms of state, and King's and Queen's bed-chambers, and royal closets, (bigger than ordinary drawing-rooms) so that the whole suite must be half a mile (it may be a mile, for aught I know) in extent. From the windows you get views of the palace-grounds, broad and stately walks, and groves of trees, and lawns, and fountains, and the Thames and adjacent country beyond. The [58] walls of all these rooms are absolutely covered with pictures, including works of all the great old masters, which would require very long study before a new eye would even begin to enjoy them; and seeing so many of them at once, and such a variety, and having such a nothing of time to look at them all, I did not even try to see any merit in them. Vandyke's picture of Charles I, (on a white horse, beneath an arched gateway) made more impression on me than any other; and as I recall it now, it seems to me as if I could see the king's noble, melancholy face, and armed form, remembered not in picture, but in reality. All Sir Peter Lely's lewd women, and Kneller's too, were in these rooms; and the jolly old stupidity of George III, and his family, many times repeated, and pictures by Titian, Rubens, and ever so many famous hands, intermixed with many by West, which provokingly drew the eye away from their betters. It seems to me that a picture, of all other things, should be by itself; whereas, people always congregate them in galleries. To endeavor really to see them so, is like trying to read a hundred poems at once—a most absurd attempt. Of all these pictures, I hardly recollect any so well as a ridiculous old travesty of the [59] Resurrection and Last Judgement, where the dead people are represented as gradually coming to life at the sound of the trumpet—the flesh re-establishing itself on the bones—one man is picking up his skull and putting it on his shoulders—and all appear greatly startled, only half-awake, and at a loss what to do next. Some devils are dragging away the damned by the heels, and on sledges; and above sits the Redeemer and some angelic and sainted people, looking complacently down upon the scene.

We saw, in one of the rooms, the funereal canopy beneath which the Duke of Wellington lay in state, very gorgeous, of black velvet embroidered with silver, and adorned with escutcheons; also the state bed of Queen Anne, broad and of comfortable appearance, though it was a queen's; the material of the curtains, quilt and furniture, red velvet, still brilliant in hue. Also, King William's and his Queen Mary's beds, with enormously tall posts, and a good deal worse for time and wear.

The last apartment we entered was the Gallery containing Raphael's cartoons, which I shall not pretend to admire, nor to understand. I can conceive, indeed, [60] that there is a great deal of expression in them, and very probably they may, in every respect, deserve all their fame; but on this point I can give no testimony. To my perception, they were a series of very much faded pictures, dimly seen (for this part of the palace was now in shadow) and representing figures neither graceful nor beautiful, nor, as far as I could discern, particularly grand. But I came to them with a wearied mind and eye; and also I had a previous distaste to them through the medium of engravings.

But what a noble palace, nobly enriched, this Hampton Court is! The English government does well to keep it up, and to admit the people freely into it; for it is impossible for even a Republican not to feel something like awe—at least a profound respect—for all this state, and for the institutions which are here represented, the Sovereigns whose moral magnificence demand[s] such a residence; and its permanence, too, enduring from age to age, and each royal generation adding new splendors to those accumulated by their predecessors. If we view the matter in another way, to be sure, we may feel indignant that such dolt-heads, scamps, rowdies, and every way mean people as most of the English sovereigns [61] have been, should inhabit these stately halls, (which, by the by, they have not for a long time past,) and contrast its splendors with their littleness; but, on the whole, I readily consented within myself to be impressed for a moment with the feeling that royalty has its glorious side. By no possibility can we ever have such a place in America.

Leaving Hampton Court at about four °clock, we walked through Bushy Park—a beauti[fu]l tract of ground, well wooded with fine old trees, green with moss all up their twisted trunks—through several villages, Twickenham among the rest, to Richmond. Before entering Twickenham, we passed a lath-and plaster castellated edifice, much time worn, and with the plaster peeling off from the laths, which I fancied might be Horace Walpole's toy-castle. Not that it really could have been; but it was like the image, wretchedly mean and shabby, which one forms of such a place, in its decay. From Hampton Court, to the Star and Garter, on Richmond Hill, is about six miles. After glancing cursorily at the prospect (which is famous, and doubtless very extensive and beautiful, if the English mistiness would only let it be seen) we ate [62] a good dinner in the large and handsome coffee-room of the Hotel; and then wended our way to the rail station, and reached home between eight and nine °clock. We must have walked not far from fifteen miles in the course of the day.

MARCH 25th TUESDAY.

YESTERDAY, at one °clock, I called by appointment on Mr. Bennoch, and lunched with him and his partner and clerks. This lunch seems to be a legitimate continuation of the old London custom of the tradesman living at the same table with his apprentices. The meal was a dinner for the latter class. The table was set in an upper room of the establishment; and the dinner was a large joint of roast mutton, to which some ten people sat down, including a German silk merchant as a guest besides myself. Mr. Bennoch was at the head of the table, and one of his partners at the foot. For the apprentices there was porter to drink, and for the partners and guests some sparkling Moselle; and we had a very sufficient dinner, with agreeable conversation. Bennoch said that Grace Greenwood used to be very fond of these lunches, while in England.

After lunch, Bennoch took me round the establishment, which is very extensive, occupying, I think, two or three adjacent houses, and requiring more. He showed me in[63]numerable packages of ribbons, and other silk manufactures, and all sorts of silks, from the raw thread to the finest fabrics. He then offered to show me some of the curiosities of old London, and took me first to Barber Surgeon's Hall, in Monkwell-street. It was at this place that the first anatomical studies were instituted in England; at the time of its foundation the Barbers and Surgeons were one company; but the latter, I believe, are now the exclusive possessors of the Hall. The edifice was built by Inigo Jones; and the principal room is a very fine one, with finely carved wood-work on the cieling [sic] and walls. There is a skylight in the roof, letting down a sufficient radiance on the long table beneath, where, no doubt, dead people have been dissected, and where, for many generations, it has been the custom for the Society to hold its stated feasts. In this room hangs the most valuable picture by Holbein now in existence, representing the Company of Barber Surgeons kneeling before Henry VIII, and receiving their charter from his hands. The picture is about six feet square. The King is dressed in scarlet, and quite fills up one's idea of his aspect; the Barber-Surgeons (all portraits) are an assemblage of grave-looking personages, in dark costumes. The Company [64] has refused five thousand pounds for this unique picture; and the keeper of the hall told me that Sir Robert Peel had offered a thousand pounds for liberty to take out only one of the heads, (that of a barber or surgeon named Pen) he conditioning to have a perfect fac-simile painted in. I did not see any merit in this head over the others.

Beside this great picture hung a most exquisite portrait by Vandyke; an elderly, bearded man, of noble and refined countenance, in a rich, grave dress. I never saw a portrait that seemed to me so fine. There are many other pictures of distinguished men of the Company, in long past times, and of some of the Kings and great people of England; all darkened with age, but richly darkened, and producing a most rich and sombre effect, in this stately old hall.

Nothing is more curious in London than these ancient localities and customs of the City Companies; each trade and profession having its own hall, and its own institutions. The keeper next showed us the plate which is used at the banquets. There were two loving-cups, very elaborately wrought of silver-gilt, one presented by Henry VIII, the other by Charles II. These cups, including the covers and pedestals, are very large; but the bowl-part, for holding the wine, might not hold, perhaps, much more [65] than half-a-pint. There is a peculiar ceremony in passing the loving-cup from guest to guest, whereby the whole circle of compotators are interwoven into one chain of good-fellowship. How many lips have touched the brims of these cups, that are now dry dust! There are also two caps of state for the Warden and Junior Warden of the Company, to be worn at the festivals; caps of silver, wrought in open-work, and lined with velvet—real crowns or coronets for these city-grandees. I put the Junior Warden's cap on my own head. There is besides, a good supply of other cups and vessels of silver, and spoons and forks, and a great silver punch-bowl (which I took to be a soup-tureen) presented by some King; and all these rich things are kept in a strong-closet or cup-board, opening from the hall. I should like to be present at one of their feasts. The keeper also showed me an old vellum manuscript in black-letter, which appeared to be a record of the proceedings of the Company; and at the end, there were many pages ruled for further entries, but none had been made in this volume for three or four hundred years past. Other noteworthy things I saw, but have forgotten them in the multiplicity of things seen and worth remembering.[300]

[66] I think it was in the neighborhood of Barber Surgeon's Hall (which stands amid an intricacy of old streets, where I should never have thought of going) that I saw a row of ancient alms-houses, of Elizabethan structure, at latest. They looked woefully dilapidated. In front of one of them was an inscription, setting forth that some worthy alderman had founded this establishment for the support of six poor men; and these six, or their successors, are still supported, but no larger number, although the value of the property left for that purpose would now suffice for a much larger number.

Then Mr. Bennoch took me to Cripplegate, and entering the door of a house (which proved to be a sexton's residence) we passed by a side entrance into the church-porch of St. Giles's, of which the sexton's house seems to be an indivisible contiguity. This is a very ancient church, that escaped the great fire of London; the galleries are supported by arches, the pillars of which are cased high upward with oak; but all this oaken-work and the oaken pews are comparatively modern, though so solid and dark that they agree well enough with the general effect of the church. Proceeding to the high altar, we found it surrounded with many very curious old monuments and memorials, some in carved oak, [67] some in marble; grim old worthies, mostly in the costume of Queen Elizabeth's time. Here was the bust of Speed, the historian; here was the monument of Fox, author of the Book of Martyrs. High up on the wall, beside the altar, there was a black wooden coffin, and a lady sitting upright within it, with her hands clasped in prayer; it being her awakening moment at the resurrection. Thence we passed down the centre-aisle, and about midway, we stopped before a marble bust, fixed against one of the pillars; and this was the bust of Milton. Yes; and Milton's bones lay beneath our feet; for he was buried under the pew, over the door of which I was leaning. The bust, I believe, is the original, or at least a fac-simile, of the one in Westminster Abbey.

We then went (treading over the tombstones of the old citizens of London both in the aisles and the porch, and within doors and without) into the churchyard, one side of which is fenced in by a portion of London Wall; very solid, and still high, though the accumulation of human dust has covered much of its base. This is the most considerable portion now remaining of the ancient wall of London. The sexton now asked us to go into the tower of the church, that he might show us the oldest part of [68] the structure; and so we did, and looking down from the organ gallery, I saw a woman sitting alone in the church, waiting for the Rector, whose ghostly consolation, I suppose, she needed.

This old church-tower was formerly lighted by three large windows—one of them of very great size—but the thrifty churchwardens of a generation or two ago, had built them up with brick, to the great disfigurement of the church. The sexton called my attention to the organ-pipe, which is large enough, I believe, to admit three men.

From Cripplegate we went to Milton-street (as it is now called) through which we walked for a very excellent reason; for this is the veritable Grub-street, where my literary kindred of former times used to congregate. It is still a shabby looking street, with old-fashioned houses, and inhabited chiefly by people of the poorer classes, though not by authors. Next, we went to Old Bread street, and being joined by Mr. Bowman, we set out for London Bridge, turning out of our direct course to see London Stone, in Watling-street. This famous stone appears now to be built into the wall of St. Swithin's Church, and is so encased that you can only see and touch the top of it through a circular hole. There are one or two long cuts or in[69]dentations in the top, which are said to have been made by Jack Cade's sword, when he struck it against the stone. If so, his sword was of a redoubtable temper. Judging by what I saw, London Stone was a rudely shaped and unhewn post.

At the London Bridge station, we took the rail for Greenwich, and it being only about five miles off, were not long in reaching the town. It was Easter Monday; and during the three first days of Easter, from time immemorial, a fair has been held at Greenwich, and this was what we had come to see. We found the streets thronged with people, mostly the riff-raff of London and the suburbs, male and female; oyster-stands, innumerable, oranges for sale, and booths covered with old sail-cloth, in which was chiefly offered gingerbread, completely gilt all over, so that I did not know what it was—these golden crowns, and glistening figures. Also toys, drums, and many other shewy and worthless things. The most striking circumstance was a sharp, angry sort of rattle which was heard everywhere and constantly, in all parts of the fair. This noise was produced by a certain little instrument called the "Fun of the Fair"— a sort of penny-rattle, consisting of a little wood[70]en wheel, the cogs of which turn against a thin slip of wood, and so produce the sound. The fun is, to draw this small machine against the backs of persons, the girls scraping the men, and the men the girls; and everybody is to laugh at the joke, and nobody be angry. This was not the only amusement, however; for there were theatres, at a penny a performance, with all the actors, in full tragic and comic costume, parading before the booths, to attract an audience; and exhibitions of pugilism, with the fighting men soliciting patronage; and jugglers, and giants, and beasts, and monsters; and booths where marks were to be shot at; and a vast many weighing machines, the owners of which continually cried out— "Come, come, know your weight to-night!" This certainly is a queer sort of amusement; but the trait is English—they want to know how solid and physical-ly ponderous they are. We got quite wedged into the crowd—a perfect squeeze—so that we could hardly move either way; and the girls exercised their rattles against our backs unmercifully. When I finally emerged, I found that my handkerchief was gone—a less penalty than I might have expected.

Thus we went through the mob-jammed town of Greenwich, occasionally passing a gruff old pensioner, looking [71] very grim amid the riot. At last we got into the park, where likewise were a great many merry-makers, but with more space for their gambols than in the streets. The most curious affair we here saw, was "Kissing in the Ring"—a sport peculiar, I suppose, to England. It is very simple. A ring is formed, (in this case it was a pretty large and well frequented one,) and any young man steps into the midst of it, looks round the circle, selects whatever girl he likes the looks of, leads her into the centre, kisses her, and retires. She, in her turn, chooses a young man, leads him into the ring, kisses him, and retires; and so it goes on in an endless chain of kisses. The girls, such of them as I saw, looked like country lasses, with cabbage-rosy cheeks, and an aspect of wholesome, vulgar, half-bashful enjoyment. I should not say that there was much harm in them; but the men seemed the shabby sediment of London life, pale, and dirtily rowdyish. It is[301]

[72] was, originally) at village festivals, where all the young men and maidens were neighbors' children. But this promiscuous kissing among perfect strangers is a sort of grossness which I do not believe any but the lower orders of English girls could be guilty of. Other girls might be much worse; but no others so coarse.

When we had seen enough of kissing in the ring, we strayed onward through the Park, which is a very beautiful one, with a surface of gentle hills, and many aged and large-trunked trees. Still there were merry-makers about us, some of whom were running races down the declivities, especially that one on which the observatory stands, and some of them getting tumbles by the way. Male and female ran and tumbled together, as in the race of life. There were oranges for sale, which were principally bought to be thrown and scrambled for by boys. Two girls, perhaps twelve years old, followed and haunted us for[302]

[73][303] petticoats; and having no mind to see any more of her, I gave the girl a sixpence, enjoining upon her never to do so again. We now left the park; but, just before we reached the gates, two ladies drew their rattles against our backs; and as I had bought one for Julian, I returned the compliment—much to their surprise—and so enjoyed my share of the fun of the fair. We emerged upon Black Heath, where the amusements of the Fair were going forward, in the shape of horseback races, men and girls partaking. Be it remembered, that, in all this scene of riot, everybody seemed perfectly good-natured, and intermingled themselves with a sort of Carnival familiarity; and nobody, so far as I saw, was drunk.[304]

Reaching Mr. Bennoch's house, we found it a pretty and comfortable one, and adorned with many works of art; for he seems to be a patron of art and literature, and a warm hearted man, of active benevolence and vivid sympathies in many directions. His face shows this. I have never seen eyes of a warmer glow than his. On the walls of one room, there were a good many sketches by Haydon, and several artist's proofs of fine engravings, presented by persons to whom he had been kind. [74][305] In the drawing-room there was a marble bust of Mrs. Bennoch, and one, I think, of himself, and one of the Queen (very good, he said, and unlike any other I have seen) intended as a gift from a number of subscribers to Miss Nightingale. Likewise, a crayon sketch of Grace Greenwood, looking rather morbid and unwholesome, as the poor lady really is. Also, a small picture of Bennoch in a military dress, as an officer, probably, of city-horse. By-and by came in a young gentleman, son of Haydon, the painter of high art; and one or two ladies staying in the house, and a Mr. Bailey, who made up the dinner party; and anon Mrs. Bennoch came down, a pleasant person, but in poor health, and looking older—at least more worn—than her husband. And so we went into dinner, which was a good, though not [an] elaborate one, befitting a prosperous tradesman of London; for I suppose that is Mr. Bennoch's rank, though he deals only by wholesale. We had roast lamb, jugged hare, and no side dishes, and port, sherry, and claret, and were attended at table by a female-servant. On formal occasions, he no doubt puts on greater state.

Bennoch is an admirable host, and warms his guests like a house-hold fire by the influence of his broad, ruddy, [75] kindly face, and glowing eyes, and by such hospitable demeanor as best suits this aspect. After the cloth was removed, came in Mr. Newton Crosland, a young man who once called on me in Liverpool; the husband of a literary lady, formerly Camilla Toulmin.[306] The lady herself, it appeared, was coming to spend the evening. The husband (and, I presume, the wife) is a decided believer in spiritual manifestations, and spoke of the subject with a quiet, self-satisfied consequence that was amusing to see. We talked of politics, and spiritualism, and literature; and, before we rose from the table, Mr. Bennoch drank the health of the ladies, and especially of Mrs. Hawthorne, in terms very kind towards her and me. I responded, on her behalf, as well as I could, and left it to Mr. Bowman, as a bachelor, to respond for the ladies generally—which he did briefly, toasting the health of Mrs. Bennoch.

We had heard the thrumming of the piano, in the drawing room, for some time past; and now adjourning thither, I had the pleasure to be introduced to Mrs. Newton Crosland, a rather tall and thin, pale, ladylike person, looking, I thought, of a sensitive charcter. She expressed, in a low tone and quiet way, great delight at seeing my distinguished self; for she is a vast admirer of the Scar[76]let Letter, and especially the character of Hester; indeed, I remember seeing a most favorable criticism of the book from her pen, in one of the London magazines. I would glady have responded by praising her own works; but, though she sent me one of them, three or four years ago, I had quite forgotten its subject, and so could not say anything greatly to the purpose. Neither would it have been easy, at any rate, to respond in due measure; for Mrs. Crosland was awfully lavish in her admiration, preferring poor me to all the novelists of this age, or I believe, any other; and she and Mr. Bennoch discussed, right across me, the uses to which I had better put my marvellous genius, as respects the mode of working up my English experiences. Oh Lord! Dear me! I suppose this may be the tone of London literary society.

At eleven ºclock, Mrs. Newton Crosland got into the littlest pony-carriage (I believe the pony was a very diminutive mule) and set forth for her own residence, with a lad walking at the pony's head, and carrying a lanthern. Mr. Bennoch, Mr. Bailey, Mr. Crosland, Mr. Bowman, and myself, walked across the heath towards Greenwich, all but Mr. Crosland with cigars in our mouths, and the odor was very agreeable after such rich incense as I had been inhaling. At a good [77] distance from his own house, Mr. Bennoch took leave and returned; Mr. Crosland, also, dropt off at his residence; and we soon reached Greenwich, where we found a considerable remnant of the mob still in the streets. The train speedily brought us back to London Bridge, whence we took a Hansom for our lodgings, and arrived precisely at midnight.

MARCH 26th TUESDAY.

YESTERDAY was not a very eventful day. After writing a good deal of journalism, I went out at about 12, and visited (for the first time) the National Gallery. It is of no use for me to criticise pictures, or to try to describe them; but I have an idea that I might get up a taste, with some little attention to the subject; for I find I already begin to prefer some pictures to others. This is encouraging. Of those that I saw yesterday, I think I liked some by Murillo best. There were a great many people in the Gallery, almost entirely of the middle, with some of the lower classes; and I should think that the effect of the exhibition must tend, at least, towards refinement. Nevertheless, the only emotion that I saw displayed was in some broad grins on the faces of a man and two women, at sight of a small picture of Venus, naked and asleep, in a most lascivious posture, with[307] [78] a Satyr peeping at her, with an expression of gross animal delight and merriment. Without being aware of it, this man and his two women were of that same Satyr breed. If I lived in London, I would endeavor to educate myself in this and other galleries of art; but, as the case stands, it would be of no use. I saw two of Turner's landscapes, but did not see so much beauty in them as in some of Claude's. A view of the Grand Canal in Venice, by Canaletto, seemed to me wonderful—absolutely perfect—a better reality; for I could see the water of the canal absolutely moving and dimpling; and the palaces and buildings, on each side, were quite as good in their way.

Leaving the Gallery, I walked down into the city, and passed through Smithfield, where I peeped at St. Bartholomew's Hospital; and between that point and St. Paul's, I went into a cook-shop and got some alamode beef and a small bottle of stout—which greatly encouraged me; for I was quite weary, and chilled with a penetrating east-wind. Then I went into St. Paul's, and walked all round the great cathedral, looking, I believe, at every monument on its floor. There is certainly nothing very wonderful in any of them; and I do wish it would not so generally happen that English warriors go into battle al[79]most stark naked; at least, we must suppose so, from their invariably receiving their death-wounds in that condition. I will not believe that a sculptor or a painter is a man of genius, unless he can make the nobleness of his subject illuminate and transfigure any given pattern of coat and breeches. Nevertheless, I never go into St. Paul's without being anew impressed with the grandeur of the edifice, and the general effect of these same groups of statuary, ranged in their niches and at the bases of the pillars, as adornments of the cathedral.

Coming homeward, I went into the enclosure of the Temple, and near the entrance, saw "Dr. Johnson's Staircase," printed over a doorway; so I not only peeped in, but went up the first flight of some broad, well worn stairs, passing my hand over a heavy, ancient-looking, oaken balustrade, on which, no doubt, Johnson's hand had often rested. It was here that Boswell used to visit him, in their early acquaintance. Before my lunch, I had gone into Bolt Court, where he died.

I reached St. James' Place, considerably tired of the London pavements, at four °clock, and spent the rest of the daylight writing my Journal. The opposite houses so overshadow us, that it is dark early here. At seven, Mr. [80] Bowman returned, and we went out and dined at the Wellington (formerly Crockford's gambling-house) in a splendid dining-room, where a great many gentlemen were at all stages of their meal. The dinner was better cooked than it would have been at most American restaurants; but there was a far less variety of dishes to select from. Wines (except the highest-priced French or German) are cheaper here than there. We came back betimes, and spent the evening at home.

This morning, there have been letters from Mr. Wilding, inclosing an invitation to me to be one of the Stewards at the Anniversary Dinner of the Literary Fund. No, I thank you, gentlemen!

MARCH 27th, THURSDAY.

YESTERDAY, I went out at about twelve, and visited the British Museum; an exceedingly tiresome affair. It quite crushes a person to see so much at once; and I wandered from hall to hall, with a weary and heavy heart, wishing (Heaven forgive me!) that the Elgin marbles and the frieze of the Parthenon were all burnt into lime, and that the granite Egyptian statues were hewn and squared into building-stones, and that the mummies had all turned to dust, two thousand years ago; and, in fine, that all the material relics of so many successive ages had disappeared with the [81] generations that produced them. The present is burthened too much with the past. We have not time, in our earthly existence, to appreciate what is warm with life, and immediately around us; yet we heap up all these old shells, out of which human life has long emerged, casting them off forever. I do not see how future ages are to stagger onward under all this dead weight, with the additions that will be continually made to it.

After leaving the Museum, I went to see Bennoch, and arrange with him our expedition of to-day; and he read me a letter from Tupper, very earnestly inviting us to come and spend a night or two with him. Then I wandered about the city, and got lost in the vicinity of Holborn; so that, for a long while, I was under a spell of bewilderment, and kept returning in the strangest way to the same point in Lincoln's Inn Fields. I must say, I wished the devil had London and them that built it, from King Lud's time downward.

We (Mr. Bowman & myself) dined at our lodgings, and went to the Princess's theatre in the evening. Charles Kean performed in Louis XI very well indeed—a thoughtful and well-skilled actor, much improved since I saw him, many years ago, in America.

[82] APRIL 1ST, TUESDAY.

AFTER my last date, on Thursday, I went out, and visited the National Gallery, where I remember fancying in myself an increasing taste for pictures. At three

°clock, or a little later, having packed up a few clothes in a travelling bag, I went to Bennoch's office and took a lunch with him; and, at about five, we took the rail from the Waterloo Station for Aldershot Camp. At Farnborough we were cordially received by Lieutenant Shaw of the North Cork Rifles, and were escorted by him (in a fly) to his quarters. The camp is a large city composed of numberless wooden barracks, arranged in regular streets, on a wide bleak heath, with an extensive and dreary prospect on all sides. Lieut. Shaw assigned me one room in his hut, and Bennoch another, and made us as comfortable as kind hospitality could; but the huts are very small, and the rooms have no size at all; neither are they air-tight, and the sharp wind whistles in at the crannies, and, on the whole, of all discomfortable places, I am inclined to reckon Aldershot camp the worst. I suppose Government has located the camp on that windy heath, and built such wretched huts, for the very purpose of rendering life as little desirable as may be, to the soldiers, so that they throw it away the more willingly.

At seven °clock, we dined at the Regimental mess, with the officers of the North Cork. The mess-room is by far the most endurable place to be found in camp. The hut is large; and the mess-room is capable of receiving between thirty and forty guests, besides the officers of the regiment, when a great dinner-party is given. As I saw it, the whole space was divided into a dining-room and two ante-rooms, by red curtains drawn across; and the second ante-room seems to be a general rendezvous for the officers, where they meet at all hours, and talk, or look over the newspapers and the army-register, which constitute the chief of their reading. The Colonel and the Lieutenant Colonel of the regiment received Bennoch and me with great cordiality, as did all the other officers, and we sat down to a splendid dinner.

All the officers of this regiment are Irishmen, and all of them, I believe, men of fortune; and they do what they can towards alleviating their hardships in camp by eating and drinking of the best. The table-service and plate were as fine as in any nobleman's establishment; the dishes numerous and admirably got up; and the wines delectable, and genuine—as they had need to be; for there is a great consumption of them. I liked these Irish officers exceedingly; not that it would be possible to live [84] long among them without finding existence a bore; for they have no thought, no intellectual movement, no ideas, that I was aware of, beyond horses, dogs, drill, garrisons, field days, whist, women, wine, cigars, and all that kind of miscellany; yet they were really gentlemen, living on the best of terms with one another, courteous, kind, most hospitable, with a rich Irish humor, softened down by social refinements— not too refined, neither, but a most happy sort of behavior, as natural as that of children, and with a safe freedom, that made me feel entirely at my ease. I think well of the Irish gentleman for their sakes; and I believe I might fairly attribute to Lieut. Colonel Stowell (next whom I sat) a higher and finer cultivation than the above description indicates. Indeed, many of them may have been capable of much more intellectual intercourse than that of the mess-table; but I suppose it would not have been in keeping with their camp life, nor suggested by it. Several of the elder officers were men who had been long in the army; and the Colonel (a bluff, hearty old soldier, with a profile like an eagle's head and beak) was a veteran of the Peninsula, and had a medal on his breast, with clasps for three famous battles, besides that of Waterloo.

[85] The regimental band played during dinner; and the Lieut. Colonel apologized to me for its not playing "Hail Columbia," the tune not coming within their musical accomplishments. It was no great matter, however, for I should not have distinguished it from any other tune; but, to do me what honor was possible, in the way of national airs, the band was ordered to play a series of Negro melodies, and I was entirely satisfied. It is really funny that the "wood notes wild"[308] of those poor black slaves should have been played, in a foreign land, as an honorable compliment to one of their white countrymen.

After dinner, we played whist, and then had some broiled bones for supper, and finally went home to our respective huts; not much earlier than four °clock, I do verily believe. But I don't wonder these gentlemen sit up as long as they can keep their eyes open; for never was there anything so utterly comfortless as their camp-beds. They are really worse than the bed of honor, no wider, no softer, no warmer, and affording not nearly so sound sleep. Indeed, I got hardly any sleep at all; and almost as soon as I did close my eyes, the bugles soun[86]ded, and the drums beat reveille, and from that moment the camp was all astir; so I pretty soon got up, and went to the mess-room for my breakfast, feeling wonderfully fresh and well, considering what my night had been.

Long before this, however, the whole regiment, and all the other regiments, had marched off to another part of the heath, to take part in a general review; and Bennoch and I followed, as soon as we had eaten a few mutton chops. It was a bright, sunshiny day, but with a strong east-wind, as piercing and pitiless as ever blew; and this wide, undulating plain of Aldershot seemed just the place where the east-wind was at home. Still, it acted, on the whole, like an invigorating cordial; and, whereas, in pleasanter circumstances, I should have lain down and gone to sleep, I now felt as if I could do without sleep for a month. In due time, we found out the place of the North Cork regiment in the general battle-array, and were greeted as old comrades by the Colonel and other officers. Soon, the soldiers (who, when we first reached them, were standing at ease, or strolling about) were called into order; and, anon, we saw a group of mounted officers riding along the lines, [87] and among them a gentleman in a civilian's round hat, and plain frock and trowsers, riding on a white horse. This group of riders turned the front of the regiment, and then passed along the rear, coming close to where we stood; and as the plainly dressed gentleman rode by, he bent towards me, and I tried to raise my hat, but did not succeed very well, because the fierce wind had compelled me to jam it tight upon my head. The Duke of Cambridge (for this was he) is a good-looking, gentlemanly man, of bluff English face, with a good deal of brown beard about it. Though a pretty tall man, he looks punchy (that is to say, puncheonlike) on horseback, being somewhat broad and round in proportion to his height. I looked at him with a certain sort of interest, and a feeling of kindness; for one does feel kindly to whatever human being is anywise marked out from the rest, unless it be by his disagreeable qualities.

The troops (there were from twelve to fifteen thousand of them on the ground) now got into marching order, and went to attack a wood, where we were to suppose the enemy to be stationed. I have seen fifty better sham-fights in America; so shall not [88] put myself to the trouble of describing this, which seemed to me rather clumsily managed, and without any striking incident or result. The officers had prophesied, the night before, that General Knowles (commanding in the camp) would make a muddle of the review; and probably he did. After the review, the Duke of Cambridge and his attendant officers took their station, and all the regiments marched in front of him, saluting as they passed. As each Colonel rode by, and as the banner of each regiment was lowered, the Duke lifted his hat; and, each time he did so, there ensued a singular and half-ludicrous transformation. For the poor Duke has suffered a good deal in his Crimean warfare, and has grown bald and gray, in consequence, although his beard and whiskers are still of a rich brown; so that, while his hat remained on his head, you saw a florid gentleman in his very prime, fringed about with the brown beard of lusty manhood; but, whenever the hat was lifted, behold! an aged head, gray, bald, forlorn. At the dinner-table, afterwards, our old Colonel told me that it was the battle of Inkerman that did him this mischief; for the Duke had been in a terrible excitement there, and, besides, Lord Raglan had be-rated him very severely for some of his conduct. The Colonel said, [89] moreover, that the Duke of Cambridge had an awfully quick temper, which breaks out whenever he is in command, and that he blows up the officers right and left, whenever anything happens not to suit him. I should have been much gratified to witness one of these explosions; but as he was merely a visitor to-day, I could not have that pleasure.

The most splendid effect of this parade was the gleam of the sun upon the long lines of bayonets; the sheen of all that steel appearing like a wavering fringe of light upon the dark length or masses of troops below. It was very fine. But I was glad when the whole thing was done, and I could go back to the mess-room, whither I carried an excellent appetite for luncheon. After this, we walked about the camp, looked at some model-tents, inspected the arrangements and modes of living in the huts of the privates; and thus gained more and more adequate ideas of the vile uncomfortableness of a military life. Finally, I returned to the mess-room, and turned over the regimental literature, (a peerage and baronetage, an army and militia register, a number of the Sporting Magazine, and one of the United Service) while Bennoch took another walk. Before [90] dinner, we both tried to catch a little nap by way of compensation for last night's deficiencies; but, for my part, the attempt was fruitless.

The dinner was as splendid and as agreeable as that of the evening before; and I believe it was nearly two °clock when Bennoch and I bade farewell to our kind entertainers. For my part, I fraternized with these military gentlemen in a way that augurs the very best things for the future peace of the two countries. They all expressed the warmest sympathies towards America; and it was easy to judge from their conversation that there is no real friendliness, on the part of the military, towards the French. The old antipathy is just as strong as ever; stronger than ever, perhaps, on account of the comparatively more brilliant success of the French in this Russian war. So, with most Christian sentiments of peace and brotherly love, we returned to our hut, and lay down each in his narrow bed. I should think a soldier would look forward with delightful anticipation to a long sleep in the bed of honor, if it were only for the sake of its vastly greater warmth, snugness, and comfort.

Early in the morning, the drums and bugles began their usual bedevilment; and shortly after six, I got up [91] and dressed, and we had breakfast at the mess-room, shook hands with Lieutenant Shaw (our more especial host) and drove off in a cab to the railway station at Ash. I know not whether I have mentioned that the villages, neighboring to the camp, have suffered terribly as regards morality from the vicinity of the soldiers. Quiet, old English towns, that, till within a little time ago, had kept their antique simplicity and innocence, have now no such thing as female virtue in them, so far as the lower classes are concerned. This is expressing the matter too strongly, no doubt; but there is too much truth in it, nevertheless; and one of the officers remarked that even ladies of respectability had grown much more free in manners and conversation than at first. I have heard observations similar to this from a Nova Scotian, in reference to moral influence of soldiers, when stationed in the provinces.

We reached Albury somewhere about ten °clock, and found, at the railway station, a boy of twelve years old, a son of Tupper, who had sent him to conduct us to his house. He was a forward, talkative, intelligent lad, and kept chattering profusely with Bennoch (whom he [92] already knew) as we walked along, in the bright, windy morning, over a pleasant, rural country, to the village of Albury. When we had entered its street, the boy exclaimed that there was his father. "Yes," said Bennoch, "there he is, as large as life!" "As small as life, you mean!" said the boy; and, indeed, Mr. Martin Farquhar Tupper's[309] size is better expressed so. He soon met us, and extended

his arms with affectionate greeting to Bennoch; and then addressing me—
"Oh, Great Scarlet Letter!" he cried. I did not know what the devil to say,
unless it were, "Oh, wondrous Man of Proverbs!"—or, "Oh, wiser Solomon!"—and as I was afraid to say either of these, I rather think I held my
tongue. I felt in an instant that Tupper was a good soul, but a fussy little
man, of a kind that always takes me entirely aback. He is a small man, with
wonderfully short legs, fat (at least very round) and walks with a kind of
waddle, not so much from corpulence of belly as brevity of leg. His hair is
curly, and of an iron gray hue; his features are good, even handsome, and his
complexion very red; a person for whom I immediately felt a kindness, and
instinctively knew to be a bore. He took me by the arm with vast cordiality,
and led me towards his [93] house; and before we reached the gate, if I
mistake not, he had asked me whom I meant by Zenobia in the Blithedale
Romance, and whether I had drawn my own character in Miles Coverdale,
and whether there really was a tombstone in Boston, with the letter A upon
it!—very posing queries, all of them.

Tupper's house is a very delightful one, standing in the centre of the
village, yet secluded from it by its own grounds and nicely arranged garden,
all encompassed by a wall. He says the house has Seven Gables, and, before
we entered, he led me round it in order to count them; but I believe we fairly
made out eight or nine. It is a house of some antiquity, and its gables make it
very picturesque, in a quiet way; and Tupper, as his family increased, has
made additions that are in good keeping with the original structure. He
inherited it from an uncle.

Mrs. Tupper, a plain, pleasant, cordial, ladylike person was now standing
at the door, with some of her children, and gave us a warm and kind welcome;
and we entered the hall, which had pictures and old cabinets in it, and communicated with the drawing-room on one [94] side, and with a parlor and a
dining-room on the other; all of them nice apartments, just such as suit a
good old country-house. Tupper's uncle was an amateur painter; and there
were some of his own pictures on the walls, and several better ones which he
had purchased, and, in the hall, two or three century-old portraits, which,
Tupper said, he called ancestral, though really they were not so. He showed
me a good many curious articles of furniture, and such things, of which I
remember only a beautiful antique cabinet, faced with polished stone, of a
peculiar kind, which, being in small squares, looked precisely like landscape-
paintings; this being the effect, at a little distance, of the natural veins of the
stone. I could not convince myself that they were not genuine pictures, without
examining them very closely.

The family had been waiting breakfast for us; so, though Bennoch and I
had eaten two chops apiece at the camp, we all sat down to table, seven
children inclusive; and I made another pretty fair meal. Tupper's three eldest
children are girls, from eighteen downward; and their cheeks were as red as

roses, and they seemed to be nice, affectionate, well-behaved young people. The father has chiefly educated them himself, and to such [95] good purpose that one of them already writes for the Magazines. Tupper is really a good man, most domestic, most affectionate, most fussy; for it appeared as if he could hardly sit down, and even if he were sitting, he still had the effect of bustling about. He has no dignity of character, no conception of what it is, nor perception of his deficiency. His son (the forward boy whom we first met) has an instinctive sense of this, and presumes upon it; and Tupper continually finds it necessary to repress him,—"Martin, do not talk so much!" he cries; for the boy really babbles without a moment's intermission. "Martin, your father was born a day or two before you were!"—and a thousand such half-pettish, half kindly admonitions, none of which have the slightest effect. The girls, however, seem to respect him and love him.

In the dining-room, there are six fine lithographic prints of the Queen's children, as large as life, and all taken at the same age; so that they would appear to have been littered at one birth, like kittens. These likenesses were presented to Tupper by her Majesty; and he is the only person who has been [96] thus honored. The Queen is a great admirer of the Proverbial Philosophy, and gives it to each of her children as they arrive at a proper age for comprehending the depths of its wisdom. I can conceive that Tupper is the man of all the world to be made most supremely happy by such appreciation as this; for he is the vainest little man of all little men, and his vanity continually effervesces out of him, as naturally as ginger-beer froths. Yet it is the least incommodious vanity I ever witnessed; he does not insist upon your expressing admiration; he does not even seem to wish it, nor hardly to know or care whether you admire him or not. He is so entirely satisfied with himself, that he takes the admiration of all the world for granted, the recognition of his supreme merit being inevitable. I liked him, and laughed in my sleeve at him, and was utterly weary of him; for certainly he is the ass of asses. Not but what he says sensible things, and even humorous ones; not but what he is a writer of strength and power; for surely the "Crock of Gold" is a very powerful tale. But, if it were not irreverent, I should say that his Creator, when He made Tupper, intended to show how easily He could turn a gifted, upright, warm-hearted, [97] and in many ways respectable person, into a jest and laughing-stock even for persons much inferior to himself.

After breakfast, Tupper, his three daughters, and his son, set out with Bennoch and me for a walk, intending to show us the meeting of a hunt. The country in this neighborhood is beautiful, swelling into long, high undulations, from the summits of which there are views of great extent. Tupper said, that from the top of one of these hills, which we ascended, the diameter of the prospect was a hundred miles. These are the Surrey Hills; and there is a legend of Saints connected with three of them, but I have forgotten it. We walked a mile or two (all the way up hill) before reaching the spot where the hunt was expected to meet; and on our way, we saw here and there a red-coated horse-man, hastening to the rendezvous. We heard now and then the sound of a horn, and the voice of a huntsman; and by and by appeared the pack, nosing along the ground and scenting into the underbrush of furze, to discover if any fox were there. The hunt followed, (perhaps a score of horsemen, some of them in red coats, and two or three ladies amongst,) but they had not yet [98] found a fox; and though we occasionally caught glimpses of the hunters, during the forenoon, and once or twice heard the cry of dogs, I doubt whether they found Reynard at all. Before we left this hill-top, Tupper shewed us some yew trees of unknown antiquity, druidical, perhaps; their trunks were of an immense size, insomuch that Bennoch, and Tupper, (but his arms are short,) and myself, could but just measure round them with all our arms outstretched. Indeed, I think Tupper's son tried to girt it along with us.

We now took our way homeward by another route, which led us through Albury Park, the seat of Mr. Drummond, one of the members of Parliament for Surrey. On the edge of the park, we came to a new Irvingite church, and at no great distance from it, but within the precincts of the park, stood another church, ancient and venerable. We obtained admittance into the new church, and found it very beautiful, with windows of stained glass admitting a soft, lovely light. A never-dying lamp hung burning before the altar; there was a vessel of holy water, and various other Catholic symbols; for these Irvingites seem to be verging nearer and nearer to Papistry, and will probably merge into it at last. But be that as it may, there was a most pleasant and soothing influence in [99] the interior of this beautiful and quiet church; and the stained windows, and the lamp, and the holy symbols, made the spectator feel religious, for the moment, at least. We next went to the old church, which, I think, is not more than a hundred yards distant. It is now no longer used as a place of worship, although it is still in excellent preservation, and, gray and time-worn as it is, might have answered its original purpose for centuries longer. Not far from this church, behind some old trees, we saw the gables and stately front of Mr. Drummond's residence; a modern structure, but in the Elizabethan style, and looking, from where we stood, antique enough to be in keeping with the rest of the scene.

Near the old church—within a few paces of its gray wall, indeed—was Tupper's burial place, belonging to the family for some generations past—and here there was a marble tombstone, finely sculptured, bearing a record of the death of two of his children, one of them two or three years old, the other of no age at all, having died at birth. Behind the tombstone was a little grave, looking like a child's garden, with a tiny fence about it, and, early as the season was, all blooming with flowers. It was easy to see that it had been constantly and carefully cultivated and [100] weeded—this little garden-grave of two dear babies. Tupper looked earnestly at it, and was quiet for a moment, and seemed pleased to see the flowers growing so finely, and said—"Ah, we must tell mamma of this!" Then he made me look into a window of the church, and catch a glimpse of a large monument to the memory of, I think, three sons of Mr. Drummond, all the male posterity this rich man had. And as we left the old churchyard, and went through Albury park, Tupper told me a story which, though of very recent date, might easily enough be worked up into a darkly impressive legend.

It seems that Mr. Drummond had been very desirous of taking down the ancient church, because he considered it an incumbrance to his park, and for whatever other reasons; and he purposed, moreover, to level all the tomb stones, and thus desecrate the ground where all the generations of the village had laid their bones, from time immemorial. As he possessed great interest with government, and with the bishop, he succeeded in obtaining permission to do so; but Tupper, who had hereditary rights in the churchyard, opposed Mr. Drummond's plan to the utmost, and fought for the church, and for the graves that belonged to him, most pertinaciously. In writing upon [101] the subject to the Bishop, he used some such expression as this—"If Mr. Drummond persists in his purpose of desecration, I trust that the building of his new church will not make good the words of Joshua, when he cursed whomsoever should re-build Jericho—'He shall lay the foundation thereof in his firstborn, and in his youngest son he shall set up the gates of it.' "[310] Well; Mr. Drummond was not to be deterred; but (I forget whether he began to take down the old church, or whether it was while he was breaking ground for the new one,) one of his sons suddenly sickened and died. Another son (and they had all three been strong and healthy young men) died while the building of the new church proceeded. The church was finished, and Mr. Drummond took down the bells from the old steeple, and set them up in the new one, and the first use of them, I think, was intended to be the ringing in of his remaining son's majority. But before this joyful peal had sounded, this last son likewise sickened and died; and the old bells in the new steeple tolled his funeral knell; and the ancient church, which his father would have levelled with the earth, became the mausoleum of his children; for he buried them all there, and thought no more of removing so much as one gray [102] stone of it! It is queer to think of little Tupper being the prophet of such a doom as this!

We went back to the village over a furzy common, very rough looking; and it is remarkable how much of this waste, unenclosed ground there is, at no great distance from the thickest populated heart of the kingdom. Reaching Tupper's house, he took me up into his study, which is a large room, with plenty of books about it, a great many of which are different editions of his own beloved works. The most remarkable object is a beautiful marble figure of a child, asleep on a cushion; a little girl of two or three years old, very delicately sculptured, enjoying a sweet repose. It is the statue of his dead child, whose grave we had seen in the old churchyard. Tupper looked at it with evident delight, as he might have done on his child alive; and it almost seemed as if, so far as his feelings were concerned, it were the real presence of his living child. He spoke about it without any reserve, and showed me the different points of view; but, for my part, though it was a very sweet little statue, I could not say much of it, feeling that a stranger's tongue had no right to infringe upon the delicacy and sanctity [103] of such a subject. But Tupper probably felt nothing of the kind; and the presence of this little marble girl seems to soothe and comfort him, and he is just as merry, when the mood serves, as if she were not there. Besides this tender marble, he showed me some certificates of honorary membership of certain American literary societies, glazed and framed, and hanging against the wall. I never heard before of any of these learned bodies. Likewise, he opened one of his book-cases, and showed it quite packed full of the various American editions of his works, all splendidly bound and gilt,—talking with evidently intense satisfaction of his American fame.

We dined early (at two °clock, I believe) the whole brood of children sitting down to table with us, and the patriarch Tupper chatting away, during the meal. A very small man seems rather out of place as the head of a large family; the dignity of the position is not in keeping with his figure and demonstrations. We had quite a good, plain dinner, in such abundance as the large appetites of seven small people rendered necessary. I sat next to Mrs. Tupper, and talking with her about her home and her [104] home [sic] and her husband, she observed that they two had played together on that spot, and gathered the nuts beneath the trees, in earliest childhood. "For we were cousins!" said she. Now, all during dinner, I had been watching a little boy who sat by her side—a boy of ten, perhaps—a pale thin, drooping little fellow, who ate not a morsel. It had been at my tongue's end to ask whether he was ill; but anon he began to twist and contort his figure in the strangest way, and to jerk and hunch, and to make fearful grimaces with his mouth and entire face, as if he were nothing less than possessed. So I though it wisest to ask no questions. But, as soon as Mrs. Tupper told me that she was her husband's cousin, I saw that this poor boy was the sickly offspring of a union on which Nature had laid a curse; and looking round at the rest of the children, I saw that some of them squinted different ways, and that the eldest boy, though apparently bright enough, was delicate and high-shouldered; and though I could see nothing amiss in the three eldest girls, yet I had little confidence in the wholesomeness and stability of their constitutions. It is wonderful what a sad[105]ness this one great misery threw over my whole contemplation of Tupper's life and character. I had already made a remark to him about the means of happiness which he had around him, and had noticed, with some surprise, that he did not respond with any heartiness. There was, for that only time, a marked reserve in his manner; a something repining in his tone. I do not see what else can be the skeleton in Tupper's house, unless it be that he has loved too well what was born too near akin.

After dinner, the pony-carriage was ordered, and Mrs. Tupper, Bennoch and myself got into it, while Tupper bestrode a horse; and we set out for Wotton, the seat of old John Evelyn at about five miles distant. Tupper breeds his own horses, and is very proud of them, though they are by no means remarkably good. One very common-place little pony he calls "Wonder," and has other fine names for all the rest. Our drive would have been a very pleasant one, but for the bitter east wind, which made our faces tingle and benumbed our fingers. Tupper rides pretty well, but his wife kept calling out to him to be careful, to go slowly down Shere Hill, and diverse other affectionate admonitions; [106] for she is truly a good woman, and loves and admires her husband just as much as if he were bigger and wiser. After passing through one or two villages, with picturesque streets of old, contiguous houses (as most English villages are built) and past an old church or two, we reached the gateway of Wotton, and drove up to the house.

Wotton stands in a hollow, near the summit of one of the long swells that here undulate over the face of the country. There is a good deal of wood behind it, as should be the case with the residence of the author of "Sylva"; but, I believe, few, if any, of these trees are known to have been planted by John Evelyn, or even to have been coeval with his time. The house is of brick, partly ancient, and consists of a front and two projecting wings, with a porch and entrance in the centre. It has a desolate, meagre aspect, and needs something to give it life, and stir, and jollity. The present proprietor is of the old Evelyn family, and is now one of the two members of Parliament for Surrey; but he is a very shy and retiring man, unmarried, sees little company, and seems either not to know how to make himself comfortable, or not to care about it. A servant told us that Mr. [107] Evelyn had just gone out; but Tupper, who is apparently on intimate terms with him, thought it best that we should go into the house, while he went in search of the master. So the servant ushered us through a hall, in which were many family pictures by Lely, and, for aught I know by Vandyke, and by Kneller, and other famous painters, up a grand staircase, and into the library, the inner room of which contained the ponderous volumes which John Evelyn used to read. Nevertheless, it was a room of most barren aspect, without a carpet on the floor, with pine-book cases, with a common white-washed ceiling, with no luxurious study chairs, without a fire. There was an open folio on the table, and a sheet of manuscript that appeared to have been recently written. I took down a book from the shelves (a volume of annals, if I remember right, connected with English history) and Tupper afterwards told me that this one single volume, for its rarity, was worth either two or three hundred pounds. Against one of the windows of this library, there grows a magnolia tree with a very large stem, and at least fifty years old.

Mrs. Tupper and I waited a good while, and then Tupper and Bennoch came back, without having found Mr. Evelyn. Tupper wished very much to show the prayer-book [108] used by King Charles at his execution, and some curious old manuscript volumes; but the servant said that his master always kept these treasures locked up, and trusted the key to nobody. We therefore had to take our leave without seeing them; and I have not often entered a house that one feels to be more forlorn than Wotton, although we did have a glimpse of a dining-room, with a table laid for three or four guests, and looking quite brilliant with plate, cut glass, and snowy napery. There was a fire, too, in this one room. Mr. Evelyn is making extensive alterations in the house, or has recently done so, and this is perhaps one reason of its ungenial meagerness and lack of finish.

On our drive home, Tupper took Bennoch's place in the pony-carriage, and Bennoch mounted Tupper's horse. Tupper asked his wife if he looked as large as Bennoch on horseback, (not he, poor little man!) and I had before seen him standing beside Bennoch, and comparing their heights, though Bennoch is a head taller. This is a characteristic trait of Tupper; for he has not the slightest idea of his own true measure in any way, either physically or intellectually.

Before our departure from Wotton, Tupper had asked [109] me to leave my card for Mr. Evelyn; but I had no mind to overstep any limit of formal courtesy in dealing with an Englishman, and therefore declined. Tupper, however, on his own responsibility, wrote his name, Bennoch's, and mine, on a piece of paper, and told the servant to show them to Mr. Evelyn. We soon had experience of the good effect of this; for we had scarcely got back before somebody drove up to Tupper's door, and one of the girls, looking out, exclaimed that there was Mr. Evelyn himself and another gentleman. He had set out, the instant he heard of our call, to bring the three precious volumes for me to see. This surely was most kind; a kindness which I should never have dreamed of expecting from a shy, cold, retiring man, like Mr. Evelyn.

So he and his friend were ushered into the dining-room, and introduced. Mr. Evelyn is a young-looking man, dark, with a moustache, rather small, and of no distinguished aspect, except that his face is rather oddly forlorn and uncomfortable in its expression. He seems to be nervous, and though he has the manners of a man who has seen the world, it evidently requires an effort in him to speak to anybody; and I could see his whole person slightly writhing itself, as it were, while he addressed me. This is [110] strange, in a man of his public position, member for the county, necessarily mixed up with life in many forms, the possessor of sixteen thousand pounds a year, and the representative of an ancient name. Nevertheless, I liked him, and felt as if I could become intimately acquainted with him, if circumstances were favorable; but, at a brief interview like this, it was hopeless to break through two great reserves; so I talked much more with his companion—a pleasant young man, fresh from college, I should imagine—than with Mr. Evelyn himself.

The three books were really of very great interest. One was an octavo volume of manuscript in John Evelyn's own hand, the beginning of his published diary, written as distinctly as print, in a small, clear, character. It can be read just as easily as any printed book. Another was a Church of England prayer-book in black-letter, with a written page of Latin prefixed, importing that this was the prayer-book which King Charles used on the scaffold, and which was stained with his sacred blood; and underneath are two or three lines in John Evelyn's hand, certifying this to be the very book. It is an octavo, or small folio, and seems to have been very little used, scarcely opened, except in one spot; its leaves elsewhere retaining their original freshness and elasticity. It [111] opens most readily at the commencement of the Communion Service; and there, on the left hand page, there is a discoloration about as large as a sixpence, of a yellowish or brownish hue, which, two hundred years ago, and a little more, was doubtless red. For, on that page, had fallen a drop of King Charles's blood.[311] The other volume was large, and contained a great many original letters, written by the King during his troubles. I had not time to examine them with any minuteness, and remember only one document, which Mr. Evelyn pointed out, and which had a strange pathos and pitifulness in it. It was a sort of due-bill, promising to pay a small sum for beer, which had been supplied to him (the King),—so soon as God should enable him, or the distracted circumstances of his kingdom make it possible, or some touching and helpless expression of that kind. Prince Hal seemed to consider it an unworthy matter, that a great prince should think of "that poor creature, small beer,"[312] at all; but that a great prince should not be able to pay for it, is far worse.

Mr. Evelyn expressed his regret that we were not staying longer in this part of the country, as he would gladly have seen me at Wotton, and he succeeded in saying something about my books; and I hope I partly succeeded in showing [112] him that I was very sensible of his kindness in letting me see those relics. I cannot say whether or no I expressed it sufficiently. It is better, with such a man—or, indeed, with any man—to say too little than too much; and, in fact, it would have been indecorous in me to take too much of his kindness to my own share, Bennoch being likewise in question.

We had a cup of coffee, and then took our leave; Tupper accompanying us part way down the village-street, and bidding us an affectionate farewell. His son went with us to the railway station, and returned in the gathering dusk of the evening. They are very kind people, all of them, and I heartily wish them well. Bennoch and I recommenced our travels, and—changing, I think, from one railway to another—reached Tunbridge Wells at nine or ten in the evening. Bennoch went out to see some friends, and I went quietly to bed at a little past eleven. The next day, Sunday, was spent at Tunbridge Wells, which is famous for a chalybeate spring, and is a watering place of note, most healthfully situated, on a high, breezy site, with many pleasant walks in the neighborhood. Bennoch's friend was a Mr. Read, of Derby, with his three womankind, who are taking the waters [113] here. We dined with them at three °clock,—previous to which they showed us some of the curiosities and pleasant aspects of the place. They likewise kept us to tea; and as Mr. Read was going to France, in the morning, we invited the three ladies to breakfast with us at the Kentish Hotel. And so they did; but as they were not very remarkable people, though agreeable and kind, I shall pass over all that matter, and get on with my further adventures as fast as I can.

From Tunbridge Wells, we transported ourselves—again passing, I believe, from one railway to another—to Battle, the village in which Battle Abbey is situated. It is a large village, with many antique houses, and some new ones; and in its principal street, on one side, with a wide green space before it, you see the gray, embattled outer wall, and great square battlemented entrance-tower (with a turret at each corner) of the ancient Abbey. It is the perfect reality of a Gothic battlement and gateway, just as solid, square, and massive, as when it was first built, though hoary and venerable with the many intervening centuries. There are only two days in the week in which visitors are allowed entrance; and this was not one of them. Neverthe[114]less Bennoch was determined to get in, and wanted me to send Lady Webster my card with his own; but this I utterly refused, for the honor of America and my own honor; because I will not do anything to increase the reputation we already have, as a very forward people. Bennoch, however, called at a bookshop, on the other side of the street, near the gateway of the castle; and making friends (as he has a marvellous tact in doing) with the bookseller, the latter offered to take in his card to the housekeeper, and see if Lady Webster would not relax her rule in our favor. Meanwhile, we went into the old church of Battle, which was built in Norman times, though subsequently to the Abbey. As we entered the church-door, the bell rang for joy at the news of peace, which had just been announced by the London papers.

The church has been whitewashed in modern times, and does not look so venerable as it ought, with its arches and pillared aisles. In the chancel stands a marble tomb, heavy, rich, and elaborate, on the top of which lie the broken-nosed statues of Sir Anthony Browne and his lady, who were the lord and lady of Battle Abbey in Henry VIII's time. The knight is in armor, and the lady in stately garb, and (save for their broken noses) they [115] are in excellent preservation. The pavement of the chancel and aisles is all laid with tombstones; and on two or three of these there were engraved brasses, representing knights in armor and churchmen, with inscriptions in Latin. Some of them are very old. On the walls, too, there are various monuments, principally of dignitaries connected with the abbey. Two hatchments, in honor of persons recently dead, were likewise suspended in the chancel. The best pew in the church is of course that of the Webster family; it is curtained round, carpeted, furnished with chairs and footstools, and more resembles a parlor than a pew; especially as there is a fireplace in one of the pointed arch-ways, which, I suppose, has been bricked up in order to form it. On the opposite side of the aisle is the pew of some other magnate, containing a stove. The rest of the parishoners have to keep themselves warm with the fervor of their own piety. I have forgotten what else was interesting; except that we were shown a stone coffin, recently dug up, in which was hollowed a place for the head of the corpse.

Returning to the bookshop, we found that Lady Webster had sent her compliments, and would be very happy to have us see the Abbey. How thoroughly kind these English people [116] can be when they like; and how often they like to be so! We lost no time in ringing the bell, at the arched entrance, under the great tower, and were admitted by an old woman, who lives, I believe, in the thickness of the wall. She told us her room used to be the prison of the abbey, and under the great arch, she pointed to a projecting beam, where, she said, criminals used to be hanged. At two of the intersecting points of the arches which form the roof of the gateway, were carved faces of stone, said to represent King Harold, and William the Conqueror. The exterior wall, of which this tower is the gateway, extends far along the village-street, and encloses a very large space, within which stands the mansion, quite secluded from unauthorized visitors, or even from the sight of those without—unless it be at very distant eye-shot. We rang at the principal door of the edifice, (it is under a deep arch, in the Norman style, but of modern date,) and a footman let us in, and then delivered us over to a respectable old lady in black. She was a Frenchwoman by birth, but had been very long in the service of the family, and spoke English almost without an accent; her French blood being indicated only by her thin and withered aspect, and a greater gentility of manner than would have [117] been seen in an Englishwoman of similar station. She ushered us first into a grand and noble hall, the arched and carved oaken roof of which ascended into the gable; it was nearly sixty feet long, and its height equal to its length—as stately a hall, I should imagine, as is anywhere to be found in a private mansion. It was lighted, at one end, by a great window, beneath which, occupying the whole breadth of the hall, hung a vast picture of the Battle of Hastings; and whether a good picture or no, it was a rich adornment to the hall. The walls were wainscoated [sic] high upward with oak; they were almost covered with noble pictures of ancestry, and of kings and great men, and beautiful women; there were trophies of armor hung aloft; and two armed figures, one in brass mail, the other in bright steel, stood on a raised dais, underneath the great picture. At the end of the hall opposite the picture, a third of the way up toward the roof, was a gallery. All these things, that I have enumerated, were perfect and beautiful, without rust, untouched by decay or injury of any kind; but yet they seemed to belong to a past age, and were mellowed, softened, not gaudy in their splendor, a little dimmed with [118] time, toned down into a venerable magnificence. Of all domestic things that I have seen in England, it satisfied me most.

Then the Frenchwoman (who, perhaps, may have been the housekeeper, but I should rather doubt whether she was of that dignity) showed us into various rooms and offices, most of which were contrived out of the old Abbey-cloisters, and the arched and vaulted cells and apartments, in which the monks used to live. If any house be haunted, I should suppose this might be. If any church-property bring a curse with it, as people say, I do not see how the owners of Battle Abbey can escape it, burrowing, as they have, right into these holy precincts, and laying their kitchen-hearth with the stones of overthrown altars. The Abbey was first granted, I believe, to Sir Anthony Browne, whom I saw asleep with his lady in the church. It was his first wife. I wish it had been his second; for she was Surrey's Geraldine. The posterity of Sir Anthony kept the place till 1719, and then sold it to the Websters, a family of baronets, who are still the owners and occupants. The present proprietor is Sir Augustus [Godfrey] Webster, whose mother is the lady who so kindly let us into the Abbey.

Mr. Bennoch gave the nice old French lady half-a-[119]crown (I should not have dared to offer less than ten shillings) and we next went round among the ruined portions of the Abbey, under the gardener's guidance. We saw two ivied towers, insulated from all other ruins; and an old refectory, open to the sky, and a vaulted crypt, supported by pillars; and we saw, too, the foundation and scanty remains of a chapel, which had been long buried out of sight of man, and only dug up within present memory—about forty years ago. There had always been a tradition that this was the spot where Harold had planted his standard, and where his body was found after the battle; and the discovery of the ruined chapel confirmed this to be true. Well; I might have seen a great deal more, had there been time; and I have forgotten much of what I did see; but it is an exceedingly interesting place. There is an old avenue of yew-trees & I rather think they were ivy, though growing unsupported; which meet on top like a cloistered arch; and this is called the Monk's Walk. As we were retiring, the gardener suddenly stopt, as if he were alarmed, and motioned us to do the same, saying, "I believe it is my lady!" And so it was, a tall and stately old dame in black, trimming shrubs in the garden; but she bowed to us very graciously, we raised our hats, and [120] thus we met and parted without more ado. As we went through the arch of the entrance-tower, Bennoch gave the old female warder a shilling, and the gardner followed us to get half-a-crown, we having exhausted our silver.

We took a car and driver from the principal hotel in Battle, and drove off for Hastings about seven miles distant. Hastings is now a famous watering and sea-bathing place, and seems to be well sheltered from the winds, though open to the sea, which here stretches off towards France. We climbed a high and steep hill, terraced round its base with streets of modern lodging-houses, and crowned on its summit with the ruins of a castle, the foundation of which was anterior to the Conquest. This castle had no wall towards the sea, the precipice being too high and sheer to admit of attack on that side. I have quite exhausted my descriptive faculty, for the present; so shall say nothing of this old castle, which indeed (the remains being somewhat scanty and straggling) is chiefly picturesque and interesting from its bold position on such a headlong hill.

Clambering down the hill on another side from that of our ascent, we entered the town of Hastings, which [121] seems entirely modern, and made up of lodging-houses, shops, hotels, parades, and all such makings-up of watering-places generally. We took a delightful warm bath, washing off all our weariness and naughtiness, and coming out new men. Then we walked to St Leonard's, (a part of Hastings, I believe, but a mile or two from the castle) and there called at the lodgings of two friends of Bennoch. These were Mr. Martin, the author of Bon Gaultier's ballads, and his wife, the celebrated actress, Helen Faucit.³¹³ Mr. Martin is a barrister, a gentleman whose face and manners suited me at once; a simple, refined, sincere, not too demonstrative person. His wife, too, I liked; a tall, dark, even sallow, but fine and ladylike woman, with the simplest manners, that give no trouble at all, so must be perfect. With these two persons I felt myself, almost in a moment, on friendly terms, and in fine accord; and so I talked, I think, more than I have at any time since coming to London; and I am very sure that I made a good impression on them, the better that I only said what came out of my mind and fancy of its own accord. We took a pleasant lunch at their house; and then they walked with us to the Rail[122]way-station, and there they took leave of Bennoch affectionately, and of me hardly less so; for, in truth, we had grown to be almost friends in this very little while. And as we rattled away, I said to Bennoch earnestly—"What good people they are!"— and Bennoch smiled, as if he had known perfectly well that I should think and say so. And so we rushed onward to London; and I reached St. James's place between 9 and 10 °clock, after a very interesting tour, the record of which I wish I could have kept as we went along, writing each day's history before another day's adventures began.

APRIL 4ᵗʰ, FRIDAY.

ON Tuesday, I went to No. 14, Ludgate Hill, to dine with Bennoch at the Milton Club; a club recently founded for dissenters, nonconformists, and people whose ideas, religious or political, are not precisely in train with the establishment in church and state. I was shown into a large reading-room, well provided with periodicals and newspapers, and found two or three persons there; but Bennoch had not yet arrived. In a few moments, a tall gentleman with white hair came in—rather a fine and intelligent looking man—whom I guessed to be one of the party who were to meet me. He walked about, glancing [123] at the periodicals; and soon entered little Tupper, and, without seeing me, exchanged warm greetings with the white-haired gentleman. "I suppose," began Tupper, "you have come here to meet,—" Now, conscious that my name was going to be spoken, and not knowing but the excellent Tupper might say something which he would not quite like for me to overhear, I advanced at once, with outstretched hand, and saluted the man of Proverbs. He expressed great joy at the recognition, and immediately introduced me to Mr. S. C. Hall; whereupon, that venerable personage, in a tone audible to the whole reading-room, began to express his admiration for me as the first—yes; it was really so—the very first writer of the age. He said that he had written fifty thousand (I think that was the number) criticisms of books, but that, in all his vocation as critic, he had never felt such delight as in recording his judgment of my merits. In short, I cannot possibly overstate what he said, and, for very shame, prefer not to record it any further; and it was all said in the most fluent, irrepressible, and yet quiet way, with a volubility of fine phrases, and with a calm benignity of face. I have never met so smooth an Englishman as Mr. S. C. Hall.[314] He likewise presented me with a flower—a perfectly beautiful camellia— [124] which his wife had sent me; for it seems her admiration is of the same intensity as her husband's. Good Heavens! What is a man to do in a case like this?

Other guests of the dinner-party now came in, to several of whom I was introduced; and by-and-by entered Bennoch himself, and taking me by the arm, led the way to the dining-room. I dreaded lest he should place Mr. S. C. Hall in the next chair to mine, and besought him most earnestly to give me any other neighbor rather than he, for that I could not bear his incense. Bennoch admitted that Mr. S. C. Hall was a little too demonstrative—that it was his nature—but said that perhaps my tendency was rather too much in the contrary direction. However, he did put Dr. Charles Mackay[315] (author of the 'Good Time Coming') between me and Mr Hall; notwithstanding which the latter besmeared me with a great deal more butter and treacle, before the dinner was over. God forbid that I should be otherwise than grateful for any true appreciation; but was this true?—did he speak, because the fulness of his heart compelled him?— could he have said less, if he had tried to restrain himself?—for, if he could, he was utterly unpardonable for saying what he did. I verily believe that he had it all on his tongue, and nowhere else.

[125] The dining-room was pretty large and lofty, and there were sixteen guests at table, most of them authors, or people connected with .the press; so that the party represented a great deal of the working intellect of London, at this present day and moment—no very eminently distinguished persons, but the men whose plays, whose songs, whose articles, are just now in vogue. Mr. Tom Taylor[316] was one of the very few whose writings I had known anything about; he is a tall, slender, dark young man, not English looking, and wearing colored spectacles, so that I should readily have taken him for an American literary man. I did not have much opportunity of talking with him, nor with anybody else except Dr. Mackay, who seemed a shrewd, sensible man, with a certain slight acerbity of thought. He is editor of the Illustrated News; and the proprietor of that widely circulated journal, Mr. Herbert Ingram[317] (recently elected member of parliament) was likewise present, and sat on Bennoch's left.

It was a very good dinner, and abundance of wine, which Bennoch sent round faster than was for the next day's comfort of his guests. It is queer that I should thus far have quite forgotten William Howitt,[318] whose books I know better than those of any other person there. He is a silver[126]headed, stout, firm-looking, and rather puckery-faced old gentleman, whose temper, I should imagine, was not the very sweetest in the world. There is an abruptness—a kind of sub-acidity, if not bitterness—in his address; he seemed not to be, in short, so genial as I should have anticipated from his books; but his flavor was really delightful when contrasted with that of Mr. Hall, while they were both talking to me before dinner.

As soon as the cloth was removed, Bennoch, without rising from his chair, made a speech in honor of his eminent and distinguished guest, which illustrious person happened to be sitting in the self-same chair that I myself occupied. I have no sort of recollection of what he said, nor of what I said in reply; but I remember that both of us were cheered and applauded much more than we deserved. Then followed about fifty other speeches; for every single individual at table was called up, (as Tupper said, 'toasted and roasted') and, for my part, I was done entirely brown. Mr. S. C. Hall, from his inexhaustible resources, poured several more gallons of molasses on my head; and everybody said something kind, not a word or idea of which can I find in my memory. Certainly, if I never get any more soft soap in my life, I have had enough [127] of it for once. I made another little bit of a speech, too, in response to something that was said in reference to the present difficulties between England and America, and ended with (as a proof that I deemed war impossible) drinking success to the British Army, and calling on my friend Lieutenant Shaw, of the Aldershot Camp, to reply. I am afraid I must have said something very wrong; for the applause was vociferous, and I could hear them whispering about the table, "Good! Good." "Yes; he is a fine fellow!"—and other such ill-earned praises; and I took shame to myself, and held my tongue (publicly) for the rest of the evening. But, in such cases, something must be allowed to the excitement of the moment, to the wine, to the effect of kindness and good-will, so broadly and warmly displayed; and even a sincere man must not be held to speak as if he were under oath.

We separated, in a blessed state of contentment with one another, at about eleven; and (lest I should starve before morning) I went with Mr. Dallas[319] to take supper at his house in Park lane. Mr. D. is a pale young gentleman, of American aspect, being a West Indian by birth. He is one of the principal writers of editorials for the Times; and we were accompanied in the cab by another gentle[128]man, Mr. MacDonald,[320] who is connected with the management of the same paper. He wrote the letters from Scutari, which drew so much attention to the state of the hospitals. Mr. Dallas is the husband of Miss Glyn,[321] the actress; and when we reached his house, or lodgings, we found that she had just come home from the theatre, and was taking off her stage-dress. Anon, she came down to the drawing-room; a seemingly good, simple, and intelligent lady, not at all pretty, and, I should think, older than her husband. She was very kind to me, and told me that she had read one of my books—"The House of the Seven Gables"—thirteen years ago; which I thought remarkable, because I did not write it till eight or nine years afterwards.

The principal talk during supper (which consisted of Welsh rabbit, and biscuits, with champagne and soda-water) was about the Times; and the two contributors expressed vast admiration of a Mr. De Lain [Delane][322] (I never heard his name before, and do not know how to spell it; perhaps he is the husband of Mrs. Mousselin de Laines [mousseline de laine])[323] who has the chief editorial management of the paper. It is odd to find how little we outsiders know of men who really exercise a vast influence on affairs; for this [129] Mr. De Lain is certainly of far more importance in the world than a minister of state. He writes nothing himself; but the character of the Times seems to depend upon his intuitive, unerring judgment, and if ever he is absent from his post, even for a day or two, they say that the paper immediately shows it. In reply to my questions, they appeared to acknowledge that he was a man of expediency, but of a very high expediency, and that he gave the public the very best principles which it was capable of receiving. Perhaps it may be so; the Times' articles are certainly not written in so high a moral vein as might be wished; but what they lack in height, they gain in breadth. Every sensible man in England finds his own best common-sense there; and, on the whole, I think its influence is wholesome.

Our party broke up, I believe, soon after midnight; and Mr. & Mrs. Dallas (but the lady retains her own name, and I do not know whether I should call her Mrs. D) made me promise to come again on Saturday, to meet Mr. Charles Reade. In respect of my severe criticism of Mr. S. C. Hall's deportment, I ought to say that Bennoch strenuously affirms that he is a good and honest man, though with some absurdities of manner; [130] and he says that he has positively known both Hall and his wife to make greater personal sacrifices for the welfare of art and literature, than he has known any other persons to make. Douglas Jerrold, on the other hand, and Doctor Mackay, think him an arrant humbug; and I believe there is no doubt of his having been the original of Dickens's Mr. Pecksniff, in Martin Chuzzlewit.[324] What a wretched piece of injustice is this, if he is really a true man!

Apropos of public speaking, Doctor Mackay said that Sir Lytton Bulwer asked him—(I think the anecdote was personal to himself)—whether he felt his heart beat when he was going to speak? "Yes!" "Does your voice frighten you?" "Yes!" "Do all your ideas forsake you?" "Yes!" "Do you wish the floor to open and swallow you?" "Yes!" "Why then you'll make an orator!" Mackay told of Canning, too, how once, before rising to speak in the house of Commons, he bade his friend feel of his pulse, which was throbbing terrifically. "I know I shall make one of my best speeches," said Canning "because I'm in such an awful funk!" President Pierce, who has a great deal of oratorical power, is subject to similar horror and reluctance.

[131] APRIL 5th SATURDAY.

ON Thursday, at 6 °clock, I went to the Reform Club to dine with Doctor Mackay. The waiter admitted me into a great basement hall, with a tessellated, or mosaic, or somehow figured floor of stone, and lighted from a dome of lofty height. In a few minutes, Dr. Mackay appeared, and showed me about the edifice, which is very noble, and of a substantial magnificence that was most satisfactory to behold; no wood-work imitating better materials, but pillars and balustrades of marble, and everything what it purported to be. The reading-room is very large, and luxuriously comfortable, and contains a beautiful library; there are rooms and conveniences for every possible purpose; and whatever material for enjoyment a bachelor may need, or ought to have, he can surely find it here, and on such reasonable terms that a small income will do as much for him, as a far greater one on any other system. In a colonnade, on the first floor, surrounding the great basement hall, there are portraits of distinguished reformers, with blank niches for others yet to come. Joseph Hume, I believe, is destined to fill one of these blanks; but I remarked that the larger part of the portraits already hung up are of men of high rank; the Duke of Sussex, for instance, Lord Durham, Lord Grey,—and, indeed, I remember no com[132]moner. In one room, I saw on the wall the Fac-simile, so common in the United States, of our declaration of Independence.

Descending again to the basement-hall, an elderly gentleman came in, and was warmly welcomed by Doctor Mackay. He was a very short man, but with breadth enough, and a back excessively bent—bowed almost to deformity; very gray hair, and a face and expression of remarkable briskness and intelligence. His profile came out pretty boldly, and his eyes had the prominence that indicates, I believe, volubility of speech; nor did he fail to talk, from the instant of his appearance; and in the tone of his voice, and in his glance, and in the whole man, there was something racy—a flavor of the humorist. His step was that of an aged man, and he put his stick down very decidedly at every step; though, as he afterwards told us that he was only fifty-two, he need not yet have been infirm. But perhaps he has had the gout; his feet, however, are by no means swollen, but unusually small. Dr Mackay introduced him as Mr. Douglas Jerrold,[325] and we went into the coffee-room to get our dinner.

The coffee-room occupies one whole side of the edifice, and is provided with a great many tables, calcu[133]lated for three or four persons to dine at; and we sat down at one of these, and Doctor Mackay ordered some mulligatawney [*sic*] soup and a bottle of white French wine. The waiters in the coffee-room were very numerous, and most of them dressed in the livery of the club, comprising plush-breeches and white silk stockings; for these English reformers do not seem to include Republican simplicity of manners in their system. Neither, perhaps, is it anywise essential. After the soup, we had turbot, and by-and-by a bottle of Chateau Margaux, very delectable; and then some lambs' feet, delicately done, and some cutlets of I know not what peculiar type; and finally, a ptarmigan, which is of the same race of birds as the grouse, but feeds high up towards the summits of the Scotch mountains. Then, some cheese, and a bottle of Chambertin. It was a very pleasant dinner, and my companions were both very agreeable men; both taking a shrewd, satirical, yet not ill-natured view of life and people; and as for Mr. Douglas Jerrold he often reminded me of Ellery Channing, in the richer veins of the latter, both by his face and expression, and by a tincture of something at once wise and humorously absurd in what he said. But I think he has a kinder, more genial, wholesomer nature than Ellery; and under a very thin crust of [134] outward acerbity, I grew sensible of a very warm heart, and even of much simplicity of character in this man, born in London, and accustomed always to London life.

I wish I had any faculty whatever of remembering what people say; but, though I appreciate anything good, at the moment, it never stays in my memory; nor do I think, in fact, that anything definite, rounded, pointed, separable, and transferrable [sic] from the general lump of conversation, was said by anybody. I recollect that they laughed at Mr. S. C. Hall, and at his shedding a tear into a Scottish river, on occasion of some literary festival. The great Tupper too (when I told them that the Queen gave the Proverbial Philosophy to each of her children, as they arrived at a proper age) came in for a smile; Douglas Jerrold intimating that he thought Solomon might have answered as good a purpose. They spoke approvingly of Bulwer, as valuing his literary position, and holding himself one of the brotherhood of authors, and not so approvingly of Charles Dickens, who, born a plebeian, aspires to aristocratic society. But I said that it was easy to condescend, and that Bulwer knew he could not put off his rank, and that he would have all the advantages of it in spite of his authorship. We talked about the position of men of letters in England; and they said that [135] the aristocracy hated, and despised, and feared them; and I asked why it was that literary men, having really so much power in their hands, were content to live unrecognized in the state. Douglas Jerrold talked of Thackeray and his success in America, and said that he himself purposed going, and had been invited thither to lecture. I asked Douglas Jerrold whether it was pleasant to a writer of plays to see them performed; and he said it was intolerable, the presentation of the author's idea being so imperfect; and Doctor Mackay observed that it was excruciating to hear one of his own songs sung. Jerrold spoke of the Duke of Devonshire with great warmth, as a true, honest, simple, most kind hearted man, from whom he himself had received great courtesies and kindnesses, (not, as I understood, in the way of patronage, or essential favors;) and I (Heaven forgive me!) queried within myself, whether this English reforming author would have been quite so sensible of the Duke's excellence, if he had not been a Duke. But, indeed, a nobleman, who is at the same time a true and whole-hearted man, feeling his brotherhood with men, does really deserve some credit for it. In the course of the evening, Jerrold spoke with high appreciation of Emerson; and of Longfellow, whose Hiawatha he considered a wonderful per[136]formance; and of Lowell, whose "Fable for the Critics," he especially admired.

I mentioned Thoreau, and proposed to send his works to Dr. Mackay, who, being connected with the Illustrated News, and otherwise a critic, might be inclined to draw attention to them. Douglas Jerrold asked why he should not have them, too. I hesitated a little; but as he pressed me, and would have an answer, I said that I did not feel quite so sure of his kindly judgment on Thoreau's books; and it so chanced that I used the word "acrid," for lack of a better, in endeavoring to express my idea of Jerrold's way of looking at men and books. It was not quite what I meant; but, in fact, he often *is* acrid, and has written pages and volumes of acridity, though, no doubt, with an honest purpose, and from a manly disgust at the cant and humbug of the world. Jerrold said no more, and I went on talking with Dr. Mackay; but, in a moment or two, I became aware that something had gone wrong, and looking at Douglas Jerrold, there was an expression of pain and emotion in his face. By this time, we had begun upon a second bottle of Burgundy (Clos Vougeot, the best the club could produce, and far richer than the Chambertin,) and that warm and potent wine may have had something to do with [137] the depth and vivacity of Mr. Jerrold's feelings. But he was indeed greatly hurt by that little word "acrid"; he knew, he said, that the world considered him a sour, bitter, ill-natured man; but that such a man as I should have the same opinion, was almost more than he could bear. As he spoke, he threw out his arms, sank back in his seat, and I was really a little apprehensive of his actual dissolution into tears. Hereupon, I spoke, as was good need, and (though, as usual, I have forgotten everything I said) I am quite sure it was to the purpose, and went to this good fellow's heart, as it came warmly from my own. I do remember saying that I felt him to be as genial as the glass of Burgundy which I held in my hand; and I think that touched the very rightest spot, for he smiled, and said he was afraid the Burgundy was better than he, but yet was comforted. Dr. Mackay said that he himself likewise had a reputation for bitterness; and I assured them, if I might venture to join myself in the brotherhood of two such men, that I was considered a very ill-natured person by many people in my own country. Douglas Jerrold said he was glad of it.

We were now in sweetest harmony; and Jerrold spoke more than it would become me to say in praise of [138] my own books, which he said he admired, and that he found the man more admirable than his books. I hope so, certainly. The Clos Vougeot, alas! being now exhausted, we went to the Haymarket Theatre, where Douglas Jerrold is on the free list; and after seeing a ballet by some Spanish Dancers, we separated, and betook ourselves, I suppose, to our several homes or lodgings. I like Douglas Jerrold very much.[326]

APRIL 8th TUESDAY.

ON Saturday evening, at ten °clock, I went to a supper-party at Mr. Dallas's (husband of Miss Glyn) and there met five or six people—Mr. Faed,[327] a young and distinguished artist; Dr Elliotson,[328] a dark, sombre, taciturn, powerful-looking man, with coal-black hair, and a beard as black, fringing round his face; Mr. Charles Reade[329] (author of Christie Johnstone, and other novels, and many plays) a tall man, rising of thirty, fair haired, in good flesh, and not of an especially intellectual aspect, but of agreeable talk and demeanor. Miss Glyn was not there when I arrived, but soon came in, hot and wearied from the stage; and when she shook hands with me, her own was moist, and gave me a strong idea of how exhausting stage-exertions are.[330] She is not pretty at all, either in face or figure, which is broad and full, with a short [139] neck; but I can conceive that she may have a good deal of power in her acting. She is more haunted by the trick, tone, and glance of the actress than either of the other distinguished ladies whom I have met; but I should say that she still retains a native goodness and simplicity. Sitting next her at supper, she alluded to her statement, a few evenings ago, that she had read the Seven Gables thirteen years since, and inquired if she had not made a little mistake. I said that she had, but that I felt much flattered by it, because it could only have arisen from the book having made itself so much a part of the permanent furniture of her mind, that she could not tell when she first became acquainted with it. She laughed, and seemed a little confused, as well she might. I went home at about ½ past 12.

On Sunday morning, at ten and a quarter, I went to the Waterloo Station, and there meeting Bennoch and Dr. Mackay, took the rail for Woking, where we found Mr. S. C. Hall's carriage waiting to convey us to Addlestone, about five miles off. On arriving, we found that Mr. and Mrs. Hall had not yet returned from Church. Their place (which they call Firfield) is an exceedingly pretty one, and arranged in very good taste. The house is not [140] large, but is filled, in every room, with fine engravings, statuettes, ingenious prettinesses, or beautifulnesses, in the way of flower-stands, cabinets, and things that seem to have flowered naturally out of the characters of the occupants. There is a conservatory connected with the drawing-room, and enriched with beautiful plants, one, at least, of which, has a certain interest, as being the plant on which Coleridge's eyes were fixed, when he died. This Conservatory is likewise beautified with several very fine casts of statues by modern sculptors, among which was the Greek Slave of Powers, which my English friends criticised as being too thin and meagre; but I defended it as in accordance with American ideas of feminine beauty. From the Conservatory we passed into the garden, but did not minutely examine it, knowing that Mr. Hall would wish to lead us through it in person. So, in the meantime, we took a walk in the neighborhood, over styles [sic], and along by-paths, for two or three miles, till we reached the old village of Chertsey. In one of its streets stands an ancient house, gabled, and with the second story projecting over the first, and bearing an inscription to the purport that the poet Cowley had once resided, and, I think, [141] died, here. Thence we passed on till we reached a bridge over the Thames, which, at this point (about twenty-five miles from London) is a narrow river, but looks clean and pure, and unconscious what abominations the city-sewers will pour into it anon. We were caught in two or three showers in the course of our walk, but got back to Firfield without being very much wetted.

Our host and hostess had by this time returned from Church; and Mrs. Hall came frankly and heartily to the door to greet us, scolding us for having got wet. She is a dame of ripe age, midway beyond fifty, but is still an agreeable object to look at, and must once have possessed beauty. Her husband loves beautiful things, and chose his wife, no doubt, on the same principle—in part, at least—that guides him in other matters. She is tall, and large, and rotund—but not too rotund—and was dressed in black, and is a good figure of a woman, not shapeless, and massive of flesh, as so many English dames, at her time of life, are apt to be. I liked her simple, easy, gentle, quiet, kindly manners;—and liked her husband, too, a great deal better than on our first acquaintance. I believe that Dickens has greatly wronged him in that odious character of Peck[142]sniff. The man has his ridiculous side; and I cannot exactly judge what the depth of his heart may be; it may possibly be all surface, for aught I know; but still I do not think him insincere, even if it be all surface. He has a wide and quick sympathy, and expresses it freely—too freely, perhaps—but yet the world is the better for him.

The shower being now over, we went out upon the beautiful lawn, before his house, where there are a good many trees, of various kinds, many of which have been set out by persons of great or small (generally rather moderate) distinction, and are labelled with their names. Thomas Moore's name was appended to one; Maria Edgeworth's to another; likewise, Fredrika Bremer's; Jenny Lind's; also, Grace Greenwood's, and I know not who besides. This is really a pleasant method of enriching one's grounds with memorials of friends; nor is there any harm (though it seems a little absurd) in making a shrubbery of celebrities. Three holes were already dug, and three new trees lay ready to be planted; and for me there was a sumach to plant—a tree I never liked; but Mr. Hall said that they had tried to dig up a hawthorn, but found it cling too fast to the soil. So, [143] since better might not be, (and telling Mr Hall that I supposed I should have a right to hang myself on this tree whenever I chose) I seized a spade, and speedily shoveled in a great deal of dirt; and there stands my sumach, an object of interest to posterity. Bennoch, also, and Dr. Mackay, set out their trees; and, indeed, it was, in some sense, a joint affair, for the rest of the party held up each tree, while its godfather shovelled in the earth; but, after all, the gardener had more to do with it than we. After this important business was over (or before, for I have forgotten which) Mr. Hall led us about his grounds, which are very nicely planned and ordered; and all this he has bought, and built, and laid out, from the profits of his own and his wife's literary exertions.

We dined early, and had a very pleasant meal; and after the cloth was removed, Mr. S. C. Hall was graciously pleased to drink my health, following it with an outrageously long tribute to my genius—which I did not particularly listen to, and only cared about it because it was necessary to say something in reply. So I answered briefly; and one half of my short speech, in all probability, was foolish, and the other half (God forgive me!) false. [144] After the ladies (there were three of them, one being a girl of seventeen, with rich auburn hair the adopted daughter of the Halls) had retired, Dr. Mackay, having been toasted himself, proposed Mrs. Hall's health. Hereupon, her husband returned thanks in another very long speech, enlarging upon her merits, giving an account of their courtship and engagement, and early marriage, and subsequent happiness, and incidentally treating upon the excellence of Mrs. Hall's mother, who had lived with them upwards of thirty years, and was only recently deceased. If there were any good in him, he said, he owed it to these two women; and there certainly is good, mixed up with a vast heap of nonsense and flummery.

I did not have a great deal of conversation with Mrs. Hall, but enough to make me think her a genuine and good woman, unspoilt by a literary career, and retaining more sentiment (for I will not call it sentimentalism) than most girls keep beyond seventeen. She told me that it had been the dream of her life to see Longfellow and myself! Good Heavens! What an object to live for! Well; her dream is half-accomplished now; and as they say Longfellow is coming over, this summer, the remainder may soon be rounded out. On taking leave, our kind hosts [145] presented me with some beautiful flowers, and with three volumes of a work, by themselves, on Ireland; and Dr. Mackay was favored also with some flowers, and a plant in a pot, which I am afraid he wished had been given to the devil rather than himself; and Bennoch, too, had his hands full of flowers; and we went on our way, rejoicing, and laughing at Mr. S. C. Hall, and acknowledging that his wife is truly a nice woman. God bless her; for I think so.

APRIL 13th SUNDAY.

I REMEMBER nothing particular that happened the day after our visit to Firfield, until about five °clock, when I went to Bennoch's; for he was to accompany me to dine at the Mansion-House, in compliance with the Lord Mayor's invitation. We went thither at ½ past six, and were received in a great entrance-hall by some of the most gorgeously dressed footmen I ever saw. Their livery is blue and buff, and they look something like American revolutionary generals, only far more splendid. Two officers of his Lordship's household were busy in assigning to the guests the seats that they were to occupy in the dining-room; a list of all the guests and their places lying on the table before them. These two officers were dressed in scarlet coats, with epaulets, and looked precisely like military men. In fact [146] there is a great deal of state and ceremony in this palace of the city-king; and the Mansion House itself (which I believe was built in Queen Anne's time) is worthy of its inhabitant, were he really the greatest man of this great city. After finding out where our places were to be, we passed into the reception-room; and our names being announced, the Lord Mayor[331] met me and shook hands with me, close by the door; introducing me also to the Lady Mayoress, whom (as she will never hear what I think of her) I shall be bold to call a short and ugly old Jewess. As for his lordship, he is a tall, hard-looking, white-headed old Jew, of plain deportment, but rather hearty than otherwise in his address. He said little to me, except that I must hold myself in readiness to respond to a toast which he meant to give; and though I hinted that I would much rather be spared, he showed no signs of mercy.

There are two reception-rooms, or one large one, connected by folding-doors; and, though in an old style, they are very handsome apartments, with carved cielings [sic] and walls, and at each end a magnificent fire-place of marble, ornamented with wreaths of flowers and foliage, and other sculpture. Both rooms were crowded with guests, principally, I suppose, city-magnates with their wives or daughters; and, [147] however it may have happened, I must own that I saw here more comeliness of womankind than I have before seen in England. I soon met with Mr. S. C. Hall, who introduced me to all the noted people he knew. The only one I had heard of before was the Rev. Mr. Gleig,[332] Chaplain General of the Army; a tall, rather stern-looking, military man of God, in clerical attire. Mrs. Hall was likewise present, and it was arranged that we were to sit together. The company consisted of about three hundred; and at a given signal, we all found our way into an immense hall (called, I know not why, the Egyptian Hall, though its architecture is classic) brilliantly lighted, and presenting quite a splendid spectacle, when all the tables were full. A band (but Mrs Hall said the music was very bad) played inspiringly; and truly there were all the circumstances and accompaniments of a stately feast. There was a cross-table, and two others (at one of which I sat) extending along the length of the hall.

The first thing produced, after a blessing had been asked, was, of course, turtle-soup, of which everybody was allowed to help themselves twice, or, no doubt, as many times as they chose, and could get it. Being not very fond of turtle-soup, I took it only once, although it must be supposed to [be] better (such a civic dainty as this) at the Lord Mayor's table than [148] anywhere else. With the soup was taken a small sip of rum-punch, in a very little tumbler. The rest of the dinner was catalogued upon a bill of fare, printed within a border of gold and green on delicate white paper, and was very good, and of variety enough, though not better than those given by the Mayors of Liverpool, or perhaps, those [by] the landlords of American Hotels. I do not remember eating anything but some red mullets, some potted ptarmigan, and some stewed mushrooms; and I have often enjoyed a mutton-chop (or, in my vegetable days, some roasted potatoes and salt) as much as I did these delicacies. The dishes were all put upon the table, and helped by guests at the table; an inconvenient arrangement in so great a party. There were decanters of sherry, from which the guests helped themselves, on the table; and the servants came round pretty frequently with champagne and hock. The band kept playing, at intervals, all the time; and, when not talking with Mrs. Hall, or my neighbor on the other side (some city dignitary) my eyes were mostly drawn to a young lady who sat nearly opposite me, across the table. She was, I suppose, dark, and yet not dark, but rather seemed to be of pure white marble, yet not white; but the purest and finest complexion, (without a shade of color in it, yet anything but sallow or sickly) that I ever beheld. Her hair was a wonder-[149]ful deep, raven black, black as night, black as death; *not* raven black, for that has a shiny gloss, and her's [*sic*] had not; but it was hair never to be painted, nor described—wonderful hair, Jewish hair. Her nose had a beautiful outline, though I could see that it was Jewish too; and that, and all her features, were so fine that sculpture seemed a despicable art beside her; and certainly my pen is good for nothing. If any likeness of her could be given, it must be by sculpture, not painting. She was slender, and youthful, but yet had a stately and cold, though soft and womanly grace; and, looking at her, I saw what were the wives of the old patriarchs, in their maiden or early married days—what Rachel was, when Jacob wooed her seven years, and seven more—what Judith was; for, womanly as she looked, I doubt not she could have slain a man, in a good cause—what Bathsheba was; only she seemed to have no sin in her— perhaps what Eve was, though one could hardly think her weak enough to eat the apple. I never should have thought of touching her, nor desired to touch her; for, whether owing to distinctness of race, my sense that she was a Jewess, or whatever else, I felt a sort of repugnance, simultaneously with my perception that she was an admirable creature. But, at the right hand of this miraculous Jewess,[333] there sat the very Jew of Jews; the distilled essence of all the Jews that have [150] that have [*sic*] been born since Jacob's time; he was Judas Iscariot; he was the Wandering Jew; he was the worst, and at the same time, the truest type of his race, and contained within himself, I have no doubt, every old prophet and every old clothesman, that ever the tribes pro- duced; and he must have been circumcised as much [as] ten times over. I never beheld anything so ugly and disagreeable, and preposterous, and laughable, as the outline of his profile; it was so hideously Jewish, and so cruel, and so keen; and he had such an immense beard that you could see no trace of a mouth, until he opened it to speak, or to eat his dinner,—and then, indeed, you were aware of a cave, in this density of beard. And yet his manners and aspect, in spite of all, were those of a man of the world, and a gentleman. Well; it is as hard to give an idea of this ugly Jew, as of the beautiful Jewess. He was the Lord Mayor's brother, and an elderly man, though he looked in his prime, with his wig and dyed beard; and Rachel, or Judith, or whatever her name be, was his wife! I rejoiced exceedingly in this Shylock, this Iscariot; for the sight of him justified me in the repugnance I have always felt towards his race.

The dishes being removed, grace was said; and then an official personage, behind the Lord Mayor's chair, made a proclamation. I ought to have mentioned that there stood a man in a helmet, in [151] accordance with an ancient custom of the city, behind his lordship's chair, but it was not he who now made the proclamation. In the first place, he enumerated the names of the principal guests, comprising two or three noblemen, some baronets, members of parliament, aldermen, and other of the illustrious, (among whom was enrolled a certain gentleman of consular rank) and ended in some such way as this—"and all others, gentlemen and ladies, here present, the Lord Mayor drinks to you all in a Loving Cup, and sends it round among you." And forthwith the Loving Cup (or rather two of them, on either side of the table) came slowly down, with all the antique ceremony. The fashion of it is thus;—the Lord Mayor presents the covered cup to the guest at his elbow, standing up, in order that the guest should remove the cover; his lordship then drinks, the guest replaces the cover, takes the cup into his own hands, and presents it to his next neighbor, for the cover to be again removed, so that he may take his own draught. His next neighbor goes through the same form with the person below him; and thus the whole company are finally interlinked in one long chain of love. When the cup came to me, I found it to be an old and richly ornamented goblet of silver, capable of containing about a quart of wine; and, indeed, there was nearly that quantity in it, for I doubt whether the guests do much [152] more than make a pretense of drinking; so that the goblets never need replenishing. I drank a sip, however, being curious to know what the liquor was, and found it to be claret, spiced and sweetened, and hardly preferable to sweetened water.

After this, the toasts began, and there were several very poor speeches; one from the young Earl of Grannard [Granard], his maiden speech, and promising nothing very wonderful in future; and I forget who else spoke, but all as dull as could well be. Before each toast, the man behind the Lord Mayor made proclamation that his Lordship was going to give a toast; after the toast, and his Lordship's accompanying remarks, the band played an appropriate tune; then the herald, or whatever he was, proclaimed that such a person was about to respond to the Lord Mayor's toast and speech; then another air, I think, from the band; and then the doomed person got up and proceeded to make a fool of himself. Now I had by no means forgotten his lordship's threat of calling me up, and conscious that, if toasted at all, it would be discourteous not to do it early in the evening, I bethought me, in some trepidation, what could be said in reply; and this was rather difficult, because I did not know what the drift of the [153] Lord Mayor's remarks might be. However, I communicated my dilemma to Mr. S. C. Hall,[334] who sat next his wife; and if I had sought the whole world over, I could not have found a better artist in whip-syllabub and flummery; and, without an instant's hesitation, he suggested a whole rivulet of lukewarm stuff, which I saw would be sufficiently to the purpose, if I could but remember it. Really, he is one of the kindest and best men in the world, and I felt grateful to him in my heart.

Well; in due time, the Lord Mayor began some remarks which I quickly perceived to be drifting in my direction; and after paying me some high compliments in reference to my works (I don't believe he ever read a word of them) he drank prosperity to my country, and my own health, which was received with great applause. Then, I suppose, the band played "Hail Columbia," (but it might have been 'God Save the Queen,' without my being the wiser) the herald proclaimed that I was going to respond, and I rose amid much cheering, so screwed up to the point that I did not care what happened next. The Lord Mayor might have fired a pistol, instead of a speech, at me, and I should not have flinched. As a starting point, I took some of Mr. Hall's flummery, and clothing it in my own words, it really did very well indeed; [154] and this I joined and interwove with two or three points of my own, and thus tinkered up and amalgamated a very tolerable little speech, which was much helped along by the cheers that broke in between the sentences. Certainly, there was a very kind feeling in the audience; and it is wonderful how conscious the speaker is of sympathy, and how it warms and animates him. When I sat down, Bennoch, and Mr. and Mrs. Hall were loud in their praises, and so were many other persons, in the course of the evening; and I was glad to have got out of the scrape so well. But one quickly cools down after these efforts; and I soon felt—indeed, I had never ceased to feel—that I, like the other orators of the evening, had made a fool of myself, and that it is altogether a ridiculous custom to talk in one's cups. Nor has this feeling been lessened, since I have read various reports[335] of what I said, none of them correct, all obliterating the best points, and all exaggerating the sentiment of international kindness, which I myself had too strongly expressed. This speech was sent down to Liverpool by electric telegraph, posted in the exchange, and has since been printed all over the kingdom; and, in the shape in which it appears before the public, it is nothing short of ridiculous. But it is an absurd world; so let [155] this absurdity pass with the rest. I should not care for England; but America will read it too.

Shortly after this great event of the evening, the ladies retired from table. There were a good many more toasts and speechifyings among the gentlemen; but I think we all went to get our coffee by eleven °clock, or thereabouts. Losing Bennoch and my other acquaintances, in the crowd, I took my departure; and not being able to find a cab, rode homeward as far as Charing Cross in an omnibus.[336]

I think nothing further of interest took place, until two °clock the next day, when I went to lunch with Bennoch, and afterwards accompanied him to one of the government offices in Downing-street. He went thither, not on official business, but on a matter connected with a monument to Miss Mitford, in which Mr. Harness (a clergyman, and some sort of a government-clerk) is interested. I gathered from their conversation that there is no great enthusiasm about the monumental affair, among the British public. It surprised me to hear allusions indicating that Miss Mitford was not the invariably amiable person that her writings would suggest; but the whole drift of what they said tended, nevertheless, towards the idea that she was an excellent and generous person, loved most by those who knew her best.

[156] From Downing-street, we crossed over and entered Westminster Hall, and passed through it, and up the flights of steps at its further end, and along the avenue of statues into the vestibule of the House of Commons. It was now somewhat past five; and we stood at the inner entrance of the House to see the members pass in, Bennoch pointing out to me the distinguished ones. I was not much impressed with the appearance of the members generally; they seemed to me rather shabbier than English gentlemen generally, and I saw, or fancied, in many of them, a certain self-importance, as they passed into the interior, betokening them to be very full of their dignity. Some of them looked more American—more like American politicians—than most Englishmen do. There was now and then a gray-headed country-gentleman, the very type of stupidity; and two or three city-members came up and spoke to Bennoch, and showed themselves quite as dull, in their aldermanic way, as the country squires. I suppose there are not ten men in the entire six hundred, who would be missed. Bennoch pointed out Lord John Russell; a little, very short, elderly gentleman, in a brown coat, and so large a hat—not large of brim, but large like a peck measure—that I saw really no face beneath it. By and by, came a rather tall, slender person, in a black frock, buttoned up, and black [157] pantaloons, taking long steps, but, I thought, rather feebly or listlessly. His shoulders were round; or else he had a habitual stoop in them. He had a prominent nose, a thin face, and a sallow, very sallow, complexion, and was a very unwholesome looking person; and had I seen him in America, I should have taken him for a hard-worked editor of a newspaper, weary and worn with night-work and want of exercise; shrivelled, and withered, before his time. It was Disraeli, and I never saw any other Englishman look in the least like him; though, in America, his appearance would not attract notice, as being unusual. I do not remember any other noteworthy person whom we saw enter; in fact, the house had already been some time in session, and most of the members were in their places.

We were to dine in the refectory of the house, with Mr. Ingram, the new member for Boston; and, meanwhile, Bennoch obtained admittance for us into the speaker's gallery, whence we had a view of the members, and could hear what was going on. A Mr. Muntz was speaking on the Income Tax, and he was followed by Sir George Cornewall Lewis, and others; but it was all very uninteresting, without the slightest animation, or attempt at oratory— which indeed would have been quite out of place. We saw Lord Palmerston, but at too great a distance to distinguish anything but a gray head. The House had daylight in it [158] when we entered, and for some time afterwards; but, by and by the roof, which I had taken to be a solid and opaque cieling [sic], suddenly brightened, and showed itself to be transparent; a vast expanse of tinted and figured glass, through which came down a great, mild radiance upon the members below. The character of the debate, however, did not grow more luminous or vivacious; so we went down into the vestibule, and there waited for Mr. Ingram, who soon came and led us into the refectory. It was very much like the coffee-room of a club. The strict rule forbids the entrance of any but members of parliament; but it seems to be winked at, although there is another room, opening beyond this, where the law of exclusion is strictly enforced.

Mr. Ingram's dinner was good—not remarkably so, but good enough—a soup, some turbot or salmon, some cutlets, and I know not what else; and a bottle of claret, a bottle of sherry, and a bottle of port; for, as he said, he did not wish to be stingy. Mr. Ingram is a self-made man, and a strong instance of the difference between the Englishman and the American, when self-made, and without early education. He is no more a gentleman now, than when he began life, not a whit more refined, either outwardly or inwardly; while the American would have been, after the same [159] experience, in no whit distinguishable, outwardly, and perhaps as refined within, as nine-tenths of the gentlemen born, in the House of Commons. And, besides, an American comes naturally to any distinctions to which success in life may bring him; he takes them as if they were his proper inheritance, and in no wise to be wondered at. Mr. Ingram, on the other hand, took evidently a childish delight in his position, and felt a childish wonder in having arrived at it; nor did it seem real to him, after all. He made his first fortunes, I believe, by inventing a quack-pill, and he established the Illustrated News, as a medium of advertising this pill. The pill succeeded marvellously, and the Illustrated News had likewise an independent success of its own; so that he had recently been offered eighty-thousand pounds for it. Mr. Ingram is a man of liberal politics, of a kindly nature, of the homeliest personal appearance and manners. He will have no shadow of influence in the House of Commons, beyond his own vote; and, to say the truth, I was a little ashamed of being entertained by such a very vulgar man, especially as I was recognized by Mr. Bramley-Moore, and some other Liverpool people. This was really snobbish in me.

While we were drinking our wine, we again saw Disraeli, another adventurer, who has risen from the people by modes per[160]haps as quackish as those of Mr. Ingram. He came, and stood near our table, looking at the bill of fare, and then sat down on the opposite side of the room, with another gentleman, and ate his dinner. He don't [sic] look as if he had a healthy appetite. Bennoch says that he makes himself up with great care, and spends a long time plucking the white hairs from among his sable locks. He is said to be poor; and though he had property with his wife, it is all gone. The story of his marriage (which Bennoch told me, but which I do not remember well enough to record it) does him much credit; and, indeed, I am inclined to like Disraeli, as a man who has made his own place good among a hostile aristocracy, and leads instead of following them.

From the House of Commons we went to Albert Smith's exhibition, or lecture, of the ascent of Mont Blanc, to which Bennoch had orders. It was very amusing, and in some degree instructive. We remained in the saloon, at the conclusion of the lecture; and when the audience had dispersed, Mr. Albert Smith made his appearance, and we fraternized. He is a gentleman of about forty, of the Dickens school, a little flashy and rowdyish, but a good-hearted man, and an agreeable companion. We went—Bennoch, Albert Smith, and I—first to an oyster-shop, and afterwards to Evans's supper-rooms, [161] where there was a crowded audience, drinking various liquors, smoking, eating Welsh rabbits, and listening to songs and other entertainments. I was introduced to various persons—among others to the musical critic of the Times, and to Mr. Edwin [Frederick] Lawrence, author of the Life of Fielding, and who seems to be a barrister in Gray's Inn, or the Temple. But the queerest introduction was that of the Superintendent of the rooms a Mr. Green, who expressed himself in the highest degree honored by my presence, and said if he could only have Emerson, likewise, and Channing (the deceased Doctor, I presume), and Longfellow, the dream of his life would be fulfilled. I got away from this place, between one and two °clock. It is a very good place to see London life in, and I mean, sometime or other, to go there again—perhaps with Longfellow.[337]

Nothing of moment happened the next day; at least, not till two °clock, when I went with Mr. Bowman to Birch's (it is not Birch's now, but this was the name of the original founder, who became an alderman, and has long been in glory) eating-house, for a basin of turtle-soup. It was very rich, very good, better than we had at the Lord Mayor's, and the best I ever ate. The price, too, was good—three and six-pence for a moderate soup-plate full. It was accompanied with [162] an exquisite glass of punch, as bright and clear as liquid gold; and soup and punch together refreshed me wonderfully.

In the evening—or on the edge of evening, about half past six—Mr. J. B. Davies (formerly our Secretary of Legation) called to take me to dine at Mr. Henry Stevens's,[338] at Camden Town. Mr. Stevens calls his residence Vermont House; but it hardly has a claim to any separate title, being one of the centre houses of a block. I forget whether I mentioned his calling on me. He is a Vermonter, a graduate of Yale College, who has been here several years, and has established a sort of book-brokerage, buying libraries for those who want them, and rare works and editions for American collectors. His business naturally brings him into relations with literary people; and he is himself a kindly and pleasant man. On our arrival, we found the junior Mr. Dallas and one of his sisters already there; and soon came a Mr. Peabody, who, if I mistake not, is one of the Salem Peabodies, a son of Frank, and has some sort of connection with the present eminent London Peabody. At any rate, he is a very sensible, well instructed, and widely and long-travelled man. Tom Taylor was also expected; but, owing to some accident or mistake, he

did not come for above an hour, all which time our host waited; though, methinks, a truer sense of [163] what was due to his guests and himself would
have made him order dinner within the first fifteen minutes. But Mr. Tom
Taylor—a wit, a satirist, and a famous diner-out—is too formidable and too
valuable a personage to be treated cavalierly.

In the interim, Mr. Stevens showed us some rare old books which he has
in his private collection; a black-letter edition of Chaucer, and other specimens
of the early English printers; and I was impressed, as I have often been, with
the idea that we have made few, if any, improvements in the art of printing,
though we have greatly facilitated the mode of it. He showed us Dryden's
translation of Virgil, with Dr. Johnson's autograph in it; and a large collection
of Bibles, of all dates, Church Bibles, family Bibles, of the common translation, and elder ones. He says he has written, or is writing, a history of the
Bible—as a printed work, I presume. Many of these Bibles had, no doubt, been
in actual and daily use from generation to generation; but they were now
all splendidly bound, and were likewise very clean and smooth;—in fact,
every leaf had been cleansed by a delicate process, a part of which consisted
in soaking the whole work in a tub of water, during several days. Mr. Stevens
is likewise rich in manuscripts, having a Spanish Document with the signature of the son of Columbus; a whole [164] little volume in Franklin's handwriting, being the first specimen of it; and (without my trying to remember
others) the original manuscripts of many of the songs of Burns. Among these
I saw Auld Lang Syne, and Bruces Address to his Army. We amused ourselves with these matters as long as we could; but, at last, as there was to be
a party in the evening, dinner could no longer be put off; so we took our
seats at table, and, immediately afterwards, Tom Taylor made his appearance,
with his wife and another lady.

The dinner was very well. Tom Taylor is reckoned a brilliant conversationist, but I suppose he requires somebody to draw him out and assist him;
for I could see nothing that I thought very remarkable, on this occasion. He
is not a kind of man whom I can talk with, or greatly help to talk; so, though I
sat next him, nothing came of it. He told some stories of his life in the Temple,
little funny incidents that he afterwards wrought into his dramas; in short,
not to bother longer with him, a sensible, active-minded, clearly perceptive
man, with a humorous way of showing up men and matters, but without originality, or much imagination, or dance of fancy. I wish I could know exactly what
the English style good conversation. Prob[165]ably it is something like plum-
pudding—as heavy, but seldom so rich.

After dinner, Mr. Tom Taylor and Mr. Dallas, with their respective ladies,
took their leave; but when we returned to the drawing-room (which is rather
small) we found it thronged with a good many people. Mr. S. C. Hall was there,
with his wife, whom I was glad to see again, for this was the third time of
meeting her, and, in this whirl of new acquaintances, I felt quite as if she

were an old friend. Mr. William Howitt was also there, and introduced me to his wife,[339] a very natural, kind, and pleasant lady; and she presented me to one daughter, and, I rather think, two. Mr. Marston,[340] the dramatist, was likewise introduced to me; and Mr. Arthur Helps,[341] a thin, scholarly, cold sort of a man. Dr Mackay and his wife were there, too; and a certain Mr. Jones,[342] a sculptor, a jolly, corpulent, elderly fellow, with a twinkle in his eye. Also, a Mr. Godwin,[343] who impressed me as quite a superior person, gentlemanly, cultivated, a man of sensibility; but it is quite impossible to take a clear imprint from any one character, when so many are stamped upon one's notice at once. This Mr. Godwin, as we were discussing Thackeray, said that he is most beautifully tender and devoted to his insane wife, whenever she temporarily emerges from her madness, and can be sensible of his [166] attentions. He says that Thackeray, in his real self, is a sweet, sad man. I grew weary of so many people, especially the ladies, who were rather superfluous in their oblations at my shrine,—quite stifling me, indeed, with the incense that they burnt under my nose. So far as I could judge, they had all been invited there to see me. It is ungracious—even hoggish—not to be gratified with the interest they expressed in me; but, then, it is really a bore, and one does not know what to do or say. I felt like the hippopotamus, or, to use a more modest illustration, like some strange bug imprisoned under a tumbler, with a dozen eyes watching whatever I did. By-and-by, Mr. Jones the sculptor relieved me by standing up against the mantel-piece and telling an Irish story, not to two or three auditors, but to the whole drawing-room, all attentive as to a set exhibition. This seems to be what he is invited for; this faculty of telling Irish stories; and he gave us another in the course of the evening. It was very funny. About eleven °clock, I took my leave, and gladly came away; and on the whole, of all my London experiences, I think this evening was the most tiresome.

The next day after this, I went with Mr. Bowman to call on Mr. Dallas, our minister, and found that he, and four [167] of the ladies of his family, with his son, had gone to the Drawing Room. We lunched at the Wellington, and spent an hour or more in looking out of the window of that establishment, at the carriages, with their pompous coachmen and footmen, driving to and from the palace of St. James's, and at the horse-guards, with their bright cuirasses, stationed along the street. At about four °clock, I took a cab for the Euston Station, where, at five, I bade farewell to Mr. Bowman, and took the rail for Liverpool, and arrived at eleven. Mrs. Blodget had no chamber for me, as I was one day earlier than she expected; so I took my travelling bag, and went to the Waterloo Hotel, where I slept and breakfasted. While I was still at table, Julian came in, ruddy-cheeked, smiling, very glad to see me, and looking, I thought, a good deal taller than when I left him. And so ended my London excursion, which has certainly been rich in incident and character, though my account of it be but meagre.[344]

Mrs. Blodget to Mr. Crane, reproaching him for coming late to the dinner-table—"You're a pretty young man!" Mr. Crane answers, "I always knew that, Mrs. Blodget." "Well," responds Mrs. Blodget, "I'm sure your glass never told you so!"

[168] FRIDAY, MAY 10th '56.

LAST Friday (May 2^d) I took the rail, with Mr. Bowman, from the Lime-street Station, at about two °clock, for Glasgow. There was nothing of much interest along the road, except that, when we got beyond Penrith, we saw snow on the tops of some of the hills. Twilight came on, as we were entering Scotland; and I have only a recollection of bleak and bare hills, and villages dimly seen; until, nearing Glasgow, we saw the red blaze of furnace-lights at frequent iron-foundries. We put up at the Queen's Hotel, where we arrived sometime about ten °clock; a better hotel than I have anywhere found in England—new, well-arranged, with brisk attendance, and reminding me of American hotels.

In the morning, I rambled largely about Glasgow, and found it to be a chiefly modern-built city, with streets mostly wide and regular, and handsome houses and public edifices of a dark gray stone. In front of our hotel, in an enclosed green space, stands a tall column surmounted by a statue of Sir Walter Scott; a good statue, I should think, as conveying the air and personal aspect of the man. There is a bronze equestrian statue of the Queen in one of the streets, and one or two more equestrian or other statues of eminent persons. I passed through the Trongate and the Gallow-gate, and visi[169]ted the Salt Market, and saw the steeple of the Tolbooth, all of which Scott has made interesting; and I went through the gate of the University, and penetrated into its enclosed courts, around which the college edifices are built. They are not Gothic, but of the age, I suppose, of James I, with odd-looking, conical-roofed towers, and here and there the bust of a benefactor in niches around the courts, and heavy stone-staircases ascending from the pavement outside of the edifices, all of dark gray granite, cold, hard, and venerable. The University stands in High-street, in as dense a part of the town as any, and a very old and shabby part, too. I think the poorer classes of Glasgow excel even those of Liverpool in the bad eminence of filth, uncombed and unwashed children, drunken[n]ess, disorderly deportment, evil smell, and all that makes city-poverty disgusting. In my opinion, however, they are a better-looking people than the English (and this is true of all classes) more intelligent of aspect, with more regular features, altogether more American. I looked for the high-cheeked bones, which have been attributed as a characteristic feature to the Scotch, but could not find them. What most distinguishes them from the English, and assimilates them to the Americans, is the regularity of the nose, which is straight, or perhaps a little curved inward; whereas, the English nose has no law whatever, but disports itself [170] in all manner of irregularity. I very soon learned to recognize the Scotch face; and, when not too Scotch, it is a handsome one. I now perceive that Miss Glyn's face (which certainly did not impress me by its beauty) is a Scotch one—broad Scotch.

In another part of the High street, up a pretty steep slope, and on one side of a public green, near a large edifice which I think is a medical college, stands Saint Mungo's Cathedral. It is hardly of cathedralic dimensions, though a large and fine old church. The price of a ticket of admittance is two-pence; so small that it might be as well to make the entrance free. The interior is in excellent repair, with the nave and side-aisles, and clustered pillars, and intersecting arches, that belong to all these old churches; and a few monuments along the walls. I was going away without seeing any more than this; but the verger (a friendly old gentleman, with a hearty Scotch way of speaking) told me that the crypts were what chiefly interested strangers; and so he showed me down into the foundation-story of the church, where there is an intricacy and entanglement of immensely massive and heavy arches, supporting the edifice above. The view through these arches, among the great shafts of the columns, was [171] very striking. In the central part is a monument; a recumbent figure, if I remember rightly, but it is not known whom it commemorates. There is also a monument to a Scotch prelate, which seems to have been purposely defaced, probably in covenanting-times. These intricate arches were the locality of one of the scenes in "Rob Roy," where Rob gives Frank Osbaldistone some message or warning, and then escapes from him into the obscurity behind.[345] In one corner is Saint Mungo's well (I do not know the history of it) secured with a wooden cover; but I should not care to drink water that comes from among so many old graves.

After viewing the Cathedral, I got back to the hotel just in time to go from thence to the steamer-wharf, and take passage up the Clyde. There was nothing very interesting in this little voyage. We passed many small iron steamers, and some large ones; and green fields along the river-shores, villas, villages, and all such suburban objects; neither am I quite sure of the name of the place we landed at, though I think it was Bowling. Here we took the railway for Balloch; and the only place or thing I remember, during this transit, was a huge bluff or crag, rising abruptly from a river side, and looking (in connection with its vicinity to the Highlands) just such a site as would be taken for the foundation of a castle. On inquiry, it turned out that [172] this abrupt and double-headed hill (for it has two summits, with a cleft between) is the site of Dumbarton Castle, for ages one of the strongest fortresses in Scotland, and still kept up as a garrisoned place. At the distance and point of view at which we passed it, the castle made no show.

Arriving at Balloch, we found it a small village with no marked features, and a hotel, where we got some lunch, and then took a stroll over the bridge across the Leven, while waiting for the steamer to take us up Loch Lomond. It was a beautiful afternoon, warm and sunny; and after walking about a mile, we had a fine view of Loch Lomond, and the mountains around and beyond it—

Ben Lomond among the rest. It is vain, at a week's distance, to try to remember the shapes of mountains; so I shall attempt no description of them, and content myself with saying that they did not quite come up to my anticipations. In due time, we returned to our hotel, and found in the coffee-room a tall, white-haired, venerable gentleman, and a pleasant-looking young lady, his daughter. They had been eating lunch; and the young lady helped her father on with his outside garment, and his comforter, and gave him his stick, just as any other daughter might—all of which I mention, because he was a nobleman; and moreover had engaged all the post-horses at the inn, so that we could not continue our travels by land, along the side of Loch Lom[173]ond, as we had first intended. At four °clock, the railway train arrived again, with a very moderate number of passengers, who (and we among them) immediately em-barked on board a neat little steamer which was waiting for us.

The day was bright and cloudless; but there was a strong, cold breeze blow-ing down the lake, so that it was impossible, without vast discomfort, to stand in the bow of the steamer and look at the scenery. I looked at it, indeed, along the sides, as we passed, and on our track behind; and no doubt it was very fine; but, from all the experience I have had, I do not think scenery can be well seen from the water. At any rate, the shores of Loch Lomond have faded completely out of my memory; nor can I conceive that they really were very striking. At a year's interval, I can recollect the cluster of hills around the head of Lake Windermere; at twenty years' interval, I remember the shores of Lake Cham-plain; but of the shores of this Scottish lake, I remember nothing—except some oddly shaped rocks, called the "cob[b]ler and his daughter," on a mountain-top, just before we landed. But, indeed, we had very imperfect glimpses of the hills along the latter part of the course, because the wind had grown so very cold that we took shelter below, and merely peeped at Loch Lomond's sublimities from the cabin-windows.

[174] The whole voyage up Loch Lomond is, I think, about thirty-two miles; but we landed at a place called Tarbet, much short of the ultimate point. There is here a large hotel; but we passed it, and walked onward, a mile or two, to Arrochar, a secluded glen among the hills, where is a new hotel, built in the old manor-house style, and occupying the site of what was once a castle of the chief of the MacFarlanes. Over the portal is a stone taken from the former house, bearing the date 1697. There is a little lake near the house; and the hills shut in the whole visible scene so closely that there appears no outlet, nor communication with the external world; but, in reality, this little lake is connected with Loch Long, and Loch Long is an arm of the sea; so that there is water-communication between Arrochar and Glasgow. We found this a very beautiful place; and being quite sheltered from all winds that blew, we strolled about late into the long twilight, and admired the outlines of the surrounding hills, and fancied resemblances to various objects in the shapes of the crags against the evening sky. The sun had not set till nearly or quite eight °clock;

and before the daylight had quite gone, the Northern lights streamed out, and I do not think that there was much darkness over the glen of Arrochar [175] that night. At all events, before the darkness came, we withdrew into the coffee-room, and took each a tumbler of hot whisky-toddy, which was brought to us in large goblets, with little silver ladles for conveying it into the small glasses from which we drank it. I cannot say I greatly love whisky-toddy; but being a Scotch drink, and pre-eminently that of the Highlands, we chose to drink it at Arrochar. Two other parties were at different tables in the coffee-room, quaffing the same liquor.

We had excellent beds and sleeping-rooms in this new hotel; and I remember nothing more till morning, when we were astir betimes, and had some chops for breakfast. Then our host, Mr. Macgregor (who is also the host of our hotel at Glasgow, and has many of the characteristics of an American land-lord, claiming to be a gentleman, and the equal of his guests) took us in a drosky, and drove us to the shore of Loch Lomond, at a point about four miles from Arrochar. The lake is here a mile and a half wide; and it was our object to cross to Inversnaid on the opposite shore; so first we waved a handkerchief, and then kindled some straw on the beach, in order to attract the notice of the ferryman at Inversnaid. It was half-an-hour before our signals and shoutings resulted in the putting-off of a boat, with [176] two oarsmen, who, however, made the transit pretty speedily; and thus we got across Loch Lomond. At Inversnaid there is a small hotel; and over the rock, on which it stands, a little waterfall tumbles into the lake—a very little one, though I believe it is reckoned among the other picturesque features of the scene.

We were now in Rob Roy's country; and at the distance of a mile or so, along the shore of the lake, is Rob Roy's cave, where he and his followers are supposed to have made their abode, in troublous times. While lunch was getting ready, we again took the boat and went thither. Landing beneath a precipitous, though not very lofty crag, we clambered up a rude pathway, and came to the mouth of the cave, which is nothing but a fissure, or a connection of fissures, among some great rocks that have tumbled confusedly together. There is hardly an[y]where room for half a dozen persons to crowd themselves to-gether, nor room to stand upright; on the whole, it is no cave at all, but only a crevice, and, in the deepest and darkest part, you can look up and see the sky. It may have sheltered Rob Roy for a night, and might partially shelter any Christian during a shower.

Returning to the hotel, we had some bread and cheese and a pint of ale, and then started in a drosky (I do not [177] know whether this is the right name of the vehicle, or whether it has a right name; but it is a carriage in which four persons sit back to back, two before, and two behind) for Aberfoyle. The mountain-side ascends very steeply from the inn-door, and not to damp the horse's courage at the outset, we went up on foot. The Guide-Book says that the prospect from the summit of this ascent is very fine; but I really believe we forgot to turn round and look at it. All through our ride, however, we had mountain-views in plenty, especially of great Ben Lomond, with his snow-covered head, around which, since our entrance into the Highlands, we had been making a circuit. Nothing can possibly be drearier than the mountains at this season; bare, barren, and bleak, with black patches of withered heath variegating the dead brown of the herbage on their sides; and as regards trees, the hills are just as naked as the day that God made them. There were no frightful precipices, no boldly picturesque features, along our road, but high, weary slopes, showing miles and miles of heavy solitude, with here and there a highland hut, built of stone and thatched, and, in one place, an old, gray, ruinous fortress, a station of the English troops after the rebellion of 1745; and once or twice a village of huts, the inhabitants [178] of which, old and young, ran to their doors to stare at us. For several miles after we left Inversnaid, the mountain-stream, which makes the waterfall, brawled along the roadside. All the hills are sheep-pastures; and I never saw such wild, rough, and ragged-looking creatures as the sheep, with their black faces, and tattered wool. The little lambs were very numerous, poor things, coming so early in the season into this inclement region; and it was laughable to see how invariably, when startled by our approach, they scampered to their mothers and immediately began to suck. It would have seemed as if they sought a draught from the maternal udder wherewith to fortify and encourage their poor little hearts; but I suppose their instinct merely drove them close to their dams, and, being there, they took advantage of the opportunity to suck. These sheep, old and young, must lead a hard life during the winter; for they are never fed nor sheltered.

The day was sunless and very uncomfortably cold; and we were not sorry to walk, whenever the steepness of the road gave us opportunity. I do not remember what °clock it was, but not far into the afternoon, when we reached the Bailie Nicol Jarvie Inn, at Aberfoyle; a scene which is [179] much more interesting in the pages of "Rob Roy," than we found it in reality. Here we got into a sort of cart, and set out, over another hill-path, as dreary, or drearier than the last, for the Trossachs. On our way, we saw Ben Venue, and a good many other famous Bens, and two or three lochs; and when we reached the Trossachs, we should probably have been very much enraptured, if our eyes had not already been weary with other mountain-shapes. But, in truth, I doubt if anybody ever does really see a mountain, who goes for the set and sole purpose of seeing it. Nature will not let herself be seen, in such cases. You must patiently bide her time; and, by and-by, at some unforeseen moment, she will quietly and suddenly unveil herself, and, for a brief space, let you look right into the heart of her mystery. But if you call out to her peremptorily— "Nature, unveil yourself, this very instant!"—she only draws her veil the closer; and you may look with all your eyes, and imagine you see all that she can show, and yet see nothing. Thus, I saw a wild and confused assemblage of heights, crags, precipices, which they call the Trossachs, but I saw them calmly and coldly, and was glad when the drosky was ready to take us on to Callander. The hotel at the Trossachs, by-the-by, is a very splendid one, in the form of an old [180] feudal castle, with towers and turrets. All among these wild hills, there is set preparation for enraptured visitants; and it seems strange that the wild and savage features do not subside of their own accord, and that there should still be cold winds, and snow on the top of Ben Lomond, and rocks, and heather, and ragged sheep, now that there are so many avenues by which the common-place world is sluiced in among the Highlands. I think that this fashion of the picturesque will pass away.

We drove along the shore of Lake Vennachar, and onward to Callander, which, I believe, is either the first point in the Lowlands, or the last in the Highlands. It is a large village on the river Teith. We stopt here to dine, and were some time in getting any warmth into our benumbed bodies, for, as I said before, it was a very cold day. Looking from the window of the hotel, I saw a young man in Highland dress, with bare thighs, marching through the village-street, towards the Lowlands, with a martial and elastic step, as if he were going forth to conquer and occupy the world. I suppose he was a soldier who had been absent on leave, returning to the garrison at Stirling. I pitied his poor thighs and further bareness,[346] though he certainly did not look uncomfortable. After dinner, as dusk was coming on and [181] we had still a long drive before us, (eighteen miles, I believe) we took a close carriage and two horses and set off for Stirling. The twilight was too obscure to show many things along the road; and by the time we drove into Stirling, we could but dimly see the houses in the long street, in which stood our hotel. There was a good fire in the coffee-room, which looked like the drawing-room in a large, old-fashioned mansion, and was hung round with engravings of the portrait of the county-member, and a master of fox-hounds, and other pictures. We made ourselves comfortable with some tea, and went to bed at about eleven.

In the morning, we were stirring betimes, and found Stirling to be a pretty large town, of rather ancient aspect, with many gray stone houses, the gables of which are notched on either side like a flight of stairs. The town stands on the slope of a hill, at the summit of which, crowning a long ascent, up which the paved street reaches all the way to its gate, is Stirling Castle. Of course, we went thither, and found free entrance, although the castle is garrisoned by five or six hundred men, among whom are bare-legged Highlanders, (I must say that their costume is very fine, and becoming, though their thighs did look blue and frost-bitten) and also some soldiers of other Scotch regiments, with tartan trowsers. Almost immediately on passing the gate, we found an [182] old artilleryman, who undertook to show us round the castle. Only a small portion of it seems to be of great antiquity. The principal edifice within the castle wall is a palace that was either built or renewed by James

VI; and it is ornamented with strange old statues, one of which is his own. The old Scottish parliament-house is likewise here. The most ancient part of the castle is the tower (as it is called, though it is really little more than the gable-end of a small stone-house) where one of the earls of Douglas was stabbed by a king, and afterwards thrown out of the window. In reading this story, one imagined a lofty turret, and the dead man tumbling headlong from a great height; but, in reality, the window is not more than fifteen or twenty feet from the garden into which he fell. This part of the castle was burned, last autumn; but is now under repair, and the wall of the tower is still staunch and strong. We went up into the chamber where the murder took place, and looked through the historic window.

Then we mounted the castle wall, where it broods over a precipice of many hundred feet perpendicular, looking down upon the level plain below, and forth upon a landscape, every foot of which is richly studded with historic events. There is a small peep-hole in the wall, which Queen Mary is said to have been in the habit of looking through. It is a most splen[183]did view; in the distance, the blue Highlands, with a variety of mountain-outlines that I could have studied unweariably; and in another direction, beginning almost at the foot of the Castle hill, were the Links of Forth, where, over a plain of miles in extent, the river meandered, and circled about, and returned upon itself, again, and again, and again, as if knotted into a silver chain, which it was difficult to imagine to be all one stream. The history of Scotland might be read from this castle-wall, as on a book of mighty page; for here, within the compass of a few miles, we see the field where Wallace won the battle of Stirling, and likewise the battlefield of Bannockburn, and that of Falkirk, and Sheriffmuir, and I know not how many besides.

Around the castle-hill there is a walk, with seats for old and infirm persons, at points sheltered from the wind. We followed it downward, and I think we passed over the site where the games used to be held, and where, this morning, some of the soldiers of the garrison were going through their exercises. I ought to have mentioned, that, passing through the inner gateway of the castle, we saw the round tower and peeped into the dungeon, where the Roderic[k] Dhu of Scott's poem was left to die.[347] It is one of the two round towers between which the portcullis rose and fell.

[184] At eleven ºclock, or some other seasonable hour, we took the rail for Edinburgh; and I remember nothing more (except that the cultivation and verdure of the country were very agreeable, after our experience of Highland barrenness and desolation) until we found the train passing close at the base of the rugged crag of Edinburgh castle. We established ourselves at a hotel (the Queen's, I believe) in Prince's street, and then went out to view the city. The monument to Sir Walter Scott (a rather fantastic and not very impressive affair, I thought) stands almost directly in front of our hotel. We went along Prince's street, and thence, by what turns I know not, to the

palace of Holyrood, which stands on a low and sheltered site, and is a venerable edifice. Arthur's Seat rises behind it, a high hill, with a plain between. As we drew near the palace, Mr. Bowman (who has been here before) pointed out the windows of Queen Mary's apartments, in a circular tower on the left of the gateway. On entering the enclosed quadrangle, we bought tickets for sixpence each, admitting us to all parts of the palace that are shown to visitors; and first we went into a noble hall, or gallery, a long and stately room, hung with pictures of ancient Scottish kings; and though the pictures are none of them authentic, they at least answer an excellent purpose in the way of upholstery. It was [185] here that the young Pretender gave the ball, which makes one of the scenes in "Waverl[e]y."[348]

Thence we passed into the old historic rooms of the Palace; Darnley's and Queen Mary's apartments, which everybody has seen and described. They are very dreary and shabby-looking rooms, with bare floors, and here and there a piece of tapestry, faded into a neutral tint, and carved and ornamented cielings [sic], looking shabbier than plain whitewash. We saw Queen Mary's old bedstead, low, with four tall posts, and her looking-glass, which she brought with her from France, and which has often reflected the beauty that set everybody mad; and some needlework and other womanly matters of hers; and we went into the little closet, where she was having such a cosey supper-party with two or three friends, when the conspirators broke in and stabbed Rizzio before her face. We saw, too, the blood-stains at the threshold of the door in the next room, opening upon the stairs. The body of Rizzio was flung down here, and the attendant told us that it lay in that spot all night. The blood-stain covers a large space—much larger than I supposed—and it gives the impression that there must have been a great puddle and sop of blood on all the spot covered by Rizzio's body, staining the floor deeply enough never to be washed out. It is now of a [186] dark brown hue; and I do not see why it may not be the genuine, veritable stain. The floor, thereabouts, appears not to have been scrubbed much; for I touched it with my finger and found it slightly rough; but it is strange that the many footsteps should not have smoothed it in three hundred years. One of the articles shown us in Queen Mary's apartments was the breastplate, supposed to have been worn by Lord Ruthven, at the murder; a heavy plate of iron, and doubtless a very uncomfortable waistcoat.

From the palace we passed into the contiguous ruin of Holyrood Abbey; which is roofless, although the front, and some broken columns along the nave, and fragments of architecture here and there, afford hints of a magnificent Gothic church, in bygone times. It deserved to be magnificent; for here have been stately ceremonials, marriages of kings, coronations, investitures, before the high altar, which has now been overthrown or crumbled away; and the floor—so far as there is any floor—consists of tombstones of the old Scottish nobility. There are likewise monuments bearing the names of illustrious Scotch families, and inscriptions in the Scotch dialect, on the walls. In one of the front

towers—the only remaining one, indeed—we saw the marble tomb of a nobleman, Lord Belhaven, who is represented reclining on the top, with a bruised
nose, of course. Except [187] in Westminster Abbey, I do not remember ever
to have seen an old monumental statue, with the nose entire. In all political
or religious outbreaks, the mob's first impulse is to hit the illustrious dead on
their noses. At the other end of the abbey, near the high altar, is the vault where
the old Scottish kings used to be buried; but peeping in through the window,
I saw only a vacant space, no skull, nor bone, nor the least fragment of a
coffin. In fact, I believe the royal dead were turned out of their last home, on
occasion of the Revolutionary movements at the accession of William III.

Quitting the Abbey and the Palace, we turned into the Canon-gate, and
passed thence into High street (which, I think, is a continuation of it;) and
being now in the old town of Edinburgh, we saw those immensely tall houses,
seven stories high, where the people live in tiers, all the way from earth to
middle air. They were not so quaint and strange-looking as I expected; but
there were some houses of very antique individuality, and among them that of
John Knox, which looks still in good repair. One thing did not in the least fall
short of my expectations—the evil odor, for which Edinburgh has an immemorial renown, nor the dirt of the inhabitants, old and young. The town,
to say the truth, when you are in the midst of it, has a very sordid, grimy,
shabby, [188] unswept, unwashen aspect, grievously at variance with all
poetic and romantic associations.

From the High-street we turned aside into the Grass market, the scene of
the Porteous mob;[349] and we found in the pavement a cross on the site where
the execution of Porteous is supposed to have taken place. Returning then
to the High street, we followed it up to the Castle, which is nearer the town,
and of more easy access from it, than I had supposed. There is a large yard,
or parade, before the castle-gate, with a parapet on the abrupt side of the
hill, looking towards Arthur's Seat and Salisbury-craigs, and overleaning a
portion of the old town. As we leaned over this parapet, my nose was conscious
of the bad smell of Edinburgh, although the streets, whence it must have come,
were hundreds of feet below. I have had some experience of this ugly fragrance in the poor streets of Liverpool; but I think I never smelt it before
crossing the Atlantic. It is the odor of an old system of life; the scent of the
pine-forests is still too recent with us for it to be known in America.

The castle of Edinburgh is free (as appears to be the case with all garrisoned
places in Great Britain) to the entrance of any peaceable person. So we went
in, and found a large space enclosed within the walls, and dwellings for officers,
and [189] accommodations for soldiers, who were being drilled, or loitering
about; and as the hill still ascends, within the external wall of the castle, we
climbed to the summit, and there found an old soldier whom we engaged to be
our guide. He showed us Mons Meg, a great old cannon, broken at the breech,
but still aimed threat[e]ningly from the highest ramparts; and then he ad-

mitted us into an old chapel (said to have been built by a Queen of Scotland, the sister of Harold, King of England) occupying the very highest point of the hill. It is the smallest place of worship I ever saw, but of venerable architecture, and of very solid construction. The old soldier had not much more to show us; but he pointed out the window, whence one of the kings of Scotland is said, when a baby, to have been lowered down the whole height of the castle, to the bottom of the precipice on which it stands, a distance of seven hundred feet.

After the soldier had shewn us to the extent of his jurisdiction, we went into a suite of rooms, in one of which I saw a portrait of Queen Mary, which gave me, for the first time, an idea that she was really a very beautiful woman. In this picture she is wonderfully so—a tender womanly grace, which was none the less tender and graceful for being equally imbued with queenly dignity and spirit. It was too lovely a head to [190] be cut off. I should be glad to know the authenticity of this picture.

I do not know that we did anything else worthy of note, except to eat our dinners, before leaving Edinburgh. There is matter enough, in and about the town, to interest the visitor for a very long time; but when the visit is calculated on such brevity as ours was, we get weary of the place before even these few hours come to an end. Thus, for my part, I was not sorry when, in the course of the afternoon, we took the rail for Melrose, where we duly arrived, and put up at the George Inn. Melrose is a village of rather antique aspect, situated on the slope and at the bottom of the Eildon Hills, which, from this point of view, appear like one hill with a double summit. The village, as I said, has an elderly look, though many of the houses have at least been re-fronted at some recent date; but others are as old, I suppose, as the days when the Abbey was in its splendor—a rustic and peasant-like antiquity, however, low-roofed and straw-thatched. There is an ancient cross of stone in the centre of the town.

Our first object, of course, was to see the Abbey, which stands just on the outskirts of the village, and is attainable (the interior, that is) only by applying at a neighboring house, the inhabitant of which probably supports himself [191] (and most comfortably too) as a showman of the ruin. He unlocked the wooden gate and admitted us into what is left of the abbey, comprising only the ruins of the church, although the refectory, the dormitories, and the other parts of the establishment, formerly covered the space now occupied by a dozen village-houses. Melrose Abbey is a very satisfactory ruin, all carpeted along its nave and transepts, with green grass; and, if I rightly remember, there are some well grown trees within the walls. We saw the window (now empty) through which the tints of the painted glass fell on the tombstone of Michael Scott, and the tombstone itself, broken in three pieces, but with a cross engraven along its whole length. It must have been the monument of an old monk, or abbot, rather than a wizard. There, too, is still the "marble stone," on which the monk and warrior sat them down, and which is supposed to mark the resting-place of Alexander of Scotland. There are remains, both without and within the Abbey, of most curious and wonderfully minute old sculpture; foliage, in places where it is almost impossible to see them, and where the sculptor could not have supposed that they would be seen, but which yet are finished faithfully to the very veins of each leaf, in stone; and a continual variety of this accurate toil. On the exterior of the [192] edifice, there is equal minuteness of finish, and a great many niches for statues, all of which, I believe, are now gone; although there are carved faces at some points and angles. The grave-yard around the Abbey is still the only one which the village has, and is populous with grave stones, among which I read the inscription of one, erected by Sir Walter Scott to the memory of Thomas Purdy [Purdie], one of his servants. Some sable birds—either rooks or jackdaws—were flitting about the ruins, inside and out.

Mr. Bowman and I talked about revisiting Melrose by moonlight; but, luckily, there was to be no moon, that evening. I do not myself think that daylight and sunshine make a ruin less effective than twilight or moonshine. In reference to Scott's description, I think he deplorably diminishes the impressiveness of the scene, by saying that the alternate buttresses, seen by moonlight, look as if made of "ebon and ivory."[350] It suggests a small and very pretty piece of cabinet-work; not these gray, rough walls, which Time has gnawed upon for a thousand years without eating them away.

Leaving the Abbey, we took a path, or a road, which led us to the river Tweed, perhaps a quarter of a mile off; and we crossed it by a foot-bridge—a pretty wide stream, a dimpling breadth of transparent water, flowing between low banks, [193] with a margin of pebbles. We then returned to our Inn, and had tea, and passed a quiet evening by the fireside. This is a good, unpretentious Inn; and its Visitors' book indicates that it affords general satisfaction to those who come here. In the morning, we breakfasted on broiled salmon, taken, no doubt, in the neighboring Tweed. There was a very coarse-looking man at table with us, who informed us that he owned the best horse anywhere round the Eildon Hills, and could make the best cast for a salmon, and catch a bigger fish than anybody, with other self-laudation of the same kind. The waiter afterwards told us that he was the son of an Admiral in the neighborhood; and soon, his horse being brought to the door, we saw him mount and ride away. He sat on horseback with ease and grace, though I rather suspect— early as it was—that he was already in his cups. The Scotch seem to me to get drunk at very unseasonable hours. I have seen more drunken people than during all my residence in England, and generally early in the day. Their liquor, so far as I have observed, makes them good-natured and sociable, imparting a perhaps needed geniality to their cold natures.

After breakfast we took a drosky, or whatever these fore-and-aft seated vehicles are called, and set out for Dry[194]burgh Abbey, three miles distant. It was a cold, though rather bright morning, with a most shrewd and bitter wind, which blew directly in my face, as I sat beside the driver. An English wind is bad enough; but methinks a Scotch one is rather worse;—at any rate, I was half-frozen, and wished Dryburgh Abbey in Tophet, where it would have been warmer work to go and see it. Some of the border-hills were striking, especially the Cowden Knowe[s], which ascends into a prominent and lofty peak. Such villages as we past did not greatly differ from English villages. By and by, we came to the banks of the Tweed, at a point where there is a ferry. A carriage was on the river-bank, the driver waiting beside it; for the party, who came in it, had already been ferried across to see the Abbey. The ferryman here is a young girl; and stepping into her boat, she shoved off, and so skilfully took advantage of the eddies of the stream (which is here deep and rapid) that we were soon on the other side. She was by no means an uncomely maiden, with pleasant Scotch features, and a quiet intelligence of aspect, gleaming into a smile when spoken to; much tanned with all kinds of weather, and, though slender, yet so agile and muscular, that it was no shame for a man to let himself be rowed by her.

[195] From the ferry, we had a walk of half-a mile, more or less, to a cottage, where we found another young girl, whose business it is to show the Abbey. She was of another mould than the ferry-maiden—a queer, shy, plaintive sort of a body—and answered all our questions in a low, wailing tone. Passing through an apple-orchard, we were not long in reaching the Abbey, the ruins of which are much more extensive and more picturesque than those of Melrose, being much over-run with bushes and shrubbery, and twined about with ivy, and all such vegetation as belongs naturally to old walls. There are remains of the refectory, and other domestic parts of the Abbey, as well as the church, and all in a delightful state of decay—not so far gone but that we had hints of its former grandeur, in the columns, and broken arches, and in some portions of the edifice that still retain a roof. In the chapter-house—I think it was—we saw a marble statue of Newton, woefully maltreated by damps and weather; and though it had no sort of business there, it fitted into the ruins picturesquely enough. There is another statue, I forget of whom, equally unauthorized; both having been placed here by a former Earl of Buchan, who seems to have been a little astray in his wits.

[196] On one side of the Abbey Church, within an arched recess, are the monuments of Sir Walter Scott and his family; three ponderous tombstones of Aberdeen granite, polished, but already dimmed and dulled by the weather. The whole floor of the recess is covered by these monuments, that of Sir Walter being the middle one, with Lady (or, as the inscription calls her, "Dame") Scott beyond him, next to the church-wall, and some one of his sons or daughters on the hither side. The effect of his being buried here is, to make the whole of Dryburgh Abbey his monument. There is another arched recess, twin to the Scott burial-place, and contiguous to it, in which are buried a Pringle [? Erskine] family; it being their ancient place of sepulture. The spectator

almost inevitably feels as if they were intruders, although their rights here are of far elder date than those of Scott.

Dryburgh Abbey must be a most beautiful spot, of a summer afternoon; and it was beautiful even in this not very genial morning, especially when the sun blinked out, upon the ivy, and upon the shrubberied path that wound about the ruins. I think I recollect the birds chirruping in the neighborhood of it. After viewing it sufficiently—sufficiently for this one time—we went back to the ferry, and being set [197] across by the same Undine, we drove back to Melrose. No longer riding against the wind, I found it not nearly so cold as before. I now noticed that the Eildon Hills, viewed from this direction, rise from one base into three distinct summits, ranged in a line. According to the "Lay of the Last Minstrel,"[351] they were cleft into this shape by the magic of Michael Scott. Reaching Melrose, we drew up at the inn-door, and drank some ale, fortified with which, and without alighting, we set out for Abbotsford, three miles off. The neighborhood of Melrose, on the road leading to Abbotsford, has many handsome residences of modern build, and very recent date; suburban villas, each with its little lawn and garden-ground, such as we see in the vicinity of Liverpool. I noticed, too, one castellated house, of no great size, but old, and looking as if its tower was built not for show, but for actual defence in the old border warfare.

We were not long in reaching Abbotsford. The house (which is more compact, and of considerably less extent than I anticipated) stands in full view from the road, and at only a short distance from it, lower down towards the river. Its aspect disappointed me; but so does everything. It is but a villa, after all; no castle, nor even a large manor[198]house, and very unsatisfactory when you consider it in that light. Indeed, it impressed me not as a real house, intended for the home of human beings—a house to die in, or to be born in— but as a plaything, something in the same category as Horace Walpole's Strawberry Hill. The present owner seems to have found it insufficient for the actual purposes of life; for he is adding a wing which promises to be as extensive as the original structure.

We rang at the front-door (the family being now absent) and were speedily admitted by a middle-aged or somewhat elderly man—the butler, I suppose, or some upper servant—who at once acceded [*sic*] to our request to be permitted to see the house. We stept from the porch immediately into the entrance-hall; and having the great hall of Battle Abbey, I believe, in my memory, and the ideal of a baronial hall in my mind, I was quite taken aback at the smallness, and narrowness, and lowness of this—which, however, is a very fine one, on its own little scale. In truth, it is not much more than a vestibule. The cieling [*sic*] is carved; and every inch of the walls is covered with claymores, targets, and other weapons and armor, or old-time curiosities, tastefully arranged, many of which, no doubt, have a history attached to them—or had, in Sir Walter's own [199] mind. Our attendant was a very intelligent person, and pointed out much that was interesting; but, in such a multitudinous variety, it was almost impossible to fix the eye upon any one thing. Probably the apartment looked smaller than it really was, on account of being so wainscoted [*sic*] and festooned with curiosities. I remember nothing particularly, unless it be the coal-grate in the fireplace, which was one formerly used by Archbishop Sharpe [Sharp], the prelate whom Balfour of Burley [Burleigh] murdered.[352] Either in this room or the next one, however, there was a glass-case, containing the suit of clothes last worn by Scott— a short green coat, somewhat worn, with silvered buttons, a pair of gray tartan trowsers, and a white hat. It *was* in the hall that we saw these things; for there, too, I recollect, were a good many walking sticks that had been used by Scott, and the hatchet with which he was in the habit of lopping branches from his trees, as he walked among them.

From the hall we passed into the study, a small room lined with the books which Sir Walter, no doubt, was most frequently accustomed to refer to; and our guide pointed out some volumes of the Moniteur, which he used while writing the History of Napoleon. Probably these were the dryest and dullest volumes in his whole library. About mid-height of the walls [200] of the study, there is a gallery with a short flight of steps, for the convenience of getting at the upper books. A study table occupies the centre of the room, and at one end of the table stands an easy chair, covered with morocco, and with ample space to fling one's self back. The servant told me that I might sit down in this chair, for that Sir Walter sat there while writing his romances; "and perhaps," quoth the man, smiling, "you may catch some inspiration!" What a bitter word this would have been, if he had known me to be a romance-writer! "No, I never shall be inspired to write romances," I answered, as if such an idea had never occurred to me. I sat down, however. This study quite satisfies me, being planned on principles of common sense, and made to work in, and without any fantastic adaptation of old forms to modern uses.

Next to the study is the library, an apartment of respectable size, and containing as many books as it can hold, all protected by wirework. I did not observe what or whose works were here; but the attendant showed us one whole compartment, full of volumes having reference to ghosts, witchcraft, and the supernatural generally. It is remarkable that Scott should have felt interested in such subjects, being such a worldly and earthly man as he [201] was; but, then, indeed, almost all forms of popular superstition do clothe the ethereal with earthly attributes, and so make it grossly perceptible. The library, like the study, suited me well—merely the fashion of the apartment, I mean—and I doubt not it contains as many curious volumes as are anywhere to be met with, within a similar space. The drawing-room adjoins it; and here we saw a beautiful ebony cabinet, which was presented to Sir Walter by George IV; and some pictures of much interest—one of Scott himself, at thirty five, rather portly, with a heavy face, but shrewd eyes, which seem to observe you closely. There is a full length of his eldest son, an officer of dragoons, leaning on his charger; and a portrait of Lady Scott, a brunette, with black hair and eyes, very pretty, warm, vivacious, and un-English in her aspect. I am not quite sure whether I saw all these pictures in the drawing-room, or some of them in the dining-room; but the one that struck me most—and very much indeed—was the head of Mary Queen of Scotts [sic], literally, the head, cut off, and lying in a dish. It is said to have been painted by an Italian or French artist, two days after her death. The black hair curls or flows all about it; the face is of a deathlike hue, but has an expression of quiet after much pain and trouble, very beauti[202]ful, very sweet and sad; and it affected me strongly with the horror and strangeness of such a head being severed from its body. Methinks I should not like to have it always in the room with me. I thought of the lovely picture of Mary that I had seen at Edinburgh Castle, and thought what a symbol it would be—how expressive of a human being having her destiny in her own hands—if that beautiful young Queen were painted as carrying this vessel, containing her own woeful head, and perhaps casting a curious and pitiful glance down upon it, as if it were not her own.

Also, in the drawing-room, (if I mistake not,) there was a plaster-cast of Sir Walter's face, taken after death; the only one in existence, as our guide assured us. It is not often that one sees a hom[e]lier set of features than this; no elevation, no dignity, whether bestowed by nature, or thrown over them by age or death; sunken cheeks, the bridge of the nose depressed, and the end turned up; the mouth puckered up, and no chin whatever, or hardly any. The expression was not calm and happy, but rather as if he were in a perturbed slumber, perhaps nothing short of nightmare. I wonder that the family allow this cast to be shown; the last record that there is of Scott's personal reality, and conveying such a wretched & unworthy idea of it

[203] Adjoining the drawing-room is the dining-room, in one corner of which, between two windows, Scott died. It is now a quarter of a century since his death; but it seemed to me that we spoke with a sort of hush in our voices, as if he were still dying here, or but just departed. I remember nothing else in this room. The next one is the armory, which is the smallest of all that we had passed through; but its walls gleam with the steel blades of swords, and the barrels of pistols, matchlocks, firelocks, and all manner of deadly weapons, whether European or oriental; for there are many trophies here of East Indian warfare. I saw Rob Roy's gun, rifled, and of very large bore; and a beautiful pistol, formerly Claverhouse's; and the sword of Montrose, given him by King Charles, the silver hilt of which I grasped. There was also a superb claymore, in an elaborately wrought silver sheath, made for Sir Walter Scott, and presented to him by the Highland Society, for his services in marshalling the clans, when George IV came to Scotland. There were a thousand other things, which I knew must be most curious, yet did not ask nor care about them; because so many curiosities drive one crazy, and fret one's heart to death. On the whole,

there is no simple and great impression left by Abbotsford; and I felt angry and [204] dissatisfied with myself for not feeling something which I did not and could not feel. But it is just like going to a museum, if you look into particulars; and one learns from it, too, that Scott could not have been really a wise man, nor an earnest one, nor one that grasped the truth of life;—he did but play, and the play grew very sad towards its close. In a certain way, however, I understand his romances the better for having seen his house; and his house the better, for having read his romances. They throw light on one another.

We had now gone through all the show-rooms; and the next door admitted us again into the entrance-hall, where we recorded our names in the visitor's book. It contains more names of Americans, (I should judge, from casting my eyes back over last years record) than of all other people in the world, including Great Britain. Bidding farewell to Abbotsford, I cannot but confess a sentiment of remorse for having visited the dwelling-place—as, just before, I visited the grave—of the mighty minstrel and romancer, with so cold a heart, and in so critical a mood;—*his* dwelling-place and *his* grave, whom I had so admired and loved, and who had done so much for my happiness, when I was young. But I, and the world generally, now look at him from a [205] different point of view; and, besides, these visits to the actual haunts of famous people, though long dead, have the effect of making us sensible, in some degree, to their human imperfections, as if we actually saw them alive. I felt this effect, to a certain extent, even with respect to Shakespeare, when I visited Stratford-on-Avon. As for Scott, I still cherish him in a warm place, and I do not know that I have any pleasanter anticipation (as regards books) than that of reading all his novels over again, after we get back to the Wayside.[353]

It was now one or two °clock, and time for us to take the rail across the borders. Many a mile behind us, as we rushed onward, we could see the three-fold Eildon Hill; and probably every pant of the engine carried us over some spot of ground which Scott has made fertile with poetry. For Scotland—cold, cloudy, barren, insignificant little bit of earth that it is—owes all the interest that the world feels in it to him. Few men have done so much for their country as he. However, having no Guide Book, we were none the wiser for what we saw out of the window of the rail-carriage; but, now and then, a castle appeared, on a commanding height, visible for miles around, and seemingly in good repair; now, in some low and sheltered spot, the gray walls of an abbey; now, on a little eminence, the ruin [206] of a border fortress, and, near it, the modern residence of the laird, with its trim lawn and shrubbery. We were not long in coming to Berwick—a town which seems to belong both to England and Scotland, or perhaps is a kingdom by itself; for it stands on both sides of the boundary river, the Tweed, where it empties into the German ocean. From the railway-bridge, we had a good view over the town, which looks ancient, with red roofs on all the gabled houses; and, it being a sunny afternoon, though bleak and chill, the sea-view was very fine. The Tweed is here broad, and looks deep, flowing far beneath the bridge, between high banks. This is all that I can say of Berwick (pronounced Berrick,) for though we spent above an hour at the station, waiting for the train, we were so long in getting our dinner that we had no time for anything else. I remember, however, some gray walls that looked like the last remains of an old castle, near the railway-station.

We next took the train for Newcastle, the way to which, for a considerable distance, lies within sight of the sea; and in close vicinity to the shore we saw Holy Isle, on which are the ruins of an Abbey. Norham castle must be somewhere in this neighborhood, on the English shore of the Tweed. It was pretty late in the afternoon—almost nightfall—when we reached Newcastle, over the roofs of which, as over [207] those of Berwick, we had a view from the railway; and, like Berwick, it was a congregation of mostly red roofs; but, (unlike Berwick, the atmosphere over which was clean and transparent) there came a gush of smoke from every chimney, which made it the dimmest and smokiest place I ever saw. This is partly owing to the iron-foundries and furnaces; but each domestic chimney, too, was smoking on its own account; coal being so plentiful there, no doubt, that the fire is always kept freshly heaped with it, reason or none. Out of this smoke cloud rose tall steeples; and it was discernible that the town stretched widely over an uneven surface, on the banks of the Tyne, which is navigable up hither (ten miles from the sea) by pretty large vessels.

We established ourselves at the Station Hotel, and then walked out to see something of the town; but I remember only a few streets of duskiness and dinginess, with a glimpse of the turrets of a castle, to which we could not find our way. So, as it was getting twilightish, and very cold, we went back to the Hotel, which is a very good one—better than any one I have seen, in the south of England, and almost or quite as good as those of Scotland. The coffee-room is a spacious and handsome apartment, adorned with a full length portrait of Wellington, and other pictures; and in [208] the whole establishment there was a kind of well ordered alacrity and liberal provision for the guest's comfort that one seldom sees in English inns. There are a good many American guests in Newcastle, and through all the North; and it is well to suppose that they have been the hotel-reformers. We found a smoking-room, too, and tolerably good cigars, and, on the whole, were pretty comfortable till bedtime. An old Newcastle gentleman and his friend came into the smoking-room, while we were there, and drank three glasses of hot whiskey toddy a-piece, and were still going on to drink more when we left them. It is delightful to see how little progress tee-totalism has yet made in these parts; these respectable persons probably went away drunk, that night, yet thought none the worse of themselves or one another for it. It is like returning to times twenty years gone by, for a New Englander to witness such simplicity of manners.

The next morning (which I believe was Wednesday, May 8th) I rose and breakfasted betimes, and took the rail soon after eight °clock, leaving Mr. Bowman behind; for he had business in Newcastle, and would not follow till some hours afterwards. There is no use in trying to make a narrative of anything that one sees along an English railway. All I remember of this tract of country is, that one of the [209] stations, at which we stopt for an instant, is called "Washington"; and this is no doubt the old family-place, where the de Wessyngtons, afterwards the Washingtons, first settled themselves in England. Before reaching York, first one old lady, and then an old Quaker lady, got into the carriage along with me; and they seemed to be going to York on occasion of some fair or celebration; this was all the company I had, and their advent the only incident. It was about eleven °clock, when I beheld York Cathedral rising huge above the old city, which stands on the river Ouse, separated by it from the railway station, but communicating by a ferry (I think, two) and a bridge. I wandered forth and found my way over the latter into the ancient and irregular streets of the town—crooked, narrow, or of unequal width, puzzling, and many of them bearing the name of the particular gate, in the old walls of the city, to which they lead. There were no such fine, ancient, stately houses as some of those in Shrewsbury, nor such an aspect of antiquity as in Chester; but still York is a quaint old place, and what looks most modern is probably (as elsewhere in England) only something old, hiding itself behind a new front.

I found my way, by a sort of instinct, as directly as [210] possible to the Cathedral. It stands in the midst of a small open space—or a space that looks small, in comparison with the vast bulk of the edifice. I was not so much impressed by its exterior as I have usually been by Gothic buildings, because it is rectangular in its general outline, and in its towers, and seems to lack the complexity, and mysterious plan, which perplexes and wonderstrikes me in most cathedrals. Doubtless, however, if I had known better how to admire it, I should have found it wholly admirable. At all events, it has a satisfactory hugeness. Seeking my way in, I at first intruded upon the Registry of Deeds (if that be the name of the office) which occupies a building patched up against the mighty side of the Cathedral, and hardly discernible, so small the one, and so large the other. I finally hit upon the right door; and, if I rightly remember, I felt no disappointment, in my first glance around, at the immensity of enclosed space;—at least, I see now in my mind's eye a dim length of nave, a breadth in the transepts like a great plain, and such an airy height beneath the central tower, that a worshipper could certainly get a good way towards Heaven without rising above the Cathedral. I only wish that the screen, or whatever they call it, between the choir and nave could be thrown down, so as to give us leave to take in [211] the whole vastitude at once. I never could understand why, after building a great church, they choose to sunder it in halves by this mid-partition. But let me be thankful for what I got, and especially for the height and massiveness of the clustered pillars that support the arches, on which rests the central tower. I remember, at Furness Abbey, I saw two tall pillars, supporting a broken arch, and thought it the most majestic fragment of architecture that could possibly be. But these pillars have a nobler height, and these arches a grander sweep. What nonsense, to try to write about a cathedral!

There is a great, cold bareness and bleakness about the interior of this Cathedral; for there are very few monuments, and those seem to be chiefly of ecclesiastical people. I saw no armed knights asleep on the tops of their tombs; but there was a curious representation of a skeleton, at full length, under the table-slab of one of the monuments. The walls are of a grayish hue, not so agreeable as the rich, dark tint of the inside of Westminster Abbey; but a great many of the windows are still filled with ancient painted glass, the very small squares and pieces of which are composed into splendid designs of Saints, and Angels, and scenes from Scripture, and I know not what. There were a few watery [212] blinks of sunshine, out of doors, and whenever these came through the old painted windows, some of the more vivid colors were faintly thrown upon the pavement of the Cathedral;—very faintly, it is true, for, in the first place, the sunshine was not brilliant; and painted glass, too, fades in the course of the ages, like all man's other works. There were two or three windows of modern manufacture, and far more magnificent, so far as brightness of color, and material beauty, go, than the ancient ones; but yet they looked vulgar, glaring, and impertinent, in comparison, because such revivals or imitations of a long disused art cannot have the good faith and earnestness of the originals. Indeed, in the very coloring, I felt the same difference as between heart's blood and a scarlet dye. It is a pity, however, that the old windows cannot be washed, both inside and out, for now they have the dust of centuries upon them.

The screen, or curtain, between the nave and choir, has eleven—unless I counted them amiss—eleven carved figures, at full length, which appeared to represent Kings, some of them wearing crowns, and bearing sceptres or swords. They were in wood, and wrought by some Gothic hand. These carvings, and the painted windows, and the few monuments, are all the details that the mind can catch hold of, in the immensity of this [213] void Cathedral; and I must say that it was a dreary place, in that cold, cloudy day. I doubt whether a Cathedral is a sort of edifice suited to the English climate; the first edifices of the kind were probably built by people who had bright and constant sunshine, and who desired a shadowy awfulness—like that of a forest, with its arched wood-paths—into which to retire, in their religious moments. In America, in a hot summer's day, how delightful its cool and solemn depths would be. The painted windows, too, were evidently contrived, in the first instance, by persons who saw how effective they would be, when a vivid sun shone through them. But, in England, the interior of a Cathedral, nine days out of ten, is a vast sullenness, and as chill as death and the tomb; at any rate, it was so to-day, and so thought one of the old vergers, who kept walking as briskly as he could along the width of the transepts. There were several of these old gentlemen when I first came in, but they went off, to their dinners, I suppose—all but this one—before I departed. None of them said a word to me, nor I to them; and admission to the Cathedral appears to be entirely free.

After emerging from this great gloom, I wandered to-and-fro about York, and contrived to go astray within [214] no very wide space. If its history be authentic, it is an immensely old city, having been founded about a thousand years before the Christian era. There used to be a palace of the Roman Emperors here; and the Emperor Severus died here, as did some of his successors; and Constantine the Great was born here. I know not what, if any, relics of those earlier times there may be; but York is still partly surrounded with a wall, and has several gates, which the city-authorities seem to take pains to keep in repair. I grew weary in the endeavor to find my way back to the railway, and inquired it of one of the good people of York—a respectable, courteous, gentlemanly person—and he told me to walk along the walls. Then he went on a considerable distance, but seemed to repent of not doing more for me; so he waited till I came up, and walking along by my side, pointed out the castle, (now the jail,) and the place of execution, and directed me to the principal gateway of the city, and instructed me how to reach the ferry. The path along the walls leads, in one place, through the room over the arch of a gateway; a low, thick-walled stone apartment, where doubtless the gatekeeper used to lodge, and to parley with those who desired entrance.

I found my way to the ferry over the Ouse, according [215] to this kind Yorkist's instructions. The ferryman told me that the fee for crossing was a half-penny, which seemed so ridiculously small that I offered him more; but this unparalleled Englishman declined taking anything beyond his rightful half-penny. This seems so wonderful to me that I can hardly trust my own memory. Reaching the station, I got some dinner; and at four o'clock, just as I was starting, came Mr. Bowman, my very agreeable and sensible travelling-companion. Our journey (so far as keeping one another company) was ended here; for he was to keep on to London, and I to return to Liverpool. So we parted; and I took the rail westward across England, through a very beautiful, and, in some degree, picturesque tract of country, diversified with hills, through the valley and vistas of which goes the track of the railway, with dells diverging from it on either hand, and streams, and arched bridges, and old villages, and a hundred pleasant English sights. After passing Rochdale, however, the dreary monotony of Lancashire succeeded this variety. Nothing else happened worthy of record; and, between nine and ten °clock, I reached the Tithebarn station in Liverpool, and took cab for Mrs. Blodget's. Ever since until now (½ past seven °clock, Saturday, May 17th) I [216] have employed my leisure moments in scribbling off this Journal of my tour; but it has lost immensely by not having been written day by day, as the scenes and occurrences were fresh. The most picturesque points can be seized in no other way; and the hues of the affair fade as quickly as those of a dying dolphin, or as, according to Audubon, the plumage of a dead bird does.[354]

One thing, that struck me as much as anything else, in the Highlands, I have forgotten to put down. In our walk at Balloch, along the road within view of Loch Lomond and the neighboring hills, it was a brilliant, sunshiny afternoon; and I never saw any atmosphere so beautiful as that among the mountains;—it was a clear, transparent, ethereal blue, as distinct as a vapor, and yet by no means vaporous, but a pure, crystalline medium. I have witnessed nothing like this among the Berkshire hills, nor elsewhere.

York is full of old churches, some of them very antique in appearance, the stones weather-worn, their edges rounded by time, blackened, and with all the tokens of sturdy and age-long decay; and in some of them I noticed windows quite full of old painted glass, a dreary kind of minute patchwork, all of one dark and dusty hue, or nearly so, when seen from the outside. Yet, had I seen them from the interior of the church, [217] there would doubtless have been rich and varied apparitions of saints, with their glories round their heads, and bright-winged angels, and perhaps even the Almighty Father Himself, so far as conceivable and representable by human powers. It is a good symbol of religion; the irreligious man sees only the pitiful outside of the painted window, and judges it entirely from that view; but he who stands within the holy precincts, the religious man, is sure of the glories which he beholds. And to push the simile a little farther, it requires light from Heaven to make them visible. If the church were merely illuminated from the inside— that is, by what light a man can get from his own understanding—the pictures would be invisible, or wear at best but a miserable aspect.[355]

"Oh that somebody would invent a new Sin," cried Bulwer, as reported by Dr. Mackay, "that I might go in for it!"

MAY 24th, SATURDAY.

DAY before yesterday, I had a call at the Consulate from one of the Potentates of the Earth—a woolly-haired mulatto man, rather thin and spare, between forty and fifty years of age, plainly dressed, at [218] the first glimpse of whom I could readily have mistaken him for some ship's steward, seeking to enter a complaint of his captain. However, this was President Roberts,[356] of Liberia, introduced by a note from Mrs. O'Sullivan, whom he has recently met in Madeira. I was rather favorably impressed with him; for his deportment was very simple, and without any of the flourish and embroidery which a negro might be likely to assume, on finding himself elevated from slavery to power. He is rather shy—reserved, at least, and undemonstrative, yet not harshly so— in fine, with manners that offer no prominent points for notice or criticism; although I felt, or thought I felt, that his color was continually before his mind, and that he walks cautiously among men, as conscious that every new introduction is a new experiment. He is not in the slightest degree (so far as I discovered in a very brief interview) an interesting man, apart from his position and history; his face is not striking, nor so agreeable as if it were jet-black; but there may be miles and miles of depth in him, which I saw nothing of. Our conversation was of the most unimportant character; for he had called merely to deliver Mrs. O'Sullivan's note, and sat only a few minutes, during which he merely responded to my observations, and origina[219]ted no remark. Intelligence, discretion, tact—these are probably his traits; not force of character and independence.

The same day, at three °clock, I took the rail from the Lime-street Station for Manchester, to meet Bennoch, who had asked me thither to dine with him. I had never visited Manchester before, though now so long resident within thirty miles of it; neither is it particularly worth visiting, unless for the sake of its factories, which I did not go to see. It is a dingy and heavy town, with very much the aspect of Liverpool, being, like the latter, built almost entirely within the present century. I stopt at the Albion Hotel; and, as Bennoch was out, I walked forth to view the city, and made only such observations as are recorded above. Opposite the Hotel stands the Infirmary, a very large edifice, which, when erected, was on the outskirts—or perhaps in the rural suburbs—of the town, but is now almost in its centre. In the enclosed space before it stands a statue of Peel, and sits a statue of Dr. Dalton, the celebrated chemist, who was a native of Manchester.

Returning to the Hotel, I sat down in the room where we were to dine; and, in due time, Bennoch [220] made his appearance, with the same glow and friendly warmth in his face that I had left burning there, when we parted in London. If this man has not a heart, then no man ever had. I like him inexpressibly, for his heart, and for his intellect, and for his flesh and blood; and if he has faults, I do not know them, nor care to know them, nor value him the less if I did know them. He went to his room to dress; and, in the meantime, a middle-aged, dark man, of pleasant aspect, with black hair, black eyebrows, and bright dark eyes, came in, limping a little, but not much; he seemed not quite a man of the world, a little shy or uncouth in manner, yet addressed me kindly and sociably. I guessed him (and rightly, as it proved) to be Mr. Charles Swain,[357] the poet, whom Mr. Bennoch had invited to dinner. Soon came another guest, whom Mr. Swain introduced to me as Mr. Ireland,[358] Editor of the Manchester Examiner. Then came Bennoch, who made us all regularly acquainted, or took for granted that we were so; and lastly appeared a Mr. Watson, a merchant in Manchester, and a very intelligent man—and the party was complete. We had a nice dinner; and the hotel being famous for its wines, we fared well in that respect.

[221] Mr. Swain, the poet, is not a man of fluent conversation; he said, indeed, very little, but gave me the impression of amiability and simplicity of

character, much feeling, no great energy, good sense, of which latter quality he makes, perhaps, but little use in his own behalf. Not that I take him to be, in any degree, one of those literary men who make their very moderate talent a plea for immoderate self-indulgence. I think him an irreproachable man, but probably an inefficient one. If we had been alone together, or with only Bennoch, I should have made him out more effectually; but these are about all my conclusions from what I saw of him. He is an engraver, I believe, by profession; and as to his poetry, though I had the volume, a year or two ago, I do not well recollect its contents.

Mr. Ireland, the Editor, is a Scotchman by birth, and saw Mr. Emerson, there, on his first visit to Europe, and directed him how to find Carlyle. When Emerson was again on this side of the water (some eight or ten years ago) Ireland asked him to Manchester, and made him his guest, and Emerson spent some time with him. Mr. Ireland is a very sensible, and seems to be a very good man, and talked earnestly in favor of the Maine Liquor law, while quaffing [222] sherry, champagne, hock, port, and claret. He is one of the few men (almost none, indeed,) who have read Thoreau's books; and he spoke of Margaret Fuller, too, and of the Dial, of which he was a reader from the beginning. Somehow or other, this vein of literary taste does not augur very great things, in Englishmen or Scotchmen; and, on the whole, I think the illiberals, the conservatives, the men who despise and hate new things and new thoughts, are the best worth knowing. The others, with all their zeal for novelty, do not seem to originate anything; and one feels, as it were, a little disgusted to find them setting forth their poor little views of progress, especially if one happens to have been a Brook Farmer. The best thing a man, born in this island, can do, is to eat his beef and mutton, and drink his port and porter, and take things as they are, and think thoughts that shall be so beef-ish, mutton-ish, port-ish, and porter-ish, that they shall be [indecipherable word] rather material than intellectual. In this way, he is natural, wholesome, and good; a being fit for the present time and circumstances, and entitled to let the future alone.

Mr. Watson is a very sensible man; he has spent [223] two or three years in America, and seems to have formed juster conclusions about us than most of his countrymen do. He is the only Englishman, I think, whom I have ever met, who fairly acknowledged that the English do cherish doubt, jealousy, suspicion, in short, an unfriendly feeling, towards the Americans. It is wonderful how every American, whatever class of the English he mingles with, is conscious of this feeling, and how no Englishman—except this sole Mr. Watson—will confess it. He expressed some very good ideas, too, about the English and American press, and the reasons why the "Times" may fairly be taken as the exponent of British feeling towards us, while the New York Herald—immense as its circulation is—can be considered, in no similar degree or kind—the American exponent.

We sat late at table; and after the other guests had retired, Bennoch and I had some very friendly talk; and he proposed that, on my wife's return, we should take up our residence in his house at Black Heath, while Mrs. Bennoch and himself are absent, for two months, on a trip to Germany. If his wife and mine ownest ratify the idea, we will do so.

We breakfasted at about 9, next morning, and then [224] went out to see the Exchange, and whatever was noticeable about the streets. Time being brief, I did not visit the Cathedral, which, I believe, is a thousand years old. There are many handsome shops in Manchester; and we went into one establishment, (the heads of which are Bennoch's acquaintances) devoted to pictures, engravings, and decorative art generally, which is much the most extensive and perfect that I have ever seen. The firm, if I remember, is that of the Messrs. Agnew; and though originating here, they have now a house in London. Here I saw some interesting objects purchased by them at the recent sale of the Rogers collection; among other things, a slight pencil and water-colored sketch by Raphael. An unfinished affair, done in a moment, as this must have been, seems to bring us closer to the hand that did it, than the most elaborately painted picture can. Were I to see the Transfiguration, Raphael would still be at the distance of centuries. Seeing this little sketch, I had him very near me. I know not why—perhaps it might be fancied that he had only laid down the pencil for an instant, and would take it up again in a moment more. I likewise saw a copy of a handsome, illustrated edition of Childe Harold, present[225]ed by old John Murray to Mr. Rogers, with an inscription on the flyleaf, purporting that it was a token of gratitude from the publisher, because, when everybody else thought him imprudent in giving 400 guineas for the poem, Mr. Rogers told him it would turn out the best bargain he ever made. There was a new picture by Millais, the distinguished Pre-Raphaelite artist, representing a melancholy parting between two lovers, or a husband and wife. The lady's face had a great deal of sad and ominous expression; but an old brick wall, over-run with foliage, was so exquisitely and elaborately wrought, that it was hardly possible to look at the personages of the picture. Every separate leaf of the climbing and clustering shrubbery was painfully made out; and the wall was reality itself, with the weather-stains, and the moss, and the crumbling lime between the bricks. It is not well to be so perfect in the inanimate, unless the artist can likewise make man and woman as lifelike—and to as great a depth too—as the Creator does.

Bennoch left town for some place in Yorkshire, at ten °clock, and I for Liverpool, at ½ past 11. I asked him to come and dine with me at the Adelphi, meaning to ask two or three people to meet him; but he had [226] other engagements, and could not spare a day, at present, though he promises to come before long.

Dining at Mr. Rathbone's, one evening last week (Wednesday, May 21st) it was mentioned that Borrow, author of the "Bible in Spain," is supposed to be of Gipsey [*sic*] descent by the mother's side. Hereupon Mr. Martineau mentioned that he had been a schoolfellow of Borrow, and that, though he had never heard of his having Gipsey [*sic*] blood, he thought it probable, from Borrow's traits of character. He said that Borrow had once run away from school, and carried with him a party of other boys, meaning to lead a wandering life. They were intercepted and sent back, however; and when Borrow was flogged for this offence, he was "horsed" on Mr. Martineau's back. Mr M. is of opinion that the accuracy of Borrow's statements on any subject is not to be depended on; not that he means to be untrue, but that his imagination misleads him.

In my description of the Lord Mayor's dinner, I ought to have mentioned, that, at the point of the festival when finger-glasses are usually introduced, a large silver basin [227] was carried round to the guests, containing rose-water, in which we dipped our napkins. The same fashion was followed in Bennoch's Manchester dinner. It is doubtless an old custom.

If an Englishman were individually acquainted with all our twenty-five millions of Americans—and liked every man of them, and believed that each man of those millions was a Christian, honest, upright, and kind,—he would doubt, despise, and hate them in the aggregate, however he might love and honor the individuals.

Captain Devereux and his wife Oakum;—they spent an evening at Mrs. Blodget's. The Captain is a Marblehead man by birth, not far from sixty years old; very talkative, and anecdotic in regard to his adventures, funny, good-humored, and full of various nautical experience. Oakum (it is a nickname which he gives his wife) is an inconceivably tall woman—taller than he—six feet at least, and with a well-proportioned largeness in all respects, but looks kind and good, gentle, smiling—a fine old girl; and almost any other woman might sit like a [228] baby on her lap. She does not look at all awful and belligerent, like the massive Englishwomen whom one often sees. You at once feel her to be a benevolent giantess, and apprehend no harm from her. She is a lady, and perfectly well-mannered, but with a sort of naturalness and simplicity that becomes her well; for any the slightest affectation would be so magnified in her vast personality, that it would be absolutely the height of the ridiculous. This wedded pair have no children, and Oakum has so long accompanied her husband on his voyages that, I suppose, by this time, she could command a ship as well as he. In case of a mutiny, she would be a host by herself. What a vast amount of connubial bliss she[359] They sat with us till pretty late, diffusing cheerfulness all about them; and then "Come, Oakum," cried the Captain, "we must hoist sail!"—and uprose Oakum to the cieling [*sic*], and moved towerlike to the door, looking down with a benignant smile on the poor little pigmy women around her. "Six feet," did I say? Why she must be seven, eight, nine—and whatever be her size, she is good as she is great.

JUNE 11th WEDNESDAY.

[229] MONDAY night, just as I was going to bed, I received a telegraphic message announcing Sophia's arrival at Southampton. So, the next day, I arranged the consular business for an absence of ten days, and set forth with Julian by the five °clock train, and reached Birmingham between eight and nine. We put up at the Queen's Hotel, an immense establishment, contiguous to the railway. Next morning, we left Birmingham at nine °clock, and made our first stage to Leamington, where we had to wait the better part of an hour, which we spent in wandering through some of the streets that had been familiar to us, last year. Leamington is certainly a beautiful town, new, bright, clean, and as unlike as possible to the business towns of England. Moreover, the sun was burning hot, and I could almost have fancied myself in America. From Leamington, we took tickets to Oxford, where we had to make another stop of two hours; and these we employed to what advantage we could, riding up into the town per omnibus, and straying hither and thither, till Julian's weariness weighed upon me, and I adjourned with him to a hotel. Oxford is an ugly old town, of crooked and irregular streets; gabled houses, mostly plastered of a buff or yellow hue; some new fronts, and as for the buildings of the University, they [230] seem to be scattered at random, without any reference among one another. I passed through the old gateway of Christ Church, and looked at its enclosed square; and that is, in truth, pretty much all I have seen of the University of Oxford. From Christ Church, we rambled along a street that led us to a bridge across the Isis; and we saw many row-boats lying in the river—the lightest craft imaginable, unless it were an Indian canoe. The Isis is but a narrow stream, and with a sluggish current. I believe the students of Oxford are famous for their skill in rowing.

To me, as well as to Julian, the hot streets (it was as hot a day as ever I saw in England) were terribly oppressive; so we went into the Roebuck Hotel, where we found a cool and pleasant coffee-room. The entrance to this hotel is through an arch, opening from High-street (I think) and giving admission into a paved court, the buildings all around being part of the establishment— old edifices with pointed gables, and old-fashioned projecting windows, but all in fine repair, and wearing a most quiet, retired, and comfortable aspect. The court was set all round with flowers, growing in pots or large pedestalled vases; on one side was the coffee-room, and all the other public apartments; and [231] the other side seemed to be taken up by the sleeping chambers and parlours of the guests. This arrangement of an inn, I presume, is very ancient; and it resembles what I have seen in the Hospitals, free schools, and other charitable establishments in the old English towns; and, indeed, all large houses were arranged on somewhat of the same principle.

I ordered luncheon—some cold beef (which Julian and I found remarkably good) and some ale, which was not so much to my liking. By-and-by, two or three young men came in, in wide-awake hats, and loose, blouse-like, summerish garments; and from their talk, I found them to be students of the University, although their topics of conversation were almost entirely horses and boats. One of them sat down to the cold beef and a tankard of ale; the other two drank a tankard of ale together, and went away without paying for it—rather to the waiter's discontent. Students are very much alike, all the world over, and, I suppose, in all time; but I doubt whether many of my fellows at college would have gone off without paying for their beer. At two °clock, we returned to the railway station, and, crossing from one line to another, and meeting with some accidental de[232]lays, we reached Southampton between seven and eight °clock. I cannot write to-day.

JUNE 15th, SUNDAY.

THE first day after we reached Southampton was sunny and pleasant; but we made little use of the fine weather, except that Sophia and I walked once along the High Street, and Julian and I took a little ramble about town, in the afternoon. The next day, there was a high and disagreeable wind, and I did not once stir out of the house. The third day, too, I kept entirely within doors; it being a storm of wind and rain. The Castle Hotel stands within fifty yards of the waterside; so that this gusty day showed itself to the utmost advantage—the vessels pitching and tossing, at their moorings, the waves breaking white out of a tumultuous gray surface, the opposite shore glooming mistily, at a distance of a mile or two; and on the hither side, boatmen and seafaring people scudding about the pier in water-proof clothes; and in the street, before the hotel-door, a cabman or two standing drearily beside his horse. But we were sunny within doors.

Yesterday, it was breezy, sunny, shadowy, showery; and we ordered a cab at half-past eleven to take us to Clifton Villa, to call on Mrs. Hume, a friend of Bennoch's, who [233] called on us the day after our arrival. Just as we were ready to start, Mrs. Hume again called, and accompanied us back to her house. It is in Shirley, about two miles from Southampton; and is a pleasant suburban villa, with a pretty ornamented lawn and shrubbery about it. Mrs. Hume is an instructress of young ladies; and at Bennoch's suggestion, she is willing to receive us for two or three weeks, until my wife is ready to go to London. She seems to be a pleasant and sensible woman; and tomorrow we shall decide whether to go there. There was nothing very remarkable, on this drive; and, indeed, my stay hereabouts, thus far, has been very barren of sights and incidents externally interesting, though the inner life has been rich.

Southampton is a very pretty town, and has not the dinginess to which I have been accustomed in English towns. The High Street reminds me very much of American streets, in its general effect, the houses being mostly stuccoed white, or light, and cheerful in aspect; though, doubtless, they are centuries old, at heart. The old gateway (which I presume I have mentioned in describing my former visit to Southampton) stands across High Street, about in the centre of the town, and is almost the only token of antiquity that [234] presents itself to the eye.

JUNE 17th TUESDAY.

YESTERDAY morning, at ½ past nine, wife, Mrs. Hume, and I, took the rail for Salisbury, where we duly arrived, without any accident, or anything noticeable—except the usual verdure and richness of an English summer-landscape. From the railway-station, we walked up into Salisbury, with the tall spire (400 feet high, the tallest in England) of the cathedral before our eyes. Salisbury is an antique city, but with more regular streets than most old towns have; and the houses have a more picturesque aspect than Oxford, for instance, where almost all are mean-looking alike. Through one of the streets, if not more, there was a swift, clear little stream, which, being close to the pavement, and bordered with stone, may be called, I suppose, a kennel, though possessing the transparent purity of a rustic rivulet. It is a brook in city garb.

We passed under the pointed arch of a gateway, which stands across one of the principal streets, and soon came in front of the Cathedral. I do not remember any cathedral with so fine a site as this, rising up out of the centre of a beautiful green, extensive enough to show its full proportions, relieved and insulated from all other patch-work and imperti[235]nence of rusty edifies. It is of gray stone, and looks as perfect as when just finished, and with a perfection, too, that could not have come in less than six centuries, of venerableness, with a view to which these edifices seem to have been built. A new cathedral would lack the last-touch to its beauty and grandeur; it needs to be mellowed and ripened, like some pictures; although, I suppose, this awfulness of antiquity was supplied, in the minds of the generation who built cathedrals, by the sanctity which they attributed to them. Salisbury Cathedral is far more beautiful than that of York, the exterior of which was really disagreeable to my eye; but this mighty spire, and these multitudinous gray pinnacles and towers, ascend towards Heaven with a kind of natural beauty, not as if man had contrived them; they might be fancied to have grown up, just as the spires of a tuft of grass do, at the same time that they have a law or propriety and regularity among themselves. The tall spire is of such admirable proportion that it does not seem gigantic; and, indeed, the effect of the whole edifice is of beauty, rather than weight and massiveness. Perhaps the bright, balmy sunshine, in which we saw it, contributed to give the edifice a tender glory, and to soften a little its majesty.

[236] When we went in, the organ was playing, the forenoon service being

just about concluding. If I had never seen the interior of York Cathedral, I should have been quite satisfied, no doubt, with the spaciousness of this nave, and these side-aisles, and the height of these arches, and the girth of these pillars; but with that recollection in my mind, they fall a little short of grandeur. The interior is seen to disadvantage, and in a way the builder never meant it to be seen; because there is little or no painted glass, nor any such mystery as it makes, but only a common, colorless daylight, revealing everything without remorse. There is a general light hue, moreover, like that of white-wash (which I believe has really been applied) over the whole of the roof and walls of the interior, pillars, monuments, and all; whereas, originally, every pillar was polished, and the cieling [sic] was ornamented in brilliant colors, and the light came many-hued through the windows, on all this elaborate beauty; in lieu of which there is nothing now but space.

Between the pillars that separate the nave from the side aisles, there are ancient tombs, most of which have recumbent statues on them. One of these is Longsword, Earl of Salisbury, son of Fair Rosamond, in chain-mail; and there [237] are many other warriors, and bishops, and one cross-legged Crusader, and, on one tomb-stone, a recumbent skeleton, which I have likewise seen in two or three other Cathedrals. The pavement of the aisles and nave is laid, in great part, with flat tombstones, the inscriptions on which are half obliterated; and on the walls, especially in the transepts, there are tablets, among which I saw one to the poet Bowles, who was a canon of this Cathedral. The ecclesiastical dignitaries bury themselves, and monument themselves, to the exclusion of almost everybody else, in these latter times; though still, as of old, the warrior has his place. A young officer, slain in the Indian wars, was memorialized by a tablet, and may be remembered by it, six hundred years hence, as we now remember the old knights and crusaders. It deserves to be mentioned that I saw one or two noses still unbroken, among these recumbent figures. Most of the antique statues, on close examination, proved to be almost entirely covered with names and initials, scratched over the once polished surface. The Cathedral and its relics must have been far less carefully watched, at some former period, than now.

[238] Between the nave and the choir, as usual, there is a screen, that half destroys the majesty of the Cathedral, by abridging the spectator of the long vista which he might otherwise have, of the whole interior at a glance. We peeped through this barrier, and saw some elaborate monuments in the chancel beyond; but the doors of the screen are kept locked, so that the vergers may raise a revenue by showing strangers through the richest part of the Cathedral. By and by, one of these vergers emerged through the screen, with a gentleman and lady whom he was taking round, and we joined ourselves to the party. He showed us into the cloisters, which had long been neglected and ruinous, until the time of Bishop Dennison [Denison], the last prelate, who has been but a few years dead. This bishop has repaired and restored the cloisters,

in faithful adherence to the original plan; and they now form a most delightful
walk about a pleasant and verdant enclosure, in the centre of which sleeps good
Bishop Dennison, with a wife on either side of him, all three beneath broad,
flat stones. Most cloisters are darksome and grim; but these have a broad,
paved walk, beneath the vista of arches, and are light, airy, and cheerful; and
from one corner, you can get the best possible view of the whole [239]
height and beautiful proportion of the Cathedral spire. One side of this cloistered walk seems to be the length, or nearly the length, of the nave of the
Cathedral; there is a square of four such sides; and of all places for meditation,
grave, yet not too sombre, it seemed to me one of the best. While we staid
there, a jackdaw was walking to-and-fro across the grassy enclosure, and
haunting around the good Bishop's grave. He was clad in black, and looked
like a feathered ecclesiastic; but I know not whether it was Bishop Dennison's
ghost, or that of some old monk.

On one side of the cloisters, and contiguous to the main body of the Cathedral, stands the Chapter House. Bishop Dennison had it much at heart
to repair this part of the holy edifice, and, if I mistake not, did begin the
work; for it had been long ruinous, and in Cromwell's time, his dragoons
stabled their horses there. Little progress, however, had been made in the
repairs, when the Bishop died; and it was decided to restore the building,
in his honor, and by way of monument to him. The repairs are now nearly completed; and the interior of this Chapter House gave me the first idea, anywise adequate, that I ever had, of the splendor of these [240] Gothic church-
edifices. The roof of the building is sustained by one great central pillar
of polished marble (small pillars, clustered about a great central column)
which rises to the cieling [*sic*] and there gushes out into various beauty, that
overflows all the walls; as if the fluid idea had sprung out of that fountain,
and grown durable in what we see. The pavement is elaborately ornamented;
the cieling [*sic*] is to be brilliantly gilded and painted, as it was of yore; and the
tracery and sculptures around the walls are to be faithfully renewed from
what remains of the original patterns.

After viewing the Chapter House, the verger (an elderly man, of grave,
benign manner, clad in black, and talking of the Cathedral and the monuments
as if he loved them) led us again into the nave of the Cathedral, and thence
within the screen of the choir. The screen is as bad as possible, mere barren
wood-work, without the least attempt at beauty. In the chancel, there are some
meagre patches of old glass, and some of modern date, not very well worth
looking at. We saw several interest[ing] monuments in this part of the
Cathedral; one, belonging to the ducal family of Somerset, and erected in
the reign of James I—of marble, extremely splendid and elab[241]orate,
with kneeling figures, and all manner of magnificence, more than I ever saw
in any monument, except that of Mary of Scotland, in Westminster Abbey.
The more ancient tombs are also very numerous, and among them that of the

bishop who founded the Cathedral. Within the screen, too, against the wall, is erected a monument by Chantrey to the Earl of Malmesbury; a full length statue of the Earl, in a half recumbent position, holding an open volume, and looking upward—a noble performance,—a calm, wise, thoughtful, firm, and not unbenignant face. Beholding its expression, it really was impossible not to have faith in the high character of the individual thus represented; and I have seldom felt this effect (which, I presume, is always aimed at) from any monumental bust or statue.

I am weary of trying to describe Cathedrals; it is utterly useless; there is no possibility of giving the general effect, or any shadow of it; and it is miserable to put down a few items of tombstones, and a bit of glass from a painted window, as if the gloom and glory of the edifice were thus to be re-produced. Cathedrals are almost the only things (if even those) that have quite [242] filled out my ideal, here in the old world; and Cathedrals often make me miserable from my inadequacy to take them wholly in; and, above all, I despise myself when I sit down to describe them.

Emerging from the great, old edifice, we walked around the Cathedral Close, which is surrounded by some of the quaintest and comfortablest ecclesiastical residences, that can be imagined. These are the dwelling-houses of the dean, and the canons, and whatever other high officers compose the bishop's staff; and there was one large brick mansion, old, but not so ancient as the rest, which we took to be the bishop's palace. I never beheld anything—I must say again—so cozy, so indicative of domestic comfort for whole centuries together —houses so fit to live in, or to die in, and where it would be so pleasant to lead a young maiden wife beneath the antique portal, and dwell with her, till husband and wife were patriarchal—as those delectable old houses. They belong naturally to the Cathedral, and have a necessary relation to it; and its sanctity is somehow thrown over them all, so that they do not quite belong to this world, though they look full to overflowing of whatever earthly things are good for man. These are places, however, in which [243] mankind makes no progress; the rushing tumult of human life here subsides into a deep, quiet pool, with perhaps a gentle circular eddy, but no onward movement. The same identical thought, I suppose, goes round, in a slow whirl, from one generation to another, as I have seen a withered leaf do, in the pool of a brook. In front of the Cathedral, there is a most stately and beautiful tree, which flings its verdure upward to a very lofty height; but, far above it, rises the tall spire, dwarfing the great tree by comparison. I wonder whether the clouds do not sometimes envelope the upper half of this spire.

When the Cathedral had sufficiently oppressed us with its beauty, we returned to sublunary matters, and went wandering about Salisbury in search of a luncheon, which we finally took in a confectioner's shop. Then we inquired, hither and thither, at various livery-stables, for a conveyance to Stonehenge, and at last took a one-horse fly from the Lamb Hotel. The ride

was by a turnpike, for the first seven miles, over a bare, ridgy country, showing little to interest us. We passed a party of seven or eight men, in a coarse
uniform dress, resembling that worn by convicts, and apparently [244] under
the guardianship of a stout, authoritative, yet rather kindly-looking man, with
a cane. Our driver said that they were lunatics from a neighboring asylum, out
for a walk. Seven miles from Salisbury, we turned aside from the turnpike, and
drove two miles or so across Salisbury plain, which is an apparently boundless
extent of uninclosed land, treeless, and houseless. It is not exactly a plain, but
a green sea of long and gentle swells and subsidences, affording views of
miles upon miles, to a very far horizon. We passed large flocks of sheep, with
the shepherds watching them; but the dogs seemed to take most of the care
of the flocks upon their own shoulders, and would scamper to turn the sheep,
when they inclined to stray whither they should not; and then arose a thou-
sand-fold bleating, not unpleasant to the ear, for it did not appear to indicate
any fear or discomfort on the part of the flock. The sheep and lambs are all
black-faced, and have a very funny expression.

As we drove over the plain (my seat was beside the driver) I saw, at a distance, a cluster of large gray stones, mostly standing upright, and some of
them slightly inclined towards each other—very irregular, and, so far off,
forming [245] no very picturesque or noteworthy spectacle. Of course, I knew
at once that this was Stonehenge, and also knew that the reality was going
to dwindle woefully within my ideal, as almost everything else does. When
we reached the spot, we found a pic-nic party just finishing their dinner, on
one of the overthrown stones of the druidical temple; and within the sacred
circle, an artist was painting a wretched daub of the scene; and an old
shepherd (I suppose, the very Shepherd of Salisbury Plain[360]) sat erect in the
centre of the ruin.

There never was a ruder thing than Stonehenge made by mortal hands; it is
so very rude, that it seems as if Nature and man had worked upon it with one
consent, and so it is all the stranger and more impressive from its rudeness.
The spectator wonders to see art and contrivance, and a regular and even
somewhat intricate plan, beneath all the uncouth simplicity of this arrangement
of rough stones; and, certainly, whatever was the intellectual and scientific ad-
vancement of the people who built Stonehenge, no succeeding architects will
ever have a right to triumph over them; for nobody's work, in after times, is
likely to endure till it becomes a mystery who built [246] it, and how, and
for what purpose. Apart from the moral considerations suggested by it, Stonehenge is not very well worth seeing. Materially, it is one of the poorest of
spectacles; and when complete, it must have been even less picturesque
than now—a few huge, rough stones, very imperfectly squared, standing on
end, and supporting a third huge stone on their two tops; other stones, of
the same pattern, overthrown, and tumbled one upon another; and the whole
comprised within a circuit of about a hundred feet diameter;—the short,

sheep-cropt grass of Salisbury plain growing among all these uncouth boulders. I am not sure that a misty, lowering day would not have better suited
Stonehenge, as the dreary mid-point of the great, desolate, trackless plain;—
not literally trackless, however, for the London and Exeter road passes within
fifty yards of the ruins, and another road intersects it.

After we had been there about an hour, there came a horseman within the
druid's circle;—evidently a clerical personage by his white neckcloth, though
his loose gray riding pantaloons were not quite in keeping. He looked at us
rather earnestly, and at last addressed Mrs. Hume, and [247] announced
himself as Mr. Hinchman—a clergyman whom she had been trying to find in
Salisbury, in order to avail herself of him as a cicerone; and he had now
ridden hither to meet us. He told us that the artist, whom we found here, could
give us more information than anybody, about Stonehenge; for, it seems, he
has spent a great many years here, painting and selling his poor sketches
to visitors, and also selling a book which his father wrote about the remains.
This man showed, indeed, a pretty accurate acquaintance with these old stones,
and pointed out what is thought to be the altar stone, and told us of some relation between this stone, and two other stones, and the rising of the sun
at midsummer, which might appear to indicate that Stonehenge was a temple
of solar worship. He pointed out, too, to how little depth the stones were
planted in the earth; insomuch that I have no doubt the American frosts
would overthrow Stonehenge in a single winter; and it is wonderful that it
should have stood so long, even in England. I have forgotten what else he said;
but I bought one of his books, and find it a very unsatisfactory performance,
being chiefly taken up with an attempt to prove these remains to be an ante-
diluvian work, construc[248]ted, I think the author says, under the super-
intendence of Father Adam himself! Before our departure, we were requested
to write our names in the Album, which the artist keeps for the purpose; and
he pointed out President Fillmore's autograph, and that of one or two other
Americans, who have been here within a short time. It is a very curious
life that this artist leads, amid the great solitude, and haunting Stonehenge
like the ghost of a druid; but he seems a brisk little man, and very communicative on his one subject.

Mr. Hinchman rode with us over the plain, and pointed out Salisbury spire,
visible close to Stonehenge. Under his guidance, we returned by a different
road from that which brought us thither—and a much more delightful one.
I think I never saw such a succession of sylvan beauty as this road showed
us, passing through a good deal of woodland scenery—fine old trees, standing
each within its own space, and thus having full liberty to outspread itself and
wax strong and broad, for ages, instead of being crowded, and thus stifled
and emaciated, as human beings are here, and forest-trees are in America.
Hedges, too; and the rich, rich verdure of England; and villages, full of picturesque old hovels, thatched, and ivied, or per[249]haps overrun with roses;

and a stately mansion in the Elizabethan style; and a quiet stream, gliding onward without a ripple from its own motion, but rippled by a large fish, darting across it;—and over all this scene, a gentle, friendly sunshine, not ardent enough to crisp a single leaf or blade of grass. Nor must the village church be forgotten, with its square, battlemented tower, dating back to the epoch of the Normans. We called at a house where one of Mrs. Hume's pupils was residing with her aunt; a thatched house of two stories high, built in what was originally a sand-pit, but which, in the course of a good many years, had been transformed into the most delightful and homelike little nook, almost, that can be found in England. A thatched cottage suggests a very rude dwelling indeed; but this cottage had a pleasant parlor and drawing-room, and chamber with lattice-windows opening close beneath the thatched-roof; and the thatch itself gives an air to the place as if it were a bird's nest, or some such simple and natural habitation. The occupants are an elderly clergyman (retired from professional duty) and, I think, his sister; and having nothing else to do, and sufficient means, they employ them[250]selves in beautifying this sweet little retreat, planting new shrubbery, laying out new walks around it, and helping Nature to add continually another charm; and Nature is certainly a more genial playfellow in England than in my own country. She is always ready to lend her aid to any beautifying purpose.

Leaving these good people (who were very hospitable, giving the ladies some tea, and offering me some wine) we reached Salisbury in time to take the train at half-past six.

JUNE 18th WEDNESDAY.

YESTERDAY, we left the Castle Hotel, after paying a bill of about £ 20 for a little more than a week's board. In America, we could not very well have lived so simply; but we might have lived luxuriously for half the money. This Castle Hotel, or a portion of it, was once a castle, (an old Roman castle, the landlord says) and the circular sweep of the tower is still seen towards the street, although, being painted white, and built up with modern additions, it would not be taken for an ancient structure. There is a dungeon beneath it, in which the landlord keeps his wine.

Julian and I, on quitting the hotel, walked towards [251] Shirley along the water-side, leaving Mamma and the rest of the family to follow in a fly. There are many traces, along the shore, of the fortifications by which Southampton was formerly defended, towards the water; and, very probably, their foundations may be as ancient as Roman times. Our hotel was no doubt connected with this chain of defences, which seems to have consisted of a succession of round towers, with a wall extending from one to another. We saw two or three of these towers, still standing, and likely to stand, though ivy-grown, and ruinous at the summit, and intermixed and even amalgamated with pot-houses and mean dwellings; and often through an antique arch there was a narrow door-way, giving access to the home of some sailor, or laborer, or artisan, and his wife gossiping at it with her neighbor, or his children playing about it.

After getting beyond the precincts of Southampton, our walk was not very interesting, except to Julian, who kept running down to the verge of the water (or rather, the mud, for the tide was low) looking for shells and sea-insects. We reached Mrs. Hume's house between six and seven °clock; and my wife and the [252] rest of us arrived soon afterwards. We purposed boarding with Mrs Hume (that is, Sophia and the children, and myself whenever I could leave Liverpool) for some weeks; but, looking a little more closely at the lady and her environment, I do not feel quite sure that the scheme will be acted out. She seems to be a good and well-meaning little woman, with spirit, energy, and self-dependence; and being at the head of a respectable school for young ladies, it would be natural to suppose her cultivated and refined. But (at this stage of our acquaintance) I should pronounce her underbred, shallow, affected, (not through a natural lack of simplicity, but because her position impels her to pretend to qualities which she does not possess,) and, on the whole, a wearisome and unintentionally annoying sort of person. As mistress of a school, her faculties must be administrative, rather than instructive. If she fed us better, I suppose I might be more lenient in my judgments; but eight months at Mrs. Blodget's table have not been a very good preparation for the schoolgirls' bread and butter, morning and night, and the simple joint of mutton, at two °clock, which this good lady sets before us.

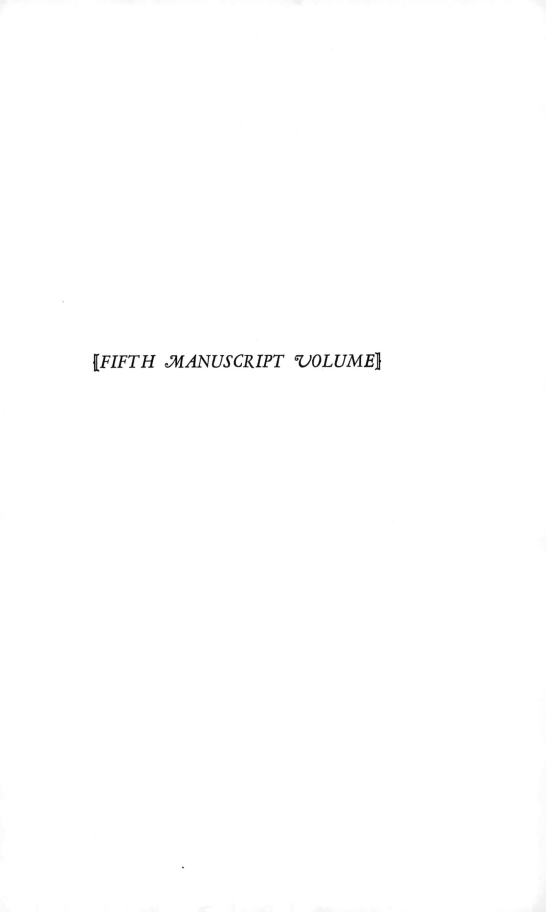

⟦*FIFTH MANUSCRIPT VOLUME*⟧

1856

JUNE 29th 1856, SATURDAY.

ON Friday, at 1 ¼, I left Liverpool from the Lime-street Station; an exceedingly hot day, for England, insomuch that the rail carriages were really uncomfortable. I have now passed over the London and Northwestern Railway so often, that the northern part of it, near Liverpool, is very wearisome; especially as it has few features of interest, even to a new observer. At Stafford, I think (no, at Wolverhampton) we diverged to a track which I have passed over only once before. We stopt an hour and a quarter at Wolverhampton, and I walked up into the town, which seems to be large and old—old, at least, in its plan, or lack of plan; the streets being irregular, and straggling over an uneven surface. Like many of the English towns, it reminds me of Boston, though dingier. The sun was so hot in Wolverhampton that I actually sought the shady sides of the streets; this, of itself, is one long step towards establishing a resemblance between an English town and an American one.

English railway carriages seem to me more tiresome than ours; and I suppose it is owing to the greater [2] motion arising from their more elastic springs. A slow train, too, like that which I was now in, is more tiresome than a quick one; at least to the spirits, whatever it may be to the body. We loitered along, through afternoon and evening, stopping at every little station, and nowhere getting to the top of our speed; till, at last, in the late dusk (at about ten ºclock) we reached Gloucester, and I put up at the Wellington Hotel, which is but a little way from the Station. I took tea and a slice or two of ham in the Coffee Room, and had a little talk with two people there; one of whom, on learning that I was an American, said—"But I suppose you have now been in England some time?" He meant (finding me not absolutely a savage) that I must have been caught a good while ago. Then I went into the smoking-room, where a number of the citizens of Gloucester were drinking ale and smoking pipes; and I left them still at it, when I went to bed. Under the chamber in which I slept, there were some people singing songs, and I believe it was after midnight before these boon-companions wended their way homeward, singing as they went.

The next morning, I went into the city (the hotel [3] being on its outskirts) and rambled about in search of the Cathedral. Some church-bells were chiming and clashing for a wedding, or other festal occasion; and I followed the sound, supposing that it might proceed from the Cathedral; but this was not the case. It was not till I had got to a bridge over the Severn, quite out of the town, that I saw again the tower of the Cathedral (which I had already seen from the vicinity of the railway) and knew how to shape my course towards it.

I did not see much that was strange or interesting in Gloucester; it is old, with a good many of those antique Elizabethan houses, with two or three peaked gables on a line together; several old churches, which seem always to cluster about a cathedral, like chickens round a hen; a hospital for decayed tradesmen; another for blue-coat boys; a great many butcher's shops scattered in all parts of the town, open in front, with a counter, or dresser, on which to display the meat, just in the old fashion of Shakspeare's house. It is a large town, and has a good deal of liveliness and bustle, in a provincial way. In fact, judging by the sheep, [4] cattle, and horses, and the people of agricultural aspect that I saw about the streets, I should think it must have been market-day. I looked here and there for the old Bell Inn, because, unless I mis-remember, Fielding brings Tom Jones to this Inn, while he and Partridge were travelling together.[361] It is still extant; for, on my arrival, the night before, a runner from it had asked me to go thither; but I forgot its celebrity, at the moment. Well; I saw nothing of it, in my rambles about Gloucester; but, at last, I found the Cathedral, though there is no point (at least, I found none) from which a very good view of the exterior can be gained.

It has a very rich and beautiful outside, however, and a lofty tower, very large and ponderous, but so finished off, and adorned with pinnacles, and all manner of architectural devices—wherewith these old builders knew how to alleviate their massive structures—that it seems to sit lightly in the air. The porch was open, and some workmen were trundling barrows into the nave; so I followed, and found two young women sitting just within the porch, one of whom offered to show me round the Cathedral. There was a great [5] dust in the nave, arising from the operations of the workmen. They had been laying a new pavement, I believe, and scraping away the plaister [sic] which had heretofore been laid over the pillars and walls. The pillars come out from this process as good as new; great, round, massive columns, not clustered like those of most Cathedrals; they are twenty-one feet in circumference, and support semicircular arches. I think there are seven of these columns on each side of the nave, which did not impress me as very spacious; and the dust and racket of the work-people quite destroyed the effect which should have been produced by the aisles and arches; so that I hardly stopt to glance at this part of the Cathedral, though I saw some mural monuments, and recumbent statues, along the walls.

The choir is separated from the nave by the usual screen, and now by a sail-cloth, or something of that kind, drawn across, in order to keep out the dust, while the repairs are going on. When the young woman conducted me hither, I was at once struck by the magnificent eastern window, the largest in England, [6] which fills, or looks vast enough to fill, all that end of the cathedral; a most splendid window, full of old painted glass, which looked as bright as sunshine, though really the sun was not then shining through it. The roof of the choir, too, is very fine, of oak, and as much as ninety-feet high. There are chapels opening from the choir, and within them the monuments of the eminent people who built them, and of others, benefactors or prelates of the Cathedral, or otherwise illustrious in their day. My recollection of what I saw here is very dim and confused; more so than I anticipated. I remember, in one of the chapels—or, at any rate, somewhere within the choir— the tomb of Edward II with himself upon the top of it, in a long robe, with a crown on his head, and ball and sceptre in his hand; likewise, a statue of Robert, son of the Conqueror, carved in Irish oak, and painted; he lolls in an easy posture on his tomb, with one leg crossed lightly over the other, to denote that he was a Crusader. There are several monuments of mitred abbots, who formerly presided over the Cathedral. A cavalier and his wife, with the dress of the period elaborately represented, lie [7] side by side, in excellent preservation; and it is remarkable that, though their noses are very prominent, they have come down from the past without any wear and tear. The date of the Cavalier's death is 1639; and I think his statue could not have been sculptured until after the Restoration; else he and his dame would hardly have come through Cromwell's time unscathed. Here, as in all the other churches in England, Cromwell is said to have stabled his horses, and broken the windows, and belabored the old monuments.

There is one large and beautiful Chapel, styled the Lady's Chapel, which is indeed a church by itself, being ninety feet along, and comprising everything that appertains to a place of worship. Here, too, there are monuments; and under foot are many old bricks and tiles, with inscriptions on them, or Gothic devices; and flat tombstones, with coats of arms sculptured into them, as, indeed, there are everywhere else about the Cathedral, except in the nave, where the new pavement has obliterated them. After viewing the choir and the chapels, the young woman led me down into the crypts below, where [8] the dead persons, commemorated in the upper region, were buried. The low, ponderous pillars, and arches of these crypts are supposed to be older than the upper portions of the Cathedral; they are about as perfect, I suppose, as when new, but very damp, dreary, and darksome, and the arches intersect one another so intricately that, if the girl had deserted me, I might easily have got lost there. There are chapels in the crypts, where masses used to be said for the souls of the deceased; and my guide said that a great many sculls [*sic*] and bones have been dug up here. No doubt, a vast population has been deposited here, in the course of a thousand years. I saw two white sculls [*sic*], in a niche, grinning, as sculls [*sic*] always do, though it is impossible to see the joke. These crypts—or crypts like these—are doubtless what Congreve calls the "aisles and monumental caves of Death," in that passage which Dr. Johnson admired so much.[362] They are very singular—something like a dark shadow or dismal repetition of the church, below ground.

Ascending from the crypts, we went next into the cloisters, which are in a very perfect state, and form [9] an unbroken square about the green grass plot enclosed within. Here, it is said, Cromwell stabled his horses; but, if so, they were remarkably quiet beasts; for tombstones, which form the pavement, are not broken nor cracked, nor have any hoof-marks; all around the cloisters, too, the stone-tracery that shuts them in, like a closed curtain drawn carefully, remains as it was in the days of the monks; insomuch that [it] is not easy to get a glimpse of the green enclosure. Probably there used to be painted glass in the larger apertures of this stone-work; otherwise it is perfect, and has required very little renewal or repair. These cloisters are very different from the free, open, and airy ones, which we saw at Salisbury; but they are more in accordance with one's notions of monkish habits, and even at this day, if I were a canon of Gloucester, I would put that dim ambulatory to a good use. The library of the Cathedral (I peeped into it, and saw some rows of folios and quartos) is adjacent to the Cloisters. I have nothing else to record about Gloucester Cathedral; though, if I were to stay there a month, I suppose it might then [10] begin to grow interesting. It is wicked to look at these solemn old churches in a hurry. By the by, it was not built in a hurry, but in full four hundred years; having been begun in 1088, and only finished in 1498, not a great many years before Papistry and Cathedrals began to go out of vogue in England.

From Gloucester, at about ½ past eleven, I took the rail for Basingstoke, where the Great Western route intersects with that from London to Southampton. The first part of the journey was through as beautiful a tract of country as I have seen in England; hilly, but not wild; a tender and graceful picturesqueness—fine trees, and clumps of trees, and sometimes wide woods, scattered over the landscape, and filling the nooks of the hills with luxuriant foliage. Old villages scattered frequently along our track, looking very peaceful, with the peace of past ages lingering about them; and a rich, rural verdure of antique cultivation, everywhere. Old country-seats—specimens of the old English hall, or manor-house—appeared on the hill-sides, with park-scenery about them; and the gray churches rose in the midst of all the little towns. The beauty of En[11]glish scenery makes me desperate, it is so impossible to describe it, or in any way to record its impression, and such a pity to leave it undescribed; and, moreover, I always feel that I do not get from it a hundredth or a millionth part of the enjoyment that there really is in it, hurrying past it thus. I was really glad when we rumbled into a tunnel, piercing a long distance through a hill; and emerging on the other side, we found ourselves in a comparatively level and uninteresting tract of country, which lasted till we reached Southampton. English scenery, to be appreciated, and to be re-produced with pen or pencil, requires to be dwelt upon long, and to be wrought out with the nicest touches. A coarse and hasty brush is not the instrument for such work.

JULY 6th SUNDAY.

MONDAY, June 30th, was a warm and beautiful day; and my wife and I took a cab from Southampton and drove to Netley Abbey, about three or four miles. The remains of the Abbey stand in a sheltered place, but within view of Southampton Water; and I have never seen a more picturesque or perfect ruin;

all ivy-grown, of course, and with great trees where the pillars [12] of the nave used to stand; and in the refectory, and the cloister-court; and so much soil on the summit of the broken walls, that weeds flourish abundantly there, and grass, too; and there was a wild rose-bush, in full bloom, as much as thirty or forty feet from the ground. Sophia and I ascended a winding stair leading up within a round tower, the steps much foot-worn; and reaching the top, we emerged at the height where a gallery had formerly run round the church, in the thickness of the wall. The upper portions of the edifice were now chiefly thrown down; but I followed a foot-path, on the top of the remaining wall, quite to the western entrance of the church. Since the time when the Abbey was taken from the Monks, it has been a private property; and the possessor, in Henry VIII's days, or subsequently, built a residence for himself within its precincts, out of the old materials. This has now entirely disappeared, all but some unsightly old masonry, patched into the original walls. Large portions of the ruin have been removed, likewise, to be used as building materials elsewhere; and this is the Abbey (mentioned, I think, by Dr. Watts) concerning which a Mr. William Taylor had a dream, while he was contemplating pulling it down. He dreamed [13] that a part of it fell upon his head; and, sure enough, a piece of the wall did come down and crush him. In the nave, I saw a large mass of conglomerated stone, that had fallen from the wall between the nave and cloisters, and thought that perhaps this was the very mass that killed poor Mr. Taylor.[363]

The ruins are extensive and very interesting; but, I have put off describing them too long, and cannot make a distinct picture of them now; moreover, except to a spectator skilled in architecture, all ruined abbies [sic] are pretty much alike. As we came away, we noticed some women making baskets at the entrance; and one of them urged us to buy some of her handiwork; for that she was the gypsey [sic] of Netley Abbey, and had lived among the ruins these thirty years. So I bought one for a shilling. She was a woman with a prominent nose, and weather-tanned, but not very picturesque or striking. There is a small hotel near the Abbey; and we got some lunch there, of cold beef and ham and bitter beer—a very satisfactory and by no means needless refreshment, after such short commons as Mrs. Hume had kept us upon.

[14] I never was more tired of a house than of Clifton Villa; and for Mrs. Hume's sake, I shall forever retain a detestation of thin slices of buttered bread. She is an awfully thrifty woman, and nobody can sit at her table without feeling that she both numbers and measures every mouthfull that you eat; and the consequence is, that your appetite is discouraged and deadened, without ever being satisfied. She brews her own beer, and it is inexpressibly small, and is served out (only to the more favored guests) in one very little tumbler, with no offer or hint of a further supply. There is water in the milk; and she puts soda into the tea-pot, thereby to give the tea a color, without adding to its strength. Human life gets cold and meagre, under such a system; and I

must say that I cordially hate Mrs. Hume—a little, bright, shallow, sharp, capable, self-relying, good woman enough. She seems to have a conscience; for she charged only four pounds a week for our whole family; whereas we had paid nearly at the rate of twenty, at the Castle Hotel. The fare, I suppose, is a fair sample of the way of living in English boarding-houses, or possibly, in economical English families generally.

[15] On Wednesday, we left Clifton Villa, with our immense luggage, by the omnibus, and took our departure from Southampton by the 11:30 train. The main street of Southampton, though it looks pretty fresh and bright, must be really antique, there being a great many projecting windows, in the old-time style; and these make the vista of the street very picturesque. I have no doubt that I missed seeing many things more interesting than the few that I saw. Our ride to London was without any remarkable incident; and at the Waterloo Station, we found one of Mr. Bennoch's clerks, under whose guidance we took two cabs for the East Kent Station, at London Bridge, and thence railed to Blackheath, where we arrived about five °clock. Mr. Bennoch's house not being so big as his heart, his poor lady (who is in infirm health) was somewhat put to her trumps by such an influx of guests; and had we fairly understood the circumstances, we certainly should not have come. After the first night, however, we took rooms in another house for Nurse, Una, and Rosebud, and they now constitute a separate family, and live and eat by themselves, with only a daily visit or two [16] to us old folks.

On Thursday, I went into London by one of the morning trains, and wandered about, all day—visiting the exhibition of the Royal Academy, and Westminster Abbey, and Saint Paul's, the two latter of which I have already written about, in former Journals. On Friday, Sophia, Julian, and I, walked over the heath, and through the Park, to Greenwich, and spent some hours in the Hospital. The Painted Hall is really splendid, and struck me much more than at my first view of it; very beautiful, indeed; and I never saw anything so magnificent as the rich effect of its frescoed cieling [sic], without meaning thereby to praise the painter's design or execution, but only the assemblage of glowing hues, producing a general result of splendor. Thence we went into the Chapel, which is chaste and cold; and over the altar there is a strangely confused picture by West, out of which I could not have made head or tail without the help of a catalogue. After this, we rambled about Greenwich in quest of a dinner, and at last were directed by policeman No. 38 to Orchard's dining-rooms, where, he said, by mentioning that he sent us, we should ensure the very best reception. A shabby-[17]looking room, hung round with oil-pictures by the landlord's brother; a dirty table-cloth; forks of steel and German silver; and, for the bill of fare, roast pork and roast beef, rice pudding, and gooseberry tarts. I made a good dinner enough (having sat at many a worse table), and so did Julian; but Sophia was more nice and wise, and let herself be bothered by the general griminess of the establishment. Having dined, we went shopping a little, and then took a cab back to Blackheath, after a day of considerable enjoyment. I perceive, however, that I have made a mistake in my dates; it was on Tuesday that we left Clifton Villa—on Wednesday that I went to London— and on Thursday that we walked to Greenwich. On Friday, nothing particular happened; except that I went to the Park with all the three children, but was soon forced to return by Rosebud's being tired and thirsty. In the evening, however, Mr. Bennoch and his lady, and I, went to a conversazione at Mrs. Newton Crosland's, who lives on Blackheath. I was quite weary of it, but met with one person who interested me—Mr. Bailey,[364] the author of Festus; —and I was surprised to find my[18]self already acquainted with him. It is the same Mr. Bailey whom I met a few months ago, when I first dined at Bennoch's;—a dark, handsome, rather picturesque looking man, about forty, with a gray beard, and dark hair a little dimmed with gray. He is of quiet and very agreeable deportment, and I liked him and believed in him. Bennoch says that he has a small property, but just enough to support him, and hinted that he is unhappily married, though himself a most irreproachable husband. There is sadness glooming out of him, but no unkindness or asperity. Mrs. Newton Crosland's conversazione was enriched with a supper, and terminated with a dance, in which Bennoch joined with heart and soul; but Mrs. Bennoch went to sleep in her chair, and I would gladly have followed her example—if I could have found a chair to sit upon. It was two °clock before we got to bed. In the course of the evening, I had some talk with a pale, nervous young lady, who has been a noted spiritual medium.

Yesterday, I went into town by the steamboat from Greenwich to London Bridge, with a nephew of Bennoch's; and calling at Bennoch's place of business, he procured us a [19] tasting order from his wine-merchants, by means of which we were admitted into the vaults at the London Docks. We there joined parties with an acquaintance, whom we found going with two French gentlemen into the vaults. It is a good deal like going down into a mine; each visitor being provided with a lamp at the end of a stick, and following the guide along dismal passages, running beneath the streets, and extending away interminably—roughly arched overhead with stone, from which depend festoons (stalactites, as it were) of a sort of black fungus, caused by the exhalations of the wine. Nothing was ever uglier than this fungus; it is strange that the most ethereal effervescence of rich wine can produce nothing better. The first series of vaults, which we entered, were filled with port-wine, and occupied a space variously estimated at from eleven to sixteen acres—which, I suppose, would hold more port wine than ever was made. At any rate, however, the pipes and butts were so thickly piled, that, in some places, we could hardly squeeze past them. We drank from two or three vintages; but I was not impressed with any especial excellence in the wine. We were not the [20] only visitors; for, far in the depths of the vault, we passed a gentleman and two young ladies, wandering about like the ghosts of defunct wine-bibbers, in a tophet specially prepared for them. People employed in these vaults sometimes go astray, and, their lamps being extinguished, remain long in this everlasting gloom. We went likewise to the vaults of sherry wine, which have the same characteristics as those just described, but are less extensive. I drank two or three specimens of sherry, but finally emerged into daylight, not at all the worse for my potations. It is no guarantee for the excellence, or even for the purity of the wine, that it is kept in these vaults under the lock and key of the government; for the merchants are allowed to mix different vintages according to their own pleasure, and, I believe, to doctor it as they like. Very little of the wine, probably, comes out as it goes in, or is exactly what it pretends to be.

I went back to Bennoch's office; and we drove together to make some calls, jointly and separately.—I went alone to Mrs. Heywood's; afterwards with Bennoch to the American Minister's, whom we found at home; and I requested of him (on the part of the Americans at Liver[21]pool) to tell me the facts about the American gentleman being refused admittance to the Levee.[365] Mr. Dallas did not seem to me to make his point good for having withdrawn with the rejected guest. We next called on Mr. Durham, the sculptor, and saw a good many busts and some ideal works; and finally we went to the Wellington, where Bennoch dined with me.

JULY 7th MONDAY.

YESTERDAY was another pretty warm and sunny day. Nothing happened worth noticing. Mr. & Mrs. Bennoch went to town; Archie (the nephew) took Julian to church; and Mamma and I staid at home. We dined at half past two; and when dinner was nearly over, Dr. Simpson came in. He is a physician eminent in diseases of the throat and lungs, and I rather think Bennoch had invited him here partly with a view to his seeing Sophia. He is about forty years old, a very pleasant, cultivated, quickly perceptive, easy and genial-mannered man. Bennoch produced some excellent Burgundy and claret; and when the decanters were emptied, the Doctor resumed his professional character, and, after due examination, gave hopeful opinions [22] respecting Sophia's case, and ordered some allopathic medicines—which she has great scruples of conscience and judgment about taking. But, for my part, I am inclined to put faith in what is tangible.

After tea, we accompanied (that is Bennoch, his nephew, Julian, and I) accompanied [sic] Dr. Simpson across the heath; and from one point, we had a fine, dusky view of immense London, with Saint Paul's in the midst, and the towers of the two houses of Parliament, four or five miles off.[366] It was rather too misty, and too near evening, to see it distinctly; but, on a bright morning, it must form a splendid picture. We parted with the Doctor, and afterwards called on Mrs. Newton Crosland, who was not at home. Then we walked through the town of Greenwich, and entered the Park, in which were many parties, groups, and couples, wandering about, or sitting on the benches beneath the old trees, and decorously enjoying their Sunday holiday. A preacher, in one of the hollows, was delivering a discourse to a tolerable audience, comprising young men and girls, some soldiers, and an old pensioner or two in cocked hats; all of them very quiet and orderly.[367] Con[23]tinuing our ramble about the Park, Bennoch led us to some ancient barrows, beneath which we supposed to be buried the slain of a great battle, that was fought in the plain below, two or three centuries after Christ. They are small mounds, ten or twelve feet in diameter, elevated only a few feet, and with a shallow depression on the summit; and it seems to be pretty certain that they are as much as sixteen hundred years old. When one of them was opened, not long ago, nothing was found but a tuft of hair and some small jewels—no bones, nor aught besides.[368] On our way home, we passed through a wicket-gate, opening through the park-wall, close by Vanbrugh House—a large, castellated and round-towered edifice of brick, erected by Sir John Vanbrugh for his own residence. It is now occupied as a boarding-house.

JULY 9th, WEDNESDAY.

WE were invited, yesterday evening, to Mrs. S. C. Hall's, where Jenny Lind was to be; so Bennoch, Sophia, and I, left here at about 8 °clock in a Brougham, and reached Ashley-place as the dusk was gathering—that is to say, at past 9. The Halls have let Fir[24]field, and now reside in a handsome set of apartments, arranged on the new system of flats—each story constituting a separate tenement, and the various families having an entrance-hall and some other conveniences in common. The plan is borrowed from the Continent, and seems rather alien to the traditionary habits of the English; though, no doubt, a good degree of seclusion is compatible with it. M[r] Hall received us with the greatest cordiality, before we entered the drawing-room; and I really think I have done him some injustice in suggesting, heretofore, that he may not be altogether sincere in his demonstrations of regard. Good, round (for she is very round) Mrs. Hall, too, greeted us with most kindly warmth; and there can be no question about her sincerity. Jenny Lind had not yet arrived; but I found Dr. Mackay there, and I was introduced to Miss Catherine Sinclair,[369] who seems to be a literary lady, though none of her works happen to be known to me. She is a tall, pale, fair-haired, mature and homely gentlewoman, pitted, I think, with the small-pox; as to her inside, I did not have talk enough with her to judge anything about it. Soon, the servant announced Madam Goldschmidt; and this [25] famous lady made her appearance, looking quite different from what I expected. Mrs. Hall established her in the inner-drawing room, where was a piano and a harp; and, shortly after, our hostess came to me and announced that Madam Goldschmidt wished to be introduced to me. There was a kind of gentle peremptoriness in the summons, that made it something like being commanded into the presence of a princess; a great favor, no doubt, but yet a little humbling to the recipient. However, I acquiesced with due gratitude, and was presented accordingly. She made room for me on the sopha [*sic*], and I sat down and began to talk.

Jenny Lind is rather tall—quite tall, for a woman—and not in the least plump; extremely light hair, a longish nose, tending upward at the end,—a face without any color at all—pale, and a little scrawniness about the neck; certainly no beauty, but with sense and self-reliance in her aspect and manners. She was suffering under a severe cold, and seemed worn down besides; so probably I saw her under disadvantages. Her conversation is quite simple, and I should have great faith in her [26] sincerity; but still there is about her the manner of a person who knows the world, and has conquered it. She said something or other about the Scarlet Letter; and on my part, I paid her such compliments as a man could pay, who had never heard her sing, nor greatly cared to hear her. Her conversational voice is an agreeable one, rather deep, and not particularly smooth. She talked about America, and about our unwholesome modes of life as to eating and exercise, and the ill-health especially of our women; but I opposed this view, as far as I could with any truth, insinuating my opinion that we are about as healthy as other people, and affirming for a certainty that we live longer. In good faith, so far as I have any knowledge of the matter, the women of England are as generally out of health as those of America; always, something has gone wrong with their clockwork; and as for Jenny Lind, she looks wan and worn enough to be an American herself. This charge of ill-health is almost universally brought forward against us, now-a-days; and, taking the whole country together, I do not believe the statistics will bear it out.

On the whole, I was not very greatly interested in Madam Goldschmidt, nor sorry to take an early opportunity of resigning my seat to somebody else. The rooms (which were respectably filled when we arrived) were now getting quite full. I saw Mr. Stevens, the American man of libraries, and had some talk with him; and Durham,[370] the sculptor; and Mr. & Mrs. Hall introduced me to various people, some of whom, I believe, were of note;—for instance, Sir Emerson Tennent,[371] a stiff-mannered man of the world, of some Parliamentary distinction, wearing a star, which needed burnishing; Mr. Samuel Lover,[372] a most good-natured, pleasant Irishman, with a shining and twinkling visage; Miss Jewsbury,[373] a mature young lady, with a thin face and large nose, reddish of hue, whom I found very conversible. She is known in literature, but not to me. We talked about Emerson, whom she seems to have been well acquainted with, while he was in England; and she mentioned that Harriet Martineau had given him a lock of hair; it was not her own hair, but a mummy's. After our return, Mrs. Bennoch told us that Miss Jewsbury had written, among [28] other things, three histories; and, as she asked me to introduce her to Sophia, and means to cultivate our acquaintance, it would be well to know something of these. We were told that she is now employed in some literary undertaking of Lady Morgan's, who, at the age of ninety, is still circulating in society, and as brisk in faculties as ever. I should like to see her ladyship;—that is, I should not be sorry to see her; for distinguished people are so much on a par with others, socially, that it would be foolish to be overjoyed at seeing anybody whomsoever.

Leaving out the illustrious Jenny, I suspect that I was myself the greatest lion of the evening; for a good many persons sought the felicity of knowing me, and had little or nothing to say, when that honor and happiness was conferred on them. It is surely very wrong and ill-mannered in people to ask for an introduction, unless they are prepared to make talk; it throws too great an expense and trouble on the wretched lion, who is compelled, on the spur of the moment, to concoct a conversible substance out of thin air, perhaps for the twentieth time that evening. On the whole, I am sure [29] I did not say—and I think I did not hear said—one remarkable word, in the course of this evening; though, nevertheless, it was rather an agreeable one. In due season, ices and jellies were handed about; and some ladies and gentlemen— professional, I suspect—were kind enough to sing unintelligible songs, and play on the piano and harp; while, in the rear, people went on with whatever conversation they had in hand. Then came supper; but there were so many people to go into the small supper-room that we could not all crowd thither together; and, coming late, I got nothing but some sponge-cake and a glass of champagne—neither of which I care for. After supper, Mr. Lover sang some Irish songs (his own, in music and words) with rich humorous effect, to which the comicality of his face contributed almost as much as his voice. I believe there is nothing else to be recorded; except that the Lord Mayor looked in for a little while, and though a hard-featured Jew enough, was much the most picturesque-looking person there. We came away at about half-past twelve.

[30] July 10ᵗʰ Thursday.

Mrs. Heywood had invited me to dinner, last evening; and at 6 ºclock, I took the rail for London; but as the invitation was for 8 ¼, I had to while away nearly an hour at the Station, before it was time to go to her house. So I read Punch till after 7, and then took a cab. Mrs. Heywood's house is very finely situated, overlooking Hyde Park, and not a great way from where Tyburn-tree used to stand. When I arrived, there were no guests but Mr. and Mrs. Denmar (the latter, Mrs. Heywood's sister, and a plump and pretty woman;) but by and by came Mr. Monckton Milnes and lady, the Bishop of Lichfield, Mr. Tom Taylor, Mr. Ewart,[374] M.P., Sir Somebody Somerville[375] (who, I think, wore a blue coat and buff underclothes, looking very odd amid everybody's black) Mr. & Mrs. Musgrave, and I forget who besides. Mr. Milnes, whom I have not seen for more than a year, greeted me very cordially, and so did Tom Taylor, who had a very pretty wife with him. I took Mrs.

Musgrave into dinner. She is an Irish lady; and Mrs. Heywood had recommended her to me as being very conversible; but I did not find her particularly so, and had a good deal more talk with Mrs. Milnes (with whom I was al[31]ready acquainted) than with her. She is of noble blood, and therefore less snobbish than most English ladies—in fact, quite unaffected, gentle, sweet, and easy to get on with; reminding me of the best-mannered American women. It was not a very interesting dinner; indeed, how can anything characteristic be said or done among a dozen people sitting at table in full dress. Speaking of full dress, the Bishop wore small clothes and silk stockings, and entered the drawing room with a kind of three-cornered hat, flattened out, which he kept under his arm. He asked the briefest blessing I ever heard; and, sitting at the other end of the table, I heard nothing further from him, till he officiated as briefly before the cloth was withdrawn. Mrs. Milnes talked about Tennyson, with whom her husband was at the University, and whom he continues to know intimately. She says that he considers Maude [*sic*] his best poem. He now lives in the Isle of Wight, spending all the year round there, and has recently bought the place on which he resides. She was of opinion that he would have been gratified by my calling on him, which I had wished to do, while [32] we were at Southampton; but this is a liberty that I should hardly venture upon with a shy, humorsome man, like Tennyson— more especially as he might perhaps suspect me of doing it on the score of my own literary character. But I should like much to see him. Mrs. Milnes spoke of his wife, a wise and tender woman, such as ought to be entrusted with such a fragile affair as Tennyson's comfort and happiness. Mr. Tom Taylor, during dinner, seemed to make some fun for the benefit of the ladies on either side of him. I liked him very well, this evening, finding him quite cordial in his greeting to myself; but he is a gentleman of very questionable aspect— un-English—tall, slender, colorless, with a great beard of soft black, and, methinks, green goggles over his eyes.

At ten °clock, when the ladies had not long been gone, and after the wine had once gone round, I asked Mr. Heywood to make my apologies to his wife, and withdrew; all London lying betwixt me and the London-bridge station, whence I was to take the rail homeward. At the station, I found Bennoch, who had been dining with the Lord Mayor, to meet Sir William [33] Williams; and we railed to Greenwich, and reached home by cab precisely at twelve °clock. Mr. and Mrs. Bennoch have set out on their Continental journey to-day, leaving us, for a little space, in possession of what will be more like a home than anything that we shall hereafter find in England.

This afternoon, I had taken up the fourth volume of Jerdan's Autobiography (wretched twaddle, though it records such constant and apparently intimate intercourse with distinguished people) and was reading it, between asleep and awake, on the sofa, when Mr. Jerdan himself was announced. I saw him, in company with Bennoch, nearly three years ago, at Rock Park, and wondered then what there was in so uncouth an individual to get him so freely into polished society. He now looks rougher than ever; time-worn, but not reverend;

a thatch of gray hair on his head; an imperfect set of false teeth; a careless apparel, checked trowsers, and a stick; for he had walked a mile or two, from his own dwelling. I suspect (and long practice at the [34] Consulate has made me keen-sighted) that Mr. Jerdan contemplates some benefit from my purse; and, to the extent of a sovereign or so, I would not mind contributing to his comfort. He spoke of a secret purpose of Bennoch and himself to obtain me a degree or diploma in some Literary Institution—what one, I know not, and did not ask; but the honor cannot be a high one, if this poor old fellow can do aught towards it. I am afraid he is a very disreputable senior, but certainly not the less to be pitied on that account; and there was something very touching in his stiff and infirm movement, as he resumed his stick and took leave, waving me a courteous farewell, and turning upon me a smile grim with age, as he went down the steps. In that gesture and smile, I fancied some trace of the polished man of society, such as he may have been once; though time and hard weather have roughened him, as they have the once polished marble pillars which I saw so rude in aspect, at Netley Abbey.

Speaking of Dickens, last evening, Mrs. Milnes mentioned his domestic tastes, how he preferred [35] home-enjoyments to all others, and did not willingly go much into society. Mrs. Bennoch, too, the other day, told us how careful he was of his wife, taking on himself all possible trouble as regards his domestic affairs, making bargains at butchers and bakers, and doing, as far as he could, whatever duty pertains to an English wife. There is a great variety of testimony, various and variant, as to the character of Dickens. I must see him before I finally leave England.

JULY 13th, SUNDAY.

ON Friday morning at 9 °clock (having first fortified myself with some coffee and cold beef) I took the rail into town, to breakfast with R. M. Milnes. As he had named a little after ten as the hour, I could not immediately proceed to his house; and so walked moderately over London bridge and into the city, meaning to take a cab from Charing Cross, or thereabouts. Passing through some street or other, contiguous to Cheapside, I saw in a courtyard the entrance to the Guildhall, and stepped in to look at it. It is a spacious hall, about 150 feet long, and perhaps half as broad, paved with flag-stones, which look worn, and some of them cracked [36] across; the roof is very lofty, and was once vaulted, but has been shaped anew in modern times. There is an immense window, partly filled with painted glass, extending quite across each end of the hall, and a row of arched windows on either side, throwing their light from far above downward upon the pavement. This fashion of high windows, not reaching within twenty or thirty feet of the floor, serves to give great effect to the large enclosed space of an antique hall. Against the walls are several marble monuments; one to the Earl of Chatham, a statue of white marble, with various allegorical contrivances, fronting an obelisk or pyramid of dark marble; and another to his son, William Pitt, of somewhat

similar design, and equal size; each of them occupying the whole space, I
believe, between pavement and cieling [*sic*]. There is likewise a statue of
Beckford, a famous Lord Mayor, the most famous except Whittington, and
him who killed Wat Tyler; and, like those two, his fame is perhaps somewhat
mythological, though he lived and bustled within less than a century past. He
is said to have made a bold speech to the King; but this I will not believe of
any Englishman—at least, of any plebeian Englishman—until I hear it. But
there stands his stat[37]ue in the Guildhall, in the act of making his speech,
as if the monstrous attempt had petrified him. Lord Nelson, too, has a monument; and so, I think, has some other modern worthy. At one end of the
hall, under one of the great painted windows, stand three or four old statues
of medi-aeval kings, whose identities I forget; and, in the two corners of the
opposite end, are two gigantic absurdities of painted wood, with grotesque
visages, whom I quickly recognized as Gog and Magog. They stand each on
a pillar, and seem to be about fifteen feet high, and look like enormous playthings for the children of giants; and it is strange to see them in this solemn
old hall, among the memorials of dead heroes and statesmen. There is an
annual banquet in the Guildhall, given by the Lord Mayor and sheriffs; and
I believe it is the very acme of civic feasting.

After viewing the hall, as it still lacked something of ten, I continued my
walk through that entanglement of city-streets, and quickly found myself
getting beyond my reckoning. I cannot tell whither I went; but I passed through
a very dirty region, and I remember a long, narrow, evil-odored street, cluttered
up with stalls on which were [38] vegetables and little bits of meat for sale;
and there was a frowzy multitude of buyers and sellers. Still I blundered on,
and was getting out of the density of the city, into broader streets, but still
shabby ones, when, looking at my watch, I found it to be past ten, and no
cab-stand within sight. It was a quarter past, when I finally got into one; and
the driver told me that it would take half an hour to go from thence to Upper
Brook-street; so that I was likely to exceed the license implied in Mr. Milnes's
invitation. Whether I was quite beyond rule, I cannot say; but it did not lack
more than ten minutes of eleven when I was ushered up stairs, and I found
all the company assembled. However, it is of little consequence, except that,
if I had come early, I should have been introduced to many of the guests,
whom now I could only know across the table. Mrs. Milnes greeted me very
kindly; and Mr. Milnes came towards me with an old gentleman in a blue coat
and gray pantaloons—with a long, rather thin, homely visage, exceedingly
shaggy eyebrows, though no great weight of brow, and thin gray hair—and
introduced me to the Marquess of Lansdowne. The Marquess had his right
hand wrapt up in a black silk handkerchief; so he [39] gave me his left, and,
from some awkwardness in meeting it, when I expected the right, I gave him
only three of my fingers;—a thing I never did before to any person, and it is
queer that I should have done it to a Marquess. He addressed me with **great**

simplicity and natural kindness, complimenting me on my works, and speaking, if I remember aright, about the society of Liverpool in former days. Lord Lansdowne was the friend of Moore, and has about him the fragrance communicated by the memories of many illustrious people, with whom he has associated.

Mr. Ticknor,[376] the Historian of Spanish Literature, now greeted me. He looks greyer than when I saw him in Boston, but in good preservation. Mr. Milnes introduced me to Mrs. Browning, and assigned her to me to conduct into the breakfast-room; she is a small, delicate woman, with ringlets of black hair, (I think they were ringlets, and am sure they were black) a pleasant, intelligent, sensitive face, and a low, agreeable voice. She is more youthful and comely than I supposed, and very gentle and ladylike. And so we proceeded to the breakfast-room, which is hung round with pictures; [40] and in the middle of it stood an immense round table, worthy to have been King Arthur's, and here we seated ourselves without any question of precedence or ceremony. On one side of me was an elderly lady, with a very fine countenance, and altogether more agreeable to look at than most English dames of her age; and, in the course of breakfast, I discovered her to be the mother of Florence Nightingale. One of her daughters (not *the* daughter) was likewise present. Mrs. Milnes, Mrs. Browning, Mrs. Nightingale, and her daughter, were the only ladies at table; and I think there were as many as eight or ten gentlemen, whose names—as I came so late—I was left to find out for myself, or to leave unknown.

It was a pleasant and sociable meal; and, thanks to my cold beef and coffee at home, I had no occasion to trouble myself much about the fare; so I just ate some delicate chicken, and a very small cutlet, and a slice of dry toast, and thereupon surceased from my labors. Mrs. Browning seems to be a vegetarian; at least, she ate nothing but an egg. We talked a good deal during breakfast; for she is of that quickly appreciative [41] and responsive order of women, with whom I can talk more freely than with any men; and she has, besides, her own originality wherewith to help on conversation; though, I should say, not of a loquacious tendency. She introduced the subject of spiritualism, which, she says, interests her very much; indeed, she seems to be a believer. Her husband, she told me, utterly rejects the subject, and will not believe even in the outer manifestations, of which there is such overwhelming evidence. We also talked of Miss Bacon; and I developed something of that lady's theory respecting Shakspeare, greatly to the horror of Mrs. Browning and that of her next neighbor—some nobleman, whose name I did not know. On the whole, I like her the better for loving the man Shakspeare with a personal love. We talked, too, of Margaret Fuller, who spent her last night in Italy with the Brownings; and of William Story, with whom they have been intimate, and who, Mrs. Browning says, is much stirred up about Spiritualism. Really, I cannot help wondering that so fine a spirit as hers should not reject the matter, till, at least, it is forced upon her. But I [42] like her very much—a great deal better than her poetry, which I could hardly suppose to have been written by such a quiet little person as she.

Mrs. Nightingale had been talking at first with Lord Lansdowne, who sat next her; but by and by she turned to me, and began to speak of London smoke. She is a nice old lady, very intelligent—that is, very sensible—but with no saliency of ideas; a lady born and bred, evidently, for—unless with that advantage—all English women have a certain nonsense about them, even more inevitably than the men. Then (there being a discussion about Lord Byron, on the other side of the table) she spoke to me about Lady Byron, whom she knows intimately, characterizing her as a most excellent and exemplary person, high-principled, unselfish, and now devoting herself to the care of her two grandchildren; their mother (Byron's daughter) being dead. Lady Byron, she says, writes beautiful verses. Somehow or other, all this praise, and more of the same kind, gave me the idea of an intolerably irreproachable person; and I asked Mrs. Nightingale if Lady Byron was warm-hearted. With some hesitation, or mental reservation—[43] at all events, not quite out-spokenly— she answered that she was.

I was too much engaged with these personal talks to attend much to what was going on elsewhere; but all through breakfast, I had been more and more impressed by the aspect of one of the guests, sitting next to Milnes. He was a man of large presence—a portly personage—gray haired, but scarcely as yet aged; and his face had a remarkable intelligence, not vivid nor sparkling, but conjoined with great quietude; and if it gleamed or brightened, at one time more than another, it was like the sheen over a broad surface of sea. There was a somewhat careless self-possession, large and broad enough to be called dignity; and the more I looked at him, the more I knew that he was somebody, and wondered who. He might have been a minister of state; only there is not one of them who has any right to such a face and presence. At last—I do not know how the conviction came—but I became aware that it was Macauley [*sic*], and began to see some slight resemblance to his portraits. But I have never seen [44] any that is not wretchedly unworthy of the original. As soon as I knew him, I began to listen to his conversation; but he did not talk a great deal— contrary to his usual custom, for I am told he is apt to engross all the talk to himself. Probably he may have been restrained by the presence of Ticknor, and Mr. Palfrey,[377] who were among his auditors and interlocutors; and as the conversation seemed to turn much on American subjects, he could not well have assumed to talk them down. Well, I am glad to have seen him—a face fit for a scholar, a man of the world, a cultivated intelligence.

After we got up from table, and went into the library, Mr. Browning[378] introduced himself to me; a younger man than I expected to see, handsome, with dark hair, a very little frosted. He is very simple and agreeable in manner, gently impulsive, talking as if his heart were uppermost. He spoke of his pleasure in meeting me, and his appreciation of my books; and (which has not often happened to me) mentioned that the Blithedale Romance was the one he admired most. I wonder why. I hope I showed as much pleasure at his praise as he [45] did at mine; for I was glad to see how pleasantly it moved him. After this I talked with Ticknor and Milnes, and with Mr. Palfrey, to whom I had been introduced, very long ago, by George Hillard, and had never seen him since. We looked at some autographs, of which Mr. Milnes has two or three large volumes. I recollect a leaf from Swift's Journal to Stella; a letter from Addison; one from Chatterton, in a most neat and legible hand; and a characteristic sentence or two and signature of Oliver Cromwell, written in a religious book. There seemed to be many curious volumes in the library; but I had not time to look at them.

I liked greatly the manners of almost all—yes, all, as far as I observed—all the people at this breakfast; and it was doubtless owing to their being all people either of high rank, or remarkable intellect, or both. An Englishman can hardly be a gentleman, unless he enjoys one or the other of these advantages; and perhaps the surest way to give him good manners is, to make a lord of him—or rather, of his grandfather, or great-grandfather. In the third generation—[46] scarcely sooner—he will be polished into simplicity and elegance, and his deportment will be all the better for the homely material out of which it is wrought and refined. The Marquess of Lansdowne, for instance, would have been a very common-place man in the common ranks of life, but it has done him good to be a nobleman. Not that I consider his tact quite perfect. In going up to breakfast, he made me precede him; in returning to the library, he did the same, although I drew back, till he impelled me up the first stair, with gentle persistence. By insisting upon it, he showed his sense of condescension, much more than if—when he saw me unwilling to take precedence—he had passed forward, as if the point were not worth either asserting or yielding. Heaven knows, it was in no humility that I would have trod behind him. But he is a kind old man, and I am willing to believe of the English aristocracy generally that they are kind, and of beautiful deportment; for certainly there never can have been mortals in a position more advantageous for becoming so. If any, they must be Americans; and, really, I hope there may come a time when we shall be so, and I already know Ameri[47]cans whose noble and delicate manners may compare well with any I have seen.

I left the house with Mr. Palfrey. He has come to England to make some researches in the State Paper office, for the purposes of a work which he has in hand. He mentioned to me a letter which he had seen, written from New England in the time of Charles II, and referring to the order sent by the Minister of that day for the appearance of Governor Bellingham and my ancestor, on this side of the water. The signature of this letter is an anagram of my ancestor's name; the letter itself is a very bold and able one, controverting the propriety of the measure above indicated; and Mr. Palfrey feels certain that it was written by my aforesaid ancestor. I mentioned my wish to ascertain the place, in England, whence the family emigrated; and Mr. Palfrey took me to the Record office, and introduced me to Mr. Joseph Hunter, a venerable and courteous gentleman, of antiquarian pursuits. The office was fragrant with musty parchments, hundreds of years old. Mr. Hunter received me with great kindness, and gave me various old records and rolls [48] of parchment, in which to seek for my family name; but I was perplexed with the crabbed characters, and soon grew weary, and gave up the quest. He says that it is very seldom that an American family, springing from the early settlers, can be satisfactorily traced back to their English ancestry.

JULY 16th, WEDNESDAY.

MONDAY morning, at 10;20, I took the rail from Blackheath to London. It is a very pleasant place, Blackheath, and far more rural than one would expect, within five or six miles of London; a great many trees, making quite a mass of foliage in the distance; green enclosures; pretty villas, with their nicely kept lawns, and gardens with grass-plots and flower-borders; and village-streets, set along the sidewalks with ornamental trees, and the houses standing a little back, and separate one from another—all this within what is called the Park, which has its gateways, and the sort of semi-privacy with which I first became acquainted at Rock Park. Then there is the bare, open, breezy heath, where, at this season, there are the tents of cricket-players, rival sets, between whom a great match, involving the credit of different counties, may be going on; elsewhere, there are butts, [49] and bows and arrows, at so many shots for a penny; and the game of throwing the stick; and donkeys for the children to ride, and ponies and horses for larger people—all this upon the heath, which, during the summer-months, seems to be a continual pleasure-ground for the Londoners. Schools of girls and boys are sometimes brought out here, and spend the day in the open air.[379] Within an easy walk (not more than a mile) of our house is Greenwich Park, with its avenue of old trees, planted by Kings and Queens, and its deer, which are tamer than sheep;—altogether, a very nice place is Blackheath; so near London, too, and costing but one and sixpence to go thither and back.

From the London bridge station, I took a cab for Paddington, and then had to wait above two hours before a train started for Birkenhead. Meanwhile, I walked a little about the neighborhood, which is very dull and uninteresting; made up of crescents, and terraces, and rows of houses that have no individuality; and second-rate shops—in short, the outskirts of the vast city, where it begins to have a kind of village-character, but no rurality or sylvan aspect, as at Blackheath. My jour[50]ney, when at last we started, was quite unmarked by incident, and extremely tedious;—it being a slow train, which plods on without haste and without rest. At about ten °clock, we reached Birkenhead, and thence crossed the familiar and detestable Mersey, which, as usual, had a cloudy sky brooding over it. Mrs. Blodget received me most hospitably, but was compelled, by surfeit of guests, to put me into a little back chamber, looking into the court, and formerly occupied by my predecessor General Armstrong[380]—where he has often gone through the horrors of delirium tremens. She expressed a hope that I might not see his ghost—nor have I, as yet. It is a better room to sleep in than my former front-chamber, where the rattling of wheels used to disturb my sweetest slumbers.

Speaking of ghosts, Mr. Bright told me a singular story, to day, of an apparition that haunts the Times Office, in Printing House Square. A Mr. Wetherell is the engineer of the establishment, and has his residence in the edifice, which is built, I believe, on the site of Merchant Taylor's School—an old house that was no longer occupied for its original purpose, and, being supposed to be haunted, was left untenanted. The [51] father-in-law of Mr. Wetherell, an old sea-captain, came on a visit to him and his wife, and was put into their guest-chamber, where he passed the night. The next morning, assigning no very satisfactory reason, he cut his visit short, and came away. Shortly afterwards, a young lady came to visit the Wetherells; but she, too, went away the next morning—going first to make a call, as she said, on a friend, and sending thence for her trunks. Mrs. Wetherell wrote to this young lady, asking an explanation—thinking of no worse cause than that perhaps she had been made uncomfortable by bugs and fleas—as, by the way, is often the case in English houses. But the young lady replied, and gave a singular account of an apparition;—how she was awakened in the night by a bright light, shining, I think, through the window, which was parallel to the bed; then, if I remember rightly, her curtains were drawn, and a shape looked in upon her—a woman's shape, she called it; but it was a skeleton, with lambent flames playing about its bones, and in and out among the ribs. Other persons have since slept in the chamber, and some have seen the shape, others not. Mr. Wetherell himself has slept there, without seeing anything. He has [52] had investigations by scientific people, apparently under the idea that the phenomena might have been caused by some of the Times workpeople, playing tricks on the magic lanthern principle; but nothing satisfactory has thus far been elucidated. Mr. Bright had this story from Mrs. Gaskell, and seems to consider it matter of fact. Supposing it a ghost, nothing else is so remarkable as its choosing to haunt the precincts of the Times newspaper.

Mr. Bright tells me that the respectable old Marquess of Lansdowne, as I innocently considered him, is a most disreputable character, and that he is the original of Thackeray's Lord Steyne. I thought that honor belonged to the Marquess of Hertford.[381] Lord Lansdowne[382] But the truth of such rumors, respecting prominent men, ought not, I presume, to be taken for granted without proof. In reference to the nobility, the whole snobbism of England is in the position of the inhabitants of an American country-village, gossiping about the village-magnates, and always spicing their lies with malice. It is queer how the English uphold their nobility as an institution, yet ridicule and abuse the individual members.

[53] July 29th Tuesday.

On Saturday, at 11 1/4, I took the rail, from the Lime-street station, for London, via the Trent Valley; and reached Blackheath at about half-past nine in the evening. The journey was quite without incident; and I have now got so accustomed to English scenery that the panorama, as viewed from the railway carriage, suggested nothing for description.

Sunday morning, between 10 & 11, wife and I, with Julian, railed into London, and drove to the Essex-street Chapel, where Mr. Channing was to preach. The Chapel is the same place where Priestley and Belsham used to preach; one of the plainest houses of worship I ever was in, as simple and undecorated as the faith there inculcated. They retain, however, all the form and ceremonial of the English established church, though so modified as to meet the doctrinal views of the Unitarians. There may be good sense in this, inasmuch as it greatly lessens the ministerial labor to have a stated form of prayer, instead of a necessity for extempore outpourings; but it must be, I should think, excessively tedious to the [54] congregation—especially as, having made alterations in these prayers, they cannot attach much idea of sanctity to them.

After the service, we drove to the Zoological Gardens, Regent's Park, and spent several hours very wearily in wandering about and looking at the animals—for Julian's pleasure, not our own. There is a peculiar disagreeableness, to me, in exhibitions of animals. I either naturally lack the taste, or have lost it. Julian is insatiable of such things; and it even overpowered his sense of hunger, though we could get no refreshment (it being Sunday) at the Gardens, and ate nothing till we reached home, at about six °clock.

Yesterday, at about ten, I walked across the heath, and through Greenwich Park, to the Thames' side, and took the Steamer to town. The trip up the river to London Bridge, occupies about half an hour, or perhaps less. From the bridge, I walked through Thames street, as far as, I think, Blackfriars bridge, and then turned into Fleet-street, and so on [to] the National Gallery, where I spent an hour or so. Then I [55] called at Morley's Hotel, on Mr. Henry Stevens, whom I did not find in; and thence I walked through Pall Mall, and along Piccadilly, towards Hyde Park, whence I took a cab to Miss Bacon's[383] lodgings, 12, Spring-street, Sussex Gardens. It is a pleasant part of London enough, at no great distance from the Park, and seems to be modern. The basement of the house, where Miss B. lodges, is occupied by a grocer, who is likewise her landlord—a portly, middle-aged, civil and kindly man, who seemed to feel a personal kindness towards his lodger. At least, this was the impression made on me by the few words I had from him, when I stept into the shop to inquire if she lived there.

The girl of the house took up my card, and then ushered me up two (and, I rather believe, three) pair of stairs, into a parlor—plain, but neat enough—and told me that Miss Bacon would come soon. There were a number of books on the table; and, looking into them, I found that every one had some reference to her Shaksperian theory;—there was a volume of Raleigh's History of the World, a vol[56]ume of Montaigne, a volume of Bacon's letters, a volume of Shakspeare's plays;—and, on another table, there was the manuscript of part of her work. To be sure, there was a pocket-Bible; but everything else referred to this one idea of hers; and, no doubt, as it has engrossed her whole soul, the Bible has reference to it likewise. I took up Montaigne (it was Hazlitt's translation) and read his Journey to Italy for a good while, until I heard a chamber on the same floor open, and Miss Bacon appeared. I expected to see a very homely, uncouth, elderly personage, and was rather pleasantly disappointed by her aspect. She is rather uncommonly tall, and has a striking and expressive face— dark hair, dark eyes, which shone as she spoke; and, by and by, a color came into her cheeks. She must be over forty years old—perhaps, towards fifty—and, making allowance for years and ill health, she may be supposed to have been handsome once. There was little or no embarrassment in her manner; and we immediately took a friendly and familiar tone together, and began to talk as if we had known one another a long while. Our previous correspon[57]dence had smoothed the way; and we had a definite topic, in my proposal to offer her book to Routledge. She thought well of this, and at once acceded.

She was very communicative about her theory, and would have been more so, had I desired it; but I thought it best to repress, rather than to draw her out. Unquestionably, she is a monomaniac; this great idea has completely thrown her off her balance; but, at the same time, it has wonderfully developed her intellect, and made her what she could not otherwise have been. I had heard, long ago, that she believed that the confirmation of her theory was to be found buried in Shakspeare's grave. Recently, as I understood her, this idea has been modified and fully developed in her mind; she now believes that she has found, in Lord Bacon's letters, the key and clue to the whole mystery—definite and minute instructions how to find a will and other documents, relating to this new philosophy, which are concealed in a hollow space in the under surface of Shakspeare's grave-stone. These instructions, she intimates, go completely and precisely to the point, and [58] obviate all difficulties in the way of coming at the treasure, and even, I believe, secure her from any troublesome consequence likely to result from disturbing the grave. All that she now stays in England for—indeed, the object for which she came here, and which has kept [her] here these three years past—is, to discover these material and unquestionable proofs of the truth of her theory.

She communicated all this strange matter in a low, quiet tone, and, for my part, I listened as quietly, and without any expression of dissent. It would have shut her up at once, and without in the least weakening her faith in the existence of these things; and, if it were possible to convince [her] of their non-existence, I apprehend that she would collapse and die at once. She says herself that she cannot now bear the society of those who do not sympathize with her; and, finding little sympathy or none, she entirely secludes herself from the world. In all these years, she has seen Mrs. Farrar a few times, but has long ago given her up; Carlyle, once or twice, but not of late; Mr. Buchanan, while minister, once called on her; and General Campbell two or three [59] times, on business;—with these exceptions, she has lived in complete solitude. She never walks out; she suffers much from neuralgia; she is in difficult circumstances, pecuniarily; and yet, she tells me, she is perfectly happy. I can well conceive of this; for she feels sure that she has a great object to accomplish, and that Providence is specially busy, not only in what promotes her progress, but in what seems to impede it. For instance, she thinks that she was providentially led to this lodging-house, and put in relation with this landlord and his family; and, to say the truth, considering what London lodging-house keepers usually are—and in view of her pecuniary embarrassments—the kindness of this man and his household is little less than miraculous. Evidently, too, she thinks that Providence has brought me forward at this critical juncture, when she could not have done without me.

For my part, I would rather that Providence would have employed some other instrument; but still I have little or no scruple or doubt about what I ought to do. Her book is a most remarkable one, and well [60] deserves publication; and towards that end, she shall have every assistance that I can render. Her relatives are endeavoring to force her home, by withholding from her all means of support in England; but, in my opinion, if taken from England now, she would go home as a raving maniac, and I shall write to them and suggest this view of the case. Meanwhile, as she must be kept alive, it devolves on me to supply her with some small means for that purpose. As to her designs on Shakspeare's grave, I see no way but to ignore them entirely, and leave Providence to manage that matter in its own way. If I had it in my power to draw her out of her delusions, on that point, I should not venture to do so;—it is the condition on which she lives, in comfort and joy, and exercises great intellectual power; and it would be no business of mine to annihilate her, for this world, by showing her a miserable fact. I am not quite sure, that she will not be practically wiser, in this particular matter, than her theory seems to indicate;—there is a ladylike feeling of propriety, and a New England orderliness, and [61] probably a sturdy common sense at bottom, which may begin to act at the right time. And, at all events, it is still the safest course to allow her her own way, till she brings up against an impossibility.

My interview with her may have lasted about an hour, and she flowed out freely, as to the first friend whom she had met in a long while. She is a very good talker, considering how long she has held her tongue for want of a listener—pleasant, sunny and shadowy, often piquant, suggesting all a woman's various moods and humors; and beneath all there is a deep under-current of earnestness, which does not fail to produce, on the listener's part, something like a temporary faith in what she believes so strongly.

From her own account, it appears she did at one time lose her reason; it was on finding that the philosophy, which she found under the surface of the plays, was running counter to the religious doctrines in which she had been educated. I think there is no other instance of anything like this; a system growing up in a person's mind without the volition—contrary to the volition—and substituting itself in place of everything that originally [62] grew there. It is really more wonderful that she should have fancied this philosophy, than if she had really found it.

AUGUST 2ᵈ SATURDAY.

ON Wednesday, at 11 1/4 °clock, I took the rail for London, with wife and Julian—a very warm day, even according to our American notions. We got into an omnibus at the Station, and rode as far as Charing Cross, whence we walked to Marlborough House, to see the Vernon Gallery of pictures. They are the works, almost entirely, of English artists of the last and present century, and comprise many famous paintings; and I must acknowledge that I had more enjoyment of them than of those portions of the National Gallery which I had before seen—comprising specimens of the grand old masters. My comprehension has not yet reached their height. I think nothing pleased me more than a picture by Sir David Wilkie—the Parish Beadle, with a vagrant boy and a monkey in custody; it is exceedingly good and true, throughout, and especially the monkey's face is a wonderful production of genius, comprising within itself the whole moral and pathos of the picture. Marl[63]borough House was the residence of the great Duke, and is to be that of the Prince of Wales, when another place is found for pictures. It adjoins St. James's palace. In its present state, it is not a very splendid mansion; the rooms (what we saw of them) being small, though handsomely shaped, with vaulted cielings [sic], and carved, white marble fireplaces. I left Sophia here, after an hour or two, and walked forth into the hot and busy city, with Julian.

We had some mutton-chops at Anderton's Hotel, in a dark coffee-room, with the roar of Fleet-street sweeping past the windows; and, afterwards, I called at Routledge's bookshop, in hopes to make an arrangement with him about Miss Bacon's business. But Routledge himself is making a journey in the north, and neither of the partners was in; so that I shall have to go thither some other day. Then we stept into St. Paul's Cathedral to cool ourselves, and it was delightful so to escape from the sunny, sultry turmoil of Fleet street and Ludgate, and find ourselves at once in this remote, solemn, shadowy seclusion, marble-cool. Oh that we had Cathedrals in Amer[64]ica, were it only for this sensuous luxury! We strolled round the Cathedral, and I delighted Julian much by pointing out the monuments of three British generals who were slain in America, in the last war—the naughty and blood-thirsty little man! We then went to Guildhall, where I thought Julian would like to see Gog and Magog; but he had never heard of those illustrious personages, and took no interest in them. Thence we strolled and went astray through various dingy and ugly thoroughfares—hot, hot, hot—till we crossed London-bridge, and took the rail homeward, where we arrived two hours sooner than mamma.

The two days since intervening have been excessively hot, and I have spent them at Blackheath, only once leaving our own house and garden for a little bit of a walk, with Sophia, Julian, and Rosebud. It is very pleasant here, very quiet, very homelike, after our long, unsettled way of life. The garden is but a little space, some thirty or fifty yards square—Oh, less than that—with the house on one side, a hedge-fence on another, and a brick-wall, with trees and shrubbery against it, on the two others;—a grassy lawn, decorated with flower-[65]beds; and rose-bushes in profusion, all about the garden, and geraniums, pinks, poppies, sweet-peas, and many other scarlet, yellow, blue, and purple blossoms; and a few fruit trees; and, over all the outer region, beyond the garden-walls, we see an abundant cloud of foliage, or separate clouds tossed upward from old trees. It is wonderfully sylvan and rural, being so nigh the great city. Two houses, to be sure, are in a range with us, though not contiguous, and overlook our garden from their chamber-windows; but still we feel at home and secluded there; and I read my book (which, in these hot days, has been Dombey & Son) or play with the children, or scold at them, as freely as if this little Cockney villa were the "Way-side." When the sun passes off the lawn (I never thought, before, of avoiding the sunshine, in England) we play at bowls—Julian, Una, and I—and, if Sophia's health were a little more rugged, I should not stint to say I am as happy as the English summer day is long. And yet there is a sort of weight or sting in my conscience for not spending this fine weather in making expeditions to see a thousand interesting objects.

[66] August 5ᵗʰ Tuesday.

Saturday and Sunday were as hot as the preceding days—not a cloud to be seen, from morning till night, and scarcely a breath of wind; the sun almost as scorching as in America, but with a less diffusive heat, so that in the shade the temperature was perfectly delicious. There never was nor can be, in Eden itself, more delightful weather than this, to sit still in; and I have spent these days almost wholly in the garden, sitting in the shadow of the shrubbery, and following the shade as it shifts beneath the sunshine. Very quiet days were these, loitering slowly through "Dombey & Son," intermingled with much talk, and broken in upon often by the children, with their sports[384] but, on the whole, with a Sabbath quietude slumbering through the long, sunny hours; and I think I felt the quiet all the more from hearing, at brief intervals, the galloping sweep of the train passing by, within a quarter of the mile, and its screech as it reached the station.[385]

On Saturday, after ten, my wife, and Julian, and I, walked in Greenwich Park, through those noble [67] avenues of old trees; scarcely so beautiful, however, nor so stately, as an avenue of American elms, because these English trees have not such tall, columnar trunks, but are John Bullish in their structure—mighty of girth, but short between the ground and the branches, and round-headed. Our trees, "high over-arched, with echoing walks between,"[386] have the greater resemblance to the Gothic aisle of a cathedral. In Greenwich Park, there are herds of deer, very beautiful objects, and so tame that they come to nibble cake out of the spectator's hand; and yet there is a quiet apprehensiveness lingering from their wild nature, so that a slight motion will send them scampering away, as easily as a breath of wind scatters the winged seeds of a dandelion. Sunday afternoon, I took another walk in the Park with Una and Julian, and found it pretty well thronged with visitors, who were lounging on the seats, or lying on the grass; principally young men and girls, and, in many cases, fathers and mothers, with all their progeny about them. The Greenwich pensioners, too, in their three-cornered hats, and long blue frock coats, with bright [68] buttons—a costume that assimilates them all to one's idea of an old admiral—were seen among the crowd; and outside of the Park a Methodist, mounted on a cart, was holding forth to a small congregation, and suffering martyrdom, I should think, in the hot sun. The English sun, when it shines in earnest, is awfully hot. These open-air preachers are not unusual, on Sundays; and I have always observed soldiers among their auditors. Soldiers, now-a-days, and hereabouts—so near Woolwich—make a part of every crowd; and some of them have as many as half a dozen medals on the breasts of their scarlet coats.[387]

Yesterday, as the day promised to be rather cooler than the preceding ones, and the morning sun being veiled, I walked through the Park to the pier at Greenwich, and took the steamer for London Bridge. While waiting at the pier, I saw a Regatta. It appears to be an ancient institution at Greenwich; this being, I think, the seventy-fourth anniversary; and it is a contention among the watermen—the Free Watermen of Greenwich, the advertisement said—for prizes, under the patronage of the Lord Mayor and [69] other distinguished individuals. On this occasion, there were six candidates, and the chief prize was a boat, the other prizes being small amounts of money. The contest appeared to excite very great interest in the spectators on the pier, and in steamers and row-boats on the river. I saw but little of it—nothing, indeed, except one or two very light boats, in each of which a single rower, (with bare arms, and little apparel save a shirt and drawers) was exerting himself to the utmost. The man, whom I most particularly noticed, looked pale and earnest, and had every muscle on the stretch; and, from his aspect, I immediately caught an interest in the affair; for it stirs one's sympathy immensely, and is even awful, to see a man doing his best—putting forth all he has in him—staking himself entirely on the turn of the moment. I do not know how the contest terminated; for the steamer went off in the height of it, and we absoluely broiled and roasted, all the way up to London Bridge; and afterwards I went broiling through the city-streets, and stept into St. Paul's (as on a [70] previous occasion) to cool myself. Truly, I am grateful to the piety of elder times for raising this vast, cool canopy of marble, in the midst of the feverish city. I wandered quite round the Cathedral, and saw, in a remote corner, a monument to the officers of the Coldstream Guards, slain in the Crimea; it was a mural tablet, with the names of the officers on an escutcheon; and two privates of the Guards (in marble, and bas-relief, not in reality) were mourning over them. Over the tablet hung two silken banners, new and glossy, with the battles, in which the regiment has been engaged, inscribed on them—not merely Crimean, but Peninsular battles. These banners will hang there, till they drop away in tatters.

After thus refreshing myself in the Cathedral, I went to Routledge's in Farringdon-street, and saw one of the partners—a Mr. Warner, I believe he called himself. He expressed great pleasure at seeing me, as indeed he ought, having published and sold (without any profit on my part) uncounted thousands of my books. I introduced the subject of Miss Bacon's work; and he expressed the utmost wil[71]lingness to do everything in his power towards bringing it before the world, but thought that his firm (it being their business to publish for the largest circle of readers) was not the most eligible for the publication of such a book. Very likely, this may be so. At all events, however, I am to send him the manuscript, and he will, at least, give me his advice and assistance in finding a publisher. He was good enough to express great regret that I had no work of my own to give him for publication; and truly I regret it too, since, being a resident in England, I could now have all the publishing privileges of a native author. He presented me with a copy of an illustrated edition—very pretentious, but incredibly poor, as far as the pictures go—of Longfellow's poems; and I took my leave.

Thence I went to the Picture Gallery at the British Institution, where there are three rooms full of paintings by the first masters, the property of private persons. Every one of them, no doubt, was worth studying for a long, long time; and I suppose I may have given, on an average, a minute [72] to each. What an absurdity it would seem, to pretend to read two or three hundred poems, of all degrees between an epic and a ballad, in an hour or two! And a picture is a poem, only requiring the greater study to be felt and comprehended, because the spectator must necessarily do much for himself towards that end. I saw many beautiful things—among them, some landscapes by Claude, which, to the eye, were like the flavor of a rich, ripe melon to the palate.

Then I called on Mr. Palfrey (19, Regent-street, St James's) and found him gone away for a fortnight. It being altogether too hot to do anything—so hot, in London-streets, that it took away all my energy—I strolled slowly down towards the city, getting what shade I could from the buildings. After passing Temple Bar, I stept into Dick's Coffee House, and got some roast mutton in a low, dark room, with cross-beams overhead—a room, very likely, of two centuries old, though the front of the house is modern. Then I kept on my course—diverging, however, into the Temple, and thence into Whitefriars, the ancient [73] Alsatia but now a most unpicturesque and commonplace region, retaining none of its wild characteristics—unless it be an unusual number of beer and spirit shops. And so, at last, half dead with heat, and wretchedly tired, I crossed London Bridge, and, at five °clock, took the train for Blackheath.

AUGUST 7th, THURSDAY.

YESTERDAY, at about eleven, my wife and I took the rail for London; it being a fine sunny day, though not so very warm as many of the preceding days have been. From the Railway Station, we got into an omnibus, which carried us through Holborn to Tottenham Court Road, whence we walked along Oxford street to Regent street, adown the whole length of which we sauntered; thence along Piccadilly, as far as the Egyptian Hall. It is quite remarkable how comparatively quiet the town has become, even to an outsider's perception, now that the season is over. One can see the difference in all the region west of Temple Bar; and, indeed, either the hot weather or some other cause seems to have operated in assuaging the turmoil in the city itself. I never saw London Bridge so little thronged as yesterday.

[74] At the Egyptian Hall, or in the same edifice, there is a gallery of pictures, the property of Lord Ward, who allows the public to see them, five days of the week, without any trouble or restriction;—a great kindness on his Lordship's part, it must be owned. It is a very valuable collection, I presume, containing specimens of many famous old masters; some of the early, stiff and hard pictures by Raphael, and his masters, and fellow pupils—very curious and nowise beautiful; a perfect, sunny glimpse of Venice, by Canaletto, and Saints, and naked women, and scriptural, allegorical, and mythological people, by Titian, Guido, Correggio, and many more names than I can remember. There is likewise a dead Magdalen by Canova, and a Venus by the same, very pretty, and with a vivid light of joyous expression in her face, making her far preferable to that cold little woman of stone, the Venus de Medici; also Powers's Greek Slave, in which I see little beauty or merit, and two or three other statues. It seems to me time to leave off sculpturing men and women naked; they mean nothing, and might as well bear one name as anoth[75]er, and belong to the same category as the ideal portraits in Books of Beauty, or in the windows of print-shops. The art does not naturally belong to this age; and the exercise of it, I think, had better be confined to the manufacture of marble fireplaces.

Coming out of the picture-gallery, we were retracing our steps along Piccadilly, and thinking of getting an ice-cream, when somebody spoke close to my ear. I took no notice, thinking the remark, whatever it might be, was intended for some other person; but again the same voice spoke, and looking round, who should it be but the Great Tupper!—he had been muttering "Scarlet Letter" in my ear. What an absurd little man! I introduced him to my wife; and then he produced Mrs. Tupper, and his eldest son, and likewise the boy whom I had noticed, when visiting Tupper, as being afflicted with a disease of twitches and contortions. Tupper himself really looked like anything but a poet, or a scholar, or a gentleman; a red-faced, round, little person, with iron-gray curls, and an odd familiarity of aspect and address. He and his wife, like me and mine, were [76] thinking of ices; so we all went into a confectioner's shop, close at hand, and ordered what we liked—Tupper taking care to tell the attendant that we were two distinct parties. It is not so customary in England as it is in America, for gentlemen to offer these little hospitalities to their friends; and I think the English custom preferable to our own. Tupper showed his bustling and good-naturedly intrusive characteristics, even in eating ice-creams; for he advised

Sophia and me to get them of two different kinds—pine-apple and biscuit—and to mix them together, for the improvement of the flavor; and he even showed us how to make the mixture. He and Mrs. Tupper ate their ice-creams in a most loving and conjugal fashion, putting their spoons, at pleasure, each into the other's glass. Tupper appears to be a most good-natured man; and yet there is an indescribable kind of waywardness and eccentricity about him—or, at least, in his manner—which makes me feel as if he might possibly go mad.

They were now, as it happened, on their way to Blackheath, where the eldest boy is to be put to [77] school. He is certainly a very intelligent lad, and did not put himself quite so much forward in conversation, as when I met him at home. Mrs. Tupper was good and kind, as usual.

After parting from these excellent people, we walked as far as the Haymarket, and then got into a cab and drove to Ashley Place, Victoria-street, to call on Mrs. S. C. Hall, whom we found at home. In fact, Wednesday is her reception-day; although, as everybody is now out of town, we were the only callers. She is an agreeable and kindly woman, and if she have faults and follies, such as are incident to literary people, I have not yet found them out. She told us that her husband and herself propose going to America, next year; and I heartily wish that they may meet with a warm and friendly reception, though I cannot but fear that it will not quite come up to their expectations. Among literary people, it is only the very first in celebrity, for whose sake Americans make fools of themselves. But she is a good woman. I have seldom been more assured of the existence of a heart, than in her; also, a good [78] deal of sentiment, passing sometimes into sentimentality, and showing itself in little gifts and tributes of flowers, for instance, gathered from somebody's grave, or strewn upon it—and other such prettinesses, not to be looked for in a rotund English dame of ripe years. She had been visiting Bessy, the widow of Moore, at Sloperton, and gave Sophia a rose from his cottage. Such things, no doubt, are very true and unaffected in her; the only wonder is, that she has not long ago written away such girlish freshness of feeling as prompts them. We did not see Mr. Hall; he having gone to the Crystal palace.

Taking our leave, we returned on foot along Victoria street—a new street, penetrating through what was recently one of the worst parts of the town, and now bordered with large blocks of building, in a dreary, half-finished state, and left so for want of funds—till we came to Westminster Abbey. We went in, and spent an hour there, wandering all round the nave and aisles, admiring the grand old edifice itself, but finding more to smile at than to admire, in the monuments. Nevertheless, they express very satisfactorily [79] the successive generations and ages that placed them there; and I should be very sorry to see better monuments substituted for them. The interior view of the Abbey is better than can be described; the heart aches, as one gazes at it, for lack of power and breadth enough to take its beauty and grandeur in. The effect was heightened by the sun shining through the painted window, in the western end, and by the bright sunshine that came through the open portal, and lay on the pavement—that space so bright, the rest of the vast floor so solemn and sombre. At the western end, in a corner from which spectators are barred out, (I know not why) there is a statue of Wordsworth, which I do not recollect seeing at any former visit. Its only companion, I believe, in the same nook, is Pope's friend, Secretary Craggs.

Downing-street, that famous official precinct, took its name from Sir George Downing, who, I believe, was proprietor or lessee of property there. He was a native of my own old native town; and his descendants (collateral, I suppose) still reside there, and follow the dry-goods business.

[80] AUGUST 10th SUNDAY.

I LEFT Blackheath on Friday at 9 °clock, and the Paddington Station at 11, and journeyed to Liverpool, via Chester. There was a rainy day in the wind; but we kept in advance of it, as it slowly worked its way northward, not reaching Liverpool, probably, till twenty-four hours later than London had it. It was a warm day along the road; and people were on the move for the watering places in Wales and elsewhere. One sees a considerable variety of climate, temperature, and season, in a ride of two hundred miles, north and south, through England;—near London, for instance, the grain was reaped, and stood in sheaves in the stubble-fields, over which parties of girls and children might be seen gleaning; farther north, the golden, or greenish gold, crops, were waving in the wind. In one part of our ride, the atmosphere was hot [and] dry; at another part, it had been cooled and refreshed by a heavy thunder shower, the pools of which still lay along our track. It seems to me that local varieties of weather are more common in this island, and within narrower precincts, than in America. I am now so accustomed to England scenery, that I saw nothing to make a description of; but I never saw England of such a dusky and dusty green before, almost sun[81]browned, indeed. Sometimes the green hedges formed a marked frame-work to a broad sheet of golden grain-field. As we drew near Oxford, just before reaching the station, I had a good view of its domes, towers, and spires,—better, I think, than when Julian and I rambled through the town, a month or two ago.

My weight, a few weeks ago, was thirteen stone.

Mr Frank Scott Haydon (of the Record Office, London) writes me, date August 12th, that he has found a "Henry atte Hawthorne," on a roll which he is transcribing, of the 1st, Edward III. He belonged to the Parish of Aldremeston, in the Hundred of Blakenhurste, Worcester County. But, searching a directory, I can find no Parish nor hundred of those names, or any name similar.

AUGUST 21st, THURSDAY.

YESTERDAY, at twelve ⁰clock, I took the steamer for Runcorn, from the Pier Head. In the streets, I had noticed that it was a breezy day; but on the river, there was a very stiff breeze from the north-east, right a-head, blowing directly in our face, the whole way; and truly this river Mersey is never without a breeze, and generally in the direc[82]tion of its course—an evil-tempered, unkindly, blustering wind too, like the worst temper of an Englishman—a wind that you cannot face without being exasperated by it. As it came right against us, it was impossible to find a shelter anywhere on deck, except it were behind the stove-pipe; and besides, the day was overcast, and threatening rain. I have undergone very miserable hours on the Mersey—where, in the space of two years, I voyaged thousands of miles—and this trip to Runcorn reminded me of them, though it was less disagreeable, after more than a twelve-month's respite. We had a good many passengers on board, most of whom were of the second-class, and congregated on the forward deck; more women than men, I think, and some of them with their husbands and children. Several produced lunch and bottles, and victualled themselves very soon after we started. By and by, the wind became so disagreeable that I went below, and sat in the cabin, only occasionally looking out to get a peep at the shores of the river, which I had never before seen above Eastham. However, they are not worth looking at, level and monotonous, without trees, or beauty of any kind—here and there a village, and a modern church; on the low ridge behind, perhaps, a windmill, which the gusty day had set busily to work. The river continues very wide—[83] no river, indeed, but an estuary —almost the whole distance to Runcorn; and nearly at the end of our voyage, we approached some abrupt and prominent hills, which, many a time, I have seen on my passages to Rockferry, looking blue and dim, and serving for prophets of the weather; for when they can be distinctly seen, adown the river, it is a token of coming rain. We met many vessels, and passed many which were beating up against the wind, and which heeled over, so that their decks must have dipt—schooners, and vessels that come from the Bridgewater Canal. We shipt a sea ourselves, that gave the fore-deck passengers a wetting.

Before reaching Runcorn, we stopt to land some passengers at another little port, where there was a pier, and a light-house, and a church on the pier, within a few yards of the riverside—a good many of the river craft, too, in dock, forming quite a crowd of masts. About ten minutes further steaming brought us to Runcorn, where were two or three tall, manufacturing chimneys, with a pennant of black smoke from each; two vessels, of considerable size, on the stocks; a church or two; and a meagre, uninteresting, shabby, brick-built town, rising from the edge of the river, with irregular streets, not village-like, but paved, and looking like a dwarfed, stunted city. [84] We cannot conceive, in America, of anything so unpicturesque as this little English town. I wandered through it, till I came to a tall, high pedestalled windmill, on the

outer-verge, the vans of which were going briskly round. Thence retracing my
steps, I stopt at a poor hotel and got some lunch—a round of cold beef, and a
cold ham, and a pint of bitter ale—and finding that I was in time to take the
steamer back, I hurried on board, and we set sail (or set steam) at a quarter
to three. I have heard of an old castle at Runcorn, but could discover nothing
of it. It was well that I returned so promptly; for we had hardly left the
pier before it began to rain, and there was a real downfall, throughout the
voyage homeward. Runcorn, I believe, is about fourteen miles from Liverpool, and is the farthest point to which a steamer runs. I had intended to
come home by railway—a circuitous route—but the advice of the landlady
of the hotel, and the aspect of the weather, and a feeling of general discouragement, prevented me.

An incident in S. C. Hall's "Ireland," of a stone cross, buried in Cromwell's
time to prevent its destruction by his soldiers. It was forgotten, and became
a mere doubtful tradition; but one old man [85] had been told by his father,
and he by his father &c. that it was buried near a certain spot; and, at last,
two hundred years after the cross was buried, the vicar of the parish dug in
that spot, and found it.[388] In my romance, an American might bring this tradition from over the sea, and so discover the cross, which had been altogether
forgotten.

AUGUST 24th SUNDAY

DAY before yesterday, I took the rail for Southport, at half past two—
a cool, generally overcast day, with glimpses of faint sunshine. The ride is
through a most uninteresting tract of country;—at first, glimpses of the river,
with the thousands of masts in the docks; the dismal outskirts of a great town,
still spreading onward, with beginnings of streets, and insulated brick buildings
and blocks; farther on, a wide monotony of level plain, and here and there
a village and a church; almost always, a windmill in sight, there being plenty
of breeze to turn its sails, on this windy coast. The railway skirts along the
sea, the whole distance, but is shut out from the sight of it by the low sandhills which seem to have been heaped up by the waves. There are one or
two light-houses on the shore. I have not seen a drearier landscape, even in
Lancashire.

[86] Reaching Southport at ½ past three, I rambled about with a view to
discover whether it is a suitable residence for Sophia and the children, during
September. It is a large village—or rather more than a village—which seems
to be almost entirely made up of lodging-houses, and, at any rate, has been
created by the influx of summer visitors;—a sandy soil, level, and laid out
with well-paved streets, the principal of which are enlivened with bazaars,
markets, shops, hotels of various degrees, and a showy vivacity of aspect;
there are a great many donkey-carriages, large vehicles, drawn by a pair
of donkeys; bath-chairs, with invalid ladies; refreshment-rooms in great

number;—a place where everybody seems to be a transitory guest, nobody at home. The main street leads directly down to the sea shore, along which there is an elevated embankment, with a promenade on the top, and seats, and a toll of one penny. The shore itself (the tide being then low) stretched out interminably seaward, a wide waste of glistening sands; and on the dry border, people were riding on donkeys, with the drivers whipping behind; and children were digging with their little wooden spades; and there were donkey carriages far out on the sands, a pleasant and breezy drive. A whole city of bathing-machines were stationed near the shore, [87] and I saw others far out seaward. The sea-air was refreshing and exhilirating [*sic*]; and if Sophia needs a sea-side residence, I should think this might do as well as any other.

I saw a large brick edifice, enclosed within a wall, and with somewhat the look of an almshouse or hospital; and it proved to be an infirmary, char-itably established for the reception of poor invalids, who need sea-air, and cannot afford to pay for it. Two or three of such were sitting under its windows. I do not think that the visitors of Southport are generally of a very opulent class, but middling people from Manchester and other parts of this northern region. The lodging-houses, however, are of sufficiently handsome style and arrangement; and inquiring the prices, at one of them, I found the weekly charge to be half a guinea for each bed, and fifteen shillings for a parlour. I staid less than two hours, and left by 5¼ train.

AUGUST 31st, SUNDAY, AT OXFORD.

ON Tuesday last, I left Liverpool at 11¼, and reached London and Black-heath, without anything particularly interesting or describable; unless it were an Englishman's movement towards dispossessing a young lady of his seat, which she [88] had taken without being aware of his prior claim. "Do you very greatly prefer that seat?" he asked; but, the young lady making no reply, he succumbed, and sat down elsewhere. As a trait of English character, I should have been glad had he persevered in turning her out.

Nothing wonderful happened, the rest of the week. Bennoch spent one evening with us, and we sat up late, he and I, talking. He told me something about Tupper that gives him an aspect of pathos and heroic endurance, very little in accordance with the ludicrous attitude in which I have sketched him. The thing is not [to] be recorded; but Tupper is a patient, tender, Chris-tian man. On Friday, I walked through Greenwich Park with Julian, and took boat to London, and up the Thames as far as Hungerford Market. We rambled about London, took a mutton-chop at the Cheshire Cheese, just aside from Fleet-street, called on Bennoch, and boated back to Greenwich, from London Bridge.

Yesterday, at twelve, my wife and I took the rail to London, and drove across the city to the Paddington Station, where we met Bennoch, and set out with him, [89] at two ⁰clock, for Oxford. I do not quite understand the matter; but it appears that we were expected guests of Mr. Spiers,[389] a very hospitable gentleman, an ex-Mayor of Oxford, and a friend of Bennoch's and of the Halls. Mr. S. C. Hall met us at the Oxford Station, and under his guidance, we drove to a quiet, comfortable house in Giles-street, where rooms had been taken for us. Durham, the sculptor, whom I have before met, is likewise of the party.

After establishing ourselves at these lodgings, Bennoch, Mr. Hall, Sophia, and I, walked forth to take a preliminary glimpse of the city; and Mr. Hall being familiar with the localities, served admirably as a guide. If I remember aright, I spoke very slightingly of the exterior aspect of Oxford, as I saw it with Julian, during an hour or two's stop here, on my way to Southampton. I am bound to say, that my impressions are now very different, and that I find Oxford exceedingly picturesque, and rich in beauty and grandeur, and in antique stateliness. I do not remember very particularly what we saw; gray, weather-stained, and picturesquely time-worn fronts of famous [90] colleges and halls of learning, everywhere about the streets, with arched entrances, passing through which, we found grassy quadrangles within, with perhaps a cloistered walk around; old gray towers and turrets, ivy grown; quaint bits of sculpture from monkish hands, the most grotesque and ludicrous faces, as if the slightest whim of these old carvers took shape in stone, the material being so soft and manageable by them; an ancient stone pulpit in the quadrangle of Maudlin College, one of only three now extant in England; a splendid— or not splendid, but dimly magnificent chapel, belonging to the same college, with painted windows, of rare beauty, not brilliant with diversified hues, but of a sombre tint. In this Chapel, there is an alabaster monument—a recumbent figure of the founder's father, as large as life—which, though several centuries old, is as well preserved as if fresh from the chisel. But I cannot separate these things in my recollection; they are all jumbled together, pretty much as if the antiquities of Oxford were tossed together into one heap of gray stones.

In the High-street—which, I suppose, is the noblest old street in England— Mr. Hall pointed out the Crown [91] Inn, where Shakspeare used to spend the night, and be most hospitably welcomed by the pretty hostess, in his journeys between Stratford and London—whereby Sir William Davenant came wrongfully into the world. It is a three story house, with other houses contiguous; an old timber-mansion, though now, I think, plastered, and painted of a yellowish hue. The ground floor is occupied as a shoe-shop; but the rest of the house seems to be still kept as a tavern, and I saw one or two young women sitting at a latticed window.

It is not now term-time, and Oxford loses one of its most characteristic features, by the absence of the gownsmen; but still there is a good deal of liveliness in the streets. We walked as far as a bridge beyond Maudlin (properly Magdalen) college; and thence turned back, and took a cab homeward, on Sophia's account. At six, we went to dine with the hospitable ex-Mayor, whose house is nearly opposite our lodgings, across the wide, tree-bordered street. The ex-Mayor is a gentlemanly and intelligent person, and the father of thirteen children, the eldest eighteen years old. He is in business, and wealthy, and was Mayor two years [92] ago, and has done a great deal to make peace between the University and the Town, who had heretofore been bitter enemies. His house—such portion of it as I saw—is adorned with pictures, and drawings, and he seems to have an especial taste for art. His wife has lately been confined with her thirteenth or fourteenth child, and looked rather feeble and worn, as might be expected in such a multitudinous mother; nevertheless, she was in the drawing-room, and also dined with us, as became a lady to whom child-birth was an every day matter. I sat by Mrs. S. C. Hall, and next to Mr. Spiers. The company were those whom I have mentioned, and a Doctor Corfe,[390] (not a physician, but a musical doctor, and organist of one of the colleges) and Mr. Spiers's eldest son, and one or two young men of no account.

Mrs. Hall is not a conversible person—at least, I never have found her so— though I like her very well. We got on, I fancy, rather poorly at dinner; neither had Mrs. Spiers much gift of talk. The ex-mayor's champagne and claret were excellent wines. The table was adorned with pieces of plate, vases and other matters, which were presented to him as tokens of public or friendly re[93]gard, and approbation of his conduct in the mayoralty. After dinner, too, he produced a large silver snuff-box, which had been given him on the same account; in fact, the inscription said, I believe, that it was one of five pieces of plate so presented. The vases are really splendid, one of them as much as two feet high, and richly ornamented; it will hold five or six bottles of wine, and he said that it had been filled, and I believe, sent round as a loving-cup, at some of his entertainments. He evidently enjoys these things, and is not without a kindly vanity, which, intermixed with genuine benevolence, produces all this excellent hospitality.

On account of Sophia's health, we retired at about ten, and I should have gone forthwith to bed; but Bennoch proposed a walk; and he, and Durham, and I, set forth. We rambled pretty extensively about the streets, sometimes seeing the shapes of old edifices, dimly and doubtfully, it being an overcast night; or catching a partial view of a gray wall, or a pillar, or a Gothic arch-way, by lamp-light. Two girls, of the frail sisterhood, persecuted us a little, with proposals to give them a glass of [94] wine, but Bennoch got rid of them with a shilling. Durham told about the sittings he had for his bust of the Queen, and how it was contrary to etiquette for her Majesty to address him directly, but only through the medium of the lady in waiting. She sometimes broke through this rule, however, as did the sculptor on his part; and, indeed, it is an odd idea that an observation needs to be filtered, as it were, before passing from a subject's mind into the sovereign's. When the bust was nearly finished, the Queen proposed that a considerable thickness of clay should be removed from the shoulders of the model; thereby improving the bust, though injuring the likeness. We walked about the streets for above an hour, in various talk, into which, as usual, Bennoch threw a great many outrageous puns; and the clock had sometime ago struck eleven, when we were passing under a long extent of antique wall and towers, which Durham said were those of Balliol College. He led us into the middle of the street, and showed us a cross which was paved into it, on a level with the rest of the pavement. This was the spot where Latimer and Ridley, and another bishop, were martyred in Bloody Mary's time. There is a memorial to [95] them in another street; but this, where I set my foot at nearly midnight, was the very spot where their flesh turned to ashes, and their bones whitened. Thence we went homeward, and to bed.

This has been a most beautiful morning, and I have seen few pleasanter scenes than this street in which we lodge, with its spacious breadth, its two rows of fine old trees, with side-walks as wide as the whole width of ordinary streets, and, on the opposite side, the rows of houses, some of them ancient, with picturesque gables, partially disclosed through the intervening foliage. My wife being overwearied, and somewhat affected with the headache, I left her in bed, and went to breakfast with the hospitable Mr. Spiers. In his drawing-room, he has pictures by Etty; amongst others, a naked woman, of course, but, to my eye, scrawny and ill-conditioned. During breakfast, plans for seeing Oxford and the neighborhood were developed and discussed; and if the weather prove good, and nothing else go wrong, there is promise of a very rich time for us. The rest of the party have gone to church; but Sophia's indisposition was a sufficient plea for my staying at home.

[96] *Half-past 8 P.M.* Sophia lay in bed all the forenoon; and, after writing my journal, I aroused her; and, at one °clock, we went over to Mr. Spiers to lunch. This street of St. Giles, as I said before, is of noble breadth, and has beautiful ranges of trees, dividing it into three almost equal spaces, of which the carriage-way is hardly more than equal to either footpath. From our window, we have a slantwise glimpse to the right of the walls of St. John's College; and the general aspect of the street is of an antiquity not to shame those mediaeval halls. Our own lodgings are in a house that seems to be very old, with panelled walls, beams across the cieling [sic], lattice-windows in the chambers, and a musty fragrance, such as old houses inevitably have. Nevertheless, everything is extremely neat, clean, and comfortable; and, in term-time, our apartments are occupied by a Mr. Stebbing (son of Rev. William Stebbing, known in literature by some critical writings) who, I believe, is a graduate, and an admirable scholar. There is a book-case of five shelves, containing his books, mostly standard works, and indicating a safe and solid taste, but with no indications of a remarkable young man.

[97] After lunch—by the way, there was a new article of drink at lunch, being hop-champagne; it seemed, judging by the taste, to be a hybrid between cider and ale, and scarcely so palatable as either, and is drunk out of a silver tankard—after lunch, we set forth in an open barouche (Mrs Hall, her adopted

daughter Fanny, Sophia, and I, with the ex-mayor on the box) to see the remarkables of Oxford; while Bennoch, Durham, Mr. Parker, a Mr. Addison,
and one or two sons of Mr. Spiers, went on foot. We first drew up at New
College, (a strange name for such an old place, but it was new, I think, sometime since the Conquest) and went through its quiet, sunny quadrangles, and
into its sunny and shadowy gardens. I am in despair about the architecture and
old edifices of these Oxford colleges; it is so impossible to express them in
words. They are themselves—as the architect left them, and as Time has
modified and improved them—the expression of an idea, which does not
admit of being otherwise expressed, or translated into anything else. Those
old battlemented walls, around the quadrangles—the Gothic ornaments, and
quaint devices—the many gables—the towers, the [98] windows, with stone
mullions, so very antique, yet some of them adorned with fresh flowers in
pots, a very sweet contrast—the ivy, mantling the gray stone—and the infinite repose, both in sunshine and shadow—it is as if half a dozen by-gone
centuries had set up their rest here, and as if nothing of the present time ever
passed through the deeply recessed arch-way that shuts in the college from
the street. Not but what people have very free admittance; and many parties
of young men and girls, and children, came into the gardens while we were
there.

These gardens of New College are indescribably beautiful; not gardens, in
our American sense, but lawns of the richest green, and softest velvet grass,
shadowed over by ancient trees, that have lived a quiet life here for centuries, and have been nursed and tended with such care, and so sheltered
from the rude winds, that certainly they must have been the happiest of all
trees. Such a sweet, quiet, sacred, stately seclusion—so age-long as this has
been, and, I hope, will continue to be—cannot exist anywhere else. One
side of the garden-wall is formed by the ancient wall of the city, which Cromwell's artillery [99] battered, and which still retains its pristine height and
strength. At intervals, there are round towers, that formed the bastions of the
wall; that is to say, on the exterior of the wall, they are round towers, but, in
the garden of the college, they are semi-circular recesses, with iron garden-
seats arranged round them. The loop-holes, through which the archers and
musketeers used to shoot, still pierce through deep recesses in the wall, which
is here about six feet thick. I do wish I could put into one sentence the whole
impression of this garden, but it could not be done in ever so many pages.

We looked also at the outside of the wall; and Mr. Parker—he is a graduate
of Oxford, and son of the University Printer, and deeply skilled in the
antiquities of the spot—showed us a weed growing upon the wall, here in little
sprigs, there in large and heavy festoons, hanging plentifully downward
from a shallow root. It is called the Oxford plant, being found only here,
and not easily, if at all, introduced anywhere else. It bears a small and pretty
blue flower, not altogether unlike the forget-me-not; and Sophia and I took
some of it [100] away with us for a memorial. We went into the chapel

of New College, which is in such fresh condition that I think it must be modern; and yet this cannot be, since there [are] old brasses, inlaid into tombstones in the pavement, representing mediaeval ecclesiastics and college-dignitaries; and busts against the walls, in antique garb; and old painted windows, unmistakable in their antiquity. But there is likewise a window, lamentable to look at, which was painted by Sir Joshua Reynolds, and exhibits strikingly the difference between the work of a man who performed it merely as a matter of taste and business, and what was done religiously and with the whole heart;—at least, it shows that the artists and public of the last age had no sympathy with Gothic art. In the Chancel of this church, there are some more painted windows, which I take to be modern too, though they are in much better taste, and have an infinitely better effect, than Sir Joshua's. At any rate, with the sunshine through them, they looked very beautiful, and tinted the high altar and the pavement with beautiful hues.

The sexton—or whatever the keeper of a college-chapel is called—opened a tall and narrow little recess in the wall [101] of the Chancel and showed it entirely filled with the Crosier of William of Wickham. It appears to be made of silver-gilt, and is a most rich, beautiful, and elaborate relic, at least six feet high. Modern art cannot—or at least, does not—equal the chasing and carving of this splendid crosier, which is enriched with figures of saints and apostles, and various Gothic devices, very minute, but all done as faithfully as if the artist's salvation had depended on every notch he made in the silver. I thought of the ex-mayor's golden goblets, which he had shown us in the morning; and the handiwork is rude and boyish, in comparison. Leaving New College, Bennoch and I, under Mr. Parker's guidance, walked round Christ Church meadows, part of our way lying along the banks of the Cherwell, which, I believe, unites with the Isis to form the Thames. The Cherwell is a narrow and remarkably sluggish stream; but is deep in spots, and capriciously so, so that a person may easily step from knee-deep to fifteen feet in depth. Mr. Parker used a queer expression in reference to the drowning of two college men;—he said it was an "awkward" affair. I think this is equal to [102] Longfellow's story of the Frenchman, who avowed himself very much "displeased" at the news of his father's death. At the confluence of the Cherwell and Isis, we saw a good many boats, belonging to the students of the various colleges, or to other individuals; some of them being very large and splendid barges, capable of accommodating a numerous party, with room on board for dancing and merry-making. Some of these barges are calculated to be drawn by horses, in the manner of canal-boats; others are propellable by oars. It is practicable to perform the voyage between Oxford and London—a distance of about 130 miles—in three days. The students of Oxford are famous boatmen; there is a constant rivalship, on this score, among the different colleges; and annually, I think, there is a match between Oxford and Cambridge. The Cambridge men beat the Oxonians, in this year's trial.

On our return into the city, we passed through Christ Church, which, as regards the number of students, is the most considerable college of the University. It has a stately dome; but my remembrance is confused with battlements, towers, and gables, and Gothic staircases, and cloisters; so that [103] I have little or nothing to say about the edifices of this college. But, if there had been nothing else in Oxford but this one establishment, my anticipations would not have been disappointed. The bell was tolling for worship in the chapel; and Mr. Parker told us that Dr. Pusey is a Canon, or in some sort of dignity, in Christ Church, and would probably soon make his appearance in the quadrangle, on his way to Chapel; so we walked to and fro, waiting our opportunity to see him. A gouty old dignitary, in a white surplice, came hobbling along from one extremity of the quadrangle; and, by and by, from the opposite corner, appeared Dr. Pusey, also in a white surplice, and with a lady by his side. We met him, and I stared pretty fixedly at him, as I well might, for he looked on the ground, as if conscious that he would be stared at. He is a man past middle life, of sufficient breadth and massiveness, with a pale, intellectual, manly face; he was talking with the lady, and smiled, but not jollily. Mr. Parker, who knows him, personally, says that he is [a] man of kind and gentle affections. The lady, who accompanied him, is a niece.

Thence, we went through High street and Broad [104] street; and passing by Balliol College (it is a most satisfactory pile and range of old towered and gabled edifices) we came to the cross in the pavement, which is supposed to mark the spot where the Bishops were martyred. But Mr. Parker told us the mortifying fact that he had ascertained that this could not possibly have been the genuine spot of martyrdom, which must have taken place at a point within view, but considerably too far off to be moistened by any tears that may be shed here. It is too bad. We concluded the rambles of the day, by visiting the gardens of Saint John's College; and I desire, if possible, to say even more in admiration of them, than of the gardens of New College;—such beautiful lawns, with tall, ancient trees, and heavy clouds of foliage, and sunny glimpses through archways of leafy branches, where, to-day, we could see parties of girls, making cheerful contrast with the sombre walls and solemn shade. The world surely has not another place like Oxford; it is a despair to see such a place, and ever have to leave it; for it would take a lifetime, and more than one, to comprehend and enjoy it satisfactorily.

[105] At five °clock, we went again to dine with Mr. Spiers, and met pretty much the same party as yesterday, with the addition, at one or another period of the dinner, of all the thirteen children of our excellent host. The vases, too, were all ranged on the table, the largest and central one containing a most magnificent bouquet of dahlias and other bright-hued flowers. Nothing very material passed at table, except that Bennoch made so vile a pun that not one of us could in the least comprehend it. Sophia had a headache, on which account she retired early, and I too, in attendance on her; and from that time till now (½ past ten) I have employed myself in this wretched attempt to

record some of the wondrous sights of the day. Tomorrow, we have other scenes in expectation.

SEPTEMBER 2ᵈ, TUESDAY.

YESTERDAY morning (about ½ past nine, I think) we set out on an excursion to Blenheim—Mr. Spiers, Mr. & Mrs. Hall & Fan[n]y, Bennoch, my wife and I, Mr. Spiers, Junior, Mr. Addison, Mr. Durham, all in and about a four-horse carriage. Mr. Durham and I sat on the box in front, and Bennoch and somebody else in the dicky behind; the rest inside. We had no coachman, but two postillions in short jackets [106] and drab small-clothes, with top-boots; and, all the way along, we had the interesting spectacle of the up-and-down bobbing of their rears. It was a sunny and beautiful day, a specimen of the perfect English weather, just warm enough for comfort,—a little too warm, perhaps, in the noontide sun—but yet retaining a little austerity that made it the more enjoyable. The country between Oxford and Blenheim is not particularly interesting; being almost level, or undulating, very slightly; nor is this, agriculturally, a rich part of England. We saw one or two hamlets, and I remember a picturesque old gabled-house, at a turnpike-gate, and, altogether, the wayside-scenery had an aspect of old English life; but there was nothing very interesting till we reached Woodstock, and stopt to water the horses at the Black Bear. This is called New Woodstock; but it has by no means a bran-new appearance, being a large village of stone-houses, most of them pretty well time-worn. The Black Bear is an ancient inn, large and respectable, with balustraded staircases, and intricate passages and corridors; and queer old pictures and engravings hanging in the entries and apartments. We ordered lunch to be ready for our return, and then resumed our drive to Blenheim.

[107] The park-gate of Blenheim is closed at the end of the village-street of Woodstock; and immediately on entering it, we saw the stately palace, at a distance;—but we made a wide circuit of the park, before approaching it. This park contains three thousand acres, and is fourteen miles in circumference; and having been (in part, at least) a royal domain before it was given to the Marlborough family, it contains many very ancient trees, and has doubtless been the haunt of game and deer for centuries. We saw pheasants in abundance feeding on the open lawns and glades, and the stags tossed their antlers, and bounded away, as we drove by. It is a noble park, not too tamely kept, but vast enough to have lapsed into nature again, after all the pains that were taken with it, when the domain of Blenheim was first laid out; and the great, knotted, aslantwise trunks of the old oaks do not look as if man had had much to do with them. The trees, that were set out in the great Duke's time, are arranged on the same plan as the order of battle of the English troops at Blenheim; but the space is so large, that the spectator is not conscious that they stand [108] in this military array. It must have been very formal, a hundred and fifty years ago, but does not seem so now, though, I suppose, the trees have kept their ranks very faithfully.

One of the park-keepers, on horseback, rode beside our carriage, pointing out the choice views, and glimpses at the palace, as we drove through the park. There is a very large artificial lake, (in fact, it seemed to me worthy of being compared with the Welsh lakes, at least, if not with those of Cumberland,) which was created by Capability Brown, and fills its valley just as if Nature had poured it out. This is a very beautiful object, whether at a distance, or directly on its banks; for the water is very pure, being supplied by a small river which was turned hitherward for the purpose. Blenheim owes not merely this water-scenery, but almost all its other beauties, to the help of man; for its natural features are not striking. But art has done wonderful things here; a skilful painter hardly does more for his blank sheet of canvas, than the landscape-gardener, the planter, the arranger of trees, has done for the monotonous surface of Blenheim; making the most of every undulation, putting [109] in beauty wherever there was a niche for it, opening views to every point that ought to be seen, throwing the foliage around what should be hidden; and then the long lapse of time has softened the harsh outline of all his labors, and given the place back to Nature again, with the addition of all that art has done for it.

After driving a good way—but in what direction I know not—we came to a battlemented tower and house, which had been the residence of the Ranger of Woodstock Park, before the Duke of Marlborough had it. The keeper opened the door for us, and, in the entrance-hall, we found various things that had to do with the chase and woodland-sports. We mounted the staircase, through several stories, up to the top of the tower, whence we had a view of Oxford, and of points much farther off; very indistinctly, however, as is usual through the misty distances of England. Returning again to the ground floor, we saw the room in which Wilmot, the wicked Earl of Rochester (who was ranger of the Park in Charles II's time) died. It is a low and bare little room, with a window in front, and a smaller one behind. In the entrance-room, there were the remains of an old-bedstead; and, for aught I know, Rochester [110] may have died under its canopy. I should like to have this Lodge for my own residence, with a study in the upper room, and all this seclusion of cultivated wilderness to ramble in.

Then we drove on, still getting glimpses of the palace, in new points of view; and, by and by, we came to Rosamond's Well. The spring gushes out from a bank, through some stonework, and makes a little cascade (that is to say, as much as one could turn out of a large pitcher) into a pool, whence it steals away towards the lake, which is but a little way off. The water is very pure and cold, and is fancied, I believe, to possess medicinal virtues. There were two or three old women and some children in attendance, with tumblers, which they present to visitors, full of Rosamond's water; but most of us filled the tumblers for ourselves, and drank.

From Rosamond's Well, we drove to the triumphal-pillar, erected in honor of Marlborough, and on the summit of which he stands, in a Roman garb, holding a winged figure of Victory in his hand, as one would hold a bird. It is a tall column, I know not how many feet high, but lofty enough to lift the Great Duke far above the rest of the world, [111] and to be visible a long way off; so, wherever he wandered about his grounds, and especially as he issued from his own mansion, he was reminded of his glory. In truth, till I came to Blenheim, I never had so positive and material an idea of what fame is—of what the admiration of his country can do for a successful warrior—as I now have. On the huge tablets, inlaid into the pedestal of the column, the entire act of Parliament, bestowing Blenheim on the Duke of Marlborough and his posterity, is engraved in deep letters, painted black on the white ground. The pillar stands exactly a mile from the principal front of the palace, and in a straight line with the centre of its entrance-hall;so that it was the Duke's principal point of view.

If I am not mistaken, our visit to the column came before we had been to Rosamond's Well; but these many new scenes make a jumble in my memory. At any rate, after seeing the Well and the Pillar, we proceeded to the palace-gate, which is very lofty and stately, a great pillared arch-way, giving admittance into a spacious quadrangle. It was funny, that a stout, elderly, and rather surly footman in livery appeared at the gate, and [112] took possession of whatever canes he could get hold of, in order to claim sixpence when we went away. There is much outcry against the meanness of the present Duke in his arrangements for the admission of visitors, his own countrymen, to view this noble palace which their forefathers bestowed upon the family. He sells tickets, admitting six persons, at ten shillings; if only one person enters the gate, he must pay for six, and if there be seven, it requires two tickets to admit them. Mr. Spiers, when Mayor, once came hither with a party of sixty, for whom he had bought ten tickets; he himself happened to make sixty-one, and another ten shillings was insisted upon. The attendants, in the park and grounds, seem to expect fees on their own private accounts, their master pocketing the ten shillings entire. This parsimony reminds one of the miserliness attributed to the hero of Blenheim.

We waited in the court-yard, while Mrs. Hall went into the porter's lodge to sew a rent in Fanny's gown; and then we passed through a gateway on the opposite side, and had before us the noble, classic front of the palace, with its two projecting wings. Mr. Spiers had gone to make some arrangements about our admission; and while we waited, an open barouche [113] drove through the courtyard to the front entrance, and, after a short stay, returned. There was a lady in it—a high-featured, light-haired, not very distinguished-looking personage—whom we found to be the Marchioness of Blandford, daughter-in-law of the present Duke. Mr. Spiers soon returned, and we were admitted into the entrance-hall, which is of noble height, not much short of seventy feet, being the whole height of the edifice. It is lighted by windows in the upper story, and, it being a clear, bright day, was very radiant with lofty sunshine, amid which a swallow was flitting to and fro. The cieling [*sic*] is painted, by Sir James Thornhill, in some allegorical design which I have forgotten; but I find these painted cielings [*sic*] to be most splendidly and effectively ornamental. The hall is paved with marble,—

SEPTEMBER 5, FRIDAY.

I WAS interrupted just at the above comma; and the rest of my time at Oxford was too much occupied to afford space for journalizing—whereby the sharp points, or most of them, will have been obliterated from my memory. But I resume the narration of our day at Blenheim.

We were guided through the show-rooms of the pal[114]ace by a very civil person, who (Mr. Spiers having procured a special order to that effect) allowed us to take pretty much our own time in looking at the pictures. The collection is exceedingly valuable; and many of them were presented to the great Duke by the crowned heads of England or the continent. One room was all a-glow with pictures by Rubens; and there were works by Raphael, and every other famous painter, any one of which would have illustrated the house that held it. I remember none of them, however, so well as a large picture of Charles I, on horseback, with a figure and face of melancholy dignity, such as never by any other hand was put on canvas. Yet, on considering this face of Charles (which I find often repeated, in half lengths) I doubt whether he was really a handsome or striking-looking man; a high nose, a meagre, hatchet-face, and reddish hair and beard. It is the painter's art that has thrown this pensive and shadowy grace around him.

While we were passing through this beautiful suite of apartments, we saw, through the vista of open door-ways, a boy of ten or twelve years old coming towards us from the farther rooms. He had on a straw hat, a linen sack that must have been washed and re-washed for a summer or two, and gray [115] trowsers a good deal worn—a dress, in short, that Julian's mother would have thought rather shabby for her darling. He was rather pale, but had pleasant eyes, and an intelligent look. This was Lord Sunderland, grandson of the present Duke, and heir of the title and estate. Mrs. Hall happened to be acquainted with some lady who knew this little nobleman; so she spoke to him, and he responded graciously, but kept his straw hat on his head—which, methought, was scarcely courteous, whether in peer or peasant. His tutor, a very ordinary looking person, was in attendance on him. The duke is on ill-terms with his son, and the latter never comes to Blenheim. He is said however, to possess talents, and to be an estimable man. The present Duke, also, is a man of natural ability, but has all [of his] life been addicted to drink, and is now only restrained from absolute sottishness by dread of the consequences to his health. We saw his portrait in one of the rooms, a man of about sixty.

We turned back, after passing through this suite of rooms, and were conducted through the corresponding suite on the opposite side of the great entrance-hall. These latter apartments are most richly adorned with tapestries, wrought [116] and presented to the great Duke by some Flemish nuns; they look like great, glowing pictures, and completely cover the walls of the rooms, representing the Duke's battles and sieges; and everywhere we see the hero himself, as large as life, gorgeous in scarlet and gold, with three-cornered hat and flowing wig, extending his leading-staff in the attitude of command, and reining in his horse. Prince Eugene is the next most prominent figure. In the way of upholstery, there never was anything so gorgeous, and, merely as works of art, they have as much merit as nine pictures out of ten.

One whole wing of the palace is occupied by the library, a most noble room, with a vast perspective length from end to end. It is more lightsome and cheerful than most libraries—perhaps more so than a library should be— being all painted white, both walls and cieling [sic], and with elaborate door- ways and fireplaces of white marble. The floor is of oak, so highly polished that our feet slipt upon it. At one end of this room stands a statue of Queen Anne in her royal robes, so elaborately finished that the spectator has a strong conception of her royal dignity, while her face, fleshy and feeble, doubtless conveys a suitable idea of her personal character. The marble of this statue is as white as [117] snow just fallen. As to the books of the library, they were wired within the cases; and, for the rest of the adornments of the apartment, I have forgotten all about them. Nor do I remember anything else in the palace, except the chapel, into which we were conducted last, and where [we] saw a magnificent monument to the first duke and duchess, sculptured by Rysbrach, at the cost, it is said, of £40,000! It includes, I believe, the statues of the deceased dignitaries, and various allegorical flourishes and confusions; and beneath sleep the great Duke and his proud wife, their veritable bones and dust, and, I suppose, all the Marlboroughs that have died since. It is not quite a comfortable idea, that they are still in the house where their successors spend the passing day.

It had been our purpose to return to the Black Bear at Woodstock for lunch, and then to come back to see the private gardens; but the attendants told us that we could not be permitted to enter them after two ºclock, and it now lacked but little of that hour. So, (as it is a difficult matter to obtain tickets for these gardens, and as most of us would never have another op- portunity) we proceeded to view them now. An old Scotch under gardener [118] led the way, and by-and-by a respectable man, also Scotch, appeared, and accompanied us, talking scientifically and lovingly of trees and plants, of which there is every variety that can be made capable of English cultivation. Really, the garden of Eden could not be more beautiful than this garden of Blenheim, which contains three hundred acres, and by the artful circumlocution of the paths, and the undulations, and the clumps of trees, might be supposed limitless. The world is not the same within that garden fence, that it is without; it is a finer, lovelier, more harmonious Nature; and the great Mother seems to lend herself kindly to the gardener's will, knowing that he will give her ideal beauty, and allow her to take all the credit and praise to herself. The lawns and glades are like the memory of places where one has wandered, when first in love. What a good and happy life might be spent there! And yet, at that very moment, the besotted Duke was in that very garden, (for the guide told us so, and cautioned our young people not to be uproarious) and perhaps was thinking of nothing nobler than how many ten-shilling tickets had that day been sold! Republican as I am, I should still love to think that noblemen lead noble lives, and that all this [119] stately and beautiful environment may serve to elevate them a little above the rest of us. Even a hog, eating the acorns under those magnificent oaks, would be cleanlier and of better habits than common hogs.

I think the finest trees here were cedars, of which I saw one—and there may have been many more—immense in girth, and as much as three centuries old. I likewise saw a vast heap of laurel, two hundred feet in circumference, all growing from one root; and there was another, which we might have seen, of twice that size. If the great Duke had been buried beneath, there could not have been a more plentiful crop of laurel.

Well; all this is pitifully meagre as a description of Blenheim, and I hate to leave it without some better expression of the noble edifice, with its rich domain, all as I saw them in that beautiful sunshine; for if a day had been chosen out of a hundred years, it could not have been a finer one. But we had to come away at last; nor can I get the impression down on paper; so I shall merely say that we went back to the Black Bear, and had a plentiful cold collation, and ale, and wine, and ate and drank abundantly.[391] After attending to these matters, we visited a [120] house in the village, not far from the park-gate, which stands on the site of a house where Chaucer formerly resided. The lady who resides there is a friend of Mr. Spiers, and received us very cordially, ushering us into her garden, where a part of an outhouse, or at least some of the stones, is supposed to have constituted a portion of Chaucer's dwelling. At any rate, there is a small, narrow window, (built into the gable of a pantry or shed,) which was one of the poet's windows. From this lady's garden, we had a glimpse of old Woodstock, at a distance.

We now took coach again, and returned to Oxford; nor did our late lunch prevent us from playing the man (and the woman) at Mr. Spiers' dinner-table; for sight-seeing is an excellent appetizer. Bennoch and Durham left us early, to take the train for London; and, as they are both inveterate punsters, we have had a quieter time ever since. Mr. Durham expressed an earnest desire to model my bust; and as my wife makes a decided point of it, I suppose it must be done.

On Tuesday, I believe, our first visit (Mr. Spiers, Mr. Spiers, Jr., Mr. Addison, Mrs. Hall, Fanny, wife and I) was to Christ Church, where [we] saw the large and stately hall, above a hundred feet long [121] by forty wide, and fifty to the top of its carved oaken roof, which is ornamented with festoons, as it were, and pendants, of solid timber. The walls are panelled with oak, perhaps half way upward, and above are the rows of arched windows on each side; but, near the upper end of the hall, two great windows come nearly to the floor. There is a dais, where the great men of the college, and the distinguished guests, sit at table, and the tables of the students are arranged along the length of the hall. All around, looking down upon those who sit at meat, are the portraits of a multitude of illustrious personages who were members of this learned fraternity in times past; not a portrait being admitted there, (unless it be a king; and I remember only Henry VIII) save of those who were actually students on the foundation, receiving the ele[e]mosynary aid of the college. Most of them seem to have been Divines; but there are likewise many statesmen, eminent during the last three hundred years, and among many earlier ones, the Marquis of Wellesley and Canning. It is an excellent idea, for their own glory, and as exemplars to the rising generations, to have this multitude of men, who have done good and great things, before the eyes of those who ought to do as well as they, in their own time; Archbishops, Prime [122] Ministers, Poets, deep scholars;—but, doubtless, an outward success has generally been their claim to this position, and Christ Church may have forgotten a better man than the best of them. It is not, I think, the tendency of English life, nor of the education of these colleges, to lead young men to high moral excellence, but to aim at illustrating themselves in the sight of mankind. Nevertheless, it is a grand old hall, and I should like to. eat a dinner there myself. I did not see it at a favorable moment; for workmen were there, making some repairs.

Thence we went into the kitchen, which is arranged very much as it was three centuries ago, with two immense fireplaces, which look capable of roasting a hundred joints at once. There was likewise a gridiron, which, without any exaggeration, was large enough to have served for the martyrdom of Saint Lawrence. The college-dinners are good, but plain, and cost the students one shilling and eleven pence each, being rather cheaper than a similar dinner could be had at an eating-house. There is no provision for breakfast or supper in commons; but they can have these meals sent to their rooms, from the buttery, at a charge proportioned to the dishes they order. There seems to be no [123] necessity for a great expenditure on the part of Oxford students.

From the kitchen we went to the chapel, which is the Cathedral of Oxford, and well-worth seeing, if there had not been so many other things to see. It is now under repair; and there was a great heap of old woodwork and panelling, lying in one of the aisles, which had been stript away from some of the ancient pillars, leaving them as good as new. There is a shrine of a saint, with a wooden canopy over it; and some painted glass, old and new; and a statue of Cyril Jackson, with a face of shrewdness and insight; and busts, and mural monuments; and I know not what besides.

Our next visit was to Merton College, which, though not one of the great Colleges, is as old as any of them, and looks exceedingly venerable. We were here received by a friend of Mr. Spiers, a Mr. Eaton, who came to receive us in his academic cap, but without his gown, which is not worn except in term time. He is a very civil gentleman, and showed us some antique points of architecture, such as a Norman archway, with a passage over it through which the Queen of Charles I'st used to go to chapel; and an edifice of the thirteenth century, with [124] a stone roof, which is considered to be very curious. It is impossible to put into words the antique aspect of these college quadrangles; so gnawed by time as they are, so crumbly, so blackened, and so gray where they are not black; so quaintly shaped too, with here a line of battlement, and there a row of gables; and here a turret, with probably a winding stair inside; and then the lattice-windows, with stone mullions, and the little panes of glass set in lead; and the cloisters, with a long arcade looking upon the green or pebbled quadrangle. The quality of the stone has a great deal to do with the apparent antiquity; it is a stone found in the neighborhood of Oxford, and very soon begins to crumble and decay, superficially, when exposed to the weather; so that twenty years do the work of a hundred, so far as appearances go. If you strike one of the old walls with a stick, a portion of it comes powdering down. The effect of this decay is very picturesque, and is especially striking, I think, on edifices of classic architecture, such as some of the Oxford colleges are, greatly enriching the Grecian columns, which look so cold when the outlines are hard and distinct. The Oxford people, however, are tired of this crumbly stone, and when repairs are necessary, they use [125] a more durable material, which does not well assort with the antiquity into which it is intruded.

Mr Eaton showed us the library of Merton College. It occupies two sides of an old building, and has a very delightful fragrance of ancient books. The halls containing it are vaulted, and roofed with oak, not carved and ornamented, but laid flat, so that they look very like a grand and spacious old garret. All along, there is a row of alcoves, on each side, with rude benches and reading desks, in the simplest style, and nobody knows how old. The books look as old as the building. They were formerly (some of the more valuable, at least) chained to the bookcases; and a few of them have not yet broken their chain. It was a good emblem of the dark and monkish ages, when learning was imprisoned in their cloisters and chained in their libraries, in the days when the schoolmaster had not yet gone abroad. Mr. Eaton showed us a very old copy of the Bible, and a vellum manuscript, most beautifully written in black-letter, and illuminated, of the works of Dun[s] Scotus, who was a scholar of Merton College.

He then showed us the chapel, a large part of which has been renewed, and ornamented with pictured windows and other [126] ecclesiastical finery, and paved with encaustic tiles, according to the Puseyite taste of the day; for Merton has adopted the Puseyite doctrines, and is one of their chief strongholds in Oxford. If they do no other good, they at least do much for preservation and characteristic restoration of the old English churches; but perhaps, even here, there is as much antiquity spoiled as retained. In the portion of the chapel not yet restored, we saw the rude old pavement, inlaid with gravestones, in some of which were ancient brasses, with the figures of the college-dignitaries and ecclesiastics, whose dust slumbered beneath; and I think it was here that I saw the tombstone of Anthony-a-Wood, the gossiping biographer of the learned men of Oxford.

From the chapel we went into the college-gardens, which are very pleasant, and possess the advantage of looking out on the broad verdure of Christ Church meadows, and the river beyond. We loitered here awhile, and then went to Mr. Eaton's rooms, to which the entrance is by a fine old staircase. They had a very comfortable aspect, a wainscotted parlor and bed-room, as nice and cosy as a bachelor could desire, with a good collection of theological books; and on a peg hung his gown, with a red border about it, denoting him to be a pro-proctor. He [127] was kind enough to order a lunch (the best the buttery could supply, out of term-time) consisting of bread and cheese, college-ale, and a certain liquor called Arch Deacon, in honor of the dignitary who first taught these erudite worthies how to brew it. It is a superior kind of ale, with a richer flavor, and of a mightier spirit. We ate and drank, and were much strengthened by the blood of the Arch Deacon;[392] and bidding farewell to good Mr. Eaton, we pursued our way to the Radcliffe Library.

This is a very handsome edifice, of a circular shape; the lower story consisting altogether of arches, open on all sides, as if to admit everybody to the learning here stored up. I always see great beauty and lightsomeness in these classic and Grecian edifices, though they seem cold and intellectual, and not to have had their mortar moistened with human life-blood, nor to have the mystery of human life in them, as Gothic structures do. The library is in a large and beautiful room, in the story above the basement, and, as far as I saw, consisted chiefly or altogether of scientific works. I saw Silliman's Journal[393] on one of the desks, being the only trace of American science, or American learning or ability in any department, which I discovered in the University of Oxford. [128] After viewing the Library, we went to the top of the building, whence we had an excellent view of Oxford and the surrounding country. Then (or whether it was then, or in some other succession of events, I cannot precisely remember) we went to the Convocation hall, and afterwards to the Theatre, where my wife sat down in the Chancellor's chair, which is very broad-bottomed, and ponderously wrought of oak. I remember little here, except the amphitheatre of benches, and the roof, which seems to be supported by golden ropes, and, on the wall opposite the door, some full length portraits, among which one of that ridiculous old coxcomb, George the Fourth, was the most prominent. These kings thrust themselves impertinently forward, by bust, statue, and picture, on all occasions; and it is not wise in them to show their shallow foreheads among men of mind.

Mr. Spiers tried to get us admittance to the Bodleian Library; but this is just the nick of time when it is closed for the purpose of being cleaned; so we missed seeing the principal halls of the library, and were only admitted into what is called the Picture Gallery. This, however, satisfied all my desires, so far as the backs of books are concerned; for they extend through a gallery, running around three sides of a [129] quadrangle, making an aggregate length of more than four hundred feet—a solid array of bookcases, full of books, within a protection of open wirework. Up and down the gallery, there are models of classic temples, and other architectural works; and about midway in its extent stands a brass statue of Earl Pembroke, who was Chancellor of the University in James I'sts [sic] time; not in scholarly garb, however, but in plate and mail, looking indeed like a thunderbolt of war. I rapped him with my knuckles, and he seemed to be solid metal, though, I should imagine, hollow at heart. A thing which interested me as much as anything else was the lanthern of Guy Faux [Fawkes]; it was once tinned, no doubt, but is now nothing but rusty iron, partly broken. As this is called the picture Gallery, I must not forget the pictures, which are ranged in long succession over the bookcases, and include almost all Englishmen whom the world has ever heard of, whether in statesmanship or literature. I saw a canvas, on which had once been a lovely, and, I believe, unique portrait of Mary of Scotland; but it was consigned to a picture-cleaner to be cleansed; and, discovering that it was painted over another picture, he had the curiosity to clean poor Mary quite away, thus revealing a wishy-washy wo[130]man's face, which now hangs in the gallery. I am so tired of seeing notable things, that I almost wish that whatever else is remarkable in Oxford could be obliterated in some similar manner.

From the Bodleian we went to the Taylor Institute, which was likewise closed; but the woman, who had it in charge, had formerly been a servant of Mr. Spiers; and he so overpersuaded her (rather to my regret) that she finally smiled, and let us in. It would truly have been a pity to miss it; for here, on the basement-floor, are the original models of Chantrey's busts and statues, great and small; and in the rooms above are a far richer treasure—a large collection of original drawings by Raphael, and by Michael Angelo. These are far better, for my purpose, than their finished pictures;—that is to say, they bring me much closer to the hands that drew them, and the minds that imagined them. It is like looking into their brains, and seeing the first conception, before it took shape outwardly. I noticed one of Raphael's drawings, representing the effect of eloquence; it was a man speaking in the centre of a group, between whose ears and the orator's mouth connecting lines were drawn. Raphael's idea must have been, [131] to frame his picture in such a way that their auricular organs should not fail to be in a proper relation with the eloquent voice; and though this relation would not have been individually traceable, in the finished picture, yet the general effect—that of deep and entranced attention—would have been produced.

In another room, there are some copies of Raphael's cartoons, and some queer mediaeval pictures, as stiff and ugly as can well be conceived, yet successful in telling their own story. We looked a little while at these, and then (thank Heaven!) went home and dressed for dinner. I can write no more to-day. Indeed, what a mockery it is, to write at all!

SEPT^r 7th SATURDAY

THE next day (which was Wednesday) Mr. Spiers and his son Richard, Mr. & Mrs. Hall, Mr. Addison, my wife and I, set forth betimes, in two flies, on a tour to some interesting places in the neighborhood of Oxford. It was a beautiful day; and, in truth, every day has been so pleasant that it seemed as if it must have been the very last of such delightful weather; and yet the long succession has given us confidence in more to come. We first drove to Cumnor, about six miles from Oxford; and alighted at the [132] entrance of the church, which stands a little removed from the roadside; and here, while waiting for the keys, we looked at an old wall of the churchyard, piled up of loose gray stones, which are said to have once formed a portion of Cumnor Hall. The Hall must have been in very close vicinity to the church, not more than twenty yards off; and I waded through the long, dewy grass of the churchyard, and tried to peep over the wall, to see if there were any traceable remains of it. But the wall was just too high to be overlooked, and difficult to clamber over without tumbling down some of the stones; so I took the word of Mr. Hall (who has been here before) that there is nothing interesting on the other side. The churchyard is in rather a neglected state, and seems not [to] have been mown; it contains a good many gravestones, but I remember none of them, except some upright ones of slate, to the memory of a family of Tabbs. Soon came a woman with the key of the church-door, and we entered the simple and bare old edifice, which has the old stone pavement of lettered tombstones, the pillars and arches, and other characteristics of a country church; one or two pews better furnished than the rest, but all in a simple style. Near the high altar, in the holiest place, there is a[n] oblong square tomb of blue mar[133]ble, against the wall, surmounted by a carved canopy of the same marble; and over the tomb, and beneath the canopy, are two monumental brasses, such as we see inlaid into the pavements of churches. They are the figures of a gentleman in armor, and a lady in antique garb, each about a foot high, devoutly kneeling in prayer; and, likewise engraven in brass, there is a long Latin inscription, bestowing the highest eulogies on the character of Anthony Forster, who, with his dame, lies buried beneath this tombstone. His is the knightly figure that kneels above; and if Sir Walter ever saw this tomb, he must have had an even greater than common disbelief in laudatory epitaphs, to have ventured on depicting Anthony Forster in such hues as blacken him in the Romance.[394] What nonsense it is, this care of ours for good fame or bad fame after death! If it were of the slightest real moment, our reputations would have been placed by Providence more in our own power, and less in other people's, than they now are.

We did not remain long in the church, as it contains nothing else of interest; and driving through the village, we passed a pretty large and rather antique-looking inn, bearing the sign of the Bear and the Ragged Staff. It could not be so old, however, by at least a hundred years, as Giles Gosling's time; nor [134] is there any other object to remind the visitor of the Elizabethan age, unless it be a few old cottages, that are perhaps of still earlier date. Cumnor is not nearly so large a village, nor a place of such mark, as one anticipates; but, being still inaccessible by railway, it has retained a sylvan character that I scarcely find elsewhere in England. The road is narrow, in its neighborhood, and bordered with grass, and sometimes interrupted by gates; the hedges grow in untrimmed luxuriance; there is not that close-shaven neatness and trimness that characterizes other English landscapes. It conveys the idea of seclusion and remoteness. We met no travellers, whether on foot or otherwise.

I cannot trace out very distinctly this day's peregrinations; but I think that, after leaving Cumnor a few miles behind us, we came to a ferry across the Thames, where an old woman served as ferryman, and pulled a boat across by means of a rope stretched from one shore to the other. Our two vehicles were thus ferried across, one after the other; and we resumed our drive; first glancing, however, at the old woman's old fashioned cottage, with its stone floor, and the circular settle round the kitchen-fireplace, which Mr. Hall said was quite in the old English style. The next place we stopt at was Stanton Har[135]court, where we were hospitably received at the parsonage of Mr. Welsh, with whom we had dined, the other evening, at Mr. Spiers' table. He had on a wide-awake hat, frock coat, and gray pantaloons, and seemed a much more free and easy man than any English clergyman I have seen; for, however worldly at heart, they are generally strict enough as respects external clericalities. He asked me whether I was the author of "The Red Letter A"; and after some consideration (for I really did not recognize my own book, at first, under this queer title) I answered that I was. He inquired, furthermore, whether I had spent much time in America; appearing to think that I must have had an English breeding, if not birth, to be so much like other people. This English narrowness is very queer, and is just as much a characteristic of gentlemen of education and culture, as of clowns.

Stanton Harcourt is a very curious old place; it was formerly the seat of the ancient family of Harcourt, which is now seat[ed] at Nuneham, a few miles off. The parsonage is a relic of the family mansion, or castle, other portions of which are close at hand; for behind it, across the garden, rise two gray towers, both of them ex[136]ceedingly venerable, and interesting for more than their antiquity. One of these towers was the kitchen of the castle, and is still used for domestic purposes, although it has not, nor ever had, any chimney; being itself, indeed, an immense chimney, as much as thirty feet square. There are two huge fireplaces within; and the interior walls of the tower are blackened with the smoke that used to gush forth from them, and climb upward, seeking an exit through some apertures in the conical roof of the tower. These apertures were capable of being so arranged, with reference to the wind, that the cooks were never troubled by the smoke. The inside of the tower is very dim and sombre, (being nothing but bare, rough stone-walls, lighted only from the apertures above) and has still a pungent odor of smoke and soot, very like that of any other kitchen-chimney.[395]

Thence we proceeded to the church, which is close by, and quite as ancient as the remnants of the castle. We found in it some very interesting monuments of the Harcourts, in the chapel or side aisle dedicated to the family; for instance, recumbent on a tombstone, an armed knight of the Lancastrian party, and slain in the wars of the Roses. His features, dress, and armor, were painted in colors, still wonderfully fresh; and [137] the symbol of the Red Rose denoted the party to which he adhered. His head rested on a marble or alabaster helmet; and on the tomb lay (I presume) the veritable helmet which he wore in his battles—a ponderous iron case, with the visor complete, and remnants of the gilding which once covered it. The crest was a large peacock, not of metal, but wood. Possibly, this helmet was but a heraldic adornment of his tomb; and, indeed, it seems strange that it has not been stolen before now, especially during Cromwell's time, when knightly tombs were not much respected, and when armor was in request. However, let it be the old knight's actual iron pot, since there is nobody to refute the story. Leaning against the wall, at the foot of his tomb, is the shaft of a spear, with a woefully tattered and utterly faded banner appended to it; the knightly banner beneath which he marshalled his followers in the field. As it is absolutely falling to pieces, I tore off one little bit, no bigger than my finger-nail, and put it in my waistpocket; but, seeking it, just now, I cannot find it. The sculptured face of this knight represents a very handsome man.

On the opposite side of the little chapel, two or three yards from this tomb, is another, on which lie side by side another knightly Harcourt and his lady. The tradition of the [138] family is, that this knight was the standard-bearer of Henry of Richmond, in the battle of Bosworth field; and a banner (it is to be supposed, the very same that he carried) is placed against the wall, at the foot of his tomb. It [is] just such a colorless silk rag as the one already described. The knight has the order of the garter on his knee, and the lady wears it on her left arm—an odd place enough for a garter; but, if she were to wear it in its proper position, it might as well be any other garter as that. The complete preservation and good condition of these statues is miraculous; their noses are entire, and the minutest adornment of the sculpture. Except in Westminster Abbey, among the chapels of the kings, I have seen none so well preserved. Perhaps they owe it to the loyalty of Oxfordshire (diffused throughout its neighborhood by the loyal University) during the great civil war and the rule of the Parliament. It speaks well, too, methinks, for this old family, that the peasantry, among whom they had lived for ages, did not desecrate their tombs, when it might have been done with impunity.

There are other and more recent memorials of the Harcourts; one of which is the tomb of the last lord, who [139] died about a hundred years ago. His figure, like that of his ancestors, lies on the top of the tomb, clad not in armor, but in his robes as a peer; and on the wall is a long eulogistic inscription, which, for aught I know, may have been merited. The title is now extinct, but the family survives in a younger branch, and still owns this estate, though they have long since quitted it as a residence.

We next, I believe, went to see the old fish-ponds appertaining to the mansion, and which used to be [of] great dietary importance to the family, in Catholic times, and when fish was not otherwise attainable. There are two or three, or more, of them, one of which is of very good size, large enough, indeed, to be really a picturesque object, with its grass-grown borders, and the trees drooping over it, and the towers of the castle and the church reflected within its smooth mirror; and a sweet fragrance, as it were, of ancient time and present quiet and seclusion, breathing all around. These ponds are said still to breed abundance of such fish as love deep and quiet waters; but I only saw some minnows, and one or two snakes, which were lying among the weeds, on the top of the water, sunning and bathing themselves, at once. Young Richard Spiers tried to cap[140]ture one of the snakes, but cut his finger so grievously in the attempt, that he nearly or quite fainted away, and had to return home. This cut of his little finger was the only accident that marred our delightful day—the only jewel that we sacrificed to the malevolent powers.

I mentioned that there were two towers remaining of the old castle. The most interesting one is yet to be described. It is some seventy feet high, gray and reverend, but in excellent, indeed, perfect, repair, though I could not perceive that anything had been done to renovate it. The basement story was once the family-chapel, and is of course a consecrated spot. At a corner of the tower, from the ground upward, rises a circular turret, within which a narrow staircase, the stone steps much worn, winds round and round, giving access to the chamber on each floor of the tower, and finally emerging on the battlemented roof. Good Mrs. Hall, being somewhat larger and heavier than altogether befits a poetess, did not climb the narrow turret-stair; but my wife did, being of no inconvenient bulk, and so did I, and the rest of us; and the third story, we came to a chamber, not large, though occupying the whole area of the tower, and lighted by a window on each side. It was wainscotted from floor to [141] cieling [sic] with dark oak, and had a little fireplace in one of the corners. The window panes were small, and set in lead. The curiosity of this room is, that it was once the residence of Pope, and that here he wrote a considerable part of his translation of Homer; and there was formerly a record by himself, scratched with a diamond on one of the window-panes— purporting that he had finished the fifth volume, or book, of the Iliad, on such a day. The glass has been removed for safer preservation. I never in my life saw a place that I should better like for a study than this;—so comfortably small, in such a safe and inaccessible seclusion, at that airy height, and with a varied landscape from each window. One window looks upon the church, close at hand, and the green churchyard reaching almost to the foot of the tower; the others have wide views over a gently undulating tract of country. About a dozen steps more of the turret-stair brought us to the top of the tower, where Pope used to come, no doubt, in the summer days, and peep— poor little figure that he was—through the embrasures of the battlement.

Descending from the tower, we found a most abundant and hospitable lunch provided for us, in the par[142]lor, and Mr. Welsh, with some sisters and friends, waiting to dispense it to us. We were pressed for time, but contrived, nevertheless, to do some little justice to the cold meats and brown sherry; and then setting forth again, we drove, I forget how far, to a point where a boat was waiting for us upon the Thames. We were now some miles above Oxford, and, I should imagine, pretty near the source of England's mighty river; for, at all events, it was little more than wide enough for the boat, with extended oars, to pass; shallow, too, and bordered with bull-rushes and water weeds, which, in some places, quite overgrew the surface of the river, from bank to bank. The shores are flat and meadowlike, and sometimes, the boatman told us, are overflowed by the rise of the stream. The water looked clean and pure, but is not particularly transparent, though enough so to show us that the bottom is very much weed-grown; and Mr. Hall told me that [it] is an American [weed], (brought to England with imports of timber) that is choking up the Thames and other English rivers. Why does it not choke up our own?

It was an open boat, with cushioned-seats astern, comfortably accommodating our party; the day was sunny and warm, and perfectly still; the boatman, well-trained [143] to his business, managed his oars skilfully and vigorously; and we went down the stream quite as swiftly as it was desirable to go, the scene being so pleasant, and the present hour so agreeable. The river grew a little wider and deeper, perhaps, as we glided on, but still it was only an inconsiderable stream, having a good deal more than a hundred miles to meander through, before it shall bear fleets on its bosom, and reflect the palaces, and towers, and dingy and sordid piles of various structure, as it rolls to and fro with the tide, dividing London asunder; not, in truth, that I ever really saw any edifice whatever reflected in its turbid breast, at London. Once, on our passage, we had to land, while the boatman and some other persons drew our skiff round some rapids, which we could not otherwise have passed; another time, we went through a lock;—at least the boat did. We, meanwhile, stept ashore, to examine the ruins of the old monastery of Godstowe, where Fair Rosamond secluded herself, after being separated from her royal lover. There is a long line of ruinous wall, and a shattered tower at one of the angles, the whole much ivy-grown, brimming over, indeed, with clustering ivy, rooted inside of the walls. The monastery [144] is now, I believe, under lease by the city of Oxford, who have converted its precincts into a barn-yard. It was locked up, and Mr. Spiers had not the key; so that we saw only the outside, and soon resumed our places in the boat.

At three °clock, or thereabouts—or sooner or later—we reached Folly Bridge, at Oxford; and here leaving our open boat, we crossed the bridge, and took possession of a spacious barge, with a house in it—and a comfortable dining-room, or drawing-room, within the house, and a level roof, where we could sit at ease, or dance, if so inclined. These barges are common at Oxford; some very splendid ones, as I have before said, being owned by the students of the different colleges, or by clubs. They are drawn by horses, like canal-boats; and a horse being attached to our barge, he trotted off at a reasonable pace, and we glided after, with a gentle and pleasant motion, which, save for the constant change of delightful scene, was like no motion at all. It was life without the trouble of living; nothing was ever more quietly agreeable. There was a table ready laid in the interior of our barge; so, while Mr. Spiers' butler and footman were getting dinner ready, we ascended to the roof, and looked out on Christ Church meadows, and at the receding [145] towers and spires of Oxford, and on a good deal of pleasant life along the banks—young men rowing, or fishing, country houses, cottages, inns, all with some[thing] fresh about them, as not being sprinkled with dust of the highway. We were a large party now; for Richard Spiers, Jr. had had his little finger dressed by a surgeon, and had taken heart, and joined us at Folly Bridge, and so had Mr. Addison, who had gone home to take care of him; and we had also picked up Mr. De la Motte, a famous photographist, who was wandering about Oxfordshire to take sketches; and Mr. Bruton, an architect; and Mr. Harvey,[396] an artist of landscapes, who took a sketch as we glided on. I remember no particular incident, before dinner, except that a swarm of wasps came aboard of us however, attracted by the scent of the pomatum which Mr. Addison had rubbed into his hair; and they persecuted the poor young man till he was almost ready to leap overboard.

The dinner being ready, we sat down and ate as if we had been twice as many, though it was early for a dinner, and we had lunched so recently;—cold ham, cold fowl, cold pigeon-pie, cold beef, and tarts, and cakes, and pears and plums; for Mr. Spiers takes excellent [146] care of the commissariat, though by no means a *bon vivant* in his own person—and sherry and port, and stout, and bitter ale, which, being mingled with ginger-beer, forms a compound of singular vivacity and sufficient body. So we made an excellent dinner, and were very merry, and in exceedingly good case.

By the time dinner was over (if I do not mis-remember) we had arrived at that part of the Thames, which passes by Nuneham-Court[e]nay, an estate belonging to the Harcourts, and the present residence of the family. The representative, at this time, is Mr. Harcourt, an old gentleman who has been fifty years in Parliament, and who is married to the Countess Waldegrave, but has no children by her. Mr. Spiers had met this lady at dinner, the evening before, and she kindly signified a desire that he would bring the party to see the estate and house. So we landed, and climbed a steep slope from the riverside, and stopt, a moment or two, to look at an architectural object, called the Carfax, the purport of which I do not well understand; and thence we proceeded onward, through the loveliest park and woodland scenery I ever saw, and amid as beautiful a declining sunshine as God ever shed over the earth, to the [147] stately mansion-house. We found tea ready for us in the drawing-room; but the Countess being out in the park, Mr. Spiers sat down and poured it out. By-and-by, Lady Waldegrave made her appearance, whereupon good Mr. Spiers was immediately transfigured and transformed—like an English snob as he is, worthy man—and looked humbler than he does in the presence of his Maker, and so respectful and so blest, that it was pleasant to behold him. Nevertheless, she is but a Brummagem kind of countess, after all—being the daughter of Braham, the famous singer, and married first to an illegitimate son of an Earl Waldegrave, next to the legitimate son, and possessor of the title (he being her first love,) and, lastly, after the death of those two, to the present old Mr. Harcourt.

She is still in her summer, even if it be waning, a lady of fresh complexion, and light hair, a Jewish nose, (to which her descent entitles her,) a kind and generous expression of face, but an officer-like figure and bearing. There seems to be a peculiarity of manner, a lack of simplicity, a self-consciousness, which I suspect would not have been seen in a lady born to the rank which she has attained. But, anyhow, she was kind to all of us, and complimentary to me; and [148] she showed us some curious things that had formerly made part of Horace Walpole's collection at Twickenham;—a missal, for instance, splendidly bound and beset with jewels, but of such value as no setting could increase; for it was exquisitely illuminated by the own hand of Raphael himself. I held this precious volume in my grasp; though I fancy (and so does my wife) that the Countess scarcely thought it safe out of her own grasp. In truth, I suppose any virtuoso would steal it if he could; and Lady Waldegrave has some reason to look to the safe-keeping of her treasures, as she exemplified by telling us a story, while exhibiting a little silver-case. This case once contained a portion of the heart of Louis XIV, (how the devil it was got, I know not) and she was showing it, one day, to Buckland, Dean of Westminster, when, to her horror and astonishment, she saw him open the case, and swallow the royal heart![397] Ate ever man such a morsel before? It was a symptom of insanity in the Dean; and I believe he is since dead, insane. Mr. Harcourt, too, a grayheaded, stiff mannered, but agreeable English gentleman enough, was very attentive, and showed us the autograph of Pope, on the Stanton Harcourt pane of glass. It is [149] very distinct and elaborate, and is set in a frame, and kept with great care in a locked-up cabinet.

There was a young Mr. Harcourt also present, a nephew, and heir-presumptive to the estate; tall, fine-looking, with a gracious, free, and kindly superiority of bearing. There is nothing better, in the English style of good breeding, than his deportment; and, no doubt, there are a thousand gentlemen of England, with manners good as his. He showed me the library, which is a fine large apartment, and all hung round with portraits of eminent literary men, principally of the last century, most of whom were familiar guests of the Harcourts. The house itself is about eighty years old, and is in the classic style; the grounds were laid out, in part, by Capability Brown, and they seemed to me more beautiful than Blenheim. There is a part of the garden, which was laid out by Mason, the Poet. Of the whole place, I will say, that it seemed to me as perfect as anything earthly can be; utterly and entirely finished; as if the years and generations had done all for it, that the heart and mind of the possessors could think of, for a place they loved;—and, finally, that very evening, the sweet [150] departing sunshine fell among the clumps of ancient trees, with a soft and solemn radiance, and gave the scene the last and perfect grace—and it was so happy a touch, that I felt as if it could last only for a moment. Let it pass; there is no use trying to give the charm of an English park to one who has not seen it. And yet, Mr. Hall insisted that there are [a] hundred places in England, equal to Nuneham Court[e]nay, and many better; it being but a second or third rate residence.

After this, we descended to the river side, to see some pleasant cottages; and methought the quiet, slothful river, without a perceptible current, or a ripple on its breast, looked, in the twilight, like our own river in Concord, at the foot of our orchard, near the Old Manse. But I have written till I am weary, and to no very good purpose; so will only say, that we found our vehicles waiting for us, when we went back to the house. After as agreeable a day as I ever spent, we reached Oxford between eight and nine.[398]

SEPT[r] 9th TUESDAY.

THE morning after our excursion on the Thames (it was Thursday) was as bright and beautiful as many preceding ones had been. We breakfasted at Mr. Spiers' house; and [151] then my wife and I walked a little about the town, and bought Thomas à Kempis, in a French translation, and also in English; Sophia being of opinion it will be particularly good for Una to read. This done, and having taken a parting glimpse at the exterior of some of the old edifices, we returned to our friends. Mr. De la Motte, the photographist, whom we picked up yesterday, had breakfasted with us; and Mr. Spiers wished him to take a photograph of the whole party. So, in the first place, before the rest were assembled, he made an experimental group of such as were there; and I did not like my own aspect very much. Afterwards, when we were all come, he arranged us under a tree, in the garden—Mr. & Mrs. Spiers, with their eldest son, Mr. & Mrs. Hall, Fanny, Mr. Addison, my wife and me—and stained the glass with our figures and faces, in the twinkling of an eye; not my wife's face, however, for she turned it away, and left only a pattern of her bonnet and gown; and Mrs. Hall, too, refused to countenance the proceeding, otherwise than with her back. But all the rest of us were caught, to the life; and I was really a little startled at recognizing myself so apart from myself, and done so quickly too.

This was the last important incident of our visit to Oxford, except that Mr. Spiers was again most hospitable, at lunch. [152] Never did anybody attend more faithfully to the creature-comforts of his friends, than does this good gentleman. But he has shown himself most kind, in every possible way; and I shall always feel truly grateful. No better way of showing our sense of his hospitality, and all the trouble he has taken for us, has occurred to Sophia and me, than to present him with a set of my tales and Romances; so, by the next steamer, I shall write to Ticknor to send them, elegantly bound, and Sophia will emblazon his coat of arms, in each volume. He accompanied us and the Halls to the railway-station; and Sophia says the tears were almost in his eyes, when he bade us farewell. We left Oxford at two °clock, and reached London at four, and Blackheath between five and six.

It had been a very pleasant visit; and all the persons whom we met were kind and agreeable, and disposed to look at one another in a sunny aspect. I saw a good deal of Mr. Hall, and feel bound to say that I repent of the harsh view which I took of his character, when we first became acquainted. I now acknowledge him to be a thoroughly genuine man, of kind heart and true affections, a gentleman of taste and refinement; not a very wise person, perhaps; too vain of his wife (though she is certainly a wife to be proud of) and of himself; saying [153] many things that he had better hold his tongue about; talking altogether too much of himself, his affairs, and his achievements; telling his Irish stories over too often to the same auditors, though he tells them well;—but still a most estimable man, and full of honor. By-the-by, he is a man of honor in a technical sense; for he told me (laughing at the folly of the affair, but, nevertheless, fully appreciating his own chivalry) how he and Charles Lever, about ten years since, had been on the point of fighting a duel. The quarrel was made up, however, and they parted good friends; Lever returning to Ireland, whence Mr. Hall's challenge had summoned him. Mr. H. is a religious man, after the manner of the Church of England; and he was continually getting into disputes with Mr. Addison (a student of the Dublin University, and a devoted Puseyite) about the Popish tendencies of a portion of the English church. This subject, judging by what I have witnessed, seems to come up for discussion very often, in Oxford society.

On the Saturday, after our return to Blackheath, Sophia and I, with Julian, went to Hampton Court, about which, as I have already recorded a visit to it, I need say little here. But I was again impressed with the stately grandeur of Wolsey's [154] Great Hall, with its great window at each end, and one side-window descending almost to the floor, and a row of windows, on each side, high towards the roof, and throwing down their many-colored light on the stone-pavement, and on the Gobelin tapestry, which must have been so gorgeously rich, when the walls were first clothed with it. I fancied, then, that no modern architect could produce so fine a room; but, oddly enough, in the great entrance-hall of the Euston Railway Station, yesterday, I could not see how this last fell very much short of Wolsey's Hall, in grandeur. I was quite wearied, and Sophia was altogether over-wrought, in passing through the endless suites of rooms, in Hampton Court, and gazing at the thousands of pictures; it is too much for one day—almost enough for one life, in such measure as life can be bestowed on pictures. It would have refreshed us had we spent half the time in wandering about the grounds, which, as we glimpsed at them from the windows of the palace, seem very beautiful, though laid out with an antique formality of straight lines, and broad, gravelled paths.

Before the central window, there is a beautiful sheet of water, and a fountain up-shooting itself and plashing into it, with a continuous and pleasant sound. How beautifully the royal [155] robe of a monarchy is embroidered! Palaces, pictures, parks! They do enrich life; and kings and aristocracies cannot keep these things to themselves—they merely take care of them for others. Even a king, with all the glory that can be shed around him, is but the liveried and bedizened footman of his people, and the toy of their delight. I am very glad that I came to this country, while the English are still playing with such a toy.

Yesterday, Julian and I left Blackheath at eleven, London at two, and reached Liverpool at eleven, last night. My wife, and the rest of us, will follow in a few days; and so finishes our residence at Bennoch's house, where I, for my part, have spent some of the happiest hours that I have known since we left our American home. It is a strange, vagabond, gypsy sort of life, this that we are leading; and I know not whether we shall finally be spoilt for any other, or shall enjoy our quiet Wayside as we never did before, when once we reach it again.

SEPTEMBER 11th, THURSDAY.

I DINED, last night, at the Monk's Ferry Hotel, with Mr. Henry Bright, who is staying there while his father and family are in Scotland. The only other guest at table was a Mr. Crawley, who is somehow [156] connected with Mr. Bright's office, but was formerly at Oxford. Speaking of our excellent friend Spiers, Mr. Crawley affirmed that he began life as a hairdresser, and had often cut his own hair; that he was afterwards an unprincipled adventurer, on the Continent, and had made money in most questionable ways; but that, growing wealthy, he had put on respectability, and, he doubted not, was now an honest man. I never should have suspected this beforehand; yet, now that I know it, it reconciles itself well enough with what I have seen of Mr. Spiers. There is a kind of ease and smartness in his manners, which I have never seen in any English gentleman; there is a trimness in his aspect, very suitable for a hair-dresser, and he wears what must be a wig, yet, if so, such an artful and exquisite one, that no unprofessional man could so well have suited himself; in the presence of Lady Waldegrave, he behaved like a footman;—in short, I accept Mr. Crawley's statement, except as regards his deficient honesty. Well;—his morality may have been scanty and ragged once, and have been pieced and mended as he rose in life. An Englishman, with such facility and adaptiveness, so ready, so neat in his action, so devoid of the national clumsi-ness, is a kind of monster to begin with. [157] On the other hand, the English are probably less tolerant than ourselves of men who attain wealth by any other than the ordinary and regular methods, and may accuse them of dis-honesty, when they have only been dext[e]rous and shifty. Mr. Spiers would be altogether more at home, and more in keeping with the society around him, in America, than here. Come what may, I shall always feel him to be, at least, a kind and hospitable man; and, hairdresser or not, he was a gentleman to us.

I supt to-night with Mr. Wilding, my clerk, at New Brighton. His salary is less than a thousand dollars; but it certainly does more for him than the same sum could do in the United States; a small, but comfortable house, with a good space of ornamented lawn, and a kitchen garden, behind it; a piano; a fair collection of books; a wife and child. To be sure, he is temperate—abstemious, I should think—and has no expenses outside of this little home.

The evening set in misty and obscure; and it was dark, almost, when Julian and I arrived at the Landing Stage, on our return, at ½ past seven. I was struck with the picturesque effect of the high tower and tall spire [158] of Saint Nicholas, rising upward with dim outline into the duskiness; while midway of its height, the dial plates of an illuminated clock blazed out, like two great eyes of a giant.

Shandy-gar, or gaf—I forget which [shandy-gaff]—is the Oxford name for a half-and-half mixture of bitter ale and ginger beer.

SEPTEMBER 18th, THURSDAY.

On Saturday, my wife with all her train arrived at Mrs. Blodget's; and, on Tuesday—vagabonds as we are—we again struck our tent and set out for Southport. I do not know what sort of character it will form in the children, this unsettled, shifting, vagrant life, with no central home to turn to, except what we carry in ourselves. It was a windy day, and judging by the look of the trees, on the way to Southport, it must be almost always windy, and with the blast in one prevailing direction; for invariably their branches, and the whole contour and attitude of the tree, turned from seaward, with a strangely forlorn aspect. Reaching Southport, we got into an omnibus, and, under the driver's guidance, came to a tall stone-house, fronting on the sands, and styled "Brunswick Terrace"; and here we made a bargain for three chambers and a parlor with a tall, thin, muscular, dark, [159] shrewd, and shabby-looking mistress—ten and sixpence for each bed, and twelve and sixpence for the parlor, with the option of a better parlor at the week's end. This English system of lodging-houses has its good points; but it is, nevertheless, a contrivance for carrying the domestic cares of home about with you, whithersoever you go; and immediately you have to set about providing your own bread and cheese and tea and coffee, and eggs and chops, and all such necessaries—even to the candles you burn, and the soap on your wash-stands. However, Fanny took most of this trouble off our hands, though there was inevitably the stiffness and discomfort of a new housekeeping, on the first day of our arrival; besides that it was cool, and the wind whistled, and grumbled, and eddied into the chinks of the house; nor did we conclude to have a fire, till next morning.

Meanwhile, in all my experience of Southport, I have not yet seen the sea, but only an interminable breadth of sands, stretching out to the horizon—brown or yellow sands, looking pooly or plashy in some places, and barred across with drier reaches of sand; but no expanse of water. It must be miles and miles, at low water, to the veritable [160] sea-shore. We are about twenty miles north of Liverpool, on the border of the Irish sea; and Ireland and, I suppose, the Isle of Man, intervene betwixt us and the broad ocean, not much to our benefit; for the air of the English coast, under ocean influences, is said to be milder than where it comes across the land—milder, therefore, above or below Ireland, because then the gulf-stream ameliorates it.

Betimes, the forenoon after our arrival, I had to take the rail to Liverpool, but got back a little after five, in the midst of a rain; still, low water and interminable sands; still, a dreary, howling blast. We had a cheerful fireside, however, and should have had a pleasant evening, only that the wind or the sea made us excessively drowsy. So we went to bed; and, this morning, we awoke to hear the wind still blustering, and blowing up clouds, with fitful little showers, and soon blowing them away again, and letting the brightest of sunshine fall over the plashy waste of sand. My wife and I (for I do not go to Liverpool to-day) have already walked forth, on the shore, with Julian and Rosebud, who pick up shells, and dig wells in the sand with their little wooden spades; but soon we saw [161] a rainbow on the western sky, and then a shower came spattering down upon us, in good earnest. We first took refuge under the bridge that stretches between the two portions of the promenade; but, as there was a chill draft there, we made the best of our way home. And here, while I have been writing, the sun has again come out brightly, though the wind is still tumbling a great many clouds about the sky.

I suppose our parlor deserves description, as a fair enough specimen of what lodging-house parlors generally are, in England. Fifteen feet square, covered with an old carpet, which has a patched covering of drugget in the middle; a square centre-table; half a dozen chairs, two of which purport to be easy-chairs, but turn out not to be hospitable nor kindly, when you sit down in them; a sofa, shabby, and not very soft, but long and broad, and good to recline upon; a beaufet, in which we keep some of our household affairs, and a little bit of a cupboard, in which we put our bottle of wine, both under lock and key. On the mantel-piece are two little glass vases, and over it a looking-glass (not flattering to the in-looker); and above hangs a colored view of some lake, or seashore; and, on each side, a cheap colored print of [162] Prince Albert, and one of Queen Victoria; and really I have seen no picture, bust, or statue of Her Majesty, which I feel so certain to be a good likeness, as this cheap print. You see the whole line of Guelphs in it—fair-haired, blue-eyed, shallow-brained, common-place, yet with a simple kind of heartiness and truth, that makes one somewhat good-natured towards them.

After writing the above, I walked out with Una; and looking seaward, we saw the foam and spray of the advancing tide, tossed about by the wind, on the verge of the horizon—a long line, like the crests and gleaming helmets of an army. Returning, in about half an hour afterwards, we found almost the whole waste of sand covered with water, and white waves breaking out all over it; but the bottom being so nearly level, and the water so shallow, there was little of the spirit and exaltation of the sea in a strong breeze. Of the long line of bathing-machines, one after another was hitched to a horse, and trundled forth into the water, where, at a long distance from shore, the bathers found themselves hardly middle-deep. It is the custom here for men, not women, to attend, and immerse the ladies. Yesterday, a man stark naked was seen dipping a lady. Oh, decorous English!

September 19th, Friday.

THE wind grumbled and made itself miserable, all last night; and, this morning, it is still howling as ill-naturedly as ever, and roaring and rumbling in the chimneys. The tide is far out; but, from our upper window, I fancied, at intervals, that I could see the flash of the surf-wave, on the distant limit of the sand; perhaps, however, it was only a gleam on the sky. Constantly, there have been sharp spatters of rain, hissing and rattling against the windows; while, a little before or after, or perhaps simultaneously, a rainbow, somewhat watery of texture, paints itself on the western clouds. Gray, sullen clouds hang about the sky, or sometimes cover it with a uniform dullness; at other times, the portions towards the sun gleam almost lightsomely; now, there may be an airy glimpse of clear blue sky, in a fissure of the clouds; now the very brightest of sunshine comes out, all of a sudden, and gladdens everything. The breadth of sands has a various aspect, according as there are pools, or moisture enough to glisten, or a drier tract, and where the light gleams along a yellow ridge, or bar, it is like sunshine itself. Certainly, the temper of the day shifts, but the smiles come far the seldomest; and its frowns and angry tears are most reliable. By seven °clock, pedestrians began to walk along the promenade, close buttoned against the blast; later a [164] single bathing-machine got under way (by means of a horse) and travelled forth seaward; but within what distance it finds the invisible margin, I cannot say;—at all events, it looks like a dreary journey. Just now, I saw a sea-gull wheeling on the blast, close in towards the promenade.

Septr 21st Sunday.

YESTERDAY morning was bright, sunny, and windy, and cool, and exhilarating. I went to Liverpool, at eleven; and returning at five, found the weather still bright and cool. This temperature, methinks, must soon diminish the population of Southport, which, judging from appearances, must be mainly made up of temporary visitors. There is a newspaper—"The Southport Visitor &c"— published weekly, and containing a register of all the visitants in the various hotels and lodging-houses. It covers more than two sides of the newspaper, to the amount of some hundreds. The guests seem to come chiefly from Liverpool, Manchester, and the neighboring country-towns, and belong to the middle-classes. It is not a fashionable watering-place. Only one nobleman's name, and those of two or three baronets, adorn the list. The people, whom we see loitering along the beach and the promenade, have, at best, a well-to-do tradesmanlike air. I do not find that there are any public amusements, or contrivances for pastime; nothing but strolling [165] on the sands, donkey-riding, or drives in donkey-carts; and solitary visitors must needs find it a dreary place. Yet one or two of the streets are brisk and lively, and, being well-thronged, have a holiday-aspect. There are no carriages in town (an omnibus or two excepted) save donkey-carts, some of which are drawn by three donkies [sic] abreast, and are large enough to hold a whole family. These conveyances will take you far out on the sands, through wet and dry. The beach is haunted by the "Flying Dutchman"—a sort of boat on wheels, schooner-rigged with sails, and which sometimes makes pretty good speed, with a fair wind.

This morning, my wife and I, with Julian and Rose, have been walking out, over the "ribbed sea-sands,"[399] a good distance from shore. Throughout the week, the tides will be so low as not to cover the shallow basin of this bay— if a bay it be. The weather is sullen, with now and then a faint gleam of sunshine lazily tracing our shadows on the sand; the wind rather quieter than on preceding days, but now again beginning to howl.

SEPTEMBER 28th, SUNDAY.

THE weather has been very showery, through the greater part of last week; yesterday was rainy throughout; and to-day is lowering, with now and then a [166] sullen tear or two. I have been to Liverpool, and back, every day but one, and so have seen little of the daily life of Southport;—only the bare, pool-strewn waste of sands, every morning and evening; and the bathing-machines, with the mer-men and mer-women, watching for their victims. In the sunshine, the sands seem to be frequented by great numbers of gulls, who begin to find the northern climates too wintry;—you see their white wings in the sunshine, but they become almost, or quite, invisible in the shade. We shall soon have an opportunity of seeing how a watering-place looks, when the season is quite over; for we have concluded to remain here till December, and almost everybody else will take flight in a week or two.

A short time ago, in the evening, in a street of Liverpool, I saw a decent man, of the lower orders, taken much aback by being roughly brushed against by a rowdy fellow. He looked after him, and exclaimed indignantly—"Is that a Yankee?" It shows the kind of character we have here.

OCTOBER 7th, TUESDAY.

ON Saturday evening, I gave a dinner to Bennoch at the Adelphi Hotel; Mr. Swain, Mr. Pollock, [167] Mr. Bright, Mr. Melly, Mr. Mott, Mr. Babcock, Mr. Holland, and Mr. Ely, being present. It was an excellent dinner, and cost me over £ 20; but the chief point, as characteristic of English manners, was, that Mr. Radly, our landlord, himself attended at table, and officiated as chief-waiter. He has a fortune of £ 100,000—half a million of dollars—and is an elderly gentleman of good address and appearance. In America, such a man would very probably be in Congress;—at any rate, he would never conceive the possibility of changing a plate, or passing round the table with hock and champagne. Some of his hock, by the way, was a most rich and imperial wine, such as can hardly be had on the Rhine itself;—and of a most deceptive potency.

A donkey, the other day, stubbornly refusing to come out of a boat which had brought him across the river; at last, after many kicks had been applied, and other persecutions of that kind, a man stept forward, addressing him affectionately—"Come along, Brother!"

OCTOBER 26th, SUNDAY.

ON Thursday, instead of taking the [168] rail for Liverpool, I set out, about eleven °clock, for a long walk, all by myself. It was an overcast morning, such as, in New England, would have boded rain; but English clouds are not nearly so portentous, in that respect. Accordingly, the sun soon began to peep through crevices, and I had not gone more than a mile or two, when it shone a little too warmly for comfort—yet not more than I liked. It was very much like our pleasant October days at home; indeed, the climates of the two countries, I think, more nearly coincide during the present month, than at any other season of the year. The air was almost perfectly still; but, once in a while, it stirred, and breathed coolly in my face; it is very delightful, this latent freshness in a warm atmosphere.

The country about Southport has as few charms as it is possible for any region to have. In the close neighborhood of the shore, it is nothing but sand-hillocks, covered with coarse grass; and this is the original nature of the whole site on which the town stands, although it is now paved, and has been covered with soil enough to make gardens, and to nourish here and there a few trees. A little further inland, the surface seems to have been marshy, but has been drained by ditches, across the fields and along the roadside; and the fields them[169]selves are embanked on all sides with parapets of earth, which appear as if intended to keep out inundations. In fact, Holland itself cannot be more completely on a level with the sea—a flat expanse and monotony, as far as the eye can see. The only dwellings are the old, white-washed stone cottages, with thatched roofs, on the brown straw of which grow various weeds and mosses, brightening it with green patches, and sprouting along the ridge-pole; the homeliest hovels that ever mortals lived in, and which they share with pigs and cows at one end. Hens, too, run in and out of the door. One or two of these hovels bore signs, "licensed to sell beer, ale, and tobacco"; and generally there was an old woman and some children visible. In all cases, there was a ditch full of water close at hand, stagnant, and often quite covered with a growth of water-weeds; very unwholesome, one would think, in the neighborhood of a dwelling; and in truth the children and grown people did look pale.

In the fields, along the roadside, people were harvesting their carrots and other root crops, and women as well as men were at work, especially digging potatoes;—the pleasantest of all farm labor, in my opinion, there be[170]ing such a continual interest in opening up the treasures of each hill. As I went on, the country began to get almost imperceptibly less flat, and there was some little appearance of trees. I had determined to go to Ormskirk, but soon got out of the way, and came to a little hamlet that looked somewhat antique and picturesque, with its small houses of stone and brick, built with the one material, and repaired with the other, perhaps ages afterward. Here I inquired my way of a woman, who told me, in broad Lancashire dialect, that I "maun" go back, and turn to my left till I came to a finger-post; and so I did, and soon came to another little hamlet, the principal object in which was a public house, with a large sign representing a dance round a may-pole. It was now about one °clock; so I entered, and being ushered into what I suppose they called the coffee-room, I asked for some cold meat and ale. There was a jolly, round, rather comely woman for a hostess, with a free, hospitable, yet rather careless manner.

The coffee-room smelt rather disagreeably of bad cigar-smoke, and was shabbily furnished with an old sofa, and flag-bottomed chairs, and adorned with a print of "Old Billy," a horse famous for a longevity of about six[171]ty years; and also with colored engravings of old fashioned hunting-scenes, conspicuous with scarlet-coats. There was a very little bust of Milton on the mantel-piece. By and by, the remains of an immense round of beef, three quarters cut away, were put on the table; then some smoking-hot potatoes; and, finally, the hostess told me that their own dinner was just ready, and so she had brought me some hot chops, thinking I might prefer them to the cold meat. Well; I did prefer them; and they were stewed or fried chops, instead of broiled, and were very savory. There was household bread, too, and some rich cheese, and a pint of ale, homebrewed, not very mighty, but good to quench thirst; and, by way of condiment, some pickled cabbage;— so instead of a lunch, I made quite a comfortable dinner. Moreover, there was a cold pudding on the table; and I called for a clean plate, and the hostess wiped on a napkin the knife and steel fork which I had already used, and I helped myself to some pudding. It seemed to be of rice, and was strewn over, rather than intermixed, with some kind of berries, the nature of which I could not exactly make out. Finally, I paid a shilling and ten pence for my dinner, left the odd two pence for the waiter; [172] (who was a slipshod girl) and set forth again. It was still sunny and warm; and I rather think I walked more slowly than before dinner—in fact, I did little more than lounge along, smoking a cigar, and sitting down, at last, on the stone parapet of a bridge, to enjoy it.

The country grew more pleasant, more sylvan, and though still of a level character, not so drearily flat. Soon appeared the first symptom that I had seen of a gentleman's residence; a lodge at a park-gate; then a long extent of wall, with a green lawn, and afterwards, an extent of wooded land; then another gateway, with a neat lodge on each side of it, and lastly another extent of wood. The hall or mansion-house, however, was nowhere apparent, being doubtless secluded deep and far within its grounds. I inquired of a boy who was the owner of the estate, and he answered "Mr. Scarybrick." There is a hotel called the "Scarisbrick Arms," in Southport; and no doubt it is a family of local eminence. I do not remember anything else of narratable interest, along the road; an old inn; some aged stone houses, built for merely respectable occupants; a canal, with two canal-boats, heaped up with a cargo of potatoes; two little [173] girls, who were watching lest some cows should go astray, and had their two little chairs by the roadside, and their doll and other playthings, and so followed the footsteps of the cows, all day long. I met two boys, coming from Ormskirk, mounted on donkeys, with empty panniers, in which they had carried vegetables to market. Finally, between two and three °clock, I saw the great tower of Ormskirk church, with its spire, not rising out of the tower, but sprouting up close beside it; and entering the town, I directed my steps first to this old church.

It stands on a gentle eminence, sufficient to give it a good site, and has a pavement of flat grave-stones in front. It is doubtless, as regards its foundation, a very ancient church, but has not exactly a venerable aspect, being in too good repair, and much restored in various parts; not ivy-grown, either, though green with moss, here and there. The tower is immensely square and massive, and might have supported a very lofty spire; so that it is the more strange that what spire it has should be so strangely stuck beside it, springing out of the church-wall. I should have liked well enough to enter the church, as it is the burial-place of the Earls of Derby, and perhaps [174] may contain some interesting monuments; but as it was all shut up, and even the iron gates of the church-yard were closed and locked, I merely looked at the outside, and came away.

From the church, a street leads to the market-place, in which I found a throng of men and women, it being market-day; wares of various kinds, tin, earthen, and cloth, set out on the pavements; droves of pigs; ducks and fowls; baskets of eggs; and a man selling quack medicines, recommending his nostrums as well as he could, but with nothing like the invention and humor that a Yankee would have shown. The aspect of the crowd was very English; portly and ruddy women; yeomen, with small clothes; broad brimmed hats, all very quiet and heavy, good-humored, and many of them, no doubt, boozy. Their dialect was so provincial that I could not readily understand more than here and there a word.

But, after all, there were few traits that could be made a note of. I soon

grew weary of the scene, and of the dulness of one or two ale-house taps
into which I stept; so I went to the railway station, and waited there near an
hour for the train to take me to Southport. I got into a [175] second-class
carriage, and remarked that the railway officials thrust in their heads much
more familiarly, and speak in a more off-hand way, than to the occupants of
first-class carriages. I have nothing more to say of Ormskirk, except that it
is famous for its gingerbread, which women sell to the railway passengers, at
a sixpence for a rouleau of a dozen little cakes.

NOVEMBER 20th, THURSDAY.

A WEEK ago last Monday, Herman Melville came to see me at the Consulate,
looking much as he used to do (a little paler, and perhaps a little sadder), in
a rough outside coat, and with his characteristic gravity and reserve of
manner. He had crossed from New York to Glasgow in a screw steamer,
about a fortnight before, and had since been seeing Edinburgh and other
interesting places. I felt rather awkward at first; because this is the first time
I have met him since my ineffectual attempt to get him a consular appointment
from 'General Pierce. However, I failed only from real lack of power to serve
him; so there was no reason to be ashamed, and we soon found ourselves on
pretty much our former terms of sociability and confidence. Melville has not
been well, of late; he has been affected with neuralgic complaints in his head
and limbs, and no doubt has [176] suffered from too constant literary occupation, pursued without much success, latterly; and his writings, for a long while
past, have indicated a morbid state of mind. So he left his place at Pittsfield,
and has established his wife and family, I believe, with his father-in-law in
Boston, and is thus far on his way to Constantinople. I do not wonder that he
found it necessary to take an airing through the world, after so many years
of toilsome pen-labor and domestic life, following upon so wild and adventurous
a youth as his was. I invited him to come and stay with us at Southport, as
long as he might remain in this vicinity; and, accordingly, he did come, the
next day, taking with him, by way of baggage, the least little bit of a bundle,
which, he told me, contained a night-shirt and a tooth-brush. He is a person
of very gentlemanly instincts in every respect, save that he is a little heterodox
in the matter of clean linen.

He stayed with us from Tuesday till Thursday; and, on the intervening day,
we took a pretty long walk together, and sat down in a hollow among the sand
hills (sheltering ourselves from the high, cool wind) and smoked a cigar.
Melville, as he always does, began to reason of Providence and futurity, and
of everything that lies beyond human ken, and informed me [177] that he had
"pretty much made up his mind to be annihilated"; but still he does not seem
to rest in that anticipation; and, I think, will never rest until he gets hold of a
definite belief. It is strange how he persists—and has persisted ever since I
knew him, and probably long before—in wandering to-and-fro over these
deserts, as dismal and monotonous as the sand hills amid which we were

sitting. He can neither believe, nor be comfortable in his unbelief; and he is too honest and courageous not to try to do one or the other. If he were a religious man, he would be one of the most truly religious and reverential; he has a very high and noble nature, and better worth immortality than most of us.

He went back with me to Liverpool, on Thursday; and, the next day, Henry Bright met him at my office, and showed him whatever was worth seeing in town. On Saturday, Melville and I went to Chester together. I love to take every opportunity of going to Chester; it being the one only place, within easy reach of Liverpool, which possesses any old English interest. It was a fitful and uncertain day; and began to shower just as we left the Landing Stage in crossing the Mersey; but, arriving at Chester, we had glimpses [178] of sunshine, and walked round the wall with hardly a spatter of rain. Chester wall is as interesting a promenade as can be found in England. Starting from the East Gate, and turning to the left, we soon come to the old Cathedral, with its churchyard, its great tower, its buttresses, of red freesone, with patches of reparation that look square and angular, but generally with an aspect as if it were thawing, or as if it were a sugar toy, and had been sucked in a child's mouth; so much have the storms of ages worn away this soft material. Passing onward, we look down from the wall into a precipitous depth, at the bottom of which creeps a canal, with long and narrow canal-boats moored in it. A little further, stands the town, uprising beside the wall, from the top of which King Charles beheld his army defeated on Rowton Moor—which is now well covered with houses, and most unlike a battlefield. Farther on, at an angle of the wall, is another tower, and a ruinous and ivy-grown outwork. From this part of the wall, we see the Welsh hills, blue in the distance; and the air from these hills comes freshly down upon Chester, making it a healthful place of residence, aged and mouldering though it be. Then comes the Roodee, the [179] modern race-course, and which the Romans are supposed to have hollowed out and used for the same purpose; a green, circular space, outside of the wall, whence its whole circumference can be taken in. Within the wall, at nearly the same point, is the castle, almost entirely a modern structure, although there is one old tower, said to have been built by Julius Caesar, I believe—at all events, by the Romans. Here the wall makes another angle, and we come in sight of the Dee, which, just as we were passing along, had a bright silvery sheen of sunshine, and a breezy ripple. At this spot, the wall passes close beneath the castle, and beneath a prison which forms a part of it, and which is built of a cold, gray granite, most fit for prisons. Next we see an old bridge, with arches, and on the hither side, some tall, decayed edifices, with hundreds of broken windows, and all powdered duskily with flour; for these are ancient mills, and are still as busily employed as ever. The view across the Dee, and on the other side, is here very picturesque and beautiful; and the dam, stretching across the river, is almost a cascade. Adown the river, we see pleasure boats, some of them with awnings, and a

small steamer. Turning another angle of the wall, we see or[180]chards beneath us, on the outer side, the trees of which, though tall, do not reach up to
a level with our feet; and gardens, cultivated close up to the old stone foundation; and all the domestic smugness of old established houses and grounds,
that have been laid out within the centuries since Chester wall ceased to be
a warlike rampart. On the city-side, the houses abut upon the wall, and rise
directly up from it, with doors opening upon the walk; the other side of the
house fronting upon one of the city-streets. It is very curious and pleasant to
see how the city has swelled, and overflowed the girdle that once kept it in;
although some of the exterior houses look almost as ancient as any of those
within. Beyond the wall, too, we saw the tower of St John's church, with
a statue in a niche over the door, looking (to repeat my simile of the Cathedral)
like a sugar image which a child had sucked in its mouth; so much is it worn
and defaced. And now, between edifices overtopping the wall, and shutting
it in on either side, we come back to the East Gate, and descend by a stone
staircase into the bustling street. The whole circuit of the wall is estimated at
two miles, and there is a paved walk the whole way, broad enough for two to
walk abreast, g[u]arded by a railing on the inside, and [181] a parapet of
stone externally. Of course, the upper portion has undergone many repairs;
but the stones of the foundation were probably laid by Roman hands.

It being now one °clock, or thereabouts, we walked through some of the
Rows, in quest of a dinner, and found one in a confectioner's shop; these
establishments being a frequent resort of Englishmen—and especially of
Englishwomen—for hasty refection, in preference to a hotel. We were shown
upstairs, into an antique room fronting on the street, with cross-beams,
panelled walls, a large table and some smaller ones, and a good fire. The waiting
maid brought us some little veal-pies on a tray, and some damson tarts on
another tray; and we had, besides, some Bass's ale, and made a very comfortable meal at the cost of a shilling and two-pence each. And then we went
to the Cathedral, which I had occasion to describe, I think, or at least to talk
about, several times before. Its gray nave seemed to impress me more than at
any former visit. Passing into the cloisters, an attendant—he did not seem to be
a verger, or other solemn personage, but was a very intelligent and ready-
witted man—took possession of us, and showed us about the Cathedral.

Within the choir, there is a profusion of very rich oaken [182] carving, both
on the screen that separates it from the nave, and on the seats, and on the
walls; very curious, and most elaborate, and lavished most wastefully, where
nobody would think of looking for it—where, indeed, amid the dimness of
the Cathedral, the exquisite detail of their elaboration could not possibly be
seen. Our guide lighted some of the gas-burners (of which there are many
hundreds in the Cathedral) to help us see them; but it required close scrutiny,
even then. It must have been out of the question, when the whole means of
illumination were a few smoky torches or candles. There was a row of niches,
where the monks used to stand for hours together, in the performance of some

of their services; and to relieve them a little, they were allowed partially to sit on a projection of the seats, which were turned up in the niche for that purpose; but if they grew drowsy, so as to fail to balance themselves, the seat was so contrived as to slip down, thus bringing the monk to the floor. These projections on the seat are each and all of them carved with curious devices, no two alike. The guide showed us one, representing, apparently, the first quarrel of a new-married couple, wrought with wonderful expression. Indeed, the artist never failed to bring out his idea in the [183] most striking manner; as for instance, Satan under the guise of a lion, devouring a sinner bodily, and again in the figure of a dragon, with a man half-way down his gullet, the legs hanging out. The carver may not have seen anything grotesque in this, nor have intended it at all by way of joke; but certainly there would appear to be a sort of grim mirthfulness in some of the designs. One does not see why such fantasies should be strewn about the holy interior of a Cathedral, unless it were intended to contain everything that belongs to the heart of man, both upward and downward.

In a side aisle of the choir, we saw a tomb, said to be that of the Emperor Henry Fourth, of Germany, though on very indistinct authority. This is a square, oblong tomb, carved, and, on one side, painted with bright colors, and gilded. During a very long period, it was built and plastered into the wall of the Cathedral, and the exterior side was whitewashed; but, on being removed, the inner side was found to have been ornamented with gold and color, in the manner in which we now see it. If this was customary with tombs, it must have added vastly to the gorgeous magnificence to which the painted windows, and polished pillars, and [184] ornamented cielings [sic], contributed so much. In fact, a Cathedral in its fresh estate seems to have been like a pavilion of the sunset, all purple and gold; whereas now it more resembles deepest and grayest twilight.

Afterwards, we were shown into the ancient Refectory, which is now used as the City Grammar School, and was furnished with the usual desks and seats for the boys. In one corner of this large room was the sort of pulpit, or elevated seat, (with a broken staircase of stone ascending to it,) where one of the monks used to read to his brethren, while sitting at their meals. The desks were cut and carved with the scholars' knives, just as they used to be in the schoolrooms where I was a scholar. Thence we passed into the Chapter House; but, before that, if I rightly remember, we went through a small room, in which Melville opened a cupboard and discovered a dozen or two of wine-bottles; but our guide told us that they were now empty, and never were meant for jollity, having held only sacramental wine. In the Chapter House we saw the library, some of the volumes of which were antique folios, though most of them might have fitted other shelves as well as these. There were two dusty and tattered banners hanging on the wall, belonging to a regiment that was raised in Cheshire; and the attendant promised to make [185] us laugh by something that he would tell us about them. The joke was, that these two banners had been in the battle of Bunker Hill; and our countrymen, he said, always smiled at hearing this. He had discovered us to be Americans by the notice we took of a mural tablet in the choir, to the memory of a Lieutenant Governor Clarke, of New York, who died in Chester before the Revolution. From the Chapter House, he ushered us back into the Nave, ever and anon pointing out some portion of the edifice more ancient than the rest, and showing pillars, or pedestals, or parts of the walls, that varied several hundred years in antiquity from other parts close beside them. And when I asked him how he knew this, he said that he had learnt it from the Archaeologists, who could read off such things like a book. This guide was a lively, quick-witted man, and did his business less by rote, and more with a vivacious interest, than any guide I ever met.

After leaving the Cathedral, we sought out the Yacht Inn, near the Water Gate. This was, for a long period of time, the principal inn of Chester, and was the house at which Swift once put up, on his way to Holyhead, and where he invited the clergy of the Cathedral to come and sup with him. We sat down in a small snuggery, behind the bar, and smoked a cigar [186] and drank some stout, conversing the while with the landlord. The Chester people, according to my experience, are very affable, and fond of talking with strangers about the antiquities and picturesque characteristics of their town. It partly lives, the landlord told us, by its visitors, and many people spend the summer here, on account of the antiquities and the good air. When our cigars were out, and our tumblers empty, he showed us a broad, balustraded staircase, into a large, comfortable, old fashioned parlor, with windows looking on the street, and on the Custom House that stood right opposite. This was the room where Swift expected to receive the clergy of Chester; and on one of the window panes (about the size of eight inches by ten) were two acrid lines, written with the diamond of his ring, satirizing those reverend gentlemen, in revenge for their refusing his invitation. The first line begins rather indistinctly; but the writing grows fully legible as it proceeds. I have forgotten the purport—which is the less matter, as it is preserved in the guide books.[400]

The Yacht Tavern is a very old house, in the gabled style. The landlord told us that the timbers and frame-work are still perfectly sound. In the same street is the Bishop's [187] house (so called as having been the residence of a prelate, long ago) which is covered with curious sculptures, representing Scriptural scenes. And, I believe, in the same neighborhood is the County Court, accessible by an archway through which we penetrated, and found ourselves in a passage way, very ancient and dusky, overlooked from the upper story by a gallery, to which an antique staircase ascended, with balustrades, and square landing-places. A printer saw us here, and asked us into his printing-office, and talked very affably; indeed, he could hardly have been more civil, if he had known that both Melville and I have given a good deal of employment to the brethren of his craft.

We left Chester at about four °clock; and I took the rail for Southport at half-past six, parting from Melville at a street-corner in Liverpool, in the rainy evening. I saw him again on Monday, however. He said that he already felt much better than in America; but observed that he did not anticipate much pleasure in his rambles, for that the spirit of adventure is gone out of him. He certainly is much overshadowed since I saw him last; but I hope he will brighten as he goes onward. He sailed from Liverpool in a steamer on Tuesday, leaving his trunk behind [188] him at my consulate, and taking only a carpet-bag to hold all his travelling-gear. This is the next best thing to going naked; and as he wears his beard and moustache, and so needs no dressing-case—nothing but a tooth-brush—I do not know a more independent personage. He learned his travelling habits by drifting about, all over the South Sea, with no other clothes or equipage than a red flannel shirt and a pair of duck trowsers. Yet we seldom see men of less criticizable manners than he.[401]

DECEMBER 15th SUNDAY.

An old gentleman has recently paid me a good many visits; a Kentucky man, who has been a good deal in England, and Europe generally, without losing the freshness and unconventionality of his earlier life. He was a boatman, and afterwards Captain of a steamer, on the Ohio and Mississippi, but has gained property, and seems now to be the owner of mines of coal and iron, which he is endeavoring to dispose of here in England. A plain, respectable, well-to-do looking personage, of more than seventy years; very free of conversation, and beginning to talk with everybody as a matter of course; tall, stalwart, a dark face, with white curly hair, and keen eyes;—an expression shrewd, yet kindly and benign. He fought through the whole war of 1812, beginning with [189] General Harrison at the battle of Tippecanoe, which he described to me. He says that at the beginning of the battle, and for a considerable time, he heard Tecumseh's voice, loudly giving orders. There was a man named Wheatley in the American camp, a strange, incommunicative person, a volunteer, making war entirely on his own hook, and seeking revenge for some relatives of his who had been killed by the Indians. In the midst of the battle, this Wheatley ran at a slow trot past Richardson, (my informant,) trailing his rifle, and making towards the point where Tecumseh's voice was heard. The fight drifted onward, and Richardson along with it; and by-and-by he reached a spot where Wheatley lay dead with his head on Tecumseh's breast. Tecumseh had been shot with a rifle, but, before expiring,[402] appeared to have shot Wheatley with a pistol, which he still held in his hand. Richardson affirms that Tecumseh was flayed by the Kentuckymen, on the spot, and his skin converted into razor-strops. I have left out the most striking point of the narrative, after all, as Richardson told it;—viz. that, soon after Wheatley passed him, he suddenly ceased to hear Tecumseh's voice, ringing through the forest, as he gave his orders.

[190] He was at the battle of New Orleans, and gave me the story of it from beginning to end; but I remember only a few particulars in which he was personally concerned. He confesses that his hair bristled upright—every hair in his

head—when he heard the shouts of the British soldiers before advancing to the attack. His uncomfortable sensations lasted until he began to fire—after which he felt no more of them. It was in the dusk of the morning, or a little before sunrise, when the assault was made; and the fight lasted about two hours and a half—during which Richardson fired twenty-four times;—"and," said he, "I saw my object distinctly, each time, and I was a good rifle-shot." He was raising his rifle to fire the twenty-fifth time, when an American officer (General Carroll, I think) pressed it down, and bade him fire no more. "Enough is enough," quoth the General; for there needed no more slaughter, the British being in utter rout and confusion. In their retreat, many of the enemy would drop down among the dead, then rise, run a considerable distance, and drop again, thus confusing the riflemen's aim. One fellow had thus got about 450 yards from the American line; and thinking himself secure, he displayed his rear to the [191] Americans, and clapt his hand on it derisively. "I'll have a shot at him, any how!" cried a rifleman; so he fired, and the poor devil dropt.

Richardson himself, with one of his twenty-four shots, hit a British officer, who fell forward on his face, about thirty paces from our line; and as the enemy were then retreating (they advanced and were repelled, two or three times) Richardson ran out, and turned him over on his back. The officer was a man of about thirty-eight, tall and fine looking; his eyes were wide open, clear and bright, and were fixed full on Richardson, with a somewhat stern glance; but there was the sweetest and happiest smile over his face that could be conceived. He seemed to be dead;—at least, Richardson thinks that he did not really see him, fixedly as he appeared to gaze. The officer held his sword in his hand; and Richardson tried in vain to wrest it from him, until suddenly the clutch relaxed. Richardson still keeps the sword, hung up over his mantel-piece. I asked him how the dead man's aspect affected him; he replied that he felt nothing, at the time; but that, ever since, in all trouble, in uneasy sleep, and whenever he is out of sorts, or waking early, or lying [192] awake at night, he sees this officer's face, with the clear bright eyes, and the pleasant smile, just as distinctly as if he were still bending over him. His wound was in the breast, almost exactly on the spot that Richardson had aimed at, and bled profusely. The enemy advanced in such masses, he says, that it was impossible not to hit them, unless by purposely firing over their heads.

After the battle, Richardson leapt over the rampart, and took a prisoner, who was standing unarmed in the midst of the slain, having probably dropt down, during the heat of the action, to avoid the hail-storm of rifle-shots. As he led him in, the prisoner paused and pointed to an officer, who was lying dead beside his dead horse, with his foot still in the stirrup. "There lies our General!" said he. The horse had been killed by a grape-shot, and Packenham [Pakenham] himself, apparently, by a six pounder ball, which had first struck the earth, covering him from head to foot with mud and clay, and had then entered his side and gone upward through his breast. The face was all besmirched with the moist earth. Richardson took the slain General's foot out of the stirrup, and then went to report his death.

[193] Much more he told me, being an exceeding talkative old man, and seldom, I suppose, finding so good a listener as myself. I like the man; a good-tempered, upright, bold, and free old fellow, of a rough breeding, but sufficiently smoothed by society to be of pleasant intercourse. He is as dogmatic as possible, having formed his own opinions—often on very disputable grounds—and hardened in them; taking queer views of matters and things, and giving shrewd, and yet ridiculous reasons for them;—but with a keen, strong sense at the bottom of his character. Only America could have produced just such a man as this.[403]

Philip Richardson, of Louisville, Kentucky (such being his name and address) took passage in the Steamer for New York, yesterday—which he could hardly have done without my help, inasmuch as he had run short of cash.

A little while ago, I met an Englishman in a railway carriage, who suggests himself as a kind of contrast with [194] this warlike and vicissitudinous backwoodsman. He seemed to be about the same age as Richardson, but had spent, apparently, his whole life in Liverpool, and has long occupied the post of Inspector of Nuisances;—a rather puffy and consequential man, as Englishmen, in whatever official station, seldom fail to be; gracious, however, and affable even to casual strangers like myself. The great contrast betwixt him and the American lies in the narrower circuit of his ideas; the latter talking about matters of history of his own country and the world—glancing over the whole field of politics, propounding opinions and theories of his own, and showing evidence that his mind has[404] [operated for better or worse on almost all conceivable matters; while the Englishman was odorous of his office, strongly flavored with that, and otherwise most insipid. He began his talk by telling me of a dead body which] he had lately discovered, in a house in Liverpool, where it had been kept about a fortnight by the relatives, partly from want of funds for the burial, and partly in expectation of the arrival of some friends from Glasgow. There was a plate of glass in the coffin-lid, through which the Inspector of Nuisances, as he told us, had looked, and seen the dead man's [195] face, in an ugly state of decay—which he minutely described. However, his conversation was not altogether of this quality; for he spoke about larks, and how abundant they are, just now (from sixpence to a shilling per dozen) and what a good pie they make; only they must be skinned, else they will have a bitter taste. We have since had a lark-pie ourselves; and, I believe, it was really very good in itself, only the recollection of the nuisance-man's talk was not a very agreeable flavor. A very racy, and peculiarly English character might be made out of a man like this, having his life-concern wholly with the disagreeables of a great city. He seemed to be a good and kindly person, too, but earthy—even as if his frame had been moulded of earth impregnated with the draining of slaughterhouses and moistened with the rank liquid of common sewers. I think a Yankee, in the same position, would not have been so flavored with his business; he would have dealt with it intellectually, but not have been thus affected by it morally.

DECEMBER 21st SUNDAY.

ON Thursday evening, I dined for the first time with the new mayor (Mr. Sharp) at the Town Hall. I did not observe much that was [196] new, or that I have not already described, probably, in my records of similar festivities. I want to preserve all the characteristic traits of such banquets; because, being peculiar to England, these municipal feasts may do well to picture in a novel. There was a big old silver tobacco-box (nearly or quite as large round as an ordinary plate) out of which the old dignitaries of Liverpool used to fill their pipes, while sitting in council, or after their dinners. The date of 1690 was on the lid. It is now used as a snuff-box, and wends its way from guest to guest, around the table. We had turtle, and various other good things; among them, American canvas-back ducks. The wines were good, and the glasses (those for port and sherry, at least) of a generous size, and with frequent opportunities of filling them. The town, I believe, provides some of the wines, and has store of them. I don't remember trying the port; it ought to be old and good. These dinners are certainly a good institution, and likely to be promotive of good feeling; the mayor giving them often, and inviting in their turn all the respectable or eminent citizens, of whatever political bias. About fifty gentlemen were present, this evening. I had the post of [197] honor, at the Mayor's right hand; but France, Turkey, and Austria were toasted before the Republic; for, as the Mayor whispered me, he must first get his allies out of the way. The Turkish consul (Mr. Massabine, a Greek) and the Austrian, both made better English speeches than any Englishman, during the evening; for it is inconceivable what ragged and shapeless utterances Englishmen are content to give vent to—without attempting anything like a shape and a wholeness, but putting on a patch here and a patch there, and finally getting out what they want to say, indeed, but in some such disorganized guise as if they had vomited it. No American could make such bad speeches; not even I. Indeed, my speech took effect better than any other; the Mayor having given me a good clue by alluding to the Bark Resolute.[405] I can conceive of very high enjoyment in making a speech; one is in such a curious sympathy with his audience, feeling instantly how every sentence affects them, and wonderfully excited and encouraged by the sense that it has gone to the right spot. Then, too, the imminent emergency (when a man is overboard, and must swim or sink) sharpens, concentrates, and invigorates the mind, and causes matters of thought and [198] sentiment to assume shape and expression, though perhaps it seemed hopeless to try to express them, just before you rose to speak. Yet I question much whether public speaking tends to elevate the orator, intellectually or morally; the effort, of course, being to say what can be immediately received by the audience, and produce its effect on the instant. I don't quite see how an honest man can be a good and successful orator; but I shall hardly undertake to decide this question on my merely post-prandial experience.

The Mayor toasted his guests by their professions—the merchants, for instance, the bankers, the solicitors; and while one of the number responded, his brethren also stood up, each in his place, thus giving their assent to what he said. I think the very worst orator was a Major of Artillery, who spoke in a meek, little, nervous voice, and seemed a good deal more discomposed than, probably, he would have been in the face of the enemy.[406] The final toast was, "the Ladies"; to which an old bachelor responded. Previously, the Mayor's lady had been toasted; and the Mayor himself responded on the topic of his domestic felicity.

[199] December 31st Wednesday.

Thus far we have come through the winter, on this bleak and blasty shore of the Irish sea, where, perhaps, the drowned body of Milton's friend Lycidas might have been washed ashore, more than two centuries ago. This would not be very likely, however; so wide a tract of sands, never deeply covered by the tide, intervening betwixt us and the sea. But it is an awfully windy place, especially here on the Promenade; always a whistle and a howl— always an eddying gust through the passages and chambers—often a patter of rain, or hail, or snow, against the windows; and, in the long evenings, the sounds outside are very much as if we were on shipboard in mid-ocean, with the waves dashing against the vessel's sides. I go to town almost daily, starting at about eleven, and reaching Southport again at a little past five; by which time it is quite dark, and continues so till nearly eight in the morning.

Christmas-time has been marked by few characteristics. For a week or so, previous to Christmas day, the newspapers contained rich details respecting market-stalls and butchers' shops, what magnificent carcasses of prize oxen and sheep they displayed; for Englishmen really like to think and talk of butcher's meat, and gaze at it with artistic delight, and [200] they crowd through the avenues of the market-houses, and stand enraptured around a dead ox. They are very earthy people. They love to eat, and to anticipate good fare, and even to hear the details of other people's good dinners.

The Christmas Waits came to us on Christmas eve, and on the day itself, in the shape of little parties of boys or girls, singing wretched dogg[e]rel, rhymes, and going away well-pleased with the guerdon of a penny or two. Last evening came two or three elder choristers, at pretty near bedtime, and sang some carols (they were psalm-tunes, however) at our door. Everybody, with whom we have had to do, in any manner of service, expects a Christmas-box; but, in most cases, a shilling seems to be quite a satisfactory amount. We have had holly and mis[t]letoe stuck up on the gas-fixtures, and elsewhere about the house, but no such kissing-licenses as last Christmas at Mrs. Blodget's.

On the mantel-piece, in the Coroner's Court, the other day, I saw corked and labelled phials, which, it may be presumed, contained samples of poisons that have brought some poor wretches to their deaths—either by murder or suicide. This Court might be wrought into a very good and [201] pregnant description, with its grimy gloom, illuminated by a conical skylight, constructed to throw daylight down on corpses; its greasy Testament, covered over with millions of perjured kisses; the Coroner himself, whose life is fed on all kinds of unnatural death; its subordinate officials, who go about scenting murders, and might be supposed to have caught the scent in their own garments; its stupid, loutish juries, settling round corpses like flies; its criminals, whose guilt is brought face to face with them here, in closer contact than at the subsequent trial.

Orson Pratt, the famous Mormonite, called on me, a little while ago;— a short, black-haired, dark complexioned man, somewhere about forty years of age; a shrewd, intelligent, but unrefined countenance, exceedingly unprepossessing; an uncouth gait and deportment—the aspect of a person in comfortable circumstances, and decently behaved, but of a vulgar nature and destitute of early culture. I think I should have taken him for a shoemaker, accustomed to reflect, in a rude, strong, evil-disposed way, on matters of this world and the next, as he sat on his bench. He said that he [202] had been residing in Liverpool about six months; and his business with me was to ask for a letter of introduction that should gain him admittance to the British Museum, he intending a visit to London. He offered to refer me to respectable people for his character; but I advised him to apply to Mr. Dallas, as the proper person for his purpose.

I heard some of the railway passengers talking, yesterday, about Mr. Scarisbrick, of Scarisbrick Hall, who is the landlord of Southport. He is an eccentric man, they said, and there seems to be an obscurity about the early part of his life; according to some reports, he kept a gambling-house in Paris, before succeeding to the estate. Neither is it a settled point whether or no he has ever been married; some authorities utterly ignoring the point; others affirming that he has legitimate children, who are now being educated in Paris. He is a Catholic, but is bringing up his children, they say, in the Protestant faith. He is a very eccentric and nervous man, and spends all his time at this secluded Hall, which stands in the midst of mosses and marshes; and sees nobody, not even his own Steward. He might be an interesting person to [203] become acquainted with; but, after all, his character, as I have just sketched [it], turns out to be one of the common-places of novels and romance.

MARCH 1st 1857.

ON the night of last Wednesday week, our house was broken into by robbers. They entered by the back window of the school-room, breaking a pane of glass, so as to undo the wooden fastening. I have a dim idea of having heard a noise through my sleep, but, if so, it did not more than slightly disturb me. Una heard it, too, she being kept awake by Rosebud, who had burnt her leg; and Julian, being unwell with a cold, was also wakeful, and thought the noise was of the family moving about, below. Neither did the idea of robbers occur to Una. Julian, however, called to his mother, and the thieves probably thought we were bestirring ourselves, and so took flight. In the morning, the cook and housemaid found the hall-door and the school-room window open; some silver-cups, and some other trifles of plate, were gone, and there were tokens that the whole lower part of the house had been ransacked; but the thieves had evidently gone off in a hurry, leaving some articles which they would have taken, had they been more at leisure.

[204] We gave information to the Police; and an Inspector and constable soon came to make investigations, making a list of the missing articles, and informing themselves as to all particulars that could be known. I did not much expect ever to hear any more of the stolen property; but, on Sunday, a constable came to request my presence at the Police-Office, to identify the stolen property. The thieves had been caught in Liverpool, and some of the property found upon them, and other articles at a pawnbrokers, where they had pledged them. The Police Office is a small, dark room, in the basement-story of the Town Hall of Southport; and over the mantel-piece, hanging one upon another, there are innumerable advertisements of robberies in houses, and on the highway,—murders, too, I suppose—garrottings, and offences of all sorts; not only in this district, but wide away, and forwarded from other police stations. Being thus aggregated together, one realizes that there are a great many more offences than the public generally takes note. Most of these advertisements were in pen and ink, with minute lists of the articles stolen, but the more important were in print; and there, too, I saw the printed advertisement of our own robbery, not for public circulation, but [205] to be handed about privately among police-officers and pawnbrokers. A rogue has a very poor chance in England, the police being so numerous, and their system so well organized.

In a corner of the police-office stood a contrivance for precisely measuring the height of prisoners; and I took occasion to measure Julian, and found him four feet, seven inches and a half high. A set of rules for the self-government of police-officers was nailed or pasted on the door, between twenty and thirty in number, and composing a system of constabulary ethics. The rules would be good for men in almost any walk of life; and I rather think the police-officers conform to them with tolerable strictness. They appear to be subordinated to one another on the military plan; the ordinary constable does not sit down in the presence of an Inspector, and this latter seems to be half a gentleman;—at least such is the bearing of our Southport Inspector, who wears a handsome uniform of green and silver, and salutes the principal inhabitants, on meeting them in the street, with an air of something like equality. Then, again, there is a superintendent (and, for aught I know, other grades [206] between him and the Inspector) who certainly claims the rank of a gentleman, and has perhaps been an officer in the army. The superintendent of this district was present on this occasion; a well-mannered person enough.

The thieves were brought down from Liverpool, on Tuesday, and examined in the Town Hall. I had been notified to be present; but, as a matter of courtesy, the police-officers refrained from calling me as a witness, the evidence of the two servants being sufficient to identify the property. The thieves were two young men, seemingly not much over twenty, (James and John Macdonald, brothers, I think,) terribly shabby, dirty, jail-bird like, yet intelligent of aspect, and one of them handsome. The police knew them already; and they seemed not much abashed by their position. There were [a] half-dozen magistrates on the bench, idle old gentlemen of Southport and the vicinity, who lounged into the court more as a matter of amusement than anything else, and lounged out again, at their own pleasure; for these magisterial duties are a part of the pastime of the country-gentlemen of England. They wore their hats on the bench. There were one or two of them more active than their fellows; but the real duty was done by the [207] Clerk of the Court. The seats within the bar were occupied by the witnesses, and around the great table sat some of the more respectable people of Southport; and without the bar were the commonalty in great numbers; for this is said to be the first burglary that has occurred here within the memory of man, and so it has caused a great stir.

There seems to be a strong case against the prisoners. A boy, attached to the railway, testified to having seen them at Birchdale on Wednesday afternoon, and directed them on their way to Southport; Peter Pickup recognized them as having applied to him for lodgings, in the course of that evening; a pawnbroker swore to one of them as having offered my great coat for sale or pledge, in Liverpool; and my boots were found on the feet of one of them—all this, in addition to other circumstances of pregnant suspicion. So they were committed for trial at the Liverpool assizes, to be holden sometime in the present month. I rather wished them to escape.

Day before yesterday, (February 27th) coming along the promenade, a little before sunset, I saw the moun[208]tains of the Welsh coast, shadowed very distinctly against the horizon. Mr. Channing told me that he had seen these mountains, once or twice, during his stay at Southport; but, though constantly looking for them, they have never before greeted my eyes, in all the months that we have spent here. It is said that the Isle of Man is likewise discernible, occasionally; but, as the distance must be between sixty and seventy miles, I should doubt it. How misty is England! I have spent four years in a gray gloom. And yet it suits me pretty well.

APRIL 10th, FRIDAY, AT SKIPTON.

WE (my wife, Julian, and I) left Southport today, at half past one, for a short tour to York and that neighborhood. The weather has been exceedingly disagreeable, for weeks past; but yesterday and today have been pleasant, and we take advantage of the first glimpses of spring-like weather. We came by Preston, along a road that grew rather more interesting as we proceeded to this place, which is about sixty miles from Southport, and where we arrived between five and six °clock. First of all, we got some tea with mutton-chops, and then, as it was a pleasant sunset, we set forth from our old-fashioned inn to take a walk.

[209] Skipton is an ancient town, and has an ancient, though well repaired aspect, the houses being built of gray stone, but in no picturesque shapes; the streets well-paved; the site irregular, and rising gradually towards Skipton Castle, which overlooks the town, as an old lordly castle ought to overlook the feudal village which it protected. The castle was built shortly after the Conquest by Robert de Romeli [Romille], and was afterwards the property and residence of the famous Cliffords. We met an honest man, as we approached the gateway, who kindly encouraged us to apply for admittance, notwithstanding it was Good Friday, telling us how to find the housekeeper, who would probably show us over the castle. So we passed through the gate, between two embattled towers; and in the castle-yard, we met a flock of young damsels who seemed to have [been] rambling about the precincts. They likewise directed us in our search for the housekeeper; and my wife (being bolder than I in such assaults on feudal castles) led the way down a dark archway, and up an exterior castle [stairway?], and knocking at a back door, immediately brought the housekeeper to a parley.

[210] She proved to be a nowise awful personage, but a homely, neat, kindly and intelligent, middle-aged body, with, I think, an old-maidish deportment. She seemed to be all alone in this great old castle, and at once consented to show us about, being no doubt glad to see any Christian visitors. The castle is now the property of Sir R[ichard] Tufton; but the present family do not make it their permanent residence, and have only occasionally visited [it]. Indeed, it could not well be made an eligible or comfortable residence, according to modern ideas; the rooms occupying the several stories of great round towers, and looking gloomy and sombre, if not dreary—not the less so for what has been done to modernize them; for instance, modern paper hangings, and, in some of the rooms, marble fireplaces. They need a great deal more light, and higher cielings [sic]; and I rather imagine that the warm, rich effect of glowing tapestry is essential to keep one's spirits cheerful in these ancient rooms. Modern paper-hangings are too superficial and wishy-washy for the purpose. Tapestry, it is true, there is, completely covering the walls of several of the rooms, but all faded into ghastliness; nor [211] could some of it have been otherwise even in its newness; for it represented persons suffering various kinds of torture, with crowds of monks and nuns looking

on. In another room, there was the story of Solomon and the Queen of Sheba, and other subjects, not to be readily distinguished in the twilight that was gathering in these antique chambers. We saw, too, some very old portraits of the Cliffords and the Thanets, in black frames, and the pictures themselves terribly faded and neglected. The famous Countess Anne, of Pembroke, Dorset, and Montgomery, was represented on one of the leaves of a pair of folding-doors, and her husband, I believe, on the other leaf. There was the picture of a little idiot lordling, who had choked himself; and a portrait of Oliver Cromwell, who battered down this old castle, together with almost every other English or Welsh castle that I ever saw or heard of. The housekeeper pointed out the grove of trees, where his cannon were planted during the siege. There was but little furniture in the rooms; amongst other articles, an antique chair, in which Mary Queen of Scots is said to have rested.

[212] The housekeeper next took us into the part of the castle which has never been modernized since it was repaired, after the siege by Cromwell. This is a dismal series of cellars above ground, with immensely thick walls, letting in but scanty light; and dim staircases of stone; and a large hall with a vast fireplace, where every particle of heat must needs have gone up [the] chimney—a chill and heart-breaky place enough. Quite in the midst of this part of the castle is the court-yard, a space of some thirty or forty feet in length and breadth, open to the sky, but shut completely in on every side by the edifices of the castle, and paved over with flat stones. Out of this pavement, however, grows a yew tree, ascending to the tops of the towers, and completely filling with its branches and foliage the whole open space between them. Some small birds—quite a flock of them—were twittering and fluttering among the upper branches. We went upward through two or three stories of dismal rooms —among others, through the ancient guard-room—till we came out on the roof of one of the towers, and had a very fine view of an amp[h]i-theatre of ridgy-hills, which shut in and seclude [213] the castle and the town. The upper foliage of the old yew tree was within our reach, close to the parapet of the tower; so we gathered a few twigs as memorials. The housekeeper told us that this yew tree is supposed to be eight hundred years old; and comparing it with other yews that I have seen, I should judge that it must measure its antiquity by centuries, at all events. It still seems to be in its prime.

I remember nothing else about the Castle, except that, along its base, on the opposite side to the entrance, flows a stream, sending up a pleasant murmur from among some trees. The housekeeper said it was not a stream, but only a "wash," whatever that may be; and I conjecture that it creates the motive power of some factory-looking edifices, which we saw on our first arrival at Skipton. We now took our leave of the housekeeper (I wished we had asked about her inmates, if she has any, and surroundings, for she surely cannot live alone in these dreary dungeons,) and came homeward to our inn; where I have written the foregoing pages by a bright fire; but I think I write better descriptions after letting the subject lie in my mind a [214] day or two. It is too raw to be properly dealt with, immediately after coming from the scene.

The castle is not at all crumbly, but in excellent repair, though so venerable. There are rooks cawing about the shapeless patches of their nests, in the tops of the trees, about the precincts. In the castle-wall, as well as in the two round towers of the gate-way, there seem to be little tenements, perhaps inhabited (probably so) by the servants and dependents of the family. They looked in very good order, with tokens of present domesticity about them. The whole of this old castle, indeed, was as neat as a new, small dwelling, in spite of an inevitable musty fragrance of antiquity. My wife says that the Countess of Pembroke &c was represented on both leaves of the folding door, at different ages.

APRIL 11th, SATURDAY, AT YORK.

THIS morning at a little before ten, we took a fly and two horses and set out for Bolton Priory, a distance of about six miles. The morning was cool, with breezy clouds, intermingled with sunshine, and, on the whole, as good as nine tenths of English mornings. Julian sat beside the driver, and mamma and I in the carriage, all closed but one window. As we drove through Skipton, the little town had a livelier as[215]pect than the day before, when it wore its Good Friday's solemnity; but now its market-place was thronged principally with butchers (displaying their meat under little moveable penthouses) and their customers. We passed along by the castle wall, and noticed the escutcheon of the Cliffords or the Thanets, or some other of its inheritors, carved in stone over the portal, with the motto, *Désormais,* the application of which I do not well see; these ancestral devices usually referring more to the past than the future. There is a large, old church, just at the extremity of the village, and just below the castle, on the slope of the hill. The grey wall of the castle extends along the road, a considerable distance, in good repair, with here and there a buttress, and the semi-circular bulge of a tower.

The scenery along the road was not particularly striking, long slopes descending from ridges; a generally hard outline of country, with not many trees, and those as yet destitute of foliage. It needs to be softened with a good deal of wood. There were stone farm-houses, looking ancient, and able to last till twice as old. Instead of the hedges, so universal [216] in other parts of England, there were stone fences, of good height and painful construction, made of small stones, which I suppose have been picked up out of the fields through hundreds of years. They reminded me of old Massachusetts, though very unlike our rude stone walls, which, nevertheless, last longer than anything else we build. Another New England feature was the little brooks, which here and there flowed across our road, rippling over the pebbles, clear and bright. I fancied, too, an intelligence and keenness in some of the Yorkshire physiognomies, akin to those characteristics in my countrymen's faces.

We passed an ancient, many gabled inn, large, low, and comfortable, bearing the name of the "Devonshire House," as does our own hotel; for the Duke of Devonshire is a great proprietor in these parts. A mile or so beyond, we came to a gateway, broken through what, I believe, was the old wall of the priory-grounds; and here we alighted, leaving our driver to take the carriage to the inn. Passing through this hole in the wall, we saw the ruins of the Priory, at the bottom of the beautiful valley, about a quarter of a mile off; and, well as the [217] monks knew how to choose the sites of their establishments, I think they never chose a better site than this, in the green lap of protecting hills, beside a stream, and with peace and fertility looking down upon it from every side. The view down the valley is very fine; and, for my part, I am glad that some peaceable and comfort-loving people possessed these precincts for many hundred years, when nobody else knew how to appreciate peace and comfort.

The old gateway-tower, beneath which was formerly the arched entrance into the domains of the Priory, is now the central part of a hunting-seat of the Duke of Devonshire; and the edifice is completed by a wing of recent date, on each side. A few hundred yards from this hunting-box are the remains of the Priory, consisting of the nave of their old church, which is still in good repair, and used as the worshipping place of the neighborhood, (being a perpetual curacy of the parish of Skipton) and the old ruined choir, roofless, with broken arches, ivy-grown, but not so rich and rare a ruin, as either Melrose, Netley, or Furness. Its situation makes its charm. It stands [218] near the river Wharfe, a broad and rapid stream, which hurries along between high banks, with a sound that the monks must have found congenial to their slumbrous moods. It is a good river for trout, too; and I saw two or three anglers, with their rods and baskets, passing through the ruins towards its shore. It was in this river Wharfe that the Boy of Egremond[407] was drowned, at the Strid, a mile or two higher up the stream.

In the first place, we rambled round the exterior of the ruins; but, as I have said, they are rather bare and meagre, in comparison with other Abbeys, and I am not sure that the especial care and neatness, with which they are preserved, does not lessen their effect on the beholder. Neglect, wildness, crumbling walls, the climbing & conquering ivy, masses of stone lying where they fell, trees of old date growing where the pillars of the aisles used to stand; these are the best points of ruined Abbeys. But everything here is kept with such trimness that it gives you the idea of a petrifaction. Decay is no longer triumphant; the Duke of Devonshire has got the better of it. The precincts around the church and the ruins are still used as a burial-ground; and [219] there are several flat tombstones, and altar tombs, with crosiers engraved or carved upon them, which, at first, I took to be the memorials of bishops or abbots, and wondered that the sculpture should still be so distinct. On one, however, I read the date of 1850, or thereabouts, and the name of a layman; for the tombstones were all modern, (the humid English atmosphere giving them their mossy look of antiquity,) and the crosier had been assumed only as a pretty device.

Close beside the ruins, there is a large, old stone farm-house, which must have been built on the site of a part of the priory—the cells, dormitories, refectory, and other portions pertaining to the monks' daily life, I suppose—and built, no doubt, with the sacred stones. I should imagine it would be a haunted house, swarming with cowled spectres. We wanted to see the interior of the church, and procured a guide from this farm-house, the Sexton probably, a gray-haired, ruddy, cheery, and intelligent man, of familiar, though respectful address. The entrance of the church was undergoing improvement, under the last of the Abbots, when the reformation broke out; and it has ever since remained in [220] an unfinished state, till now it is mossy with age, and has a beautiful tuft of wall-flowers growing on a ledge over the Gothic arch of the doorway. The body of the church is of much anterior date, though the oaken roof is supposed to have been renewed in Henry VIII's time. This, as I said before, was the nave of the old Abbey-church, and has a one sided and unbalanced aspect, there being only a single aisle, with its row of sturdy pillars. The pavement of the church is covered with pews of old oak, very homely and unor[na]mental; on the side opposite the aisle there are two or three windows of modern stained glass, somewhat gaudy and impertinent; there are likewise some hatchments and escutcheons, over the altar and elsewhere. On the whole, it is not an impressive interior; but, at all events, it had the true musty smell which I never conceived of till I came to England—the smell of dead men's decay, garnered up and shut in, and kept from generation to generation; not disgusting nor sickening, because it is so old, and of the past.

On one side of the altar, there was a small square chapel—or what had once been a chapel—separated [221] from the chancel by a partition, about a man's height, if I remember right. Our guide led us into it, and observed, that, some years ago, the pavement had been taken up in this spot, for burial purposes, but it was found that it had already been used in that way, and that the corpses had been buried upright. Inquiring further, I learned that it was the Clapham family, and another that he called Morley, that were so buried; and then it occurred to me that this was the vault Wordsworth refers to in one of his poems,[408] the burial place of the Claphams and Mauleverers, whose skeletons, for aught I know, were even then standing upright under our feet. It is but a narrow precinct, perhaps a square of ten feet. We saw little or nothing else that was memorable; unless it were the signature of Queen Adelaide[409] in a visitor's book of some years since.

On our way back to Skipton, it rained and hailed; but the sun again shone out before we arrived. We took the train for Leeds at half-past ten, and arrived there at about three, passing the ruined abbey of Kirkstall on our way. The ruins looked more interesting than [222] those of Bolton, though not quite so delightfully situated, and now in the close vicinity of manufactories, and only two or three miles from Leeds. We took a plate of soup, and spent a miserable hour in and about the railway station of Leeds; whence we departed at a little after four, and reached York in an hour or two. We put up at the Black Swan, and, before tea, went out, on the cool, bright edge of evening, to get a glimpse of the Cathedral, which impressed me more grandly than when I first saw it, nearly a year ago. Indeed, almost every object gains upon me at the second sight. I have spent the evening, writing up my Journal—an act of real virtue.

After walking round the Cathedral, we went up a narrow and crooked street, very old and shabby, but with an antique house projecting as much as a yard over the pavement, on one side—a timber-house it seemed to be, plaistered [sic] over, and stained yellow or buff. There was no external door, affording entrance into this edifice; but about midway of its front, we came to a low, Gothic, stone archway, passing right through the house; and as it looked much time worn, and was scul[p]tured with untraceable devices, we went through. There was [223] an exceedingly antique, battered and shattered pair of oaken leaves, which used doubtless to shut up the passage in former times, and keep it secure; but, for the last hundred years, probably, there has been free ingress and egress. Indeed, this portal-arch may never have been closed, since the reformation. Within, we found a quadrangle, of which the house upon the street formed one side, the three others being composed of ancient houses with gables in a row, all looking upon the paved quadrangle through quaint windows of various fashion. An elderly, neat, pleasant looking woman now came in beneath the arch, and as she had a look of being acquainted here, we asked her what the place was; and she told us, that, in the old popish times, the prebends of the Cathedral used to live here, to keep them from doing mischief in the town. The establishment, she said, was now called the College, and was let in rooms and small tenements to poor people. On consulting the York Guide, I find that her account was pretty correct; the establishment having been founded in Henry VI's time, and called Saint William's College, the statue of the patron saint being sculptured over the arch; it was intended for the residence of the parsons and priests of the Cathedral, who had formerly caused [224] troubles and scandals by living promiscuously among the wives and maidens of the town.

We returned to the front of the Cathedral, on our way homeward; and an old man stopped us to inquire if we had ever seen the Fid[d]ler of York. We answered in the negative, and said that we had no time to see him now; but the old gentleman pointed up to the highest pinnacle of the southern front, where stood the Fid[d]ler of York—one of the Gothic quaintnesses which pimple out over the grandeur and solemnity of this and other cathedrals.

APRIL 12th SUNDAY.

THIS morning was bleak, and most ungenial; a chilly sunshine, a bleak wind, a prevalence of watery cloud—April weather, without the tenderness that ought to be half-revealed in it. This is Easter Sunday, and service at the Cathedral commenced at half past ten; so we set out betimes, and found admittance into the vast nave, and thence into the choir, where an attendant ushered my wife and Julian to a seat at a distance from me, and then gave me a place in one of the seats, or stalls, where the monks used to sit or kneel, while chanting the services. I think these seats are now appropriated to the prebends. They are of modern carved oak, much less elaborate and wonderfully [225] wrought than those of Chester Cathedral, where all was done with head and heart, each in a separate device, instead of cut by machinery, like these. The whole effect of this carved work, however, lining the quire with its light tracery and pinnacles, is very fine. The whole quire from the roof downward, except the old stones of the outer walls, is of modern renovation; it being but few years since this part of the Cathedral was destroyed by fire. The arches, and pillars, and lofty roof, however, have been well restored; and there was an immense east-window, full of painted glass, which, if it be modern, is wonderfully chaste and Gothic like. All the other windows have painted glass, which does not flare and glare, as if newly painted. But the light, white washed aspect of the general interior of the choir has a cold and dreary effect. There is an immense organ, all clad in rich oaken carving, of similar pattern to that of the stalls. It was communion-day; and near the high altar, within a screen, I saw the glistening of the gold vessels wherewith the services were to be performed.

The choir was respectably filled with a pretty numerous congregation, among whom I saw some offi[226]cers in full dress, with their swords by their sides; and one old white-bearded warrior, who sat near me, seemed very devout at his religious exercises. In front of me, and on the corresponding benches on the other side of the choir, sat two rows of white robed choristers, twenty in all; and these, with some women, performed the vocal part of the music. It is not good to see musicians, for they are usually coarse and vulgar people, and so the auditor loses faith in any fine and spiritual tones that they may breathe forth.

The services of Easter Sunday, I believe, comprehend more than the ordinary quantity of singing and chanting; at all events, nearly an hour and a half were thus employed, with some intermixture of prayers and reading of scriptures; and being almost congealed with cold, I thought it never would come to an end. The spirit of my Puritan ancestors was mighty in me, and I did not wonder at their being out of patience with all this mummery, which seemed to me worse than papistry because it was a corruption of it. At last, a Canon gave out the text, and preached a sermon of about twenty minutes long, the coldest, dryest, most superficial rubbish; for this gorgeous setting of the magnificent Cathedral, the elaborate [227] music, and the rich ceremonial, seems inevitably to take the life out of the sermon—which, to be anything, must be all. The Puritans showed their strength of mind and heart, by preferring a sermon of an hour and a half long, into which the preacher put his whole soul and spirit, and lopping away all these externals, into which religious life had first gushed and flowered, and then petrified.

After the service, while waiting for my wife in the nave, I was accosted by a young gentleman who seemed to be an American, and whom I have certainly seen before, but whose name I could not recollect. This he said was his first visit to York; and he was evidently inclined to join me in viewing the curiosities of the place; but not knowing his identity, I could not introduce him to my wife, and so had to make a parting salute. After dinner, we set forth and took a promenade along the wall, and a ramble through some of the crooked streets—noting the old, jutting storied houses, story above story, and the old churches, gnawed like a bone by the teeth of Time—till we came suddenly to the Black Swan, before we expected it, but not too soon for my wife's strength. [228] I rather imagine that I must have noted most of the external peculiarities, at my former visit, and therefore need not make another record of them in my Journal. In the course of our walk, we saw a two-and-two procession of about fifty charity-schoolboys, in flat caps, each with a pair of bands under his chin, and a green collar to his coat, all looking unjoyous, and as if they had no home, nor parents' love. They turned into a gateway, which closed behind them; and as the adjoining edifice seemed to be a public institution—at least, not private—we asked what it was, and found it to be a hospital or residence for Old Maids, founded by a gentlewoman of York, I know not whether herself of the sisterhood. It must be a very singular institution, and worthy of intimate study, if it were possible to make one's way within the portal. My wife had a glimpse of one of these ancient virgins at a window, very aged, thin, and uncomely; but I had not the luck to see her.

After writing the above, Julian and I went out for another ramble before tea; and taking a new course, we came to a grated iron fence and gateway, through which we could see the ruins of St. Mary's Abbey. They are very extensive, and situated quite in the midst of the city, and the wall and then a tower of the Abbey seem to border more than one of the [229] streets. Our walk was interesting, as it brought us unexpectedly upon several relics of antiquity; a loopholed [sic] and battlemented gateway, and, at various points, fragments of the old Gothic stonework, built in among more recent edifices, which themselves were old; grimness, intermixed with quaintness and grotesqueness; old fragments of religious or warlike architecture mingled with queer domestic structures—the general effect sombre, sordid, and grimy, but yet with a fascination that makes me fain to linger about such scenes, and come to them again.

We passed round the Cathedral, and saw jackdaws fluttering round the pinnacles, while the bells chimed the quarters, and little children playing on the steps under the grand arch of the entrance. It is very stately, very beautiful, this Minster, and doubtless would be very satisfactory, could I only know it long and well enough; so rich as its front is, even with almost all the niches empty of their statues; not stern in its effect, which I suppose must be owing to the elaborate detail with which its great surface is wrought all over, like the chasing of a lady's jewel-box—and yet so grand! There seems to be a dwelling-house on one side, gray with antiquity, which has apparently grown out of it [230] like an excrescense; and though a good sized edifice, yet the Cathedral is so large that its vastness is not in the least deformed by it. If it be a dwelling-house, I suppose it is inhabited by the person who takes care of the Cathedral. This morning, while listening to the tedious chanting and lukewarm sermon, I depreciated the whole affair, Cathedral and all; but now I do more justice at least to the latter, and am only sorry that its noble echoes must follow at every syllable, and reverberate at the commas and semi-colons, such poor discourses as the Canon's. But, after all, it was the Puritans who made the sermon of such importance, in religious worship, as we New Englanders now consider it; and we are absurd in considering this magnificent church and all those embroidered ceremonies only in reference to it.

Before going back to the hotel, I went again up the narrow and twisted passage of College-street, to take another peep at St. William's College. I underestimated the projection of the front over the street; it is considerably more than a yard, and is about eight or nine feet above the pavement. The little statue of St. William is an alto relievo over the arched entrance, and has an escutcheon of arms on each side; all much defaced. In the interior of the quadrangle, the houses have not gables or [231] peaked fronts, but have peaked windows on the red-tiled roof. The door-way opposite the entrance-arch is rather stately; and on one side is a large, projecting window, which is said to belong to the room where the printing-press of Charles I was established, in the days of the Parliament.

The waiter, to-day, finding that we are Americans, brought us a book in which are inscribed the names of all the Americans who have put up at the Black Swan, for seven years past. We saw many names that we knew.

MONDAY, APRIL 13th, AT MANCHESTER.

THIS morning was chill (as every day had been, since we left home;) and, worse still, it was showery; so that our purposes to see York were much thwarted. At about ten °clock, however, we took a cab and drove to the Cathedral, where we arrived while service was going on in the choir; and ropes were put up as barriers between us and the nave; so that we were limited to the South Transept, and a part of one of the aisles of the Choir. It was dismally cold. We crept cheerlessly about within our narrow precincts (narrow, that is to say, in proportion to the vast length and breadth of the Cathedral) gazing up into the hollow height of the central tower, and looking at a [232] monumental brass, fastened against one of the pillars, representing a be-ruffed lady of the Tudor times, and at the canopied tomb of Archbishop de Grey, who ruled over the diocese in the thirteenth century. Then we went into the side aisle of the choir, where there were one or two modern monuments; and I was appalled to find that a sermon was being preached by the ecclesiastic of the day, nor were there any signs of an imminent termination. I am not aware that there was much pith in the discourse; but there certainly was a good deal of labor and earnestness in the preacher's mode of delivery, although, when he came to a close, it appeared that the audience was not more than some half a dozen people.

The barriers being now withdrawn, we walked adown the length of the nave, which did not seem to me so dim and vast as the recollection which I have had of it, since my visit of a year ago. But my pre-imaginations and my memories are both apt to play the deuce with all admirable things, and so create disappointments for me, while perhaps the thing itself is really far better than I imagine or remember it. We engaged an old gentleman, one of the attendants pertaining to the Cathedral, to show [233] us round; and he showed us first the stone screen in front of the Choir, with its sculptured kings of England; and then the tombs in the North Transept, one of a modern Archbishop, and another of an ancient one, behind which latter the insane person, who set fire to the Cathedral, a few years since, hid himself at nightfall. Then our guide unlocked a side door, and led us into the Chapter House, an octagonal hall, with a vaulted roof, a tessel[l]ated floor, and seven arched windows of old painted glass, the richest that I ever saw or imagined, each looking like an inestimable treasury of precious stones, with a gleam and glow even in the sullen light of this gray morning. What would they be with the sun shining through them! With all their brilliancy, moreover, they were as soft as rose-leaves. I never saw any piece of human architecture, so beautiful as this Chapter House; at least, I thought so while I was looking at it, and think so still; and it owed its beauty in very great measure to the painted windows. I remember looking at these windows from the outside, yesterday, and seeing nothing but an opaque old crust of conglomerated panes of glass; but now that gloomy mystery was radiantly [234] solved.

Returning into the body of the Cathedral, we next entered the Choir, where, instead of the crimson cushions and draperies which we had seen yesterday, we found everything clad in black. It was a token of mourning for one of the Canons, who died on Saturday night. The great East window, seventy-five feet high, and full of old painted glass, in many exquisitely wrought and imagined Scriptural designs, is considered the most splendid object in the Cathedral. It is a pity that it is partially hidden from view, even in the Choir, by a screen before the high altar; but, indeed, the Gothic architects seem first to imagine beautiful and noble things, and then to consider how they may best be partially screened from sight. A certain secrecy and twilight effect belong to their plan. We next went round the side aisles of the choir, which contain many interesting monuments, of prelates, and other old dignitaries; and a specimen of the very common Elizabethan design of an old gentleman in double ruff and trunk breeches kneeling in prayer, and each of his two wives kneeling on either side of him, and their conjoint children, in two rows, kneeling in the lower compartments of the [235] tomb. We saw, too, a rich marble monument of one of the Strafford family, and the tomb-stone of the famous Earl himself, a flat stone in the pavement of the aisle, covering the vault where he was buried, and with four iron rings fastened into the four corners of the stone, whereby to lift it.

And now the guide led us into the vestry, where there was a good fire burning in the grate; and it really thawed my heart, which was congealed with the dismal chill of the Cathedral. Here we saw a good many curious things; for instance, two wooden figures in knightly armor, which had stood centinels [sic] beside the ancient clock, before it was replaced by a modern one; and, opening a closet, the guide produced an old iron helmet, which had been found in a tomb, where a knight had been buried in his armor; and three gold rings, and one brass one, taken out of the graves, and off the finger-bones, of medi-aeval archbishops, one of them with ruby set in it; and two silver-gilt chalices, also treasures of the tombs; and a wooden head, carved in human likeness, and painted to the life, likewise taken from a grave where an archbishop was supposed to have been buried. They found no veritable [236] skull or bones, but only this block-head—as if death had betrayed the secret of what the poor prelate really was. We saw, too, a canopy of cloth, wrought with gold threads, which had been borne over the head of King James I, when he came to York on his way to receive the English crown. We saw some old brass dishes, in which pence used to be collected, in the monkish times. Over the door of this vestry room there hung two banners of a Yorkshire regiment, tattered in the Peninsular wars, and inscribed with the names of the battles through which they had been borne triumphantly; and Waterloo was among them. The vestry, I think, occupies that excrescential edifice, which I noticed yesterday as having grown out of the Cathedral.

After looking at these things, we went down into the crypts under the choir; these were very interesting, as far as we could see them, being more antique than anything above ground, but as dark as any cellar. There is here, in the midst of these sepulchral crypts, a spring of water, said to be very pure and delicious (owing to the limestone of the Cathedral, through which the rain that feeds its source is filtered. Near it, there was a stone trough, in which the monks used to wash their hands.

[237] April 14th, Wednesday, at Southport.

I do not remember anything more that we saw in the Cathedral; and at about twelve, we returned to the Black Swan, and in due time had luncheon. The rain still continued; so that my wife could not share in any more of our rambles; but Julian and I went out, and discovered the Guildhall. It is a very ancient edifice (of Richard II's time, I think) and has a statue over the entrance which looks time-gnawed enough to be of coeval antiquity, although in reality it is only a representation of George II, in his royal robes. We went in and found ourselves in a large and lofty hall, with an oaken roof, and a stone pavement; and the further end was parti[ti]oned off as a court of Justice. In that portion of the hall, a judge was on the bench, and a trial was going forward; but in the hither portion, a mob of people, with their hats on, were lounging and talking, and enjoying the warmth of two stoves. The window over the judgment-seat had painted glass in it, and so, I think, had some of the side-windows; at the end of the hall hung a great picture of Paul defending himself before Agrippa, where the Apostle looked like an athlete, and had a remarkably bushy black beard. Between two of the windows hung an Indian bell, from Burmah [sic], pon[238]derously thick and massive. Both the picture and the bell had been presented to the city as tokens of affectionate remembrance, by its children; and it is pleasant to think that such feelings exist, in these old, stable communities, and that there are permanent localities where such gifts can be kept from generation to generation.

We saw nothing else noticeable in York; and at four o'clock we left the city, still in a pouring rain. The Black Swan, where we had been staying, is a good specimen of the old English inn, sombre, quiet, with dark staircases, dingy rooms, curtained beds, all the possibilities of a comfortable life, and good English fare, in a fashion which cannot have been much altered for half a century past. It is very homelike, when one has one's family about him, but must be prodigiously stupid for a solitary man.

We took the train for Manchester, over pretty much the same route, I think, that I travelled last year. Many of the higher hills in Yorkshire were white with snow, which, in our lower region, softened into rain; but as we approached Manchester, the western sky reddened, and gave promise of better weather. We arrived at nearly eight °clock, and put up at the Palatine Hotel. In the evening, I scrawled [239] away at my Journal till past ten °clock; for I have really made it a matter of conscience to keep a tolerably full record of my travels, though conscious that everything good escapes in the process. In the morning, we went out and visited the Manchester Cathedral, a particularly black and grimy old edifice, containing some genuine old wood carvings within the choir. We staid a good while, in order to see some people married. One couple, with their groomsman and bridesmaid were sitting within the choir; but when the clergyman was robed and ready, there entered five other couples, each attended by groomsman and bridesmaid. They all seemed to be of the lower orders; one or two respectably dressed, but most of them poverty-stricken; the men in their ordinary loafer's or laborer's attire; the women with their poor, shabby shawls drawn closely about them; faded untimely, wrink[l]ed with penury and care; nothing fresh, virginlike, or hopeful about them; joining themselves to their mates, with the idea of making their own misery less intolerable by adding another's to it. All the six couple stood up in a row before the altar, with the groomsmen and bridesmaids in a row behind them; and the clergyman proceeded to marry them in such a way that [240] it almost seemed to make every man and woman the husband and wife of every other. However, there were some small portions of the service directed towards each separate couple; and they appeared to assort themselves in their own fashion afterwards, each man saluting his bride with a kiss. The clergyman, the sexton, and the clerk, all seemed to find something funny in this affair; and the woman, who admitted us into the church, smiled, too, when she told us that a wedding-party was waiting to be married. But I think it was the saddest thing we have seen since leaving home; though funny enough, if one likes to look at it from the ludicrous point of view.[410]

This ended the memorable things of our tour; for my wife and Julian left Manchester for Southport at a quarter past eleven, and I for Liverpool, twenty minutes afterwards.

This mob of poor marriages was caused by the fact that no marriage fee is paid, during Easter.

APRIL 19th, SUNDAY.

On Wednesday last (the 15th) having been invited to attend at the laying of the corner-stone of Mr. Brown's Free Library, I went to the Town Hall, according to the programme, at 11 °clock. There was already a large number of people (invited guests, [241] members of the Historical Society, and other local associations) assembled in the great ball-room; and one or other of these seemed to be delivering an address to Mr. Brown, when I entered. Approaching the outer edge of the circle, I was met and cordially greeted by Monckton Milnes, whom I like, and who always reminds me of Longfellow; though his physical man is more massive, and, since I saw him last, his chin has magnified itself considerably. While we were talking together, a young man approached him with a pretty little expression of surprise and pleasure at seeing him there; he had a sort of mincing, slightly affected or made up manner; and was rather a comely young man, in a brown frock, and pantaloons plaided of a very large pattern. On a casual observation, I should have taken him, I think, to be a salesman in a dry-goods establishment, or belonging to some other genteel line of business; but Mr. Milnes introduced him to me as Lord Stanley. Hereupon, of course, I observed him more closely; and I must say that I was not long in discovering a gentle dignity and half imperceptible reserve in his manner; but still my first impression was quite as real as my second one. He [242] occupies, I suppose, the foremost position among the young men of England, and has the fairest prospect of a high course before him; nevertheless, he did not impress me as possessing the native qualities that could entitle him to a high public career. He has adopted public life as his hereditary profession, and makes the very utmost of all his abilities, cultivating himself to a determined end, knowing that he shall have every advantage towards attaining his object. His natural disadvantages must have been, in some respects, unusually great; his voice, for instance, is not strong, and appeared to me to have a more positive defect than mere weakness, owing, I should think, to some slight malformation of his mouth; so that he speaks in a puffy kind of a tone.[411] Doubtless, he has struggled manfully against this defect; and it made me feel a certain pity and sympathy, and indeed a friendliness, for which he would not at all have thanked me, had he known it. I felt, in his person, what a burthen it is upon human shoulders, the necessity of keeping up the fame and historical importance of an illustrious house; at least, when the heir to its honors has sufficient intellect [243] and sensibility to feel the claim that his country, and his ancestors, and his posterity, all have upon him. Lord Stanley is fully capable of feeling these claims; but I would not care, methinks, to take his position, unless I could have considerably more than his strength.

In a little while, we formed ourselves into a procession, four in a row, and set forth from the Town Hall through James-Street, Church Street, Lord Street; Lime Street; all the way through a line of policemen and a throng of people; and the windows were alive with heads; and I never before was so conscious of a great mass of humanity, though perhaps I may often have seen as great a crowd. But a procession is the best point of view from which to see the crowd that collects together. The day, too, was very fine, even sunshiny, and the streets dry; a blessing which cannot be overestimated, for we should have been in a strange pickle for the banquet, had we been compelled to wade through the ordinary mud of Liverpool. The procession itself could not have been a very striking object. In America, it would have had a hundred picturesque and perhaps ludicrous features; the symbols of the different trades, ban[244]ners with strange devices, flower-shows, children, volunteer soldiers, cavalcades, and every suitable and unsuitable contrivance; but we were merely a trail of ordinary-looking individuals, in great coats, and with precautionary umbrellas. The only characteristic or professional costumes, as far as I noticed, was that of the Bishop of Chester, in his flat cap and black silk gown, and that of Sir Henry Smith (the general of the District) in full uniform, with a star and half-a-dozen medals on his breast. Mr. Brown himself, the hero of the day, was the plainest, and simplest man of all; an exceedingly unpretending old gentleman in black, small, withered, white haired, pale, quiet, and respectable. I rather wondered why he chose to be the centre of all this ceremony, for he did not seem either particularly to enjoy it, or to be at all incommoded by it, as a more nervous and susceptible man might.

The site of the projected edifice is on one of the streets bordering on St. George's Hall; and when we came within the enclosure, the corner stone (a large square of red-free stone) was already suspended over its destined place. It had a brass-plate let into it, [245] with an inscription, which perhaps will not be seen again till the present English type has grown as antique as black-letter. Two or three photographs were now taken of the site, the corner-stone, Mr. Brown, the distinguished guests, and the crowd at large; then ensued (or followed, I forget which) a prayer from the Bishop of Chester, and speeches from Mr. Holmes, Mr. Brown, Lord Stanley, Sir John Packington, Sir Henry Smith, and as many others as there was time for. I was amused at Sir Henry Smith, who thrust himself prominently forward, with a view to being called for by the crowd, and then said some pre-considered nothings with a martial force of utterance. Lord Stanley acquitted himself very creditably, though brought out unexpectedly (at that time) and with evident reluctance. I am convinced that men, liable to be called on to address the public, keep a constant supply of common-places in their minds, which, with little variation, can be adapted to one subject about as well as to another; and thus they are always ready to do well enough; though seldom to do particularly well.

From the scene of the corner-stone, we went to [246] St. George's Hall, where a drawing-room and dressing-room had been prepared for the principal guests. Before the banquet, I had some conversation with Sir James Kay Shuttleworth,[412] who has known Miss Bronte very intimately, and bore testimony to the wonderful fidelity of Mrs. Gaskell's life of her. He seemed to have had an affectionate regard for her, and said that her marriage promised to have been productive of great happiness; her husband being not a remarkable man, but with the merit of an exceeding love for her. Mr. Brown now took me up into the gallery, which by this time was full of ladies; and thence we had a fine view of the noble hall, with the tables laid, in readiness for the banquet. I cannot conceive of anything finer than this hall; it needs nothing but painted windows to make it perfect, and those, I hope, it may have, one day or another.

At two °clock, or a little after, we sat down to the banquet, which hardly justified that epithet, being only a cold collation, though sufficiently splendid in its way. In truth, it would have been impossible to provide a hot dinner for 900 people, in a place remote from kitchens. [247] The principal table extended lengthwise of the hall; and was a little elevated above the other tables, which stretched across, about twenty in all. Before each guest, besides the bill of fare, was laid a programme of the expected toasts, among which appeared my own name, to be proposed by Mr. Monckton Milnes. These things do not trouble me quite so much as they did, though still it sufficed to prevent much of the enjoyment which I might have had, if I could have felt myself merely a spectator. My left hand neighbor was Colonel Campbell of the artillery; my right hand one was Mr. Picton, of the Library Committee; and I found them both companionable men, especially the Colonel, who had served in China, and in the Crimea, and owned that he hated the French. We did not make a very long business of the eatables; and then came the usual toasts of ceremony, and afterwards those more peculiar to the occasion, one of the first of which, I think, was "The House of Stanley," to which, of course, Lord Stanley responded. It was a noble subject, giving scope for as much eloquence as any man could have brought to bear upon it; and capable of being so wrought [248] out as to develope [sic] and illustrate any sort of conservative or liberal tendencies which the speaker might entertain; there could not be a richer opportunity for reconciling and making friends betwixt the old system of society and the new; but Lord Stanley did not seem to make anything of it. I remember nothing that he said, except his statement of the fact, that his family had been five hundred years connected with the town of Liverpool. I wish I could have responded to the "House of Stanley," and his lordship could have spoken in my behalf. None of the speeches were remarkably good; the Bishop of Chester's perhaps the best, though he is but a little shrimp of a man, in aspect, not at all filling up one's idea of a bishop. Lord Talbot was common-place; Sir John Packington heavy and frowsy, and the rest on an indistinguishable level, though, being all from practised speakers, they were less hemmy and haw-y than English oratory ordinarily is.

I was really tired to death before my own turn came, sitting all that time, as it were, on the scaffold with the rope round my neck. At last, Monckton Milnes was called up, and made a speech of which, [249] to my dismay, I could hardly hear a single word, owing to his being at a considerable distance on the other side of the chairman, and flinging his voice (which is a bass one) across the hall, instead of a-down it in my direction. I could not distinguish one word of any allusions to my works, nor even, when he came to the toast, did I hear the terms in which he put it, nor whether I was toasted on my own basis, or as representing American literature, or as Consul of the United States. At all events, there was a vast deal of clamor; and uprose peers and bishop, general, mayor, knights, and gentlemen, everybody in the hall, greeting me with all the honors. I had uprisen, too, to commence my speech; but had to sit down again till matters grew more quiet, and then I got up and proceeded to deliver myself with as much composure as ever I felt at my own fireside. It is very strange, this self-possession and clear-sightedness which I have once or twice experienced when standing before an audience; it showed me my way through all the difficulties resulting from my not having heard Monckton Milnes's speech, and, on since reading the latter, I do not see how I [250] could have answered it better. Upon my word, I think my speech was about the best of the occasion; and certainly it was better cheered than any other, especially one passage, where I made a colossus of poor little Mr. Brown, at which the audience grew so tumultuous in their applause, that they drowned my figure of speech before it was half out of my mouth.

After rising from table, Lord Stanley[413] and I talked about our respective oratorical performances; and he really appeared to have a perception that he is not naturally gifted in this respect. I like Lord Stanley, and wish that it were possible that we might know one another better. If a nobleman has any true friend, out of his own class, it ought to be a republican. Nothing further of interest happened at the banquet; and the next morning came out the newspapers, with vile reports of my speech, attributing to me a variety of forms of ragged nonsense, which (poor speaker as I am) I was quite incapable of uttering.[414]

MAY 10th 1857, SUNDAY.

THE winter is over; but as yet we scarcely have what ought to be called spring;—nothing but cold east-winds, accompanied with sunshine, however, as east-winds generally are, in this country. All milder winds [251] seem to bring rain. The grass has been green for a month past; indeed, it has never been entirely brown; and now the trees and hedges are beginning to be in foliage. Weeks ago, the daisies bloomed, even in the sandy grass-plot bordering on the promenade, beneath our front-windows; and, in the progress of the daisy-bud towards its consummation, I saw the propriety of Burns's epithet—

"Wee, modest, *crimson tipped* flower"[415]—its little white petals, in the bud, being fringed all round with crimson, which fades into pure white when the flower blooms. At the beginning of this month, I saw fruit-trees in blossom, stretched out flat against stone-walls, reminding me of a dead bird nailed against the side of a barn. But it has been a backward and dreary spring; and I think Southport, in the course of it, has lost its advantage over the rest of the Liverpool neighborhood, in point of milder atmosphere. The east-wind feels even rawer here than in the city.

Nevertheless, the columns of the "Southport Visitor" begin to be well replenished with the names of guests, and the little town is assuming its aspect of summer-life. To say the truth, except where cultivation has done [252] its utmost, there is very little difference between winter and summer in the mere material aspect of Southport; there being nothing but a waste of sand, intermixed with plashy pools, to seaward, and a desert of sand-hillocks on the land-side. But now the brown, weather hardened donkey-women haunt people that stray along the beaches; and delicate persons face the cold, rasping, ill-tempered blast, on the promenade; and children dig in the sands; and, for want of something better, it seems to be determined that this shall be considered Spring.

Southport is as stupid a place as ever I lived in; and I cannot but bewail an ill fortune, to have been compelled to spend these many months on these barren sands, when almost every other square yard of England contains something that would have been historically or poetically interesting. Our life here has been a blank. There was, indeed, a shipwreck, a month or two ago, when a large ship came ashore within a mile from our windows, the larger portion of the crew landing safely on the hither sands, while six or seven betook themselves to the boat, and were lost in attempting to gain the shore on the other side of the Ribble. After a lapse of several weeks, two or three [253] of their drowned bodies were found floating in this vicinity, and brought to Southport for burial; so that it really is not at all improbable that Milton's Lycidas floated hereabouts in the rise and lapse of the tides, and that his bones may be still whitening among the sands. In the same gale that wrecked the above-mentioned vessel, a portion of a ship's mast was driven ashore, after evidently having been a very long time in and under water; for it was covered with great barnacles, and torn sea-weed, insomuch that there was scarcely a bare place along its whole length; rays, too, were sticking to it, and clusters of sea-anemones, and I know not what strange marine-productions besides. Julian at once recognized the sea-anemones, knowing them by his much reading of Gosse's Aquarium; and though they must have now been two or three days high and dry out of water, he made an extempore aquarium out of a wash-bowl, and put in above a dozen of these strange creatures. In a little while, they bloomed out wonderfully, and even seemed to produce young anemones; but, from some fault in his management, they afterwards grew sickly [254] and died. My wife thinks that the old storm-shattered mast, so studded with the growth of the ocean-depths, is a relic of the Spanish Armada, which strewed its wreck along all the shore of England; but I hardly think it would have taken three hundred years to produce this crop of barnacles and sea-anemones. A single summer might probably have done it.

Yesterday, we all of us, except Rosebud, went to Liverpool to see the performances of an American Circus Company. I had previously been, a day or two before, with Julian, and had been happy to perceive that the fact of its being an American establishment, really induced some slight swelling of the heart within me. It is ridiculous enough, to be sure; but I like to find myself not wholly destitute of this noble weakness, patriotism. As for the Circus, I never was fond of that species of entertainment, nor do I find in this one the flash, and glitter, and whirl, which I seem to remember in American exhibitions.

FRIDAY, MAY 22ᵈ, AT LINCOLN.

WE had been intending a tour in this direction for some time past, but have put it off on account of the bleak and bitter weather, which has made this spring even unusually late and disagreeable. We meant to have [255] started yesterday, but were prevented by the rain. This morning, however, was bright and sunny—the sunshine mingled with water, as it were, and tempered with an east-wind—so we set out at a little past eleven, and made our first stage to Manchester. Lancashire is a dreary county—at least, in all except the hilly portions of it, and I have never passed through it without wishing myself anywhere but in that particular spot where I happened to be. There were a few spots on our route historically interesting; as, for instance, Bolton, which was the scene of many remarkable events in the Parliamentary Wars, and where one of the earls of Derby was beheaded. But we saw only the never failing green fields, hedges, and monotonous features of an ordinary English landscape, along the wayside; and, often, little factory villages, or larger towns, with their tall chimneys, and their smoke, and their uglinesses of brick, and their heaps of refuse matter, which seems to be the only sort of stuff that Nature cannot take back to herself, and resolve into the elements, when man throws it by. So these little hillocks of waste and effete mineral are seen round manufacturing-towns, hardly made decent with even a little grass [256] after many years. We reached Manchester shortly after one, and drove across the city to the London Road station, seeing on our way the principal square, where, I think, a Statue of the Duke of Wellington has been put up since I was in Manchester. All the omnibuses, today, bore advertisements of the Art-Exhibition.

At a quarter to two, we left Manchester by the Sheffield and Lincoln railway; and the scenery grew rather better than that through which we had hitherto passed, though by no means very striking; in truth, except in the show-districts—such as the lakes—English scenery is not very well-worth looking at it [*sic*] as a picture or a spectacle. It has a real, homely charm of its own, no doubt; but—as Wordsworth said of a poet—You must love it before it will seem to deserve your love,[416] although the rich verdure and thorough finish, added by human art, is as striking to an American as any stronger feature could be. Our ride to-day, however, between Manchester and Sheffield, was not through a rich tract of country, but along a valley walled in by bleak, ridgy hills, extending straight as a rampart, and black moor-land, with here and there a plantation [257] of trees; sometimes, long and gradual ascents, spreading out a wide surface—miles on every side—to be taken in by the eye at once; very bleak and windy it must be, when there is any wind stirring. Old stone or brick farm-houses, and, once in a while, an old church-tower, are too common objects, almost, to be noticed in an English landscape. I imagine, however, that, on a railway, we see what little we do see of the country quite amiss; it never being intended to be looked at from any point of view in that line; so that it is like looking at the wrong side of a piece of tapestry. The road (unless it were a turnpike) no doubt adapted itself by a natural impulse to the physiognomy of the country, and everything that men erected within view of it had some subtle reference to the highway; but the line of the railway is perfectly arbitrary, and puts all precedent things at sixes and sevens. At all events, be the cause what it may, there is seldom anything worth looking at, within the scope of a railway-traveller; and, if there be, he has no chance to look at it.

At Penistone—(the station is near an ancient-looking village, nestling round a church, on a wide, [258] open moor-land, we saw a tall old lady in black, who seemed to have just alighted from the railway. My wife said that she must once have been beautiful; that did not impress me, for I am not very apt to see the beauty of the past, in human faces; but this poor old lady struck me by a singular movement of the head, constantly repeated, and at regular intervals, as if she were making a stern and solemn protest against some action that was developing itself before her eyes, and were foreboding great evil, if it should be persisted in. Of course, it was nothing but a paralytic or nervous affection; yet one might fancy that it had its origin in some great wrong that was perpetrated, half a life-time ago, in this old gentlewoman's presence, and either against herself or some body whom she loved still better. Her features had a singular sternness, which, I suppose, was caused by her habitual effort to compose and keep them quiet, and thus to counteract the tendency to paralytic movement. The slow, regular, and inexorable character of the motion—her look of force and self-control, which seemed to make this motion a part of itself—have stamped this face and gesture on my memory.

[259] The train stopped a minute or two, to allow the tickets to be taken, just before entering the Sheffield Station; and thence I saw all that I have seen of the famous town of cutlery. My impressions are very vague and misty—or rather smoky—for Sheffield seems to me smokier than Manchester, Liverpool, Birmingham—smokier than all England besides, unless Newcastle be the exception. Every where, uprose the smoke, not in dark, dense volumes, but rather

in a general fog; and this is all I know of Sheffield. By the by, we approached it, as it were, through the Valley of the Shadow of Death; for on the way from Manchester—as I should have mentioned, only that the poor, palsy-stricken lady drew me aside—we passed through a tunnel three miles in length, quite traversing the breadth and depth of a mountainous hill.

The scenery became softer, gentler, yet more picturesque, after we had passed Sheffield; and, at one point, we saw what I believe to be the utmost northern verge of Sherwood Forest; not consisting, however, of thousand-year oaks, extant from Robin Hood's [260] days, but of young and thriving plantations, which it will take a century or so, to ripen. Earl Fitzwilliam's property lies along in this neighborhood, and probably his castle was hidden among some soft depth of foliage, not far off. Proceeding onward, the country grew quite level around us, whereby I judged that we were now in Lincolnshire; and shortly after six °clock, we caught the first glimpse of the Cathedral towers, though, truth to say, they at first looked scarcely huge enough for our idea of them. Drawing nearer, however, we saw that it must really be the Cathedral, and by the time we reached the city, we recognised that it must indeed be a great edifice.

At the railway-station, we found no cab—such appearing not to be the custom of Lincoln—but only a[n] omnibus, belonging to the Saracen's Head, which the driver told us was the best in the city, and took us hither accordingly. It stands in the principal street, and within a very short distance is one of the ancient city-gates arched across the public way, with two smaller arches for foot-passengers on either side; gray, time-gnawn, ponderous, shadowy. The street was narrow, and sufficiently antique [261] to be picturesque, though, certainly, English domestic architecture seems to have lost its most striking features, in the course of the last hundred years. Shrewsbury is the finest old town that I have seen, in this respect, retaining more of the stately and quaint old houses; but, everywhere else, there is a monotony of fronts, that has obliterated the best antiquity of the street.

The Saracen's Head received us hospitably enough, though there is an evil smell of gas, or some other abomination, about our parlor. The house appears to be of an old fashion, with the entrance into its court, through an arch, in the side of which is the house door. There are long corridors, and an intricate arrangement of passages, and up and down meandering of staircases. We had a supper of cold beef, a cold trout, and a cold boiled crab, and then walked out to pay our first visit to the Cathedral. It wants but twenty minutes of eleven, and I am at the end of my volume; so I shall not begin a new one till morning.

1857

AFTER supper, and between seven and eight °clock, last evening, we set out (as I said at the close of the preceding volume) to pay a preliminary visit to the exterior of the Cathedral. Leaving the Saracen's Head, we passed through the Stone Bow, as the gate close by is called, and ascended a street which grew steeper and narrower as we advanced. At last, it got to be the steepest street I ever saw; so steep that any carriage, if left to itself, would rattle downward much faster than it could possibly be drawn up. Indeed, I can hardly think that wheel-carriages pass at all up this difficult acclivity. The houses on each side looked considerably old, but not exactly antique or venerable, except one with an arched stone portal, with carved ornaments; a dwelling place now for poor people, but which may have been a handsome edifice in its long past day. As well as I can make out from the guide, this is called the Jewess's House, being inhabited by a woman of that faith who was hanged many hundred years ago.

Still the street grew steeper and steeper; and certainly the Bishop and clergy of Lincoln ought not to be fat men, if they have to climb this hill to perform [2] their ecclesiastical duties. It is a real penance, and was probably performed as such, in monkish times. Formerly, the Guide says, the Bishop used to ascend the hill barefoot, on the day of his installation. Still, we were cheered onward by glimpses of the Cathedral towers, and, finally, getting upward to an open square, we saw an old Gothic gateway to the left hand, and another to the right; the latter being, apparently, an exterior defence of the Cathedral, the west front of which rose behind it. We passed through one of the side-arches of this portal, and found ourselves in the Cathedral-close, a wide, level space, where the great old Minster has fair room to sit, and to look down on the ancient edifices surrounding it, all of which, in former times, were doubtless the habitations of its dignitaries and officers. In fact, I presume many of them still are so, though some seem too ill-cared for to belong to such an establishment. Unless it were Salisbury-close, however (which is incomparably fine in its specimens of old domestic architecture) I remember no such comfortably picturesque precincts round any other Cathedral.

The Cathedral is built of a yellowish brown[3]stone, which seems either to have been largely restored, or else does not assume the hoary, crumbly surface which gives such a venerable aspect to most ancient churches and castles, in England. In many parts, the recent restoration was quite evident; but other [parts], and much the larger portion, can scarcely have been touched for centuries; for there are the gargoyles, perfect, or with broken noses, as the case may be, and the innumerable niches, up the whole height of the towers, and all over the walls—far the greater portion of them empty, but a few with the remains of statues, generally headless. The effect of the West Front is exceedingly rich, being covered and fretted all over with the minutest detail of sculpture and carving; at least, it was so once, and the impression remains even now that much of the artistic detail has vanished. I have seen a cherry-stone carved all over by a monk so minutely that it must have cost him half a life time of labor; and this Cathedral front seems to have been elaborated, in a monkish spirit, like that cherry-stone. Not that the result is in the least petty, but wonderfully grand, and all the more so even for the faith[f]ul beauty of the smal[4]lest details.

An elderly man, seeing us looking up at the West Front, came to the door of an adjacent house, and called to inquire if we wished to go into the Cathedral; but as it would have a dusky twilight within, we declined. So we merely walked round the exterior, and thought it more beautiful than York; though, on recollection, I hardly deem it so majestic and mighty as that. It is in vain to attempt a description, or even to record the feeling which the edifice inspires; it does not seem exactly an inanimate object, but something that has a vast, quiet life of its own—a thing which man did not build, though it belongs somehow to human nature. In short, I only talk nonsense by trying to give my sense of this and other Cathedrals.

While we stood in the close, at the eastern end of the Cathedral, the clock chimed the quarters, and then Great Tom told us it was eight °clock, in far the sweetest and mightiest accents that I ever heard from any bell—slow, too, and solemn, and allowing the reverberations of each stroke to die away before the succeeding one fell. It was still broad [5] daylight, and would be so for some time longer; but the air was getting sharp and cool; so we descended the steep street, Julian running before us and getting such headway that I fully expected him to bring up short against some wall. By-the-by, he brought off as a relic a fragment of stone from the Cathedral, which he says he picked up off the ground; but I suspect that he had knocked it[417] off from an angle. On our way homeward, we went into a stationer's shop, and into an apothecary's, to make some small purchases, and found the Lincoln people to be affable and kindly folks, readily and familiarly talking with strangers, and telling us what they were.

After writing the above, we took a fly, at about eleven °clock, and drove up to the Minster, by a road rather less steep and abrupt than that which led us thither, last evening. We alighted before the West Front; and the driver went in quest of the Verger, but, as he was not immediately to be found, a girl let us into the nave, which we found to be very grand, of course, but not so grand, we thought, as that of York, especially beneath the great central tower of the latter. Unless it be a professedly architectural description, there is but [6] one set of phrases in which to talk of all the cathedrals in England, and elsewhere. They are alike in their grand features—an acre or two of stone flags for a pavement, rows of vast columns supporting a vaulted roof, great windows. sometimes dimmed with ancient or modern stained glass, an elaborately carved screen between the nave and chancel, breaking the vista which might be of such glorious length, which is further choked up by an organ—and through these obstructions, the immense, variegated glimmer of the painted east-window. Then, within the screen, the old carved oak of the stalls; the bishop's throne, the altar, and whatever else furnishes out the holy of holies; then the range of chapels, and of old monuments, in the side aisles of the chancel; then the chapter-house, which, here at Lincoln, as at Salisbury, is supported by one central pillar, from which the roof grows forth like branches from a tree. In the Chancel, we saw an immense slab of stone, being the monument of Catherine Swynford, John of Gaunt's wife, and some tombs of prelates and warriors, and also the shrine of the little Saint Hugh—the Christian child who was fabled to have been crucified [7] by the Jews of Lincoln. The Cathedral is not rich in monuments; for it suffered great outrage and dilapidation both at the Reformation and in Cromwell's time. The soldiers of the latter stabled their steeds in the nave, and hacked and hewed the monkish sculptures at their wicked pleasure. Nevertheless, there are some most exquisite and marvellous specimens of flowers, foliage, grape-vines, and miracles of stone twined about arches, as if it had been as soft as wax in the sculptor's hands; the leaves represented with all their veins, so that you might almost think it, not art, but petrified nature. Here, too, were those grotesque faces that always grin at you from the projections of monkish architecture. Originally, it is supposed, all the pillars of the edifice, and all these magic sculptures, were polished to the utmost degree; nor is it unreasonable to think that the artists would have taken these further pains, when they had already bestowed so much labor in working out their ideas. But, at present, the whole interior of the Cathedral has been smeared over with a yellowish wash; the very meanest hue imaginable.

Adjacent to the Chapter House are the Cloisters [8] the walks of which seem to be paved with lettered tombstones; and some, the relics of Catholic times, with crosses engraved upon them, have been made to serve for memorials to dead persons of more modern date. In the centre of the green, around which the Cloisters perambulate, is a small, mean brick building, with a locked door. Our guide—(I forgot to say, that we had soon been joined by a verger, in black, and with a white tie, but of a lusty and jolly aspect)—our guide unlocked this door, and disclosed a flight of steps. At the bottom appeared what I should have taken to be a large square of dim, worn, and faded oil-carpet, which might once have been painted of rather a·gaudy pattern. This was a Roman tessel[l]ated pavement, made of small, colored bricks, or pieces of burnt clay. It had been accidentally discovered here, and had not been meddled with, except by uncovering it. Nothing else occurs to me; just now, to be recorded in respect to the Cathedral, except a place where the stone pavement was worn away by the feet of pilgrims, scraping upon it as they knelt down before a shrine of the Virgin.

[9] Leaving the Cathedral, we went (on foot, for we had dismissed our fly) along a street of high, peaked-roof houses, covered with red earthen tiles, to a Roman arch, which strides across the street. This is about four hundred yards

from the Cathedral; and it is to be noticed that there are Roman remains in all this vicinity, some above ground, and doubtless innumerably more beneath it. It was a Roman station while they held the country; and we saw in the Minster a Roman altar that was recently found on that site of Christian sanctity. This archway, which I am speaking about, is rude and massive, and, save that Time has gnawed it externally, seems about as stalwart as it was two thousand years ago, and likely to endure as much longer. I should not have observed any difference between it and the Norman or Gothic arches which we see hereabouts; except that it was perhaps a little more roughly built. After viewing this, we went towards the Castle-gate, but could not get in; the Castle, or some part of its precincts, being used as a prison. The gate-way and towers are huge and stalwart, but are closed by a modern gate of wood. We now [10] rambled about on the broad back of the hill, which, besides the Minster and the ruined castle, has many stately and queer old houses, and many mean little hovels; but I suspect that all, or most, of the life of the present day has subsided into the lower town, and that only priests, poor people, and prisoners, dwell in these upper regions.

The day was chill and dim; but, had it been bright and sunny, we might have had a most extensive and delightful prospect, from a street, or terrace, winding along the brow of the hill, and looking out over level Lincoln, and far beyond. As mist blurred it all, however, I may fairly excuse myse[l]f from attempting a description. Above our heads, rose the great, broad, ponderous ruin of the Castle-Keep, heaving its huge gray mass of stone out of a bank of green foliage and ornamental shrubbery, such as lilacs and other flowering plants, in which its foundations were quite hidden. This was very picturesque; the gloomy old Keep bathing its feet in all that flowery verdure. We walked quite round the Castle, the greater part of the circuit being a high wall of stone, battlemented, but modern, and having, as it ought, not so much a [11] castellated as a prison-like aspect. In the wide, dry moat, at the base of the wall, are clustered whole colonies of small houses, some of brick, but a large portion built of old stones which once made part of the Castle, or of Roman structures that existed before William the Conqueror's Castle was dreamed about. I forgot to mention that, within the enclosure of the Keep, are buried the bodies of executed criminals; and I believe they are hanged on its summit. There could not be a better position to publish the deed of retribution, both to earth and heaven. We now—so far as I remember—saw nothing further that was absolutely noteworthy, but came back to the Saracen's Head and got our dinner.

The weather was very unpropitious, and it sprinkled a little, now and then; so that my wife did not go out again. Julian and I took a walk along the High-Street, in the direction opposite to the Cathedral. It is a long, level, village-street, with not many remar[ka]ble houses along it; none particularly so, except an old barnlike edifice of stone, which bears the name of John of Gaunt's stables, but is supposed to have been anciently the Guild hall. At any [12] rate, it is a medi-aeval structure, and seems to be now used as the premises of a coal-dealer. Looking behind me, I could see the Minster, appearing to bet[t]er advantage at a distance than from the foot of the hill; but it appears to me that the largest tower is not sufficiently weighty and massive to give full character to the edifice. It formerly had a spire upon it, as had the two inferior towers; but I believe they were only of wood, and were either taken down or tumbled down. After tea, in the approach of twilight, Julian and I again strolled out, and ascended the hill to get another view of the Cathedral. It was the most impressive view we have had; for a mist was hovering about the upper height of the great central tower, so as to dim and half obliterate its battlements and pinnacles, even when we stood in the close beneath it; though the whole lower part of the edifice was seen with perfect distinctness. It was really and literally a "cloud-capt tower."[418] The whole effect was very grand.

After that, we came back to our hotel; and in the street, beneath our window, there was a great bustle and turmoil of people, all the evening, because it [13] was Saturday night; and they had got through their week's labors, and received their wages, and were enjoying themselves a little, and making their purchases against Sunday. A band of music passed to-and-fro, several times; a spirit-shop, opposite the hotel, was much thronged; and a dealer in hot-coffee sold his commodity in the open air. The whole breadth of the street, between the Stone Bow and the bridge across the Witham, was thronged and overflowing, and humming with human life.

SUNDAY, MAY 24th, LINCOLN.

THE morning opened with decided rain, plashing in the balcony before our parlor window and in the street beneath; so that I employed the early part of the forenoon in writing up my journal. It held up, however, about eleven °clock, and then Julian and I sallied forth; but as he complained that it hurt his stomach to walk, I sent him in, and continued my own ramble up the hill, along its brow, and around the Castle, taking in the view across the wide plain on which [is] the lower town, and which spreads far and near around it. Then I went through the Roman arch, and observed that its rough and broken top is crowned with grass and weeds, and that tufts of yellow flowers grow on projections [14] and spots of vantage up and down its sides. On one side, it is joined to an old brick dwelling house, and on the other to a gabled house of stone, the walls of which look almost as ancient as itself. I walked on a good distance past the Arch, along a pleasant and level road, bordered with dwellings of various character; one or two houses of gentility, with delightful and shadowy lawns before them; many with high, red-tiled roofs, ascending into acutely pointed gables; and some pleasant-looking cottages, very sylvan and rural, with hedges so thick and high, fencing them in, as almost to hide them up to the eaves. Before one of these, I saw various images, crosses, and relics of antiquity, among which were fragments of ancient catholic tombstones, disposed by way of ornament.

After passing a church, I turned back, and again walked round the Cathedral, viewing it unweariedly, and loving it the better the longer I looked. Its exterior is certainly far more beautiful than that of York; and I think its more interesting effect is owing to the many peaks into which the structure ascends, and to the pinnacles which, as it were, repeat and re-echo them. York Minster is too square and angular in its general effect; [15] but here there is a continual mystery of variety; so that there [is] always a change, and a disclosure of something new, yet harmonious, at every step. The West Front is wonderfully and unspeakably grand and rich, and may be read over and over again, and still be new, like a great, broad page of marvellous meaning in black-letter; so many sculptures [are] there, and statues which you did not see before, and empty niches, and a thousand canopies, beneath which carved images used to be, or might have been. I may as well leave it here. Descending the Steep Hill (so is aptly called the street that climbs to the open space before the Exchequer Gate, which fronts the Cathedral,) I returned to the Hotel. The Stone Bow, near which the hotel stands, is the Guildhall; the room used for the meetings of the city-council occupying the space over the arch-way, and looking up and down the street, on either side. On one side of the basement-story, under the arch, is a butcher's stall, and on the other a fishmonger's; and there is a shop built in with the structure of the gateway. It is pleasant to see the old Gothic edifice used in these modern times for such homely [16] purposes. There is a clock, illuminated at night, at the summit of the gate.

This afternoon, it cleared up beautifully, and at five °clock we drove out in a fly, and saw Lincoln and its vicinity, both above and below the hill. It was very delightful, the foliage and verdure being now in the prime of its virgin richness, and the atmosphere fresh and invigorating; but I think I shall here cease trying to describe Lincoln, and begin my ineffectual efforts upon some other site. On our drive back, however, I thought that the castle-keep, and the towers of the Minster, showed to better advantage than ever; for hitherto we had seen them only in one, unvaried, sombre tint; but now the sunshine and shadow were contrasted, and gave them a picturesque effect which we immediately felt (but only felt it now) to have been wanting to their perfect beauty. I never saw anything so stately and so soft as they now appeared.

MONDAY, MAY 24th, BOSTON.

SEEING in a local guide-book, which we bought at Lincoln, that a steamer runs on the river Witham, between Lincoln and Boston, I inquired of the waiter at the Saracen's Head, and learned that she was to [17] start this morning at ten °clock. Thinking it might be an interesting trip, and a good variation of our mode of travel, we determined to adopt it. The Witham flows through Lincoln, and crosses the street under an arched bridge, of Gothic construction, a little below the Saracen's Head. It has more the appearance of a canal, in its passage through the town, than of a river, being bordered with stone on each side, and provided with one or two locks. The waiter had assured me that the Steamer was a very good boat, but she proved to be small, dirty, and altogether inconvenient. The early morning had been bright; but it now looked rather sulky, and we had not long got off before we found an ugly wind blowing right in our teeth. There were a number of passengers on board, country-people, such as would travel by third class on the railway; for I suppose nobody but ourselves ever dreamt of taking the steamer for the sake of what we might happen upon in the way of river-scenery.

We bothered a good while about getting through a preliminary lock; nor, when fairly under way, did we accomplish, I think, six miles an hour. Constant delays were caused, too, by stopping to take up passengers, not [18] at regular landing-places, but anywhere along the banks, where the people chose to come down and beckon to us; also, we stopt about twenty minutes to take in some bundles of willow-twigs for basket-manufacture. With such impediments we were more than six hours on the voyage, and certainly gained no advantage which we might not have had by railway, except the drawling, snail-like sloth-fulness of our progress, which allowed us time enough and to spare for the objects along the banks. The scenery, indeed, was identical with that of the railway; because the latter runs along, throughout the whole distance, by the river-side, or no where departs from it except to make a short cut across some sinuosity. Furthermore, there was nothing, or next to nothing, to be seen; the country being one unvaried level over the whole thirty or forty miles of our passage—not a hill either near or far, except that on the summit of which we had left Lincoln Cathedral. And the Cathedral was our landmark for four hours, or more, and at last rather faded out than was hidden by any intervening object. I never saw a tamer landscape in my life; but it would have been a pleasantly lazy day enough, if the chill and bitter wind had not blown directly in our faces, and chilled us through, in spite of the sunshine that soon suc[19]-ceeded a sprinkle or two of rain. It was, at all events, an English landscape; a green luxuriance of early grass; old, high-roofed farm houses, surrounded by their stone-barns, and ricks of hay and grain; ancient villages, with the square, gray tower of a church seen afar over the level country, in the midst of the red earthen roofs; here and there a shadowy grove of ancient trees, surrounding what was once perhaps a hall, though now it looked more like a farm house; once, too, we saw the tower of an ancient castle, that of Tattershall, built by a Cromwell, but whether of the Protector's family I cannot tell. But the gentry do not seem to have settled multitudinously in this tract of country; nor is it to be wondered at, for a lover of the picturesque would as soon think of settling in Holland. The river retains its canal-like aspect all along, and only in the latter part of its course does it become more than wide enough for the Steamer to turn itself round;—and at broadest, not more than twice that width. We sat despondent on the deck, facing the ill-tempered breeze. My wife took shelter in the cabin during the little shower, but was quickly driven out by nausea. I had one little season of comfort, smoking a cigar in the steerage; otherwise, [20] it was a cheerless day. The only memorable incident, was, when a mother-duck was leading her little fleet of five ducklings across the river, just when our steamer was swaggering by. I saw the imminent catastrophe, and hastened to the stern of the boat to witness, since I could not prevent it. The poor ducklings uttered their baby quacks, and strove with all their might to escape; four of them, I believe, were washed aside and thrown off unhurt from the steamer's prow; but the fifth must have gone under her whole length, and never could have come up alive.

At last, in mid-afternoon, we saw the tall tower of St. Botolph's Church (three hundred feet high, the same elevation as the tallest tower of Lincoln cathedral) looming in the distance. At about half past four, we reached Boston, and were taken by a cab to the Peacock, in the market-place, this being, the Captain of the Steamer told us, the best hotel in town. It seems to be a poor one enough, however; and we were shown into a little, stifled parlour, musty, and smelling of stale tobacco-smoke—tobacco-smoke two days old, for the waiter assured us it had not more recently been smoked in. A very grim waiter he is, and apparently a genuine des[21]cendant of the old Puritans of Boston, who peopled their daughter-city in New England. Having had nothing to eat (save some cakes and biscuits) since breakfast, we got some refreshment of tea, and cold ham and corned beef, and then went out to take a view of St. Botolph's church. Our parlour, by the way, has the one recommendation of looking upon the market-place, and affording a sidelong glimpse of the tall spire. We went into a bookseller's shop and bought some prints of localities in Lincoln and this town, and into a jeweller's shop and bought a gold pen for my wife; then we walked round the noble old church, which I certainly shall not describe, to-night, but perhaps may, tomorrow. The town seems to be very proud of it, and with good cause.

My wife and Julian then returned to the hotel, and I took a ramble by myself about the town; and chance led me towards the river-side, at that part where the port is situated. Here were large buildings of an old fashioned aspect, apparently ware-houses, with high roofs, and windows in them. The Custom House seemed to be accommodated within an ordinary dwelling-house. Two or three large schooners were moored along the river's brink, which had a stone margin; another large and handsome [22] schooner was evidently just finished, rigged, and equipped for her first voyage; the rudiments of another were on the stocks, in a ship-yard bordering the river. Another, while I was looking on, came up the stream, and lowered her mainsail, from a foreign voyage. An old man on the bank hailed her and inquired what her cargo was; but the Lincoln-shire people have a queer accent, and I could not understand the reply. Still another vessel—a good-sized brig—was further down the river, but approaching rapidly under sail. The whole scene made an odd impression of bustle, and sluggishness, and decay, and a little remnant of wholesome life; and I could not but contrast it with the mighty activity of our own Boston, which was once the feeble infant, of this old English town—itself, perhaps, almost stationary ever since that day.

Tuesday, May 26th, Boston.

This being a bright morning, I walked out in the early sunshine (the sun must have been shining nearly four hours, however, for it was eight °clock) and in the first place visited the Church. The market-place of Boston is an irregular square, into one end of which the Chancel of the church slightly projects. The church-yard gates were open and free to all passengers, and the common footway of the [23] townspeople seems to lie to-and-fro across it. It is paved with flat tomb-stones, and there are also raised or altar-tombs, some of which have armorial bearings. One clergyman has caused himself and his wife to be buried right in the middle of the stone-bordered path that traverses the church yard, so that none of the many, who pass along this public way, can help trampling over him and her. The scene was very cheerful in the morning-sun; people going to their labor in the day's primal freshness; children with milk-pails loitering over the burial-stones; the simple old town preparing for its day, that would be like myriads of other days which had passed over it, but yet a day that would be worth living through. And down on the church-yard, where were buried many generations whom it remembered in their day, looked the stately tower; and it is good to think of such an age-long giant, connecting the present epoch with a long past, and getting quite imbued with human nature by being so long connected with men's knowledge and interests. It is a noble tower; and the jackdaws live a delightful life up among its topmost windows, and flitting and cawing about its pinnacles and flying buttresses. I should like to be a jackdaw myself, for the sake of living up there.

[24] In front of the church, not more than twenty yards distant, and with a low brick wall between, flows the river Witham; on the hither bank, a boatman was washing his boat; and another skiff, with her sail lazily half-hoisted, lay on the opposite shore. The stream is about of such width that, if the tall tower were to fall over flat on its face, its top-stone might perhaps reach to the middle channel. On the farther shore, there is a line of antique-looking houses, with roofs of red-tile, and windows opening out of them; some of these dwellings being so ancient, that the Rev. Mr. Cotton must have seen them with his own bodily eyes, when he used to issue from the front portal of the church, after service. Indeed, there must be very many houses here, and even some streets, which bear very much the aspect that they did in his day.

After gazing a little while up at the tower, and across the river, and at the cheerful life and not uncheerful death of the church-yard (it is really a pleasant thing to make an old church-yard an essential part of the public square, as this is) I took a ramble about the outskirts of the town. Returning, I called in at a bookseller's shop to inquire if he had any description of Boston for sale. He offered me (or rather produced, for he did not expect that I would buy it) [25] a quarto history of the town, published by subscription, nearly forty years ago.[419] The bookseller showed himself a well-informed and affable man, and a local antiquary, to whom an inquisitive stranger was a godsend. He has met with several Americans, who have made pilgrimage to this place, and has been in correspondence with others. He showed me several curious old things, and invited me to call by and by, and he would show me some more; and as we have left behind us a letter of introduction from Bennoch to a Boston man, we shall take advantage of this good gentleman's kindness.

The above being written, we set out, at about eleven °clock, to pay our visit to the kind bookseller, whose shop is in a street that passes off from one of the corners of the market-place, and who appeared at its door as we approached. He greeted us in very courteous fashion, and led us immediately through the shop, up stairs into the private part of his establishment. Really, it is one of the rarest adventures I ever met with, to find this treasure of a man, with his treasury of antiquities and curiosities, veiled behind the poor-looking front of a bookseller in a very moderate line of village-business. The two up-stair rooms into which he introduced us were hung round with pictures and old engravings, many of which [26] must have been very valuable. Then, premising that he was going to show us something very curious, he went into the next room and returned with a counterpane of fine linen, elaborately embroidered with silk, which so profusely covered the linen that the general effect was as if the main texture were silken. It was stained, and seemed very old, and had an ancient fragrance. Among other devices of the embroidery were the initials "M.R."—or "M.S." for I am not sure which; but, at all events, "M" was one of the letters; and then he told us that that [sic] this embroidery was done by the hands of Mary Queen of Scots, during her imprisonment at Fotheringay Castle! There can hardly be many more precious relics than this, in the world. As a counterpart, he produced some of the handiwork of a former Queen of Otaheite, who had presented it to Captain Cook. Next he brought out a blue silk embroidered waistcoat, of very antique fashion, and made Julian put it on, telling us that it had been the vestment of Queen Elizabeth's Lord Burleigh; he traced its pedigree, too, if I mistake not, until it came into his hands; but, I must say, I do not consider its authenticity absolutely settled. Then he produced some curiously engraved drinking-glasses, with a view of St. Botolph's steeple on one of them, and other Boston edi[27]fices, public or domestic, on the other two. I think they had been a present from the scholars of an old master of the free-school to their preceptor. He kept bringing out one unexpected and wholly unexpectable thing after another, as if he were a magician; and in old drawings he was especially rich—producing two or three by Raphael, one by Salvator, and others by hands almost as famous; and, besides what he showed us, he seemed to have endless stores in reserve. On the wall, too, hung a crayon drawing of Sterne, never engraved, representing him as rather a young man, blooming and not uncomely; the worldly face of a man fond of pleasure, but without that ugly, keen, sarcastic, odd expression that we see in his only engraved portrait. Yet I fancied a likeness to that one. This portrait—being, as Mr. Porter avers, an original—must needs be very valuable. There was likewise a crayon portrait of Sterne's wife, looking so haughty and unamiable that it is not to be wondered at that he quarrelled with her.

After looking at these, and a great many more things, above stairs, we went down to a parlour, where he introduced us to Mrs. Porter; a plain, kindly woman, who intimated that she did not strongly sympathize with her husband's antiquarian and virtuoso tastes. He now opened a curious old cabi[28]net, with numberless drawers, and looking just fit to be the repository of such knick-knacks as Mr. Porter had stored up in it. He seemed to have more things than he himself knew of, or knew where to find; but rummaging here and there, he brought forth things new and old[420]—rose-nobles, Victoria crowns, double sovereigns of George IV. Two guinea pieces of George II, angels;—marriage medals of Napoleon, only forty-five of which were ever struck off, and of which even the British Museum does not possess one like this, in gold;—an old brass medal, three or four inches in diameter, of some Roman emperor;—together with buckles, bracelets, amulets, and I know not what besides. One of the most curious things (both in itself, and as indication of the possessor's character) was a green silk (I think it was green) tassel from the drapery of Queen Mary's bed, at Holyrood House. This Mr. Porter (with a quiet chuckle, and humorous self-gratulation) told us he had personally stolen; and really, for my part, though I hope I would not have done it myself, I thought it no sin in him—such valuables being attracted by a natural magnetism towards such a man. He obeys, in stealing them, a higher law than he breaks. I should like to know precisely what portion of his rich and rare collection, he has obtained in a similar manner. But far be it from me to speak unkindly or sneeringly of this [29] good man; for he showed us great kindness, and obliged us so much the more by being greatly and evidently pleased with the trouble that he took in our behalf. While we talked together, a great yellow tom[?][421]-cat, looking just like some who used to be inmates of my mother's house, jumped up to the window of the yard, and seemed anxious to be let in. Mrs. Porter seemed to take more interest in this yellow puss than in any of her husband's curiosities; and I took some little, myself.

The jolly bookseller (like most antiquaries, I believe, he looked as if he had a taste for old port,) at length shut up his cabinet, and accompanied us to the Church, showing us an old-fashioned, timber-and-plaster house—one of the few, he said, in what he called the French style, now remaining in Boston. He says that the antiquity of the town has very much diminished, within his memory. I must not leave his house, without recording that I enjoyed its hospitality in the shape of a glass of wine. He is a most pleasant man; rather, I imagine, a virtuoso than an antiquarian; for he seemed to value the Queen of Otaheite's gew-gaw about as much as Queen Mary's embroidered quilt, and to have a showman's omnivorous appetite for everything rare. But it is singular that a [30] private individual, in a humble rank of life, should have amassed such a collection; and an odd coincidence that I, just when I needed such a man, should chance to stumble upon him. Leaving his house with him (it was an old house, small and comfortable, low-studded, and built around a little court-yard) he led us—as I began to say—to the Church. On one side of the right-hand aisle, they are restoring an ancient chapel, which is to be dedicated to John Cotton (founder of our American Boston) and will contain a painted, memorial window, dedicated to him. There is to to [sic] [be] a celebration of this event, here, next July; to which I have been invited by Mr. Pishey Thomson, of this town. On the pathway through the church-yard, two gentlemen stood talking, one of whom Mr. Porter told us was the present vicar of Boston. Here, I remember, that, before showing us the Cotton chapel, Mr. Porter pointed out to us the vicarage, an old brick dwelling bordering on the church-yard, and then led us to a vacant spot of ground where old John Cotton's dwelling stood till within a very short time since. According to Mr. Porter's description, it was a humble habitation, of the cottage order, of brick, and, I think, with a thatched roof—though more probably, of late years, with an earthen tiled one. Before the present vicarage was built, it was probably situated [31] on the border of the church-yard. It was now rudely fenced in, and weed-grown.

After we emerged from the Cotton chapel, Mr. Porter approached us with the vicar, to whom he had been speaking, and to whom he now introduced us. He was a gentleman of about thirty, comfortable and well-to-do, evidently a scholar, a Christian, and a man who takes life easily and makes the most of it, without prejudice to the life to come. Mr. Porter now took his leave; and the vicar accompanied us into the Church, the interior of which we found very fine and satisfactory—stately, chaste, and repaired—so far as repairs had been necessary—in a noble taste. The eastern window was of modern painted glass, but the richest and tenderest modern window that I have ever seen. From vestibule to Chancel, there was nothing to break the long vista of the church, which was almost a Cathedral, and had such garniture of carved oak as I have only seen elsewhere in Cathedrals. Around the walls, there were old engraved brasses, and a stone coffin, and a marble knight of Saint John, and a marble lady, each recumbent at full length, and many things else of the monumental kind. The vicar now took his leave, and Julian and I essayed to climb the lofty tower, leaving mamma to repose and medi[32]tate in the church below. Up we went, winding and winding around the circular stairs in the corner of the tower, till we came to the gallery beneath the stone-roof of the tower, where we could look down and see the font, and my Talma lying on one of the steps, where I had left it, and looking about as big as a pocket-handkerchief. We called to mamma; but she had gone into the chancel, and could neither see nor hear us. Then up again, up, up, up, through yet a smaller staircase, till we emerged into another stone-gallery, above the jackdaws, and far above the roof, beneath which we had before made a halt. Then up another flight, which led us into a pinnacle, but not into the highest tower; so retracing our steps, we took the right turret, this time, and emerged into the highest lantern, whence we saw level Lincolnshire, far and near, with a haze on the circular horizon, and dusty roads, and a river, and canals, converging towards Boston, which—a congregation of red-tiled roofs—lay beneath our feet, with pigmy people creeping to-and-fro beneath it. Having seen this, we des[c]ended the corkscrew turret-stairs, (winding round till it set Julian's head a spinning) and found Mamma still sitting in the Chancel. We left her there, and returned to the Hotel, where, about two °clock, she joined us.

[33] At half past two we dined, and afterwards Mamma and Julian took a drive about the neighborhood, and I walked away by myself, crossing the river by a bridge above the church; going a considerable distance up the river, and then down along its bank opposite the church, and so gaining an excellent view of the tower. Then I rambled about the town, on that side, and that [sic] the larger part of Boston seemed to be there; and the crooked streets and narrow lanes reminded me much of the North End of American Boston—Hanover street and Ann street—as I remember that region in my early days. It is singular what a home-feeling, and sense of kindred, this connection of our New England metropolis gives me, and how reluctant I am to leave this old town, on that account. It is not unreasonable to suppose that the local habits and recollections of the first settlers may have had some influence on the physical character of the streets and houses in our Boston; at any rate, here is a similar intricacy, and numbers of the same old peaked and projecting-storied dwellings, some of which I used to see there.

This was a very warm and pleasant afternoon, and continued so into the evening. After supper, Julian and I walked out again, and got a letter at the Post Office from Una, and then sauntered down by the river-side, where the sea-faring [34] people were leaning on the railings, and sitting on planks under the lee of warehouses, as they are accustomed to do in sea-ports of little business; and the boys were sailing boats in the river, and the young girls and women chatting, and children playing about in the summer twilight, and all apparently idle and happy enough. They give one the idea of taking life easily and comfortably here. I saw boys playing marbles, to day, across the flat tombstones in the church-yard. I think I shall not write anything more about Boston, except that we saw a small bird in the church, which seemed to be at home and familiar there. I will likewise record, that £500 has been contributed by persons in the United States, principally in Boston, towards the repair and restoration of the side-chapel which is to be dedicated to John Cotton's memory. By the by, on looking again at the site of his dwelling, I see that it is not weed-grown (as I believe I stated) but a carefully kept vegetable garden. To reach it, the passage is under an archway, through some charity houses, and it is situated in the rear of the present vicarage. It is singular how many errors one makes in his first hasty sketch and narrative of observation and travel; but yet there is a truth in these earliest impressions, perhaps more vivid than any one better acquainted with the subject could [35] attain. Among my impressions of Boston, I must mention that, as in other old towns, I have been struck by the frequency of ancient men about the streets; but it might well happen that this sunny day has brought them out. Another feature is the charity scholars, who walk about in antique blue coats and knee breeches, and with bands at their necks, perfect and grotesque pictures of the costume of a century or two ago.

WEDNESDAY, MAY 27th, BOSTON.

THIS morning (a sunny one) when I looked into the market-place from our parlor-window, its irregular space was already well covered with booths, and more were being put up; poles, covered with sailcloth—it being market-day. The dealers were arranging their ware, consisting chiefly of vegetables, the bulk of which seemed to be cabbages. Later in the forenoon, there is a much greater variety of merchandise—basket-work, both for fancy and use; twig-brooms, beehives, oranges, rustic attire; and all sorts of things that are ever sold in a rural fair. I heard the lowing of cattle, too, and the bleat of sheep; and there is a market of cows, oxen, and pigs, in another part of the town. I strolled round the church, again, and noticed that there were originally two statues, on one [sic] each side of the door-way under the tower, the canopies still remaining, and the pedestals being about a yard from the ground. [36] This door way is now much dilapidated, but must once have been very rich, and of a peculiar fashion. The door opens its archway through a great square tablet of stone, reared against the front of the tower. On all the projections about the church there are gargoyles of true Gothic grotesqueness—fiends, beasts, angels, and combinations of all three. In restoring portions of the edifice, the modern sculptors have tried to imitate these fantasies, but with very poor success. I shall here drop Boston, which we shall leave for Peterborough a little after noon.⁴²²

PETERBOROUGH, ¼ 9 °CLOCK, P.M. WE left Boston by railway at 12:25, and arrived here in about an hour and a quarter, and have put up at the Railway Hotel; a hotel of the modern fashion, rather resembling American hotels than the old-world ones at which we have lived since leaving home. At about four °clock, after dinner, we walked into the town to see the Cathedral, of the towers and arches of which we had already had a glimpse from our parlor-window. Perhaps I ought to say something of our journey from Boston hitherward; it was through a perfectly level country—the fens of Lincolnshire—green, green, and nothing else, with old villages and farm houses, and old church-towers; very pleasant, and rather wearisomely monotonous. To return to Peterborough, it is a town of ancient aspect; and [37] we passed, on our way towards the market-place, a very ancient looking church, with a very far-projecting porch, opening in front and on each side through arches of broad sweep. The street, by which we approached from our hotel, led us into the market-place, which had what looked like an old Guild hall on one side. On the opposite side, above the houses, appeared the towers of the Cathedral; and a street leads from the market-place to its front through an arched gate-way, which, I suppose, used to be the external entrance of the Abbey, of which the Cathedral was formerly the church. The front of this Cathedral is very striking, and unlike any other that I have seen; being formed by three lofty and majestic arches, in a row, with three gable-peaks above them, forming a sort of colonnade, within which is the western entrance of the nave. The towers are massive, but low in proportion to their bulk; there are no spires, but pinnacles, and statues, and all the rich detail of Gothic architecture, the whole of a venerable gray hue. It seemed in perfect repair, and not to have suffered, externally, except by the loss, no doubt, of multitudes of statues, gargoyles, and miscellaneous eccentricities of sculpture, which used to smile, frown, laugh, and weep, over the faces of these old structures.

[38] We entered through a side portal, and sat down on a bench in the Nave, and kept ourselves quiet, for the organ was playing and the choristers were chanting in the choir. The Nave and transepts are very noble, with clustered pillars, and Norman arches, and a great height under the central-tower; the whole, however, being covered with plaster and whitewash, except the roof, which is of painted oak. This latter adornment has the merit, I believe, of being veritably ancient; but certainly I should prefer the oak of its native hue, for the effect of the paint is to make it appear as if the cieling [sic] were covered with imitation mosaic-work, or an oil-cloth carpet.

After sitting a while, we were invited by a verger, who came from within the screen, to enter the choir and hear the rest of the service. We found the choristers there, in their white garments, and an audience of some half a dozen people, and had time to look at the interior of the choir. All the carved woodwork of the tabernacle, the bishop's throne, the prebendal stalls, and whatever else, is modern; for this Cathedral seems to have suffered terribly from Cromwell's soldiers, who hacked and hewed at the old oak, and hammered and pounded upon the marble tombs, till nothing of [39] the first, and very few of the latter, remain. It is wonderful how suddenly the English people lost their sense of the sanctity of all manner of externals in religion, without losing their religion too. The French, in their Revolution, underwent as sudden a change; but they became pagans and atheists, and threw away the substance with the shadow. I suspect that the interior arrangement of the choir and the chancel has been greatly modernized; for it is quite unlike anything that I have seen elsewhere. Instead of one vast eastern window, there are rows of windows, lighting the Lady-Chapel, and seen through rows of arches in the screen of the chancel; the effect being, whoever is to have the credit of it, very rich and beautiful. There is, I think, no stained glass in the windows of the nave, though some of recent date, and some fragments of veritable antique, in the windows of the chancel. The effect of the whole interior is grand, expansive, and both ponderous and airy; not dim, mysterious, and contracted, as Gothic interiors often are, the roundness and openness of the arches being opposed to this latter effect.

When the chanting came to a close, a verger took his stand at the entrance of the choir, and another stood further [40] up the aisle, and then the door of a pew opened—a prebendal stall, rather—and forth came a clerical dignity, of much breadth and substance, and aged and infirm—and was ushered out of the choir with a great deal of ceremony. We took him for the bishop, but he proved to be only a canon. We now engaged an attendant to show us through the Lady Chapel, and the other penetralia, which it did not take him long to accomplish. One of the first things he showed us was the tombstone, in the pavement of the southern aisle, beneath which Mary Queen of Scots had been originally buried, and where she lay a quarter of a century, till borne to her present resting-place in Westminster Abbey. It is a plain marble slab, with no inscription. Near this, there was a Saxon monument of the date of 870, with sculpture in relief upon it; the memorial of an abbot Hedda, who was killed by the Danes when they destroyed the monastery that preceded the abbey and church. I remember, likewise, a recumbent figure of a prelate, whose face has been quite obliterated by puritanic violence; and I think that there is not a single tomb, older than the parliamentary wars, which has not been in like manner battered and shattered; except the Saxon abbot's, just measured [mentioned]. The most pretentious monument remaining is that of a Mr. Deacon, a gen[41]tleman of George I'st's time, in wig and breeches, leaning on his elbow, and resting one hand upon a scull [sic]. In the north aisle, precisely opposite to that of Queen Mary, the attendant pointed out to us (by putting his foot on it,) the slab beneath which lie the ashes of Catherine of Aragon, the divorced queen of Henry VIII. There was an old stone coffin or two, and little or nothing else of special interest in this part of the Cathedral.

In the Nave, the attendant showed us the ancient font, a venerable and beautiful relic, which has been repaired not long ago, but in such a way as not to violate its individuality. This sacred vessel suffered especial indignity from Cromwell's soldiers; insomuch that if anything could possibly destroy its sanctity, they would have effected that bad end. On the eastern wall of the Nave, and near the entrance, hangs the picture of old Scarlett, the Sexton, who buried both Mary of Scotland and Catherine of Aragon, and not only these two queens, but everybody else in Peterborough twice over. I think one feels a sort of enmity and spite against these grave diggers, who live so long, and seem to contract a sort of kindred and partnership with Death, being booncompanions with him, and taking his part against mankind. In a chapel, or some side apartment, there were two pieces [42] of tapestry, wretchedly faded, having been the handiwork of two nuns, and copied from two of Raphael's cartoons. There was nothing else to show us; for the Chapter House was destroyed—no doubt by those devilish soldiers of Cromwell.

We now emerged from the Cathedral, and walked round its exterior, admiring it to our utmost capacity, and all the more because we had heard little or nothing of it beforehand, and expected to see nothing so huge, majestic, grand, and gray. And of all the lovely churchyards that I ever beheld, that of Peterborough Cathedral seems to me the most delightful; so quiet it is, so solemnly and nobly cheerful, so verdant, so sweetly shadowed, and so presided over by the noble Minster, and surrounded by quiet, ancient, and comely habitations of Christian men. The most delightful place, the most enviable as a residence, in all this world, seemed to me that of the Bishop's secretary, standing in the rear of the Cathedral, and bordering on the churchyard; so that you seem to pass through hallowed precincts in order to come at it, and find it a sort of Paradise, the holier and sweeter for the dead men that sleep so near. We looked through the gateway into the lawn, which really looked as if it hardly belonged to this world, so bright and soft the sunshine was, so fresh the grass, so lovely [43] the trees, so trained and refined, and softened down, was the whole nature of the spot; and so shut in and guarded from all intrusion. It is in vain to write about it; nowhere but in England can there be such a spot, nor anywhere but in the the [*sic*] close of Peterborough Cathedral.

MAY 28th, PETERBOROUGH.

I WALKED up into the town, about eight °clock, this morning (an overcast, and rather chill, east-windy morning) and again visited the Cathedral. On the way, I observed the "Falcon Inn," a very old-fashioned hostelry, with a thatched roof, and what looked like the barn-door, or stable-door, in a side-front. Very likely it may have been an Inn ever since Queen Elizabeth's time. The Guild Hall (as I suppose it to be) in the market-place, has a basement-story entirely open on all sides, but from its upper story it seems to communicate with a large, old house in the rear. I have not seen an older-looking town than Peterborough; but there is little that is picturesque about it, except within the precincts of the Cathedral. It was very fortunate for the beauty and antiquity of those precincts, that Henry VIII did not suffer the monkish edifices of the Abbey to be overthrown and utterly destroyed, as was the case with so many Abbeys, at the Reformation; but, converting the Abbey church into a Cathedral, he seems to have preserved much of the other arrangement of [44] the buildings connected with it. And so it happens that, to this day, we have the massive and stately gateway, with its great pointed arch, still keeping out the world from those who have inherited the habitations of the old monks; for though the gate is never closed, one feels himself in a sacred seclusion, the instant he passes under the archway. And everywhere, there are old houses that appear to have been adapted from the monkish residences, or from their spacious offices, and made into convenient dwellings for ecclesiastics, or vergers, or great or small people connected with the Cathedral; and, with all modern comfort, they still retain much of the quaintness of the elder time—arches, even rows of arcades, pillars, walls beautified with patches of Gothic sculpture, not wilfully put on by modern taste, but lingering from a long past; deep niches, let into the fronts of houses, and occupied by images of saints; a growth of ivy overspreading walls, and just allowing the windows to peep through; so that no novelty, nor anything of our hard, ugly, or actual life, comes into these limits, through the defences of the gateway, without being modified and mollified. Except in some of the old colleges of Oxford, I have not seen any other place that impressed me in this way; and the precincts of Peterborough Cathedral have the advantage over even the Oxford colleges, inasmuch as the life is here [45] domestic, that of the family, that of the affections—a natural life, which, one deludes oneself with imagining, may be made into something sweeter and purer in this beautiful spot than anywhere else. Doubtless, the inhabitants find it a stupid and tiresome place enough, and get morbid, and sulky, and heavy, and obtuse of head and heart, with the monotony of their life. But still, I must needs believe that a man with a full mind, and objects to employ his affection, might be very happy here. And perhaps the forms and appliances of human life are never fit to make people happy, until they cease to be used for the purposes for which they were directly intended, and are taken, as it were, in a sidelong application. I mean that the old monks, probably, never enjoyed their own edifices, while they were a part of the actual life of the day, so much as these present inhabitants now enjoy them, when a new use has grown up apart from the original one.

½ past 2, P.M. Peterborough. At eleven °clock, we all walked into the town again, and, on our way, went into the old church, with the projecting portal, which I mentioned yesterday. A woman came hastening with the keys, when she saw us looking up at the door. The interior had an exceeding musty smell, and looked very ancient, with side aisles opening by a row of pointed arches into the nave, and a gallery on each side, of wood, and built across the two rows of arches. [46] It was paved with tombstones, and I suppose the dead people contributed to the antique fragrance; very naked and unadorned it was, except with a few mural monuments of no great interest. We staid but a little while, and amply rewarded the poor woman with a sixpence. Thence we proceeded to the Cathedral, pausing by the way to look at the old Guildhall, which is no longer a Guildhall, but a butter-market; and then we bought some prints of exterior and interior views of the Cathedral, of which there are a great variety, on note-paper, letter-sheets, large engravings, and lithographs. We have likewise bought two Guides; and with these, and our personal inspection, ought to have some little acquaintance with the Cathedral. It is very beautiful; there seems to be nothing better than to say this over again. We found the doors most hospitably open, and every part of the edifice entirely free to us; a kindness and liberality which we have nowhere else experienced (whether as regards Cathedrals or whatever other public building) in England. My wife sat down to draw the font, and I walked through the Lady Chapel all by myself, pausing over the empty bed of Queen Mary, and the grave of Queen Catherine; and looking at the rich and beautiful roof, where a fountain, as it were, of groins of arches spouts from numberless pilasters, and intersect one another in glorious [47] intricacy. This, I believe, is modern. Under the central tower, opening to either transept, to the Nave, and to the choir, are four majestic arches, which I think must equal in height those of which I saw the ruins, and one all but perfect, at Furness Abbey. They are about eighty feet high.

I may as well give up Peterborough here; though I hate to leave it undescribed, even to the tufts of yellow flowers which grow on the projections, high out of reach, where the winds have sown their seeds in soil made by the aged decay of the edifice. I could write a page, too, about the rooks or jackdaws (for I know not which they are) that flit and clamor about the pinnacles, and dart in and out of the eyelet-holes, the windows, the piercings, whatever they are called, in the turrets and buttresses. On our way back to the hotel, Julian saw an advertisement of some knights in armor that were to tilt to-day; so he and I waited, and by and by a procession appeared, passing through the antique market-place, and in front of the abbey-gateway, which might have befitted the same spot, three hundred years ago. They were about twenty men-at-arms on horseback, with lances and banners. We were a little too near for the full enjoyment of the spectacle; for, though some of the armor seemed real, I could not help observing that other suits were made of silver paper, or gold [48] tinsel. A policeman (a queer anomaly in reference to such a mediaeval spectacle) told me that they were going to joust and run at the ring, in a field a little beyond the bridge.

MAY 28th ½ PAST 9, P.M. NOTTINGHAM.

WE left Peterborough at ½ past four, this afternoon; and however reluctant to leave the Cathedral, we were glad to get away from the Railway Hotel; for, though outwardly pretentious, it is a wretched and uncomfortable place, with scanty table, poor attendance, and enormous charges. The first stage of our journey, to-day, was to Grantham, through a country the greater part of which was as level as the Lincolnshire landscapes have been, throughout our experience of them. We saw several old villages, gathered round their several churches; and one, at least, of these little communities—"Little Byforth," I think it was called—had a very primitive appearance; a group of twenty or thirty dwellings, of stone and thatch, without a house among them that could be so modern as a hundred years. It is a little wearisome to think of people living from century to century in the same spot, going in and out of the same doors, cultivating the same fields, meeting the same faces, and marrying one another over and over again; and going to the same church, and lying down in the same churchyard—to appear again and go [49] through the same monotonous round in the next generation.

At Grantham, our route branched off from the main line; and there was a delay of about an hour, during which we walked up into the town to take a nearer view of a tall, gray steeple, which we saw from the Railway station. The streets that led from the station were poor and commonplace; and, indeed, a railway seems to have the effect of making its own vicinity mean. We noticed nothing remarkable until we got to the market-place, in the centre of which there is a market-cross, doubtless of great antiquity, though it is in too good condition not to have been recently repaired. It consists of an upright pillar, with a pedestal of half-a-dozen stone steps, which are worn hollow by the many feet that have scraped their hob-nailed shoes upon them. Among these feet, it is highly probable, may have been those of Sir Isaac Newton, who was a scholar at the free-school in this town; and when Julian scampered up the steps, we told him so. Visible from the market place, likewise, stands the Angel Inn, which seems to be a wonderfully old establishment, being adorned with gargoyles and other antique sculpture, and with projecting windows, and with [50] an arched entrance, and presenting altogether a frontispiece of so much venerable state, that I feel curious to know its history. Had I been aware that the chief hotel of Grantham was such a time-honored establishment, I should have arranged to pass the night there; especially as there were interesting objects enough in the town to occupy us pleasantly. The church—the steeple of which is seen over the market-place, but is removed from it by a street or two—is very fine; the tower and spire being adorned with arches, and canopies and niches—twelve of the latter, for the twelve apostles, all of whom have now vanished—and with fragments of other Gothic ornaments. The jackdaws had taken up their abodes in the crevices and crannies of the upper half of the steeple.

We left Grantham at nearly seven, and reached Nottingham just before eight. The castle, situated on a high and precipitous rock, right over the edge of which look the walls, was visible as we drove from the station to our hotel. We followed the advice of a railway attendant in going first to the May Pole, which proved to be a commercial inn, with the air of a drinking-shop, in a by-alley; and, furthermore, they could not take us in. So we drove to the "George the Fourth", which seems to be an excellent house; and here I [51] have remained quiet, the size of the town discouraging [me] from going out, in the twilight which was just coming on, after tea. These are glorious long days for travel; daylight fairly between four in the morning and nine at night, and a margin of twilight on either side.

MAY 29th, FRIDAY, NOTTINGHAM.

AFTER breakfast, this morning, I wandered out and lost myself, but at last found the Post Office, and a letter from Mr. Wilding with some perplexing intelligence. Nottingham is an unlovely and uninteresting town. The castle I did not see; but I happened upon a large and stately old church, almost cathedralic in its dimensions. On returning to the hotel, I found my wife deliberating on the mode of getting to Newstead Abbey; and we finally decided on taking a one-horse fly; in which conveyance, accordingly, we set out at about a quarter before twelve. It was a slightly overcast day, about half intermixed of shade and sunshine, and rather cool, but not so cool that we could exactly wish it warmer. Our drive to Newstead lay through what was once a portion of Sherwood Forest, though all of it, I believe, has now become private property, and is converted into fertile fields, except where the owners of estates have set out plantations. We have now passed out of the fen-country, and the land rises and falls in gentle swells, presenting a pleasant, but not striking character of scenery. [52] I remember no remarkable object on the road; here and there an old inn; a single gentleman's seat, of moderate pretension; a great deal of tall and untrimmed hedge-fence; a quiet English greenness and rurality; till, drawing near Newstead, we began to see copious plantations principally of firs, larches, and trees of that order, looking very sombre, though with some intermixture of lighter foliage. It was, I think, about ½ past one, when we reached "The Hut", a small, modern wayside Inn, almost directly across the road from the entrance gate of Newstead Abbey. The post-boy calls the distance ten miles from Nottingham.

The post-boy averred that it was forbidden to drive visitors within the grounds; so we left the fly at the Inn, and set out to walk from the entrance-gate to the house. There is no porter's lodge; and the grounds, in this outlying region, had not the appearance of being very trimly kept, but were well wooded with evergreens, and much overgrown with ferns, serving for cover to hares which scampered in and out of their hiding places. The road went winding gently along, and, at the distance of nearly a mile, brought us to a second gate, through which we likewise passed, and walked onward a good way farther, seeing much wood, but as yet nothing of the Abbey. At last, through the trees, we caught a glimpse of its [53] battlements, and saw, too, the gleam of water; and then appeared the Abbey's venerable front. It comprises the western wall of the church, which is all that remains of that edifice; a great central window, entirely empty, without tracery or mullions; the ivy clambering up on the inside of the wall, and hanging over in front. The front of the inhabited part of the house extends along on a line with this church-wall, rather low, with battlements along its top, and all in good keeping with the ruinous remnant. We met a servant, who replied civilly to our enquiries about the mode of gaining admittance, and bade us ring a bell at the corner of the principal entrance-porch. We rang accordingly, and were forthwith let into a low, vaulted basement, ponderously wrought with intersecting arches, dark and rather chilly, just like what I remember to have seen at Battle Abbey; and after waiting here a little while, a respectable elderly gentlewoman appeared, of whom we requested to be shown round the Abbey. She courteously acceded, first presenting us with a book in which I inscribed our names.

I suppose ten thousand people (three-fourths of them Americans) have written descriptions of Newstead Abbey; and none of them, so far as I have read, give any true idea of the place; neither will my description, if I write one. In fact, I forget very much that I saw, and especially [54] in what order the objects came. In the basement, was Byron's bath, a dark, and cold, cellar-like hole, which it must have required good courage to plunge into; in this region, too, or near it, was the Chapel, which Colonel Wildman has decorously fitted up, and where service is now regularly performed, but which was used as a dog-kennel in Byron's time. After seeing this, we were led to Byron's own bedchamber, which remains just as when he slept in it, the furniture, as well as all the other arrangements, being religiously preserved. It was in the plainest possible style—homely, indeed, and almost mean—an

ordinary paper-hanging, and everything so common-place that it was only
the deep embrasure of the window that made the place look unlike a bed-
chamber in a middling-class lodging-house. It would have seemed difficult,
beforehand, to fit up a room in that picturesque old edifice so that it should
be utterly devoid of picturesqueness; but it was effected in Byron's bedchamber;
and I suppose it is a specimen of the way in which old mansions used to be
robbed of their antique character, and adapted to modern tastes, before
mediaeval antiquities came into fashion. Some prints of the Cambridge colleges, and other pictures indicating Byron's predilections at the time, and which
he himself had hung there, were on the walls. This, the housekeeper told us,
had been the Abbot's chamber, in the monastic time. Adjoining it is the
haunted chamber, where the ghostly monk, whom Byron [55] introduces into
Don Juan,[423] is said to have his lurking-place. The chamber is fitted up in
the same style as Byron's, and used to be occupied by his valet. No doubt, in
his lordship's day, these were the only comfortable chambers in the Abbey;
and by the housekeeper's account of what Colonel Wildman has done, it is
to be inferred that the place must have been in a most wild, shaggy, tumble-
down condition, inside and out, when he bought it.

It is very different now. After showing us these two chambers of Byron and
his servant, the housekeeper led us from one to another, and another, magnificent chamber, fitted up in antique style, with oak panelling, and heavily carved
bedsteads of Queen Elizabeth's time, or of the Stuarts, hung with rich tapestry-
curtains of similar date, and with beautiful old cabinets, of carved wood,
sculptured in relief, or tortoise-shell and ivory; very pictures and realities, the
apartments were, of stately comfort; and they were called by the names of
Kings;—King Edward's chamber—King Charles II's chamber—King Henry
VII's chamber. They were hung with beautiful pictures, many of them portraits of historic people. The chimney-pieces were carved and emblazoned; and
all, so far as I could judge, was in perfect keeping, so that if a prince or noble
of three centuries ago were to come to lodge at Newstead Abbey, he would
hardly know that he had strayed out of his own century. And yet he might
have known by one token; for [56] there are volumes of poetry and light literature on the tables in some of these royal bedchambers, and in that of Henry the
Seventh, I saw the "House of the Seven Gables, and the Scarlet Letter, in
Routledge's cheap edition.

Certainly, the house is admirably fitted up; and there must have been something very excellent and comprehensive in the domestic arrangements of the
monks, since they adapt themselves so well to a state of society entirely different from that in which they originated. The library is a very comfortable
room, and provocative of studious ideas, though lounging and luxurious; it is
long, and rather low, furnished with soft couches, and, on the whole, though
a man might dream of study, I think he would be most likely to read nothing
but novels. I know not what this room was, in monkish times, but it was waste
and ruinous in Lord Byron's. Either here, or in some other room, the house-

keeper unlocked a beautiful cabinet, and took out the famous skull which Byron transformed into a drinking-goblet. It has a silver rim and stand; but still the ugly skull is bare and evident, and the naked inner bone receives the wine. I should think it would hold at least a quart,—enough to overpower any living head into which this death's head should transfer its contents; and a man must be either very drunk, or very thirsty, before he would taste wine out of such a goblet. I think Byron's [57] freak was outdone by that of a cousin of my own, who once solemnly assured me that he had a spittoon made out of the skull of one of his enemies. The ancient coffin, in which the goblet-skull was found, was shown us in the basement of the Abbey.

There was much more to see, in the house, than I had any previous notion of; but, except the two bedchambers already noticed, nothing remained in the least as Byron left it; yes, one other place there was, his own small dining-room, with a table of moderate size, where, no doubt, the skull-goblet has often gone its rounds. Colonel Wildman's dining-room was Byron's shooting-gallery, and the original refectory, the housekeeper says, of the monks; it is now magnificently arranged, with a vaulted roof, a music gallery at one end, suits of armor and weapons on the walls, and mailed arms extended, holding candelabras. There is one—I think, two—pointed windows, commemorative of the peninsular war, and the battles in which the Colonel and his two brothers fought; for these Wildmen seem to have been mighty troopers, and Colonel Wildman is represented as a fierce-looking, mustachioed hussar, at two different ages. The housekeeper spoke of him affectionately, but says that he is now getting into years, and that they fancy him failing. He has no children. He appears to have been on good terms with Byron, and had the latter ever re[58]turned to England, he was under promise to make his first visit to his old home; and it was [in] such an expectation, that Colonel Wildman had kept Byron's private apartments in the same condition in which he found them. Byron was informed of all the Colonel's fittings up and restorations, and, when he introduces the Abbey, in Don Juan, the poet describes it, not as he himself left it, but as Colonel Wildman has restored it. There is a beautiful drawing-room; and all these apartments are adorned with pictures, the collection being especially rich in portraits by Sir Peter Lely, that of Nell Gwyn (one of the few beautiful women whom I have seen on canvas) being one.

We parted with the housekeeper (and I with a good many shillings) at the door by which we entered; and our next business was to see the private grounds and gardens. A little boy attended us through the first part of our progress; but then appeared the veritable gardener, a shrewd and sensible old man, who seems to have been very many years on the place. There was nothing of special interest, as concerning Byron, until we entered the original old monkish garden, which is still laid out in the same fashion as the monks left it, with a large oblong piece of water in the centre, and terraced banks rising at two or three different [59] stages, with perfect regularity, around it; so that the sheet of water looks like the plate of an immense looking glass, of which the terraces form the frame. It seems as if, were there any giant large enough, he might raise up this mirror and set it on end. In the monks' garden there is a marble statue of Pan, which, the gardener told us, was brought by the "wicked lord" (Byron's great uncle) from Italy, and was supposed by the country people to represent the devil, and to be the object of his worship; a natural idea enough, in view of his horns, and cloven feet, and tail, though this indicates, at all events, a very jolly devil. There is also a female statue, beautiful from the waist upward, but shaggy and cloven-footed below, and holding a little cloven-footed child by the hand. This the old garden[er] assured us was Pandora, wife of the above-mentioned Pan, with her son. Not far from this spot, we came to the tree on which Byron carved his own name and that of his sister Augusta. It is a tree of two twin-stems—a beech-tree, I think—growing up, side by side. One of the stems still lives and flourishes, but that on which he carved the two names is quite dead, as if there had been something fatal in the inscription that has made it forever famous. The names are still very legible, although the letters had partly [60] been closed up by the growth of the bark, before the tree died. They must have been deeply cut, at first.

There are old yew trees, of unknown antiquity, in this garden, and many other interesting things; and among them may be reckoned a fountain of very pure water, called the Holy Well, of which we drank. There are several fountains, besides the large mirror in the centre of the garden; and these are mostly inhabited by carp, the genuine descendants of those who peopled the fish-ponds in the days of the monks. Coming in front of the Abbey, the gardener showed us the oak that Byron planted, now a vigorous young tree, and the monument which he erected to his Newfoundland dog, and which is larger than most Christians get; being composed of a marble altar-shaped tomb, surrounded by a circular area of steps, as much as twenty feet in diameter. The gardener said, however, that Byron intended this not merely as the burial-place of his dog, but for himself, too, and his sister. I know not how this may have been; but this inconvenience would have attended his being buried there, that, on transfer of the estate, his mortal remains would have become the property of some other man.

We had now come to the empty space—a smooth green [61] lawn, where had once been the abbey-church. Its length, the gardener said, had been sixty-four yards. Within his remembrance, there had been many remains of it, but now they are quite removed, with the exception of the one ivy grown western wall, which, as I mentioned, forms a picturesque part of the present front of the Abbey. Through a door in this wall the gardener now let us out. My wife found that the walk to the Hut would be rather too much for her; so I left her and Julian at the second gateway, and returned alone to the Hut, whence I sent our post-boy to take them up. Meantime I drank some ale, and looked at some engravings on the wall, one of Colonel Wildman, and another of the guests at the Waterloo banquet, where I suppose the Colonel figured.

In the evening, our landlady (who seems to be [a] very intelligent woman of a superior class to most landladies) came into our parlor, and talked about the present race of Byrons and Lovelaces, who have often been at our [her] house. There seems to be a taint in the Byron blood, which makes those who inherit it wicked, mad, and miserable. Lady Lovelace, Byron's daughter, was a strangely eccentric woman, and gambled immensely, losing £40,000 at one time. Her [62] sons are dissolute young men. The present Lord Byron is poor, and his heir is either insane or imbecile. Even Colonel Wildman comes in for a share of this ill-luck; for he has almost ruined himself by his expenditures on the estate, and by his lavish hospitality, especially to the Duke of Sussex, who liked the Colonel and used often to visit him during his lifetime; and the Duke's gentlemen ate and drank Colonel Wildman almost up. So says our good landlady. At any rate, looking at this miserable race of Byrons, who held the estate so long, and at Colonel Wildman, whom it has ruined in forty years, we might see grounds for believing in the evil fate which is supposed to attend confiscated church-property. Nevertheless, I would accept the estate, were it offered me.

While we were looking at the names carved on the tree, the gardener told us that, when Barnum was there, he offered £500, just for that little piece of dead tree on which the names are cut.[424] The gardener himself was the bearer of the proposal to Colonel Wildman, who replied that £5000 would not buy the piece of wood, and that Barnum ought to have been flogged for proposing it. Glancing back, I see that I have omitted some items that were curious, in describing the house; for instance, one of the cabinets had been the personal property of Queen Eliza[63]beth. It seems to me that the fashions of modern furniture have nothing to equal these old cabinets, for beauty and convenience. In the state-apartments, the floors were so highly waxed and polished, that we slid on them, as if on ice, and could only make sure of our footing by treading on strips of carpeting that were laid down.

SUNDAY, JUNE 7th, SOUTHPORT.

WE left Nottingham on Saturday (a week ago, yesterday) and made our first stage to Derby, where we had to wait an hour or two at a great, bustling, pell-mell, crowded railway-station. It was much thronged with second and third class passengers, coming and departing in continual trains; for these were the Whitsuntide holidays, which seem to set all the lower orders of English people astir. This time of festival was evidently the origin of the old " 'Lection" holidays, in Massachusetts; the latter occurring at the same period of the year, and being celebrated (so long as they were so) in very much the same way, with games, idleness, merriment of set purpose, and drunkenness. After a weary while, we took the train for Matlock, via Ambergate, and arrived at the former place late in the afternoon. The village of Matlock is situated on the banks of the Derwent, in a delightful little nook among the hills, which rise above it in steeps, and [64] in precipitous crags, and shut out the world so effectually that I wonder how the railway ever found it out. Indeed, it does make its approach to this region through a long tunnel. It was a beautiful, sunny afternoon, when we arrived; and my present impressions are, that I have never seen anywhere else such exquisite scenery as that which surrounds the village. The street itself, to be sure, is common-place enough, and hot, dusty, and disagreeable; but if you look above it, or on either side, there are the green hills descending abruptly down, and softened with woods, amid which are seen villas, cottages, castles; and, beyond the river, are a line of crags, perhaps three hundred feet high, clothed with shrubbery, in some parts, from top to bottom, but in other places presenting a sheer precipice of rock, over which tumbles, as it were, a cascade of ivy and creeping plants. It is very beautiful, and, I might almost say, very wild; but yet it has those characteristics of finish, and of being redeemed from nature, and converted into a portion of the adornment of a great garden—which I find in all English scenery. Not that I complain of this; on the contrary, there is nothing that delights an American more in contrast with the roughness and ruggedness of his native scenes;— to which, also, he might be glad to return, after a while.

[65] We put up at the old Bath Hotel, an immense house, with passages of such extent that, at first, it seemed almost a day's journey from parlour to bedroom. The house stands on a declivity; and after ascending one pair of stairs, we came, in travelling along the passage-way, to a door that opened on a beautifully arranged garden, with arbors and grottoes, and the hill-side rising steep above. All the time of our stay at Matlock, there was brilliant sunshine; and the grass and foliage being in their freshest and most luxuriant phase, the place has left as bright a picture as I have anywhere in my memory.

The morning after our arrival, we took a walk, and, following the sound of a church bell, entered what appeared to be a park, and passing along a road at the base of a line of crags, soon came in sight of a beautiful church. I rather imagine it to be the place of worship of the Arkwright-family, whose seat is in this vicinity; the descendants of the famous Arkwright, who contributed so much towards turning England into a cotton-man[u]factory. We did not enter the church, but passed beyond it, and over a bridge, and along a road that ascended among the hills and finally brought us by a circuit to the other end of Matlock village, after a walk of three or four miles. [66] In the afternoon, we took a boat across the Derwent (a passage which half a dozen strokes of the oars served to accomplish) and reached a very pleasant seclusion called "the Lovers' Walk." A ferriage of two pence pays for the transit across the river, and gives the freedom of these grounds, which are threaded with paths that meander and zig-zag to the top of the precipitous ridge, amid trees and shrubbery, and the occasional ease of rustic seats. It is a sweet walk for lovers, and was so for us; although Julian, with his scramblings, and disappearances, and shouts from above, and headlong scamperings down the precipitous path, occasionally frightened his mother. After gaining the heights, the path skirts along the precipice, allowing us to see down into the village-street, and, nearer, the Derwent winding through the valley, so close beneath us that we might have flung a stone into it. These crags would be very rude and harsh, if left to themselves; but they are quite softened, and made sweet and tender, by the great deal of foliage that clothes their sides, and creeps and clambers over them, only letting a stern face of rock be seen here and there, and in a smile rather than a frown.

The next day, Monday, we went to see the Grand Cavern. The entrance is high up on the hill-side, whither we [67] were led by a guide, of whom there are many, all of whom pay tribute, I believe, to the proprietor of the cavern. There is a small shed, by the side of the cavern-mouth, where the guide provided himself and us with tallow-candles, and then led us into the darksome and ugly pit, the entrance of which is not very imposing; for it has a door of rough pine-boards, and is kept under lock and key. This is the disagreeable phase—one of the disagreeable phases—of man's conquest over nature, in England; cavern-mouths shut up with cellar-doors, cataracts under lock and key, precipitous crags compelled to figure in ornamented gardens—and all accessible at a fixed amount of shillings or pence. It is not quite possible to draw a full, free breath, under such circumstances. When you think of it, it makes the wildest scenery look like the artificial rockwork, which Englishmen are so fond of displaying, in the little bit of grass-plot under their suburban parlor windows. However the cavern was dreary enough, and wild enough, though in a mean sort of way; for it is but a long series of passages and crevices, generally so narrow that you scrape your elbows, and so low that you hit your head. It never has any lofty height, though sometimes it broadens out into ample space, but never into [68] grandeur; the roof being always within reach, I believe, and in most places smoky with the tallow candles that have been held up to it. A very dirty, sordid, disagreeable burrow, more like a cellar gone mad than anything else; but it served to show us how the crust of the earth is moulded. This cavern was known to the Romans, and used to be worked by them as a lead-mine. Derbyshire spar is now taken from it; and in some of its crevices, the gleam of the tallow-candles is faintly reflected from the crystallizations; but, on the whole, I felt like a mole as I went creeping along, and was glad when we came into the sunshine again. I rather think my idea of a cavern is taken from the one in the Forty Thieves,[425] or in Gil Blas; a vast, hollow womb, roofed and curtained with obscurity. This reality is very mean.

Leaving the cavern, we went to the guide's cottage, situated high above the village, where he showed us specimens of ornaments and toys, manufactured by himself from Derbyshire spar and other materials. There was very pretty mosaic-work, flowers of spar, and leaves of malachite; and miniature copies of Cleopatra's Needle, and other Egyptian monuments; and vases, of graceful pattern; brooches, too, and many other things. The most valuable spar [69] is called Blue John, and is only to be found in one spot, where, also, the supply is said to be growing scant. We bought a number of articles, and then came homeward, still with our guide, who showed us, on the way, the Romantic Rocks. These are some crags, which have been rent away and stand insulated from the craggy hill-side, affording a pathway between it and them; while the places can yet be seen, where the sundered crags would fit into the rocky hill, if there were but a Titan strong enough to adjust them again. It is a very picturesque spot, and the price for seeing it is two-pence; though, in our case, it was included in the four shillings which (I think) we had paid for seeing the cavern. The representative men of England are the showman and the policeman; both very good people in their way.

Returning to the hotel, Julian and mamma went through the village to the river, near the railway, where the old boy set himself to fishing, and caught three minnows. I followed, after a while, to call them back; and my wife and I called into one or two of the many shops, in the village, which have articles manufactured of the spar for sale. Some of these are nothing short of magnificent. There was an inlaid table, valued, if I [70] remember, at sixty guineas, and splendid enough for any drawing-room; another inlaid with the squares of a chess-board. We heard of a table in the possession of the Marquis of Westminster, the value of which is three hundred guineas. It would be easy and pleasant to spend a great deal of money on such things as we saw there; but all our purchases in Matlock did not amount to more than twenty shillings, invested in brooches, shawl-pins, little vases, and toys, which will be valuable to us as memorials, on the other side of the water. After this, mamma and Julian visited a petrifying cave, of which there are several hereabouts. The process of petrifaction requires some months, or perhaps a year or two, varying with the size of the article to be operated upon. The articles are placed in the cave, under the drippings from the roof, and a hard deposit is formed upon them, and sometimes—as in the case of a bird's nest—makes a curious result—every straw and hair being immortalized and stiffened into stone. A horse's head was in the process of petrifaction; and Julian bought a broken eggshell for a penny, though larger articles are expensive. The process would appear to be entirely superficial—a mere crust on the outside of things—but we saw some [71] specimens of petrified oak, where the stony substance seemed to be intimately incorporated with the wood, and to have really changed it into stone. These specimens were immensely ponderous, and capable of a high polish, which brought out beautiful streaks and shades.

One might spend a very pleasant summer in Matlock, and I think there can be no more beautiful place in the world; but we left it that afternoon, and railed to Manchester, where we arrived between ten and eleven at night. The next day, I left mamma to go to the Art Exhibition, and took Julian with me to Liverpool, where I had an engagement that admitted of no delay. Thus ended our tour; in which we had seen but a little bit of little England, yet rich with variety and interest. What a wonderful land! It is our forefathers' land; our land; for I will not give up such a precious inheritance. We are now back again, in flat and sandy Southport, which, during the past week, has been thronged with Whitsuntide people, who crowd the streets, and pass to-and-fro along the promenade, with a universal and monotonous air of nothing-to-do and very little enjoyment. It is a pity these poor folks cannot employ their little hour of leis[72]ure to better advantage, in a country where the soil is so veined with gold.

These are delightfully long days. Last night, at half past nine, I could read with perfect ease in parts of the room remote from the window; and at nearly half past eleven, when I went to bed, there was a broad sheet of daylight in the west, gleaming brightly over the plashy sands. I question whether there is any total night, at this season.

JUNE 21st, SUNDAY, SOUTHPORT.

SOUTHPORT, I presume, is now in its most vivid aspect; there being a multitude of visitors here, principally of the middling-classes, and a frequent crowd whom I take to be working people from Manchester and other factory towns. It is the strangest place to come to, for the pleasures of the sea, of which we scarcely have a glimpse from month's end to month's end, nor any fresh, exhilarating breath from it, but a lazy, languid atmosphere, brooding over the waste of sands; or even if there be a sulky and bitter wind, blowing along the promenade, it still brings no salt elixir. I never was more weary of a place in all my life, and never felt such a disinterested pity as of the people who come here for pleasure. Nevertheless, the town has its amuse[73]ments; in the first-place, the day-long and perennial one of donkey-riding along the sands, large parties of men and girls pottering along together; the Flying Dutchman (a great clumsy boat on wheels) trundles hither and thither, when there is breeze enough; an archery man sets up his targets on the beach; the bathing-houses stand by scores and fifties along the shore, and likewise on the bank of the Ribble, a mile seaward; the hotels have their billiard-rooms; there is a theatre every evening; from morning till night, comes a succession of organ-grinders, playing interminably under your window; and a man with a bassoon, and a monkey, who takes your pennies and pulls off his cap in acknowledgment; and wandering minstrels, with guitar and voice; and a highland bagpiper, squealing out a tangled skein of discord, together with a highland maid who dances a hornpipe; and Punch and Judy; in a word, we have specimens of all manner of vagrancy that infests England. In these long days, and warm and pleasant ones, the promenade is at its liveliest about nine °clock, which is but just after sundown; and our Rosebud finds it difficult to go to sleep amid so much music as comes to her ears from bassoon, bag-pipe, organ, guitar, and now and then a military band. One feature of the place is the sick and in[74]firm people, whom we see dragged along in Bath-chairs, or dragging their own limbs languidly; or sitting on benches; or meeting in the streets, and making acquaintance on the strength of mutual maladies; pale men leaning on their ruddy wives; cripples, three or four together, in a ring, and planting their crutches in the centre. I don't remember whether I have ever mentioned, among the notibilities [sic] of Southport, the Town Crier, a meek-looking old man, who sings out his messages in a most doleful tone, as if he took his title in its literal sense, and were really going to cry in the world's behalf. One other stroller; a foreigner with a dog, shaggy around the head and fore-shoulders, and closely shaven behind. The poor little beast jumped through hoops, ran about on two legs of a side, danced on its hind-legs, and on its fore-paws; with its hind ones straight up in the air—all the time keeping a watch on his master's eye, and evidently mindful of many a beating.

JUNE 25th 1857.

THE war-steamer Niagara came up the Mersey, a few days since; and, day before yesterday, Captain Hudson called at my office, a somewhat meagre, elderly gentleman, of simple and hearty manners and address, having his Purser, Mr. Eldredge, with him, who, I think, rather prides himself upon having a Napoleonic profile. The Captain is an old acquaintance of Mrs. Blodget, and had come ashore principally [75] with a view to calling on her; so, after we had left our cards on the Mayor, I showed these naval gentlemen the way to her house. Mrs. Blodget and Miss Williams were prodigiously glad to see him; and they all three began to talk of old times and old acquaintances; for when Mrs. Blodget was a rich lady, at Gibraltar, she used to have our whole navy-list at her table—young midshipmen and lieutenants then, perhaps, but old gouty, paralytic Commodores now, if still even partly alive. It was arranged that Mrs. Blodget, with as many of the ladies of her family as she chose to bring, should accompany me on my official visit to the Ship, the next day; and yesterday we went accordingly—Mrs. Blodget, Miss Williams, and six or seven American Captains' wives, their husbands following in another boat. I know too little of ships to describe one, or even to feel any great interest in the details of this or any other ship; but the nautical people seemed to see much to admire. She lay in the Sloyne,[426] in the midst of a broad basin of the Mersey, with a pleasant landscape of green England (now warm with summer sunshine) on either side, with churches, and villa-residences, and suburban and rural beauty. The officers of the ship are gentlemanly men, externally very well-mannered, although [76] perhaps not polished and refined to any considerable depth. At least, I have not found naval men so, in general; but still it is pleasant to see Americans who are not stirred by such motives as usually interest our countrymen—no hope or desire of growing rich, but planting their claims to respectability on other grounds, and therefore acquiring a certain nobleness, whether it is inherent in their nature or no. It always seems to me they look down upon civilians with quiet and not ill-natured scorn, which one has the choice of smiling or being provoked at. It is not a true life which they lead, but shallow and aimless, and unsatisfactory, it must be, to the better minds among them; nor do they appear to profit by what would seem the advantages presented to them in their world-wide, though not world-deep, experience. They get to be very clannish too.

After seeing the ship, we landed, all of us, ladies and Captains, and went to the gardens of the Rock Ferry Hotel, where Julian and I stayed behind the rest.

JUNE 28th, SUNDAY, MAUCHLINE.

ON Friday, at 10 °clock, Mamma, Julian, and I, left Southport, taking the train for Preston, and as we had to stop an hour or two before starting for Carlisle, I walked up into the town. The street through which [77] most of my walk lay was brick-built, lively, bustling, and not particularly noteworthy; but turning a little way down another street, the town seemed to have a more ancient aspect. The day was intensely hot, the sun lying bright and fervid as ever I remember it in an American city; so that I was glad to get back again to the shade and shelter of the depôt. The heat and dust, moreover, made our journey to Carlisle intensely uncomfortable. It was through very pretty, and sometimes picturesque scenery, being on the confines of the hill country, which we could see on our left, dim and blue; and likewise we had a refreshing breath from the sea, in passing along the verge of Morecambe Bay. We reached Carlisle, I think, about five °clock, and after taking tea at the Bush Hotel, set forth to look at the town.

The notable objects were a castle and cathedral; and we first found our way to the castle, which stands on elevated ground, on the side of the city towards Scotland. A broad, well-constructed path winds round the castle, at the base of the wall, on the verge of a steep descent to the plain beneath, through which winds the river Eden. Along this path we walked quite round the castle, a circuit of perhaps half a mile, (more or less, but probably less) very [78] pleasant, being shaded by the castle's height and by the foliage of trees. The walls have been so much re-built and restored, that it is only here and there that we see an old buttress, or a few time-worn stones intermixed with the new facing with which the aged substance is overlaid. The material is red free-stone, which seems to be very abundant in this part of the country. We found no entrance to the castle, till the path had led us from the free and airy country into a very mean part of the town, where the wretched old houses thrust themselves between us and the castle-wall; and then, passing through a narrow street, we walked up what appeared like a by-lane, and the portal of the castle was before us. There was a sentry-box just within the gate, and a centinel [sic] was on guard; for Carlisle Castle is a national fortress, and, I believe, has usually been a depôt for arms and ammunition. The sergeant, or corporal of the guard, sat reading within the gateway; and, on my request for admittance, he civilly appointed one of the soldiers to conduct us over the castle. As I recollect, the chief gateway of the castle, with the guard-room in the thickness of the wall, is situated some twenty yards behind the first entrance, where we met the centinel [*sic*]. [79] It was an intelligent young soldier who showed us round the castle, and very civil, as I always find soldiers to be. He had not anything particularly interesting to show, nor very much to say about it; and what he did say, so far as it referred to the history of the castle, was probably apocryphal. The castle has an inner and outer ward, on the descent of the hill, and included within the circuit of the exterior wall. Having been always occupied by soldiers, it has not been permitted to assume the picturesque aspect of a ruin, but the buildings of the interior have either been constantly repaired, as they required it; or have been taken down when past repair. We saw a small part of the tower where Mary Queen of Scots was confined, on her first coming to England; these remains consist only of a portion of a winding stone-staircase, at which we peeped through a window. The keep is very large and massive, and no doubt old, in its inner substance. We ascended to the castle-walls, and looked out over the river, towards the Scottish hills, which are visible in the distance; the Scottish border being not more than eight or nine miles off. Carlisle Castle has stood many sieges, and witnessed many battles under its walls. There are now, on its ramparts, only some half-a-dozen old fash[80]ioned guns, which our soldier told us had gone quite out of use in these days; they were long iron twelve pounders, with one or two carronades. The soldier was of an artillery regiment, and wore the Crimean medal; he said the garrison now here consists only of about twenty men, all of whom had served in the Crimea, like himself. They seem to lead a very dull and monotonous life, as indeed it must be, without object, or much hope, or any great enjoyment of the present, like prisoners, as indeed they are. Our guide showed us, on the rampart, a place where the soldiers had been accustomed to drop themselves down, at night, hanging by their hands from the top of the wall, and alighting on their feet close beside the path on the outside. The height seemed at least that of an ordinary house; but the soldier said that, nine times out of ten, the fall might be ventured without harm; and he spoke from experience, having himself got out of the Castle in this manner. The place is now boarded up, so as to make egress difficult or impossible.

   The castle, after all, was not particularly well worth seeing. The soldier's most romantic story was of a daughter of Lord Scroope, a former governor of the Castle when Mary of Scotland was confined here. She attempted to assist [81] the Queen in escaping, but was shot dead in the gateway, by the warder; and the soldier pointed out the very spot where the poor young lady fell and died; all [of] which would be very interesting, were there a word of truth in the story. But we liked our guide for his intelligence, simplicity, and for the pleasure which he seemed to take, as an episode of his dull daily life, in talking to strangers. He observed that the castle walls were solid (and indeed there was breadth enough to drive a coach and four along the top) but the artillery of the Crimea would have shelled them into ruins in a very few hours. When we got back to the guard-house, he took us inside and showed the dismal and comfortless rooms where soldiers are confined for drunkenness and other offences against military laws; telling us that he himself had been confined there, and almost perished with cold. I should not much wonder if he were to get into durance again, through misuse of the fee which I put into his hand at parting.

The Cathedral is at no great distance from the castle; and though the streets are mean and sordid in the vicinity, the close has the antique repose and shadowy peace, at once domestic and religious, which seem peculiar and universal in Cathedral closes. The founda[82]tion of this Cathedral church is very ancient, it having been the church-portion of an old abbey, the refectory and other remains of which are still seen around the close. But the whole exterior of the cathedral, except here and there a buttress, and one old patch of gray stones, seems to have been renewed within a very few years, with a beautiful red free-stone; and, really, I think it is all the more beautiful for being new—the ornamental parts being so sharply cut, and the stone, moreover, showing beautiful shadings, which will dis[ap]pear when it gets weatherworn. There is a very large and fine east-window, of recent construction, wrought with beautiful stone-tracery. The door of the south transept stood open, though barred by an iron-grate; we looked in, and saw a few monuments on the wall, but found nobody to give us admittance. The portal of this entrance is very beautiful, with wreaths of stone foliage and flowers round the arch, recently carved; yet not so recently but that the swallows have given their sanction to it, as if it were a thousand years old, and have built their nests in the deeply carved recesses. While we were looking, a little bird flew into the little opening between between [sic] two of these petrified flowers, behind which was his nest, quite out of [83] sight. After some attempts to find the verger, we left the Cathedral, and found our way back to the hotel, where I refreshed and soothed myself with a cigar, after this feverishly hot and weary day.

In the morning, Mamma and Julian went back to see the interior of the Cathedral; while I strayed at large about the town, again passing round the castle-hill, and thence round the town, where I found some inconsiderable portions of the wall which once girt it about. It was market-day in Carlisle, and the principal streets were much thronged with human life and business, on that account; and, in as busy a street as any, stands a marble statue in robes of antique state, fitter for a niche in Westminster Abbey than for the thronged street of a town. It is a statue of the Earl of Lonsdale, a Lord Lieutenant of Cumberland, who died about twenty years ago.

We left Carlisle a little past eleven, and, within a quarter of an hour, were at Gretna Green; a spot which many people have visited to their woe.[427] Thence we rushed onward into Scotland, through a flat and dreary country, consisting greatly of desert and bog, where, I suppose, the moss-troopers used to take [84] refuge after their raids into England. Anon, however, the hills hove themselves up to view, some to a height which might almost be called mountainous; and, in about two hours, we reach[ed] Dumfries, and alighted at the station there. It was an awfully hot day; not a whit less so than the day before; but we boldly adventured through the burning sunshine up into the town, inquiring our way to the residence of Burns. The street which brought us from the station is called Shakspeare-street, and at its extremity we saw "Burns Street" on a corner-house; the lane so designated having formerly been called "Mill Hole Brae." It is a vile lane, paved with small hard stones from side to side, bordered by cottages or mean houses, built of stone and whitewashed, and one joining to another through the whole length of the street, not a tree, not a blade of grass between the paving-stones, hot as Tophet, reeking with a genuine Scotch stink, dirty, and infested with dirty children, and women who seemed to be hopelessly scrubbing the thresholds of their wretched dwellings. I never saw an outskirt of a town, in which it would be more miserable to live. We inquired for Burns's house; and a woman pointed across a narrow street to a two-story house, built of stone and white-washed, [85] like the rest, not a separate house, but contiguous with its neighbor; perhaps a little more decent-looking than most of the houses there, though I hesitate in saying so. I saw no inscription on the door, bearing reference to Burns, though there was one which designated it as being now occupied either as a ragged or industrial school, I forget which. We were instantly admitted, on knocking, by a servant-girl who smiled intelligently when we told our errand; and she showed us into a little, low, very plain parlor, not more than twelve or fifteen feet square. A young woman (a teacher in the school, I think,) soon appeared, and told us that this had been Burns's usual sitting-room, and that he had written many of his songs here. She then led us up a narrow staircase into a little bed-chamber, over the parlor. Connecting with it, there is a very small room, or windowed closet, which, she said, Burns had used as a study; and the bed-chamber was the one in which he slept in his life time, and died at last. Altogether, it is a very poor and unsuitable place for a pastoral and rural poet to live or die in; and it is even more unsatisfactory than Shakspeare's house, which has a certain picturesqueness. The [86] narrow lane, the paving-stones, and the brotherhood of wretched hovels, are depressing even to remember.

It was an infernally hot day. After leaving the house (which I wish were worthier of its consecration) we found our way to the principal street of the town, which is of very different aspect from this wretched outskirt. Here we entered a hotel, and ordered luncheon, meanwhile reading a Dumfries guide-book which we found there. It informed us, among other things, that Prince Charles Edward had once spent a night in this very hotel. When we had rested and refreshed ourselves, we again set forth, and inquired the way to the Mausoleum of Burns; and coming to St. Michael's church, we saw a man digging a grave, and he let us into the church-yard, which was crowded full of monuments. Their general shape seems peculiar to Scotland, being a tablet of marble or other stone, within a frame, something like that of a looking-glass, and standing upright, sometimes to the height of ten, fifteen, twenty feet, all over the churchyard, and forming quite an imposing collection of monuments to the memory of people of no great significance. In Scotland, it is the custom to put the occupation of the buried person (as "skinner," "shoe-maker," "flesher") on his tomb[87]stone; and wives are buried under their maiden names, instead of those of their husbands.

There was a footpath through the churchyard sufficiently well-worn to guide us to the grave of Burns; but soon a woman came behind us, who, it appears, keeps the key of the Mausoleum and is privileged to show it to strangers. The monument is a sort of Grecian temple, with pillars, or pilasters, and a dome, covering a space, I suppose, of twenty feet square. It was formerly open to the atmosphere, but its sides are now glazed with large squares, each the size of the whole side of the edifice, of rough glass. The woman unlocked the door, and admitted us into the interior. Inlaid into the floor of the building, is the grave-stone of Burns, the one that was laid over his grave by Jean Armour, before this monument was built. Stuck against the wall of the mausoleum there is a marble statue of Burns at the plough, surprised by a visit from the Genius of Caledonia; not very good, methinks. The plough is better than the man, and the man rather better than the goddess, being somewhat heavy and cloddish, though though [sic] the woman said that it is certified by an old man of ninety, who knew Burns, to be very like the original. The bones [88] of the poet, and of Jean Armour, and of some of their children, are in the vault over which we stood. The woman (who was intelligent, in her plain way, and very pleasant to talk with) said that the vault was opened, about three weeks ago, when the eldest son of Burns was buried, and that the bones were found, and that the skull of the poet was taken out, and kept for several days by a doctor of the town. It has since been been [sic] put in a new leaden coffin, and restored to the vault. She told us that there is a daughter surviving of the eldest son, and daughters by the two younger sons; and that there is an illegitimate son (named Robert Burns) and daughter, still extant in Dumfries by the eldest son, who was a man of disreputable life in his younger days. This son seems to have inherited his father's failings, with but a shadow of the great qualities that make the world tender of his vices and weaknesses. Seeing his poor, mean dwelling and surroundings, and picturing his outward presenti-ment from these, one does not so much wonder that the people of his day should have failed to recognize what was immortal in a disreputable, drunken, shabbily clothed and shabbily housed man, consorting with associates of ill reputation, and, as his only ostensible occupation, gauging liquor-casks. It is [89] much easier to know and honor a poet when his fame has taken shape in marble, than when he comes staggering before you plastered over and besmeared with all the sordidness of his daily life. I only wonder that his honor came so soon; there must have been something very great in his immediate presence to have caused him to seem like a demi-god so soon.

As we went back through the churchyard, we saw a spot where nearly four hundred inhabitants of Dumfries were buried during the cholera-year; and also some curious old monuments, with raised letters, the inscriptions of which were not sufficiently legible to induce us to puzzle them out; but I believe they marked the resting places of old covenanters, some of whom were killed by Claverhouse and his associates. The church is of red-freestone, and was built about a hundred years ago on an old Catholic foundation. Our guide admitted us into it, and showed us, in the porch, a very pretty little marble figure of a child asleep, with a drapery over the lower part of the figure, from beneath which appeared its two baby-feet. It was a truly a [*sic*] sweet little figure; and the woman told us that it represented a child of the sculptor (a Mr. Dunbar, whom my wife remembers to have heard of, as a sculptor of some reputation) and that the baby, here still [90] in its marble infancy, had died more than twenty-six years ago. Many ladies, she said, especially those who had lost a child, had shed tears over it. It was very pleasant to think of the sculptor bestowing the best of his genius and art to re-create his little, tender child in stone, and to make it as soft and sweet as the original; but the conclusion of the story was not quite so agreeable. A gentleman from London had seen the figure, and been so much delighted with it that he bought it of the father-artist, after it had stood above a quarter of a century in the church-porch. So this was not the real statue that came out of his heart; he had sold *that* for a hundred guineas, and sculptured this one to re-place it. The first figure was entirely naked; this, as I have mentioned, has a drapery over its lower limbs. After all, the sleeping baby may be as fitly reposited in the drawing-room of a con[n]ois-seur as in a cold church-porch.

We went into the church, which is very plain and naked, and unlike English churches; no altar-decorations, and the floor quite covered with wooden pews. The woman led us to a pew cornering on one of the side-aisles, and told us that it used to be Burns's pew, and showed us his seat, which is in the corner by the aisle, so situated that a sturdy [91] pillar hid him from the pulpit; for "he was no great friends with the ministers," said she. This touch—his seat behind the pillar, and he himself nodding, or observant of profane things—brought him before us to the life. In the corner-seat of the next pew, right before Burns, and not more than two feet off, sat the young lady on whom the poet saw the louse![428] The woman could not tell us her name. This was the last thing that we saw in Dumfries, worthy of record; and from the church we went to the railway-station, where we spent more than a weary hour waiting for the train. At last, it came, and took us on to Mauchline.

At the Mauchline-station we took an omnibus (a very small one, carrying only four passengers) and drove about a mile to the village, and established ourselves at the Loudoun hotel, one of the veriest country-inns which we have found in Great Britain. The village of Mauchline, one of the places redolent of Burns, consists principally, so far as I have seen it, of a street of contiguous cottages, mostly white-washed and with thatched roofs; as ugly a place as mortals could contrive to make, and with nothing sylvan or rural in the im-mediate village. The fashion of paving the village-street, and patching one mean house on to another, quite shuts out all verdure and pleas[92]antness; but I suppose we are not likely to see anything more like a genuine old Scotch village, such as it was in Burns's time and long before, than this of Mauchline. The greater part of the houses are built of red free stone, as is likewise the church, which stands about mid-way up the street, and has a square tower, with pinnacles. This church was the scene of Burns's poem—the "Holy Fair"— and almost directly opposite its gate, across the village-street, stands Posie Nansie's inn, where the "Jolly Beggars" congregated. This latter is a two-story, red-stone, thatched house, looking old, but not venerable, like a drunken patriarch; it has small windows, and may well be centuries old, though, sixty or seventy years ago, I should have thought it might have been something better than a beggar's ale-house. The whole town of Mauchline is rusty and time-worn, even the newer houses, of which there are several, being shadowed by the general aspect of the house [place?]. When we arrived, all the dirty little houses seemed to have vomited forth their inhabitants into the warm summer evening; and everybody was chatting with everybody on familiar terms, and the little bare-legged children playing about with riot and uproar; the boys coming freely, too, and looking into the window of our parlor. After [93] tea, we walked out, and were followed by the gaze of the whole town, people standing in the door-ways, old women popping their heads from the windows, and men—idle on Saturday at e'en, after their week's work—cluster-ing at the street-corner. We passed two or three shops, one a chemist's and druggist's, another the post-office, combined with a variety-store; but I believe the chief business of Mauchline consists in the manufacture of snuff-boxes. We find that another street crosses the head of the longer one, which we first entered; and, just beyond the extremity of the cross-street, is the entrance to a gentleman's seat. A man and woman were sweeping the shady avenue, and told us that Lord Chief Justice Hope resided at the place; but his house was not visible from the road.

This forenoon, my wife and Julian attended church; and, it being Sacrament Sunday, and they happening to be wedged into the farther end of a closely filled pew, they had to stay through the preaching of four several sermons, and came back perfectly exhausted and desperate. My wife, however, is some-what consoled by finding that she has witnessed a scene identical with that of Burns's Holy Fair, in the very spot where he located [94] it. We had a Scotch dinner to-day, so far as the first course went, being a sheep's head with the broth; and, at five °clock, we took a fly and set out for Moss Giel.

It is not more than a mile from Mauchline, and the road lies over a high ridge of land, with a view of far hills and slopes on either side. Just before we reached the farm, the driver stopt and pointed out a hawthorn, growing by the wayside, which he said was Burns's "Lousie Thorn"; and I got out of the fly and plucked a branch, though I do not remember where or how Burns has celebrated it. We then turned into a rude gateway, and almost immediately came to the farm-house of Moss Giel, standing some fifty yards removed from the highway, behind a tall hedge of hawthorn, and considerably shadowed by trees. The house is a white-washed stone cottage, like hundreds of others in England and Scotland, with a thatched roof, on which grow grass and weeds; there is a door and one window in front, besides another little window that peeps out from the thatch. Close by the cottage, extending back at right angles from it, so as to enclose the farm yard, are two other buildings of the same size, shape, and general appearance as the house; either of the three looks just as fit to be a human habitation as the others, and [95] all look more suitable for donkey stables or pigsties. We drove into the farm-yard, surrounded on three sides by these three hovels; and a large dog began to bark at us, and some women and children made their appearance, but appeared to demur about admitting us, because the master and mistress were very religious people, and had gone to the Sacrament.

However, it would not do to be turned back from Robert Burns's threshold; so, as the women seemed to be merely straggling visitors, and as nobody, at all events, had a right to send us away, we went into the back-door, and turning to the right, entered a kitchen. It was deplorably mean and filthy, and in it there were three or four children, one of whom, a little girl of eight or nine years old, had a baby in her arms. She said she was the daughter of the people of the house, and she gave us what leave she could to look about us. Thence we we [*sic*] stept across the little mid-passage of the house, into the only other room below, a sitting room, where we found a young man eating bread and cheese. He said he did not live there, and he had probably only called in to refresh himself on his way home from church. This room, too, was a poor one, and besides being all that the cot[96]tage had to show for a parlor, it was a sleeping apartment, having two beds, which might be curtained off on occasion. The young man gave us liberty (as far as in him lay) to go up stairs; so up we crept, and a few steps brought us to the top of the staircase, where, over the kitchen, we found the wretchedest little sleeping-chamber in the world, with a sloping roof, under the thatch, and containing two beds on the floor, I think. This, most probably, was Burns's sleeping-room, or it might have been that of his mother's maid; and in either case, the poet was familiar with it. On the opposite side of the passage was the door of another attic-chamber, opening which, I saw a considerable number of cheeses on the floor. It was very depressing to think that anybody—not to say Burns, but any human being—should sleep and spend their domestic lives in such a miserable hovel as this. The driver says that the present occupant of the farm lives here, and it indicates a degree of barbarism which I did not imagine to exist in Scotland, that the tiller of broad fields should live in a pig-sty.

The whole place was pervaded with a frowzy smell, and also a dunghill smell; and one does not well understand how the atmosphere of such a dwelling can be any better mor[97]ally than it is physically. No virgin can keep a holy awe about her, stowed higgledy-piggledy into this narrowness and filth; it must make beasts of men and women. We were glad to get out of the house, and out of the farm yard too. On second thought, I suppose the women, whom we found there, may be the hired people of the farm and dairy, and may have their lodgings in one or other of the supplementary hovels. Before we drove off, the young man, above-mentioned, came out and showed us a large plane-tree, on one side of the house, under which, he said, Burns used to sit and make songs. The biographers talk of the farm of Moss Giel as being damp and unhealthy;[429] but I do not see why it should be either. It occupies a high, broad ridge, sloping far downward before any marshy soil can be reached, and enjoys surely whatever benefit can come of a breezy site. The high hedge, and the trees beside the cottage give it a pleasant aspect enough, to one who does not know the grimy secrets of the interior; and the summer afternoon was so bright that I shall remember the scene with a good deal of sunshine over it.

Leaving the cottage, we drove through a field which the driver told us was that in which Burns turned up [98] the mouse's nest;[430] it is the enclosure nearest the cottage, and seems now to be a pasture; at least, it is not ploughed, and looks like poor land. It was whitened with an immense multitude of daisies—daisies, daisies, everywhere—and, in answer to my inquiry, the man said that this was likewise the field where Burns ran his plough over the daisy. If so, the soil seems to have been consecrated to daisies by the song which he bestowed on that first immortal one.[431] I alighted and plucked a whole handful of these flowers, which will be precious to many friends in our own country as coming from Burns's farm, and as being of the same race and lineage as that daisy which he turned into an amaranthine flower, while seeming to destroy it.

From Mossgiel we drove through various pleasant scenes, some of which were known to us by their connection with Burns. We skirted, too, along a portion of the estate of Auchinleck, which still belongs to the Boswell family, the present possessor being Sir James Boswell, a grandson of Johnson's friend, and son of the Sir Alexander who was killed in a duel. Our driver spoke of Sir James as a kind, free-hearted man, but addicted to races and such pastimes, and also given to drink; so that Bozzy's booziness [99] appears to have become hereditary with his posterity. There is no male heir to the estate of Auchinleck, and it will be divided among daughters at Sir James's death. The part of the estate which we saw is covered with wood, and (so the driver said) is quite undermined with rabbit-warrens; nor, though it covers a wide extent, is the income large. By-and-by, we came to the spot where Burns saw Miss Alexander, the Lass of Ballochmyle. It was on a bridge which (or else a bridge that has succeeded to it, and which is made of iron) crosses the road, high in the air, from bank to bank; so that she may have looked to Burns like a creature beneath [between?] earth and sky. Thence the driver pointed out the course which she took, through the shrubbery, to a rock on the banks of the Lugar. This is a very picturesque and beautiful scene, the river flowing over its pebbly bed, sometimes hidden deep in verdure, sometimes gleaming into the sun, and here and there eddying at the foot of a high, precipitous cliff. This estate of Ballochmyle is still possessed by the Alexander family, whom

Burns's song[432] has made famous; and I do not think that any family ever gained renown on cheaper terms—merely by a young lady's chancing to walk out, and cross the path of a neighboring farmer, one summer afternoon. [100] After all, I do not much admire this song, nor wonder that Miss Alexander saw little in it.

Two or three miles, at least, our road lay along by these pleasant woods of Ballochmyle, which would appear to be a rich estate; and the driver told me that the present owner, I believe, has erected a splendid mansion on it. I should like to know him, and ascertain what value, if any, he puts upon the celebrity which those four or five warm, rude,—at least, not refined—rather ploughmanlike verses, have shed upon his whole race. Burns has written a thousand better things. In these verses, he seems to me to have injured the poetry by attempting to make them fine; and yet a coarseness has crept in.

We passed through Catrine, which is known hereabouts as the "clean village of Scotland." It seems to be a manufacturing place, and quite modern, being built on a regular plan of rectangular streets, broad, and certainly cleaner than village-streets elsewhere in Scotland. Thence we drove home without seeing anything else remarkable. All the way, there were many young men and girls, in their Sunday clothes, returning from church, whither everybody makes a point of going on Sacrament Sunday, as in Burns's time.

[101] I ought to note down, that the little girl at Mossgiel shrank, at first, from accepting a shilling which I held out to her. Also, the woman who showed St. Michael's church, at Dumfries, declined some money offered her by my wife, because I had already paid her. She was not a Scotch woman, but from Cumberland.

MONDAY, JUNE 29th, AYR.

THERE was a rain-storm, last night; and this morning, the rusty, old, sloping street, of Mauchline was glistening with wet, and frequent showers came spattering down. The intense heat of many days past was changed for a chilly atmosphere, very suitable to one's ideas of what Scotch temperature ought to be. We found, after breakfast, that the first train northward had already gone by, and that we must wait till nearly two °clock for the next. No excursions were to be thought of in such uncertain weather, showering every other minute; so we kept within doors, writing up our journals,[433] and reading the poems and Cunningham's biography of Burns, which has been our sole indoor occupation since we came hither. Burns will live with more reality as a man for us, and be better appreciated as a poet, hereafter; for certainly one meets his ghost among these scenes where he loved and sang. I do not remember any writer whose personal char[102]acter has so much to do with his fame, and throws such a necessary light on what he has produced. Every thing he wrote (so far as it is good) has his own personal warmth in it. The Scotch people, I think, appreciate him in a kind of a personal way, as if he were a man with whom they had shaken hands and talked, and whom they had seen drunk and sober.

I merely went out once, this forenoon, and took a brief walk through the village, in which I have left little to describe. There are perhaps five or six shops, or more, including those which appear to be licensed to sell only tea and tobacco; the best of them have the characteristics of village-stores in America, dealing in a small way with an extensive variety of articles. I looked rather longingly at Posie Nansie's Change-House,[434] but forbore to go in. The gate of the churchyard was open, and I peeped in there, and saw that the ground seemed to be absolutely stuffed with dead people, and the surface crowded with gravestones, both perpendicular and horizontal. All Burns's old Mauchline acquaintance were doubtless there. The Armour family (so the driver told me yesterday) are now extinct in Mauchline.

Arriving at the Station, we found a tall, elderly, comely [103] gentleman, walking to-and-fro, and waiting for the train. He proved to be a Mr. Alexander —it may fairly be presumed, the Alexander of Ballochmyle, a blood-relation of the Lovely Lass. These Alexanders, by-the-by, are not an old family on the Ballochmyle estate, the father of the lass having made a fortune in trade, and been the first of his name here. The original family was named Whitefoord. Our ride to Ayr presented nothing very interesting; and, indeed, a cloudy and rainy day takes a varnish off the scenery, and makes a wonderful difference in the beauty and impressiveness of every thing we see. The principal part of our way lay along the coast, in a southerly direction; and much of the landscape unpleasantly reminded us of the sandhills of Southport. We reached Ayr, in the midst of rain, at about three °clock, and, after waiting some time for a cab, drove to the King's Arms Hotel. In the intervals of showers, I have twice walked out (the second time, with Julian) and taken peeps at the town, which appears to have many modern, or modern fronted, edifices, although there are likewise tall gray houses, or gabled and quaint-looking ones, here and there, and in the by-streets, which betoken an ancient place. The town lies on both sides of the river [104] Ayr, which is here broad and stately, and bordered with houses that look from their windows directly down into the river, so that Julian thought he might catch fish from them. We crossed the river by a modern and handsome stone-bridge of five arches, and re-crossed, at a little distance, by an old one of four arches; but whether these are Burns's New and Old Briggs,[435] I cannot say. I have little doubt as to the ancient one, but the other seems too modern to have been built in his day. The old one is steep and narrow, and is paved like a street with small stones, and bordered with a parapet of red free-stone. It has mean old shops at the two ends; and being too narrow for carriages to pass, it is now traversed only by foot-passengers, posts being placed midway to prevent any other passage. Nothing else has thus far impressed me in Ayr, except the tall steeple of a modern church, standing nearly opposite our parlor windows at the King's Arms. It being rainy, the women and girls go about the streets of Ayr barefooted, to save their shoes.

TUESDAY, JUNE 30th, AYR.

THIS morning looked lowering, like one of many consecutive days of storm. After breakfast, however (a very good Scotch breakfast, of fresh herrings and eggs) we took a fly, and started at a little past ten for the banks of [105] the Doon. On our way, about two miles, I should think, from the hotel, we drew up at a wayside-cottage, on which was an inscription to the effect that Robert Burns had been born here. It is now a public house; and of course we alighted, and entered, in the first place, the little sitting-room. This, as we at present see it, is a small, neat apartment, with a cieling [sic]; which was not the case in former times. The walls are much over-scribbled with names of visitors; and the wooden door of a cupboard in the wall, as well as all the other woodwork of the room is cut with initial letters. So, likewise, are two tables, and these last, being varnished over the inscriptions, form really curious and interesting articles of furniture. Set into the wall, in one corner, is a portrait on a panel of Burns, a copy from Nasmyth's original picture, I believe. The floor of this room is of boards, which have probably been a modern substitute for the ordinary flags of a peasant's cottage. There is but one other room pertaining to Burn's [sic] genuine birth-place; and that is the kitchen, into which we now went. It has a flooring of flag-stones even ruder than those of Shakspeare's house, though perhaps not so strangely cracked. A new window has been made through the wall, towards the road, but through the opposite wall there is the little, original window of only four small panes. At the side of the room op[106]posite the fireplace is a recess, as seems to be usual in Scotch cottages, in which is a bed, which can be hidden with curtains. These two rooms, as I have said, made up the whole sum and substance of Burns's birth-place; for there were no chambers, not even attics, the thatched roof being the only cieling [sic] of kitchen and sitting-room, which were each of the height of the whole house. There is not a speck of dirt to be seen now; but when Burns was born, and for the nine years that he lived here, and doubtless through all the years since, until this hovel came to be one of the famous mansions of the world, I suppose it was as filthy as the cottage at Mossgiel now is.

These two rooms are the whole of the original cottage; but it appears to join on to another cottage, as these little habitations often do; and, moreover, a splendid addition has been made to it, since the poet's renown has drawn visitors to the wayside alehouse. When we had sufficiently looked at the kitchen and sitting-room, the old woman of the house led us through an entry, and showed a vaulted hall, of no great size, to be sure, but marvellous[ly] large and splendid as compared with what might be expected from the outside aspect of the cottage. It was hung round with pictures and engravings, principally illus[107]trative of the life and poems of Burns, and had also a bust of him.

In this part of the house, too, there was a parlour, fragrant with tobacco-smoke; and no doubt many a noggin of whiskey is here quaffed to the memory of the bard who professed to draw some of his inspiration from that liquor.

We bought some engravings of Kirk Alloway, the Bridge of Doon, the Monument, and such matters, of the old woman, and took our leave, after giving her a shilling. A very short drive farther brought us within sight of the monument, and to the hotel which stands close at the entrance of the ornamental grounds within which it is enclosed. We rang the bell at the gate of the enclosure; but had to wait some time, because the old man, who superintends the spot, had gone to assist at the laying of the corner-stone of a new kirk. By-and-by, he came, unlocked the iron gate and let us in, but then immediately hurried away to be present at the conclusion of the ceremonies, leaving us locked up with Burns. The enclosure around the monument is beautifully laid out as an ornamental garden, and abundantly provided with rare flowers and shrubbery, all tended with loving care. The [108] monument stands on an elevated site, and consists of a massive basement-story, three-sided, above which rises a light and elegant Grecian temple; a mere dome, supported on Corinthian pillars, and open to all the winds. I do not know what peculiar appropriateness such an edifice may have, as the monument of a Scottish rural poet; but it is very beautiful in itself. The door of the basement story stood open, and entering, we saw a bust of Burns, in a niche, looking keener, more refined, but no[t] so warm and whole-souled, as his pictures do. I think the likeness cannot be good. Also, in the centre of the room, there was a glass case, in which are reposited the two volumes of the little pocket-Bible which Burns gave to Highland Mary, when they pledged their troth to one another. It is poorly printed, on coarse paper. A verse of scripture, referring to the solemnity and awfulness of vows, is written within the cover of each volume in the poet's own hand; and a lock of Highland Mary's golden hair is fastened to one of the covers. This Bible had been carried to America by one of her relatives, but was sent back to be treasured here.

There is a staircase within the monument, by which we ascended to the top, and had a view of both Briggs [109] of Doon; the scene of Tam O'Shanter's adventure being close at hand. Descending, we wandered through the enclosed garden, and came to a little building in a corner, entering which, we found the two statues of Tam and Sutor Wat [Johnie?]—ponderous sculptures enough, yet permeated, in a good degree, with living hilarity. From this part of the garden, too, we had a view of the old Brigg of Doon, over which Tam galloped in such awful peril; it is a beautiful object in the landscape, with one high, graceful arch, ivy-grown, and shadowed around with foliage.

When we had waited a good while, the old gardener came, telling us that the prayer at laying the corner stone had been excellent. He now gave us some roses and sweet-briar, and let us out. We immediately hastened to Kirk Alloway, which is within two or three minutes walk of the monument. A few steps ascend from the roadside, through a gate, into the old graveyard, in the midst of which stands the kirk. It is but a ruin, though care seems to have been taken to secure what remains of it; and probably it will never be allowed to fall to the ground, as long as patching and plaistering [*sic*] can secure it. The edifice is wholly roofless; but [110] the side-walls and gable-ends are quite entire, though evidently portions of them have been restored. Never was there a plainer little church than this, with less architectural pretension; no New England meeting-house has more simplicity, in its very self, though poetry and fun have clambered and clustered so wildly over it. By-the-by, I do not understand why Satan and an assembly of witches should have held their revels in a consecrated edifice; it may have been quite according to rule and custom, however. The interior of the kirk is now put to quite as impertinent a use; for it is divided in the midst by a wall of stone-masonry, and in each compartment there is the burial-place of a family. The name on one monument is Crawfurd; the other bore no inscription. It is impossible not to feel that these good people had no business to lay their bones in a spot [which] belongs to the world, and where their presence jars with the emotions—be they sad or gay—which one brings thither. They shut us out from the precincts, too; for each of the two doorways of the kirk is barred by an iron-grate. The kirk is inconceivably small, considering how large a space it fills in one's imagination before we see it. I paced its length, outside its wall, and found it [111] only seventeen of my paces, and not more than ten of them in breadth. There seem to have been but very few windows, and all of them, I think, are now blocked up with mason-work of stone. One tall and narrow, mullioned window, in the eastern gable, might have [been] seen by Tam O'Shanter, blazing with devilish light, as he approached along the road from Ayr; there was another small, square window, on the side of the kirk nearest the road, into which he might have looked, as he sat on horseback. Indeed, I could easily have looked through as I stood on the ground, had not the opening been blocked up. There [is an] odd kind of belfry at the peak of one of the gables, and the small bell still hangs there; and this [is] all I remember of Kirk Alloway, except that the stones are gray and irregular.

The road from Ayr keeps past Alloway Kirk and crosses the Doon by the new bridge, without swerving much from a straight line. To reach the old bridge, it appears to have made a bend, shortly after passing the Kirk, and then to have turned sharply upon the bridge. The new Bridge stands within a minute's walk of the monument, and we walked thither, and, leaning over its parapet, admired the beautiful Doon, flowing wildly and [112] sweetly between its deep and wooded banks. I never saw a lovelier scene; and yet this might have been even lovelier if the sun had shone upon it. The ivy-grown old bridge, with its high arch, giving a picture of the river and green banks beyond, was absolutely the most picturesque object, in a quiet and gentle way, that I ever beheld; and I shall always remember "Bonny Doon," with its wooded banks, and the boughs dipping into the water. We could not go away without crossing the very bridge of Tam's adventure; so we went round thither, only a few moments' walk, over a now disused portion of the road, and stood on the centre of the arch, and gathered some ivy-leaves from that sacred spot. This done, we returned as speedily as might be to Ayr, whence we have taken the rail to Glasgow; and I conclude this day's record at the George Hotel.

After leaving Ayr, we saw Ailsa Craig, rising like a pyramid out of the sea. Drawing near Glasgow, Ben Lomond hove in sight (at least, I have [no] doubt it was big Ben) with a dome-like height, supported by a shoulder on each side.[436]

JULY 1st, WEDNESDAY, GLASGOW.

IMMEDIATELY after our arrival, yesterday, we went out and inquired our way to the Cathedral, which we reached through a good deal of Scotch dirt, and [113] a rabble of Scotch people of all sexes and ages. The women of Scotland have a faculty of looking exceedingly ugly, as they grow old. The Cathedral I have already noticed, in the record of my former visit to Scotland. I did it no justice then, nor shall do it any better now; but it is a fine old place, although it makes a colder and severer impression than most of the Gothic architecture which I have elsewhere seen. I do not know why this should be so; for portions of it are wonderfully rich, and everywhere there are arches opening beyond arches, and clustered pillars, and groined roofs, and vistas lengthening along the aisles. The person who shows this Cathedral is an elderly man, of jolly aspect and demeanor; he seems to be enthusiastic about the edifice, and to make it the thought and object of his life; and being such a merry sort of man, always saying something mirthfully, and yet, in all his thoughts, words, and actions, having a reference to this solemn cathedral, he has the effect of one of the corbels or gargoyles—those ludicrous, strange sculptures—which the Gothic architects appended to their arches.

The upper portion of the Cathedral, though very stately and beautiful, is not nearly so extraordinary as the crypts. Here the intricacy of the arches (and yet the profound system on which they are arranged) is inconceivable, even when you see [114] them;—a whole company of arches uniting in one keystone; arches uniting to form a glorious canopy over the shrine or tomb of a prelate; arches opening through and beyond one another, whichever way you look—all amidst a shadowy gloom, yet not one detail wrought out the less beautifully and delicately, because it could scarcely be seen. The wreaths of flowers, that festoon some of the arches, are cut in such relief that they do but just adhere to the stone on which they grow. The pillars are massive, and the arches very low, the effect being a twilight which, at first, leads the spectator to imagine himself under ground; but, by and by, I saw that the sunshine came in through the narrow windows, though it scarcely looked like sunshine then. For many years, these crypts were used as a burial-ground, and earth was brought in for the purpose of making graves; so that the noble columns were half-buried, and the beauty of the architecture quite lost and forgotten. Now, the dead men's bones, and the earth that covered them, have all been removed, leaving the original pavement of the crypt, or a new one in its stead, with only the old relics of saints, martyrs, and heroes, underneath; where they have lain so long that they have become a part of the spot. My wife was greatly delighted with the architecture of the crypt, and staid so long to draw some [115] curiously wrought arches that I was chilled quite through. The old keeper of the Cathedral regretted that we had not come during the late hot weather, when the everlasting damp and chill of the spot would have made us entirely comfortable. These crypts originated in the necessity of keeping the floor of the upper Cathedral on one level; the edifice being built on a declivity, and the height of the crypt being measured by the descent of the site.

On our way home, we walked down High-street, and looked into the gray quadrangles of the University, which, I suppose, I have described elsewhere.

10 °CLOCK, P.M. DUMBARTON.

AFTER writing the above, my wife and I walked out, and saw something of the newer portion of Glasgow; and really I am inclined to think it the stateliest city I ever beheld. The Exchange, and other public buildings, and the shops, especially in Buchanan-street, are very magnificent; the latter, especially, excelling those of London. There is, however, a pervading sternness and grimness, resulting from the dark gray granite, which is the universal building material both of the old and new edifices. Later in the forenoon, we again walked out, and went along Argyle-street, and through the Trongate and the Saltmarket. The two latter were formerly the principal [116] business-streets, and, with the High-street, the abode of the rich merchants and other great people of the town. The High street, and still more the Saltmarket, now swarm with the lower orders, to a degree which I never witnessed elsewhere; so that it is difficult to make one's way among the sallow and unclean crowd, and not at all pleasant to breathe in the noisomeness of the atmosphere. The children seem to have been unwashed from birth, and perhaps they go on gathering a thicker and thicker coating of dirt till their dying days. Some of the gray houses appear to have been stately and handsome in their day, and have their high gable-ends notched at the edges, like a flight of stairs. We saw the Tron-steeple, and the Statue of King William Third, and searched for the old Tolbooth; but are not quite certain whether we found the remains of it or no. On the authority of an old man, whom my wife questioned, we suppose that a tall, antique tower (called, I think, the market-cross) standing near the end of the High-street, appertained to the Tolbooth. The sidewalk, along which we went, passes right through this tower.

Wandering up the High-street, we turned once more into the quadrangle of the University, and ascended a broad stone-staircase, which ascends, square, and with right an[117]gular turns, on one corner, on the outside of the edifice. It is very striking in appearance, being ornamented with a balustrade, on which are large globes of stone, and a great lion and unicorn, curiously sculptured, on the opposite sides. While we waited here, staring about us, a man approached, and offered to show us the interior. He seemed to be in charge of the college-edifices. We accepted his offer, and were led first up this stone-staircase, and into a large and stately hall, panelled high towards the cieling [*sic*] with dark oak, and adorned with elaborately carved cornices and other wood-work. There was a long reading-table, towards one end of the hall, on which were laid pamphlets and periodicals; and a venerable old gentleman, with white head and bowed shoulders, sat there reading a newspaper. This was the Principal of the University; and as he looked towards us, graciously, yet as if expecting some explanation of our entrance, I approached and apologized for intruding, on the plea of our being strangers and anxious to see the college. He made a courteous response, though in exceedingly decayed and broken accents, being now eighty-six years old, and gave us free leave to inspect everything that was to be seen. This hall was erected two years after the Restoration of Charles II, and has [118] been the scene, doubtless, of many ceremonials and high banquettings, since that period; and among other illustrious personages, Queen Victoria has honored it with her presence. Thence we went into several recitation or lecture-rooms, in various parts of the college-buildings; but they were all of an extreme plainness, very unlike the rich old Gothic libraries, and chapels, and halls, which we saw in Oxford. Indeed, the contrast between this Scotch severity and that noble luxuriance and antique majesty, and rich and sweet repose, of Oxford, is very remarkable, both within the college-edifices and without. But we saw one or two curious things; for instance, a chair of mahogany, elaborately carved with the arms of Scotland and other devices, and having a piece of the kingly stone of Scone inlaid into its seat. This chair is used by the Principal on certain high occasions; and we ourselves, of course, sat down in it. Our guide assigned to it a date preposterously earlier than could have been the true one, judging either by the character of the carving, or by the fact that mahogany has not been known or used much more than a century and a half.

Afterwards he led us into the Divinity Hall, where, he said, there were some old portraits of historic people, and among [119] them an original picture of Mary Queen of Scots. There was, indeed, a row of old portraits at each end of the hall; for instance, Zachariah Boyd, who wrote the rhyming version of the Bible, which is still kept, safe from any critical eye, in the library of the University, to which he presented this, besides other more valuable benefactions, for which they have placed his bust in a niche, in the principal quadrangle; also, John Knox makes one of the row of portraits; and a dozen or two more of Scotch worthies, all very dark and dingy. As to the picture of Mary of Scotland, it proved to be not her's [*sic*] at all, but a picture of Queen Mary, the consort of William the Third, whose portrait, together with that of her sister, Queen Anne, hangs in the same row. We told our guide this, but he seemed unwilling to accept it as a fact. There is a Museum belonging to the University; but this, for some reason or other, could not be shown to us just at this time;

and there was little else to show. We just looked into the college-gardens; but, though of large extent, they are so meagre and bare—so unlike that lovely shade of the Oxford gardens—that we did not care to make further acquaintance with them.

Then we went back to our Hotel; and, if there were not [120] already more than enough of description, both past and to come, I should describe George's Square, on one side of which the Hotel is situated. A tall column rises in the grassy centre of it, lifting far into the upper air a fine statue of Sir Walter Scott, whom we saw to great advantage, last night, relieved against the sunset-sky, and there are statues of Sir John Moore, a native of Glasgow, and of James Watt, at corners of the square. Glasgow is certainly a noble city. We lunched (one of the most important events of a traveller's day, after all,) and embarking on board the steamer, at four °clock, came up the Clyde. Ben Lomond, and other Highland hills soon appeared on the Horizon; we passed Douglas Castle, on a point of land projecting into the river; and passing under the precipitous height of Dumbarton Castle, which we had long before seen, came to our voyage's end at this village, where we have put up at the Elephant Hotel. It is now late, and I must leave the narrative of our further sightseeing till to-morrow.

JULY 2ᵈ, MONDAY, DUMBARTON.

AFTER tea, not far from seven °clock, it being a beautiful decline of day, we set out to walk to Dumbarton Castle, which stands apart from the town, and is said to have been once surrounded by the waters of the Clyde. The rocky height on [121] which the Castle stands, is a very striking object, bulging up out of the Clyde, with abrupt decision, to the height of five hundred feet. Its summit is cloven in twain, the cleft reaching nearly to the bottom on the side towards the river, but not coming down so deeply on the landward side. It is precipitous all around; and wherever the steepness admits, or does not make assault impossible, there are gray ramparts around the hill, with cannon threatening the lower world. Our path led us beneath one of these precipices, several hundred feet sheer down, and with an ivied fragment of ruined wall at the top. A soldier, who sat by the wayside, told us that this was called the Lover's Leap, because a young girl (in some love-exigency or other) had once jumped down from it and came safely to the bottom. We reached the Castle-gate, which is near the shore of the Clyde, and there found another artillery-soldier, who guided us through the fortress. He said that there were but about a dozen soldiers now stationed in the Castle, and no officer.

The lowest battery looks towards the river, and consists of a few twelve pound cannon; but probably the chief danger of attack was from the land, and the chief pains have been taken to render the castle densifable [defensible] in that quarter. There are flights of stone-stairs, ascending up through the natural [122] avenue in the cleft of the double-summited rock; and about midway of the height, there is an arched door-way, beneath which there used to be a portcullis; so that, if an enemy had won the lower part of the fortress, the upper portion was still inaccessible. Where the cleft of the rock widens into a gorge, there are several buildings, old, but not appertaining to the ancient castle, which has almost entirely disappeared. We ascended both summits, and reaching the loftiest point on the right, stood upon the foundation of a tower that dates back to the fifth century, whence we had a glorious prospect of Highlands and Lowlands; the chief object being Ben Lomond, with its great dome, among a hundred other blue and misty hills, with the sun going down over them; and in another direction, the Clyde winding far downward, through the plain; with the height of Dumbuck close at hand, and Douglas Castle at no great distance. On the ramparts beneath us, the soldier pointed out the spot where Wallace scaled the wall, climbing an apparently inaccessible precipice, and taking the castle. The principal parts of the ancient castle appear to have been on the other and lower summit of the hill; and thither we now went, and traced the outline of its wall, although none of it is now remaining. Here is the magazine, still containing some powder, and here is a battery of eighteen pound [123] guns, with pyramids of balls all in readiness against an assault; which, however, hardly any turn of human affairs can hereafter bring about. The appearance of a fortress is kept up merely for ceremony's sake; and these cannon have grown antiquated. Moreover, as the soldier told us, they are now seldom or never fired even for purposes of rejoicing or salute, because their thunder produces the singular effect of depriving the garrison of water. There is a large tank, and the concussion causes the rifts of the stone to open, and thus lets the water out. Above this battery, and elsewhere about the fortress, there are warders' turrets or sentry-boxes, of stone, resembling great pepper-boxes. When Doctor Johnson visited the Castle, he introduced his bulky person into one of these narrow receptacles, and found it difficult to get out again. A gentleman who accompanied him was just stepping forward to offer his assistance; but Bozzy whispered him to take no notice, lest Johnson should be offended; so they left him to get out as he could. He did finally extricate himself; else we might have seen his skeleton in this narrow receptacle. Boswell does not tell this story, which seems to have been handed down by local tradition.

The less abrupt declivities of the rock are covered with [124] grass, and afford food for a few sheep, who scamper about the heights, and seem to have attained the dexterity of goats in clambering. I never knew a purer air than this seems to be, nor a lovelier, golden sunset.

Descending into the gorge again, we went into the armory, which is in one of the buildings occupying the space between the two hill-tops. It formerly contained a large collection of arms; but these have been removed (to the tower of London, I believe) and there are now only some tattered banners, of which I do not know the history, and some festoons of pistols, and some grenades, shells, and grape and cannister [sic] shot, kept merely as curiosities; and, far more interesting than the above, a few battle-axes, daggers, and spear-heads, from the field of Bannockburn; and, far more interesting than the above, the sword of William Wallace. It is a formidable-looking weapon, made for being swayed with both hands, and, with its hilt on the floor, reached about to my chin; but the young girl, who showed us the armoury, said that about nine inches had been broken off the point. The blade was not massive, but somewhat thin, compared with its great length; and I found that I could brandish it (using both hands) with perfect ease. It is two edged, without any gaps, and is quite brown and lustreless with old rust, from [125] point to hilt.

These, so far as I now remember, were all the memorables of our visit to Dumbarton Castle, which is a most interesting spot, and connected with a long series of historical events. It was first besieged by the Danes, and had a prominent share in all the warfare of Scotland, so long as the old warlike times and manners lasted. Our soldier was very intelligent and courteous, but, as usual with these guides, was somewhat apocryphal in his narrative; telling us that Mary Queen of Scots was confined here before being taken to England, and that the cells, in which she then lived, are still extant under one of the ramparts. The fact is, she was brought here when a child of six years old, before going to France, and doubtless scrambled up and down these heights as freely and merrily as the sheep whom we saw. We now returned to our Hotel, (a very nice one,) and found the street of Dumbarton all alive in the summer evening, with the sports of children and the gossip of grown people. There was almost no night; for, at twelve °clock, there was still a golden daylight, and Yesterday, before it died, must have met its Morrow.

In the lower part of the fortress of Dumbarton, there is a large sundial of stone, which was made by a French offi[126]cer, imprisoned here during the Peninsular War. It still numbers faithfully the hours that are sunny, and is a lasting memorial of him in the stronghold of his enemies. Dumbarton is the Balclutha of Ossian.[437]

Nearly 9, P.M. Inverarnan. After breakfast, at Dumbarton, I went out to look at the town, which seems to be of considerable size, and to possess both commerce and manufactures. There was a screw steamship at the pier; and many sailor-looking people are seen about the streets. There are very few old houses, though still the town retains an air of antiquity which one does not well see how to account for, when everywhere there is a modern front, and all the characteristics of a street built to-day. Turning from the main-street, I crossed a bridge over the Clyde, and gained from it the best view of the cloven hill of Dumbarton Castle that I had yet found. The two summits are wider apart, more fully relieved from each other, than when seen from other points; and the highest ascends into a perfect pyramid, the lower one being obtusely rounded. There seem to be iron-works, or some kind of manufactory, on the farther side of the bridge; and I noticed a quaint, chateau-like mansion, with hanging turrets, standing apart from the street, probably built by some [127] person enriched by business. These are all the remarks I shall stop to make about

Dumbarton, which we left at about 1/2 past twelve °clock, taking the rail to Balloch, and the steamer to the head of Loch Lomond.

Wild mountain scenery is not very good to describe; nor do I think that any distinct impressions are ever conveyed by such attempts; so I mean to be brief in what I say about this part of our tour, especially as I suspect that I have said whatever I knew how to say, in the record of my former visit to the Highlands. As for Loch Lomond, it lies amidst very striking scenery, being poured in among the gorges of steep and lofty mountains, which nowhere stand aside to give it room, but, on the contrary, seem to do their best to shut it in. It is everywhere narrow, compared with its length of thirty miles; but it is the beauty of a lake to be of no greater width than to allow of the scenery of one of its shores being perfectly enjoyed from the other. The scenery of the Highlands (so far as I have seen them) cannot properly be called rich, but stern and impressive, with very hard outlines, which are unsoftened almost by any foliage, though at this season they are green to their summits. They have hardly flesh enough to cover their bones—hardly earth [enough] to lie over their rocky substance—as may be seen by the [128] minute variety—the, as it were, notched and jagged appearance of the profile of their sides and summits; this being caused by the scarcely covered rocks wherewith these great hills are heaped together.

Our little steamer stopped at half-a-dozen places on its voyage up the lake, most of them being stations where Hotels have been established for the effectual fleecing of summer tourists. Morally, the Highlands must have been more completely sophisticated by the invention of railways and steamboats, than almost any other part of the world; but physically, it can have wrought no great change. These mountains, in their general aspect, must be very much the same as they were a thousand years ago; for their sides never were capable of cultivation, nor ever, with such a soil and so bleak an atmosphere, have been much more richly wooded than we see them now. They seem to me to be among the unchangeable things of Nature, like the sea and sky; but there is no saying what use human ingenuity may hereafter put them to. At all events, I have no doubt in the world that they will go out of fashion in due time; for the taste for mountains and wild scenery is, with most people, an acquired taste; and it was easy to see, to-day, that nine people in ten really care noth[129]ing about them. One group of gentlemen and ladies (men and women, at least) spent the whole time in listening to a trial for murder, which was read aloud by one of their number from a newspaper. I rather imagine that a taste for trim gardens is the most natural and universal taste, as regards landscape. But perhaps it is necessary for the health of the human mind and heart that there should be a possibility of taking refuge in what is wild, and uncontaminated by any culture; and so it has been ordained that science shall never alter the aspect of the sky, whether stern, angry, or beneficent, nor of the awful sea, either in calm or tempest, nor of these rude Highlands. But they will go out of general fashion, as I have said; and perhaps the next fashionable taste will be for Cloud Land—

that is, looking skyward, and observing the wonderful variety of scenery, that now constantly passes unnoticed among the clouds.

At the head of the lake, we found that there was only a horse-cart to convey our luggage to the Hotel at Inverarnan, and that we ourselves must walk, the distance being two miles. It had sprinkled, occasionally, during our voyage, but was now sunshiny, and not excessively warm; so we set forth contentedly enough, and had an agreeable walk along [130] an almost perfectly level road; for it is one of the beauties of these hills, that they descend abruptly down, and leave off at angle with the vallies [sic] between them, instead of undulating away forever. There were lofty heights on each side of us, but not so lofty as to have won a distinctive name; and adown their sides we could see the rocky pathways of cascades, which, at this season, are either quite dry, or were trickles of a rill. The hills and vallies [sic], hereabouts, abound in streams, sparkling through pebbly beds, and forming here and [t]here a dark pool; and they would be populous with trout, if all England, with one fell purpose, did not come hither to fish them. A fisherman must find it difficult to gratify his propensities, in these days; for even the lakes and streams in Norway are now preserved. Julian, by-the-by, threatens ominously to be a fisherman. He rode the latter portion of the way to the Hotel on the luggage-cart; and when we arrived, we found that he had already gone off to catch fish (or to attempt it, for there is as much chance of his catching a whale as a trout;) in a mountain-stream near the house. I went in search of him, but without success, and was somewhat startled at the depth and blackness of some of the pools into which the stream settled itself and slept. Finally, he came [131] in while we were at dinner. We afterwards walked out with him to let him play at fishing, and discovered, on the bank of the stream, a wonderful oak, with as much as a dozen stems, springing either from close to the ground or within a foot or two of it, and looking like at least twelve separate trees instead of one.

INVERSNAID, JULY 3ᵈ, FRIDAY.

LAST night seemed to close in clear, and even at midnight it was still light enough to read, but this morning rose on us misty and chill, with spattering showers of rain. Clouds momentarily settled and shifted on the hill-tops, shutting us in even more completely than these steep and rugged green walls would be sure to do, even in the clearest weather. Often, these clouds came down and enveloped us in a drizzle, or rather a shower of such minute drops that they had not weight enough to fall. This, I suppose, was a genuine Scotch mist; and as such, it is well enough to have experienced it, though I would willingly never see it again. Such being the state of the weather, my wife did not venture out at all, but wrote courageously, all the morning, and made great progress with the history of our adventures which she sends constantly by post to Una. I strolled about the yard, in the intervals of rain-drops [132] gazing up at the hill-sides, and recognizing that there is a vast variety of shape, of light and shadow, and incidental circumstance, even in what looks so monotonous at first as the green slope of a hill. The little rills that come down from the summits were rather more distinguishable than yesterday, having been refreshed by the night's rain; but still they were very much out of proportion with the wide pathways of bare rock, adown which they ran. These little rivulets, no doubt, often lead through the wildest scenery that is to be found in the Highlands or anywhere else, and to the formation and wildness of which they have greatly contributed, by sawing away for countless ages, and thus deepening the ravines.

I suspect the American clouds are more picturesque than those of Great Britain, whatever our mountains may be; at least, I remember the Berkshire hills looking grander, under the influence of mist and cloud, than the Highlands did to day. Our clouds seem to be denser and heavier, and more decided, and form greater contrasts of light and shade. I have remarked in England that the cloudy firmament, even on a day of settled rain, always appears thinner than those I had been accustomed to at home; so as to deceive me with constant expectations of better weather. [133] It has been the same to-day. Whenever I looked upward, I thought it might be going to clear up; but, instead of that, it began to rain more in earnest, after mid-day; and at 1/2 past two, we left Inverarnan in a smart shower. At the head of the lake, we took the steamer, with the rain pouring heavier than ever, and landed at Inversnaid under the same dismal auspices. We left a very good Hotel behind us, and have come to another that seems also good. Indeed, I have hardly met so comfortable accommodations anywhere on this side of the water, as in some of the Scotch inns, and here in the Highlands they are certain to be good. We are more picturesquely situated at this spot than at Inverarnan, our Hotel being within a short distance of the lake shore, with a glen just across the water which will doubtless be worth looking at, when the mist permits us to see it. A good many tourists were standing about the door, when we arrived, and looked at us with the curiosity of idle and weather-bound people. The lake is here narrow, but a hundred fathoms deep; so that a great part of the height of the mountains, which beset it round, is hidden beneath its surface.

JULY 4th SATURDAY, INVERSNAID.

THIS morning opened still misty; but with a more hopeful promise than yesterday; and when [134] I went out, after breakfast, there were gleams of sunshine here and there on the hill-sides, falling, one did not exactly see how, through the volumes of cloud. Close beside this Hotel of Inversnaid, is the waterfall where Wordsworth saw the Highland Maid on whom he wrote some pretty verses;[438] all night, my room being on that side of the house, I had heard the voice of the falling water; and now I ascended beside it to a point where it is crossed by a wooden bridge. There is thence a view, upward and downward, of the most striking descents of the river, as I believe they call it; though it it [sic] is but a mountain stream which tumbles down an irregular and broken staircase, in its headlong haste to reach the lake. It is very picturesque, however, with its ribbons of white foam over the precipitous steps, and its deep b[l]ack pools, overhung by black rocks, which reverberate the rumble of the falling water. Julian and I ascended a little distance along the cascade, and then turned aside, he going up the hill, and I taking a path along its side which gave me a view across the lake. I rather think this particular stretch of Loch Lomond, in front of Inversnaid, is the most beautiful lake and mountain view that I have ever seen. It is so shut in that you can see nothing beyond, nor would suspect anything more to exist than this watery vale among the hills; except that directly opposite there is the beautiful glen of Inveruglas, which [135] winds away among the feet of Ben Crook [?], Ben Ein [An?], Ben Vane, Ben Voirlich, and other nameless heights, standing mist-wreathed together. The mists, this morning, had a very soft and beautiful effect, and made the mountains tenderer than I have hitherto felt them to be; and they lingered about their heads like morning dreams, flitting and returning, and letting the sunshine in, and snatching it away again. My wife came up the hillside, and we enjoyed it together till the steamer came smoking its pipe along the loch, stopt to land some passengers, and steamed away again. While we stood there, a Highlander passed by us, with a very dark tartan, and bare shanks most enormously calved. I presume he wears the dress for the sole purpose of displaying those stalwart legs; for he proves to be no genuine Gael, but a manufacturer named Hewson, who has a shooting-box, or a share in one, on the hill above the Hotel.

We now engaged a boat, and were rowed to Rob Roy's Cave, which is perhaps half a mile distant, up the lake. The shores look much more striking from a row-boat, creeping along near the margin, than from a steamer in the middle of the loch; and the ridge, beneath which Rob's Cave lies, is precipitous with gray rocks and clothed, too, with thick foliage. Over the cave itself, there is a huge ledge of rock, from which immense frag[136]ments have tumbled down, ages and ages ago, and fallen together in such a way as to leave a large, irregular crevice between them, with a small opening to the outer air; and this irregular crevice is Rob Roy's cave. We scrambled up to its mouth by some natural stairs, that occasionally required an inconveniently long stride; and scrambled down into its depth, by the aid of a ladder. I suppose I have already described this hole, in the record of my former visit. Certainly, Rob Roy—and Robert Bruce, who is said to have inhabited it before him—were not to be envied their accommodations; yet these were not so very intolerable when compared with a Highland cabin, or with cottages such as Burns inhabited.

Julian had chosen to remain in the boat to fish. On our return from the cave, we found that he had caught nothing; but just as we stept into the boat, a fish drew his float far under water, and Julian tugging at one end of the line and the fish at the other, the latter escaped with the hook in his mouth. Julian avers that he saw the fish, and gives its measurement at about eighteen inches; but the fishes that escape us are always of tremendous size. The boatman thought it might have been a pike.

July 5th, Sunday, The Trossachs Hotel, Ardcheanochrochan.

WE had luncheon before two °clock, and, not being able to get a post-chaise, took [137] places in the omnibus for the head of Loch Katrine. Going up to pay a parting visit to the waterfall, before starting, I met with Miss Cumberland (as she lately was) who is now on her wedding-tour as Mrs. Booth. She was painting the falls in oil, with good prospect of a successful picture. She came down to the hotel to see my wife; and soon afterwards Julian and I set out to ascend the steep hill that comes down upon the lake at Inversnaid, leaving the omnibus to follow at leisure. The highlander, who took us to Rob Roy's cave, had foreboded rain from the way in which the white clouds hung about the mountain-tops; nor was his augury at fault, for just at three °clock (the time he foretold) there were a few rain-drops, and a more defined shower during the afternoon, while we were on Loch Katrine. The few drops, however, did not disturb us; and reaching the top of the hill, Julian and I turned aside to examine the old stone fortress which was erected in this mountain-pass to bridle the Highlanders, after the rebellion of 1745. It stands in as desolate and dismal a situation as I ever saw, at the foot of long, bare, slopes, on mossy ground, in the midst of a disheartening loneliness, only picturesque because it is so exceedingly ungenial and unlovely. The chief interest of this spot is in the fact that Wolfe, in his earlier military career, was stationed here. The fortress was a very plain structure, built of rough stones, in the form of a par[138]ralelogram [sic], the sides of which (one side, at least) I paced, and found it, I think, between thirty and forty of my paces. The two ends have fallen down; the two sides that remain are about the height of an ordinary two story house, and have little portholes for defence, but no openings of the size of windows. The roof is gone, and the interior space overgrown with grass. Two little girls were at play in one corner; and going round to the rear of the ruin, I saw that a little highland cabin had been built against the wall. A dog sat in the doorway, and gave notice of my approach, and some hens kept up their peculiarly domestic converse about the door.

We kept on our way, after looking back towards Loch Lomond, and wondering at the grandeur which Ben Vane and Ben Voirlich, and the rest of the Benfraternity, had suddenly put on. The mists, which had hung about them all day, had now descended lower, and now lay among the depths and gorges of the hills, where also the sun shone softly down among them, and filled those deep mountain-laps, as it were, with a dimmer sunshine. Ben Vane, too, and his brethren, had a veil of mist all about them, which seemed to render them really transparent; and they had unaccountably grown higher, vastly hig[h]er, than when we viewed them from the shore of the lake. It was as if we were viewing them through the medium of a poet's imagination. All along the road, since we left [139] Inversnaid, there had been the stream which there forms the waterfall, and which here was brawling down little declivities, and sleeping in black pools, which we disturbed by flinging stones into them from the roadside. We passed a drunken old gentleman, who civilly bade me good

day; and a man and woman at work in a field, the former of whom shouted to
inquire the time of day; and we had come in sight of little Loch Arklet before
the omnibus came up with us. It was about five °clock when we reached the
head of Loch Katrine, and went on board the steamer Rob Roy; and setting
forth on our voyage, a Highland piper made music for us the better part of
the way.

We did not see Loch Katrine, perhaps, under its best presentment, for the
surface was roughened with a little wind, and darkened even to inky blackness by the clouds that overhung it. The hill-tops, too, had as dark a frown
as I ever saw hill-tops wear. A lake of this size cannot be terrific, and is therefore seen to best advantage when it is beautiful. The scenery of its shores
is not altogether so rich and lovely as I had pre-imagined; not equal, indeed,
to the best parts of Loch Lomond; the hills being lower, and of a more
ridgy shape, and exceedingly bare, at least towards the lower end. But they
turn the lake aside with headland after headland, and shut it in closely, [140]
and open one vista after another, so that the eye is never weary, and least
of all as we approach the end. The length of the loch is ten miles, and at its
termination it meets the pass of the Trossachs, between Ben An and Ben
Venue, which are the rudest and shaggiest hills that I have anywhere seen
among the Highlands. The steamer passes Ellen's isle, but to the right,
which is the side opposite to that on which Fitz-James must be supposed to have
approached it.[439] It is a very small island, situated where the loch narrows,
and is perhaps less than a quarter of a mile distant from either shore; it looks
like a lump of rock, with just soil enough to support a crowd of dwarf oaks,
birches, and firs, which do not grow high enough to be shadowy trees. Our
voyage being over, we landed, and found two omnibusses [sic], which took us
through the famous pass of the Trossachs, a distance of a mile and a quarter,
to a hotel, erected in castellated guise by Lord Willoughby d'Eresby. We were
put into a parlour within one of the round towers, panelled all around, and with
four narrow windows, opening through deep embrasures. No play-castle was
ever more like the reality, and it is really a very good hotel, like all that we
have had experience of, in the Highlands. After tea, we walked out, and visited
a little Kirk that stands near the shore of Loch Achray, at a good point of view
for seeing the hills roundabout; and, about ten or eleven °clock, I [. . .]
with a glass of whiskey.[440] [141] This morning opened cloudily; but after
breakfast (salmon, boiled eggs, and coffee) I set out alone and walked through
the pass of the Trossachs, and thence by a path along the right shore of the
lake. It is a very picturesque and beautiful path, following the windings of the
lake, now along the beach, now over an impending bank, until it comes opposite
to Ellen's isle, which, on this side, looks more worthy to be the island of the
poem, than as we first saw it. Its shore is craggy and precipitous; but there
was a point where it seemed possible to land, nor was it too much to fancy that
there might be a rustic habitation among the shrubbery of this rugged spot.
It is foolish to look into these matters too strictly. Scott evidently used as

much freedom with his natural scenery as he did with his historic incidents; and he could have made nothing of either one or the other, if he had been more scrupulous in his arrangement and adornment of them. In his description of the Trossachs, he has produced something very beautiful, and as true as possible, though certainly its beauty has a little of the scene-painter's gloss in it; Nature is better, no doubt; but Nature cannot be exactly re-produced on canvas or in print; and the artist's only resource is to substitute something that may stand in stead of and suggest the truth.

The path still kept onward, after passing Ellen's isle; and [142] I followed it, finding it wilder, more shadowy with o'er hanging foliage of trees old and young, more like a mountain-path in Berkshire or New Hampshire—yet still with an old-world restraint and cultivation about it—the farther I went. At last, it came to some bars; and though the track was still seen beyond, I took this as a hint to stop, especially as I was now two or three miles from the Hotel, and it just then began to rain. My umbrella was a poor one at best, and had been tattered and turned inside out, a day or two ago, by a gust on Loch Lomond; but I spread it to the shower and furthermore took refuge under the thickest umbrage I could find. The rain came straight down, and bubbled in the loch; the little rills gathered force and plashed merrily over the stones; the leaves of the trees condensed the shower into larger drops, and shed them down upon me where I stood. Still, I was comfortable enough in a thick Skye-tweed, and waited patiently till the shower abated; then took my way homeward, and admired the pass of the Trossachs more than when I first traversed it. If it has a fault, it is one that few scenes in Great Britain share with it—that is, the trees and shrubbery, with which the steeps and precipices are shagged, conceal them a little too much. A crag, streaked with black and white, here and there shows its head aloft, or its whole height from base to summit, and suggests that more of such sublimity is hid[143]den than revealed. I think, however, that it is this unusual shagginess which made the Trossachs a favorite scene with Scott and with the people on this side of the water generally. There are many scenes as good in America, needing only their poet.

July 6th, Monday, Brig of Allan.

We dined, yesterday, at the Ordinary, at the suggestion of the butler, in order to give less trouble to the servants of the Hotel, and afford them an opportunity to go to Kirk. The dining-room is in accordance with the rest of the architecture and fittings-up of the house, and is a very good reproduction of an old baronial hall, with high panellings and a roof of dark, polished wood. There were about twenty guests at table; and if they and the waiters had been dressed in medi-aeval costume, we might have imagined ourselves banqueting in the middle-ages.

After dinner, my wife, and Julian, and I, all took a walk through the Trossachs-pass again, and by the right-hand path along the lake, as far as Ellen's Isle. It was very pleasant; there being gleams of calm evening sunshine, gilding the mountain sides, and putting a golden crown occasionally on the head of Ben Venue. It is wonderful how many aspects a mountain has; how many mountains there are in every single mountain!—how they vary, too, in apparent altitude and bulk. When we reached the lake, its surface was almost unruffled, except by [144] now and then the narrow pathway of a breeze as if the wing of an unseen spirit had just grazed it in flitting across. The scene was very beautiful; and, on the whole, I do not know that Walter Scott has overcharged his description, although he has symbolized the reality by symbols and images which it might not precisely suggest to other minds. We were reluctant to quit the spot, and cherish still a hope (though it does not seem very likely to be gratified) of seeing it again.

This was a lowering and sullen morning; but, soon after breakfast, I took a walk in the opposite direction to Loch Katrine, and reached the Brig of Turk, a little beyond which is the New Trossachs Hotel, and the little, rude village of Duncraggan, consisting of a few thatched hovels of stone, at the foot of a bleak and dreary hill. To the left, stretching up between this and other hills, is the valley of Glenfinlas, a very awful region, in Scot[t]'s poetry and in Highland tradition, as the haunts of spirits and enchantments. I never saw a more desolate prospect than it presented. The walk back to the Trossachs showed me Ben Venue and Ben An under new aspects, the bare summit of the latter rising in a perfect pyramid, whereas, from other points of view, he looks like quite a different mountain. Sometimes a gleam of sunshine came out upon the rugged side of Ben Venue, but his prevailing mood, like [145] that of the rest of the landscape, was stern and gloomy. I wish I could give an idea of the variety of surface upon one of these hill-sides, so bulging out and hollowed in, so bare where the rock breaks through, so shaggy in other places with heath, and then perhaps a thick umbrage of birch, oak, and ash, ascending from the base high upward. When I think I have described them, I remember quite a different aspect, and find it equally true, and yet lacking something to make it the whole or an adequate truth.

Julian had gone with me, part of the way, but stopt to fish with a pin-hook in Loch Achray, which bordered along our path. When I returned, I found him much elated at having hooked a fish, which, however, had got away, carrying his pinhook along with it. Then he had amused himself with taking some lizards by the tail, and had collected several in a small hollow of the rocks. We now walked home together, and lunched, in anticipation of our departure, which was to take place at ½ past three. At that hour, we took our seats in a genuine old-fashioned stage-coach, of which there are few specimens now to be met with. The coachman was smartly dressed in the Queen's scarlet, and was a very pleasant and affable personage, conducting himself towards the passengers with courteous authority. Inside, we were [146] four including Julian, but on top there were at least a dozen; and I would willingly have been there too, but had taken an inside place under apprehension of rain, and was not allowed to change it. Our drive was not marked by much describable incident. On changing horses, at Callander, we alighted, and saw Ben Ledi behind us, making a picturesque back ground to the little town, which seems to be the meeting-point of the Highlands and Lowlands. We again changed horses at Doune, an old town which would doubtless have been worth seeing, had time permitted. Thence we kept on till the coach drew up at a spacious hotel, where we alighted, fancying that we had reached Stirling, which was to have been our journey's end; but, after fairly establishing ourselves in our parlour, we found that it was the Brig of Allan. The place is three miles short of Stirling. Nevertheless, we did not much regret the mistake, finding that the Brig of Allan is the principal Spa of Scotland, and a very pleasant spot, to all outward appearance. After supper, we walked out, both up and down the village-street; and across the bridge, and up a gently ascending street beyond it, whence we had a fine view of a glorious plain, out of which rose several insulated headlands. One of these was the height on which stands Stir[147]ling Castle, and which reclines on the plain like a hound, or a lion, or a sphinx, holding the castle on the highest part, where its head should be. A mile or two distant from this picturesque hill rises another, still more striking, called the Abbey Craig, on which is a ruin, and where is to be built the monument to William Wallace. I cannot conceive of a nobler or more fitting pedestal. The sullenness of the day had vanished; the air was cool, but invigorating; and the cloud scenery was as fine as that below it.

After this, I smoked a cigar at the hotel; and though it was nearly ten °clock, the boys of the village were in full shout and play; for these long and late summer evenings appear to keep the children out of bed interminably.

July 7th, Tuesday, Linlithgow.

We bestirred ourselves early, this morning, sat down to a breakfast of broiled salmon, whitings, mutton-chop, and eggs (the broiled salmon, however, is but a reminiscence of yesterday's breakfast,) and took the rail for Stirling at about five minutes before eight. It is but a few minutes' ride; so that doubtless we were even earlier on the field than if we had slept at Stirling. After arrival, our first call was at the post-office, where I found a large package containing letters from America, principally for my wife, but none from Una. We then went to a bookseller's shop and bought some views of Stirling [148] and the neighborhood; and it is surprising what a quantity and variety of engravings there are of every noted place that we have visited. At two bookseller's shops, you seldom find two sets alike. It is rather nauseating to find that what you came to see has already been viewed in all its lights, over and over again, with thousandfold repetition; and, beyond question, its depictment in words has been attempted still oftener than with the pencil. It will be worth while to go back to America, were it only for the chance of finding a still virgin scene.

We ascended along the steep slope of the Castle Hill, occasionally passing an antique-looking house, with a high, notched gable; perhaps with an ornamented front, until we came to the carved, sculptured, and battlemented wall, with an archway, that stands just below the castle. I believe the Earl of Mar had something to do with the erection of this. A shabby-looking man now accosted us, and could hardly be shaken off (I have met with several such burrs, in my experience of sight seeing,) keeping along with us in spite of all hints to the contrary, and insisting on pointing out objects of interest. He showed us a house in Broad-street, below the castle and the cathedral, which he said had once been inhabited by Henry Darnley, Queen Mary's husband. There was little or nothing peculiar [149] in its appearance; a large, gray, gabled-house, standing lengthwise to the street, with three windows in the roof, and connected with other houses on each side. Almost directly across the street, too, from the Earl of Mar's edifice, he pointed to an archway through the side of a house, I think; and peeping through it, we found a soldier on guard in a courtyard, the sides of which were occupied by an old mansion of the Argyle family, having towers at the corners, with conical tops, like those re-produced in the Hotel at the Trossachs. It is now occupied as a military hospital. Shaking off our self-inflicted guide, we now found our way to the castle-parade, and to the gateway, where a soldier (with a tremendously red-nose, and two medals) at once took charge of us.

Beyond all doubt, I have quite as good a description of the Castle and Cärse of Stirling, in a former volume of my Journal, as I can now write. We passed through the outer rampart of Queen Anne; through between [*sic*] the old round gate-towers of an earlier day, and beneath the vacant arch where the portcullis used to fall, thus reaching the inner region, where stands the old palace on one side, and the old parliament-house on the other. The former looks aged, ragged, and rusty, but makes a good appearance enough pictorially, being adorned all roundabout with statues (they may have been white marble once, but [150] are as gray as weatherbeaten granite now) which look down from between the windows above the basement-story. A photograph would give the idea of very rich antiquity, but as it really stands, looking on a gravelled court-yard, and with *"Canteen"* painted on one of its doors, the spectator does not find it very impressive. The great hall of this palace, the soldier told us, is now parti[ti]oned off into two or three rooms; and the whole edifice is arranged to serve as barracks; of course, no trace of ancient magnif[ic]ence, if anywise destructible, can be left in the interior. We were not shown into this palace; nor into the Parliament House; nor into the tower where King James stabbed the Earl of Douglas. When I was here a year ago, I went up the old staircase and into the room where the murder was committed; although it had then recently been the scene of a fire, which consumed as much of it as was inflammable. The window, whence the Earl's body was thrown, then remained, and I looked out of it; but now the whole tower seems to have been renewed, leaving, so far as I could see, only the mullions of the historic window.

We merely looked up at the new, light-colored free-stone of the restored tower, in passing, and ascended to the ramparts, where we found one of the most splendid views, morally and materially, that this world can show. Indeed, I think [151] there cannot be such another landscape as the Cärse of Stirling, set in such a frame as it is—the highlands, comprehending our friends Ben Lomond, Ben Venue, Ben An, and the whole Ben fraternity, with the Grampians, surrounding it to the westward and northward; and in other directions some range of prominent objects to shut it in; and the plain itself so worthy of the richest setting, so fertile, so beautiful, so written over and over again with histories. The silver Links of Forth are as sweet and gently picturesque an object as a man sees in a lifetime. I do not wonder that Providence made great things happen on this plain; it was like choosing a good piece of canvas to paint a great picture upon. Bannockburn (which we saw beneath us, with the Gillie's Hill, on the right,) could not have been fought upon a meaner plain; nor the field of Wallace's victory; and if any other great historic act still remains to be done, in this country, I should imagine the Cärse of Stirling as the future scene of it. Scott seems to me hardly to have done justice to this landscape, or to have bestowed pains enough in putting it in strong relief before the world; although it is from the light shed on it, on so much other Scottish scenery, by his mind, that we chiefly see it and take an interest in it.

Probably, in my account of my last visit, I mentioned the [152] peep-hole, through which Queen Mary used to look down from the ramparts upon the games in the archery ground, herself unseen. I do not remember seeing the hill of execution before; a mound on the same level as the castle's base, looking towards the Highlands. A solitary cow was now feeding there. I should imagine that no person could ever have been unjustly executed there; the spot is too much in the sight of heaven and earth, to countenance injustice.

Descending from the ramparts, we went into the Armory, which I did not see on my former visit. The superintendent of this department is an old soldier of very great intelligence, vast communicativeness, and quite absorbed in thinking of and handling weapons; for he seems to be a practical armorer. He had few things to show us that were very interesting; a helmet or two, a bomb and grenade, from the Crimea; also, some muskets from the same quarter, one of which, with a sword at the end, he spoke of admiringly, as the best weapon in the collection; its only fault being its extreme weight. He showed us, too, some Minie rifles, and whole ranges of the oldfashioned Brown Bess, which had helped to win Wellington's victories; also, the oldfashioned halberts of sergeants, now laid aside; and some swords that had been used at the battle of Sheriff Muir. These latter were very short, not reaching to the [153] floor when I held one of them, point downward, in my hand. This brevity of the blade, and consequent closeness of the encounter, must have given the weapon a more dagger-like murderousness. Hanging in the hall of arms, there were two tattered banners that had gone through the Peninsular battles, one of them belonging to the gallant 42^d regiment. The armorer gave my wife a rag from each of these banners, consecrated by so much battle-smoke; also, a piece of old oak, half burned to charcoal, which had been rescued from the panelling of the Douglas Tower. We saw better things, moreover, than all these rusty weapons and ragged flags; namely, the pulpit and communion-table of John Knox. The frame of the former, if I remember rightly is complete; but one or two of the panels are knocked out and lost, and, on the whole, it looks as if it had been shaken to pieces by the thunder of his holdings-forth—much worm-eaten, too, is the old oak wood, as well it may be, for the letters M.D. (1500) are carved on the front. The communiontable is polished, and in much better preservation.

Then the armorer showed us a Damascus blade, of the kind that will cut a delicate silk handkerchief while floating in the air; and some inlaid matchlock guns. A child's little toy-gun was lying on a work bench among all this array of weapons; and when I took it up and smiled, he said that it was his son's. So he called [154] in a little fellow of four years old, who was playing in the castle-yard, and made him go through the musket-exercise, which he did with great good-will. This small Son of a Gun, the father assured us, cares for nothing but arms, and has attained all his skill with the musket merely by looking at the soldiers on parade. What else the armorer showed us I have forgotten; but truly he is a man whose heart is in his business and who fits well into his position.

Our soldier (who had resigned the care of us to the armorer,) met us again at the door, and led us round the remainder of the ramparts, dismissing us finally by the gate at which we entered. All the time we were in the castle, there had been a great discordance of drums and fifes, caused by the musicians who were practising just under the walls; likewise the sergeants were drilling their squads of men, and putting them through strange gymnastic motions. Most, if not all, [of] the garrison belongs to a Highland regiment, and those whom we saw on duty, in full costume, looked very martial and gallant. Emerging from the castle, we took the broad and pleasant footpath which circles it about, midway on the grassy steep which descends from the rocky precipice on which the walls are built. This is a very beautiful walk, and affords a most striking view of the castle, right above our heads, the height of its walls forming [155] one line with the precipice. The grassy hill side is almost as precipitous as the dark gray rock that rises out of it to form the foundation of the castle; but wild rose bushes, both of a white and red variety, are abundant here, and all in bloom; nor are these the only flowers. There is also shrubbery, in some spots, tossing up green waves against the precipice; and broad sheets of ivy, here and there, mantle the headlong rock, which also has a growth of weeds, and even of rose bushes, in its crevices. The castle walls above, however, are quite bare of any such growth. Thus, looking up at the old, storied fortress, and looking abroad over the wide, historic plain, we wandered half way round the castle, and then retracing our steps, entered the town close by an old hospital.

An hospital it was, or had been intended for; but the authorities of the town had made some convenient arrangement with those entitled to the charity, and had appropriated the ancient edifice to themselves. So said a boy, who showed us into the Guildhall, an apartment with a vaulted oaken-roof, and otherwise of antique aspect and furniture; all of which, however, were modern restorations. We then went into an old church, or Cathedral, which was divided into two parts; one of them, in which I saw the royal arms, being probably for the Church of England service, and the other for the Kirk of Scotland. I re-member little or [156] nothing of this edifice, except that the Covenanters had uglified it with pews and a gallery, and white-wash; though I doubt not it was a stately Gothic church, with innumerable enrichments and incrustations of beauty, when it passed from popish hands into theirs. Thence we wandered downward through a back-street, amid very shabby houses, some of which bore tokens of having once been the abode of courtly and noble personages. We paused before one that displayed, I think, the sign of a spirit-retailer, and looked as disreputable as a house could, yet was built of stalwart stone and had two circular towers in front, once, doubtless, crowned with conical tops. We asked an elderly man whether he knew anything of the history of this house; but he said that he had been acquainted with it for almost fifty years, but never knew anything noteworthy about it. Reaching the foot of the hill, along whose back the streets of Stirling run, and which blooms out into the Castle craig, we returned to the railway, and, at about ½ past twelve, took leave of Stirling.

I forgot to tell the things that, I believe, awakened rather more sympathy in me than any other objects in the castle-armory. These were some rude weapons—pikes, very roughly made, and old rusty muskets, broken and other-wise out of order, and swords, by no means with Damascus blades—that had been taken from some poor weavers and other handicraft men, who rose against [157] the government in 1820. I pitied the poor fellows much, seeing how wretched were their means of standing up against the cannon, bayonets, swords, shot, shell, and all manner of murderous facil[i]ties possessed by their oppressors. Afterwards, our guide showed, in a gloomy quadrangle of the castle, the low windows of the dungeons where two of the leaders of the insurrectionists had been confined, before their execution. I have not the least shadow of doubt that these men had a good cause to fight for; but what availed it with such weapons, and so few even of those.

It is now half past ten °clock; and I believe I cannot go on to recount any further, this evening, the experiences of to-day. It has been a very rich day; only that I have seen more than my sluggish powers of reception can well take in at once. After quitting Stirling, we came in somewhat less than an hour to Linlithgow, and, alighting, took up our quarters at the Star and Garter Hotel, which, like almost all the Scottish Caravansaries of which we have had experience, turns out a comfortable one. As my wife had already exerted herself much in seeing Stirling, and as it had already rained a little, and threatened more, we staid within doors for an hour or two; and I busied myself with writing up my Journal. At about three, however, the sky brightened a little, and we set forth [158] through the ancient, rusty, and queer-looking town of Linlithgow, towards the palace, and the ancient church, which latter was one of Saint David's edifices, and both of which stand close together, a little removed from the long street of the village. But I can never describe them worthily, and shall make nothing of the description if I attempt it now; so good-night.

JULY 8th, WEDNESDAY, EDINBURGH.

AT about three °clock, yesterday, as I said, we walked forth through the ancient street of Linlithgow, and coming to the market-place, (I suppose it was) stopt to look at a heavy and elaborate stone-fountain, which we found by an inscription to be a fac-simile of an ancient one that used to stand on the same site. Turning to the right, the outer entrance to the palace fronts on this market-place, if such it be; and close to it, a little on one side, is the ancient church. A young woman, with a key in her hand, offered to admit us into the latter; so we went in, and found it divided by a wall across the middle into two parts. The hither portion, being the nave, was white-washed, and looked as bare and uninteresting as an old Gothic church, of Saint David's epoch, possibly could. The interior portion, being the former choir, is covered with pews over the whole floor, and further defaced and decorated by galleries, that unmercifully cut midway across the stately and beautiful arches. It is like[159]wise whitewashed. There were, I believe, some mural monuments of Baillies and other such people, stuck up about the walls; but nothing that much interested me except an ancient oaken chair, which the girl said was the chair of Saint Crispin, and which was fastened to the wall in the holiest part of the church. I know not why it was there; but as it had been the chair of so distinguished a personage, we all sat down in it. It was in this church that the apparition of Saint James appeared to King James IV, to warn him against engaging in that war which resulted in the battle of Flodden, where he and the flower of his nobility were slain. The young woman showed us the spot where the apparition spake with him; a side-chapel, with a groined roof, at the end of the choir next to the nave. The covenanters seem to have show[n] some respect to this one chapel, by refraining from drawing the gallery across its height; so that, except for the white wash, and the loss of the painted glass in the window, and probably of a good deal of rich architectural detail, it looks as it did when the ghostly saint entered beneath its arch, while the king was kneeling there.

We staid but a little while in the church, and then proceeded to the palace, which, as I said, is close at hand. [160] On entering the outer enclosure, through an ancient gateway, we were surprised to find how entire the walls seemed to be; but the reason is, I presume, that the ruins have not been used as a stone-quarry, as has almost always been the case with old abbeys and castles. The palace took fire and was consumed, so far as consumable, in 1745, while occupied by the soldiers of General Hawley; but even yet the walls appear so stalwart that I should imagine it quite possible to rebuild and restore the stately rooms, on their original plan. It was a noble palace, 175 feet in length, by 165 in breadth, and though destitute of much architectural beauty, externally, (for it seems to be a mere, unadorned parallelogram, with windows little ornamented, and irregularly placed,) yet its aspect from the quadrangle, which the four sides en[c]lose, is venerable and sadly beautiful. At each of the interior angles there is a circular tower, ascending the whole height of the edifice and overtopping it, and another in the centre of one of the sides; all containing winding staircases. The walls, facing upon the enclosed quadrangle, are pierced with many windows, and have been ornamented with sculpture, rich traces of which still remain over the arched entrance-ways; and in the grassy centre of the square there is the ruin and broken fragments of a [161] fountain, which once used to play for the delight of the king and queen, and lords and ladies, who looked down upon it from hall and chamber. Many old carvings that belonged to it are now heaped together there; but the water has disappeared, though, had it been a natural spring, it would have outlasted all the heavy stonework.

As far as we were able, and could find our way, we went through every room of the palace, all round the four sides of the quadrangle. From the first-floor upward, it is entirely roofless; in some of the chambers, there is an accumulation of soil and a goodly crop of grass; in others, there is still a flooring of flags or brick-tiles, though damp and moss-grown, and with weeds sprouting between the crevices. Grass and weeds, indeed, have found soil enough to flourish in, even on the highest ranges of the walls, though at a dizzy height above the ground; and it was like an old and trite touch of romance, to see how the weeds sprouted on the many hearthstones and aspired under the chimney flues, as if in emulation of the long extinguished flame. It was very mournful; very beautiful; very delightful, too, to see how Nature takes back the palace, now that kings have done with it, and adopts it as part of her great garden.

On one side of the quadrangle, we found the roofless cham[162]ber where Mary Queen of Scots was born, and, in the same range, the bed-chamber that was occupied by several of the Scottish Jameses; and in one corner of this latter apartment, there is a narrow, winding staircase, down which I groped, expecting to find a door either into the enclosed quadrangle, or to the outside of the palace. But it ends in nothing, unless it be a dungeon; and one does not well see why the bedchamber of the king should be so convenient to a dungeon. In one account of the palace, it is said that King James III once escaped down this secret stair and lay concealed from some conspirators who had entered his chamber to murder him. This range of apartments is terminated, like the other sides of the palace, by a circular tower enclosing a staircase, up which we mounted, winding round and round, and emerging at various heights, until at last we found ourselves at the very topmost point of the edifice; and here there is a small pepper-box of a turret, almost as entire as when the stones were first laid. It is called Queen Margaret's bower, and looks forth on a lovely prospect of mountain and plain, and on the old red roofs of Linlithgow town, and on the little loch that lies within the palace-grounds. The cold north wind blew chill upon us through the empty window frames, which very likely were never glazed; but it must be a delightful nook in [163] a calmer and warmer summer evening, and if I lived in the palace, I would make this bower my writing [?] room.[441]

Descending from this high perch, we walked along ledges, and through arched corridors, and stood contemplative in the dampness of the banquetting[sic]-hall; and sat down in the window-seats that still occupy the embrasures of the deep windows. In one of the rooms, the sculpture of a huge fireplace has recently been imitated and restored, so as to give an idea of what the richness of the adornments must have been when the edifice was perfect. We burrowed down too (a little way, at least,) in the direction of the cells where prisoners used to be confined; but these were too ugly and too impenetrably dark to tempt us far. One vault, right beneath a queen's very bedchamber, was designated as a prison. I should think bad dreams would have steamed up and made her pillow an uncomfortable one.

There seems to be no certain record as respects the date of this palace, except that the most recent part (the side of the quadrangle in which were the kitchens and other domestic offices,) was built by James I[st] of England, and bears the figures 1620 on its central tower. In Robert Bruce's time, there was a castle here, instead of a palace; and an ancestor of our friend Bennoch was the means of taking it from [164] the English by a stratagem in which valour went halves. For centuries afterwards, it was a royal residence, and might still have been nominally so, had not Hawley's dragoons lighted their fires on the floors of the magnificent old rooms; but, on the whole, I think it more valuable as a ruin than if it were still perfect. Scotland, and the world, needs only one Holyrood; and Linlithgow, were it still a palace, must have been second in interest to that, from its lack of association with historic events so grand and striking.

After tea, we took another walk, and this time went along the High Street of Linlithgow, in quest of the house whence Bothwellhaugh fired the shot that killed the Regent Murray. It has been taken down, however; or, if any part of it remain, it has been built into and incorporated with a small house of dark stone, which forms one range with two others, that stand a few feet back from the general line of the street. It is as mean-looking and common-place an edifice as was anywhere to be seen, and is now occupied by one Steele, a tailor. We went under a square arch (if an arch can be square) that goes quite through the house, and found ourselves in a little yard; but it was not easy to identify anything as connected with the historic event; so we did but glance about us, and returned into [165] the street. It is here narrow; and as Bothwellhaugh stood in a projecting gallery, the Regent must have been within a few yards of the muzzle of his carbine. The street looks as old as any that I have seen, except perhaps a vista here and there in Chester; the houses all of stone, many of them tall, with notched gables, and with stone staircases ascending on the outside, the steps much worn by feet now dust; a pervading ugliness, which yet does not fail to be picturesque; a general filth, and evil odor of gutters and people, suggesting sorrowful ideas of what the inner houses must be, when the outside looks and smells so badly;—and finally, a great rabble of the inhabitants, talking, idling, sporting, staring, about their own thresholds and those of dram-shops, the town being most alive in the long twilight of the summer evening. There was nothing uncivil in the deportment of these dirty people, old or young; but they did stare at us most unmercifully.

We walked very late, entering, after all that we had seen, into the palace-grounds, and skirting along Linlithgow loch, which would be very beautiful if its banks were much shadowy with trees, instead of being almost bare. We viewed the palace on the outside, too, and saw what had once been the principal entrance, but now looked like an arched window pretty high in the wall; for it had not been accessi[166]ble except by a drawbridge. I might spend pages in telling how venerable the ruin looked, as the twilight fell deeper and deeper around it; but we have had enough of Linlithgow, especially as there have been so many old palaces and old towns to talk about, and will still be more. We left Linlithgow at half past eight, this morning, and reached Edinburgh in half an hour. Tomorrow I suppose I shall try to set down what I have seen; at least, some few points of it.

JULY 9th, THURSDAY, EDINBURGH.

ARRIVING at Edinburgh, and acting under advice of the cabman, we drove to Addison's Alma Hotel, which we find to be in Prince's street, having Scott's monument a few hundred yards below, and the Castle Hill about as much above. The Edinburgh people seem to be accustomed to climb mountains within their own houses; so we had to mount several staircases before we reached our parlor, which, with the adjacent bedrooms, is a very good one, and commands a beautiful view of Prince's street, and of the picturesque Old Town, and the valley between, and of the Castle on its hill.

Our first visit was to the Castle, which we reached by going across the causeway that bridges the valley, and has some edifices of Grecian architecture on it, contrasting strangely with the non-descript ugliness of the Old

Town, into which we immediately pass. As this is my second [167] visit to Edinburgh, I surely need not dwell upon describing it at such length as if I had never been here before. After climbing up through the various wards of the castle, to the topmost battery, where Mons Meg holds her station (looking like an uncouth dragon, with a pile of huge stone balls beside her, for eggs) we found that we could not be admitted to Queen Mary's apartments, nor to the Crown-room, till twelve °clock; moreover, that there was no admittance to the Crown-room without tickets from the Crown Office in Parliament Square. There being no help for it, I left my wife and Julian to wander through the fortress, and came down through the High-street in quest of Parliament Square, which I found after many inquiries of police-men and others, and after first going to the Justiciary Court, where there was a great throng endeavoring to get into court; for the trial of Miss Smith, for the murder of her lover, is causing great excitement just now. There was no difficulty made about the tickets; and returning I found Sophia and Julian; but the latter grew tired of waiting, and set out to return to our Hotel, through the great, strange city, all by himself. My wife had made acquaintance with an attendant, through whose means we were admitted into Queen Margaret's little chapel, on the top of the rock; and there we sat down in such shelter as we could find (for there was a keen wind blowing through the embrasures of the ramparts) and waited as pa[168]tiently as we could.

Twelve °clock came, and we went into the Crown Room with a throng of other visitors; so many that they could only be admitted in seperate [sic] squads. The Regalia of Scotland lie on a circular table, within an iron railing, around which the visitors pass, gazing with all their eyes. The room was dark, however, except for the dim twinkle of a candle or gas-light; and the Regalia did not show to any advantage, though I believe there are some rich jewels set in their ancient gold. The articles consist of a two handed sword, with a hilt and scabbard of gold, and a sceptre, likewise of gold, ornamented with gems, and a mace, with a silver handle, all very beautifully made; besides the golden collar and jewelled badge of the Garter, and something else which I forget. Why they keep the room so dark, I cannot tell; but it is a poor show, and gives the spectator an idea of the poverty of Scotland, and the minuteness of her sovereignty, which I had not gathered from her royal palaces.

Thence we went into Queen Mary's room, and saw that beautiful portrait—that very Queen and very woman—with which I was so much impressed at my last visit. It is wonderful that this picture does not drive all the other portraits of Mary out of the field, whatever may be the comparative proofs of their authenticity. I do not know the history of this one; except that [169] the picture in the Castle is a copy by Sir William Gordon of a picture by an Italian, preserved at Dunrobin Castle.

After seeing what the Castle had to show (which is but little, except itself, its rock, and its old dwellings of princes and prisoners) we came down through the High street, inquiring for John Knox's house. It is a strange looking old edifice, with gables on high, projecting far, and has some sculpture and inscriptions, referring to Knox. There is a tobacconist's shop in the basement-story, where I bought some cigars, and[442] learned that the house used to be shown to visitors, till within three months, but is now closed for some reason or other. Thence we crossed a bridge into the new town, and came back through Prince's street to the hotel, and had a good dinner as preparatory to fresh wearinesses; for there is no other weariness at all to be compared with sight-seeing.

In mid-afternoon, we took a cab and drove to Holyrood palace, which I have already described, as well as the Chapel, and do not mean to meddle with either of them again. We looked at our faces in the old looking-glasses, that Queen Mary brought from France with her, and which had often reflected her own lovely face and figure; and I went up the winding stair through which the conspirators ascended. This, I think, was not accessible at my former visit. Before leaving the palace, one of the attendants advised us to see some pictures in the apartments occupied [170] (during the Queen's residences here) by the Marquis of Breadalbane. Here we found some fine old portraits and other pictures of Vandyke, Sir Peter Lely, Sir Godfrey Kneller, and a strange head by Rubens, amid which I walked wearily, wishing that there were nothing worth looking at, in this whole world. My wife differs altogether from me, in this matter; her body gets tired, but never her mind; whereas I hold out physically better than mentally; but we agreed, on this occasion, in being tired to death. Just as we got through with the pictures, I became convinced of what I had been dimly suspecting, all the while;—namely, that, at my last visit to the palace, I had seen these self-same pictures, and listened to the self-same woman's civil answers, in just the self-same miserable weariness of mood.

We left the palace, and toiled up through the dirty Canongate, looking vainly for a fly, and employing our time as well as we could in looking at the squalid mob of Edinburgh, and peeping down the horrible vistas of the Closes, which were swarming with dirty human life as some mouldy and half-decayed substance might swarm with insects;—vistas down alleys where sin, sorrow, poverty, drunkenness, all manner of sombre and sordid earthly circumstances, had imbued the stone, brick, and wood of the habitations, for hundreds of years. And such a multitude of children, too;—that was a most striking feature.

[171] After tea, I went down into the valley between the old town and the new, which is now laid out as an ornamental garden, with grass, shrubbery, flowers, gravelled walks, and frequent seats. Here, while I smoked a cigar,[443] the sun was setting, and gilded the Old Town with its parting rays, making it absolutely the most picturesque scene that I ever beheld. The mass of tall, ancient houses, heaped densely together, looked like a Gothic dream; for there seemed to be towers, and all sorts of stately architecture, and spires ascended

out of the mass; and above the whole was the Castle, with a crown of gold on its topmost turret. It wanted less than a quarter of nine when the last gleam faded from the windows of the old town, and left the mass of buildings dim and indistinguishable; to reappear on the morrow in squalor, lifting their meanness skyward, the home of layer upon layer of unfortunate humanity. The change symbolized the difference between a poet's imagination of life in the past—or in a state which he looks at through a colored and illuminated medium—and the sad reality.

This morning, we took a cab, and set forth between ten and eleven to see Edinburgh and its environs, driving past the University, and other noticeable objects in the Old Town, and thence out to Arthur's Seat. Salisbury Crags are [a] very singular feature of the outskirts. From the heights, beneath Arthur's [172] Seat, we had a fine prospect of the sea, with Leith and Portobello in the distance, and of a fertile plain at the foot of the hill. In the course of our drive, our cabman pointed out Dumbiedikes's house; also the cottage of Jeanie Deans (at least, the spot where it formerly stood,) and Muschat's Cairn, of which a small heap of stones is yet remaining. Near this latter object are the ruins of St. Anthony's Chapel, a roofless gable and other remains, standing on the abrupt hillside. We drove homeward past a parade ground, on which a body of cavalry were exercising, and we met a party of infantry on their route thither. Then we drove near the Calton Hill, which seems to be not a burial-ground, although the site of stately monuments. In fine, we passed through the Grass-Market, where we saw the cross in the pavement of the street, marking the spot where Porteous was executed. I think I remember planting my foot on that cross, on my former visit. Thence we passed through the Cow-gate, all the latter part of our drive being amongst the tall, quaint edifices of the old town, alike venerable and squalid. From the Grass Market, the rock of the Castle looks more precipitous than as we had hitherto seen it, and its prisons, palaces or barracks, approach close to its headlong verge, and form one steep line with its descent. We drove quite round the Castle Hill, and returned down Prince's Street to our Hotel. There can [173] be no other town in the world that affords such splendid scenery, both natural and architectural, as Edinburgh.

Then I went with my wife to St Giles's Cathedral, (which I shall not describe, it having been kirkified into three interior divisions by the Covenanters,) and left her there to take drawings; while Julian and I went to Short's Observatory, near the entrance of the Castle. Here we saw a Camera Obscura, which brought before us, without our stirring a step, almost all the striking objects which we had been wandering to-and-fro to see. We also saw the mites in cheese, gigantically magnified by a solar microscope; likewise, some dioramic views; with all which Julian was mightily pleased, and for myself, being tired to death of sights, I would as lief have seen them as any thing else. We found, on calling for mamma at Saint Giles's, that she had gone [a]way; but she rejoined us, between four and five °clock, at our hotel, where the next thing we did was to dine. Again, after dinner, mamma and I walked out, looking at the shop-windows of jewellers, where ornaments made of Cairn Gorm pebbles are the most peculiar attraction. As it was our wedding-day, and as our union has turned out to the utmost satisfaction of both parties, after fifteen years trial, I gave her a golden backed and blue [174] bodied Cairn Gorm beetle.[444] Then we sat awhile in the Prince's street gardens, and thence came home.

JULY 10th, FRIDAY, EDINBURGH.

LAST evening, I walked from our Hotel round the Castle-rock, and through the Grass-market, where I stood on the inlaid cross in the pavement, marking the scene of the Porteous execution; thence down the High-street beyond John Knox's house. The throng in that part of the town was very great. There is a strange fascination in these old streets, and in the peeps down the closes; but it would doubtless be a great blessing were a fire to sweep through the whole of ancient Edinburgh. This system of living on flats, up to I know not what story, must be most unfavorable to cleanliness, since they have to bring their water up all that distance towards Heaven, and how they get rid of their slops is best known to themselves.

My wife has gone to Roslin, this morning; and since her departure (at 9 °clock) it has become drizzly; so that Julian and I, after a walk through the new part of the town, are imprisoned in our parlour, with little resource except to look across the valley to the Castle, where Mons Meg is plainly visible on the upper platform, and the lower ramparts zigzagging about the edge of the precipice, which, nearly in front of us, is concealed or softened by a great deal of shrubbery, but, farther off, descends steep down to the grass below. Somewhere on this side of the rock was the point [175] where Claverhouse, on quitting Edinburgh before the battle of Killiecrankie, clambered up to hold an interview with the Duke of Gordon. What an excellent thing it is to have such striking and indestructible landmarks and time-marks, that they serve to affix historical incidents to, and thus, as it were, nail down the Past for the benefit of all future ages!

The Old Town of Edinburgh appears to be situated, in its densest part, on the broad back of a ridge, which rises gradually to its termination in the precipitous rock on which stands the Castle. Between the Old Town and the new, is the valley which runs along at the base of this ridge, and which, in its natural state, was probably rough and broken, like any mountain gorge. The lower part of the valley, adjacent to the Canongate, is now a broad, hollow space, filled up with dwellings, shops, or manufactories; the next portion, between two bridges, is converted into an ornamental garden free to the public, and contains Scott's beautiful monument, an edifice of Gothic arches and a fantastic spire, beneath which he sits, thoughtful and observant of what passes in the contiguous street; the third portion of the valley, above the last bridge, is another ornamental garden, open only to those who have pass keys. It is an admirable park or garden, with a great variety of surface, and extends far around the castle-rock, with paths that lead [176] up to its very base, among leafy depths of shrubbery, and wind beneath the sheer, black precipice. Julian and I walked there, this forenoon, and took refuge from a shower beneath an overhanging jut of the rock, where a bench had been placed, and where a curtain of hanging ivy helped to shelter us. On our return to the hotel, we found Mamma just alighting from a cab. She had had very bad fortune in her excursion to Roslin, having had to walk a long distance to the Chapel, and being caught in the rain; and, after all, she could spend only seven minutes in viewing the beautiful Roslin architecture.

JULY 11th, SATURDAY, DURHAM.

WE left Edinburgh (where we had found, at Addison's, 87, Prince's Street, the most comfortable Hotel in Great Britain) and came to Melrose, where we put up at the George. This is all travelled ground with me; so that I need not much bother myself with further description; especially as it is impossible, by any repetition of attempts, to describe Melrose Abbey. We went thither immediately after tea, and were shown over the ruins by a very rich and delectable old Scotchman, incomparably the best guide that I ever met with. I think he must take pains to speak the Scottish dialect; he does it with such pungent felicity and effect; and it gives a flavor to everything he says like the mustard and vinegar in a salad. This is not [177] the man I saw when here before. The Scotch is still, in a greater or less degree, universally prevalent in Scotland, insomuch that we generally find it difficult to comprehend the answers to our questions, though more, I think, from the unusual intonation than either from strange words or pronunciation. But this old man, though he spoke the most unmitigated Scotch, was perfectly intelligible—perhaps because his speech so well accorded with the classic standard of the Waverley novels. Moreover, he is thoroughly acquainted with the Abbey, stone by stone; and it was curious to see him, as we walked among its aisles, and over the grass beneath its roofless portions, pick up the withered leaves that had fallen there, and do other such little things as a good housewife might to her parlour. I have met with two or three instances where the guardian of an old edifice seemed really to love it; and this was one, although the old man evidently had a Scotch Covenanter's contempt and dislike of the faith that founded the Abbey. He repeated King James's dictum, that King David the First was a "sair saint for the crown," as bestowing so much wealth on religious edifices; but really, unless it be Walter Scott, I know not any Scotchman who has done so much for his country as this same Saint David. As the [178] founder of Melrose, and many other beautiful churches and abbeys, he left magnificent specimens of the only kind of poetry which the age knew how to produce; and the world is the better for him to this day—which is more, I believe, than can be said of any hero or statesman in Scottish annals.

We went all over the ruins, of course, and saw the marble stone of King Alexander, and the spot where Bruce's heart is said to be buried, and slab

of Michael Scott, with the cross engraved upon it; also, the exquisitely
sculptured kail-leaves, and other foliage and flowers, with which the Gothic
artists enwreathed this edifice, bestowing more minute and faithful labor than
an artist of these days would in the most delicate piece of cabinet-work. We
came away sooner than we wished, because my wife was tired, and also afraid
of the dampness of the evening; but she hoped to return thither this morning;
and, for my part, I cherish a presentiment that this will not be our last visit to
Scotland and to Melrose. After leaving Mamma at the hotel, Julian and I
walked to the Tweed, where we saw three or four people angling, with naked
legs, or trowsers turned up, and wading among the rude stones that make something like a dam over the wide and brawling [179] stream. I could not observe
that they caught any fish; but Julian was so fascinated with the spectacle that
he pulled out his poor little fishing-line and wanted to try his chance forthwith.
I never saw the angler's instinct stronger in anybody. We walked across the
foot-bridge that here spans the Tweed; and Julian observed that he did not see
how William of Deloraine[445] could have found so much difficulty in swimming
his horse across so shallow a river. Neither do I. It now began to sprinkle, and
we hastened back to the hotel.

It was not a pleasant morning; but we started immediately after breakfast
for Abbotsford, which is but about three miles distant. The country between
Melrose and that place is not in the least beautiful, nor very noteworthy—one
or two old, irregular villages; one tower, that looks principally domestic, yet
partly warlike, and seems to be of some antiquity; and an undulation, or
rounded hilly surface of the landscape, sometimes affording wide vistas between
the slopes. These hills (I suppose they are, some of them, on the Abbotsford
estate) are partly covered with woods, but of Scotch fir or some tree of that
species, which creates no softenened [sic] undulations, but overspreads the
hill like a tightly fitting wig. It is a cold, dreary, dishearten[180]ing neighborhood, that of Abbotsford; at least, it has appe[a]red so [to] me at both of my
visits; one of which was on a bleak and windy May morning, and another on
a chill, showery morning of mid-summer.

The entrance-way to the house is somewhat altered since my last visit;
and we now, following the direction of pointed fingers on the wall, went round
to a back-door in the basement-story, where we found an elderly man waiting
as if [in] expectation of visitors. He asked me to write our names in a book,
and told us that the desk, on the leaf of which it lay, was the one in which
Sir Walter found the forgotten manuscript of Waverley, while looking for
some fishing-tackle. There was another desk in the room, which had belonged
to the Colonel Gardiner who appears in Waverley. The first apartment, into
which our guide showed us, was Sir Walter's study, where I again saw his
clothes, and remarked how the sleeve of his old green coat was worn at the
cuff—a minute circumstance that seemed to bring Sir Walter very near me.
Thence into the library; thence into the drawing-room; whence, methinks,
we should have entered the dining-room, the most interesting of all, as being

the room where he died. But this room seems not to be shown now. We saw the armory, with the gun of Rob Roy, into the muzzle of which [181] I put my finger, and found the bore very large; the beautifully wrought pistol of Claverhouse, and a pair that belonged to Napoleon; the sword of Montrose, which I grasped, and drew half out of the scabbard; and Queen Mary's iron jewel-box, six or eight inches long, and two or three high, with a lid rounded like that of a trunk, and much corroded with rust. There is no use in making a catalogue of these curiosities. The feeling in visiting Abbotsford is not that of awe; it is little more than going to a museum. I do abhor this mode of making pilgrimage to the shrines of departed great men; there is certainly something wrong in it, for it seldom or never produces (in me, at least,) the right feeling. It is a queer truth, too, that a house is forever after spoiled and ruined, as a house, by having been the abode of a great man. His spirit haunts it, as it were, with a malevolent effect, and takes hearth and hall away from the nominal possessors, giving all the world (because he had such intimate relations with all) the right to enter there.

We had intended to go to Dryburgh Abbey; but as the weather more than threatened rain, and my wife was suffering from her forced march to Roslin, we gave up the idea; so took the rail for Berwick at a little past one. On our road, we passed several ruins in Scotland, and some [182] in England; one old Castle, in particular, beautifully situated beside a deep-banked stream. The road lies, for many miles, along the coast, affording a fine view of the German Ocean, which was now blue, sunny, and breezy, the day having risen out of its morning sulks. We waited an hour or more at Berwick, and Julian and I, after lunch, took a hasty walk into the town. It is a rough and rude-looking assemblage of rather mean houses, some [of] which are thatched. There seems to have been a wall about the town, at a former period, and we passed through one of the gates. The view of the river Tweed here is very fine, both above and below the railway bridge, and especially where it flows, a broad tide, and between deep banks, into the Sea. Thence we went onward along the coast, as I have said, pausing a few moments in smoky Newcastle, and reaching Durham about eight °clock.

I wandered out in the dusk of the evening (the dusk comes on comparatively early, as we draw southward) and found a beautiful and shadowy path, along the river-side, skirting its high banks, up and adown which grow noble elms. I could not well see, in that obscurity of twilight boughs, whither I was going, or what was around me, but I judged that the castle or cathedral, or both, [183] crowned the highest line of the shore, and that I was walking at the base of their walls. There was a pair of lovers in front of me, and I passed two or three or [sic] other tender couples. The walk appeared to go on interminably, by the river side, through the same sweet shadow; but I turned aside, and found my way into the Cathedral close, beneath an ancient archway, whence emerging again, I inquired my way to the Waterloo Hotel, where we had put up.

We saw the Norham Castle of "Marmion," at a short distance from the station of the same name. Viewed from the railway, it has not a very picturesque appearance; a high, square ruin of what I presume was the keep. At Abbotsford, treasured up in a glass-case, in the drawing-room, were memorials of Sir Walter Scott's servants and humble friends; for instance, a brass snuff-box of Tom Purdy [Purdie]—these, too, among precious reliques of illustrious persons. In the armoury, I grasped with some interest the sword of Sir Adam Fergus[s]on, which he had worn in the Peninsular war. Our guide said, of his own knowledge, that he was a "very funny old gentleman." He died only a year or two since.

JULY 14th TUESDAY, SOUTHPORT.

THE morning after our arrival in Durham, being Sunday, my wife and I attended service in the Cathedral; that being our only opportunity of see[184]ing the Cathedral. We found a tolerable audience seated on benches, within and in front of the Choir; and people continually strayed in and out of the sunny churchyard, and sat down, or walked softly and quietly up and down the side-aisle. Sometimes, too, one of the vergers would come in with a handful of little boys, whom, I suppose, he had caught playing among the tombstones. Durham Cathedral has one advantage over all others which I have seen; there being no organ-screen, nor any sort of partition between the Choir and Nave; so that we saw its entire length, nearly five hundred feet, in one vista. The pillars of the Nave are immensely thick, but hardly of proportionate height; and they support the round Norman arch; nor is there, so far as I remember, a single pointed arch in the Cathedral. The effect is, to give the edifice an air of heavy grandeur. It seems to have been built before the best style of church-architecture had established itself; so that it weighs upon the soul, instead of helping it to aspire. First there are these round arches, supported by gigantic columns; then, immediately above, another row of round arches, behind which is the usual gallery that runs, as it were, in the thickness of the wall, around the nave of a Cathedral; then above all, another row of round arches, enclosing the windows of the clerestory. The great pillars are ornamented in various ways; some with a great spiral groove running from [185] bottom to top; others with two spirals, ascending in opposite directions, so as to criss-cross over one another; some are fluted or channelled, straight up and down; some are wrought with chevrons like those on the sleeve of a police-inspector. There are zigzag cuttings and carvings, which I do not know how to name scientifically, round the arches of the doors and windows; but nothing that seems to have flowered out spontaneously, as natural incidents of a grand and beautiful design. The remains of old glass, if any, are very few. In the Nave, between the columns of the side aisles, I saw one or two monuments, but had not an opportunity to examine them.

The Cathedral service is immensely long; and though the choral part of it is pleasant enough, I though[t] it not best to wait for the sermon; especially as it would have been quite unintelligible, so remotely as I sat in the great space. So I left my seat, and, after strolling up and down the aisle, a few times, issued forth into the church-yard. On the Cathedral door there is a curious old knocker, in the form of a monstrous face, which was placed there centuries ago for the benefit of fugitives from justice, who used to be entitled to sanctuary here. The exterior of the Cathedral, being huge, is therefore grand; it has a great central tower, and two at the western end; and reposes in vast and heavy length, without, [186] as I remember, the multitude of niches and crumbling statues, and richness of detail, that makes the towers and fronts of some Cathedrals so endlessly interesting. One piece of sculpture I recollect; a carving of a cow, a milkmaid, and, I think, a monk; in reference to the legend that the site of the Cathedral was, in some way, determined by a woman bidding her cow go home to Dunholme. Cadmus was guided to the site of his destined city in some such way as this.

It was a very beautiful day, and though the shadow of the Cathedral fell on this side, yet, being about noontide, it did not cover the church-yard entirely, but left many of the graves in sunshine. There were not a great many monuments, and these were chiefly horizontal slabs, some of which look aged, but, on closer inspection, proved to be mostly of the present century. I observed one old stone figure, however, half worn away, which seemed to have something like a bishop's mitre on its head, and may perhaps have lain in the proudest chapel of the Cathedral, before occupying its present bed among the grass. About fifteen paces from the central tower, and within its shadow, I found a weather-worn slab of marble, seven or eight feet long, the inscription on which interested me somewhat; it was to the memory of Robert Dodsley, the bookseller, Johnson's acquaintance, who, as his tomb-stone rather [187] superciliously remarks, had made a much better figure as an author than "could have been expected from one in his rank of life." But, after all, it is inevitable that a man's tombstone should look down on him, or, at all events, comport itself towards him *de haut en bas*. I love to find the graves of men connected with literature, and find that they interest me more, even though of no great eminence, than those of persons far more illustrious in other walks of life. I know not whether this is because I happen to be one of the literary kindred, or because all men feel themselves akin and on terms of intimacy with those whom they know, or might have known, in books. I rather believe that the latter is the case.

My wife had staid in the Cathedral; but, as it was Sacrament day, she came out at the end of the sermon, and told me of two little birds who had got into the vast interior, and were in great trouble at not being able to find their way out again. Thus, two winged souls may often have been imprisoned within a faith of heavy ceremonials. We went round the edifice, and passing into the Close, penetrated through an arched passage into the crypt, which, methought, was in a better style of architecture than the nave and choir. At one end, stood a crowd of venerable figures, leaning against the wall, being stone [188] images of bearded saints, apostles, patriarchs, kings—personages of great dignity, at all events, who had doubtless occupied conspicuous niches in and about the Cathedral, till finally imprisoned in this cellar. I looked at every one, and found not an entire nose among them, nor quite so many heads as they once had. Thence we went into the Cloisters, which are entire, but not particularly interesting; indeed, this Cathedral has not taken hold of my affections, except in one aspect where it was exceedingly grand and beautiful.

After looking at the crypt and the cloisters, we returned through the close and the church-yard, and went back to the hotel by the path along the river-side. This is the same dim and dusky path through which I wandered, the night before; and in the sunshine it looked quite as beautiful as I knew it must—a shadow of elm-trees, clothing the high bank, and overshadowing the paths above and below; some of the elms growing close to the waterside, and flinging up their topmost boughs not nearly so high as where we stood, and others climbing upward and upward, till our way wound among their roots; while, through the foliage, the quiet river loitered along, with this lovely shade on both its banks, to pass through the centre of the town. The stately Cathedral rose high above us, and farther onward, in a line with it, the battlemented walls of the old Norman [189] Castle, gray and warlike, though now it has become a University. This delightful walk terminates at an old bridge, in the heart of the town; and the castle hangs right over its busiest street. On this bridge, last night, in the embrasure or just over the pier, where there is a stone-seat, I saw some old men seated, smoking their pipes and chatting. In my judgment, a river flowing through the centre of a town, and not too broad to make itself familiar, nor too swift, but idling along as if it loved better to stay than go, is the pleasantest imaginable piece of scenery; so transient as it is, and yet enduring just the same from life's end to life's end; and this river Wear, with its sylvan wildness, and yet so sweet and placable, is the best of all little rivers—not that it is so very small, but with a bosom broad enough to be crossed by a three-arched bridge. Just above the Cathedral, there is a mill upon its shore, as ancient as the times of the Abbey.

We went homeward through the market-place, and one or two narrow streets; for the town has the irregularity common to all ancient settlements; and, moreover, undulates upward and down again, and is also made more unintelligible, to a stranger, in its points and bearings, by the tortuous course of the river. After dinner, Julian and I walked along the bank, opposite to that on which the Cathedral stands, and found [190] the paths there equally delightful with those which I have attempted to describe. We went onward, while the river gleamed through the foliage beneath us, and passed so far beyond the Cathedral that we began to think that we were getting into the country, and that it was time to return; when, all at once, we saw a bridge before us, and beyond that, on the opposite bank of the Wear, the Cathedral itself! The stream had made a circuit without our knowing it. We paused upon the bridge, and admired and wondered at the beauty and glory of this scene, with those vast, ancient towers rising out of the green shade, and looking as if they were based upon it. The situation of Durham Cathedral is certainly a noble one, finer even than that of Lincoln, though the latter stands even at a more lordly height above the town. But, as I saw it then, it was grand, venerable, and sweet, all at once; and I never saw so lovely and magnificent a scene, nor (being content with this) do I care to see a better. The Castle beyond came also into the view, and the whole picture (I presume, for I do not actually remember) was mirrored in the tranquil stream below. And so, crossing the bridge, the path led us back through many a bower of hollow shade; and we quitted the hotel, and took the rail for York, where we arrived at about ½ past nine.

[191] We put up at the Black Swan, with which we had already made acquaintance at our previous visit to York. It is a very ancient hotel; for, in the Coffee Room, I saw on the wall an old, printed advertisement, announcing that a stage-coach would leave the Black Swan in London, and arrive at the Black Swan in Coney-street, York, with God's permission, in four days. The date was 1706; and still, after a hundred and fifty years, the Black Swan receives travellers in Coney-street. It is a very good hotel, and was much thronged with guests when we arrived, as the Sessions come on, this week. We found a very smart waiter, whose English faculties have been brightened by a residence of several years in America; and it seem[s] to have made him the very perfectest of waiters.

In the morning, before breakfast, I strolled out and walked round the Cathedral, passing on my way the Sheriff's javelin-men, in long gowns of faded purple, embroidered with gold, carrying halberds in their hands; also, a gentleman in a cocked hat, gold-lace, and breeches, who, no doubt, had something to do with the ceremonial of the Sessions. I saw, too, a procession of a good many old cabs and other carriages, filled with people, and a banner flaunting above each vehicle. These were the piano-forte makers [192] of York, who were going out of town to have a jollification together.

After breakfast, we all went to the Cathedral; and no sooner were we within it, than we found how much our eyes had recently been educated, by the power of appreciating this magnificent interior; for it impressed both my wife and me with a joy that we never felt before. Julian felt it, too, and insisted that the Cathedral must have been altered and improved, since we were last here. But it is only that we have seen much splendid architecture, since then, and so have grown in some degree fitted to enjoy it. York Cathedral (I say it now, for it is my present feeling) is the most wonderful work that ever came from the hands of man. Indeed, it seems like a "house not made with hands,"[446] but rather to have come down from above, bringing an awful majesty and sweetness with it; and it is so light and aspiring, with all its vast columns and pointed arches, that one would hardly wonder if it should ascend back to heaven again, by its mere spirituality. Positively, the pillars and arches of the choir are so very beautiful that they give the impression of being exquisitely polished, though such is not the fact; but their beauty throws a gleam around them. [193] I thank God that I saw this Cathedral again, and thank Him that he inspired the builder to make it, and that mankind has so long enjoyed it.

We left York at twelve °clock, and were delayed an hour or two at Leeds, waiting for a train. I strolled up into the town, and saw a fair, with puppet-shows, booths of penny actors, merry-go-rounds, clowns, boxers, and other such things as I saw, above a year ago, at Greenwich fair, and likewise at Tranmere during the Whitsuntide holidays. We resumed our journey, and reached Southport in pretty good trim at about 9 °clock. It has been a very interesting tour. We find Southport just as we left it, with its regular streets of little lodging-houses, where the visiters [sic] perambulate to-and fro without any imaginable object. The tide, too, seems not to have been up over the waste of sands, since we went away; and far seaward stands the same row of bathing-machines, and, just on the verge of the horizon, a gleam of water—even this being not the sea, but the mouth of the river Ribble seeking the sea amid the sandy desert. But we shall soon say "Good bye" to Southport.

Scotch speech is so common that we generally found it difficult to understand, or to be understood.

[194] JULY 22ᵈ, THURSDAY, OLD TRAFFORD.

WE left Southport for good on Tuesday, and have established ourselves at this place, in lodgings that had been provided for us by our friend Mr. Swain; our principal object being to spend a few weeks in the proximity of the Arts Exhibition. We are here, about three miles from the Victoria Railway Station, in Manchester, on one side, and perhaps nearly a mile from the Exhibition on the other. This is a suburb of Manchester, and consists of a long street, called the Stratford road, bordered with brick-houses, two stories high, such as are usually the dwellings of tradesmen or respectable mechanics, but which are now in demand for lodgings, at high prices, on account of the Exhibition. It seems to be rather a new precinct of the city; and the houses, though ranged along a contin[u]ous street, are but a brick border along the green fields in the rear. Occasionally, you get a glimpse of this country-aspect, between two houses; but the street itself, even with its little grass-plots and bits of shrubbery under the front-windows, is as ugly as only the English know how to make it. Some of the houses are better than I have described; but the brick here used for building is very unsightly in hue and surface.

Betimes in the morning, the Exhibition omnibuses begin to trundle along this street, and pass at intervals of two-and-a half minutes through the day; immense vehicles constructed to carry thirty-[195]nine passengers, and generally with a good part of that number inside and out. They (the omnibuses) are painted scarlet, bordered with white, have three horses abreast, and a conductor in a red coat. They perform the journey from this point into town in about half an hour; and, yesterday morning, being in a hurry to get to the railway-station, I found that I could outwalk them, taking into account their frequent stoppages.

We have taken the whole house (except some inscrutable holes into which the family creep) of a respectable couple who have never kept lodgings until this juncture. Their furniture, however, is of the true lodging-house pattern, sofas and chairs which have no possibility of repose in them; ricketty [sic] tables; an old piano, and old music, with Lady Helen Elizabeth Somebody's name written on it. It is very strange how nothing but a genuine home can ever look homelike. They appear to be good people here; a little girl of twelve, a daughter, waits on table, and there is an elder daughter, who yesterday answered the door-bell, looking very like a young lady, besides five or six smaller children, who make less uproar of grief or merriment than could possibly be expected. The husband of the house is not apparent, though I see his hat in the entry. The house is new, and has a trim, light-colored interior of half-gentility. I suppose the rent, in ordinary times, might [196] be £25 per annum; but we pay £6.10 per week for the part which we occupy. This, like all the other houses in the neighborhood, was evidently built to be sold or let; the builder never thought of living in it himself, and so that subtile element, which would have enabled him to create a home, was entirely left out.

About ten °clock, to-day, Julian and I set out on a walk, first towards the edifice of the Arts Exhibition, which looked small, compared with my idea of it, and seems to be of the Crystal Palace order of architecture—only with more iron to its glass. Its front is composed of three round arches in a row. We did not go in, this being the half-crown day; so that it was a matter of thrift to wait till tomorrow. Turning to the right, we walked onward two or three miles, passing the Botanic Garden, and thence along by suburban villas, Belgrave Terraces, and other such English prettinesses, in the modern Gothic or Elizabethan style, with prettily ornamented flower-plots before them; thence, by hedgerows and fields, and through two or three villages, with here and there an old, plaster-and-timber built, thatched house, among a street of modern brick fronts, the ale-house or rural inn being generally the most ancient house in the village. It was a sultry, heavy day, and I walked without much enjoyment of the air and [197] exercise. We crossed a narrow and swift river, flowing between deep banks; it must have been either the Mersey, still an infant-stream, and little dreaming of the thousand mighty ships that float on its farther tide, or else the Irwell, which empties into the Mersey. We passed thro' the village beyond this stream, and after drinking a glass of ale at a wayside inn, went to the railway station, and, for sixpence, were brought back to Old Trafford, and deposited close by the Exhibition.

It has showered, this afternoon; and I beguiled my idle time, for half an hour, by setting down the vehicles that went past; not that they were particularly numerous, but for the sake of knowing the character of the travel along this road. Here is the first quarter of an hour;—A man wheeling a small hand-cart in the direction from Manchester; an omnibus, pretty full, to do; a cab to do; a man on horseback, leading another horse, from do; a one-horse chaise from do; a dog-cart to do; a two-horse carriage to do; a two horse carriage to do; a cab to do; an omnibus to do; a two-horse cab from do; a two-horse cab to do; a one-horse carriage from do; a one horse carriage also from do; an omnibus from do; a two horse chaise from do; an [198] [omnibus] from do; an omnibus to do, full; an omnibus from do, nearly empty; a cab from do; a two-horse carriage to do; another two-horse carriage to do; a one horse carriage to do; a Hansom cab to do; a cab from do; an omnibus to do, full; a one-horse chaise to do; a cab to do; another cab to do; a one-horse market-cart to do; an empty furniture cart to do; a sulky gig to do; an omnibus to do, full; a one-horse chaise to do; a two horse barouche to do; an omnibus from do; a two-horse carriage to do; a cab to do; an omnibus to do, full; a carriole to do; a Hansom cab to do; an omnibus from do, empty; a Hansom cab from do; a cab from do; an omnibus from do, empty. All, except those set down as omnibuses, Hansoms, or cabs, were private of [sic] carriages, open or close, chariots, barouches, dog-carts, britzkas, and I know [not] what besides, these being in larger number to day than on ordinary days, because the half-crown price brings out the gentlefolks. The showery day probably increased the number of cabs. It was about six °clock, or perhaps a little earlier; and I thought the travel rather scantier than it had been. The private carriages do not generally strike [199] me by their lightness and elegance, but many of them are models of ease and comfort. Some have a servant, and often two, in livery, behind, or on the box with the coachman.

July 26th, Sunday, Old Trafford.

Day before yesterday, I went with my wife to the Arts Exhibition, of which I do not think that I have a great deal to say. The edifice, being built more for convenience than show, appears better in the interior than from without—long vaulted vistas, lighted from above, extending far away, all hung with pictures, and, on the floor below, statues, knights in armour, cabinets, vases, and all manner of curious and beautiful things, in a regular arrangement. Scatter five thousand people through the scene; and I do not know how to make a better outline sketch. I was unquiet, from a hopelessness of being able fully to enjoy it. Nothing is more depressing than the sight of a great many pictures together; it is like having innumerable books open before you at once, and being able to read a sentence or two in each. They bedazzle one another with cross-lights. There never should be more than one picture in a room, nor more than one picture to be studied in one day; galleries of pictures are surely the greatest absurdities that ever were contrived; there [200] being no excuse for them, except that it is the only way in which pictures can be made generally available and accessible. We went first into the gallery of British Painters, where there were hundreds of pictures; any one of which would have interested me by itself; but I could not fix my mind on one more than another; so I left my wife there, and wandered away by myself, to get a general idea of the exhibition. Truly it is very fine; truly, also, every great show is a kind of humbug. I doubt whether there were half a dozen people there who got the kind of enjoyment that it was intended to create; very respectable people they seemed to be, and very well behaved, but all skimming the surface, as I did, and none of them so feeding on what was beautiful as to digest it, and make it a part of themselves. Such a quantity of objects must be utterly rejected, before you can get any real profit from one! It seemed like throwing away time to look twice even at whatever was most precious; and it was dreary to think of not fully enjoying this collection, the very flower of Time, which never bloomed before, and never by any possibility can bloom again. Viewed hastily, moreover, it is somewhat sad to think that mankind, after centuries of cultivation of the beautiful arts, can produce no more splendid spectacle than this. It is not so very grand, although, poor as it is, I lack capacity to take [201] in even the whole of this.

What gave me most pleasure (because it required no trouble or study to come at the heart of it) were the individual relics of antiquity, of which there are some very curious ones in the cases, ranged along the principal saloon, I think, or nave of the building. For example, the dagger with which Felton killed the Duke of Buckingham; a knife with a bone handle, and a curved blade, not more than three inches long,—sharp-pointed, murderous looking, but of very coarse manufacture. Also, the Duke of Alva's leading-staff of iron; and the target of the Emperor Charles V, which seemed to be made of hardened leather, with designs artistically engraved upon it and gilt. I saw Wolsey's portrait, and, in close proximity to it, his veritable cardinal's hat, in a richly ornamented glass-case, on which was an inscription to the effect that it had been bought by Charles Kean at the sale of Horace Walpole's collection. It is a felt hat, with a brim about six-inches wide all round, and a rather high crown; the color was doubtless a bright red, originally, but now it is mottled with a greyish hue; and there are cracks in the brim, as if the hat had seen a good deal of wear. I suppose a far greater curiosity than this is the signet-ring of one of the Pharaohs[447] who reigned over Egypt during Joseph's prime ministry; a [202] large ring (to be worn on the thumb, if at all) of massive gold, seal part and all, and inscribed with some characters that looked like Hebrew. I had seen this before, in Mr. Mayer's collection, at Liverpool. The medi-aeval and English relics, however, interested me more; such as the golden and enamelled George, worn by Sir Thomas More; or the embroidered shirt of Charles the First, the very one, I presume, which he wore at his execution. There are no blood-marks on it, it being very nicely washed and folded. The texture of the linen cloth—if linen it be—is coarser than any peasant would wear, at this day; but the needle work is exceedingly fine and elaborate. Another relic of the same period is Sir Jacob Astley's (the Cavalier general) buff-coat, with his belt and sword; the leather of the buff-coat (for I took it between my fingers,) is about a quarter of an inch thick, of the same material as a wash-leather glove, and by no means smoothly dressed, though the sleeves are covered with silver lace. Of old armour there are admirable specimens; and it makes one's head ache to look at the iron pots which men used to thrust their heads into;—indeed, at one period, they seem to have worn an inner iron cap underneath the helmet. I doubt whether there ever was any age of chivalry; it certainly was no chivalric sentiment that made men case themselves in impenetrable iron, and ride [203] about in iron prisons, fearfully peeping at their enemies through little slits and gimlet-holes. The unprotected breast of a private soldier must have shamed his leaders, in those days. The point of honor is very different now.

I mean to go, again and again, many times more, to the exhibition, and will take each day some one department, and so endeavor to get some real use and improvement out of what I see. Much that is most valuable must be immitigably rejected; but something (according to the measure of my poor capacity) will really be taken into my mind. After all, it was an agreeable day, and I think the next one will be more so.

Wednesday, July 28th, Old Trafford.

Day before yesterday, I paid a second visit to the Exhibition, and devoted the day mainly to seeing the works of British painters, which fill a very large space—two or three great saloons on the right side of the nave. Among the earliest are Hogarth's pictures, including the Sigismunda, which I remember to have seen before, with her lover's heart in her hand, looking like a monstrous strawberry; and the March to Finchley, than which nothing truer to English life and character was ever painted, nor ever can be; and a large, stately portrait of Captain Coram, and several others, all excellent in proportion as they come near to ordinary life, and are wrought out through [204] its forms. All English painters seem to resemble Hogarth in this respect; they cannot paint anything high, heroic, and ideal, and their attempts in that direction are wearisome to look at; but they sometimes produce good effects by means of awkward figures in ill-made coats and small-clothes, and hard, coarse-complexioned faces, such as they might see anywhere in the street. They are strong in homeliness and ugliness; weak in their efforts at the beautiful. Sir Thomas Lawrence, for instance, attains a sort of grace, which you feel to be a trick, and therefore get disgusted with it. Reynolds is not quite genuine, though certainly he has produced some noble and beautiful heads. But Hogarth is the only English painter, except in the landscape department; there is no other (unless it be some of the modern pre-Raphaelites) who interprets life to me at all. Pretty village-scenes of common life—pleasant domestic passages, with a touch of easy humor in them—little pathoses and fancynesses— are abundant enough; and Wilkie, to be sure, has done more than this, though not a great deal more. His merit lies, not in a high aim, but in accomplishing his aim so perfectly. It is unaccountable that their achievements should be so much inferior to those of the English poets, who have really elevated the human mind; but, to be sure, painting has only become an English art subsequently to the epochs of the greatest poets, and since the beginning of the last century, [205] during which England had no poets. I respect Haydon more than I did, (not for his pictures, they being detestable to see,) but for his heroic reflection of whatever his countrymen and he himself could really do, and his bitter resolve to achieve something higher—failing in which, he died.

No doubt, I am doing vast injustice to a great many gifted men, in what I have here written; as, for instance, Copley, who certainly has painted a slain man to the life; and to a crowd of landscape-painters, who have made wonderful reproductions of little English streams and shrubbery, and cottage-doors, and country-lanes. And there is a picture called the "Evening Gun" by Danby, a ship of war on a calm, glassy tide, at sunset, with the cannon-smoke puffing from her port-hole; it is very beautiful, and so effective that you can even hear the report, breaking upon the stillness with so grand a roar that it is almost like stillness too. As for Turner, I care no more for his light-colored pictures than for so much lacquered ware, or painted gingerbread. Doubtless, this is my fault—my own deficiency—but I cannot help it; not, at least, without sophisticating myself by the effort. The only modern pictures that accomplish a higher end than that of pleasing the eye—the only ones that really take hold of the mind (and they do it with a kind of acerbity, like unripe fruit)—are the works [206] of Hunt, and one or two other painters of the pre-Raphaelite school. They seem wilfully to abjure all beauty, and to make their pictures disagreeable out of mere malice; but, at any rate, for the thought and feeling which are ground up with the paint, they will bear looking at, and disclose a deeper value the longer you look. Never was anything so stiff and unnatural as they appear; although every single thing represented seems to be taken directly out of life and reality, and, as it were, pasted down upon the canvas. They almost paint even separate hairs. Accomplishing so much, and so perfectly, it seems unaccountable that the picture does not live; but Nature has an art beyond these painters, and they leave out some medium—some enchantment that should intervene, and keep the object from pressing so baldly and harshly upon the spectator's eyeballs. With the most lifelike reproduction, there is no illusion. I think if a semi-obscurity were thrown over the picture, after finishing it to this nicety, it might bring it nearer to Nature. I remember a heap of Autumn leaves, every one of which seems to have been stiffened with gum and varnish, and then put carefully down into the stiffly disordered heap. Perhaps these artists may hereafter succeed in combining their truth of detail with a broader and higher truth. Coming from such a depth as their pictures do, and having really an idea as the seed of them, it is strange that they should look like the most made-up [207] things imaginable. One picture of Hunt's, that greatly interested me, was of some sheep that had gone astray among heights and precipices; and I could have looked all day at these poor lost muttons—so true was their meek alarm and hopeless bewilderment, their huddling together without the slightest confidence of mutual help; all that the courage and wisdom of the bravest and wisest of them could do, being to bleat, and only a few having spirits enough even for this.

After going through these modern masters (among whom were some French painters, who did not interest me at all) I did a miscellaneous business, chiefly among the water-colours and photographs, and afterwards among the antiquities and works of ornamental art. I have forgotten what I saw, except the breast plate and helmet of Henry of Navarre, of steel, engraved with designs that have been half-obliterated by scrubbing. I remember, too, a breastplate of an Elector of Saxony, with a bullet-hole through it. He received his mortal wound through that hole, and died of it, two days afterwards, three hundred years ago.

There was a crowd of visitors, insomuch that it was difficult to get a satisfactory view of the most interesting objects. They were almost entirely middling-class people; the exhibition, I think, does not reach the lower classes at all; in fact, it could not reach them, nor their betters either, without a [208] good deal of study to help it out. I shall go again to-day, and do my best to get profit out of it.

THURSDAY, JULY 30th OLD TRAFFORD.

WE all, even Rosebud and Nurse, went to the Exhibition yesterday, and spent the day there; not Julian, however, for I remember he went to the Botanical Gardens. After some little skirmishing with other things, I devoted myself to the Historical Portraits (which hang on both sides of the great nave) and went through them pretty faithfully. The oldest are pictures of Richard II and Henry IV, and Edward IV and Jane Shore, and seem to have little or no merit as works of art, being cold and stiff, the life having perhaps faded out of them; but these elder painters were trustworthy inasmuch as they had no idea of making a picture, but only of getting the face before them on canvass [sic], as accurately as they could. All English History scarcely supplies half a dozen portraits before the time of Henry VIII; after that period, and through the reigns of Elizabeth and James, there are many ugly pictures by Dutchmen and Italians; and the collection is wonderfully rich in portraits of the time of Charles Ist and the Commonwealth. Vandyke seems to have brought portrait-painting into fashion; and very likely the King's love of art diffused a taste for it throughout the nation, and remotely suggested even to his enemies to get their pictures painted. Eliza[209]beth has perpetuated her cold, thin, old-maidish visage on many canvasses [sic], and generally with some fantasy of costume that makes her ridiculous to all time. There are several of Mary of Scotland, none of which have a gleam of beauty; but the stiff old brushes of these painters could not catch the beautiful. Of all the older pictures, the only one that I took pleasure in looking at was a portrait of a Lord Deputy Falkland, by Vansomer, in James Ist's time; a very stately, full length figure in white, looking out of the picture as if he saw you. The catalogue says that this

portrait suggested an incident in Horace Walpole's Castle of Otranto; but I
do not remember it.[448]

I have a haunting doubt of the value of portrait-painting; that is to say,
whether it gives you a genuine idea of the person purporting to be represented.
I do not remember ever to have recognized a man by having previously seen
his portrait. Vandyke's pictures are full of grace and nobleness, but they do
not look like Englishmen—the burly, rough, wine-flushed and weather-reddened
faces, and sturdy flesh and blood, which we see [in] them even at the present
day, when they must naturally have become a good deal refined from either
the country gentleman or courtier of the Stuart's time. There is an old, fat
portrait of Gervase Holles, in a buff-coat, a coarse, hoggish, yet manly man.
The painter is unknown, [210] but I honor him, and Gervase Holles too, for
one was willing to be truly rendered, and the other dared to do it. It seems to
be the aim of portrait painters generally (especially of those who have been
most famous) to make their pictures as beautiful and noble as can anywise
consist with retaining the very slightest resemblance to their sitter. They seldom
attain even the grace and beauty which they aim at, but only hit some temporary
or individual taste. Vandyke, however, achieved graces that rise above time
and fashion; and so did Sir Peter Lely, in his female portraits; but the doubt
is, whether the works of either are genuine history. Not more so, I suspect,
than the narrative of a historian who should seek to make poetry out of the
events which he related, rejecting those which could not possibly be thus
idealized.

I observe, furthermore, that a full-length portrait has seldom face enough;
not that it lacks its fair proportion by measurement; but the artist does not
often find it possible to make the face so intellectually prominent as to subordinate the figure and drapery. Vandyke does this, however. In his pictures of
Charles Ist, for instance, it is the melancholy grace of the visage that attracts
the eye, and it passes to the rest of the picture only by an effort. Earlier and
later pictures are but a [211] few inches of face to several feet of figure and
costume, and more insignificant than the latter, because seldom so well done;
and I suspect the same would generally be the case now, only that the present
simplicity of costume gives the face a chance to be seen. I was interrupted here,
and cannot resume the thread of what I meant to say; but, considering how
much of his own conceit the artist puts into a portrait, how much affectation the
sitter puts on, and then again that no face is the same to any two spectators;
also, that these portraits are darkened and faded with age, and can seldom be
more than half seen, being hung too high, or somehow or other inconvenient—
on the whole, I question whether there is much use in looking at them. The
truest test would be, for a man well-read in English history and biography, and
himself an insighted observer, to go through the series, without knowing what
personages they represented, and write beneath each the name which the portrait vindicated for itself.

After getting through the portrait-gallery, I went among the engravings and photographs, and then glanced along the Old Masters, but without seriously looking at anything. While I was among the Dutch painters, a gentleman accosted me; it was Mr. Ireland, the Editor of the Manchester Examiner, whom I once met at dinner with Bennoch. He told me that [212] the Poet Laureate (and it was rather English that he should designate him by this fantastic dignity, instead of by his name) was in the Exhibition Rooms; and as I expressed great interest, Mr. Ireland was good enough to go in quest of him. Not for the purpose of introduction, however; for he was not acquainted with Tennyson, and I was rather glad of it than otherwise. Soon, Mr. Ireland returned to tell me that he had found the Poet Laureate; and going into the saloon of Old Masters, we saw him there, in company with Mr. Woolner, whose bust of him is now in the Exhibition. Tennyson is the most picturesque figure, without affectation, that I ever saw; of middle-size, rather slouching, dressed entirely in black, and with nothing white about him except the collar of his shirt, which methought might have been clean the day before. He had on a black wide-awake hat, with round crown and wide, irregular brim, beneath which came down his long black hair, looking terribly tangled; he had a long, pointed beard, too, a little browner than the hair, and not so abundant as to incumber any of the expression of his face. His frock coat was buttoned across the breast, though the afternoon was warm. His face was very dark, and not exactly a smooth face, but worn, and expressing great sensitiveness, though not, at that [213] moment, the pain and sorrow which is seen in his bust. His eyes were black; but I know little of them, as they did not rest on me, nor on anything but the pictures. He seemed as if he did not see the crowd nor think of them, but as if he defended himself from them by ignoring them altogether; nor did anybody but myself cast a glance at him. Mr. Woolner was as unlike Tennyson as could well be imagined; a small, smug man, in a blue frock and brown pantaloons. They talked about the pictures, and passed pretty rapidly from one to another, Tennyson looking at them through a pair of spectacles which he held in his hand, and then standing a minute before those that interested him, with his hands folded behind his back. There was an entire absence of stiffness in his figure; no set-up in him at all; no nicety or trimness; and if there had been, it would have spoilt his whole aspect. Gazing at him with all my eyes, I liked him well, and rejoiced more in him than in all the other wonders of the Exhibition.

Knowing how much my wife would delight to see him, I went in search of her, and found her and the rest of us under the music-gallery; and we all, Fanny and Rosebud included, went back to the saloon of Old Masters. So rapid was his glance at the pictures, that, in this little interval, Ten[214]nyson had got half-way along the other side of the saloon; and, as it happened, an acquaintance had met him, an elderly gentleman and lady, and he was talking to them as we approached. I heard his voice; a bass voice, but not of a resounding depth; a voice rather broken, as it were, and ragged about the edges, but pleasant to the ear. His manner, while conversing with these people, was not in the least that of an awkward man, unaccustomed to society; but he shook hands and parted with them, evidently as soon as he courteously could, and shuffled away quicker than before. He betrayed his shy and secluded habits more in this, than in anything else that I observed; though, indeed, in his whole presence, I was indescribably sensible of a morbid painfulness in him, a something not to be meddled with. Very soon, he left the saloon, shuffling along the floor with short irregular steps, a very queer gait, as if he were walking in slippers too loose for him. I had observed that he seemed to turn his feet slightly inward, after the fashion of Indians. How strange, that in these two or three pages I cannot get one single touch that may call him up hereafter![449]

I would most gladly have seen more of this one poet of our day, but forbore to follow him; for I must own that it seemed mean to be dogging him through the saloons, or even [215] to have looked at him, since it was to be done stealthily, if at all. I should be glad to smoke a cigar with him. Mr. Ireland says, that, having heard that he was to be at the Exhibition, and not finding him there, he conjectured that he must have gone into the contiguous Botanical Gardens to smoke; and, sure enough, he found him there. He told me an anecdote, which he received from Professor Pillans about Tennyson while on a visit to Paris. He had a friend with him, who could not speak very good French, any more than the poet himself. They were sitting by the fireside in their parlour at the hotel; and the friend proposed a walk about the city, and finally departed, leaving Tennyson by the fireside, and saying to the waiter, "Ne souffrez pas le faire sortir." By and by, Tennyson also rose to go out; but the waiter opposed him with might and main, and called another waiter to his assistance; and when Tennyson's friend returned, he found him really almost fit for a straight [sic] westcoat [sic]. He might well enough pass for a madman at any time, there being a wildness in his aspect, which doubtless might readily pass from quietude to frenzy. He is exceedingly nervous, and altogether as un-English as possible; indeed, an Englishman of genius usually lacks the national characteristics, and is great abnormally, and through disease. Even their great [216] sailor, Nelson, was unlike his countrymen in the qualities that constituted him a hero; he was not the perfection of an Englishman, but a creature of another kind, sensitive, nervous, excitable, and really more like a Frenchman.

Un-English as he was, and sallow, and unhealthy, Tennyson had not, however, an American look. I cannot well describe the difference; but there was something more mellow in him, softer, sweeter, broader, more simple, than we are apt to be. Living apart from men, as he does, would hurt any one of us more than it does him. I may as well leave him here; for I cannot touch the central point.

AUGUST 2ᵈ, SUNDAY, OLD TRAFFORD.

DAY before yesterday, I went again to the Exhibition, and began the day with looking at the Old Masters. Positively, I do begin to receive some pleasure from looking at pictures; but, as yet, it has nothing to do with any technical merit, nor do I think I shall ever get so far as that. Some landscapes by Ruysdael, and some portraits by Murillo, Velasquez, and Titian, were those which I seemed most able to appreciate; and I see reason for allowing (contrary to my opinion as expressed a few pages back) that a portrait may preserve some valuable characteristics of the person represented. The pictures in the English portrait-gallery are mostly very bad, and that may be the [217] reason why I saw so little in them. I saw, too, at this last visit, a Virgin and child, which appeared to me to have an expression more adequate to the subject than most of the innumerable Virgins and Children, in which we see only repetitions of simple maternity; indeed, any mother, with her first child, would serve an artist for one of them. But in this picture the Virgin had a look as if she were loving the infant as her own flesh and blood, and at the same time giving him an awful worship, as to her Creator.

While I was sitting in the central-saloon, listening to the music, a young man accosted me, presuming that I was so-and-so, the American author. He himself was a traveller for a publishing firm; and he introduced conversation by talking of Uttoxeter, and my description of it in the Keepsake.[450] He said that the article had caused a good deal of pique among the good people of Uttoxeter, on account of the ignorance which I attribute to them as to the circumstance which connects Johnson with their town. The spot where Johnson stood can, it appears, still be pointed out; it is on one side of the market-place, and not in the neighborhood of the church. I forget whether I recorded, at the time, that an Uttoxeter newspaper was sent me, containing a proposal that a statue or memorial should be erected [218] on the spot. It would gratify me exceedingly if such a result should come from my pious pilgrimage thither.

My new acqua[i]ntance, who was cockneyish, but very intelligent and agreeable, went on to talk about many literary matters and characters; among others, about Miss Bronte, whom he had seen at the Chapter Coffee House, when she and her sister Anne first went to London. He was at that time connected with the house of Smith and Elder, and he described the surprise and incredulity of Mr. Smith when this little, common-place looking woman presented herself as the author of Jane Eyre. His story brought out the insignificance of Charlotte Bronte's aspect, and the bluff rejection of her by Mr. Smith, much more strongly than Mrs. Gaskell's narrative.

CHORLTON ROAD, AUGUST 9th, SUNDAY.

WE have changed our lodgings since my last date; they being dear and inconvenient, and the woman of the house a sharp, peremptory housewife, better fitted to deal with her own family than to be complaisant to guests. We are now a little farther from the Exhibition, and not much better off as regards accommodation; but the housekeeper is a civil, pleasant sort of a woman, auspiciously named Mrs. Honey. The house is a specimen of the poorer middle-class dwellings, as built now-a-days; nar[219]row staircase, thin walls, and, being constructed for sale, very ill-put together indeed—the floors with wide cracks between, and wide crevices, admitting both air and light, over the doors; so that the house is full of drafts. The outer walls, it seems to me, are but of one brick in thickness, and the party walls certainly no thicker; and the movements, and sometimes the voices, of people in the contiguous house are audible to us. The Exhibition has temporarily so raised the value of lodgings here, that we pay five pounds per week.

Mr. Wilding having gone on a tour to Scotland, I have had to be at the Consulate every day, last week, till yesterday; when I absented myself from duty, and went to the Exhibition. Una and I spent an hour together, looking principally at the old Dutch Masters, who seem to me the most wonderful set of men that ever handled a brush. Such life-like representations of cabbages, onions, turnips, cauliflower, and peas; such perfect realities of brass kettles and kitchen crockery; such blankets, with the woolen fuzz upon them; such everything (except the human face, which moreover is fairly enough depicted) I never thought that the skill of man could produce. Even the photograph cannot equal their miracles. The closer [220] you look, the more minutely true the picture is found to be; and I doubt if even the microscope could see beyond the painter's touch. Gerard Dow seems to be the master among these queer magicians. A straw mat, in one of his pictures, is the most miraculous thing that human art has yet accomplished; and there is a metal vase, with a dent in it, that is absolutely more real than reality. These painters accomplish all they aim at—a praise, methinks, which can be given to no other men since the world began. They must have laid down their brushes with perfect satisfaction, knowing that each one of their million touches had been necessary to the effect, and that there was not one too little or too much. And it is strange how spiritual, and suggestive the commonest household article—an earthen pitcher, for example—becomes when represented with entire accuracy. These Dutchmen get at the soul of common things, and so make them types and interpreters of the spiritual world.

Afterwards, I looked at many of the pictures of the Old Masters, and found myself gradually getting a taste for pictures; at least, they give me more and more pleasure, the oftener I come to see them. Doubtless, I shall be able to pass for a man of taste, by the time I return to [221] America. It is an acquired taste, like that for wines; and I question whether a man is really any truer, wiser, or better, for possessing it. From the Old Masters, I went among the English painters, and found myself more favorably inclined towards some of them, than at my previous visits; seeing something wonderful even in Turner's lights, and mists, and yeasty waves, although I should like him still better if his pictures looked in the least like what they typify. The most disagreeable of English painters is Etty, who had a diseased appetite for woman's flesh, and spent his whole life, apparently, in painting them with enormously developed bosoms and buttocks[451]. I do not mind nudity, in a modest and natural way; but Etty's women really thrust their nakednesses upon you so with malice aforethought, and especially so enhance their posteriors, that one feels inclined to kick them.[452] The worst of it is, they are not beautiful. Among the last pictures that I looked at was Hogarth's March to Finchley; and surely nothing can be covered more thick and deep with English nature than that piece of canvass [*sic*]. The face of the tall grenadier in the center, between two women, both of whom have claims on him, and one of whom carries his unborn child, wonderfully expresses trouble [222] and perplexity; and every touch in the picture meant something and expresses what it meant.

The price of admission, after two °clock, being sixpence, the Exhibition was thronged with a class of people who do not usually come in such large numbers. It was both pleasant and touching to see how earnestly some of them sought to get instruction from what they beheld. The English are a good and simple people, and take life in earnest.

CHORLTON ROAD, AUGUST 14th, FRIDAY.

PASSING by the gateway of the Manchester Cathedral, the other morning, on my way to the Station, I found a crowd collected; and high over head the Cathedral bells were chiming for a wedding. These chimes of bells are exceedingly impressive, so broadly gladsome as they are, filling the whole air and every nook of one's heart with sympathy; they are good for people to rejoice with, and good also for a marriage, because, through all their joy, there is something solemn—a tone of that voice which we have heard so often at funerals. It is good to see how every body, up to this old age of the world, takes an interest in weddings, and seems to have a faith that now, at last, a couple have come together to make each other happy. The high, black, rough, old Cathedral tower sent out its chime of bells as earnestly as for any bridegroom and bride that came to be married five [223] hundred years ago. I went into the churchyard, but there was such a throng of people on its pavement of flat tombstones, and especially such a cluster along the pathway by which she was to depart, that I could only see a white dress waving along, and really do not know whether she was a beauty or a fright. The happy pair got into a postchaise, that was waiting at the gate, and immediately drew some crimson curtains, and so vanished into their Paradise. There were two other post-chaises and pairs, and all three had postillions in scarlet. This is the same Cathedral where, last May, I saw a dozen or two of couples married in the lump.[453]

In a railway-carriage, two or three days ago, an old merchant made rather a good point of one of the uncomfortable results of the electric telegraph. He said that, formerly, a man was safe from bad news, such as intelligence of failure of debtors, except at the hour of opening his letters in the morning; and then he was in some degree prepared for it, since, among say fifteen letters, he would be pretty certain to find one "queer" one. But since the telegraph has come into play, he is never safe, and may be hit with news of shipwreck, failure, fall of stocks, or whatever disaster, at all hours of the day.

I went to the Exhibition on Wednesday, with Una, [224] and looked at the pencil-sketches of the Old Masters; also at the pictures generally, old and new. I particularly remember a spring-landscape by John Linnell, the younger.

It is wonderfully good; so tender and fresh that the artist seems really to have caught the evanescent April and made her permanent. Here, at last, is eternal Spring.

I saw a little man behind an immense beard, whom I take to be the Duke of Newcastle; at least, there is a photograph of him in the gallery, with just such a beard. He was at the Exhibition on that day.

CHORLTON ROAD, AUGUST 16th, SUNDAY.

I WENT again to the Exhibition, day before yesterday, and looked much at both the Modern and Ancient pictures, as also at the water-colors. I am making some progress as a con[n]oisseur, and have got so far as to be able to distinguish the broader differences of style; as for example, between Rubens and Rembrandt. I should hesitate to claim any more for myself, thus far. In fact, however, I do begin to have a liking for good things, and to be sure that they are good. Murillo seems to me about the noblest and purest painter that ever lived, and his "Good Shepherd" the loveliest picture I ever saw. It is a hopeful symptom, moreover, of improving taste, that I see more merit in the crowd of painters than I was at first competent to acknow[225]ledge. I could see some of their defects from the very first; but that is the very earliest stage of con[n]oisseurship, after a primal and ignorant admiration. Mounting a few steps higher, one sees beauties. But how much study, how many opportunities, are requisite, to form and cultivate a taste! This Exhibition must be quite thrown away on the mass of spectators.

Both they and I are better able to appreciate the specimens of Ornamental Art, contained in the Oriental Room, and in the numerous cases that are ranged up and down the nave. The gewgaws of all time are here, in precious metals, glass, China, ivory, and every other material that could be wrought into curious and beautiful shapes; great basins and dishes of embossed gold, from the Queen's sideboard or those of noblemen; vessels set with precious stones; the pastoral staffs of prelates, some of them made of silver or gold, and enriched with gems, and which have been found in the tombs of the bishops; state-swords, and silver maces; the rich plate of Colleges, elaborately wrought, great cups, salvers, tureens, that have been presented by loving sons to their Alma Mater; the heirlooms of old families, treasured from generation to generation, and hitherto only to be seen by favored friends; famous [226] historical jewels, some of which are painted in the portraits of the historical men and women that hang on the wall; numerous specimens of the beautiful old Venetian glasses, some of which look so fragile that it is a wonder how they could bear even the weight of the wine that used to be poured into them, without breaking. These are the glasses that tested poison by being shattered into fragments. The strongest and ugliest old crockery, pictured over with monstrosities; the Palissy ware, embossed with vegetables, fishes, lobsters, that look absolutely real; the delicate Sevres china, each piece made inestimable by pictures from a master's hand; in short, it is a despair and misery to see so much that is curious and beautiful, and to feel that far the greater portion of it will slip out of the memory and be as if we had never seen it. But I mean to look again and again at these things. We soon perceive that the present day does not engross all the taste and ingenuity that has ever existed in the mind of man; that, in fact, we are a barren age in that respect.

CHORLTON ROAD, AUGUST 20th, THURSDAY.

I WENT to the Exhibition on Monday, and again yesterday, and measurably enjoyed both visits. I continue to think, however, that a picture cannot be fully enjoyed except by long and intimate acquaintance with it; [227] nor can I quite understand what the enjoyment of a connoisseur is. He is not usually, I think, a man of deep poetic feeling, and does not deal with the picture through his heart, nor set it in a poem, nor comprehend it morally. If it be a landscape, he is not entitled to judge of it by his intimacy with Nature; if a picture of human action, he has no experience or sympathy of life's deeper passages. However, as my acquaintance with pictures increases, I find myself recognizing more and more the merit of the acknowledged Masters in the art; but possibly it is only because I adopt the wrong principles which may have been laid down by the connoisseurs. But there can be no mistake about Murillo;—not that I am worthy to admire him yet.

Seeing the many pictures of Holy Families, and the Virgin and Child, which have been painted for Churches and Convents, the idea occurs that it was in this way that the poor monks and nuns gratified, as far as they could, their natural longing for earthly happiness. It was not Mary and her heavenly child that they really beheld, or wished for, but an earthly mother rejoicing over her baby, and displaying it proudly to the world, as an object worthy to be admired by Kings;—as Mary does in the Adoration of the Magi. Every mother, I suppose, feels as if her first child deserved everybody's worship.

[228] I left the Exhibition at about three °clock, and went to Manchester, where I sought out Mr. Charles Swain, in the dark little office of his engraver's establishment at 58, Cannon-street. He greeted me warmly; and, at five, we took the omnibus for his house at Prestwich, about four miles from town. He seems to be on pleasant terms with his neighbors; for almost every body that got into the omnibus exchanged kindly greetings with him; and indeed his kind[l]y, simple, genial nature comes out so evidently that it would be difficult not to like him. His house stands, with others, in a green park, a small, pretty, semi-detached, suburban residence of brick, with a small lawn and garden around it. In close vicinity, there is a deep clough, or dell, as shaggy and wild as a poet could wish, and with a little stream running through it, as much as five miles long. My wife and Julian had preceded me, in the forenoon, and were now just returned from the clough, where my wife had wet her feet, and Julian had tumbled down from a tree.

The interior of Swain's house is very pretty, and nicely, or even handsomely, and almost sumptuously furnished; and I was very glad to find him so comfortable. His recognition as a poet seems to have been hearty enough to give him a feeling of success; for he showed me various tokens of the estimation

[229] in which he is held—for instance, a presentation-copy of Southey's works, in which the latter had written, "Amicus amico—poeta poetae." He said that Southey had always been most kind to him. I never thought much of Southey's judgement, (as shown, for example, in the cases of Kirke White and Lucretia Davidson) and cannot accept it as final in Mr. Swain's case,[454] though I wish I could. There were various other testimonials from people of note, American as well as English. In his parlour, there is a good oil-painting of himself, and in the drawing-room a very fine crayon-sketch, wherein his face (naturally rather heavy, though handsome and agreeable) is lighted up with all a poet's ecstasy. Likewise, a large and fine engraving from the picture. The government has recognized his poetic merit by a pension of fifty pounds; a small sum, it is true, but enough to mark him out as one who has deserved well of his country. I have more than once looked at his poems with a genuine desire to find something good in them, because the man himself is so very good and loveable; but really I cannot discern his claim to hardly a single leaf of laurel. I was able to gratify him, however, by saying that I had recently seen many favorable notices of his poems in the American newspapers; an edition having been published, a few months since, [230] on our side of the water. He was much pleased at this, and asked me to send him the notices.

He has a wife (evidently a very good woman and excellent housewife,) and four daughters, cheerful, ladylike, and comely girls enough, the youngest about sixteen. Poor things! I fear they have no very bright destiny before them.

Two or three ladies came in to tea; and at a quarter before eight we took the omnibus back to Manchester and thence to our lodgings.

CHORLTON ROAD, AUGUST 30th, SUNDAY.

I HAVE been two or three times to the Exhibition, since my last date, and enjoy it more as I become familiar with it. There is supposed to be almost a third of the good pictures, here, which England contains; and it is said that the Tory nobility and gentry have contributed to it much more freely and largely than the Whigs. The Duke of Devonshire, for instance, seems to have sent nothing. Mr. Ticknor, the Spanish historian, whom I met yesterday,[455] observed that we should not think quite so much of this Exhibition as the English do, after we have been to Italy, although it is a good school in which to gain a preparatory knowledge of the different styles of art. I am glad to hear that there are better things still to be seen. Nevertheless, I should suppose that certain [231] painters are better represented here than they ever have been or will be elsewhere. Vandyke, certainly, can be seen nowhere else so well; Rembrandt and Rubens have satisfactory specimens; and the whole series of English pictorial achievement is shewn more perfectly than within any other walls. Perhaps it would be wise to devote myself to the study of this latter, and leave the foreigners to be studied on their own soil. Murillo can hardly have done better than in the pictures by him we see here. There is nothing of Raphael's that impresses me. Titian has some noble portraits, but little else that I care to see. In all these Old Masters (Murillo only excepted) it is very rare,

I must say, to find any trace of natural feeling and passion; and I am weary of naked goddesses, who never had any real life and warmth in the painter's imagination—or, if so, it was the impure warmth of the unchaste women who sat or sprawled for them.

Last week, I dined at Mr. F. Haywood's,[456] to meet Mr. Adolphus,[457] the author of a critical work on the Waverley Novels, published long ago, and intended to prove from internal evidence that they were written by Sir Walter Scott. Mr. Haywood, though a Liverpool cotton-broker, is likewise a man of literature, a translator, I be[232]lieve of Faust; he lives at Edge-lane Hall, a suburban residence, which seems to have been an old country-house, and stands in its own seclusion, on a breezy elevation, with a lawn and shrubbery about it. Two or three rooms are full of Mr. Haywood's library, which appears to contain many books in foreign languages. He has little or no note or reputation in Liverpool, that ever I heard of; and methinks it is rather singular that a man living in such good style, with a carriage and servants, in a large, old house—a man of cultivation and refinement, and even of literary performance—should not have acquired somewhat of Roscoe's celebrity in Roscoe's town. To be sure, he has no conversational ability, nor any particular warmth or suggestiveness in his social atmosphere; indeed, though he does not seem a shy or self-involved man, I never heard anybody say fewer rememberable things than he. He has a wife, a solid, elderly lady, who says little, and keeps a book in which people are to write their names and a sentence or two; and a son, who, I think, has been bred to the law. They are Tories and conservatives, as people of their class— over whom the Aristocracy immediately sit, and whom one would imagine most likely to be galled by them—are very apt to be. It is very kind of them.

[233] Mr. Adolphus is here in attendance on the assizes; for he was bred a barrister, though, Mr. Haywood told me, he has latterly ceased to practise as one, on obtaining an appointment to some commissionership or other such office. He came in, a little after I arrived, in a morning dress; a small, or rather small, and thin, and somewhat shrivellish person, approaching to sixty years of age, but not looking so old. I should hardly have taken him to be fifty; especially as I saw no gray hairs in his head, though some in his whiskers. He is of very quiet manners, and of rather scanty and unobtrusive talk; a calm, refined, scholarly person, with not quite an Englishman's share of flesh and blood. His wife was likewise of the party, a homely, well-mannered, kindly English lady; and also a young Spanish lady,[458] whose name I forget, but their niece, and daughter of a Spaniard of literary note. She herself has literary tastes and ability, and is well known to Prescott (whom I believe she has assisted in his historical researches) and also to Ticknor; and furthermore she is very handsome, and unlike an English damsel, though very youthful and maidenlike; and her manners have an ardour and enthusiasm that was pleasant to see and hear, especially as she spoke warmly of my [234] writings; and yet I should wrong her, if I left the impression of her being forth-putting and obtrusive, for it was not the fact in the least. She speaks English like a native, insomuch that I never should have suspected her to be anything else.

These good people were staying at Mr. Haywood's and the dinner party was made up by two other gentlemen of learning and culture, which did not particularly appear in any thing that was said; but it was a pleasant dinner too. I spent the night there; and though I had avoided champagne, and only taken a few glasses of sherry, and one of claret, I tossed about the wide bed, the whole night through. My nerves, recently, have not been in an exactly quiet and normal state. I begin to weary of England, and need another clime.

CHORLTON ROAD, SEPT 6th, SUNDAY.

THERE has come a begging to me, two or three times, at the Consulate, a very ragged and pitiable old fellow, who professes to be an American; shabby beyond all description, lean, depressed, hungry-looking, but with a large and somewhat red nose. He says he is in [sic] a printer, born in Philadelphia, (at 92d street, or some such locality) but that he came to England seventeen years ago, and has never been able to get back again. He wishes very [235] much to go home, and says, with great apparent simplicity, "Sir, I would rather be there than here." His manner and accent do not convince me that he is an American, and I tell him so; but he still says, "Sir, I was born and have lived in 92d street, Philadelphia"; and goes on to mention some public edifice, or other local objects, with which he used to be familiar. If I speak harshly to him, he takes no offence, still replying with the same mild depression, and insisting still on 92d street. I give him a trifle, and he goes away, appearing again after an interval of months, telling me of wanderings hither and thither, and of his getting now and then a little work, and perhaps how an American gentleman told him that if he could only have spared time he would have found him a passage home; likewise that he had nothing to eat yesterday, and how earnestly he wishes that he had never left 92d street, Philadelphia. Nevertheless, I do not half believe that he ever saw America in his life; he is only one of the shapes of English vagabondism;—perhaps not, however, and then how sad and how queer a fate!—homeless on this foreign shore, looking always towards his country, coming again and again to the point whence so many set sail for it—so many that will soon tread in 92d street—losing, in all these years, the distinctive characteristics of an American, and at last dying and giving his clay to be a portion of the soil from which he could [236] not escape in his lifetime. His story is quite as poetical as that of Ulysses.[459]

I think I paid my last visit to the Exhibition, and feel as if I had had enough of it, although I have got but a small part of the profit it might have afforded me. But pictures are certainly quite other things to me, now, from what they were at my first visit; it seems even as if there were a sort of illumination within them that makes me see them more distinctly. Speaking of pictures, the miniature of Ann of Cleaves [sic] is here, on the faith of which Henry VIII married her; also, the picture of the Infanta of Spain which Buckingham brought over to Charles I, while Prince of Wales. The latter picture has a delicate, rosy prettiness.

One rather interesting portion of the Exhibition is the Refreshment Room—

or rather rooms, for very much space is allowed both to the first and second classes. I have looked most at the latter, because there John Bull and his female may be seen in full gulp and guzzle, swallowing vast quantities of cold boiled beef, thoroughly moistened with porter or bitter ale; and very good meat and drink it is.

At my last visit, on Friday, I met Judge Pollock of Liverpool, who introduced me to a gentleman in a grey, slouched hat as Mr. Du Val,[460] an artist, resident in Manchester; and [237] Mr. Du Val invited me to dine with him at six °clock. So I went to Carlton Grove, his residence; and found it a very pretty house, with its own lawn and shrubbery about it; and was introduced to Mrs. Du Val, a round, handsome, cheerful, and kindly lady of middle-age. Mrs. Pollock was likewise there, with her husband, and another lady, besides a grown up daughter or two of the family; and there was a mellow fire in the grate, which made the drawing-room very cosy and pleasant, as the dusk came on, before dinner. Mr. Du Val looked like a artist, and like a remarkable man, with his careless dress, and broad, bold brow. He has two pictures in the Exhibition, which I had looked at several times, though, to tell the truth, not with very great pleasure. They are good pictures, but happen not to be agreeable. He himself is better than his pictures. He showed us, also, a picture on the easel,— Samuel's mother delivering him up to Ely [sic]—which seems to promise well; and the subject, I think, is a virgin one, though other parts of Samuel's career have been often painted.

We had the most sensible dinner I ever assisted at in England, because it was so comfortable, unpretending, and satisfactory for all the purposes of a friendly dinner; nothing but roast-beef and boiled fowls, with sherry and excellent port, and [238] some light claret for Mrs. Du Val's drinking; not that she liked it so well, she assured us, as either porter or port, but the Doctor had forbidden her those liquids. All at table were very sensible and natural people, truly refined, and devoid of airs; and I impute this in great measure to a predominance of the Irish element in the party; the Pollocks and Mr. Du Val being of that country. The English have not the art or the nature of meeting each other naturally, and for the uppermost purpose of social enjoyment; and so they make the dinner, which ought to be the mere method and medium of bringing them together, the great and overwhelming object, to which all true intercourse is sacrificed. We had very good talk, chiefly about the Exhibition; and Du Val spoke generously and intelligently of his brother-artists. He says that England might furnish five Exhibitions, each one as rich as the present. I find that the most famous picture here is one that I have hardly looked at; the Three Maries, by Annibale Car[r]acci. In the dining-room there were several pictures and sketches by Du Val, one of which I especially liked, a misty, moonlight picture of the Mersey, and its shores near Seacombe. I never saw such genuine moonlight. After the ladies retired, we talked a good while at table, and I inquired whether they had ever heard the cause (recently commu[239]nicated to me) of the separation of Lady Byron from her husband. None of them had;

though Judge Pollock had formerly been a literary man about town, conversant with all such gossip, and could hardly have failed to be acquainted with the story, whether true or false. He *had,* however, heard another solution of the mystery, quite as discreditable to Byron. I hope neither is true.

In the drawing-room we had some music from the young ladies and two sons of the family; and at about half past ten, I took my leave of these very kind and comfortable folks, whom I should like the better the more I got to know them. Judge Pollock told me that Du Val and his wife had married in early life, without a shilling between them, and that they had brought up, and were bringing up, twelve children on the avails of his artist's profession. Now, Du Val is certainly not a foremost man among English artists; indeed, I never remember to have heard his name before; and it speaks well for the profession that he should [be] able to live in such handsome comfort, and nourish so large a brood. I wish him all manner of success and fame.

I found my cab at the door, and my cabman snugly asleep inside of it; and when Mr. Du Val awoke him, he proved to be quite drunk, insomuch that I hesitated whether to let [240] him clamber upon the box, or to take post myself and drive the cabman home. However, I propounded two questions to him; first, whether his horse would go of his own accord; and, secondly, whether he himself was invariably drunk at that time of night, because, if it was his normal state, I should be safer with him drunk than sober. Being satisfied on these points, I got in, and was driven home without accident or adventure; except, indeed, that the cabman drew up, and opened the door for me to get out, at a vacant lot on Stratford Road, just as if there had been a house and home, and cheerful lighted windows, in that vacancy. On my remonstrance, he resumed the whip and reins, and reached Boston Terrace at last; and thanking me for an extra sixpence, as well as he could speak, he begged me to inquire for "Little John" whenever I next wanted a cab. Cabmen are, as a body, the most ill-natured and ungenial race in the world; but this poor little man was excellently good humored,—in his cups at least.

Speaking of the former rudeness of manners (now gradually refining away) of the Manchester people, Judge Pollock said that when he first knew Manchester (not many years ago, for he is but middle-aged) females meeting his wife in the street would take hold of her gown, and say—"Ah, three-and-six-[241]pence a yard!" The men were very rough, after the old Lancashire fashion. They have always, however, been a musical people, and this may have been a germ of refinement in them. They are still much more simple and natural than the Liverpool people, who love and ape the aristocracy, and whom they heartily despise. It is singular that the great Arts Exhibition should have come to pass in the rudest great town in England.

THURSDAY, SEPT^r 10th; 10, LANSDOWNE CIRCUS, LEAMINGTON.

WE had got quite weary of our small, mean, uncomfortable, and unbeautiful lodgings at Chorlton Road, with poor and scanty furniture within doors, and no better prospect from the parlor-windows than a mud-puddle, larger than most English lakes, on a vacant building-lot opposite our house. The Exhibition, too, was fast becoming a bore; for you must really love a picture, in order to tolerate the sight of it many times. Moreover, the smoky and sooty air of that abominable Manchester affected my wife's throat disadvantageously; so, on Tuesday morning, we struck our tent and set forth again, regretting to leave nothing except the kind disposition of Mrs. Honey, our housekeeper. I do not remember ever meeting with any other lodging-house keeper who did not grow hateful and fearful on short acquaintance; but I attribute this not so much to the people themselves, as primarily to the [242] unfair and ungenerous conduct of their English guests, who feel so sure of being cheated that they always behave as if in an enemy's country—and therefore they find it one.

The rain poured down upon us as we drove away in two cabs, laden with mountainous luggage, to the London Road station; and the whole day was grim with cloud and moist with showers. We went by way of Birmingham, and staid three hours at the great, dreary Station there, waiting for the train to Leamington, whither Fanny had been sent forward, the day before, to secure lodgings for us. England is a monotonous country to travel through by railway; its beauties and picturesque points are not panoramic, but require leisure and close inspection in order to be appreciated; besides, the day was so dreary that there was little temptation to look out. We all were tired and dull by the time we reached the Leamington Station, where a note from Fanny gave us the address of our lodgings. Lansdowne Circus is a nice little circle of pretty, moderate-sized, two-story houses, all on precisely the same plan, so that on coming out of any one door, and taking a turn, one can hardly tell which house is his own. There is a green space of grass and shrubbery in the centre of the Circus, and a little grass plot, with flowers, shrubbery, and well-kept hedges, before every house; and it is really delightful, after that ugly and grimy [243] suburb of Manchester. Indeed, there could not possibly be a greater contrast than between Leamington and Manchester; the latter built only for dirty uses, and scarcely intended as a habitation for man; the former so cleanly, so set out with shade-trees, so regular in its streets, so neatly paved, its houses so prettily contrived, and nicely stuccoed, that it does not look like a portion of the work-a-day world. 'Genteel' is the word for it; a town where people of moderate income may live an idle and handsome life, whether for a few weeks or a term of years. The tasteful shop-fronts on the principal streets; the Bath-chairs; the public garden; the servants whom one meets, and doubts whether they are groom, footman, or butler, or a mixture of the three; the ladies sweeping through the avenues; the nursery maids and children; all make up a picture of somewhat unreal finery; and the plan on which the houses are built, in large blocks or ranges (each tenement the repetition of its fellows, though the different ranges have great variety of style) betokens a town where the occupant does not build for himself, but where speculators build to let. The names of the streets and ranges of houses are characteristic; Lansdowne Crescent, Lansdowne Circus, Clarendon-street, Regent-street, the Upper Parade, and a hundred other grand titles of Terraces and Villas. To say the truth, unless I could [244] have a fine English country-house, I do not know a spot where I would rather reside than in this new village of midmost Old England.

LANSDOWNE CIRCUS, SEPT^r 11th, FRIDAY.

IN the forenoon, yesterday, my wife and I, with Julian, walked down through the Upper and Lower Parades (but first through Warwick-street—I like to repeat these grand names) to the Jephson Gardens, which are open to the public at the price of three-pence. The English, principally by aid of their moist climate, and not too fervid sun, excel in converting flat surfaces into beautiful scenery, through the skilful arrangement of trees and shrubbery. They do it in the little patches under the windows of a suburban villa, and on a larger scale in a tract of many acres. This Garden is named in honor of a Doctor Jephson, who first found out the virtues (if any there really be) of the well which has given Leamington its renown, and converted it from an old rural village into a smart watering-place. A short distance within the garden-gates, there is a circular temple of Grecian architecture, beneath the dome of which stands a marble statue of the Doctor, very well executed, representing him with a face of fussy activity and benevolence; just the man to build up the fortunes of his native village, or perhaps to ruin all its inhabitants by his speculations. He has now been dead many years; but I believe the [245] prosperity of Leamington is a growth of the present century.

The Garden is a beautiful pleasure ground, shadowed well with trees of a fine growth, but with spaces large enough for a breadth of sunshine, and with bright flower-beds, set like gems in the green sward; old trunks of trees, too, here and there, are formed into rustic chairs, and some of them are made into flower-pots. There is an archery-ground, with targets; and, all the time we were there, three young ladies were practising archery, and sometimes hitting the mark. The Leam, a very lazy stream, after drowsing across the principal street of the town beneath a handsome bridge, skirts along the margin of the Garden, without seeming to flow at all. Its water is by no means transparent, but has a greenish, goose-puddly hue, and yet is not unpleasant to sight; and certainly the river is the perfection of the gently picturesque, sleeping along beneath a margin of willows that droop into it, and other trees that incline lovingly over it; on the garden-side, a shadowy, secluded grove, with winding paths among its boskiness, and on the opposite side the church, with its church-yard full of tombstones and shrubbery. Two anglers were fishing from the church-yard bank. With a book and a cigar (but I rather think the garden-deities forbid smoking) I cannot conceive of a more delightful place for a summer day than this grove on the [246] margin of the Leam. Besides the river, there is another object of water-scenery in the shape of a small artificial lake, with a little green island in the midst. This piece of water is the haunt of swans. I forget whether I mentioned the swans in the Botanical Gardens at Old Trafford; how beautiful and stately was their aspect and their movement in the water, and how infirm, disjointed, and decrepit was their gait, when they unadvisedly chose to emerge, and walk upon dry land. In the latter case, they looked like a breed of uncommonly misshapen and ill contrived geese; and I record the matter here for the sake of the moral—that we should never pass judgment on the merits of any person or thing, unless we see it in the circumstances for which it is intended and adapted.

This is the pleasantest public garden I ever was in; not that it is superior to all others in its adornments and arrangements, but because it is so quiet, and, like other Leamington characteristics, so genteel. I think the better of this glossy gentility, from observing what a pleasant surface it puts upon matters here. We now emerged from this bosky seclusion and still water-side into the lively street, and walked up the Parade, looking at the shop-windows, where were displayed a great variety of pretty objects and knickknacks, indicating much idle time and some superfluous means [247] among the visitors of Leamington. They are the most brilliant ranges of shops that I have seen out of London; though I suppose that the most valuable part of the stock is displayed in the windows.[461]

In the afternoon, Julian and I went along the Holly Walk, and ascended what I believe is called the Newbold Hill to the "Lovers' Grove"; a range of tall old oaks and elms, from beneath which we can see Warwick Castle, and a wide extent of generally level, but beautiful landscape. So far, the walk was familiar to us when we were in Leamington before. Thence we took a field-path, with led us along hedge-rows, chiefly of hawthorn, but intermixed with blackberry bushes, on which the berries hung abundantly, mostly red, but with here and there a black one, which we plucked and ate. After a walk of a mile or so, our track ended in a farm-establishment, which, house and outbuildings, were entirely new, and of red brick. At a short distance, in a hollow, lay an old brick-village; and after inquiring at a house, and being barked at by a chained dog, we found our way thither, and entered its narrow, crooked, and ugly street. The village was Cubington, formerly Combeington—so named from Combe, a hollow. It is a very ancient place, though wholly destitute of ivied beauty or any kind of antique grace; its [248] houses being all of brick, which, in many cases, has been patched into the old timber-frames that still look as stable as they were in Elizabeth's time. Of all English villages, I think this is the meanest and ugliest; and, small though it was, it had two ale-houses. A little apart from this wretched street, we found the church, with its low, square, battlemented tower, perhaps of Norman antiquity; and, playing and laughing at the church-yard gate, there were some village-girls, of whom I inquired the way back to Leamington, and heard myself laughed at as I followed their instructions. We returned by the high-road, which led us through Lillington, a prettier little village than Cubington; one range of thatched cottages was very pretty indeed, with their little gardens before every door, separated by trimly luxuriant hedges, with fruit-trees, and beehives, and glimpses of brick floors, or stone ones, through the open doors; and women and children peering out at the passing wayfarers. These cottages were a range of comfortable little nests, where, I suppose, the inmates may have had a longer hereditary tenure than the owners of many a castle or manor-house. The church of Lillington is reached by a shady lane, and is not visible from the high road. Since I was here last, it has been almost entirely renewed, but, I believe, on its ancient plan; and the gray, square tower remains unchanged. I observed a stained window [249] (of recent date) in the Chancel; and it is as fine and picturesque a little church as I have seen. All over England, there seems to be a great zeal for the preservation and reverential re-edification of old churches. When I first came from America, I valued nothing but the genuine old article, the very old stones that the Saxons or Normans first laid one upon another; but I have passed through that phase of the love of antiquity, and now prize the antique idea more than the ancient material. Therefore I love to see an old church lovingly rebuilt.

We had a short walk hence into the stately avenues of Leamington. In my remarks about the town's prettiness and gentility, I have hardly done justice to some almost palatial ranges of edifices, and separate residences, which look quite equal to any in London. Among the range of thatched cottages, mentioned above, I must mention one, the garden of which was adorned in a way indicating taste and fancy in the occupant; for instance, a bee-hive curiously made of oyster-shells, a stump of a tree with flowers growing out of it.

LANSDOWNE CIRCUS, SEPT^r 13th SUNDAY.

THE weather was very uncertain through the last week; and yesterday morning, too, was misty and sunless; notwithstanding which Mamma, Una, Julian and I, took the rail for Kenilworth at a quarter to eleven. The distance from Leamington is less than [250] five miles; and at the Kenilworth Station we found a little bit of an omnibus, into which we packed ourselves, together with two ladies, one of whom, at least, was an American. I begin to agree partly with the English, that we are not a people of elegant manners; at all events, there is sometimes a bare, hard, meagre sort of deportment, especially in our women, that has not its parallel elsewhere. But perhaps what sets off this kind [of] behavior, and brings it into *alto relievo,* is the fact of such uncultivated persons travelling abroad, and going to see sights that would not be interesting except to people of some education and refinement.

We saw but little of the village of Kenilworth, passing through it sidelong fashion in the omnibus; but I learn from the Guide Book that it has between three and four thousand inhabitants, and is of immemorial antiquity. We saw a few old, gabled and timber-framed houses; but generally the town was of modern aspect, although less so in the immediate vicinity of the Castlegate, across the road from which, there was an inn, with bowling-greens, and a little bunch of houses and shops. A little apart from the high road, there is a gate-house, ancient, but in excellent repair, towered, turretted [*sic*], and battlemented, and looking like a castle in itself. Until Cromwell's time, the entrance to the castle used to be beneath an arch that passed through [251] this structure; but, the gate-house being granted to one of the Parliament officers, he converted it into a residence, and apparently added on a couple of gables, which now look quite as venerable as the rest of the edifice. Admission within the outer precincts of the castle is now obtained through a little wicket, close beside the gate-house; at which sat one or two old men, who touched their hats to us in humble willingness to accept a fee. One of them had guide-books for sale; and finding that we were not to be bothered by a cicerone, we bought one of his books.

The ruins are perhaps two hundred yards (or more, or less) from the gate-house and the road, and the space between is a pasture for sheep, which also browse in the inner court, and shelter themselves in the dungeons and state-apartments of the castle. Goats would be fitter occupants, because they could climb to the tops of the crumbling towers, and nibble the weeds and shrubbery that grow there. The first part of the castle which we reach[ed] is called Caesar's Tower, being the oldest portion of the ruins, and still very stalwart and massive, and built, (as all the rest is) of red free-stone. Caesar's Tower being on the right, Leicester's buildings (erected by Queen Elizabeth's favorite) is on the left; and between these two formerly stood stood [sic] other portions of [252] the castle, which have now as entirely disappeared as if they had never existed; and through the wide gap thus opened appears the grassy inner court, surrounded on three sides by half-fallen towers and shattered walls. Some of these were erected by John of Gaunt; and in this portion of the ruins is the banquetting[sic]-hall—or rather was—for it has now neither floor nor roof, but only the broken stonework of some tall, arched windows, and the beautiful, old, ivied arch of the entrance-way, now inaccessible from the ground. The ivy is very abundant about the ruins, and hangs its green curtains quite from top to bottom of some of the windows. There are likewise very large and aged trees within the castle, there being no roof nor pavement anywhere, except in here and there a dungeon-like nook; so that the trees, having soil and air enough, and being sheltered from unfriendly blasts, can grow as if in a nursery. Hawthorn, however, next to ivy, is the great ornament, and comforter, of these desolate ruins. I never saw so much and such thriving hawthorn anywhere else; in the court, high up on crumbly heights, on the sod that carpets roofless rooms; everywhere, indeed, and now rejoicing in plentiful crops of red berries. The ivy is even more wonderfully luxuriant; its trunks being, in some places, two or three feet across, and forming real buttresses against [253] the walls, which are actually supported and vastly strengthened by this parasite, that clung to them at first only for its own convenience, and now holds them up lest it should be ruined by their fall. Thus an abuse has strangely grown into a use; and I think we may sometimes see the same fact, morally, in English matters. There is something very curious in the close firm grip which the ivy fixes upon the wall, closer and closer for centuries. Neither is it at all nice as to what it clutches, in its necessity for support. I saw, in the outer court of the castle, an old hawthorn tree to which (no doubt a hundred years ago, at least) a plant of ivy had married itself, and the ivy-trunk and the hawthorn-trunk were now absolutely incorporated, and, in their close embrace, you could not tell which was which.

At one end of the banquetting [*sic*] hall, there are two large bay-windows, one of which looks into the inner-court, and the other affords a view of the surrounding country. The former is called, I think, Queen Elizabeth's dressing-room. Beyond the banquetting[*sic*]-hall, is what the guide-book calls the Strong Tower, up to the top of which we climbed, principally by aid of the ruins that have tumbled down from it. A lady sat half way down the crumbly descent, within the castle, on a camp-stool, and before an easel, sketching this tower, [254] on the summit of which we sat. She told my wife that it was Amy Robsart's Tower; and within it, open to the day, and quite accessible, we saw a room that we were free to imagine had been occupied by her. I do not find that these associations of real scenes with fi[c]titious events greatly heighten the charm of them.

By this time, the sun had come out brightly, and with such warmth that we were glad to sit down in the shadow of the ruins. Several sight-seers were now rambling about, and among them some schoolboys, who kept scrambling up to points whither no other animal, except a goat, would have ventured. Their shouts and the sunshine made the old castle cheerful; and what with the ivy and the hawthorn, and the other old trees, it was very beautiful and picturesque. But a castle does not make nearly so interesting and impressive a ruin as an abbey; because the latter was built for beauty, and on a plan in which deep thought and feeling were involved; and having once been a grand and beautiful work, it continues grand and beautiful through all the successive stages of its decay. But a castle is rudely piled together for strength and other material conveniences; and having served these ends, it has nothing left to fall back upon, but crumbles into shapeless masses, which are [255] often as little picturesque as a pile of bricks. Without the ivy and the shrubbery, this huge Kenilworth would not be a pleasant object, except for one or two window frames, with broken tracery, in the banquetting [*sic*] hall. Moreover (it is a small thing to say, but true nevertheless) the sheep are a nuisance and a nastiness, and commit great abominations; and, whether by their fault, or whatever else, the more secluded recesses are not pleasant to creep into.

We staid from a little past eleven °clock till two, and identified the various parts of the castle, as well as we could by the Guide Book. The ruins are very extensive, though less so than I should have imagined, considering that seven acres were included within the castle-wall. But a large part of the structure has been taken away to build houses in Kenilworth village and elsewhere, and much, too, to make roads with, and a good deal lies under the green turf in the court-yards, inner and outer. As we returned to the gate, my wife and Una went into the gate-house to see an old chimney-piece and other antiquities; and Julian and I, emerging through the gate, went a little way round the outer wall, and saw the remains of the moat, and Lunn's tower, a rent and shattered structure of John of Gaunt. The omnibus now drove up, and one of the old [256] men at the gate came hobbling up to open the door, and was rewarded with a sixpence; and we drove down to the King's Head, and got some luncheon. It consisted of a prime round of corn-beef, and some ale; real English cheer. We then walked out, and bought ten-and-sixpence worth of prints of the castle, and inquired our way to the church, and to the ruins of the priory. The latter, so far as we could discover them, are very few and uninteresting; and the church, though it has a venerable ex-terior, and an aged spire, has been so modernized within, and in so plain a fashion, as to have lost what beauty it may once have had. There were a few brasses and mural monuments, one of which was a marble group of a dying woman and her family, by Westmacott. The sexton was a cheerful little man, but knew very little about his church, and nothing of the remains of the Priory. There is nothing else particularly to be told of this day, which was spent very pleasantly amid this beautiful, green English scenery, these fine old Warwickshire trees, these broad, gently swelling fields.

At Mrs. Blodget's, Liverpool, Sept[r] 16th, Wednesday.

On Monday, a warm and bright afternoon, Julian and I took a walk to-gether to Warwick; a walk which I think I remember taking more than once, when we were at Leamington two years ago. It ap[257]peared to me that the suburbs of Warwick now stretch further towards Leamington than they did then; there being still some pretty reaches of sylvan road, with border-ing hedges and overshadowing trees, and here and there a bench for the wayfarer; but then begin the vulgar brick dwellings for the poorer classes, or the stuccoed Elizabethan imitation for those a step or two above them. Neither, in the town itself, did I find such an air of antiquity as I thought I re-membered there; though the old archway at the commencement of Jury Street looks as ancient as ever. But the hospital close by it has certainly undergone some transmogrification, the nature of which I cannot quite make out.

We turned aside, before entering the heart of the town, and went to the stone bridge over the Avon, whence such a fine view of the Castle is to be obtained. I suppose I have described it already; and therefore I have no heart to attempt describing it again; but I am certain that there is nothing more beautiful in the world, in such a quiet, sunny, summer afternoon, as those gray turrets, and towers, and high-windowed walls, softened with abundant foliage intermixed, and looking down upon the sleepy river, along which, between the bridge and the castle, the willows droop into the water. Many spectators have stood on the bridge and admired it, as is evidenced by their initials cut [258] into the soft freestone of the balustrade; and it was pretty to observe how the green moss had filled up some of these letters, as if it were taking pains to make them legible. I have observed the same

thing on tombstones; and indeed the moist air of England is always producing one beautiful effect or another.

I staid a good while on the bridge, and Julian mounted astride of the
balustrade, and jogged up and down like a postillion, thereby exciting a smile
from some ladies who drove by in a barouche. We afterwards returned towards
the town, and turning down a narrow lane, bordered with some old cottages
and one or two ale-houses, we found that it led straight to the castle-walls, and
terminated beneath them. It seemed to be the stable-entrance; and as two
gentlemen and a groom were just riding away, I felt ashamed to stand there
staring at the walls which I had no leave to look upon; so I turned back with
Julian, and went into the town. The precincts of the castle seem to be very extensive, and its high and massive outer wall shoulders up almost to the principal street. We rambled about, without any definite aim, and passed under the
pillars that support the spire of Saint Mary's church, and thence into the
market-place, where we found an omnibus just on the point of starting for
Leamington. So we got on, [259] and came home. I have never yet seen—
what those who have seen it call the finest old spectacle in England—the interior of Warwick Castle; it being shown only on Saturdays. I do not blame
the Earl; for I would hardly take his magnificent Castle as a gift, burthened
with the condition that the public should be free to enter it.

Yesterday, I took the train for Rugby, and thence to Liverpool; a dull,
monotonous, swift rush. It is wonderful how little one sees, from the railway,
in traversing England in whatever direction; not a feature keeps its hold on
the memory.

AT MRS. BLODGET'S, SEPT^r 17th, THURSDAY.

THE most noticeable character at Mrs. Blodget's, now, is Mr. Train,[462]
a Yankee who has seen the world, and gathered much information and experience already, though still a young man; a handsome man, with black, curly
hair, a dark, intelligent, bright face, and rather cold blue eyes; but a very
pleasant air and address. His observing faculties are very strongly developed
in his forehead, and his reflective ones seem to be adequate to making some,
if not the deepest use of what he sees. He has voyaged and travelled almost
all over the world, and has recently published a book of his peregrinations,
[260] which has been well received. He is of exceeding fluent talk, and sensible
talk too, though rather too much inclined to unfold the secret springs of action
in Louis Napoleon and other potentates, and to tell of Revolutions that are
coming, at some unlooked for moment, but soon. Still, I believe in his wisdom and foresight, about as much as in any other man's. There are no such
things. He is a merchant, and meditates settling in London, and making a
colossal fortune there during the next ten or twenty years; that being the
period during which London is to hold the exchanges of the world and so
continue its metropolis. After that, New York is to be the world's queen-
city.

There is likewise here a young American named Arnold, who has been at a German University, and favors us with descriptions of his student-life there, which seems chiefly to have consisted in drinking beer and fighting duels. He shows a cut on his nose as a trophy of these combats. He has with him a dog of Saint Bernard, who is a much more remarkable character than himself; an immense dog, a noble and gentle creature; and really it touches my heart that his master is going to take him from his native snow-mountain to a Southern plantation, to [261] die. Mr. Arnold says that there are now but five of these dogs extant at the Convent; there having, within two or three years, been a disease among them, of which this dog also has suffered. His master has a certificate of his genuineness, and of his being the rightful purchaser, and he says that, as he descended the mountain, every peasant along the road stopped him, and would have compelled him to give up the dog, had he not produced this proof of property. The neighboring mountaineers are very jealous of the breed being taken away, considering them of such importance to their own safety. This huge animal (the very biggest dog I ever saw, though only eleven months old, and not so high, by two or three inches, as he will be) allows Mr. Arnold to play with him and take him on his shoulders—he weighs at least a hundred pounds—like any lap-dog.

We have several ladies, who strike me as being colorless, and insipid, mentally and physically. My friend Mrs. Blodget, for whom I feel respect and affection, is as good, kind, and hospitable as ever, and I take pleasure in putting her name last in this last volume of my English journal.

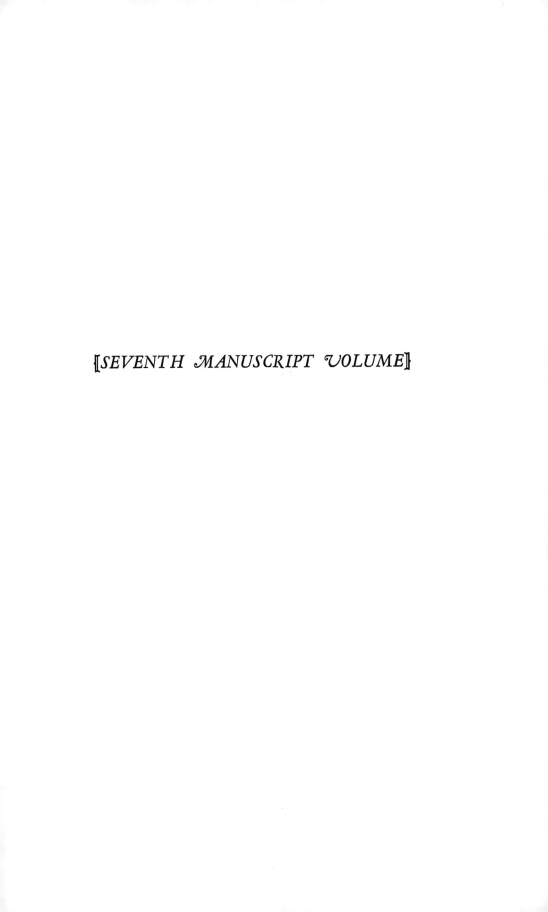

[SEVENTH MANUSCRIPT VOLUME]

1857

OCTOBER. 10, LANSDOWNE CIRCUS, LEAMINGTON.

I RETURNED hither from Liverpool on Wednesday evening of last week, and have spent the time here idly, since then, reposing myself after the four years of unnatural restraint in the Consulate. Being already pretty much acquainted with the neighborhood of Leamington, I have little or nothing new to record about this prettiest, cheerfullest, cleanest of English towns, with its beautiful elms, its lazy river, its villas, its brilliant shops—its whole smartness and gentility in the midst of green, sylvan scenery and hedgerows, and in the neighborhood of old thatched and mossgrown villages clustering each about the little, square battlemented tower of a church; villages such as Leamington itself was before Dr. Jephson transformed it into a fashionable watering-place, fifty years ago. Our immediate abode is a small, neat house, in a circle of just such houses, so exactly alike that it it [*sic*] is difficult to find one's own peculiar domicile; each with its little ornamented plot of grass and flowers, with a bit of iron fence in front, and an intersecting hedge between its grass plot and that of its next neighbor; and in the center of the Circus a little paddock of shrubbery and trees, box, yew, and much other variety of foliage, now tinged autumnally. I have [2] seldom seen, and never before lived in, such a quiet, cozy, comfortable, social seclusion and snuggery. Nothing disturbs us; it being an eddy quite aside from the stream of life. Once or twice a day, perhaps, a cab or private carriage drives round the Circus and stops at one or another of the doors; twice a day comes the red-coated postman, delivering letters from door to door; in the evening, he rings a handbell as he goes his round, a signal that he is ready to take letters for the post; in other respects, we are quite apart from the stir of the world. Our neighbors (as I learn from the list of visitors and residents in a weekly newspaper) are half-pay officers with their families, and other such quiet and respectable people, who have no great figure to make or particular business to do in life. I do not wonder at their coming here to live; there cannot be a better place for people of moderate means, who have done with hope and effort, and only want to be comfortable.

On Saturday, my wife and I took the rail for Coventry, about a half-hour's ride distant. I had been there before, more than two years ago, and my wife about a month since. No doubt I described it on my first visit; and it is not remarkable enough to be worth two descrip[3]tions; a large town of crooked and irregular streets and lanes, not looking nearly so ancient as it is, because of new brick and stuccoed fronts which have been plastered over its antiquity; although still there are interspersed the peak gables of old fashioned, timber-built houses; or an archway of worn stone, which, if you peep through it,

shows like an avenue from the present into the past; for, just in the rear of
the new-fangled aspect, lurks the old arrangement of court-yards, and rusti-
ness, and griminess, and many things that would not be suspected from the
exterior.

We went into Saint Mary's Hall, the old edifice where the municipal meetings and police-courts are held; formerly the hall of one of the guilds, where
their feasts used to be held. In the basement, there is a great, gloomy kitchen,
and a cellar, with pillars and arches like the crypt of a cathedral. Above,
there is a fine old mediaeval apartment, some sixty feet long, and broad and
lofty in proportion, lighted by six high windows of stained glass on each side,
and a large arched one at the end; the latter being of genuine ancient glass,
representing old kingly personages, and heraldic blazonries; but notwithstanding all the colored light that comes through these windows, the [4]
hall, panelled with black oak, is sombre and dark. At the end opposite
the great arched window (which is mullioned with stone) is an oaken gallery for minstrels, extending across the hall, and on the balustrade hang old
suits of armour belonging to the city. Under the gallery are arched doors,
leading to dusky rooms which are used for committees and other municipal
purposes. I have spoken of the hall as being oak-panelled; but I now remember that [it] is partly covered with tapestry of Henry VIs time, representing
historical persons; very elaborately wrought, and no doubt very rich and
magnificent in its day, though now so faded and darkened as to be hardly
distinguishable. Coats of arms were formerly painted all round the hall, but
have been obliterated by the garments of people brushing against them. I have
not seen anything in England more curious than this hall; and I must not forget its oaken roof, vaulted quite across, without any support of pillars, and
carved with figures of angels, and, I suppose, many devices which are lost
amid the duskiness that broods up aloft there like an overhanging cloud. The
floor of the hall is now covered with rows of benches. In a recess on one side,
near the entrance of what is called the Mayoress's parlour, there stood an
ancient chair of state, [5] big enough for two. Kings and queens, the guide-
book says, have sat there in former times; and my wife and I sat down as
their successors. There are full length portraits of George III and George
IV hanging in this hall, and some other portraits which I did not particularly
examine. In the Lady Mayoress's parlour, I remember, I saw many pictures at
my former visit; but there seemed to be a court in session there to-day; so
we did not inspect it.[463]

Right across the narrow street stands Saint Michael's church, with its
tall tall tower and spire, more than three hundred feet high. The body of the
church has been almost entirely recased with stone, since I was here before; but
the tower still retains its antiquity, and is decorated with statues that look down
from their lofty niches, seemingly in good preservation. The tower and spire
are most stately and beautiful; the whole church very noble. We went in,
and found that the vulgar plaster of Cromwell's time has been scraped from

the pillars and arches, leaving them all as fresh and beautiful as if just made. There are a few monuments in the church; but it seems to be paved along the aisles with flat tombstones.

[6] We looked also into Trinity Church, which stands close by St. Michael's, separated, I think, only by the church-yard. We also visited Saint John's church, which is very venerable as regards its exterior, the stone being worn and smoothed—if not roughened, rather—by centuries of storm and fitful weather. This antique wear and tear, however, has almost ceased to be a charm to my mind, comparatively to what it was when I first began to see old buildings. Within, the church is spoilt by wooden galleries built across the beautiful pointed arches.

We saw nothing else particularly worthy of remark, except Ford's Hospital, in Grey Friars' street. It has an Elizabethan front of timber and plaster, fronting on the street with two or three peaked gables in a row, beneath which is a low arched entrance, giving admission into a small paved quad-rangle, open to the sky above, but surrounded by the walls, lozenge-paned windows, and gables of the Hospital. The quadrangle is but a few paces in width, and perhaps twenty in length; and through a half-closed doorway, at the farther end, there was a glimpse into a garden. Just within the entrance, through an open door, we saw the neat and comfortable apartment of the Matron of the Hospital; and along [7] the quadrangle, on each side, there were three or four doors, through which we caught glimpses of little rooms, each containing a fireplace, a bed, a chair or two, and a little homely, domestic scene, with one old woman in the midst of it; one old woman in each room. They are destitute widows, who have their lodging and home here—a little room for every one to sleep, cook, and be at home in—and three and sixpence a week to feed and clothe themselves with; a cloak being the only garment bestowed on them. When one of the sisterhood dies, each old woman has to pay two-pence towards the funeral; and so they slowly starve and wither out of life, and claim each their two-penny contribution in turn. I am afraid they have a very dismal time. There is an old man's Hospital, in another part of the town, on a similar plan. A collection of sombre and lifelike tales might be written on the idea of giving the experience of these Hospitallers, male and female; and they might be supposed to be written down by the Matron of one—who might have acquired literary taste and practice as a Governess—and the Master of the other, a retired school-usher.

It is was [sic] market-day in Coventry, and in the Market-Place, and far adown the street leading from it, there were [8] booths and stalls, and crockery ware spread out on the ground, and apples, pears, vegetables, toys, books, (among which I saw my Twice-told Tales, with an awful portrait of myself as frontispiece,) and various country-produce, offered for sale by men, women, and girls. The scene looked lively, but had not really much vivacity in it. We lunched at the King's Head on cold beef, roast and boiled, together with half a pint of port, all of which came to six shillings and six pence; and after some rather aimless wanderings about the streets, found our way to the Station, and took the rail homeward at a quarter to five.

OCTOBER 27th, TUESDAY.

WE have had wretched weather almost ever since my last return to Leamington; cloudy, chill, always threatening rain, and sometimes actually raining; with now and then a sunny and balmy hour or two. My excursions, therefore, have been few and brief, and to places hereabouts which I have already seen and described. The autumn has advanced progressively, and is now fairly established, (as well it may be, being now more than half way towards winter,) though still there is much green foliage, in spite of many brown trees, and an immensity of withered leaves, too damp to rustle, strewing the paths—whence, however, they are continually swept up and carried off in wheelbarrows, either [9] for neatness, or for the agricultural worth as manure of even a withered leaf. The pastures look just as green as ever; a deep, bright verdure, that seems almost sunshine in itself, however sombre the sky may be. The little plots of grass and flowers, in front of our circle of houses, might still do credit to an American mid-summer; for I have seen beautiful roses here, within a day or two, and dahlias, asters, and such autumnal blossoms are plentiful; and I have no doubt that the old year's flowers will bloom till those of the new year appear. Really, the English winter is not nearly so terrible as ours.

Yesterday, the day promising better than most days now, I took the rail at half past ten for Hatton, about seven miles off; being moved to go thither, chiefly because it had been the residence of the learned Dr. Parr, and because his church is still remaining there. On reaching the Hatton station, however, I could see no signs of a neighboring village, and wandered hither and thither, a long time, in quest of it, through narrow country-lanes, bordered with untrimmed hedges. Blackberries grew plentifully in them, but were tasteless; their flavor, I suppose, having been washed out of them, besides that it is too late in the year for them to ripen sweetly. There were [10] one or two farmhouses in the first long lane through which I went, and one of them a very old, timber-framed structure, with old apple-trees about it, and the noise of a threshing-machine audible in its barn; but I could see nobody about. I walked on till I came where the lane ran into a somewhat broader road, with a broken guide-post at the corner, one finger pointing to Warwick, distant four miles, and another to some illegible town, which was not Hatton; so I retraced my steps, and tried the same lane in the opposite direction. It was still narrow, hedge-bordered, muddy, and had here and there a little grass in the midst of it; but by and by it again ran into a broader road, which looked as if it might lead somewhere or other. Behind me came a man driving a pony, harnessed into a little cart laden with boxes and packages; and he stopt at a farm house and took another package from the good woman there. When he came up with me, I inquired whither the road led; and he named some place which I could not make out, as he pronounced it; but he said it was about two miles off, and that the distance might be shortened by taking a cross-road;—so I determined to go thither, whatever the place might be.

The pony-driver seemed to be a common-carrier, and [11] stopt at every house to gather up his freight; thereby keeping in my rear. Soon, I came to a cross-road at the beginning of which was a cross-barred gate, which was wide open, however, and seemed to be permanently so. Just at the entrance, was a little old picturesque cottage, thatched, mossy, and sheltered, I think, under a shadowy bank. The door was open, and a comely young girl stood at it, but withdrew inward as I approached; and when I put my head within the door, she was standing close to the wall beside it. A tall, thin, respectable old woman was ironing, in the kitchen, parlor, and (for aught I know) bedchamber of the cottage, which looked neat and comfortable enough, though gloomy except for the fire. She told me that the cross-road led to 'Atton; so, after all, I found myself within reach of the town I had come to see, though I had now given up the hope of finding it. It was about a mile off, the old lady said. The cross-road seemed well-travelled, and led through a fertile and pleasant tract of country, with large farm-houses scattered along the way. The common-carrier came at a distance behind me, and stopt at the first farm-house so long that I saw no more of him. The day had been [12] overcast till now; but now the sun came out, and made me feel uncomfortably warm in my Talma; wherefore I took it off and carried it on my arm, but yet the wind was chill, and the sunshine fitful, insomuch that I soon put it on again. Anon, I came to the long-sought village of Hatton, if village it might any-wise be called, where there was no public-house, no shop, no contiguity of houses (as in most English villages, however small,) nor, as I at first thought, any church. The houses, however, had an ancient aspect of rural comfort and abundance; it seemed to be a community of well-to-do farmers, and I have never seen so few traces of poverty in any English scene. I remember only one building that seemed new, and in that one I thought I heard the voice of a Schoolmaster. Yes; there was one other new building, and I think that was a new church or chapel; but of the old church I had as yet seen nothing.

At last I espied it quite beyond and out of the straggling village of farm houses, and on a road that crossed at right angles and led to Warwick. It had a low, grey, battlemented, square tower; and as I approached it, the tower spoke, and told me it was twelve °clock. It was a remarkably deep-toned bell, and wonderfully impres[13]sive, considering how small it was. The church stands among its graves, a little removed from the wayside, and quite apart from any houses; a good deal shadowed by trees, and not wholly destitute of ivy. The body of the edifice, however, has been neatly covered with plaster of a yellowish tint, so as quite to destroy the aspect of antiquity except upon the tower, which wears the dark gray hue of many centuries. The chancel-window is painted with a representation of Christ upon the Cross; and all the other windows were full of painted or stained glass—but none of it ancient, nor (if it be fair to judge from without of what ought to [be] seen from within) of any great merit. I trod over the graves, and peeped in at two or three of the windows, and saw the little, snug interior of the church, fitted up with comfortable pews, where the farmers and their families repose, Sabbath after Sabbath. Those who slept under Dr. Parr's preaching now mostly sleep, I suppose, in the churchyard roundabout; but it struck me as an example of a man much misplaced—this enormous scholar, great in Greek, and making a learned tongue even of the vernacular, set here to tell of salvation to a rustic audience, to whom I do not see how he could speak one available word.[464]

[14] There are seldom any interesting tombstones in an English churchyard; the climate rendering them illegible while they are still comparatively new. Any New-England graveyard, in one of our elder towns, will gratify the curious in such matters with more ancient inscriptions. I saw none here worth noticing, except it be one to the memory of a Mr. Edwards, a chirurgeon of the last century, who seems to have owned the estate of Guy's Cliffe, and burthened it with charitable bequests to the poor of this parish. While I was looking at this tomb—a massive one, close beneath the church-tower—a man crossed the churchyard by a path leading through it to the village; and I inquired of him whether I could be admitted into the church. He pointed out the clerk's residence—a small brick-house, at some distance—but as I had already got a notion of the character of the interior by peeping through the windows, I did not think it worth while to summon him.

From the church of Hatton to Warwick is about three miles; and within about half-a mile, I was glad to find myself approaching a way side inn, which I entered and called for a glass of ale and a cigar; the [15] ale, a dark-brown liquid, harsh, and a little pricked, and almost as potent as the Arch Deacon, wherewith we made acquaintance at Oxford; the cigar, not much less potent in its way. A good many boors were quaffing ale and smoking pipes in the tap-room; so I took my refreshment in another brick-paved room, which probably served for a parlor; but a yeoman or two soon came in and took out a private store of bread and cheese;—so, fearing to incommode them with my cigar-smoke, I resumed my walk.

Guy's Cliffe, I believe, lies somewhere between Hatton and Warwick, but I knew not exactly where the entrance to this estate might be, and, in fact, felt no very great interest in seeing the spot. After walking a mile or so, the tall tower of Saint Mary's appeared at a distance; and I reached Warwick a little after one °clock, and went to a hostelrie called the "Rose and Crown," a little removed from the market-place. It seemed to be market-day in Warwick; for the tap-room was quite crowded with farmers, clowns, gentlemen's servants, and people akin to horses and cattle; and in the parlor there were two farmers drinking ale, and brandy-and water pot, and talking over their affairs. I called [16] for some luncheon; and a rosy-cheeked damsel brought me some bread and cheese, and a tankard of just such nut-brown ale as I had drunk at the wayside inn. It needs a life-time to make this beverage agreeable, but I drank it without any great repugnance. Indeed, after serving an apprenticeship to one kind of English ale, you find that you have a new variety to get acquainted with, wherever about England you happen to go; and, so far as I have experienced, they are mostly disagreeable at first.

I walked from Warwick, and reached home between three and four °clock.

OCTOBER 30th, FRIDAY.

WEDNESDAY was one of the most beautiful of all days, and gilded almost throughout with the precious English sunshine; the most delightful sunshine ever made, both for its positive fine qualities, and because we seldom get it without too great an admixture of water. However. my wife and I made no use of this day, except to walk to an "Arboretum and Pinetum" on the outskirts of the town. Una and Miss Shepard[465] made an excursion to Guy's Cliffe.

Yesterday was likewise a promising day, at the outset; the wind being from the eastward, and therefore indicative [17] of fair weather. Miss Shepard and Una, therefore, set out for Stratford-on-Avon, at 10 °clock, by stage-coach, and my wife for Warwick by the same conveyance; while Julian and I went on foot to the latter place. I like very well to visit Warwick, and, I suppose, I have described its aspect, over and over again, in the journal of our former stay in this neighborhood. The first interesting object that presents itself, on entering the town, is Saint John's Schoolhouse; a gray stone edifice, mossy and antique, with four gables in a row along its front, alternately plain and ornamented, and wide, projecting windows;—in the centre, a venerable portal, and before it a large grassy lawn, shut in by a solid stone-wall, moss-grown, like the edifice itself, and with a gateway of open iron-work, through which I peeped at the ancient school. It being, I presume, vacation-time, there was a notice on a board, in the centre of the lawn, of apartments to let. It seems to me that grown men must retain very delightful recollections of an old schoolhouse and play-place like this.

Thence we pursued our way into the interior of the old town, which certainly gives one the impression of being ancient and venerable; though, when you come to [18] analyze the streets, you find that the modern brick fronts bear a very large proportion to the old, projecting storied, gabled, timber-and-plaster built houses of past times. Soon, the east-gate appears in sight, an open archway striding half across the street, and bearing on its shoulders a gray, Gothic-looking edifice with a spire or cupola. Passing beneath or beside this archway, you find yourself in the High-street, which goes on with a gentle ascent, between shops with modern plate-glass, and ancient houses that have been re-glassed and varnished, towards another gateway, which bestrides the street at a distance of perhaps a quarter of a mile. Here, likewise, is an open archway, burrowing through the natural rock, and over the arch a Gothic chapel, with its battlemented tower, rising to the height of nearly a hundred feet; and the street divides itself, passing both beneath the archway and on one side of it, and re-uniting beyond. On the right, as you approach from the east-gate, is Leicester's Hospital, with its venerable Elizabethan front of tim-ber and plaster, in perfect repair; and being on a level with the top of the arch and foundation of the chapel, it looks down stately upon the street.

From this point, Julian and I went through some crook[19]ed cross-streets to the market-place; and soon, while we were standing under the pillars of the market-house, mamma appeared, and likewise the stage-coach, behind which, on the outside, sat Una and Miss Shepard, smiling at us very joyously. Here we divided ourselves according to our various objects; Una and Miss Shepard rumbling off in the coach towards Stratford; Julian ascend-ing to the second-floor of the market-house, where there is a Museum of Nat-ural History; and Mamma and I turning back to Leicester's Hospital, which we had come to Warwick specially to see.

Entering beneath the carved oaken portal, we were met by a man who seemed to be the steward or upper servant of the establishment. We should have preferred to be escorted by one of the twelve old soldiers, who com-pose the brotherhood of the Hospital; and, if I remember rightly, I did meet with some such guidance on occasion of my former visit. However, this man performed his part very well, and discoursed like a book (a guide-book) about the history and antiquity of the edifice, which, he said, had been a sort of religious establishment before Lord Leicester converted it into a Hospital, in 1571. All round the quadrangle, which the four [20] sides of the edifice enclose, there are rep[et]itions, large and small, of the Leicester cognizance, the Bear and the Ragged Staff, and escutcheons of the arms of families with which he was connected. I presume there is nothing else so perfect in England, in this style and date of architecture, as this interior quadrangle of Leicester's Hospital; and it probably gives an accurate idea of the appearance of a great family residence—a Hall or Manor-House—in Elizabeth's time. On one side is a corridor, on the ground-floor, is a corridor, giving admittance to the Kitchen and other offices, and above it an open gallery, looking down into the quadrangle. On the opposite side is what was formerly the Great Hall, where James the First was once feasted by one of the Earls of War-wick, as is still commemorated by an inscription at one end of the room. It is a large, barnlike apartment, with a vaulted roof, carved in oak, and a brick-floor; on one side there is a fire-place and conveniences for brewing ale, and on the other several wooden partitions, where the brethren keep their respective allotments of coal. Nevertheless, the Hall may have been very mag-nificent, when hung with rich tapestry, and gleaming with wax torches, and glittering with plate and brilliantly attired guests. [21] Then, I think, we went up the old staircase that leads to the apartments of the twelve brethren; and, in this part of the edifice, our guide showed us portions of the timber-frame-work, which are supposed to be eight or nine hundred years old. He like-wise led us into the comfortable little parlor of one of the brethren; it had a bedroom adjoining, and really seemed an abode where a warworn veteran, satiated with adventure, might spend the remnant of life as happily as anywhere else; especially as it is permitted to the married men to have the society of their wives, and as much freedom as is consistent with good order. These twelve brethren are selected from among men of good character, who have been in military service, and, by preference, natives of Warwickshire or Gloucestershire; their private resources must not exceed five pounds a year; and I suppose this regulation excludes all commissioned officers, whose half-pay would of course exceed that sum. The brethren receive from the Hospital an annuity of eighty pounds each, besides their apartments, a garment of fine blue cloth, with a silver badge, an annual quantity of ale, and a right at the kitchen fire; so that, considering the class from which they are [22] taken, few old men find themselves in such rich clover as the brethren of Leicester's Hospital. Really, bad as Leicester was, I cannot help having some hopes of his eternal salvation because he imagined such kind things for these poor people.

The little parlor, which was shown to us, had a portrait of its occupant hanging on the wall; and on a table were two swords crossed. One of them, perhaps, had been the weapon which he carried in his warfare; and the other, which I drew half out of the scabbard, had an inscription on the blade, purporting that it had been taken from the field of Waterloo. We saw none of the brethren; and I rather think, being made so comfortable and comparatively wealthy, they do not like to think themselves objects of charity, and are shy of being seen about the premises in their quaint, old-fashioned tunics. For, indeed, they become gentlemen of income, and invested with political rights; having (if I correctly understood the guide) three votes a-piece, in virtue of their brotherhood. On the other hand, they are subject to a supervision which the Master of the Hospital might make very annoying, were he so inclined, as relates to personal freedom and conduct; but, as they have all their lives been under military restraint, [23] these matters will not so much trouble them, if fairly administered; and the guide bore testimony to their being as contented and happy as old people can well be. I wish I had an opportunity to look a little into their moral and intellectual state for myself.

We next went into the Chapel, which is the Gothic edifice surmounting the gateway that stretches half across the street. Here the brethren have to attend prayers every-day, but go to the Church of Saint Mary's for public worship on Sundays. The interior of the chapel is very plain, with a picture of no merit for an altar-piece, and a single old pane of painted glass, representing the Earl of Leicester, with very much the aspect of his portrait, as I saw it at the Manchester Exhibition. We ascended the tower of the chapel, and looked down between its battlements into the street, a hundred feet below us, and at the base of the archway, with weeds growing far upward on its sides; and, also, far around us, at the rich and lovely English landscape, with many a church-spire and noble country-seat, and object[s] of historic interest. Edge Hill, where Cromwell defeated Charles the First, was in sight, far off on the horizon, and, much nearer, the house where [24] Cromwell lodged, the night before the battle. Right under our eyes, and half surrounding the town, was the Earl of Warwick's delightful park, a wide extent of sunny lawns, interspersed with great contiguities of forest-shade. The guide pointed out some of the Cedars of Lebanon, for which the Warwick estate is famous. The roofs of the town, beneath and around us, were partly slate-covered, (and these were the modern houses,) and partly covered with old red-tiles, denoting the more ancient edifices. There was a great fire, a hundred and sixty years ago, which destroyed a large portion of the town, and doubtless many structures of great antiquity; for it is said to have been founded by Shakspeare's King Cymbeline, in the year *One* of the Christian era; and Imogen and Posthumus may have strayed hand-in-hand through the country-lanes about Warwick.

The day, though it began so brightly, had long been overcast, and the clouds now spat down a few spiteful drops upon us, besides that the east-wind was very chill; so we descended the winding-tower stair, and went next into the garden, one side of which is shut in by almost the only remaining portion of the old city-wall. The garden has a grassy and ornamental part, with gravel-walks, in the centre of one of which is a beautiful stone vase, of Egyptian [25] origin, having formerly stood on the top of a Nilometer, or pillar for measuring the rise and fall of the river Nile. On the pedestal is a Latin inscription by Dr. Parr. There is likewise a vegetable garden, the lion's share of which belongs to the Master of the Hospital, and twelve little adjacent patches to the individual brethren. In the farther part of the garden is an arbor for their pleasure and convenience; and no doubt they find a good deal of occupation and amusement here. The Master's residence (forming one whole side of the quadrangle) fronts on the garden, looking at once homely and stately, and just as it may have looked two or three hundred years ago; except that then the garden may have been rather more quaint, with old-fashioned eccentricities of the gardener's art, than it is now. The Master's name is Harris, and he is a descendant of the Earl of Leicester's family, a gentleman of independent fortune, and a clergyman of the established church, as the laws of the Hospital require him to be. I do not know what his official emoluments may be; but doubtless, the brethren being so well-to-do, the Master's place must be especially comfortable and jolly. It is pleasant to think of the good life which a suitable man, in this position, must lead, linked to old customs, [26] welded in with an ancient system, never dreaming of change, and bringing all the mellowness and richness of the past down into the midst of these railway-times, which never make him or his community move one whit quicker than of yore. I wish I could know him.

From the garden we went into the kitchen, which is a fine old room, with an immense fire-place, beneath an arched oaken mantel which really seemed almost as spacious as the city gateway. The fire was burning hospitably, and diffused a genial warmth through the room. Over the hearth were crossed two ancient halberds, and some muskets hung against another part of the wall. A long table, with wooden benches on each side, stood permanently for the convenience of the brethren, who smoke their pipes and drink their ale here, in the evenings; the kitchen being prepared for their reception after a certain hour. In the daytime, each brother brings or sends what mess he will to be prepared by the Cook. There was a great, antique copper flagon for ale; also an ancient oaken cabinet; also, I think it was here that I saw, and sat down in, the oaken elbow-chair which was occupied by King James at the Earl of Warwick's banquet. Hanging up in the kitchen, too, is a piece of needle-work representing the [27] Bear and Ragged Staff, reputed to have been wrought by Amy Robsart, and which has lately been set in a carved oaken-frame, through the munificence of a countryman of my own. The guide showed us his name in the visitor's book; a Mr. Conner of the Navy. These items seem to make up the sum of what we saw in the Hospital; but the sketch is capable of being elaborated and colored into a very effective picture of a patch of old times surviving sturdily into the new.

From the Hospital we went along the High-street to an old curiosity shop, the entrance to which is near the East-gate, and is not to be found without careful search, being only denoted by the name of "Redfern" painted not very conspicuously in the toplight of the door. Immediately on entering, we found ourselves among a confusion of old rubbish and valuables, ancient armour, historic portraits (one of Charles Ist, for instance, by Dobson, which Mr. Redfern purchased at the recent sale at Alton Towers) old cabinets, clocks, china, looking-glasses, and every imaginable object that has gone out of date. The collection must have been got together at an immense cost. Some of the articles were bought at Rogers's sale; and no doubt, whenever a virtuoso's treasures are scat[28]tered abroad, some of them find their way hither. It is impossible to give any idea of the variety of articles, which were so thickly strewn about that we could hardly move without overturning some great thing or sweeping away some small one, and occupied the whole house, in three stories. The person who waited on us was exceedingly civil, and gave us his whole attention after some ladies (who were there when we came) had made their purchases and departed. Then we asked the prices of a great many things; for we wanted to buy something by way of paying an admission-fee; but it was hardly possible to find any article, however trifling, that came within our prudential views. However, we finally fixed on a little spoon of George II's time, silver-gilt and curiously wrought, which was formerly the property of Lady Blessington, and for which we paid ten shillings. I should like much (if my circumstances were in accordance) to spend a hundred pounds there.

From Redfern's we went back to the Market Place, expecting partly to find Julian at the Museum; but the keeper said that he had gone away about half an hour before, it being now a little past one. We went into the Museum, which contains the collections in Natural History &c. of a county society. It is very well arranged, and is rich in specimens of ornithology, [29] among which was an albatross, huge beyond imagination. I do not think that Coleridge could have known the size of this fowl, when he caused it to be hung round the neck of his Ancient Mariner. There were a great many humming-birds from various parts of the world; and some of their breasts actually gleamed and shone as with the brightest lustre of sunset. Also, many strange fishes, and a huge pike, taken from the river Avon, and so long that I wonder how he could turn himself about in such a little river as it is, near Warwick. A great curiosity was a bunch of skeleton leaves and flowers, prepared by a young lady, and preserving all the most delicate fibres of the plant, looking like inconceivably fine lace-work, white as snow; while the substance was quite taken away. In another room, there were minerals, shells, and a splendid collection of fossils, among which were remains of ante-diluvian creatures, several feet long. In still another room, we saw some historical curiosities, the most interesting of which were two locks of reddish brown hair, one from the head and the other from the beard of Edward IV. They were fastened to a manuscript letter, which authenticates the hair as having been taken from King Edward's tomb, in 1789. Near these relics was a seal of the great Earl of Warwick, the mighty King [30] Maker; also, a sword from Bosworth-field, smaller and shorter than those now in use; for, indeed, swords seem to have increased in length, weight, and formidable aspect, now that the weapon has almost ceased to be used in actual warfare. The short Roman sword was probably more murderous than any weapon of the same species, except the Bowie knife. Here, too, were Parliamentary cannon-balls, and many other things that have passed out of my memory.

At three °clock, my wife took the omnibus back to Leamington, and I returned by the old road, passing the castle-gate, and over the bridge across the Avon, whence I had a fine view of the castle, through the scanty autumnal foliage of its embosoming trees. I particularly remember nothing else worth recording; unless it be, that our guide showed us one of the gowns or cloaks worn by the brethren of Leicester's Hospital. The cloth was very fine, a dark blue, the skirts long, and on one sleeve was the brightly burnished silver badge of the Bear and Ragged Staff, of solid metal, and as much as four inches long. Only two of these badges (I think he said) have been lost since the foundation of the Hospital; and this was one of the original set. The Earl of Leicester certainly showed a strong desire to glori[31]fy himself and his family by causing his heraldic cognizances and his badge to be repeated so abundantly on the front of the building, all about the interior quadrangle, over the kitchen fire place, on the brethren's sleeves, and wherever else it could be painted, carved, or sewn. But I suppose this may not indicate his individual vanity, but belonged to the manners and feelings of the age; and the whole was perhaps arranged for him artistically, as a pageant would have been. In our own day, Mr. William Brown suffered himself to be feasted and profusely eulogized in public (by myself as enormously as by anybody) for a charity more splendid certainly than that of the Earl of Leicester; but I do not know that the ancient benefactor showed more vanity than the modern one, in their several ways, and according to the fashion of their times. Both wanted to do a good thing, and were willing to have the credit of it.[466]

NOVEMBER 8th, MONDAY.

ALL this month, we have had genuine, English November weather; much of it profusely rainy, and the rest overcast and foggy, making it a desperate matter to venture out for a walk. Since my last record—describing a visit to Warwick—I have taken only a few strolls up and down the Parade, or in the immediate neighborhood of the town. Yesterday afternoon, being [32] merely damp, chill, and foggy, I made a little longer stretch of my tether, and walked to Whitnash Church, with Miss Shepard, Una, and Julian. This is one of the small, old churches of the vicinity, and stands in the midst of a village that retains as much of its primitive aspect as any one that I have seen; the dwellings being mostly the old, timber and plaister [sic] cottages and farm-houses, with thatched roofs; and though there are a few new brick buildings, the air of antiquity prevails. In front of the church tower is a small, rude and irregular space, in the midst of which grows a very ancient tree, with a huge, hollow trunk, and a still verdant head of foliage growing out of its mutilated decay. I should not wonder if this tree were many centuries old, and a contemporary of the of the [sic] gray, Norman tower before which it has flourished and decayed; perhaps even older than that. The old, rustic dwellings of the village stand about the church; and the churchyard with its graves is especially central and contiguous to the living village; so that the old familiar forms and faces have had but a little way to go in order to lie down in their last sleep; and there they rest, close to their own thresholds, with their children and successors all about them, chatting, laughing, and doing business within hearing of their grave-stones. It makes death strangely familiar, and brings the centuries togeth[33]er in a lump. But methinks it must be weary, weary, weary, this rusty, unchangeable village-life, where men grow up, grow old, and die, in their fathers' dwellings, and are buried in their grandsires' very graves, the old skulls, and crossbones being thrown out to make room for them, and shovelled in on the tops of their coffins. Such a village must, in former times, have been a stagnant pool, and may be little better even now, when the rush of the main current of life has probably created a little movement. We went a few paces into the churchyard, and heard the indistinct, dull drone of the parson within the church, but thought it not best to enter the church. Passing through the village, we paused to look at a venerable farm-house—spacious and dignified enough, indeed, to have been a manor-house—with projecting bay-windows, an old, square portal, a lawn, shadowy with great trees, and an aspect of ancient peace diffused all around. It was a timber and plaster house, the timber-frame marked out in black on the white plaster, and, if I mistake not, a thatched roof, though the house was two stories high and very extensive. These thatched roofs are very beautiful, when time has made them verdant; it makes the house seem to be a part of Nature, and, so far as man has anything to do with it, as simple as a nest.[467]

[34] LONDON, 24 GREAT RUSSELL-STREET, Nov[r] 10th

WE have been thinking and negotiating about taking lodgings in London, this some time past; and this morning we left Leamington at ten °clock of a dreary day, with little mists almost amounting to rain; a very dismal day as the whole autumn has brought in its train. I rode in a second-class carriage with Julian, and Mamma, Miss Shepard, Una, and Rosebud in a first-class one; and we reached London with no other mis-adventure than that of leaving the great bulk of our luggage behind us in Leamington; the van, which we hired to take it to the railway station, having broken down under its prodigious weight, in the middle of the street. It will probably make its appearance to-morrow. On our journey, we saw nothing particularly worthy of note;— scattered villages, generally of more antique aspect than on the northern side of Birmingham, here and there an old church, and everywhere the immortal verdure of England, scarcely less perfect than in June, so far as the fields are concerned; though the foliage of the trees presents pretty much the same hues as those of our own forests, after the gaiety and gorgeousness has departed. We reached the Euston Station about two °clock; and Mamma and Rosebud took a cab to our lodgings, while the rest of us walked, inquiring our way whenever we saw [35] a person who seemed likely to give a kind response to our questions. We found our lodgings without any great difficulty, they being in close vicinity to the British Museum, and that is the greatest advantage we thus far find in them.

I felt restless and uncomfortable, and soon strolled forth, without any definite object, and walked down Oxford street and Holborn, and thence by Farringdon street into Fleet-street, and thence upward under Temple Bar, and along the Strand to Charing Cross; and so along Regent street to Oxford street again, and home. Very dull and dreary the city looked, and not in the least gay and lively, even where the throng was thickest and most brisk. As I trudged along, my reflection was, that never was there a dingier, uglier, less picturesque city than London, and that it is really wonderful that so much brick, and stone, for centuries together, have been built up, with so poor a result. Yet these old names of the city—Fleet-street, Ludgate Hill, the Strand —used to throw a glory over these homely precincts, when I first saw them, and still do so in a less degree. Where Farringdon-street empties into Fleet-street, moreover, I had a glimpse of Saint Pauls, along Ludgate-street, in the gathering dimness, and felt as if I had [36] seen an old friend. In that neighborhood (speaking of old friends) I met Mr. Parker, formerly of Boston, who told me sad news of a friend whom I love as much as if I had known him for a life time, though indeed he is but of two or three years standing. He said that Bennoch's bankruptcy is in to-day's Gazette. Of all men on earth (excepting only Ticknor, and him for selfish reasons) I had rather this misfortune should have happened to any other; but I hope and think Bennoch has sturdiness and buoyancy enough to rise up beneath it. I cannot conceive of his face otherwise than with a glow in it, like that of the sun at noonday.

Before I reached our lodgings, the dusk settled into the streets, and a mist bedewed and bedamped me, and I went astray, as is usual with me, and had to inquire my way; indeed, except in the principal thoroughfares, London is so miserably lighted that it is impossible to recognize one's whereabout. On my arrival, I found our parlour looking cheerful with a brisk fire, and the table set, with some mutton-chops and a beef-steak—which, as I had eaten only a few pears since breakfast, were very acceptable. But the first day or two, in new lodgings, is at best an uncomfortable time. Fanny has just come in with [37] more unhappy news about Bennoch. Pray Heaven it may not be true. Mrs. Stevens (our landlady) has told her that his wife died, last week, in childbirth. Troubles (as I myself have experienced, and many others before me) are a sociable sisterhood; they love to come hand in hand, or sometimes, even, to come side by side with long looked-for and hoped-for good fortune. The wedlock of the Bennoch's had been childless, owing apparently to the lady's ill health.

24, Great Russell-street, Nov[r] 11th.

This morning, Mamma and I, and Miss Shepard and the two elder children, all went to the British Museum; always a most wearisome and depressing task to me. I strolled through the lower rooms with a good degree of interest, looking at the antique sculptures, some of which were doubtless grand and beautiful in their day, though it is by no means plain to me that their merit has not been vastly overestimated. The Egyptian remains are, on the whole, more satisfactory; for, though inconceivably ugly, they are at least miracles of size and ponderosity;—for example, a hand and arm of polished granite, as much as six feet in length. The upper rooms, containing millions of specimens of Natural History, in all departments, re[38]ally made my heart ache with a pain and woe that I have never felt anywhere but in the British Museum, and I hurried through them as rapidly as I could persuade Julian to follow. We had left the rest of the party still intent on the ancient sculptures; and though Julian was much interested in the vast collections of shells, he chose to quit the Museum with me, in the prospect of a stroll about London. He seems to have my own passion for thronged streets and the intensest bustle of human life.

After leaving the Museum, we went first to the Railway Station, in quest of our luggage, which we found there, and gave directions for its being sent to our lodgings. Thence we made a pretty straight course down to Holborn, and through Newgate-street, stopping a few moments to peep through the iron fence at the Christ Church boys, in their long blue coats, and yellow petticoats and stockings. It was between twelve and one °clock; and I suppose this was their hour of play, for they were running about the enclosed space, chasing and overthrowing one another, without their caps, with their yellow petticoats tucked up, and all in immense activity and enjoyment. I never saw a healthier or handsomer set of boys than these seemed to be. Thence we went into Cheapside, where I called at Mr. Bennett's watch[39]maker's shop to inquire what are the facts about Bennoch. When I mentioned his name, Mr. Bennett (who was himself attending at the counter, and received me with great attention and kindness) shook his head and expressed great sorrow; but on further talk, I found that he referred only to the failure, and had heard nothing about Mrs. Bennoch's death. It cannot therefore be true; for Bennett lives in his neighborhood, and could not have remained ignorant of such a calamity; and moreover his own wife was adduced by Mrs. Stevens as her authority. There must be some mistake; none, however, in regard to the failure, it having been announced in The Times. Mr. Bennett is a very un-English looking man, slender, pale, and vivid in aspect, dark complexioned, with black hair.

From Bennett's shop (which is so near the steeple of Bow-church that it would tumble upon it, if it fell over) we strolled still eastward, aiming at London Bridge, but missed it, and bewildered ourselves among many dingy and frowzy streets and lanes. I bore towards the right, knowing that that course must ultimately bring me to the Thames; and, at last, emerging into a larger space, I saw before me ramparts, towers, circular, and square, with battle-mented summits, large sweeps and curves of fortifi[40]cation, as well as straight and massive walls, and chimneys behind them, all a great confusion (to my eye) of ancient and more modern structure, and four loftier turrets rising in the midst; the whole great space surrounded by a broad, dry moat, which now seemed to be used as an ornamental walk, bordered partly with trees. This was the Tower, but seen from a different and more picturesque point of view than I have heretofore gained of it. Being so convenient for a visit, I determined to go in. At the outer gate (which is not a part of the fortification) a centinel [sic] walks to and fro; besides whom there was a Warder, in the rich old costume of Henry VIII's time, looking, as I always think, like the Jack of trumps, and very gorgeous indeed—as much so as scarlet and gold can make him. We sat down in the refreshment-room, at the ticket-office, to wait for the assemblage of a party; and then one of the warders, a tall, slender, white-haired, gentlemanly person, took charge of Julian and me and half a dozen ladies, and led us first to the Armory. I have described all this before, and probably better than I should do it again; nor do I find that any particular thing in the Armory has made a deep mark in my mind. Thence we ascended a staircase, and went into that part of the White [41] Tower where Sir Walter Raleigh was confined. The whole party followed one another through the low arched doorway into his dark sleeping chamber, which was little more than big enough to contain us all. In the stone of the wall, by this doorway, there are some inscriptions engraved or scratched by prisoners, though not of illustrious name. In the large hall, opposite the dungeon-door, stands the block on which Lord Lovat was beheaded, marked with several very satisfactory cuts of an axe; there, too, was a headsman's axe, with a short handle, and long, narrow head, said to have been that which passed through the slender neck of Anne Boleyn. There can be no certainty of this; but, no doubt, it has cut off somebody's head in its day.

As Julian and I were not going to look at the Jewel Room, we loitered about in the open space, before the White Tower, while the warder led the rest of the party into that apartment. Around the White Tower, there is what one might take for a square in a town, with gabled houses lifting their peaks on one side, and various edifices enclosing the other sides, and the great White Tower (which is now more black than white) rising venerable, and rather picturesque than otherwise, the [42] most prominent object in the scene. I have no plan or available idea whatever of the Tower, in my mind; but it seems really to be a town within itself, with streets, avenues, and all that pertains to human life. There were soldiers going through their exercise in the open space; and along at the base of the White Tower lay a great many cannon and mortars, some of which were of Turkish manufacture, and immensely long and ponderous. Others, likewise of mighty size, had once belonged to the famous ship Great Harry,[468] and had lain for ages under the sea. Others were East Indian. Several were beautiful specimens of workmanship. The mortars (some so large that a fair-sized man might easily be rammed into them) held their great mouths slanting upward to the sky, and mostly contained a quantity of rain water. While we were looking at these warlike toys (for I suppose not one of them will ever thunder in earnest again) the warden reappeared with our companions, and leading us to a certain part of the open space, he struck his foot on the small stones with which it is paved, and told us that we were standing on the spot where Anne Boleyn and Catharine Parr [Howard] were beheaded. It is not exactly in the centre [43] of the Square, but on a line with one of the angles of the White Tower. The pavement I presume to be modern. I forgot to mention that the middle of the open space is occupied by a marble statue of Wellington, which appeared to me very poor, and laboriously spirited.

Lastly, the Warder led us under the Bloody Tower, and by the side of the Wakefield Tower, and showed us the Traitor's Gate, which is now closed up so as to afford no access to the Thames. No; we first visited the Beauchamp Tower, famous as the prison of many historical personages. Some of its former occupants have left their initials or names, and inscriptions of piety and patience, cut deep into the free-stone of the walls, together with devices (as a crucifix, for instance) neatly and skilfully done. This room has a large, deep fireplace, within which stands a little modern stove; it is chiefly lighted by one large window, which I fancy must have been made in recent times; but there are four narrow apertures, throwing in a little light through deep alcoves in the thickness of the octagon wall. One would expect such a room to be picturesque; but it is really not of striking aspect, being low, with a plastered cieling [sic] (the beams just showing through the plaister [sic]) [44] a boarded floor, and the walls being washed over, apparently, with buff. A

Warder sat within a railing, by the great window, with sixpenny books to sell, containing transcripts of the inscriptions on the walls.

We now left the Tower, and made our way deviously westward, passing Saint Paul's, which looked magnificently and beautifully, so huge and dusky as it was, with here and there a space, on its vast form, where the original whiteness of the marble came out like a streak of moonshine amid the blackness with which time has made it grander than in its newness. It is a most noble edifice; and I delight, too, in the statues that crown some of its heights, and in the wreaths of sculpture which are hung around it. We saw nothing else that need be recorded, but did not reach home for a considerable time, having got be-witched and bewildered (as it is so frequently my fate to be) among the streets, lanes, and passages, between Fleet-street and Holborn. We got into Covent Garden Market, and passed by Drury Lane Theatre, and went through Bow Street, and at length to Great Russell-street—but how I know not, and probably never shall know. Dinner was just ready to be put upon the table; and we were all of us ready to enjoy it, the rest of the family (except [45] Fanny and Rosebud) having spent the whole day at the British Museum, and eaten nothing since breakfast.

Yesterday and to-day, hawkers were crying a panorama of the Lord Mayor's Procession and Show, for a penny. It was a long string of coarse colored cuts.

24, GREAT RUSSELL-STREET, NOVEMBER 12th.

THE morning began with such fog, that, at the window of my chamber, lighted only from a small court-yard enclosed by high, dingy walls, I could hardly see to dress. It kept alternately darkening, and then brightening a little, and darkening again so much that we could but just see across the street; but, at eleven or thereabouts, it grew so much lighter that we resolved to venture out. Our plan for the day was to go in the first place to Westminster Abbey, and to the National Gallery if we should find time. We took the longest way round, because there was less chance for going astray, and accordingly set out (Mamma, Miss Shepard, Una, Julian, and I) along Tottenham Court Road, thence by Oxford street, Regent street, and Pall Mall, to. Parliament-street, and the Abbey. The fog darkened again as we went down Regent-street, and the Duke of York's Column was but barely discernible, looming vaguely before us; nor, from Pall Mall, was Nelson's pillar much more distinct, though methought his statue stood [46] aloft in a somewhat clearer atmosphere than ours. Passing Whitehall, however, we could scarcely see Inigo Jones' Banquet-ting [sic] House, on the other side of the street; and the towers and turrets of the new Houses of Parliament were all but invisible, as was the Abbey itself; so that we really were in some doubt whither we were going. We found our way to Poet's Corner, however (the name always reminds me of the poetical department in village-newspapers) and entered those holy precincts, which looked very dusky and grim in the smoky light.

I do not mean to attempt another description of Westminster Abbey, after at least two or three in reference to former visits. I am not aware that I had any new sensation, though I was strongly impressed with the perception that very common-place people compose the great bulk of society in this home of the illustrious dead. It is wonderful how few names there are that one cares anything about, a hundred years after their departure; but perhaps each generation acts in good faith, in canonizing its own men. It is pleasant to think of Westminster Abbey as incrusted all over, in its interior, with marble immortalities; but, looking at them more closely, you find that the fame of the buried person does not make the marble live, [47] but the marble keeps merely a cold and sad memory of a man who would else be forgotten. No man, who needs a monument, ever ought to have one. Of all the sculptures, I took particular notice only of the statue of Wilberforce, which is certainly very queer indeed. The man seems to have sunk into himself, in a sitting posture, with one thin leg crossed over the other, a book in one hand, and the other, I think, under his chin, or applied to some such familiar use; and his face twinkles at you with a shrewd complacency, as if he were looking into your eyes and twigged something there. I have no doubt the image is as like him as one pea to another; and being in modern costume, you might fancy that he had seen the Gorgon's Head, at some instant when he was in his most familiar mood, and had forthwith become stone. It shows, by its ludicrous effect, the impropriety of bestowing the age-long duration of marble upon small, characteristic individua[li]ties; the subject should be taken in a mood of broad and grand composure, which would cause all trifling peculiarities to disappear. I really felt as if the statue were impertinent, staring me in the face with that knowing complication of wrinkles; [48] and I should have liked to fling a brick-bat right at its nose, or to have broken off the foot that dangled over its knee.[469]

Una and Miss Shepard had gone through the chapels, while Mamma, Julian, and I, remained in the Nave. They now re-appeared, and we staid but little longer, reading the storied walls, and looking upward at the fog which hung half way between us and the lofty roof of the Minster. The painted windows of the Abbey, though mostly modern, are exceedingly rich and beautiful; and I do think that human art has invented no other such magnificent method of adornment as this. As we left the Abbey, a man accosted us (one of those hangers-on who always haunt around such places) and told us that we could get admission to the House of Lords by making application to Mrs. Bennett, the housekeeper. We crossed the street, accordingly, and passing under one of the arched entrances, rang at a door within the Parliamentary precincts; and a lady of dark, Italian aspect made her appearance, and after some parley, consented to show us the House of Lords. I have talked about this whole matter before; so shall only say that the lady reminded us that a "compliment" was expected, when the House [49] was shown on other than the stated days. She then passed us to the Housekeeper of the Commons, who proved to be a pleasant, homely, talkative, and well informed old lady, by whom we were permitted to sit down in the Speaker's chair, and to go through the two lobbies, and see whatever was to be shown. We made our exit through the avenue of statues into Westminster Hall, on one side of which a court was in session; and peeping in, we found it thronged with people. Up among the oaken beams of the roof of the great hall, the fog was diffused so as to render that upper region very dim. We spent but a little while, and then crossed the street again to the church-yard of Saint Peter's, on our way to the Abbey-cloisters. Our friend, who had sent us to the House of Lords, again met us, and recommended a visit to the Queen's Mews, but I declined troubling him any further, and dismissed him with a guerdon of sixpence. The cloisters are exceedingly timeworn and venerable; but as I have already written about them, (not to speak of what Addison has said) I will only mention an influx of Westminster boys, in their gowns and flat caps, who sported gaily beneath the groined arches and over the pavement of tomb-stones. [50] Our final visit, to-day, was to the National Gallery, where I came to the conclusion that Murillo's Saint John was the most beautiful picture I have ever seen; and that there never was a painter who has really made the world richer, except Murillo. On our way home, I put my wife, Miss Shepard, and Una, into a cab, and Julian and I blundered after them on foot.

24 G^t RUSSELL-ST. NOVEMBER 13th, FRIDAY.

THIS morning, about ten °clock, our party (except Fanny, Julian, and Rosebud, who were bound to the British Museum) issued forth, and found the atmosphere chill, and almost frosty, tingling upon our cheeks. A mist, or fogginess, hung somewhere between the earth and sky, and intercepted the sunshine, though it did not seem to be a cloudy day. Just at the corner of Tottenham Court Road, we got into an omnibus bound to Hungerford Market; and by it we came as far as Charing Cross, whence we walked around through the Strand. The gateway of Somerset House attracted us, and we turned in, and walked round its spacious quadrangle, encountering many Government clerks (at least, so I suppose them to be) hurrying to their various offices. This is certainly a handsome square of buildings, with its Grecian facades and pillars, and its sculptured bas-reliefs, and the group of statuary in the midst of the quadrangle. Be[51]sides the part of the edifice that rises above ground, there appear to be two subterranean stories below the surface. From Somerset House we pursued our way through Temple Bar, and intended to turn into the entrance to the Temple, but missed it, and therefore entered by the passage from what was formerly Alsatia, but which now seems to be a very respectable and humdrum part of London. We came immediately to the Temple Gardens, which we went into, and walked quite round. The grass is still green, but the trees are quite leafless, and had an aspect of not being very robust, even at more genial seasons of the year. There were, however, huge quantities of brilliant c[h]rysanthemums, golden, and of other hues, blooming gorgeously all about the borders of the garden; and several gardeners were at work, tending these flowers and sheltering them from the weather. I noticed no roses, nor even rose-bushes, in this spot where the factions of York and Lancaster plucked their two hostile flowers.

Leaving the gardens, we went, (under my wife's guidance, who had been there once before, with Henry Bright) to the Hall of the Middle Temple, where we knocked at the portal, and finding it not fastened, thrust it open. A boy appeared within; and the porter or keeper, at a distance along the [52] inner passage, called to us to enter, and, opening the door of the great hall, left us to view it till he should be at leisure to attend to us. Truly, it is the most magnificent apartment that ever I stood within; very lofty, so lofty indeed that the antique oaken roof was quite hidden, as regarded all its details, in the sombre gloom that brooded under its rafters. The hall was lighted by, I think, four great windows on each of the two sides, descending half way from the cieling [sic] to the floor, leaving all beneath enclosed by oaken panelling, which, on three sides, was carved with escutcheons of the arms of such members of the society as have held the office of reader. There is likewise, in a large recess, or transsept [sic], a great window, occupying the full height of the hall, and splendidly emblazoned with the arms of the Templars who have attained to the dignity of Chief-Justice. The other windows are pictured in like manner with coats-of-arms of legal dignitaries, connected with the Temple; and besides all these, there are arched windows, high towards the roof of the hall, at either end, full of richly and chastely colored glass; and all the light that the Great Hall had came through these glorious panes, and they seemed the richer for the sombreness in which we [53] stood. I cannot describe nor even intimate the effect of this transparent glory, glowing down upon us in that gloomy depth of the hall. The screen, at the lower end of the hall, was of carved oak, very dark and highly polished, and as antique as Queen Elizabeth's time. The keeper told us that the story of the Armada was said to be represented in these carvings; but, in the imperfect light, we could trace nothing of it out. Along the length of the hall were set two oaken tables for the students of law to dine upon; and, on the dais at the upper end, there was a cross-table for the big-wigs of the society; the latter being provided with comfortable chairs, and the former with oaken benches. From a notification, posted near the door, I gathered that the cost of dinners in this hall is two shillings to each gentleman, including, as the attendant told me, ale and a portion of wine. I do hate to leave this hall without expressing how grave, how grand, how sombre, and how magnificent, I felt it to be. As regards historical associations, the keeper told us that it was a favorite dancing-hall of Queen Elizabeth's, and that Sir C[h]ristopher Hatton danced himself into her good graces here.

We next went to the Temple Church, and finding the [54] door ajar, made free to enter beneath its Norman arch, which admitted us into a circular vestibule, very antique and beautiful. In the body of the church, beyond, we a [sic] saw a boy sitting, but nobody either forbade or invited our entrance. On the floor of the vestibule lay about half-a-score of Templars—the representatives of the warlike priests who built this church and formerly held these precincts—all in chain armour, grasping their swords, and with their shields beside them. Except two or three, they lay cross-legged, in token that they had really fought for the holy sepulchre. I think I have seen nowhere else such well-preserved monumental knights as these. We proceeded into the interior of the church, and were greatly impressed with its wonderful beauty, the roof spouting, as it were, in a harmonious and accordant fountain, out of the clustered pillars that support its groined arches; and these pillars, immense as they are, are polished like so many gems. They are of Purbeck marble, and, if [I] mistake not, had been covered with plaster for ages, until latterly redeemed and beautified anew. But the glory of the church is its old painted windows; and positively those great spaces, over the chancel, appeared to be set with all manner of precious stones; or it was as if the many colored [55] radiance of Heaven were breaking upon us, or as if we saw the wings of angels storied over with richly tinted pictures of holy things. But it is idle to talk of this wonderful adornment; it is to be seen and marvelled at, not written about. Before we left the church, the porter made his appearance, in time to receive his fee—which somebody, indeed, is always ready to stretch out his hand for. And so ended our visit to the Temple, which, by by [sic] the by, though close to the midmost bustle of London, is as quiet as if it were always Sunday there.

We now went through Fleet-street and Ludgate to Saint Paul's, of which I shall pretermit any description, having so often spoken of it before. Una and Miss Shepard ascended to the Whispering Gallery, and we, sitting under the dome, at the base of one of the pillars, saw them far above us, looking very indistinct; for those misty upper depths seemed almost to be hung with clouds. This cathedral, I think, does not profit by gloom, but requires cheerful sunshine to show it to the best advantage. The statues and sculptures in Saint Paul's are mostly covered with years of dust, and look thereby very grim and ugly; but there are few memories there from which I should care to brush away the dust, they being in [56] nine cases out of ten, naval and military heroes of second or third class merit. I really remember no literary celebrity (admitted solely on that account) except Doctor Johnson. The Crimean War has supplied two or three monuments, chiefly mural tablets; and doubtless more of the same blotches will yet break out upon the walls. One thing, that I newly noticed, was the beautiful shape of the great, covered marble vase that serves for a font.

From Saint Paul's, we went down Cheapside, and turning into King-street, visited Guildhall, which we found in process of decoration for a public ball, to take place next week. It looked rather gew-gawish than gorgeous, being hung with flags of all nations, and adorned with military trophies, and the scene was repeated by a range of looking-glass at one end of the hall. The execrably painted windows positively shocked us by their vulgar glare, after those of the Temple Hall and church; yet, a few years ago, I might very likely have thought them beautiful. Our own national banner, I must remember to say, was hanging in Guildhall, but with only ten stars, and an insufficient number of stripes.

Leaving Guildhall, we continued our walk to the Ex[57]change, through which we went, taking glimpses likewise at the Mansion House and the Bank, and at the Monument, in our further ramble, which extended as far as London Bridge. None of these matters need now be described. Returning to the Exchange, I put Mamma, Una, and Miss Shepard, into an omnibus, and myself strolled slowly homeward without any remarkable adventure.

24, G^t RUSSELL-STREET, Novr 15th, SUNDAY.

YESTERDAY morning, at 11 °clock, as usual, Mamma, Miss Shepard, Una, and I, took an omnibus from the corner of Tottenham Court Road, down Oxford street and Holborn, and all the way to London Bridge; an immense journey, which we performed for 4 pence apiece. From London Bridge, we went along Lower Thames street, and quickly found ourselves in Billingsgate Market; a dirty, evil-smelling, crowded precinct, thronged with people carrying fish on their heads, and lined with fish-shops and fish-stalls, and pervaded with a fishy odour. The footwalk was narrow (as indeed was the whole street) and filthy to tread upon; and we had to elbow our way among rough men and slatternly women, and to guard our heads from the contact of fish-trays; very ugly, grimy, and misty, moreover, is Billingsgate Market, and though we heard none of the foul language of which it is supposed to be the fountain-head, yet it has its own peculiarities of behavior. For in[58]stance, Una tells me, one man, staring at her and Miss Shepard as they passed, cried out "What beauties!"—another, looking under her veil, greeted her with "Good morning, my love!" Mamma and I were in advance, and heard nothing of these civilities. Struggling through this fishy purgatory, we caught sight of the Tower as we drew near the end of the street; and I put the party under charge of one of the Trump Cards, not being myself inclined to make the rounds of the small part of the fortress that is shown, so soon after my late visit.

When they departed, under charge of the Warder, I set out by myself to wander about the exterior of the Tower, looking with interest at what I suppose to be Tower Hill, a slight elevation of the large open space into which Great Tower-street opens; though perhaps what is now called Trinity Square (in the midst of which is an enclosure of grass and shrubbery) may have all been a part of Tower Hill, and possibly the precise spot where the executions took place. Keeping to the right, round the Tower, I found the moat quite surrounded by a fence of iron-rails, excluding me from a pleasant gravel-path, among flowers and shrubbery, on the inside, where I could see nursery maids giving children their airings. Probably these may have been the privileged inhabitants of the [59] Tower, which certainly might contain the population of a large village. The aspect of the fortress has so much that is mean and modern about it that it can hardly be called picturesque; and yet it seems unfair to withhold that epithet from such a collection of gray ramparts, turrets, and battlements, with the ancient White Tower rising prominent in the midst, though mixed up with a good deal of common-place masonry. I followed the iron fence quite round the outer precincts, till it approached the Thames; and, in this direction, the moat and the pleasure-ground terminate in a narrow graveyard, which extends beneath the ramparts of the Tower, and looks neglected, and shaggy with long grass. It appeared to contain graves enough, but only a few tombstones, of which I could read the inscription of but one; it commemorated a Mr. George Gibson, or some such name, a person of no note, nor apparently connected with the Tower. St. Katherine's Dock lies along the Thames, in this vicinity; and, while on one side of me were the Tower, the quiet gravel-path, and the shaggy grave-yard, on the other were draymen and their horses, dock-laborers, sailors, empty puncheons, and a miscellaneous spectacle of life; including organ-grinders, men roasting ches[t]nuts over small ovens on the side-walk, boys and women with boards or wheel-bar[60]rows of apples, oyster-stands, besides pedlars of small wares, dirty children at play, and other figures and things that a Dutch painter would seize upon.

I went a little way into Katherine's Dock, and found it crowded with great ships; then returning, I strolled along the range of shops that front towards this side of the Tower. They have all something to do with ships, sailors, and commerce; being for the sale of ship's stores, nautical instruments, arms, clothing, together with a tavern or grog-shop at every other door; book-stalls, too, covered with cheap novels and song-books; cigar-shops in great numbers; and everywhere were sailors, and here and there a soldier, and children at the door-steps, and women showing themselves at the doors or windows of their domiciles. These latter figures, however, pertain rather to a street up which I walked, penetrating into the interior of this region, which, I think, is Black-wall—no, I forget what its name is. At all events, it has an ancient and most grimy and shabby look, with its old gabled houses, each of them the seat of some petty trade and business in its basement-story. Among these I saw one house, with three or four peaks along its front, a second story projecting over the basement, and the whole clapboarded over, so that it [61] looked just like the houses that used to be so numerous in Ann-street, in our own Boston. There was a Butcher's stall in the lower story, with a front open to the street, in the ancient fashion, which seems to be retained only by butcher's shops. This part of London having escaped the Great Fire, I suppose there may be many relics of architectural antiquity hereabouts.

At the end of an hour, I went back to the refreshment-room within the outer-gate of the Tower, where Mamma and the other two shortly appeared. We now returned westward by way of Great Tower-street, Eastcheap, and Cannon-street, and entering St. Paul's, sat down beneath the misty dome to rest our-selves. The muffled roar of the city, as we heard it there, is very soothing, and keeps one listening to it, somewhat as the flow of a river keeps us looking at it;

it is a grand and quiet sound; and, ever and anon, a distant door slammed somewhere in the Cathedral, and reverberated long and heavily, like the roll of thunder or the boom of cannon. Every noise, that is loud enough to be heard in so vast an edifice, melts into the great quietude. The interior of the Cathedral looked very heavy and sombre, and the dome hung over us like a cloudy [62] sky. I wish it were possible to pass directly from St. Paul's into York Cathedral, or from the latter into the former; that is, if one's mind could manage to stagger under both, in the same day. There is no other way of judging of their comparative effect.

Under the influence of that great lullaby—the roar of the city—we sat for some time after we were sufficiently rested; but at last plunged forth again, and went up Newgate-street, pausing to peep through the iron railings of Christ's Hospital. The boys, however, were not at play; so we went onward in quest of Smithfield, and, on our way thither, had a greeting from Mr. Silsbee,[470] a gentleman of our own native town. He has been three or four years on this side of the water, chiefly on the Continent, and means now to spend some months in England. Parting with him, we found Smithfield, which is still occupied with pens for cattle, though I believe it has ceased to be a cattle-market. Except it be St. Bartholomew's Hospital, on one side, there is nothing interesting in this ugly and frowzy square; though, no doubt, a few feet under the pavement, there are bones and ashes as precious as anything of the kind, on earth. I wonder when men will begin to erect monuments to human error; hitherto, their pil[63]lars and statues have been only for the sake of glorification. But after all, the present fashion may be the best and whol[e]somest.

I put Mamma and the others into an omnibus in Holborn, and wended my own way deviously westward, turning aside from the Strand into Hungerford Market, and going through Spring Gardens into the Park, whence I emerged by the steps leading to the Duke of York's Column. Thence I crossed to Saint James's street, and along Piccadilly, where, seeing the gateway of Burlington House open, I stept into the enclosed space. Around three sides of a quadrangle was an edifice—or three edifices—of Classic architecture, pretty enough, but low and unimpressive. The fourth side, towards the Street, was an arcade[471] of pillars in a curved sweep on either side of the entrance. In the centre of the quadrangle was an equestrian statue, so comfortably muffled in matting that only a swollen bulk was discernible.

24 G^t Russell-St. Novr 16th, Monday.

Mr. Silsbee called yesterday, and talked a long while, principally with my wife, about matters of art, in which he is deeply interested, and which he has had great opportunities of becoming acquainted with, during three years' travel on the Continent. He is a man of great intelligence and true feeling, and absolutely brims over with ideas; [64] his conversation running in a constant stream, which it appears to be no trouble whatever to him to keep up;

but next to impossible to stop. Not to speak it unkindly, he is such a bore as only a sensible man can be; and it is a pity to think of so much knowledge, talent, and genuine sensibility, and right mindedness withal, effecting no better result than if his mind were all one platitude. He took his leave after a long call, and left with us a manuscript, describing a visit to Berlin, which I read to my wife in the evening. It was a good deal like his conversation, and very much of it was well worth reading, and needed only the practice of a writer to render the ideas worthy of public presentation. He made an engagement to go with us to the Crystal Palace, and came hither for that purpose at 10 °clock this morning.

We took an omnibus in Oxford-street as far as the Bank, and a cab thence to the London Bridge Station, where we bought return tickets, (entitling us to admission to the Palace as well as conveyance thither) for half-a-crown apiece. On our arrival, we entered the Palace by the garden-front, thus gaining a fine view of the ornamented grounds, with their fountains, and stately pathways, bordered with statues; and of the edifice itself, so vast and fairy-like, looking (in comparison with edifices of stone) as if it were bubble-like and [65] might vanish at a touch. There is as little beauty in the architecture of the Crystal Palace, however, as it was possible to attain with such gigantic use of such a material. No doubt, an architectural order, of which we have as yet little or no idea, is to be developed from the use of glass as a building-material, instead of brick and stone. It will have its own rules and its own results; but, meanwhile, even the present Palace is positively a very beautiful object. On entering, we found the atmosphere chill and comfortless; more so, it seemed to me, than the open air itself. It was not a genial day, though, now and then, the sun gleamed out, and once made fine effects in the glass work of a crystal fountain in one of the Courts.

Being under Mr. Silsbee's guidance for the day, we had no opportunity to follow our own inclinations nor to think our own thoughts; not that our visit would have been a more profitable one if we had. We looked first at the sculpture, which is composed chiefly of casts or copies of the most famous statues of all ages, and likewise of those crumbs and little fragments which have fallen from Time's jaw,—and half-picked bones, as it were, that have been gathered up from spots where he has feasted full—torsos, heads, and broken limbs, some of them half-worn away as if they [66] had been rolled over and over in the sea. I saw nothing in the sculptural way, either modern or antique, that impressed me so much as a statue of a naked mother, by a French artist. In a sitting posture, with one leg crossed over the other, she was clasping her elevated knee with both hands; and in the hollow cradle thus formed by her arms lay two sweet little babies, as snug and close to her heart as if they had not yet been born—two little love-blossoms, and the mother encircling and pervading them with love. But an infinite pathos and strange terror are given to this beautiful group, by some faint bas-reliefs on the pedestal, indicating that the happy mother is Eve, and Cain and Abel the two innocent babes.

Then we went to the Alhambra, which looks more like an enchanted palace than any thing I ever expected to see. If it had been a summer-day I should have enjoyed it more; but it was miserable to shiver and shake in the Court of the Lions, and in those chambers which were contrived as places of refuge from a fervid temperature. Furthermore, it is not quite agreeable to see such very clever specimens of stage-decoration; they are so very good that it gets to be past a joke, without becoming actual earnest. I had not a similar feeling in respect to the re-production of [67] medi-aeval statues, arches, door-ways, all brilliantly colored, as in the days of their first glory; yet I do not know but that the first is as little objectionable as the last. Certainly, in both cases, scenes and objects of a past age are here more vividly presented to the dullest mind than, without such material facilities, they could possibly be brought before the most powerful imagination. Truly the Crystal Palace, in all its departments, offers wonderful means of education. I marvel what will come of it. Among the things that I admired most was Benvenuto Cellini's Statue of Perseus, holding the head of Medusa, and standing over her headless and still writhing body, out of which, at the severed neck, gushed a vast exuberance of snakes. Likewise, a sitting statue by Michael Angelo of one of the Medici, full of dignity and grace, and reposeful might. Also the bronze gate of a Baptistery in Florence, carved all over with relievos of Scripture subjects, done in the most life-like and expressive manner. The cast itself was a miracle of art; I should have taken it for the genuine original bronze.

We then went into the House of Diomed, which seemed to me a dismal abode, affording no possibility [68] of comfort. We sat down in one of the rooms, on an iron bench, the coldness of which soon made itself very perceptible to the part of me that touched it. It being, by this time, two ºclock, we went to the refreshment-room next, and lunched on some veal-pie, some cold beef, and a bottle of ale; and before we had finished our repast, my wife discovered that she had lost her sable boa, which she had been carrying on her arm. Mr. Silsbee (who is a most kind and obliging gentleman) immediately went in quest of it, and re-visited every place where we had been before, besides the cloak-rooms and police-office, but all to no purpose. By and by, I went off in search of him, and thus a great deal of our day was spent to no purpose, until (as it was drawing towards sunset) we met again, and giving up the lost boa, set ourselves to see what we could of the wonders around us. Entering the tropical saloon, we immediately found a most welcome and delightful change of temperature, among those gigantic leaves of banyan trees and the broad expanse of water-plants, floating on pools; and spacious aviaries, where birds of brilliant plumage sported and sang amid such foliage as they knew at home. Howbeit, the atmosphere was a little faint and sickish, per[69]haps owing to the smell of the half-tepid water. The most remarkable object here was the apparent trunk of a tree huge beyond imagination; a pine-tree from California. It was the stript-off bark, which had been conveyed hither in segments, and put together again to the full height of the palace-roof; and the interior circle of the tree was large enough to contain, I should think, fifty people. We entered, and sat down in all the remoteness from one another that is attainable in a good-sized drawing-room. We ascended the gallery to get a view of this vast tree from a more elevated position, and found it looked even bigger from above. Then we went slowly along the gallery, as far as it extended, towards the entrance of the Palace, and afterwards descended into the nave, and kept still thitherward; for it was getting dark, and a horn had sounded, and a bell sounded a warning to such as loitered in the remote regions of the Palace. Mr. Silsbee again went in quest of the boa, but still without success; and at five °clock we took our seats in the rail-carriage, and taking a Paddington omnibus from the station, reached home at about six. I have not much enjoyed the Crystal Palace, but think it a great and admirable achievement.

[70] G^t RUSSELL ST. NOV^r 19th, THURSDAY.

ON Tuesday evening, Mr. Silsbee came to read some letters which he had written to his friends, chiefly giving his observations on art, together with descriptions of Venice and other cities on the continent. They were very good, and indicate much sensibility and talent; and I was glad to be able to say it, because he wishes, if possible, to work these letters up into something that may be presented to the public. I advised him, in the first instance, to work them up into a series of lectures, to be delivered in the United States. He seemed to like the idea. The audience to which he read the letters consisted, besides myself, of Miss Shepard and Una; poor Mamma having caught cold on our return from the Crystal Palace, and being confined to her bed. After the lecture, we had a little oyster-supper, and a glass or two of wine; and between 10 and 11, Mr. Silsbee took his departure for Kensington, where he resides.

I had written a note to Bennoch, and received an answer, indicating that he was much weighed down by his financial misfortunes, though there turns out to be no truth in the report of Mrs. Bennoch's death. However, he desired me to come and see him; so, yesterday morning, I wended my way down into the city, and after various reluctant circumlocutions, turned into narrow Wood-street and went to No 77. The interior of the [71] warehouse looked confused and dismal; two or three clerks seemed to be taking an account of stock; and when I inquired for Bennoch, a boy asked me to write my name on a slip of paper, and took it into his peculiar office. Then appeared Mr. Rigg, the Junior partner, looking haggard and anxious. Poor man; he is somewhat low of stature and slightly deformed; and I fancied that he felt this disgrace and trouble more on that account. But he greeted me in a friendly way, though rather awkwardly, and asked me to sit down a little while in his own apartment, where he left me. I sat a good while, reading an old number of Blackwood's Magazine, a pile of which I found on the desk, together with some well-worn ledgers and papers, that looked as if they had been pulled out of drawers or pigeon-holes and dusty corners, and were not there in the regular course of business. By and by Mr. Rigg appeared again, and telling me that I must lunch with them, conducted me up stairs, and through entries and passages, where I had been more than once before, but could not have found my way again through those extensive premises; and everywhere the packages of silk were piled up, and ranged on shelves, in paper-boxes and otherwise; a rich stock, but which had brought ruin with it. At last we came to that pleasant dining-room, hung with a picture or two, where I re[72]member enjoying the hospitality of the firm, with their clerks all at the table, and thinking that this was a genuine scene of the old life of London city, when the Master used to feed his 'prentices at a patriarchal board.

After all, the room still looked cheerfully enough; and there was a good fire, and the table was laid for four. In two or three minutes, Bennoch came in; not with that broad, warm, lustrous presence that used to gladden me in our past encounters—not with all that presence, at least—though still he was not less than a very genial man, partially bedimmed. He looked paler—it seemed to me, thinner and rather smaller—but nevertheless smiled at greeting me, more brightly, I suspect, than I smiled back at him; for, in truth, I was very sorry. Mr. Twentyman, the middle partner, now came in, and appeared as much or more depressed than his fellows in misfortune, and to bear it with a greater degree of English incommunicativeness and reserve. But he, too, met me hospitably; and I and these three poor ruined men sat down to dinner—a good dinner enough, by the by, and such as ruined men need not be ashamed to eat, since they must needs eat something. It was roast beef, and a boiled apple-pudding, and—which I was glad to see, my heart being heavy—a decanter of sherry and another of port, [73] remnants of a stock which, I suppose, will not be replenished.

They ate pretty fairly, but s[c]arcely like Englishmen, and drank a reasonable quantity, but not as if their hearts were in it, or as if the liquor went to their hearts and gladdened them. I gathered from them a strong idea of what commercial failure is, to English merchants—utter ruin, present and prospective, and obliterating all the successful past; how little chance they have of ever getting up again; how they feel that they must plod heavily onward under a burthen of disgrace—poor men, and hopeless men, and men forever ashamed. I doubt whether any future prosperity (which is unlikely enough to come to them) could ever compensate them for this misfortune, or make them, to their own consciousness, the men they were. They will be like a woman who has once lost her chastity; no after life of virtue will take out the stain. It is not so in America, nor ought it to be so here; but they said themselves they would never again have put unreserved confidence in a man who had once been bankrupt, and they could not but apply the same severe rule to their own case. I was touched by nothing more than by their sorrowful patience, without any [74] fierceness against Providence or against mankind, or disposition to find fault with any thing but their own imprudence; and there was a simple dignity, too, in their not assuming the aspect of stoicism. I could really have shed tears for them, to see how like men and Christians, they let the tears come into their own eyes. This is the true way to do; a man ought not to be too proud to let his eyes be moistened in the presence of God and of a friend. They talked of some little annoyances, half-laughingly. Bennoch has been dunned for his gas-bill at Blackheath (only a pound or two) and has paid it. Mr. Twentyman seems to have received an insulting message from some creditor. Mr. Rigg spoke of wanting a little money to pay for some boots. It was very sad, indeed, to see these men of uncommon energy and ability, all now so helpless, and, from managing great enterprises, involving vast expenditures, reduced almost to reckon the silver in their pockets.

Bennoch and I sat by the fireside a little while after his partners had left the room; and then he told me that he blamed himself, as holding the principal position in the firm, for not having exercised a stronger controlling influence over their operations. The other two mem[75]bers had recently gone into speculations, of the extent of which he had not been fully aware, and he found the liabilities of the firm very much greater than he had expected. He said this without bitterness, and said it not to the world, but only to a friend. I am exceedingly sorry for him, it is such a changed life that he must lead hereafter, and with none of the objects before him which he might heretofore have hoped to grasp. No doubt he was ambitious of civic, and even of broader public distinction, and not unreasonably so, having the gift of ready and impressive speech, and a behavior among men that wins them, and a tact in the management of affairs, and never-tiring and many-sided activity. To be Member of Parliament—to be Lord Mayor—whatever an eminent merchant of the world's metropolis may be—beyond question he had dreamed wide awake of these things. And now fate itself could hardly accomplish them, if ever so favorably inclined. He has to begin life again, as he began it twenty-five years ago, only under infinite disadvantages, and with so much of his working-day gone forever.[472] It seems to me nobody else runs such risks as a man of business, because he risks everything. Every other man, into whatever [76] depths of poverty he may sink, has still something left, be he author, scholar, handicraft man, or what not; the merchant has nothing.

We parted with a long and strong grasp of the hand, and Bennoch promised to come and see us soon. I spoke of his going to America, but he appeared to think that there would be little hope for him there. Indeed, I should be loth to see him transplanted thither, myself, away from this warm, cheerful, juicy English life into our drier and less genial sphere; he is a good guest amongst us, but might not do well to live with us.

On my way home, I called at Trübner's,[473] in Paternoster Row, to inquire about some school-books which I had asked him to import from the United States. I waited a few moments, he being busy talking with a tall, muscular, English-built man, who, after he had taken leave, Trübner told me was Charles Reade. I once met him at an evening-party, but should have been glad to meet him again now that I appreciate him so much better, after reading "Never too late to Mend." He is about publishing a new book with Trübner.

24 G^t RUSSELL-STREET, DEC^r 6th, SUNDAY.

ALL these days, since my last date, have been marked by nothing very well
[77] worthy of detail and description. I have walked the streets a great deal, in
the dull November days, and always take a certain pleasure in being in the midst
of human life—as closely encompassed by it as it is possible to be, anywhere in
this world; and, in that way of viewing it, there is a dull and sombre enjoyment
always to be had in Holborn, Fleet-street, Cheapside, and the other thronged
parts of London. It is human life; it is this material world; it is a grim and
heavy reality. I have never had the same sense of being surrounded by material-
isms, and hemmed in with the grossness of this earthly life, anywhere else;
these broad, thronged streets are so evidently the veins and arteries of an
enormous city. London is evidenced in every one of them, just as a Megatheri-
um is in each of its separate bones, even if they be small ones. Thus I never
fail of a sort of self-congratulation in finding myself, for instance, passing
along Ludgate Hill; but, in spite of this, it is really an ungladdened life, to
wander through these huge, thronged ways, over a pavement foul with mud,
ground into it by a million of footsteps; jostling against people who do not seem
to be individuals, but all one mass, so homogeneous is the street-walking aspect
of them; the roar of vehicles pervading me, wearisome cabs and omnibusses [*sic*]; everywhere, the dingy brick edifices heaving themselves up, and
shutting out [78] all but a strip of sullen cloud that serves London for a sky;—
in short, a general impression of grime and sordidness, and, at this season,
always a fog scattered along the vista of streets, sometimes so densely as almost
to spiritualize the materialism and make the scene resemble the other world of
worldly people, gross even in ghostliness. It is strange how little splendor and
brilliancy one sees in London streets; in the city, almost none, though some in
the shops of Regent-street.

My wife has had a season of indisposition, within the last few weeks; and
since her recovery, Una and Fanny have both been taken with the measles, from
which they are only now recovering; so that my rambles have generally been
solitary, or with only Julian for a companion. I think my only excursion with
my wife was a week ago yesterday, when we went to Lincoln Inn's [*sic*] Fields,
which truly are almost a field, right in the heart of London, and as retired and
secluded, almost, as if the surrounding city were a forest, and its heavy roar
were the wind among the branches. We gained admission into the noble Hall,
which is modern (finished only some ten or twelve years ago) but built in
antique style, and as stately and beautiful an interior as ever I beheld; the
most so, indeed, it seems to me. I have forgotten all but the general effect, with
its lofty oaken [79] roof, its panelled walls, with the windows high above, and
the great arched window at one end, full of painted coats of arms, which the
light glorifies in passing through them, as if each were the escutcheon of some
illustrious personage. Thence we went to the Chapel of Lincoln's Inn, where, on
entering, we found a class of young choristers receiving instruction from their
music-master, while the organ accompanied their strains. These young, clear,

fresh, elastic voices are wonderfully beautiful; they are like those of women, yet have something more birdlike and aspiring;—more like what one conceives of the singing of angels. As for the singing of saints and blessed spirits, that have once been human, it never can resemble that of these young voices; for no duration of heavenly enjoyments will ever quite take the mortal sadness out of it. In this chapel we saw some painted windows of the time of James Ist, a period much subsequent to the age when painted glass was in its glory; but the pictures of Saints and scriptural people in these windows were certainly very fine, the figures being as large as life, and the faces having much expression. The sunshine came in through some of them, and produced a beautiful effect, almost as if the painted forms were the glorified spirits of these holy personages. After leaving Lincoln's Inn, we looked [80] in at Gray's Inn, which is a great, quiet domain, quadrangle beyond quadrangle, close beside Holborn, and a large space of greensward included within its precincts. It is very strange to see so much of ancient quietude right in the Monster-city's very jaws, which yet the monster shall not eat up; right in its very belly, indeed, which yet, in all these ages, it shall not digest and convert into the same substance as the rest of its bustling streets. Nothing else in London is so like the effect of a spell, as to pass under one of these archways, and find yourself transported from the bustle, jumble, mob, tumult, uproar, as of an age of week-days intensified into the present hour, into what seems an eternal Sabbath. Thence we went into (I think it was) Staple Inn, which has a front upon Holborn of four or five ancient gables in a row, and a low arch under the impending story, admitting you into a paved quadrangle, beyond which you have the vista of another. I do not understand that the residences and chambers in these Inns of Court are now exclusively let to lawyers, though such inhabitants certainly seem to preponderate there.

Since then, I do not remember any event of special interest, unless that, on Thursday last, Julian and I walked down into the Strand, and found ourselves unexpectedly mixed up [81] with a crowd, that grew denser as we approached Charing Cross, and became absolutely impermeable when we attempted to make our way to Whitehall. The wicket in the gate of Northumberland House, by the by, was open, and gave me a glimpse of the front of the edifice within; a very partial glimpse, however, and obstructed by the solid person of a footman, who, with some women, was passing out from within. The crowd was a real English crowd, perfectly undemonstrative, and entirely decorous and well-behaved, being composed mostly of well-dressed people, and largely of women. The cause of the assemblage was the opening of Parliament by the Queen; but we were too late for any chance of seeing her. However, we extricated ourselves from the throng, and, going along Pall Mall, got into the Park by the steps at the foot of the Duke of York's Column, and thence, went to the White Hall gateway, outside of which we found the Horse Guards drawn up—a regiment of black horses and burnished cuirasses. On our way thither, an open carriage came through the gateway into the Park, conveying two ladies in court-dresses; and another splendid carriage came through the Park and passed out through the gateway;—the coachman in a cocked hat and scarlet and gold embroidery, and two other scarlet and gilt figures hanging behind. It was [82] one of the Queen's carriages, but seemed to have nobody in it. I have forgotten to mention what, I think, produced more effect on me than anything else; viz:—the clash of the bells from the steeple of Saint Martin's church, and those of Saint Margaret. Really, London seemed to cry out through them, and bid welcome to the Queen.

Yesterday forenoon, I went with Julian to the Times office, with an advertisement which Miss Shepard wished to get inserted for Mr. Fezandie.[474] There was such a throng of people on similar business, that I found great difficulty in getting to the counter. What a business this newspaper is doing! It does not deserve its prodigious success.

24, Gt Russell st, Decr 7th Monday.

This being a muddy and dismal day, and I being heavy with the dregs of a cold, I went only to the British Museum, which is but a short walk down the street. I have now visited it often enough to be on more familiar terms with it than at first, and therefore do not feel myself so weighed down by the multitude of things to be seen; the most irksome state of mind I have ever experienced. Now, I have ceased to expect, or hope, or wish, to devour and digest the whole enormous collection; so I content myself with individual things, and succeed in getting now and then a little honey from them. Unless I were [83] studying some particular branch of history or science, or art, this is the best that can be done with the British Museum. I went first, to-day, into the Townley Gallery, and so along through all the ancient sculpture, and was glad to find myself able to sympathize more than heretofore with the forms of grace and beauty which are preserved there—poor, maimed immortalities as they are—headless and legless trunks, godlike cripples, faces beautiful and broken-nosed, heroic shapes which have stood so long, or lain prostrate so long, in the open air, that even the atmosphere of Greece has almost dissolved the external layer of the marble; and yet, however much they may be worn away, or battered and shattered, the grace and nobility seems as deep in them as the very heart of the stone. It cannot be destroyed except by grinding them to powder. In short, I do really believe that there was an excellence in ancient sculpture, and that it has yet a potency to educate and refine the minds of those who look at it, even so carelessly and casually as I do. As regards the frieze of the Parthenon, I must remark that the horses represented on it, though they show great spirit and life-likeness, are rather of the pony-species, than what would be considered fine horses now. Doubtless, modern breeding has wrought a difference in the animal. [84] Flaxman, in his Outlines, seems to have imitated these classic steeds of the Parthenon, and thus has produced horses that always appeared to me affected and diminutively monstrous.

From the classic sculpture, I passed through an Assyrian room, where the walls are lined with great slabs of marble, sculptured in bas-relief with scenes in the life of Sennacherib, I believe; very ugly, to be sure, yet artistically done, in their own style, and in wonderfully good preservation. Indeed, if the chisel had cut its last stroke in them yesterday, the work could not be more sharp and distinct. In glass cases, in this room, are little relics, and scraps of utensils, and a great deal of fragmentary rubbish, dug up by Layard in his researches; things that it is hard to call anything but trash, but which yet may be of great significance as indicating the modes of life of a long past race. I remember nothing particularly, just now, except some pieces of broken glass, irridescent [*sic*] with certainly the most beautiful hues in the world—indescribably beautiful, and unimaginably, unless one can conceive of the colors of the rainbow, and a thousand glorious sunsets, and the autumnal forest-leaves of America, all condensed upon a little fragment of a glass cup; and that, too, without becoming in the least [85] glaring or flagrant, but mildly glorious, as we may fancy the shifting hues of an angel's wing to be. I think this chaste splendour will glow in my memory for years to come. It is the effect of time, and cannot be imitated by any known process of art. I have seen it in specimens of old Roman glass which have been found here in England, but never in any thing the brilliancy of these oriental fragments. How strange, that decay, in dark places, and under ground, and where there are a billion of chances to one that nobody will ever see its handiwork, should produce these beautiful effects. The glass seems to become perfectly brittle, so that it would vanish like a soap-bubble if touched.

Ascending the stairs, I went through the halls of fossil-remains (which I care little for, though one of them is a human skeleton in lime-stone,) and through several rooms of mineralogical specimens, including all the gems in the world, among which is seen—not the Koh-i-noor itself—but a fac-simile in crystal. I think the aerolites are as interesting as anything in this department; and one fragment, laid against the wall of the room, weighs about 1400 pounds of pure iron. Whence could it have come? If these aerolites are pieces of other planets, how happen they to be always iron? But I know no more of this than if I were a [86] philosopher. Then I went through rooms of shells, and fishes, and reptiles and tortoises, crocodiles and alligators, and insects, including all manner of butterflies, some of which had wings precisely like leaves a little withered and faded, even the skeleton and fibres of the leaves being imitated; and immense hairy spiders, covering with the whole circumference of their legs a space as big as a saucer;[475] and centipedes little less than a foot-long; and winged insects that look like jointed twigs of a tree. In America, I remember, while I lived in Lenox, I found an insect of this species, and at first really mistook it for a twig. It was smaller than these specimens in the Museum. I suppose every creature, almost, that runs, or swims, or creeps, or flies, is represented in this collection of Natural History; and it puzzles me to think what they were all made for; though, after all, it is quite as mysterious why man himself was made.

By and by, I entered the room of Egyptian mummies, of which there are a good many, one of which (the body of a priestess,) is unrolled, except the innermost layer of linen. The outline of her face is perfectly visible; and I saw, too, some of the small bones of her toes. Mummies of cats, dogs, snakes, and children, are in the wall-cases, together with a vast many articles of Egyptian manufacture and use, even child[87]ren's toys; bread, too, in flat cakes; grapes, that have turned to raisins, in the grave; queerest of all, methinks, a curly wig, that is supposed to have belonged to a woman, together with the wooden box that held it. The hair is brown, and the wig seems as perfect as if it had been made for some now living dowager. From Egypt, we pass into rooms containing vases and other articles of Grecian and Roman workmanship, and funeral urns, and beads, and rings; none of them very beautiful. I saw some splendid specimens, however, at a former visit, when I obtained admission to a room not indiscriminately shown to visitors. What chiefly interested me in that room, however, was a cast taken from the face of Cromwell after death, representing a wide-mouthed, long-chinned, uncomely visage, with a triangular English nose in the very centre; together with various other curiosities, which I fancied were safe in my memory, but do not know [now] come uppermost. To return to my to-day's progress through the Museum, next to the classic rooms, are the collections of Saxon and British, and early English antiquities, the earlier portions of which are not very interesting to me, possessing little or no beauty in themselves, and indicating a kind of life too remote from our own to be readily sympathized with. Who cares for glass beads, and [88] copper brooches, and knives, spear-heads, and swords, all so rusty that they look as much like pieces of old iron hoop as anything else. The bed of the Thames has been a rich treasury of antiquities, from the time of the Roman conquest downwards; it seems to preserve bronze in considerable perfection, but not iron.

Among the medi-aeval relics, the carvings in ivory are often very exquisite and elaborate. There likewise are caskets and coffers, and a thousand other old-world ornamental works; but I saw so many, and such superior, specimens of these things at the Manchester Exhibition, that I shall say nothing of them here. The seal-ring of Mary Queen of Scots is in one of the cases; it must have been a thumb-ring, judging from its size, and has a dark stone, engraved with armorial bearings. In another case is the magic glass, formerly used by Doctor Dee,[476] and in which (if I rightly remember) used to be seen prophetic visions, or figures of persons and scenes at a distance. It is a round ball of glass or crystal, slightly tinged with a pinkish hue, and about as big as a small apple, or a door-knob, or a little bigger than an egg would be, if it were perfectly round. This ancient humbug kept me looking at it perhaps ten minutes; and I saw my own face dimly [89] in it, but no other vision. Lastly, I passed through the Ethnographical rooms; but I care little for the varieties of the human race, all that is really important and interesting being found in our own variety. Perhaps equally in any other. This brought me (though I forget whether there were any other rooms between) to the head of one of the staircases, descending which I entered the library.

Here (not to speak of the noble rooms and halls) there are numberless treasures beyond all price; too valuable, in their way, for me to select any one as more curious and interesting than many others. Letters of statesmen, and warriors, of all nations and several centuries back; (among which, long as it has taken Europe to produce them, I saw none so illustrious as that of Washington, nor more so than Franklin's, whom America gave to the world in her non-age;) and epistles of poets and artists; and of Kings, too, whose chirography appears to have been much better than I should have expected from fingers so often cramped in iron gauntlets. In another case, there were the original autograph copies of several famous works; for example, that of Pope's Homer, written on the backs of letters, the direction and seals of which appear in the midst of the "tale of Troy divine,"[477] which also is much [90] scratched and interlined with Pope's corrections;—a manuscript of one of Ben Jonson's masques;—of the Sentimental Journey, written in much more careful and formal style than might be expected, the book pretending to be so harum-scarum;—of Walter Scott's Kenilworth, bearing such an aspect of straightforward diligence that I shall hardly think of it again as a romance;— in short, I may as well drop the whole matter here. All through the long vista of the King's library, we come to cases in which (with their pages open beneath the glass) we see books worth their weight in gold, either for their uniqueness or their beauty, or because they have belonged to illustrious men, and have their autographs in them. The copy of the English translation of Montaigne, containing the strange scrawl of Shakspeare's autograph, is here. Bacon's name is in another book; Queen Elizabeth's in another; and there is a little devotional volume with Lady Jane Grey's writing in it. She is supposed to have taken it to the scaffold with her. Here, too, I saw a copy, (printed on a Venetian press at the time) of the challenge which the Admirable Crichton caused to be posted on the church-door of Venice, defying all the scholars of Italy to encounter him. But if I mention one thing, I find fault with [91] myself for not putting down fifty others, just as interesting; and, after all, there is an official catalogue, no doubt, of the whole.

As I do not mean to fill any more pages with the British Museum, I will just mention the hall of Egyptian antiquities, on the ground floor of the edifice, though I did not pass through it to-day. They consist of things that would be very ugly and contemptible, if they were not so immensely magnified; but it is impossible not to acknowledge a certain grandeur, resulting from the scale on which those strange old sculptors wrought. For instance, there is an arm and hand, ten feet in length; and a granite fist of still more prodigious size, at least a yard across, and looking as if it were doubled in the face of Time, defying him to destroy it. All the rest of the statue to which it belonged, however, seems to have vanished; but this fist will certainly outlast the Museum and whatever else it contains, unless it be some similar Egyptian ponderosity.

There is a beetle, wrought out of immensely hard, black stone, as big as a hogs-head. It is satisfactory to see a thing so big and heavy. Then there are huge stone sarcophagi, engraved with Egyptian hieroglyphics within and with[92] out, all as good as new, though their age is reckoned by thousands of years; these great coffins are of vast weight and mass, insomuch that, whence [when] once the accurately fitting lids were shut down, there might have seemed little chance of its being lifted again till the Resurrection. I positively like these coffins, they are so faithfully made, and so black and stern, and polished to such a nicety, only to be buried forever; for the workmen, nor the Kings who were laid to sleep within, could never have dreamed of the British Museum. There is [a] deity named Pasht, who sits in this hall, very big, very grave, carved of black stone, and very ludicrous, wearing a dog's head. I will just mention the Rosetta Stone, with a Greek inscription and another in Egyptian characters, which gave the clue, I believe, to a whole field of history; and shall pretermit all further handling of this whole unwieldy subject.

In all the rooms, I saw people of the poorer classes, some of whom seemed to view the objects intelligently and to take a genuine interest in them. A poor man in London has great opportunities of cultivating himself, if he will only make the best of them; and such an institution as the British Museum can hardly fail to attract, as the magnet does steel, the minds that are likeliest to be [93] benefitted [sic] by it in its various departments. I saw many children there, and some ragged boys.

It deserves to be noticed, that some small figures of Indian Thugs, represented as engaged in their profession and handiwork of cajoling and strangling travellers, have been removed from the place which they formerly occupied in the part of the Museum shown to the general public. They are now in the more private room; and the reason of their withdrawal is, that, according to the Chaplain of Newgate, the practice of garrotting was suggested to the English thieves by this representation of Indian Thugs. It is edifying, after what I have written in the preceding paragraph, to find that the only lesson, known to have been inculcated here, is that of a new mode of outrage.

24 G[t] RUSSELL-ST, DEC[r] 8th, TUESDAY.

THIS morning, when it was time to get up, there was but a glimmering of daylight; and we had candles on the breakfast-table, at nearly ten °clock. All abroad, there was a dense, dim fog, brooding through the atmosphere, insomuch that we could hardly see across the street. At eleven °clock, I went out into the midst of this fog-bank, which, for the moment, seemed a little more interfused with day light; for there seem to be continual changes in the density of this dim [94] medium, which varies so much that now you can but just see your hand before you, and, a moment afterwards, you can see the cabs dashing out of the duskiness, a score of yards off. It is seldom or never, moreover, an unmitigated gloom, but appears to be mixed up with sunshine in different proportions; sometimes, only one part sun to a thousand of smoke and fog, and sometimes sunshine enough to give the whole mass a coppery hue. This would have been a bright, sunny day, but for the interference of the fog; and before I had been out long, I actually saw the sun, looking red and rayless, much like the millionth magnification of a new halfpenny.

I was bound towards Bennoch's warehouses; for he had written a note to apologize for not visiting us, last evening, and I had promised to call and see him to day. First, however, I went to Marlborough House, to look at the English pictures, which I care more about seeing, here in England, than those of foreign artists, because the latter will be found more numerously, and better, on the Continent. I saw many pictures that pleased me; nothing that impressed me very strongly. Pictorial talent seems to be abundant enough, up to a certain point; pictorial genius, I should judge, is among the rarest [95] of gifts. To be sure, I very likely might not recognize it where it existed; and yet it ought to have the power of making itself known even to the un-instructed mind, as literary genius does. If it exists only for connoisseurs, it is a very suspicious affair. I looked at all Turner's pictures, and at many of his drawings; and must again confess myself wholly unable to understand more than a very few of them. Even those few are tantalizing. At a certain distance, you discern what appears to be a grand and beautiful picture, which you shall admire and enjoy infinitely if you can get within the range of distinct vision. You come nearer, and find only blotches of color, and dabs of the brush, meaning nothing when you look closely, and meaning a mystery at the point where the painter intended to station you. Some landscapes there were, indeed, full of imaginative beauty, and of the better truth etherealized out of the pro-saic truth of Nature; only it was still impossible actually to see it. There was a mist over it; or it was like a tract of beautiful dream-land, seen dimly through sleep, and glimmering out of sight if looked upon with wide-open eyes. These were the most satisfactory specimens. There were many others which I positively could not [96] comprehend in the remotest degree; not even so far as to guess whether they purported to represent earth, sea, or sky. In fact, I should not have known them to be pictures at all, but should have supposed that the artist had been trying his brush on the canvass [sic], mixing up all sorts of hues, but principally white paints, and now and then producing an agreeable harmony of color, without particularly intending it. Now that I have done my best to understand them without an interpreter, I mean to buy Ruskin's pamphlet[478] at my next visit, and look at them through his eyes. But I do not think I can be driven out of the idea that a picture ought to have something in common with what the spectator sees in Nature.

Marlborough House may be converted, I think, into a very handsome resi-dence for the young Prince of Wales. The entrance from the court-yard is into a large, square, central hall, the painted cieling [sic] of which is at the whole height of the edifice, and has a gallery on one side, whence it would be pleasant to look down upon a festal scene below.—The rooms are of fine proportions, with vaulted cielings [sic], and with fire-places and mantel-pieces of great beauty, adorned with pillars and terminal figures of white and variega[97]ted marble; and in the centre of each mantel-piece there is a marble tablet, exquisitely sculptured with classical designs, done in such high relief that the figures are sometimes almost disengaged from the marble. One of the subjects was Androlycus [Androclus], or whatever was his name, taking the thorn out of the lion's foot. I suppose these sculptures are of the era of the great old Duke and Duchess. After all, however, for some reason or other, the house does not at first strike you as a noble and princely one, and you have to convince yourself of it by examining it more in detail.

On leaving Marlborough House, I stept for a few moments into the National Gallery, and looked, among other things, at the Turners and Claudes that hung there side by side. These pictures, I think, are quite the most comprehensible of Turner's productions; but I must say I prefer the Claudes. The latter catches the "light that never was on sea nor land,"[479] without quite taking you away from nature for it. Nevertheless, I will not be quite certain that I really care a fig for any painter but Murillo, whose Saint John I should positively like to own. As far as my own pleasure is concerned, I could not say as much for any other picture; for I [98] have always found an infinite weariness and disgust resulting from a picture being too frequently before my eyes. I had rather see a basilisk, for instance, than the very best of those old familiar pictures in the Boston Athenaeum; and most of those in the National Gallery would soon affect me in the same way.

Emerging from the Gallery, I almost groped my way towards the city; for the fog seemed to grow denser and denser as I advanced; and when I reached Saint Paul's, the sunny intermixture, above spoken of, was at its minimum, so that the smoke-cloud really grew black about the dome and pinnacles, and the statues of Saints looked down dimly from their stand-points on high, faintest, as spiritual consolations are apt to be, when the world was darkest. It was very grand, however, to see the pillars and porticoes, and the huge bulk of the edifice heaving up its dome from an obscure foundation into yet more shadowy obscurity; and by the time I reached the corner of the church-yard nearest Cheapside, the whole vast Cathedral had utterly vanished, leaving "not a wrack behind;[480]—unless those thick, dark vapours were the elements of which it had been composed, and into which it had again dissolved. [99] It is good to think, nevertheless (and I gladly accept the analogy and the moral) that the Cathedral was really there, and as substantial as ever, though these earthly mists had hidden it from mortal eyes.

I found Bennoch in better spirits than when I saw him last; but his misfortune has been too real not to affect him long and deeply. He was cheerful, however, and his face shone almost with its old lustre. It has still the cheeriest glow that I ever saw in any human countenance. He means, I think, to continue in London, and to fight the battle of life over again, even under all the disadvantages that a defeat already incurred entails upon a man, in England. I must record an anecdote that he told of Grace Greenwood. Grace, while in

London, was invited to a private reading of Shakspeare, by Charles Kemble; and she thought it behoved her to manifest her good taste and depth of feeling by going into hysterics, and finally fainting away upon the floor. Hereupon Charles Kemble looked up from his book and addressed himself to her, sternly and severely. "Ma'am," said he "this won't do! Ma'am, we are too much used to this sort of thing! Ma'am, you disturb the company! Ma'am, you expose yourself!" This last hit had the desired ef[100]fect; for poor Grace probably thought that her drapery had not adjusted itself as it ought, and that per-hap[s] she was really exposing more of her charms than were good to be imparted to a mixed company. So she came to herself in a hurry, and, after a few flutterings, subsided into a decorous listener. Bennoch says he had this story from an eye and ear-witness, and that he fully believes it; and I think it not improbable that, betwixt downright humbug and a morbid exaggeration of her own emotions, Grace may have been betrayed into this awful fix. I wonder how she survived it.

I went home by way of Holborn; and the fog was denser than ever—very black, indeed, more like a distillation of mud than anything else; the ghost of mud, the spiritualized medium of departed mud, through which the departed citizens of London probably tread in the Hades whither they are translated. So heavy was the gloom, that gas was lighted in all the shop-windows; and the little charcoal furnaces of the women and boys, roasting ches[t]nuts, threw a ruddy misty glow around them. And yet I liked it. This fog seems an at-mosphere proper to huge, grimy London; as proper as that light, neither of the sun nor moon, is to the New Jerusalem.[481] On reaching home, I found the [101] fog diffused through the parlour, though how it could have got in is a mystery. Since nightfall, however, the atmosphere is clear again.

24 G^t RUSSELL-ST. DEC^r 20th, SUNDAY.

HERE we are still in London, at least a month longer than we expected, and at the very dreariest and dullest season of the year. Had I thought of it sooner, I might have found interesting people enough to know, even when all London is said to be out of town; but meditating a stay only of a week or two, it did not seem worth while to seek acquaintances. I have been out only for one evening; and that was to Dr. Wilkinson's,[482] who had been attending the children in the measles. He is a Homeopathist, and is, I think, somehow known either in scientific or general literature, though I do not know pre-cisely in what way; at all events, a sensible and enlightened man, with an un-English freedom of mind, on some points. For example, he is a Sweden-borgian, and a believer in the whole subject of modern Spiritualism. He showed me some drawings that had been made under the spiritual influence, by a miniature-painter, who possesses no imaginative power of his own, and is merely a good mechanical and literal artist; but these drawings, representing angels and allegorical peo[102]ple, were done by an influence which directed the artist's hand, he not knowing what his next touch would be, nor what the final result. The sketches certainly did—if examined in a trustful mood—show a high and fine expressiveness. Dr. Wilkinson also spoke of Mr. Harris,[483] the American poet of spiritualism, as being the best poet of the day; and he produced his works, in several volumes, and showed me songs, and paragraphs of longer poems, in support of his opinion. They seemed to me to have a certain light and splendor, but not to possess much power, either passionate or intellectual. Mr. Harris is the medium of deceased poets, Milton among the rest, and Lord Byron; and Dr. Wilkinson said that Lady Byron (who is a devoted admirer of her husband, in spite of their conjugal troubles) pronounced some of these posthumous strains to be worthy of his living genius. Then the Doctor spoke of various strange experiences which he himself has had, in these spiritual matters; for he has witnessed the miraculous performances of Hume,[484] the American medium, and he has seen, with his own eyes, and felt with his own touch, those ghostly hands and arms, the reality of which has been certified to me by other beholders. Dr. Wilkinson tells me that they are cold [103] to the touch, and that it is a somewhat awful matter to see and feel them. I should think so, indeed. Do I believe in these wonders? Of course; for how is it possible to doubt either the solemn word or the sober observation of a learned and sensible man like Dr. Wilkinson. But, again, do I really believe it? Of course not; for I cannot consent to let Heaven and Earth, this world and the next, be beaten up together like the white and yolk of an egg, merely out of respect to Dr. Wilkinson's sanity and integrity. I would not believe my own sight or touch of the spiritual hands; and it would take deeper and higher strains than those of Mr. Harris to convince me. I think I *might* yield to higher poetry or heavenlier wisdom than mortals in the flesh have ever sung or uttered. Meanwhile, this matter of Spiritualism is surely the strangest that ever was heard of; and yet I feel unaccountably little interest in it—a sluggish disgust, and repugnance to meddle with it—insomuch that I hardly feel as if it were worth this page or two in my not very eventful journal. One or two of the ladies, present at Dr. Wilkinson's little party, seemed to be mediums.

I have made several visits to the picture-galleries, since my last date; and I think it fair to re[104]cord (fair towards my own powers of appreciation, I mean) that I begin to appreciate Turner's pictures rather better than at first. Not that I have anything to recant as respects those strange, white-grounded performances, in some of the chambers of Marlboro' House; but some of his happier productions—a large landscape illustrative of Childe Harold, for instance—seem to me to have more magic in them than any other pictures. I admire, too, that misty, morning landscape, in the National Gallery; and no doubt his very monstrosities are such as only he could have produced, and may have an infinite value for those who can appreciate the genius in them.

The shops in London begin to show some tokens of approaching Christmas; especially the toy-shops and the confectioners, the latter ornamenting their windows with a profusion of bonbons and all manner of pigmy figures in sugar; the former exhibiting Christmas trees hung with rich and gaudy fruit. At the butchers' shops, there is a great display of fat carcasses, and abundance of game at the poulterers. We think of going to the Crystal Palace to spend the festival-day and eat our Christmas-dinner; but, do what we may, we shall have [105] no home-feeling nor fireside enjoyment. I am weary, weary of London, and of England, and can judge now how the old Loyalists must have felt, condemned to pine out their lives here when the Revolution had robbed them of their native country. And yet there is still a pleasure in being in this dingy, smoky, midmost haunt of men; and I trudge through Fleet-street, and Ludgate-street, and along Cheapside, with a kind of enjoyment as great as I ever felt in a wood-path at home; and I have come to know these streets as well, I believe, as I ever knew Washington-street, in Boston, or even Essex-street in my stupid old native-town. For Piccadilly, or for Regent-street, though more brilliant promenades, I do not care nearly so much.

24 Gᵗ RUSSELL ST. DECʳ 27ᵗʰ, SUNDAY.

STILL leading an idle life, which, however, may not be quite thrown away; as I see some things, and think many thoughts. The other day, my wife and I went to Westminster Abbey, and through the chapels; and it being as sunny a day as could well be, in London, and in December, we could judge, in some small degree, what must have been the magnificence and splendor of those tombs and monuments, when first erected there. The polished marble pillars, and arches with the recumbent knights or dames beneath; the brilliancy of [106] the colors with which the statues were painted, and of the gilding that brightened their shrines; still reveal themselves in here and there a glimmer or a streak, on such a day as this, though the sunbeam, at its brightest, looks misty and covered with dust. Each one of these many tombs has been very splendid in its day, and most of them have blazed with gold and glowed with color; but as they have [been] placed there gradually, from century to century, I suppose they can never have united in producing a fresh and gorgeous effect. Henry VII's chapel, however, must have once been as magnificent as anything that human hands have made, though probably never so impressive as now, when its pavement covers the bones of a crowd of historical personages, (Addison's among them, so that you step over his remains, at the threshold) and its walls are hung with tattered banners. Yet these chapels—the most recondite portion of the Abbey—do not contain the monuments of the persons whom we remember best, either in history or literature. Rank has been the general passport to admission here; and Kings, Queens, and Dukes, lie beneath the floor in heaps, most of them little remembered and little cared for. I presume I was sufficiently minute in describing my first visit to the Chapels; so shall [107] only mention the stiff figure of a lady of Queen Elizabeth's court, re-clining on the point of her elbow, under a mural arch, through all these dusty years; the headless, wooden figure of Henry V, and on a cross-beam, high above, the saddle on which he rode, and the helmet that bore the brunt of

Agincourt; the old coronation-chair, with the stone of Scone beneath the seat, and the wood-work cut and scratched all over with names and initials. The same is the case with many, or most, of the statues, not to speak of the customary lack of noses; for nothing is so rare as for a great man to come down whether from Roman or medi-aeval times, preserving a whole nose. Emerging from the chapels, we walked through the Abbey-nave and aisles, and agreed in thinking that many of the monuments are ridiculous, and commemorative of people who might as well be forgotten. Nevertheless, these grotesque marbles, and now obscure names, have incrusted the walls by as natural a process as that which causes the growth of moss and ivy on ancient edifices; it is the historical and biographical record of each successive age, written by itself, and all the truer for its mistakes. On the whole, I should be sorry to spare one of all these monuments; and the grandeur of the Abbey is quite capable of swallowing up all these absurd in[108]dividualities, whenever it is desirable to overlook them.

I continue to go to the picture-galleries, but do not think of anything to remark about them, just now; except that I have an idea that the face of Murillo's beautiful Saint John has a certain mischievous intelligence in it. This has impressed me almost from the first. It is a boy's face, very beautiful, and very pleasant too, but with an expression that one might fairly suspect to be roguish, if seen in the face of a living boy. About equestrian statues, as those of various Kings at Charing Cross, and otherwhere about London, and of the Duke of Wellington opposite Apsley House and in front of the Exchange, it strikes me as absurd, the idea of putting a man on horseback on a place where one movement forward or backward, or sideways, of the steed, would infallibly break his own and his rider's neck. The English sculptors generally seem to have been aware of this absurdity, and have endeavored to lessen it by making the horse as quiet as a cabhorse on the stand, instead of rearing rampant, like the bronze Jackson and steed, at Washington. The statue of Wellington, at the Piccadilly corner of the Park, has a stately and imposing effect, seen from far distances, in approaching either through the Green Park, or from the Oxford-street corner of Hyde Park.

[109] 24 G^t RUSSELL-STREET, JAN^y 3^d 1858, SUNDAY.

ON Thursday, I think it was, we had the pleasure of a call from Mr. Coventry Patmore, to whom Dr. Wilkinson had given me a letter of introduction, and on whom I had called twice at the British Museum, without finding him. He has a situation in the Museum Library, and resides at Finchley, about five miles from London. We had read his Betrothal and Angel in the House with unusual pleasure and sympathy, and therefore were very glad to make his personal acquaintance. He is a man of much more youthful aspect than I had expected, looking younger than his real age, which he told us is thirty-four; a slender person, to be an Englishman, though not remarkably so, had he been an American; with an intelligent and sensitive face, pleasant, though not handsome; a man very evidently of refined feelings and cultivated mind, but, it seemed to me, not exhibiting altogether the air of an English born-and-bred gentleman. He is very simple and agreeable in his manners, however; a little shy, or rather, awkward, but yet perfectly frank, and easy to meet on real ground. He said that his wife had purposed to come with him, and had indeed accompanied him to town, but was kept away by the naughty behavior of their boy, a little fellow [110] of six years old, who refused to be of the party. We were very sorry for this, because Mr. Patmore seems to acknowledge her as the real Angel in the House, although he says she herself ignores all connection with the Poem. It is well for her to do so, and for her husband to feel that the character is her real portrait; and both, I suppose, are right. It is a most beautiful and original Poem—a poem for happy married people to read together, and to understand by the light of their own past and present life[485]—but I doubt whether the generality of English people are capable of appreciating it. I told Mr. Patmore that I thought his popularity in America would be greater than at home; and he said that it was already so, and he appeared to appreciate highly his American fame, and also our general gift of quicker and more subtle recognition of genius, than the English public. Mr. Patmore is not a man of flowing conversation—at least, not when he meets three or four strangers, for the first time;—so that the conversation sometimes dragged, during his short call, and was only set afloat again by the skill in starting new topics which I have acquired in the reception of many dry visitors, during my consular experience. But we mutually gratified each other by ex[111]pressing high admiration of one another's works; and Mr. Patmore regretted that in the few days of our further stay here, we should not have time to visit him at his home. It would really give me pleasure. His situation in the Museum occupies him from nine till two °clock, every day, and affords him four weeks of vacation, which he may take at any time of the year, either at once, or in driblets. In my new freedom, I could not help mentally pitying him for being thus confined. I expressed a hope of seeing him in Italy during our stay there; and he seemed to think it possible, as his friend, and our countryman, Thomas Buchanan Read, had asked him to come thither and be his guest. He took his leave, shaking hands with all of us, and making it (as it was pleasant to see) a matter of conscience not to neglect any one; because he saw that we were of his own people, recognizing him as a true poet. He has since sent me the new edition of his poems, with a kind note.

We are now making prepar[a]tions for our departure, which we expect will take place on Tuesday; and yesterday I went to our Minister's (Mr. Dallas) to arrange about the Passport. The very moment I rang at his door (24, Portland Place) it swung open, and the porter [112] ushered me with great courtesy into the waiting-room; not that he knew me, or anything about me, except that I was probably an American citizen. This is the deference which an American servant of the public finds it expedient to show to his sovereigns. Thank Heaven, I am a sovereign again, and no longer a servant; and really it is very queer, how I look down upon our Ambassadors, and dignitaries of all sorts, not excepting the President himself. I doubt whether this is altogether a good influence of our mode of government. I did not see—but, in fact, declined seeing, under pretence of haste—the Minister himself, but only his son Philip, the Secretary of legation, and a Dr. Patten, an American traveller, just from the Continent. He gave a fearful account of the difficulties that beset a traveller landing with much baggage in Italy, and especially at Civita Vecchia, the very port at which we intended to debark. I have now been so long in England that it seems a cold and shivery thing, to go anywhere else.[486]

NOTES

1. Henry Arthur Bright (1830-84) was born in Liverpool, and was educated at Rugby and at Trinity College, Cambridge. Being a Unitarian, he was not eligible for a Cambridge degree until after the removal of discriminatory rules against nonconformists; whereupon, he was awarded the B.A. in 1857 and the M.A. in 1860. After leaving Cambridge, he became a partner with his father in the shipping firm of Gibbs, Bright and Company, which was engaged in commerce with South America and Australia. "Henry Bright belonged," wrote Lord Houghton, "on his father's and mother's side to that aristocracy of commerce and finance which is generated by individual industry, probity, and enterprise in our great seaboard cities. The Brights of Bristol and the Heywoods of Liverpool are as distinctive in their own class and society as the Percys and Wentworths in another order." ("Henry Bright," *Philobiblon Society Miscellanies* XV.)

Not too completely immersed in business to find time for literary pursuits, Bright contributed to leading English periodicals many critical articles on contemporary books. While in America in 1852, he was introduced to Hawthorne by Longfellow as a "reader and admirer of your books." (See *Final Memorials of Henry Wadsworth Longfellow,* ed. Samuel Longfellow, Boston, 1887, p. 391.) The friendly relations between Bright and Hawthorne during the latter's residence in England are best described in the following passage from *Our Old Home* (pp. 56-7):

"Almost the only real incidents [during the days at the Consulate], as I see them "now, were the visits of a young English friend, a scholar and a literary amateur, "between whom and myself there sprung up an affectionate, and, I trust, not transitory "regard. He used to come and sit or stand by my fireside, talking vivaciously and "eloquently with me about literature and life, his own national characteristics and "mine, with such kindly endurance of the many rough republicanisms wherewith I "assailed him, and such frank and amiable assertion of all sorts of English prejudices "and mistakes, that I understood his countrymen infinitely the better for him and "was almost prepared to love the intensest Englishman of them all, for his sake. "It would gratify my cherished remembrance of this dear friend, if I could manage, "without offending him, or letting the public know it, to introduce his name upon "my page. Bright was the illumination of my dusky little apartment, as often as he "made his appearance there!"

And Longfellow declared to Bright in a letter dated July 16, 1864: ". . . I know, having heard it from his [Hawthorne's] own lips, that he liked you more than any man in England" (*Hawthorne and His Wife,* II, 350).

For his part, Bright wrote of Hawthorne in a memorial article in the *Examiner* (June 18, 1864):

"His friendship was not easy to win; for he was reserved and shy and proudly "independent, but when once the ice was broken, then that noble and gentle heart "showed itself as it truly was. . . . The more he was known, the stronger in every "case the love and admiration grew. Though delicately sensitive, no one was so little "apt to take or think offence, and the *amari aliquid,* which sometimes mingles in his "writings, never appeared in him, except, perhaps, when he suspected a personal "patronage, or fancied that his dear country was being looked down upon or despised."

2. Zachary Taylor, under whose administration Hawthorne had lost his position in the Salem Custom House in 1849, and whom he had satirized as "Old Blood-and-Thunder" in "The Great Stone Face" (1850).

3. Compare *Our Old Home*, pp. 20-22.

4. For a lively and somewhat romantic account of Mrs. Blodgett and her paradisiacal boarding-house see Julian Hawthorne, *Hawthorne and His Circle*, pp. 173-185.

5. Thomas Leonidas Crittenden (1819-93) of Kentucky was Hawthorne's predecessor at the Liverpool consulate.

6. Compare *Our Old Home*, pp. 24-5.

7. Sara Jane Clarke (1823-1904) wrote under the pseudonym, "Grace Greenwood." She was married to Leander K. Lippincott of Philadelphia in October, 1853.

Even less flattering than the present sketch were Hawthorne's remarks in letters to friends. Of Miss Greenwood's book of travels, *Haps and Mishaps of a Tour in Europe*, he said to Fields (letter dated January 30, 1854; original in the Huntington Library) : "miserable stuff—nothing genuine in the volume—I don't care a button for it." Concerning her magazine for children and its editor, he wrote to Ticknor (letter dated January 6, 1854) : "Her 'Little Pilgrim' is a humbug, and she herself is—but there is no need of telling you. I wish her well. . . . But ink-stained women are, without a single exception, detestable."

8. Compare *Our Old Home*, p. 257; and *Doctor Grimshawe's Secret*, p. 237.

9. Compare *Our Old Home*, pp. 371 ff. After "hanged," about one-fourth of a page is cut out.

10. After "also," about one-fourth of a page is cut out.

11. Compare *Our Old Home*, pp. 327 ff.

12. On August 24, Hawthorne wrote to Mrs. Wilson Auld, in New Orleans, a sympathetic and tactful letter of condolence:

"His disease was erysipelas, combined with some internal complaint. He had been "ill nearly three weeks, during the latter part of which time, he was in a state of partial "insensibility, and appeared to suffer very little. Every attention was paid to his "comfort; and you may rest assured that he received the kindest treatment from "those near him in his last moments. . . . He was buried yesterday, in the Cemetery "of Saint James in this city. [The original is in the possession of the Rev. Mr. U. S. "Milburn.]"

13. Euphrasia Fanny Haworth, a friend of Robert Browning's, was the author of *St. Sylvester's Day and Other Poems* (London, 1847) and *Stories for Idle Afternoons* (London, 1875). Browning addressed her in "Sordello" (*Complete Poems*, Cambridge ed., p. 101) as "My English Eyebright," and explained the appellation in a letter to Miss Haworth, in 1838, as follows: "I called you, 'Eyebright'—meaning a simple and sad sort of translation of 'Euphrasia' into my own language" (*Letters of Robert Browning*, ed. Thurman L. Hood, New Haven, 1933, p. 2). In a letter to F. J. Furnivall written in 1881, Browning referred to Miss Haworth as "an early sympathizer still (happily) alive" (*ibid.*, pp. 206-7).

Hawthorne's visitor was apparently infatuated with her host, for she wrote to Miss Lynch a short time after the visit, "I admire Mr. Hawthorne, as a man and as an author, more than any other human being" (Rose Hawthorne Lathrop, *Memories of Hawthorne*, Boston and New York, 1897, p. 254).

14. Anne Charlotte Lynch (1815-91), though a writer of verse (*Poems*, 1849) in which the chivalrous Poe found "evidence of at least unusual talent" (*The Literati*, Virginia ed., XV, 116), is better known as a hostess who presided over "the first important salon in the history of American letters" (*D.A.B.*). Her house in New York, both before and after her marriage to Professor Vincenzo Botta in 1855, attracted many prominent literary people. Though it seems unlikely that Hawthorne was ever a guest, references in Mrs. Hawthorne's letters (*Memories of Hawthorne*, pp. 223, 236) indicate that Miss Lynch called on the Hawthornes in Liverpool in July, 1853. And in her *Hand-Book of Universal Literature* (Boston, 1863, p. 537) she wrote a longer and more discriminating treatment of Hawthorne's productions

than of those of any other American author.

15. *Paradise Lost,* XII, 644.

16. After "legs," one line is inked out.

17. After "or," one-third of a line is inked out.

18. Compare *Our Old Home,* pp. 329 ff.

19. After "carts," two lines are inked out.

20. Compare *Our Old Home,* pp. 329 ff.

21. The parenthetical matter is inserted at the top of page [48].

22. Compare *Our Old Home,* p. 74; *Septimius Felton,* p. 324; and *Doctor Grimshawe's Secret,* pp. 224-5.

23. The phrase is, of course, a commonplace. If Hawthorne had in mind a particular literary source, the allusion was probably to Longfellow's poem "The Light of Stars" (in *Voices of the Night,* 1839), where the phrase occurs twice (ll. 8, 24).

24. Compare *Our Old Home,* p. 255.

25. William Huskisson (1770-1830) was a member of Parliament for Liverpool and a prominent advocate of liberal reforms.

26. Compare *Our Old Home,* pp. 66-8, 390-1.

27. W. D. Ticknor, Hawthorne's publisher.

28. William Nicol Burns (1791-1872) and James G. Burns (1794-1865).

29. "The Rigs o'Barley" beginning "It was upon a Lammas night."

30. "O Luve will venture in."

31. See J. G. Lockhart, *Memoirs of the Life of Sir Walter Scott, Bart.,* Edinburgh, 1838, VII, 307-8. The quotation occurs in the poem "Lines Written on Tweedside," which Scott wrote to commemorate the visit of James Glencairn Burns in 1831.

32. Hawthorne wrote to Ticknor, October 8: "I dined with two of the sons of Burns last Saturday, and got into great favor with them—partly by the affection which I showed for the whisky-bottle."

33. The following paragraph is an accurate digest of George Ormerod, *The History of the County Palatine and City of Chester . . . ,* London, 1819, I, 35-6. "They are delightful reading," observes Middleton, the American, in *The Ancestral Footstep* (p. 470), "these old county-histories, with their great folio volumes and their minute account of the affairs of families and the genealogies, and descents of estates, bestowing as much blessed space on a few hundred acres as other historians give to a principality. I fear that in my own country we shall never have anything of this kind. Our space is so vast that we shall never come to know and love it, inch by inch, as the English antiquarians do the tracts of country with which they deal. . . . I have found a pleasure that I had no conception of before, in reading some of the English local histories." Compare also *Doctor Grimshawe's Secret,* pp. 184-5.

34. Translating "magistratum omnium leccatorum et meretricum totius Cestershiriae."

35. See Ormerod, *op. cit.,* p. 97.

36. Compare *Our Old Home,* p. 343.

37. Daniel Dewey Barnard (1796-1861), graduate of Williams College, member of Congress, 1839-45, and minister to Prussia, 1850-3, under President Fillmore. He delivered the Phi Beta Kappa oration at Yale College in 1846.

38. Daniel E. Sickles was Secretary of Legation at London, 1853-4. In December, 1854, he resigned and returned to the United States (see *Works of James Buchanan,* ed. John Bassett Moore, Philadelphia, 1909, IX, 284).

39. Stephen A. Douglas (1813-1861) had been the candidate of "Young America" against "Old Fogyism" in the contest for the Democratic presidential nomination in 1852. At this time he was returning from travels in Russia and the Near East.

40. In April, 1853.

41. Hawthorne endorsed a draft for £50 by William Lilley, which proved to be noncollectable; Lilley refunded the amount, though tardily, after Hawthorne had

threatened to inform the State Department (see letters to Ticknor, December 8, 1853; February 3, and June 7, 1854). "I don't know that he is worse than many other of our foreign appointments," Hawthorne wrote to Ticknor, "who are (but don't whisper it) a set of swindlers generally. They almost always get short of money here, and never can raise a shilling without my endorsement; for the Liverpool merchants seem to know their character of old."

42. William Learned Marcy (1786-1857) was Secretary of War, 1845-9, and Secretary of State, 1853-7.

43. Compare *Our Old Home*, pp. 334-5.

44. See Ormerod, *op. cit.*, I, 535.

45. See *Memoirs, Journal, and Correspondence of Thomas Moore*, ed. Lord John Russell, London, 1853, II, 183. In Hawthorne's note, "Japan" and "Guernsey" are, as indicated, incorrectly placed; the names appear in their correct positions in Moore's diary.

46. Compare *Septimius Felton*, p. 284.

47. See Ormerod, *op. cit.*, II, 47.

48. See *ibid.*, pp. 100-1.

49. See *ibid.*, p. 171.

50. See *ibid.*, pp. 215-6. Sir Harry Wildair is the principal character in *The Constant Couple* (1699) and *Sir Harry Wildair* (1701).

51. See *ibid.*, p. 239.

52. See *ibid.*, p. 332.

53. See *ibid.*, p. 360.

54. A neighbor in Rock Park. See *Hawthorne and His Circle*, pp. 130-1.

55. Compare *Our Old Home*, p. 339.

56. See Ormerod, *op. cit.*, II, 413.

57. See *ibid.*, p. 419.

58. See *ibid.*, III, 39.

59. Hawthorne here finds the theme of "The Lily's Quest" (1839) confirmed by fact. Compare particularly *Twice-Told Tales*, p. 503.

60. See Ormerod, *op. cit.*, III, 282. The explanation is Hawthorne's.

61. See *ibid.*, pp. 309, 312.

62. Compare *Our Old Home*, p. 330.

63. G. P. R. James, *Arabella Stuart*, 1853.

64. See Ormerod, *op. cit.*, III, 344.

65. Compare *Our Old Home*, pp. 341-2.

66. Compare *Our Old Home*, pp. 35-6.

67. See *Historic Society of Lancashire and Cheshire: Proceedings and Papers*, Session IV, Liverpool, 1852, p. 117.

68. In a letter to his sister, dated February 22, 1854, William Allingham (1824-89) recorded the following impressions of Hawthorne:

"I called on him at his Consul's office, a dirty little busy place on the line of docks, "and was very kindly received. He happened to have heard my name. He is about "forty-six years old, middle sized, hair dark, forehead bald, features elegant though "American, cheeks shaved, eyes dark. He is very bashful in manner, and speaks little "and in a low tone. He has not yet had time to visit London, but intends to do so "some time in Spring, when I hope to see more of him. He looked oddly out of "place in Liverpool. [*William Allingham, A Diary*, ed. H. Allingham and D. Rad-"ford, London, 1907, pp. 70-1]."

Hawthorne transmitted to Fields review-copies of Allingham's *Poems* (London, 1850) and urged Fields (letter of April 13, 1854; original in the Huntington Library) to "try to bring him into notice." Again, in 1855, Hawthorne sent copies of *Day and Night Songs* (1854) to Ticknor, with the following comment:

"There is great merit in some of the pieces. 'Cross-Examination,' for instance, is

"wonderfully pithy. I can't say I have read them all, for I dislike poetry. But I know "the author, and should be glad to have him get an American reputation. [Letter of "August 17, 1855.]"
Hawthorne's publishers brought out an edition of Allingham's poems in 1861.

Two letters by Hawthorne to Allingham are included in *Letters to William Allingham*, ed. H. Allingham and E. Baumer Williams, London, 1911, pp. 197-8. An excerpt from a letter by Allingham to Hawthorne is quoted in *Hawthorne and His Wife*, II, 67.

69. Edward Everett (1794-1865) was Minister to the Court of St. James's, 1841-5.

70. John Hamilton Thom (1808-94) was the minister at Renshaw Street Chapel, 1831-54 and 1857-66.

71. William Roscoe (1753-1831), the historian, whose works include *The Life of Lorenzo de' Medici* and *The Life and Pontificate of Leo the Tenth*. Washington Irving wrote of Roscoe in *The Sketch Book*:
". . . the man of letters who speaks of Liverpool, speaks of it as the residence of "Roscoe. The intelligent traveller who visits it inquires where Roscoe is to be "seen. He is the literary landmark of the place, indicating its existence to the distant "scholar. He is, like Pompey's Column at Alexandria, towering alone in classic "dignity."

72. Joseph Blanco White (1775-1841), author of works on theology.

73. William Enfield (1741-97), famous for his anthology, *The Speaker, or Miscellaneous Pieces, Selected from the Best English Writers, and Disposed under Proper Heads, with a View to Facilitate the Improvement of Youth in Reading and Speaking*, London, 1774.

74. Compare *Our Old Home*, p. 116.

75. Compare *Psalms*, XVI, 6.

76. John Bramley-Moore (1800-86), chairman of the Liverpool docks, Mayor of Liverpool (1848), and Member of Parliament (1854-9, 1862-5).

77. Samuel Warren (1807-77) is remembered for his *Passages from the Diary of a Late Physician* (1838), which influenced Poe (see Margaret Alterton, *Origins of Poe's Critical Theory*, Iowa City, 1925, pp. 23 ff), and his popular novel, *Ten Thousand a Year* (1839).

78. The members of a legal firm satirized in *Ten Thousand a Year*.

79. Probably Hugh McNeile (1795-1879), Canon of Chester, 1845-68.

80. Charles Wilkins (1802-57), a Methodist preacher and strolling player, among other things, in his youth, became a prominent barrister and, in 1845, sergeant-at-law. Hawthorne records an extraordinarily favorable impression of Wilkins in *Our Old Home*, pp. 378-9.

81. The words "out . . . said" are added at the bottom of p. [154] in Mrs. Hawthorne's handwriting.

82. One leaf, pp. [155, 156], is cut out. The words in brackets are supplied from *Passages from the English Note-Books*, I, 490.

83. Compare *Doctor Grimshawe's Secret*, p. 218.

84. The words "and cigar" are inked out.

85. The words "and . . . ale" are inked out.

86. A picture by William Hogarth.

87. *Historic Society of Lancashire and Cheshire, Proceedings and Papers*, Session I, Liverpool, 1849, pp. 112-116.

88. *Ibid.*, p. 104.

89. Compare *Doctor Grimshawe's Secret*, pp. 342-3.

90. Added later.

91. John Louis O'Sullivan (1813-95), editor of *The United States Magazine and Democratic Review* (1837-46), Minister to Portugal (1854-8), and originator of the phrase "manifest destiny" (see Julius W. Pratt, "John L. O'Sullivan and Manifest

Destiny," *New York History,* XIV [July, 1933], 213-34), was for many years an intimate friend of Hawthorne's. At the time of the present visit, the O'Sullivans were on their way to Portugal.

92. *Isaiah,* IX, 5.

93. John Burke and John Bernard Burke, *A Genealogical and Heraldric History of the Extinct and Dormant Baronetcies of England, Ireland, and Scotland,* London, 1844, p. 182.

94. "Barry Cornwall" was the pseudonym of Bryan Waller Procter (1787-1874). Before the meeting here described, Procter and Hawthorne had exchanged copies of their works (see letter by Procter to Hawthorne dated November 6, 1851, *Hawthorne and His Wife,* I, 440-1; and letter by Hawthorne to Procter, dated June 17, 1852, C[oventry] P[atmore], *Bryan Waller Procter, An Autobiographical Fragment and Biographical Notes,* Boston, 1877, pp. 296-8); and in the Preface to his *Essays and Tales in Prose* (Boston, 1853) Procter had referred to Hawthorne in complimentary fashion. After seeing Hawthorne in Liverpool, Procter wrote to Fields (*Yesterdays With Authors,* p. 411): "Need I say that I like him *very* much? He is very sensible, very genial,—a little shy, I think (for an American!)—and altogether extremely agreeable." In 1855 (see below, p. *254*) Procter gave Hawthorne a letter of introduction to Leigh Hunt; and in 1864, after Hawthorne's death, he wrote to Fields (*Yesterdays With Authors,* p. 416): "He was about your best prose writer, I think. . . ."

95. Hen Pearce, the "Bristol game-chicken" (see sketch of James Belcher in *D.N.B.*). "Whether Procter made this entry into pugilism in order to overcome the disadvantages of a small and rather puny body or because it was the fashion of the day, we cannot be certain" (R. W. Armour, *Barry Cornwall,* Boston, 1935, p. 45).

96. Carlyle described Cornwall as "a decidedly rather pretty little fellow, bodily and spiritually" (*Reminiscences by Thomas Carlyle,* ed. C. E. Norton, London, 1887, II, 133).

97. John Manning, the brother of Hawthorne's mother.

98. "Though the Niagara cataract in Canada, so celebrated by travellers, is of very great breadth, and no less than 162 feet fall, yet, so far as I can judge of it from pictures, it is not by any means so picturesque as the one under notice" (Edward Parry, *The Cambrian Mirror; or, the Tourist's Companion Through North Wales,* London, 1851, p. 151). Hawthorne probably visited Niagara in 1833 or 1834 (see "My Visit to Niagara" [1835], *Sketches*).

99. Sir Thomas Joshua Platt (1790?-1862), baron of the court of exchequer, 1845-56. "Though not deeply read, he proved a sensible judge, while his blunt courtesy and amiability made him popular with the bar" (*D.N.B.*).

100. Compare *Septimius Felton,* p. 344.

101. By Maria Susanna Cummins (1827-66), an American writer. Forty thousand copies were issued within eight weeks, and seventy thousand within a year, following publication in Boston in 1854 (see S. Austin Allibone, *Dictionary of Authors,* Philadelphia, 1859). In a letter to Ticknor, dated January 19, 1855, Hawthorne commented on the popularity of *The Lamplighter* as follows: "America is now wholly given over to a d—d mob of scribbling women, and I should have no chance of success while the public taste is occupied with their trash—and should be ashamed of myself if I did succeed. What is the mystery of these innumerable editions of the Lamplighter, and other books neither better nor worse?—worse they could not be, and better they need not be, when they sell by the 100,000." For a brief, recent treatment of *The Lamplighter* and its author, see Fred Lewis Pattee, *The Feminine Fifties,* New York, 1940, pp. 110-115.

102. George Partridge Bradford (1807-90), classical scholar and Brook Farmer. For amusing additional commentary on his conscientiousness and scholarship, see Van Wyck Brooks, *The Flowering of New England,* New York, 1936, pp. 243, 247.

Hawthorne appears to have had Bradford in mind in his characterization of Colcord in *Doctor Grimshawe's Secret* (see especially pp. 64-9, 239-43).

103. *Ecclesiastes*, XII, 5.

104. Harriet Martineau (1802-1876) was the author, among numerous works, of *Illustrations of Political Economy* (1834), *Society in America* (1837), and a translation of Comte's *Philosophie Positive* (1853). Her *Autobiographical Memoir,* published posthumously, makes no mention of Hawthorne.

105. "Sassenach," according to the *N.E.D.,* is the name given by the Gaelic inhabitants of Great Britain to their "Saxon" or English neighbors. "Dim" is a negative.

106. *The Lay of the Last Minstrel,* Canto Second, ll. 3-4:
"For the gay beams of lightsome day
"Gild, but to flout, the ruins grey."

107. Hawthorne wrote to his wife at Rhyl on September 12: "We arrived safe at Rock Ferry at about ten. Emily had gone to bed, but came down in her nightclothes—the queerest figure I ever saw" (*Love Letters of Nathaniel Hawthorne,* Chicago, 1907). Emily was presumably a servant. The detail was too intimate for inclusion in Mrs. Hawthorne's edition of the Notebooks.

108. Richard Monckton Milnes, first Baron Houghton (1809-85), liberal politician, critic, verse-writer, and "literary ringmaster of London," was educated at Trinity College, Cambridge, where he was on terms of intimate friendship with Tennyson, Hallam, and Thackeray. He was an active supporter of various causes: the Anglo-Catholic revival, Miss Nightingale's Fund, the reform of the franchise. He contributed an essay on Emerson to the *Westminster Review* (XXXIII [March, 1840] 345-72) and edited, with a "Life," the poetry of Keats (1848). In 1851 he married the Hon. Annabel Crewe, daughter of the second Baron Crewe; in 1863, he was created Baron Houghton.
The relations between Hawthorne and Milnes were most cordial: they met on several occasions; they wrote letters. Of particular interest is Hawthorne's response to Milnes's request for "half a dozen good American books . . . with American characteristics, and not generally known in England" (letter to Ticknor, September 30, 1854). Hawthorne named the following works, with brief critical remarks on each, in a letter to Milnes, dated November 13, 1854 (original in the possession of the Earl of Crewe): Sylvester Judd's *Margaret* (1845), L. W. Mansfield's *Up Country Letters* (1852), Julia Ward Howe's *Passion Flowers* (1854), Anna Cora Mowatt's *Autobiography of An Actress* (1854), Thoreau's *Week* (1849) and *Walden* (1854), Lowell's *Biglow Papers* (1848) and *Fable for Critics* (1848). Later, Milnes inquired particularly "about an American book which has fallen into my hands. It is called 'Leaves of Grass,' and the author calls himself Walt Whitman. Do you know anything about him" (*Memories of Hawthorne,* p. 311)? There is no record of reply (no evidence, indeed, that Hawthorne ever read Whitman).
Lord Houghton, while visiting Emerson in October, 1875, wrote to Henry Bright: "I like to write to you from here, and fresh from a walk to Hawthorne's 'Old Manse' and grave" (T. Wemyss Reid, *The Life, Letters, and Friendships of Richard Monckton Milnes,* London, 1890, II, 318). Genuine admiration of Hawthorne's writings, if not conspicuous poetic felicity, is evidenced in the following lines from "English Critics and Present American Literature" (*Some Writings and Speeches of Richard Monckton Milnes,* London, 1888, p. 135):
". . . we knew our common history better
"In the lurid light of 'The Scarlet Letter.'
"And fully enjoyed the 'transformation'
"Of Beast into Man by Imagination."

109. Compare "Chiefly About War Matters," *Sketches,* p. 319. No such information is given concerning the "sacred ship" in R. G. Marsden, "The 'Mayflower'," *English Historical Review,* XIX (October, 1904), 669-80.

110. After "imprisoned," about two-thirds of a line is inked out.

111. Compare *Our Old Home,* pp. 66-8, 390-1; and *The Ancestral Footstep,* pp. 458, 503-5.

112. For an interesting account of this ship and its builder, see the article on Donald McKay in the *D.A.B.* by Samuel Eliot Morison.

113. The words "being . . . champagne" are inked out.

114. For Hawthorne's speech on this occasion, see Randall Stewart, "Hawthorne's Speeches at Civic Banquets," *American Literature,* VII (January, 1936), 416.

115. Compare *Our Old Home,* p. 385.

116. William Scoresby (1789-1857) made many voyages into arctic waters and published scientific works on geography, meteorology, and magnetism. He was ordained in 1825 to the curacy of Bessingby. He visited the United States in 1844, and again in 1847-8. See R. E. Scoresby-Jackson, *Life of William Scoresby,* London, 1861.

117. Compare *Our Old Home,* pp. 381-2; *Doctor Grimshawe's Secret,* p. 257.

118. After "°clock," eight lines are inked out.

119. The London *Times,* October 6, 1854, corrected the announcement of the fall of Sebastopol which had been published in the issue of October 2.

120. Hawthorne doubtless interpreted the following passages in editorials in the London *Times* as "menaces against America":
"Allied to France by the same efforts and the same triumphs, the incidents of this "war have already immeasurably increased the mutual confidence and respect of two "nations which have just shown that they are the most powerful States in the world "[October 4, 1854]."

"The lessons learned at Bomarsund and Sebastopol will not be forgotten, for they "have introduced a new era in warfare by throwing doubt on places before deemed "impregnable, and showing that the promptitude of an attack supported by the engines "of modern warfare may supersede the more protracted operations of former sieges. "The rapid triumphs which are wonderful now would have been impossible before, "and they may serve to remind States with an ill-defended coast that all their "military forces cannot save them from hostilities directed against them by a mari- "time Power [October 5, 1854]."

121. *Proverbs,* XIV, 10.

122. "1630," the correct date, is written above "1635."

123. Compare *The Ancestral Footstep,* pp. 447, 493, 510; *Doctor Grimshawe's Secret,* pp. 273, 278.

124. Robert G. Scott, a newspaper editor in Richmond, Virginia, addressed a public letter to the candidates for the Democratic nomination, asking if they would uphold the Compromise of 1850, particularly the provision for the return of fugitive slaves. The New York *Tribune* for May 26, 1852, printed Scott's letter and the replies of Cass, Douglas, and other candidates. After a strategic delay, Pierce's reply was dispatched to a friend at the Baltimore convention (see Roy F. Nichols, *Franklin Pierce,* Philadelphia, 1931, pp. 201-2). Pierce was nominated on June 5; and on June 7, the *Tribune* commented as follows:
"Scott of Virginia has proved a deadly marksman. . . . At the first crack of his "rifle, the thirteen candidates for President who answered affirmatively his demand "for a pledge to veto any serious modification of the Fugitive Slave Law have "dropped dead at his feet. . . . The Presidential nomination has fallen on one . . . "from whom he received no answer—at least, none in season to publish prior to the "nomination."

125. The *Arctic,* Captain James C. Luce, the finest of the Collins steamers, was sunk off Newfoundland on September 27, 1854, by collision with the French screw-steamer *Vesta.* Almost all on board (233 passengers and 150 crew), including Luce's son, were drowned. Luce himself and a few others were rescued. The following

portion of Luce's testimony (printed in the New York *Tribune,* October 18) shows that Hawthorne knew his man: "Mr. Baalham asked me if he should put my little boy in the boat. I said 'No; I should not allow it until other people were provided for; that he must take his chance with me.'"

126. Walter Murray Gibson (1823-88) published an account of his adventures in *The Prison of Weltevreden and a Glance at the East Indian Archipelago* (New York, 1855). Hawthorne, who was fascinated by the raconteur and his stories, included Gibson in the gallery of portraits in *Our Old Home,* pp. 36-9. For an interesting biographical sketch, see *D.A.B.*

127. For Hawthorne's interest in the question of instinctive parental affection, compare *The American Notebooks,* p. 275.

128. August Belmont (1816-90) was Minister to the Netherlands, 1853-7.

129. See Sir John Barrow, *The Mutiny and Piratical Seizure of H.M.S. Bounty* (1831).

130. *Othello,* I, iii, 145.

131. Compare *Our Old Home,* p. 343.

132. The entire paragraph is inked out.

133. William Henry Channing (1810-1884), though born and buried in Boston, spent most of his life after 1854 in England. For three years (1854-7), he was minister of the Renshaw Street Chapel (Unitarian), Liverpool.

134. Matthew Calbraith Perry (1794-1858) signed the famous treaty of commerce with Japan, March 31, 1854. His *Narrative of the Expedition of an American Squadron to the China Seas and Japan* . . . was "compiled from the original notes and journals of Commodore Perry and his officers . . . by Francis L. Hawks," and was published in Washington in 1856.

135. Apparently an error, for Perry's biographer (William Elliot Griffis, *Matthew Calbraith Perry,* Boston, 1890, pp. 377-8) asserts that Perry never wore a wig, that "his handsome and luxuriant hair grew well forward on his forehead." Griffis's inference, however, that Hawthorne, "so thoroughly at home in spiritland . . . , was not expert in judging visible things," is not at all justified. Errors like the present one are indeed rare, and the notebooks demonstrate again and again the extraordinary accuracy of Hawthorne's observation.

136. James Buchanan (1791-1868) was Ambassador to Great Britain, 1853-6, and President of the United States, 1857-61. Three letters from Hawthorne to Buchanan on consular matters are included in *The Works of James Buchanan,* ed. John Bassett Moore, Philadelphia, 1909, IX, pp. 35-6, 150, 388.

137. William Brown (1784-1864) was born in Ireland. In 1800 he went with his parents to Baltimore, where his father established the mercantile firm of Alexander Brown and Sons. In 1809 William Brown took charge of a branch of the firm in Liverpool. He was a member of Parliament, 1846-59. Brown is best known for his gift of the Free Public Library at Liverpool, which was built at a cost of £40,000 and was opened in 1860. He was created baronet in 1863.

138. Harriet Lane, an orphan whose upbringing had been at the charge of her bachelor uncle, acted as charming hostess at the American embassy in London (1854-5) and in the White House (1857-61). After her marriage in 1866 to Henry E. Johnston, she resided at "Wheatland," Buchanan's country place, near Lancaster, Pennsylvania. Selections from her letters are included in George Ticknor Curtis, *Life of James Buchanan,* New York, 1883, 2 vols.

139. Compare C. Severn, *Diary of John Ward,* 1839, p. 183: "Shakespear, Drayton, and Ben Jhonson, had a merry meeting, and itt seems drank too hard, for Shakespear died of a feavour there contracted;" and E. K. Chambers, *William Shakespeare, A Study of Facts and Problems,* London, 1930, I, 89: "There is no reason to reject this report."

140. Compare *Ecclesiastes,* VII, 2.

141. For an account, differing in some details from that given here, of the quarrel between Jackson and the Bentons, which occurred in Nashville, September 4, 1813, see J. S. Bassett, *Life of Andrew Jackson,* New York, 1911, I, 67-70.

142. Frederick Barker (1808-82), curate of St. Mary's, Edgehill, Liverpool, 1835-54, was consecrated Bishop of Sydney, New South Wales, November 30, 1854.

143. Compare *Our Old Home,* p. 362:
"Is, or is not, the system wrong that gives one married pair so immense a superfluity "of luxurious home, and shuts a million others from any home whatever? One day "or another, safe as they deem themselves, and safe as the hereditary temper of "the people really tends to make them, the gentlemen of England will be compelled "to face this question."

144. Andrew Jackson (according to Bassett, *op. cit.,* I, 4-7) was born March 15, 1767, in South Carolina, whither his father, probably of the Irish tenant class, had migrated from Ireland in 1765.
Two letters by Washington Jackson to Andrew Jackson, pertaining to various business transactions, are included in *The Correspondence of Andrew Jackson,* ed. J. S. Bassett, Washington, 1926, I, 146, 196. Washington Jackson informed his correspondent in a letter dated Natchez, December 20, 1809: "I have at length made sale of your Wench and Child."
Hawthorne evinced, on more than one occasion, an interest in, and an admiration for, Andrew Jackson.

145. Compare *Our Old Home,* p. 339.

146. For an account of the tax on windows in houses, which was operative in England from 1696 until 1851, see Stephen Dowell, *A History of Taxation and Taxes in England,* London, 1888, III, 168-77.

147. "A gentleman whom I met on my journey informed me that at the time of his visit to the whirlpool, the bodies of two English deserters, who had been drowned in attempting to swim across the river, were spinning round the cone of water, and had been so for three weeks previously" (William Chambers, *Things As They Are in America,* London, 1857 [second ed.], p. 105 [first ed., 1854]). Hawthorne's imaginative embellishment of his source is characteristic.

148. It was on this occasion that Hawthorne told the story which, upon Mrs. Heywood's request, he later wrote down as "The Ghost of Doctor Harris." The circumstances which evoked Hawthorne's oral narration are described in "The Ghost of Doctor Harris" as follows:
"We were sitting, I remember, late in the evening, in your drawing-room, where "the lights of the chandelier were so muffled as to produce a delicious obscurity "through which the fire diffused a dim red glow. In this rich twilight the feelings "of the party had been properly attuned by some tales of English superstition, and "the lady of Smithells Hall had just been describing that Bloody Footstep which "marks the threshold of her old mansion, when your Yankee guest (zealous for the "honor of his country, and desirous of proving that his dead compatriots have the "same ghostly privileges as other dead people, if they think it worth while to use "them) began a story of something wonderful that long ago happened to himself . . . "[*The Nineteenth Century,* XLVII, (January, 1900), 88]."
The manuscript of the story was sent to Mrs. Heywood with the signature, "Nathaniel Hawthorne, Liverpool, August 17, 1856," and was first published *ibid.,* pp. 88-93.
For references to the "bloody footstep" in Hawthorne's writings, see *Doctor Grimshawe's Secret,* pp. 29, 69-71, 96, 103, 186, 299, 301; *The Ancestral Footstep,* pp. 472, 510; *Septimius Felton,* pp. 326-34. Indeed, the image so impressed itself upon his mind that it became a leading motif in these stories.

149. Edward Baines, *The History of the County Palatine and Duchy of Lancaster,* London, 1868 (first ed. 1836), I, 543:
"In a passage near the door of the dining-room [in Smithell's Hall] is a natural

"cavity in a flag, somewhat resembling the print of a man's foot; and this appearance "has occasioned a tradition, that the martyr George Marsh . . . , when brought "before Mr. Barton for examination, in 1555, stamped upon the place where he "stood, in confirmation of the truth of his opinions, and that a miraculous impression "was made upon the stone with his peaked shoe, as a perpetual memorial of the "injustice of his enemies."

150. The trial of the Hopwood Will Case, which extended from April 3 to April 11, 1855, and which was reported in detail in the London *Times,* had to do with the validity of the last will of Robert Gregge Hopwood, by which he had disinherited his eldest son and had given the estate to his grandson. The decision rendered upheld the claim of the eldest son on the ground that the parent was of unsound mind at the time of the making of the will. The gossipy evidence, which aired the domestic affairs of the Hopwoods and connected families (Lady Sefton was a Hopwood), was apparently relished by Mrs. Hawthorne.

151. Hawthorne wrote to Ticknor, January 19, 1855: "I had rather hold this office two years longer; for I have not seen half enough of England, and there is the germ of a new Romance in my mind, which will be all the better for ripening slowly."

152. Austen Henry Layard (1817-94), archaeologist, published the results of his excavations in Mesopotamia in *Nineveh and Babylon* (1853). In 1854, he witnessed the battle of the Alma in the Black Sea; and in 1855, he testified concerning the state of the British army at Sebastopol before a Parliamentary Committee of Inquiry. He was knighted in 1878.

153. For Hawthorne's speech on this occasion, see Randall Stewart, "Hawthorne's Speeches at Civic Banquets," *American Literature,* VII (January, 1936) 417.

154. From Chaucer's description of the Shipman ("Prologue" to *The Canterbury Tales,* l. 406). The references to Chaucer in Hawthorne's writings are very few.

155. The word "Whoremaster" (?) is inked out.

156. Compare *Our Old Home,* pp. 40-6.

157. Several details taken from the foregoing description of the Tranmere wake were used in the account of Greenwich Fair in *Our Old Home,* pp. 279, 281.

158. Compare *David Copperfield* (1849), Chapter I: "I was born with a caul, which was advertised for sale in the newspaper, at the low price of fifteen guineas."

159. Compare *Our Old Home,* pp. 335-6.

160. Compare *Old Old Home,* pp. 30-3.

161. One leaf, pp. [113, 114], is torn out. The words in brackets are supplied from *Passages from the English Note-Books,* I, 577-8.

162. Compare *Doctor Grimshawe's Secret,* pp. 24, 217.

163. See *1 Henry IV,* V, iv, 151.

164. Hawthorne possibly remembered the dedication of George Farquhar's *The Recruiting Officer* (1706) : "To All Friends Round the Wrekin."

165. Compare *Doctor Grimshawe's Secret,* p. 170.

166. The phrase "leafy month of June" is taken from Coleridge's *Ancient Mariner,* l. 370.

167. Compare *Our Old Home,* p. 114.

168. Compare *Our Old Home,* pp. 118-9.

169. Compare *Our Old Home,* p. 69.

170. Compare *Our Old Home,* pp. 70-1.

171. Compare *Our Old Home,* pp. 71-3.

172. Compare *Our Old Home,* p. 75.

173. Compare *Our Old Home,* p. 113.

174. Compare *Our Old Home,* pp. 76-80; *Doctor Grimshawe's Secret,* pp. 218-20; *Septimius Felton,* pp. 257-8.

175. Compare *Our Old Home,* pp. 85, 88-90, 107-8.

176. "mullion" is crossed out.

177. Compare *Our Old Home,* pp. 119-20, 199.

178. Compare *Our Old Home,* pp. 120, 247.

179. Compare *Our Old Home,* pp. 120-4.

180. Compare *Our Old Home,* pp. 125-9.

181. See II, i, 21-66.

182. Compare *Our Old Home,* pp. 143-7.

183. Compare *Our Old Home,* pp. 367-9.

184. Mrs. Elizabeth Cartwright Penrose (1780-1837) wrote, under the pseudonym of "Mrs. Markham," *A History of England* (1823), which for nearly forty years was widely read in schools and families.

185. One leaf, pp. [167, 168], is cut out. Very probably, a passage describing a picture of Lady Godiva (compare *Our Old Home,* pp. 368-9) accounts for the excision. The words "in the pay and service of the city" are inserted at the bottom of p. [166] in Mrs. Hawthorne's handwriting. The bracketed words which follow are supplied from *Passages from the English Note-Books,* I, 586-7.

186. The reference is to Bablake Hospital. The probable source of Hawthorne's historical information, in this instance, was *The New Coventry Guide,* Coventry, 1849.

187. Compare *Our Old Home,* pp. 91-9; *The Ancestral Footstep,* pp. 463-4; *Doctor Grimshawe's Secret,* pp. 163, 189-94, 203.

188. Hawthorne may have remembered Johnson's tribute to Walmsley in his *Lives of the English Poets* (ed. G. B. Hill, Oxford, 1905, II, 20-1).

189. Referred to in *Our Old Home* (p. 156) as "a literary acquaintance of my boyhood."

190. Hawthorne's recollection of early reading was probably, in this instance, refreshed and perhaps supplemented by the following passage in *A Guide to the City of Lichfield* (Lichfield, 1853, p. 32):
"There are few places more interesting to a lover of literature than the walk in "front of the Palace, called the *Dean's Walk.* He stands in the avenue described by "Farquhar as leading to the house of Lady Bountiful, and in which Aimwell pretends "to faint,—at the gates of the hospitable Gilbert Walmsley, the patron of merit, "where Garrick may be supposed to have imbibed his taste for the profession he so "highly ornamented,—the favourite spot of the unfortunate André,—before the "paternal gates of the elegant Addison. . . ."

191. Compare *Our Old Home,* pp. 148-62.

192. Compare *Our Old Home,* pp. 163-4:
"But the picturesque arrangement and full impressiveness of the story absolutely "require that Johnson shall not have done his penance in a corner, ever so little "retired, but shall have been the very nucleus of the crowd,—the midmost man of "the market-place,—a central image of Memory and Remorse, contrasting with and "overpowering the petty materialism around him."
For Johnson's account of his penance, see James Boswell, *The Life of Samuel Johnson,* ed. J. W. Croker, London, 1831, V, 288.
Hawthorne had included this episode from Johnson's life in his *Biographical Stories for Children* (1842). See *Sketches,* pp. 166-76. He published accounts of his "sentimental pilgrimage" to Uttoxeter in *The Keepsake* (London, 1857), pp. 108-13, and in *Our Old Home,* pp. 162-8.

193. Compare *Our Old Home,* pp. 30-3.

194. Harriet Martineau, *A Complete Guide to the English Lakes,* London, third ed., n.d. (first ed. 1855), p. 190:
"The morals of rural districts are usually such as cannot well be made worse by "any change [such as the introduction of the railroad]. Drinking and kindred vices "abound wherever, in our day, intellectual resources are absent; and nowhere is "drunkenness a more prevalent and desperate curse than in the Lake District. Any

"infusion of the intelligence and varied interests of the townspeople must, it appears,
"be eminently beneficial . . . mental stimulus and improved education are above
"every thing wanted."

195. Thomas West, *The Antiquities of Furness*, London, 1774, is probably the
work referred to.

196. "Bekangs-Gill . . . signifying the *Solanum Lethale* or Deadly Nightshade"
(West, *op. cit.*, p. 1).

197. Compare *Our Old Home*, pp. 116-7.

198. Compare *Our Old Home*, p. 115.

199. Thomas Alcock Beck, *Annales Furnesienses*, London, 1844, is probably the
work referred to.

200. For Hawthorne's contemplated use of this passage, see *Doctor Grimshawe's
Secret*, p. 354.

201. Mrs. Hawthorne wrote to her sister, Elizabeth: "The lake surprised me by
its extreme smallness—in America we should never think of calling it a lake; but it
receives dignity from the lofty hills and mountains that embosom it, and I thought
it was irreverent in Mr. Hawthorne to say he 'could carry it all away in a porringer' "
(*Memories of Hawthorne*, pp. 318-9).

202. The reference is to the poem which begins, "In these fair vales hath many a
Tree." Wordsworth's note on the poem is as follows: "Engraven, during my absence
in Italy, upon a brass plate inserted in the Stone."

203. "The Pet-Lamb."

204. So stated by Martineau, *op. cit.*, p. 80.

205. "The Westmoreland Girl."

206. The incident, which is not included in Lockhart's account of Scott's visit to
Wordsworth in 1805 (*Memoirs of the Life of Sir Walter Scott*, Boston, 1861, II,
208-9), is taken from Martineau, *op. cit.*, pp. 96-7.

207. "The Pass of Kirkstone."

208. Compare "The Pass of Kirkstone:"
>"When, through this Height's inverted arch,
>"Rome's earliest legion passed."

209. The name as given by Martineau, *op. cit.*, p. vii, is "C. W. Rotherey Esq."

210. A rhyming *tour de force* entitled "The Cataract of Lodore; Described in
Rhymes for the Nursery."

211. Hawthorne's phrasing, so infrequently reminiscent, here seems definitely so
of Bryant's *Thanatopsis:*
>"Like one who wraps the drapery of his couch
>"About him . . ."

212. Robert Lovell was associated with Southey and Coleridge in formulating a
plan of an ideal community, or "pantisocracy," on the banks of the Susquehanna.
The three associates married sisters, respectively Mary, Edith, and Sara Fricker.

213. Southey's second marriage (to Caroline Anne Bowles, 1786-1854) occurred
in 1839, just four years before his death. According to Richard Garnett (in the
D.N.B.), the second Mrs. Southey was a congenial and devoted wife.

214. See "The Bridal of Triermain; or, The Vale of St. John, A Lover's Tale,"
I, 221-2, 242-4:
>"But, midmost of the vale, a mound
>"Arose with airy turrets crowned . . ."
>
>"Beneath the castle's gloomy pride,
>"In ample round did Arthur ride . . ."

215. See *op. cit.*, p. 100.

216. The phrase "inverted arch" is Wordsworth's; see note 208.

217. After "mother," about two-thirds of a line is inked out.

218. This sentence was, of course, added later.

219. Spencer Perceval (1762-1812), English prime minister.

220. Possibly William George Clark (1821-78), Fellow and Tutor of Trinity College, Cambridge, and contributor to the Cambridge Shakespeare (1863-6).

221. Compare the Preface to *The Life of Franklin Pierce* (*Sketches*, p. 349) :
"If this little biography have any value, it is probably . . . as the narrative of one "who knew the individual of whom he treats, at a period of life when character could "be read with undoubting accuracy, and who, consequently, in judging of the motives "of his subsequent conduct, has an advantage over much more competent observers, "whose knowledge of the man may have commenced at a later date."

222. Possibly Charles Pierre Melly (1829-88), merchant and philanthropist, who provided for the citizenry of Liverpool drinking fountains (the first in 1854), a gymnasium, playgrounds, and wayside benches.

223. See Wordsworth's "Fidelity" and Scott's "Helvellyn."

224. "How nourished here through such long time
"He knows, who gave that love sublime . . ."

225. Compare *Our Old Home*, pp. 68-9.

226. Described as "The Jingling Match" in Joseph Strutt, *The Sports and Pastimes of the People of England*, London, 1801, p. 277. Hawthorne had drawn upon this work in "The Maypole of Merry Mount" (1835).

227. For Hawthorne's adaptation of Smithell's Hall to fictional purposes, see *The Ancestral Footstep*, pp. 472 ff. and *Doctor Grimshawe's Secret*, pp. 282 ff.

228. Peter Ainsworth (1790-1870), Member of Parliament, 1835-47.

229. For Hawthorne's interest in "the bloody footstep," see note 148.

230. The story of the martyrdom of George Marsh in 1555 is told in John Foxe, *Acts and Monuments*, London, 1641, III, 223-41. Foxe includes an account of Marsh's appearance before Barton at "Smethehils" and his displeasure when Barton insisted that the defendant's brother (who was needed "at home because it was the chiefest time of seeding") be held responsible for his appearance before the Earl of Derby; but Foxe makes no mention of Marsh's having stamped his foot in protest.

231. This passage seems to have suggested some of the details in the description of Squire Eldredge in *The Ancestral Footstep* (pp. 474, 478).

232. Compare *Our Old Home*, pp. 285, 287.

233. Compare *The Marble Faun*, pp. 351-2.

234. Joseph Butler (1692-1752), author of *The Analogy of Religion, Natural and Revealed, to the Constitution and Course of Nature* (1736). But Hawthorne apparently is in error, having mistaken Samuel Butler (1774-1839), whose grave and memorial he saw at Shrewsbury, for Joseph Butler, who is buried in the Cathedral at Bristol.

235. Samuel Patch (1807-29), famous for his feats of daring, was killed when he jumped from the cliff at Genesee Falls. Hawthorne had mused whimsically upon "the story of poor Sam Patch" in *Sketches*, pp. 17-18.

236. Samuel Rogers (1763-December 18, 1855).

237. Addison was "very much pleased" with this inscription, which he quoted in *The Spectator* (No. 99).

238. Sir Peter Warren (1703-52) commanded the English fleet in the attack on Louisburg in 1745. In a biographical sketch of Sir William Pepperell (published in *The Token* for 1833) Hawthorne asserted that, although Warren's assistance "undoubtedly prevented a discomfiture" of the forces under Pepperell, "the active business, and all the dangers of the siege, fell to the share of the provincials;" and that Warren, "a rough and haughty English seaman, greedy of fame, but despising those who . . . won it for him, . . . arrogated to himself, without scruple, the whole crop of laurels gathered at Louisburg" (*Sketches*, pp. 235-45). Compare also *Grandfather's Chair*, pp. 534-40.

239. Compare *Our Old Home,* pp. 307-10.

240. Compare *Our Old Home,* p. 290.

241. Compare *Our Old Home,* pp. 270-8.

242. The words "and . . . cigar" are inked out.

243. *I Henry VI,* II, iv.

244. The words "to . . . cigar" are inked out.

245. Compare *Our Old Home,* pp. 314-8.

246. Addison's epitaph, which is taken from Thomas Tickell's "To the Earl of Warwick, on the Death of Mr. Addison," is as follows:

"Ne'er to these chambers, where the mighty rest,
"Since their foundation, came a nobler guest;
"Nor e'er was to the bowers of bliss convey'd
"A fairer spirit or more welcome shade.
"Oh, gone for ever; take this long adieu;
"And sleep in peace, next thy lov'd Montague."

For the entire poem, see *The Works of the English Poets,* ed. Alexander Chalmers, London, 1810, XI, 122. Hawthorne commented in *Our Old Home* (p. 317): "His [Addison's] gravestone is inscribed with a resounding verse from Tickell's lines to his memory, the only lines by which Tickell himself is now remembered, and which (as I discovered a little while ago) he mainly filched from an obscure versifier of somewhat earlier date." I have not been able to discover the verses "filched" by Tickell. The poet's sentiments, however, are rather commonplace; and it seems likely that Hawthorne, sharing with many others of the romantic generation, notably Poe, the glorification of "originality" and the scorn of "what oft was thought," regarded a broad similarity of ideas as sufficient ground for the charge of plagiarism.

247. Sir George Downing (1684?-1749), created a Knight of the Bath in 1732, was the grandson of the Sir George Downing (1623?-84) to whom Hawthorne refers. The latter came to Salem, Massachusetts, in 1638, and, in 1642, was graduated from Harvard College.

248. Benjamin Moran (1820-86) was a member of the American Legation at London, first as private secretary to James Buchanan (1854-7), and later as assistant secretary (1857-64) and secretary of legation (1864-74). He was Minister to Portugal, 1874-82. His voluminous diary for the years 1857-75, which except for a few excerpts is unpublished ("Extracts from the Diary of Benjamin Moran, 1860-8," *Proceedings of the Massachusetts Historical Society,* XLVIII, [1915], 431 ff.) and the manuscript of which is preserved in the Library of Congress, contains important source material for the diplomatic history of the period. He is the author also of "Contributions Towards a History of American Literature" (in Nicholas Trübner, *Bibliographical Guide to American Literature,* London, 1859, pp. xxxvii-civ). In the latter work, Moran refers to Hawthorne's novels as "among the most delightful compositions of the age," and as having secured by "their unusual merit . . . a permanent place in modern literature"; Hawthorne's writings, he adds, "are as familiar now to continental readers through the medium of translations as they are to the people of Great Britain" (p. lv).

249. In the autumn of 1855, a column devoted to comment on London happenings, with the heading "From Our Own Correspondent" and the signature "Beta," appeared frequently in the *Semi-Weekly Courier and New-York Enquirer.*

250. One of the letters referred to (dated December 11, 1852) is printed in *The Works of James Buchanan,* ed. John Bassett Moore, Philadelphia, 1909, VIII, 496-7. "One opinion I must not fail to express," Buchanan wrote, "& this is that *the Cabinet ought to be a unit.* . . . It was a regard to this vital principle of unity in the formation of his Cabinet, which rendered Mr. Polk's administration so successful." Buchanan's lack of prophetic insight is revealed in the observation: "The important Domestic questions being now nearly all settled, the foreign affairs of the Govern-

ment & especially the question of Cuba will occupy the most conspicuous place in your administration."

251. Hawthorne possibly refers to the fact that in the election of 1848, Taylor, the Whig candidate, carried six Southern states. It should be remembered that Taylor's victory cost Hawthorne his post in the Salem Custom House.

252. In a letter to Ticknor, dated April 30, 1854, Hawthorne wrote of the occasion referred to, as follows: "I had the old fellow to dine with me, and liked him better than I expected . . . he takes his wine like a true man, loves a good cigar, and is doubtless as honest as nine diplomatists out of ten."

253. John Appleton (1815-64) was born in Beverly, Massachusetts, and was graduated from Bowdoin College. He held diplomatic positions in Bolivia, England, and Russia; he was a member of Congress, 1851-3, and assistant Secretary of State, 1857-60. He is said to have been the author of the more important state papers of Buchanan's administration (see *D.A.B.*).

254. Sister of James Freeman Clarke, and friend of Mrs. Hawthorne's.

255. Robert B. Campbell had been Consul at Havana during Polk's administration.

256. William Cox Bennett (1820-95), author of *Poems* (1850), *War Songs* (1855), and other volumes of verse. For some stanzas by Bennett in praise of *Transformation,* see *Hawthorne and His Wife,* II, 253-4. His *Verdicts,* apparently modelled after Lowell's *Fable for Critics* and published anonymously in 1852, contains lines like the following:

> "William Wordsworth—a shade to be reverenced—know it
> "For that of a genuine reformer and poet,
> "One to whom more of a true hearty thanks we all owe,
> "Than perhaps we yet think and just now we all show."

Although Hawthorne deprecated this production (see below), he expressed admiration for Bennett's "verses about childhood" which he thought were "quite exquisite" (letter to Fields, December 11, 1852; original in the Huntington Library).

257. Compare *Our Old Home,* p. 310.

258. Mantle Fielding, in *Gilbert Stuart's Portraits of George Washington,* Philadelphia, 1923, lists and describes no less than thirteen full-length portraits of Washington by Stuart, but does not indicate which of these, if any, was owned by Sturgis. For the supposed history of the picture referred to by Hawthorne, see Elizabeth Bryant Johnston, *Original Portraits of Washington,* Boston, 1882, pp. 82-3.

259. See *2 Henry IV,* III, ii, 15.

260. For evidence of Hawthorne's lively interest in the *Gentleman's Magazine,* see "Books Read by Nathaniel Hawthorne, 1828-1850," *The Essex Institute Historical Collections,* LXVIII (January, 1932) 65-87.

261. Morris S. Wickersham (the surname is given in the entry of September 24), an uncle of the late George W. Wickersham, was born about 1817 and studied medicine in Philadelphia. He advocated, without success, a scheme for salvaging ships which had been sunk during the Crimean War. The greater part of his later life was spent in Italy.

262. The following notice, under the caption "Art Gossip in Boston," appeared in the New York *Evening Post,* August 27, 1855:

". . . A new name among composers of native birth was introduced to us, which we "think bids fair to be one of note. Mr. L. H. Southard brought out some new works— "two overtures. . . . Besides these were given selections from the 'Scarlet Letter,' "an unfinished opera, the story of which is taken from Hawthorne's novel of that "name, ingeniously and poetically made into a libretto, by a literary gentleman of "Cambridge, with no little dramatic skill and effect. Three scenes were given by "competent singers, with orchestral accompaniment, and I venture to say that the "audience of your Academy of Music would *come down* with hearty and enthusiastic "applause could it hear them. Rather German, Freischütz-like in general style, yet "brilliant, too, as if an Italian fancy had conceived them and created them with "more than Italian learning. . . ."

Southard's operatic score, lent by his wife to someone in New York, was lost (see "Lucien H. Southard," *Grove's Dictionary of Music and Musicians, American Supplement,* New York, 1920, p. 366).

263. The words "and perhaps . . . cigar" are inked out.

264. Compare *Our Old Home,* pp. 290-7.

265. See *The Prose Works of Jonathan Swift,* ed. Temple Scott, London, 1899, VIII, 300. Compare *Our Old Home,* p. 272.

266. Compare *Our Old Home,* p. 297. Hawthorne probably had in mind, chiefly, John Taylor (1580-1653), the "water-poet."

267. Compare *Our Old Home,* pp. 297-8.

268. Hawthorne remembered his Latin grammar, where "propria quae maribus" designated the treatment of the gender of nouns. In the present context, a pun was obviously intended.

269. See *The Spectator,* No. 26.

270. Compare *Our Old Home,* p. 270.

271. No. 26: "I Yesterday pass'd a whole Afternoon in the Church-yard, the Cloysters, and the Church, amusing myself with the Tomb-stones and Inscriptions that I met with in those several Regions of the Dead."

272. Compare *Our Old Home,* p. 300.

273. The inauguration of the newly-elected sheriffs of London (see the London *Times,* October 2, 1855).

274. Compare *Our Old Home,* p. 301.

275. Emerson's *The Problem,* l. 23. Quoted again in *Our Old Home,* p. 301.

276. Compare *Our Old Home,* pp. 302-5.

277. *Merchant of Venice,* III, i, 128.

278. See *A Treasury of Irish Poetry,* ed. Stopford A. Brooke and T. W. Rolleston, New York, 1932, pp. 32-3.

279. Compare *The Autobiography of Leigh Hunt,* ed. Roger Ingpen, London, 1903, II, 249: ". . . why (let it be asked again) so much half-beauty here and such need for completing it, if complete it is not to be?"

280. Compare *Our Old Home,* pp. 319-25. Compare, also, Myron F. Brightfield, "Leigh Hunt—American," *Essays in Criticism, Second Series* (by Members of the Department of English, University of California) Berkeley, 1934, 225-45, which finds American characteristics in Hunt's philosophy. There is no reference to Hawthorne in *The Autobiography of Leigh Hunt.*

281. "A dog [rainbow] in the morning, sailor take warning; a dog in the night is the sailor's delight" (G. L. Apperson, *English Proverbs and Proverbial Phrases,* London, 1929, p. 523).

282. For an enthusiastic account of the celebration in Liverpool, see the London *Times,* October 10, 11, 1855. The illuminated letters stand, of course, for "Victoria," "Albert," and "Napoleon."

283. Compare *Our Old Home,* p. 377.

284. Compare Henry Bright's amusing verses on the incident (Julian Hawthorne, *Hawthorne and His Wife,* II, 78-80).

285. About one-fourth of pp. [21, 22] is cut out. The two portions of text in brackets are supplied from *Passages from the English Note-Books,* II. 179, 179-80.

286. "The Traveller," l. 1.

287. The work referred to appeared as follows: Samuel F. Holbrook, *Threescore Years: An Autobiography . . .,* Boston, James French and Company, 1857.

288. See N. A. Woods, *The Past Campaign: A Sketch of the War in the East, from the Departure of Lord Raglan to the Capture of Sevastopol,* London, 1855, II, 385-6.

289. The words "when . . . Work-House" are inked out.

290. Compare *Our Old Home*, pp. 344-59.

291. Compare *Doctor Grimshawe's Secret*, pp. 80-1; *Septimius Felton*, 242.

292. George Mifflin Dallas (1792-1864) was United States Senator from Pennsylvania 1831-3, Minister to Russia 1837-9, Vice-President of the United States 1845-9, and Minister to Great Britain 1856-61. At the time of Dallas's arrival in England, President Pierce had demanded the recall of Crampton, the British Ambassador, accused of recruiting men in the United States for the British Army. When Great Britain refused to comply with Pierce's demand, Crampton was dismissed in May 1856. Hawthorne wrote to Ticknor, June 6, "Crampton ought to have been dismissed more promptly; but it is better late than never;" and again on June 20, "We have gained a great triumph over England. . . . Give Frank Pierce credit for this, at least; for it was his spirit that did it."

Dallas's achievements at the Court of St. James's show him to have been a much abler man than Hawthorne supposed (see article on Dallas by Roy F. Nichols in the *D.A.B.*).

293. Abbott Lawrence (1792-1855) was Minister to Great Britain 1849-52.

294. One line is inked out.

295. The words "drank . . . cigar" are inked out.

296. Francis Bennoch (1812-90) was head of the wholesale trading firm of Bennoch, Twentyman and Rigg, 1848-74. Hawthorne wrote of him gratefully, though anonymously, in *Our Old Home* (p. 398) as "the man to whom I owed most in England, the warm benignity of whose nature was never weary of doing me good, who led me to many scenes of life, in town, camp, and country, which I never could have found out for myself, who knew precisely the kind of help a stranger needs and gave it as freely as if he had not had a thousand more important things to live for." And Mrs. Hawthorne dedicated her *Passages from the English Note-Books* (1870) to Bennoch, "the dear and valued friend, who, by his generous and genial hospitality and unfailing sympathy, contributed so largely . . . to render Mr. Hawthorne's residence in England agreeable and homelike."

Bennoch expressed his devotion in some verses "To Nathaniel Hawthorne, On the Anniversary of his Daughter Una's Birthday," written in 1860, and printed in Francis Bennoch, *Poems, Lyrics, Songs, and Sonnets*, London, 1877, pp. 265-7.

297. William Jerdan (1782-1869) was editor, from 1817 to 1850, of the *Literary Gazette*, an influential weekly review.

298. Hawthorne wrote to Ticknor, April 11, 1856: "Fields writes me that, in case of a war between America and England, he is going to fight for the latter. I hope he will live to be tarred and feathered, and that I may live to pour the first ladleful of tar on the top of his head, and to clap the first handful of feathers on the same spot. He is a traitor, and his English friends know it; for they all speak of him as one of themselves."

299. Letitia Elizabeth Landon (1802-1838) contributed reviews and verses to the *Literary Gazette*. According to Richard Garnett (in the *D.N.B.*), "The cruel scandals which in her latter years became associated with 'L.E.L.'s' name, . . . destitute as they were of the least groundwork in fact, beyond some expressions of hers whose tenor is only known from the admission of her friends that they were imprudent, occasioned her acute misery." She died of poisoning; whether accidental or suicidal is not known.

300. Compare *Our Old Home*, pp. 369-71.

301. About one-fourth of the page is cut out.

302. About one-fourth of the page is cut out.

303. The first line is cut out, and three and one-half lines, including the words "petticoats . . . again," are inked out.

304. Compare *Our Old Home*, pp. 278-86.

305. The first line is cut out.

306. Camilla Toulmin Crosland (1812-95) wrote miscellaneously for the magazines. Her longer works include *Light in the Valley: My Experiences of Spiritualism* (1857), and *Landmarks of a Literary Life* (1893). In the latter, she recorded her personal recollections of Hawthorne:

". . . I desire to speak of Nathaniel Hawthorne as I remember him about 1854. . . .
"In society he was one of the most painfully shy men I ever knew. I never had "the privilege of an unbroken *tête-à-tête* with him, and am under the impression that "with a single listener he must have been a very interesting talker; but in the small "social circle in which I first met him—it was at the house of Mr. Bennoch . . .— "it really seemed impossible to draw him out. We were only five or six intimate "friends, sitting round the fire, and with a host remarkable for his geniality and "tact; but Hawthorne fidgeted on the sofa, seemed really to have little to say, and "almost resented the homage that was paid him. . . . Still we got on sufficiently well "for him to do us the favour of meeting a few friends one evening at our house. . . . "At the time of which I am writing, Nathaniel Hawthorne was in the mid-prime of "life, a stalwart man. . . . His blue eyes, rather small for the size of his head, had "a peculiarly soft expression (pp. 211-2)."

307. The words "naked . . . with" are inked out.

308. Milton's "L'Allegro," l. 134.

309. The works of Martin Farquhar Tupper (1810-89) include *Proverbial Philosophy* (1838), *The Crock of Gold* (1846), and *My Life as an Author* (1886). By 1881, two hundred and fifty thousand copies of *Proverbial Philosophy* had been sold in England, and a million copies in America.

Hawthorne's account of his visit at Tupper's house was omitted from Mrs. Hawthorne's *Passages from the English Note-Books;* but Julian Hawthorne included most of the account in *Nathaniel Hawthorne and His Wife* (1884, II, 108-16). In *My Life as an Author* (London, 1886, pp. 246-7), Tupper commented as follows:

". . . I am tempted here to say just one unpleasant word about the only one "of my many American guests, hospitably, nay almost affectionately treated, who wrote "home to his wife too disparagingly of his entertainer, his son having afterwards "had the bad taste to publish those letters in his father's Life [Tupper mistakenly "supposed the quoted passage to have been taken from Hawthorne's letters]. One "comfort, however, is that in 'The Memoirs of Nathaniel Hawthorne' [*Nathaniel "Hawthorne and His Wife*] that not very amiable genius praises no one of his English "hosts (except, indeed, a perhaps too open-handed London one), and that he was "not known (any more than Fenimore Cooper, whom years ago I found a rude "customer in New York) for a superabundance of good nature. When at Albury, "Hawthorne seemed to us superlatively envious: of our old house for having more "than seven gables; of its owner for a seemingly affluent independence as well as "authorial fame; even of his friends when driven by him to visit beautiful and "hospitable Wotton; and in every word and gesture openly entering his republican "and ascetic protest against the aristocratic old country; even to protesting, when we "drove by a new weather-boarded cottage, 'Ha, that's the sort of house I prefer to "see; it's like one of ours at home.' That we did not take to each other is no wonder. "This, then, is my answer to the unkindly remarks against me in print of one who "has shown manifestly a flash of genius in 'The Scarlet Letter;' but, so far as I "know, it was well-nigh a solitary one."

310. *Joshua*, 6:26.

311. Compare *Our Old Home*, p. 194.

312. *2 Henry IV*, II, ii, 13.

313. In a biography of his wife (*Helena Faucit*, London, 1900, p. 259), Sir Theodore Martin quoted Hawthorne's published record of this occasion (*Passages from the English Note-Books,* II, 224-5), and added his own recollections, as follows:

"It was impossible not to talk with 'open heart and tongue,' and, I may add, "'affectionate and true,' with Hawthorne, as he showed himself that day. We had "heard of his reserved and distant manner to strangers, but found him all cordiality "and frankness, and with a brightness and charm of thought and expression calcu- "lated to give warmth to the respect with which we had long regarded his genius. "It was our good fortune to meet him several times afterwards, and on these occa- "sions he recognized the 'almost friends' of our first meeting as friends on whose "constancy he could always rely. To my wife he sent his *Improvisatore* immediately "on its publication. [Martin confused Hawthorne's *Transformation* with Hans Chris- "tian Andersen's *Improvisatore; or, Life in Italy*, translated by Mary Howitt, 1869.]"

314. For detailed accounts of the literary activities of Samuel Carter Hall (1800-89) and of his wife Anna Maria Hall (1800-81), see the *D.N.B.* Hall wrote two brief accounts of his impressions of Hawthorne:

"He was a handsome man, of good 'presence;' reserved—nay, painfully 'shy,' and "apparently utterly unconscious of his *status* in society. He was, as is known, a most "estimable gentleman. Those who knew him intimately depose to the high qualities "of his mind and heart [*A Book of Memories of Great Men and Women of the "Age, from Personal Acquaintance*, London, 1871, p. 184]."

"Hawthorne was his [Fenimore Cooper's] very opposite. That most lovable of "writers was also—to those who knew him intimately—one of the most lovable of "men. My acquaintance with him was slight; but it has left on my mind a vivid "impression of his painful shyness in general society, and the retiring—nay, morbid "delicacy—with which he shrank from notice, instead of courting, or rather com- "manding, it, as was the manner of his brother-novelist [*Retrospect of a Long Life*, "London, 1883, II, 202)."

315. Charles Mackay (1814-89), journalist and song-writer. He was editor of the *Illustrated London News*, 1852-9, and New York correspondent of the London *Times*, 1862-5. His "lyrics" (particularly "The Good Time Coming," music by Henry Russell) were very popular.

316. Tom Taylor (1817-80) was a popular playwright and a contributor to *Punch*.

317. Herbert Ingram (1811-60) was proprietor of the *Illustrated London News*, which he had founded in 1842, and from 1856 until his death, was a Member of Parliament for Boston.

318. The voluminous works of William Howitt (1792-1879) include *Book of the Seasons, or Calendar of Nature* (1831), and a translation of Adelbert von Chamisso's *Wonderful History of Peter Schlemihl* (1844). Hawthorne may have known the latter work, for he refers to Peter Schlemihl in *Mosses from an Old Manse*, pp. 364, 556. Thoreau used Howitt's *Seasons* "as a model for his first extensive nature writing" (Henry Seidel Canby, *Thoreau*, Boston, 1939, p. 91).

319. Eneas Sweetland Dallas (1828-79).

320. John Cameron MacDonald (1822-89). His communications from Scutari, where he administered the *Times'* fund for the sick and wounded, appeared in the *Times*, January 1—March 2, 1855.

321. Isabella Dallas Glyn (1823-89).

322. John Thadeus Delane (1817-79), editor of the London *Times*, 1841-77.

323. A light fabric for dresses.

324. "In many points Samuel Carter Hall undoubtedly may be described as the prototype of Pecksniff" (John Forster, *Life of Charles Dickens*, ed. J. W. T. Ley, London, 1928, p. 318, editor's note).

325. Douglas William Jerrold (1803-57), playwright and contributor to *Punch*. His plays include *Blackeyed Susan* (1829), which ran for three hundred nights at the Surrey Theatre, and *Time Works Wonders* (1845), which ran for ninety nights at the Haymarket. His *Mrs. Caudle's Curtain Lectures*, reprinted from *Punch* in 1846, was also very popular.

J. A. Hamilton, writing in the *D.N.B.*, says of Jerrold: "He was in temperament impulsive and fiery, rarely pausing to think whether his acrid wit would give pain to friends or foes, but overflowing with scorn of meanness, and indignation at injustice."

326. In his *Forty Years' Recollections of Life, Literature, and Public Affairs* (London, 1877, II, 273-85), Charles Mackay recorded at some length his impressions of Hawthorne on this occasion, and having before him the account, substantially complete, in *Passages from the English Note-Books* (II, 229-34), he undertook to correct certain errors attributable to Hawthorne's faulty observation or lapse of memory:

"Jerrold was brilliant, as he always was; and Hawthorne threw off much of his "customary and constitutional reserve, and gambolled solemnly in his talk with the "ponderosity of an elephant attempting to be playful. . . . He [Hawthorne] remem-"bered [in his diary] the bill of fare and the wine perfectly, but he did not as "perfectly remember the conversation. When his diary was published, I became "aware that he was by no means an accurate describer, either of what he saw or "what he heard; and that the shyness of his personal manner did not affect him "when he had a pen in his hands. . . .

"Mr. Hawthorne might have known, had he enquired, that the portraits of these men "[Lord Durham and Lord Grey] were placed where he saw them, not because of "their high rank, but of their eminent services to the Liberal party and the cause of "Reform. He might also have discovered, had he looked, the portraits of Daniel "O'Connell, a commoner, and of Mr. J. W. Denison, M.P., another commoner, and an "excellent bust of John Hampden, a third commoner, more illustrious than either. . . .

"The white silk stockings were things of Mr. Hawthorne's imagination, but served to "point an innuendo against English manners and in favour of those of his own "country. . . .

"Mr. Hawthorne . . . has attempted to justify the unfortunate use of the word "'acrid,' as applied to Jerrold's wit, which he blurted out very clumsily and evidently "without the slightest suspicion of the sensitive nature that he was hurting. Jerrold "started as if stung. . . . Jerrold, however, could not but accept without rejoinder, the "attempt to make the *amende honorable* by the comparison of his geniality to that "of Burgundy, but told me some days afterwards that he thought Hawthorne one of "the heaviest and most awkward of persons he had ever met: 'But he means well,' "he added, 'as all clumsy people do.' . . .

"Mr. Hawthorne has not fully or correctly reported in his diary the conversation "about Thoreau's book. . . . Hawthorne told us that the incident of Thoreau's voluntary "seclusion afar from all human intercourse which pleased him most was that after "he had been two or three months in the woods, the wild birds ceased to be afraid "of him, and would come and perch upon his shoulder, and sometimes upon his "spade, when he was digging in the little croft that supplied him with potatoes and "pumpkins, and that Thoreau had written or said, that he deemed the honour thus "bestowed upon him by the birds to be greater than anything an Emperor could have "conferred, if he had been elevated to a dukedom.

"'That is a book I should like to read,' said Jerrold. And upon that hint, and no "other, Mr. Hawthorne undertook to send it to him. The 'pressure' alluded to existed only in Mr. Hawthorne's fancy.

"Neither has he correctly reported the conversation about the position of men of "letters in England. Nothing was said about the hatred or fear entertained of litera-"ture and its professors by the aristocracy of Great Britain, though much was said "about the superior chances afforded in the United States to men of letters who "aspired to a political or a diplomatic career."

Was Mackay very possibly piqued by Hawthorne's marked preference for Jerrold? One is glad, nevertheless, to have the report of Hawthorne's comments on Thoreau.

327. Thomas Faed (1826-1900) was a popular painter whose reputation was first established by "The Mitherless Bairn," exhibited in 1855. His characteristic subjects were "pathetic or sentimental incidents in humble Scottish life" (*D.N.B.*).

328. John Elliotson (1791-1868) resigned a professorship of medicine in the University of London in 1838 to practise mesmerism. He was the author of *Numerous Cases of Surgical Operations Without Pain in the Mesmeric State* (London, 1843).

329. Hawthorne, according to his son, had a "great liking" for some of Reade's books, and read *Griffith Gaunt* "with much interest when it was appearing serially in the *Atlantic Monthly*" (*Hawthorne and His Wife*, II, 118). The statement of Hawthorne's interest in Reade is doubtless true; but he could not have read *Griffith Gaunt*, published after his death (*Atlantic*, Dec. 1865-Nov. 1866). In October, 1857, he had read aloud to his family Reade's *It Is Never Too Late To Mend* (letter by Ada Shepard in the possession of Mr. Frederick Badger).

330. Miss Glyn's exhaustion is quite understandable, for the play was *Antony and Cleopatra:* "Miss Glyn . . . makes again of Cleopatra what she used to be, a glory of the East" (the London *Examiner*, April 12, 1856).

331. David Salomons, who was the first Jew to be elected to the office of Lord Mayor of London (see the London *Times*, October 1, 1855, and the London *Guardian*, October 3, 1855). The Lord Mayor was elected for one year, the term of office beginning on November 9.

332. George Robert Gleig (1796-1888), chaplain-general of the forces (1844-75).

333. The "miraculous Jewess" became the physical prototype of Miriam in *The Marble Faun*. Compare the following description of Miriam:

"She was very youthful, and had what was usually thought to be a Jewish aspect; "a complexion in which there was no roseate bloom, yet neither was it pale; dark "eyes, into which you might look as deeply as your glance would go, and still be "conscious of a depth that you had not sounded, though it lay open to the day. "She had black, abundant hair, with none of the vulgar glossiness of other women's "sable locks; if she were really of Jewish blood, then this was Jewish hair, and a dark "glory such as crowns no Christian maiden's head. Gazing at this portrait [Miriam's "portrait, painted by herself], you saw what Rachel might have been, when Jacob "deemed her worth the wooing seven years, and seven more; or perchance she might "ripen to be what Judith was, when she vanquished Holofernes with her beauty, and "slew him for too much adoring it [p. 65]."

Less completely, the Lord Mayor's brother, whose description follows in the text, suggested the physical appearance of Miriam's "model:" "dark, bushy-bearded" (p. 34); "a dusky wilderness of mustache and beard" (p. 45).

334. For Hall's account of his helpfulness on this occasion, see his *Retrospect of a Long Life*, London, 1883, II, 202, footnote.

335. For a newspaper report of Hawthorne's speech, see Randall Stewart, "Hawthorne's Speeches at Civic Banquets," *American Literature*, VII (January, 1936), pp. 417-8.

336. The foregoing account of the Lord Mayor's dinner appears in an expanded form in *Our Old Home*, pp. 386-403.

337. Hawthorne wrote to Longfellow, April 12, 1856:

"In London, a few evenings ago, I happened to be at Evans's Supper Rooms (a "rather rowdyish place, I am afraid, to which I was introduced by Mr. Albert Smith) "and the proprietor introduced himself to me and expressed a high sense of the honor "which my presence did him. He further said that it had been the 'dream and "romance of his life,' to see Emerson, Channing, Longfellow, and, he was kind

"enough to add, me, sitting together at a table in his rooms! I could not but smile
"to think of such a party of roisterers drinking whisky toddy or gin and water at
"one of his tables, smoking pipes or cigars, and listening to a bacchanalian catch from
"his vocalists. The band played 'Hail Columbia,' 'Yankee Doodle,' &c., in my honor;
"and several of your songs were sung; and the proprietor entreated me to lay
"this 'edition de luxe' (as he called it) of his programme 'at your feet.' You must
"certainly go there when you come to London. [Manuscript letter in the possession
"of Mr. H. W. L. Dana]."

In an informative and quite complimentary article, *Punch* (June 21, 1856) described
Evans's Supper Rooms as a "place of rational entertainment" and "unobjectionable
amusement:" "Even a bishop might give it an occasional inspection, without deroga-
tion from the decorum of his shovel hat and gaiters."

338. Henry Stevens (1819-86) was a noted bookseller, collector, and bibliographer.
His works include: *Catalogue of My English Library* (1853), *Analytical Index to
the Colonial Documents of New Jersey* (1858), *Catalogue of the American Books
in the Library of the British Museum* (1866), and *The Bibles in the Caxton Exhibition* (1878).

339. Mary Howitt (1799-1888), a voluminous writer of miscellaneous works.

340. John Westland Marston (1819-90), according to Richard Garnett in the
D.N.B., was "for a long time the chief upholder of the poetical drama on the
English stage."

341. Arthur Helps (1813-75) was known for his collection of essays, *Friends in
Council,* praised by Ruskin for their "beautiful quiet English." Helps wrote to C. E.
Norton, October 18, 1852: "I have not read the book of Hawthorne's which you
mention, but he is a most sweet, serious, and subtle writer" (*The Correspondence of
Sir Arthur Helps,* ed. E. A. Helps, London, 1917, p. 145).

342. John Edward Jones (1806-62) specialized in busts of members of the English
nobility.

343. Probably George Godwin (1815-88), who published works on the history of
art and architecture, and collected chairs formerly belonging to celebrated persons.
His collection, which was sold after his death, included chairs which had been sat
in by Shakespeare, Napoleon, Pope, Byron, Thackeray, Trollope, and Nathaniel
Hawthorne.

344. Hawthorne wrote to Ticknor from Liverpool, April 11: "I . . . returned
[from London] only last night, after having enjoyed myself gloriously—owing principally to Bennoch's kindness. I lived rather fast, to be sure; but that was not amiss,
after such a slow winter. My health and spirits are much better than when I went
away."

345. Chapter XX.

346. The words "and . . . bareness" are inked out.

347. See *The Lady of the Lake,* Canto Sixth, stanzas XII-XXI. Una Hawthorne
wrote to her aunt Elizabeth Peabody, March 16, 1855: "Papa has read the Lady
of the Lake to us. How beautiful it is! I should like to learn it very much." And
again, October 30, 1857: "I found that it was a stupendous undertaking to learn
the Lady of the Lake by heart . . . and so I contented myself with learning the
finest scenes and passages." (The originals are in the Berg Collection of the
New York Public Library.)

348. Chapter XLIII.

349. See Scott's *Heart of Mid-Lothian,* Chapters III-VII.

350. *The Lay of the Last Minstrel,* Canto Second, l. 10.

351. Canto Second, stanza XIII.

352. Hawthorne doubtless recalled Scott's use of the murder and its sequel in
Old Mortality.

353. "This Mr. Hawthorne did, aloud to his family, the year following his return

to America" (Mrs. Hawthorne's note, *Passages from the English Note-Books*, II, 274).

354. See, for example, John James Audubon, *The Birds of America*, New York, 1840, I, 22:

". . . The vivid tints of the plumage were fading much faster than I had ever "seen them in like circumstances, insomuch that Dr. Bell of Dublin, who saw it "[a Caracara Eagle] when fresh [freshly killed], and also when I was finishing the "drawing twenty-four hours later, said he could scarcely believe it to be the same "bird."

355. The same idea has been previously expressed on p. *201*.

356. Joseph Jenkins Roberts (1809-76), President of Liberia (1847-55, 1871-6).

357. Charles Swain (1801-74), engraver and writer of verse, resided in Manchester.

358. Alexander Ireland (1810-94), publisher and business manager of the Manchester *Examiner* (1846-86), is remembered chiefly as the friend and biographer of Emerson. For the relations between Emerson and Ireland, see Townsend Scudder, *The Lonely Wayfaring Man*, New York, 1936, pp. 50-4, 208.

359. Four lines, including the words "What . . . she," are inked out.

360. An allusion to Hannah More's tale, *The Shepherd of Salisbury Plain* (1798).

361. "Being arrived here, they chose for their house of entertainment the sign of the Bell, an excellent house indeed, and which I do most seriously recommend to every reader who shall visit this ancient city" (*Tom Jones*, bk. VIII, ch. VIII).

362. In "Congreve," *The Lives of the English Poets*, Johnson quotes from *The Mourning Bride* (II, i) a passage which contains the lines,

". . . the tombs
"And monumental caves of death look cold,
"And shoot a chillness to my trembling heart . . ."

and comments as follows: "If I were required to select from the whole mass of English poetry the most poetical paragraph, I know not what I could prefer to an exclamation in *The Mourning Bride*."

363. The story is told in Browne Willis, *An History of the Mitred Parliamentary Abbies . . .*, London, 1719, II, 205-6. I have not succeeded in finding the passage in the writings of Isaac Watts.

364. Philip James Bailey (1816-1902), whose *Festus* (1839) went through eleven editions in fifty years.

365. On June 25, 1856, Dennis Hart Mahan (the father of Alfred Thayer Mahan), professor of civil and military engineering at the United States Military Academy, was refused admittance to the Queen's levee by the Master of Ceremonies because his costume (West Point full-dress, apparently) did not conform to the requirements of the Court. Dallas, the American ambassador, quitted the levee prematurely, with his rejected countryman.

The incident presented another opportunity of ridiculing American "manners," which the English press utilized to the utmost. The London *Times* of June 26 commented as follows:

"When will Americans learn manners? Who shall teach our Transatlantic cousins "how to behave? Here is one of them who tried . . . to parade his republican person "before the Queen, at her levee, in a frock coat, black neckcloth, and yellow waist-"coat. . . ."

The Manchester *Guardian* of June 27 was not less castigatory:

"When our Mrs. Trollopes and Charles Dickenses go to the United States and "show up on their return the vulgarity and arrogance which they have met with in "their travels, we are always told that they have committed a gross unfairness in "judging the whole of a nation by a small part. They should have looked about "for beauties instead of deformities of character, and we are assured that they would

"have found themselves surrounded by the pink and pattern of civilized humanity.
"We are very desirous to believe that there are such premium specimens of the race
"within the republican dominion; but we cannot help wishing that stay at home
"critics could be relieved from the necessity of taking their existence entirely on
"trust. The President should at least give himself the trouble of attaching one or
"two of them to the European embassies."
The following vigorous satire appeared in *Punch* (issue of July 5):
"Messrs. Noses and Son have much pleasure in informing gents, and others connected
"with the American legation, that an outfit for attendance at the Court of Queen
"Victoria may now be had for twenty-five shillings. The suit consists of a good
"stout shooting-coat, with pockets for the hands to avoid the expense of gloves, a
"pair of coarse 'pants,' and highlows warranted to trample upon all the forms of
"decency. Wrap-rascals for Birthday Drawing-rooms made to measure on the
"lowest terms, and everything calculated to insult the British Court to be had as
"low as any house in Hounsditch."
366. Compare *Our Old Home*, p. 263.
367. Compare *Our Old Home*, pp. 268-9.
368. Compare *Our Old Home*, p. 270.
369. Catherine Sinclair (1800-64) was the author of novels, and books for children.
370. Joseph Durham (1814-77), whose busts of Jenny Lind (1848) and of Queen
Victoria (1856) "attracted much attention" (*D.N.B.*).
371. Sir James Emerson Tennent (1804-69), traveller and politician, was the
author of *Letters from the Aegean* (1829), *Christianity in Ceylon* (1850), *Wine, its
Use and Taxation* (1855), and other miscellaneous works.
372. Samuel Lover (1797-1868) was the successful author of poems, novels, and
plays on Irish subjects. He was popular also as an entertainer, his program of
"Irish Evenings" having been well received both in England and (except at Boston)
in the United States.
373. Geraldine Endsor Jewsbury (1812-80), a friend of the Carlyles, and author
of novels and books for children, was, at the time of Hawthorne's meeting her,
assisting Lady Morgan in the arrangement of her "Memoirs."
374. William Ewart (1798-1869).
375. Probably Sir William Meredyth Somerville (1802-73).
376. George Ticknor (1791-1871), Smith Professor of French and Spanish at
Harvard (1819-35), and author of the *History of Spanish Literature* (1849).
377. John Gorham Palfrey (1796-1881) is remembered chiefly for his *History of
New England* (5 vols., 1858-90).
378. Hawthorne's slight acquaintance with the Brownings in England ripened into
friendship in Florence in 1858. There is no reason to believe, however, that Hawthorne ever greatly admired the writings of either Browning or Mrs. Browning,
or that they ever greatly admired his, though Hawthorne was reading Browning's
poems in 1850 (see "Books Read by Nathaniel Hawthorne," *The Essex Institute
Historical Collections*, LXVIII [January, 1932], 87), and Browning, after Hawthorne's death, aided Una Hawthorne in deciphering the manuscript of *Septimius
Felton* (see *Septimius Felton*, p. 227).
A notable literary result of the relationship was Hawthorne's description of the
Brownings in his Italian journal (see *Passages from the French and Italian Note-
Books*, pp. 293-5), which has been praised for possessing "more true insight" than
any other contemporary portrait (W. H. Griffin and H. C. Minchin, *The Life of
Robert Browning*, New York, 1910, p. 229 note). The published passage nevertheless
suffers considerably from Mrs. Hawthorne's revisions.
379. Compare *Our Old Home*, pp. 263-5.
380. Robert Armstrong (1792-1854) served under Jackson against the Creek
Indians and against the British at New Orleans. In 1836, he was made brigadier-

general by Jackson; and in 1845, he was appointed by Polk to the consulship at Liverpool. During the greater part of his life he resided in Nashville, Tennessee.

381. Compare Lewis Melville, *William Makepeace Thackeray*, London, 1910, I, 318: "Lord Steyne undoubtedly was suggested by the second and third Marquises of Hertford. . . ." Compare also E. Beresford Chancellor, *The London of Thackeray*, London, 1923, p. 102: "All the world knows that Lord Hertford was the original, in various essentials, of the Marquis of Steyne. . . ."

382. Two and one-half lines are inked out.

383. Delia Bacon (1811-59) was the author of *The Philosophy of the Plays of Shakspere Unfolded* (London, 1857). The relationship between Hawthorne and Miss Bacon is recorded in the following pages of the journal, in *Our Old Home* (pp. 129-43), and in their correspondence, published in part in Theodore Bacon, *Delia Bacon: A Biographical Sketch* (Boston and New York, 1888, pp. 165 ff.). Hawthorne befriended Miss Bacon by giving her money, by arranging for the publication of her work (assuming full financial responsibility therefor), and by writing for the book a Preface, in which he praised the author's insight and devotion while reserving judgment on the validity of her conclusions. Despite Miss Bacon's rather difficult temperament, Hawthorne behaved toward her throughout with extraordinary tact, patience, and benevolence.

384. After "sports," two or three words are erased.

385. Compare *Our Old Home*, pp. 257-9.

386. *Paradise Lost*, IX, 1107.

387. Compare *Our Old Home*, pp. 267-9.

388. See Mr. & Mrs. S. C. Hall, *Ireland: Its Scenery, Character, &c.*, London, 1846, II, 344. The authors had previously made Hawthorne a present of this work, in three stout volumes (see p. *319*).

389. Richard James Spiers was Mayor of Oxford in 1853. In return for a lavish hospitality, Hawthorne presented to Spiers a *de luxe* edition of his complete works, with his host's name stamped on the covers (see letter to Ticknor, September 7, 1856), and made a graceful acknowledgment at the conclusion of the essay "Near Oxford" (in *Our Old Home*, pp. 229-30). The acknowledgment was anonymous, except for a pun on the name: "He has inseparably mingled his image with our remembrance of the Spires of Oxford."

390. Charles William Corfe (1814-83) was organist of Christ Church, Oxford, 1846-82.

391. Compare *Our Old Home*, pp. 201-13.

392. Compare *Our Old Home*, pp. 213-4.

393. Benjamin Silliman, *A Journal of Travels in England, Holland, and Scotland . . .*, Boston, 1810.

394. *Kenilworth*.

395. The interior just described, Hawthorne said in *Our Old Home*, pp. 219-20, seemed as familiar to him as his grandmother's kitchen from his having read Pope's description in a letter to the Duke of Buckingham (see *The Works of Alexander Pope*, ed. W. Elwin and W. J. Courthope, London, 1886, X, 150-1).

396. George Harvey (1806-76), knighted in 1864.

397. Compare *Our Old Home*, p. 194.

398. Compare the entire entry of September 7 with *Our Old Home*, pp. 214-30.

399. *The Rime of the Ancient Mariner*, l. 227.

400. Swift's "acrid lines" (according to Thomas Hughes, *The Stranger's Handbook to Chester*, Chester, n.d. [*circa* 1856], p. 60) were as follows:

"Rotten without and mouldering within,
"This place and its clergy are both near akin!"

A different version is given in *The Poems of Jonathan Swift*, ed. Harold Williams, London, 1937, II, 401:

"The Church and Clergy here, no doubt,

"Are very near a-kin;
"Both, weather-beaten are without;
"And empty both within."
But Hawthorne must have seen the version of two lines.

401. In his *Journal up the Straits* (ed. Raymond Weaver, New York, 1935, pp. 4-5), Melville wrote of his visit with the Hawthornes very briefly as follows:

"*Monday, Nov. 10th* . . . Saw Mr. Hawthorne at the Consulate. Invited me to "stay with him during my sojourn at Liverpool. . . .

"*Tuesday Nov 11* . . . Took afternoon train with Mr. Hawthorne for Southport, "20 miles distant on the seashore, a watering place. Found Mrs. Hawthorne & the "rest awaiting tea for us.

"*Wednesday Nov 12* At Southport. An agreeable day. Took a long walk by the "sea. Sands & grass. Wild and desolate. A strong wind. Good talk. In the evening "Stout & Fox & Geese.—Julian grown into a fine lad; Una taller than her mother. "Mrs. Hawthorne not in good health. Mr. H. stayed home for me.

"*Thursday Nov 13*. At Southport till noon. Mr H. & I took train then for "Liverpool. . . .

"*Friday Nov 14* . . . called at Mr. Hawthornes. . . ."

It is curious that Melville did not mention the excursion to Chester with Hawthorne on Saturday or his seeing Hawthorne again on Monday. His final comment in the *Journal* before sailing was, "Tired of Liverpool."

402. Hawthorne's informant was in error, for Tecumseh was not killed until two years later, in the battle of the Thames.

403. After "this," four lines are cut out.

404. After "has," four lines are cut out. The bracketed words which follow are supplied from *Passages from the English Note-Books*, II, 383.

405. Her Majesty's bark *Resolute* was sent to the Arctic in May, 1853, to search for Sir John Franklin. Imprisoned in ice, the vessel was abandoned by her officers and crew in May, 1854. In September, 1855, the *Resolute*, drifting aimlessly, was found by an American whaler and taken to New London, Connecticut. The Congress of the United States thereupon directed that the bark be repaired and returned to the Queen, and appropriated $40,000 to cover the costs of purchase from her captor (the English government having waived all claim to her) and of repairs. Appropriate ceremonies at Cowes, on December 16, 1856, marked the return of the *Resolute* to her original owner. Queen Victoria went on board the vessel and formally received the refurbished derelict from an American captain, who said: "Allow me to welcome Your Majesty on board the *Resolute*, and, in obedience to the will of my country-men and of the President of the United States, to restore her to you, not only as an evidence of a friendly feeling to your sovereignty, but as a token of love, ad-miration, and respect to Your Majesty personally." (See the London *Times*, December 17, 1856.)

406. Compare *Our Old Home*, pp. 381-3.

407. See Wordsworth's "The White Doe of Rylstone" (Canto I, ll. 226-230), and "The Force of Prayer."

408. "The White Doe of Rylstone," Canto I, ll. 242-7.

409. Queen Adelaide (1792-1849) was the consort of William IV of England.

410. Compare *Our Old Home*, pp. 359-61.

411. Compare *Our Old Home*, p. 382.

412. Sir James Phillips Kay-Shuttleworth (1804-77) was active in educational, sanitary, and other reforms.

413. Edward Henry Stanley, fifteenth Earl of Derby (1826-93).

414. For newspaper accounts of Hawthorne's speech on this occasion, see Randall Stewart, "Hawthorne's Speeches at Civic Banquets," *American Literature*, VII (January, 1936) 420-2.

415. "To A Mountain Daisy."

416. "A Poet's Epitaph," ll. 43-4:
> "And you must love him, ere to you
> "He will seem worthy of your love."

417. The words "but . . . it" have been partially erased, and another hand (probably Mrs. Hawthorne's) has substituted the words "and I suppose that it was knocked." In her revisions, Mrs. Hawthorne often suppressed uncomplimentary statements of fact or suspicion, regarding the behavior of the children.

418. Shakespeare's *Tempest*, IV, i, 152.

419. Pishey Thompson, *Collections for a Topographical and Historical Account of Boston . . .*, London, 1820. It is surprising that the bookseller did not show, instead of this older work, Pishey Thompson's recently published *History and Antiquities of Boston* (Boston, 1856).

420. Compare *Matthew* 13:52.

421. The word is erased.

422. The entries of May 22 through May 27 were used, with comparatively slight revision, in "Pilgrimage to Old Boston" (*Our Old Home*, pp. 169-200).

423. Canto XVI.

424. The fact is recorded in M. R. Werner, *Barnum*, New York, 1923, p. 95.

425. See "Ali Baba and the Forty Thieves," in *The Arabian Nights*.

426. The name given to that part of the Mersey which extends from Birkenhead to Rock Ferry on the Cheshire side.

427. Many runaway couples from England formerly went to Gretna Green, which is just across the border, to be married, because of the liberality of the marriage laws in Scotland.

428. See Burns's "To a Louse."

429. Allan Cunningham, whose biography of Burns Hawthorne read (see p. *506*), speaks of "the cold humid bottom of Mossgiel" (*The Life of Robert Burns*, London, 1835, p. 205).

430. See "To a Mouse."

431. See "To a Mountain Daisy."

432. "The Lass o' Ballochmyle."

433. The plural reference includes Mrs. Hawthorne's journals (see her published work, *Notes in England and Italy*, New York, 1869).

434. The scene of "The Jolly Beggars."

435. See "The Brigs of Ayr."

436. The material on pages *499-511* was used, with comparatively slight revision, in "Some of the Haunts of Burns" (*Our Old Home*, pp. 231-53).

437. Hawthorne possibly derived this information from John Glen, *History of the Town and Castle of Dumbarton, Dumbarton*, 1847, p. 21: "Many ancient authors have supposed it [Dumbarton] to have been the Balclutha of Ossian. . . ."

438. "To a Highland Girl."

439. See *The Lady of the Lake*, Canto First, stanzas XXIV-XXV.

440. The words "and . . . whiskey" are inked out; about four words have not been deciphered.

441. The words "and . . . room" are inked out.

442. The words "bought . . . and" are inked out.

443. The words "while . . . cigar" are inked out.

444. "Backed" and "blue bodied" are inked out, and another hand has added above "blue," "amethyst," and after "beetle," "with a ruby head."

445. In *The Lay of the Last Minstrel*.

446. *II Corinthians*, 5:1.

447. Compare *Our Old Home*, p. 112.

448. "The figure walking from the frame in the 'Castle of Otranto,' was suggested by this picture" (*Catalogue of the Art Treasures of the United Kingdom Collected at Manchester in 1857*, London, 1857, p. 113). In *The Castle of Otranto*,

Chap. I, the portrait of Manfred's grandfather "quit its panel, and descend[ed] on the floor with a grave and melancholy air."

449. Of interest in this connection is Emerson's description of Tennyson: "Take away Hawthorne's bashfulness, and let him talk easily and fast, and you would have a pretty good Tennyson." The statement occurs in the *Journals* (VII, 444) and also in a letter to his wife (*The Letters of Ralph Waldo Emerson*, ed. R. L. Rusk, New York, 1939, IV, 74).

450. "Uttoxeter," *The Keepsake*, London, 1857, pp. 108-113.

451. The words "and buttocks" are erased.

452. The words "and especially . . . them" are inked out.

453. Compare *Our Old Home*, pp. 361-2.

454. Southey had over-praised, Hawthorne thought, the precocious compositions of Kirke White (1785-1806) and of the American poetess, Lucretia Davidson (1808-25). Of White, Southey expressed the opinion that his early death was "not less to be lamented as a loss to English literature" than that of Chatterton (see *The Remains of Henry Kirke White . . .*, London, 1810, I, i) ; of Miss Davidson's compositions, he wrote: "In these poems, there is enough of originality, enough of aspiration, enough of conscious energy, enough of growing power to warrant any expectations, however sanguine, which the patrons and the friends, and parents of the deceased could have formed" (quoted in *Poetical Remains of the late Lucretia Maria Davidson . . .*, Philadelphia, 1841, p. 89, and in Poe's destructive review, with which Hawthorne was probably familiar, Virginia ed., X, 224).

Southey was even more extravagant, apparently, in his praise of Swain's mediocre talent: "If ever man was born to be a poet, Swain was" (quoted in the article on Swain in the *D.N.B.*). It is small wonder that the critical Hawthorne had a low opinion of Southey's judgment in literature.

455. Quite by accident, en route to Liverpool. Ticknor spoke of "having found Hawthorne in the cars, to enliven my last moments [before sailing for America]" (*Life, Letters, and Journals of George Ticknor*, Boston, 1876, II, 400).

456. Francis Haywood (1796-1858) was the author of a translation of Kant's "Critick of Pure Reason" (1838).

457. John Leycester Adolphus (1795-1862), barrister, was the author of *Letters to Richard Heber, Esq., Containing Critical Remarks on the Series of Novels Beginning with "Waverley," and an Attempt to Ascertain their Author* (1821).

458. Emilia Gayangos, whose father, Pascual de Gayangos, was of great assistance to Prescott in the collection of Spanish materials (see *Prescott: Unpublished Letters to Gayangos . . .*, ed., Clara Louisa Penney, New York, 1927, pp. 95, 194).

459. Compare *Our Old Home*, pp. 27-30.

460. Charles Allen Duval (1808-72).

461. The foregoing descriptions of Leamington appear, considerably revised, in *Our Old Home*, pp. 58-65.

462. Naturally enough, Hawthorne was impressed by the dynamic George Francis Train (1829-1904), merchant and entrepreneur extraordinary (see the *D.A.B.*). The "book of his peregrinations," referred to by Hawthorne, was *An American Mei·hant in Europe, Asia, and Australia* (New York, 1857).

463. Two passages in the journal (the foregoing passage and an earlier one on pp. *138-9*) were interwoven in the description of St. Mary's Hall in *Our Old Home* (pp. *367-9*).

464. Compare *Our Old Home*, pp. 80-2.

465. Hawthorne wrote to Ticknor, July 30, 1857: "I have engaged Miss Ada Shepard (a graduate of Mr. Mann's College at Antioch [Antioch College, at Yellow Springs, Ohio, which was founded in 1853, and of which Horace Mann, Mrs. Hawthorne's brother-in-law, was the first president]) to take charge of my children while we remain on the Continent. She is recommended to me in the highest way, as respects acquirements and character. . . . I have tried English governesses, and

find them ignorant and inefficient. Miss Shepard is to receive no salary, but only her expenses. . . ."

466. The foregoing descriptions of Warwick were used, in part, in *Our Old Home*, pp. 99-106, 111-2, and elsewhere in the chapter "About Warwick." Leicester's Hospital reappears, with fictional embellishments, in *The Ancestral Footstep*, pp. 463-4, and in *Doctor Grimshawe's Secret, passim.*

467. Two passages in the journal (the foregoing passage and an earlier one on pp. *125-7*) were interwoven in the description of Whitnash in *Our Old Home* (pp. 76-80). Whitnash reappears in *Septimius Felton*, p. 257, and in *Doctor Grimshawe's Secret*, pp. 217-220.

468. The first British war vessel, built in 1509 and destroyed by fire in 1553.

469. Compare *Our Old Home*, pp. 310-1.

470. A brief account of George Silsbee is given by Julian Hawthorne in *Hawthorne and His Circle*, p. 81.

471. "arcade" is crossed out and "colonnade" is substituted above, in another hand.

472. It is pleasant to learn from Julian Hawthorne (*Hawthorne and His Circle*, pp. 235-6) that Bennoch "lived to repay all his creditors with interest, and to become once more a man in easy circumstances, honored and trusted as well as loved by all who knew him, and active and happy in all good works to the end of his days."

473. Nicholas Trübner (1817-84), publisher and scholar. He was the author, among other learned works, of a *Bibliographical Guide to American Literature* (1855, 1859).

474. The notice, as printed in the London *Times*, December 8, 1857, advertised a "Protestant College, in Paris," of which E. Fezandie was "Director." Ada Shepard had spent several weeks at this "college" before going to England.

475. These specimens suggested to Hawthorne the enormous spider which conspicuously appears in *Septimius Felton* (see especially p. 365) and in *Doctor Grimshawe's Secret* (see especially p. 10).

476. Compare *Septimius Felton*, p. 402.

477. Milton's "Il Penseroso," l. 100.

478. *Catalogue of the Sketches and Drawings by J. M. W. Turner, R.A. Exhibited in Marlborough House in the Year 1857-8*, London, 1857. It is reprinted in *The Works of John Ruskin*, ed. E. T. Cook and A. Wedderburn, London, 1904, XIII, 235-316. Hawthorne presumably had been reading Ruskin almost a year prior to this date, for Una Hawthorne wrote to Elizabeth Peabody, December 31, 1856: "Papa brought a book from the Library called 'The Modern Painters,' by Ruskin" (manuscript letter in the Berg Collection of the New York Public Library).

479. Wordsworth's "Elegiac Stanzas, Suggested by a Picture of Peele Castle, in a Storm . . .," l. 15.

480. Shakespeare's *Tempest*, IV, i, 156.

481. See *Revelation*, 21 : 23.

482. James John Garth Wilkinson (1812-99) was the author of *Emanuel Swedenborg: a Biography* (1849), *The Human Body and its Connection with Man* (1851), and numerous other works.

483. Thomas Lake Harris (1823-1906).

484. Daniel Dunglas Home (1833-86), pronounced Hume.

485. Mrs. Hawthorne wrote to Patmore reminiscently, after the death of her husband: "Upon my return to England, after a dreary absence in Portugal, when I arrived in Liverpool and expressed my excessive fatigue and exasperation at such a long separation, my husband put 'The Angel in the House' into my hand, saying that I should be refreshed and enchanted, and forget all my vexations by reading it" (Basil Champneys, *Memoirs and Correspondence of Coventry Patmore*, London, 1900, I, 97-8).

486. The manuscript notebook continues with the entry of Paris, January 6, 1858.

INDEX

INDEX

Prepared by Miriam L. Snow